AF469269

EXPLORING NEW FRONTIERS OF THEORETICAL INFORMATICS

IFIP – The International Federation for Information Processing

IFIP was founded in 1960 under the auspices of UNESCO, following the First World Computer Congress held in Paris the previous year. An umbrella organization for societies working in information processing, IFIP's aim is two-fold: to support information processing within its member countries and to encourage technology transfer to developing nations. As its mission statement clearly states,

> *IFIP's mission is to be the leading, truly international, apolitical organization which encourages and assists in the development, exploitation and application of information technology for the benefit of all people.*

IFIP is a non-profit making organization, run almost solely by 2500 volunteers. It operates through a number of technical committees, which organize events and publications. IFIP's events range from an international congress to local seminars, but the most important are:

- The IFIP World Computer Congress, held every second year;
- Open conferences;
- Working conferences.

The flagship event is the IFIP World Computer Congress, at which both invited and contributed papers are presented. Contributed papers are rigorously refereed and the rejection rate is high.

As with the Congress, participation in the open conferences is open to all and papers may be invited or submitted. Again, submitted papers are stringently refereed.

The working conferences are structured differently. They are usually run by a working group and attendance is small and by invitation only. Their purpose is to create an atmosphere conducive to innovation and development. Refereeing is less rigorous and papers are subjected to extensive group discussion.

Publications arising from IFIP events vary. The papers presented at the IFIP World Computer Congress and at open conferences are published as conference proceedings, while the results of the working conferences are often published as collections of selected and edited papers.

Any national society whose primary activity is in information may apply to become a full member of IFIP, although full membership is restricted to one society per country. Full members are entitled to vote at the annual General Assembly, National societies preferring a less committed involvement may apply for associate or corresponding membership. Associate members enjoy the same benefits as full members, but without voting rights. Corresponding members are not represented in IFIP bodies. Affiliated membership is open to non-national societies, and individual and honorary membership schemes are also offered.

EXPLORING NEW FRONTIERS OF THEORETICAL INFORMATICS

IFIP 18th World Computer Congress
TC1 3rd International Conference on
Theoretical Computer Science (TCS2004)
22–27 August 2004
Toulouse, France

Edited by

Jean-Jacques Levy
INRIA, France

Ernst W. Mayr
Technische Universität München, Germany

John C. Mitchell
Stanford University, USA

SPRINGER SCIENCE+BUSINESS MEDIA, LLC

Library of Congress Cataloging-in-Publication Data

A C.I.P. Catalogue record for this book is available from the Library of Congress.

Exploring New Frontiers of Theoretical Informatics
Edited by Jean-Jacques Levy, Ernst W. Mayr, and John C. Mitchell

DOI 10.1007/978-1-4020-8141-5

Originally published by Kluwer Academic Publishers in 2004
MyCopy version of the original edition 2004

Printed on acid-free paper.
www.springer.com/mycopy

CONTENTS

PREFACE

IFIP TCS 2004 is the third international conference organized by IFIP TC1, whose activities cover the entire field of theoretical computer science. The major topics of the conference were chosen reflecting the current activities in theoretical computer science forming the two tracks:

Track (1) on Algorithms, Complexity, and Models of Computation,

Track (2) on Logic, Semantics, Specification, and Verification.

The program of IFIP TCS 2004 included the presentations of twenty-two contributed papers in Track (1) and twenty-four contributed papers in Track (2). The Program Committees selected them from sixty-five submissions to Track (1) and eighty-two submissions to Track (2).

The four plenary invited speakers were chosen by the Steering Committee, the Chair and the PC Co-Chairs.

This volume constitutes the record of the technical program, consisting of the contributed papers and the invited talks. We had the pleasure of chairing the conference and the program committees of the third IFIP International Conference on Theoretical Computer Science. We are extremely grateful to Jean-Claude Laprie and his staff, who helped us in preparing and announcing the call for papers, the program, and the web pages, and in putting together the proceedings.

We would like to express our thanks to the other members of the Program Committees, who are listed below, for their help in reviewing all submissions and for selecting the papers.

Jean-Jacques Lévy
Chair
Ernst W. Mayr
John C. Mitchell
Co-Chairs

PROGRAM COMMITTEE

Track (1) on Algorithms, Complexity, and Models of Computation

Farid Ablayev (State University, Kazan)
Hagit Attiya (The Technion, Haifa)
Stefano Leonardi (Universita di Roma)
Maurice Margenstern (Université de Metz)
Ernst Mayr, Chair (Technische Universität München)
Satoru Miyano (University of Tokyo)
Jean-Eric Pin (LIAFA CNRS, Paris)
Nicola Santoro (Carleton University)
Thomas Schwentick (Philipps-Universität Marburg)
Sandeep Sen (Indian Institute of Technology Delhi)
Subhash Suri (University of California Santa Barbara)
Osamu Watanabe (Tokyo Institute of Technology)

Track (2) on Logic, Semantics, Specification, and Verification

Roberto Amadio (Université de Provence, Marseille)
Luca Cardelli (Microsoft Research Cambridge)
Giuseppe Castagna (École Normale Supérieure, Paris)
Hubert Comon-Lundh (École Normale Supérieure de Cachan)
Adriana Compagnoni (Stevens Institute of Technology)
Drew Dean (SRI)
Marcelo Fiore (University of Cambridge)
Giorgio Ghelli (Università di Pisa)
Martin Hofmann (Ludwig-Maximilians-Universität, Munchen)
Alan Jeffrey (DePaul University)
Bruce Kapron (University of Victoria)
Orna Kupferman (Hebrew University)
John Mitchell, Chair (Stanford University)
George Necula (University of California Berkeley)
Catuscia Palamidessi (INRIA Futurs)
Martin Rinard (MIT)
Davide Sangiorgi (University of Bologna)

Vladimiro Sassone (University of Sussex)
Vitaly Shmatikov (SRI)
Martin Wirsing (Ludwig-Maximilians-Universität, Munchen)

THE TPI (TRNA PAIRING INDEX), A MATHEMATICAL MEASURE OF REPETITION IN A (BIOLOGICAL) SEQUENCE

Gaston H. Gonnet
Dept. of Computer Science, ETH Zurich
Swiss Federal Institute of Technology
ETH Zentrum RZ F2, CH-8092 Zurich

DNA sequences contain, among other information, the encoding of amino acids for proteins. Coding for the amino acids is redundant, that is most amino acids are coded by more than one codon (base-triplet). Usage of different codons coding for the same amino acids is called codon bias. Codon bias can be easily observed in most genomes, i.e. the probabilities of the codons is not uniform, quite skewed very often. The function of codon bias is still unknown, although error correction, DNA stability, speed of translation are usually quoted as possible reasons for it.

Different codons are translated to amino acids by different tRNA molecules. Depending on the species, codons are mapped to tRNA molecules, one-to-one or many-to-one, and tRNA molecules map to amino acids, again one-to-one or many-to-one.

One of the aspects of codon usage which is suspected of affecting the translation efficiency is whether tRNA molecules (or codons) are reused more or less frequently. To study this effect we have to design an index that will measure how much reuse of a particular tRNA (or codon) there is compared to random distribution. This is called the tPI. The tPI must be independent of particular (skewed) frequency distributions. In the end, the tPI is a probabilistic measure over a sequence of symbols from a finite alphabet.

We describe the formulation of the tPI which has the desirable properties. It is relatively straightforward to find a recursion formula to compute its values. Less straightforward is to compute the moments of its distribution, and even more complicated is to compute it efficiently. It should be noted that this is not purely a theoretical question, biologists want to compute the tPI of most sequences, so an efficient algorithm is required.

To make the computation more effective, we transformed the recursion formulas to have a desirable property that makes its computation require less intermediate storage and hence tractable. tPI indices of entire genomes have been computed.

STABILITY OF APPROXIMATION IN DISCRETE OPTIMIZATION

Juraj Hromkovič
Dept. of Computer Science, ETH Zurich
Swiss Federal Institute of Technology
ETH Zentrum RZ F2, CH-8092 Zurich
juraj.hromkovic@inf.ethz.ch

Abstract

One can try to parametrize the set of the instances of an optimization problem and look for in polynomial time achievable approximation ratio with respect to this parametrization. When the approximation ratio grows with the parameter, but is independent of the size of the instances, then we speak about stable approximation algorithms. An interesting point is that there exist stable approximation algorithms for problems like TSP that is not approximable within any polynomial approximation ratio in polynomial time (assuming P is not equal to NP). The investigation of the stability of approximation overcomes in this way the troubles with measuring the complexity and approximation ratio in the worst-case manner, because it may success in partitioning of the set of all input instances of a hard problem into infinite many classes with respect to the hardest of the particular inputs. We believe that approaches like this will become the core of the algorithmics, because they provide a deeper insight in the hardness of specific problems and in many application we are not interested in the worst-case problem hardness, but in the hardness of forthcoming problem instances.

1. Introduction

Immediately after introducing NP-hardness (completeness) [Co71] as a concept for proving intractability of computing problems [Ka72], the following question has been posed: If an optimization problem does not admit an efficiently computable optimal solution, is there a possibility to efficiently compute at least an approximation of the optimal solution? Several researchers [Jo74, Lo75, Chr76, IK75] provided already in the middle of the seventies a positive answer for some optimization problems. It may seem to be a fascinating effect if one jumps from the exponential complexity (a huge inevitable amount of physical work) to the polynomial complexity (tractable amount of physical work) due to a small change in the requirement —instead of an exact optimal solution one forces a solution whose quality differs from the quality of an optimal solution at most by $\varepsilon \cdot 100$ % for some ε. This effect is very strong, especially, if one considers problems for which this approximation concept works for any small ε (see the concept of approximation schemes in [IK75, MPS98, Pa94, BC93, Va03, Hr03]).

There is also another possibility to jump from NP to P. Namely, to consider the subset of inputs with a special, nice property instead of the whole set of inputs for which the problem is well-defined. A nice example is the Travelling Salesman Problem (TSP). TSP is not only NP-hard, but also the search of an approximation solution for TSP is NP-hard for every ε. But if one considers TSP for inputs satisfying the triangle inequality (the so-called Δ-TSP), one can even design an approximation algorithm [Chr76] with the approximation ratio $\varepsilon = \frac{1}{2}$. The situation is still more interesting, if one considers the Euclidean TSP, where the distances between the nodes correspond to the distances in the Euclidean metrics. The Euclidean TSP is NP-hard [Pa77], but for every small $\varepsilon > 0$ one can design an ε-approximation algorithm [Ar96, Ar97, Mi96] with an almost linear time complexity.

The fascinating observations of huge quantitive changes mentioned above lead us to our proposal to consider the "stability" of approximation algorithms. Let us consider the following scenario. One has an optimization problem P for two sets of inputs L_1 and L_2, $L_1 \subset L_2$. For L_1 there exists an polynomial-time ε-approximation algorithm A, but for L_2 there is no polynomial-time δ-approximation algorithm for any $\delta > 0$ (if NP is not equal to P). We pose the following question: Is the algorithm A really useful for inputs from L_1 only? Let us consider a metrics M in L_2 determining the distance between any two inputs in L_2. Now, one can consider an input $x \in L_2 - L_1$, for which there exists an $y \in L_1$ such that $distance_M(x, y) \leq k$ for some positive real k. One can look for how "good" the algorithm A is for the input $x \in L_2 - L_1$. If for every $k > 0$ and every x with the distance at most k to L_1, A computes an $\delta_{\varepsilon,k}$ approximation of an optimal solution for x ($\delta_{\varepsilon,k}$ is considered to be a constant depending on k and ε only), then one can say that A is "(approximation) stable" according to the metrics M.

The idea of this concept is similar to that of the stability of numerical algorithms. But instead of observing the size of the change of the output value according to a small change of the input value, we look for the size of the change of the approximation ratio according to a small change in the specification (some parameters, characteristics) of the set of problem instances considered. If the exchange of the approximation ratio is small for every small change in the specification of the set of problem instances, then we have a stable algorithm. If a small change in the specification of the set of problem instances causes an essential (depending on the size of the input instances) increase of the relative error, then the algorithm is unstable.

The concept of stability enables us to show positive results extending the applicability of known approximation algorithms. As we shall see later, the concept also motivates to modify an unstable algorithm A in order to get a stable algorithm B that achieves the same approximation ratio on the original set of problem instances as A has, but B can also be successfully used outside of the original set of problem instances. This concept is useful because there are a lot of problems for which an additional assumption on the "parameters" of the problem instances leads to an essential decrease in the hardness of the problem. Such effects are the starting points for trying to partition the whole set of problem instances into a spectrum of classes according to polynomial-time approximability.

As one can observe this approach is similar to the concept of parametrized complexity of Downey and Fellows [DF95, DF99] in trying to overcome the troubles caused by measuring complexity and approximation ratio in the worst-case manner. The main aim of both concepts is partitioning of the set of all instances of a hard problem into infinite many classes with respect to the hardness of particular instances. We believe that approaches like these will be the core of future algorithmics, because they provide a deeper insight in the nature of the hardness of specific problems and in many applications we are not interested in the worst-case problem hardness, but in the hardness of forthcoming problem instances.

2. Definition of the Stability of Approximation Algorithms

We assume that the reader is familiar with the basic concepts and notions of algorithmics and complexity theory as presented in standard textbooks like [BC93, GJ79, Ho96, Pa94, We93, Hr04]. Next, we give a formal definition of the notion of an optimization problem. Let $\mathbb{N} = \{0, 1, 2, ...\}$ be the set of nonnegative integers, and let $\mathbb{R}^+$ be the set of positive reals.

DEFINITION 1 *An **optimization problem** U is an 7-tuple $U = (\Sigma_I, \Sigma_O, L, L_I, \mathcal{M}, cost, goal)$, where*

(i) *Σ_I is an alphabet called **input alphabet**,*

(ii) *Σ_O is an alphabet called **output alphabet**,*

(iii) *$L \subseteq \Sigma_I^*$ is a language over Σ_I called the **language of consistent inputs**,*

(iv) *$L_I \subseteq L$ is a language over Σ_I called the **language of actual inputs**,*

(v) *$\mathcal{M}$ is a function from L to $2^{\Sigma_O^*}$, where, for every $x \in L$, $\mathcal{M}(x)$ is called **the set of feasible solutions** for the input x,*

(vi) *cost is a function, called* ***cost function****, that for every pair* (u, x), *where* $u \in \mathcal{M}(x)$ *for some* $x \in L$, *assigns a positive real number* $cost(u, x)$,

(vii) $goal \in \{minimum,\ maximum\}$.

For every $x \in L$, *we define*

$$\boldsymbol{Output_U(x)} = \{y \in \mathcal{M}(x) | cost(y) = goal\{cost(z) | z \in \mathcal{M}(x)\}\}$$

as the set of optimal solutions, and $\mathbf{Opt_U(x)}$= $cost(y)$ *for some* $y \in Output_U(x)$.

Clearly, the meaning for $\Sigma_I, \Sigma_O, \mathcal{M}$, *cost* and *goal* is the usual one. L may be considered as a set of consistent inputs, i.e., the inputs for which the optimization problem is consistently defined. L_I is the set of inputs considered and only these inputs are taken into account when one determines the complexity of the optimization problem U. This kind of definition is useful for considering the complexity of optimization problems parametrized according to their languages of actual inputs. In what follows $\boldsymbol{Language(U)}$ denotes the language L_I of actual inputs of U.

DEFINITION 2 *Let* $U = (\Sigma_I, \Sigma_O, L, L_I, \mathcal{M}, cost, goal)$ *be an optimization problem. We say that an algorithm* A *is a* ***consistent algorithm for*** $\boldsymbol{U}$ *if, for every input* $x \in L_I$, A *computes an output* $A(x) \in \mathcal{M}(x)$. *We say that* $\boldsymbol{A}$ ***solves*** $\boldsymbol{U}$ *if, for every* $x \in L_I$, A *computes an output* $A(x)$ *from* $Output_U(x)$. *The time complexity of* A *is defined as the function*

$$Time_A(n) = \max\{Time_A(x) \mid x \in L_I \cap \Sigma_I^n\}$$

from $\mathbb{N}$ *to* $\mathbb{N}$, *where* $Time_A(x)$ *is the length of the computation of* A *on* x.

DEFINITION 3 *Let* $U = (\Sigma_I, \Sigma_O, L, L_I, \mathcal{M}, cost, goal)$ *be an optimization problem, and let* A *be a consistent algorithm for* U.

For every $x \in L_I$, *the approximation ratio* $\mathbf{R_A(x)}$ ***of*** $\boldsymbol{A}$ ***on*** $\boldsymbol{x}$ *is defined as*

$$R_A(x) = \max\left\{\frac{cost(A(x))}{Opt_U(x)}, \frac{Opt_U(x)}{cost(A(x))}\right\}.$$

For any $n \in \mathbb{N}$, *we define the* ***approximation ration of*** $\boldsymbol{A}$ *as*

$$R_A(n) = \max\{R_A(x) \mid x \in L_I \cap (\Sigma_I)^n\}.$$

For any positive real δ, *we say that* A *is an* $\boldsymbol{\delta}$***-approximation algorithm for*** $\boldsymbol{U}$ *if* $R_A(x) \leq \delta$ *for every* $x \in L_I$.

For every function $f : \mathbb{N} \rightarrow \mathbb{R}$, *we say that* A *is a* $\boldsymbol{f(n)}$***-approximation algorithm for*** $\boldsymbol{U}$ *if* $R_A(n) \leq f(n)$ *for every* $n \in \mathbb{N}$.

In order to define the notion of stability of approximation algorithms we need to consider something like a distance between a language L and a word outside L.

DEFINITION 4 *Let* $U = (\Sigma_I, \Sigma_O, L, L_I, \mathcal{M}, cost, goal)$ *and* $\overline{U} = (\Sigma_I, \Sigma_O, L, L, \mathcal{M}, cost, goal)$ *be two optimization problems with* $L_I \subset L$. ***A distance function for U according to*** L_I *is any function* $h_L : L \to \mathbb{R}^+$ *satisfying the property*

$$h_L(x) = 0 \text{ for every } x \in L_I.$$

We define, for any $r \in \mathbb{R}^+$,

$$\boldsymbol{Ball_{r,h}(L_I)} = \{w \in L \mid h(w) \leq r\}.$$

Let A be a consistent algorithm for $\overline{U}$*, and let A be an* ε*-approximation algorithm for U for some* $\varepsilon \in \mathbb{R}^+$*. Let p be a positive real. We say that A is* ***p-stable according to h*** *if, for every real* $0 \leq r \leq p$*, there exists a* $\delta_{r,\varepsilon} \in \mathbb{R}^+$ *such that A is an* $\delta_{r,\varepsilon}$*-approximation algorithm for* $U_r = (\Sigma_I, \Sigma_O, L, Ball_{r,h}(L_I), \mathcal{M}, cost, goal)$.[1]

A is ***stable according to h*** *if A is p-stable according to h for every* $p \in \mathbb{R}^+$*. We say that A is* ***unstable according to h*** *if A is not p-stable for any* $p > 0$.

For every positive integer r, and every function $f_r : \mathbb{N} \to \mathbb{R}^+$ *we say that A is* $\boldsymbol{(r, f(n))}$***-quasistable according to h*** *if A is an* $f_r(n)$*-approximation algorithm for* $U_r = (\Sigma_I, \Sigma_O, L, Ball_{r,h}(L_I), \mathcal{M}, cost, goal)$.

One may see that the notion of stability can be useful for answering the question how broadly a given approximation algorithm is applicable. If one is interested in negative results then one can try to show that for any reasonable distance measure the considered algorithm cannot be extended to work for a much larger set of inputs than the original one. In this way one can search for some more exact boundaries between polynomial approximability and polynomial non-approximability.

3. Examples

We consider the well-known TSP problem that is in its general form very hard for approximation. But if one considers complete graphs in which the triangle inequality holds, then we have a 1.5-approximation algorithm due to Christofides [Chr76]. The idea of this algorithm can be shortly described as follows.

[1] Note, that $\delta_{r,\varepsilon}$ is a constant depending on r and ε only.

CHRISTOFIDES ALGORITHM

Input: A complete graph $G = (V, E)$, and a cost function $c : E \to \mathbb{N}^+$ satisfying the triangle inequality.

Step 1: Construct a minimal spanning tree T of G according to c.

Step 2: $S := \{v \in V \mid deg_T(v) \text{ is odd}\}$.

Step 3: Compute a minimum-weight perfect matching M on S in G.

Step 4: Create the multigraph $G' = (V, E(T) \cup M)$ and construct an Eulerian tour ω in G'.

Step 5: Construct a Hamiltonian tour H of G by shortening ω (i.e., by removing all repetitions of the occurrences of every vertex in ω in one run via ω from the left to the right).

Output: H.

Since the triangle inequality holds and Step 5 is executed by repeatedly shortening a path $x, u_1, ..., u_m, y$ by the edge $\{x, y\}$ (because $u_1, ..., u_m$ have already occured before in the prefix of ω) the cost of H is at most the cost of ω. Thus, the crucial point for the success of Christofides algorithm is the triangle inequality. A reasonable possibility to search for an extension of the application of this algorithm is to look for inputs that "almost" satisfy the triangle inequality. In what follows we do it in two different ways.

Let $\Delta - TSP = (\Sigma_I, \Sigma_O, L, L_I, \mathcal{M}, cost, minimum)$ be a representation of the TSP with the triangle inequality. We may assume $\Sigma_I = \Sigma_O = \{0, 1, \#\}$, L contains codes of all weight functions for edges of complete graphs, and L_I contains codes of weight functions that satisfy the triangle inequality. Let, for every $x \in L$, $G_x = (V_x, E_x, weight_x)$ be the complete weighted graph coded by x. Obviously, the Christofides algorithm is consistent for $(\Sigma_I, \Sigma_O, L, L, \mathcal{M}, cost, minimum)$.

We define for every $x \in L$,

$$dist(x) = \max\left\{0, \max\left\{\frac{weight(\{u,v\})}{weight(\{u,p\}) + weight(\{p,v\})} - 1 \,\middle|\, u, v, p \in V_x\right\}\right\}$$

For the simplicity we consider the size of x as the number of nodes of G_x instead of $|x|$.

We observe that $dist(G, c) \leq r$ implies the so-called $(1+r)$-relaxed triangle inequality

$$c(\{u, v\}) \leq (1 + r)[c(\{u, w\}) + c(\{w, v\})]$$

for all three different vertices $u, v, w \in V(G)$.

Let, for every positive real number r,

$$\Delta\text{-}TSP_r = (\Sigma_I, \Sigma_O, L, Ball_{r,dist}(L_\Delta), \mathcal{M}, cost, minimum).$$

The next results show that the CHRISTOFIDES ALGORITHM assures only a very weak approximation for instances of $\Delta\text{-}TSP_r$ for any $r \in \mathbb{R}^+$. First, we show a partially positive result and then we prove that it cannot be essentially improved.

LEMMA 5 *For every positive real number r,* CHRISTOFIDES ALGORITHM *is* $(r, O(n^{\log_2((1+r)^2)}))$*-quasistable for dist.*

Proof. Let $I = (G, c) \in Ball_{r,dist}(L_\Delta)$ for an $r \in \mathbb{R}^+$. Let T_I be the minimal spanning tree constructed in Step 1. Let ω_I be the Eulerian tour constructed in Step 4 and $H_I = v_1, v_2, v_3, \ldots, v_n, v_{n+1}$, where $v_{n+1} = v_1$, be the Hamiltonian tour constructed by shortening ω_I in Step 5.

Clearly,

$$\omega_I = v_1, P_1, v_2, P_2, v_3, \ldots, v_n, P_n, v_{n+1},$$

where P_i is a path between v_i and v_{i+1} for $i = 1, 2, \ldots, n$. To exchange a path v, P, u of a length m, $m \in \mathbb{N}^+$, for the edge $\{v, u\}$ we proceed as follows. For any $p, s, t \in V(G)$, one can exchange the path p, s, t for the edge $\{p, t\}$ by the cost increase bounded by the multiplicative constant $(1 + r)$. This means that reducing the length m of a path to the length $\lceil m/2 \rceil$ increases the cost of the connection between u and v by at most $(1 + r)$ times. After at most $\lceil \log_2 m \rceil$ such reduction steps one reduces the path v, P, u of length m to the path v, u, and

$$cost(u, v) = c(\{v, u\}) \le (1 + r)^{\lceil \log_2 m \rceil} \cdot cost(v, P, u). \tag{1}$$

Let M_I be the matching constructed in Step 3. Following the analysis of the Christofides algorithm (see Theorem 4.3.5.5 in [Hr03] for instance) we get from (1)

$$cost(M_I) \le \frac{1}{2} \cdot (1 + r)^{\lceil \log_2 n \rceil} \cdot cost(H_{Opt}), \tag{2}$$

and

$$cost(H_I) \le (1 + r)^{\lceil \log_2 n \rceil} cost(\omega_I). \tag{3}$$

Thus,

$$\begin{aligned}
cost(H_I) &\le (1 + r)^{\lceil \log_2 n \rceil} cost(\omega_I) = (1 + r)^{\lceil \log_2 \rceil} \left[cost(T_I) + cost(M_I)\right] \\
&\le (1 + r)^{\lceil \log_2 n \rceil} \left[cost(H_{Opt}) + \frac{1}{2}(1 + r)^{\lceil \log_2 n \rceil} \cdot cost(H_{Opt})\right] \\
&= (1 + r)^{\lceil \log_2 n \rceil} \left(1 + \frac{1}{2}(1 + r)^{\lceil \log_2 n \rceil}\right) \cdot cost(H_{Opt}) \\
&= O\left(n^{\log_2((1+r)^2)} \cdot cost(H_{Opt})\right).
\end{aligned}$$

Now we show that the result of Lemma 5 cannot be essentially improved. To show this, we construct an input for which the CHRISTOFIDES ALGORITHM provides a very poor approximation.

We construct a weighted complete graph from $Ball_{r,dist}(L_{\triangle})$ as follows (Figure 1). We start with the path $p_0, p_1, \ldots, p_n$ for $n = 2^k$, $k \in \mathbb{N}$, where every edge $\{p_i, p_{i+1}\}$ has weight 1. Then we add edges $\{p_i, p_{i+2}\}$ for $i = 0, 1, \ldots, n-2$ with weight $2 \cdot (1+r)$. Generally, for every $m \in \{1, \ldots, \log_2 n\}$, we define $weight(\{p_i, p_{i+2^m}\}) = 2^m \cdot (1+r)^m$ for $i = 0, \ldots, n-2^m$. For all other edges one can take maximal possible weights in such a way that the constructed input is in $Ball_{r,dist}(L_I)$.

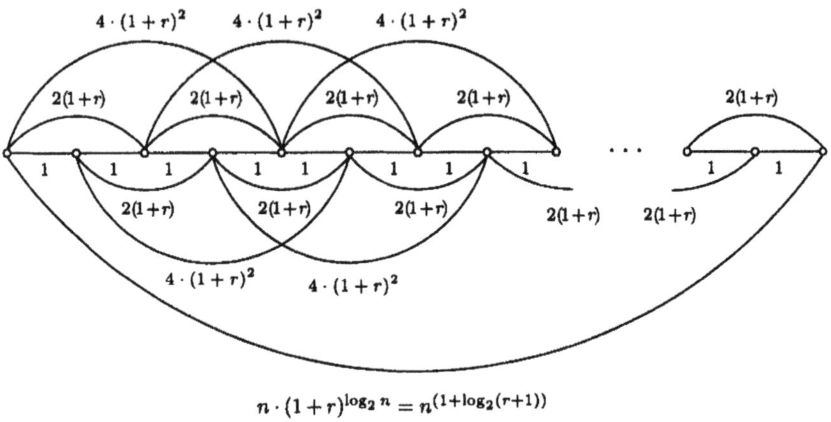

Figure 1.

Let us have a look on the work of the CHRISTOFIDES ALGORITHM on the input $(G, weight)$. There is only one minimal spanning tree that corresponds to the path containing all edges of weight 1 (Figure 1). Since every path contains exactly two vertices of odd degree, the Eulerian graph constructed in Step 4 is the cycle $D = p_0, p_1, p_2, \ldots, p_n, p_0$ with the n edges of weight 1 and the edge of the maximal weight $n \cdot (1+r)^{\log_2 n} = n^{1+\log_2(1+r)}$. Since the Eulerian tour is a Hamiltonian tour (Figure 1), the output of the CHRISTOFIDES ALGORITHM is unambiguously the cycle $p_0, p_1, \ldots, p_n, p_0$ with cost $n + n(1+r)^{\log_2 n}$. The optimal tour for this input is $H_{Opt} =$

$$p_0, p_2, p_4, \ldots, p_{2i}, p_{2(i+1)}, \ldots, p_n, p_{n-1}, p_{n-3}, \ldots, p_{2i+1}, p_{2i-1}, \ldots, p_3, p_1, p_0.$$

This tour contains two edges $\{p_0, p_1\}$ and $\{p_{n-1}, p_n\}$ of weight 1 and all $n-2$ edges of weight $2 \cdot (1+r)$. Thus, $cost(H_{Opt}) = 2 + 2 \cdot (1+r) \cdot (n-2)$ and

$$\frac{cost(D)}{cost(H_{Opt})} = \frac{n + n \cdot (1+r)^{\log_2 n}}{2 + 2 \cdot (1+r) \cdot (n-2)} \geq \frac{n^{1+\log_2(1+r)}}{2n \cdot (1+r)} = \frac{n^{\log_2(1+r)}}{2(1+r)}.$$

Thus, we have proved the following result.

LEMMA 6 *For every* $r \in \mathbb{R}^+$, *if the* CHRISTOFIDES ALGORITHM *is* $(r, f_r(n))$-*quasistable for dist, then*

$$f_r(n) \geq n^{\log_2(1+r)}/(2 \cdot (1+r)).$$

COROLLARY 7 *The* CHRISTOFIDES ALGORITHM *is unstable for dist.*

The key question is whether one can modify the Christofides algorithm to get an algorithm that is stable according to *dist*. In what follows, we give a positive answer to this question.

As we have observed, the main problem is that shortening a path $u_1, u_2, \ldots, u_{m+1}$ to the edge u_1, u_{m+1} can lead to

$$cost(\{u_1, u_{m+1}\}) = (1+r)^{\lceil \log_2 m \rceil} \cdot cost(u_1, u_2, \ldots, u_{m+1}).$$

This can increase the cost of the constructed Hamiltonian path by the multiplicative factor $(1+r)^{\lceil \log_2 n \rceil}$ in the comparison with the cost of the Eulerian tour. The rough idea, then, is to construct a Hamiltonian tour by shortening only short paths of the minimal spanning tree constructed in Step 1 of the algorithm.

To realize this idea we shall prove that, for every tree $T = (V, E)$, the graph $T^3 = (V, \{\{x, y\} \mid x, y \in V,$ there is a path x, P, y in T of a length at most $3\})$ contains a Hamiltonian tour H. This means that every edge $\{u, v\}$ of H has a corresponding unique path $u, P_{u,v}, v$ in T of a length at most 3. This is a positive development, but it still does not suffice for our purposes. The remaining problem is that we need to estimate a good upper bound on the cost of the path $P(H) = u_1, P_{u_1,u_2}, u_2, P_{u_2,u_3}, u_3, \ldots, u_{n-1} P_{u_{n-1},u_n}, u_n, P_{u_n,u_1}, u_1$ (in T) that corresponds to the Hamiltonian tour $u_1, u_2, \ldots, u_n, u_1$ in T^3. Note that in the naive 2-approximation algorithm the resulting Hamiltonian tour can be viewed as a shortening of the Eulerian tour[2] with a cost at most twice of the cost of T. But, we do not know the frequency of the occurrences of particular edges of T in $P(H)$. It may happen that the most expensive edges of T occur more frequently in $P(H)$ than the cheap edges. Observe also that $cost(T^3)$ cannot be bounded by $c \cdot cost(T)$ for any constant c independent on

[2] The Eulerian tour uses every edge of T exactly twice.

T, because T^3 may be even a complete graph for some trees T. Thus, we need the following technical lemma proving that T^3 contains a Hamiltonian tour H such that each edge of T occurs at most twice in $P(H)$.

DEFINITION 8 *Let T be a tree. For every edge $\{u, v\} \in E(T)$, let $u, P_{u,v}, v$ be the unique simple path between u and v in T.*

*Let k be a positive integer. Let $U = u_1, u_2, \ldots, u_m$ be any simple path in T^k. Then, we define the U-**path in** T as*

$$P_T(U) = u_1, P_{u_1,u_2}, u_2, P_{u_2,u_3}, \ldots, u_{m-1}, P_{u_{m-1},u_m}, u_m.$$

LEMMA 9 *Let T be a tree with $n \geq 3$ vertices, and let $\{p, q\}$ be an edge of T. Then, T^3 contains a Hamiltonian path $U = v_1, v_2, \ldots, v_n$, $p = v_1$, $v_n = q$, such that every edge of $E(T)$ occurs exactly twice in $P_T(H)$, where $H = U, p$ is a Hamiltonian tour in T^3.*

Proof. We prove this assertion by induction on the number of vertices of T.

(1) Let $n = 3$. The only tree of three vertices is

$$T = (\{v_1, v_2, v_3\}, \{\{v_1, v_2\}, \{v_2, v_3\}\})$$

and the corresponding T^3 is the complete graph of three vertices

$$(\{v_1, v_2, v_3\}, \{\{v_1, v_2\}, \{v_2, v_3\}, \{v_1, v_3\}\}).$$

Thus, the only Hamiltonian tour in T^3 is v_1, v_2, v_3, v_1. The claim of Lemma 9 is true, since $P_T(v_1, v_2, v_3, v_4) = v_1, v_2, v_3, v_2, v_1$.

(2) Let $n \geq 4$ and assume that Lemma 9 is true for trees with fewer than n vertices. Let $T = (V, E)$ be a tree, $|V| = n$. Let $\{p, q\}$ be an arbitrary edge of T. Consider the graph $T' = (V, E - \{\{p, q\}\})$ that consists of two trees T_p and T_q, where T_p [T_q] is the component of T' containing the vertex p [q]. Obviously, $|V(T_p)| \leq n - 1$ and $|V(T_q)| \leq n - 1$. Let p' and q', respectively, be a neighbor of p and q, if any, in T_p and T_q, respectively. Now, we fix some Hamiltonian paths U_p and U_q in T_p^3 and T_q^3, respectively. To do it, we distinguish three possibilities according to the cardinalities of T_p and T_q.

1 If $|V(T_p)| = 1$, then set $U_p = p = p'$.

2 If $|V(T_p)| = 2$, then set $U_p = p, p'$.

3 If $3 \leq |V(T_p)| \leq n - 1$, then we can apply the induction hypothesis. We set U_p to be a Hamiltonian path from p to p' in T_p^3 such that $P(U_p, p)$ contains every edge of T_p exactly twice.

A Hamiltonian path U_q in T_q^3 can be fixed in the same way as U_p was fixed above (Figure 2).

Now, consider the path U_p, U_q^R obtained by connecting U_p and the reverse of U_q by the edge $\{p', q'\}$. Observe, that $\{p', q'\} \in T^3$, because p', p, q, q' is a path in T. Following Figure 2, it is obvious that U_p, U_q^R is a Hamiltonian path in T^3, and that U_p, U_q^R, p is a Hamiltonian tour in T^3.

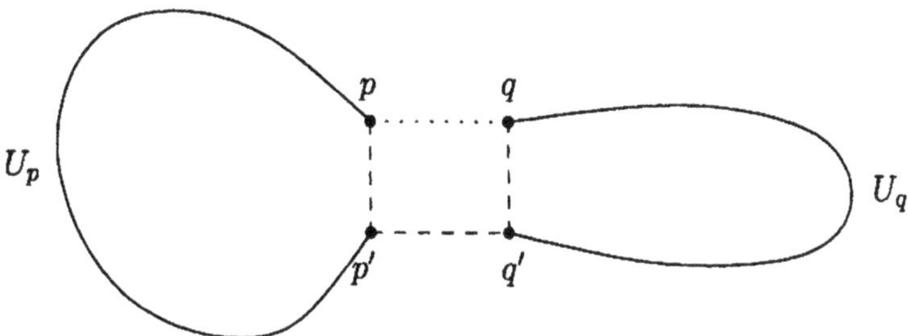

Figure 2.

Observe (by the induction hypothesis or the trivial cases with $|V(T_p)| \leq 2$) that $P_{T_p}(U_p, p')$ the Hamiltonian tour U_p, p' in T^3 contains every edge of T_p exactly twice. Thus, $P_{T_p}(U_p)$ contains every edge, but the edge $\{p, p'\}$ of T_p exactly twice. The edge $\{p, p'\}$ is contained exactly once in $P_{T_p}(U_p)$. Similarly, $P_{T_q}(U_q)$ contains every edge of T_q twice, but the edge $\{q, q'\}$ once. Finally, $P_T(U_p, U_q^R, p)$ contains every edge of T exactly twice, because

1 this is clear from the properties of U_p and U_q^R for every edge from $E - \{\{p, q\}, \{p, p'\}, \{q, q'\}\}$,

2 the edge $\{p', q'\} \in T^3$ connecting U_p and U_q (Figure 2) is realized by the path p', p, q, q' containing edges $\{p, p'\}$, $\{p, q\}$, and $\{q, q'\}$ of E, and

3 the connection of U_p, U_q^R with p is realized directly by the edge $\{p, q\}$.

SEKANINA'S ALGORITHM

Input: A complete graph $G = (V, E)$, and a cost function $c : E \to \mathbb{N}^+$.

Step 1: Construct a minimal spanning tree T of G according to c.

Step 2: Construct T^3.

Step 3: Find a Hamiltonian tour H in T^3 such that $P_T(H)$ contains every edge of T exactly twice.

Output: H.

THEOREM 10 SEKANINA'S ALGORITHM *is a polynomial-time 2-approximation algorithm for Δ-TSP.*

Proof. Obviously, Step 1 and 2 of SEKANINA'S ALGORITHM can be performed in time $O(n^2)$. Using Lemma 9 one can implement Step 3 in time $O(n)$. Thus, the time complexity of SEKANINA'S ALGORITHM is in $O(n^2)$.

Let H_{Opt} be an optimal solution for an input instance (G, c) of Δ-TSP. We have $cost(T) \leq cost(H_{Opt})$. The output H of SEKANINA'S ALGORITHM can be viewed as shortening the path $P_T(H)$ by removing repetitions of vertices in $P_T(H)$. Since $P_T(H)$ contains every edge of T exactly twice,

$$cost(P_T(H)) = 2 \cdot cost(T) \leq 2 \cdot cost(H_{Opt}). \tag{4}$$

Since H is obtained from $P_T(H)$ by exchanging simple subpaths by an edge, and c satisfies the triangle inequality,

$$cost(H) \leq cost(P_T(H)). \tag{5}$$

Combining (4) and (5) we obtain $cost(H) \leq 2 \cdot cost(H_{Opt})$.

THEOREM 11 *For every positive real number r,* SEKANINA'S ALGORITHM *is a polynomial-time $2(1+r)^2$-approximation algorithm for Δ-TSP_r.*

Proof. Since SEKANINA'S ALGORITHM always outputs a Hamiltonian tour, it is consistent for TSP. Obviously, the inequality (4) is also true for any input instance of the general TSP.

Let (G, c) be an input instance of Δ-TSP$_r$. Since $(G, c) \in Ball_{r,dist}(L_\Delta)$,

$$\begin{aligned} c(\{v_1, v_4\}) &\leq (1+r)^2 \cdot cost(v_1, v_2, v_3, v_4), \text{ and} \\ c(\{u_1, u_3\}) &\leq (1+r) \cdot cost(u_1, u_2, u_3) \end{aligned}$$

for all edges $\{u_1, u_3\}$, $\{v_1, v_4\} \in E(G)$ and every path v_1, v_2, v_3, v_4 between v_1 and v_4 and every path u_1, u_2, u_3 between u_1 and u_3. Since H is obtained from $P_T(H)$ by exchanging a simple subpath of $P_T(H)$ of length at most 3,

$$cost(H) \leq (1+r)^2 \cdot cost(P_T(H)). \tag{6}$$

Combining (4) and (6) we finally obtain

$$cost(H) \leq 2 \cdot (1+r)^2 \cdot cost(P_T(H)).$$

COROLLARY 12 SEKANINA'S ALGORITHM *is stable according to dist.*

Thus, we have reached our final aim to divide the set of all instances of TSP into an infinite spectrum in such a way that the sets of this spectrum have upper bounds on the polynomial-time approximability of their input instances. The above analysis of TSP shows that it is reasonable to measure the hardness of the TSP instances by the distance function *dist*, i.e., by the degree of violation of the triangle inequality.

4. Conclusion and an Overview

In the previous sections we have introduced the concept of stability of approximations. Here we discuss the potential applicability and usefulness of this concept.

Using this concept, one can establish positive results of the following types:

1 An approximation algorithm or a PTAS can be successfully used for a larger set of inputs than the set usually considered.

2 We are not able to successfully apply a given approximation algorithm A (a PTAS) for additional inputs, but one can simply modify A to get a new approximation algorithm (a new PTAS) working for a larger set of inputs than the set of inputs of A.

3 To learn that an approximation algorithm is unstable for a distance measure could lead to the development of completely new approximation algorithms that would be stable according to the considered distance measure.

The following types of negative results may be achieved:

4. The fact that an approximation algorithm is unstable according to all "reasonable" distance measures and so that its use is really restricted to the original input set.

5. Let $Q = (\Sigma_I, \Sigma_O, L, L_I, \mathcal{M}, cost, goal) \in NPO$ be well approximable. If, for a distance measure D and a constant r, one proves the nonexistence of any polynomial-time approximation algorithm for $Q_{r,D} = (\Sigma_I, \Sigma_O, L, Ball_{r,D}(L_I), \mathcal{M}, cost, goal)$, then this means that the problem Q is "unstable" according to D.

Thus, using the notion of stability one can search for a spectrum of the hardness of a problem according to the set of inputs. For instance, considering a hard problem like TSP or Clique Problem one could get an infinite sequence of input languages $L_0, L_1, L_2, \ldots$ given by some distance measure, where $R_r(n)$

is the best achievable approximation ratio for the language L_r. Results of this kind can essentially contribute to the study of the nature of hardness of specific problems.

The best results known for TSP instances satisfying the $\beta = (1+r)$-triangle inequality are the following ones:

1 Andreae and Bandelt [AB95] showed that the here presented Sekanina Algorithm provides a $(\beta^2 + \beta)$ approximation ratio, which is the best known for $2 \leq \beta \leq 3$;

2 Bender and Chekuri [BCh99] designed a $4 \cdot \beta$-approximation algorithm, which is the best for $\beta > 3$;

3 Böckenhauer at. al. [BHK+02] have modified the Christofides Algorithm in order to get a $\frac{3}{2} \cdot \beta^2$-approximation algorithm, which is the best for $1 < \beta < 2$.

Moreover Bender and Chekuri [BCh99] proved a lower bound on the polynomial time approximability of this TSP subproblem which grows linearly with β.

Further development of these ideas for different versions of the Hamiltonian path problem can be found by Forlizzi at. al. [FHP+04], where a few stable algorithms with respect to relaxed triangle inequality were designed.

Another possibility is to consider the so-called **α-strengthen triangle inequality**, where one requires

$$c(\{u, v\}) \leq \alpha \cdot [c(\{u, w\}) + c(\{w, v\})]$$

for an α with $1 > \alpha \geq 1/2$. Observe that for $\alpha = 1/2$ all edges have the same weight and so the problem becames trivial. Böckenhauer at. al. [BHK+00] designed three algorithms for TSP subproblems with instances satisfying the α-strengthen triangle inequality, which yield the approximation ratios starting with 1 for $\alpha = 1/2$ and growing with α to $3/2$ for $\alpha = 1$. A very strong result has been proved by Böckenhauer and Seibert [BS00] who established an explicit lower bound on polynomial time approximability of TSP with sharped triangle inequality for any $\alpha > 1/2$ and this lower bounds grows with α. Thus, the TSP instances with weights from the interval $[1, 1 + \varepsilon]$ form an APX-hard problem for arbitrary small $\varepsilon > 0$. The subproblems with sharped triangle inequality were also successfully attacked for the minimum 2-connected spanning subgraph problems in [BBH+02].

[Ar96] S. Arora: Polynomial time approximation schemes for Euclidean TSP and other geometric problems. In: *Proc. 37th IEEE FOCS*, IEEE 1996, pp. 2–11.

[Ar97] S. Arora: Nearly linear time approximation schemes for Euclidean TSP and other geometric problems. In: *Proc. 38th IEEE FOCS*, IEEE 1997, pp. 554–563.

[BC93] D. P. Bovet, C. Crescenzi: *Introduction to the Theory of Complexity*, Prentice-Hall 1993.

[Chr76] N. Christofides: Worst-case analysis of a new heuristic for the travelling salesman problem. Technical Report 388, Graduate School of Industrial Administration, Carnegie-Mellon University, Pittsbourgh, 1976.

[Co71] S. A. Cook: The complexity of theorem proving procedures. In: Proc *3rd ACM STOC*, ACM 1971, pp. 151–158.

[GJ79] M. R. Garey, D. S. Johnson: *Computers and Intractibility. A Guide to the Theory on NP-Completeness*. W. H. Freeman and Company, 1979.

[Ho96] D. S. Hochbaum (Ed.): *Approximation Algorithms for NP-hard Problems*. PWS Publishing Company 1996.

[IK75] O. H. Ibarra, C. E. Kim: Fast approximation algorithms for the knapsack and sum of subsets problem. *J. of the ACM* 22 (1975), pp. 463–468.

[Jo74] D. S. Johnson: Approximation algorithms for combinatorial problems *JCSS* 9 (1974), pp. 256–278.

[Ka72] R. M. Karp: Reducibility among combinatorial problems. In: R. E. Miller, J.W. Thatcher (eds.): *Complexity of Computer Computations*, Plenum Press 1972, pp. 85–103.

[Lo75] L.Lovasz: On the ratio of the optimal integral and functional covers. *Discrete Mathematics* 13 (1975), pp. 383–390.

[Mi96] I. S. B. Mitchell: Guillotine subdivisions approximate polygonal subdivisions: Part II — a simple polynomial-time approximation scheme for geometric k-MST, TSP and related problems. Technical Report, Dept. of Applied Mathematics and Statistics, Stony Brook 1996.

[MPS98] E. W. Mayr, H. J. Premel, A. Steger (Eds.): *Lecture on Proof Verification and Approximation Algorithms. Lecture Notes in Computer Science* 1967, Springer 1998.

[Pa77] Ch. Papadimitriou: The Euclidean travelling salesman problem is NP-complete. *Theoretical Computer Science* 4 (1977), pp. 237–244.

[Pa94] Ch. Papadimitriou: *Computational Complexity*, Addison-Wesley 1994.

[We93] I. Wegener: *Theoretische Informatik: eine algorithmenorientierte Einführung*. B.G. Teubner 1993.

[Hr04] J. Hromkovič: *Theoretical Computer Science*, Springer-Verlag 2004.

[BBH+02] H.-J. Böckenhauer, D. Bongartz, J. Hromkovič, R. Klasing, G. Proietti, S. Seibert, W. Unger: On the Hardness of constructing mininal 2-connected spanning subgraphs in complete graphs with sharped triangle inequality. In: Proc *FSTTCS?02*, pp.59-70.

[Hr03] J. Hromkovič: *Algorithmics for Hard Problems. Introduction to Combinatorial Optimization, Randomization, Approximation, and Heuristics*. Springer-Verlag 2003.

[Va03] V. V. Vazirani: Approximation Algorithms. Springer-Verlag 2003.

[DF95] R.G. Downey, M. R. Fellows: Fixed-parameter tractibility and completeness I: Basic Results. *SIAM Journal of Computing*. 24 (1995), pp. 873–921.

[DF99] R.G. Downey, M. R. Fellows: *Parametrized Complexity*. Springer-Verlag 1999.

[FHP+04] L. Forlizzi, J. Hromkovič, G. Proietti, S. Seibert: On the stability of approximation for Hamiltonian path problems. Unpublished manuscript.

[BHK+00] H.-J. Böckenhauer, J. Hromkovič, R. Klasing, S. Seibert, W. Unger: Approximation algorithms for TSP with sharped triangle inequality. *Information Processing Letters*. 75 (2000), pp. 133-138.

[BS00] H.-J. Böckenhauer, S. Seibert: Improved lower bounds on the approximability of the traveling salesman problem. *Theoretical Informatics and Applications*. 34 (2000), pp. 213-255.

[AB95] T. Andreae, H. J. Bandelt: Performance guarentees for approximation algorithms depending on parametrized triangle inequalities. *SIAM Journal on Discrete Mathematics*. 8 (1), pp. 1-16, February 1995.

[BCh99] M. Bender, C. Chekuri: Performance guarentees for TSP with a parametrized triangle inequality. In: *Proc. 6. International Workshop on Algorithms and Data Structures, WADS?99*, volume 1663 *Lecture Notes in Computer Science*. pp. 1-16, Springer, August 1999.

[BHK+02] H.-J. Böckenhauer, J. Hromkovič, R. Klasing, S. Seibert, W. Unger: Towards the notion of stability of approximation for hard optimization tasks and the traveling salesman problem. *Theoretical Computer Science*. 285 (1), pp. 3-24, July 2002.

TOWARDS A BROADER THEORY OF MOBILE PROCESSES

Robin Milner
University of Cambridge, Cambridge, UK

Bigraphs are a topographical model of reactive systems that aim to unify existing theoretical approaches to mobile communicating agents. They combine two structures orthogonally: connectivity and locality. Thus, for example, they represent both ambients and pi-calculus; the topography deals not only with (even physical) locality but also with abstract notions such as the scope of a name. In my talk I shall explain how recent joint work with Jamey Leifer on relative pushouts enables transition systems to be derived for pi-calculus and ambients (in recent work by Ole Jensen), and I shall present condition-event Petri nets as an example.

A DECIDABLE ANALYSIS OF SECURITY PROTOCOLS

Michael Rusinowitch
LORIA
54602 Villers-lés-Nancy Cedex
France

Cryptographic protocols such as IKE, SET, TLS, Kerberos have been developed to secure electronic transactions. However the design of such protocols often appears to be problematic even assuming that the cryptographic primitives are perfect, i.e. even assuming we cannot decrypt a message without the right key. An intruder may intercept messages, analyse them, modify them with low computing power and then carry out malevolent actions. This may lead to a variety of attacks such as well-known Man-in-the-Middle attacks.

Even in this abstract model, the so-called Dolev-Yao model, protocol analysis is complex since the set of states to consider is huge or infinite. One should consider messages of any size, infinite number of sessions. The interleaving of parallel sessions generates a large search space. Also when we try to relax the perfect encryption hypothesis by taking into account some algebraic properties of operators then the task gets even more difficult.

We will present translation and constraint solving techniques developed in our Cassis team for automating protocol analysis in Dolev-Yao model and some of its extensions. Protocol specifications are compiled and then passed on decision procedures for checking automatically whether they are exposed to flaws.

LOOKING INSIDE $\mathcal{AES}$ AND $\mathcal{BES}$

Ilia Toli, Alberto Zanoni
Università degli Studi di Pisa
Dipartimento di Matematica "Leonida Tonelli"
Via F. Buonarroti 2, 56127 Pisa, Italy
{toli, zanoni}@posso.dm.unipi.it

Abstract We analyze an algebraic representation of $\mathcal{AES}$–128 as an embedding in $\mathcal{BES}$, due to Murphy and Robshaw. We present two systems of equations S^* and K^* concerning encryption and key generation processes. After some simple but rather cumbersome substitutions, we should obtain two new systems $\mathcal{C}_1$ and $\mathcal{C}_2$. $\mathcal{C}_1$ has 16 very dense equations of degree up to 255 in each of its 16 variables. With a single pair (p, c), with p a cleartext and c its encryption, its roots give all possible keys that should encrypt p to c. $\mathcal{C}_2$ may be defined using 11 or more pairs (p, c), and has 16 times as many equations in 176 variables. K^* and most of S^* is invariant for all key choices.

Keywords: Advanced Encryption Standard, $\mathcal{AES}$, $\mathcal{BES}$, $\mathcal{DES}$, Cryptography, Gröbner bases, Computer Algebra

Introduction

Rijndael is a block cipher, that encrypts blocks of 128, 192, and 256 bits using symmetric keys of 128, 192, and 256 bits. It was designed with a particular attention to bit-level attacks, such as *linear* and *differential cryptanalysis*. Its resistance to such attacks is the dichotomy between operations in $\mathbf{F} = GF(2^8)$ and $GF(2)$. Since its proposal, many new bit-level attacks, such as *impossible differential* and *truncated differential* have been proposed. Most of them break with some efficiency reduced versions of Rijndael, but they are not much better than exhaustive key search in the general case. In practice they are mainly academic arguments rather than real world threats to the security of $\mathcal{AES}$. The interested reader can find an account and some references about these cryptological tools in [ODR].

Another, new, cryptological tool is the algebraic representation of the cipher [MR; FSW; CP]. In this case, an eavesdropper tries to write the whole set of operations and parameters of the cipher as a system of polynomial equations, which he/she next tries to solve. In general, the systems are enormous. Solving them using general purpose techniques, such as Gröbner bases [CLO] is considered the wrong way to face the problem. However, the systems have sometimes an intrinsic structure, and the task may get easier. Not too much research is done in the topic: in particular, $\mathcal{AES}$ seems to have been designed without considering algebraic cryptanalysis tools.

In this paper we focus on the $\mathcal{BES}$ algebraic approach, due to Murphy and Robshaw [MR]. We present some algebraic aspects of representing $\mathcal{AES}$ as a system of polynomial equations following the $\mathcal{BES}$ approach. By means of successive substitutions, we are able to eliminate all intermediate variables, obtaining two systems $S^\star$ and $K^\star$ whose solution corresponds to code breaking. Actually, they are very complicated: their resolution is not trivial at all.

1. The $\mathcal{AES}$-128 cipher

The $\mathcal{AES}$ encryption algorithm is sketched below:

- Input a cleartext $\mathbf{x}$.
  - Initialize **State** $= \mathbf{x}$.
  - perform an operation **AddRoundKey**, in which **RoundKey** is **xor**-ed with the **State**.
- For nine (first to ninth) rounds:
  - perform a substitution operation called **SubBytes** on **State**, using an $\mathcal{S}$-box.
  - perform a permutation **ShiftRows** on **State**.
  - perform an operation **MixColumns** on **State**.
  - perform **AddRoundKey**.
- The tenth (last) round:
  - perform **SubBytes**.
  - perform **ShiftRows**.
  - perform **AddRoundKey**.
- Define the ciphertext $\mathbf{y}$ to be the **State**.

All $\mathcal{AES}$ operations are byte-oriented. The cleartext, ciphertext, and each output of intermediate steps of encryption and decryption algorithms are thought of as 4×4 matrices of bytes. The operations on each

s_{00}	s_{01}	s_{02}	s_{03}
s_{10}	s_{11}	s_{12}	s_{13}
s_{20}	s_{21}	s_{22}	s_{23}
s_{30}	s_{31}	s_{32}	s_{33}

$\Longrightarrow$

s_{00}	s_{01}	s_{02}	s_{03}
s_{11}	s_{12}	s_{13}	s_{10}
s_{22}	s_{23}	s_{20}	s_{21}
s_{33}	s_{30}	s_{31}	s_{32}

Figure 1. The **ShiftRows** operation on $\mathcal{AES}$

byte are those of the finite field $\mathbf{F} = GF(2^8)$. The elements are thought of as polynomials with coefficients in $GF(2)$, mod $(m(t))$, the so-called *Rijndael polynomial* :

$$m(t) = t^8 + t^4 + t^3 + t + 1 = \texttt{11b} . \tag{1}$$

They are represented as integers pairs in hexadecimal representation. If interpreted as eight–bit binary strings, we have the $t-$term exponents.

The **SubBytes** operation substitutes each of the bytes x with $\mathcal{S}(x)$:

$$\begin{aligned} \mathcal{S}(x) &= \texttt{63} + \texttt{8f}x^{127} + \texttt{b5}x^{191} + \texttt{01}x^{223} + \texttt{f4}x^{239} + \\ &\quad \texttt{25}x^{247} + \texttt{f9}x^{251} + \texttt{09}x^{253} + \texttt{05}x^{254} \end{aligned}$$

Actually, $\mathcal{S}(x)$ is a permutation polynomial.
The **ShiftRows** operation permutes bytes in each row, see Figure 1.

The **MixColumns** operation performs a permutation of bytes in each column using a matrix in $GL(\mathbf{F}, 4)$, introduced later in Section 2.1. In practice, the columns are considered as polynomials in $\mathbf{F}[x]$, and multiplied mod $(x^4 + 1)$ by the polynomial $a(x)$:

$$a(x) = \texttt{03}x^3 + \texttt{01}x^2 + \texttt{01}x + \texttt{02}. \tag{2}$$

Now consider the key schedule. The key used in every cipher round is successively obtained by the key of the precedent one. Here is the complete procedure.

- Input a key $\mathbf{h}_0$. Initialize $\mathbf{H}_0 = \mathbf{h}_0$.
- For each round $r = 1, \ldots, 10$, permute (**RotWord**) the sub-vector formed by the last four elements (word) of $\mathbf{H}_{r-1}$, see Figure 2.
- Perform the **SubWord** ($\mathcal{S}$-box on each byte) operation on the obtained result, and add the vector $\mathbf{Rcon}_r = (t^{r-1}, 0, 0, 0)$.
- Define the other elements by means of bitwise **xor** operations in terms of the obtained result and other words from $\mathbf{H}_{r-1}$.
- Define the set of keys to be $\mathbf{h}$ to be $\{\mathbf{H}_r \mid r = 0, \ldots, 10\}$.

Figure 2. The **RotWord** operation on $\mathcal{AES}$

Consider each vector as a four-words set, indicated with a second index ranging from 0 to 3 indicating single parts. For $\mathbf{y} \in \mathbf{F}^4$ we put $\varphi_A^r(\mathbf{y}) = \mathbf{SubWord(RotWord`(y))} + \mathbf{Rcon}_r$. The rth round for $\mathcal{AES}$ key generation scheme is:

$$\mathcal{K}_A = \begin{cases} \mathbf{H}_{r0} = \varphi_A^r(\mathbf{H}_{r-1,3}) \\ \mathbf{H}_{r1} = \mathbf{H}_{r0} + \mathbf{H}_{r-1,1} \\ \mathbf{H}_{r2} = \mathbf{H}_{r1} + \mathbf{H}_{r-1,2} \\ \mathbf{H}_{r3} = \mathbf{H}_{r2} + \mathbf{H}_{r-1,3} \end{cases} \Longrightarrow \mathbf{H}_r = (\mathbf{H}_{r0}, \mathbf{H}_{r1}, \mathbf{H}_{r2}, \mathbf{H}_{r3}) \qquad (3)$$

2. The $\mathcal{BES}$ cipher

We start from the $\mathcal{BES}$ cipher, in which $\mathcal{AES}$ is embedded by a "natural" mapping. $\mathcal{BES}$ operations involve only computations in $\mathbf{F}$. This permits to describe $\mathcal{AES}$ using polynomial equation systems. Solving them means to find the key or an alias, and therefore to break the code.

The state spaces of $\mathcal{AES}$ and $\mathcal{BES}$ are respectively $\mathbf{A} = \mathbf{F}^{16}$ and $\mathbf{B} = \mathbf{F}^{128}$. The basic tool for embedding is the *conjugation* ϕ, taking for each value in $\mathbf{F}$ eight successive square powers.

$$\mathbf{F} \ni a \longmapsto \phi(a) = \tilde{\mathbf{a}} = (a^{2^0}, a^{2^1}, ..., a^{2^7}) \in \mathbf{F}^8 \qquad (4)$$

$$\mathbf{F}^n \ni \mathbf{a} \longmapsto \phi(\mathbf{a}) = \tilde{\mathbf{a}} = (\phi(a_0), ..., \phi(a_7)) \in \mathbf{F}^{8n} \qquad (5)$$

It is easily verified that (with $0^{-1} = 0$)

$$\phi(\mathbf{a} + \mathbf{a}') = \phi(\mathbf{a}) + \phi(\mathbf{a}') \qquad \text{and} \qquad \phi(\mathbf{a}^{-1}) = \phi(\mathbf{a})^{-1} \qquad (6)$$

and we define $\mathbf{B_A} = \phi(\mathbf{A}) \subset \mathbf{B}$ as the subset of $\mathbf{B}$ corresponding to $\mathbf{A}$.

Let $\mathbf{p}, \mathbf{c} \in \mathbf{B}$ be the plaintext and ciphertext, respectively; $\mathbf{w}_i$, $\mathbf{x}_i \in \mathbf{B}$ $(0 \leq i \leq 9)$ the state vectors before and after the inversion phases, and $\mathbf{h}_i \in \mathbf{B}$ the used keys.

2.1 Correspondence

The matrix $L_A : \mathbf{F} \simeq GF(2)^8 \to GF(2)^8 \simeq \mathbf{F}$ for the one-byte affine transformation in the $\mathcal{S}$-box phase can be represented by the polynomial function $f : \mathbf{F} \to \mathbf{F}$:

$$f(a) = \sum_{k=0}^{7} \lambda_k a^{2^k} \qquad (7)$$

with

$$
\begin{array}{ll}
\lambda_0 = t^2 + 1 & \lambda_4 = t^7 + t^6 + t^5 + t^4 + t^2 \\
\lambda_1 = t^3 + 1 & \lambda_5 = 1 \\
\lambda_2 = t^7 + t^6 + t^5 + t^4 + t^3 + 1 & \lambda_6 = t^7 + t^5 + t^4 + t^2 + 1 \\
\lambda_3 = t^5 + t^2 + 1 & \lambda_7 = t^7 + t^3 + t^2 + t + 1
\end{array} \tag{8}
$$

Working in $\mathbf{B}$, $L_B(a) = \phi(L_A(a)) = (f(a)^{2^0}, \ldots, f(a)^{2^7})$. The successive squares of f are needed, and the answer is given by a simple induction with basic step

$$
(f(a))^2 = \left(\sum_{k=0}^{7} \lambda_k a^{2^k} \right)^2 = \sum_{k=0}^{7} \lambda_k^2 a^{2^k \cdot 2} = \sum_{k=0}^{7} \lambda_k^2 a^{2^{k+1}} \tag{9}
$$

The resulting matrix, still indicated with L_B, is

$$
L_B = [l_{ij}]_{i,j=0,\ldots 7} \qquad \text{with} \qquad l_{ij} = \lambda^{2^i}_{(8-i+j) \bmod 8} \tag{10}
$$

The global transformation $\mathrm{Lin}_B : \mathbf{F}^{128} \to \mathbf{F}^{128}$ is the block diagonal matrix with 16 blocks equal to L_B.

The $\mathcal{AES}$ $\mathcal{S}$-box constant $c_A = 63 = t^6 + t^5 + t + 1 \in \mathbf{F}$ goes into:

$$
\begin{aligned}
\phi(c_A) \;=\; & (63, \mathtt{C2}, 35, 66, \mathtt{D3}, \mathtt{2F}, 39, 36) = (t^6 + t^5 + t + 1, t^7 + t^6 + t, \\
& t^5 + t^4 + t^2 + 1, t^6 + t^5 + t^2 + t, t^7 + t^6 + t^4 + t + 1, \\
& t^5 + t^3 + t^2 + t + 1, t^5 + t^4 + t^3 + 1, t^5 + t^4 + t^2 + t)
\end{aligned} \tag{11}
$$

The corresponding $\mathcal{BES}$ vector $\mathbf{c}_B$ is obtained using sufficient copies

$$
\mathbf{c}_B = \phi(\underbrace{c_A, \ldots, c_A}_{16}) = (\underbrace{\phi(c_A), \ldots, \phi(c_A)}_{16}) \qquad [\mathbf{c}_B]_i = [\phi(c_A)]_{i \bmod 8} \tag{12}
$$

The $\mathcal{AES}$ **ShiftRows** may be represented by $R_A : \mathbf{F}^{16} \to \mathbf{F}^{16}$.

$$
R_A = \left(\begin{array}{cccc|cccc|cccc|cccc}
1&0&0&0&0&0&0&0&0&0&0&0&0&0&0&0\\
0&0&0&0&0&1&0&0&0&0&0&0&0&0&0&0\\
0&0&0&0&0&0&0&0&0&0&1&0&0&0&0&0\\
0&0&0&0&0&0&0&0&0&0&0&0&0&0&0&1\\
\hline
0&0&0&0&1&0&0&0&0&0&0&0&0&0&0&0\\
0&0&0&0&0&0&0&0&0&1&0&0&0&0&0&0\\
0&0&0&0&0&0&0&0&0&0&0&0&0&0&1&0\\
0&0&0&1&0&0&0&0&0&0&0&0&0&0&0&0\\
\hline
0&0&0&0&0&0&0&0&1&0&0&0&0&0&0&0\\
0&0&0&0&0&0&0&0&0&0&0&0&0&1&0&0\\
0&0&1&0&0&0&0&0&0&0&0&0&0&0&0&0\\
0&0&0&0&0&0&0&1&0&0&0&0&0&0&0&0\\
\hline
0&0&0&0&0&0&0&0&0&0&0&0&1&0&0&0\\
0&1&0&0&0&0&0&0&0&0&0&0&0&0&0&0\\
0&0&0&0&0&0&1&0&0&0&0&0&0&0&0&0\\
0&0&0&0&0&0&0&0&0&0&0&1&0&0&0&0
\end{array}\right) \tag{13}
$$

"Expanding" each 1 in R_A with an identity matrix of order 8, I_8, and each 0 with a zero (8×8) matrix, we have $R_B : \mathbf{F}^{128} \to \mathbf{F}^{128}$.

The $\mathcal{AES}$ **MixColumns** may be represented by $C_A : \mathbf{F}^4 \to \mathbf{F}^4$:

$$C_A = \begin{pmatrix} t & t+1 & 1 & 1 \\ 1 & t & t+1 & 1 \\ 1 & 1 & t & t+1 \\ t+1 & 1 & 1 & t \end{pmatrix} \tag{14}$$

The $\mathcal{AES}$ transformation is given by the $\mathrm{Mix}_A : \mathbf{F}^{16} \to \mathbf{F}^{16}$ block diagonal matrix having as blocks four copies of C_A. In order to obtain the corresponding matrix we first need to compute $C_B^{(k)}$, for $k = 0, \ldots, 7$:

$$C_B^{(k)} = \begin{pmatrix} t^{2^k} & (t+1)^{2^k} & 1 & 1 \\ 1 & t^{2^k} & (t+1)^{2^k} & 1 \\ 1 & 1 & t^{2^k} & (t+1)^{2^k} \\ (t+1)^{2^k} & 1 & 1 & t^{2^k} \end{pmatrix} \tag{15}$$

where

$$\begin{array}{lll} t^{2^0} = t & t^{2^3} = t^4 + t^3 + t + 1 & t^{2^6} = t^6 + t^3 + t^2 + 1 \\ t^{2^1} = t^2 & t^{2^4} = t^6 + t^4 + t^3 + t^2 + t & t^{2^7} = t^7 + t^6 + t^5 + t^4 + t^3 + t \\ t^{2^2} = t^4 & t^{2^5} = t^7 + t^6 + t^5 + t^2 & \end{array} \tag{16}$$

from which $(t+1)^{2^k} = t^{2^k} + 1$ are immediately obtained.

In an appropriate basis, the resulting matrix $\mathrm{M}_B : \mathbf{F}^{128} \to \mathbf{F}^{128}$ is a block diagonal one, with four consecutive copies of $C_B^{(k)}$ for all possible k. The change of basis is necessary because of the different positioning of value powers in ϕ's image with respect to our needs. Indeed, if $\mathbf{a} \in \mathbf{F}^{16}$, then:

$$\phi(\mathbf{a}) = (a_0, \ldots, a_0^{2^7}, a_1, \ldots, a_1^{2^7}, \ldots, a_{15}, \ldots, a_{15}^{2^7}) \tag{17}$$

while to use the block diagonal representation, we would need:

$$\mathbf{a}' = (a_0, \ldots, a_{15}, a_0^2, \ldots, a_{15}^2, \ldots, a_0^{2^7}, \ldots, a_{15}^{2^7}) \tag{18}$$

This transformation is given by a permutation matrix $\mathrm{Perm}_B : \mathbf{F}^{128} \to \mathbf{F}^{128}$. To represent it easily, suppose to divide it into (16×8) sub-matrices P_{hk}, $h = 0, \ldots, 7, k = 0, \ldots, 15$. Each sub-matrix element (with $i = 0, \ldots, 15$, $j = 0, \ldots, 7$) is:

$$[P_{hk}]_{ij} = \begin{cases} 1 & \text{if } i = k \text{ and } j = h \\ 0 & \text{else} \end{cases} \tag{19}$$

Its inverse matrix $\mathrm{Perm}_B^{(-1)}$ is equally easy to describe: viewing it as composed of (8×16) sub-matrices $P_{hk}^{(-1)}$, with $h=0,\ldots,15$, $k=0,\ldots,7$, the generic element $[P_{hk}^{(-1)}]_{ij}$ (with $i=0,\ldots,7$, $j=0,\ldots,15$) is defined exactly as $[P_{hk}]_{ij}$ is. We have $\mathrm{Mix}_B = \mathrm{Perm}_B^{-1}\cdot M_B\cdot \mathrm{Perm}_B$.

We can avoid c_A slightly modifying the key generation scheme with respect to the original proposal. If $\mathbf{b}, (\mathbf{h}_B)_i \in \mathbf{B}$ are the state and key vectors for the generic i^{th} round of $\mathcal{BES}$, we have:

$$\begin{aligned}\mathrm{Round}_B(\mathbf{b},(\mathbf{h}_B)_i) &= \mathrm{Mix}_B(R_B(\mathrm{Lin}_B(\mathbf{b}^{-1})+\mathbf{c}_B))+(\mathbf{h}_B)_i\\ &= M_B\cdot(\mathbf{b}^{-1})+(C_B(\mathbf{c}_B)+(\mathbf{h}_B)_i)\\ &= M_B\cdot(\mathbf{b}^{-1})+(\mathbf{k}_B)_i\end{aligned} \tag{20}$$

with

$$M_B=\mathrm{Mix}_B\cdot R_B\cdot \mathrm{Lin}_B\ ,\quad C_B=\mathrm{Mix}_B\cdot R_B\ ,\quad (\mathbf{k}_B)_i=C_B(\mathbf{c}_B)+(\mathbf{h}_B)_i \tag{21}$$

For the last round, being Mix_B absent, we have

$$(\mathbf{k}_B)_i = R_B(\mathbf{c}_B)+(\mathbf{h}_B)_i \tag{22}$$

but in this particular case we have $C_B(\mathbf{c}_B)=R_B(\mathbf{c}_B)$, and for what concerns this, we can avoid to distinguish the last round from the precedent ones. The change for key generation scheme is simply the addition of a constant vector to each obtained round key, and this will be the form of the system we will work with.

Now we analyze the $\mathcal{BES}$ translation for the key generation scheme.

- The $\mathcal{AES}$ **RotWord** operation is represented by $RW_A:\mathbf{F}^4\to\mathbf{F}^4$.

$$RW_A=\begin{pmatrix}0&1&0&0\\0&0&1&0\\0&0&0&1\\1&0&0&0\end{pmatrix} \tag{23}$$

  For the $\mathcal{BES}$ version $RW_B:\mathbf{F}^{32}\longrightarrow\mathbf{F}^{32}$, replace the 1's with I_8, and 0's with the (8×8) zero matrix.

- The $\mathcal{S}$-box is here applied only to a part of the whole vector, and therefore the matrix dimension changes. The resulting block diagonal matrix $\mathrm{Lin}_B^k:\mathbf{F}^{32}\longrightarrow\mathbf{F}^{32}$ has four blocks equal to L_B.

- The constant $\mathbf{c}_B^k$ is given by just four copies of $\phi(c_A)$:

$$\mathbf{c}_B^k=\phi(c_A,c_A,c_A,c_A)=(\phi(c_A),\ldots,\phi(c_A))\ ,\quad [\mathbf{c}_B^k]_i=[\phi(c_A)]_{i \bmod 8} \tag{24}$$

- The constant vectors $\mathbf{Rcon}_i = (t^{i-1}, 0, 0, 0)$ are mapped into:

$$(\mathbf{Rcon}_B)_i = \phi(\mathbf{Rcon}_i) = (\phi(t^{r-1}), \underbrace{0, \ldots, 0}_{24}) \tag{25}$$

We keep using the matrix notation, but here in a *functional* sense. We *have* here to use constants. If $\varphi_B^i : \mathbf{F}^{32} \to \mathbf{F}^{32}$ is the $\mathcal{BES}$ i^{th}-round mapping function for a conjugated word $\mathbf{x}$:

$$\varphi_B^i(\mathbf{x}) = \mathrm{Lin}_B^k(RW_B(\mathbf{x}))^{-1} + \mathbf{c}_B^k + (\mathbf{Rcon}_B)_i \tag{26}$$

the generic $\mathcal{AES}$ and $\mathcal{BES}$ key round matrices are MK_A^i and MK_B^i :

$$MK_A^i = \begin{pmatrix} 0 & 0 & 0 & \varphi_A^i \\ 0 & I_4 & 0 & \varphi_A^i \\ 0 & I_4 & I_4 & \varphi_A^i \\ 0 & I_4 & I_4 & I_4 + \varphi_A^i \end{pmatrix}, \quad MK_B^i = \begin{pmatrix} 0 & 0 & 0 & \varphi_B^i \\ 0 & I_{32} & 0 & \varphi_B^i \\ 0 & I_{32} & I_{32} & \varphi_B^i \\ 0 & I_{32} & I_{32} & I_{32} + \varphi_B^i \end{pmatrix} \tag{27}$$

A key round is the computation of $\mathbf{h}_i = MK_B^i(\mathbf{h}_{r-1})$.

3. Polynomial Systems

We show how encryption and key generation can be represented by algebraic systems. All variables satisfy the $\mathbf{F}$-belonging equation $y^{256} + y = 0$.

3.1 Encryption

Remembering that the last round differs slightly from the other ones, with $M_B^* = R_B \cdot \mathrm{Lin}_B$, the system for codification is [MR] :

$$\begin{cases} \mathbf{w}_0 = \mathbf{p} + \mathbf{k}_0 & \\ \mathbf{x}_i = \mathbf{w}_i^{-1} & i = 0, \ldots, 9 \\ \mathbf{w}_i = M_B \mathbf{x}_{i-1} + \mathbf{k}_i & i = 1, \ldots, 9 \\ \mathbf{c} = M_B^* \mathbf{x}_9 + \mathbf{k}_{10} & \end{cases} \tag{28}$$

Let (j, m) indicate the $(8j + m)^{\text{th}}$ component of all the vectors, for $j = 0, \ldots, 15$ and $m = 0, \ldots, 7$. If no 0-inversion occurs (true for the 53% of encryptions and 85% of 128-bit keys), it is possible to expand the system as follows, for all possible values of j and m

$$\begin{cases} 0 = w_{0,(j,m)} + p_{(j,m)} + k_{0,(j,m)} & \\ 0 = x_{i,(j,m)} w_{i,(j,m)} + 1 & i = 0, \ldots, 9 \\ 0 = w_{i,(j,m)} + (M_B \mathbf{x}_{i-1})_{(j,m)} + k_{i,(j,m)} & i = 1, \ldots, 9 \\ 0 = c_{(j,m)} + (M_B^* \mathbf{x}_9)_{(j,m)} + k_{10,(j,m)} & \end{cases} \tag{29}$$

Let $\alpha, \beta \in \mathbf{F}$ indicate respectively M_B and M_B^* entries. Everything must be valid for $\mathbf{B_A}$, therefore we have (with $m+1$ considered mod 8)

$$S = \begin{cases} 0 = w_{0,(j,m)} + p_{(j,m)} + k_{0,(j,m)} & \\ 0 = w_{i,(j,m)} + k_{i,(j,m)} + \sum_{(j',m')} \alpha_{(j,m),(j',m')} x_{i-1,(j',m')} & i = 1,\dots,9 \\ 0 = c_{(j,m)} + k_{10,(j,m)} + \sum_{(j',m')} \beta_{(j,m),(j',m')} x_{9,(j',m')} & \\ 0 = x_{i,(j,m)} w_{i,(j,m)} + 1 & i = 0,\dots,9 \\ 0 = x_{i,(j,m)}^2 + x_{i,(j,m+1)} & i = 0,\dots,9 \\ 0 = w_{i,(j,m)}^2 + w_{i,(j,m+1)} & i = 0,\dots,9 \end{cases} \tag{30}$$

Let S_ℓ, $\ell = 1,\dots,6$ be the equations in the ℓth line of the system for all values of i, j and m, and I_ℓ the ideal they generate. As we see, the system is very sparse, with $S' = \{S_1, S_2, S_3\}$ linear, and the other equations in $S'' = \{S_4, S_5, S_6\}$ quadratic. If $\mathbf{k} = \{\mathbf{k}_i\}$, $\mathbf{w} = \{\mathbf{w}_i\}$, $\mathbf{x} = \{\mathbf{x}_i\}$, we have

Line	*Number of equations*	
S_1	$16 \cdot 8 =$	128
S_2	$9 \cdot 16 \cdot 8 =$	1152
S_3	$16 \cdot 8 =$	128
S_4	$10 \cdot 16 \cdot 8 =$	1280
S_5	$10 \cdot 16 \cdot 8 =$	1280
S_6	$10 \cdot 16 \cdot 8 =$	1280
S	Total =	5248

Block	*Number of variables*	
k	$11 \cdot 16 \cdot 8 =$	1408
x	$10 \cdot 16 \cdot 8 =$	1280
w	$10 \cdot 16 \cdot 8 =$	1280
	Total =	3968

3.2 Key Generation

There is an analogous system for key generation. The equations express all the $h_{i,(j,m)}$ variables in term of the $h_{0,(j,m)}$ ones. The index ranges for the equations are: $i = 1,\dots,10$, $\tilde{j}, \tilde{j}' = 0,\dots,3$ and $m, m' = 0,\dots,7$, and γ are the Lin_B^k matrix coefficients.

$$\mathcal{K}_B = \begin{cases} \tilde{\mathbf{H}}_{i0} = \varphi_B^i(\tilde{\mathbf{H}}_{i-1,3}) \\ \tilde{\mathbf{H}}_{i1} = \tilde{\mathbf{H}}_{i0} + \tilde{\mathbf{H}}_{i-1,1} \\ \tilde{\mathbf{H}}_{i2} = \tilde{\mathbf{H}}_{i1} + \tilde{\mathbf{H}}_{i-1,2} \\ \tilde{\mathbf{H}}_{i3} = \tilde{\mathbf{H}}_{i2} + \tilde{\mathbf{H}}_{i-1,3} \end{cases} = \tag{31}$$

$$= \begin{cases} z_{i,(\tilde{j},m)} & = h_{i-1,(12+[(\tilde{j}+1) \bmod 4],m)}^{254} \\ h_{i,(\tilde{j},m)} & = (\mathbf{c}_B^k + (\mathbf{Rcon}_B)_i)_{(\tilde{j},m)} + \sum_{(\tilde{j}',m')} \gamma_{(\tilde{j},m)(\tilde{j}',m')} z_{i,(\tilde{j}',m')} \\ h_{i,(4s+\tilde{j},m)} & = h_{i,(4(s-1)+\tilde{j},m)} + h_{i-1,(4s+\tilde{j},m)} \qquad s = 1,2,3 \end{cases}$$

Let $\mathbf{cR}_i = \mathbf{c}_B^k + (\mathbf{Rcon}_B)_i$ be the vector in each round, and its components δ_i. Thanks to the third equivalence of (21), with $t = 0, \ldots, 15$ and the conjugation property, we have:

$$K = \begin{cases} 0 = z_{i,(\jmath,m)} + h_{i-1,(12+[(\jmath+1) \bmod 4],m)}^{254} \\ 0 = h_{i,(\jmath,m)} + \delta_{i,(\jmath,m)} + \sum_{(\jmath',m')} \gamma_{(\jmath,m)(\jmath',m')} z_{i,(\jmath',m')} \\ 0 = h_{i,(4s+\jmath,m)} + h_{i,(4(s-1)+\jmath,m)} + h_{i-1,(4s+\jmath,m)} & s = 1,2,3 \\ 0 = k_{i,(t,m)} + (C_B(\mathbf{c_B}))_{(t,m)} + h_{i,(t,m)} \\ 0 = z_{i,(\jmath,m)}^2 + z_{i,(\jmath,m+1)} \\ 0 = h_{i,(\jmath,m)}^2 + h_{i,(\jmath,m+1)} \end{cases} \tag{32}$$

4. Resolution

We are interested in obtaining the key out of the systems S and K, that is the original key $\mathbf{h} = \phi^{-1}(\mathbf{k}^\star) = \{h_0, \ldots, h_{15}\}$, where $\mathbf{k}^\star = \{k_{0,(0,m)}, \ldots, k_{0,(15,m)}\}$.

In order to obtain relations among $\mathbf{h}$ ($\mathbf{k}$) components we eliminate all other variables. We do this:

- modifying the way the systems are presented,
- doing some "hand" substitutions, and finally
- performing Gröbner bases computations (more complicated substitutions, expansions and simplifications) to obtain the final systems.

Note that, for each variable $v \in \mathbf{k}, \mathbf{w}, \mathbf{z}, \mathbf{h}$, the conjugation property may be synthesized by the obvious following relations:

$$v_{i,(j,m)} = v_{i,(j,0)}^{2^m} \qquad m = 0, \ldots, 7 \tag{33}$$

4.1 Encryption

We rewrite S: first of all, we remove the imposed restriction about inversion, substituting S_4 with an equation expressing the true definition of the general inversion in $\mathbf{F}$. Then we use (33), to remove all the variables with index $m > 0$, obtaining:

$$S^\star = \begin{cases} 0 = w_{0,(j,0)}^{2^m} + p_{(j,0)}^{2^m} + k_{0,(j,0)}^{2^m} & \\ 0 = w_{i,(j,0)}^{2^m} + k_{i,(j,0)}^{2^m} + \sum_{(j',m')} \alpha_{(j,m),(j',m')} x_{i-1,(j',0)}^{2^{m'}} & i = 1,\dots,9 \\ 0 = c_{(j,0)}^{2^m} + k_{10,(j,0)}^{2^m} + \sum_{(j',m')} \beta_{(j,m),(j',m')} x_{9,(j',0)}^{2^{m'}} & \\ 0 = x_{i,(j,0)} + w_{i,(j,0)}^{254} & i = 0,\dots,9 \end{cases} \tag{34}$$

With the last equation we can remove all the $x_{i,(j,0)}$, and, being each line a set of successive square powers, we keep only the ones with $m = 0$:

$$S^\star = \begin{cases} 0 = w_{0,(j,0)} + p_{(j,0)} + k_{0,(j,0)} & \\ 0 = w_{i,(j,0)} + k_{i,(j,0)} + \sum_{(j',m')} \alpha_{(j,0),(j',m')} w_{i-1,(j',0)}^{254\cdot 2^{m'}} & i = 1,\dots,9 \\ 0 = c_{(j,0)} + k_{10,(j,0)} + \sum_{(j',m')} \beta_{(j,0),(j',m')} w_{9,(j',0)}^{254\cdot 2^{m'}} & \end{cases} \tag{35}$$

We note that the β coefficients do not depend on j and j', and the values are simply the coefficients of f. To simplify notations even more, we take, mod 255:

$$\begin{aligned} \omega &= (\omega_i) = 254 \cdot (2^0,\dots,2^7) = (254, 253, 251, 247, 239, 223, 191, 127)\ , \\ \omega' &= (\omega_i') = (\omega_0 - 127,\dots,\omega_7 - 127) = (127, 126, 124, 120, 112, 96, 64, 0) \end{aligned}$$

We can now avoid writing m index:

$$S^\star = \begin{cases} 0 = w_{0,j} + p_j + k_{0,j} & \\ 0 = w_{i,j} + k_{i,j} + \sum_{(j',m')} \alpha_{(j,0),(j',m')} w_{i-1,j'}^{\omega_{m'}} & i = 1,\dots,9 \\ 0 = k_{10,j} + c_j + \sum_{m'} \lambda_{m'} w_{9,j'}^{\omega_{m'}} & \end{cases} \tag{36}$$

The system has $16+9\cdot16+16 = 176$ equations in $11\cdot16+10\cdot16 = 336$ variables. Obviously, it expresses nothing but a series of successive substitutions, down to the last equation. Considering a block lexicographic (lex) order for which

$$\mathbf{k}_{10} > \mathbf{w}_9 > \mathbf{k}_9 > \cdots > \mathbf{w}_0 > \mathbf{k}_0 \tag{37}$$

we have a (not reduced) Gröbner basis [CLO], and the substitutions may be considered as the complete reduction computation. The resulting set of the last 16 equations, where all the $\mathbf{w}$ variables are no more present, is what we are looking for. If q_j^S are the resulting polynomials, we have:

$$k_{10,j} + c_j + q_j^S(\mathbf{k}_0, \ldots, \mathbf{k}_9, p) = 0 \qquad j = 0, \ldots, 15 \tag{38}$$

4.2 Key Generation

We get more informations analyzing K. We

- substitute $\mathbf{z}$ variables in the second line equations.
- use the conjugation property,
- note that $C_B(\mathbf{c_B})$ has $c_A = t^6 + t^5 + t + 1$ in the $(j, 0)$ positions, and opportune powers in the other ones. This means that the equations on the fourth line of K, K_4, may be reduced (the other ones being powers of it) to:

$$h_{i,(j,0)} + k_{i,(j,0)} + c_A = 0 \tag{39}$$

- for the above considerations, express everything directly in term of $\mathbf{k}$ variables.
- observe that Lin_B^k is a block diagonal matrix, and therefore just $\tilde{\jmath}' = \tilde{\jmath}$ is "active" for each single equation, and what remains is nothing more than the set of coefficients of the f polynomial.

We define in : $\mathbf{N} \ni n \to \mathrm{in}(n) = 12 + [(n+1) \bmod 4] \in \mathbf{N}$. After the elaboration, always remembering the $\mathbf{F}$-belonging equation, we have the following system (where $i = 1, \ldots, 10$; $s, \tilde{\jmath} = 0, \ldots, 3$ and in the last version we omit m)

$$K^\star = \begin{cases} 0 = h_{i,(\tilde{\jmath},0)} + \delta_{i,(\tilde{\jmath},0)} + \sum\limits_{(\tilde{\jmath}',m')} \gamma_{(\tilde{\jmath},0)(\tilde{\jmath}',m')} h_{i-1,(\mathrm{in}(\tilde{\jmath}'),0)}^{254 \cdot 2^{m'}} \\ 0 = h_{i,(4s+\tilde{\jmath},0)} + h_{i,(4(s-1)+\tilde{\jmath},0)} + h_{i-1,(4s+\tilde{\jmath},0)} \\ 0 = h_{i,(\tilde{\jmath},0)} + (k_{i,(\tilde{\jmath},0)} + c_A) \end{cases} =$$

$$\begin{cases} 0 = (k_{i,(\tilde{\jmath},0)} + c_A) + \delta_{i,(\tilde{\jmath},0)} + \sum\limits_{m'} \gamma_{(\tilde{\jmath},0)(\tilde{\jmath},m')} (k_{i-1,(\mathrm{in}(\tilde{\jmath}),0)} + c_A)^{\omega_{m'}} \\ 0 = (k_{i,(4s+\tilde{\jmath},0)} + c_A) + (k_{i,(4(s-1)+\tilde{\jmath},0)} + c_A) + (k_{i-1,(4s+\tilde{\jmath},0)} + c_A) \end{cases} =$$

$$\begin{cases} 0 = k_{i,\tilde{\jmath}} + (c_A + \delta_{i,(\tilde{\jmath},0)}) + (k_{i-1,\mathrm{in}(\tilde{\jmath})} + c_A)^{127} \cdot \left(\sum\limits_{m'} \lambda_{m'} (k_{i-1,\mathrm{in}(\tilde{\jmath})} + c_A)^{\omega'_{m'}} \right) \\ 0 = k_{i,4s+\tilde{\jmath}} + k_{i,4(s-1)+\tilde{\jmath}} + k_{i-1,4s+\tilde{\jmath}} + c_A \end{cases}$$

Only $\mathbf{k}$ variables remain, 160 equations in 176 variables, and by successive substitutions we can express all the ones with $i > 0$ as polynomials in the "parameters" $\mathbf{k}_0$. The equations are a Gröbner basis for several suitable lex orderings. We may obtain its complete reduction using, e.g.

$$k_{10,15} > \ldots > k_{10,0} > \cdots > k_{0,15} > \ldots > k_{0,0} \tag{40}$$

It is possible to work with $\mathbf{h}$ variables to obtain the equations following the original $\mathcal{AES}$ definition, and use (39) only at the end, in order to obtain the modified key generation scheme. In any case, the result is:

$$k_{i,j} = q^K_{i,j}(\mathbf{k}_0) \qquad i = 1, \ldots, 10 \quad , \quad j = 0, \ldots, 15 \tag{41}$$

In the final phase we merge the results. There are two possibilities, according to how many (p, c) pairs (related by the same key) are known.

One (p, c) pair : We eliminate all intermediate keys, putting together the systems $S^\star$ and $K^\star$, refining (37) with (40). We obtain the entire substitution process once and for all, summarized as follows:

$$\begin{aligned} \mathcal{C}_1 = \{\ q^K_{10,j}(\mathbf{k}_0) + c_j + q^S_j(\mathbf{k}_0, q^K_{1,j}(\mathbf{k}_0), \ldots, q^K_{9,j}(\mathbf{k}_0), p) = 0 \\ \mid\ j = 0, \ldots, 15\ \} \end{aligned} \tag{42}$$

a system of 16 equations in 16 variables, having as roots the desired keys.

More than 10 (p, c) pairs : We use a copy of (38) for each (p, c) pair, to obtain a system in 176 variables with at least 176 equations, whose roots give *all* the keys.

$$\begin{aligned} \mathcal{C}_2 = \{\ k_{10,j} + c^{(n)}_j + q^S_j(\mathbf{k}_0, \ldots, \mathbf{k}_9, p^{(n)}) = 0 \\ \mid\ n = 1, \ldots, d \quad , \quad j = 0, \ldots, 15\ \} \end{aligned} \tag{43}$$

These systems are dense, it is very difficult to write them explicitly, and even more to solve them. Using more than 11 (p, c) the $\mathcal{C}_2$ system becomes overdetermined.

5. Conclusions

$K^\star$ and most of $S^\star$ are invariant for all choices of keys. Actually, the only varying parts of $S^\star$ are the constant terms of the equations 1 to 16, and 161 to 176. Besides, for the equations 1 to 16, it can be chosen, too, if convenient.

When extended, the joint size of $K^\star$ and $S^\star$ is of about 500 Kb. Each of them is a (not reduced) Gröbner basis for several lex orderings, their union is not. Probably there exists some ordering for which the calculus of a Gröbner basis is easier. If we ever can obtain this with reasonable computational resources, then $\mathcal{AES}$ can be declared broken.

Succeeding to calculate the Hilbert series of $K^{\star} \cup S^{\star}$, we should easily obtain the number n_s of its solutions. We suspect that n_s is invariant for all key and (p, c) choices. Furthermore, we expect that n_s expresses the redundancy of the keyspace of $\mathcal{AES}$. That is, it tells us how many key choices will set up the same bijection between the cleartext space and ciphertext space. The number of such bijections is expected to be:

$$\frac{\#(\mathcal{AES}\text{ Keyspace})}{n_s} \tag{44}$$

Probably a reasonably simple canonical representation of such bijections can be found. In this case, if n_s is big enough, probably the right (unique up to the isomorphism) key can be found by means of an exhaustive search.

References

D. A. Cox, J. Little, D. O'Shea. Ideals, Varieties, and Algorithms, An Introduction to Computational Algebraic Geometry and Commutative Algebra. Springer-Verlag, New York, *1992*.

N. Courtois, J. Pieprzyk. *Cryptanalysis of block ciphers with overdefined systems of equations*. IACR eprint server `www.iacr.org`, *2002*.

J. Daemen, V. Rijmen. *AES proposal: Rijndael (Version 2)*. NIST AES website: `http://csrc.nist.gov/encryption/aes`, *1999*.

J. Daemen, V. Rijmen. *The design of Rijndael: AES - The Advanced Encryption Standard*. Springer-Verlag, *2002*.

National Institute of Standards and Technology. Advanced Encryption Standard. FIPS *197*. *26* November *2001*.

N. Ferguson, R. Schroeppel, D. Whiting. A simple algebraic representation of Rijndael. In *Selected Areas in Cryptography*, Proc. SAC *2001*, Lecture Notes in Computer Science *2259*, pp. *103-111*, Springer Verlag, *2001*.

G.-M. Greuel, G. Pfister, H. Schönemann. SINGULAR *2-0-3*. A Computer Algebra System for Polynomial Computations. Center for Computer Algebra, University of Kaiserslautern, *2003*. `www.singular.uni-kl.de`.

S. Murphy, M.J.B. Robshaw. *Essential Algebraic Structure within the AES*. M. Yung (ed.): CRYPTO *2002*, LNCS *2442*, pp. *1-16*, Springer-Verlag *2002*.

E. Oswald, J. Daemen, and V. Rijmen. *The State of the Art of Rijndael's Security*. Technical report. `www.a-sit.at/technologieb/evaluation/aes_report_e.pdf`

D. R. Stinson. CRYPTOGRAPHY, *Theory and Practice*. Chapman & Hall/CRC, *2002*. Second edition.

REMOVE KEY ESCROW FROM THE IDENTITY-BASED ENCRYPTION SYSTEM

Zhaohui Cheng, Richard Comley and Luminita Vasiu
School of Computing Science, Middlesex University
White Hart Lane, London N17 8HR, United Kingdom
{m.z.cheng,r.comley,l.vasiu}@mdx.ac.uk

Abstract Key escrow is an inherent property in the current proposed Identity-Based Encryption (IBE) systems. However the key escrow is not always a good property for all applications. In this paper, we present a scheme which removes the key escrow from the IBE system proposed by Bonch and Franklin, while at the same time maintaining some important properties of the IBE. We also present some cryptosystems based on our variant including a signature scheme and an authenticated key agreement. We finally show how to integrate our scheme into a hierarchial identity based public key encryption system.

Keywords: Identity-based encryption, Key escrow, Pairing

1 Introduction

Since the landmark paper "New directions in cryptography" [7] was published in 1976, public key systems have been playing a fundamental role in the modern information security society. To address the security threat of the "man-in-the-middle" attack, complicated public key certification systems have been developed for years. But the widespread deployment of public key systems depends heavily on the certification distribution systems which suffer from a scalability problem.

In an attempt to simplify the certification management in a Public Key Center (PKC), in 1984 Shamir [13] first formulated the concept of Identity-Based Cryptography (IBC) in which a public key is the identity (an arbitrary string) of an entity. Shamir presented an identity-based signature scheme in [13] and more signature schemes were proposed later. However constructing a practical Identity-Based Encryption (IBE) scheme has been an open problem for about twenty years. Recently Boneh and Franklin [3] and Cocks [5] presented two different systems separately. Boneh-Franklin's scheme has drawn much attention because of its provable security and efficiency in practice. Our work is based on this scheme.

In an IBE system there are four algorithms: (1) **Setup** generates the global system parameters and a master-key, (2) **Extract** uses the master-key to generate the private key corresponding to an arbitrary public key string $ID \in \{0,1\}^*$ which is the identity of an entity, (3) **Encrypt** encrypts messages using the public key ID, and (4) **Decrypt** decrypts messages using the corresponding private key.

Because an entity's identity (ID) is used as the public key directly, some interesting usages of an IBE can be naturally introduced. For example an ID can include the public key expiry time, or differentiate the entity's credentials. On the other hand a special property is inherent in the proposed IBE scheme. In Shamir's scheme, the PKC uses the **Extract** algorithm to generate a private key corresponding to the public ID. Hence the PKC knows all the entities' private keys. This property is called "*key escrow*". Because the proposed scheme [3] and [5] follow Shamir's scheme to setup systems, they also inherit the key escrow function. However the key escrow function is not necessary for all types of applications and a cryptosystem with a key escrow property has some serious disadvantages. For example once the master-key is exposed, all the entities' private keys are leaked in principle and all the prior communication information is under threat of exposure. Some mechanisms can be used to increase the security of the master-key, for example the threshold cryptography [8]. Gentry and Silverberg presented a method in a hierarchical ID-based scheme [9] to restrict the key escrow function in small areas. But the existence of a master-key is still a threat to an entity's privacy. In [1] Al-Riyami and Paterson introduced the concept of "Certificateless Public Key Cryptography" (CL-PKC) and presented a scheme which removes the key escrow property successfully. In this paper, we introduce the "*nickname*" concept and present another variant of Boneh-Franklin's IBE system without the key escrow function.

The rest of this paper is structured as follows. In section 2, we describe the original Boneh-Franklin's IBE scheme which is the basis of our variant, and we also briefly introduce the bilinear map which is the basic mathematical tool used in the scheme. In the next section, we present our scheme to show how to remove the key escrow function. A security analysis of our variant is presented in section 4. Section 5 and 6 is a signature scheme and an authenticated key agreement based on our variant separately. We show how to integrate our scheme into a hierarchial identity-based public key encryption system in section 7. Finally we make a comparison with the CL-PKC scheme.

2 Boneh-Franklin's IBE Scheme

Boneh-Franklin's IBE scheme is the first efficient and security provable identity-based encryption scheme, which is based on a "bilinear map" (pairing) $\hat{e} : \mathbb{G}_1 \times \mathbb{G}_1 \to \mathbb{G}_2$. $\mathbb{G}_1$ and $\mathbb{G}_2$ are two cyclic groups of large prime order q. The bilinear map has the following properties:

1 Bilinear: For all $P, Q, R, S \in \mathbb{G}_1$, $\hat{e}(P+Q, R+S) = \hat{e}(P,R)\hat{e}(P,S)$ $\hat{e}(Q,P)\hat{e}(Q,S)$.

2 Non-Degenerate: For a given point $Q \in \mathbb{G}_1$, $\hat{e}(Q,R) = 1_{\mathbb{G}_2}$ for all $R \in \mathbb{G}_1$ if and only if $Q = 0_{\mathbb{G}_1}$. $0_{\mathbb{G}_1}$ and $1_{\mathbb{G}_2}$ are the identity of two groups respectively. In [3], the concrete IBE uses an admissible map with a distortion map to achieve the non-degeneracy.

3 Computable: There is an efficient algorithm to compute $\hat{e}(P,Q)$ for any $P, Q \in \mathbb{G}_1$.

The modified Weil and Tate pairings [14] on elliptic curves can be used to build such bilinear maps. The security of Boneh-Franklin's scheme is based on an assumption of the hardness of the "Bilinear Diffie-Hellman" (BDH) problem.

ASSUMPTION 1 **BDH Assumption.** *Let $\mathcal{G}$ be a BDH parameter generator with a security parameter 1^k. Define*

$$Adv_{\mathcal{G},\mathcal{A}}(k) = Pr[\mathcal{A}(q, \mathbb{G}_1, \mathbb{G}_2, \hat{e}, P, aP, bP, cP) = \hat{e}(P,P)^{abc} \mid \langle q, \mathbb{G}_1, \mathbb{G}_2, \hat{e} \rangle \leftarrow \mathcal{G}(1^k), P \leftarrow \mathbb{G}_1, a, b, c \stackrel{R}{\leftarrow} \mathbb{Z}_q^*].$$

For any randomized polynomial time (in k) algorithm $\mathcal{A}$, the advantage $Adv_{\mathcal{G},\mathcal{A}}(k)$ is negligible (We say that the problem is hard to solve).

Boneh-Franklin's IBE scheme also follows the four steps proposed by Shamir. Here is the description of the scheme in detail.

Setup: Given a security parameter 1^k, the parameter generator follows the steps.

1 generate two cyclic groups $\mathbb{G}_1$ and $\mathbb{G}_2$ of prime order q and a bilinear pairing map $\hat{e} : \mathbb{G}_1 \times \mathbb{G}_1 \to \mathbb{G}_2$. Pick a random generator $P \in \mathbb{G}_1$.

2 pick a random integer $s \in \mathbb{Z}_q^*$ and compute $P_{pub} = sP$.

3 pick four cryptographic hash functions $H_1 : \{0,1\}^* \to \mathbb{G}_1^*, H_2 : \mathbb{G}_2 \to \{0,1\}^n, H_3 : \{0,1\}^n \times \{0,1\}^n \to \mathbb{Z}_q^*$ and $H_4 : \{0,1\}^n \to \{0,1\}^n$ for some integer $n > 0$.

The message space is $\mathcal{M} = \{0,1\}^n$. The ciphertext space is $\mathcal{C} = \mathbb{G}_1^* \times \{0,1\}^n \times \{0,1\}^n$. The system parameters are **params** = $\langle q, \mathbb{G}_1, \mathbb{G}_2, \hat{e}, n, P, P_{pub}, H_1, H_2, H_3, H_4 \rangle$. s is the **master-key** of the system.

Extract: Given a string $ID \in \{0,1\}^*$, **params** and the **master-key**, the algorithm computes $Q_{ID} = H_1(ID) \in \mathbb{G}_1^*$, $d_{ID} = sQ_{ID}$ and returns d_{ID}.

Encrypt: Given a plaintext $m \in \mathcal{M}$, the ID of an entity and the public parameters **params**, follow the steps:

1 pick a random $\sigma \in \{0,1\}^n$ and compute $r = H_3(\sigma, m)$.

2 compute $Q_{ID} = H_1(ID)$ and $g = \hat{e}(P_{pub}, Q_{ID})$.

3 set the ciphertext to $C = \langle rP, \sigma \oplus H_2(g^r), m \oplus H_4(\sigma) \rangle$.

Decrypt: Given a ciphertext $\langle U, V, W \rangle \in \mathcal{C}$, a private key d_{ID} and the system parameters **params**, perform the following steps.

1 compute $g' = \hat{e}(U, d_{ID})$ and $\sigma' = V \oplus H_2(g')$.

2 compute $m' = W \oplus H_4(\sigma')$ and $r' = H_3(\sigma', m')$

3 If $U \neq r'P$, reject the ciphertext, else return m' as the plaintext.

The consistency of the scheme follows from the bilinearity of $\hat{e}$. Boneh and Franklin proved that the scheme is semantically secure against the adaptive chosen ciphtertext attack (IND-CCA) [2][3] in the random oracle model [4].

3 Our Variant of Boneh-Franklin's IBE system

Based on Boneh-Franklin's scheme, we introduce another public and private key pair $\langle N_{ID}, t \rangle$ into the scheme to remove the key escrow function. The private key t, a random integer in $\mathbb{Z}_q^*$, is only owned by the entity with an identity ID (we use entity ID to refer to the entity with the identity ID in the remaining part of the paper). In our scheme the encryption and decryption operations not only depend on the public key ID (in fact Q_{ID}) and the private key d_{ID}, but also on the second public key N_{ID} and the corresponding private key t. We name the public keys $\langle ID, N_{ID} \rangle$ as $\langle ID, Nickname \rangle$ and the private keys $\langle d_{ID}, t \rangle$ as $\langle PrKeyL, PrKeyR \rangle$. Because only entity ID knows $PrKeyR$, we can prove that the key escrow function in the PKC is removed. The effect of introducing $\langle N_{ID}, t \rangle$ is discussed after the description of the scheme's details. We can find that to publish a nickname is not a serious new burden for a PKC. For simplicity we name our system as **V-IBE** and

Boneh-Franklin's scheme as **B-IBE** in the following sections.

Our scheme is specified by five algorithms: **Setup**, **Extract**, **Publish**, **Encrypt** and **Decrypt**.

Setup: As the one in Boneh-Franklin's scheme.

Extract: Identical to **Extract** in Boneh-Franklin's scheme.

Publish: Given the system parameters **params**, an entity selects a random $t \in \mathbb{Z}_q^*$, and computes $N_{ID} = \langle N_1, N_2 \rangle = \langle tP, tP_{pub} \rangle$. The entity can ask the PKC to publish this extra parameter N_{ID} or publish it by itself or via any directory service as a nickname. Note that this publishing operation has no security requirement.

Encrypt: Given a plaintext $m \in \mathcal{M}$, the identity ID, public parameters **params** and the nickname $N_{ID} = \langle N_1, N_2 \rangle$ corresponding to ID, the following steps are performed.

1 check that $N_1, N_2 \in \mathbb{G}_1^*$ and that the equality $\hat{e}(N_1, P_{pub}) = \hat{e}(N_2, P)$ holds. If not, output $\perp$ and terminate encryption.

2 pick a random $\sigma \in \{0,1\}^n$ and compute $r = H_3(\sigma, m)$.

3 compute $Q_{ID} = H_1(ID)$ and $g = \hat{e}(P_{pub} + N_1, Q_{ID})$.

4 set the ciphertext to $C = \langle rP, \sigma \oplus H_2(g^r), m \oplus H_4(\sigma) \rangle$.

Decrypt: Given a ciphertext $\langle U, V, W \rangle \in \mathcal{C}$, d_{ID}, t and system parameters **params**, follow the steps:

1 compute $g' = \hat{e}(U, d_{ID} + tQ_{ID})$ and $\sigma' = V \oplus H_2(g')$.

2 compute $m' = W \oplus H_4(\sigma')$ and $r' = H_3(\sigma', m')$.

3 If $U \neq r'P$, reject the ciphertext, else return m' as the plaintext.

The consistency of the scheme can be verified by

$$\begin{aligned} g' &= \hat{e}(U, d_{ID} + tQ_{ID}) = \hat{e}(rP, sQ_{ID} + tQ_{ID}) \\ &= \hat{e}(sP, Q_{ID})^r \hat{e}(tP, Q_{ID})^r = \hat{e}(P_{pub} + N_1, Q_{ID})^r = g^r \end{aligned}$$

Hence σ' in decryption equals σ in encryption. Thus, applying decryption on a ciphertext recovers the original message m.

Based on the BDH and another assumption stated in the next section, we can prove that the variant is secure against the adaptive chosen ciphertext attack (IND-CCA) in the random oracle model. Moreover this scheme achieves some special properties that make it different from the normal public key systems and the existing identity-based encryption schemes.

CLAIM 1 **No more key escrow.** *Without knowing the private key t (PrKeyR) of an entity, an adversary cannot decrypt a message encrypted for the entity, even with the knowledge of the master-key s.*

This claim follows from Theorem 1 in the following section.

CLAIM 2 **Partially identity-based.** *Without knowing d_{ID} (PrKeyL) of an entity identified by the ID, an adversary cannot decrypt a message encrypted for the entity even if the adversary replaces the entity's nickname N_{ID} with its own choice.*

This claim follows from Theorem 2 in the following section. Because of this property, some special usages of the original IBE are still applicable in our scheme, e.g. an entity's ID appending with expiry time or credentials.

REMARK 1 **Loosely binding nicknames.** *The extra public key parameter N_{ID} introduced in our scheme need not be bound strictly (by secure method) to the entity ID. N_{ID} can be distributed through an unsafe channel as the entity's nickname. If Alice wants to send a message to Bob, but does not know Bob's nickname, she can ask Bob directly or query the PKC or any directory service publishing Bob's nickname. Because of Claim 2, the security of the communication cannot be compromised by Eve who launches the man-in-the-middle attack and changes Bob's nickname with her own choice except that Eve is the PKC. This characteristic differentiates our scheme from the normal certification-based public key systems. In [1], a simple way is presented to thwart the PKC to impersonate another entity in the man-in-the-middle attack. The basic idea is to bind entity A's identity ID_A and nickname N_A with A's real public key Q_A by re-defining $Q_A = H_1(ID_A \| N_A)$. If the PKC impersonates entity A, there will be two valid private keys for ID_A with different nicknames which can only be generated by the PKC.*

REMARK 2 **Forward security of the master key.** *Our scheme introduces an extra public and private key pair $\langle N_{ID}, t \rangle$ and only the entity ID knows the private key t. Hence even if the master key s of the PKC is leaked, the prior communications with destination to entity ID would not be exposed, but the following communication would become vulnerable to the man-in-the-middle attack.*

4 The V-IBE's Security

Before defining the security of the scheme, we elaborate two primitive foundations of the variant.

Firstly we prove that based on the BDH assumption, it is hard for the PKC to compute g' in decryption, even though it knows the master key s. To construct g', the PKC needs to use the available information $(s, P, U = rP, Q_{ID} = aP, N_{ID} = \langle tP, tP_{pub} \rangle)$ to compute $\hat{e}(U, d_{ID} + tQ_{ID}) = \hat{e}(rP, saP + taP) = \hat{e}(P, P)^{ra(s+t)}$.

LEMMA 1 *Given* $(q, \mathbb{G}_1, \mathbb{G}_2, \hat{e}, s, P, aP, rP, tP)$, *where* $a, r, t \xleftarrow{R} \mathbb{Z}_q^*$ *and* s *is a fixed element in* $\mathbb{Z}_q^*$, *based on the BDH assumption, it is hard to compute* $\hat{e}(P, P)^{ra(s+t)}$.

Proof. The proof is straight forward. If an adversary $\mathcal{A}$ can solve the above problem, we can construct an adversary $\mathcal{B}$ using $\mathcal{A}$ as a subroutine to solve the BDH problem. Given a BDH challenge (P, aP, bP, cP), $\mathcal{B}$ randomly selects an element s from $\mathbb{Z}_q^*$ and passes (s, P, aP, bP, cP) as the challenge to $\mathcal{A}$. Upon receiving the response R from $\mathcal{A}$, $\mathcal{B}$ computes $\hat{e}(aP, bP)^{-s}$ and returns $R \cdot \hat{e}(aP, bP)^{-s}$ as the response to the BDH challenge. If $\mathcal{A}$ wins the game with non-negligible advantage, so does $\mathcal{B}$ because if $R = \hat{e}(P, P)^{ab(s+c)}$, $\mathcal{B}$'s response is $\hat{e}(P, P)^{ab(s+c)}\hat{e}(aP, bP)^{-s}$ $= \hat{e}(P, P)^{abc}$.

Secondly we show that if an adversary without the master key wants to compute $g' = \hat{e}(rP, Q_{ID})^{(s+t)}$ in decryption, it needs to solve some hard problem. Without the check step, the scheme is obviously insecure. An adversary can randomly select $j \in \mathbb{Z}_q^*$ and set $N_1 = tP = -P_{pub} + jP$ $(s + t = j \mod q)$, so as to compute $g' = \hat{e}(U, Q_{ID})^j$. But by applying the check step, the adversary needs to find $N_2 = tsP = (j - s)sP$ to pass the check step. If the adversary successfully finds N_2, then it is able to compute $s^2P = N_2 - jsP$. Given $(\mathbb{G}_1, q, P, sP)$ to compute s^2P is a squaring-DH problem in group $\mathbb{G}_1$, which is as hard as a normal DH problem because the order of $\mathbb{G}_1$ is known [12]. If an adversary $\mathcal{A}$ knows t and can compute g', we can slightly modify $\mathcal{A}$ to solve the BDH problem. Given a BDH problem (P, sP, aP, rP) where $s, a, r \xleftarrow{R} \mathbb{Z}_q^*$, after finding $N_1 = tP$, $\mathcal{A}$ computes $R = \hat{e}(P, P)^{sar}\hat{e}(tP, P)^{ra}$ but outputs $R \cdot \hat{e}(rP, aP)^{-t} = \hat{e}(P, P)^{sar}$. The output is just the solution to the BDH problem. Note that a legitimate party has t and saP to compute R. If $\mathcal{A}$ does not know t and $j = s + t \mod q$, it seems hard to find such N_1 and N_2 satisfying the check requirement and at the same time making the computation of g' easy. Based on this evaluation, we propose an assumption.

ASSUMPTION 2 *Given* $(q, \mathbb{G}_1, \mathbb{G}_2, \hat{e}, P, sP, aP)$*, where* $s, a \stackrel{R}{\leftarrow} \mathbb{Z}_q^*$*, based on the BDH assumption, it is hard to find* $N_1, N_2 \in \mathbb{G}_1^*$ *satisfying* $\hat{e}(N_1, sP) = \hat{e}(N_2, P)$ *and at the same time making computation* $\hat{e}(P,P)^{sar} \cdot \hat{e}(N_1, P)^{ra}$ *with* $rP \stackrel{R}{\leftarrow} \mathbb{G}_1$ *easy (here "easy" means existing a randomized polynomial time algorithm). (We refer to the assumption as a* **Bilinear EQuation (BEQ)** *assumption.)*

Now by defining two types of adversaries, which correspond to an adversary with and without the master-key respectively, we state the security analysis in the following two theorems.

Definition: Type-I Attack
An adversary with the *master-key* launches a Type-I attack by taking one or more of the following actions interacting with a challenger following from the IND-CCA notion.

1 Query the nickname of any entity ID_i.

2 Publish a nickname for any entity ID_i.

3 Extract $PrKeyL$ of any entity ID_i. In fact because the adversary has the master-key, it can compute $PrKeyL$ of any entity. But we still assume that the adversary issues Extract query to get the $PrKeyL$ from the challenger for simplicity.

4 Extract $PrKeyR$ of any entity ID_i but ID_{ch}. However querying $PrKeyR$ of a nickname published by the adversary is prohibited because it is unreasonable to require that the challenger knows such value which implies that the challenger can solve the discrete logarithm problem.

5 Be challenged on the chosen ID_{ch} by providing two messages m_0, m_1. Note that the nickname N_{ch} of entity ID_{ch} is not the one published by the adversary. Hence it means that although the adversary can replace N_{ch} in some phase, it must be challenged on ID_{ch}'s original nickname. Following the IND-CCA notion, the challenger randomly chooses $b \in \{0, 1\}$ and provides the ciphertext of m_b.

6 Issue a decryption query $\langle ID_i, C_i \rangle$. The adversary is prohibited from making a decryption query on the challenge ciphertext for the combination of identity ID_{ch} and the original N_{ch}.

If the adversary with the master-key also changes the nickname N_{ch} of the entity ID_{ch} on which it wants to be challenged, it knows both d_{ch} and t_{ch}. Hence the scheme cannot protect the information encrypted under

ID_{ch} and the changed nickname. In traditional public key cryptosystems this attack is not prevented either. This is the reason for the rules in the challenge phase. In the IND-CCA model, an adversary can continue to ask queries after the challenge phase. The advantage of an adversary is defined as the amount by which the probability of guessing the correct b exceeds $\frac{1}{2}$ (i.e. Advantage=max {Pr[Guessing the correct b]-$\frac{1}{2}$,0}).

THEOREM 1 *If there exists a Type-I IND-CCA adversary $\mathcal{A}$ with non-negligible advantage ϵ against V-IBE, then there exists an adversary $\mathcal{B}$ which can solve the BDHP with non-negligible advantage in the random oracle model.*

Definition: Type-II Attack
An adversary without the *master-key* launching a Type-II attack can take one or more of the following actions when interacting with a challenger.

1 Query the nickname of any entity ID_i.

2 Publish a nickname for any entity ID_i.

3 Extract $PrKeyL$ of any entity ID_i except ID_{ch}.

4 Extract $PrKeyR$ of any entity ID_i. But the adversary should not query $PrKeyR$ of a nickname published by itself.

5 Be challenged on the chosen ID_{ch} by providing two messages m_0, m_1. Note that there is no requirement on the nickname of ID_{ch}. Hence the adversary can be challenged on an entity whose nickname is published by the adversary. The challenger randomly chooses $b \in \{0, 1\}$ and provides the ciphertext of m_b.

6 Issue a decryption query $\langle ID_i, C_i \rangle$. The adversary is not allowed to query on the challenge ciphertext for the combination of identity ID_{ch} and the nickname used in the challenge query.

The adversary can query private $PrKeyL$ of any entity ID_i except ID_{ch} and can publish a nickname for any entity. The advantage is defined similarly to the one for the Type-I adversary.

THEOREM 2 *If there exists an IND-CCA Type-II adversary $\mathcal{A}$ against V-IBE with advantage ϵ, then there exits an adversary $\mathcal{B}$ which can solve the BEQ problem with non-negligible advantage in the random oracle model.*

The proofs of the above two theorems are essentially similar to the proofs of Theorem 1 and 2 in the CL-PKC [1], but with different assumptions (the authors proposed a general BDH assumption in [1]).

5 A Signature Scheme Based on Our Variant

We describe a public key signature (PKS) scheme based on a provably secure signature scheme in [10] and our variant. The PKS scheme can be specified by algorithms: **Setup, Extract, Publish, Sign** and **Verify**.

Setup: Given a security parameter 1^k, the parameter generator follows the steps.

1 generate two cyclic groups $\mathbb{G}_1$ and $\mathbb{G}_2$ of prime order q and a bilinear pairing map $\hat{e} : \mathbb{G}_1 \times \mathbb{G}_1 \to \mathbb{G}_2$. Pick a random generator $P \in \mathbb{G}_1$.

2 pick a random $s \in \mathbb{Z}_q^*$ and compute $P_{pub} = sP$.

3 pick two cryptographic hash functions $H_1 : \{0,1\}^* \to \mathbb{G}_1^*$ and $H_2 : \{0,1\}^* \times \mathbb{G}_2 \to \mathbb{Z}_q^*$.

The system parameters are **params**= $\langle q, \mathbb{G}_1, \mathbb{G}_2, \hat{e}, n, P, P_{pub}, H_1, H_2 \rangle$. s is the **master-key** of the system.

Extract: Given a string $ID \in \{0,1\}^*$, **params** and the **master-key**, the algorithm computes $Q_{ID} = H_1(ID) \in \mathbb{G}_1^*, d_{ID} = sQ_{ID}$ and returns d_{ID}.

Publish: Given the system parameter **params** and an entity ID, select a random $t \in \mathbb{Z}_q^*$, and compute $N_{ID} = \langle N_1, N_2 \rangle = \langle tP, tP_{pub} \rangle$.

Sign: To sign a message $m \in \mathcal{M}$ using the private key $\langle d_{ID}, t \rangle$ of entity ID, the following steps are performed.

1 choose an arbitrary point $P_1 \in \mathbb{G}_1^*$ and pick a random integer $k \in \mathbb{Z}_q^*$.

2 compute $r = \hat{e}(kP_1, P)$ and $v = H(m, r)$.

3 compute $Q_{ID} = H_1(ID)$ and $U = v(d_{ID} + tQ_{ID}) + kP_1$.

4 output as the signature $\langle U, v \rangle$.

Verify: To verify a signature $\langle U, v \rangle$ of entity ID with nickname $N_{ID} = \langle N_1, N_2 \rangle$ on a message $m \in \mathcal{M}$, follow the steps:

1 check that $N_1, N_2 \in \mathbb{G}_1^*$ and that the equality $\hat{e}(N_1, P_{pub}) = \hat{e}(N_2, P)$ holds. If not, output $\perp$ and terminate verification.

2 compute $Q_{ID} = H_1(ID)$.

3 compute $r' = \hat{e}(U,P)\hat{e}(Q_{ID}, -P_{pub} - N_1)^v$.

4 accept the signature if and only if $v = H(m, r')$.

The consistency of the scheme easily follows from

$$\begin{aligned} r' &= \hat{e}(U,P)\hat{e}(Q_{ID}, -P_{pub} - N_1)^v \\ &= \hat{e}(vd_{ID} + vtQ_{ID} + kP_1, P)\hat{e}(vQ_{ID}, -sP)\hat{e}(vQ_{ID}, -N_{ID}) \\ &= \hat{e}(vsQ_{ID}, P)\hat{e}(vtQ_{ID}, P)\hat{e}(kP_1, P)\hat{e}(vsQ_{ID}, -P)\hat{e}(vtQ_{ID}, -P) \\ &= \hat{e}(kP_1, P) \end{aligned}$$

6 An Authenticated Key Agreement Protocol

The following is a two-party key agreement protocol which extends Smart's protocol [15].

$$A \rightarrow B: \ xP, N_{ID}^A = (N_1^A, N_2^A) = (aP, aP_{pub}) \quad (1)$$
$$B \rightarrow A: \ yP, N_{ID}^B = (N_1^B, N_2^B) = (bP, bP_{pub}) \quad (2)$$

Upon the completion of message exchanges, A and B first check the exchanged nickname (N_{ID}^B and N_{ID}^A respectively). After that A computes $K_A = \hat{e}(Q_{ID}^B, P_{pub} + N_1^B)^x \cdot \hat{e}(d_{ID}^A + aQ_{ID}^A, yP)$, and B computes $K_B = \hat{e}(Q_{ID}^A, P_{pub} + N_1^A)^y \hat{e}(d_{ID}^B + bQ_{ID}^B, xP)$ respectively. It is easy to see that the secret key $K = K_A = K_B$ is shared between A and B.

$$\begin{aligned} K_A &= \hat{e}(Q_{ID}^B, sP + bP)^x \hat{e}(sQ_{ID}^A + aQ_{ID}^A, yP) \\ &= \hat{e}(sQ_{ID}^B + bQ_{ID}^B, xP)\hat{e}(Q_{ID}^A, sP + aP)^y \\ &= K_B \end{aligned}$$

Although A and B can use $H(K \| xyP)$ as the shared key, where H is a proper hash function to achieve forward security, Shim's protocol and its descendant [6] are vulnerable to the man-in-the-middle attack launched by the PKC. The new variant still suffers from such attack if the PKC replaces the nicknames in the two messages with its own selections. However we can use the same method mentioned in Section 3 to thwart such attacks.

7 Hierarchical PKE

In [9] Gentry and Silverberg introduced a totally collusion-resistant hierarchical ID-based infrastructure for encryption and signature. We integrate our scheme into this hierarchical system to eliminate all kinds of key escrow to any ancestor of an entity. In the system, every entity is located in one level of a hierarchical system. Except the root entity, every entity is identified by an ID-tuple which identifies every ancestor along the path to the root. The major steps of our scheme are identical to the ones in [9].

Root Setup: Given a security parameter 1^k, the parameter generator follows the steps.

1 generate two cyclic groups $\mathbb{G}_1, \mathbb{G}_2$ of prime order q and a bilinear pairing map $\hat{e} : \mathbb{G}_1 \times \mathbb{G}_1 \to \mathbb{G}_2$. Pick a random generator $P_0 \in \mathbb{G}_1$.

2 pick a random integer $s_0 \in \mathbb{Z}_q^*$ and compute $Q_0 = s_0 P_0$.

3 pick two cryptographic hash functions $H_1 : \{0,1\}^* \to \mathbb{G}_1^*$ and $H_2 : \mathbb{G}_2 \to \{0,1\}^n$ for some integer $n > 0$.

Low-lever Setup: Entity $E_t \in Level_t$ picks a random $s_t \in \mathbb{Z}_q^*$, which it keeps secret.

Extraction: Let E_t be an entity in $Level_t$ with ID-tuple $(ID_1, \dots, ID_t)$, where $(ID_1, \dots, ID_i)$ for $1 \leq i \leq t$ is the ID-tuple of E_t 's ancestor at $Level_i$. Follow the steps:

1 compute $P_t = H_1(ID_1 \| ID_2 \| \dots \| ID_t) \in \mathbb{G}_1$.

2 set E_t's secret point $S_t = S_{t-1} + s_{t-1} P_t = \sum_{i=1}^{t} s_{i-1} P_i$.

3 set $Q_i = s_i P_0$ for $1 \leq i \leq t - 1$.

Publish: For ID_t, select a random $b_t \in \mathbb{Z}_q^*$ and compute the nickname $N_t = \langle N_1^t, N_2^t \rangle = \langle b_t P_0, b_t Q_0 \rangle$.

Encryption: To encrypt $m \in \mathcal{M}$ with the ID-tuple $(ID_1, \dots, ID_t)$ and the corresponding nicknames $N_i = \langle N_1^i, N_2^i \rangle$ for $1 \leq i \leq t$, take the following steps:

1 for each $1 \leq i \leq t$, check that $N_1^i, N_2^i \in \mathbb{G}_1^*$ and that the equality $\hat{e}(N_1^i, Q_0) = \hat{e}(N_2^i, P_0)$ holds. If not output $\perp$ and terminate encryption.

2 compute $P_i = H_1(ID_1 \| ID_2 \| \dots \| ID_i) \in \mathbb{G}_1$ for $1 \leq i \leq t$.

3 choose random $r \in \mathbb{Z}_q^*$, and compute cyphertext $C = \langle U_0, U_2, \dots, U_t, V \rangle = \langle rP_0, rP_2, \dots, rP_t, m \oplus H_2(g^r) \rangle$, where $g = \hat{e}(Q_0 + N_1^t, P_1) = \hat{e}(s_0 P_0, P_1) \cdot \hat{e}(b_t P_0, P_1)$.

Decryption: To decrypt the ciphertext $C = \langle U_0, U_2, \dots, U_t, V \rangle \in \mathcal{C}_t$ for an entity in level t with the ID-tuple $(ID_1, ID_2, \dots, ID_t)$, follow the steps:

1 $g' = \frac{\hat{e}(U_0, S_t + b_t P_1)}{\prod_{i=2}^{t} \hat{e}(Q_{i-1}, U_i)} = \hat{e}(rP_0, s_0 P_1 + b_t P_1) = \hat{e}(s_0 P_0, P_1)^r \hat{e}(b_t P_0, P_1)^r$.

2 compute $m' = V \oplus H_2(g')$ as the plaintext.

8 Comparison with The CL-PKC

In the above sections we have shown that all the cryptosystems supported by the CL-PKC can be realized using our variant. In fact, the public key in the CL-PKC is essentially the same as the nickname in our scheme. Hence, our variant is an alternative implementation of the CL-PKC but based on a different hardness assumption.

Our scheme is slightly slower than the CL-PKC, because our scheme needs an extra point addition operation. However the point addition is very fast compared to the pairing computation or the scalar operation. The following table compares the complexity of the two schemes and B-IBE (P for pairing computation, S for scalar operation and E for exponentiation). We ignore the hash operation and the point addition, because the numbers of hash operations in all schemes are equal and the point addition is a very lightweight computation compared to the pairing, scalar and exponentiation operations.

Scheme	Encryption	Decryption	Key Publish
CL-PKE	3P+1S+1E	1P+1S	2 Points
V-IBE	**3P+1S+1E**	**1P+1S**	**2 Points**
B-IBE	1P+1S+1E	1P+1S	0 Point

In both schemes (CL-PKE and V-IBE) entities can save two pairing computation in the check procedure by checking an intended entity's key (the nickname in V-IBE or the public key in CL-PKE) once and save one pairing operation by pre-computing g before sending more than one message to the intended entity.

A good property of our scheme is that it cooperates seamlessly with the original IBE system. In fact, the original IBE can be deemed as a V-IBE with $\langle \mathcal{O}, \mathcal{O} \rangle$ ($\mathcal{O}$ is the identity of group $\mathbb{G}_1$) as a nickname and q as $PrKeyR$ for all entities. If an entity wants to use the "nickname" system, it can use the original IBE implementation by slightly modifying the existing functions to include the presented extension. After that, all that an entity needs to do is to select a private key t and publish $\langle tP, tP_{pub} \rangle$ by itself or via a directory service. If a peer entity does not support the nickname system in a crypto-protocol, the entities can degenerate the security scheme to the basic IBE scheme gracefully. To do this the check procedure needs a minor modification to allow $N_1, N_2 \in \mathbb{G}_1$ instead of $\mathbb{G}_1^*$.

9 Conclusion

By introducing a new concept "nickname", we modify Boneh-Franklin's IBE scheme to remove the inherent key escrow function. We find that the new scheme inherits the basic property of the IBE system to enable part of the public key to be an arbitrary string, but at the same time removes the key escrow function without necessarily increasing the PKC's burden. Using this variant we extend a signature scheme and an authenticated key agreement to remove the key escrow property. We also show one method to integrate our scheme into a hierarchial identity-based public key encryption system.

References

[1] S. S. Al-Riyami and K. G. Paterson, "Certificateless Public Key Cryptography", Advances in Cryptology-Asiacrypt '2003, LNCS 2894, 2003.

[2] M. Bellare, A. Desai, D. Pointcheval and P. Rogaway, "Relations among notions of security for public-key encryption schemes", In Advances in Cryptology CRYPTO 98, LNCS 1462, 1998.

[3] D. Boneh and M. Franklin, "Identity Based Encryption from The Weil Pairing", extended abstract in Advances in Cryptology-Crypto 2001, LNCS 2139, 2001.

[4] M. Bellare and P. Rogaway, "Random Oracles are Practical: A Paradigm for Desiging Efficient Protocols", Proc. of First ACM Conference on Computer and Communication Security, November 1993.

[5] C. Cocks, "An Identity Based Encryption Scheme Based on Quadratic Residues", Cryptography and Coding, LNCS 2260, 2001.

[6] L. Chen and C. Kudla, "Identity Based Authenticated Key Agreement from Pairings", Cryptology ePrint Archive, Report 2002/184.

[7] W. Diffie and M.E. Hellman, "New Directions in Cryptography", IEEE Transactions on Information Theory 22,1976.

[8] P. Gemmel, "An Intoduction to Threshold Cryptography", CryptoBytes, a technical newsletter of RSA Laboratories, Vol. 2, No. 7, 1997.

[9] C. Gentry and A. Silverberg, "Hierarchical ID-Based Cryptography", Proceedings of Asiacrypt 2002, LNCS 2501, 2002.

[10] F. Heβ, "Efcient Identity Based Signature Schemes Based on Pairings", In K. Nyberg and H. Heys, editors, Selected Areas in Cryptography 9th Annual International Workshop, SAC 2002, LNCS 2595, 2003.

[11] D. L. Long and A. Wigderson, "The discrete logarithm problem hides O(log n) bits", SIAM J. Computing, 17(2), April 1988.

[12] U. Maurer and S. Wolf, "Diffie-Hellman Oracles", Advances in Cryptology - CRYPTO '96 Proceedings, Springer-Verlag, 1996.

[13] A. Shamir, "Identity-Based Cryptosystems and Signature Schemes", in Advances in Cryptology-Crypto '84, LNCS 196, 1984.

[14] J. Silverman, "The Arithmetic of Elliptic Curve", Springer-Verlag, 1986.

[15] N. P. Smart, "An Identity Based Authenticated Key Agreement Protocol Based on the Weil Pairing", Electronics Letters 38 (2002), pp. 630–632, 2002

A RANDOMISED ALGORITHM FOR CHECKING THE NORMALITY OF CRYPTOGRAPHIC BOOLEAN FUNCTIONS

An Braeken, Christopher Wolf, and Bart Preneel
K.U.Leuven, ESAT-COSIC
Kasteelpark Arenberg 10
B-3001 Leuven-Heverlee, Belgium
http://www.esat.kuleuven.ac.be/cosic/
{An.Braeken, Christopher.Wolf, Bart.Preneel}@esat.kuleuven.ac.be

Abstract A Boolean function is called *normal* if it is constant on flats of certain dimensions. This property is relevant for the construction and analysis of cryptosystems. This paper presents an asymmetric Monte Carlo algorithm to determine whether a given Boolean function is normal. Our algorithm is far faster than the best known (deterministic) algorithm of Daum *et al.* In a first phase, it checks for flats of low dimension whether the given Boolean function is constant on them and combines such flats to flats of higher dimension in a second phase. This way, the algorithm is much faster than exhaustive search. Moreover, the algorithm benefits from randomising the first phase. In addition, by evaluating several flats implicitly in parallel, the time-complexity of the algorithm decreases further.

Keywords: Normality, Boolean Functions, Asymmetric Monte Carlo, Cryptography

1. Introduction

1.1 Motivation

Boolean functions and maps play a central role in cryptology. They are basic building blocks of bit-oriented block and stream ciphers. In order to construct secure cryptographic ciphers, *i.e.*, ciphers which resist all known attacks, it is important to study the structure and behaviour of Boolean functions.

Normality of a Boolean function is the property which determines if the function is constant on a flat of dimension $\lceil n/2 \rceil$. This concept was introduced by Dob94, in order to construct highly nonlinear balanced Boolean functions. Later, this property was used to distinguish different classes of bent functions. As the first bent function which is non-normal occurs for dimension 14 (Can03), we need a highly optimised algorithm for determining the normality of Boolean functions. This is non-trivial as the total number of flats increases exponentially for increasing dimension n (MWS91). Table 1 lists the number of flats of dimension $\lceil n/2 \rceil$; this clearly shows that even for moderate dimensions ($n \geq 13 \ldots 15$) establishing normality by exhaustive search is infeasible.

Table 1. The number of flats of dimension $\lceil \frac{n}{2} \rceil$ to test for different dimensions n

n	8	9	10	11	12	13	14	15	16	17	18	19	20
$\log_2$(# flats)	22	26	32	37	44	50	58	65	74	82	92	101	112

1.2 Related Work

The first attempt for determining the normality of a Boolean function, better than exhaustive search, is due to DDL03. The main idea of their algorithm is to search exhaustively all flats of small dimension on which the function is constant and then to combine these to flats of higher dimension.

1.3 Achievement

In our algorithm, we replace the exhaustive search through all flats of small dimension by a random search. This has several advantages over the algorithm of Daum *et al.* First, we do not need a unique representation of flats which means less conditions to test and therefore a lower time complexity. Second, the number of repetitions needed to determine with high probability that a function is non-normal, is far smaller than an exhaustive search on all flats of small dimension (cf Sect. 4.2). Our algorithm is of the *asymmetric Monte Carlo* type and may output "non-normal" with probability 2^{-c} for a normal function and some confidence level $c \in \mathbb{N}$. The output "normal" is always correct. This asymmetric Monte Carlo algorithm has a far smaller running time than the deterministic algorithm of DDL03 — even with a reasonable error-probability ($c = 80$ in our case).

1.4 Outline

This paper is organised as follows. In Sect. 2, we introduce the basic definitions together with a description of the main ideas in our algorithm. Sect. 3 presents more details and explains several optimisations for our algorithm. In Sect. 4, we give a detailed complexity analysis of the algorithm and compare the total time complexity of our algorithm with the time complexity of the previous algorithm from DDL03. This paper concludes with Sect. 5.

2. Background

In this section we present some definitions and a simplified algorithm to test the normality of a Boolean function.

2.1 Definitions

Before we can describe our algorithm, we need to define several objects. We start with vectors and vector spaces and finish with some definitions concerning Boolean functions.

Let a vector $\overline{u} \in \mathbb{F}_2^n$ be represented by the n-tuple $(u_{n-1}, \ldots, u_0)$ with the coefficients $u_i \in \mathbb{F}_2$ from the field with 2 elements. Let $\overline{u_1}, \ldots, \overline{u_k} \in \mathbb{F}_2^n$ be k linearly independent vectors. Then they form the base of the subspace

$$<U> := <\overline{u_1}, \ldots, \overline{u_k}> := \{\alpha_1 \overline{u_1} \oplus \ldots \oplus \alpha_k \overline{u_k} \mid \alpha_i \in \mathbb{F}_2\}.$$

Here, the dimension of $<U>$ is k. For a given vector $\overline{a} \in \mathbb{F}_2^n$, we represent the coset of this subspace by $U_{\overline{a}} := \overline{a} \oplus <U>$. Throughout this paper, we call the coset $U_{\overline{a}}$ a *flat*. The vector $\overline{a}$ of the flat $U_{\overline{a}}$ is called the *offset* of this flat. In addition, two flats are said to be *parallel* if they are cosets of the same subspace $<U>$, *i.e.*, all flats of the form $U_{\overline{a}}, \overline{a} \in \mathbb{F}_2^n$ are parallel flats by this definition. Finally, we denote the set of all flats of dimension s by Flat_s, *i.e.*,

$$\text{Flat}_s := \{U_{\overline{a}} \mid \overline{a} \in \mathbb{F}_2^n, \ <U> \subseteq \mathbb{F}_2^n, \ \dim <U> = s\}.$$

We now move on to Boolean functions. A Boolean function f is a mapping from $\mathbb{F}_2^n$ into $\mathbb{F}_2$. The property of normality for a Boolean function f is defined as follows:

DEFINITION 1 *A Boolean function $f : \mathbb{F}_2^n \rightarrow \mathbb{F}_2$ is called* normal *if there exists a flat $W_{\overline{a}} \subset \mathbb{F}_2^n$ of dimension $\lceil n/2 \rceil$ such that f is constant on $W_{\overline{a}}$, i.e., $\forall \overline{w} \in W_{\overline{a}} : f(\overline{w}) = c$ for some fixed $c \in \{0, 1\}$. We call the flat $W_{\overline{a}}$ a* witness *for the normality of the function f.*

As we see from Definition 1, the property of normality is related to the question of the highest dimension of the flats on which the function f is constant. As a consequence, it is natural to generalise the previous definition by the introduction of k-normality (Dub01; Car01):

DEFINITION 2 *For a natural number $k : 1 \leq k \leq n$, a Boolean function $f : \mathbb{F}_2^n \rightarrow \mathbb{F}_2$, is said to be "k-normal" if there exists a flat $V_{\overline{a}} \in Flat_k$ such that f is constant on $V_{\overline{a}}$, i.e., $\forall \overline{v} \in V_{\overline{a}} : f(\overline{v}) = c$ for some fixed $c \in \{0, 1\}$. We call the flat $V_{\overline{a}}$ a "k-witness" for the normality of the function f.*

Remark: It is clear that a constant function $f(\overline{x}) = c, \forall \overline{x} \in \mathbb{F}_2^n, c \in \mathbb{F}_2$ is n-normal. An affine function $f(\overline{x}) = \overline{a} \cdot \overline{x} \oplus b, \forall \overline{x}, \overline{a} \in \mathbb{F}_2^n, b \subset \mathbb{F}_2$ is $(n-1)$-normal, because it is normal on the flats $\{\overline{x} : \overline{a} \cdot \overline{x} \oplus b = 0\}$ and $\{\overline{x} : \overline{a} \cdot \overline{x} \oplus b = 1\}$ of dimension $n - 1$.

2.2 A Simple Algorithm

The previous section shows that it is important for the definition of normality and k-normality, *i.e.*, for a given dimension $e := k$ (k-normality) or $e := \lceil n/2 \rceil$ (ordinary normality), to find a witness $W_{\overline{a}} \in \text{Flat}_e$. To ease the understanding of the algorithm of Sect. 4, we start with a highly non-optimised version of it (cf Fig. 1). Both algorithms are based on the observation made by DDL03, that a Boolean function which is constant on a flat $W_{\overline{a}}$ is also constant on all flats contained in $W_{\overline{a}}$, *i.e.*, $f_{|W_{\overline{a}}} = c$ for

Figure 1. Simplified Algorithm for Checking Normality

Input: function f, start dimension s, end dimension e, repetitions r
Output: 1 if the function is e-normal
for $i \leftarrow 1$ **to** r **do**
  pick a flat $U_{\overline{a}} \in_R \text{Flat}_s$ at random
  if $f_{|U_{\overline{a}}} = c$ for some $c \in \{0,1\}$ **then** SearchFurther($U_{\overline{a}}, e$)
endfor

procedure SearchFurther($U_{\overline{a}}, e$)
  $c = f_{|U_{\overline{a}}}$
  if $\dim U_{\overline{a}} = e$ **then**
    OUTPUT 1
  endif
  forall $\overline{b} \in \mathbb{F}_2^n \setminus U_{\overline{a}}$ **do**
    if ($f_{|U_{\overline{b}}} = c$) **then** SearchFurther($\overline{a} \oplus <U, \overline{a} \oplus \overline{b}>, e$)
  endfor
endproc

some $c \in \{0,1\}$ implies $f_{|V_{\overline{b}}} = c$ for all $V_{\overline{b}} \subseteq W_{\overline{a}}$. We call the flat $V_{\overline{b}}$ a *sub-witness* of $W_{\overline{a}}$.

Our algorithm starts with a randomly chosen flat $U_{\overline{a}}$ of dimension s, the *starting dimension*. If this flat is a sub-witness, the function f must be constant on it. So, if the function f is constant on the flat $U_{\overline{a}}$, this is a possible candidate for a sub-witness and we search for a parallel flat $U_{\overline{b}}$, on which the function is constant, too. Both flats $U_{\overline{a}}, U_{\overline{b}}$ can now be combined to a flat of higher dimension, namely $\overline{a} \oplus <U, \overline{a} \oplus \overline{b}>$. We repeat this process recursively until we reach the "end dimension" e. In this case, we have found a witness $W_{\overline{a}}$ and output 1.

Depending on the "confidence level" c we want to achieve, we need to repeat the above algorithm several times. The value for r, *i.e.*, the number of repetitions, depends on c. We discuss the choice of r in Corollary 10 (cf Sect. 2).

3. Optimisations

After given a short outline of our algorithm, we show different ways of optimising it.

3.1 Complement Vector Space

There are in total $2^n - 2^s$ parallel flats $U_{\overline{a}}, \overline{a} \in \mathbb{F}_2^n \setminus <U>$ for a given subspace $<U>$ of dimension s. However, some parallel flats are equivalent as they contain the same points.

EXAMPLE 3 *Consider some parallel flats of the following subspace of dimension 2 which is defined by* $<U> := <(0,0,1),(0,1,0)> \subseteq \mathbb{F}_2^3$.

$$\begin{aligned}(1,0,0) \oplus <(0,0,1),(0,1,0)> &= (1,1,0) \oplus <(0,0,1),(0,1,0)> \\ &= (1,1,1) \oplus <(0,0,1),(0,1,0)> \\ &= (1,0,1) \oplus <(0,0,1),(0,1,0)>\end{aligned}$$

As a consequence, the parallel flats can be divided into equivalence classes. Therefore, we use the *complement* of a subspace $<U>$, *i.e.*, the subspace $<\overline{U}>$ which satisfies

$$<\overline{U}> \oplus <U> = \mathbb{F}_2^n \text{ and } <\overline{U}> \cap <U> = \{0\}.$$

This allows us to determine the representatives of the equivalence classes of the parallel flats, namely the flats $U_{\overline{a}}$, for $\overline{a} \in <\overline{U}>$. Because the dimension of $<\overline{U}>$ is equal to $n-s$, there are in total 2^{n-s} different parallel flats. To compute the complement $<\overline{U}>$ of a given subspace $<U>$ efficiently, we make use of the *Permuted Gauss Basis* (PGB) of a subspace. To define the PGB, we need to introduce the concept of left-most-one of a vector first.

DEFINITION 4 *For a given vector* $\overline{u} = (u_{n-1}, \ldots, u_0)$, *we define the* left-most-one *as the position of the left-most one in its representation:*

$$\nu(\overline{u}) := \min\{i \in \{-1, \ldots, n-1\} \mid u_j = 0 \textit{ for } i < j \leq n\}.$$

DEFINITION 5 *The vectors* $\overline{u_1}, \ldots, \overline{u_k}$ *form a PGB basis iff*

$$\nu(\overline{u_i}) \neq \nu(\overline{u_j}), \quad 0 \leq i < j < n.$$

Remark: The name Permuted Gauss Basis is motivated as follows. Thinking about the base vectors $\overline{u_1}, \ldots, \overline{u_k}$ as a matrix, we would perform Gaussian elimination on it, without swapping rows. The result would not be a triangular structure but a row permutation.

For a subspace $<U>$, we denote the set of the different left-most-ones of its elements

$$\Upsilon(<U>) := \{\nu(\overline{u}) \mid \overline{u} \in <U> \setminus \{0\}\}.$$

The complement $<\overline{U}>$ of a subspace $<U>$ where $<U>$ is in PGB can be computed as follows:

$$<\overline{U}> = \{\overline{a} \in \mathbb{F}_2^n \mid a_i = 0, \text{ where } i \in \Upsilon(<U>)\}.$$

3.2 Random Points instead of Random Bases

Instead of selecting a random flat with a PGB, we choose $(s+1)$ points at random. This is cheaper than selecting a vector space at random which satisfies the PGB-criterion. In addition, we only need to transfer a set of $(s+1)$ points into a PGB if the function f is constant on the corresponding flat. As this only happens with probability 2^{-2^s+1}, we obtain very low costs on average. For s points, we can compute

Figure 2. Algorithm for computing the PGB of a set of points

procedure ComputePGB($\overline{p}_1, \dots, \overline{p}_s$)
  Input: s points $\overline{p}_1, \dots, \overline{p}_s$
  Output: a PGB of the $\overline{p}_1, \dots, \overline{p}_s$
  for $k \leftarrow 2$ **to** s **do**
    while $\nu(\overline{p}_k) \in \{\nu(\overline{p}_1), \dots, \nu(\overline{p}_{k-1})\}$ **do**
      for $i \leftarrow 1$ **to** $k-1$ **do**
        if $\nu(\overline{p}_i) = \nu(\overline{p}_k)$ **then** $\overline{p}_k \oplus \leftarrow \overline{p}_i$
endproc

the PGB by the iterative algorithm from Fig. 2. The point $\overline{p}_0$ is the offset of the flat $\overline{p}_0 \oplus <\overline{p}_1, \dots, \overline{p}_s>$ and has to be reduced as outlined in the previous section.

Finally, we have to check whether the $(s+1)$ points form a flat of dimension s. The contrary happens only with very small probability:

$$(2^n)(2^n-1)\cdots(2^n-2^s)/2^{n\cdot(s+1)}.$$

Using the following strategy, we can reduce the running time of the algorithm further: instead of picking $(s+1)$ points at random and evaluate explicitly if they form a flat of dimension s on which the function f is constant, we do this implicitly in parallel:

- Pick $(2s+1)$ points at random
- Evaluate f on these points
- if exactly $(s+1)$ points evaluate to 1 (resp. to 0), check if the corresponding flat yields the constant 1 (resp. 0) on the function f.

This *implicit evaluation* strategy exploits different observations. First, we assume that we can form a total of *#flats* $:= \binom{2s+1}{s+1}$ independent flats of dimension s using a set of $(2s+1)$ points. This way, we can decrease the number of repetitions by this factor. In addition, we observe that a set of $(2s+1)$ points will yield at most one flat of dimension s on which the function f is constant, if $(s+1)$ points in the set evaluate to 1 (resp. 0) on the function f. However, the probability for this event is rather high, namely *Pr(only one flat)* $:= \frac{2\binom{2s+1}{s+1}}{2^{2s+1}}$.

But there is a price to pay for this strategy: we always need to perform $(2s+1)$ evaluations of the function f and also the same number of random calls.

Remark: It is natural to generalise this idea to other values than $(2s+1)$. However, in this case we do not obtain such a good trade-off between the factor *#flats* and the workload to check the corresponding flats. The choice $(2s+1)$ is optimal for the given problem.

3.3 Combining

In the original algorithm, we searched for all parallel flats and started a recursion on each of them. This is obviously superfluous as we will find the same witness several times this way. As we know from the previous section, we will obtain at least 2^{e-s} parallel flats $U_{\overline{b_i}}$ on which the function is constant. Here, e denotes the end-dimension and s the start-dimension.

To avoid this costly computation, we use a different strategy, based on DDL03: instead of recursively searching for all parallel flats of higher dimension, we combine flats of low dimension to obtain flats of higher dimension. This is based on the following observation:

$$(\overline{b}_i \oplus <U>) \cup (\overline{b}_j \oplus <U>) = \overline{b}_i \oplus <U, \overline{b}_i \oplus \overline{b}_j> .$$

Hence, we only need to consider pairs $(\overline{b}_i, \overline{b}_j) \in <\overline{U}> \times <\overline{U}>$ which lead to the same sum and then combine them recursively until we obtain a flat of dimension e. To do this efficiently, we introduce 2^n lists (depending on a vector $\overline{v} \in \mathbb{F}_2^n$) which hold an offset for each possible sum, *i.e.*, Append($L^{\overline{b}_i \oplus \overline{b}_j}, \overline{b_i}$). In the following section, we develop a branching condition for the combine method, which allows to decrease its running time even further.

3.4 Branching

Let the function f take a constant value $c \in \{0, 1\}$ on the flat $U_{\overline{a}}$ of dimension d. Denote with $P(U_{\overline{a}})$ the set of all flats parallel to $U_{\overline{a}}$ on which the function yields the same constant. The following branching condition defined by the cardinality of the set $P(U_{\overline{a}})$ has been observed by DDL03. We are able to improve their result by giving a shorter proof.

THEOREM 6 *If* $|P(U_{\overline{a}})| < 2^{e-d}$, *we can terminate the current branch of the combine-method in* $<U>$ *without violating its correctness.*

Proof: Let $W_{\overline{b}}$ be a witness and $U_{\overline{a}} \subset W_{\overline{b}}$ its subwitness. Now, there exist exactly $(e - d)$ linearly independent vectors $\overline{w_1}, \ldots, \overline{w_{e-d}} \in <W>$ with $\overline{w_1}, \ldots, \overline{w_{e-d}} \notin <U>$ and consequently $\overline{w_1}, \ldots, \overline{w_{e-d}} \in <\overline{U}>$. These vectors exist due to dimension reasons as $\dim W_{\overline{b}} = e$ and $\dim U_{\overline{a}} = d$. Therefore, for any subwitness $U_{\overline{a}} \subset W_{\overline{b}}$ exist 2^{e-d} parallel subwitnesses. This implies that $|P(U_{\overline{a}})| \geq 2^{e-d}$. As a consequence, we can stop at any step in the algorithm if this condition is violated because we will not be able to extend the flat $U_{\overline{a}}$ to a witness of dimension e. □

4. The Improved Algorithm

Using the ideas from the previous section, we obtain the algorithm of Fig. 3. The method SearchForParallelFlats can be found in Fig. 4 and the optimised version of the combine-method is presented in Fig. 5. In the following sections, we analyse this optimised algorithm.

4.1 Complexity Analysis

We start the analysis of the algorithm with determining the number r of repetitions. Then we analyse the complexity of the main loop from Fig. 3, the complexity of the SearchForParallelFlats from Fig. 4 and the complexity of the Combine-procedure from Fig. 5 in different steps.

Figure 3. Main loop for the optimised algorithm

Input: function f, start dimension s, end dimension e, repetitions r
Output: one witness if the function is e-normal
for $i \leftarrow 1$ **to** r **do**
  $S_0 \leftarrow \{\}, S_1 \leftarrow \{\}$
  for $i \leftarrow 1$ **to** $2s+1$ **do**
    $\overline{p} \in_R \mathbb{F}_2^n$
    $c \leftarrow f(\overline{p})$
    $S_c \cup \leftarrow \{\overline{p}\}$
  endfor
  if $((|S_0| \neq s+1)$ **and** $(|S_1| \neq s+1))$ **then continue**
  $c \leftarrow |S_1| - s$
  if $f|_{\overline{p}_0 \oplus <\overline{p}_0 \oplus \overline{p}_1, \ldots, \overline{p}_0 \oplus \overline{p}_s>}$ $(p_i \in S_c, i \in \{0, \ldots, s\})$ *not constant* **then continue**
  $\overline{a} \oplus <U> \leftarrow$ ComputePGB$(\overline{p_0}, \ldots, \overline{p_s})$
  if dim$<U> \neq s$ **then continue**
  SearchForParallelFlats($<U>$)
endfor

Figure 4. SearchForParallelFlats for the optimised algorithm

procedure SearchForParallelFlats($<U>$)
  $<\overline{U}> \leftarrow$ ComputeComplement($<U>$)
  $L \leftarrow \emptyset, c \leftarrow f(\overline{a})$
  for $\overline{b} \in <\overline{U}> \setminus \{\overline{a}\}$ **do**
    if $f_{|U_{\overline{b}}} = c$ **then** Append(L,$\overline{b}$)
  if $|L| \geq 2^{e-s}$ **then** Combine($<U>$,L)
endproc

Number of Repetitions.

For determining the number of repetitions, we need the following lemma from MWS91, concerning the number of subspaces and flats of a certain dimension in a vector space.

LEMMA 7 *The number of subspaces of dimension s in a vector space of dimension n is given by*

$$NS(n,s) := \prod_{i=0}^{s-1} \frac{2^{n-i}-1}{2^{s-i}-1}.$$

The number of flats of dimension s in a vector space of dimension n is given by

$$NF(n,s) := 2^{n-s} \prod_{i=0}^{s-1} \frac{2^{n-i}-1}{2^{s-i}-1} = 2^{n-s} NS(n,s).$$

Before determining a bound on r, we first introduce the term complaisant flat.

Figure 5. Combine-method for the optimised algorithm

Global Initialisation:
forall $\overline{a} \in \mathbb{F}_2^n$ **do**
    $L^{\overline{a}} \leftarrow \emptyset$

procedure Combine($<U>, L$)
    $d \leftarrow \dim <U>$
    if $d \geq e$ **then**
        Let $\overline{a} \in L$
        OUTPUT $U_{\overline{a}}$
    endif
    forall $(\overline{b_i}, \overline{b_j}) \in L \times L : i < j$ **do**
        Append($L^{\overline{b_i} \oplus \overline{b_j}}, \overline{b_i}$)
    forall $(\overline{b_i}, \overline{b_j}) \in L \times L : i < j$ **do**
        $\overline{a} \leftarrow \overline{b_i} \oplus \overline{b_j}$
        if $|L^{\overline{a}}| \geq 2^{e-d-1}$ **then**
            $L' \leftarrow \emptyset$
            forall $\overline{b} \in L^{\overline{a}}$ **do**
                if $\overline{b} \in <\overline{U, \overline{a}}>$ **then** Append($L', \overline{b}$) **else** Append($L', \overline{a} \oplus \overline{b}$)
            Combine($<U, \overline{a}>, L'$)
        endif
        $L^{\overline{a}} \leftarrow \emptyset$
    endfor
endproc

DEFINITION 8 *A flat $U_{\overline{a}}$ is called* complaisant *if the function is constant on the flat, the flat is parallel to a sub-witness, but the flat is not contained in any witness.*

THEOREM 9 *When choosing $(s+1)$ points $\overline{p}_0, \ldots, \overline{p}_s \in \mathbb{F}_2^n$ at random, the probability $PF(n, s, e)$ that the flat $U_{\overline{a}}$ formed by these $(s+1)$ points pass the first step in the algorithm is equal to*

$$PF(n,s,e) \quad = \quad Pr(U_{\overline{a}} \text{ is a sub-witness}) + Pr(U_{\overline{a}} \text{ is a complaisant flat}),$$

where

$$Pr(U_{\overline{a}} \text{ is a sub-witness}) \quad := \quad 2^{e-n} \cdot \prod_{i=1}^{s} \frac{2^e - 2^{i-1}}{2^n}$$

$$Pr(U_{\overline{a}} \text{ is a complaisant flat}) \quad := \quad 2^{-2^s+1} \cdot \frac{2^{n-e} NS(n,s) - NF(e,s)}{NS(n,s)}.$$

In the above formula, e is the dimension of the witness. The formulas for $NS(\cdot,\cdot)$ and $NF(\cdot,\cdot)$ are given in Lemma 7.

Proof: We first determine the probability that the flat $U_{\overline{a}}$ is a sub-witness. This probability is justified with an inductive argument on the dimension of the sub-witness: for one point (*i.e.*, a flat of dimension 0), the probability of being a sub-witness is $\frac{2^e}{2^n}$. Here, the witness has 2^e points. This probability is also true for extending the sub-witness from dimension $(i-1)$ to dimension i (we have $1 \leq i \leq s$). In addition, we have to consider the case $\overline{p}_i \in \overline{p}_0 + \langle \overline{p}_1, \ldots, \overline{p}_{i-1} \rangle$, *i.e.*, the new point $\overline{p}_i$ lies in the sub-witness of dimension $(i-1)$ generated by the points $\overline{p}_0, \ldots, \overline{p}_{i-1}$.

The probability that $U_{\overline{a}}$ is a complaisant flat is equal to the probability that the function is constant on $U_{\overline{a}}$ times the number of flats which are parallel with a witness but not part of a witness. This is exactly expressed in the formula. □

>From the previous theorem and the implicit evaluation strategy as described in Sect. 3.2, we can deduce the following corollary.

COROLLARY 10 *For a given start dimension s and an end dimension e, we need at most*

$$Rep(n, s, e, c) = \frac{c}{PF(n, s, e)} \cdot \frac{1}{Pr(only\, 1\, flat)\# flats}$$

repetitions to achieve a confidence of 2^{-c} *that the function f is not e-normal.*

Table 2 shows some numerical values of r in $\log_2$. In this and all following tables, we concentrate on even choices for n and fix $e = \frac{n}{2}$ as these cases are particularly relevant in cryptography.

Table 2. Number of repetitions (in $\log_2$) for different values of n and s

$s \backslash n$	8	10	12	14	16	18	20
2	15.49	18.35	21.28	24.25	27.23	30.22	33.22
3	18.68	22.31	26.14	30.06	34.02	38.00	41.99
4		26.11	30.72	35.54	40.45	45.40	50.38

Complexity of the main loop.
Obviously, picking $(2s+1)$ random points and checking if the function is constant for a given flat, will be the most expensive operations. Therefore, we start with a lemma on the average complexity for checking that a function is constant on a given set of points.

LEMMA 11 *For a given random function* $f : \mathbb{F}_2^n \to \mathbb{F}_2$ *and a given set of points* $P \subseteq \mathbb{F}_2^n$, *the algorithm from Fig. 6 needs on average 3 evaluations of f to check if this function is constant when restricted to vectors in the set P.*

Proof: The average number of evaluations depends on the number of points $p := |P|$ of this algorithm; it is given by

$$Ev(p) := \sum_{i=1}^{p-1} \frac{1}{2^i}(i+1) + \frac{1}{2^{p-1}} p = 3 - \frac{1}{2^{p-2}}.$$

Figure 6. Algorithm to determine if a function is constant on a set of points

Input: function f, a set P with $p := |P|$ points
Output: 1 if f is constant on P and 0 otherwise
Let $\overline{q}_1 \in P$, $c \leftarrow f(\overline{q}_1)$
for $\overline{q} \in P \setminus \{\overline{q}_1\}$ **do**
  if $f(\overline{q}) \neq c$ **then** OUTPUT 0
OUTPUT 1

To justify this formula, we observe that we need to evaluate f at least once to obtain the constant c. As the function is a random function by definition, we have a probability of $\frac{1}{2}$ to obtain a different constant for every further evaluation, *i.e.*, to terminate this algorithm. After checking a total of p points, the algorithm terminates. For this last check, we still have a probability of $\frac{1}{2}$ to output 0. However, the workload of outputting 0 or 1 is exactly the same, namely p evaluations. □

As a consequence, the complexity of the main loop so far depends on the costs of picking the $(2s+1)$ random points, evaluating the function f on the corresponding flat with probability *Pr(Only one flat)* and some other negligible operations whose complexity we set to one, *i.e.*, $(2s + 1 + 3\mathit{Pr(Only\ one\ flat)} + 1)r$, where r represents the number of repetitions. We obtain the following values ($\log_2$) if we evaluate the above formula numerically (cf Table 3).

Table 3. Numerical results for the time-complexity (in $\log_2$) of the main loop

n	$s=2$	$s=3$	$s=4$	$s=5$
8	18.47	21.95		
10	21.33	25.58	29.63	
12	24.26	29.41	34.24	39.12
14	27.23	33.33	39.06	44.72
16	30.21	37.29	43.97	50.53
18	33.20	41.27	48.93	56.44
20	36.20	45.26	53.90	62.40

Complexity of the SearchForParallelFlats-method.
From a computational point of view, the for-loop is very expensive, as we have to check $2^{n-s} - 1$ parallel flats every time. However, each flat costs only 3 operations on average (cf Lemma 11). In addition, we only need this for-loop in 2^{-2^s+1} of all cases as this is the probability that the function is constant on the corresponding flat. The other steps in the method are negligible in comparison to the for-loop. We therefore identify their average workload as 1. Consequently, the complexity can be approximated by $(1+3\cdot(2^{-2^s+1}\mathit{Pr(only\ one\ flat)})2^{n-2^s-s+1})r$ for the SearchForParallelFlats-method, where r denotes the number of repetitions. Numerical values for the time-complexity (in $\log_2$) of the SearchForParallelFlats-method are presented in Table 4.

Table 4. Numerical results for the time-complexity (in $\log_2$) of the SearchForParallelFlats-method

n	$s=2$	$s=3$	$s=4$	$s=5$
8	19.50	19.18		
10	24.28	23.71	26.11	
12	29.20	29.06	30.73	35.38
14	34.16	34.83	35.60	40.98
16	39.14	40.75	40.69	46.79
18	44.13	46.72	46.20	52.70
20	49.13	52.71	52.37	58.66

Complexity of the Combine-procedure.
The complexity analysis of the combine-procedure is a little more tricky. In particular, we have to deal with the problem that its complexity depends quadratically on the number of parallel flats we find, *i.e.*, the number $|P(U_{\overline{a}})|$ for a given flat $U_{\overline{a}}$. Therefore, we cannot simply take the average number of flats for this analysis as the result does not reflect the real time complexity of this algorithm. In addition, we have to deal with the branching condition (cf Sect. 3.4).

As we did not expect to find a closed formula for the time complexity of the combine-procedure, we used MAG to compute it numerically. As all computations are done with rational numbers, there are no rounding errors in MAGMA. In particular, we computed the probability for the different numbers of parallel flats we obtain in the searchForParallelFlats-method. We only took numbers $\geq 2^{e-s}$ into account (cf Thm. 6) and neglected levels of recursion which appear with too small probability ($< 2^{-40}$), due to the branching condition. In addition, we truncated the sum at points which did not contribute to the overall workload anymore (expected workload smaller than 1). We present the corresponding values ($\log_2$) for different choices of n and s in Table 5.

Table 5. Numerical results for the time-complexity (in $\log_2$) of the Combine-method

n	$s=2$	$s=3$	$s=4$	$s=5$
8	24.17	15.97		
10	31.15	22.87	≈ 0	
12	38.03	15.76	≈ 0	≈ 0
14	44.97	23.68	≈ 0	≈ 0
16	51.93	35.02	≈ 0	≈ 0
18		43.34	≈ 0	≈ 0
20		51.33	≈ 0	≈ 0

These computations were matched by our empirical results. In particular, the branching condition proved to be very powerful for $s \geq 3$ and $n \geq 12$ (note difference between $n = 10$ and $n = 12$ for $s = 3$). In these cases, we never needed a recursive call of the combine-method for non-normal functions. In addition, the probability for a function to be constant on a given flat decreases exponentially with increasing dimension of the flat. Therefore, we expect to find less than 2^{e-s} flats for $s \geq 4$ and $n \leq 20$ which means that the combine-method is never invoked in these cases (fields with ≈ 0 in the above table).

All in all, it is necessary to chose the starting dimension s correctly, *i.e.*, high enough such that the combine-method is still efficient and low enough such that Search-ForParallelFlats and the main loop do not need too much time. For dimension $n \geq 10$, the choice $s = 3$ turns out to be optimal (cf Fig. 7 for the case $n = 16$).

Figure 7. Time-complexity for the main loop (•), SearchForParallelFlats (⋆), and the combine-method (×) for dimension $n = 16$ and varying s

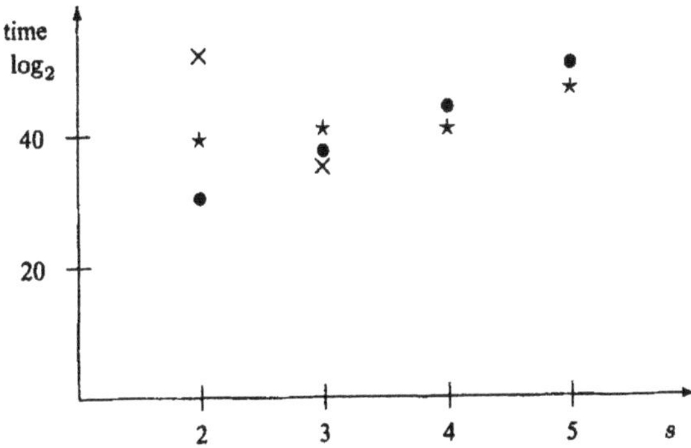

Asymptotic Analysis.

Here we sketch the asymptotical analysis of the above algorithm: we begin with the observation that for large n and subsequently large s, the running time will only depend on the number of repetitions necessary. We justify this reasoning as follows: as we saw for the combine-method, we have a very powerful branching condition, *i.e.*, asymptotically, this part will not contribute to the overall complexity. The same is true for the search of parallel flats: we have a complexity of $O(2^{(-2^s+1)(n-s)})$ here, *i.e.*, negligible for $n \to \infty$. In addition, we cannot use the implicit evaluation strategy anymore in the asymptotic case, as we obtain a rather small probability for having exactly one flat $s \to \infty$. Therefore, we drop the corresponding term in our asymptotic analysis. For our analysis, we chose $s = \frac{1}{4}n$ and $e = \frac{1}{2}n$ and obtain the following asymptotically upper bound on the number of repetitions and thus the running time of the algorithm:

$$Rep(n, \frac{1}{4}n, \frac{1}{2}n, c) \quad = \quad O(c.2^{\frac{1}{8}n^2+\frac{3}{4}n}),$$

where c is the target confidence level. To obtain this upper bound, we observe that the probability to have a complaisant flat is asymptotically very small. In addition, we notice that for large n the factor $2^{e-n+s(e-1-n)}$ is a tight lower bound on the probability $PF(n, s, e)$. Using Theorem 9 and Corollary 10 yields the result.

4.2 Comparison with the Algorithm from Daum *et al.*

In Fig. 8 and Table 6 we compare the time complexities of our algorithm with that of DDL03, for computing the normality of a function in dimension n. We are not aware of an asymptotical analysis of the algorithm from DDL03.

Figure 8. Time-complexity (in $\log_2$) of this paper ($\star$) and from DDL03 ($\bullet$)

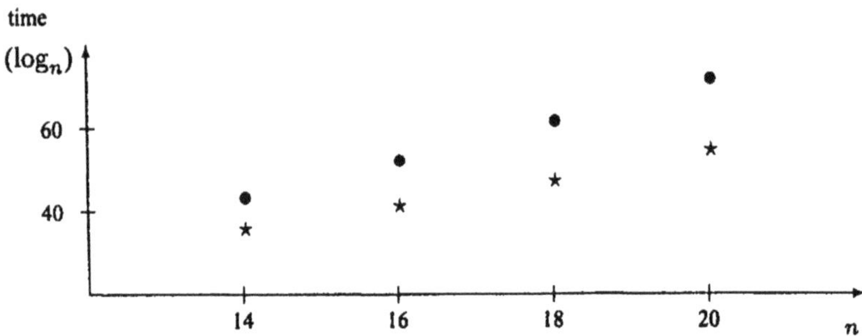

The time complexity of algorithm of DDL03, is computed using the formulas given there. According to these results, we expect that it is outperformed by our algorithm for increasing dimension n.

Table 6. Comparison of the time-complexity (in $\log_2$)

n	s	Daum *et al.*	Our alg.
14	2	**42.58**	44.97
	3	≈ 46	**35.27**
	4	≈ 52	39.18
16	2	**51.58**	51.93
	3	≈ 54	**40.88**
	4	≈ 62	44.11

n	s	Daum *et al.*	Our alg.
18	2	**61.17**	> 50
	3	**61.01**	**46.72**
	4	> 61	49.13
20	2	71.09	> 55
	3	**71.04**	> 55
	4	>71	**54.33**

4.3 Empirical Results

We have implemented our algorithm in a programme with 14,000 lines of C++ code. Checking random functions on an AMD Athlon XP 2000+, we obtained the following results for $e = \frac{n}{2}$ (normality) and $s = 3$:

n	10	12	14	16
time [min]	0.248	1.21	42.6	2880

As we see in this table, the running time gets quickly out of hand. According to DDL03, their programme needs approximately 50 h on a Pentium IV 1.5 GHz for the case $n = 14$. Our algorithm needs approximately 43 min for $n = 14$ and approximately 2 d for $n = 16$. Using the complexity analysis of DDL03, we expect a running time of more than a year for their algorithm to handle functions of dimension $n = 16$. We also estimated (empirically) the running time for the cases $n = 18, 20$ and obtain 2.5 years and 130 years, respectively.

For our C++ implementation, we have included several improvements:

Combinatorial Gray codes. In order to compute vectors more efficiently for a given basis, we used combinatorial Gray codes (Sav97) and computed all intermediate values in a Gray code like fashion. This way, we only needed one computation on average rather than $\frac{n}{2}$ when computing elements of the vector space $<\overline{U}>$.

Optimised Pseudo-Random Number Generator. As the programme spends approx. 60% of its time computing random numbers, we concluded that it could benefit from a fast way of generating pseudo-random numbers. However, due to the high number of repetitions, we still need a long period for the pseudo-random number generator. To meet both aims, we used a pseudo-random number generator from Rho which combines a multiply with carry generator and a simple multiplicative generator. It achieves a period of more than 2^{60}, has good statistical properties, and is also very fast according to our measurements. For the future, tests with the cryptographically secure pseudo-random number generator using Shamir's T-functions class (KS04) are planned.

Function storage. For the Boolean function to be checked, we can use several ways of storing it: bit-wise, byte-wise or in processor-words (32 bit). To make the best use of the internal cache of the processor, a bit-wise storage turned out to have the best performance for dimensions $n \geq 12$. For dimensions $n \leq 10$, an word-wise storage was clearly better as we do not have the overhead of retrieving single bits from a word.

5. Conclusions

In this paper, we present a fast asymmetric Monte Carlo algorithm to determine the normality of Boolean functions. It uses the fact that a function which is constant on a flat of a certain dimension is also constant on all sub-flats of lower dimension. In addition, we evaluate "parallel" flats using the implicit evaluation strategy (cf Sect. 3.2). Starting with flats of dimension s and combining them until a flat of dimension e is obtained, we achieve a far lower time-complexity than with exhaustive search on flats of dimension e.

In particular, this algorithm is far faster than the previously known algorithm (43 min in comparison to 50 h) for dimension 14 (cf 4.2). Moreover, it is the first time that the important case $n = 16$ can be computed on non-specialised hardware in 2 days (previously: more than a year). Using the fact that our algorithm can be parallelised easily, this figure can even be improved and we can even handle the case $n = 18$ (16 computers in 8 weeks). For scientific purposes and at present, $n = 20$ seems to be out of reach as it would take 128 computers about 1 year.

Acknowledgments

We want to thank the authors of DDL03, for helpful remarks and sending us both an early and an extended version of their work.

The authors were partially supported by Concerted Research Action GOA-MEFISTO-666 of the Flemish Government and An Braeken is research assistant of the Fund for Scientific research - Flanders (Belgium).

References

Canteaut, Anne; Daum, Magnus; Dobbertin, Hans; and Leander, Gregor (2003). Normal and non-normal bent functions. In WCC03. 19 pages.

Carlet, Claude (2001). On the complexity of cryptographic Boolean functions. In *6th Conference on Finite Fields and Applications, 21th – 25th May*, pages 53–69. Gary L. Mullen, Henning Stichtenoth, and Horacio Tapia-Recillas, editors, Springer.

Daum, Magnus; Dobbertin, Hans; and Leander, Gregor (2003). An algorithm for checking normality of Boolean functions. In WCC03. 14 pages.

Dobbertin, Hans (1994). Construction of bent functions and balanced Boolean functions with high nonlinearity. In *Fast Software Encryption — FSE 1994*, volume 1008 of *Lecture Notes in Computer Science*, pages 61–74. Bart Preneel, editor, Springer.

Dubuc, Sylvie (2001). *Etude des propriétés de dégénérescene et de normalité des fonctions booléennes et construction des fonctions q-aires parfaitement non-linéaires*. PhD thesis, Université de Caen.

Kipnis, Aviad and Shamir, Adi (2004). New cryptographic primitives based on multiword T-functions. In *Fast Software Encryption — FSE 2004*. Bimal Roy and Willi Meier, editors. pre-proceedings, 14 pages.

Landau, David and Binder, Kurt (2000). *A Guide to Monte Carlo Simulations in Statistical Physics*. Cambridge University Press. ISBN 0-521-65314-2.

MacWilliams, F.J. and Sloane, N.J.A. (1991). *The Theory of Error-Correcting Codes*. Elsevier Science Publisher. ISBN 0-444-85193-3.

MAGMA. *The MAGMA Computational Algebra System for Algebra, Number Theory and Geometry*. Computational Algebra Group, University of Sydney. http://magma.maths.usyd.edu.au/magma/.

Rhoads, Glenn. Random number generator in C. http://remus.rutgers.edu/~rhoads/Code/rands.c.

Savage, Carla (1997). A survey of combinatorical Gray codes. *SIAM Review*, 39(4):605--629. http://www.csc.ncsu.edu/faculty/savage/AVAILABLE_FOR_MAILING/survey.ps.

WCC (2003). *Workshop on Coding and Cryptography 2003*. Daniel Augot, Pascal Charpin, and Grigory Kabatianski, editors, l'Ecole Suprieure et d'Application des Transmissions. ISBN 2-7261-1205-6.

REVERSIBLE CIRCUIT REALIZATIONS OF BOOLEAN FUNCTIONS

Alex Brodsky
Department of Computer Science
University of Toronto, Canada
abrodsky@cs.utoronto.ca

Abstract Reversible circuits are a concrete model of reversible computation with applications in areas such as quantum computing and analysis of cryptographic block cyphers. In 1980, Toffoli showed how to realize a Boolean function by a reversible circuit, however the resulting complexity of such circuits has remained an open problem. We investigate the reversible circuit complexity of families of Boolean functions and derive conditions that characterize whether a polynomial realization is possible.

First, we derive sufficient conditions on families of Boolean functions that guarantee a polynomial-size reversible circuit realization. Namely, we show that if a Boolean function can be embedded into an even parity permutation that has a polynomial-size cycle representation, then the Boolean function can be realized by a polynomial-size reversible circuit. Furthermore, we provide a construction for the realization. Second, we provide concrete realizations for several families of Boolean functions, such as the adder, incrementor, and threshold functions, which do not necessarily satisfy the preceding condition, but still have polynomial-size realizations; this is important because such realizations will necessarily form the building blocks of quantum computers.

Keywords: Reversible computation, circuit complexity, Boolean functions

1. Introduction

Reversible circuits, introduced by Landauer [Lan61] and formalized by Toffoli and Fredkin [Tof80, FT82], are a concrete model of reversible computation that have come to prominence in the last few years; their applications range from quantum computing [BBD$^+$95], where reversibility is a prerequisite, to analysis of cryptographic block cyphers [Cle90, EG83], which use primitives that are nearly identical to those comprising reversible circuits. Reversible computation is based on a notion of equivalence between information and entropy that was formalized by Shannon and Weaver [Sha48, SW49], but dates back to Maxwell's Demon [Max71] and the work of Szilard [Szi29]. Namely, the operations comprising a reversible computation may not discard any information during the course of the computation. In this paper we investigate the reversible circuit complexity of families of Boolean functions and derive conditions that characterize whether a polynomial realization is possible.

Reversible circuits on n lines (wires) realize permutations on the Boolean cube of dimension n. In 1980, Toffoli [Tof80] showed how to embed Boolean functions into permutations and thus, be realizable by a reversible circuit. Namely, an n-adic Boolean function can be embedded into a permutation on a Boolean cube of dimension $n+1$. However, just as in the case of classical circuit complexity, the complexity of the corresponding reversible circuit is difficult to determine. Some results were obtained by Cleve [Cle90], who showed that polynomial length compositions of D.E.S.-like cipher functions—function generators, of fan-in 2—can compute $\mathbf{NC}^1$. The construction is reminiscent of Barrington's [Bar86] proof that width-5 permutation branching programs compute $\mathbf{NC}^1$. The point of Cleve's investigation was to determine if such ciphers could be used as pseudorandom generators.

Alternatively, since most Boolean functions are irreversible, the reversible circuit complexity of a Boolean function is directly related to the complexity of simulating irreversible computation reversibly. Bennett [Ben73] first described two simulation techniques, within the context of Turing machines, that used additional space to record a check-point based history of the simulation. The first simulation used $O(T)$ time and $O(S+T)$ space to reversibly simulate a computation that takes T time and S space; the second simulation used $O(T^2)$ time and $O(S\log T) \subseteq O(S^2)$ space. The latter simulation was later refined to use $O(T^{1+\epsilon})$ time and $O(S\log T)$ space [Ben89, LS90]. Although Bennett's constructions are of the same spirit as the circuit constructions of Toffoli [Tof80], it is the space parsimonious reversible simulation of a Turing machine by Lange et al. [LMT00] that mostly closely resembles the n-line reversible circuit model.

We show that any even parity permutation on an n-dimensional Boolean cube whose cycle representation is of size s can be realized by a reversible circuit of size $O(sn)$. The key corollary is that any Boolean function that can be embedded into a permutation with a polynomial size cycle representation, can be realized by polynomial size reversible circuit. Furthermore, the proof is completely constructive, yielding a simple methodology for designing reversible circuits.

In many cases this bound is not tight because there are many families of functions, such as the incrementor, whose corresponding permutations have exponentially large cycle representations, but polynomial-size circuit realizations. We exhibit several families of functions with such characteristics and derive realizations for them. Particularly, we focus on functions that are commonly implemented in hardware and will necessarily need to be implemented as part of a quantum computer, i.e., reversibly. We consider several families of functions, including incrementors, adders, consensus, and threshold functions.

In Section 2 we formally define the reversible circuit model and describe how Boolean functions are embedded within permutations on the Boolean cube. In Section 3 we prove our main result and in Section 4 we provide concrete constructions for several families of Boolean functions. Section 5 summarizes some of the techniques for constructing reversible circuits and finally, section 6 places our results in the greater context and provides some future directions.

2. Background

Reversible circuits comprise a number of wires, called **lines**, and reversible **gates** that operate on the lines. The lines carry binary values, 0 or 1, which are placed on the lines' input terminals, are modified by gates operating on the lines, and are read off the lines' output terminals; by convention, the input terminals are on the left side and the output terminals are on the right (see Figure 1). Each gate operates on at most three lines. All but one of the lines pass through the gate unmodified and are called **control lines**. The remaining line, called the **toggle line** is XORed by the gate with the conjunction of the values of the control lines. Each gate realize a bijection on the Boolean cube and each gate is also it's own inverse.

Let $B_n = \{0,1\}^n$ denote the Boolean cube of dimension n, let $x \in B_n$ denote an n-bit vector, and let x_i denote the ith bit of x. A reversible circuit C, on n lines, is specified by a sequence of m gates, $C = g_1 g_2 \dots g_m$: the gates are the NOT gate, denoted $\oplus_i$; the controlled-NOT gate, denoted $\oplus_i^j$; and the Toffoli gate, denoted $\oplus_i^{j \wedge k}$, where $j,k \in [n]$ specify the control lines and $i \in [n]$ specifies the toggle line. In the nomenclature of Coppersmith and Grossman [CG75], the three gates correspond to the 0-, 1-, and 2-functions, respectively. For example, the circuit in Figure 1 comprises two Toffoli gates and two NOT gates.

The output of circuit C on input x, is denoted $C(x)$, and the composition and inverse of circuits corresponds respectively to the concatenation and reversal of the circuits' gate sequences; we write CC' to denote the concatenation of two circuits and C^{-1} to denote the inverse of C. Each reversible circuit realizes a permutation on the Boolean cube B_n, corresponding to an element of the symmetric group S_{2^n}. We write $C \sim \sigma \in S_{2^n}$ if C realizes permutation σ and we write $C \sim C'$ if C and C' realize the same permutation, e.g., $C \sim (1\,2\,3)$. For conciseness, we assume that circuit $C_{(xyz)} \sim (xyz)$, $x,y,z \in B_n$ and in general that circuit $C_\sigma \sim \sigma$.

We often use a notion of a controlled circuit in our constructions. An **(i)-controlled** circuit, denoted $C^{(i)}$, performs two different permutations depending on the value of line i, leaving the value of line i unchanged. If line i has value 1, the circuit performs a fixed permutation, otherwise the circuit performs the identity permutation. Analogously, a **$\overline{(i)}$-controlled** circuit performs a fixed permutation only if the value of line (i) is 0. In general, a circuit is **x-controlled**, for some $x \in B_k$ and $k < n$, if the circuit, denoted C^x, is controlled by a fixed subset of control lines of size k. If the lines hold the value x, then C^x performs a fixed permutation, leaving the control lines unchanged, and performs the identity permutation otherwise. For example, the circuit in Figure 1 is a $\overline{(3)}$-controlled circuit,

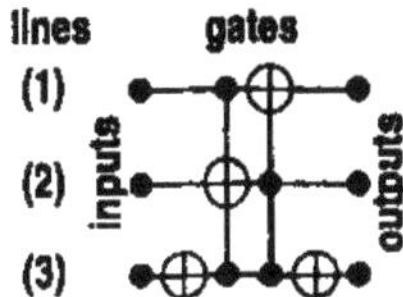

Figure 1. The circuit $C = \oplus_3 \oplus_2^{1\wedge 3} \oplus_1^{2\wedge 3} \oplus_3 \sim (1\,2\,3)$.

For conciseness, we use several schematic short forms. First, the k-line controlled Toffoli gate, $k < n-1$, which computes the conjunction of k lines and XORs the output line. A k-line controlled Toffoli (k-Toffoli) gate can be constructed using $O(k)$ Toffoli gates [BBD+95] and is illustrated in Figure 2a. Second, the controlled k-NOT, comprises k controlled-NOT gates that are all controlled by the same line. In most cases, we will be using the controlled $(n-1)$-NOT, which is illustrated in Figure 2c. Additionally, we use blocks to denote a component of a circuit: a component may either be **simple** (Figure 2e); **controlled** (Figure 2d), i.e., controlled by another line; or a **k-function** (Figure 2b), i.e., XOR a line with a Boolean function computed on k other lines. The controlled k-NOT and the k-Toffoli gate are examples of a controlled component and a k-function.

The **size** of circuit C, denoted $|C|$ is the number of gates comprising C. The **depth** of C, denoted $d(C)$ is the length of the longest path through the directed acyclic graph induced by circuit C: the lines correspond to right-oriented arcs, the gates correspond to vertices of equal indegree and outdegree, the input terminals correspond to vertices with indegree 0, and the output terminals correspond to vertices of outdegree 0. Two gates are **pairwise independent** if there is no path from one to the other in the induced graph. Since the number gates that are all pairwise independent is at most n, the depth of a circuit is at most a factor of n less than the size, i.e., $|C|/n \leq d(C) \leq |C|$. Finally, the size of the cycle representation of a permutation σ, denoted $|\sigma|$, is the number of points in the permutation that are not fixed, e.g., a transposition has size 2.

2.1 Embedding Boolean Functions

To realize a Boolean function by a reversible circuit, the function must first be embedded into a permutation, because reversible circuits can only realize permutations on the Boolean cube. In the spirit of Toffoli [Tof80], an $(n+c)$**-embedding** of an n-adic Boolean function f is a permutation σ on an $n+c$ dimensional Boolean cube such that if $y = \sigma x$, for any input x (padded with zeros), then $y_{n+c} = f(x)$. The embedding is said to be **input-preserving** if $x_i = y_i$, for all $i \in [n]$, i.e., the embedding preserves the input.

In many physical contexts, such as quantum computation, using additional lines—in addition to the n lines containing the input—is expensive. Thus, we restrict our attention to embeddings that use the minimum number of additional lines: $c \leq 2$. Unless f is linear in some variable x_i, i.e., $f(x) = g(x_1, \ldots, x_{i-1}, x_{i+1}, \ldots, x_n) \oplus x_i$, an

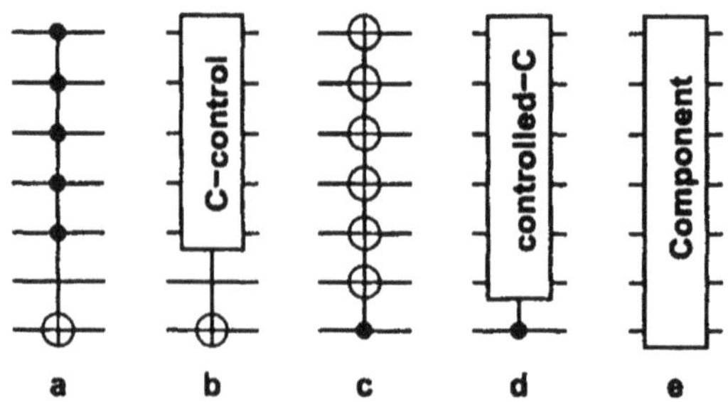

Figure 2
a) A k-Toffoli gate;
b) a k-function component;
c) a controlled n-NOT;
d) a controlled component;
e) a simple component.

input-preserving n-embedding of f does not exist; and, if f is unbalanced, there does not exist any kind of n-embedding of f [Tof80]. Thus, in most cases we consider realizations of $(n+1)$-embeddings, i.e., $c = 1$. In fact, if we require an input-preserving embedding of an unbalanced function with an odd number of satisfying assignments, only an $(n+2)$-embedding will suffice.

If f is Boolean function of the form $f : B_n \to B_k$, $1 < k \leq n$, a similar criterion can be derived. However, many such functions do not have an $(n+c)$-embedding, where c is a constant [Tof80]. For example, the multiplication function, which takes two n-bit strings and yields a $2n$ bit string, does not have a m-embedding where $m < 4n$!

On two occasions we consider functions that are of the form $f : B_n \to B_n$, e.g., the incrementor (counter) function that maps $z \to z+1 \bmod 2^n$. In this case, even if f is a bijection, a corresponding n-embedding does not exist because the corresponding permutation has odd parity. For $n > 3$, odd parity permutations cannot be realized by a reversible circuit that comprises NOT, controlled-NOT, and Toffoli gates [CG75]. However, an $(n+1)$-embedding of even parity is possible, and hence can be realized by a reversible circuit on $n+1$ lines.

The reversible circuit complexity of a Boolean function f, is the minimum over all circuit realizations of all possible embeddings of f. However, determining reversible circuit complexity of realizing a permutation is not obvious. In the next section we characterize families of permutations, and hence families of Boolean functions, that have reversible circuit complexity which is polynomial in n.

3. The Main Result

In this section we prove the following theorem:

THEOREM 1 *Any even parity permutation σ on B_n, can be realized by an n-line circuit of size $O(|\sigma|n)$.*

The proof comprises three parts: first, we prove that given a circuit that realizes a permutation that is represented by a single 3-cycle, the circuit can be modified to realize any other 3-cycle and that the modifications can be accomplished with $O(n)$ gates. Second, we show that the 3-cycle $(0\,1\,2)$ can be realized by a reversible circuit on $n > 1$ lines that is of size $O(n)$. Third, we note that any even parity permutation whose cycle representation is of size s can be factored into $O(s)$ 3-cycles. Combining these three facts yields the result. The following lemma and its corollary form the heart of the first part of the proof, which is summarized in Theorem 4.

LEMMA 2 *Let $C_{(0\,1\,2)}$ be a reversible circuit on n lines. For any $x,y \in B_n$, $x \neq y$ and $x,y \neq 0$, there exists a reversible circuit C of size $O(n)$, such that the circuit $CC_{(0\,1\,2)}C^{-1} \sim C_{(0xy)}$.*

Proof: Select two lines i and j, setting $u = x_i x_j$, $v = y_i y_j$, $u, v \in B_2$, such that $u \neq v$ and $u, v \in \{1,2,3\}$. Such a choice is possible, otherwise $x = 0$, $y = 0$, or $x = y$, none of which can happen because $(0xy)$ is a 3-cycle. Call lines i and j the control lines. The circuit C consists of three stages. Stage one comprises $|x| - |u|$ Toffoli gates plus $|y| - |v|$ Toffoli gates. The first subsequence is bracketed by a pair of NOT gates on line i (j) if x_i (x_j) is 0; the second sequence is analogously bracketed if y_i (y_j) is 0. For each $k \neq i, j$, if $x_k = 1$ a Toffoli gate $\oplus_k^{i \wedge j}$, controlled by lines i and j, toggles line k. The second subsequence of Toffoli gates is analogously specified. Thus, on input x or y, all lines but lines i and j are toggled to 0.

Stage two swaps line i with line 1 and line j with line 2. This can be done using $O(1)$ gates. Finally, stage three manipulates lines 1 and 2 since these lines now hold the value of the control lines. If $u \neq 1$ and $v \neq 2$, then stage three maps u to 1 and v to 2; this also takes $O(1)$ gates. Therefore, circuit C maps input 0 to 0, input x to 1, and input y to 2, using $O(|x| + |y|) \subseteq O(n)$ gates. The circuit may permute other points in B_n, but this is of no consequence.

Since $C \sim (x1\ldots y2\ldots)$, composing circuit C with $C_{(012)}$ in the form of a conjugate yields

$$CC_{(012)}C^{-1} \sim (x1\ldots y2\ldots)(012)(x1\ldots y2\ldots)^{-1} = (0xy) \sim C_{(0xy)},$$

which completes the proof. ■

Corollary 3 *Let $C_{(0xy)}$ be a reversible circuit on n lines. There exists a reversible circuit C of size $O(n)$, such that the circuit $CC_{(0xy)}C^{-1} \sim C_{(012)}$.*

Theorem 4 follows easily from the lemma and the corollary.

Theorem 4 (3-cycle Hardness Theorem) *If $C_{(xyz)}$ is a reversible circuit on n lines, then for any distinct $x', y', z' \in B_n$, there exists a circuit C of size $O(n)$, such that $CC_{(xyz)}C^{-1} \sim C_{(x'y'z')}$.*

Proof: Since XORing the input with a constant bit vector can be performed by $O(n)$ NOT gates, we can transform $C_{(xyz)}$ into $C_{0\bar{y}\bar{z}}$, where $\bar{y} = y \oplus x$ and $\bar{z} = z \oplus x$. Similarly, for a circuit $C_{(0\bar{y}'\bar{z}')}$, where $\bar{y}' = y' \oplus x'$ and $\bar{z}' = z' \oplus x'$, can be transformed into $C_{(x'y'z')}$ using $O(n)$ gates. Let C_x be the circuit comprising $|x|$ NOT gates such that $C_xC_{(xyz)}C_x^{-1} \sim C_{(0\bar{y}\bar{z})}$ and correspondingly let $C_{x'}$ be such that $C_{(x'y'z')} \sim C_{x'}C_{(0\bar{y}'\bar{z}')}C_{x'}{}^{-1}$.

By Corollary 3, $C_{(0\bar{y}\bar{z})}$ can be transformed into $C_{(012)}$ and by Lemma 2, this circuit can be transformed into $C_{(0\bar{y}'\bar{z}')}$, also in $O(n)$ gates. Let C_1 and C_2 be the circuits such that $C_{(012)} \sim C_1C_{(0\bar{y}\bar{z})}C_1^{-1}$ and $C_{(0\bar{y}'\bar{z}')} \sim C_2C_{(012)}C_2^{-1}$. Since

$$C_{(x'y'z')} \sim C_{x'}C_2C_1C_xC_{(xyz)}C_x^{-1}C_1^{-1}C_2^{-1}C_{x'}{}^{-1},$$

setting $C = C_{x'}C_2C_1C_x$, which is of size $O(n)$, completes the proof. ■

Thus, all 3-cycles are equally hard to realize in the sense that, given a polynomial size realization of one 3-cycle, any other 3-cycle can be realized by using an additional $O(n)$ gates. The second step of the proof, Theorem 5, shows how a 3-cycle can be realized by a reversible circuit of size $O(n)$.

Theorem 5 *For $n > 1$ there is an n-line reversible circuit $C_{(012)}$ of size $O(n)$.*

Proof: If $1 < n \leq 3$ we can construct a reversible circuit that realizes any permutation and uses a constant number of gates [CG75].

For $n > 3$, observe that permutation $(0\,1\,2)$ may be factored into $\tau_1 = (0\,1)(6\,3)$ and $\tau_2 = (0\,2)(6\,3)$. Thus, we need only demonstrate that permutations τ_1 and τ_2 can be realized in $O(n)$ gates.

First, the permutation $(0\,1)(2\,3)$ (respectively $(0\,2)(1\,3)$) may be realized by $O(n)$ gates. The circuit comprises three stages: a negation, followed by a toggling, followed by a negation; each stage requires $O(n)$ gates. Stages one and three negate the $n-2$ lines $3,\ldots,n$. The middle stage comprises an $(n-2)$-Toffoli gate, controlled by lines $3,\ldots,n$, that toggles line 1 (respectively line 2). Let $C_{(01)(23)} \sim (0\,1)(2\,3)$ and $C_{(02)(13)} \sim (0\,2)(1\,3)$ respectively.

Next, we construct a reversible circuit $C_{(01)(63)}$ that realizes permutation $(0\,1)(6\,3)$. The reversible circuit $C_{\sigma_1} = \oplus_1 \oplus_3^{1\wedge 2} \oplus_1$ realizes a permutation that transposes 2 and 6 and whose fixed-points include all points that are congruent to 0, 1, or 3 modulo 4. Since $\sigma_1(0\,1)(2\,3)\sigma_1 = (0\,1)(6\,3)$, therefore $C_{(01)(63)} = C_{\sigma_1} C_{(01)(23)} C_{\sigma_1}{}^{-1}$.

Similarly, we construct $C_{(02)(63)}$. The circuit $C_{\sigma_2} = \oplus_2 \oplus_3^{1\wedge 2} \oplus_2$ transposes points 1 and 5, with the fixed-points comprising all points that are congruent to 0, 2, and 3 modulo 4. Using conjugation, we construct circuit $C_{(02)(53)} = C_{\sigma_2} C_{(02)(13)} C_{\sigma_2}$. The circuit $C_\rho = \oplus_1^{2\wedge 3} \oplus_2^{1\wedge 3} \oplus_1^{2\wedge 3}$, switches the values of the lines 1 and 2, using line 3 as the control. Permutation ρ transposes 5 and 6; only points congruent to 5 or 6 modulo 8 are permuted. Since $\rho(0\,2)(5\,3)\rho^{-1} = (0\,2)(6\,3)$, therefore $C_{(02)(63)} = C_\rho C_{(02)(53)} C_\rho^{-1}$.

The required circuit is $C_{(012)} = C_{(01)(63)} C_{(02)(63)}$ is of size $O(n)$. ∎

In conjunction with Theorem 4, we get the following two corollaries.

COROLLARY 6 *Any 3-cycle can be realized by a reversible circuit on $n > 1$ lines of size $O(n)$.*

COROLLARY 7 *A permutation on B_n comprising two disjoint transpositions, can be realized by a reversible circuit on n lines of size $O(n)$.*

Proof: This follows from the fact that $(a\,b)(c\,d) = (a\,b\,c)(c\,a\,d)$. ∎

We note that every even parity permutation σ can be factored into $|\sigma| - 1$ transpositions and that by Corollary 7, any pair of transpositions can be realized with $O(n)$ gates. Hence, every even parity permutation σ has a reversible circuit realization of size $O(|\sigma| n)$, which is the statement of Theorem 1. Thus, any Boolean function that has an embedding with a polynomial size cycle representation can be realized by a polynomial size reversible circuit. Unfortunately, the converse is not true. There are many families of Boolean functions, such as the negation of a projection, and the incrementor, that have an exponential size cycle representation but a concise reversible circuit realization. In the next section we detail realizations for several of such families of functions.

4. Applications: Concrete Realizations

Two common families of functions that are ubiquitous in digital circuits are the incrementor family, which includes the decrementor and the adder, and the threshold family, which includes such variants as the conjunction, the disjunction, the majority, and the consensus. We first describe how to realize an incrementor, or more precisely, a near approximation of one. The adder can then be built from a number of incrementors.

The incrementor presents an interesting challenge for several reasons. First, its cycle representation is large, comprising all 2^n points of the Boolean cube. Second, even though the incrementor is a bijection, it cannot be realized (in full) by a reversible circuit because the corresponding permutation has odd parity [CG75]. Thus, at best, the incrementor can only be approximated by a reversible circuit. Even though the cycle representation is large, various approximations of the incrementor can be realized efficiently: our realization is of size and depth $O(n^2)$.

4.1 Realization of Various Incrementors

Since a full incrementor on B_n is impossible [CG75], we begin by constructing a **half-incrementor** that performs a full increment on the subspace B_{n-1} and is represented by two disjoint cycles of the form

$$\pi = (0\,1 \ldots 2^{n-1} - 1)(2^{n-1}\; 2^{n-1} + 1 \ldots 2^n - 1).$$

By concatenating this realization with another small circuit, we construct a **nigh-incrementor**, which corresponds to the permutation

$$\pi' = (0\,1 \ldots 2^{n-1} - 2),$$

i.e., performs the operation $z \rightarrow z + 1 \bmod 2^n - 1$ rather than $\bmod 2^n$.

The half-incrementor can be realized via a sequence of k-Toffoli gates, where $k = n - 2 \ldots 0$. Observe that an incrementor modifies the ith least significant bit of the input if and only if the conjunction of the $i - 1$ least significant bits of the input is equal to 1. Thus, the circuit comprises $n - 1$ components (k-Toffoli gates), where the jth gate is an $(n - 1 - j)$-Toffoli gate that negates line $n - j$ and is controlled by the lines $1 \ldots n - 2 - j$; see Figure 3.

The nth line of the circuit in Figure 3 is required in order to realize the $(n-2)$-Toffoli gate. The line is used as a temporary register and retains its original value by the end of the computation of the $(n-2)$-Toffoli gate. Via straightforward induction on n, it is easy to see that the circuit realizes permutation π. Since the realization of each k-Toffoli gate comprises $O(k)$ normal Toffoli gates (2-Toffoli gates) [BBD+95], the half incrementor may be realized in $O(n^2)$ gates. It follows that if we use an additional line, then a complete incrementor can be realized, otherwise, the best we can hope to realize is a nigh-incrementor.

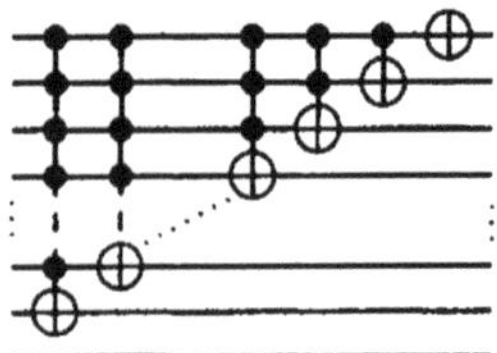

Figure 3. A half-incrementor circuit.

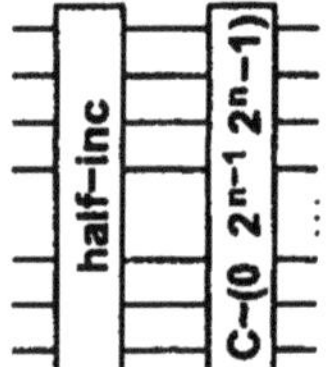

Figure 4. A nigh-incrementor circuit.

The nigh-incrementor is realized by concatenating an additional circuit onto the one that realizes a half-incrementor. Since the nigh-incrementor corresponds to the permutation π', let $\rho = \pi^{-1}\pi' = (0\ 2^{n-1}\ 2^n - 1)$, and thus the circuit $C_\pi C_\rho = C_{\pi'}$, depicted in Figure 4, realizes the nigh-incrementor. By Corollary 6, the complexity of C_ρ is $O(n)$. Hence, the circuit complexity of the nigh-incrementor is also $O(n^2)$. The half-incrementor is also the basic component in the construction of the adder.

In contrast to the incrementor, the adder requires no additional lines; this is because the adder corresponds to an even parity permutation. An adder that takes two n-bit inputs, on $2n$ lines and outputs the result on the latter n lines, $n+1,\ldots,2n$, and the first summand on the former n lines, $1,\ldots,n$. The adder comprises a sequence of n controlled half-incrementors; see Figure 5. The kth half-incrementor is controlled by line k, $k \in [n]$, and increments the $n-k$ most significant lines of the second summand, i.e., the increment is performed on lines $n+k,\ldots,2n$. This follows from the observation, that adding 2^j to an n-bit value corresponds to performing an increment on the $n-j$ most significant bits. The adder does exactly that, performing a controlled increment for each of the n bits of the first summand. Since each half-incrementor can be realized in $O(n^2)$ gates, the entire adder can be realized in $O(n^3)$ gates.

Unfortunately, there seems little that can be done to reduce this bound. For example, implementing a ripple adder is difficult because each stage of the ripple adder loses information—the preceding carry—implying that in order for a ripple adder circuit to work reversibly, all carry information needs to saved; we know of no way to accomplish this.

Realization of Threshold Functions. Quantum computing is inherently a probabilistic model of computation. Therefore, threshold functions, including the consensus function, are themselves necessarily useful in quantum computing. Except for one case—a majority of an odd number of variables—none of the threshold functions have an n-embedding. However all threshold functions have an $n+1$ embedding, and in many cases an input-preserving one. The threshold functions that are easiest to realize are the consensus, conjunction, and disjunction functions on n variables.

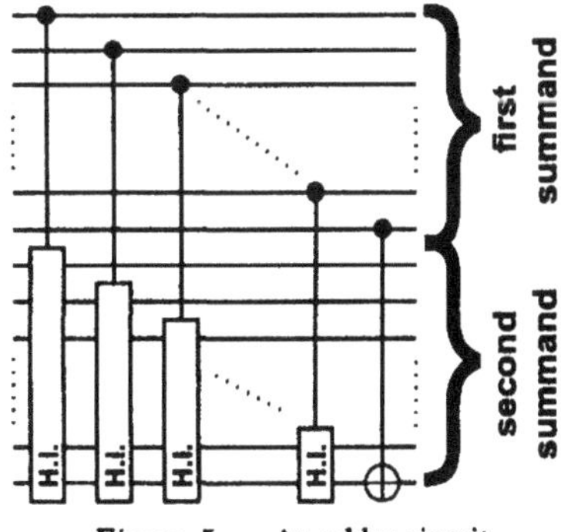

Figure 5. An adder circuit.

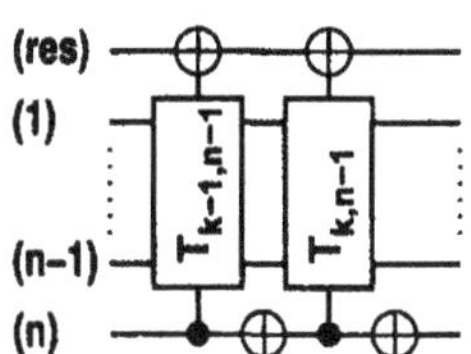

Figure 6. A $T_{k,n}$ circuit.

The consensus function evaluates to 1 if and only if all n variables have the same value. In fact, this function has input-preserving $(n+1)$-embedding comprising two transpositions: $(0\,2^n)(2^n-1\;2^{n+1}-1)$. Thus, by Corollary 7, consensus has a concise realization of size $O(n)$. On the other hand, the conjunction function—as well as its dual, disjunction—do not have an input-preserving $(n+1)$-embedding because the embedding would be an odd parity permutation, comprising one transposition: $(2^n-1\;2^{n+1}-1)$. However, there are many nearly input-preserving embeddings, like $(1\,2)(2^n-1\;2^{n+1}-1)$, whose complexity, by Corollary 7, is also $O(n)$.

More complicated threshold functions can be realized by composing the $\sum_{i=k}^{n}\binom{n}{k}$ transpositions, (xx'), where $|x|\geq k$ and $x'=2^n\oplus x$; each transposition corresponds to a 1 in the threshold's truth table. We assume that $k\geq n/2$ since computing the dual only requires an additional $O(n)$ gates. This yields realizations of size $O\left(\binom{n}{k}n\right)$ for threshold function $T_{k,n}$, $k\geq n/2$, where n is the number of variables and k is the threshold. However, the resulting realization are not necessarily obvious. We present a recursive construction that yields realizations with the same asymptotic complexity, but with a more analyzable structure.

A realization of threshold function $T_{k,n}$ comprises two simpler threshold function realizations. The two components of a realization of $T_{k,n}$ are a controlled realization of $T_{k-1,n-1}$, and a controlled realization of $T_{k,n-1}$; see Figure 6.

If line n has value 1, then the circuit needs only to check that the weight of the remaining $n-1$ lines is $k-1$ or greater. The first controlled component, which realizes $T_{k-1,n-1}$, performs this function. Otherwise, if line n has value 0, the weight of the remaining $n-1$ lines must be k or greater if the threshold is to be met. The second controlled component—a $T_{k,n-1}$ that is controlled by the negation of line n—performs this task. Each of the components are realized in the same way; the base cases, $T_{1,m}$ and $T_{m-1,m}$, are simply disjunctions and conjunctions over m variables, where $1\leq m\leq n$.

The complexity of this construction, particularly for the majority function, is exponential in n. The recurrence relation $R(k,n)=R(k-1,n-1)+R(k,n-1)$ describes the complexity of the construction—each of the two terms includes one of the two additional NOT gates. The boundary conditions are $R(1,m)=R(m,m)=cm$, where c is constant factor. Thus, the complexity of the realization of $T_{k,n}$, is $O\left(\binom{n}{k}k\right)$. Not surprisingly, the complexity of the realization is the same for both constructions. The threshold function is a prime example characterizing the application of Corollaries 6 and 7. Namely, that many Boolean functions have recursive realizations. The corollaries are useful for creating realizations of the base cases, which are then composed to yield the entire realization.

5. Techniques for Realizing Reversible Circuit

Three repeatedly used mechanisms for realizing circuits are commutators, conjugates, and "don't cares". The commutator of two circuits $[C_\sigma,C_\tau]=C_\sigma C_\tau C_\sigma^{-1}C_\tau^{-1}$—assuming that permutations σ and τ do not commute—is a mechanism for combining two circuits, which are controlled by distinct sets of control lines, into one that is controlled by union of the control lines, e.g., Barenco et al. [BBD+95] used this approach to construct $(n-2)$-Toffoli gates.

The conjugate of one circuit by another, $C_\sigma C_\tau C_\sigma^{-1}$, preserves the cycle structure realized by C_τ, but changes the points within the cycles. This mechanism is useful for massaging a circuit that does 'almost the right thing' into one that performs the required permutation. Conjugation was heavily used in the proof of the main result, particularly in the construction and transformation of 3-cycles. Conjugation decouples circuit structure from input representation, i.e., if the structure of the permutation that is realized by the circuit is correct, then the circuit can easily be adapted to work on the right set of inputs with a small amount of additional circuitry.

An input-preserving realization of the conjunction function corresponds to a singe transposition—an odd parity permutation. Since an odd parity permutation cannot be realized by a circuit on four or more wires [CG75], an even permutation, comprising two transpositions, is used. The additional permutation affects two other points of the input but does not affect the output; namely, we sacrifice the input-preserving property to achieve the realization. In a sense we take advantage of the fact that we "don't care" what the outputs of the input carrying lines is, provided that the line carrying the output value is correct. This approach is similar to the Karnaugh-maps method [Kar53], which is used for optimizing general combinational circuits.

6. Discussion

Reversible circuits are a concrete model of reversible computation that also satisfy the underpinnings of quantum computation; namely, quantum computation must be reversible. Since classical Boolean functions will necessarily comprise some building blocks of a quantum computer, determining how these functions can be reversibly realized is an important problem. We have shown that if a Boolean function f can be embedded into a permutation σ on an n-dimensional Boolean cube, such that the cycle representation of σ is of size s, then function f can be realized by a reversible circuit of size $O(sn)$. Furthermore, we showed how these results can be applied by detailing realizations of several families of Boolean functions such as incrementors and threshold functions.

One of the motivations of this work is quantum computation. One can ask how quantum circuits—which were introduced by Feynman [Fey86] and formalized by Deutch [Deu89]—compare to reversible circuit. In 1995, Barenco et al. [BBD+95] showed that quantum circuits can realize all permutations on an n-line circuit. Thus, not only are quantum circuits strictly more powerful than reversible circuits, they can also be more concise. However, the issue of whether quantum circuits are exponentially more powerful than reversible circuits remains open. Although, the famous factoring algorithm of Shor [Sho97], may indicate an affirmative answer, the result of Valiant's [Val01] indicates that in many cases the answer is negative. Since quantum circuits can simulate reversible circuits with no overhead—the Toffoli and NOT gates are commonly included in the basic set of quantum gates [BBD+95]—the results in this paper are also applicable in the quantum setting.

There is a useful analogy between our result and the fact that functions with heavily unbalanced truth tables have concise circuit realizations. Namely, if the ratio of 1s to 0s in the truth table is $O(2^{-n}n^c)$ or $\Omega(2^n n^{-c})$ for some constant c, then the number of terms in the corresponding disjunction—and the number of transpositions realized by the corresponding reversible circuit—is small. However, a function whose truth table is relatively balanced may also have a small realization.

Unfortunately, if a Boolean function f is nearly balanced and has an embedding whose cycle representation is exponentially large, there is no way to determine if f has a polynomial-size reversible circuit representation. For example, an n-line circuit comprising a single NOT gate realizes a permutation whose cycle representation comprises 2^{n-1} disjoint transpositions!

One possible approach is to partition the transpositions into equivalence classes based upon the behaviour of the transposition on a lower order Boolean cube. For example, a NOT gate on the first line of a circuit performs the permutation $(0\,1)$ on a one line circuit, $(0\,1)(2\,3)$ on a two line circuit, and $\prod_{i=0} 2^{n-1}(2i\; 2i+1)$ on an n-line circuit; all belong to the same equivalence class. Put another way, if a permutation can be projected onto a lower dimensional Boolean cube, and the sub-cube can be embedded into the original Boolean cube to yield the original permutation, then both the projection and original permutation belong to the same equivalence class. The complexity of realizing any element of the class is equal to the complexity of realizing the smallest element. In the example above, the NOT equivalence class has a complexity of 1, regardless of n. If a permutation can be factored into representatives of equivalence classes, then the complexity of realizing the permutation is simply the sum over the complexities of each of the representatives.

Even this is insufficient, because the nigh-incrementor, has a cycle representation that comprises a single exponentially large cycle. Yet, as we have shown, the nigh-incrementor has a concise realization. Unlike in the preceding case, projecting the permutation onto a lower dimensional Boolean cube does not work. Factoring a permutation into representatives is itself a difficult problem. For example, the decomposition of the nigh-incrementor into a 3-cycle and a half-incrementor is not at all obvious without a priori knowledge.

Finally, we note that a reversible realization can easily be realized by an irreversible circuit whose size and depth is only a constant factor larger than the reversible realization. In essence, a bound on the reversible complexity of a Boolean function automatically yields a bound on the classical circuit complexity of the function; the converse, is not true [LV96, LTV98, BTV01]. Thus, determining if a Boolean function has a concise reversible circuit realization remains an open an challenging problem. In fact, a simpler question should be answered first: can the n-adic majority function be efficiently realized by an $(n+c)$-line reversible circuit, where c is a constant? Alternatively, either improving the realization of the half-incrementor or proving a quadratic lower bound would also be of great interest.

References

[Bar86] D. Barrington. Bounded-width polynomial-size branching programs recognize exactly those languages in NC^1. In *Proceedings of the 18th Annual ACM Symposium on Theory of Computing*, pages 1–5, 1986.

[BBD+95] A. Barenco, C. Bennett, D. DiVincenzo, N. Margolus, P. Shor, T. Sleator, J. Smolin, and H. Weinfurter. Quantum gates and circuits. *Phys. Rev. A.*, 52:3457–3467, 1995.

[Ben73] C. Bennett. Logical reversibility of computation. *IBM Journal of Research and Development*, 17:198–200, 1973.

[Ben89] C. Bennett. Time/space trade-offs for reversible computation. *SIAM Journal on Computing*, 18(4):766–776, 1989.

[BTV01] H. Buhrman, J. Tromp, and P. Vitányi. Time and space bounds for reversible simulation. In *arXiv:quant-ph/0101133*, 2001.

[CG75] D. Coppersmith and E. Grossman. Generators for certain alternating groups with applications to cryptogaphy. *SIAM Journal on Applied Mathematics*, 29(4):624–627, 1975.

[Cle90] R. Cleve. Complexity theoretic issues concerning block ciphers related to D.E.S. In A. J. Menezes and S. A. Vanstone, editors, *Advances in Cryptology—CRYPTO '90*, volume 537 of *Lecture Notes in Computer Science*, pages 530–544. Springer-Verlag, 1990.

[Deu89] D. Deutsch. Quantum computational networks. *Proceedings of the Royal Society of London, Series A*, 425:73–90, 1989.

[EG83] S. Even and O. Goldreich. DES-like functions can generate the alternating group. *IEEE Trans. on Information Theory*, 29(6):863–865, 1983.

[Fey86] F. Feynman. Quantum mechanical computers. *Foundations of Physics*, 16(6):507–531, 1986.

[FT82] E. Fredkin and T. Toffoli. Conservative logic. *International Journal of Theoretical Physics*, 21(3/4):219–253, 1982.

[Kar53] M. Karnaugh. The map method for synthesis of combinational logic circuits. *AIEE Transactions, Part I Communication and Electronics*, 72:593–599, 1953.

[Lan61] R. Landauer. Irreversibility and heat generation in the computing process. *IBM Journal of Research and Development*, 5:183–191, 1961.

[LMT00] K. Lange, P. McKenzie, and A. Tapp. Reversible space equals deterministic space. *Journal of Computer and System Sciences*, 60(2):354–367, 2000.

[LS90] R. Levine and A. Sherman. A note on Bennett's time-space tradeoff for reversible computation. *SIAM Journal on Computing*, 19(4):673–677, 1990.

[LTV98] M. Li, J. Tromp, and P. Vitányi. Reversible simulation of irreversible computation. *Physica D*, 120:168–176, 1998.

[LV96] M. Li and P. Vitányi. Reversible simulation of irreversible computation. In *Proceedings of the 11th IEEE Computational Complexity Conference*, pages 306–306, 1996. Submitted to Physica D, 1997.

[Max71] J. Maxwell. *Theory of Heat*. Longmans, Green and Co., London, 1871.

[Sha48] C. Shannon. A mathematical theory of communication. *The Bell System Technical Journal*, 27(3):379–423, 1948.

[Sho97] P. Shor. Polynomial-time algorithms for prime factorization and discrete logarithms on a quantum computer. *SIAM Journal on Computing*, 26(5):1484–1509, 1997.

[SW49] C. Shannon and W. Weaver. *A Mathematical Theory of Communication*. University of Illinois Press, Urbana, Illinois, 1949.

[Szi29] L. Szilard. Über die Entropieverminderung in einem thermodynamischen System bei eingriffen intelligenter wesen. *Zeitschrift für Physik*, 53:829–856, 1929.

[Tof80] T. Toffoli. Reversible computing. In *Automata, Languages and Programming, 7th Colloquium*, volume 85 of *Lecture Notes in Computer Science*, pages 632–644, 1980.

[Val01] L. Valiant. Quantum computers that can be simulated classically in polynomial time. In *Proceedings of the 33rd Annual ACM Symposium on Theory of Computing*, pages 114–123, 2001.

RESOURCE BOUNDED IMMUNITY AND SIMPLICITY *

Extended Abstract

Toshio Suzuki[1] and Tomoyuki Yamakami[2]

[1] *Dept. of Math. and Inform. Sci., Osaka Prefecture University, Osaka, 599-8531 Japan*
[2] *Computer Science Program, Trent University, Peterborough, Ontario, Canada K9J 7B8*

Abstract Revisiting the thirty years-old notions of resource-bounded immunity and simplicity, we investigate the structural characteristics of various immunity notions: strong immunity, almost immunity, and hyperimmunity as well as their corresponding simplicity notions. We also study k-immunity and k-simplicity and their extensions: feasible k-immunity and feasible k-simplicity. Finally, we propose the k-immune hypothesis as a working hypothesis that ensures the existence of simple sets in NP.

Keywords: immune set, simple set, complete set, forcing, generic oracle, random oracle

1. Foundations of Immunity and Simplicity

The original notions of immunity and simplicity date back to mid 1940s. Post [17] first constructed a simple set for the class of recursively enumerable sets. The new breed of resource-bounded immunity and simplicity waited to be introduced until mid 1970s by an early work of Flajolet and Steyaert [5]. In their seminal paper, Flajolet and Steyaert constructed various recursive sets that, for instance, have no infinite DTIME$(t(n))$-subsets under the term "DTIME$(t(n))$-immune sets." Later, Ko and Moore [11] studied the polynomial-time bounded immunity, which is now preferably called P-immune sets. Subsequently, Balcázar and Schöning [2] considered P-bi-immune sets, which are P-immune sets whose complements are also P-immune. Homer and Maass [8] extensively discussed the cousin of P-immune sets, known as NP-simple sets. The importance of these notions was widely recognized in 1980s. Since these notions can be easily expanded to any complexity class $\mathcal{C}$, we begin with

*This work was in part supported by the Natural Sciences and Engineering Research Council of Canada and Grant-in-Aid for Scientific Research (No. 14740082), Japan Ministry of Education, Culture, Sports, Science, and Technology. This work was done while the first author visited the University of Ottawa between September and December of 2000.

an introduction of the general notions of $\mathcal{C}$-immune sets, $\mathcal{C}$-bi-immune sets, and $\mathcal{C}$-simple sets. These notions are further expanded in various manners in later sections.

DEFINITION 1 *Let $\mathcal{C}$ be any complexity class of languages over alphabet Σ.*

1. *A set S is* $\mathcal{C}$-immune *if S is infinite and there is no infinite subset of S in $\mathcal{C}$.*
2. *A set S is* $\mathcal{C}$-bi-immune *if S and $\overline{S}$ are both $\mathcal{C}$-immune.*
3. *A set S is* $\mathcal{C}$-simple *if S belongs to $\mathcal{C}$ and $\overline{S}$ is $\mathcal{C}$-immune.*

Note that the existence of a $\mathcal{C}$-simple set immediately implies $\mathcal{C} \neq$ co-$\mathcal{C}$; however, the separation $\mathcal{C} \neq$ co-$\mathcal{C}$ does not necessarily guarantee the existence of $\mathcal{C}$-simple sets.

Throughout this paper, we set our alphabet Σ to be $\{0,1\}$. Let $\mathbb{N}$ (or ω) denote the set of all nonnegative integers and set $\mathbb{N}^+ = \mathbb{N} - \{0\}$. All *logarithms* are taken to base 2 and a *polynomial* means a multivariate polynomial with integer coefficients. We assume a standard bijection from $\Sigma^{<\omega}$ to Σ^* that is polynomial-time computable and polynomial-time invertible, where $\Sigma^{<\omega}$ is the set of all finite sequences of strings over Σ. This bijection enables us to identify $\Sigma^{<\omega}$ with Σ^*. We use *multi-tape off-line Turing machines* (*TMs*, in short) as a model of computation. Assumed is the reader's familiarity with basic complexity classes, such as P, NP, E (linear exponential time), and EXP (polynomial exponential time). This paper focuses mostly on the complexity classes lying in the *polynomial-time hierarchy*[1] $\{\Delta_k^{\mathrm{P}}, \Sigma_k^{\mathrm{P}}, \Pi_k^{\mathrm{P}} \mid k \in \mathbb{N}\}$ [12].

We mainly use "partial" functions and all functions are presumed to be single-valued. Since total functions are also partial functions, we will define function classes as collections of *partial* functions and, whenever we need total functions, we will explicitly indicate the *totality* of functions. Now, fix $k \in \mathbb{N}^+$. The notation $\mathrm{F}\Delta_k^{\mathrm{P}}$ denotes the collection of all single-valued partial functions f such that there exist a set $B \in \Sigma_{k-1}^{\mathrm{P}}$ and a polynomial-time deterministic oracle TM M satisfying the following condition: for every x, if $x \in \mathrm{dom}(f)$ then $M^B(x)$ halts in an accepting state and outputs $f(x)$ and otherwise, $M^B(x)$ halts in a rejecting state (in this case, $f(x)$ is *undefined*). In particular, write FP for $\mathrm{F}\Delta_1^{\mathrm{P}}$.

A set A is called Δ_k^{P}*-m-reducible* to another set B via a reduction f if f is a total $\mathrm{F}\Delta_k^{\mathrm{P}}$-function from Σ^* to Σ^* and $A = \{x \mid f(x) \in B\}$. If in addition f is honest[2], then we say that A is *h-*Δ_k^{P}*-m-reducible* to B. Moreover, a set A is Δ_k^{P}*-tt-reducible* to B via a reduction triplet (ν, f, α) if (i) ν is a total $\mathrm{F}\Delta_k^{\mathrm{P}}$-function from Σ^* to $\{0\}^*$, (ii) f is a total $\mathrm{F}\Delta_k^{\mathrm{P}}$-function from Σ^* to Σ^* such that, for every x, $f(x) = \langle y_1, y_2, \ldots, y_k\rangle$ for certain strings $y_1, y_2, \ldots, y_k$, where $k = |\nu(x)|$, (iii) α is a total $\mathrm{F}\Delta_k^{\mathrm{P}}$-function from $\Sigma^* \times \Sigma^*$ to $\{0,1\}$ such that $A = \{x \mid \alpha(x, B(f(x))) = 1\}$, where $B(f(x))$ is an abbreviation of the k-bit string $B(y_1)B(y_2)\cdots B(y_k)$ when $f(x) = \langle y_1, \ldots, y_k\rangle$. If in addition f is componentwise honest[3], then A is *h-*Δ_k^{P}*-tt-reducible* to B. The notion of *completeness* can be induced from its corresponding reducibility.

---

[1]The polynomial-time hierarchy consists of the classes defined in the following fashion: $\Delta_0^{\mathrm{P}} = \Sigma_0^{\mathrm{P}} = \Pi_0^{\mathrm{P}} = \mathrm{P}$, $\Sigma_{k+1}^{\mathrm{P}} = \mathrm{NP}^{\Sigma_k^{\mathrm{P}}}$, and $\Pi_{k+1}^{\mathrm{P}} = \text{co-}\Sigma_{k+1}^{\mathrm{P}}$ for any number $k \in \mathbb{N}$.

[2]A partial function f from Σ^* to Σ^* is *polynomially honest* (*honest*, for short) if there exists a polynomial p such that $|x| \leq p(|f(x)|)$ for all strings $x \in \mathrm{dom}(f)$.

[3]A partial function from Σ^* to $\Sigma^{<\omega}$ (which is identified with Σ^*) is *componentwise honest* if there exists a polynomial p such that, for every $x \in \mathrm{dom}(f)$, $|x| \leq p(|y_i|)$ for all $i \in \{1, 2, \ldots, k\}$, provided that $f(x) = \langle y_1, y_2, \ldots, y_k\rangle$.

It is well-known that P-immune sets exist even in the class E. In particular, Ko and Moore [11] constructed a P-immune set that is also P-tt-complete for E. Note that no h-P-m-complete set for NP can be P-immune since the image of a P-immune set by a polynomial-time computable reduction is either finite or P-immune. Using a relativization technique, Bennett and Gill [3] showed that a P-immune set exists in NP relative to a random oracle with probability 1. A recursive oracle relative to which NP contains P-immune sets was later constructed by Homer and Maass [8]. Torenvliet and van Emde Boas [22] strengthened their results by demonstrating a relativized world where NP has a P-immune set which is also NP-simple.

The notion of $\mathcal{C}$-immunity is closely related to various other notions, which include complexity cores [13] and instance complexity [15]. We can naturally expand these characterizations to more general Σ_k^{P}-immune and Δ_k^{P}-immune sets. Balcázar and Schöning [2] also built a bridge between P-bi-immune sets and finite-to-one reductions. Expanding their argument, we give in Lemma 2 a characterization of $\mathcal{C}$-bi-immunity as well as $\mathcal{C}$-immunity.

For any partial function f from Σ^* to Σ^*, the set $Graph(f) = \{\langle x, f(x)\rangle \mid x \in \mathrm{dom}(f)\}$ is called the *graph* of f. Let $\Sigma_0^{\mathrm{P}}\mathrm{SV} = \mathrm{FP}$ and let $\Sigma_k^{\mathrm{P}}\mathrm{SV}$ denote the class of all single-valued partial functions f such that f is polynomially bounded[4] and $Graph(f)$ is in Σ_k^{P}. For brevity, we write NPSV for $\Sigma_1^{\mathrm{P}}\mathrm{SV}$. For any $k \in \mathbb{N}$ and any $A, B \subseteq \Sigma^*$, a single-valued partial function f from Σ^* to Σ^* is called a Σ_k^{P}-*m-quasireduction* (Δ_k^{P}-*m-quasireduction*, resp.) from A to B if (i) f is in $\Sigma_k^{\mathrm{P}}\mathrm{SV}$ ($\mathrm{F}\Delta_k^{\mathrm{P}}$, resp.), (ii) $\mathrm{dom}(f)$ is infinite, and (iii) for any string $x \in \mathrm{dom}(f)$, $x \in A$ iff $f(x) \in B$. For any string $u \in \Sigma^*$, the *inverse image* $f^{-1}(u)$ of f at u is the set $\{x \in \mathrm{dom}(f) \mid f(x) = u\}$. Notice that $f^{-1}(u) = \emptyset$ if $u \notin \mathrm{ran}(f)$.

LEMMA 2 *Let* $\mathcal{C} \in \{\Delta_k^{\mathrm{P}}, \Sigma_k^{\mathrm{P}} \mid k \in \mathbb{N}\}$ *and* $S \subseteq \Sigma^*$.

1. *S is $\mathcal{C}$-immune if and only if (i) S is infinite and (ii) for every set B, every $\mathcal{C}$-m-quasireduction f from S to B, and every u in B, $f^{-1}(u)$ is finite.*
2. *S is $\mathcal{C}$-bi-immune if and only if (i) S is infinite and (ii) for every set B, every $\mathcal{C}$-m-quasireduction f from S to B, and every u in Σ^*, $f^{-1}(u)$ is finite.*

The characterization given in Lemma 2(2) led Balcázar and Schöning [2] to introduce a stronger notion of P-bi-immunity: strong P-bi-immunity. A more general notion, called strong $\mathcal{C}$-immunity, will be introduced in Section 2.

Whether an NP-simple set exists is one of the long-standing open problems because such a set separates NP from co-NP. Nonetheless, NP-simple sets are known to exist in various relativized worlds. In early 1980s, Homer and Maass [8] and Balcázar [1] constructed relativized worlds where an NP-simple set exists. Later, Vereshchagin [24] proved that, relative to a random oracle, an NP-simple set exists with probability 1. From Theorem 9 in Section 2, for instance, it immediately follows that an NP-simple set exists relative to a generic oracle. Torenvliet [21] built an oracle relative to which a Σ_2^{P}-simple set exists. For a much higher level k of the polynomial-time

[4] A partial function f from Σ^* to Σ^* is *polynomially bounded* if there exists a polynomial p such that $|f(x)| \leq p(|x|)$ for any string $x \in \mathrm{dom}(f)$.

hierarchy, Bruschi [4] constructed an oracle relative to which Σ_k^{P}-simple sets exist using the size lower bounds of certain nonuniform constant-depth circuits.

In the rest of this section, we focus on closure properties of the class of all Σ_k^{P}-immune sets because no such closure property has been systematically studied in the literature. A complexity class $\mathcal{C}$ is said to be *closed downward under a reduction* $\leq_r$ *on infinite sets* if, for any pair of infinite sets A and B, $A \leq_r B$ and $B \in \mathcal{C}$ imply $A \in \mathcal{C}$. Here, we study three reducibilities. Let $k \in \mathbb{N}$. A set A is Δ_k^{P}*-d-reducible to* B via f if f is a total $\mathrm{F}\Delta_k^{\mathrm{P}}$-function from Σ^* to $\Sigma^{<\omega}$ (which is identified with Σ^*) and $A = \{x \mid B \cap set(f(x)) \neq \emptyset\}$, where $set(\langle y_1, y_2, \ldots, y_m\rangle) = \{y_1, y_2, \ldots, y_m\}$. By contrast, A is Δ_k^{P}*-c-reducible to* B via f if $\overline{A}$ is Δ_k^{P}-d-reducible to $\overline{B}$ via f. For any fixed $i \in \mathbb{N}^+$, A is Δ_k^{P}*-itt-reducible* to B via (f, α) if A is Δ_k^{P}-tt-reducible to B via (ν, f, α), where $\nu(x) = 0^i$ for any x. For any reducibility r using computation $\mathcal{C}$, we say that A is *h-*$\mathcal{C}$*-*r*-reducible* to B if A is $\mathcal{C}$-r-reducible to B via f (or (f, α)) such that f is componentwise honest.

Now, we claim that the class of all Σ_k^{P}-immune sets is closed downward under h-Δ_k^{P}-c-reductions on infinite sets; however, we cannot replace this conjunctive reducibility by disjunctive reducibility.

THEOREM 3 *Let* $k \in \mathbb{N}^+$.

1. *The class of all* Σ_k^{P}*-immune sets is closed downward under h-*Δ_k^{P}*-c-reductions on infinite sets.*
2. *The class of all* NP*-immune sets is not closed under h-*P*-d-reductions or h-*P*-2tt-reductions on infinite sets.*

The first claim of Theorem 3 is easy and is shown as follows. Assume that an infinite set A is h-Δ_k^{P}-c-reducible to a Σ_k^{P}-immune set B via a componentwise-honest reduction f. If A contains an infinite Σ_k^{P}-subset C, then consider the set $D = \{y \mid \exists x \in C[|x| \leq p(|y|) \wedge y \in set(f(x))]\}$, where p is a polynomial such that $|x| \leq p(|y|)$ for all x and all $y \in set(f(x))$. Clearly, D is an infinite Σ_k^{P}-subset of B, a contradiction. Therefore, A is Σ_k^{P}-immune.

How complex are Σ_k^{P}-simple sets? Intuitively, $\mathcal{C}$-simple sets are "thin" and thus cannot be "complete" for the class $\mathcal{C}$. As an immediate consequence of Theorem 3(1), we obtain the following corollary.

COROLLARY 4 *Let* $k \in \mathbb{N}^+$. *No* Σ_k^{P}*-simple set is h-*Δ_k^{P}*-d-complete for* Σ_k^{P}.

Recently, Agrawal (cited in [19]) showed, using the NP-levelability of $\overline{\mathrm{SAT}}$ (assuming SAT $\notin$ P), that no NP-simple set is h-P-btt-complete for NP, where SAT is the set of all satisfiable quantifier-free Boolean formulas. His argument will be generalized in Section 4 in connection to $\mathcal{C}$-hyperimmune sets.

2. Strong Immunity and Strong Simplicity

Following the introduction of P-bi-immunity, Balcázar and Schöning [2] stepped forward to introduce the notion of strongly P-bi-immunity, which comes from the quasireducibility-characterization of P-bi-immunity given in Lemma 2(2). While P-bi-immunity requires its quasireductions to be finite-to-one, strong P-bi-immunity requires the quasireductions to be almost one-to-one, where a quasireduction f is called *almost one-to-one on* a set S if the *collision set* $\{(x,y) \in (\mathrm{dom}(f) \cap S)^2 \mid x < y \wedge f(x) = f(y)\}$ is finite. Such strongly P-bi-immune sets are known to exist even in the class E [2].

Generalizing the notion of P-bi-immunity, we can introduce strong $\mathcal{C}$-bi-immunity for any complexity class $\mathcal{C}$ lying in the polynomial-time hierarchy. Moreover, we newly introduce the notions of strong $\mathcal{C}$-immunity and strong $\mathcal{C}$-simplicity. Recall that Σ_k^{P}-m-quasireductions are all single-valued functions in $\Sigma_k^{\mathrm{P}}\mathrm{SV}$ for each $k \in \mathbb{N}^+$.

DEFINITION 5 *Let* $\mathcal{C} \in \{\Delta_k^{\mathrm{P}}, \Sigma_k^{\mathrm{P}} \mid k \in \mathbb{N}\}$.

1. *A set S is* strongly $\mathcal{C}$-immune *if (i) S is infinite and (ii) for every set B and every $\mathcal{C}$-m-quasireduction f from S to B, f is almost one-to-one on S.*
2. *A set S is* strongly $\mathcal{C}$-bi-immune *if S and $\overline{S}$ are both strongly $\mathcal{C}$-immune.*
3. *A set S is* strongly $\mathcal{C}$-simple *if S is in $\mathcal{C}$ and $\overline{S}$ is strongly $\mathcal{C}$-immune.*

In particular, when $\mathcal{C} = \mathrm{P}$, Definition 5(2) coincides with the notion of P-bi-immunity originally given in [2].

LEMMA 6 *For any complexity class $\mathcal{C} \in \{\Delta_k^{\mathrm{P}}, \Sigma_k^{\mathrm{P}} \mid k \in \mathbb{N}\}$, every strongly $\mathcal{C}$-immune set is $\mathcal{C}$-immune and every strongly $\mathcal{C}$-simple set is $\mathcal{C}$-simple.*

A major difference between $\mathcal{C}$-immunity and strong $\mathcal{C}$-immunity is shown in the following example. For any NP-immune set A, the disjoint union[5] $A \oplus A$ is also NP-immune; on the contrary, it is not strongly NP-immune because $A \oplus A$ can be reduced to A by the almost two-to-one function f defined as $f(\lambda) = \lambda$ and $f(xb) = x$ for $b \in \{0,1\}$, where λ is the empty string. Therefore, the class of all strongly NP-immune sets is not closed under the disjoint-union operator. Historically, using the structural difference between these two notions, Balcázar and Schöning [2] constructed a set in E which is P-bi-immune but not strongly P-bi-immune.

We show a closure property of the class of strongly Σ_k^{P}-immune sets. If A is Δ_k^{P}-m-reducible to B via a one-to-one honest reduction f, we say that A is *h-Δ_k^{P}-1-reducible* to B via f.

PROPOSITION 7 *Let* $k \in \mathbb{N}^+$.

1. *The class of all strongly Σ_k^{P}-immune sets is closed downward under h-Δ_k^{P}-1-reductions on infinite sets.*
2. *The class of all strongly* NP*-immune sets is not closed downward under h-*P*-m-reductions on infinite sets.*

COROLLARY 8 *For each level $k \in \mathbb{N}^+$, there is no strongly Σ_k^{P}-simple set that is h-Δ_k^{P}-1-complete for Σ_k^{P}.*

Finally, we turn our interest to relativization. For each $k \in \mathbb{N}^+$, it is easy to show that a strongly Σ_k^{P}-simple set exists relative to a recursive oracle (similar to Proposition

[5]The *disjoint union* of A and B is the set $\{0x \mid x \in A\} \cup \{1x \mid x \in B\}$.

26). Even relative to a random oracle, there exists a strongly NP-simple set with probability 1 (similar to Proposition 27). Employing weak forcing, we now prove the following relativization result.

THEOREM 9 *A strongly* NP^G*-simple set exists relative to a generic oracle* G.

3. Almost Immunity and Almost Simplicity

We have shown in the previous section that strong $\mathcal{C}$-immunity and its simplicity strengthen the ordinary notion of $\mathcal{C}$-immunity and $\mathcal{C}$-simplicity. In contrast to these notions, Orponen [14] and Orponen, Russo, and Schöning [16] expanded P-immunity to the new notion of almost P-immunity. The complementary notion of almost P-immunity under the term P-levelability (a more general term "levelable sets" was first used by Ko [10] in a resource-bounded setting) was extensively discussed by Orponen et al. [16]. Naturally, we can generalize these notions to almost $\mathcal{C}$-immunity and $\mathcal{C}$-levelability for any complexity class $\mathcal{C}$. Furthermore, we newly introduce the notion of almost $\mathcal{C}$-bi-immunity and almost $\mathcal{C}$-simplicity.

DEFINITION 10 *Let* $\mathcal{C}$ *be any complexity class.*

1 *A set* S *is* almost $\mathcal{C}$-immune *if* S *is the union of a* $\mathcal{C}$*-immune set and a set in* $\mathcal{C}$.

2 *An infinite set is* $\mathcal{C}$-levelable *if it is not almost* $\mathcal{C}$*-immune.*

3 *A set* S *is* almost $\mathcal{C}$-bi-immune *if* S *and* $\overline{S}$ *are both almost* $\mathcal{C}$*-immune.*

4 *A set* S *is* almost $\mathcal{C}$-simple *if* S *is an infinite set in* $\mathcal{C}$ *and* $\overline{S}$ *is the union of a set* A *in* $\mathcal{C}$ *and a* $\mathcal{C}$*-immune set* B*, where the difference* $B \setminus A$ *is infinite.*

It follows from Definition 10(1) that every almost $\mathcal{C}$-immune set is infinite since so is every $\mathcal{C}$-immune set. The definition of almost $\mathcal{C}$-simplicity in Definition 10(4) is slightly different from other simplicity definitions because the infinity condition of the difference $B \setminus A$ is necessary to guarantee $\mathcal{C} \neq$ co-$\mathcal{C}$, provided that an almost $\mathcal{C}$-simple set exists.

LEMMA 11 *Let* $\mathcal{C}$ *be any complexity class closed under finite variations, finite union and finite intersection. If an almost* $\mathcal{C}$*-simple set exists, then* $\mathcal{C} \neq$ co-$\mathcal{C}$.

Lemma 11 is shown as follows. Take any set S such that $\overline{S} = A \cup B$ for a set $A \in \mathcal{C}$ and a $\mathcal{C}$-immune set B. Suppose $\mathcal{C} =$ co-$\mathcal{C}$. Note that $B \setminus A \subseteq B$ and $B \setminus A = \overline{S} \setminus A \in \mathcal{C}$. Since B is $\mathcal{C}$-immune, $B \setminus A$ must be finite.

The following lemma is immediate from Definition 10.

LEMMA 12 *For any complexity class* $\mathcal{C}$*, every* $\mathcal{C}$*-immune set is almost* $\mathcal{C}$*-immune and every* $\mathcal{C}$*-simple set is almost* $\mathcal{C}$*-simple.*

Several characterizations of almost P-immunity and P-levelability are shown in [16] in terms of maximal P-subsets and P-to-finite reductions. We can naturally expand these characterizations to almost Δ_k^{P}-immunity and Δ_k^{P}-levelability (but not to the Σ-level classes of the polynomial-time hierarchy).

To understand the characteristics of almost $\mathcal{C}$-immunity, we begin with a simple observation. It is known in [16] that any honestly paddable[6] set not in P is P-levelable. As observed in [18], the essence of this assertion is that if $A \notin \mathrm{P}$ and A is length-increasing P-m-selfreducible then A is P-levelable, where A is *length-increasing $\mathcal{C}$-m-selfreducible* if A is $\mathcal{C}$-m-reducible to A via a certain length-increasing reduction. This observation can be generalized to Δ_k^{P}-levelable sets in the following lemma.

LEMMA 13 *Let $k \in \mathbb{N}^+$ and $A \subseteq \Sigma^*$. Assuming that $A \notin \Delta_k^{\mathrm{P}}$, if A is length-increasing Δ_k^{P}-m-selfreducible, then A and $\overline{A}$ are both Δ_k^{P}-levelable. Thus, if $\Delta_k^{\mathrm{P}} \neq \Sigma_k^{\mathrm{P}}$ then Σ_k^{P} as well as Π_k^{P} has a Δ_k^{P}-levelable set.*

Most known NP-m-complete sets are known to be honestly paddable and thus, by Lemma 13, the complements of these sets are P-levelable sets, which are also NP-levelable. Therefore, most known NP-m-complete sets cannot be almost NP-simple. This result can be compared to Proposition 16.

Now, we assume a standard effective enumeration $\{\varphi_s\}_{s\in\Sigma^*}$ of all nondeterministic TMs φ_s. For each index s, define the set $W_s = \{x \mid \varphi_s(x)\downarrow = 1\}$, where "$\varphi_s(x)\downarrow$" means that φ_s eventually halts on input x. Fix $k \in \mathbb{N}$. Let $\mathrm{NP}_{(k)}$ denote the collection of all sets W_s such that, for any string $x \in W_s$, the running time of φ_s on input x is at most $|s| \cdot |x|^k + |s|$. Moreover, we set $INDEX_{(k)} = \{s \mid W_s \in \mathrm{NP}_{(k)}\}$. Note that $\mathrm{NP} = \bigcup_{k\in\mathbb{N}} \mathrm{NP}_{(k)}$.

Earlier, Ko and Moore [11] considered the resource-bounded notion of "productive sets." Another formulation based on $\mathrm{NP}_{(k)}$ was later given by Joseph and Young [9], who used the terminology of k-creative[7] sets, where k is any number in $\mathbb{N}^+$. They showed that every k-creative set is P-m-complete for NP. Orponen et al. [16] showed that, unless P = NP, every honestly k-creative set is P-levelable by demonstrating that any honestly k-creative set is length-increasing P-m-selfreducible. From Lemma 13, it follows that any honestly k-creative set and its complement are both P-levelable. Consequently, we obtain the following result.

COROLLARY 14 *For any $k \in \mathbb{N}^+$, no honestly k-creative set is almost NP-simple.*

Our notion of almost $\mathcal{C}$-simplicity is similar to what Uspenskii [23] discussed under the term "pseudosimplicity." Here, we give a resource-bounded version of his pseudosimplicity. A set S is called *$\mathcal{C}$-pseudosimple* if there is an infinite $\mathcal{C}$-subset A of $\overline{S}$ such that $S \cup A$ is $\mathcal{C}$-simple. Although $\mathcal{C}$-simple sets cannot be $\mathcal{C}$-pseudosimple by our definition, any infinite $\mathcal{C}$-pseudosimple set is almost $\mathcal{C}$-simple. The latter claim is shown as follows. Suppose that S is an infinite $\mathcal{C}$-pseudosimple set and A is a $\mathcal{C}$-subset of $\overline{S}$ for which $S \cup A$ is $\mathcal{C}$-simple. This means that $\overline{S} \setminus A$ is $\mathcal{C}$-immune. Therefore, S is almost $\mathcal{C}$-simple.

---

[6] A set S is *polynomially paddable* (*paddable*, in short) if there is an one-to-one total FP-function *pad* (called the *padding function*) from Σ^* to Σ^* such that, for all pairs $(x, y) \in \Sigma^* \times \Sigma^*$, $x \in S$ iff $pad(\langle x, y\rangle) \in S$. A set S is *honestly paddable* if it is paddable with a padding function that is componentwise honest.

[7] A set S is called *k-creative* if there exists a function $f \in \mathrm{FP}$ such that, for any index $i \in INDEX_{(k)}$, $f(i) \in S$ iff $f(i) \in W_i$. This function f is called the *productive function* for S. If in addition f is honest, S is called *honestly k-creative*.

The following theorem shows a close connection among simplicity, almost simplicity, and pseudosimplicity.

THEOREM 15 *For each $k \in \mathbb{N}^+$, the following three statements are equivalent.*

1 *There exists a Σ_k^{P}-simple set.*

2 *There exists an infinite Σ_k^{P}-pseudosimple set in* P.

3 *There exists an almost Σ_k^{P}-simple set in* P.

The most essential part of Theorem 15 is the implication from 1 to 2. Assume that S is an almost Σ_k^{P}-simple set. Let $A_1 = 1S$ and $B_1 = 1\overline{S}$. Clearly, B_1 is infinite. Note that A_1 is a Σ_k^{P}-subset of $1\Sigma^*$. Since $\overline{S}$ is Σ_k^{P}-immune and $B_1 \subseteq 1\overline{S}$, B_1 is Σ_k^{P}-immune. Since $B_1 = 1\Sigma^* \cap \overline{A_1}$, the set $0\Sigma^* \cup A_1$ is Σ_k^{P}-simple. Hence, $0\Sigma^*$ is Σ_k^{P}-pseudosimple, as required. Similarly, $1\Sigma^*$ is Σ_k^{P}-pseudosimple.

Theorem 15 indicates the importance of the structure of P in the course of the study of Σ_k^{P}-simplicity. In a relativized world where a Σ_k^{P}-simple set exists [4], since Theorem 15 relativizes, there exists an almost Σ_k^{P}-simple set within P.

Finally, we briefly discuss a closure property of the class of all almost Σ_k^{P}-immune sets under polynomial-time reductions. For each number $k \in \mathbb{N}^+$, the class of all almost Σ_k^{P}-immune sets is closed under h-Δ_k^{P}-m-reductions on infinite sets. This immediately implies the following consequence.

PROPOSITION 16 *For each number $k \in \mathbb{N}^+$, there is no almost Σ_k^{P}-simple set that is h-Δ_k^{P}-m-complete for Σ_k^{P}.*

4. Hyperimmunity and Hypersimplicity

Since Post [17] constructed a so-called *hypersimple* set, the notions of hyperimmunity and hypersimplicity have played a significant role in the progress of classical recursion theory. A resource-bounded version of these notions was first considered by Yamakami [26] and studied extensively by Schaefer and Fenner [19]. The definition of Schaefer and Fenner is based on the notion of "honest NP-arrays", which differs from the notion of "strong arrays" in recursion theory, where a strong array is a series of pairwise disjoint finite sets. For our formalization, we demand only "eventually disjointness" for sets in an array rather than "pairwise disjointness."

A binary string x is said to *represent* a finite set $\{a_1, a_2, \ldots, a_k\}$ if and only if $x = \langle a_1, a_2, \ldots, a_k \rangle$ and $a_1 < a_2 < \cdots < a_k$ in the lexicographic order on Σ^*. For convenience, we say that a set A *surpasses* another set B if there exists a string $z \in A$ satisfying $z > x$ (lexicographically) for all strings x in B.

DEFINITION 17 *Let $k \in \mathbb{N}^+$, $A \subseteq \Sigma^*$, and $\mathcal{C} \in \{\Sigma_k^{\mathrm{P}}, \Delta_k^{\mathrm{P}}\}$.*

1 *An infinite sequence $\mathcal{D} = \{D_s\}_{s\in\Sigma^*}$ of finite sets is called a* Σ_k^{P}-array *(*Δ_k^{P}-array, *resp.) if there exists a single-valued partial function f in* Σ_k^{P}SV *(*FΔ_k^{P}, *resp.) such that (i) $dom(f)$ is infinite, (ii) $D_s \neq \emptyset$ and $f(s)$ represents D_s for any string $s \in dom(f)$, and (iii) $D_s = \emptyset$ for any string $s \notin dom(f)$. This f is called the* supporting function *of $\mathcal{D}$ and the set $\bigcup_{s\in dom(f)} D_s$ is called the* support *of $\mathcal{D}$. The* width *of $\mathcal{D}$ is the supremum of the cardinality $|D_s|$ over all $s \in dom(f)$.*

2 *A $\mathcal{C}$-array $\mathcal{D}$ has an* infinite support *if the support of $\mathcal{D}$ is infinite.*

3 *A $\mathcal{C}$-array $\{D_s\}_{s\in\Sigma^*}$ via f is* polynomially honest *(honest, in short) if f is componentwise honest; namely, there exists a polynomial p satisfying that $|s| \leq p(|x|)$ for any $s \in dom(f)$ and any $x \in D_s$.*

4 *A $\mathcal{C}$-array $\{D_s\}_{s\in\Sigma^*}$ via f is* eventually disjoint *if, for every string x in $dom(f)$, there exists a string y in $dom(f)$ such that $y \geq x$ (lexicographically), D_y surpasses D_x, and $D_x \cap D_y = \emptyset$.*

5 *A $\mathcal{C}$-array $\{D_s\}_{s\in\Sigma^*}$ via f* intersects A *if $D_s \cap A \neq \emptyset$ for all $s \in dom(f)$.*

The honesty condition of an $\mathcal{C}$-array guarantees that the array is eventually disjoint. In addition, any eventually-disjoint $\mathcal{C}$-array has an infinite support because, for any element D in the array, we can always find another disjoint element D'.

A simple relationship between Σ_k^{P}-simplicity and a honest Σ_k^{P}-array is given in the following lemma, which was implicitly proven by Yamakami [26] and later explicitly stated in [19] for the case where $k = 1$.

LEMMA 18 *Let $k \in \mathbb{N}^+$ and let A be any Σ_k^{P}-simple set. For every number $\ell \in \mathbb{N}^+$, there is no honest Σ_k^{P}-array $\mathcal{D}$ such that (i) the width of $\mathcal{D}$ is at most ℓ and (ii) $\mathcal{D}$ intersects A.*

We introduce below the notions of $\mathcal{C}$-hyperimmunity and honest $\mathcal{C}$-hyperimmunity.

DEFINITION 19 *Let $\mathcal{C} \in \{\Delta_k^{\mathrm{P}}, \Sigma_k^{\mathrm{P}} \mid k \in \mathbb{N}\}$.*

1 *A set S is* (honestly) $\mathcal{C}$-hyperimmune *if S is infinite and there is no (honest) $\mathcal{C}$-array $\mathcal{D}$ such that $\mathcal{D}$ is eventually disjoint and $\mathcal{D}$ intersects A.*

2 *A set S is* (honestly) $\mathcal{C}$-bi-hyperimmune *if S and $\overline{S}$ are both (honestly) $\mathcal{C}$-hyperimmune.*

3 *A set S is* (honestly) $\mathcal{C}$-hypersimple *if $S \in \mathcal{C}$ and $\overline{S}$ is (honestly) $\mathcal{C}$-hyperimmune.*

Note that "NP-hyperimmunity" defined by Schaefer and Fenner [19] coincides with our honest NP-hyperimmunity. The following relationship between immunity and hyperimmunity can be obtained immediately from Definition 19.

LEMMA 20 *For any complexity class $\mathcal{C} \in \{\Sigma_k^{\mathrm{P}}, \Delta_k^{\mathrm{P}} \mid k \in \mathbb{N}\}$, every honestly $\mathcal{C}$-hyperimmune set is $\mathcal{C}$-immune and every honestly $\mathcal{C}$-hypersimple set is $\mathcal{C}$-simple.*

In late 1970s, Selman [20] introduced the notion of P-selective sets, which are analogues of semi-recursive sets in recursion theory. These sets connects P-immunity to P-hyperimmunity. In general, for any class $\mathcal{F}$ of *total* functions, we say that a set S is *$\mathcal{F}$-selective* if there exists a function (called the *selector*) f in $\mathcal{F}$ such that, for all pairs $(x, y) \in \Sigma^* \times \Sigma^*$, (i) $f(x, y) \in \{x, y\}$ and (ii) $\{x, y\} \cap S \neq \emptyset$ implies $f(x, y) \in S$. Recall the partial function class $\Sigma_k^{\mathrm{P}}\mathrm{SV}$. We use the notation $\Sigma_k^{\mathrm{P}}\mathrm{SV}_t$ to denote the collection of all *total* functions in $\Sigma_k^{\mathrm{P}}\mathrm{SV}$.

LEMMA 21 *Let $k \in \mathbb{N}^+$. Every Σ_k^{P}-immune $\Sigma_k^{\mathrm{P}}\mathrm{SV}_t$-selective set is honestly Σ_k^{P}-hyperimmune.*

We give the proof of Lemma 21. Assume that S is $\Sigma_k^{\mathrm{P}}\mathrm{SV}_t$-selective via a selector f and has a honest Σ_k^{P}-array $\mathcal{D} = \{D_s\}_{s\in\Sigma^*}$ intersecting S via a supporting function g. For each $y \in \mathrm{dom}(g)$, assuming $D_y = \{x_1, x_2, \ldots, x_m\}$ with $x_1 < x_2 < \cdots < x_m$, let $y_1 = x_1$ and $y_{i+1} = f(y_i, x_{i+1})$ for every $i \in \{1, 2, \ldots, m-1\}$ and then define $h(y) = y_m$. This h is honest and in $\Sigma_k^{\mathrm{P}}\mathrm{SV}$. The set $B = \{x \mid \exists y[y \in \mathrm{dom}(h) \wedge h(y) = x]\}$ is therefore infinite and in Σ_k^{P} since $\mathrm{dom}(f)$ is infinite and h is honest. Because $B \subseteq S$, B cannot be Σ_k^{P}-immune. Note that our proof relativizes.

Observe that the complement of a $\Sigma_k^{\mathrm{P}}\mathrm{SV}_t$-selective set S is also $\Sigma_k^{\mathrm{P}}\mathrm{SV}_t$-selective because the exchange of the output string of any selector for S gives rise to a selector for $\overline{S}$. It also follows from Lemma 21 that every NP-simple P-selective set is honestly NP-hypersimple since the complement of any P-selective set is also P-selective.

Next, we show that strong P-immunity does not imply honest P-hyperimmunity within the class E. Earlier, Balcázar and Schöning [2] created a strongly P-bi-immune set S in E with the density $|S \cap \Sigma^{\leq n}| = 2^{n+1} - n - 1$ for all $n \in \mathbb{N}$. For each x, let D_x consist of the first $|x| + 1$ elements of $\Sigma^{|x|}$. Clearly, D_x intersects S. This implies that S is not honestly P-hyperimmune. Therefore, we obtain the following proposition.

PROPOSITION 22 *There exists a strongly* P*-bi-immune set in* E *that is not honestly* P*-hyperimmune.*

As a main theorem, we show the P-T-incompleteness of Σ_k^{P}-hypersimple sets. Generally, we say that A is *Δ_k^{P}-T-reducible* to B if there exists an oracle Δ_k^{P}-machine M which recognizes A with access to B as an oracle. If in addition M on input x makes only queries y to B that satisfy $|x| \leq p(|y|)$, where p is a fixed polynomial, then we say that A is *h-Δ_k^{P}-T-reducible* to B via M. This reduction machine M is simply called *honest*.

THEOREM 23 *Let $k \in \mathbb{N}^+$.*

1 *No Σ_k^{P}-hypersimple set is P-T-complete for Σ_k^{P}.*

2 *No honestly Σ_k^{P}-hypersimple set is h-P-T-complete for Σ_k^{P}.*

Note that it is not clear if we can replace the P-T-completeness in Theorem 23 by the Δ_k^{P}-T-completeness. Theorem 23 follows from Lemma 24 in the following fashion. We prove only the first claim. Assume that B is a Σ_k^{P}-hypersimple set that is P-T-complete for Σ_k^{P}. Thus, $\Delta_k^{\mathrm{P}} \neq \Sigma_k^{\mathrm{P}}$. Clearly, B is in EXP and every Σ_k^{P}-set is P-T-reducible to B. By Lemma 24, every Σ_k^{P}-set is almost Δ_k^{P}-immune. This contradicts Lemma 13. Therefore, B cannot be Σ_k^{P}-hypersimple.

LEMMA 24 *Let $k \in \mathbb{N}^+$ and let A be any infinite set in Σ_k^{P}.*

1 *If A is P-T-reducible to a Σ_k^{P}-hyperimmune set in* EXP*, then A is almost Δ_k^{P}-immune.*

2 *If A is h-P-T-reducible to a honestly Σ_k^{P}-hyperimmune set, then A is almost Δ_k^{P}-immune.*

Lemma 24 needs a key idea of Agrawal (mentioned earlier), who showed that no NP-simple set is h-P-btt-complete for NP. We extend his core argument to Lemma

25. For convenience, a complexity class $\mathcal{C}$ is said to be *closed under intersection with* Δ_k^{P}*-sets* if, for any set A in $\mathcal{C}$ and any set B in Δ_k^{P}, the intersection $A \cap B$ is in $\mathcal{C}$.

LEMMA 25 *Let $\mathcal{C}$ be any complexity class containing Δ_k^{P} such that $\mathcal{C}$ is closed under intersection with Δ_k^{P}-sets. Let A be any Δ_k^{P}-levelable set in $\mathcal{C}$. If A is Δ_k^{P}-T-reducible to B via a reduction machine M, then there exists an infinite set C in $\mathcal{C}$ such that $Q(M,B,x) \cap B \neq \emptyset$ for all $x \in C$.*

Bruschi [4] demonstrated how to construct a recursive oracle relative to which a Σ_k^{P}-simple set exists. We can easily modify his proof to obtain a P-selective set that is Σ_k^{P}-simple in a relativized world. Since Lemma 21 relativizes, we obtain the following proposition.

PROPOSITION 26 *For each $k \in \mathrm{N}^+$, there exists a recursive oracle A such that a $\Sigma_k^{\mathrm{P}}(A)$-hypersimple set exists.*

As Schaefer and Fenner [19] demonstrated, it is relatively easy to prove the existence of an honest NP^G-hypersimple set relative to a generic oracle G. By contrast, Vereshchagin [24] proved the existence of an NP-simple set relative to a random oracle with probability 1. Again, we modify his proof to construct a relativized P-selective NP-simple set. From Lemma 21, the next proposition follows.

PROPOSITION 27 *With probability 1, an honestly NP^X-hypersimple set exists relative to a random oracle X.*

An important open problem is to prove that, at each level k of the polynomial-time hierarchy, honest Σ_k^{P}-hypersimple sets exist relative to a random oracle with probability 1.

5. Completeness Under Non-Honest Reductions

Immunity has a deep connection to various completeness notions. For example, there is a simple, tt-complete set; however, no simple set is btt-complete. In the previous sections, we have shown that various types of resource-bounded simple sets cannot be complete under certain polynomial-time honest reductions. This section instead focuses on the incompleteness of simple sets under non-honest reductions.

To remove the honesty condition from reductions, we often need to make extra assumptions for similar incompleteness results. In mid 1980s, Hartmanis, Li, and Yesha [6] proved that (i) no NP-immune set in EXP is P-m-hard for NP if NP $\not\subseteq$ SUBEXP and (ii) no NP-simple set is P-m-complete if NP $\cap$ co-NP $\not\subseteq$ SUBEXP. These results can be expanded to any Δ-level of the polynomial-time hierarchy and of the subexponential-time hierarchy[8]. We also improve the latter claim.

[8]The Δ-level of the subexponential-time hierarchy is defined as: $\mathrm{SUB}\Delta_0^{\mathrm{EXP}} = \mathrm{SUBEXP}$ and $\mathrm{SUB}\Delta_{k+1}^{\mathrm{EXP}} = \mathrm{SUBEXP}^{\Sigma_k^{\mathrm{P}}}$ for every $k \in \mathbf{N}$, where SUBEXP^A denotes $\bigcap_{\epsilon>0} \mathrm{DTIME}^A(2^{n^\epsilon})$ for any oracle A. When $A = \emptyset$, we simply write SUBEXP for SUBEXP^A.

To describe our expansion, we need the unambiguous complexity class $\mathrm{U}(\Sigma_k^{\mathrm{P}} \cap \Pi_k^{\mathrm{P}})$ introduced by Yamakami [25]. For any complexity class $\mathcal{C}$, a set A is in $\mathrm{U}(\mathcal{C})$ (or $\mathrm{U}\mathcal{C}$) if there exists a single-valued partial function f such that (i) f is polynomially bounded, (ii) $Graph(f) \in \mathcal{C}$, and (iii) $A = \mathrm{dom}(f)$ [25].

PROPOSITION 28 *Let j and k be any nonnegative integers.*

1 *No Σ_k^{P}-immune set in Δ_j^{EXP} is Δ_k^{P}-m-hard for Σ_k^{P} if $\Sigma_k^{\mathrm{P}} \not\subseteq \mathrm{SUB}\Delta_{\max\{j,k\}}^{\mathrm{EXP}}$.*

2 *No Σ_k^{P}-simple set is Δ_k^{P}-m-complete for Σ_k^{P} if $\mathrm{U}(\Sigma_k^{\mathrm{P}} \cap \Pi_k^{\mathrm{P}}) \not\subseteq \mathrm{SUB}\Delta_k^{\mathrm{EXP}}$.*

Note that Proposition 28(2) directly follows from Theorem 29(2).

The original result of Hartmanis et al. refers to the P-m-incompleteness of NP-simple sets. Recently, Schaefer and Fenner [19] showed a similar result for the P-1tt-completeness. They proved that no NP-simple set is P-1tt-complete for NP if $\mathrm{UP} \not\subseteq \mathrm{SUBEXP}$. A key to their proof is the fact[9] that $Sep(\mathrm{SUBEXP}, \mathrm{NP})$ implies $\mathrm{UP} \subseteq \mathrm{SUBEXP}$, where $Sep(\mathcal{C}, \mathcal{D})$ means the separation property in [25] that, for any two disjoint sets $A, B \in \mathcal{D}$, there exists a set $S \in \mathcal{C} \cap \text{co-}\mathcal{C}$ satisfying that $A \subseteq S \subseteq \overline{B}$.

The following theorem shows that the assumption $\mathrm{UP} \not\subseteq \mathrm{SUBEXP}$ in [19] can be replaced by $\mathrm{U}(\mathrm{NP} \cap \text{co-NP}) \not\subseteq \mathrm{SUBEXP}$.

THEOREM 29 *Let $j, k \in \mathbb{N}^+$.*

1 *No Σ_k^{P}-immune set in Δ_j^{EXP} is Δ_k^{P}-1tt-hard for $\mathrm{U}(\Sigma_k^{\mathrm{P}} \cap \Pi_k^{\mathrm{P}})$ if $\mathrm{U}(\Sigma_k^{\mathrm{P}} \cap \Pi_k^{\mathrm{P}}) \not\subseteq \mathrm{SUB}\Delta_{\max\{j,k\}}^{\mathrm{EXP}}$.*

2 *No Σ_k^{P}-simple set is Δ_k^{P}-1tt-complete for Σ_k^{P} if $\mathrm{U}(\Sigma_k^{\mathrm{P}} \cap \Pi_k^{\mathrm{P}}) \not\subseteq \mathrm{SUB}\Delta_k^{\mathrm{EXP}}$.*

Theorem 29 follows from the technical lemmas: Lemmas 30 and 31. The proof for its second claim proceeds as follows. Assume that B is Δ_k^{P}-1tt-complete for Σ_k^{P}. Choose an infinite set $A \in \mathrm{U}(\Sigma_k^{\mathrm{P}} \cap \Pi_k^{\mathrm{P}}) - \mathrm{SUB}\Delta_k^{\mathrm{EXP}}$, which is of the form $\{x \mid \exists y[\langle x, y\rangle \in Graph(f)]\}$ for a certain polynomially-bounded partial function f whose graph is in $\Sigma_k^{\mathrm{P}} \cap \Pi_k^{\mathrm{P}}$. Similar to [25], set $A_1 = \{\langle x, z\rangle \mid \exists y[z \leq y \wedge \langle x, y\rangle \in Graph(f)]\}$ and $A_2 = \{\langle x, z\rangle \mid \exists y[z < y \wedge \langle x, y\rangle \in Graph(f)]\}$. Clearly, A_1 and A_2 are in $\mathrm{U}(\Sigma_k^{\mathrm{P}} \cap \Pi_k^{\mathrm{P}}) - \mathrm{SUB}\Delta_k^{\mathrm{EXP}}$. Since A_1 is Δ_k^{P}-1tt-reducible to B, by Lemma 30, there exists a set $C \in \Delta_k^{\mathrm{P}}$ such that $A_1 \cap C$ is infinite and coinfinite and $A_1 \cap C$ is h-Δ_k^{P}-1tt-reducible to B. Applying Lemma 31(1), we obtain a set $D \in \Delta_k^{\mathrm{P}}$ and a total $\mathrm{F}\Delta_k^{\mathrm{P}}$-function f such that $\overline{A_1 \cap C} \cap \overline{D}$ is finite, f Δ_k^{P}-m-reduces $A_1 \cap C$ to $\overline{B}$, and f is honest on the domain D. Since $A_2 \subseteq \overline{A_1 \cap C}$, $f(A_2) \subseteq \overline{B}$. Moreover, $A_2 \cap D$ is infinite. The honesty of f on D implies that $\overline{B}$ has an infinite Σ_k^{P}-subset $f(A_2 \cap D)$.

The key idea of Hartmanis et al. [6] is to find a set that can be honestly reducible. Lemma 30 is a "1tt" version of a technical part of [6].

LEMMA 30 *Let $j, k \in \mathbb{N}^+$. Assume that $A \notin \mathrm{SUB}\Delta_{\max\{j,k\}}^{\mathrm{EXP}}$ and $B \in \Delta_j^{\mathrm{EXP}}$. If A is Δ_k^{P}-1tt-reducible to B, then there exists a set C in Δ_k^{P} such that (i) $A \cap C$ is h-Δ_k^{P}-1tt-reducible to B and (ii) $A \cap C$ and $\overline{A} \cap C$ are infinite and coinfinite.*

[9] Actually, the result of Schaefer and Fenner can be strengthened in the following way: $Sep(\mathrm{SUBEXP}, \mathrm{U}(\mathrm{NP} \cap \text{co-NP}))$ if and only if $\mathrm{U}(\mathrm{NP} \cap \text{co-NP}) \subseteq \mathrm{SUBEXP}$. This is obtained by analyzing a similar result in [25].

LEMMA 31 *Let $k \in \mathbb{N}^+$ and $A, B \subseteq \Sigma^*$. Assume that B is Σ_k^{P}-immune and A is h-Δ_k^{P}-1tt-reducible to B.*

1. *If $A \in \Sigma_k^{\mathrm{P}}$, then there exist a set $D \in \Delta_k^{\mathrm{P}}$ and a total function $f \in \mathrm{F}\Delta_k^{\mathrm{P}}$ such that $\overline{A} \cap \overline{D}$ is finite, f Δ_k^{P}-m-reduces A to $\overline{B}$, and f is honest on the domain D.*

2. *A belongs to $\Sigma_k^{\mathrm{P}} \cap \Pi_k^{\mathrm{P}}$ if and only if A belongs to Δ_k^{P}.*

6. Limited Immunity and Simplicity

Within our current knowledge, we cannot prove or disprove the existence of an NP-simple set. The difficulty comes from the fact that an NP-immune set requires *every* NP-subset to be finite. If we restrict our attention to certain types of NP-subsets, then we may overcome the difficulty. Under the name of k-immune sets, Homer [7] required only $\mathrm{NP}_{(k)}$-subsets, for a fixed number k, to be finite. He then demonstrated how to construct a k-simple set within NP using Ladner's delayed diagonalization technique.

In this section, we investigate the notions obtained by restricting the requirements for immunity and simplicity. We first review Homer's notions of k-immunity and k-simplicity.

DEFINITION 32 *Let k be any number in $\mathbb{N}^+$.*

1. *A set S is* k-immune *if S is infinite and there is no index i in $INDEX_{(k)}$ such that W_i is infinite and $W_i \subseteq S$.*
2. *A set S is* k-simple *if S belongs to* NP *and $\overline{S}$ is k-immune.*

An "effective" version of immune and simple sets, called effectively immune and effectively simple sets, has been studied in recursion theory. Effectively simple sets are known to be T-complete and there also exists an effectively simple tt-complete set. If A is strongly effectively immune, then $\overline{A}$ cannot be immune. Analogously, we consider a resource-bounded version of such effectively immune and simple sets. Here, we freely identify binary strings with natural numbers using the lexicographic order on Σ^*.

DEFINITION 33 *Let $k \in \mathbb{N}^+$.*

1. *A set S is* feasibly k-immune *if (i) S is infinite and (ii) there exists a polynomial p such that, for every index i in $INDEX_{(k)}$, $W_i \subseteq S$ implies $|W_i| \leq 2^{p(i)}$.*
2. *A set S is* feasibly k-simple *if S is in* NP *and $\overline{S}$ is feasibly k-immune.*

We can easily prove the existence of a feasibly k-immune set in Δ_2^{P} for each $k \in \mathbb{N}^+$. From Definition 33, every feasibly k-simple set is k-simple. The converse, however, does not hold since there exists a k-simple set which is not feasibly k-simple for each number k in $\mathbb{N}^+$. The theorem below is slightly stronger than this claim since any feasibly k-simple set is also feasibly 1-simple.

THEOREM 34 *For each $k \in \mathbb{N}^+$, there exists a k-simple set which is not feasibly 1-simple.*

We return to the old question of whether NP-simple sets exist. There seems no strong evidence that suggests the existence of such a set. Only relativization provides a world where NP-simple sets exist. At the same time, we can also construct another world where these sets do not exist. These relativization results clearly indicate that the question of whether NP-simple sets exist needs unrelativizable proof techniques.

In the past few decades, the Berman-Hartmanis isomorphism conjecture has served as a working hypothesis in connection to NP-complete problems. By contrast, there has been no "natural" working hypothesis that yields the existence of NP-simple sets. For example, the hypothesis $\mathrm{P} \neq \mathrm{NP}$ does not suffice since Homer and Maass [8] showed a relativized world where the assumption $\mathrm{P} \neq \mathrm{NP}$ does not imply the existence of an NP-simple set. Motivated by Homer's k-simplicity result, we propose the following working hypothesis:

- **The k-immune hypothesis:** There exists a positive integer k such that every infinite NP set has an infinite $\mathrm{NP}_{(k)}$-subset.

Under this hypothesis, we can derive the desired consequence: the existence of NP-simple sets.

LEMMA 35 *If the k-immune hypothesis holds, then there exists an* NP-*simple set.*

Assume that the k-immune hypothesis is true; that is, there exists a positive integer k such that every infinite NP-set has an infinite $\mathrm{NP}_{(k)}$-subset. Consider any k-simple set A. We claim that A is NP-simple. If A is not NP-simple, then $\overline{A}$ has an infinite NP-subset B. By our assumption, B contains an infinite $\mathrm{NP}_{(k)}$-subset. Hence, A cannot be k-simple, a contradiction. Therefore, A is NP-simple.

To close this section, we claim the following result concerning the k-immune hypothesis. The proof uses weak forcing.

PROPOSITION 36 *The k-immune hypothesis fails relative to a generic oracle.*

Final Note. All the proofs that are omitted from this extended abstract will appear in its forthcoming complete version.

References

[1] J. L. Balcázar, Simplicity, relativizations, and nondeterminism, *SIAM J. Comput.* 14 (1985) 148–157.

[2] J. L. Balcázar and U. Schöning, Bi-immune sets for complexity classes, *Math. Systems Theory* **18** (1985) 1–10.

[3] C. H. Bennett and J. Gill, Relative to a random oracle A, $\mathrm{P}^A \neq \mathrm{NP}^A \neq \text{co-NP}^A$ with probability 1, *SIAM J. Comput.* **10** (1981) 96–113.

[4] D. Bruschi, Strong separations of the polynomial hierarchy with oracles: constructive separations by immune and simple sets, *Theoret. Comput. Sci.* **102** (1992) 215–252.

[5] P. Flajolet and J. M. Steyaert, On sets having only hard subsets, in *Proc. 2nd Intern. Colloq. on Automata, Languages, and Programming*, LNCS, Springer, Vol.14, pp.446–457, 1974.

[6] J. Hartmanis, M. Li, and Y. Yesha, Containment, separation, complete sets, and immunity of complexity classes, in: *Proc. 13th Intern. Colloq. on Automata, Languages, and Programming*, LNCS, Springer, Vol.226, pp.136–145, 1986.

[7] S. Homer, On simple and creative sets in NP, *Theoret. Comput. Sci.*, **47** (1986) 169–180.

[8] S. Homer and W. Maass, Oracle-dependent properties of the lattice of NP sets, *Theoret. Comput. Sci.*, **24** (1983) 279–289.

[9] D. Joseph and P. Young, Some remarks on witness functions for nonpolynomial and noncomplete sets in NP, *Theoret. Comput. Sci.* **39** (1985) 225–237.

[10] K. Ko, Nonlevelable sets and immune sets in the accepting density hierarchy in NP, *Math. Systems Theory* **18** (1985) 189–205.

[11] K. Ko and D. Moore, Completeness, approximation and density, *SIAM J. Comput.* **10** (1981) 787–796.

[12] A. Meyer and L. Stockmeyer, The equivalence problem for regular expressions with squaring requires exponential time, in *Proc. 13th IEEE Symp. on Switching and Automata theory*, pp.125–129, 1973.

[13] N. Lynch, On reducibility to complex or sparse sets, *Journal of ACM*, **22** (1975) 341–345.

[14] P. Orponen, A classification of complexity core lattices, *Theoret. Comput. Sci.*, **47** (1986) 121–130.

[15] P. Orponen, K. Ko, U. Schöning, and O. Watanabe, Instance complexity, *Journal of ACM*, **41** (1994) 96–121.

[16] P. Orponen, D. Russo, and U. Schöning, Optimal approximations and polynomially levelable sets, *SIAM J. Comput.*, **15** (1986) 399–408.

[17] E. L. Post, Recursively enumerable sets of positive integers and their decision problems, *Bull. Am. Math. Soc.* **50** (1944) 284–316.

[18] D. A. Russo, Optimal approximations of complete sets, in *Proc. 1st Annual Conference on Structure in Complexity Theory*, LNCS, Springer, Vol.223, pp.311–324, 1986.

[19] M. Schaefer and S. Fenner, Simplicity and strong reductions, manuscript, 2000.

[20] A. Selman, P-selective sets, tally languages and the behavior of polynomial time reducibilities on NP, *Math. Systems Theory*, **13** (1979) 55–65.

[21] L. Torenvliet, A second step toward the strong polynomial-time hierarchy, *Math. Systems Theory* **21** (1988) 99–123.

[22] L. Torenvliet and P. van Emde Boas, Simplicity, immunity, relativization and nondeterminism, *Inform. and Comput.* **80** (1989) 1–17.

[23] V. A. Uspenskii, Some remarks on r.e. sets, *Zeit. Math. Log. Grund. Math.* **3** (1957) 157–170.

[24] N. K. Vereshchagin, Relationships between NP-sets, CoNP-sets and P-sets relative to random oracles, in *Proc. 8th IEEE Conf. on Structure in Complexity Theory*, pp.132–138, 1993.

[25] T. Yamakami, Structural properties for feasibly computable classes of type two, *Math. Systems Theory* **25** (1992) 177–201.

[26] T. Yamakami, Simplicity, unpublished manuscript, University of Toronto, 1995.

DEGREE BOUNDS ON POLYNOMIALS AND RELATIVIZATION THEORY*

Holger Spakowski†
Institut für Informatik
Heinrich-Heine-Universität Düsseldorf
40225 Düsseldorf, Germany
spakowsk@cs.uni-duesseldorf.de

Rahul Tripathi‡
Department of Computer Science
University of Rochester
Rochester, NY 14627, USA
rahult@cs.rochester.edu

Abstract We demonstrate the applicability of the polynomial degree bound technique to notions such as the nonexistence of Turing-hard sets in some relativized world, (non)uniform gap-definability, and relativized separations. This way, we settle certain open questions of Hemaspaandra, Ramachandran & Zimand [HRZ95] and Fenner, Fortnow & Kurtz [FFK94], extend results of Hemaspaandra, Jain & Vereshchagin [HJV93] and construct oracles achieving desired results.

Keywords: Polynomial degree bounds, complexity classes, Turing hardness, gap-definability, relativization theory

1. Introduction

1.1 Background

In this paper, we are concerned with degree bounds of polynomials representing (not necessarily boolean) functions and their applications in constructing oracles. Polynomials were used in obtaining lower bounds for constant depth

*Due to page limitations, we do not include the proofs in this paper. A detailed version with all the proofs is available at http://www.cs.rochester.edu/trs/theory-trs.html as TR820 [ST03].

†Research supported in part by a grant from the DAAD and by DFG project RO 1202/9-1. Work done in part while visiting the University of Rochester.

‡Research supported in part by grant NSF-INT-9815095/DAAD-315-PPP-gü-ab.

circuits [Smo87, AB00], proving upper bounds on the power of complexity classes [Tod91, TO92], proving closure properties of counting classes [BRS95], proving bounds on the number of queries to compute a boolean function in the quantum black-box computing model [BBC$^+$01], and in the construction of oracles in complexity theory [Tar91, dGV02, FFKL03]. See Beigel [Bei93] and Regan [Reg97] for nice surveys on the application of polynomials in circuit complexity and computational complexity theory.

In relativization theory, the technique of using degree bounds of polynomials has been extensively used in constructing oracles that separate complexity classes (see, for instance [Tar91, Bei94, dGV02]). Beigel, Buhrman and Fortnow [BBF98] and Fenner et al. [FFKL03] showed that degree bounds of polynomials can be used to obtain relativized collapses as well. In particular, [BBF98] used polynomials to construct an oracle $\mathcal{A}$ such that $P^{\mathcal{A}} = \oplus P^{\mathcal{A}}$ and $NP^{\mathcal{A}} = EXP^{\mathcal{A}}$, and [FFKL03] showed that relative to an $\mathcal{SP}$-generic oracle, AWPP (a class defined in Section 2) equals P. We demonstrate the applicability of the polynomial degree bound technique to notions such as the nonexistence of Turing-hard sets in some relativized world, (non)uniform gap-definability, and relativized separations. Before stating our contributions, we give an overview of gap-definable counting classes which will be of interest to us in the paper.

1.2 Gap-definable Counting Classes

In this paper, we will study the relativized complexity of gap-definable counting classes using lower and upper bounds on the degree of polynomials representing certain functions. Informally speaking, a gap-definable counting class is a collection of all sets such that, for any set in the class, the membership of a string in the set depends (in a way particular to the class) on the gap (difference) between the number of accepting and rejecting paths produced by some nondeterministic polynomial-time Turing machine associated with the set. (See Section 2 for the definition of classes and Figure 1 for the inclusion relationship between classes mentioned here.) Gap-definable classes like LWPP and AWPP are, for instance, interesting because of their relevance to quantum computing: LWPP is the best known classical upper bound for EQP (a quantum analog of P) and AWPP is the best known classical upper bound for BQP (a quantum analog of BPP) [FR99]. Thus the investigation of gap-definable classes may shed light on the structure of the quantum classes EQP and BQP. The gap-definable class SPP is low for several counting classes including PP, $C_=P$ and Mod_kP, and is known to contain an important natural problem—the graph isomorphism problem [AK02].

1.3 Our Contributions

The existence of complete sets in a class is a topic of interest in complexity theory. Though classes like NP, $C_=P$ and PP possess polynomial-time many-one complete sets, for several other natural classes like UP, BPP, etc., no complete set (under any weak enough to be interesting notion of reducibility) is known. This motivates the investigation of completeness for these promise classes in relativized worlds. That line of research was pursued in several papers [Sip82, HH88, HJV93]. In particular, Hemaspaandra, Jain and Vereshchagin [HJV93] showed that there is an oracle relative to which UP $\cap$ coUP, UP, FewP and Few have no polynomial-time Turing complete sets. The existence of a relativized world where promise classes like SPP, LWPP, WPP and AWPP do not have complete sets has been unresolved for a long time [HRZ95]. We use the method of symmetrization, introduced by Minsky and Papert [MP88], combined with a result from approximation theory [EZ64, RC66] to construct a relativized world in which AWPP has no polynomial-time Turing hard set for UP $\cap$ coUP. As a corollary we obtain that none of the classes SPP, LWPP, WPP and AWPP have Turing complete sets in some relativized world. This settles an open question in [HRZ95] and extends one of the main results in [HJV93]. Using a similar, though somewhat indirect, technique we construct another relativized world where AWPP has no polynomial-time Turing hard set for ZPP. The crux in both the proofs involves proving a *lower bound* on the degree of a univariate polynomial. We note that similar techniques have been used in proving a lower bound on the degree of univariate polynomials in [Bei94, NS94, BBC+01].

Fenner, Fortnow and Kurtz [FFK94] showed that SPP is low for every uniformly gap-definable class (see Section 4 for the definition of uniform and non-uniform gap-definability). Thus SPP is low for each of PP, $C_=P$, Mod_kP, and itself. Both LWPP and WPP are known to be nonuniformly gap-definable and, prior to this paper, it was an open question whether or not these classes are uniformly gap-definable. Thus [FFK94] asked whether SPP is also low for LWPP or WPP. We give a relativized answer to their question by exhibiting an oracle relative to which UP $\cap$ coUP is not low for LWPP as well as for WPP. We further relate showing the existence of a relativized world where SPP is not low for a relativized class $\mathcal{C}$ to proving that $\mathcal{C}$ is not uniformly gap-definable. As a consequence, we settle an open question of [FFK94] that both LWPP and WPP are not uniformly gap-definable.

Certain classes are known to be weak in some relativized worlds while their composition with themselves lead to powerful classes in every relativized world. $C_=P$ is a class that is immune to RP in a relativized world [STT03], but its composition with itself, i.e. $C_=P^{C_=P}$, contains the polynomial-time hierarchy in every relativized world. (In fact, $PH \subseteq P^{\#P[1]} \subseteq UP^{C_=P} \subseteq C_=P^{C_=P}$.)

Since ZPP $\not\subseteq$ WPP in some relativized world [STT03] and relative to an oracle WPP is not self-low (present paper), it is interesting to ask whether WPP, a class similar to $C_=P$, behaves in the same way as $C_=P$ when composed with itself. We use properties of low degree multilinear polynomials to construct an oracle world in which ZPP is not contained in WPP^{WPP}; thus we falsify this intuition. We also use an upper bound on the approximate degree of a boolean function to construct an oracle relative to which NP $\cap$ coNP $\not\subseteq$ AWPP.

The proof technique that we use is quite general and is applicable also to classes that are not known to be gap-definable. For instance, we use the degree lower bound of polynomials in constructing a relativized world where MIP $\cap$ coMIP has no polynomial-time Turing hard set for ZPP. This result can be viewed as an extension of a result from [HJV93], that states that relative to an oracle, IP $\cap$ coIP has no polynomial-time Turing hard set for ZPP.

2. Preliminaries

Let $\mathbb{N}$, $\mathbb{R}$ and $\mathbb{Z}$ denote the set of positive integers, real numbers and integers, respectively. Our alphabet is $\Sigma = \{0,1\}$. For any set X of variables, and for any polynomial $p \in \mathbb{R}[X]$, $\deg(p)$ denotes the total degree of p. If $f : \{0,1\}^N \to \{0,1\}$ is a boolean function and $p \in \mathbb{R}[y_1, y_2, \ldots, y_N]$ is a multilinear polynomial such that, for every $y_1, y_2, \ldots, y_N \in \{0,1\}$, $f(y_1, y_2, \ldots, y_N) = p(y_1, y_2, \ldots, y_N)$, then p is said to be a polynomial representing f. If p is a smallest degree multilinear polynomial representing a boolean function f, then we use $\deg(f)$ to denote $\deg(p)$, the total degree of p.

We assume throughout the paper that the computation paths of an oracle Turing machine include the answers from the oracle. Given a nondeterministic Turing machine N, computation path ρ and $x \in \Sigma^*$, let $\text{sign}(N, x, \rho) = +1$ if ρ is an accepting path of $N(x)$, and let $\text{sign}(N, x, \rho) = -1$ if $N(x)$ rejects along ρ. Let $\#\text{acc}_{N^A}(x)$ $(\#rej_{N^A}(x))$ denote the number of accepting (rejecting) paths of $N^A(x)$. For any oracle NPTM N and $A \subseteq \Sigma^*$, $gap_{N^A} : \Sigma^* \to \mathbb{Z}$ is defined as follows: for all $x \in \Sigma^*$, $gap_{N^A}(x) = \#\text{acc}_{N^A}(x) - \#rej_{N^A}(x)$. We define the following complexity classes relevant to this paper.

DEFINITION 1

1. *[Gup91, FFK94]* GapP $= \{g \mid (\exists \text{NPTM } N)[g = gap_N]\}$.
2. *[OH93, FFK94]* SPP $= \{L \mid (\exists g \in \text{GapP})(\forall x \in \Sigma^*)[g(x) \in \{0,1\} \wedge (x \in L \iff g(x) = 1)]$.
3. *[FFK94]* LWPP $= \{L \mid (\exists g \in \text{GapP})(\exists h \in \text{FP} : 0 \notin \text{range}(h))(\forall x \in \Sigma^*)[g(x) \in \{0, h(0^{|x|})\} \wedge x \in L \iff g(x) = h(0^{|x|})]\}$.
4. *[FFK94]* WPP $= \{L \mid (\exists g \in \text{GapP})(\exists h \in \text{FP} : 0 \notin \text{range}(h))(\forall x \in \Sigma^*)[g(x) \in \{0, h(x)\} \wedge x \in L \iff g(x) = h(x)]\}$.

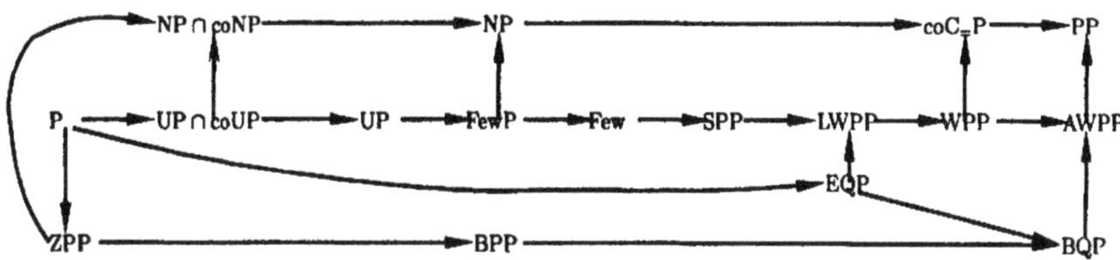

Figure 1. Complexity graph G where a node represents a complexity class and a directed edge (U, V) in G represents the fact that "class U is known to be robustly included in class V."

DEFINITION 2 ([FFKL03, FEN03]) *A language L is in* AWPP *if there exist a $g \in$ GapP, a polynomial p and $\epsilon > 0$ such that, for all $x \in \Sigma^*$,*

$$x \in L \implies \frac{(1+\epsilon)}{2} \leq \frac{g(x)}{2^{p(|x|)}} \leq 1, \text{ and}$$

$$x \notin L \implies 0 \leq \frac{g(x)}{2^{p(|x|)}} \leq \frac{(1-\epsilon)}{2}.$$

The inclusion relationship between classes considered in this paper is summarized in Figure 1. In our proofs, we use an encoding of finite sets (where the sets can be viewed as a source of a possible oracle extension at some stage of the oracle construction) defined in terms of multilinear polynomials with integer coefficients over variables representing the strings in the set. The formal description of our polynomial encoding is given below.

DEFINITION 3 *Let N be a nondeterministic polynomial-time oracle Turing machine with running time $t(.)$. Let $\mathcal{O}, \mathcal{T} \subseteq \Sigma^*$ be such that $\mathcal{O} \cap \mathcal{T} = \emptyset$, and let $x_1, x_2, \ldots, x_m$, where $m = ||\mathcal{T}||$, be the lexicographic enumeration of strings in $\mathcal{T}$. For any $x \in \Sigma^*$, a polynomial encoding of $\mathcal{T}$ w.r.t. $N^{\mathcal{O}}(x)$ is a multilinear polynomial $p \in \mathbb{Z}[y_1, y_2, \ldots, y_m]$ defined as follows: call a computation path ρ of $N^{(\cdot)}(x)$ allowable if along ρ, all queries $q \in \mathcal{O}$ have a "yes" answer, all queries $q \notin \mathcal{O} \cup \mathcal{T}$ have a "no" answer and no query $q \in \mathcal{T}$ is answered in a conflicting way. Let $x_{i_1}, x_{i_2}, \ldots, x_{i_\ell}$ be the distinct queries to strings in $\mathcal{T}$ along an allowable ρ. Create a monomial* mono(ρ) *that is the product of terms z_{i_k}, $k \in [\ell]$, where $z_{i_k} = y_{i_k}$ if x_{i_k} is answered "yes" and $z_{i_k} = (1 - y_{i_k})$ if x_{i_k} is answered "no" along ρ. Define*

$$p(y_1, y_2, \ldots, y_m) = \sum_{\rho:\rho \text{ is allowable}} \operatorname{sign}(N, x, \rho) \cdot \operatorname{mono}(\rho).$$

The polynomial $p(y_1, y_2, \ldots, y_m)$ has the following properties:

1 *for all $\mathcal{B} \subseteq \mathcal{T}$, $p(\chi_{\mathcal{B}}(x_1), \chi_{\mathcal{B}}(x_2), \ldots, \chi_{\mathcal{B}}(x_m)) = gap_{N^{\mathcal{O} \cup \mathcal{B}}}(x)$, and*
2 $\deg(p) \leq t(|x|)$.

3. Robust Hardness under Turing Reducibility

Minsky and Papert [MP88] first introduced the technique of symmetrizing a multivariate polynomial $p \in \mathbb{R}[y_1, y_2, \ldots, y_N]$ representing a function $f : \{0,1\}^N \to \mathbb{R}$. A point worth noticing is that symmetrization leads to a symmetric polynomial $p_{sym} \in \mathbb{R}[y_1, y_2, \ldots, y_N]$ with $\deg(p_{sym})$ no more than $\deg(p)$.[1] Thus p_{sym} can be used to exploit the symmetry of f within a subdomain, and thereby to get a lower bound on $\deg(p)$.

DEFINITION 4 *Let $p \in \mathbb{R}[y_1, y_2, \ldots, y_N]$ be a multilinear polynomial. The symmetrization of p is defined by*

$$p_{sym}(y_1, y_2, \ldots, y_N) = \frac{\sum_{\pi \in S_N} p(y_{\pi(1)}, y_{\pi(2)}, \ldots, y_{\pi(N)})}{N!}.$$

LEMMA 5 ([MP88]) *If $p \in \mathbb{R}[y_1, y_2, \ldots, y_N]$ is a multilinear polynomial, then there exists a univariate polynomial $\tilde{p} \in \mathbb{R}[y]$, of degree at most the total degree of p, such that for all $y_1, y_2, \ldots, y_N \in \{0,1\}$, we have*

$$p_{sym}(y_1, y_2, \ldots, y_N) = \tilde{p}(y_1 + y_2 + \cdots + y_N).$$

We use a theorem from [EZ64, RC66] to lower bound the degree of univariate polynomials that satisfy certain constraints. (See also [Bei94, NS94, BBC+01], where the same technique has been used to get a lower bound on the degree of univariate polynomials.)

LEMMA 6 ([EZ64, RC66]) *Let $p \in \mathbb{R}[y]$ be a univariate polynomial with the following properties:*

1. *for any integer $0 \le \ell \le N$, $b_1 \le p(\ell) \le b_2$, and*
2. *for some real $0 \le z \le N$, the derivative of p satisfies $|p'(z)| \ge c$.*

Then $\deg(p) \ge \sqrt{cN/(c + b_2 - b_1)}$.

The proof of Theorem 7 uses Lemma 5 and Lemma 6. We mention that [HJV93] proved, using a different combinatorial technique, that relative to an oracle, FewP contains no polynomial-time Turing hard set for UP$\cap$coUP. Theorem 7 extends this result of [HJV93] and implies that there is a relativized world where SPP has no complete sets. That answers a question raised in [HRZ95] positively.

THEOREM 7 *There exists an oracle $\mathcal{A}$ such that* $\mathrm{AWPP}^{\mathcal{A}}$ *has no* $\le_T^{p,\mathcal{A}}$*-hard set for* $\mathrm{UP}^{\mathcal{A}} \cap \mathrm{coUP}^{\mathcal{A}}$.

[1] It is well known that symmetrization may lead to a polynomial of total degree strictly smaller than that of the original polynomial. Example: Consider $p(y_1, y_2) = y_1 - y_2$.

COROLLARY 8 *There is an oracle $\mathcal{A}$ such that*

1. *for every complexity class $\mathcal{C} \in \{\mathrm{UP} \cap \mathrm{coUP}, \mathrm{UP}, \mathrm{FewP}, \mathrm{Few}\}$, $\mathcal{C}^{\mathcal{A}}$ has no $\leq_T^{p,\mathcal{A}}$-complete set [HJV93], and*
2. *for every complexity class $\mathcal{C} \in \{\mathrm{SPP}, \mathrm{LWPP}, \mathrm{WPP}, \mathrm{AWPP}\}$, $\mathcal{C}^{\mathcal{A}}$ has no $\leq_T^{p,\mathcal{A}}$-complete set.*

Through a similar, though somewhat involved, technique we show that there is a relativized world where AWPP has no polynomial-time Turing hard set for ZPP. We also have a more direct proof, that involves proving an *upper bound* on the degree of a certain multilinear polynomial, for a weaker version of Theorem 9—"existence of an oracle relative to which AWPP has no polynomial-time many-one hard set for ZPP."

THEOREM 9 $(\exists \mathcal{A})[\mathrm{AWPP}^{\mathcal{A}}$ *has no* $\leq_T^{p,\mathcal{A}}$*-hard set for* $\mathrm{ZPP}^{\mathcal{A}}]$.

COROLLARY 10 *There is an oracle $\mathcal{A}$ such that*

1. *for every class $\mathcal{C} \in \{\mathrm{ZPP}, \mathrm{RP}, \mathrm{coRP}\}$, $\mathcal{C}^{\mathcal{A}}$ has no $\leq_T^{p,\mathcal{A}}$-complete set [HJV93],*
2. $\mathrm{BPP}^{\mathcal{A}}$ *has no $\leq_T^{p,\mathcal{A}}$-complete set ([HH88] + [Amb86]), and*
3. $\mathrm{BQP}^{\mathcal{A}}$ *has no $\leq_T^{p,\mathcal{A}}$-complete set [FR99].*

Note: We obtained an alternative proof of Theorem 7 and Theorem 9 using a lemma by Vereshchagin [Ver94, Ver99] on proving whether a complexity class has a Turing-hard set for another complexity class. Fortnow and Rogers [FR99] used this lemma to prove that BQP has no polynomial-time Turing hard set for BPP in some relativized world. Since this alternative proof is also of independent interest, we sketch the proof of Theorem 9 in [ST03]. (An alternative proof of Theorem 7 can be obtained in a similar way.)

4. Lowness and Gap-Definability

The low hierarchy within NP was introduced by Schöning [Sch83] to study the inner structure of NP. Since the introduction of the low hierarchy, the concept of lowness has been generalized to arbitrary relativizable function and language classes. We now give a definition of lowness for arbitrary relativizable classes.

DEFINITION 11 (FOLKLORE) *A set $L \subseteq \Sigma^*$ is said to be low for a relativizable class $\mathcal{C}$ if $\mathcal{C}^L \subseteq \mathcal{C}$. A class $\mathcal{C}_2$ is said to be low for a relativizable class $\mathcal{C}_1$, denoted by $\mathcal{C}_1^{\mathcal{C}_2} \subseteq \mathcal{C}_1$ if every set $L \in \mathcal{C}_2$ is low for $\mathcal{C}_1$. If $\mathcal{C}_2$ is also a relativizable class then, for any $\mathcal{O} \subseteq \Sigma^*$, we say that $\mathcal{C}_2$ is low for $\mathcal{C}_1$ relative to the oracle $\mathcal{O}$, denoted by $\mathcal{C}_1^{\mathcal{C}_2^{\mathcal{O}} \oplus \mathcal{O}} \subseteq \mathcal{C}_1^{\mathcal{O}}$, if for every set $L \in \mathcal{C}_2^{\mathcal{O}}$, $\mathcal{C}_1^{L \oplus \mathcal{O}} \subseteq \mathcal{C}_1^{\mathcal{O}}$.*

Fenner, Fortnow and Kurtz [FFK94] introduced the notion of gap-definability to study the counting classes that can be defined using GapP functions alone. Since most of the well-known counting classes, like PP, $\mathrm{coC_=P}$, $\mathrm{Mod}_k\mathrm{P}$, etc., are gap-definable, any characterization for gap-definable classes carries over to these counting classes. For instance, it is known that SPP is low for every member of a particular collection of gap-definable classes, namely the collection of uniformly gap-definable classes. Thus, it follows that SPP is low for the counting classes PP, $\mathrm{coC_=P}$ and $\mathrm{Mod}_k\mathrm{P}$. The formal definition of gap-definability is given below.

DEFINITION 12 ([FFK94]) *A class $\mathcal{C}$ is gap-definable if there exist disjoint sets $A, R \subseteq \Sigma^* \times \mathbb{Z}$ such that, for any $L \subseteq \Sigma^*$, $L \in \mathcal{C}$ if and only if there exists an* NPTM *N such that for all $x \in \Sigma^*$,*

$$x \in L \Longrightarrow (x, gap_N(x)) \in A, \text{ and } x \notin L \Longrightarrow (x, gap_N(x)) \in R.$$

The class $\mathcal{C}$ is also denoted by $Gap(A, R)$.

For a relativizable class, Fenner, Fortnow and Kurtz [FFK94] introduced two ways of defining gap-definability: uniform and nonuniform. A relativizable class $\mathcal{C}$ is said to be uniformly gap-definable if it is gap-definable w.r.t. any oracle with a fixed (independent of the oracle) choice of A and R. A relativizable class $\mathcal{C}$ is said to be nonuniformly gap-definable if it gap-definable w.r.t. an oracle where the choice of A and R is dependent on the oracle. Thus, the choice of A and R may vary with different oracles in case of nonuniform gap-definability. We now give a definition that expresses the oracle (in)dependence of the pair (A, R) in the notion of gap-definability. In what follows, (A, R) is called an accepting pair if $A, R \subseteq \Sigma^* \times \mathbb{Z}$ and $A \cap R = \emptyset$.

DEFINITION 13 ([FFK94])

1 *We say that a relativizable class $\mathcal{C}$ is gap-definable relative to an oracle $\mathcal{O}$ with accepting pair (A, R) if for any $L \subseteq \Sigma^*$, $L \in \mathcal{C}^{\mathcal{O}}$ if and only if there exists an oracle* NPTM *N such that for all $x \in \Sigma^*$,*

$$x \in L \Longrightarrow (x, gap_{N^{\mathcal{O}}}(x)) \in A, \text{ and } x \notin L \Longrightarrow (x, gap_{N^{\mathcal{O}}}(x)) \in R.$$

2 *We say that a relativizable class $\mathcal{C}$ is uniformly gap-definable with accepting pair (A, R) if for any oracle $\mathcal{O} \subseteq \Sigma^*$, it holds that $\mathcal{C}$ is gap-definable relative to $\mathcal{O}$ with accepting pair (A, R).*

We observe that there is a stronger characterization of uniformly gap-definable classes than the one stated in [FFK94].

OBSERVATION 14 *If $\mathcal{C}$ is a uniformly gap-definable class, then for any $\mathcal{O} \subseteq \Sigma^*$, it holds that $\mathcal{C}^{\mathrm{SPP}^{\mathcal{O}}} = \mathcal{C}^{\mathcal{O}}$.*

In Theorem 17, we construct a relativized world in which UP ∩ coUP is not low for LWPP as well as for WPP. Since UP ∩ coUP ⊆ SPP in every relativized world, this also shows that relative to the same oracle, SPP is not low for either of LWPP or WPP. Fenner, Fortnow and Kurtz [FFK94] proved that both LWPP and WPP are nonuniformly gap-definable. However, they leave open the question whether LWPP and WPP are uniformly gap-definable. From Observation 14 and Theorem 17, we conclude that LWPP and WPP are not uniformly gap-definable. Note that the definition of uniform and non-uniform gap-definability involves relativizing a class. Therefore, they are not properties of sets in the class, but rather are the properties of machines characterizing the class. So, proving that WPP and LWPP are not uniformly gap-definable does not imply in any obvious way that these classes separate from any uniformly gap-definable class in the real world.

We use a variant of the prime number theorem, stated in Lemma 15, in the proof of Theorem 17 to estimate the number of primes between two integers.

LEMMA 15 ([RS62]) *For every $n \geq 17$, the number of primes less than or equal to n, $\pi(n)$, satisfies $n/\ln n < \pi(n) < 1.25506\, n/\ln n$.*

The following lemma, Lemma 17, was used in [STT03] to construct a relativized world in which WPP is not closed under polynomial-time Turing reductions. We found the same lemma to be useful in proving Theorem 17.

LEMMA 16 ([STT03]) *Let $N, p \in \mathbb{N}$ be such that p is a prime and $p \leq N/2$. Let $s \in \mathbb{Z}[y_1, y_2, \ldots, y_N]$ be a multilinear polynomial with $\deg(s) < p$. If for some $val \in \mathbb{Z}$, it holds that*

1. *$s(0, 0, \ldots, 0) = 0$, and*
2. *for all $y_1, y_2, \ldots, y_N \in \{0, 1\}$ with $\sum_{i=1}^{N} y_i = p$, $s(y_1, y_2, \ldots, y_N) = val$*

then $p \mid val$.

THEOREM 17 $(\exists \mathcal{A})[\mathrm{LWPP}^{\mathrm{UP}^{\mathcal{A}} \cap \mathrm{coUP}^{\mathcal{A}}} \not\subseteq \mathrm{WPP}^{\mathcal{A}}]$.

COROLLARY 18 LWPP *and* WPP *are not uniformly gap-definable.*

COROLLARY 19 *There is a relativized world $\mathcal{A}$ such that (1) for any class $\mathcal{C} \in$ {UP ∩ coUP, UP, FewP, Few, SPP, LWPP}, $\mathcal{C}^{\mathcal{A}}$ is not low for $\mathrm{LWPP}^{\mathcal{A}}$, and (2) for any class $\mathcal{C} \in$ {UP ∩ coUP, UP, FewP, Few, SPP, LWPP, WPP}, $\mathcal{C}^{\mathcal{A}}$ is not low for $\mathrm{WPP}^{\mathcal{A}}$.*

5. Relativized Noninclusion

Beigel [Bei94] constructed an oracle relative to which $\mathrm{P}^{\mathrm{NP}} \not\subseteq \mathrm{PP}$. As a consequence, there is a relativized world in which NP is not low for PP. However, in contrast to NP, it is not clear whether NP $\cap$ coNP is not low for PP in some relativized world. In [STT03], it was shown that there is an oracle relative to which ZPP is not contained in WPP, a class known to be low for PP. Thus, it follows that relative to the same oracle, NP $\cap$ coNP $\not\subseteq$ WPP. In Theorem 23, we extend this result and show that there is a relativized world where NP $\cap$ coNP $\not\subseteq$ AWPP, where AWPP is a class known to be low for PP. This supports our belief that NP $\cap$ coNP might not be low for PP in a suitable relativized world. The proof of Theorem 23 uses a property of low-degree multilinear polynomials over rings given by Tarui (Lemma 20), and the notion of approximate degree of boolean functions. The use of approximate degree of a boolean function in Theorem 23 is inspired by the proof of Theorem 6.13 (AWPP has polynomial certificate complexity) in [FFKL03]. Fenner et. al. [FFKL03] used this theorem to show that relative to an $\mathcal{SP}$-generic G, $\mathrm{P}^G = \mathrm{NP}^G \cap \mathrm{coNP}^G = \mathrm{AWPP}^G$.

LEMMA 20 ([TAR91]) *Let $\mathcal{R}$ be a ring. Let s be a multilinear polynomial in $\mathcal{R}[y_1, y_2, \ldots, y_N]$ of total degree at most d and let i be a nonnegative integer such that $0 \leq i \leq i + d \leq N$ and $s(y_1, y_2, \ldots, y_N) = 0$ for each $y_1, y_2, \ldots, y_N \in \{0,1\}$ satisfying $i \leq \sum_{j=1}^{N} y_j \leq i + d$. Then, $s \equiv 0$.*

DEFINITION 21 ([NS94]) *Given a boolean function $f : \{0,1\}^N \rightarrow \{0,1\}$ and a polynomial $p \in \mathbb{R}[y_1, \ldots, y_N]$, we say that p approximates f if there exists $0 \leq \epsilon < 1/2$ such that, for every $y_1, \ldots, y_N \in \{0,1\}$, $|f(y_1, \ldots, y_N) - p(y_1, \ldots, y_N)| \leq \epsilon$. The approximate degree of f, denoted by $\widetilde{\deg}(f)$, is the minimum integer d such that there is a polynomial of degree d that approximates f.*

Nisan and Szegedy [NS94] showed that both the degree and the decision tree complexity of a boolean function is polynomially related to its approximate degree. We use Lemma 22 to obtain an upper bound on the degree of boolean functions in the proof of Theorem 23.

LEMMA 22 ([NS94, BBC+01]) *There is a constant c such that, for any boolean function f, $\widetilde{\deg}(f) \leq \deg(f) \leq D(f) \leq c \cdot \widetilde{\deg}(f)^6$.*

THEOREM 23 $(\exists \mathcal{A})[\mathrm{NP}^{\mathcal{A}} \cap \mathrm{coNP}^{\mathcal{A}} \not\subseteq \mathrm{AWPP}^{\mathcal{A}}]$.

Certain classes are not very powerful in some relativized worlds, however their composition with themselves are found to be more powerful classes in every relativized world. For instance, [STT03] showed the existence of a relativized world in which RP is immune to $\mathrm{C_{=}P}$. But $\mathrm{C_{=}P}^{\mathrm{C_{=}P}}$ is known to contain the polynomial-time hierarchy in every relativized world. In fact in every relativized world, $\mathrm{UP}^{\mathrm{C_{=}P}}$ and $\mathrm{ZPP}^{\mathrm{C_{=}P}}$, which are subclasses of $\mathrm{C_{=}P}^{\mathrm{C_{=}P}}$, contain the polynomial-time hierarchy. Using Torán's [Tor91] combinatorial technique, [STT03] constructed an oracle relative to which ZPP $\not\subseteq$ WPP. Corollary 19 shows that there is a relativized world where WPP is not self-low, and so we cannot conclude directly from [STT03] that ZPP is not contained in $\mathrm{WPP}^{\mathrm{WPP}}$ relative to an oracle. Therefore, it is interesting to ask whether or not WPP exhibits a similar behavior as its superclass $\mathrm{C_{=}P}$. That is, whether $\mathrm{WPP}^{\mathrm{WPP}}$ is as big a class as to contain the polynomial-time hierarchy in every relativized world. We show in Theorem 24 that this is not the case by constructing a relativized world in which ZPP is not contained in $\mathrm{WPP}^{\mathrm{WPP}}$. The proof of Theorem 24 uses Lemma 20.

THEOREM 24 $(\exists \mathcal{A})[\mathrm{ZPP}^{\mathcal{A}} \not\subseteq \mathrm{WPP}^{\mathrm{WPP}^{\mathcal{A}}}]$.

For any $k \in \mathbb{N}$, let WPP^k denote the kth level of WPP hierarchy formed by composing WPP with itself up to k levels. The proof of Theorem 24 can be easily extended to show the following general result: $(\forall k \in \mathbb{N})(\exists \mathcal{A})[\mathrm{ZPP}^{\mathcal{A}} \not\subseteq \mathrm{WPP}^{k,\mathcal{A}}]$.

6. Extensions to Other Classes

In this section, we demonstrate the technique of using degree lower bound of polynomials in constructing relativized worlds for classes defined by probabilistic oracle Turing machines. Hemaspaandra, Jain and Vereshchagin [HJV93] showed that relative to an oracle, IP $\cap$ coIP has no polynomial-time Turing hard set for ZPP. We extend their result in Theorem 27 by constructing an oracle world where MIP $\cap$ coMIP has no polynomial-time Turing hard set for ZPP. In the proof, we use the characterization of MIP in terms of oracle proof systems as given by Fortnow, Rompel and Sipser [FRS94]. Note that in the real world (i.e., relative to $\emptyset$ as an oracle) $\mathrm{MIP}^{\emptyset} \cap \mathrm{coMIP}^{\emptyset} = \mathrm{NEXP} \cap \mathrm{coNEXP}$ and so, $\mathrm{MIP}^{\emptyset} \cap \mathrm{coMIP}^{\emptyset}$ contains polynomial-time Turing hard set for $\mathrm{ZPP}^{\emptyset} = \mathrm{ZPP}$. It follows that Theorem 27 does not hold in the real world.

DEFINITION 25 ([FRS94]) *We say that a set L has an oracle proof system if there exists a probabilistic polynomial-time oracle Turing machine N such that for all $x \in \Sigma^*$,*

$$x \in L \implies (\exists Q \subseteq \Sigma^*)\left[\mathrm{Prob}[N^Q(x) \textit{ accepts}\,] \geq 1 - 2^{|x|}\right] \textit{ and}$$
$$x \notin L \implies (\forall Q \subseteq \Sigma^*)\left[\mathrm{Prob}[N^Q(x) \textit{ accepts}\,] \leq 2^{-|x|}\right],$$

where the probability is over the random coin tosses done by N.

The next Theorem says that the class of sets accepted by multiprover interactive protocols (MIP) is the same as the one which contains sets that are accepted by oracle proof systems.

THEOREM 26 ([FRS94]) *A set L is accepted by an oracle proof system if and only if L is accepted by a multiprover interactive protocol.*

Since the proof of Theorem 26 relativizes, it suffices to construct a relativized world where no oracle proof system accepts a set that is Turing hard for ZPP. We construct such a relativized world in the next theorem.

THEOREM 27 *There exists an oracle $\mathcal{A}$ such that* $\mathrm{MIP}^{\mathcal{A}} \cap \mathrm{coMIP}^{\mathcal{A}}$ *has no* $\leq_T^{p,\mathcal{A}}$*-hard set for* $\mathrm{ZPP}^{\mathcal{A}}$.

COROLLARY 28 *There is an oracle relative to which*

1 ZPP, RP, coRP, IP $\cap$ coIP *have no polynomial-time Turing complete sets [HJV93],*
2 $\mathrm{BPP}^{\mathcal{A}}$ *has no* $\leq_T^{p,\mathcal{A}}$*-complete set ([HH88] + [Amb86]), and*
3 MIP $\cap$ coMIP *has no polynomial-time Turing complete sets.*

7. Conclusions

In this paper, we apply certain complexity measures (degree, approximate degree) of functions in the context of relativization theory. Likewise, Fenner et al. [FFKL03] and Vereshchagin [Ver94, Ver99] have used (related measures) certificate complexity and decision tree complexity, respectively, in constructing relativized worlds. It would be interesting to explore more connections between complexity measures of a function and relativization theory.

Acknowledgments

We are grateful to Lane Hemaspaandra for his encouragement, advice and guidance throughout the project. We thank Mayur Thakur for stimulating discussions.

References

[AB00] N. Alon and R. Beigel. Lower bounds for approximations by low degree polynomials over $\mathbb{Z}_m$. In *Proceedings of the 16th Annual IEEE Conference on Computational Complexity*, pages 184–187, Los Alamitos, CA, June 18–21 2000. IEEE Computer Society.

[AK02] V. Arvind and P. Kurur. Graph isomorphism is in SPP. In *Proceedings of the 43rd IEEE Symposium on Foundations of Computer Science*, pages 743–750, Los Alamitos, November 16–19 2002. IEEE Computer Society.

[Amb86] K. Ambos-Spies. A note on complete problems for complexity classes. *Information Processing Letters*, 23(5):227–230, 1986.

[BBC+01] R. Beals, H. Buhrman, R. Cleve, M. Mosca, and R. de Wolf. Quantum lower bounds by polynomials. *Journal of the ACM*, 48, 2001.

[BBF98] R. Beigel, H. Buhrman, and L. Fortnow. NP might not be as easy as detecting unique solutions. In *Proceedings of the 30th ACM Symposium on Theory of Computing*, pages 203–208. ACM Press, May 1998.

[Bei93] R. Beigel. The polynomial method in circuit complexity. In *Proceedings of the 8th Structure in Complexity Theory Conference*, pages 82–95, San Diego, CA, USA, May 1993. IEEE Computer Society Press.

[Bei94] R. Beigel. Perceptrons, PP, and the polynomial hierarchy. *Computational Complexity*, 4(4):339–349, 1994.

[BRS95] R. Beigel, N. Reingold, and D. Spielman. PP is closed under intersection. *Journal of Computer and System Sciences*, 50(2):191–202, 1995.

[dGV02] M. de Graaf and P. Valiant. Comparing EQP and $MOD_{p^k}P$ using polynomial degree lower bounds. Technical Report quant-ph/0211179, Quantum Physics, 2002.

[EZ64] H. Ehlich and K. Zeller. Schwankung von Polynomen zwischen Gitterpunkten. *Mathematische Zeitschrift*, 86:41–44, 1964.

[Fen03] S. Fenner. PP-lowness and a simple definition of AWPP. *Theory of Computing Systems*, 36(2):199–212, 2003.

[FFK94] S. Fenner, L. Fortnow, and S. Kurtz. Gap-definable counting classes. *Journal of Computer and System Sciences*, 48(1):116–148, 1994.

[FFKL03] S. Fenner, L. Fortnow, S. Kurtz, and L. Li. An oracle builder's toolkit. *Information and Computation*, 182(2):95–136, 2003.

[FR99] L. Fortnow and J. Rogers. Complexity limitations on quantum computation. *Journal of Computer and System Sciences*, 59(2):240–252, 1999.

[FRS94] L. Fortnow, J. Rompel, and M. Sipser. On the power of multi-prover interactive protocols. *Theoretical Computer Science*, 134:545–557, 1994.

[Gup91] S. Gupta. The power of witness reduction. In *Proceedings of the 6th Structure in Complexity Theory Conference*, pages 43–59. IEEE Computer Society Press, June/July 1991.

[HH88] J. Hartmanis and L. Hemachandra. Complexity classes without machines: On complete languages for UP. *Theoretical Computer Science*, 58:129–142, 1988.

[HJV93] L. Hemaspaandra, S. Jain, and N. Vereshchagin. Banishing robust Turing completeness. *International Journal of Foundations of Computer Science*, 4(3):245–265, 1993.

[HRZ95] L. Hemaspaandra, A. Ramachandran, and M. Zimand. Worlds to die for. *SIGACT News*, 26(4):5–15, 1995.

[MP88] M. Minsky and S. Papert. *Perceptrons: An Introduction to Computational Geometry*. MIT Press, Cambridge, Massachusetts, expanded edition, 1988. First edition appeared in 1968.

[NS94] N. Nisan and M. Szegedy. On the degree of boolean functions as real polynomials. *Computational Complexity*, 4(4):301–313, 1994.

[OH93] M. Ogiwara and L. Hemachandra. A complexity theory for feasible closure properties. *Journal of Computer and System Sciences*, 46(3):295–325, 1993.

[RC66] T. J. Rivlin and E. W. Cheney. A comparison of uniform approximations on an interval and a finite subset thereof. *SIAM Journal on Numerical Analysis*, 3(2):311–320, June 1966.

[Reg97] K. Regan. Polynomials and combinatorial definitions of languages. In L. Hemaspaandra and A. Selman, editors, *Complexity Theory Retrospective II*, pages 261–293. Springer-Verlag, 1997.

[RS62] J. Rosser and L. Schoenfeld. Approximate formulas for some functions of prime numbers. *Illinois Journal of Mathematics*, 6:64–94, 1962.

[Sch83] U. Schöning. A low and a high hierarchy within NP. *Journal of Computer and System Sciences*, 27:14–28, 1983.

[Sip82] M. Sipser. On relativization and the existence of complete sets. In *Proceedings of the 9th International Colloquium on Automata, Languages, and Programming*, pages 523–531. Springer-Verlag *Lecture Notes in Computer Science #140*, 1982.

[Smo87] R. Smolensky. Algebraic methods in the theory of lower bounds for boolean circuit complexity. In *Proceedings of the 19th ACM Symposium on Theory of Computing*, pages 77–82. ACM Press, May 1987.

[ST03] H. Spakowski and R. Tripathi. Degree bounds on polynomials and relativization theory. Technical Report TR820, Department of Computer Science, University of Rochester, November 2003.

[STT03] H. Spakowski, M. Thakur, and R. Tripathi. Quantum and classical complexity classes: Separations, collapses, and closure properties. In *Proceedings of the 23rd Conference on FSTTCS*, pages 375–386. Springer-Verlag *Lecture Notes in Computer Science #2914*, December 2003.

[Tar91] J. Tarui. Degree complexity of boolean functions and its applications to relativized separations. In *Proceedings of the 6th Annual Conference on Structure in Complexity Theory (SCTC '91)*, pages 285–285, Chicago, IL, USA, June 1991. IEEE Computer Society Press.

[TO92] S. Toda and M. Ogiwara. Counting classes are at least as hard as the polynomial-time hierarchy. *SIAM Journal on Computing*, 21(2):316–328, 1992.

[Tod91] S. Toda. PP is as hard as the polynomial-time hierarchy. *SIAM Journal on Computing*, 20(5):865–877, 1991.

[Tor91] J. Torán. Complexity classes defined by counting quantifiers. *Journal of the ACM*, 38(3):753–774, 1991.

[Ver94] N. Vereshchagin. Relativizable and nonrelativizable theorems in the polynomial theory of algorithms. *Russian Academy of Sciences–Izvestiya–Mathematics*, 42(2):261–298, 1994.

[Ver99] Nikolai K. Vereshchagin. Relativizability in complexity theory. In *L.D. Beklemishev, M. Pentus, and N. Vereshchagin, Provability, Complexity, Grammars*, volume 192 of 2, pages 87–172. AMS Translations, 1999.

THE FIRING SQUAD SYNCHRONIZATION PROBLEM WITH MANY GENERALS FOR ONE-DIMENSIONAL CA

Hubert Schmid, Thomas Worsch
IAKS Vollmar, Fakultät für Informatik
Universität Karlsruhe, Germany
worsch@ira.uka.de

Abstract The Firing Squad Synchronization Problem is one of the classical problems for cellular automata. In this paper we consider the case of more than one general. A synchronous and an asynchronous version of the problem are considered. In the latter case the generals may start their activities at different times. In the synchronous case there are optimum-time solutions. Very simple and elegant techniques for constructing one of them are the main contribution of this paper on the algorithmic side. For the asynchronous case an exact formula for the optimum synchronization time of each instance is derived. We prove that no CA can solve all instances in optimum time, but we describe a CA whose running time is very close to it; it only needs additional $\log n$ steps.

Keywords: Cellular automata, Firing Squad Synchronization Problem

Introduction

The *Firing Squad Synchronization Problem* (FSSP) is one of the most well studied algorithmic problems for cellular automata. Proposed by Myhill in 1957, first solutions date back at least to the early sixties [2].

With a few exceptions there are mainly two types of results. Part of the research is concerned with the task to find CA with as few states as possible which still solve the problem (possibly in optimum time) [7]. In other papers modifications and generalizations of the classical FSSP are investigated. The present paper is of the second type.

It is organized as follows. In Section 1 we quickly review the basic definitions of cellular automata and then proceed to describe the generalized synchronization problems we are interested in. In Section 2 an exact formula for the optimum time of any instance of the asynchronous multi-general FSSP is derived and it is shown that no CA solving the problem in general can achieve this time for all instances. Concrete CA algorithms for the synchronous and the asynchronous multi-general FSSP are the topic of Sections 3 and 4 respectively.

The results presented are part of the diploma thesis of the first author [10].

1. Basic notions

For two sets A and B we write B^A for the set of all functions $f : A \to B$. The set of integers will be denoted by $\mathbf{Z}$, the set of positive integers by $\mathbf{N}$ and the set of nonnegative integers by $\mathbf{N}_0$.

1.1 Cellular automata

We assume that the reader is familiar with the standard model of one-dimensional CA with von Neumann neighborhood of radius 1, that is we use neighborhood $N = \{-1, 0, 1\}$. We will denote by S the finite set of states and by $\delta : S^N \to S$ the local transition function.

A global configuration is a mapping $C \in S^{\mathbf{Z}}$. Given a configuration C and a cell $i \in \mathbf{Z}$ we write $C(i + N)$ for the local configuration observed by cell i which is defined as $C(i+N) : N \to S : n \mapsto C(i+n)$. The local transition function induces the global transition function $\Delta : S^{\mathbf{Z}} \to S^{\mathbf{Z}}$ as usual: For a configuration $C : \mathbf{Z} \to S$, its successor configuration $\Delta(C)$ is defined by the requirement that for all $i \in \mathbf{Z}$ one has: $(\Delta(C))(i) = \delta(C(i + N))$. If C^0 is a configuration we sometimes abbreviate $\Delta^t(C^0)$ as C^t.

We will assume that there is always a designated quiescent state $\mathtt{q}$, which for the rest of this paper is in fact even a "dead" state in the sense that $C(i) = \mathtt{q} \Longrightarrow (\Delta(C))(i) = \mathtt{q}$.

1.2 Firing squad synchronization problems

The standard FSSP. The standard formulation of the FSSP requires the existence of a designated state $\mathtt{g}$ for the "general", a designated state $\mathtt{s}$ for the "soldiers" and designated "firing" state $\mathtt{f}$.

The task is to find a CA (S, δ) with $\{\mathtt{q}, \mathtt{g}, \mathtt{s}, \mathtt{f}\} \subseteq S$ such that:

- $\delta(\ell) = \mathtt{q}$ for all local configurations such that $\ell(0) = \mathtt{q}$;
- $\delta(\ell) = \ell(0)$ for all $\ell : N \to \{\mathtt{q}, \mathtt{s}\}$, i.e. cells in state $\mathtt{s}$ don't start any activities "by themselves".

These conditions are *always* required. We will not list these requirements again, but it is to be understood that the CA for the generalized FSSPs considered below have to fulfill them, too.

- For any $n \in \mathbf{N}$ let C_n^0 denote the configuration

$$C_n^0(i) = \begin{cases} \mathtt{q} & \text{iff not } 0 \le i < n \\ \mathtt{g} & \text{iff } i = 0 \\ \mathtt{s} & \text{otherwise, i.e. iff } 1 \le i < n \end{cases}$$

Then for each n there has to be a $t \in \mathbf{N}_0$ such that the CA *fires* after t time steps when started with initial configuration C_n^0, i.e. all initially non-quiescent cells enter the firing state after the same number of steps for the first time:

- for all $0 \leq i < n$: $C_n^t(i) = \mathtt{f}$ and
- for all $0 \leq i < n$ and for all $t' < t$: $C_n^{t'}(i) \neq \mathtt{f}$.

In this case one problem instance is completely characterized by the number n of cells to be synchronized.

There are several generalizations and modifications which have been considered in the literature. These include different types of underlying "geometries", e.g. [1], the inclusion of "faulty" cells, e.g. [13], synchronization in a prescribed but non-optimum time, e.g. [6] and others. In this paper we are interested in the case of more than one general.

The synchronous multi-general FSSP. For a generalized problem which already has been investigated and solved quite some time ago, there is still one general, but its position is not known. Each problem instance is then characterized by the number n of cells and the position p, $0 \leq p < n$, of the general. The first optimum time solution for this problem is due to Moore [8]. In Section 3 we will describe a different approach which basically allows to apply any solution developed for the standard FSSP also in this generalized case.

In the present paper the restriction of having exactly one general is dropped. In the simpler case each problem instance is characterized by the number n of cells, a number $k \leq n$ of generals and arbitrary initial positions $0 \leq p_i < n$, $1 \leq i \leq k$, of the generals. In other words the initial configurations look like this:

$$C_n^0(i) = \begin{cases} \mathtt{q} & \text{iff not } 0 \leq i < n \\ \mathtt{g} & \text{iff } i \in \{p_1, \ldots, p_k\} \\ \mathtt{s} & \text{otherwise} \end{cases}$$

We call this the *synchronous multi-general FSSP*, abbreviated as S-MG-FSSP. First ideas for its (optimum-time) solution have been sketched by Hisaoka et al. [3]. In Section 3 we will present a slightly different approach.

The asynchronous Multi-General FSSP. Assume that one wants to construct the composition of two CA with local rules δ_1 and δ_2 in the following sense. Initially all cells use δ_1. After some time some cells will observe certain local configurations indicating that a first sub-goal of the algorithm has been reached and that now all (non-quiescent) cells should switch to δ_2 simultaneously. In some applications of this method of constructing new CA form old ones, different cells will note at *different* times, that the mode of operation should be switched.

Thus, what is really useful is yet another generalization of the FSSP where possibly several generals start their work at different times. We call this the *asynchronous multi-general FSSP* (where the adjective refers to the asynchronous start of the generals, of course).

In this case each problem instance $I = (n, T)$ is characterized by the number n of cells (called the *length* $\text{len}(I)$ of I), a number $k \leq n$ of generals and a set of pairs $T = \{(p_1, t_1), \ldots, (p_k, t_k)\}$, where the p_i, $0 \leq p_i < n$, are the arbitrary initial positions of the generals and each $t_i \geq 0$ is the point in time when a general "appears" at position p_i and starts to work.

We formalize this as follows. The initial configuration is

$$C_n^0(i) = \begin{cases} \mathtt{q} & \text{iff not } 0 \leq i < n \\ \mathtt{s} & \text{iff } 0 \leq i < n \end{cases}$$

Given a configuration C_n^t its successor configuration C_n^{t+1} is determined in two phases:

- First, for each p_i with $(p_i, t) \in T$ the state of cell p_i in configuration C_n^t is set to $\mathtt{g}$.
- To the resulting configuration then the global transition function is applied.

This description is not a CA. But in applications the $(p_i, t_i) \in T$ are not some "external events" but indeed result from a CA which produces certain specific local configurations observed by cells p_i at times t_i.

In order to avoid problems (which do not occur in applications anyway) we slightly restrict the set of allowed problem instances. A general must not appear in cell p_i at time t_i if that might already have entered a state different from $\mathtt{s}$. That is for any two different $(p_i, t_i) \in T$ and $(p_j, t_j) \in T$ must hold: $|t_j - t_i| < |p_j - p_i|$.

We call this the *asynchronous multi-general FSSP*, abbreviated as A-MG-FSSP. Vollmar [14, 15] has described CA solving this problem but did not investigate questions concerning the optimum time. In general Vollmar's solutions are considerably slower than the solution described below in Section 4.

1.3 Optimum time for the S-MG-FSSP and the A-MG-FSSP

Let **SP** be a solvable synchronization problem with a set $\mathcal{I}$ of instances and $f : \mathcal{I} \to \mathbf{N}$ a function. A CA A solves **SP** if for each $I \in \mathcal{I}$ as the initial configuration the CA A eventually fires. The number of steps needed for this is denoted as $T_A(I)$. We say that f is a *lower bound* for **SP** if for each CA A solving **SP** holds: $\forall I \in \mathcal{I} : f(I) \leq T_A(I)$.

If $\mathcal{A}$ denotes the set of CA solving **SP**, it is easy to see [4] that the function $T_{\min} : \mathcal{I} \to \mathbf{N}$ defined by $T_{\min}(I) = \min\{T_A(I) \mid A \in \mathcal{A}\}$ is a lower bound for **SP** and in fact is the greatest lower bound. We call $T_{\min}$ the *optimum time* for **SP**.

Note, that this definition is somewhat non-uniform, because for different I it may be that $T_{\min}(I)$ can only be achieved by different CA.

It is one of the surprises of the classical FSSP, that its optimum time can be achieved by one CA for all instances. But since one is accustomed to that it will probably come as an even greater surprise, that *each CA solving the asynchronous multi-general FSSP must solve infinitely many instances in a time which is not optimum time.* See Theorem 5 below.

Informally $T_{\min}(I)$ can be described easily for all synchronization problems considered in this paper: The optimum time for instance I is the time needed so that the leftmost and the rightmost cell can send some "information" to the other end (i.e. the rightmost or the leftmost cell respectively). This consists of $n-1$ steps needed to transmit the information plus the number of steps needed before the border cells can enter a state different from $\mathtt{s}$ for the first time. For example in the standard problem setting it takes $n-1$ steps, before a signal sent by the general at the left end has reached the rightmost cell $n-1$, resulting in an optimum time of $2n-2$.

In the asynchronous multi-general case from the general at position p_i it takes p_i steps to reach the leftmost cell 0 and $n-1-p_i$ steps to reach the rightmost cell $n-1$. This should make it plausible that one has

$$T_{\min}(I) = n - 1 + \max\left\{\min_i(t_i + p_i),\ \min_i(t_i + n - 1 - p_i)\right\} .$$

This is the first main result which we are going to prove now.

2. Optimum time for the multi-general FSSPs

THEOREM 1 *The optimum time for an instance I of the asynchronous multi-general FSSP with n cells and $T = \{(p_1, t_1), \dots, (p_k, t_k)\}$ is*

$$T_{\min}(I) = n - 1 + \max\begin{cases}\min_i(t_i + p_i)\\ n - 1 + \min_i(t_i - p_i)\end{cases}$$

Proof. We split the proof in two parts. First we show (Lemma 2) that the time given above is indeed a lower bound for the running time of CA solving the A-MG-FSSP. In Lemma 3 we show that for each I there is a CA solving the problem and needing only time $T_{\min}(I)$ for I. □

LEMMA 2 *Let A be any CA which solves the asynchronous multi-general FSSP and let I be any of its instances. Then*

$$T_A(I) \geq T_{\min}(I) = n - 1 + \max\begin{cases}\min_i(t_i + p_i)\\ n - 1 + \min_i(t_i - p_i)\end{cases}$$

Proof. The proof is by contradiction and similar to the one for the standard FSSP. Let A be any CA solving the problem and assume that I is an instance such that A needs time $t_f = T_A(I) < T_{\min}(I)$ for the synchronization. Assume that for I one has $\min_i(t_i + p_i) \leq \min_i(t_i + n - 1 - p_i)$ (the other case can be treated analogously) and let j be an index such that $t_j - p_j$ becomes minimum.

Let $D = \{(x,t) \mid 0 \leq x < n \wedge t \geq 0 \wedge x + t \leq t_f\}$ denote the set of all points in the space-time diagram for instance I which "have an influence" on cell 0 at time t_f. In particular for cell $n-1$ one has $D \cap \{n-1\} \times \mathbf{N}_0 = \{(n-1,t) \mid 0 \leq t \leq t_f - (n-1)\}$. But $t_f - (n-1) < T_{\min}(I) - (n-1) = n - 1 + t_j - p_j$ and the latter is the first time when cell $n-1$ could possible have left state $\mathtt{s}$.

Therefore for all t such that $(n-1,t) \in D$ we have $C_n^t(n-1) = \mathtt{s}$.

Now consider a new instance I' which consists of $n' = n + t_f + 1$ cells and the same set T as I. While in instance I cell $n-1$ always was in state $\mathtt{s}$ during the first $t_f - (n-1)$ steps because it had $\mathtt{q}$ as its right neighbor, in instance I' cell $n-1$ will always be in state $\mathtt{s}$ during the first $t_f - (n-1)$ steps because it has $\mathtt{s}$ as its right neighbor and again no signals can have reached it until then.

It is an easy exercise to show that as a consequence for all $(x,t) \in D$ the states in the space-time diagrams at positions (x,t) coincide for the instances I and I'. In particular for instance I' cell 0 will enter state $\mathtt{f}$ at time t_f. But *at the same time* cell $(n'-1)$ will still be in state $\mathtt{s}$ because it is t_f cells to the right of cell $(n-1)$ and hence cannot have been reached by any signal. But this is in contradiction to the requirement that always all cells have the enter state $\mathtt{f}$ simultaneously. □

LEMMA 3 *For each instance I of the asynchronous multi-general FSSP there is a CA A solving the problem for all instances and needing only $T_A(I) = T_{\min}(I)$ for instance I.*

Proof. Let I be any instance and denote by n the number of non-quiescent cells. Let A be any CA solving the A-MG-FSSP. It is clear that such CA exist. For example one can send a signal to the left from any general. As soon as the first signal arrives at the leftmost cell that one becomes the "real" general and starts an algorithm for the standard FSSP erasing all signals coming from the right.

Below we will describe a CA A_n which synchronizes all instances with $m \leq n$ cells, and these in optimum time. For instances with more than n cells the CA either never fires any cell or does fire them synchronously.

Given A_n and A one can construct a new CA A' by running those two in parallel. By definition A' fires as soon as either A or A_n would fire. A' solves the A-MG-FSSP and only needs optimum time in particular for instance I.

A_n works as follows. Each general sends a signal to the left and one to the right. Whenever two such signals meet, they erase each other. When a signal arrives at the left or right border, a counter is initialized with 0. The counter then moves to the opposite side with speed 1 and is incremented by 1 in each step. There are two possibilities:

- A counter signal reaches value n before meeting the counter signal coming from the other end. Then the counter is replaced by a state "∞", which is not the firing state and which spreads to all cells.
- The counter signals meet before they enter state ∞. Then the maximum of their values is taken and propagated to all cells with speed 1. Further-

more all cells decrement the value by 1 in each step. When 0 is reached, the cells fire.

In Figure 1 the algorithm is sketched for two instances of length 12; on the left side $T = \{(1,1),(8,0)\}$ and on the right $T = \{(1,0),(8,0)\}$. □

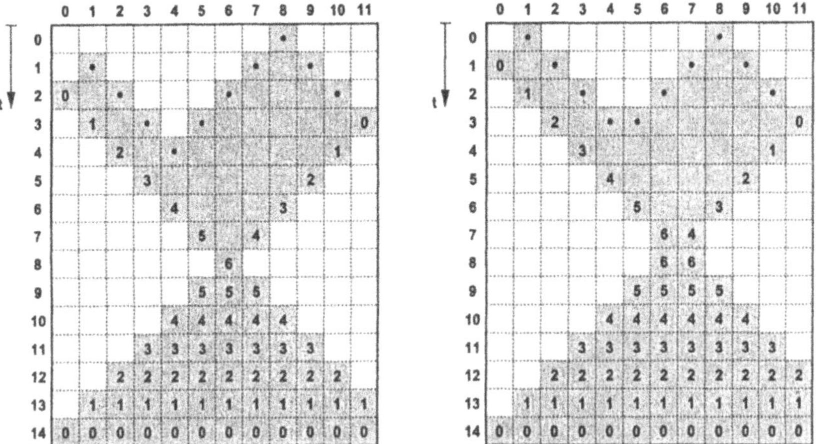

Figure 1. Solving instances of the multi-general FSSP with bounded size using a counter of finite size.

The question now is whether optimum time can be achieved for all instances by a single CA. In the synchronous case all $t_i = 0$; hence for the S-MG-FSSP holds:

$$T_{\min}(I) = n - 1 + \max\{\min_i p_i,\ n - 1 - \max_i p_i\}\ .$$

It follows from the algorithm in Section 3 that indeed one has:

THEOREM 4 *There exists a CA which solves the synchronous multi-general FSSP in optimum time for all instances.*

This has to be contrasted with the result we are going to prove now:

THEOREM 5 *For each CA with k states solving the asynchronous multi-general FSSP there are infinitely many instances I such that*

$$T_A(I) \geq T_{\min}(I) + \lfloor \log_k \text{len}(I) \rfloor\ ,$$

i.e. for which the CA does not achieve optimum synchronization time.

The main building block for the proof is the following lemma:

LEMMA 6 *Let A be a CA with k states solving the asynchronous multi-general FSSP. Then for each n there is an instance I of length n such that*

$$T_A(I) \geq T_{\min}(I) + \left\lfloor \log_k \frac{n}{2} \right\rfloor\ .$$

Proof. If $\lfloor \log_k \frac{n}{2} \rfloor \leq 0$, the statement is trivially true. Let us therefore assume that $\lfloor \log_k \frac{n}{2} \rfloor \geq 1$, i.e. $n \geq 2k$. Let $m = \lfloor \frac{n}{2} \rfloor$ and $w = \lfloor \log_k m \rfloor$. Since k is an integer, $w = \lfloor \log_k \frac{n}{2} \rfloor$ and hence $k^w \leq \frac{n}{2}$.

Let A be a CA with k states solving the asynchronous multi-general FSSP. We claim that the instance I with $T = \{(0,0),(n-1,0)\}$ has the required property. We will write t_f as an abbreviation for $T_A(I)$.

Denote by s_j the list of w states $C_n^j(j)C_n^{j+1}(j)\cdots C_n^{j+w-1}(j)$ in which a cell j, $0 \leq j < n/2$, is in w subsequent steps starting at time j. Since A has k states, there are only $k^w \leq n/2$ pairwise different lists s_j. Therefore the sequence $s_0, s_1, \ldots$ becomes periodic before there is any influence from the rightmost general. Let d denote a multiple of the period length such that $d \geq w$ and consider the instance I' of length $n' = n+d$ with $T' = \{(0,0),(n-1+d,d)\}$. It follows that $s_{n-1} = s_{n'-1}$.

Now assume by contradiction that $t_f = T_A(I) < T_{\min}(I) + \lfloor \log_k \frac{n}{2} \rfloor = T_{\min}(I)+w$. This means that s_{n-1} contains a firing state at position $t_f-(n-1)$. Therefore $s_{n'-1}$ contains a firing state, too. Since A is assumed to solve the asynchronous multi-general FSSP, it must in fact fire for instance I' at time t_f+d. But $t_f+d < T_{\min}(I)+w+d = n-1+w+d \leq n-1+d+d = n'-1+d$.

Similar to the proof of Lemma 2 this means that in particular cell 0 fires at a time when it cannot have been influenced by cell $n'-1$. Therefore increasing the length of I' to t_f+d+2 (and keeping the same T') one gets an instance I'' for which A would fail, because after t_f+d steps cell 0 would again enter a firing state but the rightmost cell would still be in state $\mathtt{s}$. □

It is now straightforward to finish this section:

Proof (of Theorem 5). It is known that even for the standard FSSP one needs at least $k \geq 5$ states [9]. For any w choose $n = k^w - 1$ and hence $\lfloor \log_k n \rfloor = w-1$. But

$$\frac{n}{2} = \frac{1}{2}(k^w - 1) \geq \frac{1}{2}(k^w - k^{w-1}) = \frac{1}{2}(k-1)k^{w-1} \geq k^{w-1}$$

and therefore $\lfloor \log_k \frac{n}{2} \rfloor \geq w - 1 = \lfloor \log_k n \rfloor$. □

3. A solution for the S-MG-FSSP

On the left side of Figure 2 an algorithm for the one-general case is depicted [16]. Compared to other solutions [8, 12] it has the advantage that any algorithm for the standard FSSP can be "plugged into" the scheme.

ALGORITHM 7 The general sends signals to both borders with speed 1. Upon arrival the border cells start a standard FSSP algorithm. The signals are reflected and meet at a point X of the space-time diagram (or at two cells at the same time; this case can be handled with the usual techniques). The left border cell starts synchronizing the segment to the left of X, the right border cell starts synchronizing the segment to the right of X, both using any algorithm for the standard FSSP.

In general there will be a longer and a shorter segment, which can be distinguished depending on whether a reflected initiation signal passes the general (point G in the space-time diagram) before meeting the other one at X or not. While the synchronization of the longer segment ends at the optimum time for the whole instance, synchronization for the shorter segment would end too early. This problem is corrected by sending two signals to the shorter segment with speed 1:

- The first is initiated at point X in the space time and "freezes" the synchronization algorithm.
- The second is "thawing" it again. That signal is triggered when another signal which is started at G and which runs with speed $1/2$ arrives at X.

The area of the space-time diagram which is frozen is shown in gray in the left part of Figure 2. A straightforward calculation yields, that as a result the synchronization for the shorter segment will end at the same time as for the longer segment.

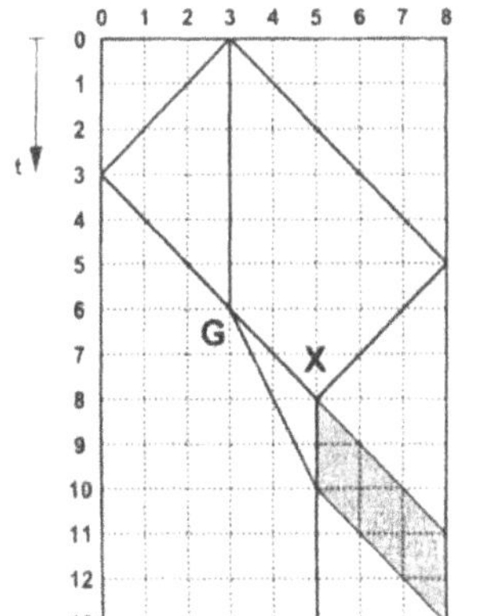

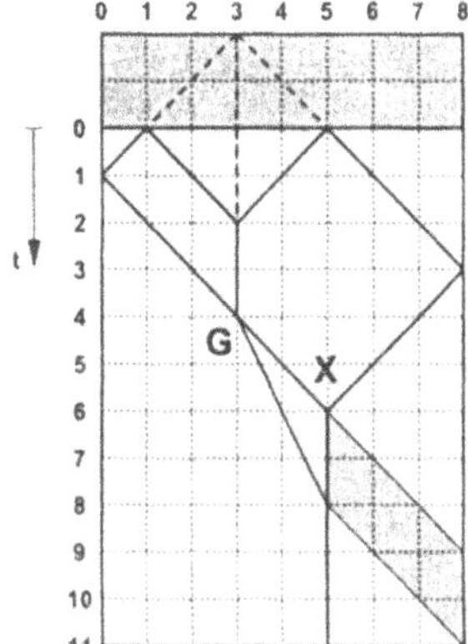

Figure 2. Synchronization using one and two generals at arbitrary positions.

An easy modification of this algorithm can be used for instances with two generals. The cell where a reflected initiation signals marks point G is determined by the meeting point of the not-yet reflected initiation signals. The right part of Figure 2 shows an example. From some time on the space-time diagram coincides with the one resulting from the case with one general at cell G. □

The transition from 2 generals to k generals can again be done in a generic way. We will briefly sketch how this can be achieved.

In the S-MG-FSSP the optimum time is $n - 1 + \max\{\min_i p_i,\ n - 1 - \max_i p_i\}$. This value is determined by the extremal positions $p_l = \min_i p_i$ and $p_r = \max_i p_i$ of generals, independently of the others. The following algorithm exploits this fact and makes sure that each cell will work after a certain number of steps as if only the outermost generals were present.

ALGORITHM 8 Assume that $A = (S, \delta)$ is a CA solving the FSSP for 2 generals with the usual states s and g. For the new CA $A' = (S', \delta')$ we write s' and g' for its soldier and general state. It basically uses 3 registers R_l, R_r and R_m. We will first describe the use of R_l. The use of R_r is analogous to R_l, but preferring information from the opposite direction (right instead of left). At last R_m will be explained.

Register R_l consists of a bit indicating the presence (*) or absence (-) of a signal and a state $x \in S$. Initially (*, g) is induced here by state g' of A'. Using algorithm *LeftChoice* described below it is made sure that the state $x \in S$ of R_l of a cell always holds the state the corresponding cell of A would have as long as that only has been influenced by the leftmost of those generals which may have had an influence on it.

This can be realized by sending a signal from each general to the right with speed 1. In the left part of Figure 3 the signals are indicated by stars *. Depending on whether a cell observes a * signal arriving from its left neighbor it can act appropriately: Whenever its left neighbor has a *, a cell behaves as if itself and its right neighbor are in s; otherwise if a cell has * itself, it behaves as if its right neighbor is in s. In the remaining cases the cell behaves "normally".

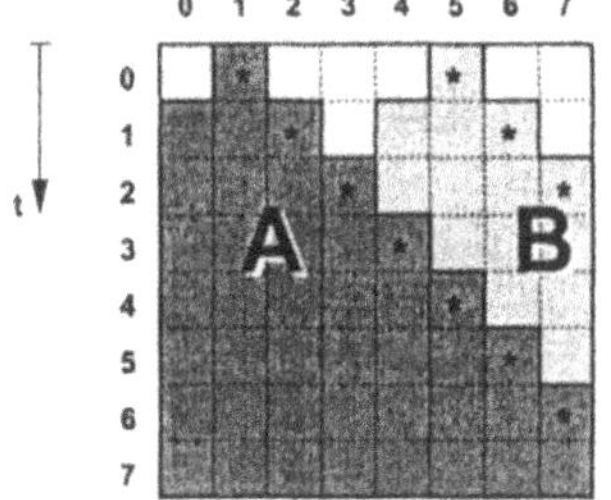

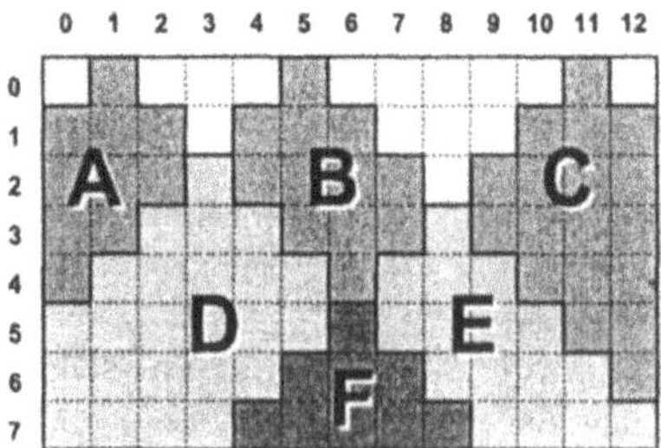

Figure 3. Left: R_l for preferring the left general. Right: R_m for choosing the "currently outermost" generals.

The transition rule for R_l can be described by the following table:

left	center	right	new center
$(*, x_l)$	y_m	y_r	$(*, \delta(x_l, s, s))$
$(-, x_l)$	$(*, x_m)$	y_r	$(-, \delta(x_l, x_m, s))$
$(-, x_l)$	$(-, x_m)$	$(?, x_r)$	$(-, \delta(x_l, x_m, x_r))$

Analogous rules for preferring the right hand side are used for R_r.

It is now easy to use register R_m to simulate the behavior of the cells as it would happen whenever the state in R_l is from the leftmost general and the state in R_r is from the rightmost general: For R_l call a cell q in the neighborhood of a cell p *relevant* for p, iff register R_l of cell q is really used (see the rule table above); similarly for R_r. The new state of R_m of a cell p is computed from 3 states z_{p-1}, z_p and z_{p+1} each stemming from one of the registers of cells $p-1$, p and $p+1$ respectively. For $i \in \{p-1, p, p+1\}$ state z_i is chosen as follows:

If i is relevant for *both*, R_l and R_r (of cell p), then z_i is taken from register R_m if cell i. If i is relevant for exactly one of R_l and R_r (of cell p), then z_i is taken from *that* register of cell i. Otherwise a quiescent state is used.

As a result of these rules one gets for example the situation depicted the right part of Figure 3. Denote by A, B and C also the generals in the corresponding parts of the space-time diagram. Then in part D of the diagram the R_m registers of the cells "behave" as if there were only generals A and B and in part E they behave as if there were only generals B and C. And in part F all states of registers R_m are the same as for the case when there are only generals A and C.

Thus an instance is fired after the same number of steps needed for the simpler instance where all generals except the leftmost and rightmost one are deleted, which is the optimum time (see the remark on the S-MG-FSSP right before Theorem 4). □

4. A solution for the A-MG-FSSP

We remind the reader of the CA A_n which were used in the proof of Lemma 3. A_n is able to fire all instances of A-MG-FSSP of length $m \leq n$ in optimum time.

Below we describe the main aspects of a CA which solves any instance I of A-MG-FSSP in time $T_{\min}(I) + \log n$. In the light of Theorem 5 this is "close to optimal". The idea is to generalize the A_n to a CA A_∞ where there is no upper bound for the counters. Of course unbounded contents of counters cannot be stored in a single cell. Instead we use segments consisting of $\log_b x$ cells to represent a value x in b-adic representation. A well-known technique introduced by Vollmar [14] and used in several contexts [5, 11] are counters with the following properties:

- The initial value of the counter is 0, stored as a single digit.
- In each step the least-significant digit of the counter moves from one cell to next one, the other digits are following.
- In each step the content of the counter is incremented by 1 in such a way that the sequence of counter digits passing a cell c forms the representation of the distance of this cell from the one where the counter started.
- When incrementing a counter an overflow at the currently most-significant digit may happen. In this case the length of the counter is increased by 1 at the end.

Analogously, given a counter with a value $x > 0$ it is possible to decrement it in each cell while moving. But in this case the *length* of the counter is *not* decreased (otherwise speed 1 would be impossible for the counters). Instead zeroes at the most-significant positions are used. Such counters are used in the following CA algorithm.

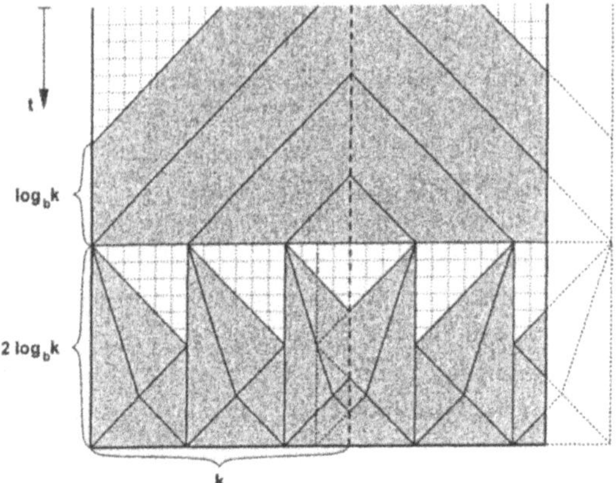

Figure 4. Solving instances of the multi-general FSSP with distributed counters.

ALGORITHM 9 Whenever a general "appears", it sends a signal to the left and one to the right. Whenever two such signals meet, they erase each other. When a signal arrives at the left or right border, a counter as described above is initialized with 0. The counters then move to the opposite sides with speed 1 and are incremented by 1 in each step.

Denote by X the cell where both counters meet. When they arrive at X they are not incremented any longer. Instead their contents are compared digit by digit. This is straightforward, since the least-significant digits arrive first and the other follow step by step. Both counters are kept until it is known which one stores the larger value. This one is used further on, the other one is destroyed.

Let k denote the larger value and K the counter, i.e. the "data structure", storing it. When K arrives at X it starts cycling as follows:

- K is reflected. Its digits move back until the least significant digit meets the most significant one in cell Y, which is $\frac{1}{2} \log k$ cells away from X.
- At Y the counter is reflected again, so that from then on all digits are moving back and forth between X and Y.

After coming back to X for the first time, it is clear that K has stored the larger value.

Now K is decremented in each step. And it is not only cycling, but copies are sent to both sides starting at X. These copies are also decremented in each step. In the upper part of Figure 4 the area where the copies of K are moving is shaded gray. Solid diagonal lines mark the boundaries between two copies.

Additionally each cell checks whether all digits of a counter passing through it are zero. This takes time $\log k$. At some point in time simultaneously some cells discover that this is the case. On both sides of X these cells are $\log k$ cells apart, and their positions are symmetrical with respect to X. The leftmost such cell is cell 0.

These cells start an algorithm for the 1-general FSSP (directed towards X) synchronizing the segment up to the next such cell. This is indicated in the lower part of Figure 4. As can be seen there, problems may arise in two areas:

- At the rightmost cell there may be a segment of unsuitable length. It would be nice if there were a few more cells at the right end as indicated by the dotted lines. Even though the cells are missing, by "folding around" that part of the space-time diagram their actions can easily be simulated in additional registers of the present cells.
- A similar trick can be used at X. The actions of the missing cells which one would have to add to make the lengths of the adjacent segments equal to that of other segments can be simulated in the registers used by the cells between X and Y for the cycling counter.

From the discussion of the above algorithm one immediately gets:

THEOREM 10 *There is a CA which solves any instance I of length n of the A-MG-FSSP in time $T_{\min}(I) + \log_b n$ for some $b \in \mathbb{N}$.*

5. Summary and outlook

Two variants of the generalized FSSP with several generals have been considered for 1-dimensional CA. Using a few simple and elegant techniques, it is possible to design a CA which solves the problem for all instances in optimum time, when all generals start to act synchronously.

When the generals may start their work asynchronously, the optimum time for an instance depends on the starting times, but it can still be computed exactly. Contrary to the case of synchronous generals, there is no longer one CA which can achieve optimum running time for all problem instances. However, we have described a CA whose firing times are quite close to the optimum; it needs only $\log n$ steps longer.

Of course, the problems can also be considered for CA working on 2- or higher-dimensional grids. Even for the synchronous multi-general case the situation becomes considerably more complicated. For example the choice of the neighborhood, e.g. Moore or von Neumann type, not only has an influence on the value of the optimum synchronization times. While for one neighborhood a CA always achieving optimum time is known, for the other neighborhood none has been found until now. This will be discussed in a follow-up paper.

References

[1] K. Čulik and S. Dube. An efficient solution of the firing mob problem. *Theoretical Computer Science*, 91:57–69, 1991.

[2] E. Goto. A minimum time solution of the Firing Squad Problem. Dittoed course notes for Applied Mathematics 298, Harvard University, 1962.

[3] M. Hisaoka, H. Yamada, M. Maeda, Th. Worsch, and H. Umeo. A design of firing squad synchronization algorithms for multi-general problems and their implementations. Unpublished manuscript, 2003.

[4] K. Kobayashi. On the minimal firing time of the firing squad synchronization problem for polyautomata networks. *Theoretical Computer Science*, 7:149–167, 1978.

[5] M. Kutrib and R. Vollmar. Minimal time synchronization in restricted defective cellular automata. *Journal of Information Processing and Cybernetics*, EIK 27:179–196, 1991.

[6] S. La Torre, M. Napoli, and M. Parente. Synchronization of a line of identical processors at a given time. *Fundamenta Informaticae*, 34:103–128, 1998.

[7] J. Mazoyer. A six-state minimal time solution to the firing squad synchronization problem. *Theoretical Computer Science*, 50:183–238, 1987.

[8] F. R. Moore and G. G. Langdon. A generalized firing squad problem. *Information and Control*, 12:17–33, 1968.

[9] P. Sanders. Suchalgorithmen auf SIMD-Rechnern — Weitere Ergebnisse zu Polyautomaten. Diploma thesis, Fakultät für Informatik, Universität Karlsruhe, 1993.

[10] H. Schmid. Synchronisationsprobleme für zelluläre Automaten mit mehreren Generälen. Diploma thesis, Fakultät für Informatik, Universität Karlsruhe, 2003.

[11] M. Stratmann and Th. Worsch. Leader election in d-dimensional CA in time $diam \cdot \log(diam)$. *Future Generation Computer Systems*, 18(7):939–950, 2002.

[12] H. Szwerinski. Time optimal solution of the firing squad synchronization problem for n-dimensional rectangles with the general at an arbitrary position. *Theoretical Computer Science*, 19:305–320, 1982.

[13] H. Umeo. A simple design of time-optimum firing squad synchronization algorithms with fault-tolerance. *IEICE Transactions on Information and Systems*, E87-D:733–739, 2004.

[14] R. Vollmar. Yet another generalization of the firing squad problem. Technical report, Technische Universität Braunschweig, Braunschweig, 1976.

[15] R. Vollmar. On two modified problems of synchronization in cellular automata. *Acta Cybernetica*, 3:293–300, 1977.

[16] Th. Worsch. Algorithmen in Zellularautomaten. Course notes, Fakultät für Informatik, Universität Karlsruhe, 2003.

A MATRIX Q-ANALOGUE OF THE PARIKH MAP

Omer Egecioglu*
Department of Computer Science
University of California, Santa Barbara
CA 93106, USA
omer@cs.ucsb.edu

Oscar H. Ibarra†
Department of Computer Science
University of California, Santa Barbara
CA 93106, USA
ibarra@cs.ucsb.edu

Abstract We introduce an extension of the Parikh mapping called the *Parikh q-matrix mapping*, which takes its values in matrices with polynomial entries. The morphism constructed represents a word w over a k-letter alphabet as a k-dimensional upper-triangular matrix with entries that are nonnegative integral polynomials in variable q. We show that by appropriately embedding the k-letter alphabet into the $(k+1)$-letter alphabet and putting $q = 1$, we obtain the extension of the Parikh mapping to $(k+1)$-dimensional (numerical) matrices introduced by Mateescu, Salomaa, Salomaa, and Yu. The Parikh q-matrix mapping however, produces matrices that carry more information about w than the numerical Parikh matrix. The entries of the q-matrix image of w under this morphism is constructed by *q-counting* the number of occurrences of certain words as scattered subwords of w.

Keywords: Parikh mapping, Parikh matrix mapping, scattered subword, injectivity, morphism, q-analogue.

1. Introduction

Parikh's theorem [7] says that every context-free language is "letter-equivalent" to a regular language. More precisely, the commutative image of any context-free language is always a semilinear set, and is therefore also the commutative

* Work done in part while on sabbatical at Sabanci University, Istanbul, Turkey during 2003-2004.
† Supported in part by NSF Grants IIS-0101134 and CCR02-08595.

image of some regular set. Consider the alphabet $\Sigma_k = \{a_1 < a_2 < \cdots < a_k\}$ and for $w \in \Sigma^*$, define by $|w|_{a_i}$ the number of occurrences of a_i in w. The *Parikh mapping* is a morphism

$$\Psi : \Sigma^* \to \mathbb{N}^k$$

where $\mathbb{N}$ denotes nonnegative integers and $\Psi(w) = (|w|_{a_1}, |w|_{a_2}, \cdots, |w|_{a_k})$.

The Parikh mapping is a very important concept in the theory of formal languages. Various languages accepted (generated) by automata (grammars) more powerful than pushdown automata (context-free grammars) have been shown to have effectively computable semilinear sets. For example, it is known that every language accepted by a pushdown automaton augmented with reversal-bounded counters (i.e., each counter can be incremented/decremented by one and tested for zero, but the number of alternations between nondecreasing and nonincreasing modes is bounded by a fixed constant) has a semilinear Parikh map [4]. The fact that the emptiness problem for semilinear sets is decidable implies that the emptiness problem for these automata (grammars) is decidable. This decidability of emptiness has been used to show the decidability of many decision questions in formal languages (e.g., [3]) and formal verification (e.g., [5]).

The *Parikh matrix mapping* introduced in [6] is a morphism

$$\Psi_{\mathcal{M}_k} : \Sigma^* \to \mathcal{M}_{k+1}$$

where $\mathcal{M}_{k+1}$ is a collection of $(k+1)$-dimensional upper-triangular matrices with nonnegative integral entries and unit diagonal. The classical Parikh vector $\Psi(w)$ appears in the image matrix as the second diagonal.

The *Parikh q-matrix mapping* introduced in this paper is a morphism

$$\Psi_q^k : \Sigma^* \to \mathcal{M}_k(q)$$

where $\mathcal{M}_k(q)$ is a collection of k-dimensional upper-triangular matrices with nonnegative integral polynomials in q as entries. The diagonal entries of $\Psi_q^k(w)$ are

$$(q^{|w|_{a_1}}, q^{|w|_{a_2}}, \ldots, q^{|w|_{a_k}})$$

which readily encodes the Parikh vector. Moreover if we embed Σ_k into Σ_{k+1} in the obvious way, and put $q = 1$, then we obtain the matrices of the Parikh matrix map of [6]. Thus, viewing $w \in \Sigma_k$ as a word in Σ_{k+1} with $|w|_{a_{k+1}} = 0$, the Parikh q-matrix $\Psi_q^{k+1}(w)$ evaluated at $q = 1$ is precisely the $(k+1)$-dimensional numerical Parikh matrix $\Psi_{\mathcal{M}_k}(w)$.

It is a basic property of the Parikh matrix mapping that two words with the same Parikh matrix have the same Parikh vector, but two words with the same Parikh vector in many cases have different Parikh matrices [1]. Thus, the Parikh matrix gives more information about a word than the Parikh vector. The injectivity of the Parikh matrix mapping is investigated in [1]. From our construction it is easy to see that two words with the same Parikh q-matrix have the same Parikh matrix (and therefore the same Parikh vector), but there are cases in which two words with the same Parikh matrix have different q-matrices. Thus the Parikh q-matrix gives more information about a word than the Parikh matrix.

The basic idea in the construction of the entries of the Parikh q-matrix image of w is *q-counting* the number of occurrences of certain words as scattered subwords of w.

The paper has five sections in addition to this section. Section 2 gives some basic notation and definitions. Section 3 recalls the notion of a Parikh matrix mapping introduced in [6] and the fundamental theorem concerning these mappings. Section 4 presents our new Parikh mapping, called q-matrix mapping, that generalizes the Parikh matrix mapping: whereas the latter produces matrices with nonnegative integer entries, the former produces matrices with nonnegative integral polynomials (in variable q) entries. This extended mapping produces matrices that carry more information about the mapped words than the numerical matrices produced by the Parikh matrix mapping. Section 5 presents the main results, including Theorem 8, which gives the main properties of a q-matrix mapping. Section 6 looks at some matrix operations such as injectivity and inverse concerning q-matrix mapping.

2. Definitions

We start with some basic notation and definitions. Most of these are as they appear in references [6] and [1]. The set of all nonnegative integers is denoted by $\mathbb{N}$. We denote by $\mathbb{N}[q]$ the collection of polynomials in the variable q with coefficients from $\mathbb{N}$. $\mathbb{Z}$ denotes integers, and $\mathbb{Z}[q]$ denotes the ring of polynomials in the variable q with integral coefficients. For an alphabet Σ, we denote the set of all words over Σ by Σ^* and the empty word by λ. We use "ordered" alphabets. An ordered alphabet is an alphabet $\Sigma = \{a_1, a_2, \ldots, a_k\}$ with a relation of order ("$<$") on it. If for instance $a_1 < a_2 < \cdots < a_k$, then we use the notation

$$\Sigma = \{a_1 < a_2 < \cdots < a_k\}.$$

If $w \in \Sigma^*$ then $|w|$ denotes the length of w. For $a_i \in \Sigma$ and $w \in \Sigma^*$ the number of occurrences of the letter a_i in w is denoted by $|w|_{a_i}$. Accordingly $|w| = |w|_{a_1} + |w|_{a_2} + \cdots + |w|_{a_k}$.

Let $\Sigma = \{a_1 < a_2 < \cdots < a_k\}$ be an ordered alphabet. The Parikh vector of $w \in \Sigma^*$ is the vector of occurrences $(|w|_{a_1}, |w|_{a_2}, \cdots, |w|_{a_k})$. The Parikh mapping

$$\Psi : \Sigma^* \to \mathbb{N}^k$$

is defined by setting

$$\Psi(w) = (|w|_{a_1}, |w|_{a_2}, \cdots, |w|_{a_k}).$$

Let v, w be words over Σ. As defined in [6], the word v is called a *scattered subword* of w if there exists a word u such that $w \in u \sqcup\!\sqcup v$, where $\sqcup\!\sqcup$ denotes the shuffle operation. If $v, w \in \Sigma^*$, then the number of occurrences of v in w as a scattered subword is denoted by $|w|_{scatt-v}$. Partially overlapping occurrences of a word as a scattered subword of a word are counted as distinct occurrences. For example, $|acbb|_{scatt-ab} = 2$, $|acba|_{scatt-ab} = 1$.

Notation: We shall also find it useful to denote $|w|_{scatt-v}$ by $S_{w,v}$. Using this notation, we write $S_{acbb,ab} = 2$, $S_{acba,ab} = 1$, and $S_{w,a_i} = |w|_{a_i}$ for any letter $a_i \in \Sigma$.

Notation: Consider the ordered alphabet $\{a_1 < a_2 < \cdots < a_k\}$ where $k \geq 1$. As in [6], we denote by $a_{i,j}$ the word $a_i a_{i+1} \cdots a_j$ where $1 \leq i \leq j \leq k$.

For motivation and further issues about the Parikh mapping as well as language-theoretic notions not considered here, we refer the reader to [8].

3. Parikh matrix mapping

We first describe the extension of the Parikh mapping to matrices as originally defined in [6]. The extension involves special types of triangular matrices. These are square matrices $m = (m_{i,j})_{1 \leq i,j \leq k}$ such that $m_{i,j} \in \mathbb{N}$, for all $1 \leq i, j \leq k$, $m_{i,j} = 0$, for all $1 \leq j < i \leq k$, and moreover, $m_{i,i} = 1$, for all $1 \leq i \leq k$. The set of all these matrices of dimension k is denoted by $\mathcal{M}_k$. Thus $\mathcal{M}_k$ is the collection $k \times k$ upper-triangular matrices with entries from $\mathbb{N}$ and unit diagonal. The set $\mathcal{M}_k$ is a monoid with respect to multiplication of matrices and has a unit which is the matrix I_k.

The main notion introduced in [6] is as follows:

DEFINITION 1 *Let $\Sigma = \{a_1 < a_2 < \cdots < a_k\}$ be an ordered alphabet, where $k \geq 1$. The Parikh matrix mapping, denoted by $\Psi_{\mathcal{M}_k}$, is the morphism:*

$$\Psi_{\mathcal{M}_k} : \Sigma^* \to \mathcal{M}_{k+1},$$

defined as follows:

If $\Psi_{M_k}(a_l) = (m_{i,j})_{1 \leq i,j \leq (k+1)}$, then for each $1 \leq i \leq k+1$, $m_{i,i} = 1$, $m_{l,l+1} = 1$ and all other elements of the matrix $\Psi_{M_k}(a_l)$ are zero.

EXAMPLE 2 Let Σ be the ordered alphabet $\{a < b < c\}$. Then the Parikh matrix mapping Ψ_{M_3} represents each word over Σ^* as a 4×4 upper triangular matrix with unit diagonal with nonnegative integral entries. We compute some special cases.

$$\begin{aligned}\Psi_{\mathcal{M}_3}(ab^2) &= \Psi_{\mathcal{M}_3}(a)\Psi_{\mathcal{M}_3}(b)\Psi_{\mathcal{M}_3}(b) \quad \text{and} \\ \Psi_{\mathcal{M}_3}(abca) &= \Psi_{\mathcal{M}_3}(a)\Psi_{\mathcal{M}_3}(b)\Psi_{\mathcal{M}_3}(c)\Psi_{\mathcal{M}_3}(a).\end{aligned}$$

Thus

$$\begin{aligned}\Psi_{\mathcal{M}_3}(ab^2) &= \begin{bmatrix} 1 & 1 & 0 & 0 \\ 0 & 1 & 0 & 0 \\ 0 & 0 & 1 & 0 \\ 0 & 0 & 0 & 1 \end{bmatrix}\begin{bmatrix} 1 & 0 & 0 & 0 \\ 0 & 1 & 1 & 0 \\ 0 & 0 & 1 & 0 \\ 0 & 0 & 0 & 1 \end{bmatrix}\begin{bmatrix} 1 & 0 & 0 & 0 \\ 0 & 1 & 1 & 0 \\ 0 & 0 & 1 & 0 \\ 0 & 0 & 0 & 1 \end{bmatrix} \\ &= \begin{bmatrix} 1 & 1 & 2 & 0 \\ 0 & 1 & 2 & 0 \\ 0 & 0 & 1 & 0 \\ 0 & 0 & 0 & 1 \end{bmatrix}\end{aligned}$$

and

$$\begin{aligned}\Psi_{\mathcal{M}_3}(abca) &= \begin{bmatrix} 1 & 1 & 0 & 0 \\ 0 & 1 & 0 & 0 \\ 0 & 0 & 1 & 0 \\ 0 & 0 & 0 & 1 \end{bmatrix}\begin{bmatrix} 1 & 0 & 0 & 0 \\ 0 & 1 & 1 & 0 \\ 0 & 0 & 1 & 0 \\ 0 & 0 & 0 & 1 \end{bmatrix}\begin{bmatrix} 1 & 0 & 0 & 0 \\ 0 & 1 & 0 & 0 \\ 0 & 0 & 1 & 1 \\ 0 & 0 & 0 & 1 \end{bmatrix}\begin{bmatrix} 1 & 1 & 0 & 0 \\ 0 & 1 & 0 & 0 \\ 0 & 0 & 1 & 0 \\ 0 & 0 & 0 & 1 \end{bmatrix} \\ &= \begin{bmatrix} 1 & 2 & 1 & 1 \\ 0 & 1 & 1 & 1 \\ 0 & 0 & 1 & 1 \\ 0 & 0 & 0 & 1 \end{bmatrix}\end{aligned}$$

and consequently

$$\Psi_{\mathcal{M}_3}(ab^2abca) = \begin{bmatrix} 1 & 1 & 2 & 0 \\ 0 & 1 & 2 & 0 \\ 0 & 0 & 1 & 0 \\ 0 & 0 & 0 & 1 \end{bmatrix}\begin{bmatrix} 1 & 2 & 1 & 1 \\ 0 & 1 & 1 & 1 \\ 0 & 0 & 1 & 1 \\ 0 & 0 & 0 & 1 \end{bmatrix} = \begin{bmatrix} 1 & 3 & 4 & 4 \\ 0 & 1 & 3 & 3 \\ 0 & 0 & 1 & 1 \\ 0 & 0 & 0 & 1 \end{bmatrix}$$

Remark: The Parikh matrix mapping is not an injective mapping. For instance over the ordered alphabet $\{a < b < c\}$ one has

$$\Psi_{\mathcal{M}_3}(acb) = \Psi_{\mathcal{M}_3}(cab) = \begin{bmatrix} 1 & 1 & 1 & 0 \\ 0 & 1 & 1 & 0 \\ 0 & 0 & 1 & 1 \\ 0 & 0 & 0 & 1 \end{bmatrix}$$

Conditions for two words α and β to possess the same Parikh matrix was studied for the binary alphabet in [1]. We will discuss some of these conditions later in the paper.

The main property of the Parikh matrix mapping proved in [6] is the following theorem:

THEOREM 3 *([6], Theorem 3.1) Let $\Sigma = \{a_1 < a_2 < \cdots < a_k\}$ be an ordered alphabet, where $k \geq 1$ and assume that $w \in \Sigma^*$. The matrix $\Psi_{M_k}(w) = (m_{i,j})_{1 \leq i,j \leq (k+1)}$, has the following properties*

1. $m_{i,j} = 0$, *for all* $1 \leq j < i \leq (k+1)$,
2. $m_{i,i} = 1$, *for all* $1 \leq i \leq (k+1)$,
3. $m_{i,j+1} = S_{w,a_{i,j}}$, *for all* $1 \leq i \leq j \leq k$.

As a corollary

COROLLARY 4 *([6], Corollary 3.1) Let $\Sigma = \{a_1 < a_2 < \cdots < a_k\}$ The matrix $\Psi_{M_k}(w)$ has the second diagonal (i.e., the vector $(m_{1,2}, m_{2,3}, \ldots, m_{k,k+1})$) the Parikh vector of w, i.e.,*

$$(m_{1,2}, m_{2,3}, \ldots, m_{k,k+1}) = \Psi(w) = (|w|_{a_1}, |w|_{a_2}, \cdots, |w|_{a_k}).$$

4. q-counting scattered subwords

Next we introduce a collection of polynomials $S_{w,a_{i,j}}(q)$ indexed by pairs of words $a_{i,j}, w \in \Sigma^*$, with $j \leq k-1$. These polynomials will "q-count" the quantities $S_{w,a_{i,j}}$ defined above for general v and w as will be explained shortly in the case $a_{i,j}$ is a scattered subword of w. To construct $S_{w,a_{i,j}}(q)$, we consider each factorization

$$w = u_i a_i u_{i+1} a_{i+1} \cdots u_j a_j u_{j+1} \tag{1}$$

with $u_s \in \Sigma^*$ for $i \leq s \leq j+1$, and construct the corresponding monomial

$$q^{|u_i|_{a_i} + |u_{i+1}|_{a_{i+1}} + \cdots + |u_j|_{a_j} + |u_{j+1}|_{a_{j+1}}} \tag{2}$$

in $\mathbb{N}[q]$, and add up these monomials. Note that $a_{j+1} \in \Sigma$ since $j < k$, so that the last term in the exponent in (2) is defined. Thus

$$S_{w,a_{i,j}}(q) = \sum_{w = u_i a_i \cdots u_j a_j u_{j+1}} q^{|u_i|_{a_i} + |u_{i+1}|_{a_{i+1}} + \cdots + |u_j|_{a_j} + |u_{j+1}|_{a_{j+1}}} \tag{3}$$

EXAMPLE 5 Suppose $\Sigma = \{a < b < c < d\}$ and $i = 2, j = 2$. Then $a_{i,j} = b$ and for $w \in \Sigma^*$,

$$S_{w,b}(q) = \sum_{w = xby} q^{|x|_b + |y|_c}$$

For example for $w = baccbcdab$, the relevant factorizations of w are

$$(\lambda)b(accbcdab), \quad (bacc)b(cdab), \quad (baccbcda)b(\lambda),$$

and therefore

$$S_{w,b}(q) = q^{0+3} + q^{1+1} + q^{2+0} = 2q^2 + q^3.$$

EXAMPLE 6 Suppose $\Sigma = \{a < b < c < d\}$ and $i = 2, j = 3$. Then $a_{i,j} = bc$ and for $w \in \Sigma^*$,

$$S_{w,bc}(q) = \sum_{w=xbycz} q^{|x|_b+|y|_c+|z|_d}$$

For example for $w = baccbcdab$, the relevant factorizations of w are

$(\lambda)b(a)c(cbcdab)$, $(\lambda)b(ac)c(bcdab)$, $(\lambda)b(accb)c(dab)$, $(bacc)b(\lambda)c(dab)$,

and therefore

$$S_{w,bc}(q) = q^{0+0+1} + q^{0+1+1} + q^{0+2+1} + q^{1+0+1} = q + 2q^2 + q^3.$$

EXAMPLE 7 Suppose $\Sigma = \{a < b < c < d\}$ and $i = 1, j = 3$. Then $a_{i,j} = abc$ and for $w \in \Sigma^*$,

$$S_{w,abc}(q) = \sum_{w=taxbycz} q^{|t|_a+|x|_b+|y|_c+|z|_d}$$

For example for $w = baccbcdab$, the only relevant factorization of w is

$$(b)a(cc)b(\lambda)c(dab),$$

and therefore

$$S_{w,abc}(q) = q^{0+0+1} = q.$$

Since the summation in the definition (3) is over all occurrences of $a_{i,j}$ in w as a scattered subword, the following proposition is immediate:

PROPOSITION 1 *Let* $\Sigma = \{a_1 < a_2 < \cdots < a_k\}$ *and* $1 \leq i \leq j < k$. *Then*

$$S_{w,a_{i,j}}(1) = S_{w,a_{i,j}} (= |w|_{scatt-a_{i,j}}).$$

This is the sense in which the polynomials $S_{w,a_{i,j}}(q)$ "q-count" the number of occurrences of $a_i a_{i+1} \cdots a_j$ as a scattered subword of w. These polynomials are the "q-analogues" of the numbers $S_{w,a_{i,j}}$.

5. Parikh q-matrix mapping

We denote by $\mathcal{M}_k(q)$ the collection of k-dimensional upper-triangular matrices with entries in $\mathbb{N}[q]$. Let I_k denote the identity matrix of dimension k. The matrix $\Psi_q(a_l)$ corresponding to a $a_l \in \Sigma$ is defined as the matrix obtained from I_k first by changing the l-th diagonal element from 1 to q. Then if $l < k$, we also change the entry immediately to the right of the q from 0 to a 1. Thus if $\Psi_q(a_l) = (m_{i,j})_{1 \le i,j \le k}$, then

1. $m_{l,l} = q$,
2. $m_{i,i} = 1$ for $1 \le i \le k, i \ne l$,
3. $m_{l,l+1} = 1$ if $l < k$,
4. all other entries of the matrix $\Psi_q(a_l)$ are zero.

When the alphabet is $\Sigma = \{a < b < c\}$, then

$$\Psi_q(a) = \begin{bmatrix} q & 1 & 0 \\ 0 & 1 & 0 \\ 0 & 0 & 1 \end{bmatrix}, \Psi_q(b) = \begin{bmatrix} 1 & 0 & 0 \\ 0 & q & 1 \\ 0 & 0 & 1 \end{bmatrix}, \Psi_q(c) = \begin{bmatrix} 1 & 0 & 0 \\ 0 & 1 & 0 \\ 0 & 0 & q \end{bmatrix}$$

We extend the mapping from Σ to Σ^* by setting

1. $\Psi_q(\lambda) = I_k$,
2. $\Psi_q(w_1 w_2 \cdots w_n) = \Psi_q(w_1)\Psi_q(w_2) \cdots \Psi_q(w_n), w_i \in \Sigma, 1 \le i \le n$

We will refer to $\Psi_q = \Psi_q^k$ as the Parikh q-matrix mapping. Note that the parameter k, which is $|\Sigma|$ is implicit in our notation.

Remark: Just as the Parikh mapping is a morphism from the monoid $(\Sigma^*, \cdot, \lambda)$ to the monoid $(\mathbb{N}^k, +, (0, 0, \ldots, 0))$, the set of matrices $\mathcal{M}_k(q)$ is a monoid with respect to matrix multiplication and I_k as its unit.

Thus the Parikh q-matrix mapping is a morphism

$$\Psi_q : \Sigma^* \to \mathcal{M}_k(q).$$

As examples, we have

$$\Psi_q(ab^2) = \Psi_q(a)\Psi_q(b)\Psi_q(b) \text{ and } \Psi_q(abca) = \Psi_q(a)\Psi_q(b)\Psi_q(c)\Psi_q(a).$$

Thus

$$\Psi_q(ab^2) = \begin{bmatrix} q & 1 & 0 \\ 0 & 1 & 0 \\ 0 & 0 & 1 \end{bmatrix} \begin{bmatrix} 1 & 0 & 0 \\ 0 & q & 1 \\ 0 & 0 & 1 \end{bmatrix} \begin{bmatrix} 1 & 0 & 0 \\ 0 & q & 1 \\ 0 & 0 & 1 \end{bmatrix} = \begin{bmatrix} q & q^2 & 1+q \\ 0 & q^2 & 1+q \\ 0 & 0 & 1 \end{bmatrix}$$

$$\Psi_q(abca) = \begin{bmatrix} q & 1 & 0 \\ 0 & 1 & 0 \\ 0 & 0 & 1 \end{bmatrix} \begin{bmatrix} 1 & 0 & 0 \\ 0 & q & 1 \\ 0 & 0 & 1 \end{bmatrix} \begin{bmatrix} 1 & 0 & 0 \\ 0 & 1 & 0 \\ 0 & 0 & q \end{bmatrix} \begin{bmatrix} q & 1 & 0 \\ 0 & 1 & 0 \\ 0 & 0 & 1 \end{bmatrix} = \begin{bmatrix} q^2 & 2q & q \\ 0 & q & q \\ 0 & 0 & q \end{bmatrix}$$

Consequently, for $w = ab^2abca$, we compute that

$$\Psi_q(w) = \begin{bmatrix} q & q^2 & 1+q \\ 0 & q^2 & 1+q \\ 0 & 0 & 1 \end{bmatrix} \begin{bmatrix} q^2 & 2q & q \\ 0 & q & q \\ 0 & 0 & q \end{bmatrix}$$

$$= \begin{bmatrix} q^3 & 2q^2+q^3 & q+2q^2+q^3 \\ 0 & q^3 & q+q^2+q^3 \\ 0 & 0 & q \end{bmatrix}$$

Remark: For the Parikh q-matrix mapping it is not true that if $\mathcal{L}$ is a context-free language, then its image is some suitable extension of the notion of semi-linearity to matrices over $\mathbb{N}[q]$. This is a direct consequence of Theorem 9 and the negative result concerning the Parikh matrix mapping ([6], Remark 3.2).

PROPOSITION 2 *Let* $\Sigma = \{a_1 < a_2 < \cdots < a_k\}$ *and* $w \in \Sigma^*$. *Then the vector of diagonal entries of the matrix* $\Psi_q(w)$ *is*

$$(q^{|w|_{a_1}}, q^{|w|_{a_2}}, \cdots, q^{|w|_{a_k}}) \in \mathbb{N}[q]^k.$$

Proof The matrices $\Psi_q(a_l)$ are all upper-triangular. It is easy to see that the diagonal entries of a product of two upper-triangular matrices depend only on the diagonal elements of each of the matrices. Since diagonal matrices commute, and each occurrence of the letter a_l in w has the effect of multiplying the l-th diagonal entry of the k-dimensional identity matrix I_k by q, the result follows immediately. •

Remark: We note that the Parikh vector of w is given by the formal derivative of

$$(q^{|w|_{a_1}}, q^{|w|_{a_2}}, \cdots, q^{|w|_{a_k}}) \in \mathbb{N}[q]^k$$

with respect to q at $q = 1$.

THEOREM 8 *Let* $\Sigma = \{a_1 < a_2 < \cdots < a_k\}$ *be an ordered alphabet, where* $k \geq 1$ *and assume that* $w \in \Sigma^*$. *The matrix* $\Psi_q(w) = (m_{i,j}(q))_{1\leq i,j\leq k}$, *has the following properties*

1. $m_{i,j} = 0$, *for all* $1 \leq j < i \leq k$,
2. $m_{i,i} = q^{|w|_{a_i}}$, *for all* $1 \leq i \leq k$,
3. $m_{i,j+1} = S_{w,a_{i,j}}(q)$, *for all* $1 \leq i \leq j < k$.

Proof The proof of the parts 1. and 2. are immediate. We now prove property 3. Assume that $|w| = n$. The proof is by induction on n. If $n \leq 1$, the assertion holds. Assume now that part 3. holds for all words of length n and let w be of length $n+1$. Write $w = w'a_j$ where $|w'| = n$ and $a_j \in \Sigma$. Then

$$\Psi_q(w) = \Psi_q(w')\Psi_q(a_j)$$

Assume that

$$\Psi_q(w') = \begin{bmatrix} q^{|w'|_{a_1}} & m'_{1,2} & \cdots & \cdots & m'_{1,k} \\ 0 & q^{|w'|_{a_2}} & \cdots & \cdots & m'_{2,k} \\ \vdots & \vdots & \vdots & \vdots & \vdots \\ \vdots & \vdots & \vdots & \vdots & m'_{k-1,k} \\ 0 & 0 & \cdots & \cdots & q^{|w'|_{a_k}} \end{bmatrix} = M'$$

By the inductive hypothesis the matrix $\Psi_q(w')$ has property 3. The proof has two cases depending on whether $j = k$, or $j < k$. For $j < k$, we have

$$\Psi_q(a_j) = \begin{bmatrix} 1 & 0 & & \cdots & & 0 \\ \vdots & \vdots & \vdots & \vdots & \vdots & \vdots \\ 0 & \cdots & q & 1 & \cdots & 0 \\ \vdots & \vdots & \vdots & \vdots & \vdots & \vdots \\ 0 & 0 & & \cdots & & 1 \end{bmatrix}$$

where the matrix differs from I_k only in two entries: The entry in position (j, j) is q, and the entry in position $(j, j+1)$ is 1. Let $M = \Psi_q(w)$. Then

$$M = \begin{bmatrix} q^{|w'|_{a_1}} & m'_{1,2} & \cdots & \cdots & m'_{1,k} \\ 0 & q^{|w'|_{a_2}} & \cdots & \cdots & m'_{2,k} \\ \vdots & \vdots & \vdots & \vdots & \vdots \\ \vdots & \vdots & \vdots & \vdots & m'_{k-1,k} \\ 0 & 0 & \cdots & \cdots & q^{|w'|_{a_k}} \end{bmatrix} \begin{bmatrix} 1 & 0 & & \cdots & & 0 \\ \vdots & \vdots & \vdots & \vdots & \vdots & \vdots \\ 0 & \cdots & q & 1 & \cdots & 0 \\ \vdots & \vdots & \vdots & \vdots & \vdots & \vdots \\ 0 & 0 & & \cdots & & 1 \end{bmatrix}$$

If $M = (m_{p,q})_{1 \leq p,q \leq k}$, then

$$\begin{aligned} m_{i,j} &= q m'_{i,j} \; for \; 1 \leq i \leq j, \\ m_{i,j+1} &= m'_{i,j} + m'_{i,j+1} \; for \; 1 \leq i \leq j \end{aligned}$$

and for all other indices, $m_{p,q} = m'_{p,q}$. But these are immediate from the definition of the polynomials $S_{w,a_{i,j}}(q)$ which satisfy

$$\begin{aligned} S_{w'a_j,a_{i,j-1}}(q) &= q S_{w,a_{i,j-1}}(q) \; for \; 1 \leq i \leq j, \\ S_{w'a_j,a_{i,j}}(q) &= S_{w',a_{i,j-1}}(q) + S_{w',a_{i,j}}(q) \; for \; 1 \leq i < j \end{aligned}$$

and are unchanged otherwise. In the case $j = k$ the only change that appears in going from M' to M is that the last column M is obtained from M' by multiplying the elements of the last column of M' by q. This corresponds to the fact that the number of occurrences of a_k in u_{k+1} in any factorization of the form (1) is increased by 1: i.e.,

$$S_{w'a_k, a_{1,k-1}}(q) = qS_{w', a_{1,k-1}}(q)$$

and the proof follows by induction. •

Remark: The structure of how the polynomials in the matrix are indexed can be mnemonically recorded as shown below in the case of the four-letter alphabet $\Sigma = \{a_1 < a_1 < a_3 < a_4\}$:

$$\begin{matrix} a_1 \\ a_2 \\ a_3 \\ a_4 \end{matrix} \begin{bmatrix} q^{|w|_{a_1}} & a_1 & a_1a_2 & a_1a_2a_3 \\ 0 & q^{|w|_{a_2}} & a_2 & a_2a_3 \\ 0 & 0 & q^{|w|_{a_3}} & a_3 \\ 0 & 0 & 0 & q^{|w|_{a_4}} \end{bmatrix}$$

As an example, the entry in second row and the fourth column is a shorthand for the polynomial $S_{w,a_2a_3}(q)$, the q-count of the number of occurrences of a_2a_3 as a scattered subword of w as developed in section 4.

PROPOSITION 3 *Let* $\Sigma = \{a_1 < a_2 < \cdots < a_k\}$ *and* $w \in \Sigma^*$. *Suppose the vector of super diagonal entries of the matrix* $\Psi_q(w)$ *is*

$$(m_{1,2}(q), m_{2,3}(q), \cdots, m_{k-1,k}(q)) \in \mathbb{N}[q]^{k-1}.$$

Then at $q = 1$, *this vector evaluates to*

$$(|w|_{a_1}, |w|_{a_2}, \cdots, |w|_{a_{k-1}}).$$

Proof This proposition is a special case of a stronger result that characterizes the whole matrix $\Psi_q(w)$ at $q = 1$ that we give as Theorem 9. •

THEOREM 9 *Suppose* $\Sigma = \{a_1 < a_2 < \cdots < a_k\}$ *and* $w \in \Sigma^*$. *Consider* w *as a word over* $\Gamma = \{a_1 < a_2 < \cdots < a_k < a_{k+1}\}$ *and let* $\Psi_q(w)$ *be the resulting Parikh q-matrix in* $\mathbb{N}[q]^{k+1}$. *Then* $\Psi_q(w)$ *evaluated at* $q = 1$ *is the Parikh matrix* $\Psi_{\mathcal{M}_k}(w)$.

Proof Combine Theorem 8, Theorem 3, and Proposition 1. •

6. Injectivity, inverse, and further remarks

Just as the Parikh matrix mapping, the Parikh q-matrix mapping is not an injective mapping either. For instance over the ordered alphabet $\{a < b < c\}$ one has

$$\Psi_q(acb) = \Psi_q(cab) = \begin{bmatrix} q & q & 1 \\ 0 & q & 1 \\ 0 & 0 & q \end{bmatrix}$$

However, there are instances in which two words can have the same Parikh matrix, but distinct Parikh q-matrices.

The injectivity of the Parikh matrix mapping was studied in [1]. In particular it was proved that over a binary alphabet Σ, a pair of *palindromic amiable* words α, β have the same Parikh matrix image. The definition of palindromic amiable pair is as follows:

1. Both α and β are palindromes,

2. α and β have the same Parikh vector, i.e., $\Psi(\alpha) = \Psi(\beta)$.

For example the words $\alpha = aba^2ba$ and $\beta = ba^4b$ over $\Sigma = \{\mathrm{a} < \mathrm{b}\}$ are palindromic amiables. Therefore as proved in [1], they have the same 3×3 Parikh matrix image. We calculate directly that indeed

$$\Psi_{\mathcal{M}_2}(\alpha) = \begin{bmatrix} 1 & 4 & 4 \\ 0 & 1 & 2 \\ 0 & 0 & 1 \end{bmatrix} = \Psi_{\mathcal{M}_2}(\beta) \tag{4}$$

The corresponding matrices given by the Parikh q-matrix mapping Ψ_q are calculated over the alphabet $\{a < b < c\}$ in accordance with Theorem 9. These are also 3×3 upper-triangular matrices, but with entries from $\mathbb{N}[q]$. They are given by

$$\Psi_q(\alpha) = \begin{bmatrix} q^4 & 2q^2 + 2q^3 & 1 + 2q + q^2 \\ 0 & q^2 & 1 + q \\ 0 & 0 & 1 \end{bmatrix} \tag{5}$$

$$\Psi_q(\beta) = \begin{bmatrix} q^4 & q + q^2 + q^3 + q^4 & 1 + q + q^2 + q^3 \\ 0 & q^2 & 1 + q \\ 0 & 0 & 1 \end{bmatrix} \tag{6}$$

Clearly, these two distinct matrices reduce to $\Psi_{\mathcal{M}_2}(\alpha) = \Psi_{\mathcal{M}_2}(\beta)$ given in (4) as guaranteed by Theorem 9. Thus the matrices obtained by the Parikh q-matrix mapping contains finer information that is able to distinguish words that are equal under the ordinary Parikh matrix map. An alternate generalization of the Parikh matrix mapping with additional injectivity properties using a different q-analogue of scattered-subwords appears in [2].

The notion of the alternate (signed) Parikh matrix developed in [6] has the nice property that the inverse of the matrix $\Psi_{\mathcal{M}_k}(w)$ is the alternate Parikh matrix of the mirror image $mi(w)$ of w. This property also carries over to the case of the Parikh q-matrix mapping with some modifications. Let $\Sigma = \{a_1 < a_2 < \cdots < a_k\}$. We define a morphism (called the *alternate Parikh q-matrix mapping*) $\overline{\Psi}_q = \overline{\Psi}_q^k$ from Σ^* to a collection of k-dimensional upper-triangular matrices over $\mathbb{Z}[q]$. $\overline{\Psi}_q$ is defined on Σ as follows: If $\overline{\Psi}_q(a_l) = (m_{i,j})_{1 \le i,j \le k}$, then

1. $m_{l,l} = 1$,
2. $m_{i,i} = q$ for $1 \le i \le k, i \ne l$,
3. $m_{l,l+1} = -1$ if $l < k$,
4. all other entries of the matrix $\Psi_q(a_l)$ are zero.

EXAMPLE 10 When the alphabet is $\Sigma = \{a < b < c\}$, then

$$\overline{\Psi}_q(a) = \begin{bmatrix} 1 & -1 & 0 \\ 0 & q & 0 \\ 0 & 0 & q \end{bmatrix}, \overline{\Psi}_q(b) = \begin{bmatrix} q & 0 & 0 \\ 0 & 1 & -1 \\ 0 & 0 & q \end{bmatrix}, \overline{\Psi}_q(c) = \begin{bmatrix} q & 0 & 0 \\ 0 & q & 0 \\ 0 & 0 & 1 \end{bmatrix}$$

Note that $\Psi_q(a)\overline{\Psi}_q(a) = \Psi_q(b)\overline{\Psi}_q(b) = \Psi_q(c)\overline{\Psi}_q(c) = qI_3$. As an example, for $w = ab^2abca$, we compute that

$$\overline{\Psi}_q(mi(w)) = \begin{bmatrix} q^4 & -2q^3 - q^4 & 2q^3 + 2q^4 + q^5 \\ 0 & q^4 & -q^4 - q^5 - q^6 \\ 0 & 0 & q^6 \end{bmatrix}$$

Then the following result holds.

THEOREM 11 *Suppose* $\Sigma = \{a_1 < a_2 < \cdots < a_k\}$ *and* $w \in \Sigma^*$. *If* Ψ_q *and* $\overline{\Psi}_q$ *are the Parikh q-matrix, and the alternate Parikh q-matrix mappings from* Σ^* *to upper-triangular integral matrices over* $\mathbb{Z}[q]$, *then the k-dimensional matrix identity*

$$\Psi_q(w)\overline{\Psi}_q(mi(w)) = \begin{bmatrix} q^{|w|} & 0 & \cdots & & 0 \\ 0 & q^{|w|} & 0 & \cdots & 0 \\ \vdots & & \ddots & & \vdots \\ 0 & \cdots & & 0 & q^{|w|} \end{bmatrix} \quad (7)$$

holds.

Proof Omitted. •

It can also be shown that the identity (7) reduces to the matrix inverse identity of the Parikh matrix mapping of [6] when we extend the alphabet as in Theorem 9 and put $q = 1$.

References

[1] Atanasiu, A., Martin-Vide, C., Mateescu, A.: On the injectivity of the Parikh matrix mapping. Fundamenta Informaticae, 49 (2002) 289-299.

[2] Egecioglu. O.: A q-Matrix Encoding Extending the Parikh Matrix Mapping. Proc. Int. Conf. on Computers and Communications (ICCC 2004), Oradea, Romania, May, 2004.

[3] Harju, T., Ibarra, O., Karhumaki, J., Salomaa, A: Some decision problems concerning semilinearity and commutation. J. Computer and System Sciences, 65 (2002), 278-294.

[4] Ibarra, O.: Reversal-bounded multicounter machines and their decision problems. J. Assoc. Comput. Mach., 24 (1978) 123-137.

[5] Ibarra, O., Su, J., Dang, Z., Bultan, T., Kemmerer, R.: Counter machines and verification problems. Theoretical Computer Science, 289 (2002) 165-189.

[6] Mateescu, A., Salomaa, A., Salomaa K., Yu, S.: A sharpening of the Parikh mapping. Theoretical Informatics and Applications, 35 (2001) 551-564.

[7] Parikh, R.J.: On context-free languages. J. Assoc. Comput. Mach., **13** (1966) 570-581.

[8] Rozenberg, G., Salomaa, A. (eds): Handbook of Formal Languages. Springer, Berlin, 1997.

THE INHERENT QUEUING DELAY OF PARALLEL PACKET SWITCHES

(Extended Abstract)

Hagit Attiya* and David Hay
Department of Computer Science
Technion — Israel Institute of Technology
Haifa 32000, Israel
{hagit,hdavid}@cs.technion.ac.il

Abstract The *parallel packet switch (PPS)* is extensively used as the core of contemporary commercial switches. This paper investigates the inherent queuing delay and delay jitter introduced by the PPS's demultiplexing algorithm, relative to an optimal work-conserving switch.

We show that the inherent queuing delay and delay jitter of a symmetric and fault-tolerant $N \times N$ PPS, where every demultiplexing algorithm dispatches cells to all the middle-stage switches is $\Omega(N)$, if there are no buffers in the PPS input-ports. If the demultiplexing algorithms dispatch cells only to part of the middle-stage switches, the queuing delay and delay jitter are $\Omega(N/S)$, where S is the PPS speedup. These lower bounds hold unless the demultiplexing algorithm has full and immediate knowledge of the switch status. When the PPS has buffers in its input-ports, an $\Omega(N/S)$ lower bound holds if the demultiplexing algorithm uses only local information, or the input buffers are small relative to the time an input-port needs to learn the switch global information.

Keywords: Inverse multiplexing, Leaky-bucket traffic, Packet switching, Clos networks, Queuing delay, Delay jitter, Load balancing

1. Introduction

The need to support a large variety of applications with *quality of service (QoS)* guarantees demands high-capacity high-speed switching technologies [5]. An $N \times N$ *packet switch* routes packets arriving on N input-ports at rate R to N output-ports working at rate R. Packets are stored and transmitted in the

*Part of the work was performed while this author was at Dune Networks.

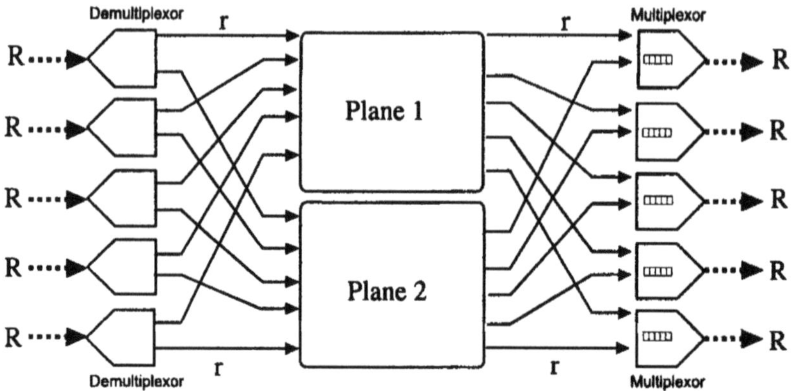

Figure 1. A 5×5 PPS with 2 planes in its center stage, without buffers in the input-ports

switch as fixed-size *cells*; fragmentation and reassembly are done outside of the switch. Cells arrive to the switch as a collection of *flows* from one input port to the same output-port; the switch should preserve the order of cells within a flow and not drop cells. Since there may be conflicts between different flows, certain amount of buffering within the switch may be needed. The location of the buffers, their sizes, and their management, depend on the specific architecture of the switch.

Switching cells in parallel is a natural approach to build switches with very high external line rate, and with large number of ports. A prime example of this approach is the *parallel packet switch* (in short, PPS) model [14], which is based on an architecture used in *inverse multiplexing* systems [12, 11], and especially on the *inverse multiplexing for ATM (IMA)* technology [2, 6]. The feasibility of the PPS and IMA architectures motivated commercial vendors to implement them at the heart of their switching architecture.

A *parallel packet switch (PPS)* is a three-stage Clos network [8], with $K < N$ switches in its center stage, also called *planes*. Each plane is an $N \times N$ switch operating at rate $r < R$, and is connected to all the input-ports on one side, and to all the output-ports on the other side (see Figure 1). The *speedup* S of the switch is the ratio of the aggregate capacity of the internal traffic lines, connected to an input- or output-port, to the capacity of its external line, namely, $S = \frac{Kr}{R}$. Iyer and McKeown [15] consider a variant of the PPS architecture, called *input-buffered* PPS, having finite buffers in its input-ports in addition to buffers in its output-ports.

Perhaps the key issue in the design of a PPS is balancing the load of switching operations among the middle-stage switches, and by that utilizing the parallel capabilities of the switch. Load balancing is performed by a *demultiplexing algorithm*, whose goal is to minimize the concentration of a disproportional number of cells in a small number of middle-stage switches.

Demultiplexing algorithms can be classified according to the amount and type of information they use. The strongest type of demultiplexing algorithms are *centralized algorithms*, in which every demultiplexing decision is done based on global information about the status of the switch. Unfortunately, these algorithms must operate at a speed proportional to the aggregate incoming flows rate, and therefore, they are impractical. At the other extreme, *fully-distributed demultiplexing algorithms* rely only on the local information in the input-port.[1] Due to their relative simplicity, they are common in contemporary switches. A middle ground is what we call *u Real-time distributed (u-RT) demultiplexing algorithms*, in which a demultiplexing decision is based on the local information and global information older than u time slots. Obviously, every fully distributed algorithm is also a u real-time distributed algorithm.

1.1 Evaluating PPS Performance. Switch architectures are evaluated by their ability to provide different QoS guarantees. Important figures are the maximum/average queuing delay of cells (i.e., delay resulting from queuing cells within the switch) and the switch's throughput. Another interesting performance number is the *per-flow delay jitter* (or *cell delay variation*), namely, the maximal difference in queuing delay between two cells in the same flow [25, 24, 20].

The performance of a PPS is measured by comparison to an optimal *work-conserving (greedy)* switch, operating at rate R [7, 19, 18]. A work-conserving switch guarantees that if a cell is pending for output port j at time-slot[2] t, then some cell leaves from output-port j at time-slot t. This property prevents an output-port from being idle unnecessarily, and by that, maximizes the switch throughput and minimizes its average cell delay.

The switch used for the comparison is called a *shadow* switch or a *reference* switch, and it receives exactly the same stream of flows as the PPS; namely, at any given time, the two switches receive the same cells, with the same destinations, on the same input-ports. We assume that this reference switch minimizes the queuing delay of cells (or minimizes the delay jitter, in case we measure the relative delay jitter). A primary candidate for a reference switch is an output-queued switch operating at rate R. This is the reason this comparison is sometimes referred to as the ability of the PPS to mimic an output-queued switch [14, 15, 21].

The *relative queuing delay* considers only the delay resulting from queuing within the PPS switch and neglects factors such as different propagation delays over the PPS and the reference switche, or the different number of stages. It captures the influence of the parallelism of the PPS on the performance of the switch, depending on the different demultiplexing algorithms, and ignores the specific PPS *hardware* implementation.

---

[1] These are also called *independent demultiplexing algorithms* [13].

[2] A *time-slot* is the time required to transmit a cell at rate R.

1.2 Our Results. Our main contributions are lower bounds on the relative queuing delay and relative delay jitter of the PPS when the switch is not flooded. We employ ***leaky-bucket constrained flows*** [23] to restrict the arrival of cells to the switch: In every time interval of length τ, the number of cells arriving to the switch and sharing the same input-port or the same output-port is bounded by $\tau R + B$, where B is a fixed *burstiness* factor [5]. Comparison between a PPS and a flooded output-queued switch is vague, since the flooded switch either introduces unbounded queuing delay or drops cells. In Section 5, we show that the lower bounds do not hold for certain classes of non leaky-bucket flows that flood the switch.

A *bufferless PPS* (i.e., without buffers at the input-ports) with fully-distributed demultiplexing algorithm induces the highest relative queuing delay and relative delay jitter. If some plane is utilized by all the demultiplexors, we prove a lower bound of $\left(\frac{R}{r} - 1\right) N$ time slots on the relative queuing delay and relative delay jitter. Even in the unrealistic and failure-prone case where the demultiplexing algorithm statically partitions the planes among the demultiplexors, the relative queuing delay and relative delay jitter are at least $\left(\frac{R}{r} - 1\right) \frac{N}{S}$ time-slots. Both lower bounds employ leaky-bucket flows with no bursts.

A bufferless PPS with u-RT demultiplexing algorithm (for any u) has relative queuing delay and relative delay jitter of at least $\left(1 - \overline{u}\frac{r}{R}\right) \frac{\overline{u}N}{S}$ time-slots, under leaky-bucket flows with burstiness factor of $\overline{u}^2 \frac{N}{K} - \overline{u}$, where $\overline{u} = \min\{u, \frac{1}{2}\frac{R}{r}\}$. In contrast, Iyer et al. [14] show that there is a bufferless PPS with centralized demultiplexing algorithm with zero relative queuing delay, provided that the switch has speedup $S \geq 2$.

An *input-buffered PPS* can support more elaborate demultiplexing algorithms, since an arriving cell can either be transmitted to one of the middle stage switches, or be kept in the input-buffer. Under a u-RT demultiplexing algorithm, a switch with speedup $S \geq 2$ and input-buffers larger than u, can employ a centralized algorithm (e.g., [14]). This demonstrates that a lower bound of $\Omega(N/S)$ time-slots does not hold when the input-buffers are sufficiently large. In contrast, a fully-distributed demultiplexing algorithm introduces relative queuing delay and relative delay jitter of at least $\left(1 - \frac{r}{R}\right) \frac{N}{S}$ time-slots, for any buffer size under leaky-bucket flows with no bursts.

Our lower bound results show that the PPS architecture does not scale with increasing number of external ports. This is significant since great effort is currently invested in building switches with a large number of ports (where $N = 512$ or even 1024). Note that large relative queuing delays usually imply that the buffer sizes at the middle-stage switches or at the external ports should be large as well, so that the cells can be queued.

Note that due to space limitations proofs are omitted throughout the paper. For detailed proofs and further discussion, the reader is referred to [3].

1.3 Related Work. The CPA centralized demultiplexing algorithm [14] allows a PPS with speedup $S \geq 2$ to mimic an FCFS output-queued switch with zero relative queuing delay. This algorithm is impractical for real switches, because it gathers information from all the input-ports in every scheduling decision. A fully-distributed version of this algorithm [15] mimics a FCFS output-queued switch with relative queuing delay of $\lceil N\frac{R}{r}\rceil$ time-slots.

Another family of fully-distributed algorithms, called *fractional traffic dispatch (FTD)* [17], works with switch speedup $S \geq \frac{K}{\lceil K/2 \rceil}$, and their relative queuing delay is at least $2NR/r$ time-slots. An extension to the FTD algorithms is introduced in Section 5, in which there is zero relative queuing delay as long as all the queues in all the planes are not empty.

Arbitrated crossbar switches [22] are prime examples of $u-RT$ demultiplexing algorithms. In these switches, a request is made by the input-port, and the cell is sent once a grant is received back from the arbiter. This implies that global information is used by the arbiter, with a certain delay. Cells are queued in the input-port buffers while waiting for a grant. Input-port buffers should operate at the external line rate R, and therefore must reside on chip. This limits their size and causes large values of u to be impractical.

Earlier research presents lower bounds on the speedup required for an input-queued switch to *exactly* mimic a reference output-queued switch. Chaung et al. [7] show that a combined input-output-queued switch needs speedup $\geq 2 - \frac{1}{N}$ in order to mimic an output-queued switch. This worst-case lower bound proof does not assume any statistical distribution on the arrival of packets to the switch; it uses specific input-flows with burstiness factor N.

2. Formal Model for Parallel Packet Switches

To prove lower bounds on the behavior of the PPS, a formal model of the switch is needed.

We assume that cells arrive to the switch and leave it in discrete *time-slots.* Since a time-slot is the time it takes to transmit a cell at rate R, in each time-slot at most one cell arrives to each input-port, and at most one cell leaves any output-port. The internal lines of the switch operate at lower rate $r < R$; for simplicity, we assume that $\frac{R}{r} = \lceil \frac{R}{r} \rceil$, and denote this value by r'. This lower rate r enforces constraints on the switch [14]: A cell sent from an input-port i to a plane k, is transmitted over r' time-slots; transmission takes place in the first time-slot of this period, and then the line between i and k is not utilized in the next $r' - 1$ time-slots. We refer to this constraint as the *input constraint.* Violating it causes a traffic rate greater than r on the internal line between an input-port and a plane. The *output constraint* is defined analogously, on the internal lines between the planes and the output-ports.

Recall that the relative queuing delay includes only queuing effects and excludes the different propagation delay between the two switches. This is achieved by assuming that cells are transmitted from/to the plane in the first time-slot. To neglect delays caused by the additional stage of the PPS, a cell can leave the PPS in the same time-slot it arrives to the output-port, provided that no other cell is leaving the same output-port on this time-slot.

The behavior of the dispatching algorithm in every input-port is modeled as a deterministic state machine, called *demultiplexor*. Demultiplexors in different input-ports may have different states set; we denote by $\mathbf{S}_i$ the states sets of the demultiplexor residing in input-port i. A state is *applicable* if it can be reached in execution of the demultiplexor.

A *switch configuration* is comprised of states of all the demultiplexors, and the content of all the buffers in the switch at a given time. A configuration is *applicable* if it can be reached in a legal execution of the switch. Since the switch does not have a predetermined initial configuration, we assume that for every pair of applicable configurations C_1, C_2, there is an incoming traffic that causes the switch to transit from C_1 to C_2 (i.e, the set of applicable configurations induces strongly-connected graph).

When there are no buffers in the input-ports, a cell arriving to the switch is immediately demultiplexed to one of the center stage switches, as modeled by the following definition:

DEFINITION 1 *The demultiplexing algorithm of the demultiplexor residing at a bufferless input-port i is the function $D_i : \{1,\ldots,N\} \times \mathbf{S}_i \rightarrow \{1,\ldots,K\}$, which gives a plane number, according to the incoming cell destination and the demultiplexor's state.*

This definition is extended for the input-buffered PPS variant: When a cell arrives, the demultiplexor either sends the cell to one of the planes or keeps it in its buffer. In every time-slot, the demultiplexor sends any number of buffered cells to the planes, provided that the rate constraints on the lines between the input-port and any plane are preserved.

We refer to the buffer residing at input-port i with finite size s as a vector $b_i \in \{1,\ldots,N,\perp\}^s$. An element of this vector contains the destination of the cell stored at the corresponding place in the buffer. Empty places in the buffer are indicated with $\perp$ in the vector. The size of the buffer at input-port i is denoted $|b_i|$.

The demultiplexor state machine is changed to include the state of the input-port buffer. $\mathbb{B}$ denotes the set of the applicable buffer's states, and $\mathbb{B}_i$ includes the applicable states of the buffer residing in input-port i. We refer to the set of states of the ith demultiplexor as $\mathbf{S}_i \times \mathbb{B}_i$. A switch configuration describes also the input-buffers content.

DEFINITION 2 *The demutliplexing algorithm of the demultiplexor residing at input-port i with input-buffer, is the function $D_i : \{1,\ldots,N,\perp\} \times \mathbf{S}_i \times \mathbb{B}_i \rightarrow \{1,\ldots,K,\perp\}^{|b_i|+1}$.*

This function receives as input the destination of the incoming cell ($\perp$ if no cell arrives), and the state of the demultiplexor. The function returns a vector of size $|b_i| + 1$ stating through which plane to send the cell in the corresponding place in the buffer; the last element of the vector refers to the incoming cell; $\perp$ indicates that the corresponding cell remains in the buffer.

3. The Relative Queuing Delay of a Bufferless PPS

The relative queuing delay of a PPS heavily depends on the information available to the demultiplexing algorithm. CPA [14] is a centralized demultiplexing algorithm with zero relative queuing delay, assuming the PPS has speedup $S \geq 2$ and the reference output-queued switch follows a global FCFS discipline.[3] Practical demultiplexing algorithms must operate with local, or out-dated, information about the status of the switch: flows waiting at other input-ports, contents of the planes' buffers, etc. As we shall see, such algorithms incur non-negligible queuing delay.

Our lower bounds are obtained using feasible flows that do not flood the switch, obeying the *leaky-bucket constrained flows* model [23]. We require only that the combined rate of flows sharing the same input-port or the same output-port does not exceed the external rate of that port by more than a fixed bound B, which is independent of time [5].

DEFINITION 3 *An* (R, B) leaky-bucket traffic *satisfies the following expression for every time-slot* t*, integer* $\tau \geq 1$*, input-port* i*, and output-port* j*:*

$$A_i(t, t+\tau) \leq \tau R + B \quad \textit{and} \quad B_j(t, t+\tau) \leq \tau R + B$$

where $A_i(t_1, t_2)$ *is the number of cells arriving to input-port* i *during time interval* $[t_1, t_2)$*, and* $B_j(t_1, t_2)$ *is the number of cells destined for output-port* j*, arriving to the switch during time-interval* $[t_1, t_2)$.

The burstiness factor of the traffic B is also an upper bound on the size of the buffer needed for any work-conserving switch [9].

In our lower bounds, the relative queuing delay is exhibited when cells that are supposed to leave the optimal reference switch one after the other, are concentrated in a single plane. We describe the concentration scenario by the following lemma:

LEMMA 4 *Assume output-port* j*'s buffer is empty at time* t*, and that* m *cells destined for the same output-port* j *arrive to the switch during time-interval* $[t, t+s)$*, out of them* $c \leq m$ *are sent through the same plane. Assume also that the incoming traffic is* (R, B) *leaky-bucket, and no cells destined for* j *arrive to the switch during time interval* $[t+s, t+m)$*. Then:*
(1) The relative queuing delay of the PPS is at least $c\frac{R}{r} - (s+B)$ *time-slots.*
(2) The relative delay jitter of the PPS is at least $c\frac{R}{r} - (s+B)$ *time-slots.*

Proof: We compare the queuing delay of the cells in the PPS and in the reference switch. Since the reference switch is work-conserving, all m cells leave the switch exactly m time-slots after the first cell is dispatched. On the other hand, a PPS completes this execution after at least cr' time-slots,

[3] i.e., cells should leave the switch in the same order they arrived, regardless of the flow they are in.

because c cells are sent to the same plane, and only one cell can be sent from this plane to the output-port every r' time-slots. Hence, the relative queuing delay is at least $cr' - m$ time-slots. Since the incoming traffic is (R, B) leaky-bucket, $m \leq s + B$. Because $r' = \frac{R}{r}$, the relative queuing delay is at least $cr' - m \geq cr' - (s + B) = c\frac{R}{r} - (s + B)$ time-slots, proving (1).

Let a be the last of the c cells sent from the plane to the output-port and let i' be the input-port from which a is sent. By the definition of a, it arrives to the PPS no later than time-slot $t + s - 1$, and leaves the PPS not before time-slot $t + cr'$.

Now assume that there is a cell a', in the same flow (i', j), which arrives to the PPS when all the buffers are empty. Clearly, if no other cell destined for output-port j arrives with cell a', a' leaves the PPS exactly one time-slot after its arrival. Hence, the delay jitter introduced by the PPS is at least $[(t + cr') - (t + s - 1)] - 1 = cr' - s$ time-slots.

Recall that the maximum buffer size needed for any work-conserving switch to work under (R, B) leaky-bucket traffic is B. Therefore a work-conserving switch, which serve the incoming cells in a FCFS manner (e.g. FCFS output-queued switch) introduces queuing delay, and therefore also delay jitter, of at most B time-slots. Thus, the relative delay jitter between the PPS and the reference switch is at least $(cr' - s) - B = c\frac{R}{r} - (s + B)$ time-slots, proving (2).
■

The concentration scenario, described in Lemma 4, does not depend on the scheduling policies of the planes, which may be optimal. It only assumes that cells are not dropped.

We start by considering the most practical demultiplexing algorithm, in which every input-port makes independent dispatching decisions.

DEFINITION 5 *A* fully-distributed demultiplexing *algorithm demultiplexes a cell, arriving at time t, according to the input-port's local information in time interval* $[0, t]$.

The state transition function of the ith bufferless demultiplexor operating under fully-distributed demultiplexing algorithm is $S_i : \mathbb{S}_i \times \{1, \ldots, N\} \to \mathbb{S}_i$. That is, the demultiplexor state transitions depend only on the previous state of the demultiplexor and the destination of the incoming cell. If no cell arrives to a specific input-port in bufferless PPS, its demultiplexor does not change its state.

The relative queuing delay of a PPS with fully-distributed demultiplexing algorithm strongly depends on the number of demultiplexors that can send a cell, destined for the same output-port, through the same plane. To capture this switch characteristic, we call a demultiplexing algorithm *d-partitioned* if there is a plane k and an output-port j, such that at least d demultiplexors send a cell destined for output-port j through plane k in one of their applicable configurations.

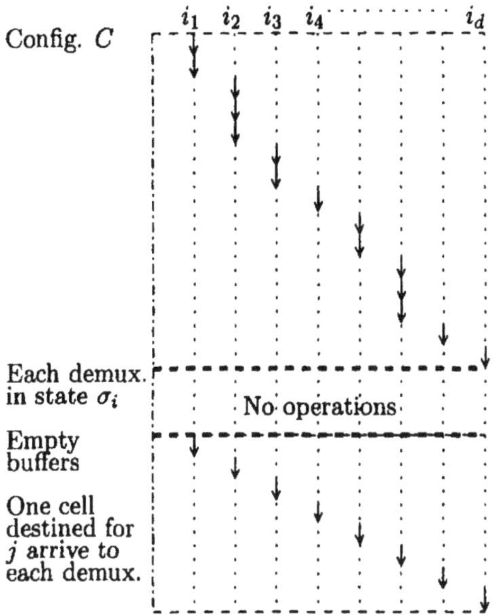

Figure 2. Schematic view of the proof of Theorem 6.

THEOREM 6 *A bufferless PPS, with d-partitioned fully-distributed demultiplexing algorithm, has relative queuing delay and relative delay jitter of* $\left(\frac{R}{r}-1\right)d$ *time-slots, under traffic without bursts.*

Proof: By the definition of a d-partitioned demultiplexing algorithm, there is an output-port j and a plane k, so that at least d demultiplexors send a cell destined for j through k in some applicable configuration. Let $I=\{i_1,i_2,\ldots i_d\}$ be the set of these demultiplexors, and let $\sigma_i \in \mathbf{S}_i$ be the state of demultiplexor $i \in I$ in configuration C_i, just before a cell is sent to plane k.

Consider traffic A from an arbitrary applicable configuration C which leads the switch to configuration C_i; such traffic exists since C and C_i are applicable, and recall that there is a traffic that causes the switch to transit between any two applicable configurations. Let A_i be a traffic in which cells arrive to input-port i exactly in the same time-slots as in traffic A. Since the demultiplexing algorithm is fully-distributed, demultiplexor i transits into σ_i. Note that in A_i at most one cell arrives to the switch in every time-slot, therefore this traffic has no bursts.

Now consider LB, a sequential composition of the traffics A_i, where $i \in I$. LB begins from configuration C, and sequentially for every $i \in I$, the same cells arrive to the switch in the same time-slots as in traffic A_i, until demultiplexor i reaches state σ_i. Then, no cells arrive to the switch until all the buffers in all the planes are eventually empty. Finally, d cells destined for output-port j arrive, one after the other, to different input-ports $i \in I$ (one cell in each time-slot). Since the demultiplexing algorithm is fully-distributed, each demultiplexor $i \in I$ remains in state σ_i, and all the cells are sent through the same plane k (see Figure 2).

LB has no bursts, and the last d cells that arrive to the switch under traffic LB arrive during d consecutive time-slots. By substituting in Lemma 4, we get that the relative queuing delay and relative delay jitter are at least $\left(\frac{R}{r} - 1\right) d$ time-slots. ∎

Statically partitioning the planes among the different demultiplexors is failure-prone. For example, if demultiplexor sends cells only through $d < K$ planes, a damage in one plane (or the internal lines connected to it) causes more cell dropping than if all K planes are utilized. Therefore, fault tolerance dictates each demultiplexor may send a cell destined for any output-port through any plane. For such *unpartitioned* (or N*-partitioned*) *fully-distributed demultiplexing algorithms*, Theorem 6 immediately implies:

COROLLARY 7 *A bufferless PPS, with unpartitioned fully-distributed demultiplexing algorithm, has relative queuing delay and relative delay jitter of* $\left(\frac{R}{r} - 1\right) N$ *time-slots, under leaky-bucket traffic without bursts.*

Iyer and McKeown [15] present an unpartitioned fully-distributed demultiplexing algorithm, which allows a bufferless PPS with speedup $S \geq 2$ to mimic a FCFS output-queued switch with a relative queuing delay of $\lceil \frac{NK}{S} \rceil = \lceil \frac{R}{r} N \rceil$ time-slots. This result implies that $\Theta\left(\frac{R}{r} N\right)$ is a tight bound on the relative queuing delay of a bufferless PPS with speedup $S \geq 2$ operating under a fully-distributed demultiplexing algorithm.

Even with static partitioning, the PPS input constraint implies that each demultiplexor must send incoming cells through at least r' planes[4]. This implies that each plane is used by $r' \frac{N}{K}$ demultiplexors, on the average. Hence, there is a plane k that is used by at least $r' \frac{N}{K} = \frac{R}{r} \frac{N}{K}$ demultiplexors in order to dispatch cells destined for a certain output-port j. These observations imply the following lower bound:

THEOREM 8 *A bufferless PPS, with fully-distributed demultiplexing algorithm, has relative queuing delay and relative delay jitter of* $\left(\frac{R}{r} - 1\right) \frac{N}{S}$ *time-slots, under leaky-bucket traffic without bursts.*

Note that centralized demultiplexing algorithms and fully-distributed demultiplexing algorithms are both extreme considering the amount of global information they use. The first kind has perfect knowledge of the switch status, and the second uses no global information at all. An interesting middle-ground is the following class of demultiplexing algorithms:

DEFINITION 9 *A* u real-time distributed (u-RT) demultiplexing algorithm *is an algorithm that demultiplexes a cell, arriving at time* t*, according to the*

[4] In this extreme case, failure even in one plane, immediately causes cells dropping

input-port's local information in time interval $[0, t]$, *and to the switch's global information in time interval* $[0, t-u]$.

The state transition function of the ith bufferless demultiplexor operating under u-RT demultiplexing algorithm is $S_i(t) : \mathbb{S}_i \times \mathbb{C}^{t-u+1} \times \{1, \ldots, N\} \rightarrow \mathbb{S}_i$, where t is the time-slot in which S_i is applied, $\mathbb{C}$ is the set of all applicable switch configurations, and $\mathbb{C}^{t-u+1}$ is the cross-product of $t-u+1$ such sets, one for each time-slot in the interval $[0, t-u]$. Note that a demultiplexor state transition may depend on other demultiplexors' state transitions, and on incoming flows to other input-ports, as long as these events occurred u time-slots before the state transition. A state of demultiplexor can change even if no cell arrives to the input-port.

The additional global information reduces the relative queuing delay. For example, when a 1-RT demultiplexing algorithm is operating under $(R, 0)$ leaky-bucket traffic, it practically has full information about the switch status, and therefore it can emulate a centralized algorithm. Yet, lack of information about recent events yields non-negligible relative queuing delay, caused by leaky-bucket traffic with a non-zero burst:

THEOREM 10 *A bufferless PPS, with u-RT demultiplexing algorithm has relative queuing delay and relative delay jitter of* $\left(1 - \overline{u}\frac{r}{R}\right)\frac{\overline{u}N}{S}$, *under leaky-bucket traffic with burstiness factor* $\overline{u}^2\frac{N}{K} - \overline{u}$, *where* $\overline{u} = \min\{u, \frac{1}{2}\frac{R}{r}\}$.

By substituting the minimal value $u = 1$, we get the following general result for any real-time distributed demultiplexing algorithm:

COROLLARY 11 *A bufferless PPS, with any real-time distributed demultiplexing algorithm, has relative queuing delay and relative delay jitter of* $\left(1 - \frac{r}{R}\right)\frac{N}{S}$ *time-slots, under leaky-bucket traffic with burstiness factor* $\frac{N}{K} - 1$.

4. The Relative Queuing Delay of an Input-Buffered PPS

When measuring relative queuing delay in an input-buffered PPS, the queuing of cells both in the input-ports' buffers and the planes' buffers of the PPS should be compared to the queuing of cells in the output-ports' buffers of the reference switch. Generally, input buffers increase the flexibility of the demultiplexing algorithms, which leads to weaker lower bounds.

The size of the input-buffers affects the relative queuing delay in an input-buffered PPS under u-RT demultiplexing algorithms. A PPS that can store u cells in each input-port is able to support a u-RT demultiplexing algorithm that guarantees relative queuing delay of at most u time-slots, by simulating the CPA algorithm [14].

THEOREM 12 *There is a u-RT demultiplexing algorithm for an globally FCFS input-buffered PPS, with buffer size* $\geq u$ *and speedup* $S \geq 2$, *and a relative queuing delay of at most u time-slots.*

This reduction gives an algorithm that may be impractical; yet, it demonstrates that a lower bound of $\Omega(N/S)$ time-slots does not hold when the input-buffers are sufficiently large. When buffers are smaller than u, it can be shown that a globally FCFS input-buffered PPS has relative queuing delay of $\left(1 - \frac{r}{R}\right)\frac{N}{S}$ time-slots, under leaky-bucket traffic with burstiness factor $u(\frac{N}{K} - 1)$.

The following lower-bound holds for any fully distributed demultiplexing algorithm, regardless of buffer size:

THEOREM 13 *An input-buffered PPS, with a fully-distributed demultiplexing algorithm, has relative queuing delay and relative delay-jitter of* $\left(1 - \frac{r}{R}\right)\frac{N}{S}$ *time-slots, under leaky-bucket traffic without bursts.*

5. The Relative Queuing Delay in Congested Periods

In this section we introduce a parameterized fully-distributed demultiplexing algorithm for bufferless PPS that has zero relative queuing delay in *congested periods*. A time period $(t_1, t_2]$ is *congested* if for a certain output-port j, all the queues of cells destined for this output-port in all the planes, are continuously backlogged.

THEOREM 14 *A bufferless PPS has a parameterized fully-distributed demultiplexing algorithm, which introduce no relative queuing delay in congested periods, after a certain warm-up period.*

The algorithm is an extension of the *fractional traffic dispatch (FTD)* demultiplexing algorithm [17]. In this fully-distributed demultiplexing algorithm, each flow (i, j) is segmented into *blocks* of size $h\lceil R/r \rceil$, where $h > 1$ is a parameter of the specific algorithm. The cells in the flow (i, j) are dispatched, so that two cells from the same block are not sent through the same plane.

This algorithm requires speedup $S \geq h$ in order to operate correctly. During an initial *warm-up* period there is still relative queuing delay. This period can be shortened by enlarging h. (See [3] for detailed analysis of this algorithm).

In the following proposition we show that the above proof does not contradict Theorem 8 since the traffic which causes the congestion is not an (R, B) leaky-bucket traffic:

PROPOSITION 15 *Any traffic that causes congestion in a PPS, under any demultiplexing algorithm described in the proof of Theorem 14, is not an* (R, B) *leaky-bucket traffic, for any* B *independent of time and the duration of the congested period.*

Note that the definition of congestion depends on both the incoming traffic to the switch, and the demultiplexing algorithm. Characterizing the non leaky-bucket traffics that can cause congestion under certain demultiplexing algorithms, and does not introduce relative queuing delay, is an open question.

6. Discussion

This paper studies the worst-case queuing delay and delay jitter induced by the demultiplexing algorithm of a parallel packet switch, *relative* to an optimal work-conserving switch. This *competitive* approach, typically used to evaluate on-line algorithms, is appealing because it does not require stochastic characterization of the incoming traffic.

Our results use Leaky-bucket traffic [5, 23] is used to avoid flooding the switch. One can also use the metaphor of an adversary controlling the injection of cells, as was done in the context of switching networks. Two models were suggested to restrict the injected flows from flooding the network [1, 4]; our flows satisfy these stronger restrictions as well.

Traffic shaping with low jitter may prefer non-work-conserving switches [10, 25], and therefore it is interesting to compare with such switches. When cells are not dropped within the switch, a non-work-conserving reference switch can degrade to work at rate r, making the comparison meaningless.

Jitter regulators that capture jitter control mechanisms, use an internal buffer to shape the traffic [20, 16, 26]; in particular, Mansour and Patt-Shamir [20] present competitive analysis of jitter regulators with bounded internal buffer size. It might be possible to translate our lower bounds on the relative queuing delay to bounds on the size of this internal buffer.

We are currently looking for demultiplexing algorithms that match the lower bounds presented in this paper. Our lower bounds present worst-case traffics also for randomized demultiplexing algorithms, but it would be interesting to study the distribution of the relative queuing delay when randomization is employed.

References

[1] M. Andrews, B. Awerbuch, A. Fernandez, J. Kleinberg, T. Leighton, and Z. Liu. Universal stability results for greedy Contention-Resolution protocols. *Journal of the ACM*, 48(1):39–69, 2001.

[2] The ATM Forum. *Inverse Multiplexing for ATM (IMA) specification*, March 1999. Version 1.1, AF-PHY-0086.001.

[3] H. Attiya and D. Hay. The inherent queuing delay of parallel packet switches. Technical Report CS-2004-02, Technion - Israel Institute of Technology, 2004.

[4] A. Borodin, J. Kleinberg, P. Raghavan, M. Sudan, and D. P. Williamson. Adversarial Queueing Theory. *Journal of the ACM*, 48(1):13–38, 2001.

[5] A. Charny. *Providing QoS guarantees in input buffered crossbar switches with speedup*. PhD thesis, Massachusetts Institute Of Technology, September 1998.

[6] F. M. Chiussi, D. A. Khotimsky, and S. Krishnan. Generalized inverse multiplexing of switched atm connections. In *IEEE Globecom*, 1998.

[7] S. Chuang, A. Goel, N. McKeown, and B. Prabhakar. Matching output queueing with a combined input output queued switch. In *IEEE Conference on Computer Communications (INFOCOM)*, pages 1169–1178, 1999.

[8] C. Clos. A study of non-blocking switching networks. *Bell System Technical Journal*, pages 406–424, 1953.

[9] R. L. Cruz. A calculus for network delay, part I: Network elements in isolation. *IEEE Transactions on Information Theory*, 37(1):114–131, January 1991.

[10] K.J. Chen C.S. Wu, J.C. Jiau. Characterizing traffic behavior and providing end-to-end service guarantees within ATM networks. In *IEEE Conference on Computer Communications (INFOCOM)*, pages 336–344, 1997.

[11] J. Duncanson. Inverse multiplexing. *IEEE Communications Magazine*, 32(4):34–41, April 1994.

[12] P. Fredette. The past, present, and future of inverse multiplexing. *IEEE Communications Magazine*, 32(4):42–46, April 1994.

[13] S. Iyer. Analysis of a packet switch with memories running slower than the line rate. Master's thesis, Stanford University, May 2000.

[14] S. Iyer, A. Awadallah, and N. McKeown. Analysis of a packet switch with memories running at slower than the line rate. In *IEEE Conference on Computer Communications (INFOCOM)*, pages 529–537, 2000.

[15] S. Iyer and N. McKeown. Making parallel packet switches practical. In *IEEE Conference on Computer Communications (INFOCOM)*, pages 1680–1687, 2001.

[16] S. Keshav. *An Engineering Approach to Computer Networking*. Addison-Wesley Publishing Co., 1997.

[17] D. Khotimsky and S. Krishnan. Stability analysis of a parallel packet switch with bufferless input demultiplexors. In *IEE International Conference on Communications (ICC)*, pages 100–106, 2001.

[18] L. Kleinrock. *Queuing Systems, Volume II*. Jhon Wiley&Sons, 1975.

[19] P. Krishna, N. S. Patel, A. Charny, and R.J. Simcoe. On the speedup required for work-conserving crossbar switches. *IEEE Journal on Selected Areas in Communications*, 17(6):1057–1066, June 1999.

[20] Y. Mansour and B. Patt-Shamir. Jitter control in Qos networks. *IEEE/ACM Transactions on Networking*, 9(4):492–502, August 2001.

[21] B. Prabhakar and N. McKowen. On the speedup required for combined input and output queued switching. *Automatica*, 35(12):1909–1920, December 1999.

[22] Y. Tamir and H.C. Chi. Symmetric crossbar arbiters for VLSI communication switches. *IEEE Transactions on Parallel and Distributed Systems*, 4(1):13–27, January 1993.

[23] J. S. Turner. New directions in communications (or which way to the information age?). *IEEE Communications Magazine*, 24(10):8–15, October 1986.

[24] H. Zhang. Providing end-to-end performance guarantees using non-work-conserving disciplines. *Computer Communications: Special Issue on System Support for Multimedia Computing*, 18(10), October 1995.

[25] H. Zhang. Service disciplines for guaranteed performance service in packet-switched networks. *Proceedings of the IEEE*, 83(10):1374–1396, October 1995.

[26] H. Zhang and D. Ferrari. Rate-controlled service disciplines. *Journal of High Speed Networks*, 3(4), 1994.

EFFICIENT PROTOCOLS FOR COMPUTING THE OPTIMAL SWAP EDGES OF A SHORTEST PATH TREE

Paola Flocchini,[1] Antonio Mesa Enriques,[2] Linda Pagli,[3] Giuseppe Prencipe,[3] and Nicola Santoro[4]

[1] *University of Ottawa, Canada,* [2] *Universidad de la Habana, Cuba,* [3] *Università di Pisa, Italy,* [4] *Carleton University, Canada*

Abstract We consider the problem of computing the *optimal swap edges* of a shortest-path tree. This theoretical problem arises in practice in systems that offer *point-of-failure shortest-path rerouting* service in presence of a single link failure: if the shortest path is not affected by the failed link, then the message will be delivered through that path; otherwise, the system will guarantee that, when the message reaches the node where the failure has occurred, the message will then be re-routed through the shortest-path to its destination. There exist highly efficient serial solutions for the problem, but unfortunately because of the structures they use, there is no known (nor foreseeable) efficient distributed implementation for them. A distributed protocol exists only for finding swap edges, not necessarily optimal ones.

We present two simple and efficient distributed algorithms for computing the optimal swap edges of a shortest-path tree. One algorithm uses messages containing a constant amount of information, while the other is tailored for systems that allow long messages. The amount of data transferred by the protocols is the same and depends on on the structure of the shortest-path spanning-tree; it is no more, and sometimes significantly less, than the cost of constructing the shortest-path tree.

Keywords: Fault-Tolerant Routing, Point of Failure Rerouting, Shortest Path Spanning Tree, Weighted Graphs, Distributed Algorithms, Data Complexity

1 Introduction

Consider an undirected graph $G = (V, E)$ with weighted edges. Let T_r be the shortest-path spanning-tree of G rooted in $r \in V$. The removal of any edge e of T_r will disconnect T_r into two subtrees. If G is biconnected, there will always be at least an edge $e' \in E(G) \setminus E(T_r)$ that would join the two disconnected subtrees forming a new spanning tree T' of G. Any such an edge is called a *swap* edge for e; let $S_r(e)$ denote the set of swap edges for e. An *optimal swap edge* (or *bridge*) for $e = (u, v)$ is any swap edge for e such that the distance from u to the source r in the new tree

T' is minimized; more precisely, the optimal swap edge for $e = (u, v)$ is the swap edge $e' = (u', v') \in S_r(e)$ such that $d_{T'}(u, r) = d_{T_r}(u, u') + |(u', v')| + d_{T_r}(v', r)$ is minimum.

The *(optimal) swap edges problem* for a shortest-path tree $T(r)$ is the one of determining for each edge in T_r an (optimal) swap edge. We are interested in the distributed solution of the optimal swap edge problem.

The Framework and Previous Work

This problem arises in the context of static fault-tolerant routing; specifi cally, it arises within the larger problem of augmenting the information of the shortest-path routing tables so to make them operate in spite of the fact that, at any time, one link (not necessarily the same at all time) might be down.

Consider a network where the routing tables contain information enabling shortest-path routing between any two nodes in the network. In this context, if one wants to continue to offer shortest-path routing after the failure of an arbitrary single link, a service called *shortest-path rerouting* (SR), the amount of additional information that needs to be stored in the tables might be formidable. This is because the failure of a single edge can dramatically change *all* the shortest-path information.

To reduce the amount of communication and of storage, a simple and convenient alternative is to offer, after the failure of an arbitrary *single* link, a lower quality service called *point-of-failure rerouting* (PR): if the shortest path is not affected by the failed link, then the message will be delivered through that path; otherwise, the system will guarantee that, when the message reaches the node where the failure has occurred (the "point of failure"), the message will then be re-routed to its destination. This approach has clearly the advantage that there is no need to broadcast a link failure and its subsequent reactivation (if any).

The amount of *storage* of the PR approach will depend on what type of information is being kept at the nodes to do the rerouting.

An effi cient solution has been recently presented. In fact Ito *et al* [6] showed that the amount of storage can be reduced by precomputing for each possible link failure a *swap* edge to replace the failed one, for every possible destination, and storing this information in the tables. In particular, for each destination, a node stores only one link in addition to the one in the fault-free shortest-path [6]. Its implementation requires to solve n instances of the *swap edges problem*, one for each choice of $s \in V$. A sequential algorithm to solve the swap edge problem has been presented [6]; this algorithm can possibly be effi ciently implemented in a distributed setting.

A basic drawback of the *point-of-failure rerouting* service is that, if the failure occurs, the system does not make any guarantee other than message delivery. Although acceptable in some contexts, this level of service might not be tolerable in general. On the other hand, the *shortest-path rerouting* service that always guarantee optimal routing, is too costly to implement. In a sense, SR and PR are two extreme approaches.

In between there two extreme, there is another type of service, the *point-of-failure shortest-path rerouting* (PSR), that has some of the service quality of SR while keeping all the space and communication advantages of PR. In PSR, if the shortest path is not affected by the failed link, then the message will be delivered through that path; otherwise, the system will guarantee that, when the message reaches the node where the failure has occurred, the message will then be re-routed through the *shortest-path* to its destination. This improved quality of service can be achieved by precomputing for each possible link failure a *optimal swap* edge, to replace the failed one, for each possible destination, and storing this information in the tables. In particular, it is enough for a node just to know (how to reach) an optimal swap edge for each possible destination. In other words, PSR can be achieved with the same amount of storage as PR: for each destination, a node stores only one link in addition to the one in the fault-free shortest-path.

For its implementation, PSR requires the solution of n instances of the more difficult *optimal swap edges problem*, one for each choice of $s \in V$.

The problem of computing all the optimal swap edges for a shortest-path tree has been attacked by Nardelli, Proietti, and Widmayer [8]. They showed that the problem can be solved sequentially in $O(m \cdot \alpha(m, n))$ time, where $\alpha(m, n)$ is the functional inverse of Ackermann's function. This bound is achieved using Tarjan's sophisticated technique for union-find, which requires the construction of *transmuters* [10]. Unfortunately, there is currently no efficient distributed implementation of this sequential technique; since in a distributed network setting the construction of transmuters requires complete global network information at some node, it is doubtful whether this approach will become feasible at all.

Summarizing, *optimal swap edges problem* is both an interesting graph-theoretic problem on its own (studied as such in [8]) and a crucial component to implement a *point-of-failure shortest-path rerouting* strategy (described in [6]). Currently, there is no distributed solution (in [6], the problem is posed but no solution given). Clearly any such a solution should not add significantly to the overall cost of constructing the final routing tables. In particular, the computation should not require more messages (at least in order of magnitude) than those used to construct the shortest-path tree.

Our Contribution

In this paper we present an efficient distributed solution to the optimal swap edges problem.

Given a shortest-path spanning-tree T_r, the proposed protocol determines at each node x the optimal swap edge for e_x. The algorithm uses $O(n_r^*)$ messages of *constant* size, where n_r^* is the size of the transitive closure of $T_r \setminus \{r\}$; observe that $0 \leq n_r^* \leq (n-1)(n-2)/2$.

If longer messages are allowed, the same strategy can be modified to construct a different algorithm that uses only $O(n)$ such messages.

Providing a uniform comparison between protocols using different sized messages, the *data complexity* of a protocol measures the total amount of data exchanged during the execution; in our context, a node, an edge, a label, a weight, and a distance are each a unit of data. Both algorithms have an overall data complexity of $O(n_r^*)$.

Notice that this cost is always less, and oftentimes substantially so, than the cost of constructing a shortest-path spanning-tree. We actually conjecture that such a cost is *optimal*.

Further notice that the information assumed available by our algorithms can be acquired during the shortest-path spanning-tree construction, without increasing the order of magnitude of the message and information complexity of that process. Should this information not be provided, it can be easily acquired with an $O(m)$ data complexity.

The paper is organized as follows. In the next section we introduce some definitions and terminology. The new distributed algorithm for constructing all the optimal swap edges for a given shortest-path spanning-tree using constant-size messages is described and analyzed in Section 3. In Section 4, we present a more efficient algorithm for systems allowing long messages. The concluding remarks and open problems are in Section 6.

2 Definitions and Terminology

Let $G = (V, E)$ be a simple undirected graph, with $n = |V|$ vertices and $m = |E|$ edges. A *subgraph* $G' = (V', E')$ of G is any graph where $V' \subseteq V$ and $E' \subseteq E$. If $V' \equiv V$, G' is a *spanning* subgraph. A *path* $P = (V_p, E_p)$ is a subgraph of G, such that $V_p = \{v_1, \ldots, v_s\} | v_i \neq v_j$, for $i \neq j$, and $(v_i, v_{i+1}) \in E_p$, for $1 \leq i \leq s-1$. If $v_1 = v_s$ then P is a *cycle*. A graph G is *connected* if, for each pair $\{v_i, v_j\}$ of its vertices, there exists a path connecting them. A graph G is *biconnected* if, after the removal of anyone of its edges it remains connected. A *tree* is a connected graph with no cycles.

A non negative real value called *weight* (or *length*) and denoted by $|e|$ is associated to each edge e in G. Given a path P, the length of the path is the sum of the lengths of its edges. The *distance* $d_{G'}(x, y)$ between two vertices x and y in a connected subgraph G' of G, is the length of the shortest path from x to y in G'. For simplicity, in the following we will denote $d_G(x, y)$ simply by $d(x, y)$.

For a given vertex r, called *source*, the *shortest path tree* (SPT) of r is the spanning tree T_r rooted at r such that the path in T_r from r to any node v is the shortest possible one; i.e., $\forall x \in V \; d_{T_r}(x, r) = d(x, r)$.

The removal of any edge e of T_r will disconnect T_r into two subtrees. If G is biconnected, there will always be at least an edge $e' \in E(G) \setminus E(T_r)$ that will join the two disconnected subtrees forming a new spanning tree T' of G. Any such an edge is called a *swap* edge for e; let $S_r(e)$ denote the set of swap edges for e.

An *optimal swap edge* (or *bridge*) for $e = (u, v)$ is any swap edge for e such that the distance from u to the source r in the new tree T' is minimized; more precisely, an optimal swap edge for $e = (u, v)$ is a swap edge $e' = (u', v') \in S_r(e)$ such that $d_{T'}(u, r) = d_{T_r}(u, u') + |(u', v')| + d_{T_r}(v', r)$ is minimum. As an example, consider the biconnected weighted graph G shown in Figure (1.a), and the shortest-path spanning tree T_A rooted shown in Figure in (1.b). It is easy to verify that the optimal swap edge for (C, A) is (F, B).

The *optimal swap edges problem* for $T(r)$ is the problem of determining an optimal swap edge for each edge in T_r.

As already mentioned, a sequential algorithm solving this problem was given in [8]. We are interested in the distributed solution of the optimal swap edge problem. We consider a *distributed computing system* with communication topology G. Each computational entity x is located at a node of G, has local processing and storage capabilities, has a distinct label $\lambda_x(e)$ from a totally ordered set associated to each of its incident edges e, knows the weight of its incident edges, and can communicate with its neighboring entities by transmission of bounded sequence of bits called messages.

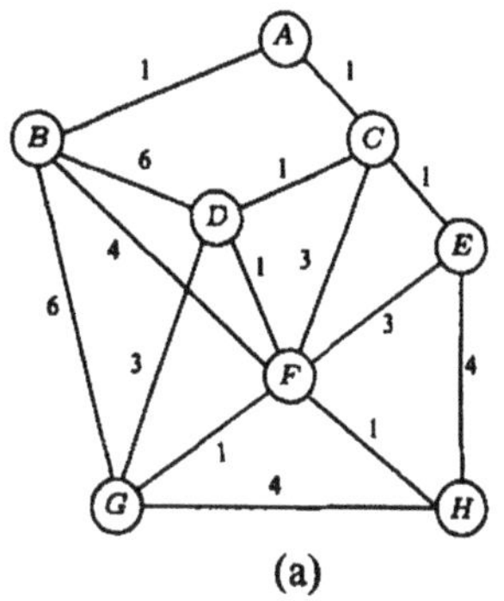

(a)

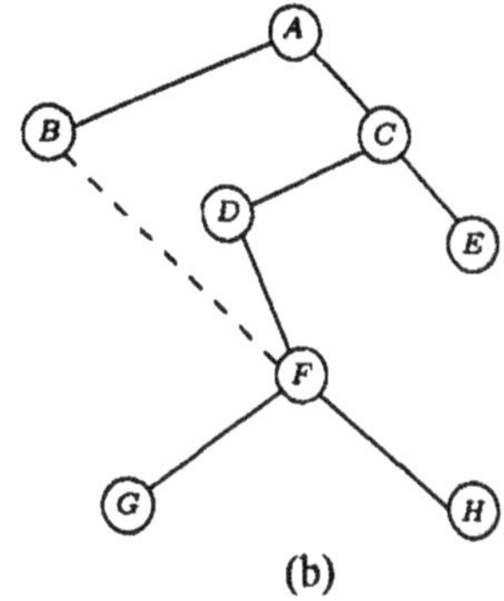

(b)

Figure 1. (a) A biconnected weighted graph G. (b) The shortest-path spanning tree T_A rooted in A; the dotted edge (F, B) is the optimal swap edge for (C, A).

The communication time includes processing, queueing, and transmission delays, and it is finite but otherwise unpredictable. In other words, the system is *asynchronous*. All the entities execute the same set of rules, called distributed algorithm.

In the following, when no ambiguity arises, we will use the terms entity, node and vertex as equivalent; analogously, we will use the terms link, arc and edge interchangeably.

3 Computing All Optimal Swap Edges

We now present a solution to the problem of distributively computing all optimal swap edges for a given shortest-path spanning tree T_r.

Basic Properties and Tools

In our algorithm we make use of some known properties of rooted trees. In T_r each node except the root r has a unique *parent*, and each edge connects a node to its parent.

PROPERTY 1 *The partial order induced by the relation* parent *has dimension at most* 2.

Consider in fact the labelling $\alpha : V \to \{1, \ldots, n\}^2$ defined as follows. Given T_r, for $x \in V$ let $\alpha(x) = (a, b)$, where a is the numbering of x in the *preorder* traversal[1] of T_r; and b is the numbering of x in the *inverted preorder* traversal of T_r, i.e., when the order of the visit of the children is inverted. The labels associated to the nodes in the tree of Figure 1.b are shown in Figure 2.a.

Let $T_r[x]$ denote the subtree of T_r rooted in x. Any node y in the subtree $T_r[x]$ is said to be a *descendant* of x. Let $Desc_r(x)$ be the set of the descendants of x in T_r; note that, by definition, $x \in Desc_r(x)$. Interestingly, the *lexicographic order* $\succ$ between the labels assigned by α completely characterizes the *descendant* relationship in a rooted tree:

[1] Since the labelling of the incident links is drawn from a totally ordered set, this numbering is unique.

PROPERTY 2 *A node y is descendant of a node x in T_r* if and only if $\alpha(y) \succeq \alpha(x)$.

Property 2 can be easily verified and it is known as a folklore method to check relationships among nodes in trees.

Furthermore, there exists a simple relationship between swap edges and the descendants.

PROPERTY 3 *An edge $(u, v) \in E \setminus E(T_s)$ is a swap for $e_x \in E(T_s)$* if and only if *only one of u and v (but not both) is in $Desc_r(x)$.*

For brevity, we will denote the set $S_r(e_x)$ of all swap edges for e_x simply by $S(x)$, and by $InS(x) \subseteq S(x)$ the set of those that are incident on x. The last useful property states that the swap edges for e_x consists only of all the swap edges incident to x and to its descendants.

PROPERTY 4 *For all $x \in V$ $S(x) = \bigcup_{y \in (Desc_r(x)} InS(y)$.*

Properties 2, 3, and 4 provide a powerful computational tool for determining which edges are possible candidate for being optimal swap edges. We will now see how to efficiently use this tool.

The Algorithm

By definition, a node x knows the weight of all its incident links, and can distinguish those that are part of T_s from those that are not; of those that are part of T_s, x can distinguish the one that leads to its parent from those leading to its children.

We assume that each node x knows its distance from r, the distances of its neighbors from r, its own pair $\alpha(x)$, as well the pairs of its neighbors. If not available, this information can be easily and efficiently acquired.

In the proposed algorithm, each node x computes an optimal swap edge for e_x, i.e., the swap edge for e_x in the shortest path from x to r in $E \setminus \{e_x\}$. We shall denote such an edge as b_x and call it the *bridge of x*. A node x also contributes, if necessary, to the computation of the bridges of other nodes.

Computing its bridge.
To compute its bridge b_x, a node x:

1 It determines which of its incident edges are swaps for e_x; i.e., it constructs the set $InS(x)$. It then sets $L(x) = InS(x)$.

2 If x is not a leaf (and if it does not have the information already),

  (a) it requests from each child y a swap edge (if any) for e_x that is incident on a descendent of y, and among all edges satisfying the above, the distance from y to r using this swap edge instead of e_x is minimized.

  (b) It waits until it receives a reply from all its children. It adds each received edge to the set $S(x)$.

3 For each $e \in L(x)$, x computes its distance from r using e instead of e_x (i.e., in $T_r - \{e_x\} \cup \{e\}$). It then sorts $L(x)$ so that the corresponding distances are in

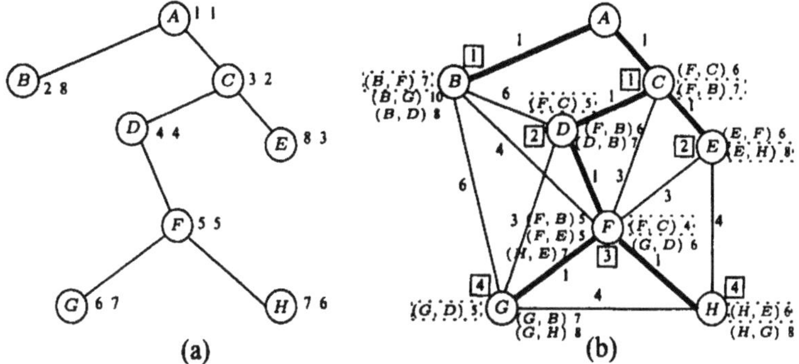

Figure 2. Computing all the optimal swap edges in the graph G of figure 1 for the SPT rooted in A. (a) For each node x there is shown $\alpha(x)$. (b) For each node x there are shown: the distance of x from the root (in the solid box): the elements of $L(x)$, among which b_x (in the dotted box).

non-decreasing order. Let min_x be the smallest edge in the sorted $L(x)$; then $b_x = min_x$.

Each node x also contributes to the calculation of the bridge of its predecessors. It does so as following.

Cooperating with the other nodes.

1 As soon as its bridge b_x has been computed, x sends it to its parent.

2 If requested by its parent to fi nd the best swap edge feasible with some edge e, then:

   (a) It creates a set $L(x, e)$ by removing from $L(x)$ all the incident links that are not swap edges for e;

   (b) if the link in $L(x)$ sent by child y is not a swap for e, then x removes it from $L(x, e)$, requests y to send its best swap edge for e, waits to receive such an edge (or notifi cation that none exists), and adds it to $L(x, e)$

   (c) x sorts $L(x, e)$ and sends the new min_x to its parent (it will send NIL if $L(x, e) = \emptyset$).

Note that, because of Properties 2 and 3, to determine if an edge is a swap edge is suffi cient to examine the relationship "descendant", which in turn is uniquely determined by the mapping α. Hence, in the following, we shall use the term "feasible for $\alpha(x)$" to mean "swap edge for e_x" without any loss of precision.

Algorithm ALL BRIDGES, reported below, describes the state-event-action set of rules: it specifi es what action must a node perform if in a given state.

Initially, all nodes are in state `COMPUTING` and start the execution. Each node x maintains a list $L(x)$ of possible swap edges. Initially $L(x)$ contains all the links incident on x that are not in the tree.

Algorithm 1 ALL BRIDGES (G, T_r) for node x

```
Input: Children of x in T_r, parent of x in T_r, pair α(x) = (a,b) of labels associated
   to x in T_r, neighbors of x in G. edge (u',v').
States: S = {COMPUTING, SWAPPED, WAITING}.
  COMPUTING
      count := 0;
      If leaf Then
         (mybridge, d) := ChooseMin(a,b);
         send ("Choice",mybridge, d) to parent;
         become SWAPPED;
      If internal Then
         Receiving ("Choice",edge, distance);  \* it comes from a child *\
         If Feasible(edge, (a,b)) Then
            count := count + 1;
            choice[sender] := (edge, distance);
            If count = |children| Then
               (mybridge, d) := ChooseMin(a,b);
               send ("Choice",mybridge, d) to parent;
               become SWAPPED;
            If Not Feasible(edge, (a,b)) Then send ("Request", (a,b)) to sender.
  SWAPPED
      Receiving ("Request", (p,q));
      (edge, d) = ChooseMin(p,q);
      If leaf Then send ("Choice",edge, d) to parent .
      Else
         check := 0;
         For All y ∈ Children Do
            If Not Feasible(swap[y], (p,q)) Then
               send ("Request",(p,q)) to y;
               check := check + 1;
         If check > 0 Then become WAITING .
         Else
            (edge, d) := ChooseMin(p,q);
            send ("Choice",edge, d) to parent.
  WAITING
      Receiving ("Choice",edge, distance);
      choice[sender] := (edge, distance);
      check := check − 1;
      If check = 0 Then
         (edge, d) :=ChooseMin(p,q);
         send (edge, d) to parent;
         become SWAPPED.
```

To each $e = (w, z) \in L(x)$, where w is a descendent of x (possibly, $x = w$), there is associated the pair $\alpha(z)$ as well as the distance

$$d[e] = d(x, w) + |(w, z)| + d(z, r).$$

The set $L(x)$ is kept sorted w.r.t. the distances. Note that while each node knows its distance from the root, the distances $d[e]$ must be computed. This can be easily done: when a swap edge e is transmitted by a child to a parent along (u, v), together with a distance d, node v will increment the distance by $|(u, v)|$.

Function `ChooseMin`(a, b) determines the swap edge with minimum distance in $L(x)$ that is feasible with (a, b) (for the leaves all the swap edges are feasible), its output is (e, d), where e is such an edge and d is the distance between x and r using e as a swap edge. If no such an edge exists, function `ChooseMin`(a, b) returns NIL.

The Boolean function `Feasible(edge,` (a, b)`)` determines whether *edge* is feasible with the pair of labels (a, b); by defi nition, if $edge = NIL$, `Feasible` is always TRUE, regardless of (a, b). Let $e = (z, w)$. The feasibility of the swap edge e is checked by comparing the pair (a, b) with the pair corresponding to w.

It is understood that when sending information about an edge e, as in the "Choice" messages, this information include the pairs of labels associated to the end nodes of e.

Example. As an example consider the SPT of the graph of Figure 1, shown in Figure 2. According to the algorithm, the leaf nodes B, G, H, and E compute their bridges directly and become SWAPPED. Node F receives swap edges from G and H and can computes its bridge $[(F, C), 4]$ becoming SWAPPED. Node D receives the swap edge $[(F, C), 5]$ from its only child F, and this becomes its bridge. Node C instead receives non feasible edges from both D and E; it then sends to both of them a request for a feasible edge. Node E does not have edges feasible with C; hence it sends NIL. As for D, as the swap link it had received from F is not feasible for C, it will forward the request to F. Since the swap edge known to F ((F, C)) is not feasible for C, F forwards the request to the leaves G and H. At this point there is a propagation of swap edges feasible with C. In fact, G sends up $[(G, B), 7]$, H sends up NIL, F chooses as minimum $[(F, B), 5]$ and returns this information to D which sends it to C. Receiving NIL from E and $[(F, B), 6]$ from D, node C can conclude its computation selecting $[(F, B), 7]$ as its bridge.

Analysis

The correctness of Algorithm ALL BRIDGES is established by the following Theorem.

THEOREM 1 *In algorithm ALL BRIDGES:*

(i) each node u correctly computes b_u;

(ii) if so requested by its parent, each node u will determine among the swap edges incident to its subtree and feasible with $\alpha(e) = (p, q)$, if any, one edge e' that minimizes the distance between u and r in $T_r - \{e\} \cup \{e'\}$.

Proof Removal of e_u partitions T_r in two subtrees, one rooted in r the other in u. By defi nition, any feasible swap edge, and hence b_u, must have an endpoint in each component. The proof will be by induction on the height $h(u)$ of the subtree of T_r rooted in u.

Basis. $h(u) = 0$; i.e., u is a leaf. In this case, one components contains only u, while the other contains all the other nodes. In other words, the only possible swap edges are incident on u. Thus, u correctly computes b_u, proving (i); it can also immediately determine the feasibility of any of those links with respect to any pair of labels, and thus answer correctly any received query, proving (ii).

Induction step. Let the theorem hold for all nodes v with $k - 1 \geq h(v) \geq 0$; we will now show that it holds for u with $h(u) = k$. Since u is not a leaf, the subtree $T_r[u]$ rooted at u contains at least two nodes. Consider the set $S(u)$ of all feasible swap edges for e_u; clearly, if $e = (w, z) \in S(u)$ then one of its end point, say w, is in $T_r[u]$ (and thus a descendent of u), while the other say z, is not.

Let v be a child of u; then $h(v) < k$. It follows that, by inductive hypothesis, when asked by u, v will send to u the edge in $Swap(v)$ that, among those feasible with e_u, minimizes the distance between v and r. We will now show that this information is suffi cient for u to correctly determine its optimal swap edge b_u.

By defi nition of bridge, b_u is the edge $e = (w, z)$ in $S(u)$ that minimizes the quantity $d_u[e] = d(u, w) + |(w, z)| + d(z, r)$. By Property 4, the optimal swap edge is either incident on u or on a strict descendent of u. Clearly u can locally determine its distance from r for any of its incident swap edges, and determine the minimum one. If e is not incident on u, it is in the subtree $T_r[v]$ rooted in a child v of u; furthermore, e is the swap edge in $S(v)$ that, among those feasible with e_u, minimizes the distance between v and r. In other words, once u obtains from each child v' the swap edge $e' \in S(v')$ that, among those feasible with e_u, minimizes the distance between v_i and r, u can determine the minimum one. Since, by inductive hypothesis, every child of u sends this information to u, it follows that u can correctly determine its optimal swap edge, proving Part (i) of the Theorem.

To prove Part (ii), it is suffi cient to observe that, by Property 3, u can determine which of its incident swap edges are feasible with a given pair (p, q); furthermore, since the height of its children in T_r is less than k, then by inductive hypothesis it can obtain from them the "best" swap edge in their subtree feasible with (p, q). Therefore, u can determine among the swap edges incident to its subtree and feasible with (p, q), if any, one that minimizes the distance between u and r, proving Part (ii).

□

Let us now examine the message complexity of the proposed algorithm. Let n_r^* be the number of edges of the transitive closure of $T_r \setminus \{r\}$; observe that $0 \leq n^* \leq (n-1)(n-2)/2$.

THEOREM 2 *The message complexity of Algorithm ALL BRIDGES is at most* $2n^* + n - 1$.

Proof Each node, once computed its optimal swap edge, sends a message to its parent, for a total of $n - 1$ "Choice" messages. To compute its optimal swap edge, a node x might send a "Request" message to all its children (if the original information provided by them is not feasible), which in turn might send to their children (if no feasible information was received), and so on. Thus, in the worst case, each descendent of x will receive a "Request" and reply a "Choice" for a total of $2|Desc(x)|$ messages.

Since each node, except the root, must compute its optimal swap edge, this process will require at most

$$\sum_{x \neq r} 2|Desc(x)| = \sum_{x} 2(|Ance(x)| - 1) = 2n_r^*,$$

where $Ance(x)$ denotes the set of ancestors of x. □

A node, an edge, a label, a weight, and a distance are all unit of data. To evaluate the overall data complexity of the algorithm we need to consider the message size; since each message contains only a constant number of units of information, we have:

THEOREM 3 *The data complexity of the distributed Algorithm ALL BRIDGES is* $O(n_r^*)$.

Observe that the data complexity needed by our algorithm to compute all the optimal swap edges of a shortest-path spanning-tree is no more (and very often dramatically less) than the one of computing the shortest-path spanning-tree itself [3, 4, 2].

4 An O(n) Messages Algorithm

In this section, we discuss how the algorithm of Section 3 can be modified in order to reduce the message complexity to $O(n)$ in case that longer messages are allowed. The overall information complexity of the new algorithm remains of $O(n_r^*)$.

The idea is now that each node simultaneously computes the "best" feasible swap edges, not only for itself, but also for all its ancestors in the SPT. The modified algorithm will be described only at high level. It consists simply of a *broadcast* phase started by the children of the root, followed by a *convergecast* phase started by the leaves.

THEOREM 4 *Each node* $u \neq r$*:*

(i) correctly computes b_u*;*

(ii) determines for each ancestor $v \neq r$ *the best swap edge feasible with* $\alpha(v)$*, if any.*

Proof First observe that, as a result of the broadcast, every node will receive the pair associated to each of its ancestors (except r); hence it can determine feasibility, for

Algorithm 2 ALL BRIDGES-2

[Broadcast.]

1 Each child x of the root starts the broadcast by sending a list containing $\alpha(x)$ to its children.

2 Each node y, adds $\alpha(y)$ to the received list and sends it to its children.

[Convergecast.]

1 Each leaf z first computes its own bridge. It then computes the best feasible swap edge for each of its ancestors, and sends the list of those edges to its parent (if different from r).

2 An internal node y waits until it receives the list of best swap edges from each of its children. Based on the received information and on $InS(y)$, it computes its bridge b_y. It also computes the best feasible swap edge for each of its ancestors, and sends the list of those edges to its parent (if different from r).

---

each ancestor, of any available set of swap edges. The proof is by induction on the height $h(u)$ of the subtree of T_r rooted in u.

Basis. $h(u) = 0$; i.e., u is a leaf. In this case, one components contains only u, while the other contains all the other nodes. In other words, the only possible swap edges are incident on u. Thus, u correctly computes b_u, proving (i); it can also immediately determine the feasibility of any of those links with respect to any pair of labels, and thus answer correctly any received query, proving (ii).

Induction step. Let the theorem hold for all nodes x with $k - 1 \geq h(x) \geq 0$; we will now show that it holds for u with $h(u) = k$. By inductive hypothesis, it receives from each child y the best feasible swap edge for each ancestor of y, including u itself. Hence, based on these lists and on the locally available set $InSwap(u)$, u can correctly determine its optimal swap edge, as well as its best feasible swap edge for each of its ancestors.

□

The functioning of the Algorithm ALL BRIDGES-2 can be followed in the example of Figure 2.b and in particular through the convergecast, starting from the two leaves G and H. After Phase 1, G and H know their ancestors, namely: F, D, C. Node G computes its bridge as $((G, D), 5)$, and the minimum swap edge for each of its ancestor, namely: $((G, D), 5)$ for F, $((G, D), 5)$ for D and $((G, B), 7)$ for C, and sends these values to F. Similarly H computes its bridge as $((H, E), 6)$, and the minimum swap edge for each ancestor, namely: $((H, E), 6)$ for F, $((H, E), 6)$ for D and NIL for C, and sends these values to F. F computes its optimal swap edge as the minimum among its incident edges, that is, $((F, C), 4)$, the edge coming from G, (G, D), having now distance 6, and the edge coming from H, (H, E), having now distance 7. Hence it selects $((F, C), 4)$, as bridge and computes the minimum feasible swap edge for each of its ancestor, namely: $((F, C), 4)$ for D, and $((F, B), 5)$ for C, and sends these values to F. D selects as bridge the edge coming from F, with distance incremented by 1, that is $((F, C), 5)$, and sends $((F, B), 6)$ for C. C can finally selects its bridge, considering the information coming from D and that coming from E which is NIL, as $((F, B), 7)$.

Let us now analyze the complexity of the algorithm:

THEOREM 5
The message complexity of Algorithm ALL BRIDGES-2 is exactly $2(n - 1 - \delta(r))$, *where* $\delta(r)$ *is the degree of* r.

Proof In the broadcast phase, every node except the root and its children receives a message. In the convergecast phase, every node except the root and its children sends a message. □

THEOREM 6 *The data complexity of Algorithm ALL BRIDGES-2 is exactly* $2n_r^*$.

Proof In the broadcast phase, every node (except the root and its children) receives the labels of all its ancestors. In the convergecast phase, every node (except the root and its children) sends a swap edge for each of its ancestors. □

5 Concluding Remarks

In this paper we have presented simple and efficient distributed algorithms for computing the optimal swap edges of a shortest-path tree. One algorithm uses messages containing a constant amount of information, while the other is tailored for systems that allow long messages. Both algorithms exchange a quantity of information which is no more, and often significantly so, than that required to construct the shortest-path spanning-tree; also, they require information that can be acquired, with no increase in order of magnitude, during the shortest-path spanning-tree construction.

Among the possible development of this study, we mention that would be interesting to study how to recover from multiple link failures, following the same strategy of storing in the routing tables the information useful for finding alternative paths. The problem appears much more complex. In addition, the size of the routing tables is limited [9], hence the additional information to store in order to compute alternative paths in presence of faults must be also be small.

The proposed algorithms allow for the efficient construction of point-of-failure shortest-path rerouting service. To do so, the proposed computation must be carried out for the n shortest path trees, each having as root a different vertex of the graph. In this regards, an interesting open problem is whether it is possible to achieve the same goal in a more efficient way than by performing n independent computations. For example, it is known that the constructions of all-pairs shortest-paths can be done more efficiently than n independent constructions of a single shortest-path spanning-tree (e.g., [1]); the research question is whether something similar holds also in this context.

Acknowledgments

Part of this work was carried out while the the fi rst and last authors were visited by the others at the University of Ottawa and at Carleton University. This work was supported in part by the Natural Sciences and Engineering Research Council of Canada, and by "Progetto ALINWEB: Algoritmica per Internet e per il Web", MIUR Programmi di Ricerca Scientifi ca di Rilevante Interesse Nazionale.

References

[1] Y. Afek, M. Ricklin Sparser: a paradigm for running distributed algorithms. *Journal of Algorithms*, 14:316-328, 1993.

[2] B. Awerbuch, R. Gallager A new distributed algorithm to find breadth first search trees. *IEEE Transactions on Information Theory*, 33:315–322, 1987.

[3] K. M. Chandy, J. Misra Distributed computation on graphs: shortest path algorithms. *Communication of ACM*, 25:833–837, 1982.

[4] G. N. Frederikson A distributed shortest path algorithm for planar networks. *Information and Computation*, 86:140-159, 1990.

[5] P. Humblet. Another adaptive distributed shortest path algorithm. *IEEE/ACM Transactions on Communications*, 39(6):995–1003, 1991.

[6] H. Ito, K. Iwama, Y. Okabe, T. Yoshihiro Polynomial-time computable backup tables for shortest-path routing. *Proc. of 10th Colloquium on Structural Information and Communication Complexity* (SIROCCO 2003), 163–177, 2003.

[7] P. Narvaez, K.Y. Siu, H.Y. Teng New dynamic algorithms for shortest path tree computation *IEEE Transactions on Networking*, 8:735–746, 2000.

[8] E. Nardelli, G. Proietti, P. Widmayer Swapping a failing edge of a single source shortest paths tree is good and fast. *Algoritmica*, 35:56–74, 2003.

[9] L. L. Peterson, B. S. Davie. *Computer Networks: A Systems Approach, 3rd Edition*. Morgan Kaufmann, 2003.

[10] R. E.Tarjan Application of path compression on balanced trees. *Journal of ACM*, 26:690–715, 1979.

TRUTHFUL MECHANISMS FOR GENERALIZED UTILITARIAN PROBLEMS

G. Melideo[1], P. Penna,[2] G. Proietti,[1,3] R. Wattenhofer,[4] and P. Widmayer[5]

[1] *Dipartimento di Informatica, Università di L'Aquila, via Vetoio, 67010 L'Aquila, Italy*
{melideo,proietti}@di.univaq.it

[2] *Dipartimento di Informatica ed Applicazioni "R.M. Capocelli", Università di Salerno via S. Allende 2, I-84081 Baronissi (SA), Italy* *
penna@dia.unisa.it

[3] *Istituto di Analisi dei Sistemi ed Informatica, CNR, Viale Manzoni 30, 00185 Roma, Italy* †

[4] *Institut für Pervasive Computing, Departement Informatik, ETH Zentrum IFW A 47.2, Haldeneggsteig 4, 8092 Zürich, Switzerland*
wattenhofer@inf.ethz.ch

[5] *Institut für Theoretische Informatik, Departement Informatik, ETH Zentrum CLW building, Clausiusstrasse 49, 8092 Zürich, Switzerland*
widmayer@inf.ethz.ch

Abstract In this paper we investigate extensions of the well-known Vickrey-Clarke-Groves (VCG) mechanisms to problems whose objective function is not utilitarian and whose agents' utilities are not quasi-linear. We provide a generalization of utilitarian problems, termed *consistent* problems, and prove that every consistent problem admits a *truthful mechanism*. These mechanisms, termed *VCG-consistent* (VCGc) mechanisms, can be seen as a natural extension of VCG mechanisms for utilitarian problems.

We then investigate extensions/restrictions of consistent problems. This yields three classes of problems for which (i) VCGc mechanisms are the only truthful mechanisms, (ii) no truthful VCGc mechanism exists, and (iii) no truthful mechanism exists, respectively. Showing that a given problem is in one of these three classes is straightforward, thus yielding a simple way to see whether VCGc mechanisms are appropriate or not.

Finally, we apply our results to a number of basic non-utilitarian problems.

Keywords: Algorithmic Mechanism Design, Algorithms for the Internet, Game Theory

*Supported by the European Project IST-2001-33135, Critical Resource Sharing for Cooperation in Complex Systems (CRESCCO). Work partially done while visiting ETH Zentrum.
†Supported by the Research Project GRID.IT, partially funded by the Italian Ministry of Education, University and Research. Work partially done while visiting ETH Zentrum.

1. Introduction

In the Internet a multitude of heterogeneous entities (e.g., providers, autonomous systems, universities, private companies, etc.) offer, use, and even compete with each other for resources. As the Internet is emerging as the platform for distributed computing, new solutions should take into account the new aspects deriving from a multi-agent system in which agents cannot be assumed to be either *honest/obedient* (i.e., to follow the protocol) or *adversarial* (i.e., to "play against"). Indeed, the entities involved in the computation are driven by different goals (e.g., minimizing *their own* costs) and they may act *selfishly*. In this case, agents cannot be assumed to follow the protocol, though they respond to *incentives* (e.g., a payment received to compensate the costs).

In essence, game theory is the study of what happens when independent agents act selfishly (for a more extensive discussion of applications of game theoretic tools and micro economics to the Internet we refer the reader to [8, 16]). Mechanism design asks how one can design systems so that agents' selfish behavior results in the desired system-wide goals. In a nutshell, each agent i has a function $u_i(\cdot)$ which expresses her *utility* derived from the system outcome. For instance, if the system computes a solution X and provides agent i with a payment P_i, then the corresponding utility is equal to $u_i(X, P_i, t_i)$, where t_i is another parameter called the *type* of agent i. The difficulty here is that the type t_i is *not known to the system* and is also part of the input required to construct the desired solution X^* (e.g., t_i represents the speed of a router and the system goal is to forward packets optimally). This piece of information is known to agent i which may report a different (false) type $r_i \neq t_i$ in order to improve her utility: on input r_i, the system computes a solution X' and provides a payment P' such that $u_i(X', P'_i, t_i) > u_i(X^*, P_i, t_i)$, where P_i is the payment that i would have received if reporting t_i. Notice that the computed solution X' is not the desired one since the input provided to the underlying algorithm is not the correct one. Therefore, one should design a suitable payment rule $p(\cdot)$ such that, for every possible t_i, agent i cannot improve her utility by reporting $r_i \neq t_i$. Moreover, this should hold also when some other agent j does not act rationally and reports $r_j \neq t_j$. The combination of an algorithm $\mathcal{A}$ and a payment rule $p(\cdot)$ that guarantees this property, for every agent, is called *truthful mechanism* with dominant strategies.

A central question in (algorithmic) mechanism design is the study of which system goals are achievable via truthful mechanisms, that is, if algorithm $\mathcal{A}$ is required to produce a certain output (e.g., an optimal solution for a combinatorial optimization problem) does a payment function $p(\cdot)$ exist such that the resulting mechanism $(\mathcal{A}, p)$ is truthful?

A large body of the existing literature focuses on the class of problems in which the utilities are *quasi-linear*, that is, agent i's utility factors into $u_i(X, P_i, t_i) = v_i(X, t_i) + P_i$, where $v_i(X, t_i)$ represents the valuations of agent i of solution X. For such problems, the celebrated Vickrey-Clarke-Groves (VCG) mechanisms [4, 10, 18] guarantee the truthfulness under the hypothesis that the algorithm $\mathcal{A}$ maximizes the function $\sum_i v_i(X, t_i)$. VCG mechanisms have been successfully applied to a multitude of optimization problems involving selfish agents with applications to networking [1, 2, 7, 14, 17] and electronic commerce [5, 11]. All these works assume that the problem is *utilitarian*, that is, the utility functions are quasi-linear and the objective maximization function can be written as the sum above. Moreover, even though Nisan and Ronen [13] first focused on problems whose objective function is not utilitarian, their n-approximation mechanism is nothing but a VCG mechanism for a related utilitarian problem. Actually, VCG mechanisms remain the only general technique to design truthful mechanisms (see Sect. 1 for a discussion on previous related work).

Unfortunately, there are problems for which (i) the objective function is not the sum of the agents' valuations and/or (ii) the utility function is not quasi-linear. Consider the following basic problem (see Sect. 3.2 for a more detailed description). In a communication network, each link e can successfully transmit a message with probability $q_e \in (0, 1)$. We want to select a *most reliable path*, i.e., a path between two given nodes which maximizes the probability that none of its links fails. Links are owned by selfish agents which are asked to report a (possibly uncorrect) probability $q'_e \in (0, 1)$. We provide to a chosen link e a payment specified by a function $p_e(\cdot)$ if and only if link e performed the transmission correctly. Each agent tries to maximizes the *expected* amount of money received.[1] Hence, *both* the objective and the utility functions can be expressed by means of the common "operator" '·'. The MOST RELIABLE PATH (MRP) problem just described can be easily reduced to a utilitarian problem by considering the logarithms of both the optimization function and of the utility functions, thus implying the existence of a truthful mechanism. It is then natural to ask whether this is just "good chance", or this problem (and others) has some "similarities" with the class of utilitarian problems.

In this paper we address this question by defining a class of problems, termed *consistent* problems (see Sect. 2), which admit truthful mechanisms. The main advantages of our approach are that: (i) it provides an answer to the following question: which mathematical properties guarantee the existence of truthful mechanisms? Moreover, for a given problem, it is easy to see whether it satisfies these properties (while reducing the problem to a utilitarian one may not be as simple as for the MRP); (ii) it provides a more intuitive interpretation of the payments, e.g., for problems like the MRP described above.

We define *VCGc* mechanisms as a natural extension of the VCG mechanisms and show that they are truthful for consistent problems. We then consider possible extensions of our result and provide both positive and negative answers depending on which property we add/drop from the definition of consistent problems. In particular, we identify four classes of problems:

$C^{\text{vcgc}}_{\text{only}}$. This class is a natural restriction of consistent problems. In particular, VCGc mechanisms are the only truthful mechanisms for problems in this class (Theorem 8).

$C^{\text{vcgc}}_{\text{vp}}$. This is a subclass of consistent problems. We prove that every problem in this class admits a truthful VCGc mechanism which also satisfies the *voluntary participation* condition (Theorem 10).

$C^{\text{vcgc}}_{\text{none}}$. This is a class of non-consistent problems in which the set of feasible solutions *depends* on the private part of the input, thus not satisfying one of the constraints of the definition of consistent problem (see Constraint (1) in Def. 4). We show that every VCGc mechanism for such a problem is not truthful (Theorem 15).

$\mathsf{C}_{\mathsf{none}}$. This is a subclass of $\mathsf{C}^{\mathsf{vcgc}}_{\mathsf{none}}$ whose problems do not admit truthful mechanisms (Theorem 20). As this class in non-empty (see Sect. 4.1), our assumption on the set of feasible solutions is necessary (indeed, removing this assumption would give a *superclass* of $\mathsf{C}_{\mathsf{none}}$).

Other problems to which we apply our results are α-RENT TASK SCHEDULING (see Sect. 3.2) and KNAPSACK (see Sect. 4.1).

α-RENT TASK SCHEDULING is a variant of the TASK SCHEDULING problem considered in [13] obtained by modifying the (quasi-linear) utility functions. The resulting problem is consistent, though straightforward reductions to a utilitarian problem do not seem to exist. This shows that the non-existence of an exact mechanism in [13] is due to the "combination" of quasi-linear utilities with a non additive objective function (i.e., the makespan). Finally, the problem does not admit a truthful mechanism satisfying voluntary participation, thus implying that $\mathsf{C}^{\mathsf{vcgc}}_{\mathsf{vp}}$ is a proper subclass of consistent problems.

Concerning KNAPSACK, we consider three variants of this problem depending on which part of the input is held by the agents (namely, the item profits, the item sizes, or both). The corresponding versions belong to $\mathsf{C}^{\mathsf{vcgc}}_{\mathsf{vp}}$, $\mathsf{C}^{\mathsf{vcgc}}_{\mathsf{none}}$ and $\mathsf{C}_{\mathsf{none}}$, respectively. This basic problem has applications to scheduling, resource allocation and to a problem of web advertising [6].

Further related work. Green and Laffont [9] showed that for certain utilitarian problems VCG mechanisms are the only truthful mechanisms. Nisan and Ronen [14] considered the approximability of NP-hard optimization problems via *VCG-based* mechanisms: these mechanisms are obtained from VCG ones by replacing an optimal algorithm $\mathcal{A}$ with a (polynomial-time) non-optimal one $\mathcal{A}'$. Archer and Tardos [3] considered so called *one-parameter* agents: here the valuation functions factor as $v_i(X, t_i) = w_i(X) \cdot t_i$. The authors provided a technique which allows to obtain truthful mechanisms (A, p) whenever A satisfies a "monotonicity" property. To the best of our knowledge this is the only technique other than the VCG one. All above mentioned results apply to the case of quasi-linear utility functions only.

Organization of the paper. We present some basic definitions and notation in Sect. 2. In Sect. 3 we provide the definition of consistent problem, VCGc mechanisms and prove our main positive results. Sect. 3.1 deals with the voluntary participation condition, while Sect. 3.2 contains some applications of our positive results. Finally, we prove the negative results in Sect. 4 where we also apply these results to some of the above mentioned problems. Conclusions and open problems are in Sect. 5. Due to lack of space some details concerning the problems formulation and some proofs are omitted (see also [12]).

2. Preliminaries

Informally, in a mechanism design problem one can imagine that the input $\mathcal{I} = (I_P, I)$ is split into a public and into a private part held by k agents. Public valuation and utility functions express the agents' preferences and how each agent "responds" to incentives. We next provide a formal setting. Without loss of generality, we present the definition for maximization problems.

Given any vector $I = \langle y_1, \ldots, y_k \rangle \in \Theta_1 \times \ldots \times \Theta_k$, let $I_{-i} = \langle y_1, \ldots, y_{i-1}, y_{i+1}, \ldots, y_k \rangle$ and $\langle I_{-i}, x_i \rangle = \langle y_1, \ldots, y_{i-1}, x_i, y_{i+1}, \ldots, y_k \rangle$. Moreover, if $\mathcal{I} = (I_P, I)$, we let $\langle \mathcal{I}_{-i}, x_i \rangle = (I_P, \langle I_{-i}, x_i \rangle)$.

DEFINITION 1 *A* Mechanism Design Maximization (MDMax) *problem is specified as follows:*

- Private instance. *Each agent a_i has available a* private input type $t_i \in \Theta_i$, *where Θ_i denotes the type space of agent a_i which is public knowledge. Given the part of the instance I_P which is* public knowledge, $\mathcal{I}_T = (I_P, I_T)$ *is the* private (or true) instance *specified by the true agents' types $I_T = \langle t_1, \ldots, t_k \rangle$.*
- Reported instance. *Each agent a_i makes public a reported type $r_i \in \Theta_i$; then, for $I_R = \langle r_1, \ldots, r_k \rangle$, the* reported instance $\mathcal{I}_R = (I_P, I_R)$ *is the input provided to the algorithm.*

  In the following, we will often write $\mathcal{I} = (I_P, I)$, for a vector $I = \langle y_1, \ldots, y_k \rangle \in \Theta_1 \times \ldots \times \Theta_k$ to denote any possible input of the algorithm (i.e., any "reportable" instance) as opposed to $\mathcal{I}_T$ and $\mathcal{I}_R$ representing the specific private and reported instances, respectively.
- Feasible solutions. *Given any instance $\mathcal{I} = (I_P, I)$, $\Phi(\mathcal{I})$ denotes the set of feasible solutions, and $\overline{\Phi}(I_P) = \bigcup_{I' \in \Theta_1 \times \ldots \times \Theta_k} \Phi(I_P, I')$. The set of feasible solutions does not depend on the private part of the input, i.e.,*

$$\forall I_P \ \forall I \in \Theta_1 \times \ldots \times \Theta_k, \quad \Phi(I_P, I) = \overline{\Phi}(I_P). \tag{1}$$

- Objective function. *A function $\mu(X, \mathcal{I})$ expresses the measure of a solution X, given any instance $\mathcal{I}$.*
- Valuation functions. *For every agent a_i, a function $v_i(X, t_i)$ expresses the* valuation *of a_i of a solution X, given any value $t_i \in \Theta_i$. The function $v_i(\cdot, \cdot)$ is public knowledge, while one of its arguments is not (namely, the type t_i).*

  We say that a solution X does not involve agent a_i *if $v_i(X, y_i) = v_i^0$, for a fixed value v_i^0 and for every $y_i \in \Theta_i$. We assume that v_i^0 is public knowledge and that, for every X, it is possible to decide whether X does not involve a_i.*
- Agent payments and utility functions. *For every agent a_i it is possible to define a* payment function $p_i(\cdot)$, *representing some sort of incentive for agent a_i. Then, a function $u_i(X, t_i, P_i)$ expresses the* utility *of a_i of a solution X, given its (true) type t_i and given $p_i(\cdot) = P_i$ (this value represents how much a_i benefits if a solution X is output and a_i receives a payment[2] equal to P_i). This function depends only on the values $v_i(X, t_i)$ and P_i, and represents what agent a_i tries to maximize.*

We use the symbol P^0 to denote the fact that a_i receives no payment. In this case, for every X, we have that $u_i(X, t_i, P^0) = v_i(X, t_i)$.

- Goal. *Find an optimal solution for the true instance, that is, a solution $X^* \in \Phi(\mathcal{I}_T)$ such that*

$$\mu(X^*, \mathcal{I}_T) = \max\{\mu(X, \mathcal{I}_T) \mid X \in \Phi(\mathcal{I}_T)\}. \qquad (2)$$

Observe that, because of Constraint (1), it is always possible to obtain a feasible solution. However, our goal is to find an optimal one, which *depends* on the agents' types (i.e., the true instance). In order to solve a **MDMax** problem we need a suitable combination of a payment scheme and an algorithm which guarantees that (i) no agent has an incentive in misreporting her type and (ii) the algorithm, once provided with the true instance $\mathcal{I}_T$, returns an optimal solution for that. In particular, the usual underlying assumption in mechanism design is that an agent misreports her type only in the case this might improve her utility (see e.g. [15]).

DEFINITION 2 (TRUTHFUL MECHANISM) *A* mechanism *for a* **MDMax** *problem is a pair $\mathcal{M} = (\mathcal{A}, \mathcal{P})$, where $\mathcal{A}$ is an algorithm computing a solution $\mathcal{A}(\mathcal{I}_R)$ and $\mathcal{P}(\mathcal{I}_R) = \langle p_1(\mathcal{I}_R), \ldots, p_k(\mathcal{I}_R)\rangle$ is the payment scheme. A mechanism $\mathcal{M} = (\mathcal{A}, \mathcal{P})$ for a* **MDMax** *problem is* truthful *if, for all i,*

$$\forall I_{-i}\ \forall r_i \neq t_i \quad u_i(\mathcal{A}\langle \mathcal{I}_{-i}, t_i\rangle, t_i, p_i\langle \mathcal{I}_{-i}, t_i\rangle) \geq u_i(\mathcal{A}\langle \mathcal{I}_{-i}, r_i\rangle, t_i, p_i\langle \mathcal{I}_{-i}, r_i\rangle).$$

Observe that truthful mechanisms guarantee that, for every a_i, reporting $r_i = t_i$ is the best strategy even when some other agents misreport their type (i.e., $I_{-i} \neq \langle t_1, \ldots, t_{i-1}, t_{i+1}, \ldots, t_k\rangle$).

Another relevant feature of a mechanism is that of guaranteeing that a truthfully behaving agent a_i incurs in a utility which is not worse than the utility she would obtain if not "participating in the game", that is, if a solution X not involving a_i is computed and a_i receives no payment (see Sect. 3.1):

DEFINITION 3 (VOLUNTARY PARTICIPATION) *A mechanism $\mathcal{M} = (\mathcal{A}, \mathcal{P})$ for a* **MDMax** *problem satisfies the* voluntary participation condition (VP) *if*

$$\forall a_i \quad \forall I_{-i} \quad u_i(\mathcal{A}\langle \mathcal{I}_{-i}, t_i\rangle, t_i, p_i\langle \mathcal{I}_{-i}, t_i\rangle) \geq v_i^0.$$

Given an instance $\mathcal{I}$, for the sake of simplicity, we denote by $\mathcal{I}_{-i}$ the instance $\langle \mathcal{I}_{-i}, \perp\rangle$, where $\perp \notin \Theta_i$ is a "dummy" value which makes unfeasible every feasible solution involving agent a_i. In the rest of the paper we consider *optimal mechanisms*, that is, mechanisms $\mathcal{M} = (\mathcal{A}, \mathcal{P})$ that use an algorithm $\mathcal{A}$ computing an optimal solution w.r.t. the *reported instance*. A truthful optimal mechanism provides a solution for a **MDMax** problem: the truthfulness guarantees that the agents, being rational, report their types t_i and then algorithm $\mathcal{A}$ computes a solution $X^* = \mathcal{A}(\mathcal{I}_T)$ satisfying Eq. 2.

3. Truthful mechanisms for consistent problems

In this section we first introduce the class of *consistent problems* (Def. 4) and a family of mechanisms for this class which we call *VCGc mechanisms* (Def. 5). We show that VCGc mechanisms are truthful for consistent problems (Theorem 6) and prove that, under some natural assumptions, VCGc mechanisms are the only truthful mechanisms for consistent problems (Theorem 8).

DEFINITION 4 (CONSISTENT PROBLEM) *A* MDMax *problem is* consistent *if (i) μ is a consistent objective function, i.e., for any instance $\mathcal{I} = (I_P, I)$, with $I = \langle y_1, \ldots, y_k \rangle$, and for any $X \in \Phi(\mathcal{I})$, it holds that $\mu(X, \mathcal{I}) = \bigoplus_i v_i(X, y_i)$, where '$\oplus$' is a suitable operator which enjoys the following properties: associativity, commutativity and monotonicity in its arguments; (ii) the utility function is such that*

$$\forall a_i \quad \forall X \in \overline{\Phi}(I_P) \quad \forall P_i \quad u_i(X, t_i, P_i) = v_i(X, t_i) \oplus P_i.$$

The class of all consistent problems is denoted as consistent.

DEFINITION 5 (VCGC MECHANISMS) *A (optimal) mechanism $(\mathcal{A}, \mathcal{P})$ for a consistent problem is a* VCGc mechanism *if, for all i, there exists a function $h_i(\mathcal{I}_{-i})$ such that, denoted $\mu_{-i}(X, \mathcal{I}) = \bigoplus_{j \neq i} v_j(X, y_j)$:*

$$p_i(\mathcal{I}) = \mu_{-i}(\mathcal{A}(\mathcal{I}), \mathcal{I}) \oplus h_i(\mathcal{I}_{-i}). \tag{3}$$

The following theorem generalizes the (proof of the) analogous result in [10] about the truthfulness of VCG mechanisms for utilitarian problems (i.e., the case '$\oplus$'='$+$'). Noticeably, it exploits Constraint (1) (see [12]).

THEOREM 6 *A VCGc mechanism for a consistent problem is truthful.*

We next show that, under some natural assumptions, VCGc mechanisms are the only truthful mechanisms for consistent problems.

DEFINITION 7 (THE CLASS $\mathsf{C}^{\mathsf{vcgc}}_{\mathsf{only}}$.) *A consistent problem Π belongs to $\mathsf{C}^{\mathsf{vcgc}}_{\mathsf{only}}$ if its operator enjoys the following properties: identity element $i_\oplus$, inverse and strict monotonicity,*[3] *and the type spaces are complete, (i.e., $\forall \mathcal{I}$, $\forall i$, $\{v_i(\cdot, y_i) \mid y_i \in \Theta_i\} = \{f : \Phi(\mathcal{I}) \mapsto \mathbb{R}\}$).*

The proof of the following theorem is a non-trivial adaptation of the proof of a similar result for (a subclass of) utilitarian problems in [9] (see [12]). However, our result is stronger since it shows that *every* consistent problem in $\mathsf{C}^{\mathsf{vcgc}}_{\mathsf{only}}$ has essentially a "unique" truthful mechanism: the VCGc mechanism in Def. 5, where the only degree of freedom is on the definition of the function $h_i(\cdot)$.

THEOREM 8 *Let $(\mathcal{A}, \mathcal{P})$ be a truthful mechanism for a problem $\Pi \in \mathsf{C}^{\mathsf{vcgc}}_{\mathsf{only}}$. Then, $(\mathcal{A}, \mathcal{P})$ is a VCGc mechanism for Π.*

3.1 The voluntary participation condition

In practical applications, agents have the freedom/right to put themselves out of the "game" if the final mechanism outcome (i.e., the utility) turns out to be disadvantageous for them. For example, consider the case in which the valuation $v_i(X, t_i)$ represents a cost required to a_i in order to implement the solution X and $p_i(\mathcal{I}_R)$ is the amount of money that a_i receives for that. Agent a_i has the freedom to refuse the payments and to not implement the solution, if the utility deriving from $v_i(X, t_i)$ and $p_i(\mathcal{I}_R)$ is less than 0 (i.e., the utility in case agent a_i does not perform any work nor receives money).

DEFINITION 9 (THE CLASS C_{vp}^{vcgc}.) *A consistent problem* Π *belongs to* C_{vp}^{vcgc} *if the operator enjoys the following properties: identity element, inverse and strict monotonicity, and*

$$\forall a_i \quad \emptyset \neq \Phi(\mathcal{I}_{-i}) \subseteq \Phi(\mathcal{I}). \tag{4}$$

The following theorem gives a sufficient condition for the existence of VCGc mechanisms which satisfies VP (see Def. 3).

THEOREM 10 *Let* Π *be a consistent problem in* C_{vp}^{vcgc} *and* $(\mathcal{A}, \mathcal{P})$ *be the VCGc mechanism for* Π *with* $h_i(\mathcal{I}_{-i}) = \mu_{-i}(\mathcal{A}(\mathcal{I}_{-i}), \mathcal{I}_{-i})^{-1}$. *Then* $(\mathcal{A}, \mathcal{P})$ *satisfies VP.*

Proof. Consider $X = \mathcal{A}\langle\mathcal{I}_{-i}, t_i\rangle$ and $P_i = p_i\langle\mathcal{I}_{-i}, t_i\rangle$, for any $\mathcal{I}_{-i}$. Since $\mathcal{A}(\mathcal{I}_{-i}) \in \Phi(\mathcal{I}_{-i})$, it holds that $\mu(\mathcal{A}(\mathcal{I}_{-i}), \langle\mathcal{I}_{-i}, t_i\rangle) = \mu_{-i}(\mathcal{A}(\mathcal{I}_{-i}), \mathcal{I}_{-i}) \oplus v_i^0$. Moreover, by Def.s 4 and 5, $u_i(X, t_i, P_i) = v_i(X, t_i) \oplus \mu_{-i}(X, \langle\mathcal{I}_{-i}, t_i\rangle) \oplus h_i(\mathcal{I}_{-i})$, and, by associativity, monotonicity and existence of the inverse:

$$\begin{aligned} u_i(X, t_i, P_i) &= \mu(X, \langle\mathcal{I}_{-i}, t_i\rangle) \oplus \left(\mu_{-i}(\mathcal{A}(\mathcal{I}_{-i}), \mathcal{I}_{-i})^{-1} \oplus (v_i^0)^{-1} \oplus v_i^0\right) \\ &= \mu(X, \langle\mathcal{I}_{-i}, t_i\rangle) \oplus \mu(\mathcal{A}(\mathcal{I}_{-i}), \langle\mathcal{I}_{-i}, t_i\rangle)^{-1} \oplus v_i^0. \end{aligned} \tag{5}$$

>From Condition 4 and from the optimality of $\mathcal{A}$, if follows that $\mu(X, \langle\mathcal{I}_{-i}, t_i\rangle) \geq \mu(\mathcal{A}(\mathcal{I}_{-i}), \langle\mathcal{I}_{-i}, t_i\rangle)$. From the monotonicity of '$\oplus$', we obtain $\mu(X, \langle\mathcal{I}_{-i}, t_i\rangle) \oplus \mu(\mathcal{A}(\mathcal{I}_{-i}), \langle\mathcal{I}_{-i}, t_i\rangle)^{-1} \geq i_\oplus$. This, Eq. 5, the monotonicity of '$\oplus$' yield $u_i(X, t_i, P_i) \geq v_i^0$. Hence the theorem follows. □

3.2 Applications to non-utilitarian problems

We now provide two examples of non-utilitarian consistent problems whose operator is '$\oplus$'='$\cdot$' (the MRP problem) and '$\oplus$'=' min' (the α-RENT TASK SCHEDULING problem).

The MOST RELIABLE PATH **(MRP) problem.** Before introducing the MRP problem, let us consider a general framework in which a truthful mechanism has to be designed on a directed weighted graph $G = (V, E, w)$ that has an edge weight $w_e \in \Theta$ associated with each edge $e \in E$. We are given $s, t \in V$, called the source and the destination, respectively The goal is to find a path from s to t which maximizes the product of the edge weights. Each edge e is owned by a distinct selfish agent a_e [4] which knows the weight $w_e \in \Theta$ (i.e., her type). In the following, we will refer to this problem as a LONGEST MULTIPLICATIVE PATH problem (LMP[Θ]).

The LMP[Θ] problem can be formalized as a consistent problem whenever the valuation functions $v_e(\cdot)$ and the utility functions $u_e(\cdot)$ satisfy

$$v_e(\pi, y_e) = \begin{cases} v_i^0 = 1 & \text{if } e \text{ is not on the path } \pi, \\ y_e & \text{otherwise,} \end{cases} \tag{6}$$

and $u_e(\pi, w_e, P_e) = v_e(\pi, w_e) \cdot P_e$. Since the set of feasible solutions depends ont the topology of the graph only, for 2-connected graphs,[5] Constraint 4 is met. Moreover, for every $\Theta \subseteq \mathbb{R}^+$, the standard product operator is strictly monotone, thus implying that LMP$[\Theta] \in \mathsf{C}_{\mathsf{vp}}^{\mathsf{vcgc}}$. Hence, by Theorem 10 we obtain the following:

COROLLARY 11 *For every $\Theta \subseteq \mathbb{R}^+$, there exists a truthful mechanism $(\mathcal{A}, p)$ for* LMP$[\Theta]$ *which, for 2-connected graphs, also meets VP. In this case, for every $e \in E$, if $X = \mathcal{A}(\mathcal{I}_T)$ and $X_{-e} = \mathcal{A}(\mathcal{I}_{T-e})$:*

$$p_e(\mathcal{I}) = \frac{\mu_{-e}(\mathcal{A}(\mathcal{I}), \mathcal{I})}{\mu_{-e}(\mathcal{A}(\mathcal{I}_{-e}), \mathcal{I}_{-e})} \tag{7}$$

$$u_e(X, t_e, p_e(\mathcal{I}_T)) = \frac{\mu(X, \mathcal{I}_T)}{\mu_{-e}(X_{-e}, \mathcal{I}_{T-e})}. \tag{8}$$

In the following we apply the above result to the MRP problem discussed in Sect. 1. In particular, the message is forwarded from one node to the next one until either (i) the message reaches the destination t or (ii) the link fails. In the latter case, the transmission is lost and a "dummy" message is forwarded throughout the selected path in place of the original one.

In order to satisfy Eq. 6, we use the following rule for the agents' payment. If edge e is not on the chosen path, then the corresponding agent receives a payment equal to $P_e = 1$. Moreover, an agent in the selected path is rewarded after (and only if) her link has *successfully* forwarded the message. Hence, the *true* agent's expected utility is $q_e P_e$. It is easy to see that the MRP problem is the LMP$[(0,1)]$ problem. Corollary 11 implies the existence of a truthful mechanism $(\mathcal{A}, \mathcal{P})$ which, if at least two disjoint st-paths exists, also meets VP. In this case, Eq.s 7 and 8 yield the following intuitive interpretation of payments and of utilities, respectively:

$$p_e(\mathcal{I}_T) = \frac{Pr[\text{no link in } \pi \text{ fails} | \text{ e does not fail}]}{Pr[\text{no link in } \pi_{-e} \text{ fails}]}$$

$$u_e(\pi, q_e, p_e(\mathcal{I}_T)) = \frac{Pr[\text{no link in } \pi \text{ fails}]}{Pr[\text{no link in } \pi_{-e} \text{ fails}]},$$

where π is the best st-path and π_{-e} denotes the best st-path not containing e.

>From Corollary 11 it is possible to obtain analogous results for the ARBITRAGE problem, which is discussed in [12].

The α-RENT TASK SCHEDULING problem. We are given k tasks which need to be allocated to n machines, each of them corresponding to one agent. Let t_j^i denote the minimum amount of time machine i is capable of performing task j and let X_i be the the set of tasks allocated to agent a_i. The goal is to minimize the makespan, that is, the maximum, over all machines, completion time. The type of agent i is given by $t_i = \langle t_1^i, \ldots, t_k^i \rangle$, thus implying $I_T = \langle t_1, \ldots, t_n \rangle$, $I_P = \langle k, n \rangle$ and $\mathcal{I}_T = (I_P, I_T)$. The set of feasible solutions $\Phi(\mathcal{I})$ is the set of all partitions $X = X_1, \ldots, X_n$ of the tasks, where X_i denotes the tasks allocated to agent a_i. For any $\mathcal{I}$, we define

$v_i(X, t_i) = -\sum_{j \in X_i} t_j^i$, that is, the completion time of machine i. Agent a_i is not involved in the solution X if $X_i = \emptyset$. In this case, $v_i(X, \cdot) = 0 = v_i^0$.

We consider the following variant of the TASK SCHEDULING problem defined in [13]. An assignment has to be computed according to the reported types. Each machine i that has been selected (i.e., $X_i \neq \emptyset$) is *rented* for the duration required to perform the tasks assigned to it. The corresponding agent must then receive an amount of money *not larger* than $\alpha - \sum_{j \in X_i} t_j^i = \alpha + v_i(X, t_i)$, where α is a fixed constant equal for all machines. Incentives are provided by defining, for each machine/agent, a *maximum* payment M_i that the machine i will receive if used. In particular, each rented machine is then payed the *minimum* between M_i and $\alpha + v_i(X, t_i)$.

The utility of an agent i is naturally defined as the amount of money derived from the renting of her machine, that is, $\min\{\alpha + v_i(X, t_i), M_i\}$. By letting $P_i := M_i - \alpha$, the previous quantity can be rewritten as

$$\min\{\alpha + v_i(X, t_i), M_i\} = \alpha + \min\{v_i(X, t_i), P_i\}.$$

To formalize the problem as a consistent problem with operator '$\oplus$'='min' it suffices to define $u_i(X, t_i, P_i) = \min(v_i(X, t_i), P_i)$, and to observe that $\mu(X, \mathcal{I}) = \max_{i=1}^n -v_i(X, y_i) = \min_{i=1}^n v_i(X, y_i)$. Hence Theorem 6 implies the following:

COROLLARY 12 *The* α-RENT TASK SCHEDULING *problem is consistent. Hence, it admits a truthful mechanism.*

The fact that the only difference between the α-RENT TASK SCHEDULING problem and the TASK SCHEDULING problem in [13] is on the utility function provides an interesting comparison, since in [13] the authors proved that no exact (or even 2-approximate non-polynomial-time) truthful mechanism exists. Corollary 12 shows that this is due to the fact that the utility functions are quasi-linear.

REMARK 3.1 (ON THE VOLUNTARY PARTICIPATION) *Observe that no mechanism for the* α-RENT TASK SCHEDULING *problem can guarantee the VP condition. Indeed, it suffices to consider instances for which* $\min\{t_j^i\} > \alpha$, *in which case the utilities are always negative. Hence,* α-RENT TASK SCHEDULING $\notin \mathsf{C}_{\mathsf{vp}}^{\mathsf{vcgc}}$.

4. Impossibility results

In this section we investigate extensions of our positive result (Theorem 6) to problems obtained by removing Constraint (1) in the definition of consistent:

DEFINITION 13 (RELAXED CONSISTENT PROBLEM) *A problem is a* relaxed consistent problem *if it satisfies all constraints of Def. 1 except for Constraint (1), as well as the two items in Def. 4. The class of all relaxed consistent problems is denoted as* relaxed consistent.

In Sect.s 4.1 and 4.2 we define two subclasses of relaxed consistent and show that problems in these two classes do not admit truthful VCGc mechanisms (Theorem 15) and truthful mechanisms (Theorem 20), respectively. We also prove that the latter class in included in the former (Theorem 20).

4.1 A class with no truthful VCGc mechanisms

Intuitively speaking, we next consider a class of problems for which some non-feasible solution $\hat{X}$ has a measure strictly better than any feasible solution. Moreover, such an unfeasible solution can be output when reporting a false input $\hat{\mathcal{I}}$, that is, $\hat{X} = \mathcal{A}(\hat{I}) \in \Phi(\hat{\mathcal{I}})$. Formally, we have the following:

DEFINITION 14 (THE CLASS $\mathsf{C}^{\mathsf{vcgc}}_{\mathsf{none}}$.) *A problem Π is said to be in the class $\mathsf{C}^{\mathsf{vcgc}}_{\mathsf{none}}$ if it is relaxed consistent and the following holds: (i) the operator '$\oplus$' satisfies* strict monotonicity; *(ii) there exist i, $\widetilde{I} = \langle \widetilde{y}_1, \ldots, \widetilde{y}_k \rangle$ and $\widehat{y}_i \in \Theta_i$ ($y_i \neq \widehat{y}_i$) such that, for $\widetilde{\mathcal{I}} = (I_P, \widetilde{I})$ and $\widehat{\mathcal{I}} = \langle \mathcal{I}_{-i}, \widehat{y}_i \rangle$, it holds that*

$$\mathcal{A}(\widehat{\mathcal{I}}) \notin \Phi(\widetilde{\mathcal{I}}) \text{ and } \mu(\mathcal{A}(\widehat{\mathcal{I}}), \widetilde{\mathcal{I}}) > \mu(\mathcal{A}(\widetilde{\mathcal{I}}), \widetilde{\mathcal{I}}). \tag{9}$$

THEOREM 15 *No problem $\Pi \in \mathsf{C}^{\mathsf{vcgc}}_{\mathsf{none}}$ admits a truthful VCGc mechanism.*

Proof. Let $(\mathcal{A}, \mathcal{P})$ be a VCGc truthful mechanism for Π and be $\widetilde{X} = \mathcal{A}(\widetilde{\mathcal{I}})$ and $\widehat{X} = \mathcal{A}(\widehat{\mathcal{I}})$. Then: $u_i(\widetilde{X}, \widetilde{y}_i, p_i(\widetilde{\mathcal{I}}))$ = (by Def.s 4, 5) $v_i(\widetilde{X}, \widetilde{y}_i) \oplus (\mu_{-i}(\widetilde{X}, \widetilde{\mathcal{I}}) \oplus h_i(\widetilde{\mathcal{I}}_{-i}))$ = (by associativity of '$\oplus$' and by Def. 4) $\mu(\widetilde{X}, \widetilde{\mathcal{I}}) \oplus h_i(\widetilde{\mathcal{I}}_{-i})$ < (by Eq. 9 and strict monotonicity of '$\oplus$') $\mu(\widehat{X}, \widetilde{\mathcal{I}}) \oplus h_i(\widetilde{\mathcal{I}}_{-i})$ = (by Def.s 13, 14) $u_i(\widehat{X}, \widetilde{y}_i, p_i(\widehat{\mathcal{I}}))$. This contradicts the truthfulness of $(\mathcal{A}, \mathcal{P})$. □

In the following we provide two examples of problems in the class $\mathsf{C}^{\mathsf{vcgc}}_{\mathsf{none}}$ which, by Theorem 15, do not admit a truthful VCGc mechanism: KNAPSACK and the 2ND SHORTEST PATH.

The KNAPSACK problem. We consider the so called variant 0-1 KNAPSACK of the classical optimization problem, which can be described as follows. We are given a set of n items $\{1, \ldots, n\}$, each one characterized by a *profit* π_i and a *size* σ_i. The goal is to find a set of items such that its total occupancy does not exceed a given capacity B and the total profit is maximized. Hence, the set of feasible solutions is $\Phi(\mathcal{I}) = \{X \in \{0,1\}^n \mid \sum_{i=1}^{n} X_i \sigma_i \leq B\}$ and the total profit of a solution $X \in \Phi(\mathcal{I})$ is given by $\mu(X, \mathcal{I}) = \sum_{i=1}^{n} X_i \pi_i$.

Each item i is associated with an agent a_i that holds a part of the instance and derives from the outcome a utility $u_i(X, t_i, P_i) = P_i + v_i(X, t_i)$, where $v_i(X, y_i) = X_i \pi_i$. Depending on how the private part of the instance is defined we distinguish the following three problem versions, which have have a natural application to the use of a shared communication channel of limited capacity and to a problem of "selling" part of a web page (typically, a marginal strip of fixed width/height) for putting some advertisements (see [6] for a description of the model):

- KNAPSACK[π], where each agent a_i only holds the profit $\pi_i = t_i$ associated with each item i, whereas every size σ_i is public knowledge.
- KNAPSACK[σ], where each agent a_i only holds the size $\sigma_i = t_i$ associated with each item i, whereas every profit π_i is public knowledge.
- KNAPSACK[π, σ] where each agent a_i holds both the profit π_i and the size σ_i associated with each item i, that is, $t_i = \langle \pi_i, \sigma_i \rangle$.

It is worth noticing that only KNAPSACK[π] meets Constraint (1), as sizes are public knowledge and $\Phi(\mathcal{I})$ is constant. Then, this proves Theorem16. On the contrary, KNAPSACK[σ] and KNAPSACK[π, σ] satisfy Def. 4 except for Constraint (1). In these case we can state Theorem17.

THEOREM 16 KNAPSACK[π] $\in \mathsf{C}_{\mathsf{vp}}^{\mathsf{vcgc}}$. *Hence, it admits a truthful mechanism which also meets VP.*

THEOREM 17 KNAPSACK[σ], KNAPSACK[π, σ] $\in \mathsf{C}_{\mathsf{none}}^{\mathsf{vcgc}}$. *Hence, they do not admit a truthful VCGc mechanism.*

The 2ND SHORTEST PATH **problem.** Let us consider an undirected weighted graph $G = (V, E, w)$ and two nodes $s, t \in V$. The objective is to find a path whose length is minimal among all st-paths that have no minimal length in G. More formally, for any instance $\mathcal{I} = G$, if Φ_{st} is the set of all st-paths in (V, E) and $X_1^*(\mathcal{I}) \subseteq \Phi_{st}$ is the subset of the shortest st-paths, $\Phi(\mathcal{I}) = \Pi_{st}(\mathcal{I}) \setminus X_1^*(\mathcal{I})$. Similarly to the SHORTEST PATH problem mentioned in [13], the valuation function of the agent owing edge e is equal to

$$v_e(\pi, \mathcal{I}_R) = \begin{cases} -r_e & \text{if } e \in \pi, \\ 0 & \text{otherwise.} \end{cases}$$

Utilities are quasi-linear and the objective function is the total weight of the path, that is, $\sum_{e \in \pi} r_e$. By letting $\mu(\pi, \mathcal{I}_R) = \sum_{e \in \pi} -r_e$, and by observing that $\mu(\pi, \mathcal{I}_R) = \sum_{e \in \pi} v_e(\pi, \mathcal{I}_R)$, we can easily prove the following result:

THEOREM 18 *The* 2ND SHORTEST PATH *problem is in* $\mathsf{C}_{\mathsf{none}}^{\mathsf{vcgc}}$. *Hence, It does not admit a truthful VCGc mechanism.*

In the next section we will strengthen the results of Theorem 17 and of Theorem 18.

4.2 A class with no truthful mechanisms

We next provide a general technique to prove the non-existence of truthful mechanisms for a given problem. We will then apply this result to the KNAPSACK[π, σ] and to the 2ND SHORTEST PATH problems and show that the reason why VCGc mechanisms fail is not due to its weakness.

DEFINITION 19 (THE CLASS $\mathsf{C}_{\mathsf{none}}$.) *A problem Π is said to be in the class $\mathsf{C}_{\mathsf{none}}$ if it relaxed consistent and the following holds: (i) the operator '$\oplus$' satisfies strict monotonicity; (ii) there exist i, ν, $\widetilde{I} = \langle \widetilde{y}_1, \ldots, \widetilde{y}_k \rangle$ and $\widehat{y}_i \in \Theta_i$ ($y_i \neq \widehat{y}_i$) such that, for $\widetilde{\mathcal{I}} = (I_P, \widetilde{I})$ and $\widehat{\mathcal{I}} = \langle \widetilde{\mathcal{I}}_{-i}, \widehat{y}_i \rangle$, it holds that*

$$\begin{aligned} \mathcal{A}(\widehat{\mathcal{I}}) \notin \Phi(\widetilde{\mathcal{I}}) \wedge v_i(\mathcal{A}(\widehat{\mathcal{I}}), \widetilde{y}_i) > v_i(\mathcal{A}(\widehat{\mathcal{I}}), \widehat{y}_i) \wedge \\ v_i(\mathcal{A}(\widehat{\mathcal{I}}), \cdot) \neq \nu \wedge v_i(\mathcal{A}(\widetilde{\mathcal{I}}), \cdot) = \nu. \end{aligned} \tag{10}$$

The class $\mathsf{C}_{\mathsf{none}}$ enjoys the properties stated by the following theorem (see [12]):

THEOREM 20 *The class* $\mathsf{C}_{\mathsf{none}}$ *is included in* $\mathsf{C}^{\mathsf{vcgc}}_{\mathsf{none}}$. *Moreover, no problem* $\Pi \in \mathsf{C}_{\mathsf{none}}$ *admits a truthful mechanism.*

The next result show that, in the case of the 2ND SHORTEST PATH and KNAPSACK$[\pi, \sigma]$ problems, VCGc mechanisms do not fail because inappropriate. Indeed, it can be proved that:

THEOREM 21 *Both the* 2ND SHORTEST PATH *and the* KNAPSACK$[\pi, \sigma]$ *problems are in* $\mathsf{C}_{\mathsf{none}}$. *Hence, none of them admits a truthful mechanism.*

REMARK 4.1 (NECESSITY OF CONSTRAINT (1)) *Observe that if we remove Constraint (1) from the definition of consistent problems, then we obtain the class* relaxed consistent *(Def. 13). Theorem 21 implies that* $\emptyset \neq \mathsf{C}_{\mathsf{none}} \subseteq$ relaxed consistent. *Hence, Constraint (1) is necessary for guaranteeing the existence of truthful mechanisms.*

5. Conclusions and open problems

In the following figure we summarize the results obtained in this work. In particular, we have isolated several classes of problems involving selfish agents which are defined according to some mathematical properties. The inclusions mostly follow

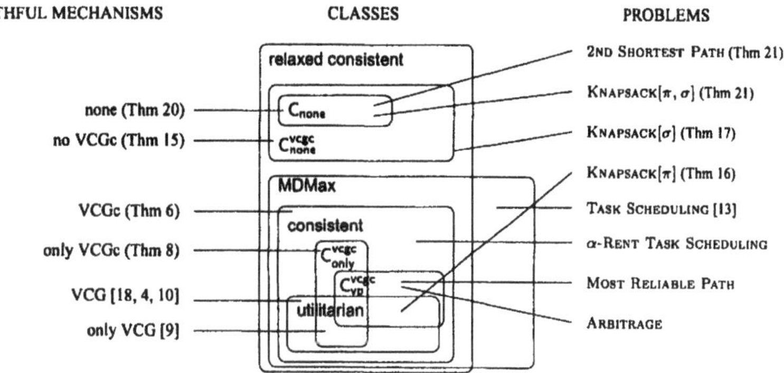

from the definitions, except for the result of Theorem 20. Moreover, the results on the α-RENT TASK SCHEDULING problem and the fact that $\mathsf{C}_{\mathsf{none}} \neq \emptyset$ imply that $\mathsf{C}^{\mathsf{vcgc}}_{\mathsf{vp}} \subsetneq$ consistent $\subsetneq$ relaxed consistent. Since the TASK SCHEDULING problem in [13] can be formulated as a MDMax problem, the negative results in [13] also implies that consistent $\subsetneq$ MDMax. It would be interesting to prove analogous separation results among the classes. For instance, if KNAPSACK$[\sigma]$ had a truthful mechanism, then we would obtain $\mathsf{C}_{\mathsf{none}} \subsetneq \mathsf{C}^{\mathsf{vcgc}}_{\mathsf{none}}$. Combinatorial auction is a classic utilitarian problem (see e.g. [14]) which admits VCG mechanisms only. If would be interesting to find a *non-utilitarian* problem in $\mathsf{C}^{\mathsf{vcgc}}_{\mathsf{only}}$. Comparing $\mathsf{C}^{\mathsf{vcgc}}_{\mathsf{only}}$ and $\mathsf{C}^{\mathsf{vcgc}}_{\mathsf{vp}}$ would be also worthwhile. Investigating classes for which mechanisms that use non-optimal algorithms $\mathcal{A}$ remain truthful is an important issue. Interestingly, Theorem 6 also holds when algorithm $\mathcal{A}$, though non-optimal, is *maximal in its range* (see [14]), thus generalizing one of the results in [14] for utilitarian problems.

Notes

1. We assume that the costs for transmitting are negligible, say equal 0.

2. The term 'payment' does not necessarily mean money as it actually denotes any form of incentive.

3. The inverse of x is denoted by x^{-1} and satisfies $x \oplus x^{-1} = i_{\oplus}$. We say that an operator $\oplus$ satisfies *strict monotonicity* if for every a,a' and b, with $a < a'$, it holds that $a \oplus b < a' \oplus b$.

4. The existence of truthful mechanisms easily extends to a more general setting where each agent owns multiple edges.

5. If the graph is not 2-connected then the problem breaks down to independent subproblems (2-connected components). In this case, it is easy to see that the VP condition cannot be fulfilled.

References

[1] C. Ambuehl, A. Clementi, P. Penna, G. Rossi, and R. Silvestri. Energy Consumption in Radio Networks: Selfish Agents and Rewarding Mechanisms. In *Proc. of SIROCCO*, 1–16, 2003.

[2] L. Anderegg and S. Eidenbenz. Ad hoc-VCG: A Truthful and Cost-Efficient Routing Protocol for Mobile Ad Hoc Networks with Selfish Agents. In *Proc. of ACM MobiCom*, 2003.

[3] A. Archer and E. Tardos. Truthful mechanisms for one-parameter agents. In *IEEE Symposium on Foundations of Computer Science*, 482–491, 2001.

[4] E. Clarke. Multipart pricing of public goods. *Public Choice*, 8:17–33, 1971.

[5] P. Cramton. The fcc spectrum auction: an early assessment. *Journal of Economics and Management Strategy*, 6:431–495, 1997.

[6] B. Dean and M. Goemans. Improved approximation algorithms for minimum-space advertisement scheduling. In *Proc. of ICALP*, LNCS 2719:1138–1152, 2003.

[7] J. Feigenbaum, C.H. Papadimitriou, and S. Shenker. Sharing the cost of multicast transmissions. *Journal of Computer and System Sciences*, 63(1):21–41, 2001.

[8] J. Feigenbaum and S. Shenker. Distributed algorithmic mechanism design: Recent results and future directions. In *Proc. of the 6th International Workshop on Discrete Algorithms and Methods for Mobile Computing and Communications*, 1–13. ACM Press, 2002.

[9] J. Green and J.J. Laffont. Characterization of satisfactory mechanisms for the revelation of preferences for public goods. *Econometrica*, 45(2):727–738, 1977.

[10] T. Groves. Incentives in teams. *Econometrica*, 41(4):617–631, 1973.

[11] K. McMillan. Selling spectrum rights. *Journal of Economic Perspectives*, 145–162, 1995.

[12] G. Melideo, P. Penna, G. Proietti, R. Wattenhofer, and P. Widmayer. *Truthful Mechanisms for Generalized Utilitarian Problems*. Technical report, European Project CRESCCO, available at `http://www.ceid.upatras.gr/crescco/`, 2004.

[13] N. Nisan and A. Ronen. Algorithmic Mechanism Design. In *Proc. of STOC*, 1999.

[14] N. Nisan and A. Ronen. Computationally feasible VCG mechanisms. In *ACM Conference on Electronic Commerce*, 242–252, 2000.

[15] M.J. Osborne and A. Rubinstein. *A course in game theory*. MIT Press, 1994.

[16] C. H. Papadimitriou. Algorithms, Games, and the Internet. In *Proc. of STOC*, 2001.

[17] P. Penna and C. Ventre. Sharing the cost of multicast transmissions in wireless networks. In *Proc. of SIROCCO*, 2004. To appear.

[18] W. Vickrey. Counterspeculation, auctions and competitive sealed tenders. *J. Finance*, 16:8–37, 1961.

THE DRIVING PHILOSOPHERS*

S. Baehni
Distributed Programming Laboratory
EPFL, Switzerland

R. Baldoni
Dipartimento di Informatica e Sistemistica
Università di Roma "La Sapienza", Italy

R. Guerraoui
Distributed Programming Laboratory
EPFL, Switzerland

B. Pochon
Distributed Programming Laboratory
EPFL, Switzerland

Abstract We introduce a new synchronization problem in mobile ad-hoc systems: the Driving Philosophers. In this problem, an unbounded number of driving philosophers (processes) access a round-about (set of shared resources organized along a logical ring). The crux of the problem is to ensure, beside traditional mutual exclusion and starvation freedom at each particular resource, gridlock freedom (i.e., a cyclic waiting chain among processes). The problem captures explicitly the very notion of process mobility and the underlying model does not involve any assumption on the total number of (participating) processes or the use of shared memory, i.e., the model conveys the ad-hoc environment. We present a generic algorithm that solves the problem in a synchronous model. Instances of this algorithm can be fair but not concurrent, or concurrent but not fair. We derive the impossibility of achieving fairness and concurrency at the same time as well as the impossibility of solving the problem in an asynchronous model. We also conjecture the impossibility of solving the problem in an ad-hoc network model with limited-range communication.

*The work presented in this paper was supported by the National Competence Center in Research on Mobile Information and Communication Systems (NCCR-MICS), a center supported by the Swiss National Science Foundation under grant number 5005-67322 and by the Federal Office for Education and Science (OFES) for the PALCOM IST project (Framework VI), under grant number 03.0495-1. Roberto Baldoni has been partially supported by the ministry of the italian universities and research (MIUR) in the context of the project IS-MANET.

Introduction

Whilst 98% of the computers in the world are embedded devices, most research on synchronization is done with the 2% left in mind [7]. One possible reason might be the lack of precisely defined problems for the former case.

In 1971, Dijkstra introduced an intricate synchronization paradigm, the Dining Philosophers problem [6]. The problem crystallizes the difficulty of accessing shared resources, by posing orthogonal constraints, in terms of mutual exclusion, starvation-freedom, and deadlock-freedom. In Dijkstra's problem, the number of processes (i.e., philosophers) is known, as well as the arrangement of processes. Hence the pairs of processes in which conflicts may appear are known. Variants of this problem, in particular the Drinking Philosophers [5], traditionally make the same assumptions.

The motivation behind the Driving Philosophers is to define a problem that crystallizes the difficulty of accessing shared resources amongst mobile processes that communicate through ad-hoc networks. The Driving Philosophers problem was inspired by the practical issue of synchronizing cars in a round-about. Like in the Dining Philosophers, asynchronous processes compete on a set of resources. Unlike in the Dining Philosophers however, the processes do so (a) without a priori knowing the number of participating processes, how many resources they might require, nor how many are available, (b) following a specific order amongst the resources that the processes request (i.e., the resources model the portions of the road in the round-about; the processes are in this sense mobile), and (c) in a system model with no shared memory or any communication medium which would make it possible to reach all processes in the system (ad-hoc network).

In this paper we first precisely define the Driving Philosophers problem. We then give a generic canvas to solve the problem. By instantiating the generic canvas with a set of predicates, we present different modular solutions to the Driving Philosophers in a synchronous model. Synchrony assumptions can be met in practice assuming a typical wireless network, and processes equipped with local GPS receivers. The genericity of our approach allows for investigating several algorithmic flavors. In particular, we introduce the notions of *concurrent* and *fair* algorithms. Roughly speaking, a concurrent algorithm is one that does not deny concurrent accesses to distinct resources, whereas a fair algorithm grants requests following the arrival time. In a precise sense, we show that concurrency and fairness are two antagonistic notions.

We also show that even if no failure is allowed, the Driving Philosophers problem is impossible without assumptions on communication delays and process relative computation speeds (asynchronous model), or specific assumptions on space or arrival rate of participating processes. We also conjecture the impossibility of solving the Driving Philosophers in a synchronous model in which communication is local, i.e., a model in which processes may communicate only using a restricted communication range. We give a proof of this conjecture in a restricted case, and leave the generalization open.

The rest of the paper is organized as follows: In Section 1, we first introduce some basic terminology, then the Driving Philosophers specification. In Section 2, we give our generic canvas solving the Driving Philosophers in a synchronous model. We instantiate our canvas with three different sets of predicates, and introduce our notion of concurrency. In Section 3, we introduce our notion of fairness, and give a new algorithm that complies with this notion. We prove then that concurrency and fairness are antagonistic. In Section 4, we prove the impossibility of solving the Driving Philosophers in the asynchronous model, and we conjecture the impossibility of solving the problem in a model with only limited-range communication. We prove this conjecture in a restricted case. In Section 5, we discuss possible variants of our problem, and present some related works. For space limitations, we postpone all proofs to a companion technical report [2].

1 The Driving Philosophers

Definitions

Processes. We consider a set of processes (philosophers) $\Omega = \{p_0, p_1, \ldots\}$. No process is a priori required to take part in the Driving Philosophers problem. More precisely, we consider that the processes take part to the problem in an uncoordinated manner (i.e, a process may be leaving the problem while another process simultaneously joins the problem). We denote by *participating* processes the set of processes which take part in the problem *at a specific point in time*. Note that the set of participating processes typically changes over time, e.g., when new processes take part in the problem. Every process has a unique identity. Processes communicate by message-passing using the primitives send and receive. The primitive send allows a process to send a message to the current participating processes, whereas the primitive receive allows a process to receive a message sent to it, that it has not yet received. Communication is reliable in the following sense: (*validity*) if a correct process sends a message to a correct process, the message is eventually received, (*no duplication*) each message is received at most once, and (*integrity*) the network does not create nor corrupt messages.

Resources. We consider a set of k resources $\Theta = \{r_0, r_1, \ldots, r_{k-1}\}$. Resources are organized in our case along a ring: $r_{i \oplus 1}$ follows r_i, where $a \oplus b$ (resp. $a \ominus b$) is defined as $(a + b)$ *mod* k (resp. $(a - b)$ *mod* k). Processes ignore the number of resources. Access to any resource may only take place within a *critical section* of code [6]. Before and after executing the critical section of code, any process executes two other fragments of code, respectively the *entry* and *exit* sections. Our problem is to design entry and exit sections, in order to adequately schedule the accesses to resources. A process is mobile in the sense it may request and access different resources at different times. We consider that the entry (resp. exit) section for resource r_s is invoked by process p_i using the primitive *entry*(i, s) (resp. *exit*(i, s)). When a process invokes a procedure for an entry or exit section, this process blocks until the procedure returns. We say that a resource r_s is *requested* by p_i upon the invocation of *entry*(i, s), *granted* to p_i upon returning from *entry*(i, s), and *released* by p_i upon the invocation of *exit*(i, s). We say that a process p_i *owns* a resource r_j at time t if there exists an invocation *entry*(i, s) which returns before time t, such that no invocation *exit*(i, s) occurs between the invocation of *entry*(i, s) and time t. Note that a process may own a resource for a finite but arbitrarily long period of time before releasing it (i.e., it is a "philosopher" in the sense that it may "think" for arbitrarily long).[1] We say that a process p_i is *new*, if p_i does not own any resource prior to invoking *entry*(i, s), for some resource r_s. At any point in time, at most one new process p_i may be requesting a resource r_s. The interaction between a process and its *entry* and *exit* sections are illustrated in Figure 1.

Problem

The Driving Philosophers problem is defined for a set of processes and a set of resources. Informally, any process which takes part in the problem has to access an *ordered* sequence of resources, starting from any resource, such that any resource is accessed by at most a single process at any time. Formally, an algorithm solves the Driving Philosophers problem if, for each of its execution, the following properties hold:[2]

(P1) (Mutual exclusion) No two processes own the same resource at the same time.
(P2) (No starvation) Any requested resource is eventually granted.

Processes are assumed to well behave in the sense that they respect the following conditions.

(B1) A process may request a resource r_s only if it *(i)* owns $r_{s\ominus 1}$ or *(ii)* does not own any resource.
(B2) After releasing every resource it owns, no process ever requests a resource.
(B3) If any process obtains every resource it requests, it eventually releases any resource it owns.

Property B1 defines the *ordering* relation among resources. Property B2 denotes the fact that a process may only take part in the problem at most once. Property B3 ensures that every process eventually releases every resource it owns.

We note that a traditional mutual exclusion algorithm, used to access each resource separately, will ensure properties P1, but may fail to ensure P2. The problem that may arise is *gridlock*, i.e., a situation in which (1) every resource is owned by a process, (2) every process would like to acquire the next resource, and (3) no process releases its current resource (i.e., no process desires to leave the round-about). We explain the gridlock problem in more details in the next paragraph.

Driving versus Dining Philosophers

Our problem differs in several aspects from the Dining Philosophers. Due to the mobility assumption, every process in the Driving case competes for different resources at different times. This fundamentally differs from the Dining case, in which each process repeatedly competes for a single critical section. The processes request resources following a specific order in the Driving case.

[1]Note that this is different from the speed of the cars, on which we make no assumption.
[2]Following [1, 14], our problem specification is broken into safety and liveness properties, as well as well-behaviorness of processes.

Process p_i

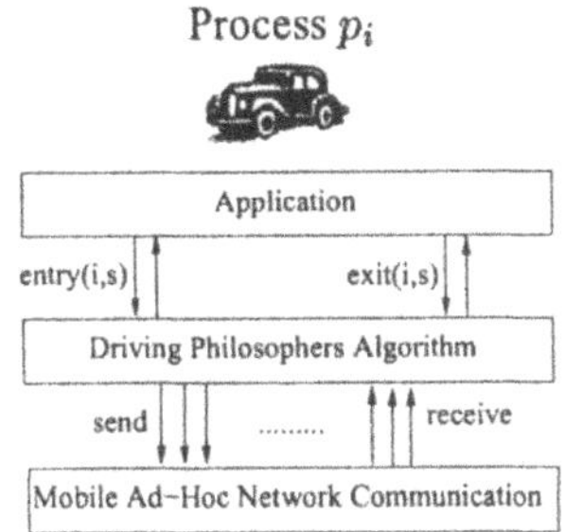

Figure 1. Component layout at process p_i

The major impact of considering mobile processes is the possibility of gridlock. Interestingly this case cannot occur in the Dining case because accessing a critical section first necessitates to acquire both adjacent tokens, which prevents two adjacent processes to access their critical section simultaneously. On the other hand, in the Dining case, processes may deadlock, if every process has acquired the left token and is waiting on the right one to be released. There is no such risk of a deadlock in the Driving case, because two simultaneous accesses to two adjacent resources are not directly conflicting.

In other words, the main difference between the Driving Philosophers problem and the Dining Philosophers lies in the fact that conflicts are not always between the same processes in the Driving case (processes are mobile). One may see the Dining Philosophers as resource-driven (resources are "applied" on a set of processes), whereas the Driving Philosophers is process-driven (processes are "applied" on a set of resources).

2 A Generic Algorithm

A generic algorithm solving the Driving Philosophers problem is presented in this section. We design this algorithm with the analogy between the Driving Philosophers and a round-about in mind, as shown in Figure 2. In this sense we assume that any process p_i which takes part in the problem invokes the entry and exit section procedures in such a way that p_i releases resource r_s, i.e., invokes $exit(i, s)$ before requesting $r_{s\oplus 2}$ (if p_i ever requests $r_{s\oplus 2}$). In this way, any process holds at most two resources at a time. This is an assumption on process well behavior, which could be described together with properties B1, B2 and B3. As such, the algorithm presented in Figure 3 solves a constrained variant of the Driving Philosophers problem.

System Model. We consider a synchronous model,[3] where there exists a known bound on (i) the time it takes for a process to execute a step, and (ii) on the message propagation delay. Computation proceeds in a round-based manner, i.e., processes interact in a synchronous, round-based computational way [14].[4] Roughly speaking, in each synchronous round, every process goes through three phases: in the first

[3]Mobile devices can typically be equipped with a GPS receiver that provides them with the synchrony assumption.

[4]Note that philosophers are still "asynchronous thinkers".

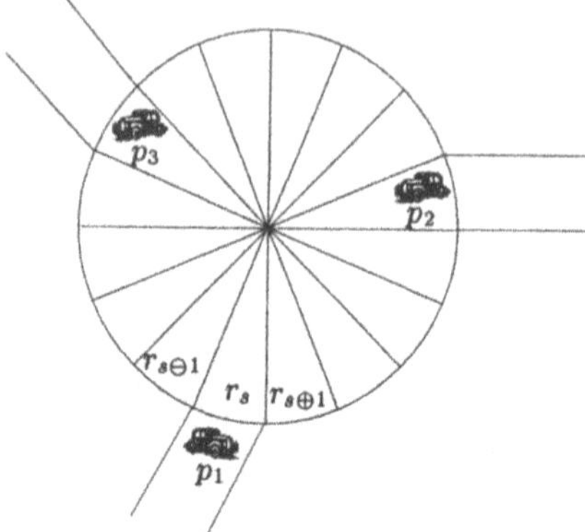

Figure 2. Analogy of the Driving Philosophers problem with a round-about

(send) phase, the process sends a message to the participating processes; in the second (receive) phase, the process receives all messages sent to it; in the third (computation) phase, the process computes the message to send in the next round. Compared with [14], our model differs in the sense that the set of participating processes (in a given round) is not necessarily the whole set of processes, not even necessarily the set of processes that ever take part to the problem.

Configurations and Runs. A *configuration* is an instantaneous cut of the state of the system at the end of a round. Roughly speaking it represents the state of resources and processes participating in the problem at the end of a round. More precisely, a configuration of the system at the end of round r is a tuple $C = \langle Waiting, Driving \rangle$. $Waiting : \Theta \rightarrow 2^{\Omega}$ is a function which gives information about processes in their trying state at the end of round r: for any resource $r_s \in \Theta$, $Waiting(s)$ is the set of processes in the entry section for r_s,[5] and is $\emptyset$ if no process has requested this resource. $Driving : \Theta \rightarrow \Omega \cup \{\perp\}$ is a function which gives information about resources that are occupied at the end of round r: for any resource $r_s \in \Theta$, $Driving(s)$ is the process that owns r_s in C, or $\perp$ if no process owns r_s. A *run* R is a (possibly infinite) sequence of configurations, ordered according to global time, starting from some initial configuration C. We say that a configuration $C = \langle Waiting, Driving \rangle$ is *gridlocked* if $\forall r_s \in \Theta : Driving(s) \neq \perp$.

The Canvas. We first give a generic canvas for the Driving Philosophers problem in Figure 3. Key to this canvas is a predicate that defines when processes are allowed to effectively access a resource. We instantiate this canvas to various algorithms: each algorithm A corresponds to a predicate $pred(A)$. The description of the canvas is divided between the mechanisms ensuring mutual exclusion and starvation freedom.

As far as mutual exclusion is concerned, any process maintains two local sets *pendingRequests.init* and *pendingRequests.transit* of pending requests of processes,

[5]This may represents at most two processes: one in the round-about, transiting through this resource, and one new process.

```
Critical section procedures for p_i:
1: init := true
2: pendingRequests := (∅, ∅)            {(pendingRequests.init, pendingRequests.transit)}
3: starvers := (∅, ∅)                   {(starvers.init, starvers.transit)}
4: resources := ∅
5: acquiring := entryRound := ⊥
6: res_0 := res_1 := ⊥

7: procedure entry(i, s)                 {Entry section for process p_i and resource r_s}
8:    entryRound := r ; acquiring := s   {r is the round number at which entry(i, s) is invoked}
9:    if init then
10:      pendingRequests.init := pendingRequests.init ∪ {(i, s, entryRound)}
11:   else
12:      pendingRequests.transit := pendingRequests.transit ∪ {(i, s, entryRound)}
13:   wait until beginning of next round {To ensure we send our init or transit message}
14:   wait until acquiring = ⊥
15:   return

16: procedure exit(i, s)                 {Exit section for process p_i and resource r_s}
17:   if res_0 = s then res_0 := ⊥ else res_1 := ⊥
18:   return

19: upon beginning of a round r do
20:   resources := ∅
21:   for all j ∈ {0, 1} : res_j ≠ ⊥ do send (RESOURCE, i, res_j, r) to all participating processes
22:   for all (j, s', r') ∈ pendingRequests.init do send (INIT, j, s', r') to all participating processes
23:   for all (j, s', r') ∈ pendingRequests.transit do send (TRANSIT, j, s', r') to all participating processes

24: upon receiving msg = (RESOURCE, j, s', r') do
25:   resources := resources ∪ {(j, s', r')}
26: upon receiving msg = (INIT, j, s', r') do
27:   pendingRequests.init := pendingRequests.init ∪ {(j, s', r')}
28: upon receiving msg = (TRANSIT, j, s', r') do
29:   pendingRequests.transit := pendingRequests.transit ∪ {(j, s', r')}

30: upon end of a round r do
31:   for all (j, s', r) ∈ resources do  {Old init and transit messages are removed}
32:      pendingRequests.init := pendingRequests.init \ {(j, s', *)}
33:      pendingRequests.transit := pendingRequests.transit \ {(j, s', *)}
34:      starvers.init := starvers.init \ {(j, s', *)}
35:      starvers.transit := starvers.transit \ {(j, s', *)}
36:   if ∃(j, s', r') ∈ pendingRequests.init and r' < Starving(entryRound) then
37:      starvers.init := starvers.init ∪ {(j, s', r')}
38:   if ∃(j, s', r') ∈ pendingRequests.transit and r' < Starving(entryRound) then
39:      starvers.transit := starvers.transit ∪ {(j, s', r')}
40:   if acquiring ≠ ⊥ then
41:      if pred(A) then
42:         if res_0 = ⊥ then res_0 := acquiring else res_1 := acquiring
43:         acquiring := ⊥; init := false
```

Figure 3. Canvas for our Driving Philosophers algorithms, instantiated with predicate $pred(A)$

respectively new or in transit.[6] The union of the two sets is denoted by *pendingRequests*. Both sets are updated at the end of each round, with the messages received during the round. Each message consists of a tuple, where the first field is the type of the message (i.e., RESOURCE, INIT, or TRANSIT), the second field is the identifier of the process sending the message, the third field is the identifier of the resource involved, and the fourth field is the round number in which the message is sent. We assume that the sets

[6] A process is *in transit* as soon as it owns a resource.

automatically eliminate duplicate entries. A process p_i that wishes to access a resource sends a message INIT or TRANSIT (depending on whether p_i is new or in transit) with its process identifier and its entry round. When a process p_i owns a resource r_s, p_i announces to the other participating processes that it holds r_s, by sending a message RESOURCE in every subsequent round in which p_i holds r_s. Processes record the set of busy resources in the set *resources*.

As far as starvation freedom is concerned, any process p_i maintains two local sets, *starvers.init* and *starvers.transit*, with the identity of "starving" processes, respectively new or in transit. *starvers* denotes the union of the two sets. To decide whether a process is starving, p_i uses a function $Starving : \mathbf{N} \to \mathbf{N}$, which p_i applies to its own entry round (i.e., the round at which p_i invokes the entry section), stored in variable *entryRound*, and then compares the result with the entry round of other processes. At the end of any round, p_i adds to *starvers* the processes which are waiting since earlier than *Starving*(*entryRound*). Process p_i removes a process from its set *starvers* as soon as p_i receives a message RESOURCE from this process. We let function *Starving* be $Starving(r) = r - \Delta$, where Δ is a constant, for instance $\Delta = 10, 15, 20, \ldots$. Different choices are possible for function *Starving*.

Before accessing any resource, predicate *pred*(A) must hold true for a process to enter. *pred*(A) is defined in a generic way as:

$$
\begin{aligned}
pred(A) \;\triangleq\;\; & predMutex \wedge \\
& [(predInit(A) \wedge \neg predStarvers \wedge \neg predGridlock_i) \vee \neg init\ ] \wedge \\
& [\ predTransit(A) \vee init\ ],
\end{aligned}
$$

where *predInit*(A) and *predTransit*(A) are defined separately for each instance of the canvas, and are respectively evaluated by new processes and processes in transit, as part of *pred*(A). *predMutex* and *predStarvers* are defined as:

$$
\begin{aligned}
predMutex &\triangleq (*, s, r) \notin resources \\
predStarvers &\triangleq starvers \neq \emptyset \wedge (i, *) \neq min_{r',j}\{(j, r') | (j, s', r') \in starvers\},
\end{aligned}
$$

where function *min* (resp. *max*) takes as subscript the variable for which the minimum (resp. the maximum) is considered (in the order of appearance of the variables if more than one). *predMutex* ensures mutual exclusion at the resource and is generic to both new processes and processes in transit. *predStarvers* ensures starvation freedom, by preventing new processes to access a free resource, when there is a starving process (unless the starving process is the process evaluating *predStarvers* itself). $predGridlock_i$ avoids a gridlock, by preventing a new process to access a free resource, when this process could create a cyclic chain of waiting processes. The index i in $predGridlock_i$ allows a process p_j distinct from p_i to evaluate *predGridlock* with p_i's identity. In contrast, the predicates *predMutex* and *predStarvers* are always evaluated by and concerning a single process p_j.

Roughly speaking, $predGridlock_i$ is described as "there may remain no free resource in next round **and** i is the highest process id in INIT messages for free resources with the shortest waiting time **and** p_i does not only receive its own INIT message."

More precisely, let s_{max} be the highest resource identifier process p_i is aware of, from the messages received in previous rounds.[7] *predGridlock*$_i$ is defined as:

$$\begin{aligned} predGridlock_i \triangleq\ & \forall s \in [0, s_{max}] : (*, s, *) \in pendingRequests \cup resources \wedge \\ & (i, *) = max_{r',j}\{(j, r') | (j, s', r') \in pendingRequests.init \wedge \\ & (*, s', *) \notin resources\} \wedge pendingRequests \cup resources \neq \{(i, *, *)\}. \end{aligned}$$

Predicting a gridlock is not easy, because the number of ressources. The idea used in the predicate is to make sure the new configuration always contains at least a free resource. We state a preliminary lemma, in sight of proving the mutual exclusion property of the Driving Philosophers problem, separately from any specific instance of the canvas.

LEMMA 1 *If process p_i owns resource r_s in round r, no process but p_i may own r_s in round $r+1$.*

A Simple Sequential Algorithm. Clearly there are solutions to the Driving Philosophers problem in the synchronous model. A simple algorithm consists in allowing a single process at a time in the round-about. A process p_i, that wishes to access resource r_s, sends a request message to all other participating processes, as soon as p_i takes part in the problem. Process p_i enters the critical section if and only if (a) in the previous round, there was no message from any process in the critical section, and (b) p_i is the process in *pendingRequests.init* which has been waiting for the longest period of time. The algorithm, denoted Serial, is obtained by instantiating the canvas in Figure 3 with the following predicates:

$$\begin{aligned} predInit(\text{Serial}) \triangleq\ & (i, *) = min_{r',j}\{(j, r') | (j, s', r') \in pendingRequests.init\} \wedge \\ & (*, *, r) \notin resources \\ predTransit(\text{Serial}) \triangleq\ & true. \end{aligned}$$

In the next paragraph, we refine our problem. Indeed we forbid such solutions by requiring an additional property to the Driving Philosophers problem.

Concurrency. To avoid sequential solutions such as the one described above, we add a concurrency property to our Driving Philosophers problem. We reformulate the definition of concurrency from [5] in our settings:[8]

(P3) From any configuration C,[9] any invocation of an entry section *entry*(i, s) by p_i for r_s is granted within the minimum number of steps for any entry section

[7] In Figure 3, maintaining s_{max} up-to-date when new messages are received is not shown.

[8] Indeed the very same definition of concurrency ("The solution does not deny the possibility of simultaneous drinking from different bottles by different philosophers") does not apply in our case. In our case for instance, a process cannot enter the round-about if its presence might cause a gridlock, although it may not be in direct conflict with any other process.

[9] Note that in a given configuration C, no process may be starving. Starvation appears when we consider a sequence of configurations, i.e., a run.

invocation to return in any run, unless (1) there is a concurrent entry section invocation for the same resource (contention on r_s), or (2) the configuration resulting if all concurrent yet non-conflicting entry section invocations are granted (including p_i's one) may be gridlocked.

Looking ahead, we introduce a relation $>_c$ to compare different algorithms with respect to their degree of concurrency.

DEFINITION 2 *Let A_1 and A_2 be any two distinct Driving Philosophers algorithms. We say that A_1 is more concurrent than A_2, denoted $A_1 >_c A_2$, if (1) for any configuration C in which any new process p_i has invoked entry(i, s) for resource r_s and pred(A_2) is true at p_i (i.e., for any process p_i which is in its trying section and is going to enter its critical section), then pred(A_1) is true at p_i, and (2) there is a configuration C_0 such that pred(A_1) is true and pred(A_2) is false, at p_i.*

Algorithm Concur1. Roughly speaking, the idea of our first concurrent algorithm, is that processes initially compete to access their first resource; once a process owns a resource, it has priority on the next resource over a new process. The algorithm is defined with the following predicates:

$$\begin{aligned} predInit(\text{Concur1}) &\triangleq (*, s, *) \notin pendingRequests.transit \\ predTransit(\text{Concur1}) &\triangleq true. \end{aligned}$$

THEOREM 3 *Concur1 solves the Driving Philosophers problem, and is concurrent.*

Algorithm Concur2. Roughly speaking, in our second concurrent algorithm, a new process p_i has priority over a process that already owns a resource, unless p_i detects a potential gridlock or a starving process (distinct of p_i). The algorithm is defined by the following predicates:

$$\begin{aligned} predInit(\text{Concur2}) &\triangleq true \\ predTransit(\text{Concur2}) &\triangleq (*, s \oplus 1, *) \notin pendingRequests.init \lor \\ &\quad (\exists (j, s \oplus 1, *) \in pendingRequests.init \land predGridlock_j) \lor \\ &\quad (\exists (j, s', *) \in starvers.init \land s' \neq s \oplus 1). \end{aligned}$$

THEOREM 4 *Concur2 solves the Driving Philosophers problem, and is concurrent.*

3 Local Fairness

It is appealing to define a notion of fairness that takes into account the *position* of a process with respect to the resource(s) it owns. In this section we introduce a new notion of fairness, denoted x-fairness, defined only within a proximity scope, and propose a locally fair algorithm. We relate concurrency with fairness, and prove that our locally fair algorithm cannot be concurrent for most locality values. We first introduce

Δ-starvation,[10] to crystallize the notion of starvation in local fairness. We also introduce, for any resource r_s and any $h \in \mathbf{N}$, a set of resources denoted by $cluster(s, h)$, corresponding to the resources neighboring r_s within a radius of h resources. Finally, we define the resources neighboring the location of a process p_i as $neighborhood(i)$. Formally, we have:

DEFINITION 5 *For any resource r_s, a process p_i is* Δ-starving *if it invokes entry(i, s) in round r, and does not return from the invocation before round $r + \Delta$.*

DEFINITION 6 *For any resource r_s and any $h \in \mathbf{N}$,*
$cluster(s, h) = \{r_{s\ominus\lfloor\frac{h}{2}\rfloor}, \dots, r_s, \dots, r_{s\oplus\lfloor\frac{h-1}{2}\rfloor}\}$.

DEFINITION 7 *For any process p_i, neighborhood$(i) \supseteq \{r_{s\ominus 1}, r_s, r_{s\oplus 1}\}$ if p_i owns r_s or invokes entry(i, s).*

DEFINITION 8 *A Driving Philosophers algorithm is* x-fair *if no new process p_i, before returning from entry(i, s), waits more than any other process that invokes any entry section after p_i to access its first resource within cluster(s, x), unless (1) the configuration resulting if all concurrent yet non-conflicting entry section invocations are granted (including p_i's one) may be gridlocked, or (2) there is (at least) a Δ-starving process.*

THEOREM 9 *There is no concurrent, x-fair algorithm to the Driving Philosophers problem, for any $2 \leq x \leq k$.*

Algorithm x-Fair. This algorithm is x-fair according to Definition 8. In case of possibility of a gridlock or Δ-starvation, processes in transit have a static priority over new processes. The algorithm is defined by the following predicates:

$$predInit(\text{x-Fair}) \triangleq (entryRound, i) \leq min_{r',j}\{(r', j) | \; [(j, s', r') \in pendingRequests.init \wedge s' \in cluster(s, x)] \vee [(j, s', r') \in pendingRequests.transit \wedge s' = s \ominus \lfloor\frac{x}{2}\rfloor]\}$$

$$predTransit(\text{x-Fair}) \triangleq$$
$$\left[(entryRound, i) < min_{r',j}\{(r', j) | (j, s \oplus \lfloor\frac{x}{2}\rfloor, r') \in pendingRequests.init\}\right] \vee$$
$$\left[\exists (j, s \oplus \lfloor\frac{x}{2}\rfloor, r') \in pendingRequests.init \wedge (r', j) < (entryRound, i) \wedge predGridlock_j\right] \vee$$
$$\left[\exists (j, s', *) \in starvers.init \wedge s' \neq s \oplus \lfloor\frac{x}{2}\rfloor\right].$$

Roughly speaking, a new process may access its first resource only if it has been waiting for a longer time than a process in transit, trying to access the same resource. This general rule cannot be satisfied in all cases. More precisely, when there is a risk

[10] In Figure 3, Δ-starvation is hidden behind function *Starving*.

of gridlock or when a new process is starving, any other new process must refrain from accessing the resource, and must give way to processes in transit.

THEOREM 10 *x-Fair solves the Driving Philosophers problem, and is x-fair for any $1 \leq x \leq k$.*

COROLLARY 11 *x-Fair is not concurrent, for any $2 \leq x \leq k$.*

THEOREM 12 *1-Fair is concurrent.*

THEOREM 13 *Concur2 $>_c$ 1-Fair $>_c$ Concur1 $>_c$ Serial.*

4 Impossibility Results

Asynchrony

We consider here an asynchronous model, where the time taken by any process p_i to execute a step is finite but unknown, the time taken by p_i to use any resource r_s is finite but unknown, and processes do not fail. Communication is reliable, in the sense that any message sent is eventually delivered, no spurious messages are created, and no messages are duplicated. Communication is asynchronous in the sense that the message propagation time is finite but unknown, and may be arbitrarily large. Intuitively, mutex is not solvable in this model because we do not know from which processes we may receive messages, and how long we may wait before considering that there is no process to communicate with. The mutex impossibility automatically implies the impossibility of the Driving Philosophers problem in such a model, as the (non-concurrent variant of the) Driving Philosophers reduces to mutex.

THEOREM 14 *There is no solution to the mutex problem in an asynchronous model amongst an arbitrarily large set of processes.*

COROLLARY 15 *There is no solution to the Driving Philosophers problem in an asynchronous model amongst an arbitrarily large set of processes.*

Locality

In this section, we investigate the solvability of the Driving Philosophers problem with *local* communication, revisiting the assumption that all participating processes may directly communicate with each other, but considering that processes may communicate only with *nearby* processes. This local communication assumption is motivated by the limited communication range of typical ad-hoc mobile devices. We conjecture the impossibility of a solution to the Driving Philosophers problem with local communication, and prove it for a restricted case. Informally, we say that communication is h-local for any process p_i, or that p_i h-communicates, if p_i may communicate only with processes whose neighborhood are in the cluster of any resource within p_i's neighborhood. More precisely, let $Scope_i$ be the set of processes to which p_i may send a message, or from which p_i may receive a message. For any process p_i, resource r_s and $h \in \mathbb{N}$, we say that communication is h-local, if $\forall p_j \in Scope_i$, $\exists r_s \in neighborhood(i)$, such that $neighborhood(j) \cap cluster(s, h) \neq \emptyset$.

CONJECTURE 16 *In any Driving Philosophers algorithm, there exists a run of A, for which there exist a process p_i and a resource r_s such that, for any $h \in \mathbb{N}$, between the invocation entry(i, s) and its return, there exists $H > h$ such that p_i H-communicates.*

We prove a weaker proposition, Proposition 18, which corresponds to Conjecture 16 restricted to algorithms belonging to a class we introduce and we denote by ConservativeAlgorithms.

DEFINITION 17 *An algorithm solving the Driving Philosophers belongs to* ConservativeAlgorithms *if any new process p_i may return from its first invocation to entry(i, s) only if no process owns any resource in cluster(s, h).*

PROPOSITION 18 *In any Driving Philosophers algorithm $A \in$ ConservativeAlgorithms, there exists a run of A, for which there exist a process p_i and a resource r_s such that, for any $h \in \mathbb{N}$, between the invocation entry(i, s) and its return, there exists $H > h$ such that p_i H-communicates.*

5 Concluding Remarks

Since Dijkstra's seminal paper [6] which first stated the mutual exclusion (mutex) problem and solved it in a system where processes communicate using shared memory, many mutex solutions have been given. In the message passing model, mutex was first solved by Lamport [12]. Other papers have refined his result, improving the performance of mutex algorithms (e.g. [13]). Several variants of mutex have later appeared in the literature, for instance group mutual exclusion [11], and l-exclusion [8]. In the Dining Philosophers, a fixed set of processes is organized as a ring. The Drinking Philosophers generalizes the ring of the Dining Philosophers to an arbitrary graph of processes, whereas [3] generalizes all philosophers problem as *neighborhood-constrained* problems. [3] however assumes a static configuration of processes and resources. Interestingly, the same generalizations can be made to the Driving Philosophers. This generalization is however orthogonal to the issues raised in this paper, and is subject to future work.

To our knowledge, all attempts to address mutex kind of problems in mobile ad-hoc networks [4, 16] consider weak variants of the problem where mutual exclusion is ensured only when the network is "stable" for a certain period of time.

In fact, another seminal problem in distributed computing, namely consensus, has recently been considered in a model with an unbounded number of processes [15], more precisely, where the participation of any process to the algorithm is not required. The underlying model however assumes a shared memory. Interestingly, consensus is in fact not solvable in our system model (no shared memory), even if we consider strong synchrony assumptions. This conveys an interesting difference between the consensus and mutual exclusion problems, in the kinds of models we consider.

In the channel allocation problem [9], a known set of fixed processes (nodes) communicate through point-to-point asynchronous message passing. Each node knows the list of free resources (frequency bands) in its area and the list of processes' requests for these frequencies. Any node has to grant requests of any process, but not simultaneously with an adjacent node, and for the same frequency. The problem does however not consider starvation issues, as these frequency allocations occur for calls that can be dropped. In the multi-robot grid (MRG) problem [10], a fixed set of robots has to move on a grid to reach specific targets. The number of robots is known and no new robot may enter the grid. Furthermore to reach its target, a robot does not need to follow a specific path.

Acknowledgments

We would like to thank Hagit Attiya for pointing out to us the terminology of gridlock freedom.

References

[1] H. Attiya and J. Welch. *Distributed Computing*. McGraw-Hill, 1998.

[2] S. Baehni, R. Baldoni, R. Guerraoui, and B. Pochon. The Driving Philosophers. Technical Report IC/2004/15, EPFL, Lausanne, 2004.

[3] V. Barbosa and E. Gafni. Concurrency in heavily loaded neighborhood-constrained systems. *ACM Transactions on Programming Languages and Systems*, 11(4):562–584, 1989.

[4] M. Benchaïba, A. Bouabdallah, N. Badache, and M. Ahmed-Nacer. Distributed mutual exclusion algorithms in mobile ad-hoc networks. *ACM Operating Systems Review*, 38(1):74–89, January 2004.

[5] K. M. Chandy and J. Misra. The drinking philosophers problem. *ACM Transactions on Programming Languages and Systems*, 6(4):632–646, 1984.

[6] E. W. Dijkstra. Hierarchical ordering of sequential processes. *Acta Informatica*, 1(2):115–138, 1971.

[7] D. Estrin, R. Govindan, and J. Heidemann. Embedding the internet. *Communication of the ACM*, 43(5):39–41, 2000.

[8] M. Fischer, N. Lynch, J. Burns, and A. Borodin. Resource allocation with immunity to limited process failure. In *IEEE Symposium on Foundations of Computer Science*, pages 234–254, 1979.

[9] N. Garg, M. Papatriantafi lou, and P. Tsigas. Distributed long-lived list colouring: How to dynamically allocate frequencies in cellular networks. *ACM Wireless Network*, 8(1):49–60, 2002.

[10] R. Grossi, A. Pietracaprina, and G. Pucci. Optimal deterministic protocols for mobile robots on a grid. *Information and Computation*, 173:132–142, 2002.

[11] Y. Joung. Asynchronous group mutual exclusion. In *Proceedings of the* 17th *ACM Symposium on Principles of Distributed Computing (PODC'98)*, pages 51–60, 1998.

[12] L. Lamport. The mutual exclusion problem. *Journal of the ACM*, 33(2):313–348, 1985.

[13] L. Lamport. A fast mutual exclusion algorithm. *ACM Transactions on Computer Systems*, 5(1):1–11, February 1987.

[14] N. A. Lynch. *Distributed Algorithms*. Morgan-Kaufmann, 1996.

[15] M. Merritt and G. Taubenfeld. Resilient consensus for infi nitely many processes. In *Proceedings of the* 17th *International Symposium on Distributed Computing (DISC'03)*, pages 1–15, October 2003.

[16] J. Walter, J. Welch, and N. Vaidya. A mutual exclusion algorithm for ad hoc mobile networks. *Wireless Networks*, 9(6):585–600, 2001.

ENGINEERING AN EXTERNAL MEMORY MINIMUM SPANNING TREE ALGORITHM*

Roman Dementiev, Peter Sanders, Dominik Schultes
Max-Planck-Institut f. Informatik, 66123 Saarbrücken, Germany
{dementiev,sanders}@mpi-sb.mpg.de,mail@dominik-schultes.de

Jop Sibeyn
Universität Halle, Institut für Informatik, 06099 Halle, Germany
jopsi@informatik.uni-halle.de

Abstract We develop an external memory algorithm for computing minimum spanning trees. The algorithm is considerably simpler than previously known external memory algorithms for this problem and needs a factor of at least four less I/Os for realistic inputs.

Our implementation indicates that this algorithm processes graphs only limited by the disk capacity of most current machines in time no more than a factor 2–5 of a good internal algorithm with sufficient memory space.

Keywords: secondary memory, random permutation, time forward processing, external priority queue, external graph algorithm

1 Introduction

The high capacity and low price of hard disks makes it increasingly attractive to process huge data sets using cheap PC hardware. However, the large access latency of such mechanical devices requires the design of external memory algorithms that achieve high locality of access. A simple and successful model for external memory assumes a limited fast memory of size M and a large memory that can be accessed in consecutive blocks of size B in one I/O step [2].

While simple algorithmic problems like sorting have very efficient external algorithms, even simple graph problems are quite difficult to solve for general graphs. For example, depth first search has no efficient external solution. Refer to [14, Chapters 3–5] for an overview. One of the most important exceptions is the minimum spanning tree (MST) problem: Consider an undirected connected graph G with n nodes and m edges. Edges have nonnegative weights. A minimum spanning tree

*This work was partially supported by DFG grant SA 933/1-1 and the IST Programme of the EU under contract number IST-1999-14186 (ALCOM-FT).

of G is a subset of edges with minimum total weight that forms a spanning tree of G. If the graph is not connected, most algorithms are easily adapted to find a *minimum spanning forest* (MSF), i.e., a minimum spanning tree of each connected component. The MST problem can be solved in $\mathcal{O}(\text{sort}(m))$ expected I/O steps [1] where $\text{sort}(N) = \mathcal{O}(N/B \log_{M/B} N/B)$ denotes the number of I/O steps required for external sorting [2]. Section 3 gives more details on previous work. We are not aware of any implementations of external MST algorithms. One reason may be that even the simplest previous I/O efficient MST algorithms turn out to be quite complicated to implement. In the full paper we take a more detailed look at some implementation details of previous algorithms and the resulting I/O overheads.

In this paper we describe the design, analysis, implementation, and experimental evaluation of a very simple randomized algorithm for external memory minimum spanning trees.

We begin in Section 4 with a discussion of *semi-external* algorithms that are applicable if $n = \mathcal{O}(M)$, i.e., there is enough internal memory to store a constant number of words for each node. We choose a simple adaptation of Kruskal's algorithm [1] that needs only a single machine word for each node.

If $n > M$, all known external algorithms reduce the number of nodes by *contracting* MST edges: If $e = (u, v) \in E$ is known to be an MST edge, we can remove u from the problem by outputting e and identifying u and v, e.g., by removing node u and renaming an edge of the form (u, w) to a new edge (v, w). By remembering where (v, w) came from, we can reconstruct the MST of the original graph from the MST of the smaller graph. Our main algorithmic innovation is a very simple randomized node reduction algorithm that removes one node at a time from the graph. Section 5 develops this idea from an abstract algorithm over an external realization using priority queues to a bucket based implementation that reduces internal overhead. Besides being simpler and faster than previous node reduction algorithms, our algorithm needs to store each edge only once, whereas previous algorithms store an edge $\{u, v\}$ twice, once as (u, v) and once as (v, u).

The semiexternal algorithm from Section 4 and the node reduction from Section 5 can be combined to an external MST algorithm with expected I/O complexity $\mathcal{O}(\text{sort}(m) \lceil \log(n/M) \rceil)$. This seems to be inferior by a factor of $\log(n/M)$ to the best previous algorithms. However, in Section 2 we argue that $n/M \leq 16$ for any problem that runs on a "well balanced" machine. Hence, $\log(n/M)$ will be a small constant. A comparison with previous algorithms in the full paper indicates that for all such inputs our algorithm uses at least a factor four less I/Os than all previous algorithms. Moreover, if n/M should really get large, our node reduction algorithm could be used to speed up asymptotically better algorithms by a similar constant factor. For graphs that are *sparse under edge contraction* in the sense of [6] (e.g., planar graphs or graphs with bounded tree width), our algorithm achieves asymptotically optimal performance of $\mathcal{O}(\text{sort}(m))$ I/Os.

In Section 7 we report about an implementation using `<stxxl>`,[1] an external implementation of the C++ STL library. Using a PC and 4 cheap disks, the implementation

[1] `http://www.mpi-sb.mpg.de/~rdementi/stxxl.html`

can solve instances with up to 2^{32} nodes using about $5\mu s$ per edge. (About $2.5\mu s$ per edge when the semi-external algorithm suffices.) The best internal algorithm for very sparse graphs — Kruskal's algorithm — needs about 1–1.5 μs per edge for the largest inputs our machine can handle.

2 "Realistic" Input Sizes

In the past few years, the cost ratio between main memory and the same amount of hard disk space has consistently been between 100 and 200. Hence, in a balanced system, the ratio between hard disk capacity and main memory size will be of the same order. Let us assume a disk capacity of $128M$. To represent an edge, algorithms based on edge contraction need at least four words to describe the incident nodes, the edge weight, and the original identity of the edge. Hence, the largest graph we may ever want to process on a balanced machine will have $m \approx 128M/4 = 32M$. If we further assume that the sparsest "interesting" graphs have about $2n$ edges we get $n \leq 16M$. A semiexternal implementation of Kruskal's algorithm needs one machine word per node so that we need node reduction by a factor of at most 16. This factor might be up to five times smaller (non-inplace sorting, edge $\{u, v\}$ stored as (u, v) *and* (v, u) in previous algorithms, five words per edge) or larger (somewhat unbalanced machine, even more sparse graphs). However, the complexity of simple external algorithm as ours only depends logarithmically on this factor so that the error is not very big. We have also slightly "tuned" this discussion in favor of previous algorithms. For example, Boruvka's algorithm is most efficient compared to ours if the reduction factor is a power of two.

3 Related Work

Boruvka's algorithm [4, 17] was the first MST algorithm. Interestingly it is the basis of most "advanced" MST algorithm. Conceptually, the algorithm is very simple: Assume that all edge weights are different. In a *Boruvka phase*, find the lightest incident edge for each node. The set C of these edges can be output as part of the MST. Now contract these edges, i.e., find a representative node for each connected component of (V, C) and rename an edge $\{u, v\}$ to $\{\text{componentId}(u), \text{componentId}(v)\}$. This routine at least halves the number of nodes.

One Boruvka phase can be implemented externally to run with $\mathcal{O}(\text{sort}(m))$ I/Os [1, 3]. To achieve a node reduction by a factor two, our algorithm needs the same asymptotic I/O complexity. However, a detailed analysis in the full paper [8] shows that our algorithm is both simpler and needs a factor around four less I/Os then the most efficient external realization of a Boruvka phase that we could find [3].

Boruvka's original (internal memory) algorithm repeatedly applies Boruvka phases until only a single node remains. In this paper, when we talk about Boruvka's algorithm as an external algorithm, we assume that only $\mathcal{O}(\log(n/M))$ phases are executed before switching to a semiexternal algorithm as described in Section 4. This choice of base case should probably be considered as folklore.

Boruvka phases are also an ingredient of the asymptotically best internal algorithm [10] that runs in expected linear time. This algorithm additionally contains a component for reducing the number of edges based on random sampling. An external implementation of this approach yields an I/O complexity of $\mathcal{O}(\text{sort}(m + n))$ [1]. The authors also discuss a deterministic, recursive, external implementation of Kruskal's algorithm that works in $\mathcal{O}\big(\text{sort}(m) + \frac{m}{n}\text{sort}(n)\log(n/M)\big)$ I/Os. The base case is a graph with $\mathcal{O}(M)$ edges. The full paper gives more details of these algorithms [8].

Several deterministic external algorithms are described by Arge, Brodal, and Toma [3]. They start with an interesting alternative base case. Rather than reducing the number of nodes until a semiexternal algorithm can be used they make the graph so dense that the average node degree is B. Then an external implementation of the Jarník-Prim algorithm [9, 18] takes over that stores edges in a priority queue. The algorithm needs one random I/O for each node but for very dense graphs this I/Os step can be amortized over B edge accesses. We have not used this base case since for current disk technology (a block stores around 2^{16} edges) the semiexternal case is reached much earlier than a case with $E/V \geq B$. Although both our algorithm and the external Jarník-Prim algorithm use an edge priority queue, they are quite different. Our algorithm is a node reduction that does little else than priority queue accesses whereas the external Jarník-Prim algorithm is a base case whose limiting factor are random node accesses. The two algorithms also use different priorities. In particular, our algorithm can be modified to use only a single node index for the priority whereas the external Jarník-Prim algorithm needs to compare edge weights. This can translate into a logarithmic factor difference in internal work. The main result in [3] is an algorithm that reduces the number of nodes by a factor r in $\mathcal{O}(\text{sort}(m+n)\log\log r)$ I/Os rather than $\mathcal{O}(\text{sort}(m+n)\log r)$.

4 Semi-External Algorithms

The base case of our external MST algorithm is a *semiexternal* algorithm that is applicable once the number of nodes is reduced to $\mathcal{O}(M)$. Abello, Buchsbaum, and Westbrook [1] describe two such algorithms.

The simplest one is an adaptation of Kruskal's algorithm: First sort the edges by weight using external sorting. Then the edges are processed in order of increasing weight. Kruskal's algorithm maintains a minimum spanning forest (MSF) F of the edges seen so far. An edge $\{u, v\}$ is put into F if it joins two components in F and is discarded otherwise. The necessary operations can be implemented very efficiently using a union-find data structure [24] if nodes are numbered $0..n-1$.[2] This data structure can be implemented using a *single* array of integers $a[0..n-1]$. If node i is the representative of its component then $a[i] \geq n$ and $a[i] - n$ is its merging rank. Otherwise $a[i]$ stores an index of another node in the component. The pointers of nodes in a component form a tree rooted at the component representative. Since the merging depths reach at most $\lceil \log n \rceil$,[3] a w bit word can represent node indices in the range $0..2^w - w$. For example, using 32 bit words we can represent up to 4 294 967 264 nodes.

The second algorithm needs even less I/Os since it scans the edges in their original, unsorted order. Using dynamic trees [23] it is still possible to maintain the MSF F of the edges seen so far using space $\mathcal{O}(n)$ and time $\mathcal{O}(\log n)$ per edge. However, the

[2] In this paper we use $i..j$ as a shorthand for $\{i, \ldots, j\}$.

[3] In this paper, $\log x$ stands for $\log_2 x$.

constant factors involved make this algorithm not very promising for a practical implementation. Not only are dynamic tree operations much more costly than operations on a union find data structure, but also the savings in I/O volume can be deceptive. For example, the LEDA [13] implementation of dynamic trees needs at least ten times more space for each node than an efficient implementation of the union-find data structure. This means that our algorithm would need $2 \cdot \mathrm{sort}(m) \ln 10$ additional I/Os to reduce the number of nodes sufficiently to make the dynamic tree algorithm applicable.

A scanning based algorithm is still attractive for computing MSTs of fairly dense graphs where the number of nodes is small enough for direct semiexternal treatment. We have not included such graphs into the present study since the I/O aspects of finding MSTs for them are not very interesting. However, it is worth noting that *any* internal MST algorithm with running time $T(n, m)$ can be transformed into a semiexternal MST algorithm that scans the edges once and has internal overhead $\mathcal{O}(\frac{m}{n}T(n, \mathcal{O}(n)))$: The unsorted edges are processed in batches C of size $\Theta(n)$ and we remember the MSF F of the edges seen so far. In each iteration, we set $F := \mathrm{MSF}(C \cup F)$. In practice, one would use Krukal's algorithm or the Jarník-Prim algorithm. A theoretically interesting observation is that together with the linear time randomized algorithm [10] we get a semiexternal MST algorithm with internal overhead $\mathcal{O}(m + n)$.

5 Efficient Node Reduction

Similar to Boruvka's algorithm, our *sweeping algorithm* is based on edge contraction. But the difference is that we identify only one MST edge at a time. The most abstract form of the algorithm is very simple. In each iteration, we remove a random node u from the graph. We find the lightest edge $\{u, v\}$ incident to u. By the well known cut-property that underlies most MST algorithms, $\{u, v\}$ must be an MST edge. So, we output $\{u, v\}$, remove it from E, and *contract* it, i.e., all other edges $\{u, w\}$ incident to u are replaced by edges $\{v, w\}$. If we store the original identity of each edge, we can reconstruct the MST from the edges that are output.

THEOREM 1 *The expected number of edges inspected by the abstract algorithm until the number of nodes is reduced to n' is bounded by $2m \ln \frac{n}{n'}$.*

Proof: In the iteration when i nodes are left (note that $i = n$ in the first iteration), the expected degree of a random node is at most $2m/i$. Hence, the expected number of edges, X_i, inspected in iteration i is at most $2m/i$. By the linearity of expectation, the total expected number of edges processed is

$$\sum_{n'<i\leq n} \mathbb{E}[X_i] \leq \sum_{n'<i\leq n} \frac{2m}{i} = 2m \sum_{n'<i\leq n} \frac{1}{i} = 2m\left(\sum_{1\leq i\leq n} \frac{1}{i} - \sum_{1\leq i\leq n'} \frac{1}{i}\right)$$

$$= 2m(H_n - H_{n'}) \leq 2m(\ln n - \ln n') = 2m \ln \frac{n}{n'}$$

where $H_n = \ln n + 0.577 \cdots + \mathcal{O}(1/n)$ is the n-th harmonic number. ∎

As a first step towards an external implementation, we replace random selection of nodes by *sweeping* the nodes in an order fixed in advance. We assume that nodes

```
ExternalPriorityQueue: Q
foreach (e = (u,v), c) ∈ E do Q.insert(((π(u), π(v)), c, e))          -- rename
currentNode := -1                                        -- node currently being removed
i := n                                                   -- number of remaining nodes
while i > n' do
    ((u,v), c, e_old) := Q.deleteMin()
    if u ≠currentNode then                               -- lightest edge out of a new node
        currentNode := u                                 -- node u is removed
        i--
        relinkTo := v
        output e_old                                     -- MST edge
    elsif v ≠ relinkTo then Q.insert((v, relinkTo), c, e_old)-- relink non-self-loops
```

Figure 1. An external implementation of the sweeping algorithm using a priority queue.

are numbered $0..n-1$. We first rename the node indices using a random permutation $\pi : 0..n-1 \rightarrow 0..n-1$ and then remove renamed nodes in the order $n-1$, $n-2$, $\ldots, n'$.

THEOREM 2 *The sweeping algorithm is equivalent to the abstract node reduction algorithm.*

Proof: In each iteration, the abstract algorithm can be viewed as fixing one value of a random permutation of node indices. It does that by choosing one of the remaining nodes uniformly at random. This exactly emulates the most commonly used algorithm for generating uniformly distributed random permutations [12]. ■

Note that the sweeping algorithm produces a graph with node indices $0..n'-1$, i.e., it can be directly used as input to our semiexternal Kruskal algorithm from Section 4.

5.1 A Priority Queue Implementation

There is a very simple external realization of the sweeping algorithm based on priority queues of edges. Edges are stored in the form $((u,v), c, e_{\text{old}})$ where (u,v) is the edge in the current graph, c is the edge weight, and e_{old} identifies the edge in the original graph. The queue normalizes edges (u,v) in such a way that $u \geq v$. We define a priority order $((u,v), c, e_{\text{old}}) < ((u',v'), c', e'_{\text{old}})$ iff $u > u'$ or $u = u'$ and $c < c'$. With these conventions in place, the algorithm can be described using the simple pseudocode in Figure 1. If e_{old} is just an edge identifier, e.g. a position in the input, an additional sorting step at the end can extract the actual MST edges. If e_{old} stores both incident vertices, the MST edge and its weight can be output directly.

THEOREM 3 *The sweeping algorithm can be implemented to work with $O(\lceil m'/m \rceil \operatorname{sort}(m))$ I/Os if it processes m' edges during its execution. It processes the same number of edges as the abstract algorithm from Theorem 1.*

Proof: Renaming using a random permutation can be done using $\mathcal{O}(\mathrm{sort}(n+m))$ I/Os (e.g. [19]).[4] The algorithm performs only $m + m'$ insertions and the queue size never exceeds m. External priority queues can be implemented to do this using $\frac{m+m'}{m}\mathrm{sort}(m) = \mathcal{O}(\lceil m'/m \rceil\,\mathrm{sort}(m))$ I/Os [5]. Outputting the MST edges takes $\mathcal{O}(n/B)$ I/Os. ■

5.2 A Bucket Implementation

The priority queue implementation unnecessarily sorts the edges adjacent to a node where we really only care about the smallest edge coming first. We now describe an implementation of the sweeping algorithm that has internal work linear in the total I/O volume. We first make a few simplifying assumptions to get closer to our implementation.

The representation of edges and the renaming of nodes works as in the priority queue implementation. As before, in iteration i, node i is removed by outputting the lightest edge incident to it and relinking all the other edges. We split the node range $n'..n-1$ into $k = \mathcal{O}(M/B)$ equal sized *external buckets*, i.e., subranges of size $(n-n')/k$ and we define a special external bucket for the range $0..n'-1$. An edge (u, v) with $u > v$ is always stored in the bucket for u. We assume that the current bucket (that contains i) completely fits into main memory. The other buckets are stored externally with only a write buffer block to accommodate recently relinked edges.

When i reaches a new external bucket, it is distributed to *internal buckets* — one for each node in the external bucket. The internal bucket for i is scanned twice. Once for finding the lightest edge and once for relinking. Relinked edges destined for the current external bucket are immediately put into the appropriate internal bucket. The remaining edges are put into the write buffer of their external bucket. Write buffers are flushed to disk when they become full.

When only n' nodes are left, the bucket for range $0..n'-1$ is used as input for the semi-external Kruskal algorithm from Section 4.

A more general implementation needs a special case for internal buckets that correspond to very high degree nodes. However, although this somewhat complicates the implementation, it will not have a negative effect on running time. On the contrary, nodes with very high degree can be moved to the bucket for the semiexternal case directly. These nodes can be assigned the numbers $n'+1, n'+2, \ldots$ without danger of confusing them with nodes with the same index in other buckets. To accomodate these additional nodes in the semiexternal case, n' has to be reduced by at most $\mathcal{O}(M/B)$ since for $m = \mathcal{O}(M^2/B)$ there can be at most $\mathcal{O}(M/B)$ nodes with degree $\Omega(M)$.

If the overall number of edges gets so large that even an average size external bucket does not fit into internal memory, one has to switch to multi-level distribution schemes. However, the added complexity for this is needed even for sorting so that we remain I/O optimal and work optimal.

[4] In Appendix 1 we give an algorithm that produces pseudorandom permutations directly without additional I/Os.

5.3 Parallel Edges and Sparse Graphs

The basic sweeping algorithm described above can produce parallel edges by relinking. These edges remain parallel during subsequent relinking operations. Parallel edges can be removed relatively easily. When scanning the internal bucket for node i, the edges (i, v) are put into a hash table using v as a key. The corresponding table entry only keeps the lightest edge connecting i and v seen so far.

This leads to an asymptotic improvement for planar graphs, graphs with bounded tree width and other classes of graphs that remain sparse under edge contraction:

THEOREM 4 *Consider a graph that has $\mathcal{O}(n - i)$ edges after any sequence of i edge contractions. Then the sweeping algorithm with removal of parallel edges runs using $\mathcal{O}(\mathrm{sort}(n))$ I/Os.*

Proof: We charge the cost for inspecting (and immediately discarding) a parallel edge to the relinking operation that created the parallel edge. This demonstrates that the algorithm performs only a constant factor more work than an algorithm where parallel edges are not even generated. Since the graph is sparse under edge contraction, $\mathcal{O}(\mathrm{sort}(n))$ I/Os suffice to reduce the number of nodes *and edges* by a factor at least two. Hence, the I/O steps needed for the algorithm obey the recurrence $W(n) \leq \mathcal{O}(\mathrm{sort}(n)) + W(n/2)$. This recurrence has the solution $W(n) = \mathcal{O}(\mathrm{sort}(n))$. ■

6 Implementation

Our external implementation makes extensive use of **<stxxl>**, an external implementation of the C++ standard template library STL. The semiexternal Kruskal and the priority queue based sweeping algorithm become almost trivial using external sorting [7] and external priority queues [20]. The bucket based implementation uses external stacks to represent external buckets. The stacks have a single private output buffer and they share a common pool of additional output buffers that facilitates overlapping of output and internal computation. When a stack is switched to reading, it is assigned additional private buffers to facilitate prefetching.

The internal aspects of the bucket implementation are also crucial. In particular, we need a representation of internal buckets that is space efficient, cache efficient, and can grow adaptively. Therefore, internal buckets are represented as linked lists of small blocks that can hold several edges each. Edges in internal buckets do not store their source node because this information is redundant.

Our implementation deviates in three aspects from the previous description. Edges are stored as 5-tuples of 32 bit integers and store both endpoints of the original edge directly. This saves an additional sorting phase at the end for collecting missing information on the MST edges and it allows us to process more then 2^{32} edges without resorting to cumbersome packed representations with 40 bit edge-ids. Our implementation of the Union-Find data structure uses a separate byte for the merging rank. We have not implemented the special case treatment for nodes of very high degree outlined in Section 5.2 because this case does not occur for the graph families studied in [15]. We saw also no reason to invent or find such graph families since with the special case treatment we could expect them to be easier to solve than other graphs.

In any case, our priority queue based implementation covers this case and performs reasonably well for a single disk.

A more detailed account of the implementation is given in [21] and on the web `http://www.dominik-schultes.de/emmst/`.

7 Experiments

Our starting point for designing experiments was the study by Moret and Shapiro [15]. We have adopted the instance families for *random* graphs with random edge weights and random *geometric* graphs where random points in the unit square are connected to their d closest neighbors. In order to obtain a simple family of planar graphs, we have added *grid* graphs with random edge weights where the nodes are arranged in a grid and are connected to their (up to) four direct neighbors. We have not considered the remaining instance families in [15] because they define rather dense graphs that would be easy to handle semiexternally or they are specifically designed to fool particular algorithms or heuristics. We have chosen the parameters of the graphs so that m is between $2n$ and $8n$. Considerably denser graphs would be either solvable semiexternally or too big for our machine.

The experiments have been performed on a low cost PC-server (around 3000 Euro in July 2002) with two 2 GHz Intel Xeon processors, 1 GByte RAM and 4×80 GByte disks (IBM 120GXP) that are connected to the machine in a bottleneck-free way (see [7] for more details on the hardware). This machine runs Linux 2.4.20 using the XFS file system. Swapping was disabled. All programs were compiled with g++ version 3.2 and optimization level `-O6`. The total computer time spend for the experiments was about 25 days producing a total I/O volume of several dozen Terabytes.

Figure 2 summarizes the results for the bucket implementation. Tables with detailed numerical data can be found in Appendix 2. The internal implementations were provided by Irit Katriel [11]. The curves only show the internal results for random graphs — at least Kruskal's algorithm shows very similar behavior for the other graph classes. Our implementation can handle up to 20 million edges. Kruskal's algorithm is best for very sparse graphs ($m \leq 4n$) whereas the Jarník-Prim algorithm (with a fast implementation of pairing heaps) is fastest for denser graphs but requires more memory. For $n \leq 160\,000\,000$, we can run the semiexternal algorithm and get execution times within a factor of two of the internal algorithm.[5] The curves are almost flat and very similar for all three graph families. This is not astonishing since Kruskal's algorithm is not very dependent on the structure of the graph. Beyond 160 000 000 nodes, the full external algorithm is needed. This immediately costs us another factor of two in execution time: We have additional costs for random renaming, node reduction, and a blowup of the size of an edge from 12 bytes to 20 bytes (for renamed nodes). For random graphs, the execution time keeps growing with n/M as predicted by the upper bound from Theorem 1.

[5] Both the internal and the semiexternal algorithm have a number of possibilities for further tuning (e.g., using integer sorting or a better external sorter for small elements). But none of these measures is likely to yield more than a factor of 2.

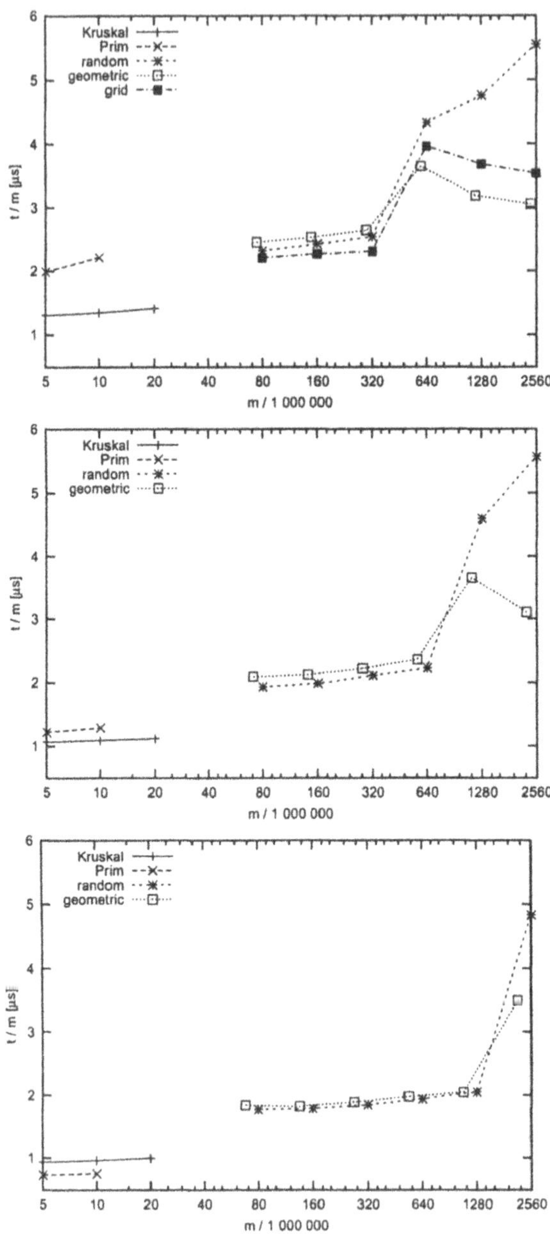

Figure 2. Execution time per edge for $m \approx 2 \cdot n$ (top),$m \approx 4 \cdot n$ (center), $m \approx 8 \cdot n$ (bottom).

The behavior for grid graphs is much better than predicted by Theorem 4. It is interesting that similar effects can be observed for geometric graphs. This is an indication that it is worth removing parallel edges for many nonplanar graphs.[6] Interestingly, the time per edge *decreases* with m for grid graphs and geometric graphs. The reason is that the time for the semiexternal base case does not increase proportionally to the number of input edges. For example, $5.6 \cdot 10^8$ edges of a grid graph with $640 \cdot 10^6$ nodes survive the node reduction, and $6.3 \cdot 10^8$ edges of a grid graph with twice the number of edges.

Another observation is that for $m = 2560 \cdot 10^6$ and random or geometric graphs we get the worst time per edge for $m \approx 4n$. For $m \approx 8n$, we do not need to run the node reduction very long. For $m \approx 2n$ we process less edges than predicted by Theorem 1 even for random graphs simply because one MST edge is removed for each node.

We have made a few runs with even larger graphs. The largest one was a grid graph with $n = 2^{32}$ which takes 96GByte just to represent the input. Even this graph that required an I/O volume of about 830 GByte was processed in about 8h 40min.

The following small table shows running time in μs per edge for random graphs with $n = 320 \cdot 10^6$ and $m = 640 \cdot 10^6$ where we varied the number of disks and where we compare the priority queue implementation with the bucket implementation:

	1 disk	4 disks
bucket implementation	6.7	4.3
priority queue implementation	11.0	8.9

Since the speedup for the bucket algorithm after quadrupling the number of disks is only 1.56, one can conclude that even with a single disk and the internally efficient bucket algorithm, the computation is not I/O-bound. This explains why the bucket implementation brings a considerable improvement over the priority queue implementation. Considering its simplicity, the priority queue implementation is still interesting since it also achieves reasonable performance for a single disk.

8 Conclusions

We have demonstrated that massive minimum spanning tree problems filling several hard disks can be solved "overnight" on a PC. The key algorithmic ingredient for this result is the sweeping paradigm that yields simpler and faster algorithms than previous approaches. This paradigm is also useful for other problems like connected components, list ranking, tree rooting, ... [22]. The efficient and relatively simple implementation profits from the `<stxxl>` library that implements external sorting, priority queues, and other basic data structures in an efficient way using parallel disks, overlapping of I/O and computation, DMA directly to user space, ...

An interesting challenge for the future is whether we can solve even larger MST problems using parallel processors and external memory together. Here, the sweeping paradigm seems to break down and other simplifications of existing algorithms are sought for.

[6] Very few parallel edges are generated for random graphs. Therefore, switching off duplicate removal gives about 13 % speedup for random graphs compared to the numbers given.

Acknowledgments

We would like to thank Irit Katriel for providing the internal implementations and some of the graph generators. Ulrich Meyer was very helpful navigating previous work.

References

[1] J. Abello, A. Buchsbaum, and J. Westbrook. A functional approach to external graph algorithms. *Algorithmica*, 32(3):437–458, 2002.

[2] A. Aggarwal and J. S. Vitter. The input/output complexity of sorting and related problems. *Communications of the ACM*, 31(9):1116–1127, 1988.

[3] L. Arge, G. Brodal, and L. Toma. On external memory MST, SSSP and multi-way planar graph separation. In *7th Scandinavian Workshop on Algorithm Theory*, volume 1851 of *LNCS*, pages 433–447. Springer, 2000.

[4] O. Boruvka. O jistém problému minimálním. *Pràce, Moravské Prirodovedecké Spolecnosti*, pages 1–58, 1926.

[5] Gerth Stølting Brodal and Jyrki Katajainen. Worst-case efficient external-memory priority queues. In *6th Scandinavian Workshop on Algorithm Theory*, number 1432 in LNCS, pages 107–118. Springer Verlag, Berlin, 1998.

[6] Y.-J. Chiang, M. T. Goodrich, E. F. Grove, R. Tamassia, D. E. Vengroff, and J. S. Vitter. External-memory graph algorithms. In *Proceedings of the Sixth Annual ACM-SIAM Symposium on Discrete Algorithms*, pages 139–149, 1995.

[7] R. Dementiev and P. Sanders. Asynchronous parallel disk sorting. In *15th ACM Symposium on Parallelism in Algorithms and Architectures*, pages 138–148, San Diego, 2003.

[8] R. Dementiev, P. Sanders, D. Schultes, and J. Sibeyn. Engineering an external memory minimum spanning tree algorithm — full paper. `http://www.mpi-sb.mpg.de/~sanders/papers/emstfull.ps.gz`, 2004.

[9] V. Jarník. O jistém problému minimálním. *Práca Moravské Přírodovědecké Společnosti*, 6:57–63, 1930. In Czech.

[10] D. Karger, P. N. Klein, and R. E. Tarjan. A randomized linear-time algorithm for finding minimum spanning trees. *J. Assoc. Comput. Mach.*, 42:321–329, 1995.

[11] I. Katriel, P. Sanders, and J. L. Träff. A practical minimum spanning tree algorithm using the cycle property. In *11th European Symposium on Algorithms (ESA)*, number 2832 in LNCS, pages 679–690. Springer, 2003.

[12] D. E. Knuth. *The Art of Computer Programming — Seminumerical Algorithms*, volume 2. Addison Wesley, 2nd edition, 1981.

[13] K. Mehlhorn and S. Näher. *The LEDA Platform of Combinatorial and Geometric Computing*. Cambridge University Press, 1999.

[14] U. Meyer, P. Sanders, and J. Sibeyn, editors. *Algorithms for Memory Hierarchies*, volume 2625 of *LNCS Tutorial*. Springer, 2003.

[15] B.M.E. Moret and H.D. Shapiro. An empirical assessment of algorithms for constructing a minimum spanning tree. *DIMACS Series in Discrete Mathematics and Theoretical Computer Science*, 15:99–117, 1994.

[16] M. Naor and O. Reingold. On the construction of pseudorandom permutations: Luby-Rackoff revisited. *Journal of Cryptology: the journal of the International Association for Cryptologic Research*, 12(1):29–66, 1999.

[17] J. Nešetřil, H. Milková, and H. Nešetřilová. Otakar boruvka on minimum spanning tree problem: Translation of both the 1926 papers, comments, history. *DMATH: Discrete Mathematics*, 233, 2001.

[18] R. C. Prim. Shortest connection networks and some generalizations. *Bell Systems Technical Journal*, pages 1389–1401, November 1957.

[19] P. Sanders. Random permutations on distributed, external and hierarchical memory. *Information Processing Letters*, 67(6):305–310, 1998.

[20] P. Sanders. Fast priority queues for cached memory. In *ALENEX '99, Workshop on Algorithm Engineering and Experimentation*, number 1619 in LNCS, pages 312–327. Springer, 1999.

[21] D. Schultes. External memory minimum spanning trees. Bachelor thesis, Max-Planck-Institut f. Informatik and Saarland University, `http://www.dominik-schultes.de/emmst/`, August 2003.

[22] J. F. Sibeyn. External connected components. In *12th Scandinavian Workshop on Algorithm Theory*, Springer LNCS, 2004. to appear.

[23] D. D. Sleator and R. E. Tarjan. A data structure for dynamic trees. *Journal of Computer and System Sciences*, 26(3):362–391, 1983.

[24] R. E. Tarjan. Efficiency of a good but not linear set merging algorithm. *Journal of the ACM*, 22:215–225, 1975.

Appendix

1 Fast Pseudo Random Permutations

For renaming nodes, we need a (pseudo)random permutation $\pi : 0..n-1 \rightarrow 0..n-1$. Assume for now that n is a square so that we can represent a node i as a pair (a, b) with $i = a + b\sqrt{n}$. Our permutations are constructed from *Feistel* permutations, i.e., permutations of the form $\pi_f((a,b)) = (b, a + f(b) \bmod \sqrt{n})$ for some random mapping $f : 0..\sqrt{n}-1 \rightarrow 0..\sqrt{n}-1$. Since $\sqrt{n}$ is small, we can afford to implement f using a lookup table filled with random elements. For example, for $n = 2^{32}$ the lookup table for f would require only 128 KByte. It is known that a permutation $\pi(x) = \pi_f(\pi_g(\pi_h(\pi_l(x))))$ build by chaining four Feistel permutations is "pseudorandom" in a sense useful for cryptography. The same holds if the innermost and outermost permutation is replaced by an even simpler permutation [16]. In our implementation we use just two stages of Feistel-Permutations. It is an interesting question what provable performance guarantees for the sweep algorithm or other algorithmic problems can be given for such permutations.

A permutation π' on $0..\lceil\sqrt{n}\rceil^2 - 1$ can be transformed to a permutation π on $0..n-1$ by iteratively applying π' until a value below n is obtained. Since π' is a permutation, this process must eventually terminate. If π' is random, the expected number of iterations is close to 1 and it is unlikely that more than three iterations are necessary for *any* input.

2 Detailed Measurement Data

Table A.1. (Semi-)External test cases. n: nodes, m: edges, t: elapsed time, p: processed edges, $E(p)$: expected value of p according to Theorem 1, d: duplicates removed.

type	$n/10^6$	$m/10^6$	$t[s]$	$t/m[\mu s]$	$p/10^6$	$p/E(p)$	d/m
grid	40	80	177	2.21			
grid	80	160	362	2.27			
grid	160	320	738	2.31			
grid	320	640	2 535	3.96	750	85 %	4 %
grid	640	1 280	4 712	3.68	2 492	70 %	13 %
grid	1 280	2 560	9 056	3.54	6 167	58 %	22 %
random	40	80	185	2.32			
random	80	160	388	2.42			
random	160	320	813	2.54			
random	320	640	2 773	4.33	766	86 %	0 %
random	640	1 280	6 098	4.76	2 752	78 %	0 %
random	1 280	2 560	14 202	5.55	7 676	72 %	0 %
random	20	80	155	1.94			
random	40	160	318	1.99			
random	80	320	676	2.11			
random	160	640	1 427	2.23			
random	320	1 280	5 889	4.60	1 651	93 %	0 %
random	640	2 560	14 248	5.57	6 284	89 %	0 %
random	10	80	142	1.77			
random	20	160	286	1.79			
random	40	320	591	1.85			
random	80	640	1 242	1.94			
random	160	1 280	2 627	2.05			
random	320	2 560	12 370	4.83	3 426	97 %	0 %
geometric	40	75	183	2.45			
geometric	80	149	377	2.53			
geometric	160	298	787	2.64			
geometric	320	596	2 175	3.65	644	78 %	7 %
geometric	640	1 190	3 797	3.18	1 949	59 %	13 %
geometric	20	71	148	2.09			
geometric	40	141	300	2.13			
geometric	80	282	627	2.22			
geometric	160	564	1 333	2.36			
geometric	320	1 130	4 126	3.66	1 275	82 %	18 %
geometric	10	68	124	1.84			
geometric	20	135	246	1.82			
geometric	40	270	511	1.89			
geometric	80	540	1 067	1.98			
geometric	160	1 080	2 209	2.04			

SCHEDULING WITH RELEASE TIMES AND DEADLINES ON A MINIMUM NUMBER OF MACHINES *

Mark Cieliebak[1], Thomas Erlebach[2], Fabian Hennecke[1], Birgitta Weber[1], and Peter Widmayer[1]

[1] *Institute of Theoretical Computer Science, ETH Zurich, 8092 Zurich, Switzerland*

cieliebak, hennecke, weberb, widmayer @inf.ethz.ch

[2] *Computer Engineering and Networks Laboratory (TIK), ETH Zurich, 8092 Zurich, Switzerland*

erlebach@tik.ee.ethz.ch

Abstract In this paper we study the SRDM problem motivated by a variety of practical applications. We are given n jobs with integer release times, deadlines, and processing times. The goal is to find a non-preemptive schedule such that all jobs meet their deadlines and the number of machines needed to process all jobs is minimum. If all jobs have equal release times and equal deadlines, SRDM is the classical bin packing problem, which is $\mathcal{NP}$-complete. The *slack* of a job is the difference between its release time and the last possible time it may be started while still meeting its deadline. We show that instances consisting of jobs with slack at most one can be solved efficiently. We close the resulting gap by showing that the problem already becomes $\mathcal{NP}$-complete if slacks up to 2 are allowed. Additionally, we consider several variants of the SRDM problem and provide exact and approximation algorithms.

1. Introduction

In this paper we study the SCHEDULING WITH RELEASE TIMES AND DEADLINES ON A MINIMUM NUMBER OF MACHINES (SRDM) problem: Given n jobs, each associated with a release time, a deadline, and a processing time, what is the minimum number of identical machines that a non-preemptive schedule needs such that all jobs meet their deadlines?

* Work partially supported by the EU Thematic Network APPOL II, IST-2001-32007, with funding provided by the Swiss Federal Office for Education and Science.

The task to process all given jobs within certain time frames and minimize the number of needed machines has recently gained new interest [5] and applies to many practical applications. For example, consider a workshop with a variable number of repairmen. In the morning the boss gets a number of requests from customers. Each customer has a certain time window in which a repairman is allowed to visit. If there is no traveling time between customers, the SRDM problem is equal to finding the minimum number of repairmen needed for this day. If all time windows are equal, SRDM is the classical bin packing problem [8, 10]. On the other hand, if the time window of each customer is exactly the repair time, the number of needed repairmen is the same as the clique number of the corresponding interval graph.

The variant of SRDM where the goal is to decide whether all jobs can be scheduled on one machine is known as "sequencing with release times and deadlines". It is strongly $\mathcal{NP}$-complete [10]. This implies that there cannot be an approximation algorithm for SRDM with ratio $2 - \varepsilon$ for any $\varepsilon > 0$.

Related Work Machine scheduling problems have been the subject of extensive research and numerous publications (see [11] for references). Recently two variants of machine scheduling problems have gained a lot of interest: real-time scheduling [1–3], and the job interval selection problem (JISP) [6, 9, 14]. For the real-time scheduling problem the input consists of n jobs and k machines. Each of the jobs is associated with a release time, a deadline, a weight, and a processing time on each of the machines. The goal is to find a non-preemptive schedule that maximizes the sum of the weights of the jobs that meet their deadlines. The input of the JISP consists of a set of n jobs and an integer value m. Each job consists of a number of intervals on the real line. The goal is to select a subset of intervals with maximum cardinality such that at most one interval is selected for each job, and for any point x on the real line at most m intervals containing x are selected. An optimum schedule for these two problems in general just processes a subset of all jobs.

For the real-time scheduling problem constant approximation algorithms are known. In [2] Bar-Noy et al. presented an LP-based approach, whereas in [1] and [3] Bar-Noy et al., and Berman and DasGupta proposed combinatorial algorithms. If the number of machines for the JISP is one, Spieksma proved in [14] MAXSNP-hardness for this problem and proved that a greedy algorithm gives a 2-approximation. In [6] Chuzhoy et al. presented an $e/(e-1)$-approximation algorithm for JISP.

Very recently Chuzhoy and Naor [5] have studied the machine minimization problem for sets of alternative processing intervals. The input consists of n jobs and each of them is associated with a set of time intervals. A job is scheduled by choosing one of its intervals. The objective is to schedule all jobs on a minimum number of machines. Chuzhoy and Naor [5] have shown that their machine minimization problem is $\Omega(\log\log n)$-hard to approximate unless $\mathcal{NP} \subseteq DTIME(n^{O(\log\log\log n)})$.

Model and Notation Each job of the input is associated with a release time r, a deadline d, and a processing time p, where r, d, and p are integers and $d - r \geq p > 0$. The interval $[r, d)$ is the window in which an interval of size p will be placed. If the size $d - r$ of the window is equal to p, the job occupies the whole window. If the window of a job is larger than its processing time, the choice of a schedule implies for each considered job shifting an interval (the processing interval) into a position within a larger interval (the window). Therefore, we use the notation of interval graphs and *shiftable intervals* [12] $J = \langle r, d, p\rangle$. The difference $\delta = d - r - p$ is the *slack* and corresponds to the maximum amount the interval can be moved within its window. The *flexibility* of an interval in its window is described by the ratio $\tau = \frac{d-r}{p}$.

For every interval we have to select a legitimate position within its window. This position is described by a *placement* $\phi \in \{0, .., \delta\}$. The processing interval according to a placement ϕ is denoted by $J^{\phi} = [r + \phi, r + \phi + p)$. The range within the window that the interval has to occupy for every placement is the *core*. If the slack is smaller than the processing time, the core is the interval $[d - p, r + p)$, otherwise the core is empty.

For an n-tuple $\mathcal{S} = (J_1, .., J_n)$ of shiftable intervals, $\Phi = (\phi_1, .., \phi_n)$ defines a placement, where for $1 \leq i \leq n$ the value ϕ_i is the placement of the shiftable interval J_i. Both $\mathcal{S}$ and Φ together describe a finite collection of intervals $\mathcal{S}^{\Phi} = \{J_i^{\phi_i} \mid i = 1, .., n\}$ and can be interpreted as an interval graph G. For the definition of interval graphs see [4]. Since one machine can process only one job at a time, the maximum number of overlapping intervals corresponds to the minimum number of machines needed to process all jobs. This value is equal to the size of a maximum clique of the interval graph G and can be determined by a sweepline algorithm in time $O(n \log n)$.

The *domain* D of the input is the interval $[r_{\min}, d_{\max})$, where $r_{\min}$ is the earliest release time and $d_{\max}$ is the latest deadline. Let $h(\mathcal{S}^{\Phi}, x)$ be the number of overlapping intervals at point $x \in D$. The maximum number of overlapping intervals over all possible $x \in D$ is the *height of* $\mathcal{S}^{\Phi}$, which is denoted by $h(\mathcal{S}^{\Phi})$. We denote the *minimum height* over all placements by $\widehat{h}(\mathcal{S})$.

The SCHEDULING WITH RELEASE TIMES AND DEADLINES ON A MINIMUM NUMBER OF MACHINES (SRDM) problem is defined as follows:

INSTANCE:	An n-tuple $\mathcal{S}$ of shiftable intervals.
SOLUTION:	A placement Φ.
MEASURE:	The height of the interval set $\mathcal{S}^{\Phi}$.

The decision version of the problem is SRDM(m). An instance is a yes-instance, if and only if a placement Φ exists such that the height of the corresponding set of intervals is less or equal to m.

The interval graph of all non-empty cores of the shiftable intervals in S is the *core graph*. Analogously, the *window graph* is the interval graph of the windows of S. The maximum cliques of the core and window graphs obviously determine lower and upper bounds for $\widehat{h}(S)$.

In this paper we will present algorithms which use the *maximum slack* ($\delta_{\max}$) and *maximum flexibility* ($\tau_{\max}$) over all shiftable intervals. The *height function of a placement* Φ *for* S is a function $D \to \mathbb{N}_0$, where $x \in D$ is mapped to the number of intervals of S^{Φ} which contain the point x.

Our Contribution In this paper, we give several exact and approximation algorithms for the SRDM problem and special cases of it. We start with presenting exact algorithms for the SRDM problem. In Section 2.1 we give a polynomial time algorithm for instances with $\delta_{\max} = 1$. Then we develop two dynamic programs for the decision version SRDM(m). The first one considers instances where the maximum slack is smaller than the minimum processing time. Its running time is exponential in m. The second can be used for any instance. Its running time is exponential in the maximum number of overlapping windows.

In Section 3 we describe several approximation algorithms. We explain how filling machine by machine leads to a $\Theta(\log n)$-approximation to SRDM. For restricted instances we develop algorithms with a constant approximation ratio. We show that for small windows even an arbitrary placement is a good approximation. The Greedy Best Fit algorithm is an asymptotic 9-approximation for instances with equal processing times. This algorithm can be extended for instances with a restricted ratio of processing times. For the general case we show that the number of machines determined by this algorithm can differ from the optimum value by a factor of $\Omega(\log n)$. In addition we study a few special cases. We present an asymptotic 4.62-approximation algorithm for SRDM instances where all jobs have equal release times. If the window graph is a clique we present an asymptotic 14.9-approximation.

Since the SRDM problem is easy to solve if $\delta_{\max}$ is 0 or 1, we aim to understand instances where the slack is bounded. We will prove in Section 4 that the problem is already $\mathcal{NP}$-hard for instances with every fixed $\delta_{\max} \geq 2$.

A full version of this paper can be found in [7].

2. Efficient Solutions for Special Cases

Although the SRDM problem is $\mathcal{NP}$-hard in general, some problem instances can be solved efficiently. In this section we propose a polynomial time algorithm for cases with $\delta_{\max} = 1$ and we present two dynamic programs for restricted instances of SRDM. The first approach deals with instances with small slack compared to the processing times, whereas the second has a polynomial running time if the maximum number of overlapping windows is constant.

2.1 A Polynomial Time Algorithm for SRDM with Maximum Slack 1

Next we present a polynomial time algorithm for SRDM instances with $\delta_{\max} = 1$.

THEOREM 1 *The* SRDM *problem with maximum slack at most* 1 *can be solved in polynomial time.*

Proof. We solve the decision version SRDM(m) and use binary search to determine the minimum value for m. Let the input instance $\mathcal{S} = (J_1, .., J_n)$ with domain D contain k shiftable intervals with slack 1, and $n - k$ shiftable intervals with slack 0. If the height of the cores is greater than m, SRDM(m) is a no-instance.

The placement of a shiftable interval $J = \langle r, d, p \rangle$ with slack 1 is either 0 or 1. Hence, the corresponding interval contains either the point r ($\phi = 0$) or $d-1$ ($\phi = 1$). This observation leads to the following network flow formulation. Initially, the network contains nodes s and q, representing the source and the sink. For every shiftable interval J_i in $\mathcal{S}$ $(1 \leq i \leq n)$ with slack 1 we add a node s_i. Next we introduce a node q_x for every integer value $x \in D$ where the number of overlapping windows at point x is strictly larger than the number of overlapping cores at x. The number of q_x is at most $2k$. The source s is connected by an edge of capacity 1 to all nodes s_i representing a shiftable interval $\langle r_i, d_i, d_i - r_i - 1 \rangle$. The node s_i has two outgoing edges, having capacity 1, to the nodes q_{r_i} and $q_{d_i - 1}$. There is an edge from every q_x to the sink q. Its capacity is the difference between m and the height of the cores at x.

A flow on edge (s_i, q_x) determines a unique placement of the shiftable interval J_i such that it contains x. The capacity on edge (q_x, q) guarantees that $h(\mathcal{S}^\Phi, x)$ is at most m for all $x \in D$. Thus, a maximum flow of size k from s to q returns a placement Φ for the input $\mathcal{S}$ such that $h(\mathcal{S}^\Phi) \leq m$. If the maximum flow is less than k, $\widehat{h}(\mathcal{S})$ is greater than m. The decision version SRDM(m) can be solved in time $O(n^2 \log n)$ using the maximum flow algorithm presented by Sleator and Tarjan [13]. ■

2.2 Dynamic Program for Rather Stiff Instances

In the following we only consider instances $\mathcal{S}$ for SRDM(m) where the maximum slack $\delta_{\max}$ is less than the minimum processing time $p_{\min}$. For those instances the sequence of the jobs on one machine is already determined by their release dates. Thus, if the shiftable intervals $(\langle r_1, d_1, p_1 \rangle, .., \langle r_n, d_n, p_n \rangle)$ are ordered by non-decreasing r_i values, then it is possible to schedule the first

k jobs on m machines if and only if the first $k-1$ jobs can be scheduled in such a way that there exists at least one machine with enough remaining idle time to process the k-th job afterward.

We recursively compute table F, where $F_k(t_1,..,t_m)$ indicates for $k \geq 1$ whether it is possible to schedule the first k jobs such that for all j, $1 \leq j \leq m$, machine j finishes its last job no later than t_j. We start with $F_0(t_1,..,t_m) =$ TRUE for all integers $t_1,..,t_m$ within the domain and recursively define

$$\begin{aligned} &F_k(t_1,..,t_m) = \\ &\quad \bigvee_{j=1}^{m}((F_{k-1}(t_1,..,t_{j-1},t_j-p_k,t_{j+1},..,t_m) \;\wedge\; r_k+p_k \leq t_j \leq d_k) \\ &\qquad \vee(F_{k-1}(t_1,..,t_{j-1},d_k-p_k,t_{j+1},..,t_m) \;\wedge\; t_j > d_k)). \end{aligned}$$

The value of $F_n(d_{\max},..,d_{\max})$, where $d_{\max}$ is the right endpoint of the domain, indicates if all jobs can be scheduled on m machines. If L denotes the width of the domain of the given shiftable intervals, the total effort to calculate the whole table is $O(n \cdot L^m \cdot m)$, where the last factor m results from evaluating the right hand side of the recursion above. So we have the following theorem:

THEOREM 2 *For an instance of* SRDM(m) *with* $\delta_{\max} < p_{\min}$ *there exists a dynamic program that computes the optimum solution with running time* $O(n \cdot L^m \cdot m)$, *where* L *denotes the width of the domain of the instance.*

2.3 Dynamic Program for Bounded Number of Overlapping Windows

THEOREM 3 *The problem* SRDM(m) *can be solved in time* $O(n \cdot (\delta_{\max} + 1)^H \cdot H \log H)$, *where* H *is the maximum number of overlapping windows and* n *the number of shiftable intervals.*

Proof. W.l.o.g. we assume that the window graph for a given n-tuple S of shiftable intervals $\langle r_1,d_1,p_1\rangle,..,\langle r_n,d_n,p_n\rangle$ is connected. Let $\{t_1,..,t_s\}$ be the sorted set of all distinct left window endpoints, with $s \leq n$. For $i = 1,..,s$ let $S_i = \{j \mid r_j \leq t_i < d_j\} \subseteq \{1,..,n\}$ be the set of all indices of shiftable intervals whose windows contain t_i. A local placement P for t_i is a mapping $S_i \to \mathbb{N}_0$ where $P(j) \leq d_j - r_j - p_j$ describes job j's placement.

We say that a local placement P for t_i is feasible if the resulting height of the local placement is at most m, and either $i = 1$ or there exists a feasible local placement Q for t_{i-1} such that $Q(j) = P(j)$ for all $j \in S_{i-1} \cap S_i$.

The program checks for increasing $i = 1,..,s$ the feasibility of all possible local placements for t_i. The information which is relevant for the next step is stored in a table. Assume there exists a feasible local placement P_s for t_s. If $s = 1$ then P_s is a placement of all jobs in S. Otherwise there exists a feasible local placement P_{s-1} for t_{s-1} such that P_s and P_{s-1} place the jobs with indices from $S_{s-1} \cap S_s$ in the same way. Iteratively we know there exists a sequence $P_1,..,P_s$ of feasible placements for $t_1,..,t_s$ which represents a placement for all jobs. On the other hand, if we are given a placement Φ for the input $\mathcal{S}$ such that $h(\mathcal{S}^\Phi) \leq m$, the restriction of Φ to S_s gives a feasible local placement for t_s. Details of the running time analysis are omitted due to space restrictions. ∎

3. Approximation Algorithms for SRDM

In this section, we develop and analyze approximate solutions. We start with an intuitive approach of iteratively filling machines. We show that an arbitrary placement is a good approximation if $\frac{\delta_{max}}{p_{min}}$ is small. We develop the Greedy Best Fit algorithm, which is a good approximation for instances where the processing times do not differ very much. A lower bound for this algorithm is presented as well. Finally, we study approximation algorithms for instances where all windows have one common point.

3.1 A $\Theta(\log n)$-Approximation Algorithm

A greedy 2-approximation algorithm for the job interval selection problem (JISP) is presented in [14]. To solve the SRDM problem we use this algorithm and successively load machines with jobs until no job is left over.

THEOREM 4 *Iteratively filling the machines using a constant approximation algorithm for JISP leads to a* $\Theta(\log n)$*-approximation algorithm for* SRDM.

3.2 Instances with Small Windows

If the ratio of the maximum slack δ_{max} and the minimum processing time p_{min} is small, an arbitrary placement of all shiftable intervals is already a good approximation for SRDM.

THEOREM 5 *An arbitrary placement is a* $(k+1)$*-approximation for* SRDM, *where* $k = \lceil \frac{2\delta_{max}}{p_{min}} \rceil$.

Proof. The proof is by contradiction. Assume that, for an n-tuple $\mathcal{S}$ of shiftable intervals with $\delta_{max} \leq \frac{k}{2} \cdot p_{min}$, there exists a placement Φ and a point x such that $h(\mathcal{S}^\Phi, x) \geq (k+1) \cdot \widehat{h}(\mathcal{S}) + 1$.

Let $\mathcal{T} \subseteq \mathcal{S}$ be the subset of shiftable intervals whose windows contain x. Using an optimum solution, this subset can be partitioned into at most $\widehat{h}(\mathcal{S})$ sets $\mathcal{T}_1,..,\mathcal{T}_t$ such that the height of $\mathcal{T}_i$ is 1. By Φ_i for $i = 1,..,t$ we denote the restriction of Φ to the set $\mathcal{T}_i$. Using an averaging argument we know that for the placement Φ there exists one $v \in \{1,..,t\}$ with $h(\mathcal{T}_v^{\Phi_v}, x) \geq k+2$. The number s of elements in $\mathcal{T}_v$ must be at least $k+2$. Consider a placement Ψ of the shiftable intervals in $\mathcal{T}_v$ with $h(\mathcal{T}_v^\Psi) = 1$. W.l.o.g. we assume the elements in $\mathcal{T}_v$ are sorted such that $r_i + \psi_i < r_{i+1} + \psi_{i+1}$ for $i = 1,..,s-1$.

We consider the points $L = r_1 + p_1 + \psi_1 \geq d_1 - \delta_1$ and $R = r_s + \psi_s \leq r_s + \delta_s$. By definition of $\mathcal{T}_v$ at least k intervals can be placed between L and R, hence $R - L \geq k \cdot p_{\min}$. Since all windows in $\mathcal{T}_v$ contain x we know $d_1 > x \geq r_s$. We obtain $k \cdot p_{\min} \leq R - L \leq r_s + \delta_s - (d_1 - \delta_1) < \delta_s + \delta_1 \leq 2 \cdot \delta_{\max}$, which contradicts our hypothesis. ∎

3.3 The Greedy Best Fit Algorithm

If the ratio between the longest and shortest processing time is bounded we propose the Greedy Best Fit (GBF) algorithm. This algorithm processes the shiftable intervals $\mathcal{S}$ in order of increasing window size. For a job J the algorithm calculates for every placement ϕ the maximum height inside the interval J^{ϕ}. From the subset of placements which lead to the lowest height, it chooses the leftmost.

> $\mathcal{I} = \emptyset$
> **for** $J = \langle r, d, p \rangle \in \mathcal{S}$ in order of increasing window size **do**
>   **for** $\phi = 0, .., r - d - p$ **do** $h_{\max}[\phi] = \max_{x \in J^{\phi}} h(\mathcal{I}, x)$ **end for**
> $h_{\min} = \min\{h_{\max}[\phi] \mid \phi = 0, .., r - d - p\}$
> $\psi_J = \min\{\phi \mid \phi = 0, .., r - d - p \text{ and } h_{\max}[\phi] = h_{\min}\}$
>   add J^{ψ_J} to $\mathcal{I}$
> **end for**

Algorithm 1: GBF-Algorithm

For the analysis of the GBF algorithm, we define the *work* of a set of intervals I in $[a, b]$ as the value $\int_a^b h(I, x)\, dx$. We start with the case where all processing times are equal.

THEOREM 6 *For a* SRDM *instance $\mathcal{S}$ with equal processing times the GBF algorithm returns a placement Φ such that* $h(\mathcal{S}^{\Phi}) \leq 9 \cdot \widehat{h}(\mathcal{S}) + 1$.

Proof. Let $\mathcal{I}$ be the intervals placed by the GBF algorithm. Denote $h = h(\mathcal{I})$. Consider the first shiftable interval $J = \langle r, d, p \rangle$ in $\mathcal{S}$ whose placement increases the height to h. Denote by $I \subseteq \mathcal{I}$ the set of all intervals which have been placed so far, not including J, i.e. $h(I) = h - 1$ and $h(\{J^{\phi}\} \cup I) = h$ for all placements ϕ. The size of J's window is $L = d - r$. Let $I' \subseteq I$ denote the subset of intervals whose intersection with $[r, d)$ is non-empty and denote by W the work of I' in $[r, d]$. Since the size of the windows of all intervals in I' is not greater than L, even an optimal solution has to place them between $r - L$ and $d + L$. It follows $\widehat{h}(\mathcal{S}) \geq \frac{W}{3L}$.

To obtain a lower bound on W, we construct a set of intervals I'' with the following properties: the height of I'' is $h - 1$, any placement of J increases the height to h, and the work of I'' is minimal. Since the placement of J increases the height, there is no range of length p between r and d with height at most $h-2$. Hence, there must be peaks of height $h-1$ at least every $p-1$ points within the interval $[r,d]$. Thus I'' consists of $N = \left\lceil \frac{L-(p-1)}{2p-1} \right\rceil$ peaks of height $h-1$ and width p and we get a lower bound $W \geq N \cdot (h-1) \cdot p$. From the definition of N we have $L \leq N \cdot (2p-1) + p - 1 \leq (2 \cdot N + 1) \cdot p$. Since N is a positive integer, with the bounds on L and W we have $\widehat{h}(\mathcal{S}) \geq \frac{W}{3L} \geq \frac{N(h-1)}{3 \cdot (2N+1)} \geq \frac{h-1}{9}$ ■

The idea of the proof above can be extended to instances with different processing times by constructing the peaks of intervals of size $p_{\max}$ and calculating their work as if they were of size $p_{\min}$. This results in

THEOREM 7 *GBF has asymptotic approximation ratio* $9 \cdot \frac{p_{\max}}{p_{\min}}$ *for* SRDM.

If we partition a given instance of SRDM into subinstances such that the ratios between the maximal and the minimal processing times are bounded by $e \approx 2.718$, we obtain

THEOREM 8 *There exists an asymptotic* $9e \cdot \left\lceil \ln \left(\frac{p_{\max}}{p_{\min}} \right) \right\rceil$*-approximation algorithm to* SRDM.

The GBF algorithm can be implemented using 3 nested for loops. The way we presented it in Algorithm 1 its running time depends on the size of the domain. With some changes the algorithm can be implemented in time $O(n^3)$.

Lower Bound for Greedy Best Fit. Unfortunately for general instances the GBF algorithm does not have a constant approximation ratio.

THEOREM 9 *The height of the GBF algorithm can differ from the optimum by a factor of* $\Omega(\log n)$.

3.4 Constant Approximation for Complete Window Graphs

If the release times of all shiftable intervals are equal and all deadlines are equal as well, we have the classical bin packing problem ([8, 10]). For this problem constant approximation algorithms and asymptotic polynomial time approximation schemes are known. Hence it would be interesting to generalize these results to SRDM instances with a complete window graph.

Equal Release Times. In the following we investigate the case where all release times are 0 but the deadlines differ.

THEOREM 10 *If all release times of shiftable intervals are equal the Divide Best Fit algorithm returns a placement* Φ *with* $h(\mathcal{S}^{\Phi}) < \frac{1}{2}(7+\sqrt{5}) \cdot \widehat{h}(\mathcal{S}) + 1$.

For $\tau_0 = \frac{1}{2} \cdot (1 + \sqrt{5})$ partition the given instance $\mathcal{S}$ into
$\mathcal{S}_f = \{\langle 0, d, p\rangle \in \mathcal{S} \mid \frac{d}{p} \geq \tau_0\}$ and $\mathcal{S}_s = \{\langle 0, d, p\rangle \in \mathcal{S} \mid \frac{d}{p} < \tau_0\}$.
Use the GBF algorithm for $\mathcal{S}_f$.
for $J \in \mathcal{S}_s$ **do** place J at the rightmost position **end for**

Algorithm 2: Divide Best Fit Algorithm

Proof. The Divide Best Fit algorithm splits $\mathcal{S}$ into two sets according to their flexibility values. The set $\mathcal{S}_f$ denotes relatively flexible shiftable intervals where the τ values are at least τ_0. The remaining shiftable intervals $\mathcal{S}_s$ are relatively stiff.

For the flexible set $\mathcal{S}_f$ the GBF algorithm traverses the shiftable intervals by increasing right endpoints. It places the intervals as far to the left as possible such that the height is minimized. This algorithm leads to a collection of intervals $\mathcal{I}_f$ with height ALG_f. It is not difficult to see that $\widehat{h}(\mathcal{S}_f)$ can be bounded by $\widehat{h}(\mathcal{S}_f) \geq \frac{\tau_0 - 1}{\tau_0} \cdot (\text{ALG}_f - 1)$. In the stiff set $\mathcal{S}_s$ all intervals are placed at their rightmost position. The resulting height is at most twice the optimum height.Using the lower bound on $\widehat{h}(\mathcal{S}_f)$ we obtain the stated approximation. ■

Obviously, the Divide Best Fit algorithm can be adapted to solve problem instances where the release times differ and all deadlines are equal.

Window Graph Is a Clique. Next we want to generalize the problem discussed in the previous section and consider instances $\mathcal{S} = (\langle r_1, d_1, p_1\rangle, \ldots, \langle r_n, d_n, p_n\rangle)$ of SRDM where all windows have a common point x. Thus, it holds $r_i \leq x < d_i$ for $1 \leq i \leq n$. We partition $\mathcal{S}$ into three disjoint subsets $\mathcal{S}_L$, $\mathcal{S}_R$ and $\mathcal{S}_C$. The set $\mathcal{S}_L$ contains all members J_i of $\mathcal{S}$ whose cores do not contain x and for which the part of the window left of x is larger than the part to the right of x ($x - r_i > d_i - x$). Similarly, the set $\mathcal{S}_R$ contains all members J_i of $\mathcal{S}$ whose cores do not contain x and for which $x - r_i \leq d_i - x$. The remaining shiftable intervals are in $\mathcal{S}_C$ and have cores overlapping in x. We transform $\mathcal{S}_R$ into $\mathcal{S}_{R|}$ by setting all release times to x, and $\mathcal{S}_L$ into $\mathcal{S}_{L|}$ by setting all deadlines to x. Now we use the Divide Best Fit algorithm to place $\mathcal{S}_{L|}$ and $\mathcal{S}_{R|}$ independently. Finally, we place the intervals in $\mathcal{S}_C$ arbitrarily. To analyze the approximation ratio of the described algorithm, we first show that the height of the optimum solution for $\mathcal{S}_{R|}$ is at most three times the optimal height for $\mathcal{S}_R$.

LEMMA 11 *The minimum height of $\mathcal{S}_{R|}$ can be bounded by $\widehat{h}(\mathcal{S}_{R|}) \leq 3\widehat{h}(\mathcal{S}_R)$.*

Proof. We change the optimum placement for $\mathcal{S}_R$ such that the resulting placement is feasible for the restricted instance $\mathcal{S}_{R|}$ and its height only increases by a factor of three. We change the placements for all shiftable intervals placed to the left of x. If an interval is placed completely to the left of x we replace it with its mirror image where the mirror is at x. This is feasible since the part of the window to the right of x is larger than its remaining part. This operation, carried out for all intervals to which it applies, increases the height of the placement by a factor of at most 2. If the interval is placed such that it contains x, it is shifted to the right of x. This shifting can increase the height by another $\widehat{h}(\mathcal{S}_R)$. We have a new placement where all intervals are placed to the right of x and its height is at most $3 \cdot \widehat{h}(\mathcal{S}_R)$. ∎

The analogous result holds for $\mathcal{S}_{L|}$, too. The height of the optimal placement for $\mathcal{S}$ is at least the minimum height for every single set $\mathcal{S}_L$, $\mathcal{S}_R$, and $\mathcal{S}_C$. Using Theorem 10, the placement computed by the algorithm for $\mathcal{S}_{R|}$ has height at most $\frac{1}{2}(7+\sqrt{5}) \cdot 3\widehat{h}(\mathcal{S}_R) + 1$, and similarly for $\mathcal{S}_{L|}$. Since the domains of $\mathcal{S}_{L|}$ and $\mathcal{S}_{R|}$ are non-overlapping, the height of the overall solution computed by the algorithm is at most $\frac{1}{2}(7+\sqrt{5}) \cdot \max\{3\widehat{h}(\mathcal{S}_L), 3\widehat{h}(\mathcal{S}_R)\} + 1 + |\mathcal{S}_C| \leq \frac{1}{2}(23+3\sqrt{5}) \cdot \widehat{h}(\mathcal{S}) + 1$. This gives the following theorem.

THEOREM 12 *For* SRDM *instances $\mathcal{S}$ where the window graph is a clique, there exists an approximation algorithm such that the resulting height is at most* $\frac{1}{2}(23+3\sqrt{5})\widehat{h}(\mathcal{S}) + 1$.

4. $\mathcal{NP}$-Hardness of SRDM with Maximum Slack 2

As shown in Section 2.1, the SRDM problem is easy to solve if the maximum slack is at most 1. Furthermore a very simple approximation algorithm can be found if the ratio between maximum slack and minimum processing time is small. Hence, it seems as if small slack makes the problem easy. Surprisingly, already if $\delta_{\max} = 2$ the SRDM problem is $\mathcal{NP}$-hard.

THEOREM 13 *The* SRDM *problem with $\delta_{\max} = 2$ is $\mathcal{NP}$-hard.*

Proof. This proof is by reduction from 3-SAT [10]. The input is a set U of variables and a Boolean formula $\mathcal{F}$ in conjunctive normal form. Every clause C contains 3 literals, where a literal is a variable or a negated variable in U. 3-SAT asks for an assignment to U such that $\mathcal{F}$ is satisfied. For a Boolean formula $\mathcal{F}$ having k clauses, we construct a set of shiftable intervals $\mathcal{S}$ such that $\widehat{h}(\mathcal{S}) = 3k$ if and only if $\mathcal{F}$ is satisfiable. W.l.o.g. we assume that every variable in U occurs in $\mathcal{F}$ negated and not negated.

The construction of $\mathcal{S}$ contains generators for variables, clause gadgets and gadgets for copying values of literals. We are going to explain our construction with help of Figure 1.

Generator: For every variable we construct a generator $\mathcal{G}$ with starting point g. In our example they are positioned left, indicated by light-grey boxes. A generator is built out of four shiftable intervals. Two of them have a slack of zero (are *fixed*). Both shiftable intervals with slack greater zero overlap one of

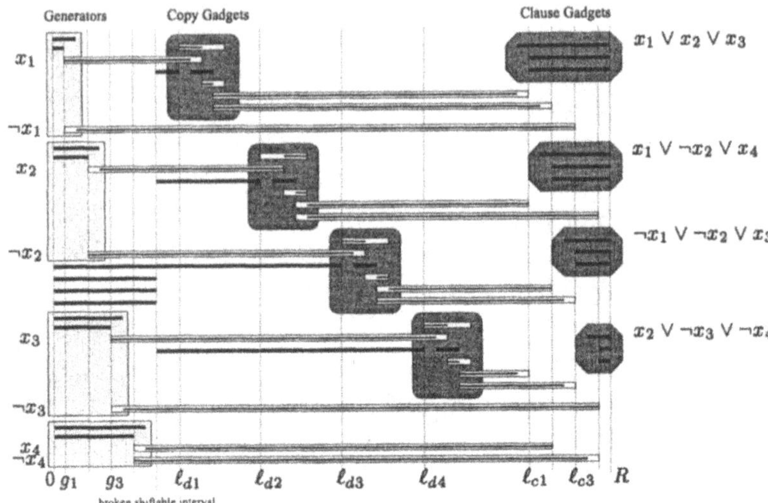

Figure 1. $(x_1 \vee x_2 \vee x_3) \wedge (x_1 \vee \neg x_2 \vee x_4) \wedge (\neg x_1 \vee \neg x_2 \vee x_3) \wedge (x_2 \vee \neg x_3 \vee \neg x_4)$

the fixed intervals by 1 unit. These two represent both literals of the variable. Only one of its literals can be TRUE. An interval in its leftmost position is interpreted as a literal set to TRUE. Otherwise the literal is set to FALSE.

$$\mathcal{G} = (\langle 0, g+1, g+1 \rangle, \langle 0, g, g \rangle, \underbrace{\langle g, r_1, r_1 - g - 1 \rangle, \langle g, r_2, r_2 - g - 1 \rangle}_{x, \neg x})$$

The endpoints r_1, r_2 of the windows are defined by a starting point of a copy gadget, or by a clause. Since $\widehat{h}(\mathcal{G}) = 2$, at least one of the intervals has to be shifted to the right and represents a literal which is FALSE. Observe that both shiftable intervals starting at g can be shifted to the right, and thus represent false. Then the corresponding variable will not contribute to the result.

Copy Gadget for Values of Literals: In $\mathcal{F}$ a literal can occur more than once. Thus, the construction of $\mathcal{S}$ has to ensure that all shiftable intervals representing the same literal have the same value. To copy values of literals a *copy gadget* with the following form is used:

$$\mathcal{D} = (\underbrace{\langle \ell, \ell_d + 2, \ell_d - \ell + 1 \rangle}_{\text{original literal}}, \underbrace{\langle 0, \ell_d, \ell_d \rangle}_{\text{place holder}}, \langle \ell_d, \ell_d + 4, 2 \rangle, \langle \ell_d + 1, \ell_d + 3, 2 \rangle,$$
$$\langle \ell_d + 2, \ell_d + 4, 1 \rangle, \underbrace{\langle \ell_d + 3, r_1, r_1 - \ell_d - 4 \rangle, \langle \ell_d + 3, r_2, r_2 - \ell_d - 4 \rangle}_{\text{two copies}})$$

In the example these gadgets are depicted by boxes with round corners. Within the copy gadget exists only one shiftable interval with slack 2. The value ℓ_d represents the starting point of the copy gadget.

To not exceed $\widehat{h}(\mathcal{D}) = 2$ the copy gadget has to work in the following way: If the original literal is placed left, both copies can also be placed left without exceeding height 2. On the other hand, if the original interval is shifted to the right, both copies have to be shifted to the right in order to obtain the minimum height for this gadget.

Observe that for every copy gadget we introduce one shiftable interval with slack zero starting at zero. To simplify Figure 1 we split some of these intervals into two parts. It is always possible to shift an interval representing a literal to its right endpoint, even if it could also be placed left. This would set the corresponding literal to FALSE. The important point is: if once a literal is set to FALSE, all copies of this literal will represent FALSE as well.

The Clause Gadget: For every clause a *clause gadget* is constructed. In Figure 1 these gadgets are octagons and placed at the right end. Every gadget is built out of three shiftable intervals representing literals and three shiftable intervals with zero slack.

$$C = (\underbrace{\langle \ell_1, \ell_c, \ell_c - \ell_1 - 1\rangle, \langle \ell_2, \ell_c, \ell_c - \ell_2 - 1\rangle, \langle \ell_3, \ell_c, \ell_c - \ell_3 - 1\rangle}_{\text{literal intervals}},$$

$$\langle \ell_c - 1, R, R - \ell_c + 1\rangle, \langle \ell_c, R, R - \ell_c\rangle, \langle \ell_c, R, R - \ell_c\rangle) \text{ for some } R > \ell_c$$

The starting points of the literals are defined either by a generator or by a copy gadget. To not exceed $\widehat{h}(C) = 3$, at most 2 of the literals can be shifted to the right (FALSE). Hence, at least one literal must not be shifted – and represents a TRUE literal. A clause gadget C has its left starting point at an appropriate position ℓ_c defined by the placement. As indicated in Figure 1, the value R has to be the same value for all clauses in $\mathcal{F}$.

Placement of Components: All gadgets have to be placed independently of each other. As shown in the example, the starting points of the generators differ and the copy gadgets have their starting points one after the other without influencing each other. At the right end of the domain the clause gadgets are placed similar to the generators on the left. The formula $\mathcal{F}$ contains n different variables, k clauses, and hence $3k$ literals. If there exists a placement Φ for $\mathcal{S}$ such that $\mathcal{S}^{\Phi}$ has height $3k$, then the 3-SAT formula $\mathcal{F}$ is satisfiable. Since we placed all gadgets independently, it is essential that all generators and copy gadgets have height two, and every clause gadget has height three. If no copy gadget has height three, all literals set to FALSE at their generators are represented by a shifted interval at the corresponding clause gadget. Observe that for every placement the height at point $R - 1$ and 0 is exactly $3k$. Because at most two intervals are allowed to be shifted at every clause gadget – to not exceed the height – at least one interval of every clause gadget must not be shifted. Thus, if the Boolean formula $\mathcal{F}$ is satisfiable, a placement Φ for $\mathcal{S}$ can be found such that $h(\mathcal{S}^{\Phi})$ is $3k$. Otherwise $\widehat{h}(\mathcal{S})$ is at least $3k + 1$. ■

In the proof of Theorem 13 the maximum flexibility $\tau_{\max}$ is 2. We can adapt the gadgets and the placements of the components such that we obtain the following result:

THEOREM 14 *The* SRDM *problem is* $\mathcal{NP}$*-hard for arbitrary* $\tau_{\max} > 1$.

5. Conclusion

We studied the SRDM problem, a scheduling problem motivated by a variety of practical applications. We presented positive and negative results, but there are still open questions. Is there an asymptotic PTAS or an approximation algorithm with a constant approximation ratio for arbitrary problem instances? Even if we cannot hope for a $(2-\varepsilon)$ - approximation algorithm, an asymptotic PTAS could still exist.

Acknowledgment We would like to thank Riko Jacob for many helpful comments and suggestions.

References

[1] A. Bar-Noy, R. Bar-Yehuda, A. Freund, J.S. Naor, and B. Schieber. A unified approach to approximating resource allocation and scheduling. *Journal of the ACM*, 48(5):1069–1090, 2001.

[2] A. Bar-Noy, S. Guha, J.S. Naor, and B. Schieber. Approximating the throughput of multiple machines in real-time scheduling. *SIAM Journal on Computing*, 31(2):331–352, 2001.

[3] P. Berman and B. DasGupta. Multi-phase algorithms for throughput maximization for real-time scheduling. *Journal of Combinatorial Optimization*, 4(3):307–323, 2000.

[4] A. Brandstädt, V.B. Le, and J.P. Spinrad. *Graph Classes: a Survey*. SIAM Monographs on Discrete Mathematics and Applications, 1999.

[5] J. Chuzhoy and S. Naor. New hardness results for congestion minimization and machine scheduling. accepted for STOC'04, 2004.

[6] J. Chuzhoy, R. Ostrovsky, and Y. Rabani. Approximation algorithms for the job interval selection problem and related scheduling problems. In *IEEE Symposium on Foundations of Computer Science*, pages 348–356, 2001.

[7] M. Cieliebak, T. Erlebach, F. Hennecke, B. Weber, and P. Widmayer. Scheduling jobs on a minimum number of machines. Technical Report 419, Institute of Theoretical Computer Science, ETH Zürich, 2003.

[8] E.G. Coffman Jr., M.R. Garey, and D.S. Johnson. Approximation algorithms for bin packing: A survey. In D. Hochbaum, editor, *Approximation Algorithms for NP-hard Problems*. PWS, 1996.

[9] T. Erlebach and F.C.R. Spieksma. Interval selection: Applications, algorithms, and lower bounds. *Journal of Algorithms*, 46(1):27–53, 2003.

[10] M.R. Garey and D.S. Johnson. *Computers and Intractability*. W.H. Freeman and Company, New York, 1979.

[11] E.L. Lawler, J.K. Lenstra, A.H.G. Rinnooy Kan, and D.B. Shmoys. Sequencing and scheduling: Algorithms and complexity. In S.C. Graves, A.H.G. Rinnooy Kan, and P. Zipkin, editors, *Handbooks in Operations Research and Management Science*, volume 4, pages 445–522. North-Holland, 1993.

[12] F. Malucelli and S. Nicoloso. Shiftable interval graphs. In *Proc. 6th International Conference on Graph Theory*, 2000.

[13] D.D. Sleator and R.E. Tarjan. A data structure for dynamic trees. *Journal of Computer and System Sciences*, 26(3):362–391, 1983.

[14] F.C.R. Spieksma. Approximating an interval scheduling problem. In *International Workshop on Approximation Algorithms for Combinatorial Optimization Problems*, volume 1444, pages 169–180. Springer-Verlag LNCS, 1998.

APPROXIMATION ALGORITHMS FOR MIXED FRACTIONAL PACKING AND COVERING PROBLEMS *

Klaus Jansen, [1]

[1] *University of Kiel*
Olshausenstr. 40, 24118 Kiel, Germany
kj@informatik.uni-kiel.de

Abstract We propose an approximation algorithm based on the Lagrangian or price - directive decomposition method to compute an ϵ-approximate solution of the mixed fractional packing and covering problem: find $x \in B$ such that $f(x) \leq (1+\epsilon)a$, $g(x) \geq (1-\epsilon)b$ where $f(x), g(x)$ are vectors with M nonnegative convex and concave functions, a and b are M - dimensional nonnegative vectors and B is a convex set that can be queried by an optimization or feasibility oracle. We propose an algorithm that needs only $O(M\epsilon^{-2}\ln(M\epsilon^{-1}))$ iterations or calls to the oracle. The main contribution is that the algorithm solves the general mixed fractional packing and covering problem (in contrast to pure fractional packing and covering problems and to the special mixed packing and covering problem with $B = \mathbb{R}_+^N$) and runs in time independent of the so-called width of the problem.

Keywords: Convex and concave optimization, approximation algorithms.

1 Introduction.

We study mixed fractional packing and covering problems (MPC_ϵ) of the following form: Given a vector $f : B \rightarrow \mathbb{R}_+^M$ of M nonnegative continuous convex functions and a vector $g : B \rightarrow \mathbb{R}_+^M$ of M nonnegative continuous concave functions, two M - dimensional nonnegative vectors a, b, a nonempty convex compact set B and a relative tolerance $\epsilon \in (0,1)$, find an approximately feasible vector $x \in B$ such that $f(x) \leq (1+\epsilon)a$ and $g(x) \geq (1-\epsilon)b$ or find a

*Research of the author was supported in part by EU Thematic Network APPOL, Approximation and Online Algorithms, IST-2001-30012, by EU Project CRESCCO, Critical resource sharing for cooperation in complex systems, IST-2001-33135 and by DFG Project, Entwicklung und Analyse von Approximativen Algorithmen für Gemischte und Verallgemeinerte Packungs- und Überdeckungsprobleme, JA 612/10-1. Part of this work was done while visiting the Department of Computer Science at ETH Zürich.

proof that no vector is feasible (that satisfies $x \in B$, $f(x) \le a$ and $g(x) \ge b$). W.l.o.g. we may assume that a and b are equal to the vector e of all ones.

The fractional packing problem with convex constraints, i.e. to find $x \in B$ such that $f(x) \le (1+\epsilon)a$, is solved in [6, 7, 10] by the Lagrangian decomposition method in $O(M(\epsilon^{-2} + \ln M))$ iterations where each iteration requires a call to an approximate block solver $ABS(p,t)$ of the form: find $\hat{x} \in B$ such that $p^T f(\hat{x}) \le (1+t)\Lambda(p)$ where $\Lambda(p) = \min_{x \in B} p^T f(x)$. Furthermore, Grigoriadis et al. [8] proposed also an approximation algorithm for the fractional covering problem with concave constraints, i.e. to find $x \in B$ such that $g(x) \ge (1-\epsilon)b$, within $O(M(\epsilon^{-2} + \ln M))$ iterations where each iteration requires here a call to an approximate block solver $ABS(q,t)$ of the form: find $\hat{x} \in B$ such that $q^T g(\hat{x}) \ge (1-t)\Lambda(q)$ where $\Lambda(q) = \max_{x \in B} q^T g(x)$. Both algorithms solve also the corresponding min-max and max-min optimization variants within the same number of iterations. Furthermore, the algorithms can be generalized to the case where the block solver has arbitrary approximation ratio [9–11].

Further interesting algorithms for the fractional packing and fractional covering problem with linear constraints were developed by Plotkin et al. [14] and Young [16]. These algorithms have a running time that depends linearly on the width ρ - an unbounded function of the input instance. Several relatively complicated techniques were proposed to reduce this dependence. Garg and Könemann [5] described a nice algorithm for the fractional packing problem with linear constraints that needs only $O(M\epsilon^{-2} \ln M)$ iterations. On the other hand, the algorithm by Grigoriadis et al. [8] is the only known algorithm that solves the fractional covering problem with a number of iterations independently on the width.

For the mixed packing and covering problem (with linear constraints and polytope B), Plotkin et al. [14] proposed also approximation algorithms where the running time depends on the width. They present an algorithm that uses $O(M^2(\ln^2 \rho)\epsilon^{-2} \ln(\epsilon^{-1} M \ln \rho) \ln \rho)$ calls to an oracle of the form: find a vertex $\hat{x} \in B$ with $f(\hat{x}) \le va$ and

$$p^T f(\hat{x}) - \sum_{m \in I(v,\hat{x})} q_m g_m(\hat{x}) = \min\{p^T f(x) - \sum_{m \in I(v,x)} q_m g_m(x) | x \text{ vertex of } B\}$$

where $I(v,x) = \{m | g_m(x) \le v b_m\}$, v is a constant and where

$$\rho = \max_{x \in B} \max_{m=1,\ldots,M} (f_m(x)/a_m, g_m(x)/b_m).$$

Young [17] described an approximation algorithm for a special mixed packing and covering problem with linear constraints with non-negative coefficients and special convex set $B = \mathbb{R}_+^N$. The algorithm has a running time of $O(M^2 \epsilon^{-2} \ln M)$. Recently, Fleischer [4] gave an approximation scheme for the optimization variant (minimizing $c^T x$ such that $Cx \geq a$, $x \leq b$ and $x \geq 0$ where a, b, and c are nonnegative integer vectors and C is a nonnegative integer matrix). Applications of the pure and mixed fractional packing and covering problems can be found in [1–5, 9–12, 14, 17]. Young [17] posed the following open problem: find an efficient width-independent Lagrangian-relaxation algorithm for the abstract mixed packing and covering problem: find $x \in B$ such that $Px \leq (1+\epsilon)a$, $Cx \geq (1-\epsilon)b$, where P, C are nonnegative matrices, a, b are nonnegative vectors and B is a polytope that can be queried by an optimization oracle (given a vector c, return $x \in B$ minimizing $c^T x$) or some other suitable oracle.

New Result: Our contribution here is an efficient width-independent Lagrangian - relaxation algorithm for the mixed packing and covering problem that uses a suitable optimization oracle of the form (given two vectors c, d, return $x \in B$, $d^T x \geq 1$, minimizing $c^T x$). Interestingly, a feasibility oracle of the form (given two vectors c, d, return $x \in B$ such that $c^T x \leq 1$ and $d^T x \geq 1$) is also sufficient. This solves the open problem by N.E. Young [17]. Interestingly, our algorithm works also for a more general problem with a convex set B and nonnegative convex packing and concave covering constraints.

The algorithm uses a variant of the Lagrangian or price directive decomposition method. This is an iterative strategy that solves (MPC_ϵ) by computing a sequence of triples (p, q, x) as follows. A coordinator uses the current vector $x \in B$ to compute two price vectors $p = p(x) \in \mathbb{R}_+^M$ and $q = q(x) \in \mathbb{R}_+^M$ with $\sum_{m=1}^M p_m + q_m = 1$. Then the coordinator calls an optimization oracle to compute a solution $\hat{x} \in B$ of the block problem (BP) of the form $\Lambda(p,q) = \min\{p^T f(y) | y \in B, q^T g(y) \geq \sum_{m=1}^M q_m\}$, and makes a move from x to $(1-\tau)x + \tau\hat{x}$ with an appropriate step length $\tau \in (0,1)$. Such a iteration is called a coordination step. For our algorithm, we only require an approximate block solver (ABS) that solves the underlying block problem (BP) to a given relative tolerance $t \in (0,1)$:

$$ABS(p,q,t): \qquad \text{compute} \quad \hat{x} = \hat{x}(p,q) \in B \text{ such that}$$

$$p^T f(\hat{x}) \leq (1+t)\Lambda(p,q) \text{ and } q^T g(\hat{x}) \geq \tfrac{1}{1+t} \textstyle\sum_{m=1}^M q_m.$$

Our main result is the following:

THEOREM 1 *There is an approximation algorithm that for any given accuracy $\epsilon \in (0,1)$ solves the mixed fractional packing and covering problem (MPC_ϵ) within*

$$N = O(M\epsilon^{-2}\ln(M\epsilon^{-1}))$$

iterations or coordination steps, where each of which requires a call to $ABS(p, q, \Theta(\epsilon))$ and a coordination overhead of $O(M \ln(M\epsilon^{-1}))$ arithmetic operations.

Alternatively, instead of using the approximate block solver an approximate feasibility oracle of the form (compute $\hat{x} \in B$ such that $p^T f(\hat{x}) \le (1 + t)\sum_{m=1}^{M} p_m$ and $q^T g(\hat{x}) \ge \frac{1}{1+t}\sum_{m=1}^{M} q_m$) is also sufficient.

Main Ideas: Our algorithm builds on approximation schemes of Grigoriadis et al. [7, 8] and Young [17]. One of the ideas is to combine two different potential functions that were proposed for pure fractional packing and covering problems [7, 8]. We associate here with the packing and covering constraints the following potential function:

$$\Phi'_t(\theta, x) = 2\ln\theta - \tfrac{t}{M}\sum_{m=1}^{M}\ln(\theta - f_m(x)) - \tfrac{t}{M}\sum_{m=1}^{M}\ln(g_m(x) - \tfrac{1}{\theta})$$

where $\theta \in \mathbb{R}_+$ and $t > 0$ is a tolerance that depends on ϵ and is used in the approximate block solver. The function Φ' can be extremely small, since there is no upper bound on the function values $g_m(x)$. Let A be a nonempty subset of $\mathcal{M} = \{1, \ldots, M\}$. To control the values of the covering functions $g_m(x)$ and to have a lower bound for the potential function, we eliminate functions g_m (and the corresponding index in A) when the function value $g_m(x)$ is larger than a prespecified threshold value T and modify the potential function. Let $A(x)$ denote the index set corresponding to a given vector $x \in B$. Then the modified potential function has the form:

$$\Phi_t(\theta, x, A(x)) = 2\ln\theta - \tfrac{t}{M}\sum_{m=1}^{M}\ln(\theta - f_m(x))$$
$$-\tfrac{t}{M}\sum_{m\in A(x)}\ln(g_m(x) - \tfrac{1}{\theta}) - \tfrac{t}{M}\sum_{m\notin A(x)}\ln(T).$$

The potential function Φ_t has an unique minimum $\theta_{A(x)}(x)$ that approximates the objective value

$$\lambda_{A(x)}(x) = \max(\max_{m\in\mathcal{M}} f_m(x), \max_{m\in A(x)} 1/g_m(x)).$$

This potential function Φ_t and the minimizer $\theta_{A(x)}(x)$ is used to define the price vectors $p = p(x)$ and $q = q(x)$ for the current vector $x \in B$ and to optimize in the correct direction. Another important parameter for the convergence of the algorithm is the reduced potential value $\phi_t(x, A(x)) = \Phi_t(\theta_{A(x)}(x), x, A(x))$ for $x \in B$ and $A(x) \subset \{1, \ldots, M\}$. Since we can not control the values of eliminated functions g_m for $m \notin A(x)$ (after the elimination), at the end of each phase s we take a convex combination over different computed vectors.

The main problem is to choose a good step length τ in order to obtain a fast and width-independent convergence. To achieve this goal we study the following four cases:

$$(1) : p^T f(x) - p^T f(\hat{x}) \geq 0 \text{ and } q^T g(\hat{x}) - q^T g(x) \geq 0,$$

$$(2) : p^T f(x) - p^T f(\hat{x}) < 0 \text{ and } q^T g(\hat{x}) - q^T g(x) \geq 0,$$

$$(3) : p^T f(x) - p^T f(\hat{x}) \geq 0 \text{ and } q^T g(\hat{x}) - q^T g(x) < 0,$$

$$(4) : p^T f(x) - p^T f(\hat{x}) < 0 \text{ and } q^T g(\hat{x}) - q^T g(x) < 0,$$

where x is the current solution and $\hat{x}$ is the block solution corresponding to the price vectors $p = p(x)$ and $q = q(x)$. Case (4) with $p^T f(x) - p^T f(\hat{x}) < 0$ and $q^T g(\hat{x}) - q^T g(x) < 0$ is not possible. In this case one of the stopping rules is satisfied and the algorithm stops with the iterate x. The step length τ is defined carefully in dependence on the cases $(1) - (3)$ and the minimizer $\theta_{A(x)}(x)$ of the potential function. In the general case, the coordinator moves from solution x to $(1-\tau)x + \tau\hat{x}$ and sets the index set $A(x') = \{m \in A(x) | g_m(x') < T\}$. In the case where $\max_{m \in A} g_m(x)(1-\tau) + g_m(\hat{x})\tau > T$ we reduce the step length from τ to $\bar{\tau}$ and use as next vector $x' = (1-\bar{\tau})x + \bar{\tau}\hat{x}$. This is important for the convergence analysis.

2 Potential function and price vectors

Let A be a nonempty subset of $\mathcal{M} = \{1, \ldots, M\}$. During a phase, we eliminate a concave function g_m (and the corresponding index in A) when the function value $g_m(x) \geq T$. Let $A(x)$ denote the index set corresponding to a given vector $x \in B$. For simplicity we use $A = A(x)$ (if the dependence is clear).

2.1 Potential function

The potential function Φ_t (given above) is well defined for $\lambda_A(x) < \theta < \infty$ where

$$\lambda_A(x) = \max\left(\max_{1 \leq m \leq M} f_m(x), \max_{m \in A} \frac{1}{g_m(x)}\right).$$

If $g_m(x) = 0$ for at least one index $m \in A$ then we define $\lambda_A(x) = \infty$. Furthermore, Φ_t has the barrier property (i.e. $\Phi_t(\theta, x, A) \to \infty$ for $\theta \to \infty$ and for $\theta \to \lambda_A(x)$). We define the reduced potential function $\phi_t(x, A)$ as the minimum value $\Phi_t(\theta, x, A)$ over $\theta \in (\lambda_A(x), \infty)$ for a given $x \in B$. The unique minimizer $\theta_A(x)$ can be determined from the first-order optimality condition:

$$\frac{t\theta}{M}\sum_{m=1}^{M}\frac{1}{\theta - f_m(x)} + \frac{t}{M\theta}\sum_{m\in A}\frac{1}{g_m(x) - 1/\theta} = 2. \tag{1}$$

The implicit function $\theta_A(x)$ approximates $\lambda_A(x)$. This is important for the further analysis.

LEMMA 2

$$\theta_A(x)/(1 + t/(2M)) \geq \lambda_A(x) \geq \theta_A(x)(1 - \frac{t}{2} - \frac{t|A|}{2M}) \geq \theta_A(x)(1 - t).$$

Lemma 2 shows that the value $\theta_A(x)$ approximates the objective value $\lambda_A(x)$ for small t. Interestingly, the reduced potential function $\phi_t(x, A)$ can be bounded also in terms of $\theta_A(x)$.

LEMMA 3 *If $g_m(x) \leq T$ for each $m \in A$ then $\phi_t(x, A) \geq (2 - t)\ln\theta_A(x) - t\ln T$. Furthermore, if $T > 1/\lambda_A(x)$ then $\phi_t(A, x) \leq 2\ln\theta_A(x) + 2t\ln(\frac{2M}{t}) + t\ln(1 + t/(2M))$.*

2.2 Price vectors

Given a vector $x \in B$ and a subset $A \subset \{1, \ldots, M\}$, the price vector $p(x, A)$ is defined by

$$p_m(x, A) = \frac{t}{2M}\frac{\theta_A(x)}{\theta_A(x) - f_m(x)} \tag{2}$$

and the price vector $q(x, A)$ is given by

$$q_m(x, A) = \begin{cases} \frac{t}{2M}\frac{1}{g_m(x)\theta_A(x) - 1} & m \in A, \\ 0 & \text{otherwise.} \end{cases} \tag{3}$$

Using the first-order condition, $\sum_{m=1}^{M} p_m(x, A) + \sum_{m=1}^{M} q_m(x, A) = 1$ and each component $p_m(x, A), q_m(x, A)$ is nonnegative.

LEMMA 4 **(a)** $p(x, A)^T f(x) = \theta_A(x)(\sum_{m=1}^{M} p_m(x, A) - t/2) \leq \theta_A(x)(1 - t/2)$,

(b) $q(x, A)^T g(x) = (\sum_{m\in A} q_m(x, A) + t|A|/(2M))/\theta_A(x) \leq (\sum_{m\in A} q_m(x, A) + t/2)/\theta_A(x) \leq (1 + t/2)/\theta_A(x)$.

Notice that Lemma 4 (a) implies that $\sum_{m=1}^{M} p_m(x, A) \geq t/2$.

3 Our approximation algorithm

In this section we describe the approximation algorithms for the mixed fractional packing and covering problem. First we suppose that there exists a feasible solution $x \in B$ with $f(x) \leq e$ and $g(x) \geq e$. Then the approximation algorithm works as follows:

(1) compute initial solution $x^{(0)}$, $s := 0$, $\epsilon_0 := 1/4$;

(2) **repeat** {scaling phase }

(2.1) $s := s+1; \epsilon_s := \epsilon_{s-1}/2; x := x^{(s-1)}; T(s) := 528(M^3/\epsilon_s^2)/\lambda_{\mathcal{M}}(x);$
$A := \{m \in \{1, \ldots, M\} | g_m(x) < T(s)\};$ $finished := false;$
$k := 0;$

(2.2) **if** $A \neq \{1, \ldots, M\}$ **then begin** k:=k+1; $x_k := x$ **end**;

(2.3) **if** stopping rule 1 is satisfied for x **then** $finished := true; y := x$
end;

(2.4) **while** $not(finished)$ **do begin**

(2.4.1) compute $\theta_A(x)$, $p(x, A)$ and $q(x, A)$;

(2.4.2) $\hat{x} := ABS(p(x, A), q(x, A), \epsilon_s/32)$;

(2.4.3) **if** one of the stopping rules is satisfied
then begin $finished := true; y := x$ **end**
else begin

(2.4.3.1) compute step length τ and $x' := (1 - \tau)x + \tau\hat{x}$;

(2.4.3.2) **if** $\max_{m \in A} g_m(x)(1 - \tau) + g_m(\hat{x})\tau > T(s)$ **then**
reduce
τ to $\bar{\tau}$ and $x' := (1 - \bar{\tau})x + \bar{\tau}\hat{x}$;

(2.4.3.3) $A' := A \setminus \{m | g_m(x') \geq T(s)\}; x := x'$;

(2.4.3.4) **if** $A \neq A'$ **then begin** $k := k + 1; x_k = x'$;
$A := A'$ **end**

end

end;

(2.5) compute convex combination of $x_1, \ldots, x_k, y$ to get $x^{(s)}$;

(2.6) **until** $\epsilon_s \leq \epsilon/2$ or $\lambda(x^{(s)}) \leq 1 + \epsilon$;

(3) return($x^{(s)}$).

The details of the algorithm are described later in this section (how to compute an initial solution, the stopping rules, the choice of the step length, and the reduction of the step length). For the case where the set of feasible solutions $\{x \in B | f(x) \leq e, g(x) \geq e\}$ is empty, we have to modify the program above. If an inequality $p(x, A)^T f(\hat{x}) > (1+t) \sum p_m(x, A)$ holds for a block solution $\hat{x}$, then we can conclude that there is no feasible solution.

3.1 Initial solution

For each $m \in \{1, \ldots, M\}$, we consider the block problem (B_m) of the form $\Lambda(p,q) = \min\{\frac{1}{M}\sum_{\ell=1}^{M} f_\ell(x) | x \in B, g_m(x) \geq 1\}$ where $p = (1/M, \ldots, 1/M)$ and $q = e_m$ is the unit vector with all zero coordinates except for its m.th component which is 1. If there is a solution $\bar{x} \in B$ with $f(\bar{x}) \leq e$ and $g(\bar{x}) \geq e$, then this solution satisfies $(1/M)\sum_{\ell=1}^{M} f_\ell(\bar{x}) \leq 1$ and $g_m(\bar{x}) \geq 1$. Let $\hat{x}^{[m]} \in B$ be an approximate solution of the block problem (B_m) with tolerance $t = 1/2$, and let $x^{(0)} = (1/M)\sum_{m=1}^{M} \hat{x}^{[m]}$. Using the convexity of B, $x^{(0)} \in B$. If the approximate solution satisfies $(1/M)\sum_{\ell=1}^{M} f_\ell(\hat{x}^{[m]}) > 1 + t$, then we conclude that the solution set of the mixed problem is empty. In the other case we can prove:

LEMMA 5 *If there exists a feasible solution of the mixed packing and covering problem, then* $\lambda(x^{(0)}) \leq 3M/2$.

3.2 Stopping rules

In the algorithm we stepwise decrease in phases the objective value λ from $3M/2$ to $1/(1-\epsilon/2)$. In the first phase we decrease $3M/2$ to $\epsilon_1 = 1/8$. After that we set $\epsilon_s = \epsilon_{s-1}/2$. The goal in phase s is to obtain a solution $x^{(s)}$ with $\lambda(x^{(s)}) \leq 1/(1-\epsilon_s)$. In order to get such a solution we need at the end of phase s a solution y with $\lambda_A(y) \leq 1/(1-\epsilon_s/4)$. This is necessary, since we eliminate covering constraints within the phases. To obtain the solution y and to show the convergence we use three stopping rules. For the first rule we simply test whether

$$\lambda_A(x) \leq 1 + \epsilon_s/4 \tag{4}$$

for the current solution x. For this rule we get immediately

LEMMA 6 *If* $\lambda_A(x) \leq 1 + \epsilon_s/4$ *then* $f_m(x) \leq 1 + \epsilon_s/4 \leq 1/(1-\epsilon_s/4)$ *for each* $m \in \{1, \ldots, M\}$ *and* $g_m(x) \geq 1/(1+\epsilon_s/4) \geq 1 - \epsilon_s/4$ *for each* $m \in A$.

For the second rule we define a parameter ν that depends on the current iterate x and the approximate block solution $\hat{x}$ as follows

$$\nu = \nu(x, \hat{x}) = \frac{p^T f(x) - p^T f(\hat{x}) + \theta(q^T g(\hat{x}) - q^T g(x))}{p^T f(x) + p^T f(\hat{x}) + \theta(q^T g(\hat{x}) + q^T g(x))} \tag{5}$$

where $p = p(x, A)$, $q = q(x, A)$ and $\theta = \theta_A(x)$. Clearly, $\nu(x, \hat{x}) \leq 1$. The Lemma below states that x is an approximate solution of the phase s corresponding to subset A, when ν is bounded by $t_s = \Theta(\epsilon_s)$.

LEMMA 7 *Suppose* $\epsilon_s \in (0,1)$ *and* $t_s = \epsilon_s/32$. *For a given* $x \in B$, *let* p, q *be computed by* $(2,3)$ *and* $\hat{x}$ *computed by* $ABS(p, q, t_s)$. *If* $\nu(x, \hat{x}) \leq t_s$, *then* $f_m(x) \leq 1 + \epsilon_s/4 \leq 1/(1-\epsilon_s/4)$ *for each* $m \in \{1,\ldots,M\}$ *and* $g_m(x) \geq 1/(1+\epsilon_s/4) \geq (1-\epsilon_s/4)$ *for each* $m \in A$.

The third stopping rule is used to control the number of iterations during one phase. Here we use a parameter ω_s that depends on the phase s:

$$\omega_s = \begin{cases} \frac{2}{3M(1-\epsilon_1/4)} & s = 1 \\ \frac{1-\epsilon_{s-1}}{1-\epsilon_s/4} & s > 1 \end{cases}$$

Then the third rule is defined by

$$\lambda_A(x) \leq \omega_s \lambda_{\mathcal{M}}(x^{(s-1)}) \tag{6}$$

where $x^{(s-1)}$ is the solution of phase $s-1$ that satisfies $\lambda(x^{(s-1)}) \leq 1/(1-\epsilon_{s-1})$.

LEMMA 8 *Let* $x^{(s-1)}$ *be the initial solution and* x *be a vector in phase* $s \geq 1$ *with* $\lambda_A(x) \leq \omega_s \lambda(x^{(s-1)})$ *for* $A \subset \mathcal{M}$. *If* $\lambda_A(x^{(s-1)}) \leq 3M/2$ *for* $s = 1$ *and* $\lambda_A(x^{(s-1)}) \leq 1/(1-\epsilon_{s-1})$ *for* $s \geq 2$, *then we obtain* $\lambda_A(x) \leq 1/(1-\epsilon_s/4)$.

3.3 Choice of the step length

In this subsection we describe the choice of the step length τ. We suppose that we have computed a vector x and an approximate block solution $\hat{x}$ in a phase s such that $\nu(x,\hat{x}) > t$, $p^T f(\hat{x}) \leq (1+t)\sum_{m=1}^M p_m$ and $q^T g(\hat{x}) \geq \frac{1}{1+t}\sum_{m=1}^M q_m$ (where $t = t_s$, $p = p(x, A(x))$ and $q = q(x, A(x))$). Let $x' = (1-\tau)x + \tau\hat{x}$. First we focus on the case where $g_m(x') < T = T(s)$ for each $m \in A(x)$. In this case we do not eliminate a component (i.e. $A(x') = A(x)$). The other case will be discussed later (in some cases we have in addition to reduce the step length). For simplification we use $\theta = \theta_{A(x)}(x)$. Since each function f_m is convex and each function g_m is concave, we get independently on the choice of τ the following inequalities

$$\begin{aligned} \theta - f_m(x') &\geq (\theta - f_m(x))(1 + \tfrac{2\tau M}{t\theta} p_m (f_m(x) - f_m(\hat{x}))), \\ g_m(x') - 1/\theta &\geq (g_m(x) - 1/\theta)(1 + \tfrac{2\tau M\theta}{t} q_m (g_m(\hat{x}) - g_m(x))) \end{aligned}$$

for each index $m \in \mathcal{M}$ or $m \in A(x)$, respectively. We call a step length τ **feasible** if $\tau \in (0,1)$ and if the following value:

$$\max\left(\max_{m\in\mathcal{M}} \left|\frac{2\tau M}{t\theta} p_m (f_m(x) - f_m(\hat{x}))\right|, \max_{m\in A(x)} \left|\frac{2\tau M\theta}{t} q_m (g_m(\hat{x}) - g_m(x))\right|\right) \tag{7}$$

is bounded by $1/2$. Suppose from now on that τ is a feasible step length. Later we will specify different step lengths τ with $\tau \in (0,1)$ to obtain the bound (7). Then using $\theta - f_m(x) > 0$ and $g_m(x) - 1/\theta > 0$ we obtain $\theta - f_m(x') > 0$ and $g_m(x') - 1/\theta > 0$ for the next computed vector $x' \in B$. This implies that the objective value $\lambda_{A(x')}(x')$ for the next vector x' is at most $\theta_{A(x)}(x)$, where here $A(x') = A(x)$.

LEMMA 9 *For any two consecutive iterations in a phase with computed vectors x, x' and $A(x') = A(x)$ and any feasible step length τ, the difference $\phi_t(x, A(x)) - \phi_t(x', A(x'))$ is at least*

$$+2\tau[(p^T f(x) - p^T f(\hat{x}))/\theta + (q^T g(\hat{x}) - q^T g(x))\theta]$$
$$-\frac{4M\tau^2}{t}[(p^T f(x) + p^T f(\hat{x}))/\theta + (q^T g(\hat{x}) + q^T g(x))\theta]^2,$$

where $\theta = \theta_{A(x)}(x)$, $p = p(x, A(x))$ and $q = q(x, A(x))$.

The proof of Lemma 9 can be found in the full version. In our algorithm we use the following step lengths:

$$\tau_1 = t\nu/(4M[(p^T f(x) + p^T f(\hat{x}))/\theta + (q^T g(\hat{x}) + q^T g(x))\theta]),$$

$$\tau_2 = t\nu/(4M[(p^T f(x) + p^T f(\hat{x})) + (q^T g(\hat{x}) + q^T g(x))\theta]),$$

$$\tau_3 = t^2/(4M[(p^T f(x) + p^T f(\hat{x}))/\theta + (q^T g(\hat{x}) + q^T g(x))\theta]),$$

$$\tau_4 = t/(12M)$$

where $\theta = \theta_A(x)$ and $\nu = \nu(x, \hat{x})$. With exception of the last case, all step lengths above are feasible for any $t \in (0, 1/2]$. The last step length τ_4 is feasible only for the case $q^T g(\hat{x}) \leq q^T g(x)$ and any $t \in (0, 1]$. Furthermore, note that each step length $\tau \in (0, \tau_i]$ is also feasible for $i \in \{1, \ldots, 4\}$. In our algorithm we use the step lengths (see Table 1) in dependence on the current vector x, the approximate block solution $\hat{x}$, the minimizer $\theta = \theta_{A(x)}(x)$ and the price vectors $p = p(x, A(x))$, $q = q(x, A(x))$.

The main goal now is to prove the following result. The proof can be found in the full version of the paper.

THEOREM 10 *For any two consecutive iterations in a phase with computed vectors x, x', index sets $A(x) = A(x')$ and $t \leq 1/224$ we obtain: $\phi_t(x, A(x)) - \phi_t(x', A(x')) \geq \Theta(\frac{t^3}{M})$.*

3.4 Reducing the step length

Let $x' = (1-\tau)x + \tau\hat{x}$ where x is the current vector, $\hat{x}$ is the block solution and τ is the step length as used in the previous subsection. Consider a phase

	$\theta \leq 2$	$2 < \theta \leq 200$	$200 < \theta$
$p^T f(x) - p^T f(\hat{x}) \geq 0$ and $q^T g(\hat{x}) - q^T g(x) \geq 0$	$\tau_1/120$	$\tau_1/120$	$\tau_1/2$
$p^T f(x) - p^T f(\hat{x}) < 0$ and $q^T g(\hat{x}) - q^T g(x) \geq 0$	τ_2	τ_2	τ_2
$p^T f(x) - p^T f(\hat{x}) \geq 0$ and $q^T g(\hat{x}) - q^T g(x) < 0$	$\tau_3/3$	$\tau_4/9$	$\tau_4/9$

Table 1. The choice of the step lengths

s with threshold value $T(s)$. For simplicity we use $T = T(s)$. If $g_m(x') \leq T$ for each $m \in A(x)$, then we use x' as the next iterate and set $A(x') = \{m \in A(x) | g_m(x') < T\}$. In this case some components may be eliminated, but we use the original step length. Now we consider the case that $g_m(x') > T$ for at least one coordinate $m \in A(x)$. Let $\gamma(\tilde{\tau}) = \max_{m \in A(x)} g_m(x)(1 - \tilde{\tau}) + g_m(\hat{x})\tilde{\tau}$ for $0 \leq \tilde{\tau} \leq 1$. If $\gamma(\tau) > T$ then we reduce the step length τ. In this case we compute $\bar{\tau} < \tau$ such that $\gamma(\bar{\tau}) = T$. Using $g_m(x) < T$ for each $m \in A(x)$ and $\gamma(\tau) > T$, there is at least one component $m \in A(x)$ such that $g_m(\hat{x}) > T$. In addition, the value $\bar{\tau}$ is unique and can be computed in $O(M)$ time. We use here $x' = x(1 - \bar{\tau}) + \hat{x}\bar{\tau}$ as next iterate and set $A(x') = \{m \in A(x) | g_m(x') < T\}$. If $\gamma(\tau) \leq T$ then we do not have to reduce the step length τ and use again $x' = x(1 - \tau) + \hat{x}\tau$. But we eliminate as above all components $m \in A(x)$ with $g_m(x') \geq T$. Notice that the case with $g_m(x') > T > g_m(x)(1 - \tau) + g_m(\hat{x})\tau$ is possible (since the functions g_m are concave). For each $m \in A(x')$ we have $g_m(x') < T$. If we use a reduced step length $\bar{\tau} < \tau$ then $A(x) \neq A(x')$. But $A(x) \neq A(x')$ can happen also when $\gamma(\tau) < T$ or $g_m(x') \leq T$ for each $m \in A(x)$. Now we consider two cases depending whether we use the original step length τ or the reduced step length $\bar{\tau}$. We can prove similar to Theorem 10 the following two results (the proofs are given in the full paper).

THEOREM 11 *For any two consecutive iterations with computed vectors x, x', index sets $A(x) \neq A(x')$, $\max_{m \in A(x)} g_m(x)(1 - \tau) + g_m(\hat{x})\tau \leq T$ and $t \leq 1/224$, we obtain $\phi_t(x, A(x)) - \phi_t(x', A(x')) \geq \Theta(\frac{t^3}{M})$.*

THEOREM 12 *For any two consecutive iterations with computed vectors x, x', index sets $A(x) \neq A(x')$, $\max_{m \in A(x)} g_m(x)(1 - \tau) + g_m(\hat{x})\tau > T$ and $t \leq 1/224$, we obtain $\phi_t(x, A(x)) - \phi_t(x', A(x')) \geq 0$.*

3.5 Convex combination of different vectors

First we can prove an upper bound for the packing constraints.

LEMMA 13 *For any iteration of the phase s with computed vector x, $\lambda_f(x) = \max_{1\leq m\leq M} f_m(x)$ is bounded by $4M/t_s$.*

Lemma 13 shows that the values $f_m(x)$ are not arbitrary large in the algorithm. Notice that this is independently from the chosen step length $\tau \in (0,1)$. We use this bound for the convex combination below. Notice that in addition the components $p_m(x, A(x))$ of the price vector $p(x, A(x))$ are not arbitrary small (i.e. $p_m(x, A(x)) > t_s/(2M)$). At the end of phase s we have computed a vector $y \in B$ with $\lambda_{A(y)}(y) \leq 1/(1-\epsilon_s/4)$. This implies $f_m(y) \leq 1/(1-\epsilon_s/4)$ for each $m \in \{1,\ldots,M\}$ and $g_m(y) \geq 1-\epsilon_s/4$ for each $m \in A(y)$. The goal is now to compute a vector $x^{(s)} \in B$ with $\lambda_{\mathcal{M}}(x^{(s)}) \leq 1/(1-\epsilon_s)$. The key idea is to use a convex combination over several vectors computed during the phase. Let $x_1,\ldots,x_k$ be the vectors in phase s where at least one function g_m is eliminated (i.e. where $g_m(x_i) \geq T(s)$). Clearly, $k \leq M$. We have $x_1 = x^{(s-1)}$ if $g_m(x^{(s-1)}) \geq T(s)$ for at least one $m \in \mathcal{M}$ (here $x^{(s-1)}$ is the solution of the previous phase). We take the following convex combination:

$$x^{(s)} = \sum_{i=1}^{k} \frac{\epsilon_s^2}{264M^2} x_i + \left(1 - \frac{k\epsilon_s^2}{264M^2}\right) y.$$

Since the set B is convex and $x_1,\ldots,x_k, y \in B$, we obtain $x^{(s)} \in B$. Our threshold value $T(s)$ is equal to $528(\frac{M^3}{\epsilon_s^2}) \cdot \frac{1}{\lambda_{\mathcal{M}}(x^{(s-1)})}$. Notice that $T(s) \leq 528M^3/\epsilon_s^2$, since $\lambda_{\mathcal{M}}(x^{(s-1)}) \geq 1$ (otherwise we are done). Then we can prove:

LEMMA 14 *The computed solution $x^{(s)}$ satisfies $\lambda_{\mathcal{M}}(x^{(s)}) \leq 1/(1-\epsilon_s)$.*

4 Analysis of the approximation algorithm

In this subsection we determine the total number of iterations of our algorithm. To do this we calculate first the number of iterations N_s in a single phase s. Let $y, \tilde{y}$ denote the initial and final iterate of phase s. Furthermore, let $\bar{y}$ be the solution after $\bar{N}_s = N_s - 1$ iterations. For consecutive iterations with computed vectors x, x' in a phase and $A(x) = A(x')$, the difference in the potential values $\phi_t(x, A(x)) - \phi_t(x', A(x')) \geq \frac{ct^3}{M}$ where c is a positive constant and $t = t_s = \epsilon_s/32$. In addition, there are at most M iterations with consecutive vectors x, x' and different subsets $A(x) \neq A(x')$ (i.e. in these iterations at least one component is eliminated). In these cases, we have $\phi_t(x, A(x)) - \phi_t(x', A(x')) \geq 0$. Therefore, $\phi_t(y, A(y)) - \phi_t(\bar{y}, A(\bar{y})) \geq \frac{ct^3}{M}(\bar{N}_s - M)$. Then we can prove the following result:

THEOREM 15 *The number of iterations N_s in phase s is at most*

$$O(M\epsilon_s^{-2}\ln(M\epsilon_s^{-1}))$$

and the total number of iterations of our algorithm is at most

$$O(M\epsilon^{-2}\ln(M\epsilon^{-1})).$$

Remark: The root $\theta_A(x)$ can often be computed only approximately, but an accuracy of $O(\epsilon^2/M)$ for $\theta_A(x)$ is sufficient to generate the above bounds on the number of iterations. With this required accuracy, the number of evaluations of the sum $\frac{t\theta}{M}\sum_{m=1}^{M}\frac{1}{\theta-f_m(x)}+\frac{t}{M\theta}\sum_{m\in A}\frac{1}{g_m(x)-1/\theta}$ is bounded by $O(\ln(M\epsilon^{-1}))$. This gives $O(M\ln(M\epsilon^{-1}))$ arithmetic operations to determine $\theta_A(x)$ approximately.

5 Concluding Remarks

In this paper we have presented an approximation algorithm for the mixed packing and covering problem that uses only $O(M\epsilon^{-2}\ln(M\epsilon^{-1}))$ calls to an oracle of the form: compute a $\hat{x}\in B$ such that $f(x)\leq 1$ and $g(x)\geq 1$. We note that probably the computation of the convex combination can be avoided and the number of calls to the oracle can be improved to $O(M(\ln M+\epsilon^{-2}\ln\epsilon^{-1}))$. The details will be given in the full paper.

References

[1] Bienstock, D. (2002). Potential function methods for approximately solving linear programming problems: Theory and practive. Boston: Kluwer.

[2] Charikar,M., Chekuri, C., Goel, A., Guha, S., and Plotkin, S. A. (1998). Approximating a finite metric by a small number of tree metrics, *Proceedings of the 39th Annual IEEE Symposium on Foundations of Computer Science*, 379-388.

[3] Caragiannis, I., Ferreira, A., Kaklamanis, C., Perennes, S., and Rivano, H. (2001). Fractional path coloring with applications to WDM networks, *Proceedings 28th International Colloquium on Automata, Languages, and Programming*, ICALP 2001, LNCS 2076, 732-743.

[4] Fleischer, L. (2004). A fast approximation scheme for fractional covering problems with variable upper bounds, *Proceedings of the 15th ACM-SIAM Symposium on Discrete Algorithms*, SODA 2004.

[5] Garg, N. and Könemann, J. (1998). Fast and simpler algorithms for multicommodity flow and other fractional packing problems, *Proceedings of the 39th IEEE Annual Symposium on Foundations of Computer Science*, FOCS 1998, 300-309.

[6] Grigoriadis, M.D. and Khachiyan, L.G. (1994). Fast approximation schemes for convex programs with many blocks and coupling constraints, *SIAM Journal on Optimization*, 4: 86-107.

[7] Grigoriadis, M.D. and Khachiyan, L.G. (1996). Coordination complexity of parallel price-directive decomposition, *Mathematics of Operations Research*, 2: 321-340.

[8] Grigoriadis, M.D., Khachiyan, L.G., Porkolab, L., and Villavicencio, J. (2001). Approximate max-min resource sharing for structured concave optimization, *SIAM Journal on Optimization*, 41: 1081-1091.

[9] Jansen, K. and Porkolab, L. (2002). On preemptive resource constrained scheduling: polynomial-time approximation schemes, *Proceedings of the 9th International Conference on Integer Programming and Combinatorial Optimization*, IPCO 2002, LNCS 2337, 329-349.

[10] Jansen, K. and Zhang, H. (2002) Approximation algorithms for general packing problems with modified logarithmic potential function, *Proceedings of the 2nd IFIP International Conference on Theoretical Computer Science*, TCS 2002, Foundations of information technology in the era of network and mobile computing, Kluwer Academic Publisher, 2002, 255-266.

[11] Jansen, K. (2004). Approximation algorithms for the general max-min resource sharing problem: faster and simpler, to appear in: *Proceedings of the 9th Scandinavian Workshop on Algorithm Theory*, SWAT 2004.

[12] Kenyon, C. and E. Remila, E. (1996). Approximate strip packing, *Proceedings 37th IEEE Symposium on Foundations of Computer Science*, FOCS 1996, 31-36.

[13] Könemann, J. (2000). Fast combinatorial algorithms for packing and covering problems, Diploma Thesis, Max-Planck-Institute for Computer Science Saarbrücken.

[14] Plotkin, S.A., Shmoys, D.B., and Tardos, E. (1995). Fast approximation algorithms for fractional packing and covering problems, *Mathematics of Operations Research*, 20: 257-301.

[15] Villavicencio, J. and Grigoriadis, M.D. (1997). Approximate Lagrangian decomposition with a modified Karmarkar logarithmic potential, *Network Optimization*, Lecture Notes in Economics and Mathematical Systems, 450: 471-485.

[16] Young, N.E. (1995). Randomized rounding without solving the linear program, *Proceedings of the 6th ACM-SIAM Symposium on Discrete Algorithms* SODA 1995, 170-178.

[17] Young, N.E. (2001). Sequential and parallel algorithms for mixed packing and covering, *Proceedings of the 42nd Annual IEEE Symposium on Foundations of Computer Science*, FOCS 2001, 538-546.

ON WEIGHTED RECTANGLE PACKING WITH LARGE RESOURCES*

Aleksei V. Fishkin,[1] Olga Gerber,[1] and Klaus Jansen[1]

[1] *University of Kiel*
Olshausenstr. 40, 24118 Kiel, Germany
{avf,oge,kj}@informatik.uni-kiel.de

Abstract We study the problem of packing a set of n rectangles with weights into a dedicated rectangle so that the weight of the packed rectangles is maximized. We consider the case of large resources, that is, the side length of all rectangles is at most 1 and the side lengths of the dedicated rectangle differ by a factor of at least $1/\varepsilon^4$, for a fixed positive $\varepsilon > 0$. We present an algorithm which finds a rectangle packing of weight at least $(1-\varepsilon)$ of the optimum in time polynomial in n. As an application we show a $(2+\varepsilon)$-approximation algorithm for packing weighted rectangles into k rectangular bins of size (a, b).

Keywords: Rectangle packing, approximation algorithms

Introduction

We address the following problem of packing rectangles with weights into a rectangle. We are given a dedicated rectangle R of width $a \geq 0$ and height $b \geq 0$, and a list L of n rectangles R_i $(i = 1, \ldots, n)$ with widths $a_i \in (0, a]$, heights $b_i \in (0, b]$, and positive integral weights w_i. For a sublist $L' \subseteq L$ of rectangles, a *packing* of L' into the dedicated rectangle R is a positioning of the rectangles from L' within the area $[0, a] \times [0, b]$, so that all the rectangles of L' have disjoint interiors. Rectangles are not allowed to rotate. The goal is to find a sublist of rectangles $L' \subseteq L$ and its packing in R which maximizes the weight of packed rectangles, i.e., $\sum_{R_i \in L'} w_i$.

The above problem is a natural generalization of the knapsack problem to the two-dimensional version.

*Supported by EU-Projekt CRESCCO, Critical Resource Sharing for Cooperation in Complex Systems, IST-2001-33135, by EU Thematic Network APPOL, Approximation and Online Algorithms, IST-2001-30012 and by DFG-Graduiertenkolleg 357, Effiziente Algorithmen und Mehrskalenmethoden.

Related results. It is well-known that the knapsack problem is just weakly NP-hard [Garey and Johnson, 1979], and admits an FPTAS [Kellerer et al., 2004; Lawler, 1979]. In contrast, already the problem of packing squares with unit weights into a rectangle is strongly NP-hard [Baker et al., 1983]. So, the problem of packing rectangles with weights into a rectangle admits no FPTAS, unless P = NP.

From another side, one can also find a relation to strip packing: Given a list L of rectangles R_i $(i = 1, \ldots, n)$ with widths $a_i \in (0, 1]$ and positive heights $b_i \geq 0$ it is required to pack the rectangles of L into the vertical strip $[0, 1] \times [0, +\infty)$ so that the packing height is minimized. In particular, this also defines the problem of packing rectangles into a rectangle of fixed width and minimum height, or the well-known two-dimensional cutting stock problem [Gilmore and Gomory, 1965].

Of course, the strip packing problem is strongly NP-hard since it includes the bin packing problem as a special case. In fact many known simple strip packing ideas come from bin packing. The "Bottom-Left" heuristic has asymptotic performance ratio equal to 2 when the rectangles are sorted by decreasing widths [Baker et al., 1980]. In [Coffman et al., 1980] several simple algorithms were studied where the rectangles are placed on "shelves" using one-dimensional bin-packing heuristics. It was shown that the First-Fit shelf algorithm has asymptotic performance ratio of 1.7 when the rectangles are sorted by decreasing height (this defines the First-Fit-Decreasing-Height algorithm). The asymptotic performance ratio of the best heuristic was further reduced to $3/2$ [Sleator, 1980], then to $4/3$ [Golan, 1981] and to $5/4$ [Baker et al., 1981]. Finally, in [Kenyon and Remila, 1996] it was shown that there exists an asymptotic FPTAS in the case when the side lengths of all rectangles in the list are at most 1. (In the above definition $a_i, b_i \in (0, 1]$ for all R_i.) For the absolute performance, the two best current algorithms have the same performance ratio 2 [Schiermeyer, 1994; Steinberg, 1997].

In contrast to knapsack and strip packing there are just few results known for packing rectangles into a rectangle. For a long time the only known result has been an asymptotic $(4/3)$-approximation algorithm for packing unweighted squares into a rectangle [Baker et al., 1983]. Only very recently in [Jansen and Zhang, 2004], several first approximability results have been presented for the packing rectangles with weights into a rectangle. The best one is a $(2 + \varepsilon)$-approximation algorithm.

Our results. In this paper we consider the case of so-called large resources, when the number of packed rectangles is relatively large. Formally, in the above formulation it is assumed that all rectangles R_i $(i = 1, \ldots, n)$ in the list L have widths and heights $a_i, b_i \in (0, 1]$, and the dedicated rectangle R has unit width $a = 1$ and quite a large height $b \geq 1/\varepsilon^4$, for a fixed positive

$\varepsilon > 0$. We present an algorithm which finds a sublist $L' \subseteq L$ of rectangles and its packing into the dedicated rectangle R with weight at least $(1 - \varepsilon)$OPT, where OPT is the optimum weight. The running time of the algorithm is polynomial in the number of rectangles n.

Our approach to approximation is as follows. At the beginning we take an optimal rectangle packing inside of the dedicated rectangle, considering it as a strip packing. We then perform several transformations that simplify the packing structure, without dramatically increasing the packing height and decreasing the packing weight, such that the final result is amenable to a fast enumeration. As soon as such a "near-optimal" strip packing is found, we apply our shifting technique. This puts the packing into the dedicated rectangle by removing some less weighted piece of the packing.

Interestingly, by considering a weekly restricted case we are able to achieve the best possible approximation ratio. This makes a significant step in understanding of approximation properties of the problem. Furthermore, the difference in the side lengths of the dedicated rectangle and the rectangles in the list yields that the number of packed rectangles is large, that can be met quite often in practice. In order to be able to cope with the problem we also design several new approximation techniques, some of them are nice combinations of various classical techniques from knapsack and strip packing. This demonstrates quite a strong relation between several variants of packing.

Applications. There recently has been increasing interest in the advertisement placement problem for newspapers and the Internet [Adler et al., 1998; Freund and Naor, 2002]. In a basic version of the problem, we are given a list of n advertisements and k identical rectangular pages of fixed size (a, b), on which advertisements may be placed. Each ith advertisement appears as a small rectangle of size (a_i, b_i), and is associated with a profit p_i $(i = 1, \dots, n)$. Advertisements may not overlap. The goal is to maximize the total profit of the advertisements placed on all k pages.

This problem is also known as the problem of packing n weighted rectangles into k identical rectangular bins. Here, as an application of our algorithm, we provide a $(2 + \varepsilon)$-approximation algorithm. The running time of the algorithm is polynomial in n for any fixed $\varepsilon > 0$.

Last notes. The paper is organized as follows. In section 1 we introduce notations and give some preliminary results. In Section 2, we present our shifting technique. In Section 3 we perform packing transformations. In Section 4 we outline the algorithm. Finally, in the last section we give an approximation algorithm to pack rectangles into k rectangular bins of size (a, b). Due to space limitations, some of the proofs are omitted.

1. Preliminaries

We are given a dedicated rectangle R of unit width $a = 1$ and height $b \geq 0$, and a list L of rectangles R_i ($i = 1, \ldots, n$) with widths $a_i \in (0, 1]$, heights $b_i \in (0, 1]$, and positive integral weights w_i. The goal is to find a sublist of rectangles $L' \subseteq L$ and its packing in R which maximizes the weight of packed rectangles, i.e., $\sum_{R_i \in L'} w_i$.

We will use the following notations. For a sublist of rectangles $L' \subseteq L$, we will write $weight(L')$, $height(L')$, and $size(L')$ to denote the values of $\sum_{R_i \in L'} w_i$; $\sum_{R_i \in L'} b_i$, and $\sum_{R_i \in L'} a_i \cdot b_i$, respectively. Also, we will write $L^{opt} \subseteq L$ to denote an optimal sublist of rectangles, and OPT to denote the optimal objective value. Thus, $weight(L^{opt}) = \text{OPT}$ and $size(L^{opt}) \leq a \cdot b = b$. Throughout of the paper we assume that $0 < \varepsilon < 1/2^{10}$, $1/\varepsilon' = (2 + \varepsilon)/\varepsilon$ is integral ($\varepsilon' = \varepsilon/(2 + \varepsilon)$), $m = 1/(\varepsilon')^2$, and the height value $b \geq 1/\varepsilon^4$.

1.1 Separating rectangles

Given a positive $\varepsilon' > 0$, we partition the list L of rectangles into two sublists: L_{narrow}, containing all the rectangles of width at most ε', and L_{wide}, containing all the rectangles of width larger than ε'.

1.2 Knapsack

In the knapsack problem we are given a knapsack capacity B and a set of items $I = \{1, 2, \ldots, n\}$, where each item $i \in I$ is associated with its size s_i and profit p_i. It is required to find a subset $I' \subseteq I$ which maximizes the profit of $\sum_{i \in I'} p_i$ subject to $\sum_{i \in I'} s_i \leq B$, i.e., it fits in a knapsack of size B.

The knapsack problem is NP-hard, but it admits an FPTAS [Garey and Johnson, 1979]. In particular, we can use any FPTAS version from [Kellerer et al., 2004; Lawler, 1979]. Given a precision $\delta > 0$, the algorithm outputs a subset $I(B) \subseteq I$ such that

$$\sum_{i \in I(B)} s_i \leq B \text{ and } \sum_{i \in I(B)} p_i > (1 - \delta)\text{OPT}(I, B), \tag{1}$$

where $\text{OPT}(I, B)$ is the maximum profit of I with respect to capacity B. For simplicity, we will write $KS(n, \delta)$ to denote the running time of the algorithm, which is polynomial in the number of items n and $1/\delta$.

1.3 Solving knapsacks with wide and narrow rectangles

We order all the wide rectangles in L_{wide} by non-increasing widths. W.l.o.g. we assume that there are n' wide rectangles $R_1 = (a_1, b_1)$, $R_2 = (a_2, b_2), \ldots,$ $R_{n'} = (a_{n'}, b_{n'})$ with widths $a_1 \geq a_2 \geq \ldots \geq a_{n'} \geq \varepsilon'$. So, for any two $1 \leq k < \ell \leq n'$, let $L_{wide}(k, \ell)$ denote the list of all wide rectangles R_i in

L_{wide} with $\ell \geq i \geq k$. Here we work with rectangles as items. However, we treat narrow and wide rectangles differently. For wide rectangles, we only pay attention to the height values. For narrow rectangles, however, we only pay attention to the size values. By solving knapsack problems, we get the following result.

LEMMA 1 *Let H and S be some positive variables. Let $L_{wide}(k, \ell)$ be the list of wide rectangles between R_k and R_ℓ. Let L_{narrow} be the list of all narrow rectangles. Then, in $O(KS(n, \varepsilon^2)$ time we can find*

- *a sublist $L_{wide}(k, \ell, H) \subseteq L_{wide}(k, \ell)$ such that the height of $L_{wide}(k, \ell, H)$ is at most H and*

$$weight(L_{wide}(k, \ell, H)) \geq (1 - \varepsilon^2/4)\mathrm{OPT}(L_{wide}(k, \ell), H),$$

  where $\mathrm{OPT}(L_{wide}(k, \ell), H)$ is the maximum weight of a subset of $L_{wide}(k, \ell)$ with a total height at most H.

- *a sublist $L_{narrow}(S) \subseteq L_{narrow}$ such that the size of $L_{narrow}(S)$ is at most S and*

$$weight(L_{narrow}(S)) \geq (1 - \varepsilon^2/4)\mathrm{OPT}(L_{narrow}, S),$$

  where $\mathrm{OPT}(L_{narrow}, S)$ is the maximum weight of a subset of L_{narrow} with area at most S.

1.4 Packing narrow rectangles: NFDH

We consider the following strip-packing problem: Given a sublist $L' \subseteq L_{narrow}$ of narrow rectangles and a strip with fixed width $1 - c$ ($c \in [0, 1]$) and unbounded height, pack the rectangles of L' into the the strip such that the height to which the strip is filled is as small as possible.

First, we order the rectangles of L' by decreasing heights. Then, we put the narrow rectangles into the strip-packing by using Next-Fit-Decreasing-Height (NFDH): The rectangles are packed so as to form a sequence of sublevels. The first sublevel is just the bottom line of the strip. Each subsequent sublevel is defined by a horizontal line drawn through the top of the rectangle placed on the previous sublevel. Rectangles are packed in a left-justified greedy manner, until there is insufficient space to the right to place the next rectangle, at that point, the current sublevel is discontinued, the next sublevel is defined and packing proceeds on the new sublevel. For an illustration see Fig. 1.

We will use the following simple result.

LEMMA 2 *Let $L' \subseteq L_{narrow}$ be any sublist of narrow rectangles ordered by non-increasing heights. If the Next-Fit-Decreasing-Height (NFDH) heuristic outputs a packing of height $NFDH(L')$, then the area covered by the narrow rectangles $AREA \geq (1 - c - \varepsilon')(NFDH(L') - 1)$.*

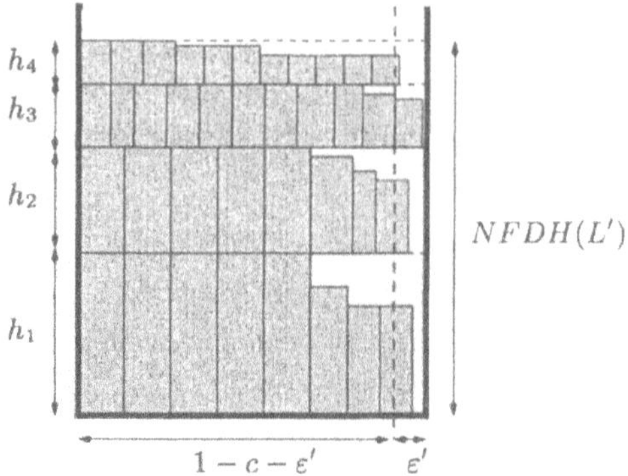

Figure 1. NFDH for narrow rectangles

1.5 Strip packing by KR-algorithm

We consider the following strip-packing problem: Given a sublist $L' \subseteq L$ of rectangles and a strip with unit width and unbounded height, pack the rectangles of L' into the the strip such that the height to which the strip is filled is as small as possible.

As we mentioned before the strip packing problem admits an asymptotic FPTAS. We will use the following result.

THEOREM 3 (KENYON AND RÉMILA, 1996) *There is an algorithm A which, given an accuracy $\varepsilon > 0$, a sublist $L' \subseteq L$ of rectangles and a strip with unit width 1 and unbounded height, packs the rectangles of L' into the the strip such that the height to which the strip is filled*

$$A(L') \leq (1+\varepsilon)strip(L') + O(1/\varepsilon^2), \tag{2}$$

where $strip(L')$ denotes the height of the optimal strip packing of L'. The running time of A is polynomial in n and $1/\varepsilon$.

For simplicity, we name such an algorithm in the theorem by the KR-algorithm. Also, we will write $KR(n, \varepsilon)$ to denote its running time. In Section 3 we will give more details on packing by the KR-algorithm.

2. Shifting

Assume that we are given a strip packing of height $(1 + O(\varepsilon))b$ for a list of rectangles whose weight is at least $(1 - O(\varepsilon))$OPT. The idea of our shifting technique is to remove some less weighted piece of height $O(\varepsilon)b$. Then, the weight value remains $(1 - O(\varepsilon))$OPT, but the height value reduces to b. This fits into the area of the dedicated rectangle $R = (a, b)$.

LEMMA 4 *Suppose we are given a strip packing of height* $(1+\delta_2)b$ *for a sublist* $L' \subseteq L$ *with weight at least* $(1-\delta_1)OPT$, *for some* $\delta_1, \delta_2 \approx O(\varepsilon)$. *If*

$$\left\lceil \frac{1}{\delta_1} \right\rceil \leq \left\lfloor \frac{(1+\delta_2)+2}{\delta_2 \cdot b + 2} \right\rfloor, \tag{3}$$

then in $O(n + 1/\varepsilon)$ *time we can find a rectangle packing of a sublist of* L' *into the area of the dedicated rectangle* $R = (a, b)$ *with the weight value at least* $(1 - 3\delta_1)$OPT.

3. Transformations of optimal solution

Here we discuss some transformations which simplify the structure of the optimal solution L^{opt}. We start with transforming a packing of L^{opt} into a well structured packing. This introduces the lists L^{opt}_{wide} of wide rectangles, L^{opt}_{narrow} of narrow rectangles, and m optimal threshold rectangles. Next, assuming the m threshold rectangles and the m height capacity values are known, we perform a transformation of the optimal lists L^{opt}_{wide} and L^{opt}_{narrow} to some lists found by solving a series of knapsacks. Then, we perform a rounding transformation which turns all the m height capacity values to some discrete points. Each of these transformations may increases the height value by $O(\varepsilon b)$, and may decrease the weight value by $O(\varepsilon\text{OPT})$. However, in the next section we show that L^{opt} can be still approximated with quite a good precision.

3.1 Well-structured packing

Here we describe a well structured packing of the optimal solution.

Separation. Let L^{opt} be the optimal solution. We define the lists of narrow and wide rectangles: $L^{opt}_{narrow} = L^{opt} \cap L_{narrow}$ and $L^{opt}_{wide} = L^{opt} \cap L_{wide}$. Clearly, $weight(L^{opt}_{wide}) + weight(L^{opt}_{narrow}) = \text{OPT}$.

Threshold rectangles. Let $R_{k_1} = (a_{k_1}, b_{k_1}), R_{k_2} = (a_{k_2}, b_{k_2}), \ldots, R_{k_m} = (a_{k_m}, b_{k_m})$ be a sequence of optimal wide rectangles in L^{opt}_{wide} such that $1 \leq k_1 < k_2 < \ldots < k_m \leq n'$. Then, we call such rectangles as the threshold rectangles. As it is defined, widths $a_{k_1} \geq a_{k_2} \geq \ldots \geq a_{k_m} \geq \varepsilon'$.

Configurations. Now we can define configurations. A configuration is defined as a multi-set of widths chosen among the m threshold widths in $\{a_{k_i} | i = 1, \ldots, m\}$ which sum to at most 1, i.e. they may occur at the same level. Their sum is called the width of the configuration.

Layers. Let q be some positive integer. Let $C_1, C_2, \ldots, C_q$ be some distinct configurations, numbered by non-increasing widths, and let C_{q+1} be an empty configuration. Let α_{ij} denote the number of occurrences of width a_{k_i} in C_j. Then, the value of $c_j = \sum_{i=1}^{m} a_{k(ij)}\alpha_{ij}$ is called the width of C_j. Therefore, $c_1 \geq c_2 \geq \ldots \geq c_q \geq c_{q+1} = 0$.

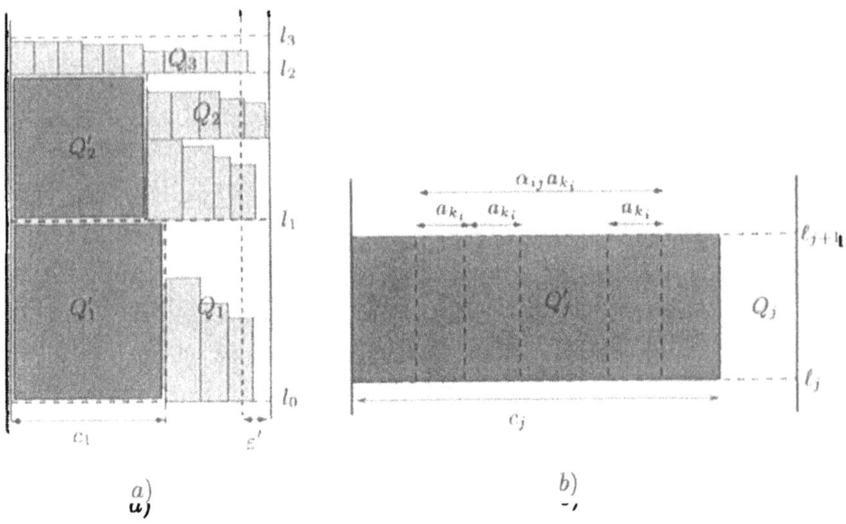

Figure 2. a) A well structured packing with 3 layers; b) Structure of layer $[0,1] \times [\ell_j, \ell_{j+1}]$

Let $0 = \ell_0 \leq \ell_1 \leq \ldots \leq \ell_q \leq \ell_{q+1} = h$ be some $q+1$ non-negative values. We define $q+1$ layers as follows. The layer $[0,1] \times [\ell_j, \ell_{j+1}]$ ($j = 0, \ldots, q+1$) corresponds to configuration C_j. It is divided into two rectangles: $Q_j = [c_j, 1] \times [\ell_j, \ell_{j+1}]$ and $Q'_j = [0, c_j] \times [\ell_j, \ell_{j+1}]$. (Notice that the last layer is $Q_{q+1} = [0,1] \times [\ell_q, \ell_{q+1}]$, as shown in Fig. 2a)

From one side, all Q_j ($j = 1, \ldots, q+1$) are empty. From another side, each Q'_j ($j = 1, \ldots, q$) consists of m vertical multi-slices, each ith of those with exactly α_{ij} identical slices of width a_{k_i}, as shown in Fig. 2b. The value of $(\ell_{j+1} - \ell_j)$ defines the height of configuration C_j, and the value of $h = \ell_{q+1}$ defines the packing height. The value of $H_i = \sum_{j=1}^{q} \alpha_{ij}(\ell_{j+1} - \ell_j)$ defines the total height of all slices of width a_{k_i}, and it is called the ith threshold capacity.

Well-structured packing. A strip packing of the optimal solution L^{opt} is called a well-structured strip packing with $q+1$ layers if all Q_j ($j = 1, \ldots, q+1$) are filled by narrow rectangles, and all the slices of width a_{k_i} ($i = 1, \ldots, m$) are greedily filled by the wide rectangles from $L^{opt} \cap L_{wide}(k_i, k_{i+1} - 1)$. (Here and further we assume w.l.o.g. that $k_{m+1} - 1 = n'$.) Now we are ready to give the following result.

THEOREM 5 (KENYON AND RÉMILA, 1996) *There exists a well-structured packing of L^{opt} with $2m+1$ layers such that its height $h \leq \max\{strip(L^{opt}_{wide})$*

$(1+1/(m\varepsilon'))+2m+1, size(L^{opt})(1+1/(m\varepsilon'))/(1-\varepsilon')+4m+1\}$, where $strip(L^{opt}_{wide})$ is the height of the optimal strip packing of L^{opt}_{wide}.

3.2 Augmentation

Now we can give the following simple result.

LEMMA 6 *If $\varepsilon' = \varepsilon/(2+\varepsilon)$, $m = (1/\varepsilon')^2$, $\varepsilon < 1/2^{10}$ and $b \geq 1/\varepsilon^4$, then there exists a well-structured packing with $2m+1$ layers of the optimal solution L^{opt} of height $h \leq (1+2\varepsilon)b$.*

3.3 Approximating wide rectangles

Our idea is to guess most profitable rectangles, knowing the optimal threshold rectangles and capacity values. Let R_{k_i} and H_i $(i = 1,\ldots,m)$ be the optimal ith threshold rectangle and capacity, respectively. Then, by solving a series of knapsacks we can find the lists $L_{wide}(k_i, k_{i+1}-1, H_i)$ of wide rectangles. These are quite good approximations for lists $L_{wide}(k_i, k_{i+1}-1) \cap L^{opt}$, and hence all together they give a good approximation of the optimal list L^{opt}_{wide} of wide rectangles.

LEMMA 7 *The value of*

$$\sum_{i=1}^{m} weight(L_{wide}(k_i, k_{i+1}-1, H_i)) \geq (1-\varepsilon^2/4)weight(L^{opt}_{wide}). \quad (4)$$

If the wide rectangles of L^{opt}_{wide} are replaced by the rectangles of all lists $L_{wide}(k_i, k_{i+1}-1, H_i)$ $(i = 1,\ldots,m)$, then the height h of the well-structured packing increases by at most $\Delta_{wide} \leq \varepsilon b$.

Proof. As it was defined, $L_{wide}(k_i, k_{i+1}-1) \cap L^{opt} \subseteq L_{wide}(k_i, k_{i+1}-1)$. In the well structured packing, the rectangles of $L_{wide}(k_i, k_{i+1}-1) \cap L^{opt}$ are placed in the slices of width a_{k_i}. The total height of all these slices is exactly the value of H_i. So, $height(L_{wide}(k_i, k_{i+1}-1) \cap L^{opt}) \leq H_i$. Hence, by Lemma 1 solving m knapsack problems we can decrease the weight by at most some factor of $(1-\varepsilon^2/4)$.

Notice that both $L_{wide}(k_i, k_{i+1}-1, H_i)$ and $L_{wide}(k_i, k_{i+1}-1) \cap L^{opt}$ have quite similar characteristics. We use it as follows. We take the well-structured packing of L^{opt} and go over all the rectangles $Q'_1, Q'_2, \ldots, Q'_{2m}$ in the $2m$ layers. Inside all the slices of widths a_{k_i} $(i = 1,\ldots,m)$ we replace the rectangles of $L_{wide}(k_i, k_{i+1}-1) \cap L^{opt}$ by the rectangles of $L_{wide}(k_i, k_{i+1}-1, H_i)$ in a greedy manner.

Since we greedily place rectangles, it may happen that some rectangles do not fit completely into the slices. We then increase the height of each layer by 1, that must create enough space for all rectangles. Since there are $2m$ layers, the height h increases by at most $\Delta_{wide} \leq 2m \leq \varepsilon b$, for $\varepsilon < 1/2^{10}$ and $b \geq 1/\varepsilon^4$. The result of lemma follows.

3.4 Approximating narrow rectangles

We use a similar idea to guess most profitable narrow rectangles, knowing the optimal configurations with heights and widths. Let c_j and ℓ_j ($i = 1, \ldots, 2m+1$) be the width and height of configuration C_j, respectively. Recall that the optimal narrow rectangles of L^{opt}_{narrow} are placed in rectangles $Q_1, Q_2, \ldots, Q_{2m}, Q_{2m+1}$. Hence we can bound the size value

$$size(L^{opt}_{narrow}) \leq \sum_{j=1}^{2m+1} (1 - c_j)(\ell_{i+1} - \ell_i). \tag{5}$$

So, by solving the knapsack problem we can find the list $L_{narrow}(S)$ of narrow rectangles, where the value of knapsack capacity

$$S = \sum_{j=1}^{2m+1} (1 - c_j)(\ell_{j+1} - \ell_j). \tag{6}$$

This is a good approximation of the optimal list L^{opt}_{narrow} of narrow rectangles.

LEMMA 8 *The value of* $weight(L_{narrow}(S)) \geq (1-\varepsilon^2/4)weight(L^{opt}_{narrow})$. *If the narrow rectangles of* L^{opt}_{narrow} *are replaced by the narrow rectangles* $L_{narrow}(S)$, *then the height h of the well-structured packing increases by at most* $\Delta_{narrow} \leq 2\varepsilon b$.

Proof. Clearly, the rectangles of L^{opt}_{narrow} must be in L_{narrow}. By (5), the area of L^{opt}_{narrow} is at most S. Hence, by Lemma 1 solving the knapsack problem can only decrease the weight by some factor of $(1 - \varepsilon^2/4)$. So, we get the weight at least $(1 - \varepsilon^2/4)weight(L^{opt}_{narrow})$.

Notice that both L^{opt}_{narrow} and $L_{narrow}(S)$ have quite similar characteristics. We use it as follows. We go over the rectangles $Q_1, Q_2, \ldots, Q_{2m}, Q_{2m+1}$ in the $2m + 1$ layers, and place the rectangles of $L_{narrow}(S)$ by using NFDH. If not all rectangles are placed, then we work with a new layer of width 1 and height Δ_{narrow}.

The new rectangle has width 1 and height Δ_{narrow}. Similar to Lemma 2, the area covered by narrow rectangles in additional layer is at least $(1-\varepsilon')(\Delta_{narrow} - 1)$. Similarly, consider the narrow rectangles packed in rectangle Q_j ($j = 1, \ldots, 2m+1$). The height of this packing is at least $\ell_{j+1} - \ell_j - 1$. The width of Q_j is $1 - c_j$. Hence, the area covered by the narrow rectangles is at least $(1 - c_j - \varepsilon')(\ell_{j+1} - \ell_j - 2)$. Combining over all layers, the area covered is at least $\sum_{j=1}^{2m+1}(1 - c_j - \varepsilon')(\ell_{j+1} - \ell_j - 2) + (1 - \varepsilon')(\Delta_{narrow} - 1)$.

Recall that the area of $L^{opt}_{narrow}(S)$ is at most $S = \sum_{j=1}^{2m+1}(1-c_j)(\ell_{j+1}-\ell_j)$. We need an upper bound on the value of Δ_{narrow}. So, it is enough to require that this size value is equal to the above bound. So, $\sum_{j=1}^{2m+1}(1-c_j-\varepsilon')(\ell_{j+1} - \ell_j - 2) + (1-\varepsilon')(\Delta_{narrow} - 1) \leq \sum_{j=1}^{2m+1}(1-c_j)(\ell_{j+1} - \ell_j)$. Hence, $(1-\varepsilon')(\Delta_{narrow} - 1) \leq 2\sum_{j=1}^{2m+1}(1-c_j-\varepsilon') + \varepsilon' \sum_{j=1}^{2m+1}(\ell_{j+1} - \ell_j)$ and from $\sum_{j=1}^{2m+1}(\ell_{j+1} - \ell_j) = h$

$$\Delta_{narrow} \leq 1 + [2\sum_{j=1}^{2m+1}(1-c_j-\varepsilon') + \varepsilon' \cdot h]/(1-\varepsilon') \leq 2\varepsilon b$$

for $\varepsilon < 1/2^{10}$, $m = 1/(\varepsilon')^2$, $\varepsilon' = \varepsilon/(2+\varepsilon)$ and $b \geq 1/\varepsilon^4$. The result of lemma follows.

3.5 Rounding

Finally, we round all values to some discrete points.

LEMMA 9 *If we round up each threshold capacity H_i ($i = 1, \ldots, m$) in $L_{wide}(k_i, k_{i+1} - 1, H_i)$ to the the closest value in*

$$CAPACITY = \{t \cdot (\varepsilon')^4 \cdot b | t = 1, 2, \ldots, 1/(\varepsilon')^6\},$$

and the value of S in $L_{narrow}(S)$ to the closest value in

$$SIZE = \{t \cdot (\varepsilon')^4 \cdot b | t = 1, 2, \ldots, 1/(\varepsilon')^5\},$$

then the height h of the well-structured packing increases by at most $\Delta_{rounding} \leq \varepsilon b$.

Proof. Consider a well structured packing of all $L_{wide}(k_i, k_{i+1} - 1, H_i)$ and $L_{narrow}(S)$ with $2m+1$ layers. Each layer is cut into slices which correspond to a configuration. The wide rectangles of $L_{wide}(k_i, k_{i+1} - 1, H_i)$ are packed in the slices of width a_{k_i} in a greedy manner. The rectangles of $L_{narrow}(S)$ are packed by the NFDH heuristic. The height of the packing is

$$h + \Delta_{wide} + \Delta_{narrow} \leq (1 + 5\varepsilon)b.$$

By rounding, we increase the value of each H_i and S by at most $(\varepsilon')^4 b$. Hence, in solving knapsacks the height of $L_{wide}(k_i, k_{i+1} - 1, H_i)$ increases by at most $(\varepsilon')^4 b$, and the area of $L_{narrow}(S)$ increases by at most $(\varepsilon')^4 b$. Next, we proceed as in approximating wide and narrow rectangles. We go over all slices of width a_{k_i} and replace all old wide rectangles by the new wide rectangles in $L_{wide}(k_i, k_{i+1} - 1, H_i)$. Also, we go over all layers and replace all old narrow rectangles by the new narrow rectangles in $L_{narrow}(S)$.

In order to accommodate all of wide and narrow rectangles we need to increase the heights of some layers (configurations). We can estimate the total increase as follows. First, we increase the height value of each layer (configuration) by $(\varepsilon')^4 b$. Then, similar to approximating wide and narrow rectangles, we can pack all the rectangles, but cutting them if they do not fit into slices or layers. Since the height value of any rectangle is at most 1, we simply increase the height of each layer by 1. This eliminates cuts. In overall, we can estimate the total increase as

$$\Delta_{rounding} \leq (2m+1)[(\varepsilon')^4 b + 1] = O(\varepsilon^2 b) \leq \varepsilon b,$$

for $m = 1/(\varepsilon')^2$, $\varepsilon' = \varepsilon/(2+\varepsilon)$, $\varepsilon \leq 1/2^{10}$ and $b \geq 1/\varepsilon^4$.

The height of the final packing is at most $(1+5\varepsilon)b + \Delta_{rounding} = (1+6\varepsilon)b$. This means that the size of all $L_{wide}(k_i, k_{i+1}-1, H_i)$ and $L_{narrow}(S)$ is at most $(1+6\varepsilon)b$. Hence, after rounding the value of S is at most $(1+6\varepsilon)b \leq b/\varepsilon'$. Since the width value of the rectangles in $L_{wide}(k_i, k_{i+1}-1, H_i)$ is at least ε', after rounding the value of H_i can be at most $(1+6\varepsilon)b/\varepsilon' \leq b/(\varepsilon')^2$. Thus, the value of t in $CAPACITY$ and $SIZE$ can be at most $1/(\varepsilon')^5$ and $1/(\varepsilon')^6$, respectively. The result of lemma follows.

4. Overall algorithm

Here we outline our algorithm and summarize all above results. We simply enumerate all possible sequences of threshold rectangles and their capacity values. Then, we solve a series of knapsack problems to get several lists of wide and narrow rectangles, and find a packing for them by using the KR-algorithm. At the end, we select the most profitable packing and apply the shifting technique to it. The final packing fits into the dedicated rectangle and its weight is near-optimal.

Rectangle Packing (RP):
Input: List L, accuracy $\varepsilon > 0$, and $\varepsilon' = \varepsilon/(2+\varepsilon)$, $m = 1/(\varepsilon')^2$.

1 Split L into L_{narrow} and L_{wide} of narrow and wide rectangles, whose widths are at most ε' and larger than ε';

2 Sort the wide rectangles of L_{wide} according to their widths;

3 For each sequence of $m = (1/\varepsilon')$ wide threshold rectangles $R_{k_1}, R_{k_2}, \ldots R_{k_m}$ from L_{wide}:

   (a) select m capacity values of $H_i \in CAPACITY$ and a value of $S \in SIZE$;

   (b) find m lists $L_{wide}(k_i, k_{i+1}-1, H_i)$ and list $L_{narrow}(S)$;

   (c) run the KR-algorithm and keep the solution (if it's height is at most $(1+16\varepsilon)b$).

4 Select a packing whose weight is maximum;

5 Apply the shifting technique.

We conclude with the following final result.

THEOREM 10 *The* RP*-algorithm outputs a rectangle packing of a sublist* $L' \subseteq L$ *in the area* $[0, a] \times [0, b]$ *of the dedicated rectangle R. The weight of the packing* $weight(L') \geq (1-\varepsilon)\mathrm{OPT}$, *where* OPT *is the optimal weight. The running time of the* RP*-algorithm is bounded by* $O(n^{1/\varepsilon^2}(1/\varepsilon^6)^{1/\varepsilon^2+1}[KS(n,\varepsilon)\cdot KR(n,\varepsilon)])$, *where* $KS(n,\varepsilon)$ *is the running time of a FPTAS for solving the knapsack problem, and* $KR(n,\varepsilon)$ *is the running time of the KR-algorithm.*

5. Packing into *k* rectangular bins

Here we consider the problem of packing weighted rectangles into k bins. Given k identical bins of size (a, b) and a list L of n rectangles R_i ($i = 1, \ldots, n$) with widths $a_i \in (0, a]$, heights $b_i \in (0, b]$, and positive integral weights w_i. The goal is to find a sublist $L' \subseteq L$ of rectangles and its packing into k bins such that the total weight of packed rectangles is maximized. We present the following algorithm:
Algorithm k-Bins:
Input: List L, accuracy $\varepsilon > 0$, k bins of size (a, b).

Case 1. $k \leq O(1/\varepsilon^4)$. Use a $(2+\varepsilon)$-approximation algorithm, that generalizes an approximation algorithm for one bin [Jansen and Zhang, 2004] to a constant number of bins (for the details we refer to a full version of this paper).

Case 2. $k > O(1/\varepsilon^4)$.

1 Take all k bins together to get the rectangle (a, kb).

2 Apply our algorithm with the PTAS to pack a subset of rectangles into a larger rectangle (a, kb), that gives us a packing with the total profit $\geq (1-\varepsilon)\mathrm{OPT}$.

3 Take the current rectangle packing. Draw $(k-1)$ vertical lines which divide the packing into k bins.

4 Split this packing into 2 solutions:

   (a) solution, which contains all rectangles which lie inside of each bin.

   (b) solution, which contains all rectangles which intersect any dividing line between two bins.

5 Take the solution which has the highest profit.

We can conclude with the following result.

THEOREM 11 *The algorithm k-Bins is a* $(2+\varepsilon)$*-approximation algorithm. Its running time is polynomial in the number of rectangles* n *for any fixed* $\varepsilon > 0$.

References

Adler, M., Gibbons, P., and Matias, Y. (1998). Scheduling space-sharing for internet advertising. Journal of Scheduling (to appear).

Baker, B., Brownand, D., and Katseff, H. (1981). A 5/4 algorithm for two dimensional packing. *J. of Algorithms*, 2:348–368.

Baker, B., Calderbank, A., Coffman, E., and Lagarias, J. (1983). Approximation algorithms for maximizing the number of squares packed into a rectangle. *SIAM Journal on Algebraic and Discrete Methods*, 4:383–397.

Baker, B., Coffman, E., and Rivest, R. (1980). Orthogonal packings in two dimensions. *SIAM J. Comput.*, 9:846–855.

Coffman, E., Garey, M., Johnson, D., and Tarjan, R. (1980). Performance bounds for level-oriented two-dimensional packing algorithms. *SIAM J. Comput.*, 9:808–826.

Freund, A. and Naor, J. (2002). Approximating the advertisement placement problem. In *Proceedings of the 9th Conference on Integer Programming and Combinatorial Optimization (IPCO'02)*, LNCS 2337, pages 415–424.

Garey, M. R. and Johnson, D. S. (1979). *Computers and intractability: A guide to the theory of NP-completeness*. Freeman, San Francisco, CA.

Gilmore, P. and Gomory, R. (1965). Multistage cutting stock problems of two and more dimensions. *Operations Research*, 13:94–120.

Golan, I. (1981). Performance bounds for orthogonal, oriented two-dimensional packing algorithms. *SIAM J. Comput.*, 10:571–582.

Jansen, K. and Zhang, G. (2004). On rectangle packing: maximizing benefits. In *Fifteenth Annual Symposium on Discrete Algorithms*, pages 197–206.

Kellerer, H., Pferschy, U., and Pisinger, D. (2004). *Knapsack problems*. Springer.

Kenyon, C. and Remila, E. (1996). Approximate strip-packing. In *Thirty-Seventh Annual Symposium on Foundations of Computer Science*, pages 31–36.

Lawler, E. (1979). Fast approximation algorithms for knapsack problems. *Mathematics of Operations Research*, 4:339–356.

Schiermeyer, I. (1994). Reverse fit : a 2-optimal algorithm for packing rectangles. *Proceedings 2nd European Symposium on Algorithms*, pages 290–299.

Sleator, D. (1980). A 2.5 times optimal algorithm for bin packing in two dimensions. *IPL*, (10):37–40.

Steinberg, A. (1997). A strip-packing algorithm with absolute performance bound 2. *SIAM Journal on Computing*, 26(2):401–409.

AN $O(n \log^2 n)$ ALGORITHM FOR A SINK LOCATION PROBLEM IN DYNAMIC TREE NETWORKS

Satoko Mamada,[1] Takeaki Uno,[2] Kazuhisa Makino,[1] and Satoru Fujishige[3]

[1] *Division of Mathematical Science for Social Systems, Graduate School of Engineering Science, Osaka University*
mamada@inulab.sys.es.osaka-u.ac.jp, makino@sys.es.osaka-u.ac.jp

[2] *Foundations of Informatics Research Division, National Institute of Informatics*
uno@nii.jp

[3] *Research Institute for Mathematical Sciences, Kyoto University*
fujishig@kurims.kyoto-u.ac.jp

Abstract In this paper, we consider a sink location in a dynamic network which consists of a graph with capacities and transit times on its arcs. Given a dynamic network with initial supplies at vertices, the problem is to find a vertex v as a sink in the network such that we can send all the initial supplies to v as quickly as possible. We present an $O(n \log^2 n)$ time algorithm for the sink location problem in a dynamic network of tree structure, where n is the number of vertices in the network. This improves upon the existing $O(n^2)$-time bound. As a corollary, we also show that the quickest transshipment problem can be solved in $O(n \log^2 n)$ time if a given network is a tree and has a single sink. Our results are based on data structures for representing tables (i.e., sets of intervals with their height), which may be of independent interest.

Keywords: Dynamic flows, location problem, tree networks.

1. Introduction

We consider dynamic networks that include transit times on arcs. Each arc a has the transit time $\tau(a)$ specifying the amount of time it takes for flow to travel from the tail to the head of a. In contrast to the classical *static* flows, flows in a dynamic network are called *dynamic*. In the dynamic setting, the capacity of an arc limits the rate of the flow into the arc at each time instance. Dynamic flow problems were introduced by Ford and Fulkerson [6] in the late 1950s (see e.g. [5]). Since then, dynamic flows have been studied extensively. One of the main reasons is that dynamic flow problems arise in a number of applications such as traffic control, evacuation plans, production systems, communication networks, and financial flows (see the surveys by Aronson [2] and Powell, Jaillet, and Odoni [14]). For example, for building evacuation [7], vertices

$v \in V$ model workplaces, hallways, stairwells, and so on, and arcs $a \in A$ model the connection link between the adjacent components of the building. For an arc $a = (v, w)$, the capacity $u(a)$ represents the number of people who can traverse the link corresponding to a per unit time, and $\tau(a)$ denotes the time it takes to traverse a from v to w.

This paper addresses the sink location problem in dynamic networks: given a dynamic network with the initial supplies at vertices, find a vertex, called a *sink*, such that the completion time to send all the initial supplies to the sink is as small as possible. In this setting of building evacuation, for example, the problem models the location problem of an emergency exit together with the evacuation plan for it.

Our problem is a generalization of the following two problems. First, it can be regarded as a dynamic flow version of the 1-center problem [13]. In particular, if the capacities are sufficiently large, our problem represents the 1-center location problem. Secondly, our problem is an extension of the location problems based on flow (or connectivity) requirements in static networks, which have received much attention recently [1, 10, 16].

We consider the sink location problem in dynamic *tree* networks. This is because some production systems and underground passages form almost-tree networks. Moreover, one of the ideal evacuation plans makes everyone to be evacuated fairly and without confusion. For such a purpose, it is natural to assume that the possible evacuation routes form a tree. We finally mention that the multi-sink location problem can be solved by solving the (single-)sink location problem polynomially many times [12]. It is known [11] that the problem can be solved in $O(n^2)$ time by using a double-phase algorithm, where n denotes the number of vertices in the given network. We show that the problem is solvable in $O(n \log^2 n)$ time.

Our algorithm is based on a simple single-phase procedure, but uses sophisticated data structures for representing tables g i.e., sets of time intervals $[\theta_1, \theta_2)$ with their height $g(\theta_1)$ to perform three operations *Add-Table* (i.e., adding tables), *Shift-Table* (i.e., shifting a table), and *Ceil-Table* (i.e., ceiling a table by a prescribed capacity). We generalize interval trees (standard data structures for tables) by attaching additional parameters and show that using the data structures, we can efficiently handle the above-mentioned operations. Especially, we can merge tables g_i in $O((\sum_i d_i) \log^2(\sum_i d_i))$ time, where we say that *tables g_i are merged* if g_i's are added into a single table g after shifting and ceiling tables are performed, and d_i denotes the number of intervals in g_i. This result implies an $O(n \log^2 n)$ time bound for the location problem. We mention that our data structures may be of independent interest and useful for some other problems which manage tables.

We remark that our location problem for general dynamic networks can be solved in polynomial time by solving the quickest transshipment problem n

times. Here the quickest transshipment problem is to find a dynamic flow that zeroes all given supplies and demands within the minimum time, and is polynomially solvable by an algorithm of Hoppe and Tardos [8]. However, since their algorithm makes use of submodular function minimization [9, 15] as a subroutine, it requires polynomial time of high degree. As a corollary of our result, this paper shows that the quickest transshipment problem can be solved in $O(n \log^2 n)$ time if the given network is a tree and has a single sink.

The rest of the paper is organized as follows. The next section provides some preliminaries and fixes notation. Section 3 presents a simple single-phase algorithm for the sink location problem, and Section 4 discusses our data structures and shows the complexity of our single-phase algorithm with our data structures. Finally, Section 5 gives some conclusions.

Due to the space limitations, some proofs have been omitted.

2. Definitions and Preliminaries

Let $T = (V, E)$ be a tree with a vertex set V and an edge set E. Let $\mathcal{N} = (T, c, \tau, b)$ be a dynamic flow network with the underlying undirected graph being a tree T, where $c : E \to \mathbf{R}_+$ is a capacity function representing the least upper bound for the rate of flow through each edge per unit time, $\tau : E \to \mathbf{R}_+$ a transit time function, and $b : V \to \mathbf{R}_+$ a supply function. Here, $\mathbf{R}_+$ denotes the set of all nonnegative reals and we assume the number of vertices in T is at least two.

This paper addresses the problem of finding a sink $t \in V$ such that we can send given initial supplies $b(v)$ $(v \in V \setminus \{t\})$ to sink t as quickly as possible. Suppose that we are given a sink t in T. Then, T is regarded as an in-tree with root t, i.e., each edge of T is oriented toward the root t. Such an oriented tree with root t is denoted by $\vec{T}(t) = (V, \vec{E}(t))$. Each oriented edge in $\vec{E}(t)$ is denoted by the ordered pair of its end vertices and is called an arc. For each edge $\{u, v\} \in E$, we write $c(u, v)$ and $\tau(u, v)$ instead of $c(\{u, v\})$ and $\tau(\{u, v\})$, respectively. For any arc $e \in \vec{E}(t)$ and any $\theta \in \mathbf{R}_+$, we denote by $f_e(\theta)$ the flow rate entering the arc e at time θ which arrives at the head of e at time $\theta + \tau(e)$. We call $f_e(\theta)$ $(e \in \vec{E}(t), \theta \in \mathbf{R}_+)$ a *continuous-time dynamic flow* in $\vec{T}(v^*)$ (with a sink v^*) if it satisfies the following three conditions, where $\delta^+(v)$ and $\delta^-(v)$ denote the set of all arcs leaving v and entering v, respectively.

(a) (Capacity constraints): For any arc $e \in \vec{E}(t)$ and $\theta \in \mathbf{R}_+$,

$$0 \leq f_e(\theta) \leq c(e). \tag{1}$$

(b) (Flow conservation): For any $v \in V \setminus \{v^*\}$ and $\Theta \in \mathbf{R}$,

$$\sum_{e\in\delta^+(v)}\int_0^{\Theta} f_e(\theta)d\theta - \sum_{e\in\delta^-(v)}\int_{\tau(e)}^{\Theta} f_e(\theta-\tau(e))d\theta \le b(v). \quad (2)$$

(c) (Demand constraints): There exists a time $\Theta \in \mathbf{R}_+$ such that

$$\sum_{e\in\delta^-(v^*)}\int_{\tau(e)}^{\Theta} f_e(\theta-\tau(e))d\theta - \sum_{e\in\delta^+(v^*)}\int_0^{\Theta} f_e(\theta)d\theta = \sum_{v\in V\setminus\{v^*\}} b(v). \quad (3)$$

As seen in (b), we allow intermediate storage (or holding inventory) at each vertex. For a continuous-time dynamic flow f, let θ_f be the minimum time θ satisfying (3), which is called the *completion time* for f. We further denote by $C(v^*)$ the minimum θ_f among all continuous dynamic flows f in $\vec{T}(v^*)$. We study the problem of computing a sink $v^* \in V$ with the minimum $C(v^*)$. This problem can be regarded as a dynamic version of the 1-center location problem (for a tree) [13]. In particular, if $c(v,w) = +\infty$ (a sufficiently large real) for each edge $\{v,w\} \in E$, our problem represents the 1-center location problem [13].

We remark that dynamic flows can be restricted to those having no intermediate storage without changing optimal sinks of our problem (see discussions in [6, 8, 11], for example).

3. A Single-Phase Algorithm

This section presents a simple $O(n^2)$ algorithm with a single phase. Because of the simplicity, it gives us a good basis for developing a faster algorithm. In fact, we can construct an $\tilde{O}(n)$ algorithm based on this framework, which is given in the next section.

The algorithm computes two tables, *Arriving Table* A_v and *Sending Table* S_v for each vertex $v \in V$. Let us assume that a sink t is given for a while, in order to explain them. Arriving Table A_v represents the sum of the flow rates arriving at vertex v as a function of time θ, i.e.,

$$\sum_{e\in\vec{E}(t):e=(u,v)} f_e(\theta-\tau(e)) + \eta_\theta(v), \quad (4)$$

where $f_e(\theta) = 0$ holds for any $e \in \vec{E}(t)$ and $\theta < 0$, and $\eta_\theta(v) = \frac{b(v)}{\Delta}$ if $0 \le \theta < \Delta$; otherwise 0. Here, Δ denotes a sufficiently small positive constant. Intuitively, $\eta_\theta(v)$ denotes the initial supply at v. Sending Table S_v represents the flow rate leaving vertex v as a function of time θ, i.e.,

$$f_{(v,w)}(\theta), \quad (5)$$

where $(v,w) \in \vec{E}(t)$.

Let us consider a table $g : \mathbf{R}_+ \to \mathbf{R}_+$, which represents the flow rate in time $\theta \in \mathbf{R}_+$. Here, we assume $g(\theta) = 0$ for $\theta < 0$. Since our problem can be solved by sending out as much amount of flow as possible from each vertex toward an optimal sink (which will be computed), we only consider the table g which is representable as

$$g(\theta) = \begin{cases} 0 & \text{if } \theta < \theta_1 \\ g(\theta_i) & \text{if } \theta_i \le \theta < \theta_{i+1} \quad \text{for } i = 1, \cdots, k-1 \\ 0 & \text{if } \theta \ge \theta_k, \end{cases} \tag{6}$$

where $\theta_i < \theta_{i+1}$ and $g(\theta_i) \neq g(\theta_{i+1})$ for $i = 1, \ldots, k$. Thus, we represent such tables g by a set of intervals (with their height), i.e.,

$$((-\infty, \theta_1), 0), \quad ([\theta_i, \theta_{i+1}), g(\theta_i)) \ (i = 1, 2, \cdots, k), \tag{7}$$

where $\theta_{k+1} = +\infty$ and $g(\theta_k) = 0$.

Intuitively, our single-phase algorithm first constructs Sending Table S_v for each leaf v to send $b(v)$ to its adjacent vertex. Then the algorithm removes a leaf v^* from T such that the completion time of S_v is the smallest, since T has an optimal sink other than v^*. If some vertex v becomes a leaf of the resulting tree T, then the algorithm computes Sending Table S_v to send all the supplies that have already arrived at v to an adjacent vertex $p(v)$ of the resulting tree T, by using Sending Tables for the vertices w ($\neq p(v)$) that are adjacent to v in the original tree. The algorithm repeatedly applies this procedure to T until T becomes a single vertex t, and outputs such a vertex t as an optimal sink.

Algorithm SINGLE-PHASE

Input: A tree network $\mathcal{N} = (T = (V, E), c, \tau, b)$.

Output: An optimal sink t that has the minimum completion time $C(t)$ among all vertices of T.

Step 0: Let $W := V$, and let L be the set of all leaves of T. For each $v \in L$, construct Arriving Table A_v.

Step 1: For each $v \in L$, construct from A_v Sending Table S_v to go through $(v, p(v))$, where $p(v)$ is a vertex adjacent to v in T. Compute the time $Time(v, p(v))$ at which the flow based on S_v is completely sent to $p(v)$.

Step 2: Compute a vertex $v^* \in L$ minimizing $Time(v, p(v))$, i.e., $Time(v^*, p(v^*))= \min_{v \in L} Time(v, p(v))$. Let $W := W \setminus \{v^*\}$ and $L := L \setminus \{v^*\}$.

If there exists a leaf v of $T[W]$ such that v is not contained in L,

then: **(1)** Let $L := L \cup \{v\}$.

(2) Construct Arriving Table A_v from the initial supply $\eta_\theta(v)$ and Sending Table S_w for the vertices w that are adjacent to v in T and have already been removed from W.

(3) Compute from A_v Sending Table S_v to go through $(v, p(v))$ where $p(v)$ is a vertex adjacent to v in $T[W]$, and compute $Time(v, p(v))$.

Step 3: If $|W| = 1$, then output $t \in W$ as an optimal sink. Otherwise, return to Step 2. □

Here $T[W]$ denotes a subtree of T induced by a vertex set W. Note that $p(v)$'s in Steps 1 and 2 are uniquely defined, since v's are leaves of $T[W]$.

We then have the following lemma, though we skip the proof.

LEMMA 1 *Algorithm* SINGLE-PHASE *outputs an optimal sink t.* □

If we construct Arriving and Sending Tables explicitly, each table g can be computed in time linear in the total number of intervals in the tables from which g is constructed. Since the number of intervals in each table is linear in n,[1] Algorithm SINGLE-PHASE requires $O(n^2)$ time. In Section 4, we present a method to represent these tables implicitly, and develop an $O(n \log^2 n)$ time algorithm for our location problem.

4. Implicit Representation for Arriving and Sending Tables

Since Algorithm SINGLE-PHASE requires $\Theta(n^2)$ time if explicit representations are used for tables, we need sophisticated data structures which can be used to represent Arriving/Sending Tables *implicitly*. We adopt interval trees for them, which are standard data structures for a set of intervals. Note that SINGLE-PHASE only applies to tables A_v and/or S_v the following three basic operations: *Add-Table* (i.e., adding tables), *Shift-Table* (i.e., shifting a table), and *Ceil-Table* (i.e., ceiling a table by a prescribed capacity). It is known that interval trees can efficiently handle operations *Add-Table* and *Shift-Table* (see Section 4). However, standard interval trees cannot efficiently handle operation *Ceil-Table*. This paper develops new interval trees which efficiently handle all the three operations.

Data Structures for Implicit Representation

This section explains our data structures for representing tables which are obtained from interval trees by attaching several parameters to handle the three operations efficiently. Let g be a table represented as

$$I_i = ([\theta_i, \theta_{i+1}), g(\theta_i)) \quad (i = 0, 1, \cdots, k), \tag{8}$$

where $\theta_0 = -\infty$, $\theta_{k+1} = +\infty$, and $g(\theta_0) = g(\theta_k) = 0$,[2] and let BT_g denote a binary tree for g. We denote the root by r^{BT} and the height of BT by *height*(BT). The binary tree BT_g has an additional parameter t_{base} to represent how much g is shifted right. This t_{base} is used for operation *Shift-Table* by updating t_{base} to $t_{base} + \mu$, where μ denotes the time to shift the table right. Moreover, each node x in BT_g has five nonnegative parameters *base*(x), *ceil*(x), $h_e(x)$, $t^r(x)$, and $t^l(x)$ with $t^l(x) \leq t^r(x)$, and each leaf has $e(x)$ in addition, where these parameters will be explained later. A leaf x is called *active* if $t^l(x) < t^r(x)$ and *dummy* otherwise. The time intervals of a table g correspond to the active leaves of BT_g bijectively. We denote by $\#(BT)$ the number of active leaves of BT.

Initially (i.e., immediately after constructing BT_g by operation MAKE-TREE given below), BT_g contains no dummy leaf and hence there exists a one-to-one correspondence between the time intervals of g and leaves of BT_g. Moreover, for each leaf x corresponding to I_i in (8), we have $t^l(x) = \theta_i$, $t^r(x) = \theta_{i+1}$, $base(x) = g(\theta_i)$ and $ceil(x) = +\infty$, and for each internal node x, $t^l(x)= \min_{y\in Leaf(x)} t^l(y)$, $t^r(x)= \max_{y\in Leaf(x)} t^r(y)$, $base(x) = 0$ and $ceil(x) = +\infty$. Here, $Leaf(x)$ denotes the set of all leaves which are descendants of x. Namely, $t^l(x)$ and $t^r(x)$, respectively, represent the start and the end points of the interval corresponding to x, and $base(x)$ and $ceil(x)$, respectively, represent the flow rate and the upper bound for the flow rate in the time interval corresponding to x.

Operation MAKETREE(g: *table*)

Step 1: Let $t_{base} := 0$.

Step 2: Construct a binary balanced tree BT_g whose leaves x_i correspond to the time interval I_i of g in such a way that the leftmost leaf corresponds to the first interval I_0, the next one corresponds to the second interval I_1, and so on.

Step 3: For each leaf x_i corresponding to interval $I_i = [\theta_i, \theta_{i+1})$, $base(x) := g(\theta_i)$, $t^l(x) := \theta_i$ and $t^r(x) := \theta_{i+1}$.

Step 4: For each internal node x, $base(x) := 0$, and $t^l(x) := \min_{y\in Leaf(x)} t^l(y)$ and $t^r(x) := \max_{y\in Leaf(x)} t^r(y)$.

Step 5: For each node x, $ceil(x) := +\infty$.

Step 6: For each leaf x, set $e(x)$, and for each node x, set $h_e(x)$, where $e(x)$ and $h_e(x)$ shall be explained later. □

We can easily compute a table g from BT_g constructed by MAKETREE. It should also be noted that a binary tree BT_g is not unique, i.e., distinct trees may represent the same table g.

As mentioned in this section, *Shift-Table* can easily be handled by updating t_{base}. We now consider *Add-Table*, i.e., constructing a table g by adding two tables g_1 and g_2, where we regard an addition of k tables as $k-1$ successive additions of two tables. Let us assume that $\#(BT_{g_1}) \geq \#(BT_{g_2})$, that is, g_1 has at least as many intervals as g_2. Our algorithm constructs BT_g by adding all intervals (corresponding to active leaves) of BT_{g_2} one by one to BT_{g_1}. Each addition of an interval $([\theta_1, \theta_2), c)$ to BT_{g_1}, denoted by $\text{ADD}(BT_1; \theta_1, \theta_2, c)$, can be performed as follows.

We first modify BT_{g_1} to $\widetilde{BT}_{g_1}$ that has (active) leaves x and y such that $t^l(x) = \theta_1$ and $t^r(y) = \theta_2$ if there exist no such leaves. Then we add an interval $([\theta_1, \theta_2), c)$ to the resulting $\widetilde{BT}_{g_1}$. One of the simplest way is to add c to all leaves of $\widetilde{BT}_{g_1}$ such that the corresponding intervals are included in $[\theta_1, \theta_2)$. However, this takes $O(n)$ time, since BT_{g_1} may have $O(n)$ such intervals. We therefore add c only to their representatives.

Note that the time interval $[\theta_1, \theta_2)$ can be represented by the union of disjoint maximal intervals in $\widetilde{BT}_{g_1}$, i.e., the set of incomparable nodes in $\widetilde{BT}_{g_1}$, denoted by $rep(\theta_1, \theta_2)$. We thus update *base* of $\widetilde{BT}_{g_1}$ as follows

$$base(x) := base(x) + c \quad \text{for all } x \in rep(\theta_1, \theta_2). \tag{9}$$

We remark that this is a standard technique for interval tree. By successively applying this procedure to new interval tree $\widetilde{BT}_{g_1}$ and each of the remaining intervals in BT_{g_2}, we can construct BT_g with $g = g_1 + g_2$.

For an interval tree BT and an active leaf x of BT, let $y_1(= x), y_2, \cdots, y_s(= r^{BT})$ denote the path from x to the root r^{BT}. The procedure given above shows that the height of an active leaf x representing the flow rate of the corresponding interval can be represented as

$$h(x) = \sum_{i=1}^{s} base(y_i). \tag{10}$$

Operation ADD$(BT_{g_1}; \theta_1, \theta_2, c)$ can be handled in O(*height*(BT_{g_1})) time, since $|rep\ (\theta_1, \theta_2)| \leq 2height\ (BT_{g_1})$. This means that BT_g can be constructed from BT_{g_1} and BT_{g_2} in O $(\#(BT_{g_2}) \log n)$ time by balancing the tree after each addition. Moreover, operations *Add-Table* in Algorithm SINGLE-PHASE can be performed in $O(n \log^2 n)$ time in total, since we always add a smaller table to a larger one (see Section 4 for the details). Thus *Add-Table* can be performed efficiently.

However, operations *Ceil-Table* in Algorithm SINGLE-PHASE require $\Theta(n^2)$ time in total, since the algorithm contains $\Theta(n)$ *Ceil-Table*, each of which requires $\Theta(n)$ time, even if we use interval trees as data structures for tables. Therefore, when we bound BT by a constant c, we omit modifying t^l, t^r, and *base*, and keep c as $ceil(r^{BT}) = c$. Clearly, this causes difficulties to overcome as follows.

First, $h(x)$ in (10) does not represent the actual height any longer. Roughly speaking, the actual height is c if $c \leq h(x)$, and $h(x)$, otherwise. We call $h(x)$ the *tentative height* of x in BT, and denote by $\hat{h}(x)$ the *actual height* of x. Let us consider a scenario that an interval $([\theta_1, \theta_2), c')$ is added to BT after bounding it by c. Let x be an active leaf such that (i) the corresponding interval is contained in $[\theta_1, \theta_2)$ and (ii) the actual height is c, immediately after bounding BT by c. Then we note that the actual height of x is $c + c'$ after the scenario, which is different from both $h(x)$ and c. To deal with such scenarios, we update *ceil* to compute the actual height $\hat{h}(x)$ efficiently (See more details in the subsequent sections). The actual height $\hat{h}(x)$ can be computed as

$$\hat{h}(x) = h(x) - \max_{y \in path(x, r^{BT})} \{0, \Big(\sum_{z \in path(x,y)} base(z)\Big) - ceil(y)\}, \tag{11}$$

where $path(x, y)$ denotes the path from x to y. Intuitively, for a node y_k in BT, $ceil(y_k)$ represents the upper bound of the height of active leaves $x \in Leaf(y_k)$

within the subtree of BT whose root is y_k. Thus $\sum_{i=1}^{k} base(y_i) - ceil(y_k)$ has to be subtracted from the height $h(x)$ if $\sum_{i=1}^{k} base(y_i) - ceil(y_k) > 0$, and the actual height $\hat{h}(x)$ is obtained by subtracting their maximum. Note that $\hat{h}(x) = h(x)$ holds for all active leaves x of a tree constructed by MAKETREE.

We next note that there exists no one-to-one correspondence between active leaves in BT and time intervals of the table that BT represents, if we just set $ceil(r^{BT}) = c$. In this case, the table is updated too drastically to efficiently handle the operations afterwards. Thus by modifying BT (as shown in the subsequent subsections), we always keep the one-to-one correspondence, i.e., the property that any two consecutive active leaves x and x' satisfy

$$\hat{h}(x) \neq \hat{h}(x'). \tag{12}$$

We finally note that, for an active leaf x, $t^l(x)$ and $t^r(x)$ do not represent the start and the end points of the corresponding interval. Let x be an active leaf in BT that does not correspond to the first interval or the last interval. For such an x, let x^- and x^+ denote active leaves in BT which are left-hand and right-hand neighbors of x, respectively, i.e.,

$$t^r(x^-) = t^l(x), \quad t^l(x^+) = t^r(x). \tag{13}$$

Then the start and the end points of the corresponding interval can be obtained by

$$\hat{t}^r(x) = t_{base} + t^r(x) + (t^r(x) - t^l(x)) \times \frac{h(x) - \hat{h}(x)}{\hat{h}(x) - \hat{h}(x^+)} \tag{14}$$

$$\hat{t}^l(x) = \hat{t}^r(x^-). \tag{15}$$

Here $\hat{t}^r(x)$ and $\hat{t}^l(x)$ are well-defined from 12. For active leaves x and y corresponding to the first interval and the last interval, we have $\hat{t}^l(x) = -\infty$, $\hat{t}^r(x) = t^l(x^+)$, $\hat{t}^l(y) = \hat{t}^r(y)$ and $\hat{t}^r(y) = +\infty$.

It follows from (11), (14), and (15) that $\hat{h}(x)$, $\hat{t}^r(x)$, and $\hat{t}^l(x)$ can be computed from *base*, *ceil*, $t^r(x)$, and $t^l(x)$ in $O(height(BT))$ time. In order to check (12) efficiently, each active leaf x has

$$e(x) = \begin{cases} \max\{0, h(x) - h(x^+)\} \times \dfrac{t^r(x^+) - t^r(x)}{t^r(x^+) - t^l(x)} & \text{if } x^+ \text{ exists,} \\ +\infty & \text{otherwise,} \end{cases} \tag{16}$$

and each node x has

$$h_e(x) = \max_{y \in Leaf_A(x)} \{ \Big(\sum_{z \in path(x,y)} base(z) \Big) - e(y) \}, \tag{17}$$

where $Leaf_A(x)$ denotes the set of active leaves that are descendants of x, and $path\ (x, y)$ denotes the set of nodes on the path from x to y. Thus we have the following lemma.

LEMMA 2 *Let BT be a binary tree in which $\hat{h}(x) \neq \hat{h}(x^+)$ holds for every active leaf x. After bounding BT by a constant c,*

(i) *$\hat{h}(x) \neq \hat{h}(x^+)$ holds for an active leaf x if and only if x satisfies $h(x) - e(x) < c$, and*

(ii) *all active leaves x in BT satisfy $\hat{h}(x) \neq \hat{h}(x^+)$ if and only if $h_e(r^{BT}) < c$.* □

Moreover, we can compute an active leaf x with $\hat{h}(x) = \hat{h}(x^+)$ in $O(height(BT))$ time by scanning $h_e(x)$ from the root r^{BT}. Note that $h_e(x)$ can be obtained by the following bottom-up computation.

$$h_e(x) = \begin{cases} base(x) - e(x) & \text{if } x \text{ is a leaf,} \\ \max\{h_e(x_1), h_e(x_2)\} + base(x) & \text{otherwise,} \end{cases} \tag{18}$$

where x_1 and x_2 denote the children of x. This means that preparing and updating h_e's can be handled efficiently.

In summary, we always keep the following conditions for binary trees BT_g to represent tables g. Note that BT satisfies the conditions.

(C0) For any node x, BT maintains $t^l(x), t^r(x), ceil(x), base(x)$, and $h_e(x)$. For any leaf x, BT maintains $e(x)$ in addition.

(C1) Any node x satisfies $t^l(x) \leq t^r(x)$. Any internal node x satisfies $t^l(x) = \min_{y \in Leaf(x)} t^l(y)$, and $t^r(x) = \max_{y \in Leaf(x)} t^r(y)$.

(C2) Any active leaf x satisfies $t^r(x) = t^l(x^+)$.

(C3) Any active leaf x satisfies $\hat{h}(x) \neq \hat{h}(x^+)$.

(C4) Any active leaf x satisfies $\hat{h}(x) \geq h(x) - e(x)$.

A binary tree BT is called *valid* if it satisfies conditions (C0)~ (C4). For example, a binary tree BT constructed by MAKETREE is valid.

Operation NORMALIZE

As discussed in Section 4, we represent a table g as a valid binary balanced tree BT. For an active leaf x, our algorithm sometimes need to update BT to get one having *accurate* x, i.e., *base* and *ceil* are updated so that

$$base(y) := \begin{cases} 0 & \text{for a proper ancestor } y \text{ of } x^- \text{ or } x \\ \hat{h}(y) & \text{for } y = x^- \text{ or } x \end{cases} \tag{19}$$

$$ceil(y) := +\infty \quad \text{for an ancestor } y \text{ of } x^- \text{ or } x \tag{20}$$

$$t^r(y) = t^l(y^+) := \hat{t}^r(y) \quad \text{for } y = x^- \text{ or } x.$$

In fact, we perform this operation, when we insert a leaf x or change the parameters $ceil(x)$, $base(x)$, $t^r(x)$, and $t^l(x)$ of a leaf x. The following operation, called NORMALIZE, updates BT as above, and also maintains the balance of BT (i.e., $height(BT) = O(\log n)$).

Operation NORMALIZE(BT, x : *an active leaf*)

Step 1: Update *base* and *ceil* by the following top-down computation along the path from r^{BT} to the parent of y for $y = x^-$ or x. For a node z on the path and its children z_1 and z_2,

$$base(z_i) := base(z_i) + base(z), \;\; ceil(z_i) := \min\{ceil(z_i) + base(z), ceil(z)\},$$
$$base(z) := 0, \;\; ceil(z) := +\infty.$$

Step 2: If x was added to BT immediately before this operation, then rotate BT in order to keep the balance of BT.

Step 3: For $y = x, x^-$, if $base(y) > ceil(y)$, then $t^r(y) = t^l(y^+) := \hat{t}^r(y)$ and $base(y) := ceil(y)$. Otherwise $ceil(y) := +\infty$.

Step 4: For $y = x^-, x, x^+$, update t^l, t^r, e, and h_e by the bottom-up computation along the path from y to r^{BT}. □

Note that nodes may be added to BT (by operation SPLIT in the next section), but are never removed from BT, although some nodes become dummy. This simplifies the analysis of the algorithm, since removing a node from BT requires the rotation of BT that is not easily implemented.

It is not difficult to see that the tree BT' obtained by NORMALIZE is valid, satisfies (20), and represents the same table as BT. Moreover, since the lengths of the paths in Steps 1 and 4 are $O(height(BT))$, BT' can be computed from BT in $O(height(BT))$ time. Thus we have the following lemma.

LEMMA 3 *Let BT be a valid binary balanced tree representing a table g, and let x be an active leaf of BT. Then BT' obtained by* NORMALIZE(BT, x) *is a valid binary balanced tree that represents g and satisfies* (20). *Furthermore, BT' is computable from BT in* $O(height(BT))$ *time.* □

Add-Table

This section shows how to add two binary balanced trees BT_{g_1} and BT_{g_2} for tables g_1 and g_2. We have already mentioned an idea of our Add-Table after describing operation MAKETREE. Formally it can be written as follows.

Input: Two valid binary balanced trees BT_{g_1} and BT_{g_2} for tables g_1 and g_2.

Output: A valid binary balanced tree BT_g for $g = g_1 + g_2$.

Step 1: If $\#(BT_{g_1}) \geq \#(BT_{g_2})$, then $BT_1 := BT_{g_1}$ and $BT_2 := BT_{g_2}$. Otherwise $BT_1 := BT_{g_2}$ and $BT_2 := BT_{g_1}$.

Step 2: For each active leaf $x \in BT_2$, compute $\hat{t}^l(x)$, $\hat{t}^r(x)$ and $\hat{h}(x)$, and call operation ADD for BT_1, $\hat{t}^l(x)$, $\hat{t}^r(x)$, and $\hat{h}(x)$. □

Operation ADD($BT, \theta_1, \theta_2, c$)

Step 1: Call SPLIT($BT, \theta_1 - t^{BT}_{base}$) and SPLIT ($BT, \theta_2 - t^{BT}_{base}$), where t^{BT}_{base} denotes the parameter t_{base} for BT.

Step 2: For a node x in $rep(\theta_1 - t^{BT}_{base}, \theta_2 - t^{BT}_{base})$, $base(x) := base(x) + c$, $ceil(x) := ceil(x) + c$, and $h_e(x) := h_e(x) + c$.

Step 3: For a node x such that $t^l(x) = \theta_1 - t^{BT}_{base}$, call NORMALIZE($BT, x$).

If $base(x^-) = base(x)$ (i.e., $\hat{h}(x^-) = \hat{h}(x)$), then

$$\begin{aligned} y &:= x^-, \\ t^r(y) = t^l(y^+) &:= t^r(y^+) \text{ (i.e., } y^+ \text{ becomes dummy).} \end{aligned} \tag{21}$$

and call NORMALIZE(BT, y) and NORMALIZE(BT, y^+).

Step 4: For a leaf y such that $t^r(y) = \theta_2 - t^{BT}_{base}$, call NORMALIZE$(BT, y)$.
If $base(y) = base(y^+)$ (i.e., $\hat{h}(y) = \hat{h}(y^+)$), then update $t^r(y)$, $t^l(y^+)$ and $t^r(y^+)$ as 21, and call NORMALIZE(BT, y) and NORMALIZE(BT, y^+). □

Steps 3 and 4 are performed to keep (12). Note that $h_e(x)$ is updated in Step 2 for all nodes in $rep(\theta_1 - t^{BT}_{base}, \theta_2 - t^{BT}_{base})$. It follows from (18) that $h_e(y)$ must be updated for all proper ancestors y of a node in $rep(\theta_1 - t^{BT}_{base}, \theta_2 - t^{BT}_{base})$. Since a proper ancestor y of some node in $rep(\theta_1 - t^{BT}_{base}, \theta_2 - t^{BT}_{base})$ is a proper ancestor of the node x such that $t^l(x) = \theta_1 - t^{BT}_{base}$ or $t^r(x) = \theta_2 - t^{BT}_{base}$, all such $h_e(y)$'s are updated in Steps 3 and 4 by operation NORMALIZE.

Operation SPLIT$(BT, t$: *a nonnegative real*)

Step 1: Find a node x such that $t^l(x) \le t < t^r(x)$.

Step 2: Call NORMALIZE(BT, x^-) and NORMALIZE(BT, x).

Step 3: If $t^l(x) = t$, then halt.

Step 4: For the node $y \in \{x^-, x\}$ such that $t^l(y) \le t < t^r(y)$, construct the left child y_1 with $t^l(y_1) := t^l(y), t^r(y_1) := t$, $base(y_1) := 0$ and $ceil(y_1) := +\infty$, and construct the right child y_2 with $t^l(y_2) := t, t^r(y_2) := t^r(y)$, $base(y_2) := 0$ and $ceil(y_2) := +\infty$.

Step 5: Call NORMALIZE(BT, y_1) and NORMALIZE(BT, y_2). □

We can see that the following two lemmas hold.

LEMMA 4 *Let BT be a valid binary balanced tree representing a table g, and let t be a nonnegative real. Then BT' obtained by operation* SPLIT(BT, t) *is a valid binary balanced tree representing g in* $O(height(BT))$ *time.* □

LEMMA 5 *Let BT be a valid binary balanced tree representing a table g, and let $I = ([\theta_1, \theta_2), c)$ be a time interval. Then* ADD$(BT, \theta_1, \theta_2, c)$ *produces a valid binary balanced tree representing the table $g + I$, and moreover, it can be handled in* $O(height(BT))$ *time.* □

Operation Ceil-Table

This section considers operation *Ceil-Table*. Let BT be a valid binary balanced tree representing a table g and let c be an upper bound of BT. As mentioned in Section 4, we set $ceil(r^{BT}) = c$, and modify BT so that $\hat{h}(x) \ne \hat{h}(x^+)$ holds for any two consecutive active leaves x and x^+.

Operation CEIL$(BT, c$: *a positive real*)

Step 1: Compute the leftmost active leaf y such that $h(y) - e(y) \ge c$ by using h_e. If BT has no such node, then go to Step 4.

Step 2: Call NORMALIZE(BT, y) and NORMALIZE(BT, y^+),

$$base(y) := \frac{base(y)(t^r(y) - t^l(y)) + base(y^+)(t^r(y^+) - t^l(y^+))}{t^r(y^+) - t^l(y)}, \text{ and}$$

$t^r(y) = t^l(y^+) := t^r(y^+)$.

Step 3: Call NORMALIZE(BT, y) and NORMALIZE(BT, y^+). Return to Step1.

Step 4: For a root r^{BT}, $ceil(r^{BT}) := c$. □

LEMMA 6 *Let BT be a valid binary balanced tree representing a table g, and let c be a nonnegative real. Then BT′ obtained by operation* CEIL(BT, c) *is a valid binary balanced tree representing the table obtained from g by ceiling it by c.* □

Step 3 concatenates two consecutive active leaves x and x^+, where x^+ becomes dummy. We notice that the active leaf x (which has already been concatenated) may further be concatenated. This means that $\hat{h}(x) = \hat{h}(x^+)$ may hold after successive concatenations, even if original BT satisfies $\hat{h}(x) \neq \hat{h}(x^+)$.

Time complexity of SINGLE-PHASE with our data structures

We can see that all operations *Add-Tables*, *Shift-Tables*, and *Ceil-Tables* can be done in $O(n \log^2 n)$ time in total, though we skip its proof.

THEOREM 7 *The sink location problem in dynamic tree networks can be solved in* $O(n \log^2 n)$ *time.* □

This implies the following corollary.

COROLLARY 8 *If a given network is tree and has a single sink,* SINGLE-PHASE *can solve the quickest transshipment problem in* $O(n \log^2 n)$ *time.* □

5. Conclusions

In this paper, we have developed an $O(n \log^2 n)$ time algorithm for a sink location problem for dynamic flows in a tree network. This improves upon an $O(n^2)$ time algorithm in [11].

We have considered continuous-time dynamic flows that allow intermediate storage at vertices. We note that optimal sinks remain the same, even if we do not allow intermediate storage, and moreover, our algorithm can also be applicable for discrete-time dynamic flows. Therefore, our sink location problem is solvable in $O(n \log^2 n)$ time for dynamic continuous-time/discrete-time flows with/without intermediate storage.

Acknowledgments

This research is partially supported by the Grant-in-Aid for Creative Scientific Research of the Ministry of Education, Culture, Sports, Science and Technology.

Notes

1. It was shown in [11] that the number of intervals is at most $3n$ for *discrete-time* dynamic flows.
2. For simplicity, we write the first interval I_0 as $([-\infty, \theta_1), 0)$ instead of $((-\infty, \theta_1), 0)$.

References

[1] K. Arata, S. Iwata, K. Makino and S. Fujishige: Locating sources to meet flow demands in undirected networks, *Journal of Algorithms*, **42** (2002) 54–68.

[2] J. E. Aronson: A survey of dynamic network flows, *Annals of OR*, **20** (1989) 1–66.

[3] L. G. Chalmet, R. L. Francis and P. B. Saunders: Network models for building evacuation. *Management Science*, **28** (1982) 86–105.

[4] L. Fleischer and É. Tardos: Efficient continuous-time dynamic network flow algorithms, *Operations Research Letters*, **23** (1998) 71–80.

[5] L. R. Ford, Jr. and D. R. Fulkerson: Constructing maximal dynamic flows from static flows, *Op. Res.*, **6** (1958) 419–433.

[6] L. R. Ford, Jr. and D. R. Fulkerson: *Flows in Networks*, (Princeton University Press, Princeton, NJ, 1962).

[7] H. W. Hamacher and S.A.Tjandra: Mathematical modelling of evacuation problems: A state of the art, In: *Pedestrian and Evacuation Dynamics*, Springer, (2002) 227–266.

[8] B. Hoppe and É. Tardos: The quickest transshipment problem, *Mathematics of Operations Research*, **25** (2000) 36–62.

[9] S. Iwata, L. Fleischer, and S. Fujishige: A combinatorial strongly polynomial algorithm for minimizing submodular functions, *Journal of the ACM*, **48** (2001) 761–777.

[10] H. Ito, H. Uehara and M. Yokoyama: A faster and flexible algorithm for a location problem on undirected flow networks, *IEICE Trans. Fundamentals*, **E83-A** (2000) 704–712.

[11] S. Mamada, K. Makino and S. Fujishige: Optimal sink location problem for dynamic flows in a tree network, *IEICE Trans. Fundamentals*, **E85-A** (2002) 1020–1025.

[12] S. Mamada, T, Uno, K. Makino, and S. Fujishige: An evacuation problem in tree dynamic networks with multiple exits, Working paper.

[13] P. B. Mirchandani and R. L. Francis: *Discrete Location Theory*, (John Wile & Sons, Inc., 1989).

[14] W. B. Powell, P. Jaillet, and A. Odoni: Stochastic and dynamic networks and routing, In: *Network Routing, Handbooks in Operations Research and Management Science* **8** (M. O. Ball, T. L. Magnanti, C. L. Monma, and G. L. Nemhauser, eds, North-Holland, Amsterdam, The Netherlands, 1995), Chapter 3, 141–295.

[15] A. Schrijver: A combinatorial algorithm minimizing submodular functions in strongly polynomial time, *J. Combinatorial Theory*, **B80** (2000) 346–355.

[16] H. Tamura, M. Sengoku, S. Shinoda, and T. Abe: Some covering problems in location theory on flow networks, *IEICE Trans. Fundamentals*, **E75-A** (1992) 678–683.

EFFICIENT ALGORITHMS FOR HANDLING MOLECULAR WEIGHTED SEQUENCES

Costas S. Iliopoulos,[1] Christos Makris,[2,3] Yannis Panagis,[2,3] Katerina Perdikuri,[2,3] Evangelos Theodoridis,[2,3] and Athanasios Tsakalidis,[2,3]

[1] *Department of Computer Science*
King's College London, Strand, London WC2R2LS
England
csi@dcs.kcl.ac.uk

[2] *Department of Computer Engineering and Informatics*
University of Patras, 26500 Patras
Greece
{makri, panagis, perdikur, theodori}@ceid.upatras.gr

[3] *Research Academic Computer Technology Institute*
61 Riga Feraiou Str., 26221 Patras
Greece
tsak@cti.gr

Abstract In this paper we introduce the Weighted Suffix Tree, an efficient data structure for computing string regularities in weighted sequences of molecular data. Molecular Weighted Sequences can model important biological processes such as the DNA Assembly Process or the DNA-Protein Binding Process. Thus pattern matching or identification of repeated patterns, in biological weighted sequences is a very important procedure in the translation of gene expression and regulation. We present time and space efficient algorithms for constructing the weighted suffix tree and some applications of the proposed data structure to problems taken from the Molecular Biology area such as pattern matching, repeats discovery, discovery of the longest common subsequence of two weighted sequences and computation of covers.

Keywords: Molecular Weighted Sequences, Suffix Tree, Pattern Matching, Identifications of repetitions, Covers.

1 Introduction

Molecular Weighted Sequences appear in various applications of Computational Molecular Biology. A molecular weighted sequence is a molecular sequence (either a sequence of nucleotides or aminoacids), where each character in every position is assigned a certain weight. This weight could model either the probability of appearance of a character or the stability that the character contributes in a molecular complex.

Thus in the first case a molecular weighted sequence can be the result of a DNA Assembly process. The key problem today in sequencing a large string of DNA is that only a small amount of DNA can be sequenced in a single read. That is, regardless of whether the sequencing is done by a fully automated machine or by a more manual method, the longest unbroken DNA substring that can be reliably determined in a single laboratory procedure is about 300 to 1000 (approximately 500) bases long [4],[5]. A longer string can be used in the procedure but only the initial 500 bases will be determined. Hence to sequence long strings or an entire genome, the DNA must be divided into many short strings that are individually sequenced and then used to assemble the sequence of the full string. The critical distinction between different large-scale sequencing methods is how the task of sequencing the full DNA is divided into manageable subtasks, so that the original sequence can be reassembled from sequences of length 500.

Reassembling DNA substrings introduces a degree of uncertainty for various positions in a biosequence. This notion of uncertainness was initially expressed with the use of "don't care" characters denoted as "$*$". A "don't care" character has the property of matching against any symbol in the given alphabet. For example the string $p = AC * C*$ matches the pattern $q = A * GCT$ under the alphabet $\Sigma = \{A, C, G, T, *\}$. In some cases though, scientists are able to go one step further and determine the probability of a certain character to appear at the position previously characterised as wildcard. In other words, a "don't care" character is replaced by a probability of appearance for each of the characters of the alphabet. Such a sequence is modelled as a *weighted sequence*.

In the second case a molecular weighted sequence can model the binding site of a regulatory protein. Each base in a candidate motif instance makes some positive, negative or neutral contribution to the binding stability of the DNA-protein complex [7], [13]. The weights assigned to each character can be thought of as modeling those effects. If the sum of the individual contributions is greater than a treshold, the DNA-protein complex can be considered stable enough to be functional.

Thus we need new and efficient algorithms in order to analyze molecular weighted sequences. A fundamental problem in the analysis of Molecular Weighted Sequences is the computation of significant repeats which represent functional and structural similarities among molecular sequences. In [10] authors presented a simple algorithm for the computation of repeats in molecular weighted sequences. Although their algorithm is simple and easy to be implemented, it is not efficient in space needed. In this paper we present an efficient algorithm, both in time and space limitations, to construct the Weighted Suffix Tree, an efficient data structure for computing string regularities in biological weighted sequences. The Weighted Suffix Tree, was firstly intoduced in [9]. In this work, which is primarily motivated by the need to efficiently compute repeats in a weighted sequence, we further extend the use of the Weighted Suffix Tree to other applications on weighted sequences.

The structure of the paper is as follows. In Section 2 we give all the basic definitions used in the rest of the paper, in Section 3 we present the Weighted Suffix Tree while

Word w

Position	1	2	3	4	5	6	7	8	9	10	11
	A	C	T	T	(A,0.5)	T	C	(A,0.5)	T	T	T
					(C,0.5)			(C,0.3)			
					(G, 0)			(G,0)			
					(T, 0)			(T,0.2)			

Figure 1. Example of a weighted word with three weighted positions. Positions consisting of a single character indicate that this character appears with probability 1.

in Section 4 we list a set of applications for the data structure. Finally in Section 5 we conclude and discuss our research interest in open problems of the area.

2 Preliminaries

Let Σ be a finite alphabet which consists of a set of characters (or symbols). The cardinality of an alphabet, denoted by $|\Sigma|$, expresses the number of distinct characters in the alphabet. A *string* or *word* is a sequence of zero or more characters drawn from an alphabet. The set of all words over the alphabet Σ is denoted by Σ^+. A word w of length n is represented by $w[1..n] = w[1]w[2]\cdots w[n]$, where $w[i] \in \Sigma$ for $1 \leq i \leq n$, and $n = |w|$ is the length of w. The empty word is the empty sequence (of zero length) and is denoted by ε; we write $\Sigma^* = \Sigma^+ \cup \{\varepsilon\}$. Moreover a word is said to be *primitive* if it cannot be written as v^e with $v \in \Sigma^+$ and $e \geq 2$.

A subword u of length p is said to occur at position i in the word w if $u = w[i..i+p-1]$. In other words u is a substring of length p occurring at position i in word w. A word has a *repeat* when it has two equal subwords.

In the case that for a given position of a word w we consider the presence of a set of characters each with a given probability of appearance, we define the concept of a weighted word w, as following:

DEFINITION 1 *A weighted word $w = w[1]w[2]\cdots w[n]$ is a sequence of positions, where each position $w[i]$ consists of a set of ordered pairs. Each pair has the form $(s, \pi_i(s))$, where $\pi_i(s)$ is the probability of having the character s at position i. For every position w_i, $1 \leq i \leq n$, $\sum_{\forall s} \pi_i(s) = 1$.*

For example, if we consider the DNA alphabet Σ = {A,C,G,T} the word w shown in Fig. 1 represents a word having 11 letters: the first four are definitely ACTT, the fifth can be either A or C each with 0.5 probability of appearance, letters 6 and 7 are T and C, and letter 8 can be A, C or T with probabilities 0.5, 0.3 and 0.2 respectively and finally letters 9 to 11 are T. Some of the words that can be produced are: $w_1 = ACTT\underline{A}TC\underline{A}TTT$, $w_2 = ACTT\underline{C}TC\underline{A}TTT$[1], etc. The probability of presence of a word is the cumulative probability which is calculated by multiplying the relative probabilities of appearance of each character in every position. For the above example, $\pi(w_1) = \pi_1(A)*\pi_2(C)*\pi_3(T)*\pi_4(T)*\pi_5(A)*\cdots*\pi_8(T) = \pi_5(A)*\pi_8(A) = 0.25$. Similarly $\pi(w_2) = \pi_5(C) * \pi_8(A) = 0.25$. The definition of subword can be easily extended to accommodate weighted subwords.

[1] underlined letters indicate the choice of a particular letter in a weighted position

The Suffix Tree

The suffix tree is a fundamental data structure supporting a wide variety of efficient string searching algorithms. In particular, the suffix tree is well known to allow efficient and simple solutions to many problems concerning the identification and location either of a set of patterns or repeated substrings (contiguous or not) in a given sequence. The reader can find an extended literature on such applications in [8].

DEFINITION 2 *We denote by $T(S)$ the suffix tree of S, as the compressed trie of all the suffixes of $S\$$, $\$ \notin \Sigma$. Let $L(v)$ denote the path-label of node v in $T(S)$, which results by concatenating the edge labels along the path from the root to v. Leaf v of $T(S)$ is labeled with index i iff $L(v) = S[i..n]$. We define the leaf-list $LL(v)$ of v as a list of the leaf-labels in the subtree below v.*

Linear time algorithms for suffix tree construction are presented in [14], [17].

3 The Weighted Suffix Tree

In this section we present a data structure for storing the set of suffixes of a weighted sequence with probability of appearance greater than $1/k$, where k is a given constant. We use as fundamental data structure the suffix tree, incorporating the notion of probability of appearance for every suffix stored in a leaf. Thus, the introduced data structure is called the *Weighted Suffix Tree* (abbrev. WST).

The weighted suffix tree can be considered as a generalisation of the ordinary suffix tree to handle weighted sequences. We give a construction of this structure in the next section. The constructed structure inherits all the interesting string manipulation properties of the ordinary suffix tree. However, it is not straightforward to give a formal definition as with its ordinary counterpart. A quite informal definition appears below.

DEFINITION 3 *Let S be a weighted sequence. For every suffix starting at position i we define a list of possible weighted subwords so that the probability of appearance for each one of them is greater than $1/k$. Denote each of them as $S_{i,j}$, where j is the subword rank in arbitrary numbering. We define $WST(S)$ the weighted suffix tree of a weighted sequence S, as the compressed trie of a portion of all the weighted subwords starting within each suffix S_i of $S\$$, $\$ \notin \Sigma$, having a probability of appearance greater than 1/k. Let $L(v)$ denote the path-label of node v in $WST(S)$, which results by concatenating the edge labels along the path from the root to v. Leaf v of $WST(S)$ is labeled with index i if $\exists j > 0$ such that $L(v) = S_{i,j}[i..n]$ and $\pi(S_{i,j}[i \cdots n]) \geq 1/k$, where $j > 0$ denotes the j-th weighted subword starting at position i. We define the leaf-list $LL(v)$ of v as a list of the leaf-labels in the subtree below v.*

We will use an example to illustrate the above definition. Consider again the weighted sequence shown in Fig. 1 and suppose that we are interested in storing all suffixes with probability of appearance greater than a predefined parameter. We will construct the suffix tree for the sequence incorporating the notion of probability of appearance for each suffix.

For the above sequence and $k \geq 1/4$ we have the following possible prefixes for every suffix:

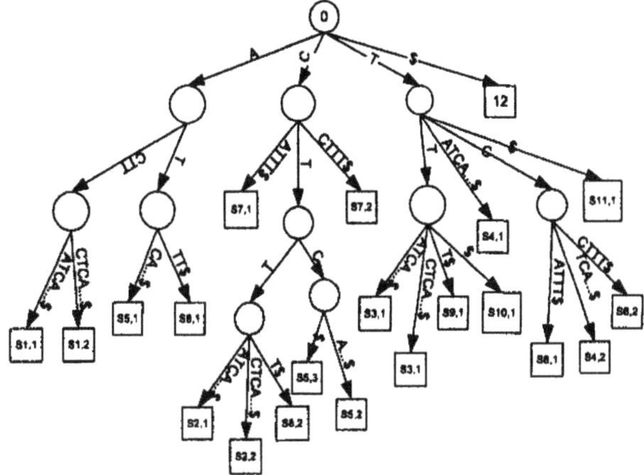

Figure 2. A Weighted Suffix Tree example.

- Prefixes for suffix $x[1 \cdots 11]$: $S_{1,1} = ACTT\underline{A}TC\underline{A}TTT$, $\pi(S_{1,1}) = 0.25$, and $S_{1,2} = ACTT\underline{C}TC\underline{A}TTT$, $\pi(S_{1,2}) = 0.25$.

- Prefixes for suffix $x[2 \cdots 11]$: $S_{2,1} = CTT\underline{A}TC\underline{A}TTT$, $\pi(S_{2,1}) = 0.25$, and $S_{2,2} = CTT\underline{C}TC\underline{A}TTT$, $\pi(S_{2,2}) = 0.25$, etc.

The weighted suffix tree for the above subwords appears in Fig. 2.

Construction of the WST

In this paragraph we describe an efficient algorithm for constructing the WST for a given weighted sequence $w = w[1..n]$, of length n. Firstly we describe the naive approach, which is quadratic in time. As already discussed the weighted suffix tree, (which consists of all subwords with probability of appearance greater than $1/k$, k is a given constant), is a generalized suffix tree (GST) that can be built as follows.

Step 1: For each i, $(2 \leq i \leq n)$, generate all possible weighted suffixes of the weighted sequence with probability of appearance greater than $1/k$.

Step 2: Construct the Generalized Suffix Tree GST, for the list of all possible weighted suffixes.

The above naive approach is not optimal since the time for construction is $O(n^2)$. In the following paragraphs we present an alternative efficient approcah. The exact steps of our methodology for construction are:

Step 1: Scan all the positions i $(1 \leq i \leq n)$ of the weighted sequence and mark each one according to the following criteria:

- mark position i *black*, if *none* of the possible characters, listed at position i, has probability of appearance greater than $1 - 1/k$,

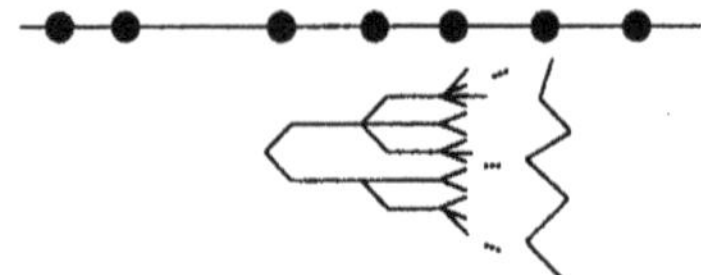

Figure 3. Producing all possible subwords from left to right

- mark position i *gray*, if *at least one* of the possible characters listed at position i, has probability of appearance greater than $1 - 1/k$,
- and finally mark position i *white*, if *one* of the possible characters has probability of appearance *equal to* 1.

Notice that the following holds: at white positions we have only one possible character appearing, thus we can call them *solid* positions, at black positions since no character appears with probability greater than $1 - 1/k$, more than one character appear with probability greater than $1/k$ hence we can call them *branching* positions. At gray positions, only one character eventually survives, since all the possible characters except one, have probability of appearance less than $1/k$, which implies that they can not produce an eligible subword (i.e. $\pi(subword) \geq 1/k$). During the first step we also maintain a list B of all black positions.

Step 2: Scan all the positions in B from left to right. At each black position i a list of possible subwords starting from this position is created. The production of the possible subwords is done as follows: moving rightwards, we extend the current subwords by adding the same single character whenever we encounter a white or gray position, only one possible choice, and creating new subwords at black positions where potentially many choices are provided. The process is illustrated in Fig. 3. At this point we define for every produced subword two cumulative probabilities π', π''. The first one measures the actual subword probabilities and the second one is defined by temporarily treating gray positions as white. The generation of a subword stops when it meets a black position and π'' (which skips gray positions) has reached the $1/k$ threshold. We call this position *extended position*. Notice that the actual subword may actually be shorter as π' (which incorporates gray positions) may have met the $1/k$ threshold earlier. For every subword we store the difference D of the actual ending position and the extended one as shown in Fig. 4. Notice that only the actual subwords need to be represented with the GST.

Step 3: Having produced all the subwords from every black position, we insert the actual subwords in the generalised suffix tree in the following way. For every subword we initially insert the corresponding extended subword in the GST and then remove from it the redundant portion D. To further illustrate the case, suppose that $X' = x[i..\ i + f' - 1]$ is the extended subword of the actual subword $X = x[i..\ i + f - 1]$ ($f \leq f'$) that begins at black position i of the weighted sequence in Fig. 4. Observe the following two facts:

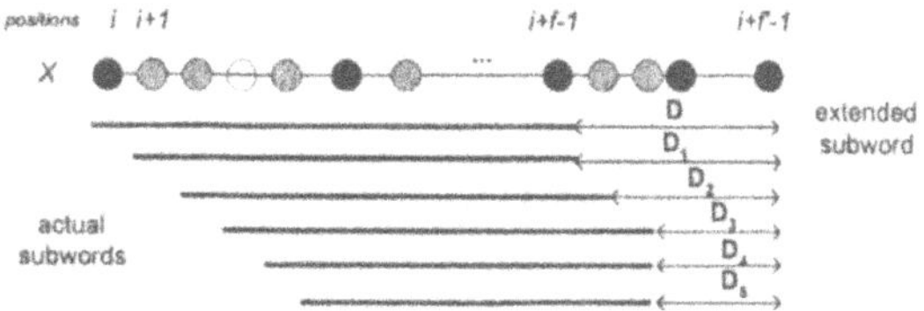

Figure 4. Insertion of subwords in the GST

- There is no need to insert every suffix of X in the GST apart from those starting to the left of the next black position i', as all the other suffixes will be taken into account when step 2 is executed for i'.
- A suffix of X' can possibly extend to the right of position $i+f-1$, where the actual subword ends, since π' does not take gray positions into account (cf. Fig. 4). No suffix can end though at a position greater than $i+f'-1$, where the extended subword ends.

We have kept every leaf storing a suffix of X', in a list L. Let D_j denote the redundant portion of suffix $X'[i+j..i+f'-1]$ of X' (cf. Fig. 4). After we have inserted the extended subword and the proper suffixes using McCreight's algorithm [14], we have to remove all the D_j's from the GST. Starting from the leaf corresponding to the entire X', we move upwards the tree by D characters. At the current position we eliminate the extra portion of X', storing X. The next redundancy of length D_1 is at the end of $X'[i+1..i+f'-1]$. We locate this suffix using the suffix link. Let $\lambda_d = |D_{d-1}| - |D_d|$, $d > 1$ and $\lambda_1 = D - D_1$. After using the suffix link we also may descend by λ_1 characters. At this position we store the correct suffix (possibly extending it up to λ_1 characters after position $i+f-1$). We continue the elimination procedure for the remaining suffixes of X', as outlined above. The entire process costs at most $\sum_{d>0} \lambda_d = O(D)$, which is the time required to complete the suffix tree construction.

Note: The above description implicitly assumes that there are no positions i where $\pi_i(\sigma) < 1/k$, $\forall \sigma \in \Sigma$. If this is not the case, the sequence can be divided into subsequences where this assumption holds and process these subsequences separately, according to the previous algorithm.

Time and Space Analysis on the Construction of the WST

The time and space complexity analysis for the construction of the WST is based on the combination of the following lemmas:

LEMMA 4 *At most* $O\left(|\Sigma|^{\log k / \log(\frac{k}{k-1})}\right)$ *subwords could start at each branching position* i *(*$1 \leq i \leq n$*) of the weighted sequence.*

Proof. Consider for example position i and the longest subword u which starts at that position. If we suppose that u is λ characters long, its cumulative probability will be $\pi(u[1..\lambda]) = \pi_i(u[1]) * \pi_{i+1}(u[2]) * \cdots * \pi_{i+\lambda-1}(u[\lambda])$. In order to produce this

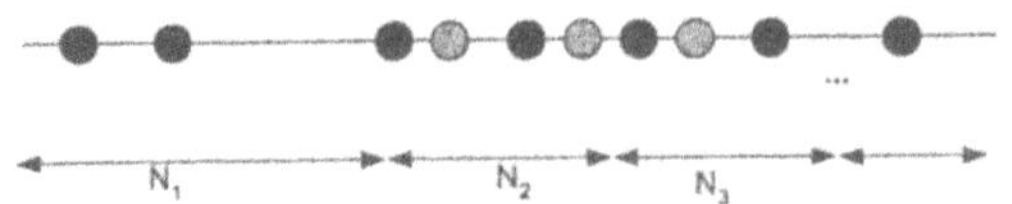

Figure 5. Time cost for step 2

subword we have to pass through l black positions of the weighted sequence. Recall that at black positions none of the possible characters has probability of appearance greater than $\hat{\pi} = 1 - 1/k$. Assuming that there are no gray positions that could reduce the cumulative probability, $\pi(u[1..\lambda])$ is less or equal to $\hat{\pi}^l$ (taking only black positions into account). In order to store this subword its cumulative probability is $\hat{\pi}^l \geq 1/k$ and thus $l \leq \log k / \log(\frac{k}{k-1})$ by taking logarithms (all logarithms are $\log_2$). For example, typical values of l are $\cong 21.9$ for $k = 20$ and $\cong 1046$ for $k = 200$.

Thus, regardless of considering or not the gray positions, u includes at most $l = O(1)$ black positions, or in other words, positions where new subwords are produced. Hence, every position i of the weighted sequence can be the starting point of at most $|\Sigma|^l$ number of subwords. ∎

LEMMA 5 *The number of subwords with probability greater than or equal to $1/k$ is at most $O(n)$.*

Proof. If every position i of the weighted sequence is the starting point of a constant number of subwords (Lemma 4), the total number of subwords is $O(n)$. ∎

LEMMA 6 *Step 2 of the construction algorithm takes $O(n)$ time.*

Proof. Suppose that the weighted sequence is divided into windows $N_j, j \geq 1$ (cf. Fig. 5). Each window contains $l = \log k / \log(\frac{k}{k-1})$ black positions. Notice that a window can contain more than l positions of all types and that $\sum_{j\geq 1} |N_j| = n$. Lets consider window N_i. Step 2 scans the black positions inside N_i. Every black position will generate $O(1)$ subwords (according to Lemma 4) and none of them is going to exceed window N_{i+1} because it can not be extended to more than l black positions. Thus, the length of subwords will be at most equal to $|N_i| + |N_{i+1}|$. Thus, for the window N_i, step 2 costs at most $O(l^2(|N_i| + |N_{i+1}|)) = O(|N_i| + |N_{i+1}|)$ time. Summing up the costs for all windows we conclude that step 2 incurs a total of $O\left(\sum(|N_i| + |N_{i+1}|)\right) = O(n)$ cost. ∎

LEMMA 7 *Step 3 of the construction algorithm takes $O(n)$ time.*

Proof. Consider again the windows scheme as in the previous lemma and in particular window N_i. In step 3 we insert the extended subwords in the WST that correspond to that window. Each one of them has length at most $|N_i| + |N_{i+1}|$. The cost to insert those extended subwords in the WST using McCreight's algorithm is $O(l \cdot |N_i| + |N_{i+1}|) = O(|N_i| + |N_{i+1}|)$ and the cost to repair the WST (as we described in step 3) is $O(l \cdot D)$. D is always smaller than $|N_i| + |N_{i+1}|$ thus for window N_i step 3 costs $O(|N_i| + |N_{i+1}|)$ time. Summing the costs for all windows, step 3 yields $O(n)$ time in total. ∎

Based on the previous lemmas we derive the following theorem.

THEOREM 8 *The time and space complexity of constructing the WST is linear to the length of the weighted sequence.*

Proof. The WST, which is a compact trie data structure, stores $O(n)$ subwords (by Lemma 5) and thus the space is $O(n)$. None of the three construction steps takes more than $O(n)$ time so the total time complexity is $O(n)$. ∎

4 Applications

In this section we present three applications of the Weighted Suffix Tree, namely: pattern matching in weighted sequences, computing repeats in weighted sequences, detection of the longest common subsequence in weighted sequences and computation of covers in weighted sequences.

Pattern Matching in Weighted Sequences

The classical pattern matching can be reformulated in weighted sequences as follows:

Problem 1. *Given a pattern p and a weighted sequence x, find the starting positions of p in x, each with probability of appearance greater than* $1/k$.

Solution. Firstly, we build the WST for x with parametre k. We distinguish two cases. If p consists entirely of non-weighted positions we spell p from the root of the tree until at an internal node v, either we have spelled the entire p, in which case we report all items in $LL(v)$, or we cannot proceed further and thus we report failure. If p contains weighted positions we decompose it into solid patterns each with $\Pr\{\text{occurence}\} > 1/k$ and match each one of them using the above procedure. Apparently, pattern matching can be solved in $O(m + \alpha)$ time, $m = |p|$ and is α the output size, with $O(n)$ preprocessing.

Computing the Repeats

A lot of work has been done for identifying the repeats in a word. In [6], [2] and [15], authors have presented efficient methods that find occurrences of squares in a string of length n in time $O(n \log n)$ plus the time to report the detected squares. Moreover in [11] authors presented efficient algorithms to find maximal repetitions in a word. In the area of computational biology, algorithms for finding identical repetitions in biosequences are presented in e.g. [12] and [16].

Using the WST we can compute in linear time the repeats of a weighted sequence. In particular, we compute the repeats of all subwords u, with $\Pr\{u\} > 1/k$, $\forall u$. This version of the problem is of particular biological interest.

Problem 2. *Given a weighted sequence x and an integer k find all the repeats of all possible words having a probability of appearance greater than* $1/k$.

Solution. We build the WST with parametre k and traverse it bottom-up. At each internal node v, with $|LL(v)| > 1$ we report the items in $LL(v)$, in pairs. This process requires $O(n)$ time by Lemma 5

In the example shown in Fig. 1 and Fig. 2, the longest repeat is the word CTT, which appears in suffixes: $(S_{2,1}, S_{8,2}), (S_{2,2}, S_{8,2})$ (with probability greater than 1/4). The time to required by the solution is $O(n + \alpha)$, where α denotes the output size.

REMARK 1 *Apart from the repeats problem the repetitions detection in weighted molecular sequences can be solved in $O(n \log n + \alpha)$ time, by extending appropriately either of the approaches in [15], [3].*

Longest Common Substring in Weighted Sequences

A classical problem in string analysis is to find the longest common substring of two given strings S_1 and S_2. Here we reformulate the *longest common substring problem* for weighted sequences.

Problem 3. *Given two weighted strings S_1 and S_2, find the longest common substring with probability of appearance greater than $1/k$ in both strings.*

Solution. An efficient and simple way to find the longest common substring in two given weighted strings S_1 and S_2 is to build a generalised weighted suffix tree for S_1 and S_2. The path label of any internal node is a substring common to both S_1 and S_2 with probability of appearance greater than $1/k$. The algorithm merely finds the node with greatest string-depth. A preorder traversal of the WST suffices to compute the longest string-depth (for details see [8]). It is easily derived that the above procedure runs in $O(n)$ time.

Computing the Covers in a Weighted Sequence

In this section we address the problem of computing the set of covers in a weighted sequence. In a more formal manner the problem can be defined as:

Problem 4 *Given a weighted sequence X of length n and an integer k, find all possible covers of X that have probability of appearance larger than $1/k$.*

A subword u of X is called a *cover* of X if and only if X can be constructed by concatenations and superpositions of w, so that every position of X lies within some occurrence of w in X. Two problems have been investigated in the computation of covers, known as the *shortest-cover* problem(finding the shortest cover of a given string of length n), and the *all-covers* problem(finding all the covers of a given string). Apostolico, Farach and Iliopoulos first introduced the notion of covers in [1] as well as that of *shortest-cover*, where a linear-time algorithm for this problem was presented.

Using the WST we can compute in $O(n \log n \log n)$ time the covers of a weighted sequence. All proper covers of X along with X itself compose the set of covers of the weighted sequence.

Solution. We build WST(S) with parametre k for the sequence S in which every subword appears with probability above $1/k$. We merely have to examine the path to $S[1..n]$. Let s_1 be the leaf storing $S[1..n]$. Let also v be an internal node of WST(S). At each such node v, let s_v denote the string spelled in the path from the root to v.

First we need to perform a depth-first search to construct at each internal node, the leaf-lists of its subtree, as those correspond to occurrences of s inside the indexed string. We organize these lists as simple linked lists, namely $LL(v)$ at a node v. We also need to maintain a gap-tree G, implemented as a van Emde Boas tree [18] over the universe $U = [1, 2, ..., n]$. The gap-tree keeps track of the indices of leaf-lists on the way from s_1 to the root and performs predecessor-successor queries. The algorithm entails moving upwards from s_1 to the root and keeping at each node encountered, the maximum distance, d_{max} of consecutive indices stored at G as well as the maximum index value i_{max}.

In order for an internal path label at node s_v on the path from root to s_1 to form a cover, it must hold that $d_{max} \leq |s_v|$ and $n - i_{max} \leq |s_v|$. More informally, $LL(v)$ of v stores several indices in $[1..n]$. These correspond to repetitive occurrences of s_v in S. Consequently, s_v is a cover whenever the maximum difference between any two starting points of these occurrences is less than the $|s_v|$.

More concretely, we start at s_1 and construct an empty van Emde Boas tree G, insert value 1 and set $d_{max} = n$ and $i_{max} = 1$. At each internal node we must check whether it forms a cover according to the conditions stated above. As moving from a node v to $father(v)$, we insert all the items of the $LL(w)$, $\forall w =$ sibling(v) to the tree G. After having inserted item i we perform an operation $succ(i)$ and $pred(i)$ in the tree and set $d_{max} = \min\{i - pred(i), succ(i) - i, d_{max}\}$. We also need to check whether $i > i_{max}$ and update d_{max} accordingly.

THEOREM 9 *Computing all covers requires $O(n \log n \log n)$ time.*

Proof. The initialisation procedure takes $O(n)$, to construct the LL lists at the children of each node in path from root to s_1. At each transition from a node v to $father(v)$ a number of insertions need to be made to the gap-tree G. The number of insertions equals the cardinality of each $LL(w)$, $\forall w =$ sibling(v). Each of these insertions costs $O(\log \log n)$ (see [18]). The item of each LL is only once inserted in G and subsequently left intact. Furthermore, each of the n positions in S occurs only once within a leaf-list, thus inserted only once in G. Each such insertion causes a predecessor and a successor operation in G which are also performed in $O(\log \log n)$ time. Hence, our algorithm incurs a total of $O(n)$ cost for constructing leaf-lists, another $O(n)$ maybe spent during the bottom up traversal of the s_1-to-root path and a total $O(n \log \log n)$ time for performing operations on G, yielding the overall time complexity. ∎

5 Conclusions

In this paper we have presented the Weighted Suffix Tree, an efficient data structure solving a wide range of problems in weighted sequences such as: pattern matching, repeats finding, least common substring in weighted molecular sequences, and computation of covers.

Our future direction is focused on using the WST for computing string regularities (like for example borders and palindromes) on weighted biological sequences. Some immediate applications in molecular biology include: using sequences containing degenerate bases, where a letter can replace several bases (for example, a B will represent a G, T or C and a H will represent A, T or C); using logo sequences which are more or less related to consensus: either from assembly or from blocks obtained by a multiple alignment program; analysis of DNA micro-arrays where expression levels of genes are recorded under different experimental.

Moreover we believe that the Weighted Suffix Tree can also be used in the analysis of weighted sequences in other applications of computer science. Weighted Sequences also appear in the field of event management for complex networks, where each event has a timestamp.

References

[1] Apostolico, A., Farach. M., Iliopoulos, C.S.: Optimal superprimitivity testing for strings, Information Processing Letters, 39, (1991) 17-20.

[2] Apostolico, A., Preparata, F.P.,: Optimal off-line detection of repetitions in a string. Theoretical Computer Science, Vol. 22. (1983) 297–315.

[3] Brodal G.S., Lyngso R.B., Storm Pedersen C.N., and Stoye J.: Finding Maximal Pairs with Bounded Gap. In Proc. 10th CPM, pp. 134–149, (1999).

[4] Celera Genomics: The Genome Sequence of Drosophila melanogaster. Science, Vol. 287. (2000) 2185–2195

[5] Celera Genomics: The Sequence of the Human Genome. Science, Vol. 291, (2001) 1304–1351.

[6] Crochemore, M.: An Optimal Algorithm for Computing the Repetitions in a Word. Inf. Proc. Lett., Vol. 12. (1981) 244–250.

[7] G. Grillo, F. Licciuli, S. Liuni, E. Sbisa, G. Pesole PatSearch: a program for the detection of patterns and structural motifs in nucleotide sequences. *Nucleic Acids Res.* **31** (2003), 3608–3612.

[8] Gusfield, D.: Algorithms on Strings, Trees, and Sequences: Computer Science and Computational Biology. Cambridge University Press, New York (1997)

[9] Iliopoulos, C., Makris, Ch, Panagis, I., Perdikuri, K., Theodoridis, E., Tsakalidis, A.: Computing the Repetitions in a Weighted Sequence using Weighted Suffix Trees, In European Conference on Computational Biology (ECCB 2003), Posters' Track.

[10] Iliopoulos, C., Mouchard, L., Perdikuri, K., Tsakalidis, A.,: Computing the repetitions in a weighted sequence, Proceedings of the Prague Stringology Conference (PSC 2003), 91-98.

[11] Kolpakov, R., Kucherov, G.,: Finding maximal repetitions in a word in linear time. In Proc. FOCS99, pp. 596–604, (1999).

[12] Kurtz, S., Schleiermacher, C.,: REPuter: fast computation of maximal repeats in complete genomes. Bioinformatics, Vol. 15, (1999) 426–427.

[13] H. Li, V. Rhodius, C. Gross, E. Siggia Identification of the binding sites of regulatory proteins in bacterial genomes *Genetics* **99** (2002), 11772–11777.

[14] McCreight, E.,M.,: A space-economical suffix tree construction algorithm. J. of the ACM, Vol. 23, (1976) 262–272.

[15] Stoye, J., Gusfield, D.,: Simple and flexible detection of contiguous repeats using a suffix tree. In Proc. 9th CPM, Vol. 1448 of LNCS, (1998) 140–152.

[16] Tsunoda, T., Fukagawa, M., Takagi, T.,: Time and memory efficient algorithm for extracting palindromic and repetitive subsequences in nucleic acid sequences. Pacific Symposium on Biocomputing, Vol. 4, (1999) 202–213.

[17] Ukkonen, E.,: On-line construction of suffix trees. Algorithmica, Vol. 14, (1995), 249–260.

[18] van Emde Boas P., R. Kaas and E. Zijlstra, Design and implementation of an efficient priority queue. *Mathematical Systems Theory*, **10**, pp. 99-127, (1977)

IMPERFECTNESS OF DATA FOR STS-BASED PHYSICAL MAPPING

Hiro Ito,[1] Kazuo Iwama,[1] and Takeyuki Tamura[1]

[1] *School of Informatics, Kyoto University*
Kyoto 606-8501, Japan
{itohiro, iwama, tamura}@kuis.kyoto-u.ac.jp

Abstract In the STS-based mapping, we are requested to obtain the correct order of probes in a DNA sequence from a given set of fragments or equivalently a hybridization matrix A. It is well-known that the problem is formulated as the combinatorial problem of obtaining a permutation of A's columns so that the resulting matrix has the consecutive-one property. If the data (the hybridization matrix) is error free and includes enough information, then the above column order determines the correct order of the probes uniquely. Unfortunately this is no longer true if the data include errors, which has been one of the popular research targets in computational biology. Even if there is no error, ambiguities in the probe order may still remain. This in fact happens by the lack of some information of the data, but almost no further investigation was made previously. In this paper, we define a measure of such imperfectness of the data as a minimum amount of additional fragments which are needed to fix the probe order uniquely. Several polynomial-time algorithms to compute such additional fragments of minimum cost are presented.

Keywords: DNA, hybridization, probe, fragment and PQ-tree

1. Introduction

The STS-based mapping is one of the most popular techniques for physical mapping of DNA sequences. In this procedure, a DNA sequence S is cloned into many copies and then they are cut into smaller, overlapped subsequences called *fragments*. An STS (sequence-tagged site), also called a *probe*, is used as a marker; each probe is supposed to appear at a unique position in the entire DNA sequence S. Now we are given a *hybridization matrix*, an *H-matrix* in short, $A = (a_{ij})$ such that $a_{ij} = 1$ if probe p_j exists in fragment f_i and $a_{ij} = 0$ otherwise. Our goal is to compute the order of probes $P=\{p_1, \ldots, p_n\}$ in the original DNA sequence S from the given H-matrix A. It is well-known that this can be formulated as the following combinatorial problem: Given an H-matrix, obtain a permutation of the columns so that the resulting matrix has the so-called *consecutive-one property*, i.e., all 1s are consecutive in each row of the matrix.

The problem can be solved in linear time by using the famous data structure called *PQ-trees* [12]. Unfortunately, there are several kinds of errors involved in experiments, which makes the data, H-matrices in our case, imperfect. Typical errors include the case that (i) an entry of the H-matrix changes from 0 to 1, and vice versa, and that (ii) two fragments which are not consecutive in the DNA sequence put together into a "chimeric" fragment [3, 4, 6–9]. In the presence of such noises, we cannot use PQ-trees any longer; the problem now becomes several optimization problems due to different assumptions of noises. Not surprizingly, they are NP-hard in most cases [3, 7, 9, 11].

Even if there are no such errors, there may still remain ambiguities in the probe order. See for example Fig. 1 (a), which illustrates an example of an H-matrix consisting of six fragments (rows) f_1 to f_6, and ten probes (columns) A to J. By exchanging columns, the matrix can be transformed into the matrix in Fig. 1 (b) which satisfies the consecutive-one property, (i.e., each row has a single block of consecutive ones). One can see however that there are several other orders of the columns, say EGBFIADHC, which also achieve the consecutive-one property. Thus we cannot fix the order of probes uniquely from the requirement of the consecutive-one property in the case of this H-matrix, which is obviously due to the imperfectness of the data. There is a few literature which mentions the existence of this fact, e.g., [2], but no further investigation was made previously.

Our contribution. In this paper, we propose a measure of such imperfectness in H-matrices. Recall that the imperfectness is due to the lack of information. For example, if we add two extra fragments to the H-matrix of Fig. 1 (a) as in Fig. 1 (c), then the order of probes is now determined uniquely as shown in Fig. 1 (d). Thus the amount of additional fragments being needed to uniquely fix the probe order looks closely related to the degree of the imperfectness. It is apparently convenient to know this quantity for conducting the STS-based physical mapping.

More formally we consider the following problem: For a given H-matrix, obtain the minimum amount of additional fragments such that there is only one order of columns for the augmented H-matrix to have the consecutive-one property. Here are some issues which should be taken into consideration: (i) The minimum amount of fragments differs according to the order of probes to be selected as a unique one among possible different orders. For example, we needed two additional fragments in Fig. 1 (d), but three additional fragments are needed to fix the column order as BGEAIDHCFJ. (ii) There are different measures for the "amount" of fragments, such as the number of fragments and the total length of them.

Our main result is to give polynomial-time algorithms which compute (1) for a given H-matrix having the consecutive-one property, the minimum number of additional fragments which are enough to fix the probe order to the current order (i.e., the order of the columns in the given H-matrix), (2) the minimum total length of additional fragments under the same setting, (3) for a given H-matrix not necessary having the consecutive-one property, the minimum number of additional fragments enough to fix the probe order uniquely (but the order itself may be arbitrary) so that the augmented H-matrix has the consecutive-one property, (4) the minimum total length of additional fragments under the same setting. We also mention a computer simulation using genes of human chromosome 20.

Related Work. As mentioned previously, if the data are perfect, then the problem can be solved in linear time by using PQ-trees [12]. Several possibilities of errors have been investigated including obtaining a sub-matrix have the consecutive-one property [1], obtaining most-likely probe orders in the presence of false position and false negative hybridization errors using a different data structure [7], using the LP-relaxation for optimizing the most-likely probe order [6], and exploiting the fact that each probe occurs at a unique position in a more sophisticated way to handle errors such as chimeric fragments [3]. Also see [4, 8–11] for other related work including parallelization of the construction of PQ-trees [5].

2. PQ-trees

PQ-trees are a convenient data structure for our problem. Fig. 3 shows an example of a PQ-tree. A PQ-tree T consists of *P-nodes* denoted by circles, *Q-nodes* denoted by rectangles, and *leaf-nodes*. $P(T)$ denotes a set of permutations of leaf-nodes that is defined by the following rules: (i) Children of a P-node may be arbitrarily permuted. (ii) Children of a Q-node must be consecutive but may be arranged in reverse order. For example, let T_0 be the PQ-tree in Fig. 3. Then $P(T_0)$=$\{BGEJAIDHCJF, EGBJIADHCF, \ldots\}$. Two PQ-trees T and T' are said to be equivalent if $P(T) = P(T')$.

There is a linear-time algorithm [12] which constructs a PQ-tree T from H-matrix A such that (i) T's leaf-nodes correspond to columns of A and (ii) A has the consecutive-one property iff A's columns are rearranged into an order in $P(T)$. (If A cannot be rearranged into any matrix having the consecutive-one property, then the algorithm can detect it. If A is an H-matrix, this does not happen unless A includes errors. Although details are omitted, the algorithm constructs a target PQ-tree by transforming PQ-trees step-by-step, begining with a PQ-tree of a single P-node. In each step, a row of the H-matrix is selected and the PQ-tree changes so that the constraint by that row is added. For example, from the H-matrix in Fig 1(a), we can construct the associated

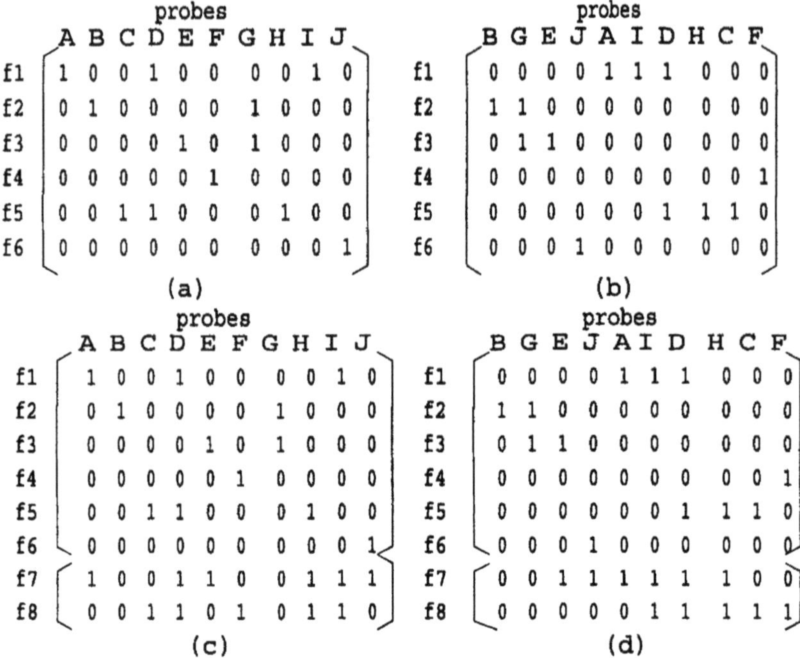

Figure 1. Permuting the (0,1)-matrix gotten by the experiment

PQ-tree as shown in Fig. 2 by selecting rows f_1 through f_6 in each step. Note that the final PQ-tree is the same as T_0 in Fig. 3 and $P(T_0)$ includes several different orders as mentioned before. For example, BGEJAIDHCF in $P(T_0)$ corresponds to the H-matrix in Fig. 2 (b) which has the consecutive-one property.

If we add two new rows (fragments) f_7 and f_8 as in Fig. 2 (c), then the PQ-tree is furthermore changed as in Fig. 4 and the final PQ-tree consists of a single Q-node (Such a PQ-tree is called a *1Q-tree.*) This means that the probe order is fixed uniquely (without its reverse order) by adding two extra fragments, which is exactly what we wanted to do. Thus our problem can be restated as follows.

Problem $FIX(T, \sigma)$: For a given PQ-tree T (made from H-matrix by the algorithm of [12]) and a probe order (leaf order) σ, obtain a set of additional fragments of a minimum cost such that T will change into a 1Q-tree of leaf order σ.

If σ is not given then the problem is denoted by $FIX(T, -)$ which requires to obtain a minimum fragments to change T into *some* 1Q-tree. As the cost of a fragment set, we consider mainly two different definitions. One is the size of fragment set, i.e., the number of fragments. The other is the sum of the lengths

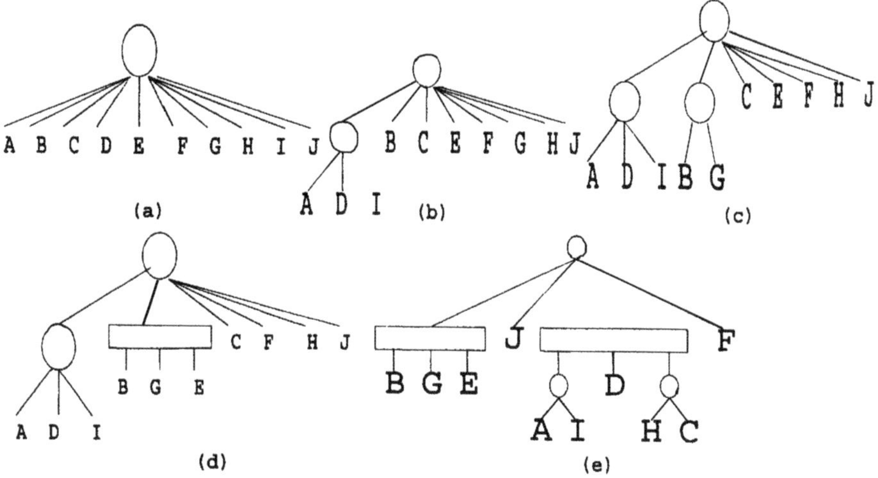

Figure 2. The process to make the input PQ-tree

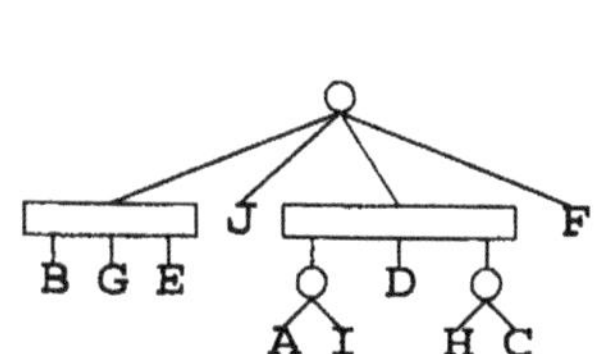

Figure 3. After adding fragment 5

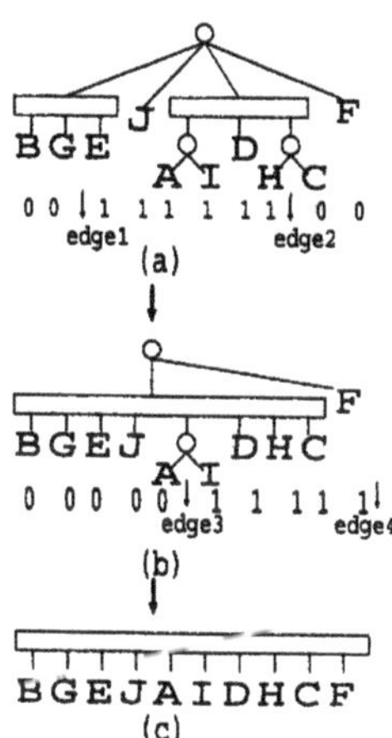

Figure 4. Making a 1Q-tree

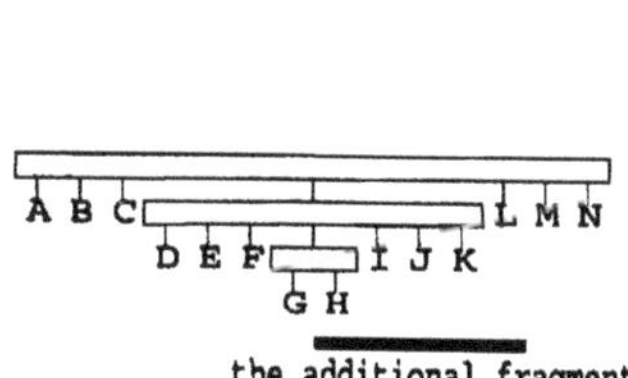

Figure 5. The number of fragment=1 the total length=5

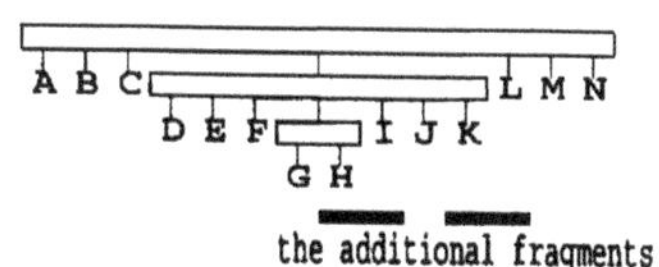

Figure 6. The number of fragment=2 the total length=4

of the fragments, where the length of a fragment is the number of 1s included in the corresponding row of the H-matrix. Those two measures sometimes conflict: As a simple example, the PQ-tree in Fig. 5 needs one fragment of length five (i.e., the fragment including probes H, I, J, K and L) for the fixing operation. The same fixing operation is also possible by using two fragments of total length four as shown in Fig. 6.

3. Minimizing the number of additional fragments

In this section, we first discuss minimizing the number of additional fragments for $FIX(T, \sigma)$ (i.e., the probe order is to be fixed to σ which is explicitly given) and then for $FIX(T, -)$ (to be fixed to an arbitrary order).

$FIX(T, \sigma)$

Suppose that the PQ-tree is given so that the leaves are arranged in the order $\sigma = p_1 p_2 \dots p_n$ of length n. Then we consider $n + 1$ different *positions*, denoted by $(-, p_1), (p_1, p_2), \dots, (p_{n-1}, p_n)$, and $(p_n, -)$. Thus a position means a "between" of two consecutive probes or the left (right) of p_1 (p_n). A position denoted by (p_i, p_{i+1}) is called an *inside* position, $(-, p_1)$ and $(p_n, -)$ an *outside* position. See Fig. 4 again. An additional fragment should have a consecutive sequence of probes, EJAIDH for example for the first added fragment in Fig. 4, which can be designated by giving two positions, its *left end-position* and *right end-position* ((G,E) and (H,C)) in the example). We sometimes say that a fragment is *terminated* by its (left and/or right) end-positions.

In Fig. 4, we selected two positions (G,E) and (H,C) to terminate the first additional fragment. As one can see later, this selection of (G,E) and (H,C) contributes to converting the PQ-tree into the final 1Q-tree efficiently. Thus among all positions, there are some "important" positions for our purpose. We call such positions "edges," since using these important positions as edges of additional fragments plays a great role in minimizing the number of additional fragments. *Edges* are divided into three types and defined as follows: A position (x, y) is called (i) an *Inside-P-type edge* if probes x and y are children of a single P-node, (ii) an *Outside-P-type edge* if probe x (or y) is $-$ and it is a child of the root P-node, (iii) a *Q-type edge* if both x and y belong to a single Q-node which is not a root Q-node and which includes only leaf-nodes. In Fig. 4 for example, (A,I) is Inside-P-type, (F,-) is Outside-P-type and (G,E) is Q-type. It should be noted that if we select two edges appropriately to terminate an additional fragment, like (G,E) and (H,C) in Fig. 4 then those two edges "disappear" in the transformed PQ-tree. ((G,E) or any other Q-type edge for the Q-node BGE. By definition, (B,G) is also a Q-type edge for the same Q-node. As described later, we only need one Q-type edge for a Q-node for the fixing operation.) Thus the key point is how to select such appropriate edges for additional fragments.

LEMMA 1 *A PQ-tree includes no edge if and only if it is a 1Q-tree.*

Proof. If a PQ-tree has two internal nodes, there is at least one edge by the definition. If a PQ-tree has only one internal node and if it is a P-node, it includes at least one P-type edge from the definition. □

LEMMA 2 *For any solution of $FIX(T, \sigma)$, every edge must be selected at least once to terminate additional fragments.*

Proof. It is proved by examing all templates for transformation of PQ-trees in each step defined in [12]. □

In Fig. 4, the first additional fragment is terminated by edges (G,E) and (H,C). After adding this fragment, edges 1 and 2 disappear. However, we cannot say that every edge always disappears when a fragment terminated by the edge is added. For example, if the first additional fragment is terminated by (A,I) and (H,C), two Inside-P-type edges seem to disappear. However, because (A,I), (I,D), (D,H) and (H,C) become Q-type edges, the number of edges which are disappeared by this additional fragment is actually only one. In Fig. 4, edges 1 and 2 have another edge, edge 3, between them. In fact, both edges always disappear in such a case as shown in the following lemma.

LEMMA 3 *Suppose that a PQ-tree T_1 has two edges e_1 and e_2, and T_1 is transformed into T_2 by adding the fragment terminated by e_1 and e_2. Then (i) at least one of e_1 and e_2 disappears in T_2 and (ii) if there is another edge, say e_3, between e_1 and e_2, then both e_1 and e_2 disappear in T_2 (iii) Furthermore no new edges are created.*

Proof. Let v be the lowest common ancestor of e_1 and e_2. Let v_l be the internal node which is an ancestor of e_1 and a child of v. Let v_r be the internal node which is an ancestor of e_2 and a child of v. Let l_1 be the leftest probe included in the subtree whose root is v_l. Let l_r be the rightest probe included in the subtree whose root is v_r. (See Fig. 7)

Assume that a fragment terminated by e_1 and e_2 is added and at most one of the two edges disappear. In this case, there are the following two cases only.

- When v is a P-node and there is not another edge except for e_1 and e_2 in the position set between l_l and l_r,
- When v is a Q-node and there is not another edge except for e_1 and e_2 in the positions included by the subtree whose root is v.

Our method avoids these cases. Hence (i) and (ii) are shown. Property (iii) can be proved by examining all templates for transformation of PQ-trees in each step defined in [12]. □

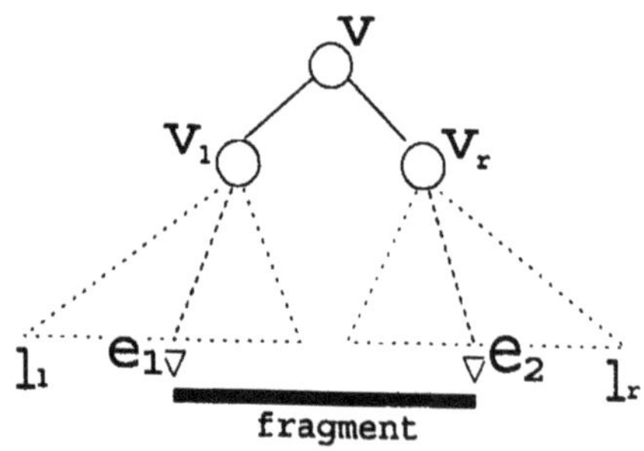

Figure 7. An additional fragment terminated by e_1 and e_2

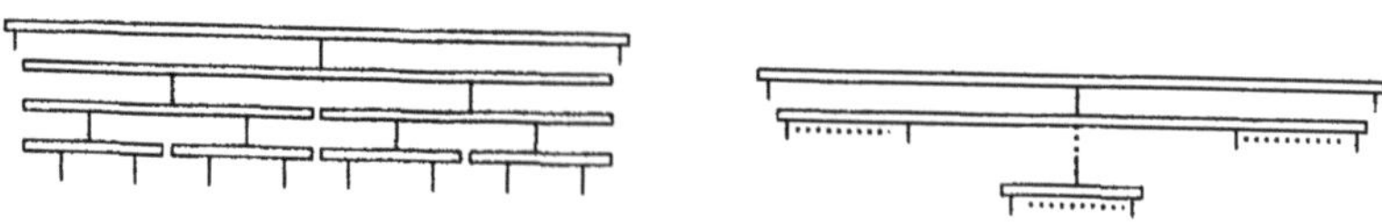

Figure 8. A PQ-tree in which $\frac{e}{2}+1$ additional fragments are necessary

Figure 9. One step before the 1Q-tree

By using Lemma 3, we can remove two edges by adding one fragment, and thus we can show that the number of necessary additional fragments for a fixing operation is about a half of the number of edges. Note that, there must be at least three edges in order to apply lemma 3. In fact, there exists a case that there are only two edges, and two fragments are needed. As the result of this, there exists a PQ-tree that has e edges and $\lceil \frac{e}{2} \rceil + 1$ additional fragments are needed. The PQ-tree in Fig. 8 is an example of it. It becomes the PQ-tree of Fig. 9 after adding $\lceil \frac{e}{2} \rceil$ fragments terminated by two.

In other words, when the number of edges is even, there are two cases, i.e., the minimum numbers of additional fragments are $\frac{e}{2}$ and $\frac{e}{2} + 1$. We can distinguish them by using a simple characterization as the following theorem.

THEOREM 4 *Let e be the number of edges and n be the number of probes of (T, σ). The minimum number of additional fragments for $FIX(T, \sigma)$ is shown as follows:*

1 *When e is odd: $\frac{e+1}{2}$.*

2 *When e is even:*

2-1. *When the root node is a Q-node and there is only one internal child node of the root: $\frac{e}{2} + 1$.*

2-2. *Otherwise: $\frac{e}{2}$.*

Moreover, a fragment set with the minimum number of additional fragments for $FIX(T, \sigma)$ can be found in $O(n^3)$ time.

For proving the theorem, we introduce the following lemma.

LEMMA 5 *Consider a PQ-tree (T, σ) that includes at least three edges and doesn't satisfy the condition of 2-1 in Theorem 1. There exists a fragment satisfying the condition of Lemma 3 (ii) such that the resultant PQ-tree (T', σ) also doesn't satisfy the condition of 2-1 in Theorem 1 after adding the fragment.*

Proof of Theorem 1.

- When e is odd:

  From Lemma 3 (ii), two edges can be decreased by adding one fragment if $e \geq 3$. Hence, by iterating this process, only one edge remains after adding $\frac{e-1}{2}$ fragments. A PQ-tree including only one edge must satisfy all of the following three conditions:

  - The root is a Q-node.
  - Every internal node has at most one internal child node.
  - The lowest internal node (the internal node which doesn't have an internal child node.) is a Q-node.

  It becomes a 1Q-tree by adding a fragment.

- When e is even:

  By using the same discussion with the odd case above, a PQ-tree including only two edges can be obtained by adding $\frac{e}{2} - 1$ fragments. From Lemma 4, if the original PQ-tree doesn't satisfy the condition of 2-1, then the resultant PQ-tree doesn't also. Hence, it is enough to consider the case that $e = 2$. It can be easily proved by examing all cases.

Because we consider only the given order of probes, there are $O(n^2)$ fragments. A transformation by each additional fragment can be done in $O(n)$ time. □

$FIX(T, -)$

The result of Theorem 1 can be used to solve $FIX(T, -)$ also. That is, $FIX(T, -)$ can be solved by finding a leaf order σ in which the number of edges is minimum. The following Lemma 6 shows how to find such σ. In the lemma, v and l mean the number of internal child nodes and the number of child probes, respectively, of the noticed P-node.

LEMMA 6 *Let a_1 be the number of Q-nodes which don't have internal child nodes. Let a_2 be the total number of $max\{|l| - |v| - 1, 0\}$ for all P-nodes which are not the root. Let a_3 be $max\{|l| - |v| + 1, 0\}$ if the root is a P-node, or 0 otherwise. The minimum number of edges for $FIX(T, -)$ is $a_1 + a_2 + a_3$.*

It can be proved by definitions of edges. See an example of Fig. 3. If probe F is moved to the space between BGE and AIDHC, the number of edges decreases by one and it is the PQ-tree yielding the minimum solution three.

THEOREM 7 *In $FIX(T, -)$, a fragment set, in which the number of additional fragments is minimum, can be found in $O(n^3)$ time, where n is the number of probes.*

Proof. It is clear from Lemma 3 and 6, and Theorem 1. □

4. Minimizing the total length of additional fragments

In this section, we pay attention another cost function, i.e., minimizing the total length of additional fragments.

$FIX(T, \sigma)$

As shown in Fig.s 5 and 6, the smallness for the number of additional fragments and the shortness for the total length of additional fragments may conflict each other. For a fixing operation, for every edge, there must be at least one fragment terminated by the edges. However, there is a case that we can shorten the total length by using a fragment which is terminated by two non-edge positions. The fragment which consists of KL shown in Fig. 6 is an example of this. As shown in this example, "edge" is a concept related to the number of fragments, and there is scarcely any relation between edges and the total lengths of fragments.

We propose an algorithm, which scans from the leaves to the root and base on a dynamic programming, for this problem. We explain the basic ideas by using simple examples. Before the explanation, we introduce some notations as follows. A fragment *covers* position (i, j) if the fragment includes both i and j. A set F of fragments *covers* a set P of consecutive probes if for each neighbor probes $i, j \in P$, F has a fragment that covers position (i, j). If a set F of fragments doesn't cover a set P of consecutive probes, then there is at least one "cut" defined as follows. A *cut* of F for P is a position (i, j) such that $i, j \in F$ and the position is not covered by any fragment in F.

We consider a PQ-tree shown in Fig. 10 (c). It consists of only one P-node and leaves. The lengths of fragments are $2, 3, 3, 3, \dots, 3, 3, 3, 2$. The numbers of 1s assigned to each probes are $1, 2, 1, 2, \dots, 2, 1, 2, 1$. Note that the set of fragments covers the set of all probes. If additional fragment set doesn't cover the set of all probes as Fig. 10 (d), the fixing operation can't be completed. However, if this is a subtree of the given PQ-tree, although the additional fragment set doesn't cover the set of all probes, there is a case that the fixing operation can be completed. In many cases, it causes to save the total length of additional fragments. In other words, a naive procedure such as to

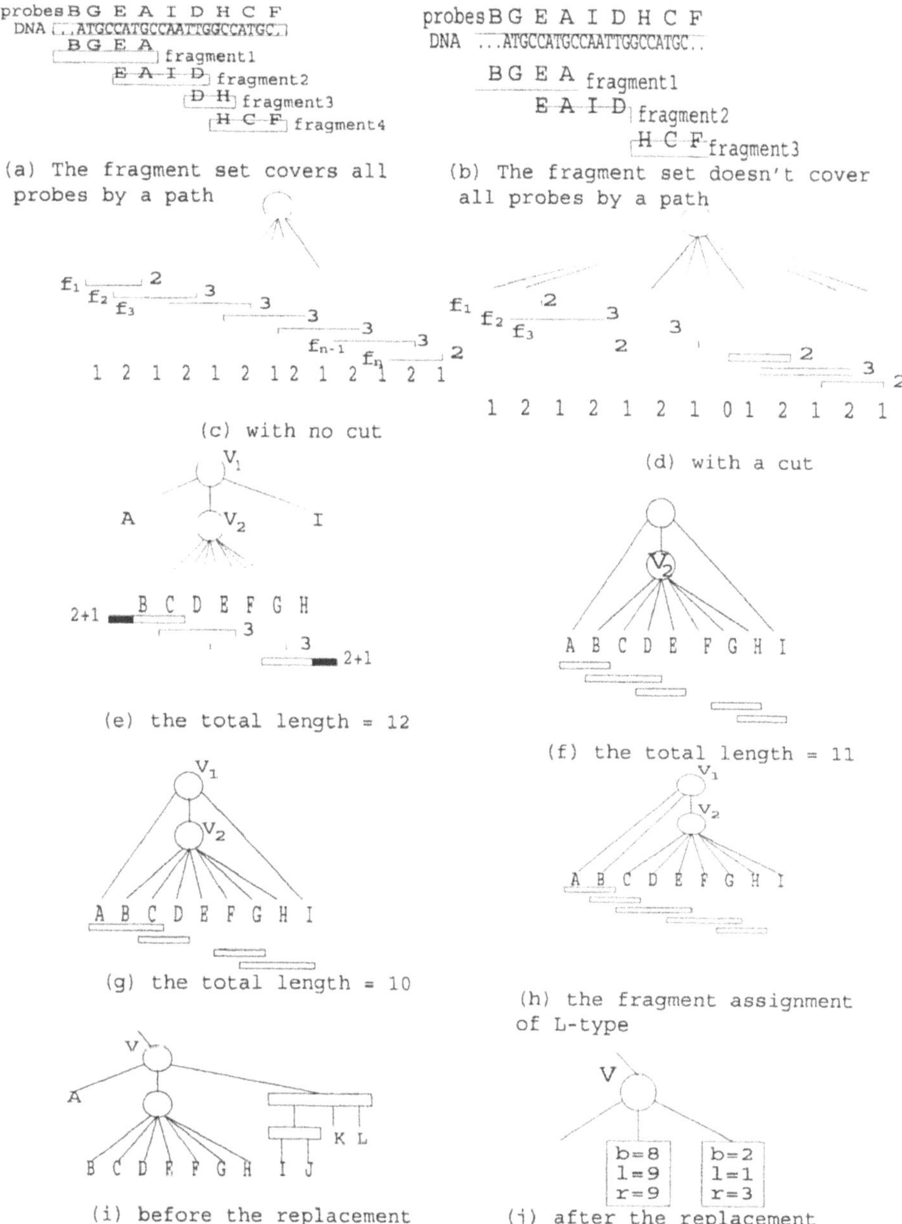

Figure 10. minimizing the total length of additional fragments

find the optimal solution in each subtree and to build them up from leaves to the root simply may not to obtain an optimal solution.

For example, if the cut is moved to F as Fig. 10 (f), the total length increases from 10 to 11.

For example, the additional fragment set shown in Fig. 10 (g) doesn't cover all probes by a path in the subtree whose root is v_2. However, the subtree is also fixed by assigning fragments to A and I which are next to the subtree as in the figure. Here, we pay attention only to the subtree v_2 (the subtree rooted by v_2) of Figures 10 (e)–(g). If additional fragments on the subtree are given as Fig. 10 (g), order of BCDE, E, and FGH cannot be fixed yet. Thus fragments A and I, which are neighbors of the subtree, must be covered by fragments.

Hence, let us say that the pair of such subtree and such fragment assignment is B-type (B means "both sides".The precise definition will be done later). Moreover, if the fragment assignment on the subtree v_2 are given as Fig. 10 (h), we have to assign a fragment to B which is the left neighbor of the subtree. Hence, let us say that the pair of such subtree and such fragment assignment is L-type. R-type is defined symmetrically. More precisely, they are defined as follows: (Note that a pair of a subtree and a fragment assignment can be two or three types at a time.)

- **R-type** A pair of a subtree and a fragment assignment, such that if there is 1 at the right neighbor probe of the subtree, the subtree can be transformed into 1Q-tree and connected to the right side.
- **L-type** A pair of a subtree and a fragment assignment, such that if there is 1 at the left neighbor probe of the subtree, the subtree can be transformed into 1Q-tree and connected to the left side.
- **B-type** A pair of a subtree and a fragment assignment, such that if there are 1s at the both neighbor probes of the subtree, the subtree can be transformed into 1Q-tree and connected to the both sides.

The minimum value of the total length of feasible fragment assignments for each of the three types can be calculated in polynomial time, since if the cut is fixed, then the minimum value can be obtained easily. By memorizing the minimum values of the total length of additional fragments for each of the three types for every subtree, we can also calculate the minimum values of them for the upper subtrees. Now, we establish an algorithm, which examines all candidates of the cut and finds the optimal fragment assignments in the three types for every sub-tree, in order to find the minimum fragment set of the whole PQ-tree.

The following example explains the algorithm more in detail. Fig. 10 (i) can be replaced with Fig. 10 (j) by calculating the optimal fragment assignments for the three types for every subtree except for v. Let b, l and r be the minimum values for the total lengths of the additional fragment sets of B-type, L-type and R-type, respectively.

By using the algorithm, we obtain the following theorem.

THEOREM 8 *A fragment set with minimum total length for $FIX(T, \sigma)$ can be found in $O(n^2)$ time, where n is the number of probes.*

Proof. We omit the proof for that the algorithm can construct the minimum fragment set correctly. The proof for the computational time is as follows. Let d_i be the degrees for each internal nodes x_i. Since, the computational time for each internal node is at most $O({d_i}^2)$, the whole computational time is at most $\sum_{x_i} O({d_i}^2) = O(n^2)$. □

FIX(T,-)

In $FIX(T, -)$, since there is no distinction between L-type and R-type, they are called *LR-type*. Let lr be the smaller one of l and r. Although, in $FIX(T, \sigma)$ a cut is scanned from left to right, in $FIX(T, -)$ a cut is fixed. However, the algorithm has to examine all candidates of nodes for both adjacent sides of the cut and the leftest node and the rightest node of the subtree. For the other nodes, the B-type assignment in which the total length of fragments is less than any other B-type assignment is used. Since the position of the cut and whether there is a cut or not are assumed in advance, the algorithm is not allowed to make a new cut by assigning fragments to nodes. However, if the B-type assignment is replaced by another assignment which is not B-type, a new cut is created.

Leaves and internal nodes should be ordered alternately as far as possible. Although the algorithm has to examine more cases, the order of the computation time doesn't become large.

THEOREM 9 *A fragment set with minimum total length for $FIX(T, -)$ can be found in $O(n^5)$ time, where n is the number of probes.*

5. Concluding Remarks

For the problem for fixing the probe order of a given PQ-tree, we showed two polynomial time algorithms. One of them minimizes the number of additional fragments. The other minimizes the total length of additional fragments. We solved not only the problems to fix probes as a given order, but also the problems to find the best order of the probes. For treating the former cost function, we introduced an idea of "edges". We showed the minimum number of additional fragments are $\lceil \frac{e}{2} \rceil$ or $\lceil \frac{e}{2} \rceil + 1$, where e is the number of edges.

For practical use, it may be difficult to make additional fragments which we want. However, if fragments are concentrated to the part where edges exist densely, the probability that fragments which our algorithm wants are generated becomes high. In other words, the probability that edges disappear becomes high and fixing operations are accelerated. Some results of computer experiments for this method are appeared on our web page addressed: http://www.lab2.kuis.kyoto-u.ac.jp/~tamura/tcs2004.html.

Acknowledgments

We appreciate Mr. D. Tsuchida and Mr. H. Kasahara for their cooperation.

References

[1] M. T. Hajiaghayi and Y. Ganjali, A note on consecutive ones submatrix problem, Information processing letters 83, pp. 163–166, 2002

[2] S. Heber, J. Hoheisel, and M. Vingron, Application of bootstrap techniques to physical mapping, Genomics 69, pp235–241, 2000

[3] F. Alizadeh, R. M. Karp, D. K. Weisser, and G. Zweig, Physical mapping of chromosomes using unique probes, Symposium on Discrete Algorithms, pp. 489–500, 1994

[4] J. Krececioglu, S. Shete, and J. Arnold, Reconstructing distances in physical maps of chromosomes with nonoverlapping probes, Proceedings of the fourth annual international conference on Computational molecular biology, pp. 183-192, 2000

[5] F. S. Annexstein and R. P. Swaminathan, On testing consecutive-ones property in parallel, Proceedings of the seventh annual ACM symposium on Parallel algorithms and architectures, pp. 234-243, 1995

[6] M. Jain and E. W. Myers, Algorithms for computing and integrating physical maps using unique probes, Proceedings of the first annual international conference on Computational molecular biology, pp. 151-161, 1997

[7] T. Christof and J. Kececioglu, Computing physical maps of chromosomes with nonoverlapping probes by branch-and-cut, Proceedings of the third annual international conference on Computational molecular biology, pp. 115-123, 1999

[8] R. Beigel, N. Alon , S. Kasif , M. S. Apaydin, and L. Fortnow, An optimal procedure for gap closing in whole genome shotgun sequencing, Proceedings of the fifth annual international conference on Computational biology, pp. 22-30 2001

[9] T. Christof, M. Jnger, J. Kececioglu, P. Mutzel, and G. Reinelt, A branch-and-cut approach to physical mapping with end-probes, Proceedings of the first annual international conference on Computational molecular biology, pp. 84-92, 1997

[10] D. B. Wilson, D. S. Greenberg, and C. A. Phillips, Beyond islands (extended abstract): Runs in clone-probe matrices, Proceedings of the first annual international conference on Computational molecular biology, pp. 320-329, 1997

[11] A. Ben-Dor and B. Chor, On constructing radiation hybrid maps (extended abstract), Proceedings of the first annual international conference on Computational molecular biology, pp. 17-26, 1997

[12] K. S. Booth and G. S. Lueker, Testing for the Consecutive Ones Property, Interval Graphs, and Graph Planarity Using PQ-Tree Algorithms, Journal of Computer and System Sciences 13, pp. 335–379, 1976.

[13] A.V.Aho, J.E.Hopcraft, and J.D.Ullman, The Design and Analysis of Computer Algorithms, Addison-Wesley, Reading, Mass., 1974.

SOLVING PACKING PROBLEM WITH WEAKER BLOCK SOLVERS *

Hu Zhang
Institute of Computer Science and Applied Mathematics
University of Kiel, Germany
hzh@informatik.uni-kiel.de

Abstract We study the general packing problem with M constraints. In [Jansen and Zhang, TCS 2002] a $c(1+\varepsilon)$-approximation algorithm for the general packing problem was proposed. A block solver $ABS(p, \varepsilon/6, c)$ with price vector p, given accuracy ε and ratio c is required. In addition, in [Villavicencio and Grigoriadis, Network Optimization (1997)] a $(1+\varepsilon)$-approximation algorithm for standard packing problem and its dual problem was studied, with a block solver $ABS(p, \varepsilon/10)$ (i.e., $c = 1$). In this paper we develop $c(1+\varepsilon)$-approximation algorithms for the general packing problem (or with its dual problem), with only weaker block solvers $ABS(p, O(\varepsilon'), c)$ with same structure as in previous algorithms, where $\varepsilon' > \varepsilon$. For both primal and dual problems we design an algorithm with an $ABS(p, \varepsilon_1/10, c)$ and $\varepsilon_1 > \varepsilon$. The bound on the number of iterations is polynomial in M, ε and c. Furthermore we show an algorithm for the primal problem with an $ABS(p, \varepsilon_3/6, c)$ and $\varepsilon_3 > \varepsilon$. And the bound on the number of iterations is polynomial in only M and ε. In both cases running times are further improved with corresponding weaker block solvers. This is the first attempt to solve the packing problem with weaker block solvers.

1. Introduction

An interesting class of optimization problems is the *packing problem* or *convex min-max resource-sharing problem* defined as follows:

$$(P) \qquad \lambda^* = \min\{\lambda | f(x) \leq \lambda e, x \in B\},$$

*This research was supported in part by the DFG Graduiertenkolleg 357, Effiziente Algorithmen und Mehrskalenmethoden, by EU Thematic Network APPOL, Approximation and Online Algorithms for Optimization Problems, IST-2001-32007, and by EU Project CRESCCO, Critical Resource Sharing for Cooperation in Complex Systems, IST-2001-33135.

where $f : B \to \mathbb{R}_+^M$ is a vector of M continuous convex functions defined on a nonempty convex set $B \subseteq \mathbb{R}^N$, and e is the vector of all ones. Without loss of generality we can assume $\lambda^* > 0$. The functions f_m, $1 \le m \le M$, are packing constraints. In addition, we denote by $\lambda(x) = \max_{1 \le m \le M} f_m(x)$ for any given $x \in B$. There are many applications of the packing problem. Typical examples include scheduling on unrelated machines, job shop scheduling, network embeddings, Held-Karp bound for TSP, minimum-cost multicommodity flows, maximum concurrent flow, bin covering, spreading metrics, approximating metric space, graph partitioning, multicast congestion in communication networks, and energy consumption problem in ad-hoc networks on general metric spaces [1–4, 7, 9, 13, 17, 19, 22].

The problem (P) could be solved exactly in polynomial time in its size usually. However, in some cases an approximate solution is enough (e.g. [16]). In addition, it is possible that the size of (P) is exponential in the size of input (e.g. [1, 15, 19]). Thus we consider fast but approximation algorithms for problem (P). Given an accuracy tolerance $\varepsilon > 0$, the approximate problem is as follows:

$$(P_\varepsilon) \qquad \text{compute } x \in B \text{ such that } f(x) \le (1+\varepsilon)\lambda^* e.$$

Grigoriadis et al. [5, 6] proposed algorithms for the above problem based on the Lagrangian duality relation $\lambda^* = \min_{x \in B} \max_{p \in P} p^T f(x) = \max_{p \in P} \min_{x \in B} p^T f(x)$, where $P = \{p \in \mathbb{R}^M \mid \sum_{m=1}^M p_m = 1, p_m \ge 0\}$. Denoting by $\Lambda(p) = \min_{x \in B} p^T f(x)$, it can be verified that a pair $x \in B$ and $p \in P$ is optimal if and only if $\lambda(x) = \Lambda(p)$. On the other hand, the corresponding approximate dual problem is:

$$(D_\varepsilon) \qquad \text{compute } p \in P \text{ such that } \Lambda(p) \ge (1-\varepsilon)\lambda^*.$$

In addition, the Lagrangian or price-directive decomposition method is applied in their algorithms, which is an iterative approach that solves (P_ε) and (D_ε) by computing a sequence of pairs x and p to approximate the exact solution from above and below, respectively. Grigoriadis and Khachiyan [6] proved that (P_ε) and (D_ε) can be solved in $O(M(\ln M + \varepsilon^{-2} \ln \varepsilon^{-1}))$ iterations or calls to a standard approximate block solver $ABS(p,t)$ that solves the block problem for a given tolerance $t = O(\varepsilon)$: to compute $\hat{x} = \hat{x}(p) \in B$ such that $p^T f(\hat{x}) \le (1+t) \min_{y \in B} p^T f(y)$. Villavicencio and Grigoriadis [18] proposed a modified logarithmic potential function to avoid the ternary search and the number of iterations is also $O(M(\ln M + \varepsilon^{-2} \ln \varepsilon^{-1}))$. In [14] the bound was improved to $O(M(\ln M + \varepsilon^{-2}))$ for both (P_ε) and (D_ε).

However, in general the block problem may be hard to approximate [1–3, 15, 19], i.e., the assumption to have a block solver with accuracy

$t = O(\varepsilon)$ is too strict. Therefore in [14] the authors considered the case that only a weak approximate block solver $ABS(p,t,c)$ is available, which is defined to compute $\hat{x} = \hat{x}(p) \in B$ such that $p^T f(\hat{x}) \leq c(1 + t) \min_{y \in B} p^T f(y)$, where $c \geq 1$ is the approximation ratio. The main goal is to solve the following primal problem (using the weak block solver):

$$(P_{\varepsilon,c}) \qquad \text{compute } x \in B \text{ such that } f(x) \leq c(1+\varepsilon)\lambda^* e.$$

And the corresponding dual problem is:

$$(D_{\varepsilon,c}) \qquad \text{compute } p \in P \text{ such that } \Lambda(p) \geq \frac{1}{c}(1-\varepsilon)\lambda^*.$$

Jansen et al. [14] developed an approximation algorithm that for any accuracy $\varepsilon \in (0,1]$ solves the $(P_{\varepsilon,c})$ in $O(M(\ln M + \varepsilon^{-2} \ln \varepsilon^{-1}))$ iterations by adding a new stopping rule. Each step calls the weak block solver $ABS(p, O(\varepsilon), c)$ once and has an overhead of $O(M \ln\ln(M\varepsilon^{-1}))$ arithmetic operations. In addition, for small ratio c with $\ln c = O(\varepsilon)$ they improved the bound to $O(M(\ln M + \varepsilon^{-2}))$.

Related results: Plotkin et al. [17] considered the linear feasibility variants of both problems: either to find a point $x \in B$ such that $f(x) = Ax \geq (1-\varepsilon)b$ or to find a point $x \in B$ such that $f(x) = Ax \leq (1+\varepsilon)b$ where A is the coefficient matrix with M rows and b is an M-dimensional vector. The problems are solved by Lagrangian decomposition with exponential potential reductions. The numbers of iterations in these algorithms are $O(\varepsilon^{-2}\rho \ln(M\varepsilon^{-1}))$ and $O(M + \rho \ln^2 M + \varepsilon^{-2}\rho \ln(M\varepsilon^{-1}))$ respectively, where $\rho = \max_{1 \leq m \leq M} \max_{x \in B} a_m^T x / b_m$ is the width of B relative to $Ax \geq b$. However, their algorithms could have only pseudo polynomial running time due to the parameter ρ. Garg and Könemann [4] proposed a $(1+\varepsilon)$-approximation algorithm for the linear packing problem within $O(M\varepsilon^{-2} \ln M)$ iterations, which is independent of the width. Unfortunately implementation results show that their algorithm is very impractical [1]. Young [20] studied also the linear case of the packing problem but weak block solvers are allowed. His algorithm uses $O(\rho'(\lambda^*)^{-1}\varepsilon^{-2} \ln M)$ calls to the block solver, where $\rho' = \max_{1 \leq m \leq M} \max_{x \in B} a_m^T x / b_m - \min_{1 \leq m \leq M} \min_{x \in B} a_m^T x / b_m$ and λ^* is the optimal value of the packing problem. Similar to [17], this result also depends on input data. Furthermore, Charikar et al. [2] noticed that the result in [17] for the packing problem can be extended also to the case of weak block solvers in the same number $O(\varepsilon^{-2}\rho \ln(M\varepsilon^{-1}))$ of iterations. For the covering problem, which is related to the packing problem, Grigoriadis et al [8] showed that the number of iterations is $O(M(\ln M + \varepsilon^{-2}))$ with $c = 1$. Jansen and Porkolab [12] studied the general covering problem with only weak approximate block solver and showed that at most

$O(M(\ln M + \varepsilon^{-2} + \varepsilon^{-3}\ln c))$ coordination steps are necessary. Recently Jansen [10] improved the bound to $O(M(\ln M + \varepsilon^{-2}\ln\varepsilon^{-1}))$, which is same as the bound in [14] for the packing problem. In addition, Young [21] proposed an approximation algorithm for a mixed linear packing and covering problem with the number of iterations $O(Md\varepsilon^{-2}\ln M)$, where d is the maximum number of constraints any variable appears in. Jansen [11] further improved the bound to $O(M\varepsilon^{-2}\ln(M\varepsilon^{-1}))$, which is also the first result independent of data for the mixed problem.

Our contribution: We notice that in [18] a $(1+\varepsilon)$-approximate solution for (P_ε) and (D_ε) can be obtained with a $(1+\varepsilon/10)$-approximate block solver, while a $c(1+\varepsilon)$-approximate solution for $(P_{\varepsilon,c})$ with a $c(1+\varepsilon/6)$-approximate block solver as well. Thus it is an interesting problem to solve $(P_{\varepsilon,c})$ with either a $c(1+\varepsilon'/10)$- or a $c(1+\varepsilon'/6)$-approximate block solver, where $\varepsilon \leq \varepsilon' \leq 1$. In this paper we develop algorithms for the above problems. First, we show a $c(1+\varepsilon)$-approximation algorithm $\mathcal{A}$ for both $(P_{\varepsilon,c})$ and $(D_{\varepsilon,c})$, with only an $ABS(p, \varepsilon_1/10, c)$, where $\varepsilon_1 = 8\varepsilon/(7-\varepsilon) > 8\varepsilon/7$ and the number of iteration is bounded by $O(Mc^2(\ln M + \varepsilon^{-4}\ln c + \varepsilon^{-3}\ln\varepsilon^{-1}))$. We then improve the coordination complexity to $O(Mc^2(\ln M + \varepsilon^{-3}\ln c + \varepsilon^{-2}\ln\varepsilon^{-1}))$ in $\mathcal{A}'$, but an $ABS(p, \varepsilon_2/10, c)$ is required, where $\varepsilon_2 = 8\varepsilon/((7+8r) - (1-8r)\varepsilon) \geq 8\varepsilon/(7+8r)$ for a constant $r \in (0, 1/8)$. Notice here $\varepsilon_2 \in (\varepsilon, \varepsilon_1)$. Furthermore, for only $(P_{\varepsilon,c})$ we develop a $c(1+\varepsilon)$-approximation algorithm $\mathcal{F}$ with an $ABS(p, \varepsilon_3/6, c)$, with $\varepsilon_3 = (43 - \sqrt{1849 - 1176\varepsilon})/12 \geq 49\varepsilon/43$. And the bound on the number of iterations is $O(M(\ln M + \varepsilon^{-4}\ln\varepsilon^{-1}))$, which is also improved to $O(M(\ln M + \varepsilon^{-2}\ln\varepsilon^{-1}))$ in $\mathcal{F}'$ with an $ABS(p, \varepsilon_4/6, c)$ for an $\varepsilon_4 \in (\varepsilon, \varepsilon_3)$. These algorithms are the first ones to solve general packing problems with only weaker block solvers.

Applications: One application is the case that the block problem only has an algorithm with a running time depending on input value power to a function of ε^{-1}, for instance, $O(n^{1/\varepsilon})$. In this case, to solve both problem $(P_{\varepsilon,c})$ and $(D_{\varepsilon,c})$, we just need a $c(1+\varepsilon'/10)$-approximate block solver, or a $c(1+\varepsilon'/6)$-approximate block solver to solve only $(P_{\varepsilon,c})$. Thus the running time of ABS can be reduced and the overall running time, which is the product of the bound on number of iterations and the running time of ABS, can decrease considerably. Another very interesting case is that the requirement of approximation ratio to block solver is too strict, i.e., only a $c'(1+\varepsilon/10)$- or $c'(1+\varepsilon/6)$-approximate block solver exists, where $c' > c$. For this case, if $c' \leq c(1+\varepsilon'/10)/(1+\varepsilon/10)$ or $c' \leq c(1+\varepsilon'/6)/(1+\varepsilon/6)$, respectively, we are able to also use our algorithms to solve the instance.

The paper is organized as follows: In Section 2 the potential function, price vector and their properties are reviewed. The algorithm $\mathcal{A}$ is presented in Section 3, as well as algorithm $\mathcal{F}$ in Section 4. Improvements of running times are also addressed. Due to the limit of space, proofs are not given in this version.

2. Modified logarithmic potential function

We use potential function to relax the packing constraints and show that an approximation of the minimum value of potential function corresponds to an approximation of λ^*. Thus the original problem can be replaced by finding a good approximate minimum point of the (smooth) potential function. The modified potential function is defined as follows [14, 18]:

$$\Phi_t(\theta, x) = \ln \theta - \frac{t}{M} \sum_{m=1}^{M} \ln(\theta - f_m(x)), \tag{1}$$

where $\theta \in \mathbb{R}_+$ and $x \in B$ are variables, and $t \in (0, 1]$ is a given tolerance parameter, which is also used in the approximate block solver $ABS(p, t, c)$. Same as [14, 18], in our algorithm, the values of t will be from $O(1)$ down to $O(\varepsilon)$, where ε is the desired accuracy tolerance. Since $\lambda(x) < \theta < \infty$ where $\lambda(x) = \max\{f_1(x), \ldots, f_M(x)\}$, the function Φ_t is well-defined. In addition, it has the *barrier property*: $\Phi_t(\theta, x) \to \infty$ for $\theta \to \lambda(x)$ and $\theta \to \infty$.

The reduced potential function is defined as the minimum of $\Phi_t(\theta, x)$ over $\theta \in (\lambda(x), \infty)$ for a fixed $x \in B$, i.e.

$$\phi_t(x) = \min_{\lambda(x) < \theta < \infty} \Phi_t(\theta, x). \tag{2}$$

It can be proved that $\theta(x)$ is the solution to the following equation:

$$\frac{t}{M} \sum_{m=1}^{M} \frac{\theta}{\theta - f_m(x)} = 1. \tag{3}$$

The function $g(\theta) = (t/M) \sum_{m=1}^{M} \theta/(\theta - f_m)$ is strictly decreasing in θ in $(\lambda(x), \infty)$. Therefore the implicit function $\theta(x)$ is the unique root of (3) in the interval $(\lambda(x), \infty)$. $\theta(x)$ and $\phi_t(x)$ are bounded by the following lemmas, same as [14, 18].

LEMMA 1 *$\lambda(x)/(1 - t/M) \le \theta(x) \le \lambda(x)/(1 - t)$ for any $x \in B$.*

LEMMA 2 *$(1 - t) \ln \lambda(x) \le \phi_t(x) \le (1 - t) \ln \lambda(x) + t \ln(\exp(1)/t)$ for any $x \in B$.*

The price vector $p(x) \in \mathbb{R}^M$ is defined as follows [14, 18]:

$$p_m(x) = \frac{t}{M} \frac{\theta(x)}{\theta(x) - f_m(x)}, \qquad m = 1, \ldots, M. \tag{4}$$

The following lemma holds:

LEMMA 3 *$p(x) \in P$ and $p(x)^T f(x) = \theta(x)(1-t)$ for any $x \in B$.*

3. Approximation algorithm $\mathcal{A}$

In this section we will study the algorithm $\mathcal{A}$, which solves both primal problem $(P_{\varepsilon,c})$ and dual problem $(D_{\varepsilon,c})$ with a weaker block solver $ABS(p, \varepsilon_1/10, c)$, where $\varepsilon_1 = 8\varepsilon/(7-\varepsilon) > 8\varepsilon/7$. Compared with that in [18], the block solver employed here is weaker.

The algorithm works as follows. We apply the scaling phase strategy. In each scaling phase an error tolerance σ is set. Based on the known pair of x and p, a solution $\hat{x}$ is delivered by the approximate block solver. Afterwards an appropriate linear combination of the old solution x and block solution $\hat{x}$ is computed as the new iterate. The iteration stops when the solution satisfies a stopping rule (defined later). After one scaling phase, the error tolerance σ is halved and the next scaling phase starts until the error tolerance $\sigma \leq \varepsilon$. The pair x and p generated by the last scaling phase solves both $(P_{\varepsilon,c})$ and $(D_{\varepsilon,c})$ (see Subsection 3.1).

The minimum dual value $\Lambda(p)$ can be approximated by $p^T f(\hat{x})$, where $\hat{x}$ is the solution computed by the weak approximate block solver for the current price vector p. Furthermore, to establish the stopping rule of the scaling phase in algorithm $\mathcal{A}$, the value of duality gap should be estimated in each iteration. Thus we define the stopping rule as follows:

$$(1 + \sigma'/4)p^T f(x) - p^T f(\hat{x}) \leq \sigma' \theta(x)/2, \tag{5}$$

where $\sigma' = 8\sigma/(7-\sigma) > 8\sigma/7$. This stopping rule is similar to that in [18] (which is only valid for a standard block solver), but with an additive term in the left hand side and σ is replaced by σ'. Only in this way can we obtain the desired solution with a weaker block solver. In addition, the stopping rule (5) is also different from the first one in [14]. We set $t = \sigma'/10$ for the error tolerance in the block solver $ABS(p, t, c)$. To run the algorithm, we need an initial solution $x_0 \in B$. Here we use the solution of the block solver $ABS(e/M, \sigma/10, c)$ as x_0, where the price vector e/M is the vector of all $1/M$'s and the initial error tolerance $\sigma = 1/2$.

Algorithm $\mathcal{A}(f, B, \varepsilon, c)$:

```
initialize: σ := 1/2, σ' := 8σ/(7 − σ), t := σ'/10, p := e/M;
x = x_0 := ABS(p, t, c), finished_scaling := false;
while not(finished_scaling) do {scaling phase}
  σ := σ/2, σ' := 8σ/(7 − σ), t := σ'/10;
  finished_coordination := false;
  while not(finished_coordination) do {coordination step}
    compute θ(x) from (3) and p = p(x) ∈ P from (4);
    x̂ := ABS(p, t, c);
    if (5) then
      finished_coordination := true;
    else
      x := (1 − τ)x + τx̂ for an appropriate step length τ ∈ (0, 1];
    end
  end
  if (σ ≤ ε) then finished_scaling := true;
end
```

We set the step length τ as $\tau = (3t\sigma')/(32Mc^2)$ here.

3.1 Analysis of algorithm $\mathcal{A}$

In this subsection we first show the correctness of algorithm $\mathcal{A}$ by proving that if the algorithm stops, the delivered pair x and p is the solution to $(P_{\varepsilon,c})$ and $(D_{\varepsilon,c})$. Afterwards, we will prove that the algorithm stops in each scaling phase after a finite number of iterations. From now on for convenience we denote $\theta = \theta(x)$, $\theta' = \theta(x')$, $f = f(x)$, $f' = f(x')$ and $\hat{f} = f(\hat{x})$ in this section. First we have the following bound on the initial solution x_0 similar to that in [14].

LEMMA 4 *If x_0 is the solution of $ABS(e/M, 1/20, c)$, then $\lambda(x_0) \leq (21/20)Mc\lambda^*$.*

Before proving the correctness of the algorithm $\mathcal{A}$, the following technical lemma is needed to show that even though there is no guarantee that the sequence of values $\lambda(x)$ computed by algorithm $\mathcal{A}$ is decreasing, $\lambda(x)$ can increases only slightly in each coordination step:

LEMMA 5 *For any two consecutive iterates x and $x' \in B$ within a scaling phase of algorithm $\mathcal{A}$, $\lambda(x') \leq \theta(x) \leq \lambda(x)/(1 - \sigma'/10)$.*

Now we show that algorithm $\mathcal{A}$ is correct.

THEOREM 6 *If algorithm $\mathcal{A}$ stops, then for any $\varepsilon \in (0, 1/2]$ the pair x and p delivered solves $(P_{\varepsilon,c})$ and $(D_{\varepsilon,c})$ with an approximate block solver $ABS(p, \varepsilon_1/10, c)$, where $\varepsilon_1 = 8\varepsilon/(7 - \varepsilon)$.*

The remaining task is to prove that the algorithm $\mathcal{A}$ will halt in finite number of iterations. In order to do so, in the next lemma we show that the reduced potential function ϕ_t decreases boundedly by a constant factor (depending on parameters t, τ and σ) in each coordination step. This helps us to prove an upper bound on the number of iterations.

LEMMA 7 *For any two consecutive iterates x, $x' \in B$ within a scaling phase of algorithm $\mathcal{A}$, $\phi_t(x') \leq \phi_t(x) - t\tau\sigma'/4$.*

THEOREM 8 *For a given accuracy tolerance $\varepsilon \in (0, 1/2]$, the number of coordination steps of algorithm $\mathcal{A}$ is bounded by $N_\varepsilon = O(Mc^2(\ln M + \varepsilon^{-4}\ln c + \varepsilon^{-3}\ln\varepsilon^{-1}))$.*

Similar to the special case of small c discussed in [14], from the Theorem 6 we immediately have the following result:

COROLLARY 9 *If $c \leq 1 + \varepsilon/8$, algorithm $\mathcal{A}$ generates a pair x and p as the solution to (P_ε) and (D_ε) with a weak block solver $ABS(p, \varepsilon_1/10, c)$ within $O(M(\ln M + \varepsilon^{-3}\ln\varepsilon^{-1}))$ iterations.*

Remark: It is worth noting that to compute price vector (4), equation (3) should be solved to obtain $\theta(x)$, while it only can be solved approximately by numerical methods. The way to avoid the influence of numerical error is discussed in [8, 14, 18]. And the numerical overhead in each coordination step can be bounded by $O(M \ln\ln(M\varepsilon^{-1}))$ with the Newton's method.

3.2 Better running time

In [14] it is mentioned that both $(P_{\varepsilon,c})$ and $(D_{\varepsilon,c})$ can be solved in $O(Mc^2(\ln M + \varepsilon^{-3}\ln c + \varepsilon^{-3}\ln\varepsilon^{-1}))$ iterations with an $ABS(p, \varepsilon/10, c)$. However, by Theorem 6 we are only able to show that the bound is $O(Mc^2(\ln M + \varepsilon^{-4}\ln c + \varepsilon^{-3}\ln\varepsilon^{-1}))$ for algorithm $\mathcal{A}$ to solve $(P_{\varepsilon,c})$ and $(D_{\varepsilon,c})$ with $ABS(p, \varepsilon_1/10, c)$. In this way we are going to develop another algorithm $\mathcal{A}'$ to obtain a better running time with a new block solver $ABS(p, \varepsilon_2/10, t)$, where $\varepsilon_2 = 8\varepsilon/((7+8r) - (1-8r)\varepsilon) \geq 8\varepsilon/(7+8r)$ for a constant $r \in (0, 1/8)$. Notice here $\varepsilon_2 \in (\varepsilon, \varepsilon_1)$.

The stopping rule of $\mathcal{A}'$ is as follows:

$$(1 + (1/4 - 2r)\sigma')p^T f(x) - p^T f(\hat{x}) \leq \sigma'\theta(x)/2, \tag{6}$$

where $\sigma' = 8\sigma/((7+8r) - (1-8r)\sigma)$. And other parts of algorithm $\mathcal{A}'$ are same as $\mathcal{A}$. Lemma 4 and 5 are still valid in this case. Then the following theorem holds:

THEOREM 10 *If algorithm $\mathcal{A}'$ stops, then for any $\varepsilon \in (0, 1/2]$ the pair x and p delivered solves $(P_{\varepsilon,c})$ and $(D_{\varepsilon,c})$ with an approximate block solver $ABS(p, \varepsilon_2/10, c)$.*

As for the running time, we have the following lemma for the bound on increase of reduced potential function similar to Lemma 7:

LEMMA 11 *For any two consecutive iterates $x, x' \in B$ within a scaling phase of algorithm $\mathcal{A}'$, $\phi_t(x') \leq \phi_t(x) - r\tau\sigma'$.*

In this way we can follow the proof of Theorem 8 to obtain the number of iterations of algorithm $\mathcal{A}'$. Since here r is a constant in $(0, 1/8)$, we have the following bound:

THEOREM 12 *For a given accuracy tolerance $\varepsilon \in (0, 1/2]$, the number of coordination steps of algorithm $\mathcal{A}'$ is bounded by $N_\varepsilon = O(Mc^2(\ln M + \varepsilon^{-3}\ln c + \varepsilon^{-2}\ln \varepsilon^{-1}))$.*

This bound is exactly the same as mentioned in [14]. But here we still get some improvement of the approximation ratio though it is not as good as algorithm $\mathcal{A}$.

4. Fast approximation algorithm $\mathcal{F}$ for $(P_{\varepsilon,c})$

In this section, based on the algorithm in [14], we will propose a fast approximation algorithm $\mathcal{F}$ only for $(P_{\varepsilon,c})$ with $ABS(p, \varepsilon_3/6, c)$, where $\varepsilon_3 = (43 - \sqrt{1849 - 1176\varepsilon})/12 \geq 49\varepsilon/43$.

The algorithm works similarly to $\mathcal{A}$. The scaling phase strategy is employed, and in each scaling phase a relative error tolerance σ_s is set. We have two stopping rules here and the iterative procedure in one scaling phase stops if any one of them is fulfilled. Then the error tolerance σ_s is halved and the new scaling phase starts in the same way as in algorithm $\mathcal{A}$, until the error tolerance $\sigma_s \leq \varepsilon$. The solution x_s delivered in the last scaling phase solves $(P_{\varepsilon,c})$ (see also Subsection 4.1).

We also estimate the duality gap to construct the stop rule. For our first stopping rule a parameter ν is defined as follows (same as [14, 18]):

$$\nu = \nu(x, \hat{x}) = \frac{p^T f(x) - p^T f(\hat{x})}{p^T f(x) + p^T f(\hat{x})}. \tag{7}$$

If $\nu = O(\varepsilon)$, then the duality gap is small. However, in the case that ν is large and close to 1, the gap may be extremely large [14]. To obtain a better bound on the number of iterations, we define another parameter to connect the function value with the solution of previous scaling phase.

Let σ_s be the relative error tolerance of the s-th scaling phase. Then similar to [14], the parameter w_s is defined as follows:

$$w_s = \begin{cases} \frac{1+\sigma_1}{(1+\sigma_0/6)M}, & \text{for the first scaling phase;} \\ \frac{1+\sigma_s}{1+2\sigma_s}, & \text{otherwise.} \end{cases} \tag{8}$$

Let x_s be the solution of s-th scaling phase. Then the two stopping rules used in the s-th scaling phase are:

$$\begin{array}{ll} \textit{Rule } 1: & \nu \le \sigma_s'^2/36; \\ \textit{Rule } 2: & \lambda(x) \le w_s \lambda(x_{s-1}), \end{array} \tag{9}$$

where $\sigma' = k_\varepsilon \sigma$ and the parameter $k_\varepsilon = (55 + \sqrt{1849 - 1176\varepsilon})/98 < 1$. The stopping rules here are similar to those in [14]. But the latter are only for the case of an $ABS(p, \varepsilon/6, c)$.

We set $t = \sigma_s'/6$ for the error tolerance in the block solver $ABS(p, t, c)$ in algorithm $\mathcal{F}$. We use the solution of the block solver $ABS(e/M, 1/6, c)$ as initial solution x_0, where the price vector e/M is still the vector of all $1/M$'s and the initial error tolerance $\sigma_0 = 1$.

Algorithm $\mathcal{F}(f, B, \varepsilon, c)$:
initialize: $s := 0$, $\sigma_1 = \sigma_0 := 1$, $\sigma_1' = \sigma_0' := k_\varepsilon \sigma_0$, $t := \sigma_0'/6$, $p := e/M$;
$x_0 := ABS(p, t, c)$ and $finished\_scaling := false$;
while $not(finished\_scaling)$ **do** $\{scaling\ phase\}$
  $s := s + 1$, $x := x_{s-1}$ and $finished\_coordination := false$;
  compute w_s from (8);
  while $not(finished\_coordination)$ **do** $\{coordination\ step\}$
    compute $\theta(x)$ from (3) and $p = p(x) \in P$ from (4);
    $\hat{x} := ABS(p, t, c)$;
    compute $\nu = \nu(x, \hat{x})$ from (7);
    if (*Stopping Rule 1 or 2*) **then**
      $x_s := x$ and $finished\_coordination := true$;
    else
      $x := (1 - \tau)x + \tau\hat{x}$ for an appropriate step length $\tau \in (0, 1]$;
    end
  end
  $\sigma_{s+1} := \sigma_s/2$, $\sigma_{s+1}' := k_\varepsilon \sigma_{s+1}$ and $t := \sigma_{s+1}'/6$;
  if $(\sigma_{s+1} \le \varepsilon/2)$ **then** $finished\_scaling := true$;
end

The step length is set as $\tau = t\theta(x)\nu/(2M(p(x)^T f(x) + p(x)^T f(\hat{x})))$, similar to [14, 18].

4.1 Analysis of the algorithm $\mathcal{F}$

We are going to analyze the algorithm $\mathcal{F}$ is this section. We will show the correctness, i.e., to prove that the solution x_s of the last scaling phase is a solution to $(P_{\varepsilon,c})$. Then we will prove that the bound on the number of iterations such that the algorithm stops is polynomial only in M and ε. From now on we denote $\theta = \theta(x)$, $\theta' = \theta(x')$, $f = f(x)$, $f' = f(x')$ and $\hat{f} = f(\hat{x})$. First we can obtain the following bound on the function value of the initial solution x_0, similar to that in [14, 18].

LEMMA 13 *If x_0 is the solution of $ABS(e/M, t, c)$ with $t = 1/6$, then $\lambda(x_0) \leq (7/6)cM\lambda^*$.*

We can prove the following theorem by showing that at the end of the s-th scaling phase the solution satisfies $\lambda(x) \leq c(1+\sigma_s)\lambda^*$:

THEOREM 14 *If algorithm $\mathcal{F}$ stops, then for any $\varepsilon \in (0,1]$ the computed solution $x \in B$ fulfils $(P_{\varepsilon,c})$ with $ABS(p, \varepsilon_3/6, c)$, where $\varepsilon_3 = (43 - \sqrt{1849 - 1176\varepsilon})/12$.*

Then we are to find the bound on the number of iterations of the algorithm $\mathcal{F}$. In the next lemma we show that the decrease of the reduced potential function ϕ_t in each iteration is lower-bounded by a parameter depending only on t, ν and M, similar to Lemma 7. This helps us to prove an upper bound on the number of iterations.

LEMMA 15 *For any two consecutive iterates x, $x' \in B$ within a scaling phase of algorithm $\mathcal{F}$, $\phi_t(x') \leq \phi_t(x) - t\nu^2/(4M)$.*

From the above bound we are able to obtain the bound on the number of iterations of algorithm $\mathcal{F}$.

THEOREM 16 *For a given relative accuracy tolerance $\varepsilon \in (0,1]$, algorithm $\mathcal{F}$ delivers a solution x satisfying $\lambda(x) \leq c(1+\varepsilon)\lambda^*$ with a weak block solver $ABS(p, \varepsilon_3/6, c)$ in $N = O(M(\ln M + \varepsilon^{-4}\ln \varepsilon^{-1}))$ coordination steps.*

Remark: The running time here is worse than that in [14]. However, a block solver $ABS(p, \varepsilon/6, c)$ is required in [14] while here we only need a $ABS(p, \varepsilon_3/6, c)$. In addition, different from Theorem 8, we have got the first algorithm with the iteration complexity independent of c in the case of weaker block solvers.

Similar to the special case of small c ($\ln c = O(\varepsilon)$) discussed in [14], we here can also design a faster algorithm $\bar{\mathcal{F}}$ with only the first stopping rule. It can be proved that $\bar{\mathcal{F}}$ can solve both primal and dual problems with a better bound on the number of iterations. Therefore we have the following result:

COROLLARY 17 *If $c \leq 1/k_\varepsilon$, the algorithm $\bar{\mathcal{F}}$ can generate a pair x and p solving both (P_ε) and (D_ε) with only the weak approximate block solver $ABS(p, \varepsilon_3/6, c)$ within $O(M(\ln M + \varepsilon^{-4}))$ iterations.*

4.2 Better running time

The number of iterations of the algorithm for primal problem in [14] is bounded by $O(M(\ln M + \varepsilon^{-2} \ln \varepsilon))$, which is better than the bound in Theorem 16. In addition, in Subsection 3.2 it has been showed that a better bound on running time can be achieved with a different weak block solver. Here we also get such an algorithm with this technique.

Similar to the cases in Subsection 3.2, we can develop an algorithm $\mathcal{F}'$ by slight modification of the stopping rules. Suppose $r \in (0,1)$ is a constant. And here a function $h(r)$ is defined as:

$$h(r) = \begin{cases} \frac{2r(1-r)}{3(1+r)^2}, & \text{if } r \geq \frac{3}{4}; \\ \frac{6(1-r)}{7(6-r)}, & \text{otherwise.} \end{cases} \tag{10}$$

And $\varepsilon_4 = ((1 - h(r)) - \sqrt{(1 - h(r))^2 - 4h(r)\varepsilon})/(2h(r)) > \varepsilon/(1 - h(r))$, and $k_{r,\varepsilon} = 1 - h(r)\varepsilon_4$. Define $\sigma'_s = k_{r,\varepsilon}\sigma_s$. Then the stopping rules of $\mathcal{F}'$ are as follows:

$$\begin{array}{ll} \textit{Rule } 1: & \nu \leq r\sigma'_s/6; \\ \textit{Rule } 2: & \lambda(x) \leq w_s \lambda(x_{s-1}), \end{array} \tag{11}$$

Lemma 13 is still valid for algorithm $\mathcal{F}'$. Similar to that for $\mathcal{F}$, we have the following theorem:

THEOREM 18 *If algorithm $\mathcal{F}'$ stops, then for any $\varepsilon \in (0,1]$ the solution x delivered satisfies $(P_{\varepsilon,c})$ with $ABS(p, \varepsilon_4/6, c)$.*

As for the running time, we have also the same bound on increase of reduced potential function for $\mathcal{F}'$ as in Lemma 15. To find the bound on number of iterations of algorithm $\mathcal{F}'$, we can just apply the similar argument to the proof of Theorem 16. Since here r is a constant in $(0,1)$, we have the following theorem:

THEOREM 19 *For a given relative accuracy $\varepsilon \in (0,1]$, the number of coordination steps of algorithm $\mathcal{F}'$ is bounded by $N = O(M(\ln M + \varepsilon^{-2} \ln \varepsilon^{-1}))$.*

This bound exactly matches the bound in [14]. But here we just need a weaker block solver.

Remark: We find that if we design the first stopping rule as $\nu \leq v$ for any $v < t$, we can always have a $\varepsilon' > \varepsilon$ for $ABS(p, \varepsilon'/6, c)$ called in algorithm. A reasonable choice, $v = t^q$ for large q, can generate a large ε'. Unfortunately this kind of improvement is very limited and the running time increases considerable for the bound on the number of iterations is $O(M(\ln M + \varepsilon^{-2q} \ln \varepsilon^{-1}))$.

5. Conclusion and open problem

In this paper we have presented the first $c(1+\varepsilon)$-approximation algorithms for the general packing problem (or with its dual problem), with only weaker block solvers. The number of iterations is bounded by polynomials in M, ε and c or even only in M and ε. We also reduced the bounds to the same as in [14].

An interesting problem is whether one can find $c'(1+\varepsilon)$-approximation algorithms for general packing problem with only an approximate block solver $ABS(p, O(\varepsilon), c)$, where $c' < c$. By the gap between $p^T f(x)$ and $p^T f(\hat{x})$ we conjecture that it is possible and the lower bound on c' is $(c+1)/2$.

References

[1] A. Baltz and A. Srivastav, Fast Approximation of Minimum Multicast Congestion - Implementation versus Theory, *Proceedings of 5th Conference on Algorithms and Complexity*, CIAC 2003.

[2] M. Charikar, C. Chekuri, A. Goel, S. Guha and S. Plotkin, Approximating a finite metric by a small number of tree metrics, *Proceedings of the 39th Annual IEEE Symposium on Foundations of Computer Science*, FOCS 1998, 379-388.

[3] G. Even, J. S. Naor, S. Rao and B. Schieber, Fast approximate graph partitioning algorithms, *SIAM. Journal on Computing*, 6 (1999), 2187-2214.

[4] N. Garg and J. Könemann, Fast and simpler algorithms for multicommodity flow and other fractional packing problems, *Proceedings of the 39th IEEE Annual Symposium on Foundations of Computer Science*, FOCS 1998, 300-309.

[5] M. D. Grigoriadis and L. G. Khachiyan, Fast approximation schemes for convex programs with many blocks and coupling constraints, *SIAM Journal on Optimization*, 4 (1994), 86-107.

[6] M. D. Grigoriadis and L. G. Khachiyan, Coordination complexity of parallel price-directive decomposition, *Mathematics of Operations Research*, 2 (1996), 321-340.

[7] M. D. Grigoriadis and L. G. Khachiyan, Approximate minimum-cost multicommodity flows in $O(\varepsilon^{-2}knm)$ time, *Mathematical Programming*, 75 (1996), 477-482.

[8] M. D. Grigoriadis, L. G. Khachiyan, L. Porkolab and J.Villavicencio, Approximate max-min resource sharing for structured concave optimization, *SIAM Journal on Optimization*, 11 (2001), 1081-1091.

[9] K. Jansen, Approximation algorithms for fractional covering and packing problems, and applications, Manuscript, (2001).

[10] K. Jansen, Approximation algorithms for the general max-min resource sharing problem: faster and simpler, *Proceedings of the 9th Scandinavian Workshop on Algorithm Theory*, SWAT 2004, LNCS.

[11] K. Jansen, Approximation algorithms for the mixed fractional packing and covering problem, *these proceedings.*

[12] K. Jansen and L. Porkolab, On preemptive resource constrained scheduling: polynomial-time approximation schemes, *Proceedings of the 9th Conference on Integer Programming and Combinatorial Optimization*, IPCO 2002, LNCS 2337 329-349.

[13] K. Jansen and R. Solis-Oba, An asymptotic fully polynomial time approximation scheme for bin covering, *Proceedings of 13th International Symposium on Algorithms and Computation*, ISAAC 2002.

[14] K. Jansen and H. Zhang, Approximation algorithms for general packing problems with modified logarithmic potential function, *Proceedings of 2nd IFIP International Conference on Theoretical Computer Science*, TCS 2002.

[15] K. Jansen and H. Zhang, An approximation algorithm for the multicast congestion problem via minimum Steiner trees, *Proceedings of 3rd International Workshop on Approximation and Randomized Algorithms in Communication Networks*, ARANCE 2002.

[16] C. Kenyon and E. Rémila, Approximate strip packing, *Proceedings of 37th Annual Symposium on Foundations of Computer Science*, FOCS 1996, 31-36.

[17] S. A. Plotkin, D. B. Shmoys and E. Tardos, Fast Approximation algorithms for fractional packing and covering problems, *Mathematics of Operations Research*, 2 (1995), 257-301.

[18] J. Villavicencio and M. D. Grigoriadis, Approximate Lagrangian decomposition with a modified Karmarkar logarithmic potential, *Network Optimization, P. Pardalos, D. W. Hearn and W. W. Hager, Eds, Lecture Notes in Economics and Mathematical Systems 450, Springer-Verlag, Berlin*, (1997), 471-485.

[19] D. Ye and H. Zhang The Range Assignment Problem in Static Ad-Hoc Networks on Metric Spaces, *Proceedings of the 11th Colloquium on Structural Information and Communication Complexity* Sirocco 2004, LNCS.

[20] N. E. Young, Randomized rounding without solving the linear program, *Proceedings of the 6th ACM-SIAM Symposium on Discrete Algorithms*, SODA 1995, 170–178.

[21] N. E. Young, Sequential and parallel algorithms for mixed packing and covering, *Proceedings of the 42nd Annual Symposium on Foundations of Computer Science*, FOCS 2001, 538-546.

[22] H. Zhang, Packing: Scheduling, Embedding and Approximating Metrics, *Proceedings of the 2004 International Conference on Computational Science and its Applications* ICCSA 2004, LNCS 3045.

ADAPTIVE SORTING WITH AVL TREES

Amr Elmasry
Computer Science Department
Alexandria University
Alexandria, Egypt
elmasry@alexeng.edu.eg

Abstract A new adaptive sorting algorithm is introduced. The new implementation relies on using the traditional AVL trees, and has the same performance limitations. More precisely, the number of comparisons performed by our algorithm, on an input sequence of length n that has I inversions, is at most $1.44n \lg \frac{I}{n} + O(n)$ [1]. Our algorithm runs in time $O(n \log \frac{I}{n})$ and is practically efficient and easy to implement.

1. Introduction

An adaptive sorting algorithm is a sorting algorithm that benefits from the presortedness in the input sequence. In the literature there are plenty of adaptive sorting algorithms. One of the commonly recognized measures of presortedness is the number of inversions in the input sequence [12]. The number of inversions is the number of pairs of input items in the wrong order. For an input sequence X, the number of inversions of X, *Inv(X)*, is defined

$$Inv(X) = |\{(i,j) \mid 1 \leq i < j \leq n \text{ and } x_i > x_j\}|.$$

An adaptive sorting algorithm is optimal with respect to the number of inversions when it runs in $O(n \log \frac{Inv(X)}{n})$ [9]. Unfortunately, most of the known theoretically optimal adaptive sorting algorithms are not practical and not easy to implement [9, 18, 3, 17, 15].

The number of comparisons is considered one of the main analytical measures to compare different sorting algorithms. The number of comparisons performed by an *Inv*-optimal sorting algorithm is at most $cn \lg \frac{Inv(X)}{n} + O(n)$ comparisons, for some constant $c \geq 1$. Among the adaptive sorting algorithms, Splitsort [13] and Adaptive Heapsort [14] guarantee $c = 2.5$. Finger trees [9, 17], though not practical, guarantee $c = 2$. Trinomialsort [6] guarantees $c = 1.89$. Recently, Elmasry and

Fredman [7] introduced an adaptive sorting algorithm with $c = 1$, and hence achieving the information theoretic lower bound for the number of comparisons.

The task of achieving the optimal number of comparisons is therefore accomplished, still with the practicality issue being open. The algorithm in [7] uses near optimal trees [1], which is a practically complicated structure that involves a large maintenance overhead. The other operations performed by the algorithm in [7] (splits, combines, coalescing and reduction operations) contribute with another overhead factor, making the algorithm not fully practical. Namely, the time bound for the operations, other than the comparisons, performed by the algorithm in [7] is $\Theta(n \log \frac{Inv(X)}{n})$. Among the adaptive sorting algorithms Splitsort [13], Adaptive Heapsort [14] and Trinomialsort [6] are the most promising from the practical point of view. As a consequence of the dynamic finger theorem for splay trees (see Cole [5]), the splay trees of Sleator and Tarjan [21] provide a simplified substitute for finger trees that achieves the same asymptotic run-time. Moffat et al. [19] performed experiments showing that Splaysort is efficient in practice.

We introduce a new adaptive sorting algorithm that uses AVL trees [2]. Our new algorithm guarantees $c = 1.44$ in the worst case, while it achieves a value of c very close to 1 (optimal) from the practical point of view [10, 11]. This result is a direct consequence of the nature of the well-known search trees known as AVL trees. The worst-case behavior of the AVL trees is achieved when the tree is a Fibonacci tree, a case that rarely pops-up in practice. The contribution of this paper is to introduce a practically efficient adaptive sorting algorithm, and to show that apart from the comparisons, the other operations performed by this algorithm take linear time; a fact that does not hold for other efficient adaptive sorting algorithms. For example: Trinomialsort, Adaptive Heapsort and Splitsort would perform a non-linear number of moves. We expect our new algorithm to be efficient, fast in practice, and easy to implement. The space utilized by our algorithm is $O(n)$.

Other methods that use AVL trees to implement adaptive sorting algorithms include the algorithm of Mehlhorn [18], and the finger trees of Tsakalidis [23]. These two algorithms require augmenting the AVL trees with extra information that make the implementation non-practical, with a larger constant for the number of comparisons.

Several authors have proposed other measures of presortedness and proposed optimal algorithms with respect to these measures [8, 4, 14, 15]. Mannila [16] formalized the concept of presortedness. He studied several measures of presortedness and introduced the concept of optimality with respect to these measures. Petersson and Moffat [20] related all of the various known measures in a partial order and established new definitions with respect to the optimality of adaptive sorting algorithms.

2. The algorithm

Consider the following method for inserting y into a sorted sequence, $x_1 < x_2 < \cdots < x_{n-1}$. For a specified value r, we first perform a linear search among the items $x_r, x_{2r}, \cdots x_{r\lfloor n/r \rfloor}$ to determine the interval of length r among $x_1 < x_2 < \cdots < x_{n-1}$ into which y falls. Next, we perform a binary search within the resulting interval of length r to determine the precise location for y. If y ends up in position i, then $\frac{i}{r} + \lg r + O(1)$ comparisons suffice for this insertion. Using the strategy of successively inserting the items $x_1, \cdots, x_n$ in reverse order (into an initially empty list), let i_j be the final position of element j after the jth insertion. The total number of comparisons required to sort would be bounded by $\sum_{1 \leq j \leq n} \frac{i_j}{r} + \lg r + O(1)) = \frac{Inv(X)}{r} + n \lg r + O(n)$. If we use $r = \frac{Inv(X)}{n}$, the required bound on the number of comparisons follows. Unfortunately, we cannot use this value of r, since the number of inversions is not known beforehand. Instead, we choose r to be a dynamic quantity that is maintained as insertions take place; r is initially chosen to be $r_1 = 1$, and during the kth insertion, $k > 1$, r is given by $r_k = \frac{1}{k-1} \sum_{1 \leq j < k} i_j$. The quantity r_k is at least 1. For completeness, we give the proof of the following lemma, which is in [7].

LEMMA 1 *Our insertion sort algorithm performs at most* $n \lg \frac{Inv(X)}{n} + O(n)$ *comparisons to sort an input* X *of length* n.

Proof. Define $E(k)$, the excess number of comparisons performed during the first k insertions, to be the actual number performed minus $k \lg(\frac{1}{k} \sum_{1 \leq j \leq k} i_j)$. We demonstrate that $E(k) = O(n)$ when $k = n$. We proceed to estimate $E(k+1) - E(k)$.

Let r' denote the average, $\frac{1}{k+1} \sum_{1 \leq j \leq k+1} i_j$, and let r denote the corresponding quantity, $\frac{1}{k} \sum_{1 \leq j \leq k} i_j$. Then

$$E(k+1) - E(k) = \lg r + \frac{i_{k+1}}{r} - (k+1) \lg r' + k \lg r + O(1),$$
$$= \frac{i_{k+1}}{r} + (k+1)(\lg r - \lg r') + O(1). \qquad (1)$$

Now write $r' = (k \cdot r + i_{k+1})/(k+1) = (k/(k+1)) \cdot r \cdot g$, where $g = 1 + i_{k+1}/(k \cdot r)$. Substituting into (1) this expression for r', we obtain

$$E(k+1) - E(k) = \frac{i_{k+1}}{r} + (k+1) \lg \frac{k+1}{k} - (k+1) \lg g + O(1).$$

The term $(k+1)\lg\frac{k+1}{k}$ is $O(1)$, leaving us to estimate $i_{k+1}/r-(k+1)\lg g$. We have two cases: (i) $i_{k+1}\le k\cdot r$ and (ii) $i_{k+1}>k\cdot r$

For case (i), using the fact that $\lg(1+x)\ge x$ for $0\le x\le 1$, we find that $i_{k+1}/r-(k+1)\lg g\le 0$ (since $\lg g\ge i_{k+1}/(k\cdot r)$ for this case). For case (ii), we bound $i_{k+1}/r-(k+1)\lg g$ from above using i_{k+1}. But the condition for case (ii), namely $i_{k+1}>k\cdot r=\sum_{1\le j\le k} i_j$, implies that the sum of these i_{k+1} estimates (over those k for which case (ii) applies) is at most twice the last such term, which is bounded by n. Since $E(1)=0$, we conclude that $E(n)=O(n)$. □

To convert the above construction to an implementable algorithm with total running time $O(n\log\frac{Inv(X)}{n})$, we utilize the considerable freedom available in the choice of the r_k values in the above construction, while preserving the result of the preceding Lemma. Let $\alpha\ge 1$ be an arbitrary constant. If we replace our choice for r_k in the above algorithm by any quantity s_k satisfying $r_k\le s_k\le\alpha\cdot r_k$, then the above lemma still holds; the cost $i_k/s_k+\lg s_k+O(1)$ of a single insertion cannot grow by more than $O(1)$ as s_k deviates from its initial value r_k while remaining in the indicated range.

Efficient Implementation

At each insertion point, the previously inserted items are organized into a list of consecutive bands from left to right. Every band has $1, 2,$ *or* 3 AVL trees. Each of our AVL trees is organized as a search tree with the data items stored only in the leaves of the tree while the internal nodes contain indexing information. A rank value is assigned to every band. The trees of a band with rank h will have heights equal to h, except for at most one tree that may have height equal to $h-1$. We call a tree whose height is one less than the rank of its band a *short* tree. We call a band that has a short tree an s-band. These conditions are referred to as the rank conditions. At any stage of the algorithm, the ranks of the bands form an increasing consecutive sequence $m, m+1, m+2, \ldots$ from left to right, with the value of m changing through the algorithm. This is referred to as the monotonicity condition.

With every insertion, the relevant tree is first identified by employing a linear search through the list of trees from left to right. After each insertion, the band list may require reorganization, though on a relatively infrequent basis. The details of this implementation is facilitated by defining the following operations:

1. Split: An AVL tree of height h can be split in constant time into two trees, one of height $h-1$ and the other of height $h-1$ *or* $h-2$, by removing the root node of the given tree.

2. Combine: Two AVL trees, one of height $h - 1$ and the other of height $h-1$ *or* $h-2$, can be combined in constant time to form an AVL tree of height h by adding a new root node. The data values of the left tree are not larger than those of the right tree.

3. Find largest: The value of the largest member of a given tree can be accessed in constant time. A pointer to the largest value is maintained in constant time after each of the other operations.

4. Tree-insertion: An insertion of a new value into an AVL tree of height h can be performed with at most h comparisons, and in time $O(h)$ [2].

Consider the cost of the single operation: inserting y into a sorted sequence $S = x_1 < x_2 < \cdots < x_{n-1}$. If S is organized, as mentioned above, in a list of trees, and y belongs to the ith tree, which is of height h, then the insertion requires no more than $i + h$ comparisons.

As a result of an insertion, the height of the trees may increase and the rank conditions are to be maintained. Such a case arises when the height of a tree, in a band of rank h, becomes $h + 1$. This tree is split into two trees. If, as a result of this split, we now have two short trees in this band, these two trees are combined. (If these two trees are not adjacent, the heights of the trees in this band must have either the pattern $h-1, h, h-1$ *or* $h-1, h, h, h-1$. In either case, we split the middle trees, whose heights are h, then combine every adjacent pair of the trees. This accounts for at most 3 splits and 3 combines.) Otherwise, if the number of trees of this band becomes 4, the two right trees are combined and the combined tree is moved to become the left tree of the next higher band. This operation is referred to as a *promote* operation. This combine/promote may be repeated several times through consecutive bands. We call such a process a *propagating promotion.*

Besides enforcing the rank conditions, we maintain the additional condition that just prior to the kth insertion the rank m of the leftmost band satisfies

$$m = \lceil \log_\theta r_k \rceil + 1, \tag{2}$$

where θ is a parameter of the algorithm whose value will be analyzed and determined later. The value of θ should satisfy $1 < \theta \leq 2$.

If, as a result of an insertion, r_k grows such that the current value of m is now equal to $\lceil \log_\theta r_k \rceil$ (note that r_k may grow by at most 1), then a *coalescing* operation is performed. The purpose of the coalescing operation is to make the rank of the leftmost band equal to $m+1$. The trees of the leftmost interval are combined to form 1 *or* 2 trees that are promoted to the next band whose rank is $m+1$ (if there were 3 trees in the leftmost band, 2 of them are combined including the short tree if it exists). If there was only one short tree of rank $m-1$ that is promoted, the leftmost two trees of the band whose rank is $m+1$ will have heights $m-1, m$ or $m-1, m+1$. In the first case, these two trees are combined. In the second case, the tree with height $m+1$ is first split producing a pattern of heights that is either $m-1$,m,m or $m-1$,$m-1$,m or $m-1$,m,$m-1$. For the first two patterns, the leftmost two trees are combined. For the second pattern, the combined tree is further combined with the tree to its right. For the third pattern, the tree, whose rank is m, is split and each of the two resulting adjacent pairs is combined (for a total of at most 2 splits and 2 combines). If, as a result of the promotion, two short trees of rank m exist in the band whose rank is $m+1$, these two trees are combined (as above). If the number of trees of this band becomes 4 *or* 5, a propagating promotion is performed and repeated as necessary through consecutive bands. As a special case, that does not affect the bounds on the operations of the algorithm, the coalescing operation is skipped when there is only one band and the number of nodes is not enough to perform the coalescing operation while maintaining the rank conditions.

If, as a result of an insertion, r_k drops such that the current value of m is now equal to $\lceil \log_\theta r_k \rceil + 2$ (note that r_k may drop by at most 1), then a *reduction* operation is performed. The purpose of the reduction operation is to make the rank of the leftmost band equal to $m-1$. A new leftmost band with rank $m-1$ is created. The leftmost tree of the old leftmost band (the band with rank m) is moved to the new band. We call this operation a *demote* operation. If this tree has height m, then it is split. If, as a result of the demotion, the band whose rank is m now has no trees, the leftmost tree of the band whose rank is $m+1$ is demoted and split if necessary. This demote/split may be repeated for several times through consecutive bands. We call such a process a *propagating demotion.*

Note that the reduction and the coalescing operations serve to preserve the rank and monotonicity conditions as well as (2).

Analysis

LEMMA 2 *Our algorithm performs at most* $n \log_\phi \frac{Inv(X)}{n} + O(n)$ *comparisons to sort an input* X *of length* n (ϕ *is the golden ratio* $= \frac{1+\sqrt{5}}{2}$).

Proof. In view of Lemma 1, it suffices to show that a given insertion, arriving in position L, requires at most

$$L/s_k + \log_\phi s_k + O(1) \tag{3}$$

comparisons, where $r_k \leq s_k \leq \alpha \cdot r_k$ and $\alpha \geq 1$ is an arbitrary constant.

Let m be the rank of the leftmost band, and m' be the rank of the band that has the tree into which the newly inserted item falls, and let i be the position of this tree (number of the tree counting the trees from the left), so that the total insertion cost is at most $i + m'$. As a result of the rank and monotonicity conditions, we have $i \geq m' - m + 1$. Next, we bound L from below as follows. Contributing to L, there is at least 1 tree in each of the bands with ranks from m to $m' - 1$. There is another $i - d - 1$ (where $d = m' - m \geq 0$) trees of heights at least $m - 1$. For any AVL tree, the size of a tree of height h is at least ϕ^h. It follows that:

$$\begin{aligned} L &> (i-d-1)\phi^{m-1} + \sum_{i=m-1}^{m'-2} \phi^i, \\ &> (i-d-2)\phi^{m-1} + \phi^{m'-1}. \end{aligned}$$

Choosing our parameter to be $\theta = \phi$, it follows from (2) that $\phi^{m-1} = s_k$. Hence

$$\frac{L}{s_k} > (i-d-2) + \phi^d.$$

This results in the following relation, which implies (3).

$$\begin{aligned} i + m' &< L/s_k + m + 2d - \phi^d + 2, \\ &< L/s_k + \log_\phi s_k + O(1). \end{aligned}$$

□

LEMMA 3 *The time spent by our algorithm, in performing operations other than comparisons, is* $O(n)$.

Proof. The primitive operations, which the algorithm performs other than comparisons, are the spit and combine operations. Each of these operations requires constant time. Excluding the propagating promotion and demotion, the number of splits and combines per insertion, coalescing or reduction is constant. Hence, the only operations that need to be investigated are the propagating promotions and demotions.

We use a potential function [22] to derive the linear bounds on these operations. Let N_s be the number of s-bands and let N_{odd} be the number of bands that have 1 *or* 3 trees. Let Φ^i be the potential function after the *ith* insertion, such that $\Phi^i = c_1 N_{odd} + c_2 N_s$, where c_1 and c_2 are constants to be determined and $c_1 > c_2$. The value of Φ^0 is 0, and the value of $\Phi^n = O(n)$. What we need to show is that the difference in potential when added to the actual amount of work during the *ith* insertion is bounded by a constant.

Consider the case where during the $i+1$ insertion a propagating promotion that involves t bands takes place. Assume first that the initiative of this propagating promotion is an insertion that causes a height of a tree to become $h+1$ in a band of rank h. As a result of a promotion in a band, the number of trees in this band should have been 3, and becomes 2 after the promotion. This should be the case for the $t-1$ bands that propagate the promotion, accounting for a decrease of $t-1$ in the value of N_{odd}. In the last band, the opposite may take place and N_{odd} may increase by 1 as a result. Except for the first band, into which the newly inserted item falls, the number of s-bands may only decrease as a result of any of these promotions. Hence, the amortized cost of the propagating promotion in this case is bounded by $O(t) - c_1(t-2) + c_2$. By selecting c_1 greater than the constant involved in the O() notation in this bound, the amortized cost of this operation is a constant. The analysis is similar if the initiative for the propagating promotion is a coalescing operation. The only difference is the first band that gets promoted trees, where the number of trees in this band may remain the same (either 2 or 3). This band may also be converted to an s-band as a result of this promotion. This leads to a bound of $O(t) - c_1(t-3) + c_2$, which is a constant as well.

Consider the case that during the $i+1$ insertion a reduction operation is performed. Assume that this reduction initiates a propagating demotion that involves t bands. A new band is created that may get 1 tree (increasing N_{odd} by 1), or 2 trees one of them may be short (increasing N_s by 1). For each of the next $t-2$ bands that involves a demotion, the number of trees in each of these bands should have been 1 before this propagating demotion. If a demoted tree was not short, it is split resulting in 2 trees. This causes N_{odd} to decrease by 1, while N_s may increase by 1. On the other hand, if a demoted tree was short, the number of trees in the corresponding band remains 1 after the demotion, while the number of s-bands decreases by 1 causing N_s to decrease by 1. In the last band, the opposite may take place, and N_{odd} may increase by 1 as a result. Hence, the amortized cost of the propagating demotion is bounded by $O(t) - (c_1 - c_2)(t - k - 2) - c_2 k + 2c_1$, for some $k \leq t - 2$. By selecting c_2 and $c_1 - c_2$ greater than the constant in the O() notation in this bound, the amortized cost of this operation is a constant. □

We have thus established the following theorem.

THEOREM 4 *The preceding insertion sort algorithm sorts an input X of length n in time* $O(n \log \frac{Inv(X)}{n})$, *and performs at most* $n \log_\phi \frac{Inv(X)}{n} + O(n)$ *comparisons. The space requirement for the algorithm is* $O(n)$.

Tuning the parameter

In the above analysis, to prove the bound for the number of comparisons, we have chosen the parameter $\theta = \phi$. In practice, this value is a too conservative value to insure the worst-case behavior. For random sequences the performance of AVL trees is very efficient, and empirical data shows that the average height of an AVL tree of n nodes is about $1.02 \log n$ [10, 11]. This motivates using a larger value of θ. Knowing that the constant factor in the height of an average AVL tree is close to 1, the parameter θ can be chosen to be closer to 2.

Notes

1. $\lg x$ is the maximum of $\log_2 x$ and 1.

References

[1] A. Andersson and T. W. Lai. *Fast updating of well-balanced trees.* Scandinavian Workshop on Algorithm Theory (1990), 111-121.

[2] G. Adelson-Velskii and E. Landis. *On an information organization algorithm.* Doklady Akademia Nauk SSSR, 146(1962), 263-266.

[3] M. Brown and R. Tarjan. *Design and analysis of data structures for representing sorted lists.* SIAM J. Comput. 9 (1980), 594-614.

[4] S. Carlsson, C. Levcopoulos and O. Petersson. *Sublinear merging and natural Mergesort.* Algorithmica 9 (1993), 629-648.

[5] R. Cole. *On the dynamic finger conjecture for splay trees. Part II: The proof.* SIAM J. Comput. 30 (2000), 44-85.

[6] A. Elmasry. *Priority queues, pairing and adaptive sorting.* 29th Int. Colloquium for Automata, Languages and Programming. In LNCS 2380 (2002), 183-194.

[7] A. Elmasry and M. Fredman. *Adaptive sorting and the information theoretic lower bound.* Symp. on Theoret. Aspect. Comput. Sc. In LNCS 2607 (2003), 654-662.

[8] V. Estivill-Castro and D. Wood. *A new measure of presortedness.* Infor. and Comput. 83 (1989), 111-119.

[9] L. Guibas, E. McCreight, M. Plass and J. Roberts. *A new representation of linear lists.* ACM Symp. on Theory of Computing 9 (1977), 49-60.

[10] L. Guibas and R. Sedgewick. *A dichromatic framework for balanced trees.* Foundations of Computer Science (1978), 8-21.

[11] P. Karlton, S. Fuller, R. Scroggs and E. Kaehler. *Performance of height-balanced trees.* Information Retrieval and Language Processing 19(1) (1976), 23-28.

[12] D. Knuth. *The art of Computer programming. Vol III: Sorting and Searching.* Addison-wesley, second edition (1998).

[13] C. Levcopoulos and O. Petersson. *Splitsort - An adaptive sorting algorithm.* Information Processing Letters 39 (1991), 205-211.

[14] C. Levcopoulos and O. Petersson. *Adaptive Heapsort.* J. Alg. 14 (1993), 395-413.

[15] C. Levcopoulos and O. Petersson. *Exploiting few inversions when sorting: Sequential and parallel algorithms.* Theoret. Comput. Science 163 (1996), 211-238.

[16] H. Mannila. *Measures of presortedness and optimal sorting algorithms.* IEEE Trans. Comput. C-34 (1985), 318-325.

[17] K. Mehlhorn. *Data structures and algorithms. Vol.1. Sorting and Searching.* Springer-Verlag, Berlin/Heidelberg. (1984)

[18] K. Mehlhorn. *Sorting presorted files.* 4th GI Conference on Theory of Computer Science. In LNCS 67 (1979), 199-212.

[19] A. Moffat, G. Eddy and O. Petersson. *Splaysort: fast, verstile, practical.* Softw. Pract. and Exper. 126(7) (1996), 781-797.

[20] O. Petersson and A. Moffat. *A framework for adaptive sorting.* Discrete App. Math. 59 (1995), 153-179.

[21] D. Sleator and R. Tarjan. *Self-adjusting binary search trees.* J. ACM 32(3) (1985), 652-686.

[22] R. Tarjan. *Amortized computational complexity.* SIAM J. Alg. Disc. Meth. 6 (1985), 306-318.

[23] A. Tsakalidis. *AVL-trees for localized search.* Inf. and Cont. 67 (1985), 173-194.

PRECISE ANALYSIS OF π-CALCULUS IN CUBIC TIME

L.Colussi, G.Filè and A.Griggio
Department of Pure and Applied Mathematics
University of Padova, Italy

Abstract It is known that a static analysis of π-calculus can be done rather simply and also efficiently, i.e. in $O(n^3)$ time. Clearly, a static analysis should be as precise as possible. We show that it is not only desirable, but also possible to improve the precision of the analysis without worsening its asymptotic complexity. We illustrate the main principles of this efficient algorithm, we prove that it is indeed cubic and we also show that it is correct. The technique introduced here appears to be useful also for other applications, in particular, for the static analysis of languages that extend the π-calculus.

Keywords: static analysis, π-calculus, algorithm complexity

Introduction

The π-calculus [11, 10] is an algebra of processes that models communications among agents that share a common channel. When an input and an output operation synchronize on a common channel, then the bound name of the input gets instantiated to the name sent by the output operation. The algebra also models mobility by allowing the exchange of channel names among agents.

In a real computation of a π-calculus process, the bound name of an input operation can be instantiated at most once. However, when one wants to compute statically all possible behaviours of the process he/she must take into account the fact that an input action can in general synchronize with many output actions (in different real computations) and therefore, a static analysis generally associates a set of names to each input bound name. Thus, in general, a static analysis applied to a process P is *correct* if it computes a function ρ that we call *name-association* such that for each input operation $B = b(v)$ of P, $\rho(v)$ contains all the names that may instantiate v as a result of the synchronization of B with some output operations of P. It is easy to see that a correct static analysis could be designed according to the following scheme:

- First compute all the input/output pairs (A, B) of P that may synchronize;
- For each such pair (A, B), where $A = \overline{a}\langle u\rangle$ and $B = b(v)$, the pair can communicate only when $\rho(a) \cap \rho(b) \neq \emptyset$ and when this condition is satisfied, one accounts for the communication from A to B by adding $\rho(u)$ to $\rho(v)$.

Such an analysis is surely very simple, but it is also bound to be very poor in terms of precision, because in general it considers many synchronizations that cannot take place in real computations. Let us consider this example.

EXAMPLE 1 *In this example we want to model the situation of a client that downloads an applet from a server and when this applet requests a connection to some host with a given IP number, accepts the request only if this IP number meets two conditions: (i) it is the same as that of the server from which the applet was downloaded and, (ii) it is in a* white list *that contains the client's trustworthy servers.*

For simplicity we assume that the client C *already shares a channel* C_S *with the server* S *and a channel* C_A *with the applet* A. *Channel* C_W *connects* C *with its white list* W. *OK is a message that client* C *sends to* A *to signal that it accepts its request. The applet* A *sends to* C *three IP numbers of hosts to which it wishes to connect. The system is the parallel composition of four processes* $C|W|S|A$ *where:*

$$\begin{aligned} C &= C_S(x).C_A(y).C_W(z).[x=y].[x=z].\overline{C_A}\langle OK\rangle \\ W &= \overline{C_W}\langle IP_1\rangle + \overline{C_W}\langle IP_2\rangle \qquad S = !\overline{C_S}\langle IP_S\rangle \\ A &= (\nu M)(\overline{C_A}\langle IP_S\rangle.C_A(x).[x=OK].\overline{IP_S}\langle M\rangle + \overline{C_A}\langle IP_1\rangle.C_A(x). \\ &\quad [x=OK].\overline{IP_1}\langle M\rangle + \overline{C_A}\langle IP_2\rangle.C_A(x).[x=OK].\overline{IP_2}\langle M\rangle) \end{aligned}$$

It should be easy to see that, each test of the client C *can be satisfied, but that they cannot be satisfied together. Therefore there is no execution of the system in which* C *sends OK to the applet* A. *For a static analysis to discover this fact, it is important that the 2 tests are considered together. The analysis presented below does this and therefore it will statically discover this fact.*

In what follows we consider an input/output pair (A, B) and we assume that A is the output action $\overline{a}\langle u\rangle$ and B the input action $b(v)$. The above example indicates that it is desirable to have static analyses that consider that pair (A, B) can synchronize only when they really **can** synchronize! More precisely, only when:

(i) there is a real computation in which A and B synchronize and moreover,

(ii) if this is the case, then we would like to model this synchronization by adding to $\rho(v)$ only the name that may instantiate u in the corresponding computation.

These two points cannot be accomplished in general as deciding point (i) is an unsolvable problem. However, during a static analysis, it is possible to use the name-association ρ that is being computed in order to approximate safely these two wishes.

Concerning point (i), we can discover that A and B can never synchronize if they are preceded by a test $[x = y]$ such that $\rho(x) \cap \rho(y) = \emptyset$. By the correctness of ρ this fact clearly implies that the test is never satisfied. As a matter of fact, it is easier to reason in the opposite direction, i.e., to conclude that the test may be satisfied in some real computation only when $\rho(x) \cap \rho(y) \neq \emptyset$. Clearly, if together with $[x = y]$ also the test $[y = z]$ precedes A and B, then both tests must be satisfied together and this is possible only when $\rho(x) \cap \rho(y) \cap \rho(z) \neq \emptyset$ and so on. The tests that precede A and B, permit to refine ρ into a more precise ρ'. For instance, $\rho'(x) = \rho'(y) = \rho'(z) = \rho(x) \cap \rho(y) \cap \rho(z)$. This refined ρ' may allow to detect that indeed the communication between A and B is impossible in real computations. This happens when $\rho'(a) \cap \rho'(b) = \emptyset$ even though $\rho(a) \cap \rho(b) \neq \emptyset$. Similarly using ρ', we may deduce that certain input actions $A = c(w)$ never synchronize with an output action: in this case $\rho'(w) = \emptyset$. The presence of an input action like A is important for the precision of the analysis because it implies that all actions that follow A will never execute. Unfortunately, ρ' does not carry an analogous information also for the output actions. In fact, the values that ρ' associates to the names used in an output action do not reveal whether the action can synchronize or not.

The aim of point(ii) is approximated by adding $\rho'(u)$ to $\rho(v)$, in place of $\rho(u)$, where ρ' is the refined name-association introduced in the previous point.

The notion of satisfaction of tests and input actions and how they can be used to refine a name-association is illustrated in the following Example 2.

EXAMPLE 2 *Consider process* $P = [a = r].a(z).[r = z].\overline{a}\langle r\rangle$ *and the name-association* ρ *such that* $\rho(a) = \{c, d\}, \rho(r) = \{d, e\}, \rho(z) = \{e, f\}$. *Clearly,* ρ *satisfies both* $[a = r]$ *and* $[r = z]$ *since* $\rho(a) \cap \rho(r) = \{d\}$ *and* $\rho(r) \cap \rho(z) = \{e\}$ *and shows that* $a(z)$ *can synchronize with some output action because* $\rho(z) \neq \emptyset$. *However,* ρ *does not satisfy the two tests together:* $\rho(a) \cap \rho(r) \cap \rho(z) = \emptyset$*! From this we can deduce that* $\overline{a}\langle r\rangle$ *can never be executed and this consideration may be useful to improve the quality of the static analysis of a process that contains* P.

Consider now a process with two concurrent processes, $P = Q \mid R$, *where* $Q = [a = r].r(z).[z = k].\overline{a}\langle r\rangle$ *and* $R = [l = a].b(v)$ *with the following name-association:* $\rho(a) = \{c, d\}$, $\rho(r) = \{d, e\}$, $\rho(z) = \{e, f\}$, $\rho(k) = \{f, g\}$, $\rho(l) = \{d, e\}$, $\rho(b) = \{c, e\}$, $\rho(v) = \emptyset$. *If we consider* Q *and* R *independently, then we would deduce that the action* $A = \overline{a}\langle r\rangle$ *of* Q *and the action* $B = b(v)$ *of* R *are both possible. However, it is easy to see that these 2 actions cannot synchronize. In fact, in order for these two actions to synchronize,* ρ *must satisfy* $[a = b]$ *together with all the tests and input actions that precede the 2 actions. Clearly this in not the case here:* $\rho(a) \cap \rho(r) \cap \rho(l) \cap \rho(b) = \emptyset$. *If, on the other hand,* $\rho(a) = \{c, d, e\}$ *(with all other values of* ρ *unchanged) then* ρ *would satisfy the condition and thus we would deduce that* $\overline{a}\langle r\rangle$ *and* $b(v)$ *may synchronize and then consider this action in our analysis of* P.

The above ideas are rather intuitive and can be used to design a precise static analysis for the π-calculus. We show that this analysis can also be implemented rather efficiently, namely, we show that its time complexity is cubic in the size of the process that is analyzed. Also [4] presents a static analysis of the π-calculus that has been shown in [14] to be cubic. However, the analysis of [4] checks the tests one by one instead of simultaneously as our analysis and therefore, it is in general less precise. For instance, it would not be able to infer that the system of Example 1 behaves safely.

In [5] a static analysis is presented for a language slightly different from that of [4] and of the present article. The main differences of the language considered inS [5] are that the repetition operator is absent and that the role of tests is played by special input actions called selective inputs. A selective input, before to accept an input, tests if the input is in a given set of names. This is in some sense equivalent to group together many tests. Thus, one could say that in [5] a complementary approach is taken with respect to the one we follow: in place of making the analysis more sophisticated by grouping together tests, the language of [5] allows to directly write protocols with more complex tests. On these protocols a simple analysis obtains results similar to those that our analysis obtains on the same protocols described with a simpler language. However, it is not difficult to show that all results obtainable with the approach of [5] can be obtained with ours, but not vice versa.

The rest of the article is organized as follows. Section 1 contains some standard definitions about π-calculus, some new notation, and a static analysis that uses the ideas explained in Example 2 for improving the precision of the analysis. This analysis is very abstract in the sense that it does not specify how its sophisticated tests are actually performed. Section 2 is devoted precisely to the illustration of how this analysis can be implemented in cubic time. This is done in 2 steps: a pre-processing step followed by the static analysis part. Subsection 2 illustrates the theoretical foundations on which the actual implementation is built. The implementation of the static analysis part is described in Subsection 2. The correctness of the efficient implementation is discussed in Section 3 and the complexity of the algorithm is discussed in Section 4. The work ends with Section 5 where we try to link our algorithm with similar proposals and we point out some directions for future investigation.

For the sake of brevity, only the proof of the main theorem 2 is reported, the proofs of all technical lemmata are given in [6]. Also the pre-processing phase of the algorithm (and the proof that also this phase is $O(n^3)$) is described in [6].

1 Preliminaries

In this section we first recall the syntax of the π-calculus, [10]. The semantics of the language is explained only intuitively by means of an Example. A complete description can be found in [10, 15]. After this we introduce some new notation and we describe a simple static analysis of the π-calculus.

DEFINITION 1 *Let $\mathcal{N}$ denote an infinite set of* names, *ranged over by $a, b, x, y, \ldots$. Let also τ be a symbol not in $\mathcal{N}$. Processes of π-calculus are constructed according to the following syntax:*

$$P ::= \mathbf{0} \mid \mu.P \mid P+P \mid P \mid P \mid (\nu c)P \mid [x=y].P \mid !P$$

where μ is either a silent action indicated with τ, or an output action $\overline{a}\langle b\rangle$, or an input action $a(b)$. In these actions a is called the subject *and b the* object *of the action. The "." operator indicates sequential execution, the "+" operator indicates nondeterministic choice and "$\mid$" denotes parallel execution. The operator "!" means replication and is very important because it replaces recursion. The (νc) operator introduces private name c. Process $\mathbf{0}$ does nothing and thus we shorten $P.\mathbf{0}$ into P.*

EXAMPLE 3 *Consider process $P = \overline{a}\langle x\rangle.x(v).[v=x].R \mid a(w).[w=x].\overline{w}\langle x\rangle$. P consists of two processes that execute concurrently and whose input and output actions can synchronize. First, $\overline{a}\langle x\rangle$ can synchronize with $a(w)$ producing $x(v).[v=x].R \mid [x=x].\overline{x}\langle x\rangle$. Note that as an effect of this synchronization step, the name x has been substituted to w and thus the test $[w=x]$ has become $[x=x]$ which is satisfied. Thus the output $\overline{x}\langle x\rangle$ can execute and synchronize with $x(v)$ producing $[x=x].R \mid \mathbf{0} = R$. Clearly, in process P, actions and tests are partially ordered by the execution order induced by the sequencing operator ".". For instance, in $\overline{a}\langle x\rangle.x(v).[v=x].R$, $\overline{a}\langle x\rangle$ is executed first, then $x(v)$, then $[v=x]$ and finally R.*

In what follows P is a π-calculus process. In our analysis private names are considered as free names. So we will just ignore them. This causes no loss of precision because the fact that a name is private is irrelevant to our analysis. We simply study how names can propagate inside P. Being able to distinguish the private names from the free ones may become an issue when considering the problem of approximating the communications of P with the "outside world". $fn(P)$ and $bn(P)$ are, respectively, the set of free names of P and that of the bound names of P. We always assume, w.l.g., that $fn(P) \cap bn(P) = \emptyset$ and we call $n(P) = fn(P) \cup bn(P)$.

DEFINITION 2 *Two actions or tests of P are said to be* in concurrent positions *when either they occur in a same replicated subprocess* $!Q$ *or they occur in opposite sides of a parallel composition* $Q \mid R$.

PAIR(P) is the set of all pairs (A, B) *of actions and tests of P that are in concurrent positions and such that A and B are not both input or both output actions. We will also assume that* $(A, B) \in PAIR(P)$ *only when A occurs to the left of B in the process P. Thus, if* $(A, B) \in PAIR(P)$ *then* $(B, A) \notin PAIR(P)$.

EXAMPLE 4 *In process P of Example 3, if we call* $A = \overline{a}\langle x\rangle$, $B = x(v)$, $C = a(w)$ *and* $D = \overline{w}\langle x\rangle$, *the pairs in concurrent positions are* (A, C) *and* (B, D). *If we consider the process* $!P$, *then we should add also* (A, B) *and* (C, D).

DEFINITION 3 *A* name-association *is a function* $\rho : \mathcal{N} \rightarrow \mathcal{PS}(\mathcal{N})$ *(where* $\mathcal{PS}$ *denotes the power set). Let K be a set of tests and actions, such that their variables are in* $\mathcal{N}$. *If* $n(K)$ *is the set of names contained in K, then the tests in K define an equivalence relation on* $n(K)$ *whose corresponding partition is denoted with* $\Pi(K)$. *We say that a name-association* ρ satisfies K, *when* $\bigcap_{x \in W} \rho(x) \neq \emptyset$ *for all* $W \in \Pi(K)$. *Observe that this condition also implies that for all input and output actions in K, if a is the subject of the action and u the object, then* $\rho(a)$ *and* $\rho(u)$ *are both not empty. That* ρ *satisfies K is denoted with* $\rho \models K$.

The refinement *of* ρ *wrt K is a new name-association* ρ' *as follows:*

$$\rho'(z) = \begin{cases} \rho(z) & \text{if } z \notin n(K) \\ \bigcap_{x \in W} \rho(x) & \text{if } z \in W \in \Pi(K) \end{cases}$$

Observe that if $\rho \not\models K$, *then for some* $x \in n(K)$, $\rho'(x) = \emptyset$. *Given any name* x, *with* $[x]_K$ *we denote the equivalence class in* $\Pi(K)$ *that contains* x. *This operation is obvious when* $x \in n(K)$. *When* $x \notin n(K)$, *conventionally* $[x]_K = \{x\}$.

Example 2 of the Introduction illustrates the above notions. The following technical fact is a basis for next results.

FACT 1 *Let K be a set of tests and W a non singleton equivalence class in* $\Pi(K)$, *let also* $S \in K$ *such that* $n(S) \cap W \neq \emptyset$ *then the following 3 statements hold:*

1. $n(S) \subseteq W$;
2. *for any name* $a \in W$, $[a]_{K\setminus\{S\}} \cap n(S) \neq \emptyset$.
3. *let* S' *be another test in K and assume that a is a name of S and* a' *one of* S' *and finally, let* W' *be the equivalence class in* $\Pi(K)$ *that contains* $n(S')$. *Then it holds that* $[a]_{K\setminus\{S'\}} \cap [a']_{K\setminus\{S\}} \neq \emptyset$ *iff* $W = W' = [a]_{K\setminus\{S'\}} \cup [a']_{K\setminus\{S\}}$

DEFINITION 4 *For any action or test X of P, with* $PRED(X)$ *we denote the set of actions and tests that precede X in P according to the execution order explained in Example 3 (observe that* $PRED(X)$ *does not contain X).* $COND(X) \subseteq$

$PRED(X)$ is the set of all the tests that precede X in P. Recall from Example 3 that the tests and actions in $PRED(X)$ are totally ordered according to their execution order. For any pair $(A,B) \in PAIR(P)$, $PRED(A,B) = PRED(A) \cup PRED(B)$ and $COND(A,B) = COND(A) \cup COND(B)$.

The following Example explains the previous Definition.

EXAMPLE 5 *Let P be the following process,*
$a(x).a(y).a(z).a(w).[x=w].\left([x=y].\bar{b}\langle x\rangle \mid [x=z].\bar{c}\langle x\rangle \mid [w=z].[w=y].d(k)\right)$
then $PRED(\bar{b}\langle x\rangle) = \{a(x), a(y), a(z), a(w), [x=w], [x=y]\}$, $COND(\bar{b}\langle x\rangle) = \{[x=w], [x=y]\}$ and the set of actions and tests in $PRED(\bar{b}\langle x\rangle) \cap PRED(d(k))$ is $\{a(x), a(y), a(z), a(w), [x=w]\}$. These actions and test precede both $\bar{b}\langle x\rangle$ and $d(k)$. Observe that all tests and actions in the above sets are listed in execution order.

This Section is concluded with a very simple but powerful static analysis for the π-calculus, that we call in fact the **Simple Analysis**.

1 Let P be the process to be analyzed and ρ_0 be the following name-association: for each free name x in P, $\rho_0(x) = \{x\}$ and for each bound name y in P, $\rho_0(y) = \emptyset$. Set $i = 1$ and proceed to the following step,
2 consider any pair $(A,B) \in PAIR(P)$, such that A is an output action $\bar{a}\langle u\rangle$ and B an input action $b(v)$. If $\rho_{i-1} \models PRED(A,B) \cup [a=b]$, let ρ'_{i-1} be the refinement of ρ_{i-1} wrt $PRED(A,B) \cup [a=b]$ (cf. Definition 3), then $\rho_i(v) = \rho_{i-1}(v) \cup \rho'_{i-1}(u)$.
3 if $\rho_i = \rho_{i-1}$ then stop with output $\rho_{SA} = \rho_i$, otherwise go back to step 2.

Even though the above analysis is very simple to describe, it contains operations that seem to require a high polynomial number of steps (in particular, the test whether $\rho_i \models PRED(A,B) \cup [a=b]$ and the computation of ρ'_{i-1} in step (2)). It is in fact fairly easy to see how to perform these operations in $O(n^5)$ steps. Observe that the operations of step (2) of the Simple Analysis that seem to be particularly complex are exactly those that perform the improvements mentioned in points (1) and (2) of the Introduction. Improving this bound was for us not easy, but we succeeded and in the following Sections we report the algorithm we found. This algorithm implements the Simple Analysis and has worst case time complexity $O(n^3)$.

The reader may wonder why in the above step (2) we consider $PRED(A,B)$ and not $COND(A,B)$. Notice that $\Pi(COND(A,B)) \subseteq \Pi(PRED(A,B))$ and in some cases the containment is proper and the difference consists of some singletons. This may happen when $PRED(A,B)$ contains some input or output action with names that do not appear in any test in $COND(A,B)$. As already observed in the Introduction (cf. Point (1)), the names in these singletons that are objects of input actions, can be exploited for improving the analysis. This explains the choice in step (2).

2 The Efficient Algorithm

In this Section we explain how the Simple Analysis of the previous Section can be implemented efficiently obtaining an algorithm that has cubic worst case time complexity. This algorithm will be called in what follows **the Efficient Algorithm**.

The problem is to perform efficiently the tests of point (2) of the Simple Analysis and the computation of a refined name-association (called ρ'_{i-1} in the Simple Analysis). The key idea is that of computing and maintaining all the necessary refined values throughout the analysis (instead of recomputing them each time they are needed as in a naive implementation of the Simple Analysis). To this end we introduce a set of new names whose role is to hold the refined values. Roughly this works as follows. Consider a pair $A = \overline{a}\langle u\rangle$ and $B = b(v)$ that may synchronize. The tests and actions that precede A and B, together with $[a = b]$, determine equivalence classes of names, cf. Example 2. Call these classes $X_1, \ldots, X_m$. For each X_i, a new name c_i is introduced and during the analysis, if ρ is the name-association computed so far, then the value of $\rho(c_i)$ will always satisfy the following relation: $\rho(c_i) = \bigcap_{y \in X_i} \rho(y)$. Thus, $\rho(c_i)$ is the refined value of each name in X_i. Namely, it is the set of names that are assigned to all the names in X_i and that satisfy all the tests and actions in $PRED(A, B)$ that have formed the class X_i. The above description is necessarily simplified. In particular, the new names that are used in the algorithm are not simply c_i. For instance, the new name that corresponds to the class that contains the subjects a and b is $c_{A,B}$ and the new name that corresponds to the class that contains the object u of the output is $c_{A\downarrow B}$. With these new names that hold the refined values of the equivalence classes, it is possible to implement the actions of point (2) of the Simple Analysis as follows :

(a) the synchronization between A and B is considered by the analysis only when each $\rho(c_i) \neq \emptyset$, this guarantees that all actions and tests in $PRED(A, B) \cup [a = b]$ can be executed/satisfied; observe that $[a = b]$ is added to check that A and B can actually communicate;

(b) the synchronization of A and B is modelled by adding $\rho(c_{A\downarrow B})$ to $\rho(v)$. Observe that this is the refined value of u, as requested in point (2) of the Simple Analysis.

The number of new names introduced is quadratic. However, maintaining the value of each of these names (and also of those in $n(P)$ that in what follows will be called *old*) takes linear time. This follows from the fact that each new name c depends on only 2 other names (new or old), say c' and c''. This dependency is as follows: when $x \in \rho(c') \cap \rho(c'')$ then x must be also in $\rho(c)$. Moreover, c' and c'' are strictly smaller than c wrt a partial order and thus there is no circularity in these dependencies. Exploiting this fact, it is possible to maintain the value of each name in linear time.

The test described in point (a) above can also be done very efficiently: a counter $Ready(c_{A\downarrow B})$ is initially set to the number of classes in $\amalg(PRED(A, B) \cup [a = b])$ and is decreased by 1 each time the value of $\rho(c_i)$ (where c_i corresponds to one of the classes) becomes not empty. When $Ready(c_{A\downarrow B}) = 0$, the test of point (a) is satisfied and thus the analysis performs the action of point (b). We have actually implemented this sophisticated static analysis algorithm. The C++ source is downloadable from the directory "www.math.unipd.it/~colussi/Analizer/".

theoretical foundations

This Section is devoted to the construction of the theoretical foundations of the Efficient Algorithm and of the proof that it is cubic in the size of P (P is always the process under analysis). It mainly contains three things:

(I) The precise definition of the new names that are needed for the Efficient Algorithm together with a partial order on them;

(II) The proof that the value of each new name v depends on that of only two other names $lc(v)$ and $rc(v)$;

(III) The proof that for each pair (A, B) of input/output action one can compute once and for all a set X of names, such that the test of point(a) above is performed by checking that for every name $x \in X$, $\rho(x) \neq \emptyset$. It is also important that $|X|$ is linear in the size of P.

Points (II) and (III) are fundamental for showing that the Efficient Algorithm is cubic in the size of P. Recall that $n(P)$ stands for the set of all the names of P, i.e., $n(P) = fn(P) \cup bn(P)$, where, w.l.g., we assume that $fn(P) \cap bn(P) = \emptyset$. In what follows these names are called *old* to distinguish them from the new ones that we are going to introduce. As explained above, each new name v stands for a set of old names that is indicated with $[v]$. This notation is extended to old names x, letting $[x] = \{x\}$. The set of new names that we create for P is denoted $new(P)$ and consists of two parts $news(P)$ and $newp(P)$. The first part contains new names that corresponds to a single test T of P ('s' stands for single), whereas the second one contains new names that correspond to pairs ('p' stands for pair) as follows: these names correspond either to pairs (A, B) of an input and an output action which are in concurrent position in P or to pairs (T, T') of tests which are in concurrent position in P.

DEFINITION 5 *For each test $T = [a = b]$ of P, $news(P)$ contains a new name c_T that stands for the set of old names $[c_T] = [a]_{COND(T) \cup T}$.*

The following is an easy consequence of Fact 1(2) that is useful for the next Lemma.

FACT 2 *Let c_T be the new name that corresponds to a test $T = [a = b]$, then $[c_T] = [a]_{COND(T)} \cup [b]_{COND(T)}$.*

It is useful to define a partial order on the set $news(P) \cup n(P)$.

DEFINITION 6 *The relation $\preceq$ on $news(P) \cup n(P)$ is defined as follows.*

- *for each $x \in news(P) \cup n(P)$, $x \preceq x$;*
- *the old names in $n(P)$ are unrelated among each other and for each $x \in n(P)$ and $y \in news(P)$, $x \preceq y$;*
- *for any two names c_T and $c_S \in news(P), c_T \preceq c_S$ iff T precedes S in the execution order.*

In what follows we will write $x \prec y$ to denote $x \preceq y$ and $x \neq y$.

In the following Lemma we show point (II) for the names in $news(P)$.

LEMMA 1 *Let c_T be a new name in $news(P)$, where $T = [a = b]$. There are two names (either old or in $news(P)$) $lc(c_T)$ and $rc(c_T)$ such that $[c_T] = [lc(c_T)] \cup [rc(c_T)]$. Moreover, $lc(c_T) \prec c_T$ and $rc(c_T) \prec c_T$.*

Names in $newp(P)$ correspond to pairs $(A, B) \in PAIR(P)$ whose names may interact in some way. Interaction may be of two types: either A and B are an output and an input action that may communicate or A and B are tests and there is a name in A and a name in B that are equated by the tests in $COND(A, B)$.

Recall from Definition 2 that pairs $(A, B) \in PAIR(P)$ are such that A is always to the left of B in P. In this way we avoid the nuisance of having a new name for (A, B) and another for (B, A), while only one of them is enough for the analysis.

DEFINITION 7 *$newp(P)$ contains the following names:*

(a) For each test/test pair $(T, T') \in PAIR(P)$, where $T = [a = c]$ and $T' = [b = d]$, and such that $[a]_{COND(T,T') \cup T} \cap [b]_{COND(T,T') \cup T'} \neq \emptyset$ a new name $c_{T,T'}$ is in $newp(P)$. This name stands for the set of old names $[c_{T,T'}] = [a]_{COND(T,T') \cup T \cup T'}$.

(b) For each input/output pair $(A, B) \in PAIR(P)$, where $\overline{a}\langle u\rangle$ is the output action and $b(w)$ is the input action, $newp(P)$ contains two new names $c_{A,B}$ and $c_{A\downarrow B}$. The name $c_{A,B}$ is intended to stand for the set $[c_{A,B}] = [a]_{COND(A,B) \cup [a=b]}$ of old names, whereas $c_{A\downarrow B}$ stands for the set $[c_{A\downarrow B}] = [u]_{COND(A,B) \cup [a=b]}$.

Notice that in point (b) of the above Definition no assumption is made on which one between A and B is input and which is output. Moreover, $[a = b]$ is not a test in P. We add it to $COND(A, B)$ to mimic the fact that the synchronization of A and B is possible only when this condition is satisfied. Observe that this is coherent with step (2) of the Simple Analysis, cf. Section 1. In what follow with $nn(P)$ we denote $n(P) \cup new(P)$. The partial order $\preceq$ is easily extended to $nn(P)$ as follows.

DEFINITION 8 *The partial order $\preceq$ is extended to $nn(P)$ adding the following points to those of Definition 6:*

- *for each name $x \in newp(P)$, $x \preceq x$;*
- *all old names are smaller than all new names of $newp(P)$;*
- *a name c_T is smaller than every name $c_{X,Y}$ and $c_{X\downarrow Y}$;*
- *if T_1 and T_2 are tests and X_1 and X_2 are either two tests or an input and output action, then $c_{T_1,T_2} \preceq c_{X_1,X_2}$ iff for each $i \in [1, 2]$ either T_i precedes X_i or $T_i = X_i$;*
- *for all name x, if $x \preceq c_{A,B} \in newp(P)$, where A and B are an input and an output action, then $x \preceq c_{A\downarrow B}$.*

FACT 3 *The relation $\preceq$ of Definition 8 is a partial order.*

We want now to show point (II) also for the names in $newp(P)$. To this end we follow the same strategy that was used in Lemma 1: for any $v \in newp(P)$, we show that $[v]$ can be split into two parts for which there are corresponding names. The following simple consequence of Fact 1(c) is useful for this.

FACT 4 *Let $c_{T,T'}$ be a new name introduced in step (a) of Definition 7 and let $T = [a = c]$ and $T' = [b = d]$. It is true that $[a]_{COND(T,T') \cup T \cup T'} = [a]_{COND(T,T') \cup T} \cup [b]_{COND(T,T') \cup T'}$.*

LEMMA 2 *Let $v \in newp(P)$, there are names $lc(v)$ and $rc(v)$ in $n(P) \cup news(P) \cup newp(P)$ such that $[v] = [lc(v)] \cup [rc(v)]$ and moreover, these names are smaller than v with respect to the partial order $\prec$.*

- A boolean array *Bound* indexed on the set $nn(P)$. $Bound[x] = 1$ if there is a name $z \in n(P)$ such that $Rho[z, x] = 1$.
- An array *Ready* of integers such that for each name $v = c_{A \downarrow B}$, $Ready[v]$ is initially set to the cardinality of $Pred(v)$. For each name $x \in Pred(v)$, there is a list isP_x that contains v and all other names having x in their $Pred$ set.
- Two arrays *Lc* and *Rc* indexed on the set $new(P)$ (to store $lc(v)$ and $rc(v)$) and for all $x \in nn(P)$ a list $isLc_x$ (for "x is Left Component of") of all names v such that $x = lc(v)$ and a list $isRc_x$ (for "x is Right Component of") of all those names v such that $x = rc(v)$.
- An array *Rho* of booleans indexed in $n(P) \times nn(P)$.

Table 1. Main data structures used by the algorithm.

The following Theorem summarizes what we have shown.

THEOREM 1 *For each name v in $new(P)$ there exist names $lc(v)$ and $rc(v)$ (possibly equal) that are strictly smaller than v wrt the partial order $\prec$ defined on $nn(P)$.*

COROLLARY 1 *The relation on $nn(P)$ defined by the $lc(v)$ and $rc(v)$ functions among names is noncircular.*

We turn now to point (III). Consider an input/output pair (A, B) and let a and b be the subjects of the two actions and u the object of the output one. As explained in (III), in order for the Efficient Algorithm to check whether the pair (A, B) can synchronize, all the refined values corresponding to the equivalence classes of $\Pi(PRED(A, B) \cup [a = b])$ should be not empty. In order to perform this test for each such class X there must exist a new or an old name x that corresponds to the class and thus that will hold its refined value. This is shown in the following Lemma.

LEMMA 3 *Let $v = c_{A \downarrow B}$ and let a and b be the subjects of the actions A and B. For each class $X \in \Pi(PRED(A, B) \cup [a = b])$ there is a name $x \in nn(P)$ such that $[x] = X$. Moreover, $x \prec c_{A \downarrow B}$.*

Let us conclude the Section with a notation that will be useful in the next one: For any name $c_{A \downarrow B}$, $Pred(c_{A \downarrow B})$ denotes the names (that were just shown to exist) that correspond to the equivalence classes of $\Pi(PRED(A, B) \cup [a = b])$.

the implementation

The Efficient Algorithm uses several data structures and is composed of two parts: a pre-processing part and the static analysis part. For the sake of brevity, we only describe the static analysis part, in Table 2, and the most important data structures used in that part, in Table 1. The pre-processing part and all other data structures used by the algorithm are described in [6]. Data structures in Table 1 have the following purpose. In the matrix *Rho* we assume that the first $|n(P)|$ columns correspond to the old names (i.e., those in $n(P)$). This matrix holds, throughout the execution of the algorithm, the name-association computed at each moment.

The name-association ρ_{Rho} on $nn(P)$ that corresponds to a given matrix *Rho* is as follows: $\forall x \in n(P)$ and $w \in nn(P)$, $x \in \rho_{Rho}(w)$ iff $Rho[x, w] = 1$. The restriction

$Compute(P)$ 1 Set to 0 all entries of arrays *Rho* and *Bound*. 2 Call $Try(u)$ for all $u \in fn(P)$ (i.e., those u that do not occur in P as the object of an input action).
$Try(u)$ 1 if $Rho[u,u] = 0$ then set $Rho[u,u] = 1$ and call $VisitIsC(u,u)$. 2 if $Bound[u] = 0$ then set $Bound[u] = 1$ and call $VisitIsP(u)$.
$Filter(u,v)$ 1 set $Rho[u,v] = 1$ and call $VisitIsC(u,v)$. 2 if $v = c_{A\downarrow B}$, $Ready[v] = 0$ and $Rho[u,w] = 0$, where w is the object of the input action in the input/output pair (A,B) associated to v, then call $Close(u,w)$. 3 if $Bound[v] = 0$ set $Bound[v] = 1$ and call $VisitIsP(v)$.
$Transmit(v,w)$ 1 call $Close(z,w)$ for all $z \in n(P)$ such that $Rho[z,w] = 0$ and $Rho[z,v] = 1$.
$Close(u,v)$ 1 set $Rho[u,v] = 1$ and call $VisitIsC(u,v)$. 2 if $Bound[v] = 0$ then set $Bound[v] = 1$ and call $VisitIsP(v)$. 3 call $Close(z,v)$ for all $z \in n(P)$ such that $Rho[z,v] = 0$ and $Rho[z,u] = 1$. 4 call $Close(u,z)$ for all $z \in n(P)$ such that $Rho[u,z] = 0$ and $Rho[v,z] = 1$.
$VisitIsC(u,v)$ 1 call $Filter(u,x)$ for all $x \in isLc_v$ such that $Rho[u,Rc[x]] = 1$ and $Rho[u,x] = 0$. 2 call $Filter(u,x)$ for all $x \in isRc_v$ such that $Rho[u,Lc[x]] = 1$ and $Rho[u,x] = 0$.
$VisitIsP(v)$ 1 for all $x \in isP_v$ set $Ready[x] = Ready[x] - 1$ and in case $Ready[x] = 0$ call $Transmit(x,w)$ where w is the object of the input action in the input/output pair (A,B) associated to x (recall that all $x \in isP_v$ are of type $x = c_{A\downarrow B}$).

Table 2. The static analysis part of the Efficient Algorithm

of ρ_{Rho} to the old names in $n(P)$ is denoted $\bar{\rho}_{Rho}$. Lc and Rc specify for each new name v the $lc(v)$ and $rc(v)$. *Bound* is used to signal when a name x is assigned a not empty value, i.e., $\rho(x) \neq \emptyset$. *Ready* is defined only for names of the form $c_{A\downarrow B}$. Its initial value is the cardinality of $Pred(c_{A\downarrow B})$. Each time a name x in this set becomes bound, then $Ready[c_{A\downarrow B}]$ is decreased by 1. On the other hand, $isLc_x$ is used to reach all those names v that have x as $lc(v)$ and similarly for $isRc_x$. isP_x lists those names of the form $c_{A\downarrow B}$ such that $x \in Pred(c_{A\downarrow B})$.

3 Correctness of the Efficient Algorithm

In what follows we show that the Efficient Algorithm computes the same name-association as the Simple Analysis of Section 1. In the following Lemma we list some important facts that are true about the Efficient Algorithm.

LEMMA 4

1 *For all $u \in n(P)$ and $z \in nn(P)$, $Rho[u,z]$ is set to 1 iff $Rho[u,v] = 1$ for all $v \in [z]$.*
2 *Consider any $v = c_{A\downarrow B}$, and let a and b be the subjects of actions A and B. The following holds: Initially $Ready[v] > 0$ and $Ready[v]$ became 0 as soon as $\rho_{Rho} \models PRED(A,B) \cup [a=b]$.*
3 *Consider any $u, w \in n(P)$ where w is the object of an input action. Initially $Rho[u,w] = 0$ and $Rho[u,w]$ is set to 1 as soon as $Rho[u,v] = 1$ and $Ready[v] = 0$ for some $v = c_{A\downarrow B}$ such that the object of the input action is w.*

Using the above facts we can now show the correctness of the Efficient Algorithm. Let ρ_{EA} be the name-association computed by the Efficient Algorithm and ρ_{SA} that computed by the Simple Analysis. Clearly, ρ_{EA} is ρ_{Rho}, where Rho is the final matrix produced by the Efficient Algorithm. Recall that $\bar{\rho}_{EA}$ is its restriction to $n(P)$.

THEOREM 2 $\bar{\rho}_{EA} = \rho_{SA}$

Proof. For this proof it is convenient to consider that ρ_{SA} is extended to $nn(P)$ by setting for each new name v, $\rho_{SA}(v) = \bigcap_{x \in [v]} \rho_{SA}(x)$. Moreover, it will be useful to consider the computation of the Efficient Algorithm and of the Simple Analysis and the sequence of name-associations produced by the two processes. With ρ_{EA_i} we denote the name-associations obtained by the Efficient Algorithm after the first i changes operated to the initial name-association which is the empty matrix Rho and thus the empty name-association. Rho_i is the corresponding matrix. Similarly, ρ_{SA_i} denotes the name-association computed by the Simple Analysis after i changes operated on the initial name-association ρ_0. Recall that ρ_0 is the identity for the free names of P and the empty set for the other names.

Let us first show that $\rho_{EA} \subseteq \rho_{SA}$. We reason by contradiction. Assume that there are old names $x, y \in n(P)$ such that $y \in \rho_{EA_{i+1}}(x)$, but that $y \notin \rho_{SA}(x)$. We assume that the (I+1)-th step introduces this difference for the first time and thus $\rho_{EA_i} \subseteq \rho_{SA}$. By Lemma 4(3), from the fact that $Rho_i[y,x] = 1$, it follows that there must be a new name $v = c_{A\downarrow B}$ such that $Rho_i[y,v] = 1$ and $Ready[v] = 0$. Let also u be the object of the output action in (A,B). From Lemma 4(2), it follows that $Ready[v] = 0 \Rightarrow \rho_{EA_i} \models PRED(A,B) \cup [a=b] \Rightarrow \rho_{SA} \models PRED(A,B) \cup [a=b]$. Let $\rho'_{SA} = \rho_{SA}|_{PRED(A,B)\cup[a=b]}$. Observe now that, since $Rho_i[y,v] = 1$, from Lemma 4(1), it follows that $y \in \rho_{EA_i}(d), \forall d \in [v] = [u]_{PRED(A,B)\cup[a=b]}$. Hence, $y \in \rho'_{SA}(u)$ and therefore, $y \in \rho_{SA}(x)$. This clearly contradicts the initial hypothesis.

Let us now prove that $\rho_{EA} \supseteq \rho_{SA}$. Observe that the Simple Analysis starts from ρ_0. It suffices to look at the function *Compute* of Table 2 to see that $\rho_{EA} \supseteq \rho_0$.

Make the following Assumption (*): for the first time at the (i+1)-th step the Simple Analysis adds y to $\rho_{SA_i}(x)$ such that $y \notin \rho_{EA}(x)$. In order to meet Assumption (*) the

Simple Analysis must consider an input/output pair (A, B). Assume that the subjects of the 2 actions are a and b, whereas the object of the output one is u, whereas that of the input, from the hypothesis, must be x. Moreover, it must be that **(A)** $\rho_{SA_i} \models PRED(A,B) \cup [a = b]$ and if $\rho'_{SA_i} = \rho_{SA_i}|_{PRED(A,B)\cup[a=b]}$, then **(B)** $y \in \rho'_{SA_i}(u)$.

From Assumption (*) and statement **(A)**, it follows that $\rho_{EA} \models PRED(A,B) \cup [a = b]$ and, by Fact 4(2), we derive that **(C)** $Ready[c_{A\downarrow B}] = 0$. From **(B)** and Assumption (*), it follows that $\forall d \in [c_{A\downarrow B}] = [u]_{PRED(A,B)\cup[a=b]}$, $Rho[y, d] = 1$, and thus, by Fact 4(1), that **(D)** $Rho[y, c_{A\downarrow B}] = 1$. From **(C)** and **(D)**, by Fact 4(3), we can conclude that $Rho[y, x] = 1$ in contradiction with our initial assumption. □

4 Complexity of the algorithm

It is quite simple to prove that the Efficient Algorithm requires time $O(n^3)$ (where n is the size of the π-expression P in input): for each function we find a bound for the number of times it is called and a bound for the time required to execute the function. The execution time of each function does not include the time required to execute the function calls it may contain. At the end it suffices to sum everything up in order to obtain a bound for the total time required by whole Efficient Algorithm.

Observe that there are at most $O(n)$ actions or tests in P and at most $O(n)$ old names in $n(P)$ while the cardinality of $nn(P)$ can be $O(n^2)$. The function $Compute$ is called only once and requires $O(n^3)$ time. This time is needed fundamentally for initializing matrix *Rho*. Try is called $O(n)$ times (at most once for each name in $n(P)$) and its execution requires time $O(1)$. $Filter$ is called $O(n^3)$ times (at most once for each entry of *Rho*) and it requires time $O(1)$. $Transmit$ is called $O(n^2)$ times (at most once for each name $c_{A\downarrow B}$) and it requires time $O(n)$. $Close$ is called $O(n^2)$ times (at most once for each pair of names in $n(P)$) and it requires time $O(n)$. $VisitIsC$ is called at most once for each pair (u, v) and requires time proportional to the length of lists $isLc_v$ and $isRc_v$. Since the sum of the lengths of all lists $isLc$ and $isRc$ is $O(n^2)$ the total time required is $O(n^3)$. For function $VisitIsP$ the reasoning is more subtle. $VisitIsP$ is called at most once for each name $v \in nn(P)$ and requires time proportional to the length of the list isP_v. Since the sum of the lengths of all lists isP_v is $O(n^3)$ (because each name in $c_{A\downarrow B}$ can be inserted in at most $O(n)$ such lists), the total time required by this function is $O(n^3)$.

Since the above functions use the data structures shown in Table 1, it is important to consider also the cost of constructing these structures in a pre-processing phase.

The pre-processing can be done in time $O(n^3)$. A detailed description of the pre-processing and the proof that it require time $O(n^3)$ is given in [6]. Here we explain why this is the case on a more intuitive level. The pre-processing consists of a double visit of the parse tree of the π-expression P in input. For each action or test A encountered in the first visit we do a second visit to find all action or test B that is in concurrent position with A. At each step we update a disjoint-set data structure cls that holds the classes in $\Pi(PRED(A, B))$. The data structure cls is augmented by the name of classes and a list $Pred$ that links names of classes in cls. Since cls and $Pred$ can be updated in many different ways, they must be copied before an update takes place. Double visiting the parse tree takes time $O(n^2)$ and copying the structures cls requires time $O(n)$. Thus the total time used is $O(n^3)$.

5 Related work and perspectives

Bodei et al. in [4] proposed a static analysis of the π-calculus that in [14] was shown to have a cubic time complexity. This analysis considers that any input/output pair (A, B) can synchronize only when all tests that precede them are satisfied by the name-association computed so far, but the tests are considered one at the time and not together as our analysis does. In [13] the analysis of [4] is extended to the $spi-$calculus [2] maintaining the same time complexity. This extended version still handles the cryptographic primitives one at the time as before.

Also Venet [17] and Feret [8, 9] have proposed static analyses of the π-calculus that are formulated in the abstract interpretation framework, [7]. They first introduce non standard semantics and then define their analyses as abstractions of these semantics. The semantics they propose are expressive enough to encompass *non uniform* analyses, that is analyses able to distinguish among the different copies of a same replicated subprocess and among the names that these copies can define and transmit. In fact, these analyses are useful, for instance, for evaluating the resource usage inside a system. These works are rather different from the present one. They focus on the expressivity of the analyses rather than on their efficient implementation.

Clearly, many other methods, different from ours and from those mentioned before, have also been used for proving properties of protocols. These methods include model checking [12], type systems [2], the use of theorem provers [3, 1]. Often these proposals try to establish more sophisticated properties of protocols than what our static analysis can compute. However, we believe that any method for inferring properties of protocols must lay on a precise knowledge of the name-association the protocol actually produces and this is precisely what our static analysis computes with high precision and also efficiently.

In the future we intend to substantiate the above statement by extending our analysis in various ways. First of all we will further enhance the precision of our analysis by including into it the detection of "blocked" output actions, i.e., outputs that cannot synchronize with any input and that, therefore, block the successive actions. Our approach improves precision by considering the global condition $COND(A) \cup COND(B) \cup [a = b]$ under which transmission of a name can take place from the output action $A = \overline{a}\langle u \rangle$ to the input action $B = b(w)$. It is possible to further improve the precision of the analysis by considering the transmission of each name through sequences of synchronizing pairs of input/output actions, evaluating together all tests that precede these actions. We obviously expect that the complexity of this improved analysis will grow with the length of the action sequences considered.

Finally, we will apply our method to the analysis of extensions of the π-calculus that include various cryptographic primitives.

References

[1] Martìn Abadi and Bruno Blanchet. Computer assisted verification of a protocol for certified email. In *Proceedings of 10th SAS*, number 2694 in LNCS, pages 316–335, 2003.

[2] Martìn Abadi and Andrew Gordon. A calculus for cryptographic protocols—the spi calculus. *Information and Computation*, 148(4):1–70, 1999.

[3] G. Bella and L.C. Paulson. Kerberos version iv:inductive analysis of the secrecy goals. In *Proceedings of ESORICS 98*, number 1485 in LNCS, pages 361–375, 1998.

[4] Chiara Bodei, Pierpaolo Degano, Flemming Nielson, and Hanne Riis Nielson. Static analysis for the π-calculus with applications to security. *Information and Computation*, 165:68–92, 2001.

[5] C. Priami C.Bodei, P.Degano and N. Zannone. An enhanced cfa for security policies. In *Proceedings of WITS'03, pp.131-145, Warszawa*, 2003.

[6] L. Colussi, G. Filè and A. Griggio. Precise Analysis of π-calculus in cubic time. Preprint n. 20 *Dipartimento di Matematica Pura ed Applicata, University of Padova*, 2003.

"www.math.unipd.it/~colussi/DMPA-Preprint20-2003.ps"

[7] Patrick Cousot and Radhia Cousot. Abstract interpretation: a unified lattice model for static analysis of programs by construction or approximation of fixpoints. In *Proceedings of 4th ACM POPL*, pages 238–252, 1977.

[8] Jérôme Feret. Confidentiality analysis of mobile systems. In *Proceedings of 7th SAS*, number 1824 in LNCS, 2000.

[9] Jérôme Feret. Occurrence counting analysis. In *Proceedings of GETCO 2000, appeared on ENTCS*, number 39, 2001.

[10] Robin Milner. *Communicating and mobile systems: the π-calculus*. Cambridge University Press, 1999.

[11] Robin Milner, Joachim Parrow, and David Walker. A calculus of mobile processes (i and ii). *Information and Computation*, 100(1):1–77, 1992.

[12] J.C. Mitchell, V. Shmatikov, and U. Stern. Finite state analysis of ssl 3.0. In *Proceedings of 7th USENIX Security Symposium*, pages 201–216, 1998.

[13] Flemming Nielson, Hanne Riis Nielson, and Helmut Seidl. Cryptographic analysis in cubic time. In *ENTCS*, number 62 in ?, 2002.

[14] Flemming Nielson and Helmut Seidl. Control flow analysis in cubic time. In *Proceedings of ESOP '01*, number 2028 in LNCS, pages 252–268, 2001.

[15] Davide Sangiorgi and David Walker. *The π-calculus: a Theory of Mobile Processes*. Cambridge University Press, 2001.

[16] R. L. Rivest T. H. Cormen, C. E. Leiserson and C. Stein. *Introduction to Algorithms*. The Mit Press, 1998.

[17] Arnaud Venet. Automatic determination of communication topologies in mobile systems. In *Proceedings of 5th SAS*, number 1503 in LNCS, pages 152–167, 1998.

PROTOTYPING PROOF CARRYING CODE

Martin Wildmoser, Tobias Nipkow
Institut für Informatik, Technische Universität München
wildmosm@in.tum.de, nipkow@in.tum.de

Gerwin Klein
National ICT Australia, Sydney
gerwin.klein@nicta.com.au

Sebastian Nanz *
Yale University, Department of Computer Science
nanz@cs.yale.edu

Abstract We introduce a generic framework for proof carrying code, developed and mechanically verified in Isabelle/HOL. The framework defines and proves sound a verification condition generator with minimal assumptions on the underlying programming language, safety policy, and safety logic. We demonstrate its usability for prototyping proof carrying code systems by instantiating it to a simple assembly language with procedures and a safety policy for arithmetic overflow.

1 Introduction

Proof Carrying Code (PCC), first proposed by Necula and Lee [11] [12], is a scheme for executing untrusted code safely. Fig. 1 shows the architecture of a PCC system. The code producer is on the left, the code receiver on the right. Both use a verification condition generator (VCG) that relies on annotations in the program to reduce the program to a logic formula. The logic used in annotations and proof is the *safety logic*, the property that is shown about the program is the *safety policy*.
It is the responsibility of the producer to generate the annotations and a proof for the formula the VCG constructs. They are then transmitted to the code receiver who again runs the VCG and uses a proof checker to verify that the proof indeed fits the formula produced by the VCG. Proof checking is much simpler and more efficient than proof searching. The framework for PCC systems we present in this paper concentrates on the safety critical receiver side. It has the following two main purposes and contributions: safety of the system and prototyping new safety logics. Proof checker, VCG,

*supported in part by NSF grant CCR-0208618.

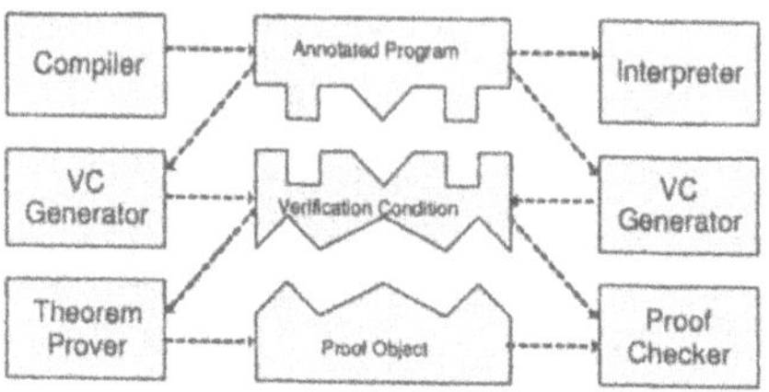

Figure 1. PCC Architecture

and safety logic constitute the trusted code base of the PCC system. Proof checkers are relatively small standard components of many logical frameworks. The VCG on the other hand is large (several thousand lines of C code in current PCC systems [6] [13]) and complex (it handles annotations, produces complex formulae, and contains parts of the safety policy). Our framework contains a VCG with a formal proof of safety, mechanically checked in the theorem prover Isabelle/HOL [16]. The VCG is not restricted to any particular machine language, safety policy, or safety logic. Additionally to the correctness of VCG and proof checker, we need the safety logic to be sound. As a recent bug [9] in the SpecialJ system [6] shows, this is not trivial. It is not even immediately clear, what exactly a safety logic must satisfy to be sound. Our framework makes the underlying assumptions on machine, policy, and logic explicit. It also makes a simple, formally clear statement what it means for a safety logic to be sound: if the formula produced by the VCG is derivable in the safety logic, the program must be safe according to the safety policy. The framework reduces the workload for showing soundness of a safety logic by giving sufficient conditions. Since the VCG is directly executable and the framework reasonably easy to instantiate, it provides a good platform for trying out, tuning, and analysing different safety policies and logics for different target platforms.

Our approach is different from other work in the formal foundation of PCC by Appel et al. [1] [2] or Hamid et al. [7] in that it works with an explicit, executable, and verified VCG and not directly on the machine semantics or a type system. The focus of the framework is on aiding logical foundations of PCC as the one started by Necula and Schneck [14] and on encouraging the analysis of safety properties other than the much researched type and memory safety. Necula and Schneck [15] also present a framework for VCGs. They work with a small, trusted core VCG that can be extended by optimised plugins. We see our work as complementary to this development: the core VCG could be proven sound within our framework, the technique of using safe, optimised extensions can then be applied to that sound core. On a broader scale, our approach is related to other techniques that impose safety policies on machine code statically: Typed Assembly Language [10], Mobile Ressource Guarantees [3] or Java Bytecode Verification [8].

There are four levels in our PCC systems. The first level, the PCC framework (§2), provides generic features and minimal assumptions. The second level is the platform (§3). Platform designers can provide a concrete instantiation of the framework with respect to a specific programming language, safety policy, and safety logic. The third level is the code producer who can now write and certify programs based on the instantiated framework. We show this by certifying a concrete program in §4. Finally, also in §4, we show how code receivers can check certified code within the framework. The formalization in this paper was carried out in Isabelle/HOL, so we inherit some of Isabelle's syntax. Most of the notation is familiar from functional programming and standard mathematics, we only mention a few peculiarities. Consing an element x to a list xs is written as $x\#xs$. Infix @ is the append operator, and $xs\ !\ n$ selects the n-th element from the list xs. The type $T1 \Rightarrow T2$ is the space of total functions from $T1$ to $T2$, and we frequently use the polymorphic option type **datatype** $'a\ option = None \mid Some\ 'a$ to simulate partiality in HOL, a logic of total functions: *None* stands for an undefined value, *Some x* for a defined value x.

2 Framework Definition

The components of a PCC system shown in Fig. 1 depend on three factors: programming language, safety policy, and safety logic. The programming language defines syntax and semantics for programs, the safety policy specifies the safety conditions programs must satisfy, and the safety logic provides a formal notation and a derivation calculus for proving these conditions. Our framework consists of skeletons and requirements for these three components and uses them to define and verify a generic VCG.

2.1 Program Semantics

Our framework expects the semantics of the underlying programming language in form of a function $effS :: 'prog \Rightarrow (('pos \times 'mem) \times ('pos \times 'mem))\ set$ which relates runtime states of a program to their immediate successor states. States are tuples (p,m) of type $'pos \times 'mem$, where p denotes the current position in the control flow graph and m is the machine's memory, e.g., heap, stack and registers. Since $'prog$, $'pos$ and $'mem$ are type variables the representation of programs, positions and memory can be instantiated as one likes.

2.2 Safety Logic

To specify and prove properties about programs we use a safety logic.

$$\llcorner True \lrcorner :: 'form \qquad \llcorner\bigwedge\lrcorner :: 'form\ list \Rightarrow 'form$$
$$\llcorner False \lrcorner :: 'form \qquad \llcorner\Longrightarrow\lrcorner :: 'form \Rightarrow 'form \Rightarrow 'form$$
$$\models :: 'prog \Rightarrow ('pos \times 'mem) \Rightarrow 'form \Rightarrow bool$$
$$\vdash :: 'prog \Rightarrow 'form \Rightarrow bool$$

Every structure having constants for the truth values $\llcorner True \lrcorner$ and $\llcorner False \lrcorner$, operators for conjunction $\llcorner\bigwedge\lrcorner$ and implication $\llcorner\Longrightarrow\lrcorner$, judgements for validity $\models$ and provability $\vdash$ of formulae can be employed as a safety logic as long as it respects the assumptions below. These assumptions only concern the semantics of the logical connectives. How formulae or their proofs look like and what they mean, is left open. This depends on how $'form$, $\vdash$ and $\models$ get instantiated.

assumptions

semTrueF: $\Pi,s \models \llcorner True \lrcorner$ *semFalseF*: $\neg\ \Pi,s \models \llcorner False \lrcorner$

semConj: $\Pi,s \models \llcorner\bigwedge\lrcorner\ Fs\ =\ (\forall\ F \in set\ Fs.\ \Pi,s \models F)$

semImpl: $\Pi,s \models (A \Longrightarrow B) = (\Pi,s \models A \longrightarrow \Pi,s \models B)$

2.3 Safety Policy

Our framework expects the safety policy to be defined by means of the safety logic. We assume that for each position p in a program Π a safety formula *safeF* Π p expresses the conditions we want to hold whenever we reach p at runtime.

safeF:: *'prog* $\Rightarrow$ *'pos* $\Rightarrow$ *'form*

In addition we assume that a safety logic formula *initF* Π characterises all states under which a program Π can be started.

initF:: *'prog* $\Rightarrow$ *'form*

Now we can give a generic notion of safety for programs: A program is safe, if all states (p,m) it reaches from some initial state are safe. That is (p,m) satisfies the safety formula *safeF* Π p, which the platform dedicates to position p.

$$isSafe\ \Pi = (\forall p_0\ m_0\ p\ m.\ \Pi,(p_0,m_0) \models initF\ \Pi \wedge ((p_0,m_0),(p,m)) \in (effS\ \Pi)^* \longrightarrow \Pi,(p,m) \models safeF\ \Pi\ p)$$

2.4 The Verification Condition Generator

The VCG is the core of our PCC framework. It takes a program Π and generates a formula *vc* in the safety logic. If this formula is provable, then the program is safe at runtime, i.e., *isSafe* Π holds. The structure of the *vc* is determined by the program's control flow graph, which is a directed graph. Nodes denote program positions and can be marked with annotations. Edges point to successor positions and are marked with branch conditions. Fig. 2 shows a control flow graph. It can be seen as an abstraction of the assembly program E, which compares two variables X and Y and eventually sets X to the maximum of these two.

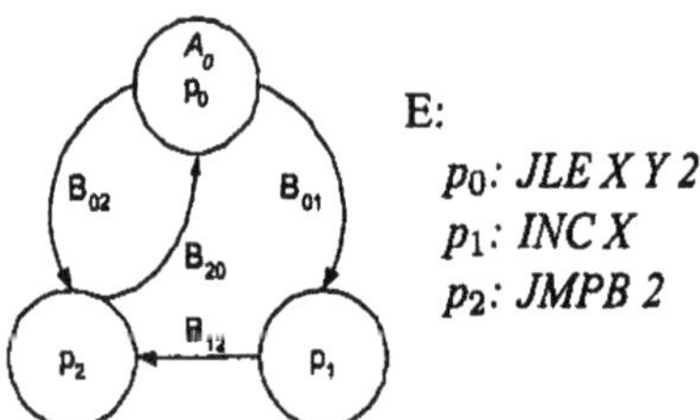

Figure 2. control flow graph

Parameters. To extract parts of the control flow graph and to express the semantics of programs by means of safety logic formulae and manipulations on these, our framework requires various parameter functions:

anF:: *'prog* $\Rightarrow$ (*'pos* $\Rightarrow$ *'form option*)
succsF:: *'prog* $\Rightarrow$ *'pos* $\Rightarrow$ (*'pos* $\times$ *'form*) *list*
wpF:: *'prog* $\Rightarrow$ *'pos* $\Rightarrow$ *'pos* $\Rightarrow$ (*'form* $\Rightarrow$ *'form*)
domC:: *'prog* $\Rightarrow$ *'pos list*   *ipc*:: *'prog* $\Rightarrow$ *'pos*

With *anF* we access the annotations; *anF* Π *p* returns *Some A* if position *p* in Π is annotated with *A*, otherwise *None*. Function *succsF* yields the edges of the control flow graph. Given a position *p* in a program Π the expression *succsF* Π *p* yields a list of pairs (p',B) where p' is a possible successor of *p* and *B* is the branch condition for the edge from *p* to p'. The branch condition *B* is a safety logic formula that characterises the situations when p' is accessible from *p*. For example if Π jumps from *p* to either p' or p'' depending on a condition *C*, then *succsF* Π *p* should return something like $[(p',C),(p'',\neg C)]$. To reflect the semantics within the safety logic we use *wpF*, a function for computing (weakest) preconditions. The formula *wpF* $\Pi\ p\ p'\ Q$ is expected to characterises those states (p,m) that have successor states (p',m') satisfying *Q*. The function *domC* is expected to yield the code domain of a program; this is a list of all positions with instructions. Finally *ipc* is used to determine the initial program counter.

Definition. The *vcg* constructs the verification condition out of so called inductive safety formulae *isafeF* Π *p*, which we generate individually for each position *p* in a program Π. We call a state (p,m) *inductively safe* if it satisfies the inductive safety formula for *p*, i.e., $\Pi,(p,m) \models$ *isafeF* $\Pi\ p$. Fig. 3 defines *isafeF* $\Pi\ p$. The wellformedness

$$
\begin{aligned}
& wf\ \Pi \longrightarrow \\
& isafeF\ \Pi\ p = if\ p \in set\ (domC\ \Pi) \\
& then\ \llcorner\bigwedge\lrcorner [safeF\ \Pi\ p]\ @ \\
& \qquad (case\ (anF\ \Pi\ p) \\
& \qquad of\ None \Rightarrow (map(\lambda(p',B).\ B \llcorner\Longrightarrow\lrcorner\ wpF\ \Pi\ p\ p'\ (isafeF\ \Pi\ p')) \\
& \qquad\qquad\qquad\qquad (succsF\ \Pi\ p)) \\
& \qquad \mid Some\ A \Rightarrow [A]) \\
& else\ \llcorner False \lrcorner
\end{aligned}
$$

Figure 3. Construction of inductive safety formulae

constraint *wf* Π ensures that every loop in Π has at least one annotation; otherwise the recursion of *isafeF* would not terminate.

When *p* lies outside the code domain *domC* Π we must never reach it at runtime. We express this formally by returning the unsatisfiable formula $\llcorner False \lrcorner$ in this case. For positions *p* within the code domain the inductive safety formula guarantees the safety formula *safeF* $\Pi\ p$. In addition, if there is an annotation *A* at *p*, we conjoin the safety formula with *A*. For example in program *E* from Fig. 2, we have the annotation A_0 at p_0. Hence, we obtain $\llcorner\bigwedge\lrcorner[safeF\ E\ p_0, A_0]$ for *isafeF* $E\ p_0$.

If *p* is not annotated, we take all successor positions p' together with their branch conditions *B* and recursively compute the inductive safety formulae *isafeF* $\Pi\ p'$. Using the *wpF* operator we construct a precondition *wpF* $\Pi\ p\ p'$ (*isafeF* $\Pi\ p'$). If this precondition holds for a state (p,m) with some successor (p',m'), then *isafeF* $\Pi\ p'$ holds for (p',m'). By constructing implications of the form $B \llcorner\Longrightarrow\lrcorner$ (*wpF* $\Pi\ p\ p'$ (*isafeF* Π p')), we design the inductive safety formula *isafeF* $\Pi\ p$ such that all states satisfying the branch condition *B* for a particular successor p' also have to satisfy the precondition above. These implications are constructed for all pairs (p',B) we get from *succsF* $\Pi\ p$. For example the positions p_1 and p_2 are not annotated in *E*. Below are their inductive safety formulae, where *safeF*, *wpF*, branch conditions and annotations are not expanded.

$$
\begin{aligned}
&isafeF\ E\ p_1 = \bigwedge [\ safeF\ E\ p_1, \\
&B_{12} \Longrightarrow wpF\ E\ p_1\ p_2\ (\bigwedge [\ safeF\ E\ p_2, B_{20} \Longrightarrow wpF\ E\ p_2\ p_0\ (\bigwedge [safeF\ E\ p_0, A_0])])]
\end{aligned}
$$

$$
isafeF\ E\ p_2 = \bigwedge [safeF\ E\ p_2, B_{20} \Longrightarrow wpF\ E\ p_2\ p_0\ (\bigwedge [safeF\ E\ p_0, A_0])]
$$

Executing a program Π with an inductively safe state (p,m) produces a trace of inductively safe states until we reach an annotated position p'. The state (p',m') under which we reach this position, is safe and satisfies the annotation. After this state the execution could become unsafe. However, this does not happen if all successor states of (p',m') are again inductively safe. This observation guides the construction of the verification condition *vcg* Π, which we show in Fig. 4. The verification condition *vcg*

$$
\begin{aligned}
vcg\ \Pi = \bigwedge ([initF\ \Pi \Longrightarrow (isafeF\ \Pi\ (ipc\ \Pi))] @ \\
& map(\lambda p_a.\ \bigwedge (map(\lambda (p',B).\ \bigwedge [isafeF\ \Pi\ p_a, B] \Longrightarrow \\
& \qquad\qquad wpF\ \Pi\ p_a\ p'\ (isafeF\ \Pi\ p')) \\
& \qquad (succsF\ \Pi\ p_a))) \\
& [p_a \in domC\ \Pi.\ anF\ \Pi\ p_a \neq None])
\end{aligned}
$$

Figure 4. Verification Condition Generator

Π demands two things: First, all initial states must satisfy the first inductive safety formula *isafeF* Π (*ipc* Π). Second, for every annotated position p_a the inductive safety formula *isafeF* $\Pi\ p_a$ and the branch condition B for all successors p' of p_a must guarantee the precondition *wpF* $\Pi\ p_a\ p'$ (*isafeF* $\Pi\ p'$). This ensures that the transitions out of annotated positions leads to inductively safe successor states. As discussed above, this proves the safety of Π. For example *vcg E* would have the following form:

$$
\begin{aligned}
&\bigwedge [initF\ E \Longrightarrow isafeF\ E\ p_0, \\
&\quad \bigwedge [isafeF\ E\ p_0, B_{01}] \Longrightarrow wpF\ E\ p_0\ p_1\ (isafeF\ E\ p_1), \\
&\quad \bigwedge [isafeF\ E\ p_0, B_{02}] \Longrightarrow wpF\ E\ p_0\ p_2\ (isafeF\ E\ p_2)]
\end{aligned}
$$

The first conjunct expresses that initial states are inductively safe. Note that *ipc* $E = p_0$. Since p_0 has two successors p_1 and p_2, which are accessible if B_{01} resp. B_{02} hold, we have two further conjuncts. One requires us to show that all states satisfying the inductive safety formula for p_0 and the branch condition B_{01} can only have successor states that satisfy the inductive safety formula for p_1. The other is analogous for p_2.

Soundness. The VCG is sound if for every well formed program Π a provable verification condition $\Pi \vdash vcg\ \Pi$ guarantees program safety, i.e., *isSafe* Π.

theorem $wf\ \Pi \wedge \Pi \vdash vcg\ \Pi \longrightarrow isSafe\ \Pi$

We have proven this theorem in Isabelle based on the requirements our PCC framework has on its parameter functions. In these assumptions, which we discuss in detail in the appendix, we require that *succsF* approximates the control flow, that *wpF* yields proper preconditions and that the safety logic is correct.

3 Framework Instantiation

In this section we instantiate the framework with a simple assembly language (SAL). We show how HOL can be instantiated as safety logic and demonstrate it on a safety policy that prohibits type errors and arithmetical overflows.

3.1 A Simple Assembly Language

SAL provides instructions for arithmetics, pointers, jumps, and procedures. We distinguish two kinds of addresses. Locations, which we model as natural numbers, identify memory cells, whereas positions identify places in a program. We denote positions as pairs (pn,i), where i is the relative position inside the procedure with name pn.

types $loc = nat, pname = nat, pos = pname \times nat$

datatype *instr* =*SET loc nat* | *ADD loc loc* | *SUB loc loc* | *MOV loc loc* |
JMPL loc loc nat | *JMPB nat* | *CALL loc pname* | *RET loc* | *HALT*

The instructions manipulate states of the form $(p,(m,e))$, where p denotes the program counter and (m,e) the system memory. Since pairs associate to the right in Isabelle/HOL we often leave out the inner brackets and write (p,m,e) to denote a state with program counter p, main memory m and environment e.

types $SALstate = pos \times (loc \Rightarrow tval) \times env$

The program counter stores the position of the instruction that is executed next. The main memory m, which maps locations to typed values, stores all the data a program works on. We have three kinds of values: Uninitialised values having type *ILLEGAL*, natural numbers *NAT n*, and positions *POS* (pn,i).

datatype *tval* = *ILLEGAL* | *NAT nat* | *POS pos*

The environment e tracks information about the run of a program. It contains a call stack *cs e*, which lists the memory contents and times under which currently active procedures have been called, and a history *h e*, which traces the values of program counters.

record $env = cs :: (nat \times (loc \Rightarrow tval))\ list$
$h :: pos\ list$

To update a field x in a record r with an expression E we write $r(\!|x{:=}E|\!)$, to access it we write $x\ r$. We use the environment like a history variable in Hoare Logic; it provides valuable information for annotations written as predicates on states. We can describe states by relating them to former states or refer to system resources,e.g., the length of *h e* is a time measure.
A SAL program is a list of procedures, which consist of a name *pname* and a list of possibly annotated instructions. Annotations are predicates on states.

types $SALform = SALstate \Rightarrow bool$
$SALprocedure = pname \times ((instr \times (SALform\ option))\ list)$
$SALprogram = SALprocedure\ list$

To access instructions we write *cmd* Π *p*, which gives us *Some ins* if Π has an instruction *ins* at *p*, or *None* otherwise.

3.2 SAL Semantics

SAL Instructions do the following: *SET X n* initialises *X* with *NAT n*. *ADD X Y* and *SUB X Y* add and subtract the values at *X* and *Y* storing the result in *X*. *MOV X Y* interprets the values of *X* and *Y* as addresses *a* and *b*; it copies the value at *a* to *b*. *JMPL X Y t* jumps t positions forward if the value at *X* is less than the value at *Y*; otherwise just one. *JMPB t* jumps *t* positions backwards. *CALL X pn* jumps into procedure *pn* leaving the return address in *X*. *RET X* leaves a procedure and returns to the address expected in *X*. Finally, *HALT* stops execution. In the instantiation of *effS* we formalise these effects.

$$effS\ \Pi = \{(s,s') \mid step\ \Pi\ s = Some\ s'\}$$

We do this with an auxiliary expression *step* Π (p,m,e), which yields *Some* (p',m',e') if the instruction *cmd* Π *p* exists and yields the successor state (p',m',e'). For example *ADD X Y* updates *X* with $(m\ X)\oplus(m\ Y)$, which is *ILLEGAL* if either *X* or *Y* contains no number or *NAT* $(a+b)$ if $m\ X = NAT\ a$ and $m\ Y = NAT\ b$. In addition the history is augmented with the current program counter. $cmd\ \Pi\ (pn,i) = Some\ ADD\ X\ Y \longrightarrow$
$step\ \Pi\ ((pn,i),m,e) =$
$= Some\ ((pn,i+1),m[X\mapsto(m\ X)\oplus(m\ Y)],e(\!|h:=(h\ e)@(pn,i)|\!))$

The other instructions can be handled in a similar fashion.

3.3 SAL Safety Policy

In initial states the program counter is $(0,0)$, the main memory only contains uninitialised values and the environment *e* has an empty history and a copy of the initial memory on its call stack.

$$initF\ \Pi = \lambda(p,m,e).\ p=(0,0) \land \forall X.\ m\ X=ILLEGAL \land h\ e=[] \land cs\ e=[(0,m)]$$

States are safe if the current instruction respects type safety and does not produce an arithmetic overflow, that is numerical results are less than *MAX*. Example:

$cmd\ \Pi\ p = Some\ (ADD\ X\ Y) \longrightarrow$
$safeF\ \Pi\ p = \lambda(p,m,e).\ (\exists n.\ (m\ X)\oplus(m\ Y)=NAT\ n \land n \leq MAX)$

For the sake of brevity we skip the remaining instructions.

3.4 SAL Safety Logic

By identifying assertions with HOL predicates, we instantiate a shallow embedded safety logic in Fig. 5. The valididy judgment $\models$ is directly defined by applying a predicate to a state. The argument Π is only there to be compatible with the generic signature of the framework. We define the provability judgment $\vdash$ directly by means of the semantics. This enables us to prove verification conditions with Isabelle/HOL's inference rules using various tactics and decision procedures as tools. Alternatively we could also use a deep embedding and define $\vdash$ with an explicit proof calculus, possibly tailored to the programming language and its safety policy. This means more effort, but could pay off in form of shorter proofs or higher degree of automation in proof search. However, this paper focuses on the framework and we rather keep the instantiation simple. According to $\vdash$ a formula F is provable iff it holds for all states

$$\begin{array}{ll} True_{\lrcorner} = \lambda s.\ True & \bigwedge_{\lrcorner} fs = \lambda s.\ \forall F \in set\,fs.\ F\ s \\ False_{\lrcorner} = \lambda s.\ False & A \Longrightarrow_{\lrcorner} B = \lambda s.\ A\ s \longrightarrow B\ s \\ \Pi,s \models F = F\ s & \Pi \vdash F = \forall s.\ s \in isafe_{\Box}\ \Pi \longrightarrow \Pi,s \models F \end{array}$$

Figure 5. Safety Logic for SAL.

in $isafe_{\Box}\ \Pi$. The inductively defined set $isafe_{\Box}\ \Pi$ contains all initial states and states that originate from a computation where all states are inductively safe.

$\Pi,(p,m) \models initF\ \Pi \longrightarrow (p,m) \in isafe_{\Box}\ \Pi$

$(p,m) \in isafe_{\Box}\ \Pi \wedge \Pi,(p,m) \models isafeF\ \Pi\ p \wedge \Pi,(p',m') \models isafeF\ \Pi\ p' \wedge$
$((p,m),(p',m')) \in effS\ \Pi \longrightarrow (p',m') \in isafe_{\Box}\ \Pi$

This constraint on states simplifies proofs and shortens annotations, because one can derive properties of a state from the fact that this state can be reached at runtime by only traversing inductively safe intermediate states.

3.5 Instantiating VCG helper functions

The instantiations of *anF*, *domC* and *ipc* are straightforward. More interesting are *wpF* and *succsF*. For the instantiation of *wpF* we use λ-abstraction to postpone substitution of formulae to the verification stage. Example:
$cmd\ \Pi\ p = Some\ (ADD\ X\ Y) \longrightarrow wpF\ \Pi\ p\ p'\ Q =$
$\lambda(p,m,e).\ let\ m'=m[X \mapsto (m\ X) \oplus (m\ Y)];\ e'=e(\!|h:=(h\ e)@p|\!)\ in\ Q\ (p',m',e')$

We compute the effect of $ADD\ X\ Y$ on some symbolic state (p,m,e) and demand that Q holds for the resulting state. Finally, we have a glimpse of the *succsF* instantiation. Here, we chose *JMPL* as example:

$cmd\ \Pi\ (pn,i) = Some\ (JMPL\ X\ Y\ t) \longrightarrow succsF\ \Pi\ (pn,i) =$
$[((pn,i+t),\lambda(p,m,e).\ \exists n\ n'.\ m\ X{=}NAT\ n \wedge m\ Y{=}NAT\ n' \wedge n{<}n' \wedge p{=}(pn,i)),$
$((pn,i+1),\lambda(p,m,e).\ \exists n\ n'.\ m\ X{=}NAT\ n \wedge m\ Y{=}NAT\ n' \wedge \neg n{<}n' \wedge p{=}(pn,i))]$

The constraint on the program counter $p{=}(pn,i)$ in the branch conditions helps to apply system invariants. These are properties that hold for all states in $isafe_{\Box}\ \Pi$ irrespective of Π. For example $\lambda((pn,i),m,e).\ cmd\ \Pi\ (pn,i) = Some\ (RET\ X) \longrightarrow (\exists k\ m'\ css.\ cs\ e = (k,m')\#css \wedge cmd\ \Pi\ (h\ e)!k = (CALL\ pn\ X))$ is a system invariant. It says that for the call time k of the current procedure the history $h\ e$ records the position of a *CALL* instruction.

3.6 Verifying Procedures

Procedure proofs should be modular. Code with procedure calls should only depend on these procedure's specifications (the annotations at entry and exit positions) and not on their code. For example $\lambda(p,m,e).\ m\ X = (\overleftarrow{m}\ e)\ X \oplus (NAT\ 1)$ might be the postcondition of a procedure that increments a location X. Here we use $\overleftarrow{m}\ e = snd\ (hd\ (cs\ e))$ to reconstruct the memory at call time.This procedure could be called from a position where X is $NAT\ 5$. The programmer expects that after the procedure X is $NAT\ 6$ and could write this into the annotation at the return point. In the verification condition we would have to prove that this follows from the procedure's postcondition. However $\lambda(p,m,e).\ m\ X = (\overleftarrow{m}\ e)\ X \oplus (NAT\ 1) \lfloor\Longrightarrow\rfloor (\lambda(p,m,e).\ m\ X = NAT\ 6)$ is not provable. The information that X has been $NAT\ 5$ at the procedures entry point is missing. We cannot add this information into the postcondition, otherwise we loose modularity. A way out is to pack call context dependent information into branch conditions, which *succsF* computes individually for each successor. If a procedure returns to $(pn',i'+1)$ and (pn',i') is annotated with Ac we can construct the branch condition $\lambda(p,m,e).\ Ac\ (\overleftarrow{pc}\ e, \overleftarrow{m}\ e, \overleftarrow{e}\ e)$, which claims that $(\overleftarrow{pc}\ e, \overleftarrow{m}\ e, \overleftarrow{e}\ e)$, the state at call time, satisfies the annotation Ac. Note that $\overleftarrow{pc}$ and $\overleftarrow{e}$, the position and environment at call time, can be defined analogously to $\overleftarrow{m}$. Since branch conditions are added to inductive safety formulas, we now obtain a provable formula: $(\lfloor\bigwedge\rfloor [\lambda(p,m,e).\ m\ X = (\overleftarrow{m}\ e)\ X \oplus (NAT\ 1)\ ,\ \lambda(p,m,e).\ (\overleftarrow{m}\ e)\ X = NAT\ 5]) \lfloor\Longrightarrow\rfloor (\lambda\ (p,m,e).\ m\ X = NAT\ 6)$. Call context dependent branch conditions involve some technicalities for the definition and verification of *succsF*. However, they fit neatly into our concept of a generic VCG. We achieve modular procedure proofs although our VCG has no notion of procedures at all.

4 Case Study: Overflow Detection

4.1 Motivating Example for Overflow Detection

The exemplary safety policy expressed the definition of *safeF* in §3.3 has two aspects: First, type safety is needed as a general property to ensure that SAL programs never get stuck. Second, the safety formula demands that the result of arithmetic operations does not exceed *MAX*, thus preventing overflows. Consider the following program fragment: *[CALL P CHECK, ADD B C]*

It might be part of an application that tries to add a credit stored as a natural number in memory location C to a balance in B—for example as part of a load transaction of a smart card purse. Before executing the addition, a procedure *CHECK* is called to ensure that the new balance in B is less than *MAX*; if it does, the credit in C will be set to zero and thus the balance remains the same as before. Special care has to be taken in the implementation of *CHECK*:

[SET M MAX, SET H 0, ADD H B, ADD H C, JMPL H M 2, SET C 0, RET P]

M represents the maximum balance considered for the application. H should contain $B + C$ after the second *ADD* statement. If the check $B + C < M$ fails, the credit is set to zero; otherwise it is left unchanged. Even this simple example contains an implementation flaw: there could be an overflow in H. And the flaw is not merely theoretical: in the case of a silent overflow as in Java it would lead to debiting the purse instead of crediting.

4.2 Annotated SAL Program

Fig. 6 shows the corrected and annotated version of our example. The main procedure and *CHECK* are now identified with 0 and 1. For better readability we write instruction/annotation pairs of the form $(ins, None)$ as just *ins* and $(ins, Some\ A)$ as $\{A\}\ ins$.

$$
\begin{aligned}
&OD = [(0,[SET\ B\ b_0,\ SET\ C\ c_0,\\
&\qquad \{\lambda(p,m,e).\ m\ B = NAT\ b_0 \wedge m\ C = NAT\ c_0\}\\
&\qquad CALL\ P\ 1,\\
&\qquad \{\lambda(p,m,e).\ m\ B = NAT\ b_0 \wedge (\exists c.\ m\ C = NAT\ c \wedge\\
&\qquad\qquad c = (if\ b_0 + c_0 < MAX\ then\ c_0\ else\ 0))\}\\
&\qquad ADD\ B\ C,\ HALT\ ])\\
&\quad (1,[\ \{\lambda(p,m,e).\ m\ P = POS\ (incA\ (\overleftarrow{pc}\ e)) \wedge (\exists b.\ m\ B = NAT\ b) \wedge\\
&\qquad\qquad (\exists c.\ m\ C = NAT\ c) \wedge (\forall X.\ X \neq P \longrightarrow m\ X = \overleftarrow{m}\ e\ X)\}\\
&\qquad SET\ M\ MAX,\ SUB\ M\ C,\ JMPL\ B\ M\ 2,\ SET\ C\ 0,\\
&\qquad \{\lambda(p,m,e).\ (\forall X.\ X \neq C \wedge X \neq M \wedge X \neq P \longrightarrow m\ X = \overleftarrow{m}\ e\ X) \wedge\\
&\qquad\qquad (\exists b\ c\ c'.\ m\ B = NAT\ b\ \wedge m\ C = NAT\ c \wedge \overleftarrow{m}\ e\ C = NAT\ c' \wedge\\
&\qquad\qquad c = (if\ b + c' < MAX\ then\ c'\ else\ 0))\}\\
&\qquad RET\ P\ ])]
\end{aligned}
$$

Figure 6. Corrected and annotated program OD.

Before execution of *CALL P 1*, the memory positions *B* and *C* contain the numbers b_0 and c_0. The annotation for *ADD B C* states that the value of *C* may have changed according to the condition $b_0 + c_0 < MAX$.
Inside the *CHECK* procedure we first set the memory location *M* to the maximum balance. The annotation states that location *P* stores the proper return address for the procedure: *incA* ($\overleftarrow{pc}$ *e*) represents the program counter of the calling procedure incremented by one. Furthermore the annotation states that there are natural numbers in both *B* and *C*, and that all memory locations except *P* are the same as in the caller. The following statements require no annotations, only the exit point of the procedure *RET P* does: it states that all values except for those in *C*, *M*, and *P* are unchanged, that there are natural numbers in both *B* and *C*, and that the new value of *C* will be changed to zero if the new balance exceeds the maximum balance.

4.3 Verification Condition

In Fig. 7 we show the part of the verification condition that is generated for the return from procedure *CHECK*. In general we get as many parts (conjuncts) as there are paths between annotated positions. That means the size of verification conditions is linear to the number of positions if all branch positions are annotated. The example demonstrates again how the VCG works. On the top-level the conditions for the annotated program positions are conjoined; the fragment refers to position p=(*1*,*4*) of our program, *1* stands for the procedure *CHECK* and *4* for the line number with the statement *RET P*. There is only one successor p'=(*0*,*2*), which is the statement *ADD B C*. Therefore the conjunction over the list of all successors collapses to one element. The verification condition fragment shown in Fig. 7 results from the expression $\bigwedge$[*isafeF OD* (*1*,*4*), *B*] $\Longrightarrow$ *wpF OD* (*1*,*4*) (*0*,*2*) (*isafeF OD* (*0*,*2*)) where *B* is the branch condition of *succsF OD* (*1*,*4*). Numbers 1–4 in Fig. 7 correspond to the assumption of the implication, numbers 5–6 to the conclusion. *isafeF OD* (*1*,*4*) results in $\bigwedge$[*safeF OD* (*1*,*4*), *Ae*] (compare Fig. 3), where *safeF OD* (*1*,*4*) corresponds to 1 and the annotation *Ae*, e.g., *anF OD* (*1*,*4*) = *Some Ae*, corresponds to 2. The branch

$$
\begin{array}{ll}
\bigwedge [& \\
1 & \bigwedge [\ \lambda(p,m,e).\ \exists pn'\,i'.\ m\ P = POS\ (pn', i'+1)\ \wedge \\
& \quad (\exists k\ m'\ cl\ css.\ cs\ e = (k, m')\#cl\#css \wedge (pn', i') = (h\ e)!k), \\
2 & \quad \lambda(p,m,e).\ (\forall X.\ X \neq C \wedge X \neq M \wedge X \neq P \longrightarrow m\ X = \overleftarrow{m}\ e\ X)\ \wedge \\
& \quad (\exists b\ c\ c'.\ m\ B = NAT\ b \wedge m\ C = NAT\ c \wedge \overleftarrow{m}\ e\ C = NAT\ c' \wedge \\
& \quad c = if\ b + c' < MAX\ then\ c'\ else\ 0], \\
3 & \bigwedge [\ \lambda(p,m,e).\ m\ P = POS\ (0,2) \wedge p{=}(1,4), \\
4 & \quad \lambda(p,m,e).((\lambda(p,m,e).\ m\ B = NAT\ b_0 \wedge m\ C = NAT\ c_0)\ (\overleftarrow{pc}\ e, \overleftarrow{m}\ e, \overleftarrow{e}\ e))] \\
] & \\
5 \Longrightarrow & \bigwedge [\ \lambda(p,m,e).\ \exists n.\ (m\ B) \oplus (m\ C) = NAT\ n \wedge n \leq MAX, \\
6 & \quad \lambda(p,m,e).\ m\ B = NAT\ b_0 \wedge \exists c.\ m\ C = NAT\ c\ \wedge \\
& \quad c = if\ b + c_0 < MAX\ then\ c_0\ else\ 0]
\end{array}
$$

Figure 7. **Fragment of the verification condition.**

condition B for $RET\ P$ appears in 3 and 4, and consists of $\bigwedge[\lambda\ (p,m,e).\ m\ P = POS\ (0,2) \wedge p{=}(1,4), \lambda(p,m,e).\ Ac\ (\overleftarrow{pc}\ e, \overleftarrow{m}\ e, \overleftarrow{e}\ e)]$ where $\lambda(p,m,e).\ Ac\ (\overleftarrow{pc}\ e, \overleftarrow{m}\ e, \overleftarrow{e}\ e)$ is the annotation of the call instruction, e.g., $anF\ OD\ (0,1) = Some\ Ac$, applied to the reconstructed state at the moment of the call, and P is the memory location of the return address. This shows again how the environment e enables us to reconstruct the call state $(\overleftarrow{pc}\ e, \overleftarrow{m}\ e, \overleftarrow{e}\ e)$ and how to transfer the information Ac of the call point to the return point. Note that this context-specific information is encoded into the branch condition B, which *succsF* computes individually for each successor. The annotation at the procedure's return point does not refer to a particular call point. Hence, the procedure and its verification are modular. The conclusion of the verification condition consists of the safety condition for *ADD* in 5 and its annotation in 6; together they form *isafeF OD (0,2)*.

4.4 Code Producer and Consumer

The code producer can write annotated programs in Isabelle. To obtain the verification condition one can generate and execute ML code for the VCG [5] or use the simplifier to evaluate *vcg* Π. Proving the verification condition is supported by powerful proof tools and a rich collection of HOL theorems. For the example in Fig. 6 the simplifier and a decision procedure for presburger arithmetic suffice to prove the verification condition. For the client side Isabelle provides (compressed) proof terms and a proof checker [4]. Proofs are encoded as λ terms having a type that corresponds to the theorem they prove (Curry Howard Isomorphism). Proof Checking becomes a type checking problem, which can be handled by a small trusted program.

5 Conclusion

Our framework can be instantiated to various programming languages, safety policies, and safety logics. As long as the requirements of the framework are satisfied, one can directly apply our generic VCG and rely on its machine checked soundness proof. In our instantiation to SAL we show how HOL can be embedded as safety logic and how this can be used to verify the absence of arithmetic overflows. Since HOL is very expressive, formulating complex assertions or safety policies is possible. Isabelle's code generator gives us an executable version of the VCG. Using the built in tools for proof search, proof terms and proof checking we can simulate producer and client activities. Before one embarks on a particular PCC implementation, one can build a prototype in our framework and prove the soundness of the safety logic. On our web page [19] we present more complex examples and instantiations of our framework. These include programs with pointer arithmetic or recursive procedures and safety policies about time and memory consumption of programs. Moreover we have instantiated a safety logic based on first order arithmetic in form of a deep embedding [18]. There, formulae are modelled as HOL datatype and can by analysed by other HOL functions. This enables us to optimise verification conditions after/during their construction. By now, we also have instantiated the PCC framework to a (downsized) version of the Java Virtual Machine [17]. For this we did not have to change the framework, thus we believe that our framework's formalisation and its requirements are reasonable, even for real life platforms.

References

[1] Appel, A. W. (2001). Foundational proof-carrying code. In *16th Annual IEEE Symposium on Logic in Computer Science (LICS '01)*, pages 247–258.

[2] Appel, A. W. and Felty, A. P. (2000). A semantic model of types and machine instructions for proof-carrying code. In *27th ACM SIGPLAN-SIGACT Symposium on Principles of Programming Languages (POPL '00)*, pages 243–253.

[3] Aspinall, D., Beringer, L., Hofmann, M., Loidl, H.W. (2003) A Resource-aware Program Logic for a JVM-like Language In Trends in Functional Programming, editor: S. Gilmore, Edinburgh

[4] Berghofer, S. and Nipkow, T. (2000). Proof terms for simply typed higher order logic. In *Theorem Proving in Higher Order Logics*, Springer LNCS vol. 1869, editors: J. Harrison, M. Aagaard

[5] Berghofer (2003). Program Extraction in simply-typed Higher Order Logic. In *Types for Proofs and Programs, International Workshop, (TYPES 2002)*, Springer LNCS, editors: H. Geuvers, F. Wiedijk

[6] Colby, C., Lee, P., Necula, G. C., Blau, F., Plesko, M., and Cline, K. (2000). A certifying compiler for Java. In *Proc. ACM SIGPLAN conf. Programming Language Design and Implementation*, pages 95–107.

[7] Hamid, N., Shao, Z., Trifonov, V., Monnier, S., and Ni, Z. (2002). A syntactic approach to foundational proof-carrying code. In *Proc. 17th IEEE Symp. Logic in Computer Science*, pages 89–100.

[8] Klein, G. (2003). *Verified Java Bytecode Verification*. PhD thesis, Institut für Informatik, Technische Universität München.

[9] League, C., Shao, Z., and Trifonov, V. (2002). Precision in practice: A type-preserving Java compiler. Technical Report YALEU/DCS/TR-1223, Department of Computer Science, Yale University.

[10] Morrisett, G., Walker, D., Crary, K., and Glew, N. (1998). From system F to typed assembly language. In *Proc. 25th ACM Symp. Principles of Programming Languages*, pages 85–97. ACM Press.

[11] Necula, G. C. (1997). Proof-carrying code. In *Proc. 24th ACM Symp. Principles of Programming Languages*, pages 106–119. ACM Press.

[12] Necula, G. C. (1998). *Compiling with Proofs*. PhD thesis, Carnegie Mellon University.

[13] Necula, G. C. and Lee, P. (2000). Proof generation in the touchstone theorem prover. In McAllester, D., editor, *Automated Deduction — CADE-17*, volume 1831 of *Lect. Notes in Comp. Sci.*, pages 25–44. Springer-Verlag.

[14] Necula, G. C. and Schneck, R. R. (2002). A gradual approach to a more trustworthy, yet scalable, proof-carrying code. In Voronkov, A., editor, *Proc.CADE-18, 18th International Conference on Automated Deduction, Copenhagen, Denmark*, volume 2392 of *Lect. Notes in Comp. Sci.*, pages 47–62. Springer-Verlag.

[15] Necula, G. C. and Schneck, R. R. (2003). A sound framework for untrustred verification-condition generators. In *Proc. IEEE Symposium on Logic in Computer Science (LICS03)*, pages 248–260.

[16] Nipkow, T., Paulson, L. C., and Wenzel, M. (2002). *Isabelle/HOL – A Proof Assistant for Higher-Order Logic*, volume 2283 of *Lect. Notes in Comp. Sci.* Springer.

[17] Klein, G. and Nipkow, T. (2004) A Machine-Checked Model for a Java-Like Language, Virtual Machine and Compiler *Technical Report*, National ICT Australia, Sydney

[18] Wildmoser, M. and Nipkow, T. (2004) Certifying machine code safety: shallow versus deep embedding. *TPHOLs 2004*

[19] VeryPCC website in Munich (2004),`http://isabelle.in.tum.de/verypcc/`.

Appendix: Requirements

Our PCC framework makes some assumptions on the functions it takes as parameters (cf. p.4). Based on these assumptions we prove the generic VCG correct. It is the task of the framework instantiator to make sure that the implementations of the parameter functions satisfy the requirements listed below. We have proven in Isabelle that these requirements hold for our instantiation to SAL. Hence, we have a PCC system for SAL with a mechanically verified trusted code base. Note that none of the requirements involves the safety policy *safeF*. Hence it is very easy to instantiate our framework to different safety policies.

Assumption *correctWpF* ensures that *wpF* computes proper preconditions. That is for every state (p,m) having a successor state (p',m'), we require that Q holds for (p',m') whenever $wpF\ \Pi\ p\ p'\ Q$ holds for (p,m). We require this property only for wellformed programs Π and for states in $isafe_\Box\ \Pi$, a set of states we introduce in §3.4.

assumption *correctWpF*:
$wf\ \Pi \wedge\ (p,m) \in isafe_\Box\ \Pi \wedge ((p,m),(p',m')) \in (effS\ \Pi) \wedge$
$\Pi,(p,m) \models (wpF\ \Pi\ p\ p'\ Q) \longrightarrow \Pi,(p',m') \models Q$

Although the set $isafe_\Box\ \Pi$ seems to complicate matters at a first sight, it simplifies the instantiator's job of proving the requirements. Only initial states and safe states originating from a safe execution must be considered. We can conclude information about these states from inductive safety formulae of previous states.

Assumption *correctIpc* demands that *ipc* and *initF* fit together:

assumption *correctIpc*: $\Pi,(p,m) \models \mathit{initF}\ \Pi \longrightarrow p = \mathit{ipc}\ \Pi$

In *succsF−complete* we assume that *succsF* covers all transitions of *effS* and yields branch conditions that hold whenever a particular transition is accessible. Again, this is only required for wellformed programs and states in $\mathit{isafe}_{\Box}\ \Pi$.

assumption *succsF-complete*:
$\mathit{wf}\ \Pi \wedge (p,m) \in \mathit{isafe}_{\Box}\ \Pi \wedge ((p,m),(p',m')) \in \mathit{effS}\ \Pi$
$\longrightarrow (\exists\ B.\ (p',B) \in \mathit{set}\ (\mathit{succsF}\ \Pi\ p) \wedge \Pi,(p,m) \models B)$

In *correctSafetyLogic* the safety logic's provability judgement is constrained such that provable formulae are guaranteed to hold for states in $\mathit{isafe}_{\Box}$.

assumption *correctSafetyLogic*:
$\Pi \vdash f \wedge (p,m) \in \mathit{isafe}_{\Box}\ \Pi \longrightarrow \Pi,(p,m) \models f$

Based on these assumptions we can prove that our VCG is sound. A provable verification condition gurantess safety of a program at runtime.

theorem *vcg-soundness*:
$[\![\ \mathit{wf}\ \Pi;\ \Pi \vdash \mathit{vcg}\ \Pi\ ]\!] \Longrightarrow \mathit{isSafe}\ \Pi$

CONTRACT ORIENTED DEVELOPMENT OF COMPONENT SOFTWARE*

Zhiming Liu[1,3], He Jifeng[1,4], and Xiaoshan Li[2]

[1] *International Institute for Software Technology, The United Nations University, Macao SAR, China*
lzm@iist.unu.edu, hjf@iist.unu.edu

[2] *Faculty of Science and Technology, The University of Macau, Macau*
xsl@umac.mo

[3] *Department of Computer Science, The University of Leicester, U.K.*

[4] *East China Normal University, Shanghai, China*

Abstract We present a model for component software. We describe how components are specified at the interface level, design level and how they are composed. From its external view, a component consists a set of interfaces, *provided* to or *required* from its environment. From its internal view, a component is an executable code that can be coupled with other components via its interfaces. The developer has to ensure that the specification of a component is met by its design and implementation. We also combine component-based and object-oriented techniques in component-based software development.

Keywords: Component, Contract, Interface, Object-Orientation, Refinement

1 Introduction

Using components to build and maintain software systems is not a new idea. However, it is today's growing complexity of these systems that forces us to turn this idea into practice [Szyperski, 2002, Cheesman and Daniels, 2001, Heineman and Councill, 2001]. While component technologies such as COM, CORBA, and Enterprise JavaBeans are widely used, there is so far no agreement on standard technologies for designing and creating components, nor on methods for composing them. Finding appropriate formal approaches for specifying components, the architectures for composing them, and the methods for component-based software construction, is correspondingly challenging. In this paper, we consider a contract-oriented approach to the specification, design and composition of components. Component specification is

*This work is partly supported by the research grant 02104 MoE and the 973 project 2002CB312000 of MoST of P.R.China.

essential as it is impossible to manage change, substitution and composition of components if components have not been properly specified.

When we specify a component, it is important to separate different views about the component. From its user's (i.e. external) point of view, a component P consists a set of *provided services* [Szyperski, 2002]. The syntactic specification of the provided services is described by an interface, defining the operations that the component provides with their signatures are. This is also called the *syntactic specification* of a component, such as COM and CORBA that use IDL, and JavaBeans that uses Java Programming Language to specify component interfaces. Such a syntactic specification of a component does not provide any information about the effect, i.e. the *functionality* of invoking an operation of a component or the *behavior*, i.e. the temporal order of the interface operations, of the component.

For the functional specification of the operations in an interface, it is however necessary to know the conceptual state of the component. Consequently, the interface specification contains a so-called *information model* [Cheesman and Daniels, 2001, Filipe, 2002]. In the context of such a model, we specify an operation *op* by a *design* $p(x) \vdash Q(x, x')$ in Hoare and He's Unifying Theories of Programming (UTP) [Hoare and He, 1998] that is seen as a *contract* between the component and its client [Cheesman and Daniels, 2001, Heineman and Councill, 2001]. This definition of a *contract* also agrees with that of [Meyer, 1992, Meyer, 1997]. To use the service *op*, a client has to ensure the pre-condition $p(x)$, and when this is true the component must guarantee the post-condition Q. We then define a *contract* of an interface by associating the interface with a set of *features* that we will call *fields* and assigning each a design $MSpec(op)$ to each interface operation *op*. The types of the fields are given in a *data/class model*.

The contract for the provided interface of a component allows the user to check whether the component provides the services required by other components in the system, without the need to know the design and implementation of the component. It also commits (or requires) the designers of the component who have to design the component's provided services. A designer of the component under consideration (*CuC*) may decide to use services provided by other components. These services are called *required services* [Szyperski, 2002] of CuC. Components that provide the required services of CuC can be built by another team or bought as a component-off-the-self (COTS). To use a component to assemble a system, one needs to know the specifications of both its provided and required services.

We will specify the design of a component by giving each operation *op* in the provided interface a program specification text $MImpl(op)$ in the object-oriented specification language (OOL) defined in [Liu et al., 2004c]. In $MImpl(op)$, calls to operations in a required interface are allowed. With the *refinement calculus of object-oriented designs* (RCOOD) in OOL [He et al., 2002, Liu et al., 2004b], we can verify whether $MImpl(op)$ refines the specification of *op* given in a contract of the provided interface. The *verifier* of a component needs to know the contracts of the provided interfaces, the contracts of the required interfaces, and the specification text for each operation *op* of the provided interface. We can thus understand a component as a relation between contracts of the required interfaces and contracts of the provided interface: given a contract for each required interface, we can calculate a design of an op from $MImpl(op)$ and check whether it conforms to the specification $MSpec(op)$ defined by the contract of the provided interface. A design of a component can be further refined into an implementation by refining the data/class model and then operation specifications $MImpl(op)$.

A component assumes an architectural context defined by its interfaces. We *connect* or *compose* two components P_1 and P_2 by linking the operations in the provided interface of one component to the matching operations of a required interface of another. For this, we have to check whether the provided interface of one component P_1 contains the operations of a required interface of another component P_2, and whether the contract of the provided interface of P_1 meets the contract of the required interface of P_2. If P_1 and P_2 match well, the composition $P_1||P_2$ forms another component. The provided interface of $P_1||P_2$ is the *merge* of the provided interfaces of P_1 and P_2. The required interfaces of $P_1||P_2$ are the union of required interfaces of P_1 and P_2, excluding (*by hiding*) the matched interfaces of P_1 and P_2. For defining composition, interfaces can be *hidden* and *renamed.*

A component is also replaceable, meaning that the developer can replace one component with another, may be *better*, as long as the new one provides and requests the same services. An component is better than another if it can provide more services, i.e. the contracts for its provided interfaces refine those of the other, with the same required services. Component replaceability is based on the notion of *component refinement.*

As a starting point, we only deal with the functional/service specification of components and deals with functional compatibility. In Section 5, we give a discussion on the alternative ways to deal with behavioral specification and compatibility. This paper is not about development processes either. However, we will give an overview on how the model can be used in a component-based development together with an object-oriented implementation.

2 Interfaces

An *interface* I is a set of *operation* (or *method*) *signatures*, of the form $op(\mathbf{in} : \underline{U}\ \underline{x}, \mathbf{out} : \underline{V}\ \underline{y}, \mathbf{inout} : \underline{W}\ \underline{z})$, where op is the *name* of the operation, $\underline{x}$ are the *value* parameters of types $\underline{U}$, $\underline{y}$ the *result* parameters of types $\underline{V}$, and $\underline{z}$ the value-result parameters of types $\underline{W}$. An interface can be specified as a family of operation signatures in the following format:

$$
\begin{array}{lll}
\mathbf{Interface}\ I\ \{ & & \\
& \mathbf{Method}: & op_1(\mathbf{in} : \underline{U}_1\ \underline{x}_1, \mathbf{out} : \underline{V}_1\ \underline{y}_1, \mathbf{inout} : \underline{W}_1\ \underline{z}_1); \\
& & \ldots; \\
& & op_k(\mathbf{in} : \underline{U}_k\ \underline{x}_k, \mathbf{out} : \underline{V}_k\ \underline{y}_k, \mathbf{inout} : \underline{W}_1\ \underline{z}_k) \\
\} & &
\end{array}
$$

Figure 1 shows the ParcelCall system in [Filipe, 2002] that has three main components:

- a *Mobile Logistic Server* (MLS): is an exchange point or a transport unit (container, trailer, freight wagon, etc). It always knows its current location via the GPS satellite positioning system.

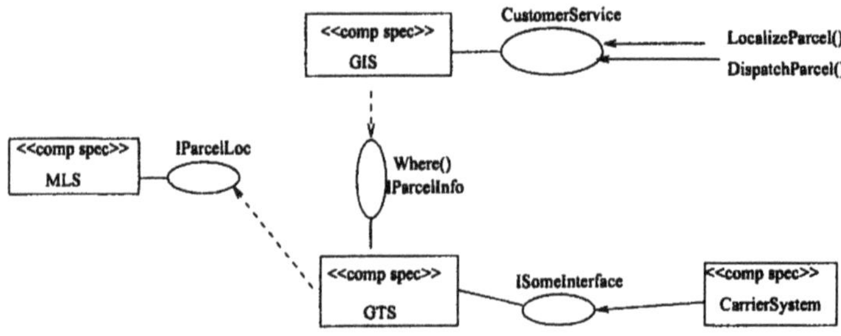

Figure 1. Architecture of ParcelCall

- a *Goods Tracing Server* (GTS): keeps track of all the parcels registered in the ParcelCall system. GTS is also the component which is integrated with the legacy systems of transport or logistic companies.
- a *Goods Information Server* (GIS): is the component which interacts with the customers and provides the authorized customers the current location of their parcel, keeps them informed in case of delivery delays, etc.

In Figure 1, UML notation for interfaces and components is used.The provided interface of GIS component will establish communication with the customer: for instance a customer can request for finding the current location of a parcel via $LocateParcel$. The specification of this interface can be described as follows, where we use $\mathbb{P}PS$ to denote the powerset of a set S

> **Interface** *CustomerService* {
> **Method** : *LocateParcel*(**in** : *PName pId*, *CName sId*), **out** : *Position location*);
> *DispatchParcel*(**in** : *PName pId*, *CName sId*)}

Merge interfaces

It is often the case that there are a number of components, each providing a part of the operations in the required interface of another component. We thus need to *merge* these components to provide one single interface to match the interface required by the other component.

Two interfaces I_1 and I_2 are *composable* provided that every operation name in both I_1 and I_2 must be assigned the same signature. This condition is not too restrictive as to use a component designed for an application in another or specialize a generic component for a special application, renaming or adding a *connector* component [Allen and Garlan, 1997, Selic, 1998] can be used to *customize* the component.

DEFINITION 1 Let $\{I_k : \mid k \in K\}$ be a finite family of composable interfaces. Their **merge** $\uplus_{k\in K} I_k$ is defined by $\uplus_{k\in K} I_k \stackrel{def}{=} \cup_{k\in K} I_k$.

3 Contracts

Only a *syntactic specification* of its interface is not enough for the use or the design of a component. We also need to specify the effect, i.e. the *functionality*, of invoking an interface operation. This requires one to associate the interface to a *conceptual state space*, and a specification of how the states are changed by the operation under certain pre-conditions. We view such a *functional specification* of an interface as a contract between the component *client* and the component *developer*. The contract is the specification of the component that the developer has to implement. The contract is also between a user of the component and a provider of an implementation of the interface: the component has to provide the services promised by the specification *provided* that the user uses the component according to the precondition [Szyperski, 2002].

Conceptual model

To define the conceptual state space of a contract for an interface and the types for the parameters of the interface operations, we assume that a type is either a primitive data type (such as the integers, the Booleans, etc.) or a class of objects (such as a Java class). This allows our framework to support both imperative and object-oriented programming in the design of a component.

The type definitions in fact form a *conceptual class diagram* [Liu et al., 2003, Liu et al., 2004c] that is a UML class diagram in which the classes have **no** methods and the associations have **no** direction of visibility or navigation. Figure 2 is an example of a conceptual model for a library system. A UML class diagram can be specified by a class declaration section of an object-oriented program in the object-oriented specification language (OOL) developed in [Liu et al., 2004b, Liu et al., 2004c] of the form

$$class_1; class_2; \ldots; class_n$$

where each $class_i$ is of the form

Class N **extends** M {
  public $U_1\, u_1, \ldots, U_k\, u_k$;
  }

where

- N and M are distinct names of classes, and M is called the direct superclass of N.

- The **public** declaration declares the public attributes of the class and their types. Initial values are set when an object is created.

Notice that we do not declare methods for the classes as they will be given in the implementation of the component. Also, we need to declare the public fields as functional specification of operations directly refer to them. In the design model of a component, methods are introduced to realize the specification and then data encapsulation can be applied to make the fields private or protected.

Consider the simple conceptual class diagram in Figure 2 as an example. It is specified as

> **Class** Lib $\{String\ name, String\ address\}$;
> **Class** Publication $\{String\ isbn, String\ title, String\ author\}$;
> **Class** Copy $\{String\ id, String\ location\}$;
> **Class** Own $\{Lib\ lib, Publication\ p\}$; // * Association
> **Class** Contain $\{Publication\ p, Copy\ c\}$; // * Association

Please see [Liu et al., 2003, Liu et al., 2004b] for details on the formalization of UML, and [Liu et al., 2004c] for the semantics of class declarations.

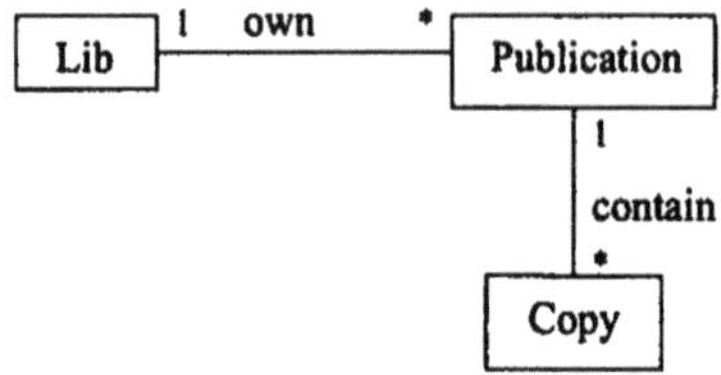

Figure 2. A conceptual class diagram

Contract

Given an interface I, a conceptual model M, a set A of variable declarations of the form $T\ x$ where T is either a primitive type or a class declared in M, called the type of x, we define the alphabet α as the union of sets of the variables, the input and output parameters of the operations of I.

$$
\begin{aligned}
in\alpha &\stackrel{def}{=} A \cup \{x \in \underline{x} \cup \underline{z} \mid op(\mathbf{in} : \underline{U}\ \underline{x}, \mathbf{out} : \underline{V}\ \underline{y}, \mathbf{inout} : \underline{W}\ \underline{z}) \in I\} \\
out\alpha &\stackrel{def}{=} A \cup \{y \in \underline{y} \cup \underline{z} \mid op(\mathbf{in} : \underline{U}\ \underline{x}, \mathbf{out} : \underline{V}\ \underline{y}, \mathbf{inout} : \underline{W}\ \underline{z}) \in I\} \\
out\alpha' &\stackrel{def}{=} \{x' \mid x \in out\alpha\}, \quad \alpha \stackrel{def}{=} in\alpha \cup out\alpha
\end{aligned}
$$

A *conceptual state* for $\langle I, M\rangle$ is a well-typed mapping from the variables α to their value spaces. It is in fact a UML object diagram of M plus values of variables in $out\alpha$ of primitive types that is a snapshot of the models consisting the current objects of the classes and links by the associations among these objects, as well as the values of variables of primitive types. A change of such a state is carried out by creating or destroying existing objects, forming or breaking links among objects, modifying values of object attributes, and changing values of some variables of primitive types. A *specification* of an operation $op(\mathbf{in} : \underline{U}\ \underline{x}, \mathbf{out} : \underline{V}\ \underline{y}, \mathbf{inout} : \underline{W}\ \underline{z})$ in an alphabet α is a *framed design* $\beta : D$ where

- β, a subset of $in\alpha$, is the *frame* of D containing the variables to be changed by D.
- $D = (b \vdash Q)$ is a design [Hoare and He, 1998] describing the behavior of the method:

$$\beta : (b \vdash Q) \stackrel{def}{=} b \wedge ok \Rightarrow Q \wedge ok' \wedge \bigwedge_{x \in in\alpha \setminus \beta}(x' = x)$$

Predicate b is the assumption on the variables and input parameters which the method can rely on when it is activated, while predicate Q is the commitment which must be true when the execution terminates. ok and ok' are used to describe the termination behavior of op. We will omit the frames in the examples by assuming that a design only changes those variables whose primed versions appear are mentioned.

The variables of $in\alpha$ are used to record the values of the variables in A and input parameters $\underline{x}$ on the activation of op, and the variables of $out\alpha$ the values of the corresponding variables and outgoing parameters $\underline{y}$ on the termination of a method. For the conceptual model in Figure 2, let

$$A \stackrel{def}{=} \{\mathbb{P}Publication\ P, \mathbb{P}Copy\ Cp, \mathbb{P}Contain\ con, Lib\ lib, \mathbb{P}Own\ own\}$$

where $\mathbb{P}S$ is the power set of S. The operation $RecordCopy()$ that records a new copy of a given publication can be specified as

$$\begin{array}{lll} \{con, Cp\}: & & \exists p \in P.p.isbn = pid \wedge < lib, p > \in own \wedge \neg \exists c \in Cp.c.id = cid \vdash \\ & & \exists c' \in Cp'.c'.id = cid \wedge \exists p \in P.p.isbn = pid \\ & \wedge & con' = con \cup \{< p, c' >\} \end{array}$$

DEFINITION 2 A **contract** is a tuple $C = (I, M, A, MSpec, Init)$ where I is an interface, M is a conceptual model, A is a set of variables, called the *fields* of C, whose types are either declared in M or as primitive types, and *MSpec* a function that maps each operation of I to a specification, and *Init* an initial condition that defines some values to fields as their initial values.

If no field is of an object type, we will omit the conceptual model from the specification of a contract.

In modular programming, a primitive contract is a specification of a module that defines the behavior of the operations in its interface. However, later we will see that contracts can be *merged* to form another contract and this corresponds to the merge of a number of modules. In object-orient programming, a primitive contract specifies an initialized class, i.e. an object, whose public methods are operations in the interface. This class *wraps* the classes in the conceptual model M, and provides the interface operations to the environment. In the Java-like OOL [Liu et al., 2004c], such a contract can be specified as

```
Interface I {Meth : {m() | m() ∈ I}};
M; // * class declarations for the conceptual model
Class C implements I {Attr : A = Init;
    Meth : {m(){MSpec(m)} | m ∈ I};
    main(){C.New(x)}
    }
```

where **main** provides the condition $Init$ when creating the new object of **C** attached to x with the initial values of the attributes in A (see Section 4.1 for this command and [?, Liu et al., 2004c] for its semantics).

Example A *contract* for interface *CustomerService* of *ParcelCall* assigns a specification to each method and can be written as follows, where *MSpec(op)* is given as the specification following the name *op* of each operation. We present a contract in a style such that the name of the interface is followed by the fields declarations, then the initial condition, and finally the operations with their specifications:

<< **Contract** >> CS
Interface *CustomerService*
  Attr : $\mathbb{P}PName\ P$; // $*$ set of parcel names
    $\mathbb{P}CName\ S$; // $*$ set of customer names
    $CName \times PName\ owns$; // $*$ $owns(s, p)$: s owns p
    $PName \longmapsto Position\ loc$; // $*$ $loc(p)$: the location of p
  Init : $P = \varnothing \wedge S = \varnothing$;
  Meth : $LocateParcel(\mathbf{in} : PName\ pId, CName\ sId, \mathbf{out} : Position\ location)$ {
    $pId \in P \wedge sId \in S \wedge owns(sId, pId) \vdash location' = loc(pId)\}$;
    $DispatchParcel(\mathbf{in} : PName\ pId, CName\ sId)$: {
    $pId \notin P \vdash (P' = P \cup \{pId\}) \wedge (S' = S \cup \{sId\}) \wedge$
    $(owns' = owns \cup \{(sId, pId)\}) \wedge (loc' = loc \cup \{pId \rightarrow (0,0)\})$
    }

Merge and refinement

Contracts of interfaces can be merged only when their interfaces are composable and the specifications of the common methods are *consistent*. This merge will be used to calculate the provided and required services when components are composed.

DEFINITION 3 Contracts $(I_i,\ M_i,\ A_i,\ MSpec_i,\ Init_i)$, $i = 1,\ 2$, are **consistent** if

1 I_1 and I_2 are composable.

2 If x is declared in both A_1 and A_2, it has the same type; and $Init_1(x) = Init_2(x)$.

3 Any class name C in both M_1 and M_2 has the same class declaration in them.

4 $MSpec_1(op) \Leftrightarrow MSpec_2(op)$ for all $op \in I_1 \cap I_2$

This definition can be extended to a finite family of contracts.

DEFINITION 4 Let $\{C_k = (I_k,\ M_k,\ A_k,\ MSpec_k,\ Init_k)\}$ be a consistent finite family of contracts. Their **merge**, (denoted by $\|_{k \in K} C_k$), is defined by

$$I \stackrel{def}{=} \uplus_k I_k, \qquad M \stackrel{def}{=} \oplus_k M_k, \qquad A \stackrel{def}{=} \oplus_k A_k,$$
$$Init \stackrel{def}{=} \oplus_k Init_k, \quad MSpec \stackrel{def}{=} \oplus_k Mspec_k$$

where $\oplus$ denotes the overriding operator, e.g. $(MSpec_k \oplus MSpec_{k+1})(op) = MSpec_{k+1}(op)$ if $op \in I_k \cap I_{k+1}$; $MSpec_k(op)$ if $op \in I_k$ but $op \notin I_{k+1}$; $MSpec_{k+1}(op)$ otherwise.

A merge of a family of contracts corresponds the construction of a conceptual model from the partial models of the application domain in the contracts. There are three cases about the partial models:

1 The contracts do not share any fields or modelling elements in their conceptual models. In this case, the system formed by the components of these contracts are most loosely coupled. All communications are via method invocations. Such a system is easy to design and maintain. Composing these components is only plug-in composition.

2 The contracts may share fields, but their conceptual models do not share any common model elements. In this case, application domain is partitioned by the conceptual models of these contracts. And components of the system are also quite loosely coupled and easy to construct and maintain. When composing these components, some simple wiring is needed.

3 The contracts share common model elements in their conceptual models. The refinement/design of the contracts has to preserve the consistency and integrity, generally specified by state invariants, of the model. The more elements they share, the more tightly the components are coupled and the more wiring is needed when composing these components.

DEFINITION 5 We say that a contract $C_1 = (I_1, M_1, A_1, MSpec_1, Init_1)$ is *(downwards)* **refined** by $C_2 = (I_2, M_2, A_2, MSpec_2, Init_2)$, denoted by $C_1 \sqsubseteq C_2$, if there is a mapping ρ from A_1 to A_2 satisfying

1 The initial state is preserved: $(\underline{x} := Init_1(\underline{x}); \rho) \sqsubseteq (\underline{y} := Init_2(\underline{y}))$, where $\underline{x}$ is the list of variables defined in A_1, and $\underline{y}$ the list of variables in A_2. Notice that we have used a UTP design to represent a refinement mapping.

2 The behavior of the operations of C_1 are preserved: every operation *op* declared in I_1 is also declared in I_2 and $(MSpec_1(op); \rho) \sqsubseteq (\rho; MSpec_2(op))$.

An *upwards refinement* relation can be similar defined in terms of a refinement mapping from A_2 to A_1.

The refinement relation between contracts will be used to define component refinement. The state mapping ρ allows that a component developed in an application domain can be used in another application domain if such a mapping can be found.

THEOREM 6 *Contract refinement enjoys the properties of program refinement.*

1 $\sqsubseteq$ *is reflexive and transitive and a pre-order.*

*2 (***An upper bound condition***) The merge of a family of contracts refines any contract in the family, i.e.* $\{C_k \mid k \in K\}$ *be a family of consistent contracts,* $C_i \sqsubseteq \|_{k \in K} C_k$ *for any* $i \in K$.

*3 (***An isotonicity condition***) The refinement relation is preserved by the merge operation on contracts, i.e. let* $\{C_k^i \mid k \in K\}$, $i = 1, 2$, *be families of consistent contracts without shared fields. If* $C_k^1 \sqsubseteq C_k^2$ *for all k, then* $\|_{k \in K} C_k^1 \sqsubseteq \|_{k \in K} C_k^2$.

We define the *equivalence relation* by $\equiv \overset{def}{=} \sqsubseteq \cap \sqsupseteq$.

4 Component

A component consists of a provided interface and optionally a required interface, and an executable code which can be coupled to the codes of other components via their interfaces.

The external behavior of a component is specified by the contracts of its interfaces. A design of a component has to reorganize the data to realize the conceptual states, and realize the conceptual models in the contract of the component by software classes. That is the conceptual model has to be transformed into a *design model.*

Design class model

We slightly generalize the definition of a contract to allow the declarations of methods in the class model that is now called a *design class model,* which is specified as a sequence of class declarations $class_1; \ldots; class_n$, each is of the form defined in OOL:

```
Class N extends M {
    private    U1 u1, ..., Uk uk;
    protected  V1 v1, ..., Vl vl;
    public     W1 w1, ..., Wm wm;
    method     m1(parameters1){c1}; ··· ; mn(parametersn){cn}
    }
```

where $parameters_i$ is of the form $< \mathbf{in} : \underline{T_{1i}}\ \underline{x_i}, \mathbf{out} : \underline{T_{2i}}\ \underline{y_i}, \mathbf{inout} : \underline{T_{3i}}\ \underline{z_i} >$ consisting of the *value, result* and *value-result* parameters of m_i, c_i of method m_i is a command called the body of m_i. We use $Meth(M)$ to denote the set of all methods declared in a design model M.

A command c is specified according to the following syntax:

$c ::=$	$\beta : p \vdash Q$	design
	$\mid skip \mid chaos$	skip and abort
	$\mid$ **var** T x=e $\mid$ **end** x	variable declaration and undeclaration
	$\mid le := e \mid c; c$	assignment and sequence
	$\mid c \lhd b \rhd c \mid b * c$	conditional choice and loop
	$\mid le.m(\underline{e}) \mid op(\underline{e})$	method call and operation call
	$\mid C.New(x)[\underline{e}]$	Creating a new object with initail values $\underline{e}$ for its attributes

where b is a Boolean expression, e is an expression, and le is an expression which may appear on the left hand side of an assignment and is of the form $le ::= x|le.a|self$ where x a simple variable and a is an attribute of an object. We use $\mathbf{if}\{(b_i \longrightarrow P_i)|1 \leq i \leq n\}\mathbf{fi}$ to denote the multiple choice statement.

Expressions, which can appear on the right hand sides of assignments, are constructed according to the rules $e ::= x|null|self|e.a|e$ **is** $\mathrm{C}|(C)e|f(e)$, where $null$ represents the special object of the special class $Null$ that is a subclass of all class and has $null$ as its unique object, $e.a$ is the a-attribute of e, $(C)e$ is the type casting, e **is** C is the type test.

Components

DEFINITION 7 A **component** P is a tuple $< O, I, M, A, MImpl, Init, R >$ where

- O is an interface, called the *provided* or (*output*) *interface* of P.
- I is an interface disjoint from O, called the *internal interface* of P
- M is a design class model.
- A is a set of fields whose types are all declared in M.
- *MImpl* maps each operation declared in $O \cup I$ to a pair $(\alpha, \mathtt{Q})$, where $\mathtt{Q}$ is a command written in the above OOL, and α is the alphabet obtained from A and the input and output parameters of the operations in $O \cup I$.
- R, is the interface that is disjoint from O and I and consists of the *operations* (not methods of classes in M) which are referenced in the program text *MImpl*(*op*) and bodies of methods in $Meth(M)$ but not in $O \cup I$, where $op \in O \cup I$. R is called the *input* or *required* interface of P.

We call $C = (O, I, M, A, \mathit{MImpl}, \mathit{Init})$ a *generalized contract*, as it has internal operations and *MImpl* provides the specification of each operation of O in terms a general OOL command.

Hence, we will use 4-tuple $P = (C, I, O, R)$ denote a component, where C is a generalized contract for the interface $O \uplus I$.

A contract for R is called a *required service* of P, and a contract of the interface O a *provided service*. Operations in R can be seen as *holes* in the component where their specifications or implementation given in other components that are to be plugged in. Therefore, the provided services of a component depends on its required services plugged in from other components. This leads to the definition of our semantics of a component.

In the above definition, we introduced private operations so that we can hide an output operation by making it a private operation. This will keep the definition *MImpl* valid as the hidden operations may be called in *MImpl*(*op*).

Method hiding

Hiding interface operations allows to offer different services to different clients.

DEFINITION 8 **(Hiding)** Let $C = (O,\ I,\ A,\ M,\ \mathit{MImpl},\ \mathit{Init})$ be a general contract, and $H \subseteq O$ a set of operations. The notation $C \backslash H$ represents the contract

$$(O \setminus H, I \cup H,\ M,\ A,\ \mathit{MImpl},\ \mathit{Init})$$

where $S \backslash S_1$ is set-subtraction.

THEOREM 9 *The hiding operator enjoys the following properties.*

1. $(C \backslash H) \sqsubseteq C$.
2. $C \backslash \emptyset \equiv C$.
3. $C \backslash H \equiv C \backslash (H \cap O)$, *where I is the interface of* C.
4. $(C \backslash H_1) \backslash H_2 \equiv C \backslash (H_1 \cup H_2) \equiv (C \backslash H_2) \backslash H_1$
5. $(\|_{k \in K} C_k) \backslash H \equiv \|_{k \in K} (C_k \backslash H)$

Semantics components

DEFINITION 10 The **semantics** of a component P is identified as a binary relation between its required services and their corresponding provided services

$$[\![P]\!](C_R, C'_O) \stackrel{def}{=} (C_R >> P) \sqsubseteq C'_O$$

where the variable C_R takes an arbitrary required service as its value, C'_O takes a provided service for O, and the notation $C_R >> P$ denotes the provided service

$$(O, F(M), A, MSpec, Init)$$

where $F(M)$ is the class model obtained from M by removing the methods of its classes, and mapping *MSpec* is defined from the given required service

$$C_R =< R, M_R, A_R, MSpec_R, Init_R >$$

by the recursive equations $MSpec(op) = \mathcal{M}(MImpl(op))$, where $\mathcal{M}$ replaces every call of $op(inexp, outvar)$ with the actual input parameters *inexp*, output parameters *outvar* and value-result parameters *vrexp* of O by its corresponding specification.

$$\begin{array}{lcl}
\mathcal{M}(op(inexp, outvar, vrexp)) & \stackrel{def}{=} & \left(\begin{array}{l}\mathbf{var}\ T_1\ x = inexp,\ T_2\ y,\ T_3\ z = vrexp;\\ MSpec_R(op); outvar, vrexp := y, z;\\ \mathbf{end}\ x,\ y,\ z\end{array}\right)\\
 & \text{if} & op(\mathbf{in}: T_1\ x, \mathbf{out}: T_2\ y, \mathbf{inout}: T_3\ z) \in R\\
\mathcal{M}(op(inexp, outvar, vrexp)) & \stackrel{def}{=} & \left(\begin{array}{l}\mathbf{var}\ T_1\ x = inexp,\ T_2\ y,\ T_3\ z = vrexp;\\ MImpl(op); outvar, vrexp := y, z;\\ \mathbf{end}\ x,\ y,\ z\end{array}\right)\\
 & \text{if} & op(\mathbf{in}: T_1\ x, \mathbf{out}: T_2\ y, \mathbf{inout}: T_3\ z) \in\\
 & & O \cup I\\
\mathcal{M}(v := e) & \stackrel{def}{=} & v := e\\
\mathcal{M}(\mathcal{F}(c)) & \stackrel{def}{=} & \mathcal{F}(\mathcal{M}(c)) \text{ for any comand } c \text{ and context } \mathcal{F}
\end{array}$$

Notice that when a component P has an empty set of required interface operations, P is a *closed component* and the notation $C_\emptyset >> P$ becomes a constant that is the semantics of the closed program P.

For a given contract C_R for the required interface of P, $C_R >> P$ is a closed component. Let C_O be a contract of the provided interface of P which serves as the specification of the component. We say that P *correctly realizes* or *implements* C_O with a given required service C_R if $C_O \sqsubseteq (C_R >> P)$.

In a modular programming paradigm, a component can be designed and implemented as a module in which each of the operations in the output interface is "programmed" using procedures or functions that are defined either locally in the module or externally in other modules. In this case, the external modules that the component calls methods from must be declared, as well as the types of the attribute values and parameters of its methods. Therefore, a component is in fact not a single module, but an artifact that contains all these declared types and modules. In an object-oriented paradigm, such as Java, a component can be seen as a class that implements the interfaces in O:

M; //* the declaration of the design model
Class P implements O {**Attr** : A;
  public : $m \stackrel{def}{=} MImpl(m)$; //* for each $m \in O$;
  private : $op \stackrel{def}{=} MImpl(op)$ //* for each $op \in I$
  }

Thus, after adding the notation for interfaces and contracts to OOL in [Liu et al., 2004b, Liu et al., 2004c], the extended language provides a formal model for components and the calculus of contract refinement and component refinements [He et al., 2003], and also extends RCOOD in [He et al., 2002, Liu et al., 2004b] to for component-based development.

Example Now we define a component GIS in the ParcelCall system to provide the services to customers. We will use some Java conventions in writing the specification, such as assignment to a variable with a method call that has an **out** parameter.

<< **Component** >> *GIS*
Output Interface *CustomerService*
  Attr : $\mathbb{P}PName\ P$; // * set of parcel names
    $\mathbb{P}CName\ S$; // * set of customer names
    $CName \times PName\ owns$; // * $owns(s,p)$: s *owns* p
    $(PName \longmapsto Position)\ loc$; // * $loc(p)$ returns the location of p
  Init : $P = \emptyset \wedge S = \emptyset$;
Meth : $LocateParcel(\mathbf{in} : PName\ pId, CNamesId, \mathbf{out} : Position\ location)\{$
    if $pId \in P \wedge sId \in S \wedge owns(sId, pId)$ //* call required method
    then $location := IParcelInfo.Where(pId)$ **else** $Abort\}$;
   $DispatchParcel(\mathbf{in} : PName\ pId, CName\ sId)\ \{$
    if $pId \notin P \wedge sId \notin S$ **then** $(P := P \cup \{pId\}; S := S \cup \{sId\};$
    $owns := owns \cup \{(sId, pId)\}; IParcelInfo.Deal(pId))$ **else** $chaos\}$;
Input Interface $Parcelinfo$
  Attr : $\mathbb{P}PName\ P$; // * set of parcel names
    $(PName \longmapsto Position)\ loc$; // * $loc(p)$ returns the location of p;
  Meth : $Where(\mathbf{In} : PName\ pId, \mathbf{out} : Coordinates\ location)\ \{$
     $Deal(\mathbf{in} : PName\ pId)\}$;
<< **Contract** >> *Parcelinfo*
$IParcelInfo :: \mathbf{Init} : P = \varnothing$;
$IParcelInfo :: Where(\mathbf{in} : PName\ pId, \mathbf{out} : Position\ location)$:
     $pId \in P \vdash location := loc(pId)$;
$IParcelInfo :: Deal(\mathbf{in} : PName\ pId) : pId \notin P \vdash loc'(pId) = (0,0)$

We can calculate $ParcelInfo >> GIS \sqsubseteq CS$. We have kept the attribute $loc : PName \longmapsto Position$ to avoid from defining a state mapping in the proof of the refinement. In the following part of the example, we provide a definition of component GTS to implement the contract $ParcelInfo$, that need the specification of a design class.

$$
\begin{array}{l}
\ll \textbf{Component} \gg GTS \\
\textbf{Class}\ Parcel\{\ PName\ id;\ Position\ location = (0,0); \\
\qquad\qquad Positionloc()\{return := location\}\}; \\
\textbf{Ouput Interface}\ IParcelInfo \\
\quad \textbf{Attr}: \mathbb{P}Parcel\ Parcels:\ ; \\
\quad \textbf{Init}: Parcels = \emptyset; \\
\quad \textbf{Meth}: Deal(\textbf{in}: PName\ pId)\{ \\
\qquad\qquad Parcel.New(p)[pId]; Parcels := Parcels \cup \{p\}; \textbf{end}\ p\}; \\
\qquad\qquad Where(\textbf{in}:\ PName\ id,\ \textbf{out}:\ Position\ location)\{ \\
\qquad\qquad \textbf{var}\ Parcel\ p = P.find(pId); location := p.loc(); \textbf{end}\ p\}
\end{array}
$$

Define the refinement mapping ρ from the attributes of $Parcel$ to those of $ParcelInfo$:

$$
\begin{array}{l}
\rho(P) \stackrel{def}{=} \{p.id \mid p \in Parcel\} \\
\rho(loc(pId)) = p.location \text{ for all } pId \in P \text{ such that } \exists p \in Parcel.p.id = pId
\end{array}
$$

Then $ParcelInfo \sqsubseteq GTS$.

Refinement and composition of components

For a component P with provided and required interfaces O and R, the semantics $[\![P]\!]$ is a binary relation between the input services and output services.

THEOREM 11 ***(Monotonicity and Upwards Closure* [Smyth, 1978])** *Let $P =< C, I, O, R >$ and $\sqsubseteq_R$ and $\sqsubseteq_O$ are the refinement relations among contracts of R and among contracts of O respectively. Then $\sqsubseteq_R \circ [\![P]\!] \circ \sqsubseteq_O \ = \ [\![P]\!]$, where $\circ$ denotes relational composition.*

Thus, for any required services $C_R \sqsubseteq C'_R$, and provided services $C_O \sqsubseteq C'_O$, then

$$[\![P]\!](C_R, C'_O) \Rightarrow [\![P]\!](C'_R, C_O)$$

A component P_1 is a *refinement* of a component P_2, denoted by $P_2 \sqsubseteq P_1$, if P_1 is a sub-relation of P_2.

DEFINITION 12 Component P_1 is a **refinement** of P_2 if

$$R_1 = R_2 \wedge O_1 = O_2 \wedge [\![P_1]\!] \Rightarrow [\![P_2]\!]$$

P_1 refines P_2 iff for any required service C_R, $(C_R \gg P_2) \sqsubseteq (C_R \gg P_1)$.

We therefore have when P_1 refines P_2, then for any given required service C_R and a contract a provided service C_O as the specification, P_1 realizes C_O with C_R if P_2 realizes C_O with C_R.

DEFINITION 13 Let $P_i = (C_i, I_i, O_i, R_i)$ be two components with contracts $C_i = (O_i \cup I_i, M_i, A_i)$, for $i = 1,2$. Assume that $I_1 \cap I_2 = \emptyset$, $O_1 \cap O_2 = \emptyset$ and $R_1 \cap R_2 = \emptyset$. The **composition** $P_1 || P_2$ is defined to merge their contracts, output interfaces and input interfaces, and to remove those input interfaces of each component that are matched by the output interfaces in another:

$$P_1 \| P_2 \stackrel{def}{=} < C_1 \| C_2, I_1 \cup I_2, O_1 \uplus O_2, R_1 \backslash O_2 \cup R_2 \backslash O_1 >$$

Let $I \stackrel{def}{=} I_1 \cup I_2$, $R \stackrel{def}{=} R_1 \backslash O_2 \cup R_2 \backslash O_1$ and $O \stackrel{def}{=} O_1 \cup O_2$. The composition of P_1 and P_2 is defined by

$$\begin{array}{rcl} [\![P_1 \| P_2]\!](C_R, C'_O) & \stackrel{def}{=} & \exists C_{R_1}, C'_{O_1}, C_{R_2}, C'_{O_2} \bullet \\ & & [\![P_1]\!](C_{R_1}, C'_{O_1}) \wedge [\![P_2]\!](C_{R_2}, C'_{O_2}) \wedge \\ & & C_{R_1} \backslash (R_1 \setminus O_2) = C'_{O_2} \backslash (O_2 \setminus R_1) \wedge \\ & & C_{R_2} \backslash (R_2 \setminus O_1) = C'_{O_1} \backslash (O_1 \setminus R_2) \wedge \\ & & C_R = C_{R_1} \backslash (R_1 \backslash O_2) \| C_{R_2} \backslash (R_2 \backslash O_1) \wedge \\ & & C'_O = C'_{O_1} \backslash (R_2 \backslash O_1) \| C'_{O_2} \backslash (R_1 \backslash O_2) \end{array}$$

This definition allows an output interface and thus part of provided service of one component to be shared among a number other components. Hiding can be used to *internalize* the part of a provided service of one component that is used in another component: $(P_1 \| P_2) \backslash (R_1 \cap O_2) \backslash (R_2 \cap O_1)$.

Example We can now compose GIS and GTS. $(GIS \| GTS) \backslash IParcelInfo$. If we do not consider the relation between GTS with other components of the Parcel-Call system, this composite component is a closed system that only provides services according to the contract of CS, but it does not have any required interface. However, to complete the ParcelCall system, we can add a required service interface to get the new location of a parcel from the Mobile Logistic Server component MLS. Alternatively, we add another provided interface $ChangLoc()$ that will be needed as a required interface of Mobile Logistic Server component MLS to update the location of a parcel.

Client-server systems are often seen as applications in component software. The architecture of such a system is organized as a layered structure and can be model with in our model as shown in the full paper [Liu et al., 2004a].

5 Conclusion

We have proposed a model for software components and defined composition and refinement of components. This allows us to use the existing calculus in [Hoare and He, 1998, Liu et al., 2004b, Liu et al., 2004c] to reason about and refine components. We have separated the different views about a component. The different views are specified at different levels of abstraction. A component is constructed to provide certain services and these services are specified in terms of the component's interface and contract. This specification is taken as the requirement specification of the component. The designer of the component has to design and implement the component to satisfy this requirement specification. A design can be specified in the object-oriented specification notation developed in, that supports incremental and step-wise construction of a component [Liu et al., 2004b, Liu et al., 2004c]. Merge and hiding of interfaces for components add more support to incremental construction of component software as well as to restrict the use of some services by certain users.

When composing components, one has to check the matchability of the provided services of one component with the specification of the required services of another; both syntactically and semantically. The syntactic check is only to check the signature of the interface methods. The semantic check is to ensure that the provided service of one component does ensure the service required by another component. This is to check the pre and post conditions of in the specification of the services.

Points of discussion The model of components is simplified in the sense that behavior or protocols of the interfaces are not described. There are several possible ways to address the problem of protocols. First, we can introduce control state variables in contracts and thus in components. This will allow us to define a contract as a state machine or statechart, e.g. [Selic, 1998, Wirsing and Broy, 2000]. Then when two components are composed, deadlock freedom needs to be verified and this is not an easy task. Second, in addition to the state information, we can add a CSP-like specification of the order of the methods in a component, e.g. [Allen and Garlan, 1997]. Again, matching between protocols in different components has to be checked and deadlock needs to be avoided. As we know from the model of CSP, this is not a trivial task either. We would like to propose a weak approach in which protocols of the provided interface and required interface of a component are described independently in terms of *regular languages* on the method names of the interfaces. To check the matchability between a provided interface with a required interface is then to check the provided interface protocol is a subset of the required interface protocol in terms of the regular languages that are defined for the protocols, and this can be automated.

Related work There is much work on the definitions of software components. We take the informal views of [Cheesman and Daniels, 2001, Szyperski, 2002] that a component both provides to and requires services from other components. We used the notion of contract for formal specification of provided and required services, A contract here is similar to that of Meyer [Meyer, 1992]. However, we have provided the notion of composition and there is a standard calculus for reason about and refine components at different levels of abstracts. A distinctive nature of our framework is the natural link of the component contract specification and its object-oriented implementation.

A contract in [Helm et al., 1990] models the collaboration and behavioral relationships between objects. In our approach, we provide the separation between the specification of a contract for an interface from the specification of the behavior of the component that realizes the contract. A contract in [Andrade and J.L.Fiadeiro, 1999] describes the coordinations among a number of partners (i.e. components or objects). Its main purpose is to support system architectural evolution and to deal with changes in business rules of the system application. Our contracts here specify the services of components while we treat interaction and coordinations as part of the implementation of the components. Our aim is to support construction of software components and component software systems.

Acknowledgement We thank the referees for their careful review and constructive and helpful comments. We also thank our colleague Dang Van Hung for his comments on the earlier version of the paper.

References

[Allen and Garlan, 1997] Allen, R. and Garlan, D. (1997). A formal basis for architectural connection. *ACM Transactions on Software Engineering and Methodology*, 6(3).

[Andrade and J.L.Fiadeiro, 1999] Andrade, L. F. and J.L.Fiadeiro (1999). Interconnecting objects via contracts. In France, R. and Rumpe, B., editors, *UML'99 - Beyond the Standard, LNCS1723*. Springer-Verlag.

[Cheesman and Daniels, 2001] Cheesman, J. and Daniels, J. (2001). *UML Components. Component Software Series*. Addison-Wesley.

[Filipe, 2002] Filipe, J. (2002). A logic-based formalization for component specification. *Journal of Object Technology*, 1(3):231–248.

[He et al., 2002] He, J., Liu, Z., and Li, X. (2002). Towards a refinement calculus for object-oriented systems (keynote talk). In *Proc. ICCI02, August 19-20, 2002, Alberta, Canada*.

[He et al., 2003] He, J., Liu, Z., and Li, X. (2003). Component calculus. In Dang, V. and Liu, Z., editors, *Proc. Proc. Workshop on Formal Aspects of Component Software (FACS'03), Satellite Workshop of FME2003, Pisa, Italy, 8-9 September, 2003*. UNU/IIST Report No 284, UNU/IIST, P.O. Box 3058, Macao.

[Heineman and Councill, 2001] Heineman, G. and Councill, W. (2001). *Component-Based Software Engineering, Putting the Pieces Together*. Addison-Wesley.

[Helm et al., 1990] Helm, R., Holland, I., and Gangopadhyay, D. (1990). Contracts: Specifying behavioral compositions in object-oriented systems. In *Proc. OOPSLA'90/ECOOP'90*, pages 169–180. ACM.

[Hoare and He, 1998] Hoare, C. and He, J. (1998). *Unifying theories of programming*. Prentice-Hall International.

[Liu et al., 2004a] Liu, Z., He, J., and Li, X. (2004a). Contract-oriented component software development. Technical Report UNU/IIST, Report No 298. http://www.iist.unu.edu/newrh/III/1/page.html.

[Liu et al., 2004b] Liu, Z., He, J., and Li, X. (2004b). Integrating and refining UML models. Technical Report UNU/IIST Report No 295, http://www.iist.unu.edu/newrh/III/1/page.html, UNU/IIST, P.O. Box 3058, Macao. Submitted for publication.

[Liu et al., 2003] Liu, Z., He, J., Li, X., and Chen, Y. (2003). A relational model for object-oriented requirement analysis in UML. Technical Report UNU/IIST, Report No 287. *Proc. ICFEM03*, 5-7 November, 2003, Singapore. Lecture Notes in Computer Science.

[Liu et al., 2004c] Liu, Z., He, J., Li, X., and Liu, J. (2004c). Unifying views of UML. Technical Report UNU/IIST Report No 288, http://www.iist.unu.edu/newrh/III/1/page.html, UNU/IIST, P.O. Box 3058, Macao. Presented at <<UML>> 2003 Workshop on Compositional Verification of UML, 21 October 2003, SF, USA. To appear in ENTCS.

[Meyer, 1992] Meyer, B. (1992). Applying design by contract. *IEEE Computer*.

[Meyer, 1997] Meyer, B. (1997). *Object-oriented Software Construction (2nd Edition)*. Prentice Hall PTR.

[Selic, 1998] Selic, B. (1998). Using UML for modelling complex real-time systems. In Mueller, F. and Bestavros, A., editors, *Language Compilers, and Tools for Embedded Systems, LNCS 1474*, pages 250–262. Springer.

[Smyth, 1978] Smyth, M. (1978). Powerdomain. *Journal of Computer Science and System Sciences*, 16:23–36.

[Szyperski, 2002] Szyperski, C. (2002). *Component Software: Beyond Object-Oriented Programming*. Addison-Wesley.

[Wirsing and Broy, 2000] Wirsing, M. and Broy, M. (2000). Algebraic state machines. In Rus, T., editor, *Proc. 8th Internat. Conf. Algebraic Methodology and Software Technology, AMAST 2000. LNCS 1816*, pages 89–118. Springer.

NEW INSIGHTS ON ARCHITECTURAL CONNECTORS*

Roberto Bruni [1], José Luiz Fiadeiro [2], Ivan Lanese [1], Antónia Lopes [3] and Ugo Montanari [1]

[1] *Computer Science Department, University of Pisa, Italy.*
{bruni,lanese,ugo}@di.unipi.it

[2] *Department of Computer Science, University of Leicester, UK.*
jose@fiadeiro.org

[3] *Department of Informatics, Faculty of Sciences, University of Lisbon, Portugal.*
mal@di.fc.ul.pt

Abstract This work is a first step toward the reconciliation of the two main approaches to composition in system modeling, namely the categorical one and the algebraic one. In particular, we present a mapping from CommUnity, which uses the categorical approach based on colimits, into the Tile Model, which uses algebraic operators for composition. Our results include a standard decomposition for CommUnity programs. We also establish a strong link between the colimit computation of the categorical approach and the abstract semantics of configurations in the algebraic approach by proving that the encoding of a CommUnity diagram is behaviorally equivalent to the encoding of its colimit.

Introduction

In this paper, we report on new insights on architectural connectors raised by the analysis of mobility aspects within software architectures for *Global Computing*. Since there is no single formalism that can best address these aspects we study the relationships between two different approaches: CommUnity [6] and the Tile Model [7]. The former is a prototype architectural description language that was developed to formalize the conceptual distinction between *computation* and *coordination* in communicating distributed systems. The latter is an operational model designed for concurrent systems. It is suited for behavioral semantics that deal uniformly with closed and open systems.

*Research supported by the FET-GC Project IST-2001-32747 AGILE.

These two frameworks can be seen as "canonical" representatives of two general approaches to the study of complex system structures: the *categorical approach* (for CommUnity) and the *algebraic approach* (for the Tile Model).

The *Categorical Approach*, which can be traced back to [8], is based on the definition of a category whose objects model system components and whose morphisms represent how systems are superposed, simulated, refined, etc. Complex systems can be modeled as diagrams in the category. Composition is achieved via universal constructions like taking the colimit, which encapsulates components and interactions in a single object. Different diagrams have the same colimit, which thus defines some sort of denotational semantics. The categorical approach is best suited for modeling systems based on shared resources (e.g., memory, channels, actions), sharing being expressed through morphisms. The main contribution of CommUnity has been to show how the categorical approach can be applied to program designs, formalizing architectural aspects.

The *Algebraic Approach*, initiated in [9, 13], is based on signatures whose constants are the basic processes and whose operations capture composition. The initial algebra of the signature defines the class of admissible systems. Typically, systems are equipped with an operational semantics based on labeled transition systems in the SOS style [14]. Abstract semantics can then be obtained by collapsing systems that are equivalent w.r.t. some observational semantics. The algebraic approach is best suited for message passing calculi. The main contribution of the Tile Model has been the support for two different dimensions of composition to co-exist, namely Computation and Distribution.

On the one hand, we are interested in capturing the "physiological" structure of architectural connectors, i.e. what they are made of and what mechanisms they put in place to coordinate required interactions, which is addressed through CommUnity. This is essential, for instance, to provide support for more abstract levels of modeling. On the other hand, we are interested in the "social" structures in which these connectors live, i.e. the laws that regulate the way they can be composed and superposed to interconnect components, as can be captured in the Tile Model. This step is essential for supporting the transition between the declarative and operational aspects of architectural configurations.

We are even more interested in relating the two approaches. In particular, the technical contribution of this paper is three-fold:

1 we define a standard decomposition for CommUnity diagrams in terms of elementary programs;

2 we define a translation from CommUnity diagrams into the Tile Model;

3 we establish a strong link between the denotational semantics of the categorical approach and the abstract semantics yielded by the algebraic approach by proving that the encoding of a CommUnity diagram is behaviorally equivalent to the encoding of its colimit.

This work has been developed in the context of FET-FP5 Project AGILE [2] on "Architectures for Mobility", that brings together different approaches to the modeling of architectural aspects of systems with the aim of complementing each other and of extending them to cope with *Global Computing*.

design P **is**
in in(V)
out out(V)
do $[]_{g \in \Gamma}$ g: G(g) $\rightarrow$ R(g)

Figure 1. CommUnity designs.

design counter **is**
in x:nat
out y:int
do inc: $true \rightarrow y := y + x$
[] dec: $y > MIN \rightarrow y := y - x$

Figure 2. The "counter" design.

Structure of the paper. In § 1 we survey CommUnity and the Tile Model. In § 2 we define the standard decomposition of CommUnity diagrams and prove colimit preservation. In § 3 we define the tile system associated to CommUnity while in § 4 we sketch the encoding and the bisimilarity result (Theorem 9). Conclusions and directions for future work are given in § 5.

1. Background

1.1 CommUnity

In this section we give a brief account of CommUnity, while referring the interested reader to [5] for full details.

CommUnity is a parallel program design language in the style of Unity [3] but based on action sharing. It was initially proposed in [6] to show how programs fit into Goguen's categorical approach to General Systems Theory [8]. Since then, it has evolved into an architectural description language, capitalizing on the fact that CommUnity takes to an extreme the separation between "computation" and "coordination" concerns.

The individual components of a system can be defined in terms of *channels* and *actions* organized in *designs*. In this paper, we consider a special class of CommUnity designs (see Figure 1), called *programs*, which are particular instances of the more general form in [5].

Channels. A design P is based on a set of (input and output) *channels* V. Input channels are read-only and are controlled by the environment while output channels are controlled locally by the component. Each channel v is typed with a sort $sort(v)$ which is part of a fixed many-sorted data algebra.

Actions. A design P exploits a pointed set of actions $\Gamma_\perp$. Actions represent possible interactions between the component and the environment. For each action name g, $G(g)$ is the enabling condition of g (a predicate on V), and $R(g)$ is a multiple assignment, assigning to output channels expressions on input and output channels. The empty assignment is denoted by *skip*.

As an example, consider the design in Figure 2. It models a component that calculates and stores an integer value. It can decrease or increment this value of x units through the execution of actions *inc* and *dec*, but decreasing is only allowed when a minimum value MIN has not been reached.

A program with a non-empty set of input channels is *open* in the sense that its execution is only meaningful in a configuration in which these inputs have been instantiated

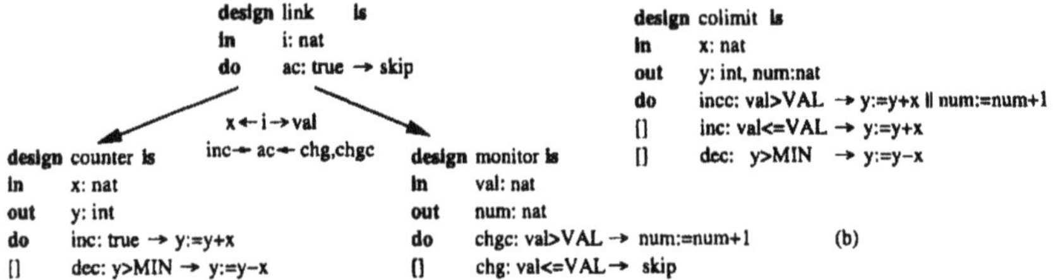

Figure 3. The "counter with monitor" diagram and its colimit.

with channels controlled by other components. A closed program behaves as follows: at each step, one of the actions whose enabling condition holds is selected, and its assignments are executed atomically.

Diagrams. The interaction between programs is based on action synchronization and interconnection of input and output channels. Name bindings are established through diagrams of the form in Figure 3(a) in a category **c-DSGN** with morphisms as follows. We may consider that the design in the middle is a program whose actions are all *true* $\rightarrow$ *skip*, called a *cable* [5].

DEFINITION 1 *A morphism of designs* $\sigma : P_1 \rightarrow P_2$ *consists of a total function* σ_{var} : $V_1 \rightarrow V_2$ *that preserves sorts and never maps an output channel to an input channel together with a pointed mapping* $\sigma_{ac} : \Gamma_{2_\perp} \rightarrow \Gamma_{1_\perp}$ *that maps a conditional multiple assignment* $G(g) \rightarrow R(g)$ *to another one with stronger condition and a superset of the assignments (up-to renamings of channels).*

EXAMPLE 2 *The diagram in Figure 3(a) defines a system with two components: a* counter *and a* monitor. *The* monitor *counts the executions of an action when channel* val *has a value greater than a fixed value* VAL. *In that case action* chgc *takes place, action* chg *is executed in the other cases. In this configuration,* chgc *and* chg *monitor the execution of action* inc *and the value of channel* x, *as shown by the interconnection of channels* x *of* counter *and* val *of* monitor *and the synchronization of action* inc *with both* chg *or* chgc. *Here* dec *is (implicitly) mapped to the* $\perp$ *action of* link *and thus not synchronized.*

The colimit construction internalizes the interactions described in a diagram **dia** and returns a program colim(**dia**) for the system as a whole. Colimits in **c-DSGN** capture a generalized notion of parallel composition in which interconnections are explicit. The colimit of the diagram in Figure 3(a) returns, up to isomorphism, the program in Figure 3(b). Only diagrams where no output channels are connected make sense. These are called *configuration diagrams*.

To conclude this overview of CommUnity, we mention star-shaped configurations (see Figure 4) which play an important role in the process of structuring systems. They can be used to represent architectural connectors as defined in [1]: the program in the center is the *glue* and the programs in the vertices are the *roles*. Each role $Role_i$ is connected to the glue by one *cable* C_i. The glue of the connector defines how the activities of the role instances are coordinated.

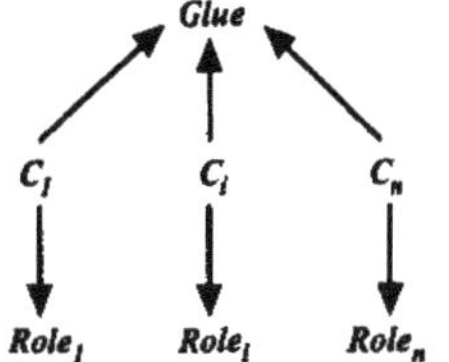

Figure 4. Star-shaped configurations.

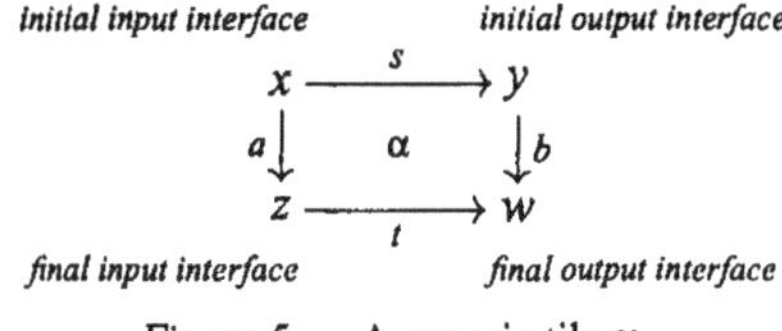

Figure 5. A generic tile α.

1.2 Tile Model

The tile model [7] relies on rewrite rules with side effects, called *basic tiles*, which are reminiscent of SOS rules and *context systems* [10], collecting ideas from *structured transition systems* [4] and *rewriting logic* [12].

A tile $\alpha : s \xrightarrow[b]{a} t$ has the graphical representation in Figure 5, stating that the *initial configuration* s can evolve to the *final configuration* t via α, producing the *effect* b; but the step is allowed only if the 'arguments' of s can contribute by producing a, which acts as *trigger*. Triggers and effects are called *observations*. Configurations and observations are represented by arrows to show that they can be composed via their interfaces.

DEFINITION 3 *A* tile system *is a tuple* $\mathcal{R} = (\mathcal{H}, \mathcal{V}, N, R)$ *where* $\mathcal{H}$ *and* $\mathcal{V}$ *are monoidal categories with the same set of objects* $O_{\mathcal{H}} = O_{\mathcal{V}}$*,* N *is a set of rule names and* $R\colon N \to \mathcal{H} \times \mathcal{V} \times \mathcal{V} \times \mathcal{H}$ *is a function such that for all* $\alpha \in N$*, if* $R(\alpha) = \langle s, a, b, t\rangle$*, then the arrows* s, a, b, t *can form a tile like in Figure 5.*

The Tile Model is designed for systems that are *compositional in space* and in *time*: tiles can be composed horizontally, in parallel, and vertically to generate larger steps. Horizontal composition coordinates the evolution of the initial configuration of α with the evolution of the environment yielding the 'synchronization' of the two rewrites. The parallel composition builds concurrent steps. Vertical composition is sequential composition of computations. Moreover, we always have the horizontal and vertical identities as auxiliary tiles (vertical identities model idle components, while horizontal identities propagate effects through identity substitutions). All this is defined in Figure 6.

Depending on the chosen tile format, $\mathcal{H}$ and $\mathcal{V}$ must satisfy certain constraints and some other auxiliary tiles are added and composed with basic tiles and identities. The set of resulting tiles defines the *tile logic* associated with $\mathcal{R}$ and we write $\mathcal{R} \vdash s \xrightarrow[b]{a} t$ if the tile is derivable.

By taking $\langle$trigger, effect$\rangle$ pairs as labels one can see tiles as a labeled transition system. The resulting notion of bisimilarity is called *tile bisimilarity*.

DEFINITION 4 *Let* $\mathcal{R} = (\mathcal{H}, \mathcal{V}, N, R)$ *be a tile system. A symmetric relation* $\sim$ *on configurations is called* tile bisimulation *if whenever* $s \sim t$ *and* $\mathcal{R} \vdash s \xrightarrow[b]{a} s'$*, then* t' *exists such that* $\mathcal{R} \vdash t \xrightarrow[b]{a} t'$ *and* $s' \sim t'$*. The maximal tile bisimulation is denoted by* $\simeq$*, and two configurations* s *and* t *are* tile bisimilar *iff* $s \simeq t$*.*

$$\frac{R(\alpha) = \langle s,a,b,t\rangle}{s \xrightarrow[b]{a} t}\ (\texttt{bas}) \qquad \frac{s \xrightarrow[b]{a} t \quad h \xrightarrow[c]{b} f}{s;h \xrightarrow[c]{a} t;f}\ (\texttt{hor}) \qquad \frac{t : x \to y \in \mathcal{H}}{t \xrightarrow[id_y]{id_x} t}\ (\texttt{vid})$$

$$\frac{s \xrightarrow[b]{a} t \quad h \xrightarrow[d]{c} f}{s \otimes h \xrightarrow[b \otimes d]{a \otimes c} t \otimes f}\ (\texttt{par}) \qquad \frac{s \xrightarrow[b]{a} t \quad t \xrightarrow[d]{c} h}{s \xrightarrow{a;c} h}\ (\texttt{ver}) \qquad \frac{a : x \to z \in \mathcal{V}}{id_x \xrightarrow[a]{a} id_z}\ (\texttt{hid})$$

Figure 6. Inference rules for tile logic.

We focus on tile systems where $\mathcal{H}$ and $\mathcal{V}$ are *categories of substitutions*. Substitutions over a signature Σ and their composition $\_;\_$ form a cartesian category for which there is an alternative presentation given by Lawvere's *algebraic theories* [11]. In Lawvere's theories cartesianity is expressed by a symmetric monoidal structure $(\otimes, \underline{0}, \gamma)$ enriched with two natural transformations, a duplicator $\nabla = \{\nabla_n : \underline{n} \to \underline{2n}\}_n$ and a discharger $! = \{!_n : \underline{n} \to \underline{0}\}_n$. The result is a freely generated cartesian category $\mathbf{Th}[\Sigma]$ whose objects are underlined natural numbers and whose arrows from $\underline{m}$ to $\underline{n}$ are in a one-to-one correspondence with n-tuples of terms of the free Σ-algebra over m variables. In particular, arrows from $\underline{0}$ to $\underline{1}$ are in bijective correspondence with the closed terms over Σ. We assume the standard naming $x_1, \ldots, x_m$ of the m input variables. For example, $f \in \Sigma_2$ defines an arrow $f(x_1, x_2) : \underline{2} \to \underline{1}$ in $\mathbf{Th}[\Sigma]$. We denote the identity arrow $\langle x_1, \ldots, x_n\rangle$ for the object $\underline{n}$ as $id_{\underline{n}}$ and the empty substitution as $id_{\underline{0}}$.

In this work we deal with substitutions on multi-sorted terms, thus instead of natural numbers we have monoids on the set of sorts. For instance, if a and b are sorts we have $\gamma_{a,b} : a \otimes b \to b \otimes a$ and $\nabla_{a \otimes b} : a \otimes b \to a \otimes b \otimes a \otimes b$.

2. Standard decomposition of CommUnity programs

In this section we present an original decomposition for CommUnity programs, which is the first step towards the definition of the mapping from CommUnity to the Tile Model. This decomposition transforms a complex program in a star-shaped configuration with simpler components. Given a CommUnity program $\mathcal{D}$ we decompose it in a diagram with four kinds of components:

- a *glue*, which has as many actions as the number of actions in $\mathcal{D}$, but each action in the glue has the form *true* $\to$ *skip*. The glue has one input channel for each input/output channel of $\mathcal{D}$;

- one *channel manager* for each output channel in $\mathcal{D}$. The channel manager for channel x has exactly one action for each action in $\mathcal{D}$, with *true* as guard and as body the assignment (if any) in the action that assigns x. The channel manager has exactly one output channel x and all the input channels needed by the assignments to x;

- one *guard manager* for each action in $\mathcal{D}$. The guard manager has exactly one action in the form $p \to$ *skip* where p is the guard of the corresponding action in $\mathcal{D}$. The guard manager has exactly the channels needed for evaluating its guard, all as input channels;

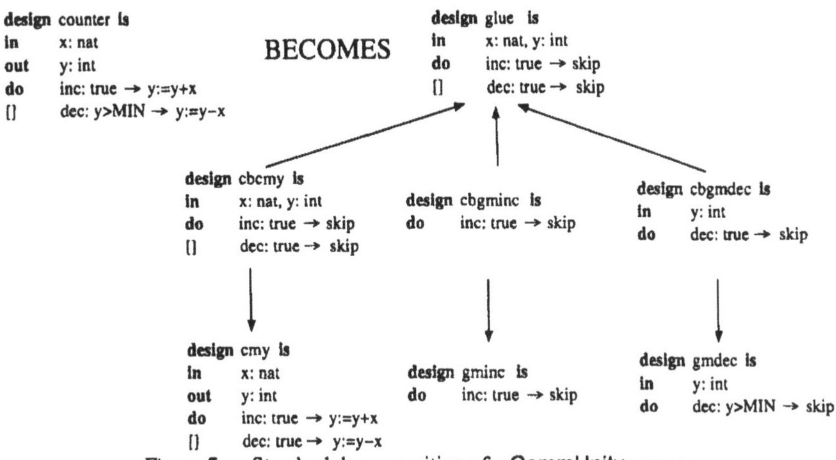

Figure 7. Standard decomposition of a CommUnity program.

- *cables* to connect each channel manager and each guard manager to the glue. Each cable has one action/input channel for each action/channel of the corresponding role, mapped to that action/channel and to the corresponding action/channel in the glue.

Roughly, letting n and m be respectively the number of output channels and of actions in $\mathcal{D}$, then the standard decomposition $\mathsf{DS}(\mathcal{D})$ of $\mathcal{D}$ is a diagram with n channel managers, m guard managers, $n+m$ cables and one glue.

Figure 7 shows a sample decomposition. In the figure we have not explicitly represented the details of morphisms, but we have just used the same name in different programs for corresponding actions and corresponding channels.

We can also define the standard decomposition of a diagram **dia**, which is a diagram obtained by substituting each role with its standard decomposition. The morphisms entering a program become morphisms entering the glue of its standard decomposition.

The correctness of the decomposition is given by the following theorem, where $\cong$ denotes the isomorphism relation in **c-DSGN**.

THEOREM 5 *For each design $\mathcal{D}$ we have* $\mathsf{colim}(\mathsf{DS}(\mathcal{D})) \cong \mathcal{D}$. *Moreover, for each diagram* **dia** *we have* $\mathsf{colim}(\mathsf{DS}(\mathbf{dia})) \cong \mathsf{colim}(\mathbf{dia})$.

3. Mapping CommUnity into the Tile Model

In this section we define the operational and abstract semantics of CommUnity by exploiting the Tile Model. The encoding maps a diagram into a tile system together with a fixed initial configuration. We consider both *anchored* systems (systems with state) and *unanchored* systems.

In order to have a clear separation between functionalities and state, each configuration is the composition of two parts: one that corresponds to the state, and the other one that corresponds to the unanchored system.

Tile objects. The typed interfaces of the tile system are tuples that contain the following elements:

- channels: these are specified by a type (boolean, integer, ...) and a modality (input or output) exactly as in CommUnity;
- a special boolean object b that is attached to the evaluation of guards;
- placeholders for actions, which play the role of synchronization objects.

We denote tuples of channels and special boolean objects with *chs* with an optional subscript to denote their cardinality and/or types, furthermore we write *ins* to specify that all channels in the tuple are input channels (or possibly special boolean objects) and similarly *outs* for outputs. We denote a synchronization object with 1 and a tuple of n synchronization objects with n.

Tile configurations. We take as horizontal category the symmetric strict monoidal category freely generated by the basic arrows below. Note that symmetries allow for rearranging the order of the objects in the interfaces.

- $state[val : typ] : 0 \to chs$ models a state where *val* is a tuple of values of types *typ* and *chs* a tuple of channels with these types; arrows of this form model the actual states of anchored configurations;
- $cm[\langle f_i \rangle_{i=1...n}] : out \otimes ins \otimes b \to n$ models a channel manager where f_is are functions on channels in $out \otimes ins$ to the output channel *out*;
- $gm[p] : ins \otimes b \to 1$ models a guard manager with predicate p that uses channels in *ins*;
- $\nabla_{chs,ins \otimes chs} : chs \to ins \otimes chs$ which are data synchronization connectors (where *ins* and *chs* have the same number of elements and the same type);
- $!_{ins} : ins \to 0$; which are hiding connectors;
- $\triangledown_n : n \to 2n$ and $!_n : n \to 0$ which are mutual exclusion and hiding connectors respectively;
- $\nabla_n : n \to 2n$ and $\Delta_n : 2n \to n$ which are synchronization connectors;
- $\bar{1} : 0 \to 1$ which is a connector that forces some actions to be performed.

The structure of the anchored configuration obtained as the translation of a generic CommUnity diagram is shown in Figure 8, using the wire-and-box notation, where arrows are represented as boxes and their composition as wiring between their interfaces.

Given a well-formed connected diagram on which we have applied the standard decomposition we want to build such an arrow in a compositional way. In order to do that we must first fix a total ordering over the programs in the diagram and we translate each of them separately. Then we use as basic operation to build up the

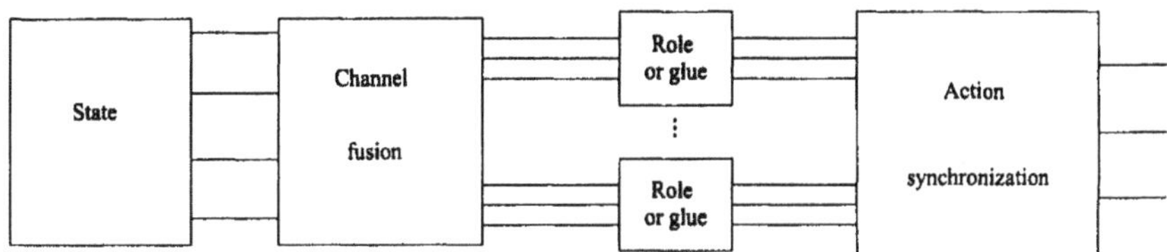

Figure 8. Initial configuration for a CommUnity program.

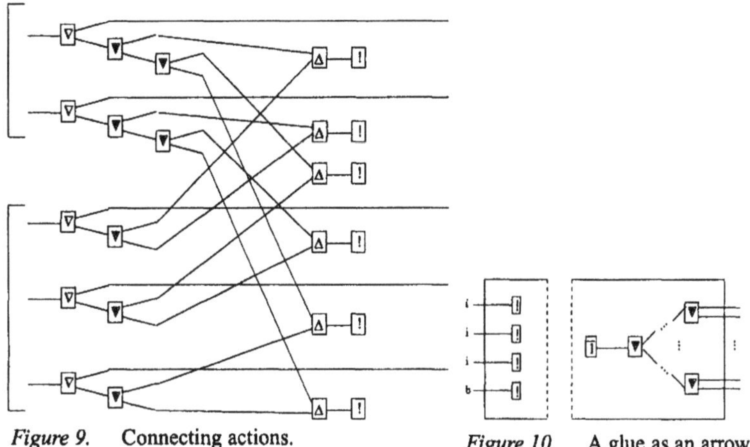

Figure 9. Connecting actions.

Figure 10. A glue as an arrow.

system the "parallel composition through one cable". Thanks to the hypothesis that the CommUnity diagram is well-formed, a sequence of operations of this kind allows to translate the whole diagram. At the end we may add the state. A main result ensures that the behavior of the resulting tile system is independent from the choice of the ordering (Proposition 8).

During the translation we have to remember which are the channels that correspond to each channel object and which is the action that corresponds to each synchronization object.

- The translation of a channel manager is a basic arrow $cm[\langle f_i \rangle_{i=1\ldots n}] : chs \otimes b \to n$ where chs contains the channels used by the channel manager and f_i is the function that is computed during the i-th action. The i-th action corresponds to the i-th synchronization object in the interface.

- The translation of a guard manager is a basic arrow $gm[p] : ins \otimes b \to 1$ where p is the guard of the only action of the guard manager.

- The translation of a glue with n actions is a tree composed by ∇ connectors with n leaves and with a $\overline{1}$ connector as root together with the ! for all its channels (plus one for a special boolean object), see e. g. Figure 10.

Note that we have a bijective correspondence between channels in a program and channel objects in the left interface of its translation and between actions of a program and synchronization objects in the right interface.

We show now how the operation of "parallel composition through one cable" is performed. Suppose we have a cable with channels $x_1,\ldots,x_n$ and actions $a_1,\ldots,a_n$. Each channel is mapped through morphisms to two groups of channels, one for each of the diagrams to be composed. Each action is the image of zero or more actions from the diagrams to be composed.

The resulting arrow is obtained by taking the parallel composition of the translations of the two components. On the left we merge, using trees of ∇ connectors (and possibly some permutations), the two special boolean objects and all the channels that are mapped to the same channel in the cable.

On the right we have to synchronize tuples of actions that are mapped to the same action in the cable. In order to synchronize a tuple t_1 of n actions with a tuple t_2 of m actions we have to duplicate each of them. Then we create using ∇ connectors n links to each object in t_2 and m links to each object in t_1. Then we merge using Δ connectors each action in the first group with each action in the second group and we close the resulting objects using ! connectors. See Figure 9 for an example (groups of two and three actions respectively).

The left interface of the resulting arrow has all the channels modulo equivalence while the right interface has all the actions in the components.

When the whole diagram has been mapped we also need to close all the synchronization objects in the output interface using ! connectors. If we want an anchored configuration, we can add the state to the left.

Tile observations. The observations of our tile system are of two kinds: in the action part we have tuples of $\mathsf{tick} : 1 \to 1$ and $\mathsf{untick} : 1 \to 1$ operators, which express that the action associated with the initial interface is either taking place or it is inhibited, respectively.

In the channel part we have as observations conditional multiple assignments where the condition is associated to the special boolean object and the assignments to the output channels (note that names are immaterial). This kind of observations can be formalized as arrows of $\mathbf{Th}[\Sigma]$ where Σ contains the data-signature, all predicate symbols, logical conjunction and also a $*$ unary operator standing for a guess on the update of input channels, on which components have no control. Graphically, observations are conveniently represented as boxes decorated with predicates and assignments over the variables in the initial and final interfaces, denoted by the x's and y's, respectively. Three sample observations are in Figure 11.

Tiles. The rules defining the behavior of the configurations in terms of allowed observations are the following. Since the structure of diagrams is fixed, we have tiles with equal initial and final configurations, except for the values in the state.

- $state[val : typ] \xrightarrow[Term]{id_0} state[val' : typ]$ where *Term* is a conditional multiple assignment whose condition is satisfied by *val* such that *val'* is obtained evaluating the assignments on *val* (the arrow *Term* involves a guess $*$ attached to each input variable);

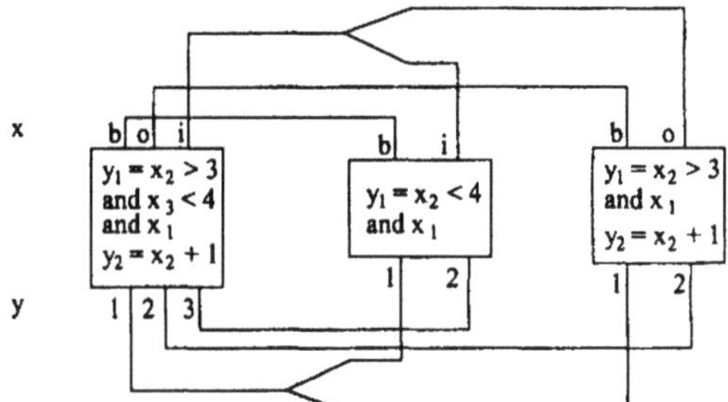

Figure 11. A sample tile for data handling.

- there are several auxiliary tiles for value handling that guarantee the consistency of distributed assignments and assumptions on shared channels (an example of tile for value handling is in Figure 11);
- there are n possible tiles for each channel manager with n actions, of the form $cm[\langle f_i \rangle_{i=1...n}] \xrightarrow[\mathsf{untick}^{i-1} \otimes \mathsf{tick} \otimes \mathsf{untick}^{n-i}]{true \to f_i} cm[\langle f_i \rangle_{i=1...n}]$ where untick^{i-1} denotes the monoidal product of $i-1$ instances of untick, and the term $true \to f_i$ assigns f_i to the output channel and has $true$ as condition;
- there are two possible tiles for each guard manager:

$$gm[p] \xrightarrow[\mathsf{tick}]{p \to skip} gm[p] \qquad gm[p] \xrightarrow[\mathsf{untick}]{true \to skip} gm[p]$$

- tiles for action connectors are as follows. They define the allowed combinations of tick and untick actions at the interfaces.

$$\nabla \xrightarrow[\mathsf{tick} \otimes \mathsf{untick}]{\mathsf{tick}} \nabla \qquad \nabla \xrightarrow[\mathsf{untick} \otimes \mathsf{tick}]{\mathsf{tick}} \nabla \qquad \nabla \xrightarrow[\mathsf{untick} \otimes \mathsf{untick}]{\mathsf{untick}} \nabla$$

$$\nabla_1 \xrightarrow[\mathsf{tick} \otimes \mathsf{tick}]{\mathsf{tick}} \nabla_1 \qquad \Delta_1 \xrightarrow[\mathsf{tick}]{\mathsf{tick} \otimes \mathsf{tick}} \Delta_1 \qquad !_1 \xrightarrow[id_0]{\mathsf{tick}} !_1 \qquad \bar{1} \xrightarrow[\mathsf{tick}]{id_0} \bar{1}$$

$$\nabla_1 \xrightarrow[\mathsf{untick} \otimes \mathsf{untick}]{\mathsf{untick}} \nabla_1 \qquad \Delta_1 \xrightarrow[\mathsf{untick}]{\mathsf{untick} \otimes \mathsf{untick}} \Delta_1 \qquad !_1 \xrightarrow[id_0]{\mathsf{untick}} !_1$$

4. The encoding and its properties

The tile system for CommUnity allows for many ill-formed configurations that have no correspondence with CommUnity diagrams, so we restrict our attention to configurations that are images of configuration diagrams as defined in § 1.1.

The operational semantics is then given by taking as transitions the tiles whose initial configuration is the image of such a diagram. The abstract semantics is given by tile bisimilarity.

Although the details of the encoding are omitted because of space limitations, the formal definition is given inductively on the size of the diagram. Let **dia** be a CommUnity configuration diagram, let DS(**dia**) be its standard decomposition, let $\leq$ be a total ordering on the programs in $\mathsf{DS}(\mathbf{dia})$, and let *val* denote the initial state; then we denote by $\mathsf{TS}(\mathbf{dia},\leq,val)$ the resulting initial anchored configuration where synchronization objects have been closed using ! connectors. We denote by $\mathsf{TS}(\mathbf{dia},\leq)$ the corresponding unanchored configuration.

Note that the configuration $\mathsf{TS}(\mathbf{dia},\leq,val)$ has empty input and output interfaces, while the input interface of $\mathsf{TS}(\mathbf{dia},\leq)$ has the form $chs \otimes b$, for *chs* the list of typed channels in $\mathsf{colim}(\mathbf{dia})$. When $\mathsf{DS}(\mathbf{dia})$ is a single program, the total order is fixed and we denote it with $\bullet$.

PROPOSITION 6 *If a tile has initial configuration* $\mathsf{TS}(\mathbf{dia},\leq,val)$, *then there exists an assignment of values val′ such that the final configuration takes the form* $\mathsf{TS}(\mathbf{dia},\leq,val')$.

We state the correctness result of our encoding w.r.t. the intended behavior of the program obtained as colimit of the diagram.

THEOREM 7 *We have a tile with* $\mathsf{TS}(\mathbf{dia},\leq,val) \xrightarrow[id_0]{id_0} \mathsf{TS}(\mathbf{dia},\leq,val')$ *iff there exists a sequence of (enabled) actions of* $\mathsf{colim}(\mathbf{dia})$ *starting from a state with values val to a state with values val′.*

It follows that the ordering considered in the encoding is immaterial.

PROPOSITION 8 *Let* **dia** *be a configuration diagram, let* $\leq$, $\leq'$ *be total orderings on the programs in* $\mathsf{DS}(\mathbf{dia})$, *and let val denote the initial state. Then,* $\mathsf{TS}(\mathbf{dia},\leq,val) \simeq \mathsf{TS}(\mathbf{dia},\leq',val)$. *Moreover, there exists a symmetry* ρ *such that* $\mathsf{TS}(\mathbf{dia},\leq) \simeq (\rho \otimes id_b);\mathsf{TS}(\mathbf{dia},\leq')$.

The symmetry ρ is needed to rearrange the input interface of $\mathsf{TS}(\mathbf{dia},\leq')$ so that channel objects that are associated to the same channel in $\mathsf{colim}(\mathbf{dia})$ have the same position in $\mathsf{TS}(\mathbf{dia},\leq)$ and $(\rho \otimes id_b);\mathsf{TS}(\mathbf{dia},\leq')$

Proposition 8 is also instrumental in proving the main result below.

THEOREM 9 $\mathsf{TS}(\mathbf{dia},\leq,val) \simeq \mathsf{TS}(\mathsf{colim}(\mathbf{dia}),\bullet,val)$. *Moreover, there exists a symmetry* ρ *such that* $\mathsf{TS}(\mathbf{dia},\leq) \simeq (\rho \otimes id_b);\mathsf{TS}(\mathsf{colim}(\mathbf{dia}),\bullet)$.

5. Concluding remarks

In this paper, we have reported on our research aimed to establish connections between CommUnity and the Tile Model in the way they address architectural concerns in the development of distributed and mobile software systems.

The main results of our investigation are:

- we have identified a standard decomposition for CommUnity programs, which separates the key aspects involved: channel managers, guard managers, coordination;
- the encoding into tiles gives an operational semantics to CommUnity programs and an abstract semantics correct w.r.t. the colimit construction;

- the separation of concerns has been exported from CommUnity to the Tile Model by separating the state from functionalities in the latter.

As already mentioned, the two frameworks are being investigated as representatives of two more general approaches to the study of complex system structures in general, and of their architectural aspects in particular: the *categorical approach* and the *algebraic approach*. It is clear that both views allow for separating *components* from *coordinators*.

In CommUnity the elementary components are channel managers and guard managers, which are boxes in the Tile Model, while coordination is expressed by cables, glues and morphisms which are connectors in the Tile Model.

As future work, we plan to extend our investigation by taking into account locality and mobility aspects and dynamic diagram reconfigurations. Furthermore we want to find a suitable axiomatization of ours connectors such that the translation of a diagram and of its colimit are equal up-to the axioms.

References

[1] R. Allen and D. Garlan. A formal basis for architectural connectors. *ACM Transactions on Software Engineering and Methodology*, 6(3):213–249, 1997.

[2] L. Andrade *et al.* AGILE: Software architecture for mobility. *Proc. of WADT 2002, LNCS* 2755, pp. 1–33. Springer Verlag, 2003.

[3] K. Chandy and J. Misra. *Parallel program design: a foundation*. Addison-Wesley, 1988.

[4] A. Corradini and U. Montanari. An algebraic semantics for structured transition systems and its application to logic programs. *Theoret. Comput. Sci.*, 103:51–106, 1992.

[5] J.L. Fiadeiro, A. Lopes, and M. Wermelinger. A mathematical semantics for architectural connectors. *Generic Programming, LNCS* 2793, pp. 190–234. Springer Verlag, 2003.

[6] J.L. Fiadeiro and T. Maibaum. Categorical semantics of parallel program design. *Science of Computer Programming*, 28:111–138, 1997.

[7] F. Gadducci and U. Montanari. The tile model. *Proof, Language and Interaction: Essays in Honour of Robin Milner*, pp. 133–166. MIT Press, 2000.

[8] J. Goguen. Categorical foundations for general systems theory. *Advances in Cybernetics and Systems Research*, pp. 121–130. Transcripta Books, 1973.

[9] C.A.R. Hoare. *Communicating Sequential Processes*. International Series in Computer Science. Prentice-Hall, 1985.

[10] K.G. Larsen and L. Xinxin. Compositionality through an operational semantics of contexts. *Proc. of ICALP '90, LNCS* 443, pp. 526–539. Springer Verlag, 1990.

[11] F.W. Lawvere. Functorial semantics of algebraic theories. *Proc. National Academy of Sciences*, 50:869–872, 1963.

[12] J. Meseguer. Conditional rewriting logic as a unified model of concurrency. *Theoret. Comput. Sci.*, 96:73–155, 1992.

[13] R. Milner. A calculus of communicating systems. *LNCS* 92. Springer Verlag, 1989.

[14] G. D. Plotkin. A structural approach to operational semantics. Technical Report DAIMI FN-19, Aarhus University, 1981.

ON COMPLEXITY OF MODEL-CHECKING FOR THE TQL LOGIC

Iovka Boneva, Jean-Marc Talbot
Laboratoire d'Informatique Fondamentale de Lille, France
INRIA team Mostrare

Abstract In this paper we study the complexity of the model-checking problem for the tree logic introduced as the basis for the query language TQL [Cardelli and Ghelli, 2001]. We define two distinct fragments of this logic: TL containing only spatial connectives and $TL^{\exists}$ containing spatial connectives and quantification. We show that the combined complexity of TL is PSPACE-hard. We also study data complexity of model-checking and show that it is linear for TL, hard for all levels of the polynomial hierarchy for $TL^{\exists}$ and PSPACE-hard for the full logic. Finally we devise a polynomial space model-checking algorithm showing this way that the model-checking problem for the TQL logic is PSPACE-complete.

1. Introduction

The development of the WEB made semi-structured data prominent. Semi-structured data can be represented by various models such as graphs [Abiteboul et al., 2000], unranked-ordered trees [Neven, 2002] (as for XML documents) or unranked-unordered trees. In [Cardelli, 2000], Cardelli noticed the similarity between this model of unranked-unordered trees and processes from the ambient calculus [Cardelli and Gordon, 2000b]. He also suggested that the ambient logic [Cardelli and Gordon, 2000a] could be a formalism for querying such data representation. Following those ideas, Cardelli and Ghelli proposed in [Cardelli and Ghelli, 2001] TQL (Tree Query Language). The main features of TQL are a semi-structured data representation based on (static) ambient processes and a query formalism based on a tree logic which is an extension of the spatial fragment of the ambient logic. The TQL logic is a very expressive logic which contains Boolean operations, spatial connectives, quantification over labels and trees and a fixed point operator.

The model-checking problem is to decide for a tree and a formula, whether the tree satisfies the formula. In the context of databases, this problem (also called Boolean query) can be used to test whether a database satisfies some integrity constraints. We focus in this paper on the model-checking problem for the TQL logic and two natural fragments of it: we investigate in particular the combined and data complexity for these fragments; we recall that the combined complexity of model-checking is the complexity of the model-checking problem when both the tree and the formula are inputs of the problem. The data complexity is the complexity considering only the tree as input of the problem.

One of our main results is that combined complexity for model-checking for the tree logic is PSPACE-complete. To prove complexity upper bound, we design a polynomial space model-checking algorithm inspired from the local model-checking of the μ-calculus [Stirling and Walker, 1991]. Combined complexity of model-checking for the tree logic is already known to be PSPACE-hard [Charatonik et al., 2001]. For the proof of this latter, the authors use quantification over labels. We show here that PSPACE-hardness of model-checking is obtained even for the smallest spatial fragment of the tree logic, that is, the fragment containing only spatial connectives and Boolean operators (we call this fragment *TL*). This result is surprising as it shows that quantification and fixed point operator, although adding expressive power to the logic, do not make model-checking harder.

Our second contribution concerns the data complexity of model-checking: we show that the data complexity is linear for the *TL* fragment and PSPACE-hard for the full logic. We obtain also an intermediate result: the data complexity of the fragment obtained by removing fixed point operators from the full logic is hard for any level of the polynomial hierarchy.

The paper is organized as follows: in Sect. 2, we introduce information trees (a representation as nested multisets for edge-labeled, unranked and unordered trees). We give also the syntax and the semantics of the tree logic proposed by Cardelli and Ghelli and define two fragments of this logic. Sect. 3 is devoted to the study of complexity lower bounds of the model-checking problem for the tree logic and its fragments. Finally, we present in Sect. 4 a polynomial space model-checking algorithm for the tree logic.

2. Definitions

2.1 The Tree Model

We consider edge-labeled, unranked and unordered trees represented, following [Cardelli and Ghelli, 2001], as nested multisets. This is a quite natural interpretation when dealing with unordered unranked trees.

We denote $\{\!\{\ \}\!\}$ the empty multiset and $\uplus$ the multiset union. We consider a countable set of labels Λ and we define the set $\mathcal{D}$ of *information trees*[1] as the

[1] In [Cardelli and Ghelli, 2001], the authors considered additionally the notion of *info-terms*, which correspond to ambient processes. They also define a denotation for info-terms in terms of information trees. Here we omit this notion of info-terms to speak directly about information trees.

least one satisfying: (i) the empty multiset $\{\!\{\}\!\}$ is in $\mathcal{D}$, (ii) if m is a label from Λ and A belongs to $\mathcal{D}$ then $\{\!\{m[A]\}\!\}$ belongs to $\mathcal{D}$ and (iii) if A, A' belong to $\mathcal{D}$ then $A \uplus A'$ belongs to $\mathcal{D}$.

For any tree A, we denote $fn(A)$ the set of labels appearing in A.

We define the *component relation* as a partial ordering relation over information trees recursively defined as follows: a tree A is a component of a tree A' (denoted $A \sqsubseteq A'$) if either A is a subset of A' or, for some element $m[B]$ in A', A is a component of B. The component relation on information trees differs from the usual subtree relation: considering the tree structure of some information tree A, a subtree can be identified by a single node in A whereas a component of A is characterized by a *set* of sibling nodes. We use a different term to avoid counter-intuitions. Note also that the number of subtrees for some tree A is linear in the size of A whereas the number of components of A may be exponential in the size of this tree.

2.2 The Tree Logics $TL^{\exists}_{\nu}$, $TL^{\exists}$ and TL

This section presents the tree logic defined in [Cardelli and Ghelli, 2001], that we denote $TL^{\exists}_{\nu}$, as well as its two fragments $TL^{\exists}$ and TL.

Syntax. We assume a countable set $\mathcal{L}$ of *label variables* ranging over by x, y, a countable set $\mathcal{T}$ of *tree variables* ranging over by X, Y and a countable set $\mathcal{R}$ of *recursion variables* ranging over by ξ. Let η be a label constant or a label variable. Formulas of the logic $TL^{\exists}_{\nu}$ are defined recursively as :

- $\mathbf{0}$ (empty tree), $\top$ (true), X (tree variable), ξ (recursion variable) and $\eta = \eta'$ (label equality test) are formulas from $TL^{\exists}_{\nu}$;
- if φ, ψ are formulas from $TL^{\exists}_{\nu}$ then $\eta[\varphi]$ (location), $\varphi \,|\, \psi$ (composition), $\neg\varphi$ (negation), $\varphi \vee \psi$ (disjunction), $\exists x.\varphi$ (quantification over label variables) $\exists X.\varphi$ (quantification over tree variables) and $\nu\xi.\varphi$ (greatest fixed point) are formulas from $TL^{\exists}_{\nu}$.

To guarantee the existence of the greatest fixed point $\nu\xi.\varphi$, we require that any occurrence of the recursion variable ξ in the formula φ is in the scope of an even number of negations.

The derived operators $\varphi \wedge \psi$, $\forall x.\varphi$, $\forall X.\varphi$ and $\mu\xi.\varphi$ are defined as usual.

Binding operators are $\exists x$ for label variables, $\exists X$ for tree variables and $\nu\xi$ for recursion variables. Let $fv(\varphi)$ be the set of free variables of the formula φ. We say that a formula is *closed* if it does not contains free variables.

We denote $fn(\varphi)$ the set of labels occurring in the formula φ. >From now on, we assume that in formulas free variables are disjoint from bounded variables and moreover, that two distinct occurrences of binders bind different variables.

Semantics and Satisfiability. We consider *valuations* ρ and δ defined over a finite subset of respectively $\mathcal{L} \cup \mathcal{T}$ and $\mathcal{R}$. The valuation ρ maps label variables to labels and tree variables to trees whereas the valuation δ maps recursion variables to subsets of $\mathcal{D}$. For ρ (resp. δ), we denote $dom(\rho)$ (resp. $dom(\delta)$) its domain.

The set of free label- and tree-variables of a formula φ under a valuation ρ denoted $fv(\varphi, \rho)$ is defined as $(fv(\varphi) \cap (\mathcal{L} \cup \mathcal{T})) \setminus dom(\rho)$. Respectively, the set of free recursion variables of a formula φ under a valuation δ denoted $fv(\varphi, \delta)$ is defined as $(fv(\varphi) \cap \mathcal{R}) \setminus dom(\delta)$. We say that a formula φ is closed under a valuation ρ, or simply ρ-closed (resp. under a valuation δ, or δ-closed) if $fv(\varphi, \rho) = \varnothing$ (resp. $fv(\varphi, \delta) = \varnothing$).

The interpretation of the formula φ is given by a mapping $\llbracket\varphi\rrbracket_{\rho,\delta}$ which associates with φ a subset of $\mathcal{D}$. This mapping is parametrized by two valuations ρ and δ such that φ is both ρ- and δ-closed. We assume that ρ is extended on labels from Λ and maps any label to itself; thus, we can write $\rho(\eta)$ for constant labels η. The valuation $\rho[x \mapsto n]$ is identical to ρ except for x which is mapped to n; the valuations $\rho[X \mapsto A]$ and $\delta[\xi \mapsto S]$ are defined in a similar way.

Interpretation of formulas

$$
\begin{array}{lcl@{\qquad}lcl}
\llbracket 0\rrbracket_{\rho,\delta} & = & \{\{\!\{\,\}\!\}\} & \llbracket \eta[\varphi]\rrbracket_{\rho,\delta} & = & \{\{\!\{\rho(\eta)[A]\}\!\} \mid A \in \llbracket\varphi\rrbracket_{\rho,\delta}\} \\
\llbracket \top\rrbracket_{\rho,\delta} & = & \mathcal{D} & \llbracket \varphi \mid \psi\rrbracket_{\rho,\delta} & = & \{A \uplus B \mid A \in \llbracket\varphi\rrbracket_{\rho,\delta}, B \in \llbracket\psi\rrbracket_{\rho,\delta}\} \\
\llbracket \neg\varphi\rrbracket_{\rho,\delta} & = & \mathcal{D} \setminus \llbracket\varphi\rrbracket_{\rho,\delta} & \llbracket \varphi \vee \psi\rrbracket_{\rho,\delta} & = & \llbracket\varphi\rrbracket_{\rho,\delta} \cup \llbracket\psi\rrbracket_{\rho,\delta} \\
\llbracket \exists x.\varphi\rrbracket_{\rho,\delta} & = & \bigcup_{n\in\Lambda} \llbracket\varphi\rrbracket_{\rho[x\mapsto n],\delta} & \llbracket \eta = \eta'\rrbracket_{\rho,\delta} & = & \mathcal{D} \text{ if } \rho(\eta) = \rho(\eta'), \varnothing \text{ otherwise} \\
\llbracket X\rrbracket_{\rho,\delta} & = & \{\rho(X)\} & \llbracket \exists X.\varphi\rrbracket_{\rho,\delta} & = & \bigcup_{A\in\mathcal{D}} \llbracket\varphi\rrbracket_{\rho[X\mapsto A],\delta} \\
\llbracket \xi\rrbracket_{\rho,\delta} & = & \delta(\xi) & \llbracket \nu\xi.\varphi\rrbracket_{\rho,\delta} & = & \bigcup\{S \subseteq \mathcal{D} \mid S \subseteq \llbracket\varphi\rrbracket_{\rho,\delta[\xi\mapsto S]}\}
\end{array}
$$

DEFINITION 1 (SATISFIABILITY) *For any tree A, any formula φ, and any valuations ρ, δ such that φ is ρ- and δ-closed, the tree A* satisfies *the formula φ under the valuations ρ and δ, written $A \models_{\rho,\delta} \varphi$, if A is in the set $\llbracket\varphi\rrbracket_{\rho,\delta}$.*

In the notations $A \models_{\rho,\delta} \varphi$ and $\llbracket\varphi\rrbracket_{\rho,\delta}$ we sometimes omit ρ (resp. δ) whenever the formula φ contains no free label- and tree-variables (resp. no free recursion variables).

Fragments of the Logic. In the following of this paper, we will consider two fragments of the tree logic $TL^{\exists}_{\nu}$; the first fragment, denoted TL, is the smallest spatial logic included in $TL^{\exists}_{\nu}$ as it is defined only with Boolean operators, the empty tree, composition and location. The second fragment, denoted $TL^{\exists}$, is obtained by removing fixed point operator from the logic $TL^{\exists}_{\nu}$. It is easy to see that $TL \subseteq TL^{\exists} \subseteq TL^{\exists}_{\nu}$.

2.3 Comparison with Other Logics

We show in this section that the monadic second-order logic over trees (MSO) is more expressive than the TL fragment but that the logic $TL^{\exists}$ can express properties that can not be expressed in MSO.

We consider $\Lambda' \subseteq \Lambda$ a finite set of labels. Let τ be the signature $\{\mathsf{label}_n \mid n \in \Lambda'\} \cup \{<\}$ where the label_n's are unary predicates and $<$ is a binary predicate. An information tree A (with $fn(A) \subseteq \Lambda'$) can be represented by a finite τ-structure $T^A = \langle E^A, \{\mathsf{label}_n^A \mid n \in \Lambda'\}, <^A\rangle$ where E^A is a finite set of edges, label_n^A associates the label n with edges, and $<^A$ is a binary relation over edges such that $u < u'$ holds iff the destination of the edge u and the source of the edge u' coincide.

We consider MSO over the signature τ. Edge variables range over u, v and set variables range over U, V. For any TL formula φ, we define an MSO formula $R_\varphi(U)$ parametrized by the set of edges U, such that for any information tree A, $A \models \varphi$ iff $T^A \models \forall U.((\forall u.u \in U) \rightarrow R_\varphi(U))$.

Encoding of *TL* in MSO

$$
\begin{array}{ll}
R_\top(U) & := \mathsf{true} \\
R_{\neg\varphi}(U) & := \neg R_\varphi(U) \\
R_{\varphi\vee\psi}(U) & := R_\varphi(U) \vee R_\psi(U) \\
R_0(U) & := (U = \varnothing) \\
R_{n[\varphi]}(U) & := \forall V, U' \,(\mathsf{src}(U,V) \wedge U' = U \setminus V) \rightarrow (\mathsf{singleton}(V) \wedge R_\varphi(U')) \\
R_{\varphi|\psi}(U) & := \exists U', U'' \,\mathsf{dunion}(U,U',U'') \wedge R_\varphi(U') \wedge R_\psi(U'') \wedge \\
 & \quad \forall V, V', V''(\mathsf{src}(U,V) \wedge \mathsf{src}(U',V') \wedge \mathsf{src}(U'',V'')) \rightarrow \mathsf{dunion}(V,V',V'') \\
\mathsf{src}(U,V) & := \forall v, v \in V \leftrightarrow (v \in U \wedge \neg(\exists v' \in U(v' < v))) \\
\mathsf{dunion}(U,U',U'') & := U' \cap U'' = \varnothing \wedge U = U' \cup U''
\end{array}
$$

Now, consider the $TL^\exists$ formula $\exists X(a[X] \mid b[X])$: it expresses that the root of the tree has two direct subtrees (reachable by a and b) and that these subtrees are isomorphic. It is well-know that this property can not be expressed in MSO.

Some other logics express properties of unranked and unordered trees: for instance, the monadic second order logic with counting (CMSO) [Courcelle, 1990b], the Presburger monadic second order logic (PMSO) [Seidl et al., 2003], the sheaves logic [Dal-Zilio and Lugiez, 2003]. We strongly believe that the tree logic we consider in this paper is strictly more powerful than those logics.

3. Complexity of Model-Checking

The model-checking problem is given an information tree A, a valuation ρ[2] and a ρ-closed formula φ without free recursion variable, decide whether $A \models_\rho \varphi$. We study in this section lower bounds of the combined complexity and the data complexity of model-checking for the tree logic $TL_\nu^\exists$ and its fragments. We establish that combined complexity is PSPACE-hard for the less expressive fragment TL and that data-complexity is linear for TL, hard for any level of the polynomial hierarchy for $TL^\exists$ and PSPACE-hard for the full logic $TL_\nu^\exists$.

For PSPACE-hardness (resp. hardness for levels in the polynomial hierarchy) proof, we use reductions of the validity problem of closed quantified

[2]The valuation ρ is considered to be empty for the logic TL.

Boolean formulas (QBF) (resp. of closed QBF with fixed quantifier alternation depth) to the model-checking problem.

3.1 Quantified Boolean Formulas

A quantified Boolean formula (QBF) is a formula $Q_1 v_1. \dots .Q_n v_n.G$ where each Q_i is a quantifier among $\exists$ and $\forall$ and G is a propositional logic formula built on the set of variables $\{v_1, \dots, v_n\}$. We can assume without loss of generality that G is in disjunctive normal form and follows the syntax:

$$G ::= \theta_1 \vee \ldots \vee \theta_k \qquad \theta ::= l_1 \wedge \ldots \wedge l_r \qquad l ::= v_i \mid \overline{v_i}, \;\; i \in \{1, \dots, n\}$$

It is well known that validity of closed QBF is a PSPACE-complete problem [Stockmeyer, 1976].

The quantifier alternation depth $depth(\mathcal{G})$ of a QBF $\mathcal{G}$ is defined as: (i) for a quantifier-free formula $\mathcal{G}$, $depth(\mathcal{G}) = 0$ and $depth(Qx.\mathcal{G}) = 1$ (for $Q \in \{\exists, \forall\}$), (ii) $depth(Qx.Q'x'.\mathcal{G}) = depth(Q'x'.\mathcal{G})$ if $Q = Q'$ and (iii) $depth(Qx.Q'x'.\mathcal{G}) = 1 + depth(Q'x'.\mathcal{G})$ if $Q \neq Q'$.

The validity problem of a closed QBF of alternation depth n whose outermost quantifier is $\forall$ (resp. $\exists$) is complete for the universal (resp. existential) n^{th} level of the polynomial hierarchy PH, that is Π_n^P-complete (resp. Σ_n^P-complete) [Stockmeyer, 1976].

3.2 Combined Complexity

The combined complexity of the model-checking problem $A \models_\rho \varphi$ is the complexity of the problem considering A, φ and ρ as inputs of the problem.

It has already been shown in [Charatonik et al., 2001] that the combined complexity of $TL^\exists$ is PSPACE-hard by encoding the validity problem of QBF into the model-checking of $TL^\exists$. This encoding uses only Boolean connectives, label comparison and existential quantification over labels. We show here that the combined complexity is PSPACE-hard even for the less expressive logic TL.

With any QBF $\mathcal{F}$, we associate the TL formula $(\!|\mathcal{F}|\!)$ defined as:

Encoding of QBF into *TL*

$(\!\mid v_i \mid\!)$	$= \mathsf{v}_i[\mathsf{t}[0]]$	$(\!\mid \overline{v_i} \mid\!)$	$= \mathsf{v}_i[\mathsf{f}[0]]$
$(\!\mid \exists v_i.\mathcal{F} \mid\!)$	$= \mathsf{v}_i[\top] \mid (\!\mid \mathcal{F} \mid\!)$	$(\!\mid \forall v_i.\mathcal{F} \mid\!)$	$= \neg(\mathsf{v}_i[\top] \mid \neg (\!\mid \mathcal{F} \mid\!))$
$(\!\mid l_1 \wedge \ldots \wedge l_k \mid\!)$	$= (\!\mid l_1 \mid\!) \mid \top \wedge \ldots \wedge (\!\mid l_k \mid\!) \mid \top$	$(\!\mid \theta_1 \vee \ldots \vee \theta_k \mid\!)$	$= (\!\mid \theta_1 \mid\!) \vee \ldots \vee (\!\mid \theta_k \mid\!)$

where t, f and the v_i are labels from Λ.

Let T and F be respectively the information trees $\{\!\{\mathsf{t}[\{\!\{\}\!\}]\}\!\}$ and $\{\!\{\mathsf{f}[\{\!\{\}\!\}]\}\!\}$. We consider in the sequel the n-variables QBF $\mathcal{G} = Q_1 v_1. \dots .Q_n v_n.G$. Let $P_\mathcal{G}$ be the constant information tree (note that the construction of $P_\mathcal{G}$ is polynomial time)

$$P_{\mathcal{G}} = \{\!\{ \mathsf{v}_1[T], \mathsf{v}_1[F], \mathsf{v}_2[T], \mathsf{v}_2[F], \ldots, \mathsf{v}_n[T], \mathsf{v}_n[F] \}\!\}$$

LEMMA 2 *For any closed quantified Boolean formula $\mathcal{G}$, $P_{\mathcal{G}} \models (\!|\mathcal{G}|\!)$ iff $\mathcal{G}$ is valid.*

We don't give here the full proof of the lemma, but just an intuitive idea about the encoding. Remark first that the tree $P_{\mathcal{G}}$ is the multiset of the elements $\mathsf{v}_i[T]$ and $\mathsf{v}_i[F]$ for all the variables v_i occurring in G. On the other hand, a valuation for the variables v_i in G can be viewed as a component P' of $P_{\mathcal{G}}$ in which each of the v_i occurs only once either as $\mathsf{v}_i[T]$ or as $\mathsf{v}_i[F]$, and T and F determine the valuation of the variable v_i. The tree P' can be constructed from $P_{\mathcal{G}}$ by n successive eliminations of one of the elements $\mathsf{v}_i[T]$ and $\mathsf{v}_i[F]$ for each i in $\{1, \ldots, n\}$. Hence, the model-checking problem $P_{\mathcal{G}} \models (\!|\mathcal{G}|\!)$ can be viewed as the construction of a valuation for the set of variables $\{v_1, \ldots, v_n\}$ by elimination of elements in $P_{\mathcal{G}}$, followed by the verification that this valuation renders the formula G true. The elimination of the element $\mathsf{v}_i[Z]$ for $Z \in \{T, F\}$ is done considering $P_{\mathcal{G}}$ as the union $\{\!\{\mathsf{v}_i[Z]\}\!\} \uplus P'$. Thus, model-checking $(\!|\exists v_i.\mathcal{F}|\!) = \mathsf{v}_i[\mathsf{T}] \,|\, (\!|\mathcal{F}|\!)$ leads us to eliminate non-deterministically one of the elements ($\mathsf{v}_i[T]$ or $\mathsf{v}_i[F]$) while model-checking $(\!|\forall v_i.\mathcal{F}|\!) = \neg(\mathsf{v}_i[\mathsf{T}] \,|\, \neg(\!|\mathcal{F}|\!))$ leads us to consider both cases in which $\mathsf{v}_i[T]$ and $\mathsf{v}_i[F]$ are eliminated.

THEOREM 3 *The combined complexity of model-checking the tree logic TL is PSPACE-hard.*

3.3 Data Complexity

The data complexity of the model-checking problem $A \models_\rho \varphi$ is the complexity of the problem for some fixed closed formula φ and valuation ρ. That is, only the tree A is considered as input for the problem. We show in the following that the data complexity of model-checking is PSPACE-hard for $TL^{\exists}_{\nu}$, hard for any level of the polynomial hierarchy for $TL^{\exists}$ and linear for TL.

Let us first introduce some objects which are in common to the next two encodings. Let $G = \theta_1 \vee \ldots \vee \theta_k$ be a Boolean formula in disjunctive normal form constructed over the set of variables $\bigcup_{i \in I}\{v_i\}$ for some finite set I. Moreover, we require that the θ_j are not trivially false, that is, for any j in $1..k$, there is no i in I such that both v_i and $\overline{v}_i$ occur in θ_j.

For any i in I, we define the sets $C_i^{\mathsf{true}} \subseteq \{1, \ldots, k\}$ and $C_i^{\mathsf{false}} \subseteq \{1, \ldots, k\}$ as: j is in C_i^{true} if the variable v_i does not occur negatively in θ_j and j is in C_i^{false} if the variable v_i does not occur positively in θ_j. Assuming that c_j, for j in $1..k$, is a label from Λ, we define the information trees $C_i^t = \biguplus_{j \in C_i^{\mathsf{true}}} \{\!\{\mathsf{c}_j[\{\!\{\}\!\}]\}\!\}$ and $C_i^f = \biguplus_{j \in C_i^{\mathsf{false}}} \{\!\{\mathsf{c}_j[\{\!\{\}\!\}]\}\!\}$.

A *valuation* γ for G is a mapping from I to $\{\text{true}, \text{false}\}$. It is easy to see that the formula G is valid for some valuation γ iff there exists some $j \in 1..k$ such that j is in $C_i^{\gamma(i)}$ for any i in I.

***$TL_\nu^\exists$*.** We show here that the data complexity of the model-checking problem for the tree logic $TL_\nu^\exists$ is PSPACE-hard, that is, there exists a fixed $TL_\nu^\exists$ formula Φ such that the model-checking problem "given the information tree A, does $A \models \Phi$ hold" is PSPACE-hard.

The PSPACE-hardness proof is done using a reduction of the validity problem of a closed QBF into the model-checking problem for $TL_\nu^\exists$. With any QBF $\mathcal{G}$, we associate the information tree $A_\mathcal{G}$ such that $A_\mathcal{G} \models \Phi$ iff $\mathcal{G}$ is valid.

Consider the n-variables QBF $\mathcal{G} = Q_1 v_1. \dots .Q_n v_n.G$. Let v_i for $i \in 1..n$, c_j for $j \in 1..k$, v_0, $\mathsf{q}_\forall$, $\mathsf{q}_\exists$, tt, ff, pred, quant and sat be labels. Let

$$A_\mathcal{G} = \{\!\{\mathsf{v}_0[\{\!\{\}\!\}], V_1^{\mathsf{true}}, V_1^{\mathsf{false}}, \dots, V_n^{\mathsf{true}}, V_n^{\mathsf{false}}\}\!\}$$

where, for any $i \in 1..n$, the trees V_i^{true} and V_i^{false} are

$$\begin{aligned} V_i^{\mathsf{true}} &= \mathsf{v}_i[\{\!\{\mathsf{tt}[\{\!\{\}\!\}], \mathsf{quant}[\{\!\{\mathsf{q}_{Q_i}[\{\!\{\}\!\}]\}\!\}], \mathsf{pred}[\{\!\{\mathsf{v}_{i-1}[\{\!\{\}\!\}]\}\!\}], \mathsf{sat}[C_i^t]\}\!\}] \\ V_i^{\mathsf{false}} &= \mathsf{v}_i[\{\!\{\mathsf{ff}[\{\!\{\}\!\}], \mathsf{quant}[\{\!\{\mathsf{q}_{Q_i}[\{\!\{\}\!\}]\}\!\}], \mathsf{pred}[\{\!\{\mathsf{v}_{i-1}[\{\!\{\}\!\}]\}\!\}], \mathsf{sat}[C_i^f]\}\!\}] \end{aligned}$$

Intuitively, for any variable v_i occurring in the QBF $\mathcal{G}$, the information tree $A_\mathcal{G}$ encodes the kind of quantification of v_i (in the component $\mathsf{quant}[\{\!\{\mathsf{q}_{Q_i}[\{\!\{\}\!\}]\}\!\}]$) and the rank of the variable (giving the previous variable in the component pred). The information trees C_i^t and C_i^f encode the formula G.

The $TL_\nu^\exists$ formula Φ is defined as

$$\Phi = \mu\xi.(\neg \mathit{IsValuation} \wedge \mathit{ConstructVal}) \vee (\mathit{IsValuation} \wedge \mathit{Valid})$$

The mechanism used here is similar to the one used to prove combined complexity lower bound of TL (Sect. 3.2). Intuitively, the formula Φ constructs all possible valuations for the variables v_i regarding their quantification in $\mathcal{G}$ and then verifies, for each valuation, whether it valuates the formula G to true.

To any valuation γ corresponds exactly a component of $A_\mathcal{G}$ denoted $A_\mathcal{G}\{\gamma\}$ and defined as $\{\mathsf{v}_0[\{\}], V_1^{\gamma(1)}, V_2^{\gamma(2)}, \dots, V_n^{\gamma(n)}\}$. Note that in $A_\mathcal{G}\{\gamma\}$, any of the v_i occurs only once. Therefore, the formula *IsValuation* verifying whether a component of $A_\mathcal{G}$ corresponds to a valuation is defined as:

$$\mathit{IsValuation} = \neg(\exists x_\mathsf{v}.x_\mathsf{v}[\mathsf{T}] \,|\, x_\mathsf{v}[\mathsf{T}] \,|\, \mathsf{T})$$

Now, a valuation can be constructed from $A_\mathcal{G}$ by n successive eliminations of one of V_i^{true} or V_i^{false}, for any $i \in \{1, \dots, n\}$. All possible valuations of the variables v_i, according to the quantifications of these variables, are enumerated by the $TL_\nu^\exists$ subformula *ConstructVal* which is the recursive part of Φ. In the following, we let $Forall(x_v) = x_v[\mathsf{quant}[\mathsf{q}_\forall[0]] \mid \top] \mid \top$ and $Exists(x_v) = x_v[\mathsf{quant}[\mathsf{q}_\exists[0]] \mid \top] \mid \top$.

$$ConstructVal = \exists x_v.FirstNonVal(x_v) \wedge \begin{pmatrix} Forall(x_v) \wedge \neg(x_v[\top] \mid \neg\xi) \\ \vee \\ Exists(x_v) \wedge x_v[\top] \mid \xi \end{pmatrix}$$

$$FirstNonVal(x_v) = \exists x'_v. \begin{pmatrix} \neg(x'_v[\top] \mid x'_v[\top] \mid \top) \\ \wedge \\ x_v[\top] \mid x_v[\top] \mid \top \\ \wedge \\ x_v[\mathsf{pred}[x'_v[\top]] \mid \top] \mid \top \end{pmatrix}$$

Finally, according to the definitions of the sets C_i^{true} and C_i^{false}, to verify the validity of G under the valuation γ amounts to test the existence of some $j \in \{1, \ldots, k\}$ such that $\mathsf{c}_j[\{\{\}\}]$ is a component of $C_i^{\gamma(i)}$ for any i. This is done by the formula *Valid* which is the base case for Φ.

$$\begin{array}{rcl} Valid & = & \mathsf{v}_0[\top] \mid \exists x_c.Everywhere(x_c) \\ Everywhere(x_c) & = & \forall x_v.\, (x_v[\top] \mid \top \rightarrow x_v[\mathsf{sat}[x_c[0] \mid \top] \mid \top] \mid \top) \end{array}$$

Lemma 4 embodies the correctness of the reduction and implies Theorem 5 simply by noticing that the size of the tree $A_{\mathcal{G}}$ is polynomial in the size of the QBF $\mathcal{G}$.

LEMMA 4 *The closed quantified Boolean formula $\mathcal{G}$ is valid iff $A_{\mathcal{G}} \models \Phi$.*

THEOREM 5 *The data complexity of model-checking the tree logic $TL_\nu^\exists$ is PSPACE-hard.*

$TL^\exists$. We show here that the data complexity of the model-checking problem for the tree logic $TL^\exists$ is hard for any level of the polynomial hierarchy PH. That is, we show that for any universal (resp. existential) level of PH Π_n^P (resp. Σ_n^P), there exists a fixed formula $\Phi_n^\forall$ (resp. $\Phi_n^\exists$) such that the model-checking problem "given the information tree A, does $A \models \Phi_n^\forall$ (resp. $A \models \Phi_n^\exists$) hold" is Π_n^P-hard (resp. Σ_n^P-hard).

To prove Π_n^P-hardness (resp. Σ_n^P-hardness), we present a reduction of the validity problem of closed QBF with alternation depth n and universal (resp. existential) outermost quantifier into the model-checking problem for $TL^\exists$ with some fixed formula $\Phi_n^\forall$ (resp. $\Phi_n^\exists$). More precisely, with any closed QBF $\mathcal{G}$ of alternation depth n we associate the information tree $A_{\mathcal{G}}$ and we show that $A_{\mathcal{G}} \models \Phi_n^\forall$ (resp. $A_{\mathcal{G}} \models \Phi_n^\exists$) iff the outermost quantifier of $\mathcal{G}$ is $\forall$ (resp. $\exists$) and $\mathcal{G}$ is valid.

Consider the closed QBF with alternation depth n ($Q_i \neq Q_{i+1}$ for i in $1..n-1$).

$$\mathcal{G} = Q_1\, v_{(1,1)} \ldots v_{(1,n_1)}.Q_2\, v_{(2,1)} \ldots v_{(2,n_2)}. \ldots .Q_n\, v_{(n,1)} \ldots v_{(n,n_n)}.G$$

Let $\mathsf{v}_{(h,i)}$ for any $h \in 1..n$ and any $i \in 1..n_h$, c_j for any $j \in 1..k$, quant, sat and q_i for any $i \in 1..n$ be labels from Λ. The information tree $A_{\mathcal{G}}$ is:

$$A_{\mathcal{G}} = \{\!\{V^{\mathsf{true}}_{(1,1)}, V^{\mathsf{false}}_{(1,1)}, \ldots, V^{\mathsf{true}}_{(1,n_1)}, V^{\mathsf{false}}_{(1,n_1)}, V^{\mathsf{true}}_{(2,1)}, V^{\mathsf{false}}_{(2,1)}, \ldots, V^{\mathsf{true}}_{(n,n_n)}, V^{\mathsf{false}}_{(n,n_n)}\}\!\}$$

where for any $h \in 1..n$ and for any $i \in 1..n_h$, $V^{\mathsf{true}}_{(h,i)}$ and $V^{\mathsf{false}}_{(h,i)}$ are

$$V^{\mathsf{true}}_{(h,i)} = \{\!\{\mathsf{tt}[\{\!\{\}\!\}], \mathsf{quant}[\{\!\{\mathsf{q}_h[\{\!\{\}\!\}]\}\!\}], \mathsf{sat}[C^t_{(h,i)}]\}\!\}$$
$$V^{\mathsf{false}}_{(h,i)} = \{\!\{\mathsf{ff}[\{\!\{\}\!\}], \mathsf{quant}[\{\!\{\mathsf{q}_h[\{\!\{\}\!\}]\}\!\}], \mathsf{sat}[C^f_{(h,i)}]\}\!\}$$

The formulas $\Phi^{\forall}_n$ and $\Phi^{\exists}_n$ are defined respectively as $\Psi^{\forall}_n(1)$ and $\Psi^{\exists}_n(1)$ where for any $h \in 1..n$, the formulas $\Psi^{\forall}_n(h)$ and $\Psi^{\exists}_n(h)$ are defined recursively:

$$\Psi^{\forall}_n(h) = \neg(\mathit{Remove}(h) \,|\, (\mathit{IsValuation}(h) \wedge \neg\Psi^{\exists}_n(h+1)))$$
$$\Psi^{\exists}_n(h) = \mathit{Remove}(h) \,|\, (\mathit{IsValuation}(h) \wedge \Psi^{\forall}_n(h+1))$$

and $\Psi^{\forall}_n(n+1) = \Phi^{\exists}_n(n+1) = \mathit{Valid}'$.

The intuition for this encoding is similar to the one used in previous section. The formulas $\Phi^{\forall}_n$ and $\Phi^{\exists}_n$ construct all possible valuations for the variables of the formula $\mathcal{G}$ according to their quantification and check, for each valuation, whether it valuates G to true. More precisely, for any $h \in 1..n$, the formula $\Psi^{\forall}_n(h)$ (resp. $\Psi^{\exists}_n(h)$) constructs all possible valuations of the variables $v_{(h,1)}, v_{(h,2)}, \ldots, v_{(h,n_h)}$ according to the universal (resp. existential) quantification and reiterates the same mechanism to $h+1$. Therefore, $\mathit{IsValuation}(h)$ and $\mathit{Remove}(h)$ are defined as:

$$\mathit{IsValuation}(h) = \neg\exists x_{\mathsf{v}}.(x_{\mathsf{v}}[\mathsf{quant}[\mathsf{q}_h[0]] \,|\, \mathsf{T}] \,|\, x_{\mathsf{v}}[\mathsf{quant}[\mathsf{q}_h[0]] \,|\, \mathsf{T}] \,|\, \mathsf{T})$$
$$\mathit{Remove}(h) = \forall x_{\mathsf{v}}.(x_{\mathsf{v}}[\mathsf{T}] \,|\, \mathsf{T} \rightarrow x_{\mathsf{v}}[\mathsf{quant}[\mathsf{q}_h[0]] \,|\, \mathsf{T}] \,|\, \mathsf{T}) \wedge \mathit{IsValuation}(h)$$

The formulas $\Psi^{\forall}_n(n+1)$ and $\Psi^{\exists}_n(n+1)$ check validity of G for some valuation, so the formula Valid' is defined as $\exists x_{\mathsf{c}}.\mathit{Everywhere}(x_{\mathsf{c}})$.

The correctness of the encoding we presented is given by Lemma 6 and the complexity result in Theorem 7 is an easy consequence of this lemma using the fact that the size of the tree $A_{\mathcal{G}}$ is polynomial in the size of the QBF $\mathcal{G}$.

LEMMA 6 *Let $\mathcal{G}$ be a closed quantified Boolean formula of alternation depth n whose outermost quantifier is universal (resp. existential). The formula $\mathcal{G}$ is valid iff $A_{\mathcal{G}} \models \Phi^{\forall}_n$ (resp. $A_{\mathcal{G}} \models \Phi^{\exists}_n$).*

THEOREM 7 *The data complexity of model-checking the tree logic $TL^{\exists}$ is hard for any level of the polynomial hierarchy.*

TL. We show here that the data complexity of the model-checking problem for the tree logic TL is linear time using the encoding of TL formulas into MSO presented in Sect. 2.3.

Remark first that by [Courcelle, 1990a], the data complexity of model-checking is linear for MSO interpreted over finite graphs of bounded tree-width which are a generalization of unranked unordered trees. Consider the model-checking problem $A \models \varphi$ where the formula φ is fixed. Let τ be the signature $\{\mathsf{label}_n \mid n \in fn(A) \cup fn(\varphi)\} \cup \{<\}$, and let T^A be the τ-structure corresponding to A. It is easy to see that the construction of T^A is linear time in the size of A. Moreover, as φ is fixed, the construction of $R_\varphi(U)$ is constant time.

THEOREM 8 *The data complexity of model-checking the tree logic TL is linear time.*

4. A Model-Checking Algorithm

Model-checking for the tree logic $TL_\nu^\exists$ is non trivial for two reasons. On one hand, the existential quantification operator quantifies label and tree variables over infinite sets. We show here how to handle this problem. On the other hand, the (greatest) fixed point operator from $TL_\nu^\exists$ differs from the kind of fixed points used to extend the first-order logic (FO) to LFP. In LFP, fixed points are defined over the lattice of relations on nodes of a tree (or graph) whereas in $TL_\nu^\exists$, fixed points are defined over the lattice of sets of trees.

We use an adaptation of the local model-checking for the modal μ-calculus given in [Stirling and Walker, 1991] to devise a polynomial space model-checking algorithm. Following the ideas from [Winskel, 1991], our algorithm will actually perform model-checking for a slight extension of $TL_\nu^\exists$: the syntax of greatest fixed point operator is now $\nu\xi(M).\varphi$ where M is a finite subset of $\mathcal{D}$ and its semantics is given by $\bigcup\{S \subseteq \mathcal{D} \mid S \subseteq [\![\varphi]\!]_{\rho,\delta[\xi \mapsto S]} \cup M\}$.

One can notice that the logic $TL_\nu^\exists$ corresponds to formulas where M is the empty set for all fixed point operators. We extend the definition of labels occurring in a formula by letting $fn(\nu\xi(M).\varphi) = fn(\varphi) \cup \bigcup_{A \in M} fn(A)$.

4.1 Properties of Satisfaction

The two propositions here after establish that only a finite number of labels and a finite number of information trees have to be considered while model-checking a formula with quantifiers.

Let $fn(S) = \bigcup_{A \in S} fn(A)$ for some $S \subseteq \mathcal{D}$, $fn(\rho) = \bigcup_{x \in dom(\rho) \cap \mathcal{L}} \{\rho(x)\} \cup \bigcup_{X \in dom(\rho) \cap \mathcal{T}} fn(\rho(X))$ for some valuation ρ and $fn(\delta) = \bigcup_{\xi \in dom(\delta)} fn(\delta(\xi))$ for some valuation δ. For a formula φ considered under some valuations ρ and δ, we define $fn(\varphi, \rho, \delta)$ as $fn(\varphi) \cup fn(\rho) \cup fn(\delta)$.

PROPOSITION 9 *Let A be a tree and $\exists X.\varphi$ be a closed formula under some valuations ρ and δ. Let n be a label which does not belong to $fn(A)$. Then $A \models_{\rho,\delta} \exists X.\varphi$ iff there exists some tree B in $\{C \mid C \sqsubseteq A\} \cup \{\{\!\{n[\{\!\{\}\!\}]\}\!\}\}$ such that $A \models_{\rho[X \mapsto B],\delta} \varphi$.*

SKETCH OF PROOF. The right-to-left implication is an easy consequence of the definition of satisfaction. For the left-to-right implication: if $A \models_{\rho,\delta} \exists X.\varphi$ then, by definition of satisfaction, there exists a tree B such that $A \models_{\rho[X \mapsto B],\delta} \varphi$. If this tree B is a component of A, then the statement is obvious. Otherwise, we show that for any tree C such that $C \not\sqsubseteq A$, it holds that $A \models_{\rho[X \to C],\delta}$ iff $A \models_{\rho[X \to B],\delta}$. As $\{\!\{n[\{\!\{\}\!\}]\}\!\} \not\sqsubseteq A$, we have $A \models_{\rho[X \mapsto \{\!\{n[\{\!\{\}\!\}]\}\!\}],\delta} \varphi$.

PROPOSITION 10 *Let A be a tree and $\exists x.\varphi$ be a closed formula under some valuations ρ and δ. Let n be a label such that $n \notin fn(A) \cup fn(\varphi, \rho, \delta)$. Then $A \models_{\rho,\delta} \exists x.\varphi$ iff there exists some label p in $fn(A) \cup fn(\varphi, \rho, \delta) \cup \{n\}$ such that $A \models_{\rho[x \mapsto p],\delta} \varphi$.*

SKETCH OF PROOF. The right-to-left direction is straightforward by the definition of satisfaction. For the left-to-right direction: as $A \models_{\rho,\delta} \exists x.\varphi$, by definition of satisfaction, there exists some label p' in Λ such that $A \models_{\rho[x \mapsto p'],\delta} \varphi$. If $p' \in fn(A) \cup fn(\varphi, \rho, \delta)$ then the property obviously holds. Otherwise, we show that for any label m such that $m \notin fn(A) \cup fn(\varphi, \rho, \delta)$, it holds that $A \models_{\rho[x \mapsto m],\delta} \varphi$ iff $A \models_{\rho[x \mapsto p'],\delta} \varphi$. Therefore, $A \models_{\rho[x \mapsto n],\delta} \varphi$.

4.2 Polynomial Space Model-checking Algorithm

We consider Δ, a (possibly empty) sequence of the form $[\xi_1 \to \varphi_1]\ldots[\xi_n \to \varphi_n]$ where the φ_i's are formulas from the tree logic and $\xi_i \neq \xi_j$ whenever $i \neq j$. For all i, $[\xi_i \to \varphi_i]$ is the substitution which, when applied to some formula ψ, replaces the free occurrences of the recursion variable ξ_i in ψ by the formula φ_i. The empty sequence is denoted ϵ and considered as the identity. The domain of a sequence of substitutions Δ (written $dom(\Delta)$) is defined as (i) $\varnothing$ if $\Delta = \epsilon$ and (ii) $\{\xi_1, \ldots, \xi_n\}$ if $\Delta = [\xi_1 \to \varphi_1]\ldots[\xi_n \to \varphi_n]$.

For a formula φ, $\Delta(\varphi)$ denotes the formula $[\xi_1 \to \varphi_1] \circ \ldots \circ [\xi_n \to \varphi_n](\varphi)$. For a sequence of substitutions Δ, $\Delta\langle\xi \leftarrow \varphi\rangle$ denotes the sequence of substitution (i) $\Delta[\xi \to \varphi]$ if $\xi \notin dom(\Delta)$ and (ii) $[\xi_1 \to \varphi_1]\ldots[\xi_i \to \varphi]\ldots[\xi_n \to \varphi_n]$ if $\Delta = [\xi_1 \to \varphi_1]\ldots[\xi_n \to \varphi_n]$ and $\xi = \xi_i \in dom(\Delta)$.

We extend the mapping fn to sequences of substitutions Δ: $fn(\epsilon) = \varnothing$ and $fn(\Delta[\xi \to \varphi]) = fn(\varphi) \cup fn(\Delta)$. For any formula φ, any valuation ρ and any sequence of substitutions Δ, we define $fn(\varphi, \rho, \Delta) = fn(\varphi) \cup fn(\rho) \cup fn(\Delta)$.

We present an algorithm $\mathsf{check}(A, \varphi, \rho, \Delta)$ with A an information tree, φ a tree logic formula, ρ a valuation for label and tree variables and Δ a sequence of substitutions. This algorithm is correct in the sense of Theorem 11 below.

Model-checking algorithm

check(A, φ, ρ, Δ) is
  case φ of
    0 : return $A = \{\!\{\}\!\}$;
    $\eta[\varphi']$: return $A = \{\!\{\rho(\eta)[A']\}\!\}$ and check($A', \varphi', \rho, \Delta$);

$\varphi' \mid \varphi''$:	for all A', A'' such that $A = A' \uplus A''$
	  if check$(A', \varphi', \rho, \Delta)$ and check$(A'', \varphi'', \rho, \Delta)$
	  then return true;
	return false;

$\top$:	return true;
$\neg\varphi'$:	return not check$(A, \varphi', \rho, \Delta)$;
$\varphi' \vee \varphi''$:	return check$(A, \varphi', \rho, \Delta)$ or check$(A, \varphi'', \rho, \Delta)$;

$\exists x.\varphi'$:	let m be a label neither in $fn(A)$ nor in $fn(\varphi', \rho, \Delta)$ in
	  for $n \in fn(A) \cup fn(\varphi', \rho, \Delta) \cup \{m\}$ do
	    if check$(A, \varphi', \rho[x \to n], \Delta))$ then return true;
	  return false;

X :	return $A = \rho(X)$;

$\exists X.\varphi'$:	let m be a label not in $fn(A)$ in
	  for $B \in \{C \mid C \sqsubseteq A\} \cup \{\{\!\{m[\{\!\{\}\!\}]\}\!\}\}$ do
	    if check$(A, \varphi', \rho[X \to B], \Delta)$ then return true;
	  return false;

$\eta = \eta'$:	return $\rho(\eta) = \rho(\eta')$;
$\nu\xi(M).\varphi'$:	if $A \in M$ then return true; else return check$(A, \varphi', \rho, \Delta\langle\xi \leftarrow \nu\xi(M \cup \{A\}).\varphi'\rangle)$;

ξ :	if $\xi \notin dom(\Delta)$ return error;
	let $[\xi \to \nu\xi(M).\varphi']$ occurring in Δ in
	  if $A \in M$ then return true;
	  else return check$(A, \varphi', \rho, \Delta\langle\xi \leftarrow \nu\xi(M \cup \{A\}).\varphi'\rangle)$;

THEOREM 11 (CORRECTNESS) *Let φ be a $TL_\nu^\exists$ formula without free recursion variable and ρ be a valuation such that φ is ρ-closed, and let A be an information tree. Then the evaluation of* check$(A, \varphi, \rho, \epsilon)$ *terminates and computes* true *if $A \models_\rho \varphi$ holds and* false *otherwise.*

PROPOSITION 12 (COMPLEXITY) *For any valuation ρ, any ρ-closed $TL_\nu^\exists$ formula φ without free recursion variables and any information tree A, the evaluation of* check$(A, \varphi, \rho, \epsilon)$ *requires polynomial space in the size of the model-checking problem $A \models_\rho \varphi$.*

SKETCH OF PROOF. Any recursive call check$(A', \varphi', \rho', \Delta')$ generated by the evaluation of check$(A, \varphi, \rho, \epsilon)$ has a polynomial-size representation. Moreover, the length of any chain of recursive calls of the algorithm check starting from check$(A, \varphi, \rho, \epsilon)$ is polynomially bounded. It is then sufficient to show that the evaluation of check$(A', \varphi', \rho', \Delta')$ can be done in polynomial space. For most of the cases of the "case" statement, it is obvious. The two non trivial cases are for φ' being $\psi' \mid \psi''$ and $\exists X.\psi$. For the former, one has to consider all couples of trees A', A'' such that $A' \uplus A'' = A$. These couples correspond to all bipartitions of the multiset A and so can be enumerated using linear space. For the latter, the set of all components of A have to be considered. Remark that a component of A corresponds to a subset of the set of nodes of A. This correspondence is not bijective, but one can determine in polynomial space whether a subset of the set of nodes of A corresponds to a component of A. Therefore, the set of all components of A can be enumerated in polynomial space. Note finally that all iterations of the evaluation loop reuse the same space. □

As a consequence of Theorem 3, Proposition 12 and the inclusion $TL \subseteq TL^{\exists} \subseteq TL^{\exists}_{\nu}$ we have

THEOREM 13 *The model-checking problem for the tree logics TL, $TL^{\exists}$ and $TL^{\exists}_{\nu}$ is PSPACE-complete.*

References

[Abiteboul et al., 2000] Abiteboul, S., Buneman, P., and Suciu, D. (2000). *Data on the Web*. Morgan Kaufmann Publishers.

[Cardelli, 2000] Cardelli, L. (2000). Semistructured Computation. In *7th International Workshop on Database Programming Languages, DBPL'99*, LNCS, pages 1–16. Springer.

[Cardelli and Ghelli, 2001] Cardelli, L. and Ghelli, G. (2001). A Query Language Based on the Ambient Logic. In *European Symposium on Programming (ESOP'01)*, volume 2028 of *LNCS*, pages 1–22. Springer.

[Cardelli and Gordon, 2000a] Cardelli, L. and Gordon, A.D. (2000a). Anytime, Anywhere: Modal Logics for Mobile Ambients. In *27th ACM Symposium on Principles of Programming Languages (POPL'00)*, pages 365–377.

[Cardelli and Gordon, 2000b] Cardelli, L. and Gordon, A.D. (2000b). Mobile Ambients. *Theoretical Computer Science*, 240:177–213.

[Charatonik et al., 2001] Charatonik, W., Dal Zilio, S., Gordon, A. D., Mukhopadhyay, S., and Talbot, J.-M. (2001). The Complexity of Model Checking Mobile Ambients. In *Foundations of Software Science and Computation Structures (FoSSaCS'01)*, volume 2030 of *LNCS*, pages 152–167. Springer.

[Courcelle, 1990a] Courcelle, B. (1990a). Graph Rewriting: An Algebraic and Logic Approach. In *Handbook of Theoretical Computer Science*, volume B. Elsevier.

[Courcelle, 1990b] Courcelle, B. (1990b). The Monadic Second-Order Logic of Graphs. I. Recognizable Sets of Finite Graphs. *Information and Computatution*, 85(1):12–75.

[Dal-Zilio and Lugiez, 2003] Dal-Zilio, S. and Lugiez, D. (2003). XML Schema, Tree Logic and Sheaves Automata. In *Rewriting Techniques and Applications, 14th International Conference, RTA 2003*, LNCS, pages 246–263. Springer.

[Neven, 2002] Neven, F. (2002). Automata, Logic and XML. In *Annual Conference of the European Association for Computer Science Logic (CSL'02)*, volume 2471 of *LNCS*, pages 2–26. Springer.

[Seidl et al., 2003] Seidl, H., Schwentick, T., and Muscholl, A. (2003). Numerical Document Queries. In *Twenty-Second ACM SIGACT-SIGMOD-SIGART Symposium on Principles of Database Systems*, pages 155–166. ACM.

[Stirling and Walker, 1991] Stirling, C. and Walker, D. (1991). Local model checking in the modal mu-calculus. *Theoretical Computer Science*, 89:161–177.

[Stockmeyer, 1976] Stockmeyer, L. J. (1976). The Polynomial-time Hierarchy. *Theoretical Computer Science*, 3(1):1–22.

[Winskel, 1991] Winskel, G. (1991). A note on model checking the modal ν-calculus. *Theoretical Computer Science*, 83:157–167.

A GENERIC FRAMEWORK FOR CHECKING SEMANTIC EQUIVALENCES BETWEEN PUSHDOWN AUTOMATA AND FINITE-STATE AUTOMATA

Antonín Kučera*
Faculty of Informatics, Masaryk University,
Botanická 68a, 60200 Brno,
Czech Republic.
tony@fi.muni.cz

Richard Mayr†
Department of Computer Science,
Albert-Ludwigs-University Freiburg
Georges-Koehler-Allee 51,
D-79110 Freiburg, Germany.
mayrri@informatik.uni-freiburg.de

Abstract We propose a generic method for deciding semantic equivalences between pushdown automata and finite-state automata. The abstract part of the method is applicable to every process equivalence which is a right PDA congruence. Practical usability of the method is demonstrated on selected equivalences which are conceptual representatives of the whole spectrum. In particular, special attention is devoted to bisimulation-like equivalences (including weak, early, delay, branching, and probabilistic bisimilarity), and it is also shown how the method applies to simulation-like and trace-like equivalences. The generality does not lead to the loss of efficiency; the algorithms obtained by applying our method are essentially time-optimal and sometimes even polynomial. The list of particular results obtained by our method includes items which are first of their kind.

Keywords: Formal verification; Pushdown automata; Semantic equivalences;

*On leave at the Institute for Formal Methods in Computer Science, University of Stuttgart. Supported by the Alexander von Humboldt Foundation and by the Grant Agency of the Czech Republic, grant No. 201/03/1161.
†Supported by Landesstiftung Baden-Württemberg, grant No. 21-655.023.

1 Introduction

The importance of *pushdown automata (PDA)* has recently been recognized also in areas different from theory of formal languages. In particular, PDA are a natural and convenient model for sequential programs with recursive procedure calls (see, e.g., [1, 2, 13, 15, 14]). Global data of such a program is stored in the finite control, and the stack symbols correspond to activation records of individual procedures. A procedure call is thus modeled by pushing a new symbol onto the stack, and a return from the procedure is modeled by poping the symbol from the stack. Consequently, a PDA is seen as a finite description of a "computational behavior" rather than a language acceptor in this context[1]. The behavior of a given PDA Δ is formally defined by the associated transition system $\mathcal{T}_\Delta$, where the states are configurations of Δ and $p\alpha \xrightarrow{a} q\beta$ if this move is consistent with the transition function of Δ. Hence, $\mathcal{T}_\Delta$ has infinitely many states.

One of the dominating approaches to formal verification of software systems is *equivalence-checking*. The idea is to compare the behavior of a given program with its intended behavior called the *specification*. Since the two behaviors are formalized as transition systems, the comparison means proving some kind of semantic equivalence between the initial states of the two transition systems. Since such proofs cannot be completed by humans for programs of realistic size, a natural question is whether the problem is decidable and what is its complexity. This question has been considered for many computational models and a large number of results have been achieved during the last decade (see [30, 11, 20, 5, 23, 7, 33] for surveys of some subfields).

In this paper we restrict our attention to the class of programs whose behavior is definable by pushdown automata, and to the class of specifications which are definable by finite-state systems. On the other hand, we consider a large class of equivalences which subsumes the linear/branching time spectrum of [40, 42].

The state of the art: Checking semantic equivalences between two pushdown automata tends to be undecidable. Special attention has been devoted to *stateless* PDA, which are often denoted BPA[2] in this context. The first result indicating that the situation is not completely hopeless is due to Baeten, Bergstra, and Klop [3] who proved that strong bisimilarity is decidable for *normed* BPA (a PDA is normed if the stack can be emptied from every reachable configuration). Simpler proofs were given later in [9, 17, 19], and there is even a polynomial-time algorithm [18]. The decidability result has been extended to all (not necessarily normed) BPA in [10], and an elementary upper complexity bound is due to [8]. Recently, **PSPACE**-hardness of this problem has been established in [34]. Strong bisimilarity was shown to be decidable also for

[1]From the language-theoretic point of view, the definition of PDA adopted in this area corresponds to the subclass of real-time PDA. It does not mean that the concept of ε-transitions vanished—it has only been replaced by "silent" transitions with a distinguished label τ which may (but does not have to) be taken into account by a given semantic equivalence.

[2]This is because stateless PDA correspond to a natural fragment of ACP known as "BPA" (Basic Process Algebra; see [4]). BPA cannot model global data, but they are sufficiently powerful to model, e.g., the interprocedural data-flow [13]. It is worth noting that the expressive power of PDA is strictly greater than the one of BPA w.r.t. most of the considered semantic equivalences.

normed PDA [36]. Later, Sénizergues proved that bisimilarity is decidable for all PDA processes [32]. For simulation-like and trace-like equivalences, the equivalence-checking problem is undecidable even for (normed) BPA; this follows directly from Friedman's result [16]. In the presence of silent moves, the situation gets even worse. Weak bisimilarity is undecidable for PDA [35], and in fact for a very modest subclass of PDA known as one-counter nets [28].

Comparing a PDA with a finite-state system is computationally easier. Strong and weak bisimilarity between a BPA and a finite-state system is decidable in polynomial time [25]. For general pushdown automata, both problems are **PSPACE**-complete [24]. Checking strong and weak simulation equivalence between a BPA and a finite-state system is **EXPTIME**-complete [24], and the same holds for general PDA. Trace-like equivalences between BPA and finite-state systems are undecidable (this is a direct consequence of the undecidability of language equivalence).

Our contribution: In this paper we consider the equivalence-checking problem between PDA and finite-state systems. More precisely, we consider the problem of checking *full* equivalence between a given PDA process $p\alpha$ and a given process f of a given finite-state system $\mathcal{T}$. The processes $p\alpha$ and f are *fully equivalent* if $p\alpha$ is equivalent to f and, in addition, every reachable state of $p\alpha$ is equivalent to some state f' of $\mathcal{T}$. In other words, the specification must define the "global" behaviour of a given program. For bisimulation-like equivalences, the extra condition about reachable states is redundant. However, for simulation-like and trace-like equivalences, this condition is fully meaningful.

We propose a unified method for deciding full equivalence between PDA and finite-state systems. The method consists of two parts. The first part is generic and works for every "reasonable" semantic equivalence (an equivalence is considered "reasonable" if it is a right PDA congruence; see Definition 4). The authors are not aware of any semantic equivalence which is not reasonable in this sense. The second part is equivalence-specific. The difference between individual equivalences is hidden in the notion of *expansion*. There are four abstract conditions which guarantee appropriateness of the designed expansion for a given equivalence. The applicability of the method to concrete equivalences is demonstrated by defining appropriate expansions for the main conceptual representatives. Special attention is devoted to bisimulation-like equivalences (we explicitly consider weak, early, delay, branching, and probabilistic bisimilarity), but we also show how to handle weak simulation equivalence and weak trace equivalence. The application part is nontrivial and most of technical tricks are hidden there.

Interestingly, the generality of the method does not lead to the loss of efficiency. For bisimulation-like and simulation-like equivalences, our method results in algorithms which are *polynomial* in the size of the PDA and the finite-state system on input, and *exponential* in the number of control states of the PDA. So, the algorithm is exponential for general PDA, but polynomial for each subclass of PDA where the number of control states is bounded by a fixed constant (in particular, this applies to BPA). Since these problems are **PSPACE**-hard for general PDA processes, the obtained algorithms are essentially time-optimal. For trace-like equivalences, the algorithm requires exponential time even for BPA, but the problem is also **PSPACE**-hard for BPA.

The list of particular results obtained by applying our method includes some items which are first results of their kind. Below we explicitly mention some of them (the subclass of PDA where the number of control states is bounded by a given k is denoted PDA^k):

(a) Branching bisimilarity [43] between PDA^k and finite-state systems is decidable in polynomial time. To the best of authors' knowledge, this is the first result about computational tractability of branching bisimilarity for systems with infinitely many states. Branching bisimilarity plays a distinguished role in the semantics of systems with silent moves [39], similarly as strong bisimilarity [31] for processes without silent moves. However, the "algorithmic support" for branching bisimilarity has been so far limited only to finite-state systems. A related concept of weak bisimilarity [29] is substantially more developed in this sense. One reason is that weak bisimilarity admits a simple game-theoretic characterization [37, 38] and consequently it is "more manageable" than branching bisimilarity. Our method treats all equivalences in the same way and consequently branching bisimilarity is equivalently manageable as weak bisimilarity in our setting (the same applies to early and delay bisimilarity; results for these equivalences are also first of their kind).

(b) Probabilistic bisimilarity [27, 41] between PDA^k and finite-state systems is decidable in polynomial time. This result applies to (fully) probabilistic extensions of PDA and finite-state systems. Probabilistic bisimilarity has so far been considered only for finite-state systems. The obtained polynomial-time algorithm indicates that one can go beyond this limit without losing efficiency.

(c) For simulation-like equivalences (represented by weak simulation equivalence), we prove that full equivalence between PDA^k and finite-state systems is decidable in polynomial time. Since the non-full variant of the problem is **EXPTIME**-complete even for BPA [24], this result shows that the extra condition about reachable states used in the definition of full equivalence actually makes the problem more tractable (rather than more complicated). The same applies to trace-like equivalences (represented by weak trace equivalence in this paper). Trace-like equivalences between BPA and finite-state systems are undecidable; this is a direct consequence of the undecidability of language equivalence. However, full trace-like equivalences between PDA and finite-state systems are decidable in exponential time (this problem is **PSPACE**-hard even for BPA).

Another generic outcome of our method is an algorithm deciding whether a given finite-state process f is the $\sim$-quotient of a given PDA process $p\alpha$ for a given semantic equivalence $\sim$. The complexity of this algorithm is essentially the same as the complexity of deciding full $\sim$-equivalence. In particular, it is polynomial for PDA^k processes when $\sim$ is simulation-like, and exponential for PDA processes when $\sim$ is trace-like. In the context of formal verification, semantic quotients are used as succinct representations of original systems. Since most (if not all) of the existing process equivalences are preserved under their respective quotients [21, 22], the information about the state-space of a given process is faithfully preserved in its $\sim$-quotient.

This paper is organized as follows. We start with basic definitions in Section 2. In Section 3, a suitable composition principle allowing to derive new pairs of equivalent processes from already existing ones is developed. This, in turn, allows to represent full equivalence between a given PDA and a given finite-state system by a finite relation called *base*. The method is related to the technique of bisimulation bases pioneered by Caucal [9], and can also be seen as a generalization of the method used in [25] to prove that weak bisimilarity between BPA and finite-state systems is decidable in polynomial time. In Section 4 we show how to compute the base. The first part of our development is again generic; we give an abstract algorithm for computing the base and identify the equivalence-specific part of the problem which is hidden in the notion of expansion. In subsequent subsections, we show how to define expansions for various concrete process equivalences.

Due to the lack of space, we had to omit all proofs and also the parts devoted to probabilistic bisimilarity, simulation-like equivalences, and trace-like equivalences. These can be found in a full version of this paper [26].

2 Basic Definitions

DEFINITION 1 *A* transition system *is a triple* $\mathcal{T} = (S, \rightarrow, \mathcal{A})$ *where* S *is a finite or countably infinite set of* states, $\mathcal{A}$ *is a finite set of* actions, *and* $\rightarrow \subseteq S \times \mathcal{A} \times S$ *is a* transition relation.

We write $s \xrightarrow{a} t$ instead of $(s, a, t) \in \rightarrow$, and we extend this notation to the elements of $\mathcal{A}^*$ in the standard way. We say that a state t is *reachable* from a state s, written $s \rightarrow^* t$, if there is $w \in \mathcal{A}^*$ such that $s \xrightarrow{w} t$. Let τ be a distinguished *silent* action, and let $\mathcal{A}_\tau = \mathcal{A} \cup \{\tau\}$. For every $a \in \mathcal{A}_\tau$ we define the relation $\stackrel{a}{\Rightarrow} \subseteq S \times S$ as follows:

- $s \stackrel{\tau}{\Rightarrow} t$ iff there is a sequence of the form $s = p_0 \xrightarrow{\tau} \cdots \xrightarrow{\tau} p_k = t$ where $k \geq 0$;
- $s \stackrel{a}{\Rightarrow} t$ where $a \neq \tau$ iff there are p, q such that $s \stackrel{\tau}{\Rightarrow} p \xrightarrow{a} q \stackrel{\tau}{\Rightarrow} t$.

From now on, a *process* is formally understood as a state of (some) transition system. Intuitively, transitions from a given process s model possible computational steps, and the silent action τ is used to mark those steps which are internal (i.e., not externally observable).

DEFINITION 2 *A* pushdown automaton (PDA) *is a tuple* $\Delta = (Q, \Gamma, \mathcal{A}, \delta)$ *where* Q *is a finite set of* control states, Γ *is a finite* stack alphabet, $\mathcal{A}$ *is a finite* input alphabet, *and* $\delta : (Q \times \Gamma) \rightarrow 2^{\mathcal{A} \times Q \times \Gamma^{\leq 2}}$ *is a* transition function *where* $\Gamma^{\leq 2} = \{\varepsilon\} \cup \Gamma \cup (\Gamma \times \Gamma)$

In the rest of this paper we adopt a more intuitive notation, writing $pX \xrightarrow{a} q\beta \in \delta$ instead of $(a, (q, \beta)) \in \delta(p, X)$. To Δ we associate the transition system $\mathcal{T}_\Delta$ where $Q \times \Gamma^*$ is the set of states (we write $p\alpha$ instead of (p, α)), $\mathcal{A}$ is the set of actions, and the transition relation is determined by $pX\alpha \xrightarrow{a} q\beta\alpha$ iff $pX \xrightarrow{a} q\beta \in \delta$.

3 A Finite Semantic Base for PDA

For the rest of this section, let us fix a pushdown automaton $\Delta = (Q, \Gamma, \mathcal{A}, \delta)$ and a finite state system $\mathcal{T} = (F, \mathcal{A}, \rightarrow)$. The symbol $F_\perp$ denotes the set $F \cup \{\perp\}$, where $\perp \notin F$ stands for "undefined".

DEFINITION 3 *For every process* $p\alpha$ *of* Δ *we define the set* $M_{p\alpha} = \{q \in Q \mid p\alpha \rightarrow^* q\varepsilon\}$. *A function* $\mathcal{F} : Q \rightarrow F_\perp$ *is* compatible *with* $p\alpha$ *iff for every* $q \in M_{p\alpha}$ *we have that* $\mathcal{F}(q) \neq \perp$. *The class of all functions that are compatible with* $p\alpha$ *is denoted* $\mathcal{C}(p\alpha)$.

For every process $p\alpha$ of Δ and every $\mathcal{F} \in \mathcal{C}(p\alpha)$ we define the process $p\alpha\mathcal{F}$ whose transitions are determined by the following rules:

$$\frac{p\alpha \xrightarrow{a} q\beta}{p\alpha\mathcal{F} \xrightarrow{a} q\beta\mathcal{F}} \mathcal{F} \in \mathcal{C}(p\alpha) \qquad \frac{\mathcal{F}(p) \xrightarrow{a} f}{p\mathcal{F} \xrightarrow{a} p\mathcal{F}[f/p]} \mathcal{F} \in \mathcal{C}(p\varepsilon)$$

Here $\mathcal{F}[f/p] : Q \to F_\perp$ is a function which returns the same result as $\mathcal{F}$ for every argument except for p where $\mathcal{F}[f/p](p) = f$. In other words, $p\alpha\mathcal{F}$ behaves like $p\alpha$ until the point when the stack is emptied and a configuration of the form $q\varepsilon$ is entered; from that point on, $p\alpha\mathcal{F}$ behaves like $\mathcal{F}(q)$. Note that if $\mathcal{F} \in \mathcal{C}(p\alpha)$ and $p\alpha \to^* q\beta$, then $\mathcal{F} \in \mathcal{C}(q\beta)$. We put $Stack(\Delta, F) = \Gamma^* \cup \{p\alpha\mathcal{F} \mid p \in Q, \alpha \in \Gamma^*, \mathcal{F} \in (F_\perp)^Q\}$, and $\mathcal{P}(\Delta, F) = \{p\alpha \mid p \in Q, \alpha \in \Gamma^*\} \cup \{p\alpha\mathcal{F} \mid p \in Q, \alpha \in \Gamma^*, \mathcal{F} \in \mathcal{C}(p\alpha)\}$.

DEFINITION 4 *We say that an equivalence $\sim$ over $\mathcal{P}(\Delta, F) \cup F$ is a* right PDA congruence *iff the following conditions are satisfied:*

- *For every process $p\alpha$ of Δ and all $w, v \in Stack(\Delta, F)$ we have that if $qw \sim qv$ for all $q \in M_{p\alpha}$, then also $p\alpha w \sim p\alpha v$.*
- *$p\mathcal{F} \sim \mathcal{F}(p)$ for every $p\mathcal{F} \in \mathcal{P}(\Delta, F)$. (This condition is satisfied by all "behavioral" equivalences which do not distinguish between isomorphic processes. However, $\sim$ can be an arbitrary equivalence, and therefore this condition is not redundant.)*

One intuitively expects that every "reasonable" semantic equivalence should be a right PDA congruence. In particular, bisimulation-like, simulation-like, and trace-like equivalences (even in their "weak" forms) are right PDA congruences. For the rest of this section, we fix a right PDA congruence $\sim$.

In this paper we consider the problem of full equivalence checking between PDA and finite-state processes. The notion of full equivalence is introduced in our next definition.

DEFINITION 5 *Let $p\alpha$ be a process of Δ and $f \in F$. We say that $p\alpha$ is* fully equivalent *to f (with respect to $\sim$), written $p\alpha \precsim f$, iff $p\alpha \sim f$ and for every $p\alpha \to^* q\beta$ there is some $f' \in F$ such that $q\beta \sim f'$. (Note that f' does not have to be reachable from f.)*

Now we formulate a composition lemma for pushdown processes.

LEMMA 6 *Let $p\alpha\mathcal{G} \precsim f$, where $\mathcal{G} \in \mathcal{C}(p\alpha)$ and $f \in F$. Further, let $\beta, \gamma \in \Gamma^*$ and $\mathcal{H} : Q \to F_\perp$. Then the following holds:*

(1) If $q\beta \precsim \mathcal{G}(q)$ for all $q \in M_{p\alpha}$, then $p\alpha\beta \precsim f$.
(2) If $\mathcal{H} \in \mathcal{C}(q\gamma)$ and $q\gamma\mathcal{H} \precsim \mathcal{G}(q)$ for all $q \in M_{p\alpha}$, then $\mathcal{H} \in \mathcal{C}(p\alpha\gamma)$ and $p\alpha\gamma\mathcal{H} \precsim f$.

DEFINITION 7 *Let $\alpha \in \Gamma^*$, $\mathcal{F}, \mathcal{G} : Q \to F_\perp$. We write*

- *$\alpha \simeq \mathcal{F}$ iff $\forall p \in Q : \mathcal{F}(p) \neq \perp \implies p\alpha \precsim \mathcal{F}(p)$;*
- *$\alpha\mathcal{G} \simeq \mathcal{F}$ iff $\forall p \in Q : \mathcal{F}(p) \neq \perp \implies \mathcal{G} \in \mathcal{C}(p\alpha) \wedge p\alpha\mathcal{G} \precsim \mathcal{F}(p)$.*

DEFINITION 8 *Let*

$$K = \{(\varepsilon, \mathcal{F}) \mid \varepsilon \simeq \mathcal{F}\} \cup \{(\mathcal{G}, \mathcal{F}) \mid \mathcal{G} \simeq \mathcal{F}\} \cup K'$$

where $K' \subseteq \Gamma \times (F_\perp)^Q \cup (\Gamma \times (F_\perp)^Q)) \times (F_\perp)^Q)$. *(That is,* K' *consists of (some) pairs of the form* $(X, \mathcal{F})$ *and* $(X\mathcal{G}, \mathcal{F})$*).*

We say that K *is* well-formed *iff* K *satisfies the following conditions:*

- *if* $(X\mathcal{G}, \mathcal{F}) \in K$ *and* $\mathcal{F}(p) \neq \perp$, *then* $\mathcal{G} \in \mathcal{C}(pX)$;
- *if* $(X, \mathcal{F}) \in K$ *(or* $(X\mathcal{G}, \mathcal{F}) \in K$*) and* $(\mathcal{F}, \mathcal{H}) \in K$, *then also* $(X, \mathcal{H}) \in K$ *(or* $(X\mathcal{G}, \mathcal{H}) \in K$, *resp.).*

It is clear that there are only finitely many well-formed sets, and that there exists the greatest well-formed set G whose size is $\mathcal{O}(|\Gamma| \cdot |F|^{2 \cdot |Q|})$. Further, observe that if $\sim$ is decidable for finite-state processes, then G is effectively constructible.

DEFINITION 9 *Let* K *be a well-formed set. The* closure of K, *denoted* $Cl(K)$, *is the least set* L *satisfying the following conditions:*

(1) $K \subseteq L$;
(2) if $(\alpha\mathcal{G}, \mathcal{F}) \in L$, $(\varepsilon, \mathcal{G}) \in K$, *and* $\alpha \neq \varepsilon$, *then* $(\alpha, \mathcal{F}) \in L$;
(3) if $(\alpha\mathcal{G}, \mathcal{F}) \in L$, $(\mathcal{H}, \mathcal{G}) \in K$, *and* $\alpha \neq \varepsilon$, *then* $(\alpha\mathcal{H}, \mathcal{F}) \in L$;
(4) if $(\alpha\mathcal{G}, \mathcal{F}) \in L$, $(X, \mathcal{G}) \in K$, *and* $\alpha \neq \varepsilon$, *then* $(\alpha X, \mathcal{F}) \in L$;
(5) if $(\alpha\mathcal{G}, \mathcal{F}) \in L$, $(X\mathcal{H}, \mathcal{G}) \in K$, *and* $\alpha \neq \varepsilon$, *then* $(\alpha X\mathcal{H}, \mathcal{F}) \in L$.

Note that $Cl(K) = \bigcup_{i=0}^{\infty} Cl^i(K)$ where $Cl^0(K) = K$ and $Cl^{i+1}(K)$ consists of exactly those pairs which are either in $Cl^i(K)$ or can be derived from K and $Cl^i(K)$ by applying one of the rules (1)–(5) of Definition 9. Another simple observation (which will be useful later) is the following:

LEMMA 10 *Let* K *be a well-formed set, and let* $(\mathcal{F}, \mathcal{H}) \in K$. *If* $(\alpha, \mathcal{F}) \in Cl^i(K)$, *then also* $(\alpha, \mathcal{H}) \in Cl^i(K)$. *Similarly, if* $(\alpha\mathcal{G}, \mathcal{F}) \in Cl^i(K)$, *then also* $(\alpha\mathcal{G}, \mathcal{H}) \in Cl^i(K)$.

For our purposes, the following well-formed set is particularly important:

DEFINITION 11 *The* base $\mathcal{B}$ *is defined as follows:*

$$\begin{aligned} \mathcal{B} &= \{(\varepsilon, \mathcal{F}) \mid \varepsilon \simeq \mathcal{F}\} \cup \{(\mathcal{G}, \mathcal{F}) \mid \mathcal{G} \simeq \mathcal{F}\} \cup \{(X, \mathcal{F}) \mid X \simeq \mathcal{F}\} \\ &\cup \{(X\mathcal{G}, \mathcal{F}) \mid X\mathcal{G} \simeq \mathcal{F}\} \end{aligned}$$

THEOREM 12 *Let* $\alpha \in \Gamma^*$ *and* $\mathcal{F}, \mathcal{G} : Q \to F_\perp$. *We have*

- $\alpha \simeq \mathcal{F}$ *iff* $(\alpha, \mathcal{F}) \in Cl(\mathcal{B})$;
- $\alpha\mathcal{G} \simeq \mathcal{F}$ *iff* $(\alpha\mathcal{G}, \mathcal{F}) \in Cl(\mathcal{B})$.

4 Computing the Base

In this section we present algorithms for computing the base $\mathcal{B}$ for various process equivalences. We start by describing the generic part of the method together with some auxiliary technical results which are also valid for every process equivalence which is a right PDA congruence. The applicability of the method to concrete process equivalences is demonstrated in subsequent subsections (due to the lack of space, we could include only a subsection devoted to bisimulation equivalences with silent moves; the other parts can be found in [26]). For the rest of this section, let us fix

- a pushdown automaton $\Delta = (Q, \Gamma, \mathcal{A}, \delta)$ of size n;
- a finite state system $\mathcal{T} = (F, \mathcal{A}, \rightarrow)$ of size m.
- a right PDA congruence $\sim$ over $\mathcal{P}(\Delta, F) \cup F$ which is decidable for finite-state processes.

In our complexity estimations we also use the parameter $z = |F|^{|Q|}$.

Let $\mathcal{W}$ be the (finite) set of all well-formed sets. Note that $(\mathcal{W}, \subseteq)$ is a complete lattice. Let $Exp : \mathcal{W} \rightarrow \mathcal{W}$ be a function satisfying the following four conditions:

(1) $Exp(\mathcal{B}) = \mathcal{B}$.
(2) Exp is monotonic, i.e. $K \subseteq L$ implies $Exp(K) \subseteq Exp(L)$.
(3) If $K = Exp(K)$, then $K \subseteq \mathcal{B}$.
(4) For every well formed set K, the membership to $Exp(K)$ is decidable.

The conditions (1) and (3) together say that $\mathcal{B}$ is the greatest fixed-point of Exp. Since Exp is monotonic and $\mathcal{W}$ is finite, we further have $\mathcal{B} = \bigcap_{i=0}^{\infty} Exp^i(G)$ where G is the greatest well-formed set. In other words, the base $\mathcal{B}$ can be computed by the algorithm of Figure 1. Observe that G is effectively computable because $\sim$ is decidable over finite-state processes.

Input: A PDA Δ, a finite-state system $\mathcal{T}$
Output: The base $\mathcal{B}$

1: $\mathcal{B}$:= the greatest well-formed set;
2: **repeat**
3: $\quad K := \mathcal{B}; \mathcal{B} := \emptyset$
4: $\quad$ **for all** $(w, \mathcal{F}) \in K$ **do**
5: $\quad\quad$ **if** $(w, \mathcal{F}) \in Exp(K)$ **then** $\mathcal{B} := \mathcal{B} \cup \{(w, \mathcal{F})\}$ **fi**
6: $\quad$ **od**;
7: **until** $\mathcal{B} = K$

Figure 1. An algorithm for computing $\mathcal{B}$

As we shall see, an appropriate Exp satisfying the conditions (1)–(4) can be designed for almost every process equivalence of the linear/branching time spectrum [40, 42]. Now we introduce further notions and results which underpin our technical constructions.

For every set of processes $\mathcal{P}$ and every action a we define the sets

- $Post_a(\mathcal{P}) = \{t \mid \exists s \in \mathcal{P} : s \xrightarrow{a} t\}$
- $Post^*(\mathcal{P}) = \{t \mid \exists s \in \mathcal{P} : s \rightarrow^* t\}$
- $Post^*_\tau(\mathcal{P}) = \{t \mid \exists s \in \mathcal{P} : s \stackrel{\tau}{\Rightarrow} t\}$

Note that if $\mathcal{P}$ is a subset of $\mathcal{P}(\Delta, F)$, then so are $Post_a(\mathcal{P})$, $Post^*(\mathcal{P})$, and $Post^*_\tau(\mathcal{P})$.

To be able to represent infinite subsets of $\mathcal{P}(\Delta, F)$ in a finite and compact way, we borrow the following concept from [6]:

DEFINITION 13 *A* multi-automaton *is a tuple* $\mathcal{M} = (S, \Sigma, \delta, Acc)$ *where*

- S *is a finite set of* states *such that* $Q \subseteq S$ *(i.e, the control states of* Δ *are among the states of* $\mathcal{M}$*);*
- $\Sigma = \Gamma \cup \{\mathcal{F} \mid \mathcal{F} : Q \to F_\perp\}$ *is the* input alphabet *(the alphabet has a special symbol for each* $\mathcal{F} : Q \to F_\perp$*);*
- $\delta \subseteq S \times \Sigma \times S$ *is a transition relation;*
- $Acc \subseteq S$ *is a set of* accepting states.

Every multi-automaton $\mathcal{M}$ *determines a unique set*

$$\mathcal{L}(\mathcal{M}) = \{pw \mid p \in Q, w \in \Sigma^*, \delta(p, w) \cap Acc \neq \emptyset\}$$

A set $\mathcal{P} \subseteq \mathcal{P}(\Delta, F)$ *is* recognized *by a multi-automaton* $\mathcal{M}$ *iff* $\mathcal{P} = \mathcal{L}(\mathcal{M})$.

A proof of the following lemma can be found, e.g., in [12].

LEMMA 14 *Let* $\mathcal{P} \subseteq \mathcal{P}(\Delta, F)$ *be a set of processes recognized by a multi-automaton* $\mathcal{M}$. *Then one can compute multi-automata recognizing the sets* $Post_a(\mathcal{P})$, $Post^*(\mathcal{P})$, *and* $Post^*_\tau(\mathcal{P})$ *in time which is polynomial in* m, n, z *and the size of* $\mathcal{M}$.

DEFINITION 15 *Let* K *be a well-formed set. For all* $f \in F$ *and* $i \in \mathbb{N}_0$ *we define the set* $Gen^i_f(K) =$

$$\begin{aligned} & \{p\alpha \mid \exists \mathcal{F} \text{ s.t. } \mathcal{F}(p) = f \text{ and } (\alpha, \mathcal{F}) \in Cl^i(K)\} \\ \cup \; & \{p\alpha\mathcal{G} \mid \exists \mathcal{F} \text{ s.t. } \mathcal{F}(p) = f \text{ and } (\alpha\mathcal{G}, \mathcal{F}) \in Cl^i(K)\} \end{aligned}$$

Further, we put $Gen_f(K) = \bigcup_{i=0}^{\infty} Gen^i_f(K)$.

LEMMA 16 *The relation* $\precsim$ *over* $\mathcal{P}(\Delta, F) \times F$ *is exactly* $\bigcup_{f \in F} Gen_f(\mathcal{B}) \times \{f\}$.

LEMMA 17 *Let* K *be a well-formed set and* $f \in F$. *The set* $Gen_f(K)$ *is recognized by a multi-automaton* $\mathcal{M}_{K,f}$ *which is constructible in time polynomial in* m, n, z.

Proof: We refer to [25] where a similar result is proven explicitly; the construction required for Lemma 17 differs from the one presented in [25] only in minor details. □

We finish this part by an auxiliary technical lemma whose proof is also independent of a concrete choice of $\sim$.

LEMMA 18 *Let* K *be a well-formed set. The following conditions hold:*

(1) If $q\beta\mathcal{G} \in Gen_g(K)$ *and* $(\varepsilon, \mathcal{G}) \in K$, *then* $q\beta \in Gen_g(K)$.
(2) If $q\beta\mathcal{G} \in Gen_g(K)$, $(X, \mathcal{G}) \in K$, *then* $q\beta X \in Gen_g(K)$.
(3) $p\mathcal{G} \in Gen_g(K)$ *iff* $\mathcal{G}(p) \precsim g$.
(4) Let $g \precsim g'$. *Then* $pw \in Gen^i_g(K)$ *implies* $pw \in Gen^i_{g'}(K)$.

4.1 Bisimulation Equivalences with Silent Moves

In this subsection we show how to compute the base $\mathcal{B}$ for bisimulation-like equivalences which take into account silent moves. We explicitly consider the main four representatives which are *weak, early, delay,* and *branching bisimilarity.* We prove that for all these equivalences, the base $\mathcal{B}$ is computable in time polynomial in m, n, z.

DEFINITION 19 *Let R be a binary relation over processes, and let* $(s,t) \in R$. *We say that a move* $t \stackrel{a}{\Rightarrow} t'$ *is* R-consistent with a move $s \stackrel{a}{\rightarrow} s'$ in a weak, early, delay, or branching style, respectively, *if one of the following conditions is satisfied:*

- $a = \tau$, $t = t'$, *and* $(s', t) \in R$;
- *the move* $t \stackrel{a}{\Rightarrow} t'$ *is of the form* $t{=}u_0 \stackrel{\tau}{\rightarrow} \cdots \stackrel{\tau}{\rightarrow} u_i \stackrel{a}{\rightarrow} v_0 \stackrel{\tau}{\rightarrow} \cdots \stackrel{\tau}{\rightarrow} v_j{=}t'$, *where* $i, j \geq 0$, *such that* $(s', t') \in R$ *and*

  (i) if the style is early or branching, then also $(s, u_i) \in R$;
  (ii) if the style is delay or branching, then also $(s', v_0) {\in} R$.

We say that $(s,t) \in R$ expands in R *(in the respective style) iff for all* $a \in Act_\tau$ *and* $s \stackrel{a}{\rightarrow} s'$ *there is a move* $t \stackrel{a}{\Rightarrow} t'$ *which is R-consistent with* $s \stackrel{a}{\rightarrow} s'$. *Furthermore, we say that* $(s,t) \in R$ b-expands in R *(in the respective style) if* (s,t) *expands in* R *and* (t,s) *expands in* R^{-1} *in the respective style.*

A binary relation R over processes is a weak, early, delay, or branching bisimulation *iff for every* $(s,t) \in R$ *we have that* (s,t) *b-expands in R in the respective style. Processes* s, t *are weakly, early, delayed, or branching bisimilar if they are related by some weak, early, delay, or branching bisimulation, respectively.*

REMARK 20 *An important fact (which will be used in the proof of Lemma 23) is that the* same *notion of weak, early, delay, and branching bisimilarity is obtained when the conditions* (i) *and* (ii) *of Definition 19 are reformulated as follows:*

(i) *if the style is early or branching, then* $(s, u_\ell) \in R$ *for* all $0 \leq \ell \leq i$;
(ii) *if the style is delay or branching, then* $(s', v_\ell) \in R$ *for* all $0 \leq \ell \leq j$,

Since our constructions are to a large extent independent of the chosen style of bisimilarity, from now on we refer just to "bisimilarity" which is denoted by $\sim$ in the rest of this subsection. It follows directly from Definition 19 that $\sim \; = \; \precsim$ over $\mathcal{P}(\Delta, F) \times F$ and therefore we do not distinguish between these two relations.

For technical reasons which become clear in (the proof of) Theorem 19, we need to assume that the transition relation of $\mathcal{T}$ is "complete" in the following sense:

DEFINITION 21 *Let* $\sim_F$ *be the relation of bisimilarity restricted to* $F \times F$. *We say that* $\mathcal{T}$ *is* complete *iff for all* $f, f' \in F$ *and* $a \in \mathcal{A}_\tau$ *the following condition is satisfied: If there is a sequence of transitions forming a* $f \stackrel{a}{\Rightarrow} f'$ *move which is* $\sim_F$*-consistent with a* hypothetical *transition* $f \stackrel{a}{\rightarrow} f'$ *(note that the condition of* $\sim_F$*-consistency with* $f \stackrel{a}{\rightarrow} f'$ *makes a clear sense even if* $f \stackrel{a}{\rightarrow} f'$ *is not a transition of* $\mathcal{T}$*), then* $f \stackrel{a}{\rightarrow} f'$ *is a* real *transition of* $\mathcal{T}$.

From now on in this subsection, we assume that $\mathcal{T}$ is complete. This assumption is not restrictive because if we add the missing transitions to $\mathcal{T}$ (which can be done in polynomial time because $\sim_F$ is computable in polynomial time), each state f of $\mathcal{T}$ stays bisimilar to itself. A pleasant consequence of this assumption is that we do not have to deal with the "$\stackrel{a}{\Rightarrow}$" moves of f; it suffices to consider the "$\stackrel{a}{\rightarrow}$" ones.

DEFINITION 22 *Let $R \subseteq \mathcal{P}(\Delta, F) \times F$ be a relation. We say that a pair $(pw, f) \in R$* quasi-expands *in R iff it satisfies the following conditions:*

- *for all $a \in \mathcal{A}$ and $pw \stackrel{a}{\rightarrow} qv$, there is $f \stackrel{a}{\rightarrow} g$ such that $(qv, g) \in R$;*
- *for all $a \in \mathcal{A}$ and $f \stackrel{a}{\rightarrow} g$, one of the following conditions is satisfied:*
  - *$a = \tau$ and $(pw, g) \in R$;*
  - *there is an R-consistent move $pw \stackrel{a}{\Rightarrow} qv$ such that $(qv, g) \in R$. Moreover, we require that if pw is of the form $p\alpha\mathcal{G}$, then the move $p\alpha\mathcal{G} \stackrel{a}{\Rightarrow} qv$ contains at most one transition of the form $r\mathcal{G} \stackrel{\tau}{\rightarrow} r\mathcal{H}$ (which can appear only at the end of the whole move).*

We say that R is a quasi-bisimulation *iff every pair of R quasi-expands in R. Processes pw and f are quasi-bisimilar iff they are related by some quasi-bisimulation.*

Every quasi-bisimulation is clearly a bisimulation. The opposite is not necessarily true, but we can prove the following (here we need the fact formulated in Remark 20 and the assumption that $\mathcal{T}$ is complete):

LEMMA 23 *The relation $\sim$ restricted to $\mathcal{P}(\Delta, F) \times F$ is a quasi-bisimulation.*

DEFINITION 24 *Let K be a well-formed set, and let $R = \bigcup_{f \in F} Gen_f(K) \times \{f\}$. The set $BExp(K)$ consists of all pairs $(w, \mathcal{F}) \in K$ such that for each $p \in Q$ we have that if $\mathcal{F}(p) \neq \bot$, then the pair $(pw, \mathcal{F}(p))$ quasi-expands in R.*

Now we prove that $BExp$ satisfies the conditions (1)–(4) formulated at the beginning of Section 4. It follows immediatelly from the definition of $BExp$ that $BExp$ is monotonic. Due to Lemma 16 and Lemma 23 we obtain $BExp(\mathcal{B}) = \mathcal{B}$. Now we prove that if $K = BExp(K)$ then $K \subseteq \mathcal{B}$. This is where we need the above introduced technicalities (completeness of $\mathcal{T}$, quasi-expansion, etc.). If the definition of $BExp$ was based "directly" on the notion of b-expansion, which seems to be the most natural possibility, the following theorem would *not* hold.

THEOREM 25 *Let K be a well-formed set. If $K = BExp(K)$, then $K \subseteq \mathcal{B}$.*

Now we show how to decide the membership to $BExp(K)$. At the same time, we perform a (rough) complexity analysis. Pairs of the form $(\mathcal{G}, \mathcal{F})$ and $(\varepsilon, \mathcal{F})$ belong to $BExp(K)$ if and only if they belong to K. Hence, they do not require any special attention. As for pairs of the form $(X, \mathcal{F})$, by Definition 24 we have that $(X, \mathcal{F}) \in BExp(K)$ iff for all $p \in Q$ such that $\mathcal{F}(p) \neq \bot$ we have that the pair $(pX, \mathcal{F}(p))$ quasi-expands in $\bigcup_{f \in F} Gen_f(K) \times \{f\}$. This means to check if

- for all $pX \stackrel{a}{\rightarrow} q\beta$ there is some $\mathcal{F}(p) \stackrel{a}{\rightarrow} g$ such that $q\beta \in Gen_g(K)$. In other words, we are interested if there is some $g \in F$ such that $\mathcal{F}(p) \stackrel{a}{\rightarrow} g$ and $q\beta \in \mathcal{L}(\mathcal{M}_{K,g})$. Since the multi-automaton $\mathcal{M}_{K,g}$ is effectively constructible in time which is polynomial in m, n, z (see Lemma 17), this condition can be also checked in time which is polynomial in m, n, z.

- for all $\mathcal{F}(p) \stackrel{a}{\rightarrow} g$, one of the following two conditions is satisfied:
  - $a = \tau$ and $pX \in Gen_g(K)$. In other words, we check whether $pX \in \mathcal{L}(\mathcal{M}_{K,g})$ which can be done in time polynomial in m, n, z due to Lemma 17.
  - there is a sequence $pX \stackrel{\tau}{\Rightarrow} q\alpha \stackrel{a}{\rightarrow} r\beta \stackrel{\tau}{\Rightarrow} s\gamma$ such that $s\gamma \in Gen_g(K)$ and
    - if the style is early or branching, then $q\alpha \in Gen_{\mathcal{F}(p)}(K)$;
    - if the style is delay or branching, then $r\beta \in Gen_g(K)$.

  Depending on whether the style is weak, early, delay, or branching, this condition can be reformulated as follows:

    - $Post_\tau^*(Post_a(Post_\tau^*(\{pX\}))) \cap Gen_g(K) \neq \emptyset$
    - $Post_\tau^*(Post_a(Post_\tau^*(\{pX\}) \cap Gen_{\mathcal{F}(p)}(K))) \cap Gen_g(K) \neq \emptyset$
    - $Post_\tau^*(Post_a(Post_\tau^*(\{pX\})) \cap Gen_g(K)) \cap Gen_g(K) \neq \emptyset$
    - $Post_\tau^*(Post_a(Post_\tau^*(\{pX\}) \cap Gen_{\mathcal{F}(p)}(K)) \cap Gen_g(K)) \cap Gen_g(K) \neq \emptyset$

  Due to Lemma 17 and Lemma 14, each of these four conditions can be checked in a purely "symbolic" way by performing the required operations directly on the underlying multi-automata. Obviously, the whole procedure takes time which is still polynomial in m, n, z.

Pairs of the form $(X\mathcal{G}, \mathcal{F})$ are handled in a similar way. So, the membership to $BExp(K)$ for a given K is decidable in time polynomial in m, n, z. This means that the algorithm of Fig. 1 terminates in time which is polynomial in m, n, z. So, we obtain the following theorem:

THEOREM 26 *The problem of weak, early, delay, and branching bisimilarity between PDA and finite-state processes is decidable in time polynomial in m, n, z. For PDA^k processes, the same problem is decidable in time polynomial in m, n (for each fixed k).*

References

[1] R. Alur, K. Etessami, and P. Madhusudan. A temporal logic of nested calls and returns. In *Proceedings of TACAS 2004*, vol. 2988 of *Lecture Notes in Computer Science*, pp. 467–481. Springer, 2004.

[2] R. Alur, K. Etessami, and M. Yannakakis. Analysis of recursive state machines. In *Proceedings of CAV 2001*, vol. 2102 of *Lecture Notes in Computer Science*, pp. 207–220. Springer, 2001.

[3] J.C.M. Baeten, J.A. Bergstra, and J.W. Klop. Decidability of bisimulation equivalence for processes generating context-free languages. *Journal of the Association for Computing Machinery*, 40:653–682, 1993.

[4] J.C.M. Baeten and W.P. Weijland. *Process Algebra*. No. 18 in Cambridge Tracts in Theoretical Computer Science. Cambridge University Press, 1990.

[5] A. Bouajjani. Languages, rewriting systems, and verification of infinite-state systems. In *Proceedings of ICALP 2001*, vol. 2076 of *Lecture Notes in Computer Science*, pp. 24–39. Springer, 2001.

[6] A. Bouajjani, J. Esparza, and O. Maler. Reachability analysis of pushdown automata: application to model checking. In *Proceedings of CONCUR'97*, vol. 1243 of *Lecture Notes in Computer Science*, pp. 135–150. Springer, 1997.

[7] O. Burkart, D. Caucal, F. Moller, and B. Steffen. Verification on infinite structures. In J.A. Bergstra, A. Ponse, and S.A. Smolka, editors, *Handbook of Process Algebra*, pp. 545–623. Elsevier, 2001.

[8] O. Burkart, D. Caucal, and B. Steffen. An elementary decision procedure for arbitrary context-free processes. In *Proceedings of MFCS'95*, vol. 969 of *Lecture Notes in Computer Science*, pp. 423–433. Springer, 1995.

[9] D. Caucal. Graphes canoniques des graphes algébriques. *Informatique Théorique et Applications (RAIRO)*, 24(4):339–352, 1990.

[10] S. Christensen, H. Hüttel, and C. Stirling. Bisimulation equivalence is decidable for all context-free processes. *Information and Computation*, 121:143–148, 1995.

[11] J. Esparza. Decidability of model checking for infinite-state concurrent systems. *Acta Informatica*, 34:85–107, 1997.

[12] J. Esparza, D. Hansel, P. Rossmanith, and S. Schwoon. Efficient algorithms for model checking pushdown systems. In *Proceedings of CAV 2000*, vol. 1855 of *Lecture Notes in Computer Science*, pp. 232–247. Springer, 2000.

[13] J. Esparza and J. Knoop. An automata-theoretic approach to interprocedural data-flow analysis. In *Proceedings of FoSSaCS'99*, vol. 1578 of *Lecture Notes in Computer Science*, pp. 14–30. Springer, 1999.

[14] J. Esparza, A. Kučera, and S. Schwoon. Model-checking LTL with regular valuations for pushdown systems. *Information and Computation*, 186(2):355–376, 2003.

[15] J. Esparza and S. Schwoon. A BDD-based model checker for recursive programs. In *Proceedings of CAV 2001*, vol. 2102 of *Lecture Notes in Computer Science*, pp. 324–336. Springer, 2001.

[16] E.P. Friedman. The inclusion problem for simple languages. *Theoretical Computer Science*, 1(4):297–316, 1976.

[17] J.F. Groote. A short proof of the decidability of bisimulation for normed BPA processes. *Information Processing Letters*, 42:167–171, 1992.

[18] Y. Hirshfeld, M. Jerrum, and F. Moller. A polynomial algorithm for deciding bisimilarity of normed context-free processes. *Theoretical Computer Science*, 158:143–159, 1996.

[19] H. Hüttel and C. Stirling. Actions speak louder than words: Proving bisimilarity for context-free processes. *Journal of Logic and Computation*, 8(4):485–509, 1998.

[20] P. Jančar and F. Moller. Techniques for decidability and undecidability of bisimilarity. In *Proceedings of CONCUR'99*, vol. 1664 of *Lecture Notes in Computer Science*, pp. 30–45. Springer, 1999.

[21] A. Kučera. On finite representations of infinite-state behaviours. *Information Processing Letters*, 70(1):23–30, 1999.

[22] A. Kučera and J. Esparza. A logical viewpoint on process-algebraic quotients. *Journal of Logic and Computation*, 13(6):863–880, 2003.

[23] A. Kučera and P. Jančar. Equivalence-checking with infinite-state systems: Techniques and results. In *Proceedings of SOFSEM'2002*, vol. 2540 of *Lecture Notes in Computer Science*. Springer, 2002.

[24] A. Kučera and R. Mayr. On the complexity of semantic equivalences for pushdown automata and BPA. In *Proceedings of MFCS 2002*, vol. 2420 of *Lecture Notes in Computer Science*, pp. 433–445. Springer, 2002.

[25] A. Kučera and R. Mayr. Weak bisimilarity between finite-state systems and BPA or normed BPP is decidable in polynomial time. *Theoretical Computer Science*, 270(1–2):677–700, 2002.

[26] A. Kučera and R. Mayr. A generic framework for checking semantic equivalences between pushdown automata and finite-state automata. Technical report FIMU-RS-2004-01, Faculty of Informatics, Masaryk University, 2004.

[27] K. Larsen and A. Skou. Bisimulation through probabilistic testing. *Information and Computation*, 94(1):1–28, 1991.

[28] R. Mayr. Undecidability of weak bisimulation equivalence for 1-counter processes. In *Proceedings of ICALP 2003*, vol. 2719 of *Lecture Notes in Computer Science*, pp. 570–583. Springer, 2003.

[29] R. Milner. *Communication and Concurrency*. Prentice-Hall, 1989.

[30] F. Moller. Infinite results. In *Proceedings of CONCUR'96*, vol. 1119 of *Lecture Notes in Computer Science*, pp. 195–216. Springer, 1996.

[31] D.M.R. Park. Concurrency and automata on infinite sequences. In *Proceedings* 5th *GI Conference*, vol. 104 of *Lecture Notes in Computer Science*, pp. 167–183. Springer, 1981.

[32] G. Sénizergues. Decidability of bisimulation equivalence for equational graphs of finite out-degree. In *Proceedings of FOCS'98*, pp. 120–129. IEEE Computer Society Press, 1998.

[33] J. Srba. Roadmap of infinite results. *EATCS Bulletin*, (78):163–175, 2002.

[34] J. Srba. Strong bisimilarity and regularity of basic process algebra is PSPACE-hard. In *Proceedings of ICALP 2002*, vol. 2380 of *Lecture Notes in Computer Science*, pp. 716–727. Springer, 2002.

[35] J. Srba. Undecidability of weak bisimilarity for pushdown processes. In *Proceedings of CONCUR 2002*, vol. 2421 of *Lecture Notes in Computer Science*, pp. 579–593. Springer, 2002.

[36] C. Stirling. Decidability of bisimulation equivalence for normed pushdown processes. *Theoretical Computer Science*, 195:113–131, 1998.

[37] C. Stirling. The joys of bisimulation. In *Proceedings of MFCS'98*, vol. 1450 of *Lecture Notes in Computer Science*, pp. 142–151. Springer, 1998.

[38] W. Thomas. On the Ehrenfeucht-Fraïssé game in theoretical computer science. In *Proceedings of TAPSOFT'93*, vol. 668 of *Lecture Notes in Computer Science*, pp. 559–568. Springer, 1993.

[39] R. van Glabbeek. What is branching time semantics and why to use it? *EATCS Bulletin*, (53):191–198, 1994.

[40] R. van Glabbeek. The linear time—branching time spectrum. *Handbook of Process Algebra*, pp. 3–99, 1999.

[41] R. van Glabbeek, A. Smolka, B. Steffen, and C. Tofts. Reactive, generative, and stratified models for probabilistic processes. In *Proceedings of LICS'90*, pp. 130–141. IEEE Computer Society Press, 1990.

[42] R.J. van Glabbeek. The linear time—branching time spectrum II: The semantics of sequential systems with silent moves. In *Proceedings of CONCUR'93*, vol. 715 of *Lecture Notes in Computer Science*, pp. 66–81. Springer, 1993.

[43] R.J. van Glabbeek and W.P. Weijland. Branching time and abstraction in bisimulation semantics. *Journal of the Association for Computing Machinery*, 43(3):555–600, 1996.

Tailoring Recursion to Characterize Non-Deterministic Complexity Classes Over Arbitrary Structures

O. Bournez,[1] F. Cucker*[2], P. Jacobé de Naurois,[1] and J.-Y. Marion[1]

[1] *LORIA, 615 rue du Jardin Botanique,BP 101, 54602 Villers-lès-Nancy Cedex, Nancy, FRANCE*

{Olivier.Bournez,Paulin.De-Naurois,Jean-Yves.Marion}@loria.fr

[2] *Department of Mathematics, City University of Hong Kong, 83 Tat Chee Avenue, Kowloon, HONG KONG*

macucker@math.cityu.edu.hk

Abstract We provide machine-independent characterizations of some complexity classes, over an arbitrary structure, in the model of computation proposed by L. Blum, M. Shub and S. Smale. We show that the levels of the polynomial hierarchy correspond to safe recursion with predicative minimization. The levels of the digital polynomial hierarchy correspond to safe recursion with digital predicative minimization. Also, we show that polynomial alternating time corresponds to safe recursion with predicative substitutions and that digital polynomial alternating time corresponds to safe recursion with digital predicative substitutions.

1 Introduction

Classical complexity can be considered as the restriction to finite structures of a more general notion of computability and complexity over arbitrary structures, see [4, 20]. To understand computability in a whole perspective, it is therefore interesting to study machine-independent characterizations of complexity classes over arbitrary structures.

We focus on function algebras characterizing classical complexity classes as initiated by Bellantoni and Cook [3], Leivant [17] and Marion [18]. This *implicit* approach, stemming on Fagin seminal logical characterization of nondeterministic polynomial time and other works [11, 6, 16, 10, 15, 21] is based on a purely syntactic distinction between different types of arguments, and

*Partially supported by City University of Hong Kong SRG grant 7001290.

avoids explicit upper bounds on computational resources or restrictions on the growth as originally done by Cobham in [7].

In a previous paper [5], based on classical characterizations in [3] and [19], we exhibited machine-independent characterizations of the classes of functions over an arbitrary structure computable in polynomial sequential or parallel time. Our aim here is to provide such machine-independent characterizations over an arbitrary structure for polynomial hierarchy and polynomial alternating time. Our characterizations need to coincide with the classical ones when restricted to a structure yielding the classical notion of computation.

Over an arbitrary structure, two kinds of nondeterminism may be considered according to whether the witness is allowed to be an arbitrary element of the structure or is restricted to be in $\{0, 1\}$. The latter is usually called *digital* and a letter D is used to denote complexity classes arising from the use of digital nondeterminism. Note that in classical complexity theory, i.e., over a finite structure, these two notions of nondeterminism coincide and they yield the same polynomial hierarchy and class of polynomial alternating time. Moreover, polynomial alternating time coincides with PSPACE and with PAR (the class of sets decided in parallel polynomial time). This need not to be so over infinite structures. For instance, over $(\mathbb{R}, +, -, *, /, \leq)$, we have the following inclusions of complexity classes [9]

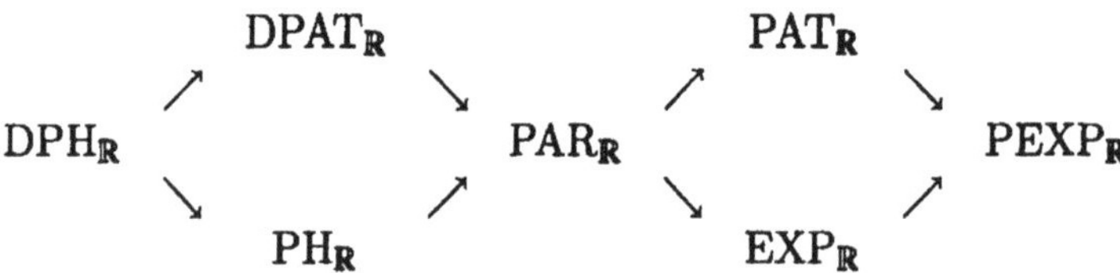

where an arrow means inclusion, $\mathrm{EXP}_\mathbb{R}$ denotes exponential time, $\mathrm{PEXP}_\mathbb{R}$ parallel exponential time, $\mathrm{PH}_\mathbb{R}$ is the polynomial hierarchy, and $\mathrm{PAT}_\mathbb{R}$ polynomial alternating time. In addition the two inclusions $\mathrm{PAR}_\mathbb{R} \subset \mathrm{PAT}_\mathbb{R}$ and $\mathrm{PAR}_\mathbb{R} \subset \mathrm{EXP}_\mathbb{R}$ are known to be strict.

Concerning classical complexity, our characterizations of PAT and DPAT, combined with our previous one of PAR in [5], provide several new original alternative characterizations of PSPACE.

Concerning complexity over arbitrary structures, we believe our characterizations to provide nice and natural definitions of complexity classes. First, our characterizations are machine-independent and avoid usual technical considerations about machines. Second, they do not require over arbitrary structure to distinguish two (not so natural) types of functions (called "number terms" and "index terms" in [14]) in order to be able to use finiteness considerations over the models even in presence of infinite underlying domains like the field of real numbers as in [13, 14].

We believe that the minimization schemes we introduce for coping with non-determinism, related to Hilbert choice operator and to the operators used to tailor recursion [1, 12] shed some light on the nature of choice operators.

Based on previous characterizations of deterministic complexity classes [5], recalled in Section 2 and 3, we provide in Section 4 a characterization of the polynomial hierarchy. Minor changes allow us to characterize the digital polynomial hierarchy in Section 5. Section 6 is devoted to a characterization of polynomial alternating time, with a similar characterization of digital polynomial alternating time in Section 7.

2 Arbitrary Structures

Definition 1

A structure $\mathcal{K} = (\mathbb{K}, \{op_i\}_{i \in I}, rel_1, \ldots, rel_l, \mathbf{0}, \mathbf{1})$ *is given by some underlying set* $\mathbb{K}$, *a family of operators* op_i, *and a finite number of relations* $rel_1, \ldots, rel_l$. *Constants correspond to operators of arity 0. While the index set* I *may be infinite, the number of operators of non-null arity needs to be finite.*

We will not distinguish between operator and relation symbols and their corresponding interpretations as functions and relations respectively over the underlying set $\mathbb{K}$. We assume that the equality relation $=$ is a relation of the structure, and that there are at least two constant symbols, with different interpretations (denoted by $\mathbf{0}$ and $\mathbf{1}$ in our work) in the structure.

An example of structure is $\mathcal{K} = (\mathbb{R}, +, -, *, =, \leq, \{c_r\}_{r \in \mathbb{R}})$. Another example, corresponding to classical complexity and computability theory, is $\mathcal{K} = (\{0, 1\}, =, \mathbf{0}, \mathbf{1})$.

We denote by $\mathbb{K}^* = \bigcup_{i \in \mathbb{N}} \mathbb{K}^i$ the set of words over the alphabet $\mathbb{K}$. The space $\mathbb{K}^*$ is the analogue to Σ^* the set of all finite sequences of zeros and ones. Words of elements in $\mathbb{K}$ will be represented with overlined letters, while elements in $\mathbb{K}$ will be represented by letters: $a.\overline{x}$ stands for the word in $\mathbb{K}^*$ whose first letter is a and which ends with the word $\overline{x}$. We denote by ϵ the empty word. The length of a word $\overline{w} \in \mathbb{K}^*$ is denoted by $|\overline{w}|$.

We assume that the reader has some familiarities with the BSS model of computation. Detailed accounts can be found in [4] —for structures like real and complex numbers— or [20] —for considerations about more general structures.

Roughly speaking, a BSS machine over $\mathcal{K}$ is a a kind of Turing machine which is able to perform the basic operations op_i and the basic tests $rel_1, \ldots, rel_l$ at unit cost, and whose tape cells can hold arbitrary elements of the underlying set $\mathbb{K}$. Operations op_i of arity 0, i.e., constants, occur in a finite number in every machine. [20, 4].

In this setting resources such as time, parallel time or alternating time can be considered allowing one to define several complexity classes. For example, a problem $P \subset K^*$ will be said polynomial iff there exists a machine that, given some word $w = a_1.a_2.\dots.a_n \in K^*$, determine whether $w \in P$ using a polynomial number in the length n of w of basic operations and basic tests. For most natural complexity classes, complete problems can be exhibited [4].

In a previous paper [5], we provided machine independent characterizations of the class of computable functions and of the class of functions computable in polynomial time. Since this work is based on the latter characterization, we next briefly recall our previous result.

3 Safe Recursive Functions

We shall define formally the set of safe recursive functions over an arbitrary structure $\mathcal{K}$, extending the notion of safe recursive functions over the natural numbers found in [3]. Safe recursive functions are defined in a similar manner as primitive recursive functions, i.e. as the closure of some basic functions under the application of some operations, among which one operation of safe recursion. However, in the spirit of [3], safe recursive functions have two different types of arguments, each of them having different properties and purposes. The first type of argument, called *normal*, can be used to make basic computation steps or to control recursion. The second type of argument, called *safe*, can not be used to control recursion. This distinction between safe and normal arguments ensures that safe recursive functions can be computed in polynomial time. Algebras of functions with this distinction between safe and normal arguments are sometimes denoted as BC functions, referring to Bellantoni and Cook [3].

To emphasize the distinction between normal and safe variables we will write $f : N \times S \to R$ where N indicates the domain of the normal arguments and S that of the safe arguments. If all the arguments of f are of one kind, say safe, we will write $\emptyset$ in the place of N. If $\overline{x}$ and $\overline{y}$ are these arguments, we will write $f(\overline{x};\overline{y})$ separating them by a semicolon ";". Normal arguments are placed at the left of the semicolon and safe arguments at its right.

Definition 2 We call *basic functions* the following four kinds of functions:

(i) functions making elementary manipulations of words over $\mathbb{K}$. For any $a \in \mathbb{K}, \overline{x}, \overline{x_1}, \overline{x_2} \in \mathbb{K}^*$

$$\begin{array}{rclcrclcrcl} \mathsf{hd}(;a.\overline{x}) & = & a & & \mathsf{tl}(;a.\overline{x}) & = & \overline{x} & & \mathsf{cons}(;a.\overline{x_1},\overline{x_2}) & = & a.\overline{x_2} \\ \mathsf{hd}(;\epsilon) & = & \epsilon & & \mathsf{tl}(;\epsilon) & = & \epsilon & & \mathsf{cons}(;\epsilon,\overline{x_2}) & = & \overline{x_2}. \end{array}$$

(ii) projections. For any $n \in \mathbb{N}, i \leq n$, $\mathsf{Pr}_i^n(;\overline{x_1},\dots,\overline{x_i},\dots,\overline{x_n}) = \overline{x_i}$.

(iii) functions of structure. For any operator (including the constants treated as operators of arity 0) op_i or relation rel_i of arity n_i we have the following initial functions (the equality relation will be denoted Equal).

$$\begin{aligned}\mathsf{Op}_i(;a_1.\overline{x_1},\ldots,a_{n_i}.\overline{x_{n_i}}) &= (op_i(a_1,\ldots,a_{n_i})).\overline{x_{n_i}}\\ \mathsf{Rel}_i(;a_1.\overline{x_1},\ldots,a_{n_i}.\overline{x_{n_i}}) &= \begin{cases}1 \text{ if } rel_i(a_1,\ldots,a_{n_i})\\ 0 \text{ otherwise.}\end{cases}\end{aligned}$$

(iv) a selector function

$$\mathsf{Select}(;\overline{x},\overline{y},\overline{z}) = \begin{cases}\overline{y} & \text{if } \mathsf{hd}(\overline{x}) = 1\\ \overline{z} & \text{otherwise.}\end{cases}$$

Definition 3 The set of *safe recursive functions* over $\mathcal{K}$, denoted by $\mathrm{SR}_{\mathcal{K}}$, is the smallest set of functions $f : (\mathbb{K}^*)^p \times (\mathbb{K}^*)^q \to \mathbb{K}^*$ containing the basic safe functions, and closed under the following operations:

(1) *Safe composition.* $g : (\mathbb{K}^*)^m \times (\mathbb{K}^*)^n \to \mathbb{K}^*$, $h_1,\ldots,h_m : \mathbb{K}^* \times \emptyset \to \mathbb{K}^*$ and $h_{m+1},\ldots,h_{m+n} : \mathbb{K}^* \times \mathbb{K}^* \to \mathbb{K}^*$ are given safe recursive functions. Their safe composition is the function $f : \mathbb{K}^* \times \mathbb{K}^* \to \mathbb{K}^*$ defined by

$$f(\overline{x};\overline{y}) = g\left(h_1(\overline{x};),\ldots,h_m(\overline{x};);h_{m+1}(\overline{x};\overline{y}),\ldots,h_{m+n}(\overline{x};\overline{y})\right).$$

(2) *Safe recursion.* $h : \mathbb{K}^* \times \mathbb{K}^* \to \mathbb{K}^*$ and $g : (\mathbb{K}^*)^2 \times (\mathbb{K}^*)^2 \to \mathbb{K}^*$ are given functions. $f : (\mathbb{K}^*)^2 \times \mathbb{K}^* \to \mathbb{K}^*$ is defined by safe recursion as follows

$$\begin{aligned}f(\epsilon,\overline{x};\overline{y}) &= h(\overline{x};\overline{y})\\ f(a.\overline{z},\overline{x};\overline{y}) &= g(\overline{z},\overline{x};f(\overline{z},\overline{x};\overline{y}),\overline{y}).\end{aligned}$$

When Φ is a set and F a complexity class, we denote by F^{Φ} the class F with oracle Φ. When G is another complexity class, F^G denotes the class F with oracles in G.

Definition 4 Given a function $\phi : \mathbb{K}^* \times \emptyset \to \mathbb{K}^*$, the set of *safe recursive functions relative to* ϕ over $\mathcal{K}$, denoted by $\mathrm{SR}_{\mathcal{K}}(\phi)$, is the smallest set of functions $f : (\mathbb{K}^*)^p \times (\mathbb{K}^*)^q \to \mathbb{K}^*$ containing the basic safe functions and ϕ, and closed under safe composition and safe recursion.

Theorem 1 *Let $\Phi \in \mathbb{K}^*$ be a decision problem over $\mathcal{K}$, and denote by $\phi : \emptyset \times \mathbb{K}^* \to \{0,1\}$ its characteristic function. Then, a function $f : \mathbb{K}^* \to \mathbb{K}^*$ is in the class $\mathrm{FP}_{\mathcal{K}}^{\Phi}$ of functions computable in polynomial time with oracle Φ if and only if $f : \mathbb{K}^* \times \emptyset \to \mathbb{K}*$ can be defined in $SR_{\mathcal{K}}(\phi)$.*

We consider only decision oracles and not functional oracles in order to avoid problems related to the output size of these oracles, see [8].

Corollary 1 ([5]) *Over any structure $\mathcal{K} = (\mathbb{K}, \{op_i\}_{i \in I}, rel_1, \ldots, rel_l, 0, 1)$, a function is computed in polynomial time by a BSS machine if and only if it is defined as a safe recursive function over $\mathcal{K}$.*

We shall now introduce a technical lemma needed further in our proofs.

Lemma 1 *Assume $f : (\mathbb{K}^*)^2 \times \emptyset \to \mathbb{K}^*$ is in $SR_{\mathcal{K}}(\phi)$. Moreover, assume that there exists a polynomial p such that, for all $\overline{x}, \overline{y} \in \mathbb{K}^*$, $f(\overline{x}, \overline{y};)$ can be evaluated in time bounded by $p(|\overline{x}|)$. Then, there exists $f' : \mathbb{K}^* \times \mathbb{K}^* \to \mathbb{K}^* \in SR_{\mathcal{K}}(\phi)$ such that $f'(\overline{x}; \overline{y}) = f(\overline{x}, \overline{y};)$.*

PROOF. The idea is to follow the proof of Corollary 1: a BSS machine, on input $\overline{z}$, can be simulated by a safe recursive function Eval such that $\mathsf{Eval}(\mathbf{0}^t; \overline{z})$ gives the content of the tape after t computation steps. Its normal argument $\mathbf{0}^t$ can be seen as a clock for the BSS machine. Assume M is a BSS-machine computing $f(\overline{x}, \overline{y};)$ in time $p(|\overline{x}|)$. Corollary 1 gives a safe recursive function $f_p : \mathbb{K}^* \times \emptyset \to \mathbb{K}^*$ such that $f_p(\overline{x};) = \mathbf{0}^{p(|\overline{x}|)}$. Consider a safe recursive function Cons such that $\mathsf{Cons}(\overline{x}; \overline{y}) = \overline{x}.\overline{y}$. Then, $f'(\overline{x}; \overline{y}) = \mathsf{Eval}(f_p(\overline{x}); \mathsf{Cons}(\overline{x}; \overline{y}))$.

4 A Characterization of $\mathrm{PH}_{\mathcal{K}}$

As in the classical settings, the polynomial hierarchy over a given structure $\mathcal{K}$ can be defined in several equivalent ways, including syntactic descriptions, or semantic definitions by successive relativizations of non-deterministic polynomial time (see [4]).

Recall some basic complexity classes:

- $\mathrm{P}_{\mathcal{K}}$ is the class of problems over $\mathcal{K}$ decided in polynomial time. We denote by $\mathrm{FP}_{\mathcal{K}}$ the class of functions over $\mathcal{K}$ computed in polynomial time.
- A decision problem A is in $\mathrm{NP}_{\mathcal{K}}$ if and only if there exists a decision problem B in $\mathrm{P}_{\mathcal{K}}$ and a polynomial p_B such that $\overline{x} \in A$ if and only if there exists $\overline{y} \in \mathbb{K}^*$ with $|\overline{y}| \leq p_B(|\overline{x}|)$ satisfying $(\overline{x}, \overline{y}) \in B$.
- A decision problem A is in $\mathrm{coNP}_{\mathcal{K}}$ if and only if there exists a decision problem B in $\mathrm{P}_{\mathcal{K}}$ and a polynomial p_B such that $\overline{x} \in A$ if and only if for all $\overline{y} \in \mathbb{K}^*$ with $|\overline{y}| \leq P_B(|\overline{x}|)$, $(\overline{x}, \overline{y})$ is in B.

Definition 5 Let $\Sigma^0_{\mathcal{K}} = \mathrm{P}_{\mathcal{K}}$ and, for $i \geq 1$, $\Sigma^i_{\mathcal{K}} = \mathrm{NP}_{\mathcal{K}}^{\Sigma^{i-1}_{\mathcal{K}}}$, $\Pi^i_{\mathcal{K}} = \mathrm{coNP}_{\mathcal{K}}^{\Sigma^{i-1}_{\mathcal{K}}}$. The *polynomial time hierarchy* over $\mathcal{K}$ is $\mathrm{PH}_{\mathcal{K}} = \bigcup_{i=0}^{\infty} \Sigma^i_{\mathcal{K}} = \bigcup_{i=0}^{\infty} \Pi^i_{\mathcal{K}}$. A function in $\mathrm{F}\Delta^i_{\mathcal{K}}$ is a polynomial time function over $\mathcal{K}$ which queries $\Sigma^i_{\mathcal{K}}$ oracles: $\mathrm{F}\Delta^i_{\mathcal{K}} = \mathrm{FP}_{\mathcal{K}}^{\Sigma^i_{\mathcal{K}}} = \mathrm{FP}_{\mathcal{K}}^{\Pi^i_{\mathcal{K}}}$. The *functional polynomial time hierarchy* over $\mathcal{K}$ is $\mathrm{FPH}_{\mathcal{K}} = \bigcup_{i=0}^{\infty} \mathrm{F}\Delta^i_{\mathcal{K}}$.

Remark Extending the classical notion of polynomial time reduction between decision problems, complete problems for every of the $\Sigma^i_{\mathcal{K}}$ and $\Pi^i_{\mathcal{K}}$ have been shown to exist [4].

In the spirit of [2], we now introduce the notion of predicative minimization (we use the terminology "minimization" taken from [2], even if this might be considered as not being a true minimization.).

Definition 6 Given $h : \mathbb{K}^* \times (\mathbb{K}^*)^2 \to \mathbb{K}^*$, we define $f : \mathbb{K}^* \times \mathbb{K}^* \to \mathbb{K}$ by *predicative minimization* as follows

$$f(\overline{x};\overline{a}) = \exists\overline{b}(h(\overline{x};\overline{a},\overline{b})) = \begin{cases} 1 & \text{if there exists } \overline{b} \in \mathbb{K}^* \text{ with } h(\overline{x};\overline{a},\overline{b}) = 0 \\ 0 & \text{otherwise.} \end{cases}$$

Remark Predicative minimization applied on functions h for which one can guarantee the existence of a $\overline{b}$ of polynomial size in the length of $\overline{x}$ when there is one, preserves (non-deterministic) computability. This consideration will assure computability of functions of our considered classes, in analogy with the "polychecking-lemma" used in [2] to guarantee computability.

We now introduce new sets of functions.

Definition 7 *Let F be a class of BC functions. The set of* restricted safe recursive functions relative to F *over $\mathcal{K}$, denoted by $RSR_{\mathcal{K}}(F)$, is the smallest set of functions containing the basic safe functions and F, and closed under the following* restricted safe composition *scheme*

$$f(\overline{x};\overline{y}) = g\left(h_1(\overline{x};),\ldots,h_m(\overline{x};);h_{m+1}(\overline{x};\overline{y}),\ldots,h_{m+n}(\overline{x};\overline{y})\right).$$

where the h_i belong to $RSR_{\mathcal{K}}(F)$ and g to $SR_{\mathcal{K}}$, and the following restricted safe recursion *scheme*

$$\begin{aligned} f(\epsilon,\overline{x};\overline{y}) &= h(\overline{x};\overline{y}) \\ f(a.\overline{z},\overline{x};\overline{y}) &= g(\overline{z},\overline{x};f(\overline{z},\overline{x};\overline{y}),\overline{y}) \end{aligned}$$

where h belongs to $RSR_{\mathcal{K}}(F)$ and g to $SR_{\mathcal{K}}$. This implies that no function in $F \backslash SR_{\mathcal{K}}$ may be involved in the definition of g.

Definition 8 Assume F is a class of functions: a function f is in $\exists$F if it is defined with one predicative minimization over a function h of F.

We define by induction the following sets:

- $F^0_{\mathcal{K}} = SR_{\mathcal{K}}$.
- $F^{i+1}_{\mathcal{K}} = RSR_{\mathcal{K}}(F^i_{\mathcal{K}} \bigcup \exists F^i_{\mathcal{K}})$, for $i \geq 0$.

We denote by $\exists PH_{\mathcal{K}} = \bigcup_{i \in N} F^i_{\mathcal{K}}$ the closure of the basic safe functions over $\mathcal{K}$ under the application of restricted safe recursion, predicative minimization and safe composition.

Lemma 2 *This notion of restricted safe recursion ensures that, for any function f in $F^i_{\mathcal{K}}$, there are at most i nested predicative minimizations. This bound does not depend on the arguments of f. In other words, there exists h in $SR_{\mathcal{K}}$ and $f_1, \ldots, f_n$ in $F^{i-1}_{\mathcal{K}}$, such that, for all $\mathbf{x} = (\overline{x_1}, \ldots, \overline{x_l})$,*

$$f(\mathbf{x};) = h(\mathbf{x}; \ni\overline{z_1}(f_1(\mathbf{x};\overline{z_1})), \ldots, \ni\overline{z_n}(f_n(\mathbf{x};\overline{z_n}))).$$

We denote this as a normal form for f.

Lemma 3 *Assume $f : (\mathbb{K}^*)^n \times \emptyset \to \mathbb{K}^*$ is a function in $\mathrm{F}\Delta^i_{\mathcal{K}}$. Then f can be defined in $F^i_{\mathcal{K}}$.*

PROOF. By induction on i. For $i = 0$, f is in $\mathrm{F}\Delta^0_{\mathcal{K}} = \mathrm{FP}_{\mathcal{K}}$ and we may apply Corollary 1. Assume now that the result holds for $i > 0$.

Let f be a function in $\mathrm{F}\Delta^i_{\mathcal{K}}$. By definition of $\mathrm{F}\Delta^i_{\mathcal{K}}$, there exist a polynomial time BSS machine M_f and a set Φ in $\Sigma^i_{\mathcal{K}}$ such that, for all $\overline{x} \in \mathbb{K}^*$, $f(\overline{x})$ is computed by M_f with oracle Φ. We are now establishing that the oracle Φ can be denoted by a function in $\mathrm{F}^i_{\mathcal{K}}$.

Since $\Phi \in \Sigma^i_{\mathcal{K}} = \mathrm{NP}^{\Sigma^{i-1}_{\mathcal{K}}}_{\mathcal{K}}$ there exist a deterministic polynomial-time BSS machine M_g over $\mathcal{K}$, a polynomial p and a set $\Psi \in \Sigma^{i-1}_{\mathcal{K}}$ such that

$$\overline{x} \in \Phi \Leftrightarrow \exists\overline{y} \text{ s.t. } M_g \text{ accepts } (\overline{x},\overline{y}) \text{ with oracle } \Psi \text{ and} |\overline{y}| < p(|\overline{x}|).$$

Denote by g the characteristic function computed by M_g with oracle Ψ and let ψ be the characteristic function of Ψ. Then, apply Theorem 1: g belongs to $\mathrm{SR}(\psi)_{\mathcal{K}}$. Since the evaluation time of M_g on $(\overline{x},\overline{y})$ is polynomial in $|\overline{x}|$, Lemma 1 gives g' in $\mathrm{SR}(\psi)_{\mathcal{K}}$ such that: $g'(\overline{x};\overline{y}) = g(\overline{x},\overline{y};)$. Therefore $\phi(\overline{x};) = \ni\overline{y}(g'(\overline{x};\overline{y}))$ decides Φ, and, since $\Sigma^{i-1}_{\mathcal{K}} \subseteq \mathrm{F}\Delta^{i-1}_{\mathcal{K}}$, we may apply the induction hypothesis on ψ to deduce that ϕ belongs to $\mathrm{F}^i_{\mathcal{K}}$ and therefore so does f.

Lemma 4 *Assume $f : (\mathbb{K}^*)^n \times \emptyset \to \mathbb{K}^*$ is a function in $F^i_{\mathcal{K}}$. Then it belongs to $\mathrm{F}\Delta^i_{\mathcal{K}}$.*

PROOF. By induction on i. For $i = 0$, the result is a straightforward consequence of Corollary 1. Assume now that the result holds for $i > 0$.

Assume f is a function in $\mathrm{F}^i_{\mathcal{K}}$. Then, as in Lemma 2,

$$f(\mathbf{x};) = h(\mathbf{x}; \ni\overline{z_1}(f_1(\mathbf{x};\overline{z_1})), \ldots, \ni\overline{z_n}(f_n(\mathbf{x};\overline{z_n}))).$$

By induction hypothesis, the functions $f_1, \ldots, f_n$ belong to $\mathrm{F}\Delta^{i-1}_{\mathcal{K}}$. The corresponding decision problems $f_1(\mathbf{x};\overline{z_1}) = 0, \ldots, f_n(\mathbf{x};\overline{z_n}) = 0$ belong to $\mathrm{P}^{\Sigma^{i-1}_{\mathcal{K}}}_{\mathcal{K}} = \Sigma^{i-1}_{\mathcal{K}}$. Indeed, they use a polynomial number of queries in $\Sigma^{i-1}_{\mathcal{K}}$. If S_{i-1} denotes a complete problem in $\Sigma^{i-1}_{\mathcal{K}}$ (see Remark 1), we can replace these different oracles by S_{i-1} (by making the oracle machine compute the reductions).

Define $g_j(\mathbf{x};) = \exists \overline{z_j}(f_j(\mathbf{x};\overline{z_j}))$ for $1 \leq j \leq n$. Then, g_j is the characteristic function of a set in $\Sigma^i_{\mathcal{K}}$. Indeed, if there exists $\overline{z_j} \in \mathbb{K}^*$ such that $f_j(\mathbf{x};\overline{z_j}) = \mathbf{0}$, since the evaluation time for $f_j(\mathbf{x};\overline{z_j})$ is bounded by $p_j(|\mathbf{x}|)$ for some polynomial p_j, only the first $p_j(|\mathbf{x}|)$ elements of $\overline{z_j}$ may possibly be taken into account. Therefore, there exists $\overline{z'_j} \in \mathbb{K}^*$ of length $p_j(|\mathbf{x}|)$ such that $f_j(\mathbf{x};\overline{z'_j}) = \mathbf{0}$, which proves the claim. Therefore, f can be computed in polynomial time using n oracles in $\Sigma^i_{\mathcal{K}}$. If S_i denotes a complete problem in $\Sigma^i_{\mathcal{K}}$, again, we can replace these n different oracles by S_i: $f \in \mathrm{FP}_{\mathcal{K}}^{\Sigma^i_{\mathcal{K}}} = \mathrm{F}\Delta^i_{\mathcal{K}}$.

This gives our first main characterization.

Theorem 2 *A function:* $(\mathbb{K}^*)^n \times \emptyset \rightarrow \mathbb{K}^*$ *belongs to* $\mathrm{F}\Delta^i_{\mathcal{K}}$ *if and only if it is defined in* $F^i_{\mathcal{K}}$.

Example Over the real numbers, an example of $\mathrm{NP}_{\mathbb{R}}$-complete problem is $4-\mathrm{FEAS}$: does a given polynomial of degree four have a zero? Assume by Corollary 1 that the safe recursive function $p(\overline{x};\overline{y})$ evaluates a polynomial encoded in $\overline{x}$ on an input encoded in $\overline{y}$. $4-\mathrm{FEAS}$ is then decided on $\overline{x}$ by $f(\overline{x};) = \exists \overline{y}(p(\overline{x};\overline{y}))$.

Corollary 2 *A decision problem over* $\mathcal{K}$ *belongs to* $\mathrm{PH}_{\mathcal{K}}$ *if and only if its characteristic function is defined in* $\exists\mathrm{PH}_{\mathcal{K}}$.

5 A Characterization of $\mathrm{DPH}_{\mathcal{K}}$

Definition 9 A set $S \subseteq \mathbb{K}^*$ belongs to $\mathrm{DNP}_{\mathcal{K}}$ if and only if there exist a polynomial p and a polynomial time BSS machine M over $\mathcal{K}$ such that, for all $\overline{x} \in \mathbb{K}^*$,

$$\overline{x} \in S \Leftrightarrow \exists \overline{y} \in \{0,1\}^* \text{ s.t. } |\overline{y}| \leq p(|\overline{x}|) \text{ and } M \text{ accepts } (\overline{x},\overline{y}).$$

Let $\mathrm{D}\Sigma^0_{\mathcal{K}} = \mathrm{P}_{\mathcal{K}}$ and, for $i \geq 1$, $\mathrm{D}\Sigma^i_{\mathcal{K}} = \mathrm{DNP}_{\mathcal{K}}^{\mathrm{D}\Sigma^{i-1}_{\mathcal{K}}}$, $\mathrm{D}\Pi^i_{\mathcal{K}} = \mathrm{coDNP}_{\mathcal{K}}^{\mathrm{D}\Sigma^{i-1}_{\mathcal{K}}}$. The *digital polynomial time hierarchy* is $\mathrm{DPH}_{\mathcal{K}} = \bigcup_{i=0}^{\infty} \mathrm{D}\Sigma^i_{\mathcal{K}} = \bigcup_{i=0}^{\infty} \mathrm{D}\Pi^i_{\mathcal{K}}$. A function in $\mathrm{DF}\Delta^i_{\mathcal{K}}$ is a polynomial time function over $\mathcal{K}$ which queries $\mathrm{D}\Sigma^i_{\mathcal{K}}$ oracles: $\mathrm{DF}\Delta^i_{\mathcal{K}} = \mathrm{FP}_{\mathcal{K}}^{\mathrm{D}\Sigma^i_{\mathcal{K}}} = \mathrm{FP}_{\mathcal{K}}^{\mathrm{D}\Pi^i_{\mathcal{K}}}$. The *functional digital polynomial time hierarchy* is $\mathrm{DFPH}_{\mathcal{K}} = \bigcup_{i=0}^{\infty} \mathrm{DF}\Delta^i_{\mathcal{K}}$.

In this digital version of the polynomial hierarchy, witnesses for a given problem are discrete choices among given values, and not arbitrary elements of the structure. As in the previous section, complete problems have been shown to exist for every level of this hierarchy [4].

Similarly to the notion of predicative minimization of the previous section, we introduce the notion of digital predicative minimization.

Definition 10 Given $h : \mathbb{K}^* \times (\mathbb{K}^*)^2 \to \mathbb{K}^*$, we define $f : \mathbb{K}^* \times \mathbb{K}^* \to \mathbb{K}$ by *digital predicative minimization* as follows

$$f(\overline{x};\overline{a}) = \exists_{\mathrm{D}}\overline{b}(h(\overline{x};\overline{a},\overline{b})) = \begin{cases} 1 & \text{if there is a } \overline{b} \in \{0,1\}^* \text{ with } h(\overline{x};\overline{a},\overline{b}) = 0 \\ 0 & \text{otherwise.} \end{cases}$$

Definition 11 Let F be a class of functions. A function f is in $\exists_{\mathrm{D}}\mathrm{F}$ if it is defined with one predicative minimization over a function h of F.

We define by induction the following sets:

- $\mathrm{dF}^0_{\mathcal{K}} = \mathrm{SR}_{\mathcal{K}}$
- $\mathrm{dF}^{i+1}_{\mathcal{K}} = \mathrm{RSR}_{\mathcal{K}}(\mathrm{dF}^i_{\mathcal{K}} \bigcup \exists_{\mathrm{D}}\mathrm{F}^i_{\mathcal{K}})$, for $i \geq 0$.

We denote by $\exists_{\mathrm{D}}\mathrm{PH}_{\mathcal{K}}$ the closure of the basic safe functions over $\mathcal{K}$ under the application of projections, restricted safe recursion, digital predicative minimization and safe composition.

The proof of Theorem 2, *mutatis mutandis*, yields the following results.

Theorem 3 *A function:* $(\mathbb{K}^*)^n \times \emptyset \to \mathbb{K}^*$ *belongs to* $\mathrm{DF}\Delta^i_{\mathcal{K}}$ *if and only if it is defined in* $dF^i_{\mathcal{K}}$.

Corollary 3 *A decision problem over* $\mathcal{K}$ *belongs to* $\mathrm{DPH}_{\mathcal{K}}$ *if and only if its characteristic function is defined in* $\exists_{\mathrm{D}}\mathrm{DPH}_{\mathcal{K}}$.

Example Over the real numbers, a problem in $\mathrm{D}\Sigma^1_{\mathbb{R}}$ is KNAPSACK: given n objects of weight $w_i \in \mathbb{R}$ and value $v_i \in \mathbb{R}$, a weight limit W and a minimal value V, can we select a subset of objects of total value greater than V and of total weight less than W? Assume by Corollary 1 that the safe recursive function $v(\overline{x};\overline{y})$ decides whether, for an instance described by $\overline{x}$ in size polynomial in n, a choice among the objects described by $\overline{y} \in \{0,1\}^n$, the requirements of weight and value are satisfied. KNAPSACK is then decided on $\overline{x}$ by $f(\overline{x};) = \exists_{\mathrm{D}}\overline{y}(v(\overline{x};\overline{y}))$. When considering finite structures, this yields naturally a characterization of the classical polynomial hierarchy alternative to the one found in [2]:

Corollary 4 *A decision problem belongs to* PH *if and only if its characteristic function is defined in* $\exists_{\mathrm{D}}\mathrm{DPH}_{\{0,1\}}$.

6 A Characterization of $\mathrm{PAT}_{\mathcal{K}}$

Definition 12 A set $S \subseteq \mathbb{K}^*$ belongs to $\mathrm{PAT}_{\mathcal{K}}$ (*polynomial alternating time*) if and only if there exist a polynomial function $q : \mathrm{N} \to \mathrm{N}$ and a polynomial time BSS machine M_S over $\mathcal{K}$ such that, for all $\overline{x} \in \mathbb{K}^*$,

$$\overline{x} \in S \Leftrightarrow \exists a_1 \in \mathbb{K}\, \forall b_1 \in \mathbb{K} \ldots \exists a_{q(|\overline{x}|)} \in \mathbb{K}\, \forall b_{q(|\overline{x}|)} \in \mathbb{K}$$
$$M_S \text{ accepts } (\overline{x}, a_1.b_1 \ldots a_{q(|\overline{x}|)}.b_{q(|\overline{x}|)}).$$

In addition, we define $\mathrm{FPAT}_{\mathcal{K}} = \mathrm{FP}_{\mathcal{K}}^{\mathrm{PAT}_{\mathcal{K}}}$.

When $\mathcal{K}$ is the classical structure $\{\{0,1\},=,0,1\}$, $\mathrm{PAT}_{\mathcal{K}}$ is PSPACE.

It is important to note that the number of quantifier alternations is not fixed, but depends on the length of the input and is polynomial in that length. It follows that $\mathrm{PH}_{\mathcal{K}} \subseteq \mathrm{PAT}_{\mathcal{K}}$.

Definition 13 Given $h : \mathbb{K}^* \times (\mathbb{K}^*)^2 \to \mathbb{K}^*$, we define $f : \mathbb{K}^* \times \mathbb{K}^* \to \mathbb{K}$ by *predicative substitution* as follows

$$f(\overline{x};\overline{a}) = \ni^{[1]}c(h(\overline{x};\overline{a},c)) = \begin{cases} 1 & \text{if there is a } c \in \mathbb{K} \text{ with } h(\overline{x};\overline{a},c) = 0 \\ 0 & \text{otherwise.} \end{cases}$$

Definition 14 Assume $h : \mathbb{K}^* \times (\mathbb{K}^*)^2 \to \mathbb{K}^*$ and $g : (\mathbb{K}^*)^2 \times (\mathbb{K}^*)^2 \to \mathbb{K}^*$ are given functions. The function $f : (\mathbb{K}^*)^2 \times (\mathbb{K}^*)^2 \to \mathbb{K}^*$ is defined by *safe recursion with predicative substitution* as follows

$$\begin{aligned} f(\epsilon,\overline{x};\overline{u},\overline{y}) &= h(\overline{x};\overline{u},\overline{y}) \\ f(a.\overline{z},\overline{x};\overline{u},\overline{y}) &= g(\overline{z},\overline{x};\ni^{[1]}c(f(\overline{z},\overline{x};c.\overline{u},\overline{y})),\overline{y}). \end{aligned}$$

Definition 15 The set $\ni^{[1]}\mathrm{PAT}_{\mathcal{K}}$ of *safe recursive functions with predicative substitutions* over $\mathcal{K}$ is the closure of the basic safe functions under the application of safe composition, safe recursion and safe recursion with predicative substitutions.

Theorem 4 *A function is computed in* $\mathrm{FPAT}_{\mathcal{K}}$ *if and only if it can be defined in* $\ni^{[1]}\mathrm{PAT}_{\mathcal{K}}$.

PROOF. Let F be a function in $\mathrm{FPAT}_{\mathcal{K}}$, and denote by G the associated oracle in $\mathrm{PAT}_{\mathcal{K}}$. There exists a polynomial time BSS machine M over $\mathcal{K}$, and a polynomial function $q : \mathbb{N} \to \mathbb{N}$ such that, for all $\overline{x} \in \mathbb{K}^*$,

$$\begin{aligned} \overline{x} \in G \quad \Leftrightarrow \quad & \exists a_1 \in \mathbb{K}\, \neg\exists b_1 \in \mathbb{K} \ \dots\ \exists a_{q(|\overline{x}|)} \in \mathbb{K}\, \neg\exists b_{q(|\overline{x}|)} \in \mathbb{K} \\ & M \text{ accepts } (\overline{x}, a_1.b_1 \dots a_{q(|\overline{x}|)}.b_{q(|\overline{x}|)}). \end{aligned}$$

Corollary 1 and Lemma 1 ensure that there exists a safe recursive function f_M over $\mathcal{K}$ such that, for any $(\overline{x},\overline{y}) \in (\mathbb{K}^*)^2$, M accepts on input $(\overline{x},\overline{y})$ if and only if $f_M(\overline{x};\overline{y}) = 1$.

Consider now the function $F_G : (\mathbb{K}^*)^2 \times \mathbb{K}^* \to \mathbb{K}^*$ deciding G. $F_G(\epsilon,\overline{x};\overline{u})$ simulates M on input $\overline{x},\overline{u}$. The recurrence parameter $a.\overline{z}$ in $F_G(a.\overline{z},\overline{x};\overline{u})$ describes the shape of the quantifier sequence. F_G is defined with quantified safe recursion as follows,

$$\begin{aligned} F_G(\epsilon,\overline{x};\overline{u}) &= f_M(\overline{x};\overline{u}) \\ F_G(a.\overline{z},\overline{x};\overline{u}) &= \mathsf{Select}(;\mathsf{Equal}(;\mathsf{hd}(;\overline{z}),1),\ni^{[1]}c(F_G(\overline{z},\overline{x};c.\overline{u})), \\ & \mathsf{Select}(;\mathsf{Equal}(;\mathsf{hd}(;\overline{z}),0),\mathsf{Select}(;\ni^{[1]}c(F_G(\overline{z},\overline{x};c.\overline{u})),0,1),f_M(\overline{x};\overline{u}))). \end{aligned}$$

In addition, let $g_q : \mathbb{K}^* \times \emptyset \to \mathbb{K}^*$ such that $g_q(\overline{x};) = (\mathbf{1.0})^{q(|\overline{x}|)}$. Since g_q is computable in polynomial time over $\mathcal{K}$, by Corollary 1, it is safe recursive. This function g_q actually gives the type of the quantifier at every level of the quantifier alternation for any input $\overline{x}$ to the problem G.

It is easy to check by induction on $|\overline{x}|$ that $F_G(\text{cons}(\mathbf{1}, g_q(\overline{x};);), \overline{x}; \mathbf{0})$ decides whether $\overline{x}$ belongs to G. Therefore, the characteristic function χ_G of G belongs to $\ni^{[1]}\text{PAT}_{\mathcal{K}}$.

Consider a polynomial time machine M' with oracle G computing F. We apply Theorem 1: F belongs to $\text{SR}_{\mathcal{K}}(F_G)$, i.e., $F \in \ni^{[1]}\text{PAT}_{\mathcal{K}}$.

The other direction of the proof is by induction on the definition of f. The only critical case is when f is defined by safe recursion with predicative substitution, as in Definition 14. In this case, $f(a.\overline{z}, \overline{x}; \overline{u}, \overline{y})$ equals $\mathbf{1}$ if and only if

$$\begin{aligned} &(\exists c \in \mathbb{K}\ f(\overline{z}, \overline{x}; c.\overline{u}, \overline{y}) = \mathbf{0} \wedge g(\overline{z}, \overline{x}; \mathbf{1}, \overline{y}) = \mathbf{1}) \\ \vee\ &(\forall c \in \mathbb{K}\ f(\overline{z}, \overline{x}; c.\overline{u}, \overline{y}) \neq \mathbf{0} \wedge g(\overline{z}, \overline{x}; \mathbf{0}, \overline{y}) = \mathbf{1}). \end{aligned}$$

If $g(\overline{z}, \overline{x}; \mathbf{1}, \overline{y}) = \mathbf{1}$ and $g(\overline{z}, \overline{x}; \mathbf{0}, \overline{y}) = \mathbf{1}$, then $f(a.\overline{z}, \overline{x}; \overline{u}, \overline{y}) = \mathbf{1}$ and there is no need for a recursive call. If $g(\overline{z}, \overline{x}; \mathbf{1}, \overline{y}) \neq \mathbf{1}$ and $g(\overline{z}, \overline{x}; \mathbf{0}, \overline{y}) \neq \mathbf{1}$, then $f(a.\overline{z}, \overline{x}; \overline{u}, \overline{y}) \neq \mathbf{1}$ and there is no need for a recursive call either. If $g(\overline{z}, \overline{x}; \mathbf{1}, \overline{y}) = \mathbf{1}$ and $g(\overline{z}, \overline{x}; \mathbf{0}, \overline{y}) \neq \mathbf{1}$, then $f(a.\overline{z}, \overline{x}; \overline{u}, \overline{y}) = \mathbf{1}$ if and only if

$$\exists c \in \mathbb{K}\ f(\overline{z}, \overline{x}; c.\overline{u}, \overline{y}) = \mathbf{0}.$$

If $g(\overline{z}, \overline{x}; \mathbf{1}, \overline{y}) \neq \mathbf{1}$ and $g(\overline{z}, \overline{x}; \mathbf{0}, \overline{y}) = \mathbf{1}$, then $f(a.\overline{z}, \overline{x}; \overline{u}, \overline{y}) = \mathbf{1}$ if and only if

$$\forall c \in \mathbb{K}\ f(\overline{z}, \overline{x}; c.\overline{u}, \overline{y}) \neq \mathbf{0}.$$

Therefore, at every level of the recursion, the choice is determined by the function g. By induction hypothesis, this can be done in $\text{FPAT}_{\mathcal{K}}$. When unfolding the recursion, we get a sequence of quantifiers $Q_1, \ldots, Q_{|\overline{z}|+1}$ and a relation symbol $r \in \{=, \neq\}$ such that

$$\begin{aligned} &f(a.\overline{z}, \overline{x}; \overline{u}, \overline{y}) = \mathbf{1} \\ \text{iff } &Q_1 c_1 \in \mathbb{K}, \ldots, Q_{|\overline{z}|+1} c_{|\overline{z}|+1} \in \mathbb{K}\ h(\overline{x}; c_1. \ldots .c_{|\overline{z}|+1}.\overline{u}, \overline{y})\ r\ \mathbf{0}. \end{aligned}$$

Apply the induction hypothesis on function h. Then, f belongs to $\text{FPAT}_{\mathcal{K}}^{\text{FPAT}_{\mathcal{K}}}$, with an oracle which computes g and gives the quantifier sequence. One just needs to note that $\text{FPAT}_{\mathcal{K}}^{\text{FPAT}_{\mathcal{K}}} = \text{FPAT}_{\mathcal{K}}$ to conclude.

7 A Characterization of $\text{DPAT}_{\mathcal{K}}$

Class $\text{DPAT}_{\mathcal{K}}$ is similar to $\text{PAT}_{\mathcal{K}}$ but with all quantified variables belonging to $\{\mathbf{0}, \mathbf{1}\}$. Similarly, we can define $\text{DFPAT}_{\mathcal{K}} = \text{FP}_{\mathcal{K}}^{\text{DPAT}_{\mathcal{K}}}$.

Similarly to the notion of predicative substitution, we define the notion of digital predicative substitution.

Definition 16 Given $h : \mathbb{K}^* \times (\mathbb{K}^*)^2 \to \mathbb{K}^*$, we define $f : \mathbb{K}^* \times \mathbb{K}^* \to \mathbb{K}$ by *predicative substitution*,

$$f(\overline{x};\overline{a}) = \ni_{\mathrm{D}}^{[1]} c(h(\overline{x};\overline{a},c)) = \begin{cases} 1 & \text{if there is } c \in \{0,1\} \text{ with } h(\overline{x};\overline{a},c) = 0 \\ 0 & \text{otherwise.} \end{cases}$$

Definition 17 Assume $h : \mathbb{K}^* \times (\mathbb{K}^*)^2 \to \mathbb{K}^*$ and $g : (\mathbb{K}^*)^2 \times (\mathbb{K}^*)^2 \to \mathbb{K}^*$ are given functions. The function $f : (\mathbb{K}^*)^2 \times (\mathbb{K}^*)^2 \to \mathbb{K}^*$ is defined by *safe recursion with digital predicative substitution* as follows

$$\begin{aligned} f(\epsilon,\overline{x};\overline{u},\overline{y}) &= h(\overline{x};\overline{u},\overline{y}) \\ f(a.\overline{z},\overline{x};\overline{u},\overline{y}) &= g(\overline{z},\overline{x};\ni_{\mathrm{D}}^{[1]} c f(\overline{z},\overline{x};c.\overline{u},\overline{y}),\overline{y}). \end{aligned}$$

Definition 18 The set $\ni_{\mathrm{D}}^{[1]}\mathrm{PAT}_{\mathcal{K}}$ of *safe recursive functions with digital predicative substitutions* over $\mathcal{K}$ is the closure of the basic safe functions under the application of safe composition, safe recursion and safe recursion with digital predicative substitution.

Again, the proof of Theorem 4 yields, *mutatis mutandis*, the following result.

Theorem 5 *A function is computed in* $\mathrm{DFPAT}_{\mathcal{K}}$ *if and only if it can be defined in* $\ni^{[1]}\mathrm{DPAT}_{\mathcal{K}}$.

When restricted to finite structures, this yields another characterization of PSPACE:

Corollary 5 *A decision problem is decided in* PSPACE *if and only if its characteristic function can be defined in* $\ni^{[1]}\mathrm{DPAT}_{\{0,1\}}$.

References

[1] A.Blass and Y. Gurevich. The logic of choice. *Journal of Symbolic Logic*, 65(3):1264–1310, Sept. 2000.

[2] S. Bellantoni. Predicative recursion and the polytime hiearchy. In Peter Clote and Jeffrey B. Remmel, editors, *Feasible Mathematics II, Perspectives in Computer Science*. Birkhauser, 1994.

[3] S. Bellantoni and S. Cook. A new recursion-theoretic characterization of the poly-time functions. *Computational Complexity*, 2:97–110, 1992.

[4] L. Blum, F. Cucker, M. Shub, and S. Smale. *Complexity and Real Computation*. Springer-Verlag, 1998.

[5] O. Bournez, F. Cucker, P. Jacobe de Naurois, and J.-Y. Marion. Computability over an arbitrary structure. sequential and parallel polynomial time. In Andrew D. Gordon, editor, *Foundations of Software Science and Computational Structures, 6th International*

Conference (FOSSACS'2003), volume 2620 of *Lecture Notes in Computer Science*, pages 185–199. Springer, 2003.

[6] P. Clote. Computational models and function algebras. In D. Leivant, editor, *LCC'94*, volume 960 of *Lecture Notes in Computer Science*, pages 98–130. Springer-Verlag, 1995.

[7] A. Cobham. The intrinsic computational difficulty of functions. In Y. Bar-Hillel, editor, *Proceedings of the International Conference on Logic, Methodology, and Philosophy of Science*, pages 24–30. North-Holland, Amsterdam, 1962.

[8] S. Cook. Computability and complexity of higher-type functions. In Y. Moschovakis, editor, *Logic from Computer Science*, pages 51–72. Springer-Verlag, New York, 1992.

[9] F. Cucker. On the complexity of quantifier elimination: the structural approach. *The Computer Journal*, 36:400–408, 1993.

[10] H.-D. Ebbinghaus and J. Flum. *Finite Model Theory*. Perspectives in Mathematical Logic. Springer-Verlag, Berlin, 1995.

[11] R. Fagin. Generalized first order spectra and polynomial time recognizable sets. In R. Karp, editor, *Complexity of Computation*, pages 43–73. SIAM-AMS, 1974.

[12] E. Gradel and Y. Gurevich. Tailoring recursion for complexity. *Journal of Symbolic Logic*, 60(3):952–969, Sept. 1995.

[13] Erich Gradel and Yuri Gurevich. Metafinite model theory. *Information and Computation*, 140(1):26–81, 10 January 1998.

[14] Erich Gradel and Klaus Meer. Descriptive complexity theory over the real numbers. In *Proceedings of the Twenty-Seventh Annual ACM Symposium on the Theory of Computing*, pages 315–324, Las Vegas, Nevada, 29 May–1 June 1995.

[15] Y. Gurevich. Algebras of feasible functions. In *Twenty Fourth Symposium on Foundations of Computer Science*, pages 210–214. IEEE Computer Society Press, 1983.

[16] N. Immerman. *Descriptive Complexity*. Springer-Verlag, 1999.

[17] D. Leivant. Predicative recurrence and computational complexity I: Word recurrence and poly-time. In Peter Clote and Jeffery Remmel, editors, *Feasible Mathematics II*, pages 320–343. Birkhauser, 1994.

[18] D. Leivant and J-Y Marion. Lambda calculus characterizations of poly-time. *Fundamenta Informaticae*, 19(1,2):167,184, September 1993.

[19] D. Leivant and J.-Y. Marion. Ramified recurrence and computational complexity II: substitution and poly-space. In L. Pacholski and J. Tiuryn, editors, *Computer Science Logic, 8th Workshop, CSL'94*, volume 933 of *Lecture Notes in Computer Science*, pages 369–380, Kazimierz, Poland, 1995. Springer-Verlag.

[20] B. Poizat. *Les Petits Cailloux*. Aleas, 1995.

[21] V. Sazonov. Polynomial computability and recursivity in finite domains. *Elektronische Informationsverarbeitung und Kybernetik*, 7:319–323, 1980.

A CALCULUS WITH LAZY MODULE OPERATORS

Davide Ancona, Sonia Fagorzi and Elena Zucca
DISI - Università di Genova
*Via Dodecaneso, 35, 16146 Genova (Italy)**
{davide,fagorzi,zucca}@disi.unige.it

Abstract Modern programming environments such as those of Java and C# support dynamic loading of software fragments. More in general, we can expect that in the future systems will support more and more forms of interleaving of *reconfiguration* steps and standard *execution* steps, where the software fragments composing a program are dynamically changed and/or combined on demand and in different ways. However, existing kernel calculi providing formal foundations for module systems are based on a *static* view of module manipulation, in the sense that open code fragments can be flexibly combined together, but all module operators must be performed once for all *before* starting execution of a program, that is, evaluation of a module component.
The definition of clean and powerful module calculi supporting *lazy* module operators, that is, operators which can be performed *after* the selection of some module component, is still an open problem. Here, we provide an example in this direction (the first at our knowledge), defining CMS^{ℓ}, an extension of the Calculus of Module Systems [5] where module operators can be performed at execution time and, in particular, are executed on demand, that is, only when needed by the executing program. In other words, execution steps, if possible, take the precedence over reconfiguration steps. The type system of the calculus, which is proved to be sound, relies on a dependency analysis which ensures that execution will never try to access module components which cannot become available by performing reconfiguration steps.

Keywords: module calculi, dynamic linking

1 Introduction

In the last years considerable effort has been invested in studying theoretical foundations and designing advanced forms of module systems [5, 15, 13, 12, 2], inspired by the unifying principle of two separate linguistic levels, a *module language* providing operators for combining software components, with their own typing rules, constructed on top of a *core language* for defining module components. In particular, module calculi such as *CMS* (Calculus of Module Systems) [5] provide a simple and powerful model allowing to express a large variety of existing mechanisms for com-

*Partially supported by Dynamic Assembly, Reconfiguration and Type-checking - EC project IST-2001-33477, and APPSEM II - Thematic network IST-2001-38957.

bining software components, hence can be used as a paradigmatic calculus for modular languages, in the same spirit the lambda calculus is used for functional programming. Indeed, modules in *CMS* are constructed from *basic modules* (of the form $[\iota; o; \rho]$ where ι, o and ρ model input, output and local components, respectively) by only three primitive operators: *sum* (merging two modules), *link* (called *freeze* in the original formulation in [5], binding an input to an output component) and *reduct* (independently renaming input and output components). As shown in previous papers [5, 4], these operators allow to express, e.g., parameterized modules similar to ML functors, extension with overriding as in object-oriented programming, and mixin modules. However, *CMS* (as other module calculi as well) is based on a *static* view of module manipulation, in the sense that open code fragments can be flexibly combined together, but before starting program execution we must eventually obtain a fully reduced, closed module.

This is formally reflected in *CMS* by the fact that *selection*, denoted $M.X$, where M is a module expression and X is the name of a module component, can only be performed when M has form $[; o; \rho]$, that is, is a basic module (no module operators remain) and, moreover, has no input components. In other words, before actually *using* a module, all *configuration* steps (that is, those concerning assembly and manipulation of code fragments) must have been performed, hence in particular all the component names must have been resolved (that is, no dependency on other fragments is allowed).

However, in widely-used programming environments, such as those of Java and C#, single code fragments are dynamically linked to an already executing program. More generally, we can expect that in the future systems will support more and more forms of interleaving of *reconfiguration* steps and standard *execution* steps, where the software fragments composing a program are dynamically changed and/or combined on demand and in different ways. To our knowledge, only a little amount of literature exists on this subject, mainly concerned with the modeling of concrete mechanisms in existing programming environments (see, e.g., the large amount of work of Drossopoulou and others on phases of dynamic linking and verification in Java-like languages [9, 10]).

In particular, what is still missing is the definition of clean and powerful module calculi supporting *lazy* module operators, that is, operators which can be performed *after* the evaluation of some module component has started, hence providing formal foundations for systems where reconfiguration and standard execution steps are interleaved (as *CMS* or other module calculi do for static module manipulation).

Here, we provide a proposal in this direction (the first to our knowledge), defining CMS^{ℓ}, an extension of *CMS* where module operators can be performed at execution time and, in particular, are executed *on demand*, that is, only when needed by the executing program. In other words, execution steps, if possible, take the precedence over reconfiguration steps.

The type system of the calculus, which is proved to be sound, relies on a dependency analysis which ensures that execution never tries to access module components which cannot become available by performing reconfiguration steps.

The rest of the paper is organized as follows. In Sect.2 we briefly revise the original *CMS* and then informally introduce CMS^{ℓ} by some examples illustrating the new possibilities offered in this calculus. In Sect.3 we give the syntax and the reduction rules, in Sect.4 the type system and in Sect.5 the results (confluence and soundness). Finally, in the Conclusion we summarize the contribution of the paper, compare the approach here with our previous work on dynamic linking [2, 11] and describe further work.

2 An informal introduction

In this section we briefly introduce *CMS* and then illustrate the new possibilities offered by CMS^{ℓ} by some examples, written by using some syntactic sugar.
A *CMS basic module* consists of *output* and *local* components, bound to an expression, and *input* components, declared but not yet defined. For instance,

```
module M1 is
 import X as x, export Y = e1[x,y], local  y = e2[x,y]
end M1
```

is a basic module with one input, one output and one local component, where `e1[x,y]` and `e2[x,y]` denote two arbitrary expressions possibly containing `x` and `y` as free variables. Note that input components are associated with both a name (as `X`) and a variable (as `x`); component names are used for accessing input and output components from the outside, while variables are used for accessing input and local components from inside the module. Local components are not visible from outside and can be mutually recursive.
Two modules can be combined by the *sum* operation, which performs the union of the input components (in the sense that components with the same name are shared), and the disjoint union of the output and local components. However, while the sets of output names must be disjoint, the disjoint union of local components can always be performed (using α-renaming of local variables when needed).
For instance, below module `M3` is defined as the sum of `M1` above and another basic module `M2`.

```
module M2 is
  import Y as y,  export X = e3[x,y],  local  x = e4[x,y]
end M2
```

Module `M3 = M1 + M2` simplifies to

```
module import X  as x, Y as y',
       export Y  = e1[x,y], X  = e3[x',y'],
       local  y = e2[x,y], x' = e4[x',y']
end
```

Note that the sum operation supports cross-module recursion: in module `M3`, the definition of `X` is needed by `M1` and is provided by `M2`, whereas the definition of `Y` is needed by `M2` and is provided by `M1`. However, in the sum above there is no connection yet between input and output names; this can be accomplished by means of the link operator described below.
The *link* operation connects input and output components having the same name inside a module, so that an input component becomes local. For instance, in

```
link X in
 (module import X  as x, export X  = e[x, ...], local  ... end)
```

which simplifies to

```
module export X = e[x, ...], local  ..., x = e[x, ...] end
```

the input name X has been effectively bound to the corresponding output component. The *reduct* operator performs a renaming of component names where input and output names are renamed independently. The input renaming is a mapping whose domain and codomain are old input names and new input names, respectively , whereas the output renaming is a mapping whose domain and codomain are new output names and old output names, respectively. For instance,

```
rename input X by X, X2 by X,  _ by X', output Y1 by Y, Y2 by Y
in module
  import X1 as x1, X2 as x2,
  export Y = e1[x1,x2,x], Y' = e2[x1,x2,x],
  local x = e[x1,x2,x]
end
```

simplifies to

```
module
  import X as x1,  X as x2,  X' as x',
  export Y1 = e1[x1,x2,x], Y2 = e1[x1,x2,x],
  local x = e[x1,x2,x]
end
```

Note that the two renamings can be non-injective and non-surjective. A non-injective input renaming allows to merge two input names (in the example X1 and X2 in X), whereas a non-surjective is used for adding dummy input names (X' in the example). A non-injective output renaming allows duplication of definitions (in the example the definition of Y is used as definition of both Y1 and Y2), whereas a non-surjective one is used for deleting output components (Y' in the example).
In the following examples M\Y denotes the application to the module M of a reduct operator s.t. the input renaming is the identity and the output renaming is the embedding of all output names of M except Y in themselves. In other words, M\Y denotes the module where the Y component has been deleted.
Output components can be accessed from the outside by means of the selection operator. In CMS^{ℓ}, selection is much more general than in CMS, where it can be performed only on basic modules with no input components.
Consider, for instance, the following configuration:

```
C = (module import X as x, export Y = e[x], local  ... end).Y
```

This configuration is well-formed in CMS^{ℓ} if the defining expression e of Y does not use the variable x, which is bound to an input component. Moreover, even in the case e uses the variable x, we can obtain a well-formed CMS^{ℓ} configuration by inserting C in a context where the input component X can become available, as shown below:

```
link X in (C + module import ... export X = ... local ...)
```

The following examples illustrate how CMS^{ℓ} allows dynamic reconfiguration of systems. First we show how CMS^{ℓ} lazy sum and link operators allow to model loading of software on demand. Consider a situation where there is a program Prg to be executed, possibly requiring other software fragments located in different sites, e.g., on the web. In CMS, this can be modeled by the following module expression, where each basic module in the sum expression intuitively corresponds to software from a different site.

```
(link X, Y in (
  module import X as x, Y as y, export Prg = e,  local  ... end +
  module import Y as y, export X = ..., local  ...  end  +
  module import X as x,  export Y = ..., local  ... end)
).Prg
```

In *CMS*, in order to select the Prg output component, the module expression must be first of all reduced to a basic module, regardless of the nature of the defining expression of Prg. Hence the program can be executed only after loading and combining software from all sites, thus requiring a not negligible amount of time. In CMS^{ℓ} the situation described above could be modeled instead by the term:

```
link X, Y in (
(module import X as x, Y as y, export Prg = e, local  ... end).Prg) +
 module import Y as y, export X = ...,  local  ... end  +
 module import X as y, export Y = ..., local  ... end)
```

In this case, execution of the program can start immediately, and the sum and link will be performed only if and when the evaluation of the expression e will need x and y.
The following example shows how CMS^{ℓ} lazy reduct operator allows to express reference to different versions of the same software fragment. Consider a situation where two versions of a component Y are available.

```
link Y in (
 (module import Y as x, export Y = e,  local  ... end).Y  \ Y +
 module  import ..., export Y = e', ...,  local  ... end)
```

The old definition e of Y is initially selected and its evaluation starts. However, if during evaluation of e the variable x is needed, then reconfiguration steps are performed and the new definition e' of Y is used. However, note that only a limited form of dynamic reconfiguration is allowed, since all reconfiguration steps are planned statically: the fact that they will be actually performed depends on the program execution (thus allowing in particular to use different versions of a component at different stages, as shown above), but it is not possible to perform *different* reconfiguration steps depending on the execution. See the Conclusion for more comments on this point.

3 Syntax and Semantics

Notations We denote by $A \stackrel{fin}{\rightarrow} B$ the set of the partial functions f from A to B with finite domain, written $\mathsf{dom}(f)$; the image of f is written $\mathsf{img}(f)$. We denote by f, g the union of two partial functions with disjoint domain, whereas we use the notation $f \cup g$ for the union of two compatible partial functions, that is, s.t. $f(x) = g(x)$ for all $x \in \mathsf{dom}(f) \cap \mathsf{dom}(g)$. Finally, $\circ$ denotes composition of partial functions.

The syntax of the calculus is given in Fig.1. We assume an infinite set Name of *names* X, an infinite set Var of *variables* x, and a set Exp of (core) expressions (the expressions of the underlying language used for defining module components). Indeed, as CMS, CMS^{ℓ} is a parametric and stratified calculus, which can be instantiated over different core calculi satisfying some (standard) assumptions specified in the sequel. In CMS^{ℓ}, however, differently from CMS, module components cannot be modules. Intuitively, names are used to refer to a module from the outside (hence they are used in reconfiguration steps), while variables are used to refer to a (basic) module from a program executing in the context of the components offered by this module.

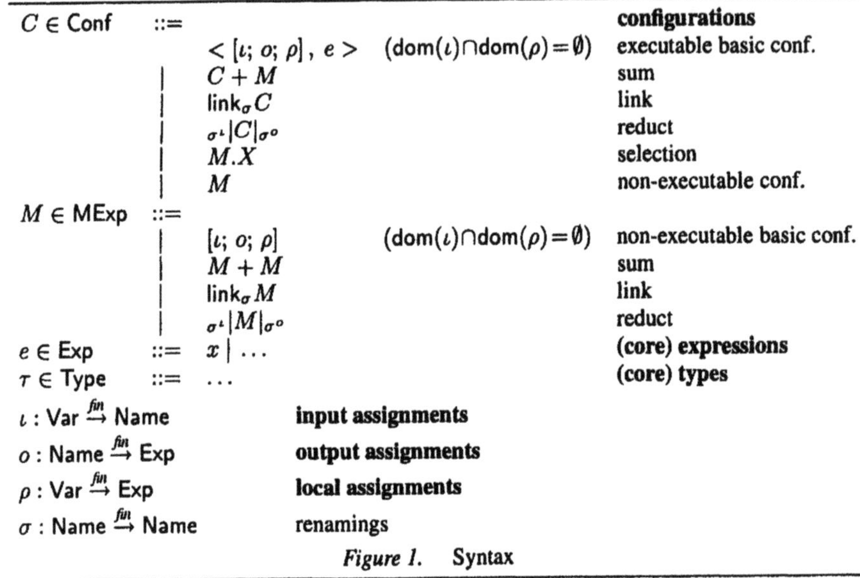

Figure 1. Syntax

This distinction between names and variables is standard in module calculi and, besides the methodological motivation explained above, has technical motivations as well, such as allowing α-conversion for variables while preserving external interfaces (see, e.g., [5] for an extended discussion of this point).

Terms of the calculus are called *configurations*. Configurations can be either *non-executable* configurations (module expressions) M, or *executable* configurations, which are constructed from *executable basic configurations* by the three primitive module operators *sum*, *link* and *reduct*. Moreover, a configuration can be obtained by selecting a component from a module expression.

An executable basic configuration is a pair $< [\iota; o; \rho], e >$, consisting of a basic module and a core expression. Basic modules are as in *CMS* and consist of three components. The ι component is a mapping from variables to names and represents the *input* interface of the module; the o component is a mapping from names into expressions and represents the *output* interface of the module; the ρ component is a mapping from variables into expressions and represents the local (that is, already linked) components. Variables in the domain of ι and ρ are called the *deferred* and the *local* variables of the basic module, respectively.

Basic (both executable and non-executable) configurations are well-formed only if the sets of deferred and local variables are disjoint.

We will explain module operators in more detail when introducing reduction rules.

Expressions of the core language are not specified; we only assume that they contain variables. For the examples in the sequel we assume that core expressions contain integer constants and the usual operations on integers.

In Fig.2 and Fig.3 we give the reduction rules of the calculus. For convenience, we first give the reduction rules for non-executable configurations (module expressions) and then those for executable configurations. By definition, the one step reduction relation $\longrightarrow$ is the relation over well-formed terms inductively defined by the rules. For this

$$(M\text{-sum})\ \frac{}{M_1 + M_2 \longrightarrow [\iota_1, \iota_2;\ o_1, o_2;\ \rho_1, \rho_2]}\ \begin{array}{l} M_i \equiv [\iota_i;\ o_i;\ \rho_i], i \in \{1,2\} \\ \mathsf{BV}(M_1) \cap \mathsf{FV}(M_2) = \emptyset \\ \mathsf{BV}(M_2) \cap \mathsf{FV}(M_1) = \emptyset \end{array}$$

$$(M\text{-link})\ \frac{}{\mathsf{link}_\sigma[\iota_1, \iota_2;\ o;\ \rho] \longrightarrow [\iota_2;\ o;\ \rho, o \circ \sigma \circ \iota_1]}\ \mathsf{img}(\iota_2) \cap \mathsf{dom}(\sigma) = \emptyset$$

$$(M\text{-reduct})\ \frac{}{{}_{\sigma^\iota}|[\iota;\ o;\ \rho]|_{\sigma^o} \longrightarrow [\sigma^\iota \circ \iota;\ o \circ \sigma^o;\ \rho]}$$

Figure 2. Reduction rules for non-executable configurations (module expressions)

reason, we have omitted all side conditions ensuring well-formedness of terms, since those are satisfied by definition.

Reduction rules for sum, link and reduct on non-executable configurations are exactly those for module expressions in CMS. We give here a brief description, referring to [5] for more detailed comments.

Sum The sum operation simply has the effect of gluing together two modules. The two explicit side conditions avoid undesired captures of free variables; $\mathsf{BV}([\iota;\ o;\ \rho])$ denotes the binding variables of $[\iota;\ o;\ \rho]$, that is, $\mathsf{dom}(\iota) \cup \mathsf{dom}(\rho)$, whereas $\mathsf{FV}([\iota;\ o;\ \rho])$ denotes the free variables (the definition of $\mathsf{FV}(e)$ depends on the core calculus) of $[\iota;\ o;\ \rho]$, that is, $(\bigcup_{X \in \mathsf{dom}(o)} \mathsf{FV}(o(X)) \cup \bigcup_{x \in \mathsf{dom}(\rho)} \mathsf{FV}(\rho(x))) \setminus \mathsf{BV}([\iota;\ o;\ \rho])$. Since the reduction is defined only over well-formed terms, the deferred and local variables of one module must be disjoint from those of the other (implicit side condition). Both the explicit and implicit side conditions above can always be satisfied by an appropriate α-conversion. For the same reason of well-formedness, the output names of the two modules must be disjoint (implicit side condition due to the fact that o_1, o_2 must be well-defined[1]); however, in this case the reduction gets stuck since this conflict cannot be resolved by an α-conversion. The only way to solve this problem is to explicitly rename the output names in an appropriate way by means of the reduct operator (see below), thus changing the term.

Link The link operator is essential for binding input with output in order to accomplish inter-connection of modules. A renaming σ explicitly specifies how resolution has to be performed, associating output to input names; the domain of σ can be a proper subset of all input names of the module so that resolution is partial

The effect of applying the link operator is that all input names that are resolved, represented by the set $\mathsf{img}(\iota_1)$, disappear and all the deferred variables mapped into them, represented by the set $\mathsf{dom}(\iota_1)$, become local. These variables are associated with the definition of the output component to which their associated (by ι_1) names are bound by σ, that is, $o(\sigma(\iota_1(x)))$, for all $x \in \mathsf{dom}(\iota_1)$). The composition is well-defined if the following implicit side conditions (needed for composition of mappings to be well-defined) are verified: $\mathsf{img}(\iota_1) \subseteq \mathsf{dom}(\sigma)$ and $\mathsf{img}(\sigma) \subseteq \mathsf{dom}(o)$. Note that this implies that only variables for which actually *exist* a corresponding definition become

[1]Note that, since ι goes "backwards", that is, from variables into names, the fact that ι_1, ι_2 must be well-formed does not prevent to share input names, but only to share deferred variables, what can be avoided by α-conversion.

Evaluation contexts

$$\begin{array}{lcl} \mathcal{C}[\,] \in \mathsf{ECCtx} & ::= & \Box \mid \mathcal{M}[\;].X \mid \mathcal{C}[\,]+M \mid C+\mathcal{M}[\;] \mid \mathsf{link}_\sigma \mathcal{C}[\,] \mid {}_{\sigma^\iota}|\mathcal{C}[\,]|_{\sigma^o} \\ \mathcal{M}[\;] \in \mathsf{NCCtx} & ::= & \Box \mid \mathcal{M}[\;]+M \mid M+\mathcal{M}[\;] \mid \mathsf{link}_\sigma \mathcal{M}[\;] \mid {}_{\sigma^\iota}|\mathcal{M}[\;]|_{\sigma^o} \\ \mathcal{E}[\,] \in \mathsf{ECtx} & ::= & \Box \mid \ldots \end{array}$$

$$(\mathcal{C}[\,]\text{-ctx})\ \frac{C \longrightarrow C'}{\mathcal{C}[C] \longrightarrow \mathcal{C}[C']} \qquad (\mathcal{M}[\;]\text{-ctx})\ \frac{M \longrightarrow M'}{\mathcal{M}[M] \longrightarrow \mathcal{M}[M']}$$

$$(\text{core})\ \frac{e \underset{e}{\longrightarrow} e'}{<[\iota;\, o;\, \rho]\,,\, e> \;\longrightarrow\; <[\iota;\, o;\, \rho]\,,\, e'>}$$

$$(\text{var})\ \frac{}{<[\iota;\, o;\, \rho]\,,\, \mathcal{E}[x]> \;\longrightarrow\; <[\iota;\, o;\, \rho]\,,\, \mathcal{E}[\rho(x)]>}\ \begin{array}{l} x \in \mathsf{dom}(\rho) \\ \mathcal{E}[x] \underset{e}{\not\longrightarrow} \end{array}$$

$$(C\text{-link})\ \frac{\mathsf{link}_\sigma[\iota;\, o;\, \rho] \longrightarrow [\iota';\, o';\, \rho']}{\mathsf{link}_\sigma <[\iota;\, o;\, \rho]\,,\, \mathcal{E}[x]> \longrightarrow <[\iota';\, o';\, \rho']\,,\, \mathcal{E}[x]>}\ \begin{array}{l} x \in \mathsf{dom}(\iota) \\ \mathcal{E}[x] \underset{e}{\not\longrightarrow} \end{array}$$

$$(C\text{-sum})\ \frac{[\iota_1;\, o_1;\, \rho_1] + [\iota_2;\, o_2;\, \rho_2] \longrightarrow [\iota;\, o;\, \rho]}{<[\iota_1;\, o_1;\, \rho_1]\,,\, \mathcal{E}[x]> + [\iota_2;\, o_2;\, \rho_2] \longrightarrow <[\iota;\, o;\, \rho]\,,\, \mathcal{E}[x]>}\ \begin{array}{l} x \in \mathsf{dom}(\iota) \\ \mathcal{E}[x] \underset{e}{\not\longrightarrow} \end{array}$$

$$(C\text{-reduct})\ \frac{{}_{\sigma^\iota}|[\iota;\, o;\, \rho]|_{\sigma^o} \longrightarrow [\iota';\, o';\, \rho']}{{}_{\sigma^\iota}|<[\iota;\, o;\, \rho]\,,\, \mathcal{E}[x]>|_{\sigma^o} \longrightarrow <[\iota';\, o';\, \rho']\,,\, \mathcal{E}[x]>}\ \begin{array}{l} x \in \mathsf{dom}(\iota) \\ \mathcal{E}[x] \underset{e}{\not\longrightarrow} \end{array}$$

$$(\text{sel})\ \frac{}{[\iota;\, o;\, \rho].X \longrightarrow <[\iota;\, o;\, \rho]\,,\, o(X)>}\ X \in \mathsf{dom}(o)$$

Figure 3. Reduction rules for executable configurations

local, thus ensuring that we cannot create modules containing undefined (that is, neither local nor deferred) variables. The explicit side condition just ensures that $\mathsf{img}(\iota_1)$ actually contains *all* the input names that have to be resolved as specified by σ.

Reduct The reduct operator performs a renaming of component names and does not change the local assignment and the variables of a module; its effect is simply a composition of maps which can be correctly performed only if $\mathsf{img}(\iota) \subseteq \mathsf{dom}(\sigma^\iota)$ and $\mathsf{img}(\sigma^o) \subseteq \mathsf{dom}(o)$ (implicit side condition). Note that input and output names are renamed independently, and that the two renamings can be non-injective and non-surjective. A non-injective map σ^ι allows sharing of input names, whereas a non-surjective one is used for adding dummy (in the sense that no variable is associated with them) input names; a non-injective map σ^o allows duplication of definitions, whereas a non-surjective map is used for hiding output components.
We describe now reduction rules for executable configurations.
The first two rules are the usual contextual closures for executable and non-executable configurations, respectively.
Rule (core) models an execution step which is an evaluation step of the core expression in the basic executable configuration (we denote by $\underset{e}{\longrightarrow}$ the reduction relation of the core calculus).

Rule (var) models the situation where the evaluation of the core expression needs a variable which has a corresponding definition in the current basic module (that is, is local). In this case, the evaluation can proceed by simply replacing the variable by its defining expression. Here and in the following rules, the side condition $\mathcal{E}[x] \not\xrightarrow[e]{}$ expresses the fact that evaluation at the core level is stuck. Note that this ensures that there is no overlapping between (core) steps and other steps, but of course does not prevent non-determinism inherited from the core level. For instance, assuming that the core expression in a configuration is $x+y$, and both x, y are local variables, variable x will be first considered for application of another rule if $x+y$ can only be seen as $\mathcal{E}[x]$ by the core context formation rules, whereas either x or y will be non-deterministically consideredif $x+y$ can be seen as both $\mathcal{E}[x]$ and $\mathcal{E}'[y]$.
The following three rules express the fact that, whenever the evaluation of the core expression needs a variable which has no corresponding definition in the module (that is, is deferred), then a *reconfiguration* step happens: more precisely, the innermost enclosing module operator is applied.
As combined effect of the above rules, execution proceeds by standard execution steps ((core) and (var) rules) until a deferred variable is encountered; in this case, reconfiguration steps are performed (from the innermost to the outermost module operator) until the variable becomes local and rule (var) can be applied.

EXAMPLE 1 *Let us write $a_1 : b_1, \ldots, a_n : b_n$ for the partial function mapping a_i to b_i for all $i \in 1..n$ (where the a_i must be different).*
$C \triangleq \mathsf{link}_{X:Y}(< [x : X; \,; y : 1] \,, \, y + x > + [; Y : 2;])$
$\longrightarrow \mathsf{link}_{X:Y}(< [x : X; \,; y : 1] \,, \, 1 + x > + [; Y : 2;])$
$\longrightarrow \mathsf{link}_{X:Y} < [x : X; Y : 2; y : 1] \,, \, 1 + x > \;\longrightarrow\; < [; Y : 2; y : 1, x : 2] \,, \, 1 + x >$
$\longrightarrow\; < [; Y : 2; y : 1, x : 2] \,, \, 1 + 2 > \;\longrightarrow\; < [; Y : 2; y : 1, x : 2] \,, \, 3 > \triangleq C'$

Note that this precedence of standard execution over reconfiguration only applies to the module operators which contain the executable configuration, whereas the remaining module operators can be evaluated non deterministically at each time during execution. However, this non determinism does not affect confluence, as will be proved in Sect.5 (Prop.3).

EXAMPLE 2 *Set $M = \emptyset|\mathsf{link}_{Z:U}[z : Z; U : 3;]|_{W:U}$ and C as in Example 1. We have $M \longrightarrow \emptyset|[; U : 3; z : 3]|_{W:U} \longrightarrow [; W : 3; z : 3] \triangleq M'$ and $C+M \xrightarrow{*} C'+ M'$ where all the reduction steps (included those in Example 1) can be arbitrarily interleaved.*

4 Type system

The type system of the calculus is given in Fig.4 and Fig.5.
The typing judgment for module expressions has form $\vdash_M M : [\pi^\iota; \pi^o; \mathcal{D}]$, meaning that M is a well-formed module expression of type $[\pi^\iota; \pi^o; \mathcal{D}]$. Types for module expressions are triples $[\pi^\iota; \pi^o; \mathcal{D}]$ where $\pi^\iota, \pi^o : \mathsf{Name} \xrightarrow{fin} \mathsf{Type}$ are the *input* and *output signature*, respectively, and $\mathcal{D}$ is a binary relation on Name called the *dependency* relation. The first two components are standard for module calculi (see [5]), while $\mathcal{D}$ keeps track of the input names an output name depends on, and will be used later in typing rules for executable configurations. Hence, typing rules for non-executable

$$(M\text{-basic})\ \frac{\{\Gamma^\iota,\Gamma^\rho \vdash_e o(X):\pi^o(X)\mid X\in\mathsf{dom}(o)\}\quad \{\Gamma^\iota,\Gamma^\rho \vdash_e \rho(x):\Gamma^\rho(x)\mid x\in\mathsf{dom}(\rho)\}}{\vdash_M [\iota;\ o;\ \rho] : \left[\pi^\iota;\ \pi^o;\ \mathcal{D}^{[\iota;\,o;\,\rho]}\right]}\quad \begin{array}{l}\mathsf{dom}(\pi^\iota)=\mathsf{img}(\iota)\\ \mathsf{dom}(\pi^o)=\mathsf{dom}(o)\\ \Gamma^\iota=\pi^\iota\circ\iota\\ \mathsf{dom}(\Gamma^\rho)=\mathsf{dom}(\rho)\end{array}$$

$$(M\text{-sum})\ \frac{\vdash_M M_1 : [\pi^\iota{}_1;\ \pi^o{}_1;\ \mathcal{D}_1]\quad \vdash_M M_2 : [\pi^\iota{}_2;\ \pi^o{}_2;\ \mathcal{D}_2]}{\vdash_M M_1+M_2 : [\pi^\iota{}_1\cup\pi^\iota{}_2;\ \pi^o{}_1,\pi^o{}_2;\ \mathcal{D}_1\cup\mathcal{D}_2]}$$

$$(M\text{-link})\ \frac{\vdash_M M : [\pi^\iota{}_1,\pi^\iota{}_2;\ \pi^o;\ \mathcal{D}]}{\vdash_M \mathsf{link}_\sigma M : [\pi^\iota{}_2;\ \pi^o;\ \mathsf{link}_\sigma\mathcal{D}]}\quad \sigma:\pi^\iota{}_1\to\pi^o$$

$$(M\text{-reduct})\ \frac{\vdash_M M : [\pi^\iota;\ \pi^o;\ \mathcal{D}]}{\vdash_M {}_{\sigma^\iota}|M|_{\sigma^o} : \left[\pi'^\iota;\ \pi'^o;\ {}_{\sigma^\iota}|\mathcal{D}|_{\sigma^o}\right]}\quad \begin{array}{l}\sigma^\iota:\pi^\iota\to\pi'^\iota\\ \sigma^o:\pi'^o\to\pi^o\end{array}$$

Figure 4. Typing rules for module expressions

configurations exactly correspond to typing rules for module expressions in *CMS* except for calculation of dependencies.

The definition of $\mathcal{D}$ as well as the corresponding operators on it defined in the sequel has been inspired by the CMS_v calculus [12]. Note, however, that here we have preferred to consider the inverse relation and that we do not need to deal with labelled multi-graphs. Intuitively, if $(Y,X)\in\mathcal{D}$ then Y depends on X, that is, Y is an output component of M associated with a core expression which (either directly or indirectly) refers to a deferred variable x which is mapped to the input component X. If $\mathcal{D}$ is a dependency relation, then we will write $Y\overset{\mathcal{D}}{\to}X$ for $(Y,X)\in\mathcal{D}$.

In rule (M-basic), we denote by $\Gamma\vdash_e e:\tau$ the typing judgment for core expressions, meaning that e is a well-formed expression of type τ in Γ, where Γ is a mapping from variables to core types. Moreover, $\mathcal{D}^{[\iota;\,o;\,\rho]}$ denotes the dependency relation induced by a basic module $[\iota;\ o;\ \rho]$, defined as follows. For $y\in\mathsf{dom}(\rho)$, $x\in\mathsf{dom}(\iota)\cup\mathsf{dom}(\rho)$, let us write $y\to_\rho x$ iff $x\in\mathsf{FV}(\rho(y))$, and denote by $\to_\rho^\star$ the transitive and reflexive closure of $\to_\rho$. Then, for all $Y\in\mathsf{dom}(o)$, $X\in\mathsf{img}(\iota)$, $Y\overset{\mathcal{D}^{[\iota;\,o;\,\rho]}}{\to}X$, iff there exist $y\in\mathsf{FV}(o(Y))$, $x\in\mathsf{dom}(\iota)$ s.t. $y\to_\rho^\star x$ and $\iota(x)=X$.

The (M-sum) typing rule allows sharing of input components having the same name and type, while preventing output components from being shared. Recall that $f_1\cup f_2$ denotes the union of two compatible partial functions, while $f_1,\ f_2$ denotes the union of two partial functions with disjoint domain. The dependency relation is the union of the dependency relations of the arguments.

In the (M-link) typing rule, the side-condition having the form $\sigma:\pi_1\to\pi_2$ ensures that the renaming σ preserves types; formally, this means that $\sigma:\mathsf{dom}(\pi_1)\to\mathsf{dom}(\pi_2)$ and $\sigma(X)=Y\Rightarrow\pi_1(X)=\pi_2(Y)$. The dependency relation $\mathsf{link}_\sigma\mathcal{D}$ is defined as follows:

$\mathsf{link}_\sigma\mathcal{D}\triangleq(\mathcal{D}\cup\mathcal{D}_{\mathsf{add}}{}^\star)\setminus\mathcal{D}_{\mathsf{remove}}$, where

$\mathcal{D}_{\mathsf{add}}\triangleq\left\{(Y,X),(X,\sigma(X)),(\sigma(X),Z)\mid Y\overset{\mathcal{D}}{\to}X\wedge\sigma(X)\overset{\mathcal{D}}{\to}Z\right\}$

$\mathcal{D}_{\mathsf{remove}}\triangleq\{(Y,X),(X,\sigma(X))\mid Y\overset{\mathcal{D}_{\mathsf{add}}}{\to}X\wedge X\in\mathsf{dom}(\sigma)\}$

The intuition behind this definition is the following: any output name Y depending on an input name X that is going to be linked (that is, $X\in\mathsf{dom}(\sigma)$) will use the definition of the output component $\sigma(X)$ to which X is linked, which in turn may depend on

$$\frac{\begin{array}{c}\{\Gamma^\iota, \Gamma^\rho \vdash_e o(X) : \pi^o(X) \mid X \in \mathsf{dom}(o)\} \\ \{\Gamma^\iota, \Gamma^\rho \vdash_e \rho(x) : \Gamma^\rho(x) \mid x \in \mathsf{dom}(\rho)\} \\ \Gamma^\iota, \Gamma^\rho \vdash_e e : \tau\end{array}}{\vdash_C < [\iota;\, o;\, \rho],\, e >: \left([\pi^\iota;\, \pi^o;\, \mathcal{D}^{[\iota;\, o;\, \rho]}],\, \mathcal{N}^{<[\iota;\, o;\, \rho],\, e>} \Rightarrow \tau\right)} \; (C\text{-basic}) \quad \begin{array}{l}\mathsf{dom}(\pi^\iota) = \mathsf{img}(\iota) \\ \mathsf{dom}(\pi^o) = \mathsf{dom}(c \\ \Gamma^\iota = \pi^\iota \circ \iota \\ \mathsf{dom}(\Gamma^\rho) = \mathsf{dom}(\rho\end{array}$$

$$\frac{\begin{array}{c}\vdash_C C : ([\pi^\iota{}_C;\, \pi^o{}_C;\, \mathcal{D}_C],\, \mathcal{N} \Rightarrow \tau) \\ \vdash_M M : [\pi^\iota{}_M;\, \pi^o{}_M;\, \mathcal{D}_M]\end{array}}{\vdash_C C + M : ([\pi^\iota{}_C \cup \pi^\iota{}_M;\, \pi^o{}_C, \pi^o{}_M;\, \mathcal{D}_C \cup \mathcal{D}_M],\, \mathcal{N} \Rightarrow \tau)} \; (C\text{-sum})$$

$$\frac{\vdash_C C : ([\pi^\iota{}_1, \pi^\iota{}_2;\, \pi^o;\, \mathcal{D}],\, \mathcal{N} \Rightarrow \tau)}{\vdash_C \mathsf{link}_\sigma C : \left([\pi^\iota{}_2;\, \pi^o;\, \mathsf{link}_\sigma \mathcal{D}],\, \mathsf{link}^{\mathcal{D}}_\sigma \mathcal{N} \Rightarrow \tau\right)} \; (C\text{-link}) \quad \sigma : \pi^\iota{}_1 \to \pi^o$$

$$\frac{\vdash_C C : ([\pi^\iota;\, \pi^o;\, \mathcal{D}],\, \mathcal{N} \Rightarrow \tau)}{\vdash_C {}_{\sigma^\iota}|C|_{\sigma^o} : \left([\pi'^\iota;\, \pi'^o;\, {}_{\sigma^\iota}|\mathcal{D}|_{\sigma^o}],\, \sigma^\iota(\mathcal{N}) \Rightarrow \tau\right)} \; (C\text{-reduct}) \quad \begin{array}{l}\sigma^\iota : \pi^\iota \to \pi'^\iota \\ \sigma^o : \pi'^o \to \pi^o\end{array}$$

$$\frac{\vdash_M M : [\pi^\iota;\, \pi^o;\, \mathcal{D}]}{\vdash_C M.X : ([\pi^\iota;\, \pi^o;\, \mathcal{D}],\, \mathcal{N} \Rightarrow \pi^o(X))} \; (\text{sel}) \quad \mathcal{N} = \{Y \mid X \overset{\mathcal{D}}{\to} Y\}$$

Figure 5. Typing rules for configurations

some input name Z; hence, in the linking process the new dependencies obtained by computing the transitive closure of $\mathcal{D}_{\mathsf{add}}$ (denoted by $\mathcal{D}_{\mathsf{add}}{}^*$) must be added. Then all the dependencies involving the linked names $X \in \mathsf{dom}(\sigma)$ are removed.
In the (M-reduct) typing rule, the dependency relation ${}_{\sigma^\iota}|\mathcal{D}|_{\sigma^o}$ is defined as follows:
${}_{\sigma^\iota}|\mathcal{D}|_{\sigma^o} \triangleq \{(Y, \sigma^\iota(X)) \mid \sigma^o(Y) \overset{\mathcal{D}}{\to} X\}$
Note that in the side-condition we again use the notation introduced in (M-link) to ensure that renamings preserve types.
The typing judgment for executable configurations has the form $\vdash_C C : ([\pi^\iota;\, \pi^o;\, \mathcal{D}],\, \mathcal{N} \Rightarrow \tau)$, meaning that C is a well-formed executable configuration of type $([\pi^\iota;\, \pi^o;\, \mathcal{D}],\, \mathcal{N} \Rightarrow \tau)$. The first component $[\pi^\iota;\, \pi^o;\, \mathcal{D}]$ has the same meaning as for module expressions, whereas $\mathcal{N} \Rightarrow \tau$, with $\mathcal{N}$ set of names and τ core type, means that the expression to be executed in the configuration has type τ providing that all (input) names in $\mathcal{N}$ can be eventually linked (with the proper type).
In rule (C-basic), $\mathcal{N}^{<[\iota;\, o;\, \rho],\, e>}$ denotes the set of input names the expression e depends on, defined as follows:
$\mathcal{N}^{<[\iota;\, o;\, \rho],\, e>} \triangleq \{X \mid y \to^*_\rho x, \iota(x) = X, y \in \mathsf{FV}(e)\}$
Since the sum operator just glues modules together without linking any input name, in rule (C-sum) the second component $\mathcal{N} \Rightarrow \tau$ remains unchanged.
In the (C-link) typing rule, the set of names $\mathsf{link}^{\mathcal{D}}_\sigma \mathcal{N}$ is defined as follows:
$\mathsf{link}^{\mathcal{D}}_\sigma \mathcal{N} \triangleq (\mathcal{N} \cup \mathcal{N}^{\mathcal{D}}_{\mathsf{sum}}) \setminus \mathsf{dom}(\sigma)$, where $\mathcal{N}^{\mathcal{D}}_{\mathsf{sum}} = \{Z \mid X \in \mathcal{N} \wedge \sigma(X) \overset{\mathsf{link}_\sigma \mathcal{D}}{\to} Z\}$.
Indeed, before removing from $\mathcal{N}$ all linked input names in $\mathsf{dom}(\sigma)$, all new dependencies reachable from $\mathcal{N}$ with respect to the relation $\mathsf{link}_\sigma \mathcal{D}$ must be added.
In the (C-reduct) typing rule, $\sigma^\iota(\mathcal{N})$ denotes the set $\{\sigma^\iota(X) \mid X \in \mathcal{N}\}$.
Finally, in (C-sel) the set $\mathcal{N}$ corresponds to all the input names the output component X depends on, whereas the type τ of the expression to be executed coincides with the type of X.

5 Results

In this section we collect all the technical results about the calculus. In particular, we state the Church Rosser property for the reduction relation and the Subject reduction and Progress properties. Clearly, these results hold providing that the corresponding properties are verified at the core level as well. Moreover, we also assume the core language to be such that: if $e \underset{e}{\longrightarrow} e'$, then $\mathsf{FV}(e') \subseteq \mathsf{FV}(e)$; if $\Gamma \vdash_e \mathcal{E}[e] : \tau$, then there exists τ' such that $\Gamma \vdash_e e' : \tau'$ and for all e' such that $\Gamma \vdash_e e' : \tau'$ we have that $\Gamma \vdash_e \mathcal{E}[e'] : \tau$.

PROPOSITION 3 *The reduction relation* $\longrightarrow$ *is confluent.*

THEOREM 4 (SUBJECT REDUCTION) *If* $\vdash_M M : [\pi^\iota; \pi^o; \mathcal{D}]$ *and* $M \longrightarrow M'$, *then* $\vdash_M M' : [\pi^\iota; \pi^o; \mathcal{D}]$. *If* $\vdash_C C : ([\pi^\iota; \pi^o; \mathcal{D}], \mathcal{N} \Rightarrow \tau)$ *and* $C \longrightarrow C'$, *then* $\vdash_C C' : ([\pi^\iota; \pi^o; \mathcal{D}], \mathcal{N} \Rightarrow \tau)$.

To state the Progress property, we have to define the set VConf of values for the terms of the calculus:

$$
\begin{array}{lll}
CV \in \mathsf{VConf} & ::= & <[\iota; o; \rho], ev> \mid CV + MV \mid \mathsf{link}_\sigma CV \mid {}_{\sigma^\iota}|CV|_{\sigma^o} \\
MV \in \mathsf{VMExp} & ::= & [\iota; o; \rho]
\end{array}
$$

where with ev we denote a value at the core level.

THEOREM 5 (PROGRESS)
If $\vdash_M M : [\pi^\iota; \pi^o; \mathcal{D}]$ *and* $M \notin \mathsf{VMExp}$, *then there exists* M' *s.t.* $M \longrightarrow M'$. *If* $\vdash_C C : ([\pi^\iota; \pi^o; \mathcal{D}], \emptyset \Rightarrow \tau)$ *and* $C \notin \mathsf{VConf}$, *then there exists* C' *s.t.* $C \longrightarrow C'$.

Note that progress for executable configurations holds only if the expression to be executed does not depend on any input name.

6 Conclusion

We have defined CMS^ℓ, an extension of *CMS* [5] where operators on modules are performed on demand, when needed by the execution of a program, rather than eagerly, before any access to module components. We have provided a sound type system for the calculus, relying on a dependency analysis which ensures that execution never needs to access module components which cannot become available by performing reconfiguration steps.

The relevance of this work is twofold. On one hand, whereas lazy evaluation has been extensively studied in the context of variants of lambda-calculus (see, e.g., [6]), there was to our knowledge no previous attempt at analyzing this feature in the context of record-based calculi or module calculi. We believe that the combination of laziness with the computational paradigm based on record selection is a stimulating subject for research, which could provide new programming patterns and be used in a wide variety of contexts. In this respect, the contribution of this paper is to provide the first step in this direction.

On the other hand, a more specific motivation for CMS^ℓ is the need for foundational calculi providing an abstract framework for dynamic reconfiguration (that is, interleaving of reconfiguration steps and execution steps). Indeed, though the area of unanticipated software evolution continues attracting large interest, with its foundations studied in, e.g., [14], there is a little amount of work at to our knowledge going toward the development of abstract models for dynamic reconfiguration, analogous to those which exist for the static case (where the configuration phase always precedes execution) [8, 15, 5]. Apart from the wide literature concerning concrete dynamic linking mechanisms in existing programming environments [9, 10], we mention [7], which presents a simple calculus modeling dynamic software updating, where modules are just records, many versions of the same module may coexist and update is modeled by an external transition which can be enforced by an update primitive in code, and [1], where dynamic linking is studied as the programming language counterpart to the axiom of choice. Finally, we have proposed in a recent paper [3] a calculus for dynamic linking (*CDL*) partly driven by the same objectives as CMS^ℓ, that is, to define a kernel calculus able to express some form of dynamic reconfiguration abstracting from the details of the particular underlying programming language. Here below we briefly compare the two proposals.

In *CDL*, we did not attempt at introducing dynamic features in a pure module calculus, but rather to combine a module calculus with explicit imperative features. Indeed, terms of *CDL* are *configurations* consisting of a *linkset* (corresponding to a module expression in the terminology used in this paper) and a command. Configurations can evolve in two ways: either by simplifying the linkset expression (that is, performing a reconfiguration step) or by performing a step in the execution of the command. In particular, classical module operators such as sum and (static) link must be performed before execution of the command starts; however, a new operator is introduced, called *dynamic link*, which is only performed on demand, after execution of the command has started. More precisely, a dynamic link operator for a component X (in *CDL* linking is performed on a per-name basis) is only performed if the execution needs a deferred variable, say x, which is associated to X.

Both *CDL* and CMS^ℓ proposals give, in our opinion, an important contribution toward the development of a framework for dynamic reconfiguration, but both have some (different) limitations. In *CDL*, only a limited form of interleaving between the reconfiguration and the execution phase is allowed, since the classical module operators, notably sum, must be performed before execution starts. Moreover, run-time reconfiguration ability is obtained by adding new ingredients (the dynamic link operator). In CMS^ℓ, on the contrary, no new operator is added to a standard module calculus, and there is true interleaving of the reconfiguration and execution phase, since no module operator needs to be performed before evaluating a module component. However, in CMS^ℓ this interleaving is handled by a fixed policy, in the sense that standard execution steps always take the precedence over reconfiguration steps, unless they are needed since execution would otherwise get stuck. Moreover, all reconfiguration steps are planned statically.

We believe that both CMS^ℓ and *CDL* can be seen as early steps towards more powerful calculi able to handle interleaving of reconfiguration and standard execution steps in a liberal way and to encode all the possibilities mentioned above. An important issue to be investigated in parallel is the expressive power of such calculi, by showing which kind of real-world reconfiguration mechanisms can be modeled and which kind cannot by each of them. Though the practical motivations of calculi for dynamic reconfiguration are certainly founded, a more detailed analysis of this connection is at a very initial stage, due to the youth of the trend toward such models itself. We have presented a preliminary attempt in [11], where we have used a particular instantiation of *CDL* to encode a toy language, called JL, which provides an abstract view of the mechanism of dynamic class loading with multiple loaders as in Java.

Acknowledgments

We warmly thank Eugenio Moggi, Joe Wells, Henning Makholm and Sebastien Carlier for useful comments on previous drafts of this work.

References

[1] Martin Abadi, Goerges Gonthier, and Benjamin Werner. Choice in dynamic linking. In *FOSSACS'04 - Foundations of Software Science and Computation Structures 2004*, Lecture Notes in Computer Science. Springer, 2004.

[2] D. Ancona, S. Fagorzi, E. Moggi, and E. Zucca. Mixin modules and computational effects. In Jos C. M. Baeten et al., editors, *International Colloquium on Automata, Languages and Programming 2003*, number 2719 in Lecture Notes in Computer Science, pages 224–238. Springer, 2003.

[3] D. Ancona, S. Fagorzi, and E. Zucca. A calculus for dynamic linking. In C. Blundo and C. Laneve, editors, *Italian Conf. on Theoretical Computer Science 2003*, number 2841 in Lecture Notes in Computer Science, pages 284–301, 2003.

[4] D. Ancona and E. Zucca. A theory of mixin modules: Basic and derived operators. *Mathematical Structures in Computer Science*, 8(4):401–446, August 1998.

[5] D. Ancona and E. Zucca. A calculus of module systems. *Journ. of Functional Programming*, 12(2):91–132, 2002.

[6] Z. M. Ariola and M.Felleisen. The call-by-need lambda calculus. *Journ. of Functional Programming*, 7(3):265–301, 1997.

[7] G. Bierman, M. Hicks, P. Sewell, and G. Stoyle. Formalizing dynamic software updating (Extended Abstract). In *USE'03 - Workshop on Unexpected Software Evolution*, 2003.

[8] L. Cardelli. Program fragments, linking, and modularization. In *ACM Symp. on Principles of Programming Languages 1997*, pages 266–277. ACM Press, 1997.

[9] S. Drossopoulou. Towards an abstract model of Java dynamic linking and verfication. In R. Harper, editor, *TIC'00 - Third Workshop on Types in Compilation (Selected Papers)*, volume 2071 of *Lecture Notes in Computer Science*, pages 53–84. Springer, 2001.

[10] S. Drossopoulou, G. Lagorio, and S. Eisenbach. Flexible models for dynamic linking. In Pierpaolo Degano, editor, *ESOP 2003 - European Symposium on Programming 2003*, pages 38–53, April 2003.

[11] S. Fagorzi, E. Zucca, and D. Ancona. Modeling multiple class loaders by a calculus for dynamic linking. In *ACM Symp. on Applied Computing (SAC 2004), Special Track on Object-Oriented Programming Languages and Systems*. ACM Press, 2004. To appear.

[12] T. Hirschowitz and X. Leroy. Mixin modules in a call-by-value setting. In D. Le Métayer, editor, *ESOP 2002 - European Symposium on Programming 2002*, number 2305 in Lecture Notes in Computer Science, pages 6–20. Springer, 2002.

[13] X. Leroy. A modular module system. *Journal of Functional Programming*, 10(3):269–303, May 2000.

[14] Tom Mens and Guenther Kniesel. Workshop on foundations of unanticipated software evolution. ETAPS 2004, http://joint.org/fuse2004/, 2004.

[15] J.B. Wells and R. Vestergaard. Confluent equational reasoning for linking with first-class primitive modules. In *ESOP 2000 - European Symposium on Programming 2000*, number 1782 in Lecture Notes in Computer Science, pages 412–428. Springer, 2000.

DYNAMIC TYPING WITH DEPENDENT TYPES

Xinming Ou, Gang Tan, Yitzhak Mandelbaum and David Walker

Department of Computer Science
Princeton University
{xou,gtan,yitzhakm,dpw}@cs.princeton.edu

Abstract Dependent type systems are promising tools programmers can use to increase the reliability and security of their programs. Unfortunately, dependently-typed programming languages require programmers to annotate their programs with many typing specifications to help guide the type checker. This paper shows how to make the process of programming with dependent types more palatable by defining a language in which programmers have fine-grained control over the trade-off between the number of dependent typing annotations they must place on programs and the degree of compile-time safety. More specifically, certain program fragments are marked *dependent*, in which case the programmer annotates them in detail and a dependent type checker verifies them at compile time. Other fragments are marked *simple*, in which case they may be annotation-free and dependent constraints are verified at run time.

1 Introduction

Dependent type systems are powerful tools that allow programmers to specify and enforce rich data invariants and guarantee that dangerous or unwanted program behaviors never happen. Consequently, dependently-typed programming languages are important tools in global computing environments where users must certify and check deep properties of mobile programs.

While the theory of dependent types has been studied for several decades, researchers have only recently begun to be able to integrate these rich specification mechanisms into modern programming languages. The major stumbling block in this enterprise is how to avoid a design in which programmers must place so many typing annotations on their programs that the dependent types become more trouble than they are worth. In other words, how do we avoid a situation in which programmers spend so much time writing specifications to guide the type checker that they cannot make any progress coding up the computation they wish to execute?

The main solution to this problem has been to explicitly avoid any attempt at full verification of program correctness and to instead focus on verification of safety properties in limited but important domains. Hence, Xi and Pfenning [12] and Zenger [13] have focused on integer reasoning to check the safety of array-based code and also on simple symbolic constraints for checking properties of data types. Similarly, in their language Vault [5], DeLine and Fahndrich use a form of linear type together with dependency to verify properties of state and improve the robustness of Windows device drivers.

These projects have been very successful, but the annotations required by programming languages involving dependent types can still be a burden to programmers, particularly in functional languages, where programmers are accustomed to using complete type reconstruction algorithms. For instance, one set of benchmarks analyzed by Xi and Pfenning indicates that programmers can often expect that 10-20 percent of their code will be typing annotations[1].

In order to encourage programmers to use dependent specifications in their programs, we propose a language design and type system that allows programmers to add dependent specifications to program fragments bit by bit. More specifically, certain program components are marked *dependent*, in which case the type checker verifies statically that the programmer has properly maintained dependent typing annotations. Other portions of the program are marked *simple* and in these sections, programmers are free to write code as they would in any ordinary simply-typed programming language. When control passes between dependent and simple fragments, data flowing from simply-typed code into dependently-typed code is checked dynamically to ensure that the dependent invariants hold.

This strategy allows programmers to employ a pay-as-you-go approach when it comes to using dependent types. For instance, when first prototyping their system, programmers may avoid dependent types since their invariants and code structure may be in greater flux at that time or they simply need to get the project off the ground as quickly as possible. Later, they may add dependent types piece by piece until they are satisfied with the level of static verification. More generally, our strategy allows programmers to achieve better compile-time safety assurance in a gradual and type-safe way.

The main contributions of our paper are the following: First, we formalize a source-level dependently-typed functional language with a syntax-directed type checking algorithm. The language admits programs that freely mix both dependently-typed and simply-typed program fragments.

Second, we formalize the procedure for inserting coercions between higher-order dependently-typed and simply-typed code sections and the generation of intermediate-language programs. In these intermediate-language programs, all dynamic checks are explicit and the code is completely dependently typed. We have proven that the translation always produces wellformed dependently-typed code. In other words, we formalize the first stage of a certifying compiler for our language. Our translation is also total under an admissibility requirement on the dependently-typed interface. Any simply-typed code fragment can be linked with a dependently-typed fragment that satisfies this requirement, and the compiler is able to insert sufficient coercions to guarantee safety at run-time.

---

[1]Table 1 from Xi and Pfenning [12] shows ratios of total lines of type annotations/lines of code for eight array-based benchmarks to be 50/281, 2/33, 3/37, 10/50, 9/81, 40/200, 10/45 and 3/18.

Finally, we extend our system with references. We ensure that references and dependency interact safely and prove the correctness of the strategy for mixing simply-typed and dependently-typed code. Proof outlines for all our theorems can be found in our companion technical report [9].

2 Language Syntax and Overview

At the core of our system is a dependently-typed lambda calculus with recursive functions, pairs and a set of pre-defined constant symbols. At a minimum, the constants must include booleans **true** and **false** as well as conjunction ($\wedge$), negation ($\neg$),and equality($=$). We use $\lambda x:\tau_1.\,e$ to denote the function $\texttt{fix}\,f(x:\tau_1):\tau_2.e$ when f does not appear free in e and $\texttt{let}\;\; x=e_1$ **in** e to denote $(\lambda x:\tau.\,e)\,e_1$.[2]

$$\begin{array}{rcl} \tau & ::= & \tau_b \mid \Pi x:\tau.\tau \mid \tau\times\tau \mid \{x:\tau_b \mid e\} \\ e & ::= & c \mid x \mid \texttt{fix}\,f(x:\tau_1):\tau_2.e \mid e\,e \\ & \mid & \langle e,\,e\rangle \mid \pi_1 e \mid \pi_2 e \mid \texttt{if}\;e\;\texttt{then}\;e\;\texttt{else}\;e \end{array}$$

The language of types includes a collection of base types (τ_b), which must include boolean type and unit type, but may also include other types (like integer) that are important for the application under consideration. Function types have the form $\Pi x:\tau_1.\tau_2$ and x, the function argument, may appear in τ_2. If x does not appear in τ_2, we abbreviate the function type as $\tau_1 \rightarrow \tau_2$. Note that unlike much recent work on dependent types for practical programming languages, here x is a valid run-time object rather than a purely compile-time index. The reason for this choice is that the compiler will need to generate run-time tests based on types. If the types contain constraints involving abstract compile-time only indices, generation of the run-time tests may be impossible.

To specify interesting properties of values programmers can use *set types* with the form $\{x:\tau_b \mid e\}$, where e is a boolean term involving x. Intuitively, the type contains all values v with base type τ_b such that $[v/x]e$ is equivalent to **true**. We use $\{e\}$ as a shorthand for the set type $\{x:\textbf{unit} \mid e\}$ when x does not appear free in e. The *essential type* of τ, $[\![\tau]\!]$, is defined below.

$$[\![\{x:\tau_b \mid e\}]\!] = \tau_b \qquad [\![\tau]\!] = \tau \;\; (\tau \text{ is not a set type})$$

The type-checking algorithm for our language, like other dependently-typed languages, involves deciding equivalence of expressions that appear in types. Therefore, in order for our type system to be both sound and tractable, we cannot allow just any lambda calculus term to appear inside types. In particular, allowing recursive functions inside types makes equivalence decision undecidable, and allowing effectful operations such as access to mutable storage within types makes the type system unsound. To avoid these difficulties, we categorize a subset of the expressions as *pure terms*. For the purposes of this paper, we limit the pure terms to variables whose essential type is a base type, constants with simple type $\tau_{b_1} \rightarrow \cdots \rightarrow \tau_{b_n}$, and application of pure terms to pure terms. Only a pure term can appear in a valid type. Note this effectively limits dependent functions to the form $\Pi x:\tau_1.\tau_2$ where $[\![\tau_1]\!] = \tau_b$[3]. A pure

[2] The typing annotations τ_2 and τ are unnecessary in these cases.

[3] Non-dependent function $\tau_1 \rightarrow \tau_2$ can still have arbitrary domain type.

term in our system is also a valid run-time expression, as opposed to a compile-time only object.

As an example of the basic elements of the language, consider the following typing context, which gives types to a collection of operations for manipulating integers (type `int`) and integer vectors (type `intvec`).

```
... -1, 0, 1, ... : int
+, -, * : int -> int -> int
<, <=   : int -> int -> bool
type nat = {x:int | 0 <= x}
length  : intvec -> nat
newvec  : Πn:nat.{v:intvec | length v = n}
sub     : Πi:nat.({v:intvec | i < length v} -> int)
```

The `newvec` takes a natural number `n` and returns a new integer vector whose length is equal to `n`, as specified by the set type. The subscript operation `sub` takes two arguments: a natural number `i` and an integer vector, and returns the component of the vector at index `i`. Its type requires `i` must be within the vector's bound.

Simple and Dependent Typing. To allow programmers to control the precision of the type checker for the language, we add three special commands to the surface language:

$$e ::= \cdots \mid \textbf{simple}\{e\} \mid \textbf{dependent}\{e\} \mid \textbf{assert}(e,\ \tau)$$

Informally, **simple**$\{e\}$ means expression e is only simply well-typed and there is no sufficient annotation for statically verifying all dependent constraints. The type checker must insert dynamic checks to ensure dependent constraints when control passes to a dependent section. For instance, suppose f is a variable that stands for a function defined in a dependently-typed section that requires its argument to have set type $\{x : \texttt{int} \mid x \geq 0\}$. At application site **simple**$\{f\ e\}$ the type checker must verify e is an integer, but may not be able to verify that it is nonnegative. To guarantee run-time safety, the compiler automatically inserts a dynamic check for $e \geq 0$ when it cannot verify this fact statically. At higher types, these simple checks become more general coercions from data of one type to another.

On the other hand, **dependent**$\{e\}$ directs the type checker to verify e is well-typed taking all of the dependent constraints into consideration. If the type checker cannot verify all dependent constraints statically, it fails and alerts the user. We also provide a convenient utility function **assert**$(e,\ \tau)$ that checks at run time that expression e produces a value with type τ.

Together these commands allow users to tightly control the trade-off between the degree of compile-time guarantee and the ease of programming. The fewer **simple** or **assert** commands, the greater the compile-time guarantee, although the greater the burden to the programmer in terms of type annotations. Also, programmers have good control over where potential failures may happen — they can only occur inside a **simple** scope or at an **assert** expression.

For instance, consider the following function that computes dot-product:

```
simple{
  let dotprod = λv1.λv2. let f = fix loop n i sum
                if (i = n) then sum
                else loop n (i+1) (sum + (sub i v1) * (sub i v2))
               in f (length v1) 0 0
    in dotprod vec1 vec2 }
```

Function dotprod takes two vectors as arguments and returns the sum of multiplication of corresponding components of the vectors. The entire function is defined within a **simple** scope so programmers need not add any typing annotations. However, the cost is that the type checker infers only that i is some integer and v1 and v2 are integer vectors. Without information concerning the length of the vectors and size of the integer, the checker cannot verify that the sub operations are in bound. As a result, the compiler will insert dynamic checks at these points.

As a matter of fact, without these checks the above program would crash if the length of vec1 is greater than that of vec2! To prevent clients of the dotprod function from calling it with such illegal arguments, a programmer can give dotprod a dependent type while leaving the body of the function simply-typed:

```
dependent {
  let dotprod = λv1:intvec, v2:{v2:intvec | length v1 = length v2}.
                  simple { ... }
   in dotprod vec1 vec2 }
```

The advantage of adding this typing annotation is that the programmer has formally documented the condition for correct use of the dotprod function. Now the type checker has to prove that the length of vec1 is equal to that of vec2. If this is not the case the error will be detected at compile time.

Even though the compiler can verify the function is called with valid arguments, it still needs to insert run-time checks for the vector accesses because they are inside a **simple** scope. To add an extra degree of compile-time confidence, the programmer can verify the function body by placing it completely in the **dependent** scope and adding the appropriate loop invariant annotation as shown below.

```
dependent {
 let dotprod = λv1:intvec, v2:{v2:intvec | length v1 = length v2}.
        let f = fix loop (n:{n:nat|n = length(v1)})
                         (i:{i:nat|i <= n}) (sum:int).
                if (i = n) then sum
                else loop n (i+1) (sum + (sub i v1) * (sub i v2))
        in f (length v1) 0 0
  in  dotprod vec1 vec2 }
```

With the new typing annotations and some simple integer arithmetic reasoning, our type checker can verify that all the dependent function applications within the function body are well-typed. Once the above code type checks, there can be no failure at run time.

As illustrated by the example, the compiler has the freedom to insert dynamic checks to explicitly verify dependent constraints at run-time. While the kind of run-

$$\frac{\mathcal{F}(c) = \tau}{\Gamma \vdash c : \tau}\ \mathit{TConst} \qquad \frac{\Gamma(x) = \tau}{\Gamma \vdash x : \tau}\ \mathit{TVar} \qquad \frac{\Gamma \vdash \tau \text{ valid}}{\Gamma \vdash \textbf{fail} : \tau}\ \mathit{TFail}$$

$$\frac{\Gamma \vdash \Pi x : \tau_1.\tau_2 \text{ valid} \qquad \Gamma, f : \Pi x : \tau_1.\tau_2, x : \tau_1 \vdash e : \tau_2}{\Gamma \vdash \mathtt{fix}\, f(x : \tau_1) : \tau_2.e : \Pi x : \tau_1.\tau_2}\ \mathit{TFun}$$

$$\frac{\Gamma \vdash e_1 : \Pi x : \tau_1.\tau_2 \qquad \Gamma \vdash e_2 : \tau_1 \qquad \Gamma \vdash_{pure} e_2}{\Gamma \vdash e_1\, e_2 : [e_2/x]\tau_2}\ \mathit{TAppPure} \qquad \frac{\Gamma \vdash e_1 : \tau_1 \to \tau_2 \qquad \Gamma \vdash e_2 : \tau_1}{\Gamma \vdash e_1\, e_2 : \tau_2}\ \mathit{TAppImPure}$$

$$\frac{\Gamma \vdash e_1 : \tau_1 \qquad \Gamma \vdash e_2 : \tau_2}{\Gamma \vdash \langle e_1,\, e_2 \rangle : \tau_1 \times \tau_2}\ \mathit{TP} \qquad \frac{\Gamma \vdash e : \tau_1 \times \tau_2}{\Gamma \vdash \pi_1 e : \tau_1}\ \mathit{TPL} \qquad \frac{\Gamma \vdash e : \tau_1 \times \tau_2}{\Gamma \vdash \pi_2 e : \tau_2}\ \mathit{TPR}$$

$$\frac{\Gamma \vdash_{pure} e : \textbf{bool} \qquad \Gamma, u : \{e\} \vdash e_1 : \tau \qquad \Gamma, u : \{\neg e\} \vdash e_2 : \tau}{\Gamma \vdash \mathtt{if}\ e\ \mathtt{then}\ e_1\ \mathtt{else}\ e_2 : \tau}\ \mathit{TIf}$$

$$\frac{\Gamma \vdash e : \tau \qquad \Gamma \vdash_{pure} e}{\Gamma \vdash e : \textbf{self}(\tau, e)}\ \mathit{TSelf} \qquad \frac{\Gamma \vdash e : \tau' \qquad \Gamma \vdash \tau' \leq \tau}{\Gamma \vdash e : \tau}\ \mathit{TSub}$$

Figure 1. Type rules for the internal language

time checks in this example are simple, one has to be careful if the objects passed between dependent and simple sections involve functions, because the dependent constraints may appear at both covariant and contravariant positions. We formalize the process of inserting dynamic checks in the type coercion judgment discussed in the next section.

3 Formal Language Semantics

We give a formal semantics to our language in two main steps. First, we define a type system for our internal dependently-typed language which contains no **dependent{}**, **simple{}** or **assert** commands. Second, we simultaneously define a syntax-directed type system and translation from the surface programming language into the internal language. We have proven that the translation always generates well-typed internal language terms. Since the latter proof is constructive, our translation always generates expressions with sufficient information for an intermediate language type checker to verify type correctness.

Internal Language Typing. The judgment $\Gamma \vdash e : \tau$ presented in Figure 1 defines the type system for the internal language. The context Γ maps variables to types and $\mathcal{F}$ maps constants to their types. Many of the rules are standard so we only highlight a few. First, the **fail** expression, which has not been mentioned before is used to safely terminate programs and may be given any type. Dependent function introduction is standard, but there are two elimination rules. In the first case, the function type may be dependent, so the argument must be a pure term (judged by $\Gamma \vdash_{pure} e$), since only pure terms may appear inside types. In the second case, the argument may be impure so the function must have non-dependent type. When type checking an `if` statement, the primary argument of the `if` must be a pure boolean term and this argument (or its negation) is added to the context when checking each branch[4].

The type system has a *selfification* rule (*TSelf*), which is inspired by dependent type systems developed to reason about modules [7]. The rule applies a "selfification" function, which returns the most precise possible type for the term, its *singleton type*. For instance, though x might have type `int` in the context, **self**(`int`, x) produces the type $\{y : \texttt{int} \mid y = x\}$, the type of values exactly equal to x. Also, the constant $+$ might have type $\texttt{int} \rightarrow \texttt{int} \rightarrow \texttt{int}$, but through selfification, it will be given the more precise type $\Pi x : \texttt{int}.\Pi y : \texttt{int}.\{z : \texttt{int} \mid z = x + y\}$, the type of functions that add their arguments. Without selfification, the type system would be too weak to do any sophisticated reasoning about variables and values. The selfification function is defined below. Notice that the definition is only upon types that a pure term may have.

$$\begin{aligned}
\textbf{self}(\tau_b, e) &= \{x : \tau_b \mid x = e\} \\
\textbf{self}(\{x : \tau_b \mid e'\}, e) &= \{x : \tau_b \mid e' \wedge x = e\} \\
\textbf{self}(\tau_b \rightarrow \tau, e) &= \Pi x : \tau_b.\textbf{self}(\tau, e\,x)
\end{aligned}$$

Finally, the type system includes a notion of subtyping, where all reasoning about dependent constraints occur. The technical report [9] gives the complete subtyping rules. The interesting case is the subtype relation between set types. As stated below, $\{x : \tau_b \mid e_1\}$ is a subtype of $\{x : \tau_b \mid e_2\}$ provided that $e_1 \supset e_2$ is **true** under assumptions in Γ. Term $e_1 \supset e_2$ stands for the implication between two boolean terms.

$$\frac{\Gamma \vdash \{x : \tau_b \mid e_1\}\ \text{valid} \qquad \Gamma \vdash \{x : \tau_b \mid e_2\}\ \text{valid} \qquad \Gamma, x : \tau_b \models e_1 \supset e_2}{\Gamma \vdash \{x : \tau_b \mid e_1\} \leq \{x : \tau_b \mid e_2\}}$$

Here, $\Gamma \models e$ is a logical entailment judgment that infers truth about the application domains. For example it may infer that $n : \texttt{int} \models n \leq n + 1$. We do not want to limit our language to a particular set of application domains so we leave this judgment unspecified but it must obey the axioms of standard classical logic. A precise set of requirements on the logical entailment judgment may be found in the technical report [9].

Surface Language Typing and Translation. We give a formal semantics to the surface language via a type-directed translation into the internal language. The translation has the form $\Gamma \vdash_w e \rightsquigarrow e' : \tau$ where e is a surface language expression and e' is the resulting internal language expression with type τ. w is a type checking mode which is either *dep* or *sim*. In mode *dep* every dependent constraint must be *statically* verified, whereas in mode *sim* if the type checker cannot infer dependent constraints statically it will generate dynamic checks. It is important to note that this judgment is a syntax-directed function with Γ, w and e as inputs and e' and τ uniquely determined outputs (if the translation succeeds). In other words, the rules in Figure 2 defines the type checking and translation algorithm for the surface language.

$$\frac{\Gamma \vdash_{pure} c \qquad \mathcal{F}(c) = \tau}{\Gamma \vdash_{w} c \leadsto c : \mathbf{self}(\tau, c)}\ \textit{ATConstSelf} \qquad \frac{\Gamma \not\vdash_{pure} c \qquad \mathcal{F}(c) = \tau}{\Gamma \vdash_{w} c \leadsto c : \tau}\ \textit{ATConst}$$

$$\frac{\Gamma \vdash_{pure} x \qquad \Gamma(x) = \tau}{\Gamma \vdash_{w} x \leadsto x : \mathbf{self}(\tau, x)}\ \textit{ATVarSelf} \qquad \frac{\Gamma \not\vdash_{pure} x \qquad \Gamma(x) = \tau}{\Gamma \vdash_{w} x \leadsto x : \tau}\ \textit{ATVar}$$

$$\frac{\begin{array}{c}\Gamma \vdash \Pi x : \tau_1.\tau_2 \ \mathbf{valid} \qquad \Gamma' = \Gamma, f : \Pi x : \tau_1.\tau_2, x : \tau_1 \\ \Gamma' \vdash_{w} e \leadsto e' : \tau_2' \qquad \Gamma' \vdash_{w} e' : \tau_2' \longrightarrow e'' : \tau_2\end{array}}{\Gamma \vdash_{w} \mathtt{fix}\ f(x : \tau_1) : \tau_2.e \leadsto \mathtt{fix}\ f(x : \tau_1) : \tau_2.e'' : \Pi x : \tau_1.\tau_2}\ \textit{ATFun}$$

$$\frac{\begin{array}{c}\Gamma \vdash_{w} e_1 \leadsto e_1' : \Pi x : \tau_1.\tau_2 \\ \Gamma \vdash_{w} e_2 \leadsto e_2' : \tau_1' \qquad \Gamma \vdash_{w} e_2' : \tau_1' \longrightarrow e_2'' : \tau_1 \qquad \Gamma \vdash_{pure} e_2''\end{array}}{\Gamma \vdash_{w} e_1\, e_2 \leadsto e_1'\, e_2'' : [e_2''/x]\tau_2}\ \textit{ATAppPure}$$

$$\frac{\begin{array}{c}\Gamma \vdash_{w} e_1 \leadsto e_1' : \Pi x : \tau_1.\tau_2 \qquad \Gamma \vdash_{w} e_1' : \Pi x : \tau_1.\tau_2 \longrightarrow e_1'' : \tau_1 \to [\tau_2]_x \\ \Gamma \vdash_{w} e_2 \leadsto e_2' : \tau_1' \qquad \Gamma \vdash_{w} e_2' : \tau_1' \longrightarrow e_2'' : \tau_1 \qquad \Gamma \not\vdash_{pure} e_2''\end{array}}{\Gamma \vdash_{w} e_1\, e_2 \leadsto e_1''\, e_2'' : [\tau_2]_x}\ \textit{ATAppImPure}$$

$$\frac{\Gamma \vdash_{w} e_1 \leadsto e_1' : \tau_1 \qquad \Gamma \vdash_{w} e_2 \leadsto e_2' : \tau_2}{\Gamma \vdash_{w} \langle e_1,\ e_2 \rangle \leadsto \langle e_1',\ e_2' \rangle : \tau_1 \times \tau_2}\ \textit{ATProd}$$

$$\frac{\Gamma \vdash_{w} e \leadsto e' : \tau_1 \times \tau_2}{\Gamma \vdash_{w} \pi_1 e \leadsto \pi_1 e' : \tau_1}\ \textit{ATProjL} \qquad \frac{\Gamma \vdash_{w} e \leadsto e' : \tau_1 \times \tau_2}{\Gamma \vdash_{w} \pi_2 e \leadsto \pi_2 e' : \tau_2}\ \textit{ATProjR}$$

$$\frac{\begin{array}{c}\Gamma \vdash_{pure} e : \mathbf{bool} \\ \Gamma, u : \{e\} \vdash_{w} e_1 \leadsto e_1' : \tau_1 \qquad \Gamma, u : \{e\} \vdash_{w} e_1' : \tau_1 \longrightarrow e_1'' : \tau_1 \sqcup \tau_2 \\ \Gamma, u : \{\neg e\} \vdash_{w} e_2 \leadsto e_2' : \tau_2 \qquad \Gamma, u : \{\neg e\} \vdash_{w} e_2' : \tau_2 \longrightarrow e_2'' : \tau_1 \sqcup \tau_2\end{array}}{\Gamma \vdash_{w} \mathtt{if}\ e\ \mathtt{then}\ e_1\ \mathtt{else}\ e_2 \leadsto \mathtt{if}\ e\ \mathtt{then}\ e_1''\ \mathtt{else}\ e_2'' : \tau_1 \sqcup \tau_2}\ \textit{ATIfPure}$$

$$\frac{\Gamma \not\vdash_{pure} e \qquad \Gamma \vdash_{w} \mathtt{let}\ \ x = e\ \mathtt{in}\ \mathtt{if}\ x\ \mathtt{then}\ e_1\ \mathtt{else}\ e_2 \leadsto e' : \tau}{\Gamma \vdash_{w} \mathtt{if}\ e\ \mathtt{then}\ e_1\ \mathtt{else}\ e_2 \leadsto e' : \tau}\ \textit{ATIfImPure}$$

$$\frac{\Gamma \vdash_{dep} e \leadsto e' : \tau' \qquad \Gamma \vdash \tau \ \mathbf{valid} \qquad \Gamma \vdash_{sim} e' : \tau' \longrightarrow e'' : \tau}{\Gamma \vdash_{dep} \mathbf{assert}(e,\ \tau) \leadsto e'' : \tau}\ \textit{ATAssert}$$

$$\frac{\Gamma \vdash_{sim} e \leadsto e' : \tau}{\Gamma \vdash_{dep} \mathbf{simple}\{e\} \leadsto e' : \tau}\ \textit{ATDynamic} \qquad \frac{\Gamma \vdash_{dep} e \leadsto e' : \tau}{\Gamma \vdash_{sim} \mathbf{dependent}\{e\} \leadsto e' : \tau}\ \textit{ATStatic}$$

Figure 2. Surface language type checking and translation

Constants and variables are given singleton types if they are pure via the selfification function (*ATConstSelf* and *ATVarSelf*), but they are given less precise types otherwise (*ATConst* and *ATVar*). To translate a function definition (*ATFun*), the function body e is first translated into e' with type τ_2'. Since this type may not match the annotated result type τ_2, the *type coercion judgment* is called to coerce e' to τ_2, possibly inserting run-time checks if the type checking mode is sim.

The type coercion judgment has the form $\Gamma \vdash_w e : \tau \longrightarrow e' : \tau'$. It is a function, which given type checking mode w, context Γ, expression e with type τ, and a target type τ', generates a new expression e' with type τ'. The output expression is equivalent to the input expression aside from the possible presence of run-time checks. We will discuss the details of this judgment in a moment.

There are two function application rules, distinguished based on whether the argument expression is judged pure or not. If it is pure, rule *ATAppPure* applies and the argument expression is substituted into the result type. If the argument expression is impure, rule *ATAppImpure* first coerces the function expression that has a potentially dependent type $\Pi x : \tau_1.\tau_2$, to an expression that has a non-dependent function type $\tau_1 \rightarrow [\tau_2]_x$. $[\tau]_x$ returns the type with all occurrences of variable x removed. It is defined on set types as follows and recursively defined according to the type structures for the other types.

$$[\{y : \tau_b \mid e\}]_x = \tau_b \quad (x \in FV(e))$$
$$[\{y : \tau_b \mid e\}]_x = \{y : \tau_b \mid e\} \quad (x \notin FV(e))$$

Note that in both application rules the argument expression's type τ_1' may not match the function's argument type so it is coerced to an expression e_2'' with the right type.

In type checking an `if` expression, the two branches may be given different types. So they are coerced to a common type $\tau_1 \sqcup \tau_2$ (*ATIfPure*). Informally, $\tau_1 \sqcup \tau_2$ recursively applies disjunction operation on boolean expressions in set types that appear in covariant positions and applies conjunction operation on those on contravariant positions. For example,

$$\{x : \mathtt{int} \mid x < 3\} \sqcup \{x : \mathtt{int} \mid x > 10\} = \{x : \mathtt{int} \mid x < 3 \lor x > 10\}$$

and

$$(\{x : \mathtt{int} \mid x > 3\} \rightarrow \mathtt{int}) \sqcup (\{x : \mathtt{int} \mid x < 10\} \rightarrow \mathtt{int})$$
$$= \{x : \mathtt{int} \mid x > 3 \land x < 10\} \rightarrow \mathtt{int}$$

The precise definition for $\tau_1 \sqcup \tau_2$ can be found in the technical report [9].

The rules for checking and translating **dependent**$\{e\}$ and **simple**$\{e\}$ expressions simply switch the type checking mode from sim to *dep* and vice versa. The rule for **assert**(e, τ) uses the type coercion judgment to coerce expression e to type τ. Note that the coercion is called with *sim* mode to allow insertion of run-time checks.

Type coercion judgment. The complete rules for the type coercion judgment can be found in Figure 3. When the source type is a subtype of the target type, no conversion is necessary (*CSub*). The remaining coercion rules implicitly assume the subtype relation does not hold, hence dynamic checks must be inserted at appropriate places. Note that those rules require the checking mode be sim; when called with mode *dep* the coercion judgment is just the subtyping judgment and the type checker is designed to signal a compile-time error when it cannot statically prove the source is a subtype of the target.

$$\frac{\Gamma \vdash \tau \leq \tau'}{\Gamma \vdash_w e : \tau \longrightarrow e : \tau'} \ CSub$$

$$\frac{\tau = \tau_b \text{ or } \tau = \{x : \tau_b \mid e_1'\}}{\Gamma \vdash_{sim} e : \tau \longrightarrow \mathtt{let}\ x = e \ \mathbf{in}\ \mathtt{if}\ e_1\ \mathtt{then}\ x\ \mathtt{else}\ \mathbf{fail} : \{x : \tau_b \mid e_1\}} \ CBase$$

$$\frac{\Gamma \vdash \tau_1' \leq \tau_1 \qquad \Gamma, y : \Pi x : \tau_1.\tau_2, x : \tau_1' \vdash_{sim} y\, x : \tau_2 \longrightarrow e_b : \tau_2'}{\Gamma \vdash_{sim} e : \Pi x : \tau_1.\tau_2 \longrightarrow (\mathtt{let}\ \ y = e \ \mathbf{in}\ \lambda x : \tau_1'.\, e_b) : \Pi x : \tau_1'.\tau_2'} \ CFunCo$$

$$\frac{\Gamma \not\vdash \tau_1' \leq \tau_1 \qquad \Gamma, x : \tau_1' \vdash_{sim} x : \tau_1' \longrightarrow e_x : \tau_1 \\ \Gamma, y : \tau_1 \rightarrow \tau_2, x : \tau_1' \vdash_{sim} y\, e_x : \tau_2 \longrightarrow e_b : \tau_2'}{\Gamma \vdash_{sim} e : (\tau_1 \rightarrow \tau_2) \longrightarrow (\mathtt{let}\ \ y = e \ \mathbf{in}\ \lambda x : \tau_1'.\, e_b) : (\tau_1' \rightarrow \tau_2')} \ CFunContNonDep$$

$$\frac{\Gamma \not\vdash \tau_1' \leq \tau_1 \qquad \tau_1 = \{x : \tau_b \mid e_1\} \qquad \tau_1' = \{x : \tau_b \mid e_1'\} \text{ or } \tau_b \\ \Gamma, y : \Pi x : \tau_1.\tau_2, x : \tau_1 \vdash_{sim} y\, x : \tau_2 \longrightarrow e_b : \tau_2' \\ e_b' = \mathtt{if}\ e_1\ \mathtt{then}\ e_b\ \mathtt{else}\ \mathbf{fail}}{\Gamma \vdash_{sim} e : \Pi x : \tau_1.\tau_2 \longrightarrow (\mathtt{let}\ \ y = e \ \mathbf{in}\ \lambda x : \tau_1'.\, e_b') : \Pi x : \tau_1'.\tau_2'} \ CFunContDep$$

$$\frac{\Gamma, y : \tau_1 \times \tau_2 \vdash_{sim} \pi_1 y : \tau_1 \longrightarrow e_1' : \tau_1' \\ \Gamma, y : \tau_1 \times \tau_2 \vdash_{sim} \pi_2 y : \tau_2 \longrightarrow e_2' : \tau_2'}{\Gamma \vdash_{sim} e : \tau_1 \times \tau_2 \longrightarrow (\mathtt{let}\ \ y = e \ \mathbf{in}\ \langle e_1',\ e_2' \rangle) : \tau_1' \times \tau_2'} \ CPair$$

Figure 3. Type coercion

Coercion for the base-type case (*CBase*) is straightforward. An `if` expression ensures that the invariant expressed by the target set type holds. Otherwise a runtime failure will occur. With the help of the logical entailment judgment, our type system is able to infer that the resulting `if` expression has the set type.

In general, one cannot directly check at run-time that a function's code precisely obeys some behavioral specification expressed by a dependent type. What we can do is ensure that every time the function is called, the function's argument meets the dependent type's requirement, and its body produces a value that satisfies the promised result type. This strategy is sufficient for ensuring run-time safety. The coercion rules for functions are designed to coerce a function from one type to a function with another type, deferring checks on arguments and results until the function is called.

There are three coercion rules for function types. In all cases the expression that generates the function is evaluated first to preserve the order of effects. Next a new function is constructed with checks on argument and result inserted when necessary. In the case where the new argument type is a subtype of the old one (*CFunCo*), we only need to convert the function body to the appropriate result type. Otherwise checks must be inserted to make sure the argument has the type the old function expects. This can be done by recursively calling the coercion judgment on the argument x to convert it to a term e_x with type τ_1. When the function's type is not dependent, it can receive e_x as an argument (*CFunContNonDep*). But when it is a dependent function, it cannot receive e_x as an argument since e_x contains dynamic checks and is impure[5]. Consequently rule *CFunContDep* uses an `if` statement to directly check the constraint on the dependent argument x. This is possible because x must be a pure term and hence has a base type. If the check succeeds, x is directly passed to the function. For all the three cases, our type system is able to prove the resulting expression has the target function type.

4 Mutable References

The addition of mutable references to our language presents a significant challenge. When sharing a reference between simple and dependent code, it is natural to wish to assign the reference a simple type in the simple code and a dependent type in the dependent code, for example `int ref` and `{x:int|x >= 0} ref`. However, the inequivalence of these types can lead to unsoundness. Therefore, in our surface language, we define two classes of references, τ **ref** and τ **dref**. The former is invariant in its typing, thereby disallowing the transfer of such references between one piece of code and another unless the supplied and assumed types are equal. The latter is more flexible in its typing, but is dynamically checked according to the following two principles: First, the recipient of such a reference is responsible for writing data that maintains the invariants of the reference's donor. Second, the recipient must protect itself by ensuring that data it reads indeed respects its own invariants.

In the internal language, the τ **dref** is implemented as a pair of functions:

$$(\mathbf{unit} \to \tau) \times (\tau \to \mathbf{unit})$$

Intuitively, the first function reads an underlying reference and coerces the value to the right type; the second one coerces the input value to the type of the underlying reference and writes the coerced value into it.

We define a type translation $(\!|\tau|\!)$ to translate surface language types to internal language types. It recursively traverses the type structure of τ and translates any appearance of dynamic references as shown above.

The coercion rules for references allow translation from an expression of τ **ref** to an expression of τ' **dref**, or from τ **dref** to τ' **dref**. But there is no coercion rule from τ **dref** to τ' **ref**, because an expression with τ **dref** will potentially incur runtime failures, while an expression with type τ **ref** will not. Further details of our solution can be found in our companion technical report [9].

5 Language Properties

In this section, we present theorems that state formal properties of our language. We leave details of the proofs and precise definitions to the technical report [9]. First, we proved type safety for the internal language based on a standard dynamic semantics with mutable references:

---

[5] We also cannot simply write `let` $z = e_x$ **in** $y\ z$ since the effects in e_x do not allow the type system to maintain the proper dependency between x and z in this case.

Theorem 1 (Type safety) *If* $\bullet \vdash e : \tau$*, then e won't get stuck in evaluation.*

The proof is by induction on the length of execution sequence, using standard progress and preservation theorems.

The soundness of the type-directed translation for the surface language is formalized as the following theorem.

Theorem 2 (Soundness of translation of surface language) *If* $\Gamma \vdash_w e \rightsquigarrow e' : \tau$*, then* $(\!|\Gamma|\!) \vdash (\!|e'|\!) : (\!|\tau|\!)$.

$(\!|e|\!)$ is the expression with every type τ appearing in it replaced by $(\!|\tau|\!)$, and $\forall x \in dom(\Gamma).(\!|\Gamma|\!)(x) = (\!|\Gamma(x)|\!)$.

For all source programs that are simply well-typed (judged by $\Gamma \vdash_0 e : \tau$), if the dependent interface Γ satisfies an admissibility requirement *co_ref*(Γ), the translation is total in *sim* mode:

Theorem 3 (Completeness of translation) *Assuming co_ref*(Γ) *and co_ref*($\mathcal{F}$)*, if* $\Gamma \vdash_0 e : \tau$*, then there exist* e' *and* τ' *such that* $\Gamma \vdash_{sim} e \rightsquigarrow e' : \tau'$.

Informally, *co_ref*(Γ) states that in Γ, unchecked reference type (τ **ref**) can only appear in covariant positions. The reason for this restriction is that we cannot coerce a checked reference (τ **dref**) to an unchecked one.

6 Related Work

In this paper, we have shown how to include fragments of *simply-typed* code within the context of a *dependently-typed* language. In the past, many researchers have examined techniques for including *uni-typed* code (code with one type such as Scheme code) within the context of a *simply-typed* language by means of soft typing ([3, 2, 4]). Soft typing infers simple or polymorphic types for programs but not general dependent types.

Necula et al. [8] have developed a soft typing system for C, with the goal of ensuring that C programs do not contain memory errors. Necula et al. focus on the problem of inferring the status of C pointers in the presence of casts and pointer arithmetic, which are either *safe* (well-typed and requiring no checks), *seq* (well-typed and requiring bounds checking) or *dynamic* (about which nothing is known). In contrast, we always know the simple type of an object that is pointed to, but may not know about its dependent refinements.

When dependent types mix with references, one has to be very careful to ensure the system remains sound. Xi and Pfenning [12] shows how to maintain soundness by using singleton types, and restricting the language of indices that appear in the singleton types. Our approach is similar in that we have designated a subset of terms as pure terms, but different in that we accommodate true dependent types. However, the distinction is minor, and the main contribution of this work is the interaction between the dependently-typed world and the simply-typed world.

Walker [11] shows how to compile a simply-typed lambda calculus into a dependently-typed intermediate language that enforces safety policies specified by simple state machines. However, he does not consider mixing a general dependently-typed language with a simply-typed language or the problems concerning mutable references.

In earlier work, Abadi et al. [1] showed how to add a special *type dynamic* to represent values of completely unknown type and a typecase operation to the simply-typed lambda calculus. Abadi et al. use type dynamic when the simple static type of data is unknown, such as when accessing objects from persistent storage or exchanging data with other programs. Thatte [10] demonstrates how to relieve the programmer from having to explicitly write Abadi et al.'s typecase operations themselves by having the compiler automatically insert them as we do. In contrast to our work, Thatte does not consider dependent types or how to instrument programs with mutable references.

In contract checking systems such as Findler and Felleisen's work [6], programmers can place assertions at well-defined program points, such as procedure entries and exits. Findler and Felleisen have specifically looked at how to enforce properties of higher-order code dynamically by wrapping functions to verify function inputs conform to function expectations and function outputs satisfy promised invariants. Our strategy for handling higher-order code is similar. However, Finder and Felleisen's contracts enforce all properties dynamically whereas we show how to blend dynamic mechanisms with static verification.

Acknowledgments. We are grateful to Daniel Wang for his comments on an earlier version of this work. ARDA grant NBCHC030106, and NSF grants CCR-0238328, and CCR-0306313 have provided support for this research. Any opinions, findings and conclusions or recommendations expressed in this material are those of the authors and do not necessarily reflect the views of ARDA or the NSF.

References

[1] Martín Abadi, Luca Cardelli, Benjamin C. Pierce, and Gordon Plotkin. Dynamic typing in a statically typed language. *ACM Transactions on Programming Languages and Systems*, 13(2):237–268, April 1991.

[2] Alex Aiken, Edward L. Wimmers, and T. K. Lakshman. Soft typing with conditional types. In *Twenty-First ACM Symposium on Principles of Programming Languages*, pages 163–173, January 1994.

[3] R. Cartwright and M. Fagan. Soft typing. In *ACM Conference on Programming Language Design and Implementation*, pages 278–292, 1991.

[4] R. Cartwright and M. Fagan. A practical soft type system for Scheme. *ACM transactions on programming languages and systems*, 19(1):87–152, January 1997.

[5] Rob Deline and Manuel Fähndrich. Enforcing high-level protocols in low-level software. In *ACM Conference on Programming Language Design and Implementation*, pages 59–69, Snowbird, Utah, June 2001. ACM Press.

[6] Robert Bruce Findler and Matthias Felleisen. Contracts for higher-order functions. In *ACM International Conference on Functional Programming*, pages 48–59, Pittsburgh, October 2002. ACM Press.

[7] Robert Harper and Mark Lillibridge. A type-theoretic approach to higher-order modules with sharing. In *Twenty-First ACM Symposium on Principles of Programming Languages*, pages 123–137, Portland, OR, January 1994.

[8] George C. Necula, Scott McPeak, and Westley Weimer. Ccured: Type-safe retrofitting of legacy code. In *ACM Symposium on Principles of Programming Languages*, London, January 2002. ACM Press.

[9] Xinming Ou, Gang Tan, Yitzhak Mandelbaum, and David Walker. Dynamic typing with dependent types. Technical Report TR-695-04, Department of Computer Science, Princeton University, 2004.

[10] S. Thatte. Quasi-static typing. In *Seventeenth ACM Symposium on Principles of Programming Languages*, pages 367–381, January 1990.

[11] David Walker. A type system for expressive security policies. In *Twenty-Seventh ACM Symposium on Principles of Programming Languages*, pages 254–267, Boston, January 2000.

[12] Hongwei Xi and Frank Pfenning. Eliminating array bound checking through dependent types. In *ACM Conference on Programming Language Design and Implementation*, pages 249–257, Montreal, June 1998.

[13] Christoph Zenger. Indexed types. In *Theoretical Computer Science*, volume 187, pages 147–165. Elsevier, November 1997.

SUBTYPING-INHERITANCE CONFLICTS: THE MOBILE MIXIN CASE*

Lorenzo Bettini[1] Viviana Bono[2] Betti Venneri[1]
[1]*Dipartimento di Sistemi e Informatica, Università di Firenze*
[2]*Dipartimento di Informatica, Università di Torino*
[1]{bettini,venneri}@dsi.unifi.it, [2]bono@di.unito.it

Abstract In sequential class- and mixin-based settings, subtyping is essentially a relation on objects: no subtype relation is defined on classes and mixins, otherwise there would be conflicts with the inheritance mechanism, creating type un-safety. Nevertheless, a width-depth subtyping relation on class and mixin types is useful in the realm of mobile and distributed processes, where object-oriented code may be exchanged among the sites of a net. In our proposal, classes and mixins become "first-class citizens" at communication time, and communication is ruled by a type-safe width-depth subtyping relation.

1. Introduction

In sequential class-based settings, and similarly in sequential mixin-based settings, subtyping is essentially a relation on objects. Either no subtype relation (as in [9]), or no non-trivial subtype relation is defined on classes and mixins, otherwise there would be conflicts with the inheritance mechanism (see [11], Chapter 5.3). Our goal is to study a subtyping relation extended to classes and mixins in the realm of mobile and distributed processes, where object-oriented code can be exchanged among the sites of a network. Classes and mixins become "first-class citizens" at communication time, and communication is ruled by the subtyping relation.

In [5], we introduced MoMi (Mobile Mixins), a core coordination calculus for mobile processes that exchange mixin-based object-oriented code. The leading idea of MoMi is that the intrinsic "incompleteness" of mixins, which are incomplete classes parameterized over a superclass [10, 2, 17], makes mixin-based inheritance more suited than classical class-based inheritance to model mobile code. The most important feature of MoMi's typing is a *subtype* relation that guarantees safe, yet flexible, code communication. We assume that the code that is communicated has been successfully compiled, and that it travels together with its static type. When the

*This work has been partially supported by EU within the FET - Global Computing initiative, project AGILE IST-2001-32747, project DART IST-2001-33477 and by MIUR project NAPOLI. The funding bodies are not responsible for any use that might be made of the results presented here.

code is received on a site (whose code also has been successfully compiled), it is accepted only if its type is subtyping-compliant with respect to the one expected. If the code is accepted, it can interact with the local code in a safe way (i.e., with no run-time errors), without any further type checking of the whole code.

The proposed subtype relation on classes and mixins is far from straightforward. In fact, it is well known that subtyping and inheritance do not interact well: problems mirroring the "width subtyping versus addition" and "depth subtyping versus override" conflicts in the object-based setting [1, 15, 8, 20] also arise in our setting. Our contribution is to solve comprehensively both conflicts in the setting of mobile mixin-based code, enforcing a correct substitution property. The effort of defining a class-mixin subtype relation and the related dynamic checking at communication time is worthwhile in a distributed setting, where it is not predictable how mobile code will be used when transmitted to different remote contexts, and, symmetrically, a certain site must allow some controlled flexibility in accepting foreign code.

2. MoMi: Mobile Mixin Calculus

			v	$::=$	$\{m_i = f_i\ ^{i\in I}\}$
				$\mid$	x
exp	$::=$	v		$\mid$	class $[m_i = f_i\ ^{i\in I}]$ end
	$\mid$	new exp			mixin
	$\mid$	$exp \Leftarrow m$			expect$[m_i : \tau_{m_i}\ ^{i\in I}]$
	$\mid$	$v \diamond exp$		$\mid$	redef$[m_k : \tau_{m_k}$ as τ'_{m_k} with $f_k\ ^{k\in K}]$
					def$[m_j = f_j\ ^{j\in J}]$
					end

Table 1. Syntax of SOOL.

The calculus MoMi has an object-oriented mixin-based component, and a coordination component including representative features for distribution, communication and mobility of processes and code. MoMi supports mixin-based class hierarchies via *mixin definition* and *mixin application*. Specific incarnations of most object-oriented notions (such as, e.g., functional or imperative nature of method bodies, object references, cloning, etc.) are irrelevant in this context, where the emphasis is on the structure of the object-oriented mobile code. Hence, we work here with a basic syntax forming the kernel calculus SOOL (*Surface Object-Oriented Language*, shown in Table 1), including the essential features a language must support to be the MoMi's object-oriented component.

SOOL expressions offer object instantiation, method call and *mixin application*; $\diamond$ denotes the mixin application operator and it associates to the right. A SOOL value, to which an expression reduces, is either an object, which is essentially a (recursive) record $\{m_i = f_i\ ^{i\in I}\}$, or a class definition, or a mixin definition, where $[m_i = f_i\ ^{i\in I}]$ denotes a sequence of method definitions, and $[m_k : \tau_{m_k}$ as τ'_{m_k} with $f_k\ ^{k\in K}]$ denotes a sequence of method re-definitions, where τ_{m_k} is the type of the original method m_k in the superclass and τ'_{m_k} is the type of the redefining method body f_k of m_k in the mixin. I, J and K are sets of indexes. Method bodies, denoted here with f (possibly with subscripts), are closed terms/programs and we abstract away from their actual form.

Another assumption we make is that methods do not accept/return classes and mixins as parameters/results, in order to keep the algorithm of Section 6 technically simpler.

A mixin is essentially an abstract class that is parameterized over a (super)class. Each mixin consists of three parts: (*i*) methods defined in the mixin; (*ii*) *expected methods*, that must be provided by the superclass; (*iii*) *redefined methods*, where *next* can be used to access the (old) implementation of the method in the superclass. The application $M \diamond C$ constructs a class, which is a subclass of C.

P	::=	nil	(null process)
	|	$a.P$	(action prefixing)
	|	$P_1 \mid P_2$	(parallel comp.)
	|	X	(process variable)
	|	def $x = exp$ in P	(def)
a	::=	send(A, ℓ)	(send)
	|	receive$(id : \tau)$	(receive)
A	::=	$v \mid P$	(send's arg.)
id	::=	$x \mid X$	(receive's arg.)
N	::=	$\ell :: P$	(node)
	|	$N_1 \parallel N_2$	(net composition)

Table 2. MoMi syntax.

MoMi's coordination component is similar to CCS [18] but also inspired by Klaim [14], since physical nodes are explicitly denoted as localities. MoMi is higher-order in that processes can be exchanged as first-entity data. A node is denoted by its locality, ℓ, and by the processes P running on it, i.e., $\ell :: P$. Informally, send(A, ℓ) sends A, that can be either a process, P, or code represented as an object-oriented value, v, to locality ℓ, where there may be a process waiting for it by means of a receive. The argument of receive, id, ranges over x (a variable of Sool) and X (a process variable).

3. Typing

The set $\mathcal{T}$ of types for Sool is defined as follows:

$$\tau ::= \Sigma \mid \mathsf{class}\langle\Sigma\rangle \mid \mathsf{mixin}\langle\Sigma_{new}, \Sigma_{red}, \Sigma_{exp}, \Sigma_{old}\rangle \qquad \Sigma ::= \{m_i : \tau_{m_i}{}^{i \in I}\}$$

Σ (possibly with a subscript) denotes a record type of the form $\{m_i : \tau_{m_i}{}^{i \in I}\}$. If $m_i : \tau_{m_i} \in \Sigma$ we say that the *subject* m_i *occurs* in Σ. $Subj(\Sigma)$ is the set of the subjects of Σ and $Meth(\Sigma)$ is the set of all the method names occurring in Σ (e.g., if $\Sigma = \{m : \{n : \tau\}\}$, then $Subj(\Sigma) = \{m\}$ and $Meth(\Sigma) = \{m, n\}$). As we left method bodies unspecified (see Section 2), we must assume that there is a type system for the underlying part of Sool that types correctly method bodies, records, and some sort of fix-point. We denote this type derivability with $\Vdash$, and $\Vdash$-statements are used as assumptions in typing values. Sool *typing environments* are sets of assumptions of the form $x : \tau$ and $m : \tau$, where x is a variable and m is a method name.

Class types $\mathsf{class}\langle\Sigma\rangle$ and mixin types $\mathsf{mixin}\langle\Sigma_{new}, \Sigma_{red}, \Sigma_{exp}, \Sigma_{old}\rangle$ are formed over record types. A class type collects the types of its methods $\{m_i : \tau_{m_i}{}^{i \in I}\}$. The typing rule for mixin values is in Table 3 (typing rules for classes and other values are straightforward and therefore omitted). A mixin type encodes the following information. Σ_{new}, Σ_{red} are the types of the mixin methods (new and redefining, respectively). Σ_{exp}, Σ_{old} are the expected types of the methods that must be supported by any class to which the mixin is applied. In Σ_{exp} there are the types of the methods that are not redefined by the mixin but expected to be supported by the superclass. In Σ_{old} there are the types assumed for the superclass bodies of the methods redefined by the mixin. We

$$\frac{\begin{array}{c}\Gamma, \bigcup_{i\in I} m_i : \tau_{m_i}, \bigcup_{k\in K} m_k : \tau'_{m_k} \vdash \{m_j = f_j{}^{j\in J}\} : \{m_j : \tau_{m_j}{}^{j\in J}\} \\ \Gamma, \bigcup_{i\in I} m_i : \tau_{m_i}, \bigcup_{k\in K} m_k : \tau'_{m_k}, \bigcup_{j\in J} m_j : \tau_{m_j}, next : \tau_{m_r} \Vdash f_r : \tau''_{m_r} \quad \tau''_{m_r} <: \tau'_{m_r} \quad \forall r \in K \\ Meth(\Sigma_{new}) \cap Meth(\Sigma_{exp}) = \emptyset \quad Meth(\Sigma_{new}) \cap Meth(\Sigma_{red}) = \emptyset \quad Meth(\Sigma_{red}) \cap Meth(\Sigma_{exp}) = \emptyset \\ \tau'_{m_k} <: \tau_{m_k} \quad \forall k \in K\end{array}}{\Gamma \vdash \begin{array}{l}\mathsf{mixin} \\ \quad \mathsf{expect}[m_i : \tau_{m_i}{}^{i\in I}] \\ \quad \mathsf{redef}[m_k : \tau_{m_k} \text{ as } \tau'_{m_k} \text{ with } f_k{}^{k\in K}] \\ \quad \mathsf{def}[m_j = f_j{}^{j\in J}] \\ \mathsf{end}\end{array} : \mathsf{mixin}\langle \Sigma_{new}, \Sigma_{red}, \Sigma_{exp}, \Sigma_{old}\rangle} \ (mixin)$$

$$\text{where} \quad \begin{array}{l}\Sigma_{new} = \{m_j : \tau_{m_j}{}^{j\in J}\}, \Sigma_{red} = \{m_k : \tau'_{m_k}{}^{k\in K}\} \\ \Sigma_{exp} = \{m_i : \tau_{m_i}{}^{i\in I}\}, \Sigma_{old} = \{m_k : \tau_{m_k}{}^{k\in K}\}\end{array}$$

Table 3. Typing rule for mixin values.

$$\frac{\Gamma \vdash exp : \{m_i : \tau_{m_i}{}^{i\in I}\} \qquad j \in I}{\Gamma \vdash exp \Leftarrow m_j : \tau_{m_j}} \ (lookup) \qquad \frac{\Gamma \vdash exp : \mathsf{class}\langle\{m_i : \tau_{m_i}{}^{i\in I}\}\rangle}{\Gamma \vdash \mathsf{new}\ exp : \{m_i : \tau_{m_i}{}^{i\in I}\}} \ (new)$$

$$\frac{\begin{array}{l}\Gamma \vdash v : \mathsf{mixin}\langle \Sigma_{new}, \Sigma_{red}, \Sigma_{exp}, \Sigma_{old}\rangle \\ \Gamma \vdash exp : \mathsf{class}\langle \Sigma_b \rangle \\ \Sigma_b <: (\Sigma_{exp} \cup \Sigma_{old}) \\ \Sigma_{red} <: \Sigma_b / \Sigma_{red} \\ Meth(\Sigma_b) \cap Meth(\Sigma_{new}) = \emptyset\end{array}}{\Gamma \vdash v \diamond exp : \mathsf{class}\langle \Sigma_d \rangle} \ (mixin\ app)$$

$$\text{where} \quad \begin{array}{lcl}\Sigma_d & = & \Sigma_b / \Sigma_{exp} \cup \Sigma_{new} \cup \Sigma_{red} \cup \Sigma_{rest} \\ \Sigma_{rest} & = & (\Sigma_b - (\Sigma_b / \Sigma_{exp} \cup \Sigma_b / \Sigma_{old}))\end{array}$$

Table 4. Typing rules for SOOL expressions.

refer to both sets of types Σ_{exp} and Σ_{old} as *expected types* since the actual superclass methods may have different types. Well-typed mixins are well formed in the sense that name clashes among the different families of methods do not happen.

The typing rules for SOOL expressions are in Table 4. The crucial rule (*mixin app*) relies strongly on a subtyping relation $<:$ whose judgments are of the form $\tau_1 <: \tau_2$. This subtyping relation depends obviously on the nature of the SOOL calculus we choose, but as an essential constraint it must contain the *width and depth subtyping* rule for record types. Our specimen record subtyping rule is an algorithmic subtyping rule as the one in [19]:

$$\frac{J \subseteq I \qquad \tau_{m_j} <: \tau'_{m_j} \ \forall j \in J}{\{m_i : \tau_{m_i}{}^{i\in I}\} <: \{m_j : \tau'_{m_j}{}^{j\in J}\}} \ (width\text{-}depth)$$

In order to formalize the (*mixin app*) rule, we introduce the following operation over record types ($m : \tau_1$ and $m : \tau_2$ are considered as distinct elements, thus $\Sigma_1 \cup \Sigma_2$ and $\Sigma_1 - \Sigma_2$ are the standard set operations):

$$\Sigma_1 / \Sigma_2 = \{m_i : \tau_{m_i} \mid m_i : \tau_{m_i} \in \Sigma_1 \ \wedge \ m_i \text{ occurs in } \Sigma_2\}$$

In the rule (*mixin app*), Σ_b contains the type signatures of all methods supported by the superclass to which the mixin is applied. Then, Σ_b / Σ_{red} are the superclass methods redefined by the mixin, Σ_b / Σ_{exp} are the superclass methods needed by the mixin methods but not redefined, and Σ_{rest} are the superclass methods not mentioned in the mixin definition at all. Notice that the superclass may have more methods than those required by the mixin constraints. The premises of the rule (*mixin app*) are as follows: (*i*) $\Sigma_b <: (\Sigma_{exp} \cup \Sigma_{old})$ requires the actual types of the superclass methods be subtypes of those expected by the mixin; (*ii*) $\Sigma_{red} <: \Sigma_b / \Sigma_{red}$ checks that the types of the methods redefined by the mixin (Σ_{red}) are subtypes of the superclass methods with the same name; (*iii*) $Meth(\Sigma_b) \cap Meth(\Sigma_{new}) = \emptyset$ guarantees that no name clash takes place during the mixin application. Intuitively, the above constraints insure that all the actual method bodies of the newly created sub-class are at least as "good" as expected. The resulting class, of type $\mathsf{class}\langle\Sigma_d\rangle$, contains the signatures of all methods forming the new class created as a result of the mixin application. Σ_b/Σ_{exp} and Σ_{rest} are inherited directly from the superclass, Σ_{red} and Σ_{new} are defined by the mixin.

Typing rules for processes are defined in Table 5. At this stage, we are not interested in typing processes in detail, therefore we will simply assign to a well-typed process the constant type proc, which means that the object-oriented code the process may contain is well typed. The set $\mathcal{T}$ of types is extended to $\mathcal{T}^* = \mathcal{T} \cup \{\mathsf{proc}\}$. Typing environments are extended with assertions $id : \tau$, where id ranges over x and X and τ ranges over $\mathcal{T}^*$.

$$\frac{}{\Gamma, X : \mathsf{proc} \vdash X : \mathsf{proc}} \ (proj) \qquad \frac{}{\Gamma \vdash \mathbf{nil} : \mathsf{proc}} \ (nil)$$

$$\frac{\Gamma \vdash A : \tau \qquad \Gamma \vdash P : \mathsf{proc}}{\Gamma \vdash \mathsf{send}(A, \ell).P : \mathsf{proc}} \ (send) \qquad \frac{\Gamma, id : \tau \vdash P : \mathsf{proc}}{\Gamma \vdash \mathsf{receive}(id : \tau).P : \mathsf{proc}} \ (receive)$$

$$\frac{\Gamma \vdash P_1 : \mathsf{proc} \qquad \Gamma \vdash P_2 : \mathsf{proc}}{\Gamma \vdash (P_1 \mid P_2) : \mathsf{proc}} \ (comp) \qquad \frac{\Gamma \vdash exp : \tau \qquad \Gamma, x : \tau \vdash P : \mathsf{proc}}{\Gamma \vdash \mathsf{def}\ x = exp\ \mathsf{in}\ P : \mathsf{proc}} \ (def)$$

Table 5. Typing rules for processes.

The rules are auto-explicative. Notice that if a process P has type proc, then all object-oriented expressions occurring in P are typed. Finally, we require that a process, in order to be executed on a site, must be closed (i.e., be without free variables), so it must be well typed under $\Gamma = \emptyset$. It is easy to verify that if a process P is closed, then, for any $\mathsf{send}(A, \ell)$ occurring in P, the free variables of A are bound by an outer def or by an outer receive. This implies that the exchanged code is closed when a send is executed. Notice also that all typing rules characterizing our calculus are in an algorithmic form.

4. Subtyping on Classes and Mixins

The key point of our approach is the introduction of a subtyping relation, $\sqsubseteq$, on class and mixin types. It is of paramount importance to notice that $\sqsubseteq$ is never used in the (local) static type inference. Only during communication the actual parameter type will be matched against the formal parameter type by $\sqsubseteq$ in order to synchronize a send action with a receive one. Therefore, in our mobile scenario, classes and mixins get a polymorphic and higher-order nature only during the mobile code exchange via $\sqsubseteq$. The subtyping relation $\sqsubseteq$ is defined in Table 6. The rule ($\sqsubseteq$ *class*) is naturally induced by the depth-and-width subtyping on record types. The rule ($\sqsubseteq$ *mixin*): (*i*) allows the subtype to define more new methods; (*ii*) requires the subtype to override the same methods; (*iii*) allows a subtype to require fewer expected methods.

$$\frac{\Sigma' <: \Sigma}{\mathsf{class}\langle\Sigma'\rangle \sqsubseteq \mathsf{class}\langle\Sigma\rangle}\ (\sqsubseteq\ \mathit{class})$$

$$\frac{\Sigma'_{new} <: \Sigma_{new} \qquad \Sigma_{exp} <: \Sigma'_{exp}}{\mathsf{mixin}\langle\Sigma'_{new}, \Sigma_{red}, \Sigma'_{exp}, \Sigma_{old}\rangle \sqsubseteq \mathsf{mixin}\langle\Sigma_{new}, \Sigma_{red}, \Sigma_{exp}, \Sigma_{old}\rangle}\ (\sqsubseteq\ \mathit{mixin})$$

Table 6. Subtype on class and mixin types.

The communication mechanism is implemented by annotating the send's argument with its type during the static type analysis. Therefore, it is possible to replace the formal parameter inside a process P with the sent code if its type is subtyping-compliant with the expected one, without requiring any further type checking. To guarantee this, we must prove that our type system enjoys a property of *substitutivity*, i.e., well-typedness is preserved under substitution by $\sqsubseteq$. Concerning this issue, width and depth subtyping raises two orthogonal problems that mirror their counterparts in the object-based setting [1, 15, 8, 20]. We solve those problems, and prove a global substitutivity property, in the sequel.

5. Width Subtyping vs Method Addition: Refreshing

Accidental overrides can occur when replacing at run-time M or C with M_1 and C_1 of smaller types in a mixin application $M \diamond C$, because of names of new methods possibly added by M_1 or C_1. This is related to the "width subtyping versus method addition" problem (well-known in the object-based setting, see for instance [15]), that in our case boils down to a careful management of such *dynamic name clashes*. Thus, we define a suitable capture-avoid-substitution, denoted with $[\ ]$, requiring possible renaming of methods with fresh names.

DEFINITION 1 (SUBSTITUTION BY REFRESH) *If x is a class variable of type* $\mathsf{class}\langle\Sigma\rangle$ *and C is a class value of type* $\mathsf{class}\langle\Sigma'\rangle$ *such that* $\mathsf{class}\langle\Sigma'\rangle \sqsubseteq \mathsf{class}\langle\Sigma\rangle$, *then $[C/x]$ denotes the replacement of C' to x, where C' is obtained from C by renaming all methods belonging to $Meth(\Sigma') - Meth(\Sigma)$ with fresh names. If x is a mixin variable of type* $\mathsf{mixin}\langle\Sigma_{new}, \Sigma_{red}, \Sigma_{exp}, \Sigma_{old}\rangle$ *and M is a mixin value of type* $\mathsf{mixin}\langle\Sigma'_{new}, \Sigma'_{red}, \Sigma'_{exp}, \Sigma'_{old}\rangle$ *such that* $\mathsf{mixin}\langle\Sigma'_{new}, \Sigma'_{red}, \Sigma'_{exp}, \Sigma'_{old}\rangle \sqsubseteq \mathsf{mixin}\langle\Sigma_{new}, \Sigma_{red}, \Sigma_{exp}, \Sigma_{old}\rangle$, *then $[M/x]$ denotes the replacement of M' to x, where M' is obtained from M by renaming all methods belonging to $Meth(\Sigma'_{new}) - Meth(\Sigma_{new})$ with fresh names. In all remaining cases, substitution is intended as a standard replacement.*

With our solution, new methods added by a class or a mixin value during substitution are hidden by renaming, for each occurrence of the variable to be replaced (this is similar to the "privacy via subsumption" of [20]). Notice that we only rename methods that do not appear in the type of the variable x. This constraint ensures that the subtyping relation is preserved by the refreshed version. This basic property is necessary for proving that the substitution is type-safe (Theorem 11).

PROPERTY 1 (REFRESHING PRESERVES SUBTYPING) *Let v be a class value or a mixin value. If $\Gamma \vdash v : \tau_1$ and $\Gamma \vdash x : \tau_2$ with $\tau_1 \sqsubseteq \tau_2$, then $\Gamma \vdash [v/x] : \tau_1'$ with $\tau_1' \sqsubseteq \tau_2$.*

From the point of view of the implementation, the above treatment of "global" fresh names can be solved with static binding for the mentioned methods. The technique of using the static types of the variables and the actual types of the substituted class or mixin definitions may recall the approach of [17] of allowing overriding, i.e., dynamic binding, only for methods declared in the mixin's *inheritance interface*.

6. Depth Subtyping vs Override: Annotating Processes

Let P be a closed process to be compiled. While reconstructing the derivation of $\emptyset \vdash P : \mathsf{proc}$ (this derivation is unique, see the typing rules), it is easy to decorate any send argument occurring in P with its type. For instance, def $x = exp$ in $\mathsf{send}(x, \ell)$ has type proc, and its compiled version is def $x = exp$ in $\mathsf{send}(x^{\tau_1}, \ell)$ if exp has type τ_1.

However, this type information is not sufficient for dynamic matching, since the presence of depth subtyping conflicts with the overriding inheritance mechanism. First, we present an example (which is directly adapted from the classical one related to the object-based case of [1]). Let us consider the following expression:

$$\mathsf{receive}(x : \mathsf{class}\langle\{m : \mathsf{int}, n : \mathsf{int}\}\rangle).(\mathsf{new}\ M \diamond x) \Leftarrow m()$$

where M is a mixin redefining n with body -3. Now, receive could accept as an actual parameter a fully-fledged class $C : \mathsf{class}\langle\{m : \mathsf{int}, n : \mathsf{posint}\}\rangle$, where the actual body of m is $\log(self \Leftarrow n)$ (i.e., it invokes the sibling method n and applies the natural logarithm to the result of the invocation), since $\mathsf{posint} <: \mathsf{int}$; however, the result of the execution of $(\mathsf{new}\ M \diamond C) \Leftarrow m()$ would raise a run-time error.

To abstract away from the details of the previous example, we consider the following situation: a variable $x : \mathsf{class}\langle\{m : \tau\}\rangle$ appearing in an expression of the form $M \diamond x$ and being the argument of a receive, with M a mixin that overrides $m : \tau_1$ with $\tau_1 <: \tau$. We might substitute dynamically to such x any received class $C : \mathsf{class}\langle\{m : \tau_2\}\rangle$, with $\mathsf{class}\langle\{m : \tau_2\}\rangle \sqsubseteq \mathsf{class}\langle\{m : \tau\}\rangle$, i.e., $\tau_2 <: \tau$. We can have three cases with respect to τ_1: (*i*) $\tau_1 <: \tau_2$; (*ii*) $\tau_2 <: \tau_1$; (*iii*) τ_1 and τ_2 are not comparable. The only case that does not create problems is case (*i*).

The same problem can arise when replacing a mixin value M to a mixin variable x, e.g., in a mixin application of the shape $M_1 \diamond (x \diamond C)$. In fact, some new method m might be of type τ_2 in the (Σ_{new} of the) type of M (see ($\sqsubseteq$ *mixin*) rule in Table 6), while it is of type τ in x and redefined by M_1 as $m : \tau_1$, with $\tau_2 <: \tau$ and $\tau_1 <: \tau$. Again, $M_1 \diamond (M \diamond C)$ is well typed if and only if $\tau_1 <: \tau_2 <: \tau$.

As a consequence, the formal parameter of a receive, if it is of type "class" or "mixin", must be annotated not only with its explicit type (which acts as an upper bound for the type of the actual parameter), but also with some information about a "lower bound", such as the above $\tau_1 <: \tau_2$. This "lower bound", in general, cannot be simply another type because a "class" or "mixin" variable can appear inside a chain of mixin applications, and this may give rise to several constraints concerning several methods. Any receive's argument of type "class" or "mixin" will be then annotated with both its type and a type assertion $\mathfrak{A}$, which will contain no lower bound if the parameter does not participate in any mixin application.

The algorithm presented in Tables 7 and 8 performs all the above type annotations while checking well-typedness of processes. We remark that the preliminary version of this algorithm sketched in [6] was a restriction of the present one, since depth subtyping was only considered on classes (not on mixins).

DEFINITION 2 *A type assertion $\mathfrak{A}$ is a property of the shape $\mathfrak{A} = \mathrm{inf}(x:\tau):\Sigma'$, where τ is either a class or mixin type and:*

- *Σ' can be empty ($\Sigma' = \emptyset$);*
- *if $\tau \equiv \mathsf{class}\langle\Sigma\rangle$,*
  - *$Subj(\Sigma') \subseteq Subj(\Sigma)$;*
  - *if $m:\tau' \in \Sigma'$ then $m:\tau \in \Sigma$ with $\tau' <: \tau$, for some τ;*
- *if $\tau \equiv \mathsf{mixin}\langle\Sigma_{new}, \Sigma_{red}, \Sigma_{exp}, \Sigma_{old}\rangle$,*
  - *$Subj(\Sigma') \subseteq Subj(\Sigma_{new})$;*
  - *if $m:\tau' \in \Sigma'$ then $m:\tau \in \Sigma_{new}$ with $\tau' <: \tau$, for some τ.*

Informally speaking, Σ' acts as an "inf" for Σ (resp. Σ_{new}), since it contains lower bounds for some (possibly none) of the types associated to methods in Σ (resp. Σ_{new}). We define *label*($\mathfrak{A}$) as follows: $label(\mathrm{inf}(x:\tau):\Sigma') = x$. We define *rectype*($\mathfrak{A}$) as follows: $rectype(\mathrm{inf}(x:\mathsf{class}\langle\Sigma\rangle):\Sigma') = \Sigma$; and $rectype(\mathrm{inf}(x:\mathsf{mixin}\langle\Sigma_{new}, \Sigma_{red}, \Sigma_{exp}, \Sigma_{old}\rangle):\Sigma') = \Sigma_{new}$.

DEFINITION 3 *Let τ be a class or mixin type and $\mathfrak{A}$ be a type assertion, $\mathfrak{A} = \mathrm{inf}(x:\tau'):\Sigma'$. We say that τ* satisfies *$\mathfrak{A}$, denoted by $\tau \models \mathfrak{A}$, if and only if*

- *$\tau \sqsubseteq \tau'$;*
- *$\tau \equiv \mathsf{class}\langle\Sigma\rangle \Rightarrow \Sigma/\Sigma' :> \Sigma'$;*
- *$\tau \equiv \mathsf{mixin}\langle\Sigma_{new}, \Sigma_{red}, \Sigma_{exp}, \Sigma_{old}\rangle \Rightarrow \Sigma_{new}/\Sigma' :> \Sigma'$.*

In other words, $\mathsf{class}\langle\Sigma\rangle \models \mathrm{inf}(x:\Sigma_1):\Sigma_2$ means that Σ is a subtype of Σ_1, but for any method m such that $m:\tau \in \Sigma$ if $m:\tau_2 \in \Sigma_2$ then $\tau :> \tau_2$. Notice that if $\Sigma_2 = \emptyset$, the second condition holds trivially. For instance, the type $\tau = \mathsf{class}\langle\{m_1:\tau_1, m_2:\tau_2, m_3:\tau_3\}\rangle$ satisfies the assertion $\mathfrak{A} = \mathrm{inf}(x:\mathsf{class}\langle\{m_1:\tau_1^b, m_2:\tau_2^b\}\rangle):\{m_1:\tau_1^{red}, m_2:\tau_2^{red}\}$, provided that $\tau_1 <: \tau_1^b$ and $\tau_2 <: \tau_2^b$, and that $\tau_1^{red} <: \tau_1$ and $\tau_2^{red} <: \tau_2$. The clause on mixins is analogous, on the component Σ_{new}. We can collect assertions for several distinct variables, therefore obtaining a *type effect*.

DEFINITION 4 *A* type effect *$\mathcal{E}$ is a set, possibly empty, of type assertions $\mathcal{E} = \{\mathfrak{A}_1, \ldots, \mathfrak{A}_n\}$, where $label(\mathfrak{A}_i) \neq label(\mathfrak{A}_j)$, $1 \leq i, j \leq n$, for $i \neq j$.*

An *annotated process*, denoted by $\overline{P}$, is a process decorated by adding: (*i*) types to the arguments of its send's; (*ii*) and types and type assertions to the arguments of its receive's. The procedure for annotating processes is described in two steps. Firstly, the algorithm *Ann* is defined on SOOL expressions: $Ann(\Gamma, exp)$ returns $\langle exp, \tau, \mathcal{E}\rangle$ where τ is the type of *exp* in Γ and $\mathcal{E}$ is the derived type effect. Then, we define $Ann(\Gamma, P)$ that returns $\langle \overline{P}, \mathsf{proc}, \mathcal{E}\rangle$: $\overline{P}$ is the annotated version of P, proc means that P is well typed in Γ and $\mathcal{E}$ is a type effect. In both cases, the algorithm fails if the expression or the process are not typable, but here we do not handle failures explicitly.

$Ann(\Gamma, v)$:
  let $\tau = \Gamma(v)$ in
  if v is a variable and τ is class or mixin type then
    $\langle v, \tau, \{\mathsf{inf}(v:\tau):\emptyset\}\rangle$
  else
    $\langle v, \tau, \emptyset\rangle$

$Ann(\Gamma, \mathsf{new}\ exp)$:
  let $\langle exp, \mathsf{class}\langle\Sigma\rangle, \mathcal{E}\rangle = Ann(\Gamma, exp)$ in
    $\langle \mathsf{new}\ exp, \Sigma, \mathcal{E}\rangle$

$Ann(\Gamma, exp \Leftarrow m)$:
  let $\langle exp, \mathsf{class}\langle\{\ldots m:\tau\ldots\}\rangle, \mathcal{E}\rangle = Ann(\Gamma, exp)$ in
    $\langle exp \Leftarrow m, \tau, \mathcal{E}\rangle$

$Ann(\Gamma, v \diamond exp)$:
  let $\langle v, \mathsf{mixin}\langle\Sigma_{new}, \Sigma_{red}, \Sigma_{exp}, \Sigma_{old}\rangle, \{\mathfrak{A}\}\rangle = Ann(\Gamma, v)$ in
  let $\langle exp, \mathsf{class}\langle\Sigma_b\rangle, \mathcal{E}\rangle = Ann(\Gamma, exp)$ in
  let $\Sigma_{rest} = (\Sigma_b - (\Sigma_b/\Sigma_{exp} \cup \Sigma_b/\Sigma_{old}))$ in
  let $\Sigma_d = \Sigma_b/\Sigma_{exp} \cup \Sigma_{new} \cup \Sigma_{red} \cup \Sigma_{rest}$ in
    $\langle v \diamond exp, \mathsf{class}\langle\Sigma_d\rangle, update(\mathcal{E}, \Sigma_{red}) \cup \{\mathfrak{A}\}\rangle$

Table 7. The annotation algorithm for expressions.

The algorithm *Ann* on expressions is in Table 7 and it is defined inductively on the structure of expressions. For simplicity, we use the notation $\Gamma(v)$ to denote the type τ such that $\Gamma \vdash v:\tau$ for any value v, not only for the variables occurring in Γ. Type assertions are neither generated nor modified by class and mixin definitions. The only values affecting them are variables of class or mixin types. When the algorithm is called on a variable x of class or mixin type τ, it creates a new assertion $\mathsf{inf}(x:\tau):\emptyset$ where the lower bound for τ is temporarily empty. This lower bound will be defined by examining the possible occurrences of x inside mixin applications present in the expression. Notice that the final type effect collected by the algorithm can consist of several type assertions, since different free variables of mixin and class types can occur inside the same expression.

Cases of new *exp* and $exp \Leftarrow m$ are simple. The only interesting case concerns mixin application expressions of the shape $x \diamond exp$. In this case, $Ann(\Gamma, x \diamond exp)$ recursively calls *Ann* on x and *exp*, therefore obtaining a type assertion $\mathfrak{A}$ and a type effect $\mathcal{E}$, respectively. Let x be of type $\mathsf{mixin}\langle\Sigma_{new}, \Sigma_{red}, \Sigma_{exp}, \Sigma_{old}\rangle$. Now $\mathcal{E}$ must be firstly updated by using Σ_{red}, and then the resulting type effect must be extended with the new type assertion $\mathfrak{A}$. The first operation is performed by the function *update*, which is formally defined in Definition 5. The function $update(\mathcal{E}, \Sigma_{red})$ enriches $\mathcal{E}$ with lower bounds associated to any method $m:\tau$ belonging to Σ_{red} in the following way: (*i*) for all assertions of $\mathcal{E}$ of the shape $\mathsf{inf}(y:\mathsf{class}\langle\Sigma\rangle):\Sigma_1$, where $m \in Subj(\Sigma)$, if m has no lower bound in Σ_1, then the new lower bound $m:\tau$ is added to Σ_1; (*ii*) analogously, for assertions $\inf(y:\mathsf{mixin}\langle\Sigma'_{new},\Sigma'_{red},\Sigma'_{exp},\Sigma'_{old}\rangle):\Sigma'_1$, where $m \in Subj(\Sigma'_{new})$.

Thus, $update(\mathfrak{E},\Sigma_{red})$ defines the lower bound associated to the method name m only if a lower bound for m had not already been defined; this guarantees that the greater lower bound for any redefined method is stored in the assertion. Finally, the assertion $\mathfrak{A}$, generated by the mixin value x, is added to the result of *update*. Notice that all this is based on the fact that mixin applications are well typed, thus, if x occurs twice in the same mixin application expression, its Σ_{new} must be empty and therefore $update(\mathfrak{E},\Sigma_{red}) \cup \{\mathfrak{A}\}$ is well defined.

DEFINITION 5 *Given an effect* $\mathfrak{E}$ *and a record type* Σ', $update(\mathfrak{E},\Sigma')$ *is the type effect* $\mathfrak{E}'$ *defined as follows:*
for each assertion $\inf(x:\tau):\Sigma_1 \in \mathfrak{E}$, *let* $\Sigma = rectype(\inf(x:\tau):\Sigma_1)$;

1. *if* $Subj(\Sigma) \cap Subj(\Sigma') \neq \emptyset$ *then* $\inf(x:\tau):\Sigma_1 \cup \Sigma_2 \in \mathfrak{E}'$, *where* $\Sigma_2 = \{m_i:\tau_i \mid m_i:\tau_i \in \Sigma' \wedge m_i \notin Subj(\Sigma_1)\}$;
2. *otherwise,* $\inf(x:\tau):\Sigma_1 \in \mathfrak{E}'$.

The algorithm *Ann* for processes is in Table 8 and is defined inductively on the structure of processes or, equivalently, on typing rules for processes. The resulting $\mathfrak{E}$ will contain type assertions for all of the variables occurring in the mixin application subterms of the process. Notice that a free variable can have different occurrences in a process P, in particular, it can occur in different sub-processes, giving raise to different type effects, one for each sub-process. Thus, when *Ann* is called on the process $P_1 \mid P_2$ (on $\mathsf{def}\ x = exp\ \mathsf{in}\ P$) type effects obtained by recursive calls on P_1 and P_2 (on *exp* and P) must be merged according to the Definition 7 of *merge*. Namely, if P_1 and P_2 (*exp* and P) produce two distinct type assertions corresponding to the same variable, then the maximum lower bound for every method is collected (which always exists by well-typedness and Definitions 6 and 7).

$Ann(\Gamma,X)$:
 if $\mathsf{proc} = \Gamma(X)$ then
 $\langle X,\mathsf{proc},\emptyset\rangle$

$Ann(\Gamma,\mathsf{send}(A,\ell).P)$:
 let $\langle \overline{A},\tau,\mathfrak{E}\rangle = Ann(\Gamma,A)$ in
 let $\langle \overline{P},\mathsf{proc},\mathfrak{E}'\rangle = Ann(\Gamma,P)$ in
 $\langle \mathsf{send}(\overline{A}^{\tau},\ell).\overline{P},\mathsf{proc},merge(\mathfrak{E},\mathfrak{E}')\rangle$

$Ann(\Gamma,\mathsf{receive}(id:\tau).P)$:
 let $\langle \overline{P},\mathsf{proc},\mathfrak{E}\rangle = Ann(\Gamma\cup\{id:\tau\},P)$ in
 $\langle \mathsf{receive}(id^{\tau|(\mathfrak{E}\downarrow id)}).\overline{P},\mathsf{proc},\mathfrak{E}-(\mathfrak{E}\downarrow id)\rangle$

$Ann(\Gamma,\mathsf{def}\ x = exp\ \mathsf{in}\ P)$:
 let $\langle exp,\tau,\mathfrak{E}\rangle = Ann(\Gamma,exp)$ in
 let $\langle \overline{P},\mathsf{proc},\mathfrak{E}'\rangle = Ann(\Gamma\cup\{x:\tau\},P)$ in
 $\langle \mathsf{def}\ x = exp\ \mathsf{in}\ \overline{P},\mathsf{proc},merge(\mathfrak{E},\mathfrak{E}')\rangle$

$Ann(\Gamma,P_1 \mid P_2)$:
 let $\langle \overline{P_1},\mathsf{proc},\mathfrak{E}_1\rangle = Ann(\Gamma,P_1)$ in
 let $\langle \overline{P_2},\mathsf{proc},\mathfrak{E}_2\rangle = Ann(\Gamma,P_2)$ in
 $\langle \overline{P_1} \mid \overline{P_2},\mathsf{proc},merge(\mathfrak{E}_1,\mathfrak{E}_2)\rangle$

Table 8. The annotation algorithm for processes.

When *Ann* is called on a $\mathsf{send}(A,\ell).P$, the argument A is annotated with its type, while the effect generated by A is merged with the one collected when annotating the continuation P. When *Ann* is called on $\mathsf{receive}(id:\tau).P$, the variable *id* is annotated with its type τ and with the assertion on the subject *id* that is possibly generated during the recursive call of *Ann* on the continuation P ($\mathcal{E} \downarrow id$ is $\inf(id:\tau):\Sigma$ if $\inf(id:\tau):\Sigma \in \mathcal{E}$, and $\emptyset$ otherwise). Since receive is a binder for *id*, it makes sense to discard the assertions for *id* from the type effect ($\mathcal{E} - (\mathcal{E} \downarrow id)$) after annotating the receive, thus the final $\mathcal{E}$ is empty when starting from a closed P.

In the following we define formally the function *merge* that takes two type effects and builds a new type effect.

DEFINITION 6 *Given the types* τ, τ_1 *and* τ_2 *we define*

$$\tau_1 \sqcap_\tau \tau_2 = \begin{cases} \max(\tau_1,\tau_2) & \text{if } \tau_1 \text{ and } \tau_2 \text{ are comparable} \\ \tau & \text{otherwise} \end{cases}$$

DEFINITION 7 *Given two type effects* $\mathcal{E}_1$ *and* $\mathcal{E}_2$, $merge(\mathcal{E}_1,\mathcal{E}_2) = \mathcal{E}$, *where* $\mathcal{E}$ *is defined as follows:*

- *for all* $\mathfrak{A}_i \in \mathcal{E}_1$,
  - *if* $label(\mathfrak{A}_i) \neq label(\mathfrak{A}_j)$ *for all* $\mathfrak{A}_j \in \mathcal{E}_2$, *then* $\mathfrak{A}_i \in \mathcal{E}$,
  - *else if* $label(\mathfrak{A}_i) = label(\mathfrak{A}_j)$ *for some* $\mathfrak{A}_j \in \mathcal{E}_2$, *let* $\mathfrak{A}_i = \inf(x:\tau):\Sigma_i$, $\mathfrak{A}_j = \inf(x:\tau):\Sigma_j$ *and* $\Sigma = rectype(\mathfrak{A}_i) = rectype(\mathfrak{A}_j)$, *then* $\mathfrak{A}' \in \mathcal{E}$ *where:*

$$\begin{aligned} \mathfrak{A}' &= \inf(x:\tau):\Sigma' \text{ and} \\ \Sigma' &= (\Sigma_i - \Sigma_j) \cup (\Sigma_j - \Sigma_i) \cup \\ &\quad \{m:\tau' \mid m:\tau \in \Sigma, m:\tau_i \in \Sigma_i, m:\tau_j \in \Sigma_j, \tau' = \tau_i \sqcap_\tau \tau_j\}; \end{aligned}$$

- *for all* $\mathfrak{A}_k \in \mathcal{E}_2$ *such that* $label(\mathfrak{A}_k) \neq label(\mathfrak{A}_i)$, *for all* $\mathfrak{A}_i \in \mathcal{E}_1$, *then* $\mathfrak{A}_k \in \mathcal{E}$.

A key property of *merge* is its *monotonicity*: merging two type effects never decreases the inf associated to variables' types.

THEOREM 8 (SOUNDNESS OF THE ANNOTATION ALGORITHM) *If* $Ann(\Gamma,P) = \langle \overline{P}, \mathsf{proc}, \mathcal{E}\rangle$ *then*

i) $\Gamma \vdash P:\mathsf{proc}$;

ii) *for any free variable x of class or mixin type occurring in P, then there is one and only one type assertion* $\mathfrak{A} \in \mathcal{E}$, *of the shape* $\inf(x:\tau):\Sigma'$, *such that:*

   (a) (correctness of lower bounds) $\mathfrak{A}$ *is well defined (according to Definition 2);*

   (b) (completeness of lower bounds) *for each* $m:\tau' \in \Sigma'$, *m is redefined by a mixin in some mixin application expression occurring in P and for each such redefinition* $m:\tau''$ *we have that* $\tau'' <: \tau'$.

COROLLARY 9 *For any well-typed closed process P,* $P \equiv \mathsf{receive}(x:\tau).P'$ ($P \equiv \mathsf{send}(A,\ell).P'$), *its compiled version* $\overline{P}$ *is of the form* $\overline{P} \equiv \mathsf{receive}(x^{\tau|\mathfrak{A}}).\overline{P'}$ ($\overline{P} \equiv \mathsf{send}(\overline{A}^{\tau},\ell).\overline{P'}$), *where* $\mathfrak{A}$ *is correct and complete w.r.t. the occurrences of x in* P' (*A is of type* τ).

LEMMA 10 (SUBSTITUTION FOR EXPRESSIONS) *Let v and exp be an object-oriented value and an object-oriented expression, respectively. If* $\Gamma, x:\tau_1 \vdash exp:\tau$

and $\Gamma \vdash v : \tau_2$*, then* $\Gamma \vdash exp[v/x] : \tau'$*, provided that the following condition* (COND) *is satisfied:*

- *if* τ_1 *is a mixin or class type: if* $Ann(\Gamma, x : \tau_1, exp) = \langle exp, \tau, \mathcal{E} \rangle$ *and there is an assertion* $\mathfrak{A} \in \mathcal{E}$ *such that* $label(\mathfrak{A}) = x$*, then* $\tau_2 \models \mathfrak{A}$*;*
- *otherwise:* $\tau_2 <: \tau_1$.

THEOREM 11 (SUBSTITUTION FOR PROCESSES) *Let v, exp and P be an object-oriented value, an object-oriented expression and a process, respectively. If* $\Gamma, x : \tau_1 \vdash P : \mathsf{proc}$ *and* $\Gamma \vdash v : \tau_2$*, then* $\Gamma \vdash P[v/x] : \mathsf{proc}$*, provided that the following condition* (COND) *is satisfied:*

- *if* τ_1 *is a mixin or class type: if* $Ann(\Gamma, x : \tau_1, P) = \langle \overline{P}, \mathsf{proc}, \mathcal{E} \rangle$ *and there is an assertion* $\mathfrak{A} \in \mathcal{E}$ *such that* $label(\mathfrak{A}) = x$*, then* $\tau_2 \models \mathfrak{A}$*;*
- *otherwise:* $\tau_2 <: \tau_1$.

7. Operational Semantics

The operational semantics of MOMI groups two sets of rules. The first one describes how to evaluate SOOL object-oriented expressions and is denoted by $\twoheadrightarrow$. We omit it here since it is standard. The second set of rules, presented in Table 9, describes the evolution of a net. It is based on a standard structural congruence $\equiv$, defined as the least congruence relation closed under the following rules:

$$N_1 \parallel N_2 = N_2 \parallel N_1 \qquad (N_1 \parallel N_2) \parallel N_3 = N_1 \parallel (N_2 \parallel N_3)$$
$$\ell :: \overline{P} = \ell :: \overline{P} \mid \mathbf{nil} \qquad \ell :: (\overline{P_1} \mid \overline{P_2}) = \ell :: \overline{P_1} \parallel \ell :: \overline{P_2}$$

Notice that the semantics is defined on annotated (compiled) processes $\overline{P}$. Actions send and receive synchronize only if the type of the delivered expression *matches* the one expected according to the following matching predicate:

$$match_{\mathfrak{A}}(\tau_1, \tau_2) = \begin{cases} \tau_1 \models \mathfrak{A} & \text{if } \tau_1 \text{ and } \tau_2 \text{ are class or mixin types} \\ \tau_1 <: \tau_2 & \text{otherwise} \end{cases}$$

The type τ_1 of the send's argument A is built statically by the annotation algorithm. The (*comm*) rule uses this type information, delivered together with the argument A, in order to check dynamically that the received item is correct with respect to the formal argument. The other rules are straightforward.

Assuming that types are preserved under $\twoheadrightarrow$, a subject-reduction property is proved by using Theorem 11, that deals with the crucial case of rule (*comm*). Then, the subject reduction property extends easily to a global type safety for nets, where a net N is *well typed* if and only if for any node $\ell :: \overline{P}$ in N, $\Gamma \vdash P : \mathsf{proc}$ for some Γ. Finally, the theorem below guarantees that merging (well-typed) code received from a remote site into local (well-typed) code does not harm local type safety.

THEOREM 12 (SUBJECT REDUCTION) *If* N *is well typed and* $N \rightarrowtail N'$*, then* N' *is well typed.*

$$\frac{match_{\mathfrak{A}}(\tau_1,\tau_2)}{\ell_1 :: \mathsf{send}(\overline{A}^{\tau_1},\ell_2).\overline{P'} \parallel \ell_2 :: \mathsf{receive}(id^{\tau_2|\mathfrak{A}}).\overline{Q} \rightarrowtail \ell_1 :: \overline{P'} \parallel \ell_2 :: \overline{Q}[\overline{A}^{\tau_1}/id]}\ (comm)$$

$$\frac{exp \twoheadrightarrow v}{\ell :: \mathsf{def}\ x = exp\ \mathsf{in}\ \overline{P} \rightarrowtail \ell :: \overline{P}[v/x]}\ (def)$$

$$\frac{N_1 \rightarrowtail N_1'}{N_1 \parallel N \rightarrowtail N_1' \parallel N}\ (par) \qquad \frac{N \equiv N_1 \quad N_1 \rightarrowtail N_2 \quad N_2 \equiv N'}{N \rightarrowtail N'}\ (net)$$

Table 9. Net and process operational semantics.

The dynamic checking during communication is the only dynamic use of types: it consists essentially in checking some subtyping relations between record, class or mixin types, which is of linear complexity on the argument types. The type analysis of processes remains totally static and performed in each site independently.

Let us go back to the example of the beginning of Section 6. The annotated versions of those processes are:
$\ell_1 :: \mathsf{send}(C^{\tau'},\ell_2)$, where $\tau' = \mathsf{class}\langle\{m:\mathsf{int}, n:\mathsf{posint}\}\rangle$, and
$\ell_2 :: \mathsf{receive}(x^{\tau \mid \mathsf{inf}(x:\tau):\{n:\mathsf{int}\}}).(\mathsf{new}\ M \diamond x) \Leftarrow m()$,
where $\tau = \mathsf{class}\langle\{m:\mathsf{int}, n:\mathsf{int}\}\rangle$.
The communication between ℓ_1 and ℓ_2 cannot take place because $\tau' \not\models \mathsf{inf}(x:\tau):\{n:\mathsf{int}\}$. In fact, $\tau' \sqsubseteq \tau$, but $\{n:\mathsf{int}\} \not<: \{m:\mathsf{int}, n:\mathsf{posint}\}/\{n:\mathsf{int}\}$.

8. Conclusions

We introduced a safe form of subtyping on classes and mixins, by offering a general and comprehensive solution both to "width subtyping versus addition" and "depth subtyping versus override" conflicts. Correctness is guaranteed by our renaming, to take care of name clashes, and by our constraints, to avoid accepting code that create override conflicts. The solution for the width-subtyping-related problem is the formal counter-part of classical implementation techniques to avoid name-clashes. The solution for the depth-subtyping-related problem is, at the best of our knowledge, the first proposal in the literature to solve such problem, and it is based on the simple observation that a method body cannot be overridden by a body whose type is bigger with respect to subtyping, i.e., is "less good".

Some future research directions look interesting: (*i*) to introduce *higher-order mixins* and *mixin composition* as presented in [17]; (*ii*) to replace structural subtyping with a form of nominal subtyping; (*iii*) to explore the possibility of applying a form of our "safe subtyping" to typed *traits* [21, 16].

In the literature, there are some proposals of combining objects with processes and/or mobile agents, such as, e.g., [13, 12]. Our approach is, however, more related to works as [22], where properties of distributed systems are enforced by a typing system equipped with subtyping. In our case the property we address is a flexible and type-safe coordination for exchanging code among processes.

Concerning the applicability of MoMi's approach, in [7] we presented O'Klaim, a mixin-oriented version of Klaim. A prototype implementation of O'Klaim is presented in [4] and freely available at `http://music.dsi.unifi.it`. This is based on the Java package `momi` [3], that implements the run-time system (or the virtual machine) for MoMi classes, mixins and objects. Code exchange in O'KLAIM exploits width subtyping only. An extended version of O'KLAIM (and relative implementation), including the annotation algorithm for dealing with depth subtyping, is work-in-progress.

References

[1] M. Abadi and L. Cardelli. *A Theory of Objects*. Springer, 1996.

[2] D. Ancona, G. Lagorio, and E. Zucca. Jam - A Smooth Extension of Java with Mixins. In *Proc. of ECOOP'00*, volume 1850 of *LNCS*, pages 145–178, 2000.

[3] L. Bettini. A Java package for class and mixin mobility in a distributed setting. In *Proc. of FIDJI'03*, volume 2952 of *LNCS*, pages 12–22. Springer-Verlag, 2003.

[4] L. Bettini. *Linguistic Constructs for Object-Oriented Mobile Code Programming & their Implementations*. PhD thesis, Dip. di Matematica, Università di Siena, 2003. Available at `http://music.dsi.unifi.it`.

[5] L. Bettini, V. Bono, and B. Venneri. Coordinating Mobile Object-Oriented Code. In *Proc. of Coordination*, volume 2315 of *LNCS*, pages 56–71. Springer, 2002.

[6] L. Bettini, V. Bono, and B. Venneri. Subtyping Mobile Classes and Mixins. In *Proc. of FOOL 10*, 2003.

[7] L. Bettini, V. Bono, and B. Venneri. O'KLAIM: a coordination language with mobile mixins. In *Proc. of Coordination*, volume 2949 of *LNCS*, pages 20–37. Springer, 2004.

[8] V. Bono and L. Liquori. A Subtyping for the Fisher-Honsell-Mitchell Lambda Calculus of Objects. In *Proc. of CSL'94*, volume 933 of *LNCS*, pages 16–30. Springer-Verlag, 1995.

[9] V. Bono, A. Patel, and V. Shmatikov. A Core Calculus of Classes and Mixins. In *Proc. of ECOOP'99*, volume 1628 of *LNCS*, pages 43–66. Springer-Verlag, 1999.

[10] G. Bracha and W. Cook. Mixin-based inheritance. In *Proc. of OOPSLA '90*, pages 303–311. ACM, 1990.

[11] K. Bruce. *Foundations of Object-Oriented Languages – Types and Semantics*. The MIT Press, 2002.

[12] M. Bugliesi, S. Crafa, and G. Castagna. Typed Mobile Objects. In *Proc. of CONCUR'00*, volume 1877 of *LNCS*, pages 504–520. Springer-Verlag, 2000.

[13] L. Cardelli. A Language with Distributed Scope. *Computing Systems*, 8(1):27–59, 1995.

[14] R. De Nicola, G. Ferrari, and R. Pugliese. KLAIM: a Kernel Language for Agents Interaction and Mobility. *IEEE Transactions on Software Engineering*, 24(5):315–330, 1998.

[15] K. Fisher and J. C. Mitchell. A Delegation-based Object Calculus with Subtyping. In *Proc. of FCT'95*, volume 965 of *LNCS*, pages 42–61. Springer-Verlag, 1995.

[16] K. Fisher and J. Reppy. A typed calculus of traits. In *FOOL 11*, 2004.

[17] M. Flatt, S. Krishnamurthi, and M. Felleisen. Classes and mixins. In *Proc. of POPL '98*, pages 171–183. ACM, 1998.

[18] R. Milner. *Communication and Concurrency*. Prentice Hall, 1989.

[19] B. C. Pierce. *Types and Programming Languages*. The MIT Press, 2002.

[20] J. Riecke and C. Stone. Privacy via Subsumption. *Information and Computation*, 172:2–28, 2002.

[21] N. Schärli, S. Ducasse, O. Nierstrasz, and A. Black. Traits: Composable units of behaviour. In *Proc. of ECOOP 2003*, volume 2743 of *LNCS*, pages 248–274. Springer, 2003.

[22] N. Yoshida and M. Hennessy. Subtyping and Locality in Distributed Higher Order Mobile Processes (extended abstract). In *Proc. of CONCUR'99*, volume 1664 of *LNCS*, pages 557–572. Springer-Verlag, 1999.

ASYMPTOTIC BEHAVIORS OF TYPE-2 ALGORITHMS AND INDUCED BAIRE TOPOLOGIES*

Chung-Chih Li
Computer Science Department
Lamar University
Beaumont, Texas, USA
licc@hal.lamar.edu

Abstract We propose an alternative notion of asymptotic behaviors for the study of type-2 computational complexity. Since the classical asymptotic notion (*for all but finitely many*) is not acceptable in type-2 context, we alter the notion of "small sets" from "finiteness" to topological "compactness" for type-2 complexity theory. A natural reference for type-2 computations is the standard Baire topology. However, we point out some serious drawbacks of this and introduce an alternative topology for describing compact sets. Following our notion explicit type-2 complexity classes can be defined in terms of resource bounds. We show that such complexity classes are recursively representable; namely, every complexity class has a programming system. We also prove type-2 analogs of Rabin's Theorem, Recursive Relatedness Theorem, and Gap Theorem to provide evidence that our notion of type-2 asymptotic is workable. We speculate that our investigation will give rise to a possible approach in examining the complexity structure at type-2 along the line of the classical complexity theory.

Keywords: Type-2 Complexity, Type-2 Asymptotic Notation, Baire Topology.

1. Introduction

A key notion involved in defining the complexity of a problem is the use of "finiteness". We say that, function f is asymptotically bounded by g if and only if *for all but finitely many* $x \in \mathbf{N}$ such that $f(x) \leq g(x)$. Namely,

$$f \leq^* g \quad \Longleftrightarrow \quad \exists x_0 \in \mathbf{N} \forall x \in \mathbf{N}[x > x_0 \Rightarrow f(x) \leq g(x)]. \tag{1}$$

* A full version with detailed proofs of the theorems in this paper is available at
`http://hal.lamar.edu/~licc/T2Asy/Full_T2AsyTCS2004.pdf`

Based on the notion above, Hartmanis and Stearns [8] gave the very first precise definition for explicit complexity classes in the following form:

$$\mathbf{C}(t) = \{\varphi_e \mid \Phi_e \leq^* t\}, \tag{2}$$

where t is a computable function and $\langle\varphi_i\rangle_{i\in\mathbf{N}}$ is an *acceptable programming system* [18] with a *complexity measure* $\langle\Phi_i\rangle_{i\in\mathbf{N}}$ associated to it [2]. The use of $\leq^*$ can also be found elsewhere, e.g., the asymptotic notations (Θ, Ω, O) in algorithm analysis. The most important consequence of using asymptotic notations, in our opinion, is not only that we can significantly simplify our notations, but that it is an indispensable tool in the theoretical study of computational complexity. Almost all nontrivial complexity theorems at the center of classical complexity theory such as the Speedup Theorem [2, 24], the Union Theorem [13], the Gap Theorem [3, 5, 24], the Compression Theorem [2], the Honesty Theorem [13], and so on (see [20] for more), are all proven by a mathematical technique called *priority method*. The method argues that the required properties (behaviors) of a required program will be fulfilled eventually in the process of its construction. In other words, we allow some finitely many violations. Likewise, the *recursive relatedness theorem* [2] is also proven based on the notion of asymptotic behaviors, which is the foundation for lifting different complexity measures into a certain degree of abstraction such as the two machine independent axioms proposed by Blum [2]. It is worth to note that the asymptotic notation is not arbitrary. Instead, it is justified by a fact that any program can be patched on some finitely many inputs by using a finite table to avoid expensive computations on those particular inputs. Thus, theoretically, we can use $\leq$ and $\leq^*$ in (2) alternatively without changing the underlying complexity structure of computable functions[1].

When we shift our attention to higher ordered computation (in particular, type-2 computation), which in many cases seems to be a better computing model for many contemporary computing problems, we soon realize that there is no general complexity theory to unify results from different approaches. A primary reason is that we do not have a reasonable notion of higher ordered asymptotic behaviors as the one involved in (2). The direct use of "for all but finitely many" in type-2 computation is not acceptable, because we cannot patch a type-2 program on a function input in general. Consequently, many techniques used in the proofs of classical complexity theorems are not applicable in type-2 context. Therefore, the present paper is intended to provide a robust notion of type-2 asymptotic behaviors so that the classical complexity theory can be advanced into type-2. Since any machine model for computation beyond type-2 seems inconceivable by intuitions, we thus focus on type-2 computation which can be intuitively modelled by the antiquity – Oracle Turing Machine (see [7] for conventions).

Notations: A type-0 object is simply a natural number. A type-1 object is a function over natural numbers. A type-2 object is a *functional* that takes and produces type-1 objects. By convention, we consider type-0 $\subset$ type-1 $\subset$ type-2. We are only interested

[1] In fact, this is an overstatement. Here we overlook the honesty property of t, which is a necessary condition for the statement. Nevertheless, the honesty condition is rather weak for most reasonable resource bounds.

in total functions, $\mathbf{N} \to \mathbf{N}$, when they are taken as inputs of functionals. For convenience, we use $\mathcal{T}$ to denote the set of total functions and $\mathcal{P}$ to denote the set of partial functions. Note that functions in $\mathcal{T}$ or $\mathcal{P}$ may not be computable. Also, we use $\mathcal{F}$ to denote the set of *finite* functions, which means $\sigma \in \mathcal{F}$ if and only if $\mathrm{dom}(\sigma) \subset \mathbf{N}$ and $\mathrm{card}(\sigma) \in \mathbf{N}$. We fix a canonical indexing for $\mathcal{F}$, and hence we are free to treat any function in $\mathcal{F}$ as a number so it can be taken as the input of a type-1 function. Unless stated otherwise, we let a, b, x, y, z range over $\mathbf{N}$, f, g, h range over $\mathcal{T}$, and F, G, H range over type-2 functionals. Here we consider some examples of type-2 functionals: $F(f,x) = f(x)$; $G(f,x) = f(f(x))$; $H(f,x) = \sum_{i=0}^{x} f(i)$; $\Gamma(f) = f \circ f$, where $\circ$ is function composition. Clearly, F, G, and H are type-2 functionals of type $\mathcal{T} \times \mathbf{N} \to \mathbf{N}$, and Γ is a type-2 functional of type $\mathcal{T} \to \mathcal{T}$. With λ-abstraction, we have $\Gamma(f) = \lambda x G(f,x)$. Since some complexity properties at type-2 can be easily proven by the same tricks used in the original proofs, we therefore keep a type-0 input in order to take this advantage. We also note that $\mathcal{T} \cong \mathcal{T} \times \mathbf{N}$ via, for example, $f \mapsto (f', f(0))$, where $f'(x) = f(x+1)$. Thus, we do not lose generality when we restrict type-2 functionals to our standard type $\mathcal{T} \times \mathbf{N} \rightharpoonup \mathbf{N}$.

Although the type-1 input itself is an infinite object in general, we observe that only a finite part of it is needed for any terminating computation. This is a trivial application of the following theorem due to Uspenskii [23] and Nerode [14]: *A functional F is continuous if and only if F is compact and monotone.* Compactness and monotonicity are defined as follows.

DEFINITION 1 *Let* $F : (\mathbf{N} \rightharpoonup \mathbf{N}) \times \mathbf{N} \rightharpoonup \mathbf{N}$. *We say that:*

(i) F is **compact** *if and only if*

$$\forall (f,x) \in (\mathbf{N} \rightharpoonup \mathbf{N}) \times \mathbf{N}\, \exists \sigma \in \mathcal{F}\, \left[F(f,x) = F(\sigma,x)\right].$$

(ii) F is **monotone** *if and only if*

$$\forall (\sigma,x) \in \mathcal{F} \times \mathbf{N}\, \left[F(\sigma,x)\downarrow \Rightarrow \forall \tau \supseteq \sigma (F(\tau,x)\downarrow = F(\sigma,x))\right].$$

Compactness and monotonicity are the key properties of computable functionals in defining our topologies for the concerned computation. We take Oracle Turing Machines (OTM here after) as our formal type-2 computing device, where the oracle is extended from a set-oracle to a function-oracle. Thus, by a *computable functional*, we mean a functional that can be computed by some OTM, where the type-1 input will be prepared as an oracle attached to the machine. Clearly, every computable functional is continuous [18]. As for classical Turing Machines, we can fix a programming system $\langle \widehat{\varphi} \rangle_{i \in \mathbf{N}}$ associated with a complexity measure $\langle \widehat{\Phi} \rangle_{i \in \mathbf{N}}$ (say, the number of steps performed) for OTM's. Blum's two axioms can be used directly without any modification. However, having Blum's axioms for type-2 complexity measures does not mean a general complexity theory immediately follows. A workable notion of type-2 asymptotic behaviors indeed is the missing part of the current type-2 complexity theory.

2. An Outlook of Present Complexity Theory at Type-2

Cook and Kapron defined *second-order polynomials* [9] in order to characterize the set of type-2 Basic Feasible Functionals (BFF here after) [6]. Their framework requires a rather artificial function called the *length function*, which is served as the type-2 analog of $|x|$, where $|x|$ is the length of the bit string representing $x \in \mathbf{N}$. For $f \in \mathcal{T}$, the length function of f is defined by

$$|f| = \lambda n.\max(\{\ell \,:\, \ell = |f(x)| \text{ and } |x| \leq n\}).$$

Thus, $|f|(n)$ is the maximum length of the values of f on input with length $\leq n$. BFF, to some degree, is seen as the type-2 analog of **P**. Inside BFF, how conceivable is the use of second-order polynomials together with the length functions? We present an easy example to show that some results may drift away from our intuition. Consider

$$\begin{aligned} F(f,x) &= \; 2^{\max\{f(2^{|x|}), f(2^{|x|}-1), \ldots, f(2^{|x|}-(|x|-1))\}}; \\ G(f,x) &= \begin{cases} 2^{2^{1000}} & \text{if } x = 0 \text{ and } f(2^{|x|}) = 0; \\ 2^{\min\{f(2^{|x|}), f(2^{|x|}-1), \ldots, f(2^{|x|}-(|x|-1))\}} & \text{otherwise.} \end{cases} \end{aligned} \tag{3}$$

Let $\widehat{\Phi}_F$ and $\widehat{\Phi}_G$ denote their cost functions (e.g., numbers of steps performed). We observe that the major cost of computing the two functionals is querying the oracle. For each query q, at least $O(|q| + |f(q)|)$ steps are needed (for placing the query and reading the answer). Thus, the max and min functions above need $|x|$ many queries and each query need $O(|x| + |f(2^{|x|})|)$ steps. In terms of length functions, both functionals are bounded by $O(|x| \times (|x| + |f|(|x|))$, and hence by a second-order polynomial p defined as $p(\ell, x) = c(x^2 + x \cdot \ell(x))$, where $c \in \mathbf{N}$. However, we also observe that, unless $x = f(2^{|x|}) = 0$, we have $\widehat{\Phi}_G(f,x) \leq \widehat{\Phi}_F(f,x)$. In other words, in *most cases* we have $\widehat{\Phi}_G(f,x) \leq \widehat{\Phi}_F(f,x)$, but we have difficulty to describe this situation in terms of second-order polynomials and length functions. What should be a formal and satisfactory notion of "most cases"? How do we formalize the concept of "most cases" so that we can forgive a "few" "affordable" exceptional cases? On what ground we can justify our intuition that G is easier than F?

For a general type-2 complexity theory to begin with, arguably, we need to have a robust notion of type-2 complexity classes along the line of Hartmanis and Stearns' definition as shown in (2). Here we consider Kapron and Cook's setting again as their work currently seems to be the most suitable framework for the study of type-2 complexity classes in terms of explicit bounds.[2] A type-2 complexity class determined by a second-order polynomial p can be formulated as follows,

$$\mathbf{C}(p) = \left\{\widehat{\varphi}_e \mid \forall (f,x) \in \mathcal{T} \times \mathbf{N} \left[\widehat{\Phi}_e(f,x) \leq p(|f|,|x|)\right]\right\}. \tag{4}$$

In [21] Seth also suggested a type-2 complexity class similar to (4) where p was extended to any type-2 computable functional. Seth speculated that some classical complexity results such as the Gap theorem and the Union theorem may be proven. However, we are skeptical about this because we notice that there is no notion of asymptotic behaviors involved in (4) and, as we mentioned earlier, the original proofs

[2] Another line for the study of higher-order complexity theory is *Implicit Computational Complexity*; no explicit resource bounds are used to name higher-order complexity classes.

of the two theorems rely on *priority arguments* in which some violations need to be tolerated. In fact, we suspect that it is impossible to prove any nontrivial complexity theorems without such tolerance.

An immediate idea is to keep the same notion of $\leq^*$ and implant it in (4) directly. However, this is problematic, because there is no corresponding Church-Turing thesis at type-2. In other words, there is no effective way to patch a program on finitely many type-1 inputs (because some of them may not be computable).

Another way to get around the problem is to consider only "seen computation". As a matter of fact, all terminating computations are finite and countable. Based on this observation, in early 70's Symes [22] presented an axiomatic approach for type-2 complexity theory. The axiomatic system was modified from Blum's. Symes required a computation (represented by a computation tree) of the concerned type-2 functionals to be explicitly provided as an input. The machine will be shut down if the provided computation is not consistent with the "actual" computation of the machine. In his proofs, $\leq^*$ was used as the context: "for all but finitely many computations". This seems to be a reasonable setup in a sense that, for every computable type-2 functionals F and G, we consider F almost-everywhere less than G (i.e., $F \leq^* G$) if there are only finitely many computations of F and G resulting in $F > G$. However, the setup is too remote for practice. No one can provide a computation tree before the computation begins. All we can do is to enumerate all possible computations only for theoretical investigation.

In the following section we introduce a new idea to define a workable type-2 almost-everywhere relation, $\leq_2^*$. As "compact" used in topology to some extent is considered as a surrogate for "finite" and "small" and "computable", our investigation begins with a study on the close relation between topology and type-2 computation.

3. Topologies and Type-2 Computation

Notations:. Let $\mathbb{N}$ be the discrete topology on $\mathbf{N}$. The space $\mathcal{T}$ is called Baire space. The Baire topology [1, 15, 18] is denoted by $\mathbb{T}$, in which a basic open set is the set of all total extensions of some finite function. Let $\mathbb{T} \times \mathbb{N}$ denote the product topology of $\mathbb{T}$ and $\mathbb{N}$. Given $F, G : \mathcal{T} \times \mathbf{N} \rightharpoonup \mathbf{N}$, we use $X_{[F \leq G]} \subseteq \mathcal{T} \times \mathbf{N}$ to denote the set $\{(f,x) | F(f,x) \leq G(f,x)\}$. Similarly, $X_{[F=X]}, X_{[F>G]}$ will be used in the same way. A type-2 functional F is said to be computable if there is an OTM with index e that computes F (i.e., $F = \widehat{\varphi}_e$). For $F, G : \mathcal{T} \times \mathbf{N} \rightharpoonup \mathbf{N}$, a straightforward analog of $\leq^*$ would be:

$$\text{"For all but finitely many } (f,x),\ F(f,x) \leq G(f,x)\text{."} \tag{5}$$

However, as we pointed out earlier, (5) is too restrictive, because in general there is no terminating computation that can recognize finitely many (f,x)'s. Thus, if we are interested in computable functionals, a better notion of $F \leq^* G$ would be something like: *"For all but finitely many computations of F and G, the result of F is less than or equal to the result of G."* This in fact is Symes' idea. We put the subscript "$_2$" in $\leq_2^*$ to reflect the type of its operands. We will use "computation" to mean "terminating computation" for the time being. A computation of a computable functional is simply a branch with finite length of its computation tree. We first state two naive objectives for an *ideal* type-2 almost-everywhere relation to achieve.

Goal 1: OTM's for F and G, respectively, such that, there are only finitely many computations of the two OTM's resulting in values such that $F > G$.

Goal 2: The type-2 relation $\leq_2^*$ should be *transitive*.

In type-1, the two objectives are rather trivial. Nevertheless, the first one assures that we can patch a program, and the second one assures that we do not lose any functions from a complexity class by increasing the resource bound. For the obvious reason, we want to preserve the two properties at type-2. Unfortunately, the two properties conflict; they hurt each other. In the end, we give up transitivity, which does not seem too essential to our primary purpose: a workable notion of type-2 asymptotic behaviors for proving theorems. The following standard theorem hints a possible way to formalize "$\leq_2^*$".

THEOREM 2 *Let $\widehat{\varphi}_e$ be total and let $S \subset \mathcal{T} \times \mathbf{N}$. If S is compact in $\mathbb{T} \times \mathbb{N}$, then there are only finitely many computations of $\widehat{\varphi}_e$ on S.* □

Thus, it seems reasonable to formalize our notion as follows: $F \leq_2^+ G$ if and only if there is a set X such that, X is $(\mathbb{T} \times \mathbb{N})$-compact and for all $(f, x) \in (\mathcal{T} \times \mathbf{N} - X)$ we have $F(f, x) \leq G(f, x)$. We restate this in the following definition.

DEFINITION 3 *Let $F, G : \mathcal{T} \times \mathbf{N} \rightharpoonup \mathbf{N}$. $F \leq_2^+ G$ if and only if $X_{[F \leq G]}$ is co-compact in $\mathbb{T} \times \mathbb{N}$.*

We change the superscript to "$+$" to reflect the conclusion we will discuss in a moment that this definition is too strong for our purposes. Nevertheless, the following theorem shows that relation $\leq_2^+$ meets our Goal 2.

THEOREM 4 *Relation $\leq_2^+$ is transitive over type-2 continuous functionals.* □

A standard property of Baire topology says that, if S is compact, then the image of any continuous functional on S is also compact. Also, every compact set in $\mathbb{N}$ is finite. We have the following corollary.

COROLLARY 5 *If F and G are continuous and $F \leq_2^+ G$, then there exists $c \in \mathbf{N}$ such that, for every $(f, x) \in \mathcal{T} \times \mathbf{N}$, $F(f, x) \leq G(f, x) + c$.* □

Thus, if $F \leq_2^+ G$, then adding some constant value c to G allows us to bound F everywhere. If we consider G as some sort of resource bound, we speculate that a constant or *linear speedup theorem* may be proven. In other words, we can patch the program for F to remove the extra constant cost c. Comparing to (1), the similarity between $f \leq^* g$ and $F \leq_2^+ G$ can be easily seen:

$$F \leq_2^+ G \iff \exists f_0 \in \mathcal{T} \exists x_0 \in \mathbf{N} \forall f \in \mathcal{T} \forall x \in \mathbf{N} \; [(f > f_0) \vee (x > x_0) \Rightarrow F(f, x) \leq G(f, x)].$$

This suggests that Definition 3 might be a right choice. However, $\leq_2^+$ has a fatal problem that discourages us to move any further. We show that $\leq_2^+$ in fact is an empty notion and any possible definition for type-2 asymptotic behaviors based on $\leq_2^+$ will not give any flexibility.

THEOREM 6 *Let $F, G : \mathcal{T} \times \mathbf{N} \to \mathbf{N}$ be continuous. $F \leq_2^+ G$ if and only if $X_{[F>G]} = \emptyset$.*

Sketch of Proof: The proof is an application of the Uspenskii-Nerode theorem that every continuous functional must be *compact* [15]. Thus, if $X_{[F>G]}$ is not empty, it must be $(\mathbb{T} \times \mathbb{N})$-open. But the only set in $\mathbb{T} \times \mathbb{N}$ that is both open and compact is the empty set. Therefore, if $X_{[F>G]}$ is not empty, it can't be compact in $\mathbb{T} \times \mathbb{N}$. □

To fix this problem, we need a topology that can provide enough compact sets for describing "small" sets. In other words, a coarser topology is needed.

4. Type-2 Almost-Everywhere Relations

In this section we define a class of topologies determined by the functionals involved in the relations. These topologies are induced from the Baire topology. On the one hand, the induced topology must be coarse enough so that the compact sets are not necessarily trivial. On the other hand, the induced topology must be fine enough so that we can differentiate two computations in terms of their type-1 inputs. Also, the formalization of the almost-everywhere relation should catch the intuitive idea stated in previous sections. Unfortunately, the two goals proposed in Section 3 are difficult to achieve at the same time. In the end, we give up transitivity in order to have a workable notion of type-2 asymptotic behaviors. Let $F(f,x)\downarrow= y$ denote the case that F is defined on (f,x) and its value is y.

DEFINITION 7 *Let $F : \mathcal{T} \times \mathbf{N} \to \mathbf{N}$ and $(\sigma, x) \in \mathcal{F} \times \mathbf{N}$. We say that (σ, x) is a **locking fragment** of F if and only if*

$$\exists y \in \mathbf{N}\, \forall f \in \mathcal{T} \left[\sigma \subset f \Rightarrow F(f,x)\downarrow= y\right].$$

*If (σ, x) is a locking fragment of F and, for every $\tau \subset \sigma$, (τ, x) is not a locking fragment of F, then (σ, x) is said to be a **minimal locking fragment** of F.*

Clearly, if F is total and computable, then for every $(f,x) \in \mathcal{T} \times \mathbf{N}$, there must exist a unique $\sigma \in \mathcal{F}$ with $\sigma \subset f$ such that (σ, x) is a minimal locking fragment of F. It is also clear that, if (σ, x) is a minimal locking fragment of F cannot be effectively decided. For convenience, we use $(\!(\sigma)\!)$ to denote the set of total extensions for any $\sigma \in \mathcal{F}$, i.e., $(\!(\sigma)\!) = \{f \in \mathcal{T} \mid \sigma \subset f\}$. We extend this notation to $(\!(\sigma, x)\!) = \{(f,x) \mid f \in (\!(\sigma)\!)\}$. For each $(\sigma, x) \in \mathcal{F} \times \mathbf{N}$, we take $(\!(\sigma, x)\!)$ as a basic open set of $\mathbb{T} \times \mathbb{N}$. We observe that, for every $\sigma_1, \sigma_2 \in \mathcal{F}$ and $x_1, x_2 \in \mathbf{N}$,

$$(\!(\sigma_1, x_1)\!) \cap (\!(\sigma_2, x_2)\!) = \begin{cases} \emptyset & \text{if } x_1 \neq x_2; \\ \left[(\!(\sigma_1)\!) \cap (\!(\sigma_2)\!)\right] \times \{x_1\} & \text{if } x_1 = x_2. \end{cases}$$

Note that $(\!(\sigma_1)\!) \cap (\!(\sigma_2)\!) = (\!(\sigma_1 \cup \sigma_2)\!)$ if σ_1 and σ_2 are consistent; otherwise, $(\!(\sigma_1)\!) \cap (\!(\sigma_2)\!) = \emptyset$. The union operation $(\!(\sigma_1, x_1)\!) \cup (\!(\sigma_2, x_2)\!)$ is conventional and an arbitrary union may result in an open set that is not basic. Given any $f, g \in \mathcal{T}$ and $a \in \mathbf{N}$, if $f \neq g$, then there exist σ, τ, and k such that, $\sigma \subset f, \tau \subset g$, $k \in \mathrm{dom}(\sigma) \cap \mathrm{dom}(\tau)$, and $\sigma(k) \neq \tau(k)$. Namely, $\mathbb{T} \times \mathbb{N}$ is a Hausdorff (T_2) topology on $\mathcal{T} \times \mathbf{N}$.

4.1 The Induced Topology $\mathbb{T}(F_1, F_2, \ldots, F_n)$ on $\mathcal{T} \times \mathbf{N}$

In stead of taking every $((\sigma, x))$ as a basic open set (this will form the Baire topology), we consider only those that are related to the concerned functionals. We introduce a class of relative topologies determined by some participated functionals.

DEFINITION 8 *Given a finite number of continuous functionals, $F_1, \ldots, F_n$, let $\mathbb{T}(F_1, \ldots, F_n)$ denote the topology determined by $F_1, \ldots, F_n$ as follows. For each $(f, a) \in \mathcal{T} \times \mathbf{N}$, let (σ_i, a) be the minimal locking fragment of F_i on (f, a). Take $((\sigma, a)) = ((\sigma_1, a)) \cap ((\sigma_2, a)) \cap \cdots \cap ((\sigma_n, a))$ as a basic open set of $\mathbb{T}(F_1, \ldots, F_n)$.*

Note that, in the definition above, we have $\sigma = \bigcup_{1 \le i \le n} \sigma_i$. Thus, if $((\sigma, a))$ is a basic open set of $\mathbb{T}(F_1, F_2, \ldots, F_n)$, then (σ, a) must be a locking fragment to each of $F_1, F_2, \ldots,$ and F_n. However, given any two functionals, F_1 and F_2, the topologies $\mathbb{T}(F_1)$ and $\mathbb{T}(F_2)$ are determined by different basic open sets, and hence the two topologies do not share the same set of compact sets. This in fact is the inherited difficulty of having a transitive relation.

4.2 Type-2 Almost-Everywhere Relation, $\le_2^*$

Now, we are in a position to define our type-2 almost-everywhere relation.

DEFINITION 9 *Let $F_1, F_2 : \mathcal{T} \times \mathbf{N} \to \mathbf{N}$ be continuous. Define*

$$F_1 \le_2^* F_2 \text{ if and only if } X_{[F_1 \le F_2]} \text{ is co-compact in } \mathbb{T}(F_1).$$

The complement of $X_{[F_1 \le F_2]}$ is $X_{[F_1 > F_2]}$. We call set $X_{[F_1 > F_2]}$ the *exceptional set* of $F_1 \le_2^* F_2$.

THEOREM 10 *There are two computable functionals $F_1, F_2 : \mathcal{T} \times \mathbf{N} \to \mathbf{N}$ such that, $F_1 \le_2^* F_2$ and, for any two OTM's that computes F_1 and F_2, respectively, there are infinitely many computations resulting in $F_1 > F_2$.*

Sketch of Proof: We simply observe that, given any two computable functionals F_1 and F_2, F_2 may not be continuous in topology $\mathbb{T}(F_1)$. Thus, $X_{[F_1 > F_2]}$ being compact in $\mathbb{T}(F_1)$ does not mean $F_2(X_{[F_1 > F_2]})$ must be compact in $\mathbb{T}(F_1)$. Also, $X_{[F_1 > F_2]}$ may not be compact in $\mathbb{T}(F_2)$, and hence $F_2(X_{[F_1 > F_2]})$ is not necessarily compact in $\mathbb{T}(F_2)$. □

Thus, Goal 1 fails,[3] but the statement of Goal 1 may be too strong in the context of type-2 computation if the real purpose behind is to patch programs. We have the following theorem to support our definition.

[3] We could have defined Definition 9 as $F_1 \le_2^* F_2$ if and only if $X_{[F_1 \le F_2]}$ is co-compact in $\mathbb{T}(F_1, F_2)$. In such a way we will have a finer topology so that every involved functional is also continuous in $\mathbb{T}(F_1, F_2)$. It follows that we can have a result opposite to Theorem 10. However, the break of Goal 1 due to the infinitely many computations of F_2 is acceptable, since F_2 mostly serves as a mathematical bound and its computation is not interested at all. Besides, the topology $\mathbb{T}(F_1, F_2)$ is still not fine enough to bring back transitivity to our type-2 almost everywhere relation. Therefore, we do not find any particular advantage of using $\mathbb{T}(F_1, F_2)$ as our reference topology for the compactness of $X_{[F_1 > F_2]}$.

THEOREM 11 *Suppose $F_1, F_2 : \mathcal{T} \times \mathbf{N} \to \mathbf{N}$ are computable. If $F_1 \leq_2^* F_2$, then there is an OTM for F_1 such that, there are only finitely many computations of the OTM on $X_{[F_1 > F_2]}$.* □

We omit the proof, which is obvious from the definition of $\leq_2^*$. If F_1 in the above theorem is the cost function of some OTM, we can patch the machine so that the complexity of the patched machine is bounded by F_2 everywhere.

THEOREM 12 *The relation $\leq_2^*$ is not transitive.*

Proof: The idea is that the relations $F_1 \leq_2^* F_2$ and $F_2 \leq_2^* F_3$ hold based on two unrelated topologies $\mathbb{T}(F_1)$ and $\mathbb{T}(F_2)$, respectively. Thus, $X_{[F_2 > F_3]}$ may not be compact in $\mathbb{T}(F_1)$. Consequently, the set $X_{[F_1 > F_3]}$, which is a subset of $X_{[F_1 > F_2]} \cup X_{[F_2 > F_3]}$ may not be compact in $\mathbb{T}(F_1)$. Consider the following example.

$$F_1(f, x) = \begin{cases} f(1) \bmod 2 & \text{if } f(0) = 0 \text{ and } x = 0, \\ 0 & \text{otherwise.} \end{cases}$$

$$F_2(f, x) = \begin{cases} 2 & \text{if } f(0) = 0 \text{ and } x = 0, \\ 1 & \text{otherwise.} \end{cases}$$

$$F_3(f, x) = \begin{cases} f(1) \bmod 3 & \text{if } f(0) = 0 \text{ and } x = 0, \\ 2 & \text{otherwise.} \end{cases}$$

It is clear that $X_{[F_1 > F_2]} = \emptyset$, and hence $F_1 \leq_2^* F_2$. Also, we have

$$X_{[F_2 > F_3]} = \{(f, 0) \mid f(0) = 0 \text{ and } f(1) \leq 1\}.$$

Since the only basic open set of $\mathbb{T}(F_2)$ that contains $X_{[F_2 > F_3]}$ is $((\sigma, 0))$ with $\sigma(0) = 0$ and $\mathrm{dom}(\sigma) = \{0\}$, it follow that $X_{[F_2 > F_3]}$ is compact in $\mathbb{T}(F_2)$, and hence $F_2 \leq_2^* F_3$. We observe F_1 and F_3 to have

$$X_{[F_1 > F_3]} = \{(f, 0) \mid f(0) = 0 \text{ and } f(1) = 3 + 6k \text{ with } k \in \mathbf{N}\}.$$

For each $i \in \mathbf{N}$, define σ_i as $\mathrm{dom}(\sigma_i) = \{0, 1\}$ and $\sigma_i(0) = 0, \sigma_i(1) = i$. Thus, for every $i \in \mathbf{N}$, $((\sigma_i, 0))$ is a basic open set of $\mathbb{T}(F_1)$. Let

$$\mathcal{O} = \{((\sigma_n, 0)) \mid n = 3 + 6k \text{ with } k \in \mathbf{N}\}.$$

Clearly, $\mathcal{O}$ is an open cover for $X_{[F_1 > F_3]}$ without finite subcover. Thus, $X_{[F_1 > F_3]}$ is not compact in $\mathbb{T}(F_1)$. Therefore, $F_1 \not\leq_2^* F_3$ □

5. Applications in Type-2 Complexity Theory

Recall the two functionals F and G defined in (3). We simply compare $\widehat{\Phi}_F$ and $\widehat{\Phi}_G$. Assume $|0| = 1$ under some coding convention. Thus, $2^{|x|} = 2$ if $x = 0$. Let $S = \{((f, 0)) \mid f(2) = 0\}$. We observe that, $X_{[\widehat{\Phi}_G > \widehat{\Phi}_F]} \subset S$. Since S is compact in

$\mathbb{T}(\widehat{\Phi}_G)^4$, it follows that $X_{[\widehat{\Phi}_G > \widehat{\Phi}_F]}$ is also compact in $\mathbb{T}(\widehat{\Phi}_G)$. Therefore, $\widehat{\Phi}_G \leq_2^* \widehat{\Phi}_F$, which indeed reflects our intuitive understanding about the complexity of G and F.

In the following, we provide some serious applications of our type-2 asymptotic behaviors. We show that the set of type-2 computable functionals asymptotically bounded by a given computable type-2 functional is recursively enumerable. In other words, every type-2 complexity class has a programming system. Also, we prove a few complexity theorems at type-2 to show that the techniques used in classical complexity theory now can be transferred under the notion of our type-2 asymptotic behaviors.

5.1 Type-2 Complexity Classes

In [12, 11] we define a special class of type-1 computable functions of type $\mathcal{F} \times \mathbf{N} \to \mathbf{N}$ called *Type-2 Time Bounds*. Under some proper *clocking scheme*, we give a type-2 complexity class $\mathbf{C}(\beta)$ determined by Type-2 Time Bound β. Since each Type-2 Time Bound β also determines a *limit functional* F_β, we can understand the complexity class $\mathbf{C}(\beta)$ by the following formula .

$$F \in \mathbf{C}(\beta) \Longrightarrow \exists e \left[\widehat{\varphi}_e = F \ \wedge \ \widehat{\Phi}_e \leq_2^* F_\beta\right]. \tag{6}$$

Note that, for every $\widehat{\varphi}$-program e, $\mathbb{T}(\widehat{\varphi}_e) = \mathbb{T}(\widehat{\Phi}_e)$. Since the way we clock an OTM not only depends on the result of F_β but also on the course of computing F_β, we do not have the converse of (6) in general. The complexity class $\mathbf{C}(\beta)$ is very sensitive to the clocking scheme and the conventions made for our OTM's. We may want to get rid of the specific knowledge of the clocking scheme in defining complexity classes. In the following, we give a more direct way in defining a type-2 complexity class, where the computable type-2 functional simply serves as the resource bound.

DEFINITION 13 *Let $T : \mathcal{T} \times \mathbf{N} \to \mathbf{N}$ be computable. Define*

$$\mathbf{C}(T) = \left\{F \mid \exists e \left[\widehat{\varphi}_e = F \ \wedge \ \widehat{\Phi}_e \leq_2^* T\right]\right\}.$$

Here we point out a fact with detailed explanation omitted that the notions of $\mathbf{C}(T)$ and $\mathbf{C}(\beta)$ are not equivalent. Nevertheless, we speculate that the type-2 almost everywhere relation involved in Definition 13 will let us directly modify the proofs given in [11] for type-2 Speedup Theorem, Gap Theorem, Union Theorem, Compression Theorem, and so on.

An analog big-O notation for type-2 algorithms can be directly given as follows:

DEFINITION 14 *Let $T : \mathcal{T} \times \mathbf{N} \to \mathbf{N}$ be computable. Define*

$$\mathbf{O}(T) = \left\{F \mid \exists c \in \mathbf{N} \ [F \leq_2^* cT]\right\}.$$

[4]Note that the topology $\mathbb{T}(\widehat{\Phi}_G)$ is determined by the locking fragments of the functional G, but not by the actual queries made during the course of the computation of a machine for G (some unnecessary queries may be made). However, an optimal program should not make unnecessary queries just as an ordinary optimal type-1 program that should not go into some unnecessary loop.

We do not know yet if there is a computable functional F such that $\mathbf{C}(F) = \mathbf{O}(T)$ in general. A positive result to this question requires a Union Theorem.

At type-1, it is easy to show that the *finite invariant* closure of a complexity class is *recursively enumerable* [3]. However, not every complexity class itself can be recursively enumerated. When the resource bound t is very small (namely, very *dishonest*), the complexity class determined by t is unlikely to be recursively enumerable [3, 10]. On the other hand, if t is big enough to bound all *finite support* functions[5] almost everywhere, then the complexity class determined by t is recursively enumerable. In particular, if t is nontrivial, i.e., $t(x) \geq |x| + 1$ for all $x \in \mathbf{N}$, then all finite support functions are contained in the complexity class determined by t (see [4], Section 9.4). The intuitive reason behind this is that, if the bound t allows to compute every finite support function almost everywhere, then we can patch a program at finitely many places with cost bounded by t almost everywhere. In such a way, we can exactly enumerate the complexity class determined by t. At type-2, we have the same situation. To recursively enumerate $\mathbf{C}(T)$, we need a notion of non-triviality for T.

DEFINITION 15 *Let $T : \mathcal{T} \times \mathbf{N} \to \mathbf{N}$ be computable. T is said to be nontrivial if and only if there is a constant $c \in \mathbf{N}$ such that, for every minimal locking fragment (τ, x) of T, we have that, if $(f, x) \in ((\tau, x))$ and $\sigma \subseteq \tau$, then $T(f, x) \geq c(|\sigma| + |x|)$.*

Note that, the constant c in Definition 15 depends on OTM's conventions. Although we may not be interested in finding out what c really is, we can't drop this constant until a linear speedup theorem is formally proven. Intuitively, a nontrivial computable resource bound T allows an OTM to check whether or not (f, x) is in $((\tau, x))$ at computational cost bounded by T as long as (τ, x) is a fixed minimal locking fragment of T. This property serves the same purpose of non-triviality of classical type-1 resource bounds. We obtain the following theorem.

THEOREM 16 *Let $T : \mathcal{T} \times \mathbf{N} \to \mathbf{N}$ be computable and nontrivial. Then, the complexity class $\mathbf{C}(T)$ is recursively enumerable.*

Sketch of Proof: Recall that every $\sigma \in \mathcal{F}$ is represented by a unique canonical index. Let $\sigma^{\sim 0} \in \mathcal{T}$ denote the zero extension of $\sigma \in \mathcal{F}$. That is, $\sigma^{\sim 0}(x) = \sigma(x)$ when $x \in \mathrm{dom}(\sigma)$; $\sigma^{\sim 0}(x) = 0$ otherwise. Let $\langle \cdot, \cdot \rangle : \mathbf{N} \times \mathbf{N} \to \mathbf{N}$ be a standard pairing function. Together with the canonical indexing of $\mathcal{F}$, we have $\langle \sigma, x \rangle \in \mathbf{N}$ for every $\sigma \in \mathcal{F}$ and $x \in \mathbf{N}$.

Let $T : \mathcal{T} \times \mathbf{N} \to \mathbf{N}$ be computable and nontrivial. Unlike the proof for its type-1 counterpart, we are not going to enumerate all finite invariants of $\mathbf{C}(T)$.[6] Instead, we directly argue that there is a recursive function g such that,

$$\mathbf{C}(T) = \{\widehat{\varphi}_{g(e,a,b)} \mid e, a, b, \in \mathbf{N}\}.$$

With a proper *S-m-n theorem* on type-0 arguments,[7] we can construct a recursive $g : \mathbf{N} \times \mathbf{N} \times \mathbf{N} \to \mathbf{N}$ such that, for every $e, a, b \in \mathbf{N}$ and $(f, x) \in \mathcal{T} \times \mathbf{N}$,

---

[5] A function f is finite support if the value of f is 0 almost everywhere.

[6] In fact, we haven't had a precise definition of finite invariant for type-2 functionals.

[7] Obviously, we do not have an *S-m-n theorem* for OTMs on type-1 arguments.

$$\widehat{\varphi}_{g(e,a,b)}(f,x) = \begin{cases} \widehat{\varphi}_e(\tau^{\sim 0},x) & \text{if } (i)\ \forall\langle\sigma,y\rangle \leq a\ [\widehat{\Phi}_e(\sigma^{\sim 0},y) \leq T(\sigma^{\sim 0},y)+b] \\ & \quad (ii)\forall\langle\sigma,y\rangle \leq \langle\tau,x\rangle\ [\forall\eta \subseteq \sigma(a < \langle\eta,y\rangle) \\ & \qquad \Rightarrow \widehat{\Phi}_e(\sigma^{\sim 0},y) \leq T(\sigma^{\sim 0},y)], \\ & \text{where } (\tau,x) \text{ is a locking fragment of } T \text{ on } (f,x); \\ 0 & \text{otherwise.} \end{cases} \tag{7}$$

Next, we shall argue: (i) If $F \in \mathbf{C}(T)$, there exist $e, a, b \in \mathbf{N}$ such that $F = \widehat{\varphi}_{g(e,a,b)}$. (ii) For every $e, a, b \in \mathbf{N}$, we have $\widehat{\varphi}_{g(e,a,b)} \in \mathbf{C}(T)$. Due to the space constrains, we omit the detailed argument. □

5.2 Type-2 Complexity Theorems – Rabin's, Recursive Relatedness, and Gap Theorems

Here we demonstrate the type-2 analogs of three interesting complexity theorems in classical complexity theory: Rabin's theorem [17], recursive relatedness theorem [2], and Gap theorem [3]. Our purpose is to show that our type-2 asymptotic approach is a reasonable one that can lead to a full scale investigation of type-2 complexity theory. Due to the space constraints, detailed proofs are removed.

A technique using diagonalization together with a priority argument with no *injury* is also known as cancellation argument [16], by which Rabin proved that, for any recursive function t, there is a recursive 0-1 valued function f such that $f \notin DTIME(t)$. We modify Rabin's proof and obtain an analogous type-2 result as follows. The proof is also given in the full version of this paper.

THEOREM 17 (TYPE-2 RABIN'S THEOREM) *For any computable $T : \mathcal{T} \times \mathbf{N} \to \mathbf{N}$, there is a 0-1 valued computable $F : \mathcal{T} \times \mathbf{N} \to \mathbf{N}$ such that $F \notin \mathbf{C}(T)$.*

As we mentioned earlier, recursive relatedness is a bridge for complexity theorems between different complexity measures [2]. A type-2 analog will be also essential if we want to further abstract away from a particular model of type-2 computation. We thus formulate a type-2 Recursive Relatedness Theorem in the following. We omit the proof since it can be obtained from the original proof with some minor modification.

THEOREM 18 (TYPE-2 RECURSIVE RELATEDNESS THEOREM) *For any two complexity measures for OTM's, $\langle\Phi\rangle_{i\in\mathbf{N}}$ and $\langle\Psi\rangle_{i\in\mathbf{N}}$, there is a computable functional $R : \mathcal{T} \times \mathbf{N} \times \mathbf{N} \to \mathbf{N}$ such that, for every $i \in \mathbf{N}$,*

$$\Phi_i \leq_2^* \lambda F,x \cdot R(F,x,\Psi_i(F,x)) \text{ and } \Psi_i \leq_2^* \lambda F,x \cdot R(F,x,\Phi_i(F,x)). \quad \square$$

The operation of an effective operator of type $\mathcal{R} \times \mathbf{N} \to \mathbf{N}$ is indeed a special case of type-2 computations where the type-1 input is restricted to $\mathcal{R}$ (recursive functions). However, the Operator Gap Theorem [5, 24] does not imply that we can directly obtain a gap theorem at type-2. In fact, we prove that if we allow the gap factor to be a type-2 computable functional (not just an operator), we can uniformly construct a type-2 computable functional that can inflate every type-2 complexity class [11]. For simplicity, here we restrict the gap factor to recursive functions. We obtain the following result.

THEOREM 19 (TYPE-2 GAP THEOREM) *For any increasing recursive function $g : \mathbf{N} \to \mathbf{N}$, there is a computable functional T such that,* $\mathbf{C}(T) = \mathbf{C}(g \circ T)$.

Sketch of Proof: To proof this theorem, we first accept a convention that the OTM has to scan (read) every bit of the oracle answer at least once; otherwise an opposite theorem can be proven [11]. In other words, the cost of a query is at least the length of the answer. This model is called *Answer-Length-Cost Model* [19]. We use the following computable predicate, $P(f, x, k)$, to determine the value of $T(f, x)$.

$P(f, x, k) \equiv$ Every computation of $\widehat{\varphi}_1, \widehat{\varphi}_2, \ldots, \widehat{\varphi}_x$ on (f, x) is either: (i) making a oracle query outside $\{0, 1, \ldots, x\}$ or (ii) halts in k steps or does not halt in $g(k)$ steps;

In the the predicate, (ii) essentially comes from the idea of the original proof. For (i), we observe that, under our convention, if $T(f, x)$ converges on a segment $\sigma \subset f$ with $\mathsf{dom}(\sigma) \subseteq \{0, 1, \ldots, x\}$, then so does $g(T(f, x))$ and no OTM e that queries beyond $\mathsf{dom}(\sigma)$ can have $\widehat{\Phi}_e \leq_2^* g \circ T$. □

6. Conclusion

As a matter of fact, a general type-2 complexity theory is still an unclear territory. Many applications of type-2 (or higher) computations (e.g., machine learning, interactive computing, real computation, and the theory of programming languages) use their own approaches to address their complexity issues. It is usually difficult to apply one approach that is developed for one particular application to another application. We believe that a workable notion of asymptotic behaviors of type-2 algorithms is the first step in the search of a standard framework for the study of type-2 complexity. And we hope that our notion of $\leq_2^*$ can provide such a step towards a general theory of type-2 complexity.

References

[1] S. Abramsky, Dov M. Gabbay, and T.S.E. Maibaum, editors. *Handbook of Logic in Computer Science*. Oxford University Press, 1992. Background: Mathematical Structures.

[2] Manuel Blum. A machine-independent theory of the complexity of recursive functions. *Journal of the ACM*, 14(2):322–336, 1967.

[3] A. Borodin. Computational complexity and the existence of complexity gaps. *Journal of the ACM*, 19(1):158–174, 1972.

[4] Walter S. Brainerd and Landweber Lawrance H. *Theory of Computation*. John Wiley & Sons, New York, 1974.

[5] Robert L. Constable. The operator gap. *Journal of the ACM*, 19:175–183, 1972.

[6] Stephen Cook and Alasdair Urquhart. Functional interpretation of feasibly constructive arithmetic. *Proceedings of the 21st Annual ACM Symposium on the Theory of Computing*, pages 107–112, 1989.

[7] Martin Davis. *Computability and Unsolvability*. McGraw-Hill, 1958. First reprinted by Dover in 1982.

[8] J. Hartmanis and R. E. Stearns. On the computational complexity of algorithms. *Transitions of the American Mathematics Society*, pages 285–306, May 1965.

[9] Bruce M. Kapron and Stephen A. Cook. A new characterization of type 2 feasibility. *SIAM Journal on Computing*, 25:117–132, 1996.

[10] L.H. Landweber and E.R. Robertson. Recursive properties of abstract complexity classes. *ACM Symposium on the Theory of Complexity*, May 1970.

[11] Chung-Chih Li. Type-2 complexity theory. Ph.d. dissertation, Syracuse University, New York, 2001.

[12] Chung-Chih Li and James S. Royer. On type-2 complexity classes: Preliminary report. *Proceedings of the Third International Workshop on Implicit Computational Complexity*, pages 123–138, May 2001.

[13] E. McCreight and A. R. Meyer. Classes of computable functions defined by bounds on computation. *Proceedings of the First ACM Symposium on the Theory of Computing*, pages 79–88, 1969.

[14] A. Nerode. General topology and partial recursive functionals. *Talks Cornell Summ. Inst. Symb. Log., Cornell*, pages 247–251, 1957.

[15] Piergiorgio Odifreddi. *Classical Recursion Theory*, volume 125 of *Studies in Logic and the Foundations of Mathematics*. Elsevier Science Publishing, North-Holland, Amsterdam, 1989.

[16] Piergiorgio Odifreddi. *Classical Recursion Theory, Volume II*, volume 143 of *Studies in Logic and the Foundations of Mathematics*. Elsevier Science Publishing, North-Holland, Amsterdam, 1999.

[17] M.O. Rabin. Degree of difficulty of computing a function and a partial ordering of recursive sets. Technical Report 2, Hebrew University, 1960.

[18] Hartley Rogers, Jr. *Theory of Recursive Functions and Effective Computability*. McGraw-Hill, 1967. First paperback edition published by MIT Press in 1987.

[19] James S. Royer. Semantics vs. syntax vs. computations: Machine models of type-2 polynomial-time bounded functionals. *Journal of Computer and System Science*, 54:424–436, 1997.

[20] Joel I. Seiferas and Albert R. Meyer. Characterization of realizable space complexities. *Annals of Pure and Applied Logic*, 73:171–190, 1995.

[21] Anil Seth. Complexity theory of higher type functionals. Ph.d. dissertation, University of Bombay, 1994.

[22] D.M. Symes. The extension of machine independent computational complexity theory to oracle machine computation and the computation of finite functions. Ph.d. dissertation, University of Waterloo, Oct. 1971.

[23] V.A. Uspenskii. On countable operations (Russian). *Doklady Akademii Nauk SSSR*, 103:773–776, 1955.

[24] Paul Young. Easy construction in complexity theory: Gap and speed-up theorems. *Proceedings of the American Mathematical Society*, 37(2):555–563, February 1973.

EFFECTIVE CHEMISTRY FOR SYNCHRONY AND ASYNCHRONY

Deepak Garg[1], Akash Lal[2], Sanjiva Prasad[3]

[1] *Carnegie Mellon University, Pittsburgh*
dg+@cs.cmu.edu

[2] *University of Wisconsin, Madison*
akash@cs.wisc.edu

[3] *Indian Institute of Technology Delhi, New Delhi*
sanjiva@cse.iitd.ernet.it

Abstract We study from an implementation viewpoint what constitutes a reasonable and effective notion of structural equivalence of terms in a calculus of concurrent processes and propose *operational effectiveness* criteria in the form of *confluence*, *coherence* and standardization properties on an oriented version of the structural laws. We revisit Berry and Boudol's Chemical Abstract Machine (CHAM) framework using operational effectiveness criteria. We illustrate our ideas with a new formulation of a CHAM for TCCS with external choice, one which is operationally effective unlike previous CHAM formulations, and demonstrate that the new CHAM is fully abstract with respect to the LTS semantics for TCCS. We then show how this approach extends to the synchronous calculus SCCS, for which a CHAM had hitherto not been proposed.

1. Introduction

Most presentations of structural operational semantics (SOS) of concurrent languages nowadays employ the notion of *structural equivalence* $\equiv$ between terms. This notion can be thought of as defining algebraic structure whereas transitions $\rightarrow$ modulo this equivalence represent computation across such structures. Typically included is a rule

$$\frac{P \equiv P' \qquad P \rightarrow Q \qquad Q \equiv Q'}{P' \rightarrow Q'}\ \textit{STRUCT}$$

which allows a term P to be readjusted into a form P' to which a specified transition rule applies. At an implementation level, however, such a rule is not "effective", in that it does not specify appropriate selections of elements within an equivalence class, nor does it bound the amount of "structural adjustment" to be performed. Indeed, there are few criteria for deciding what constitute reasonable notions of structural equivalence, beyond Milner's injunction [Mil93] that "structural laws should be digestible without concern for the dynamics of actions" and the obvious requirement that the notion be decidable. Relevant work on the latter issue concerns decidability of structural equivalence for the π-calculus with the replication operator [EG01].

In this paper, we propose formal conditions that ensure reasonable and effective notions of structural equivalence. These *operational effectiveness* conditions, discussed in §3, are in the form of *confluence* and *coherence* properties for an oriented version of the structural rules, which yield a "standardization" result for execution sequences. Our conditions are closely related to the notions of coherence developed in the context of term rewriting modulo equivalence relations [Vir95]. Also related is Noll's work exploring the notion of coherence while expressing *finite* CCS (calculus of communicating systems) with SOS inference rules in a conditional rewriting framework [Nol99].

Operational effectiveness ensures correct and complete (abstract) implementations of the specified semantics. Taken together with termination of the oriented structural rules, these conditions yield a simple but complete implementation strategy. The import of these conditions is that they simplify establishing adequacy and/or full abstraction results. Confluence and coherence of oriented "administrative" transitions are also useful in analysis and verification of encodings of concurrent systems, since they vastly reduce the state space that needs exploration (see [AP98, GS95] for use of this idea). The connection with rewriting theory has additional benefits — while establishing confluence and coherence, standard rewriting techniques such as *completion* help ensure that there are "enough" structural rules.

We motivate, develop and present our ideas in the *chemical abstract machine* (CHAM) framework proposed by Berry and Boudol [BB90, BB92], which was the inspiration for Milner's formulation of the notion of structural equivalence in [Mil90]. The CHAM framework is an intuitive *style* of presenting operational semantics (presumably also an abstract implementation), where components of a parallel system are likened to *molecules*, and interaction between them is likened to a *chemical reaction* between ions. It exploits the commutative monoidal (*ACI*) properties of parallel composition to present systems as *solutions*, essentially finite multisets of molecules, within which *reactions* are specified locally in the form of conditional rewriting rules. "Structural adjustments", accomplished via the so-called *heating-cooling* and *clean-up rules* and permutations on molecules in a solution via a *magical mixing* mechanism (which can be seen as a prototypical treatment of mobility), allow distant components to react, thus dismantling the bureaucratic rigidity imposed by syntax. We argue that operational effectiveness provides an important criterion for assessing a CHAM specification, and for realizing an abstract implementation from it. It is central in our articulation of a new perspective on the CHAM framework, namely that the essence of CHAMs is that they define operationally effective rewrite systems modulo an *AC* equational theory. We must clarify that though our presentation is in the CHAM framework, the notion of operational effectiveness applies to any style of specification based on rewriting.

Our alternative perspective on the CHAM framework makes possible using a uniform disciplined CHAM idiom for expressing constructs involving non-local interaction, such as external choice, which are problematic in an asynchronous system with purely local interaction [NP96, Pal97]. Several distributed systems and protocols employ non-local interaction via some infrastructure or exhibit some degree of synchrony with the environment, and we believe that it is important for a robust framework for specifying concurrent behaviour to be able to express such *mediated* or *catalyzed* interaction *at an appropriate level of abstraction*. Roughly speaking, our alternative formulation trades the simplicity of autarkic asynchronous computation for applicability of the CHAM idea to more complex interactions. The confluence and coherence conditions provide the necessary discipline for structuring computation and controlling the effects of non-local interaction. We illustrate this idea by focussing on concurrency combinators such as external choice in a variant of CCS and synchronous parallel composition in Milner's synchronous calculus of communicating systems (SCCS) [Mil83].

Organization of the Paper. In §2 we introduce the CHAM framework and our notation. The idea of operational effectiveness for CHAMs is described in §3. The original CHAM in [BB90, BB92] for the variant of CCS called TCCS [NH87] fails to satisfy the confluence-coherence properties, and accordingly we present a reworked CHAM for TCCS in §4. We believe that this CHAM also suffices for the π-calculus, at least the part without name-matching, since it implements scope extrusion and the other structural equivalences. Further, we show that this CHAM is in full agreement with the standard labelled transition system (LTS) semantics for TCCS, with bisimilarity as the notion of equivalence. This result improves on the full abstraction result sketched by Boudol [Bou94] in that it works for external choice contexts as well. The proof technique we use seems to be widely applicable, and relies on the confluence and coherence properties of structural rules.

We then explore a "chemistry for synchrony" in §5, providing a CHAM for a version of SCCS. This is the first synchronous CHAM of which we are aware (hitherto all CHAMs were for calculi with asynchronous process execution). Paucity of space prevents us from presenting here a treatment of choice in SCCS, which appears in the full version of this paper. The proof of correctness follows the same template as that for the TCCS CHAM. The main analysis required in all our example CHAMs involves showing that various rules commute. The TCCS and SCCS CHAM examples use mechanisms based on information-carrying tags for capturing non-local interactions in external choice and synchronous parallel composition. These tags are, however, manipulated by local rules, giving workable implementations of these constructs that involve non-local interaction. We believe that this model can be extended to distributed settings because of its compositional nature. The concluding section (§6) comments on the essence of this alternative view on CHAMs, extensions and future directions of work. The full version of this paper can be obtained from `http://www.cse.iitd.ac.in/~sanjiva`.

2. Preliminaries

A CHAM consists of a specification of its *molecules*, *solutions* and *transformation rules* on solutions. The rewriting semantics is that a rule $l \rightarrow r$ may be applied to any solution that contains substitution instances of the molecules of l, which are replaced by the instances under the same substitution of the molecules in r. Consider the following sub-language (called CCS$^-$) of CCS, where p denotes a typical process term and α a typical action defined over a set $Act = \mathcal{N} \cup \overline{\mathcal{N}}$ where $\mathcal{N}$ is a set of names and $\overline{\mathcal{N}} = \{\overline{x} \mid x \in \mathcal{N}\}$ is the set of "co-names". The "co" operation is involutive, *i.e.*, $\overline{\overline{x}} = x$.

$$p ::= 0 \mid \alpha.p \mid \nu x.p \mid p|p \mid \ldots$$

Here 0 stands for inaction, "." denotes action prefixing, "|" parallel composition and "ν" the restriction operation (written in the notation favoured in the π-calculus).

A CHAM *solution*, typically denoted S or $\{\!|m_1, \ldots, m_k|\!\}$, consists of a finite multiset of *molecules* m_i, delimited by the membrane brackets "$\{\!|\ |\!\}$". In the CHAM framework, *all* transformations are specified on solutions. *Molecules* are basically terms, extended to allow solutions within them, and certain constructions on solutions. Molecules for CCS$^-$ (typically m) are defined as follows:

$$m ::= p \mid \nu x.S \qquad S ::= \{\!|m_1, \ldots, m_k|\!\} \ \ (k \geq 0)$$

Let $\uplus$ denote multiset union on solutions, *i.e.*,

$$\{\!|m_1, \ldots, m_k|\!\} \uplus \{\!|m'_1, \ldots, m'_l|\!\} = \{\!|m_1, \ldots, m_k, m'_1, \ldots, m'_l|\!\}.$$

Rules peculiar to a calculus consist of: (a) *Reaction rules*, presented as conditional rewrite rules on solutions, which are of the form $\{\!|m_1, \ldots, m_k|\!\} \mapsto \{\!|m'_1, \ldots, m'_l|\!\}$. These basic computational steps, which may be non-deterministic, are denoted using the arrow "$\mapsto$", possibly subscripted by a rule label. (b) *Structural rules*, which are either the *reversible* "heating-cooling" rules $S \rightleftharpoons S'$ or oriented "clean-up" rules $S \leadsto S'$ that get rid of inert terms. Heating rules usually are of the form $\{\!|m|\!\} \rightharpoonup \{\!|m'_1, \ldots m'_k|\!\}$ and intuitively are intended to prepare a solution for reaction. Cooling rules, the inverses of the heating ones, usually are of the form $\{\!|m'_1, \ldots m'_k|\!\} \rightharpoondown \{\!|m|\!\}$. We use the symbol $\rightharpoondown$ to denote $\rightharpoonup^{-1}$, the symmetric inverse of the heating relation. Clean-up transitions will be denoted by $\leadsto$. Clean-up rules are distinguished, as a matter of taste, from heating rules in that they do not increase the ability of a solution to react, and their orientation is obvious.

Laws common to a variety of calculi include: (a) The *Chemical Law*, which permits rewriting within a solution according to a *locality principle* that allows reactions and adjustments to occur independently of the other molecules in a solution (here "$\rightarrow$" denotes any rewriting, whether reaction or structural):

$$\frac{S \rightarrow S'}{S \uplus S'' \rightarrow S' \uplus S''}$$

(b) The *Membrane Law*, which permits reactions to occur within reduction contexts:

$$\frac{S \rightarrow S'}{\{\!|C[S]|\!\} \rightarrow \{\!|C[S']|\!\}}$$

A reduction context $C[\,]$ is a molecule with a *solution*-shaped hole in it, that is only a solution may be placed in such a hole. Berry and Boudol also employed an *Airlock Law* in some CHAMs, particularly for implementing choice. It allows particles to be isolated from a solution, to support restricted interaction with the external context: $\{\!|m, m_1, \cdots, m_n|\!\} \rightleftharpoons \{\!|m \triangleleft \{\!|m_1, \cdots, m_n|\!\}|\!\}$. In our treatment, we drop such a law, since it does not have the desired confluence properties.

Notation. The symbol $\rightarrow$ will be used to denote the union of (*i.e.*, any of) the relations $\rightharpoonup$, $\rightharpoondown$, $\leadsto$, and $\mapsto$, whereas the symbol $\rightarrow_{\mathcal{A}}$ abbreviates $\rightharpoonup \cup \leadsto$. The symbol $\leftrightarrow_{\mathcal{A}}$ denotes the symmetric closure of $\rightarrow_{\mathcal{A}}$, and $=_{\mathcal{A}}$ its reflexive-transitive-symmetric closure. For any relation R, let $R^{\leftrightarrow}$, R^+ and R^* denote its symmetric, its transitive, and its reflexive-transitive closures, respectively. The different rewrite rules are labelled, and we will often subscript these reaction/heating/cooling/clean-up relations with the labels of the rules of interest.

The operational rules for CCS$^-$ are specified as follows. Communication is specified through the irreversible reaction rule (schema): $(R)\quad \{\!|x.p, \overline{x}.q|\!\} \mapsto \{\!|p, q|\!\}$

For the CCS$^-$ subset the structural rules are:

(P)	$\{\!|p\|q|\!\} \rightleftharpoons \{\!|p, q|\!\}$	$(0c)$	$\{\!|0|\!\} \leadsto \{\!|\,|\!\}$
(M)	$\{\!|\nu x.p|\!\} \rightleftharpoons \{\!|\nu x.\{\!|p|\!\}|\!\}$	(νc)	$\{\!|\nu x.S|\!\} \leadsto S \quad x \notin fv(S)$
(E)	$\{\!|\nu x.S, p|\!\} \rightleftharpoons \{\!|\nu x.(\{\!|p|\!\} \uplus S)|\!\} \quad x \notin fv(p)$		

All these rules are applicable whenever permitted by the Chemical and Membrane laws. The contexts to be considered are:

$$C ::= [\,] \mid C \uplus S \mid \{\!|\nu x.C|\!\}$$

The structural rules are adapted from the CHAM given by Boudol for the π-calculus [Bou94], rather than the TCCS CHAM given in [BB92]. The main difference is that the airlock mechanism is not used and instead the rule (E) is introduced which allows scope extrusion. *Note that in this specification we identify terms upto α-renaming of bound variables and swapping of consecutive restriction membranes.* The rules apply modulo an equational theory $\mathcal{E}$ (on solutions) induced by the following equalities (here M denotes a molecule or a solution):

$$\begin{array}{ll} (\alpha\text{-}cnv) & \nu x.M = \nu y.M[y/x] \;\; (y \notin fv(M)) \\ (\nu\text{-}swap) & \nu x.\{\!|\nu y.S|\!\} = \nu y.\{\!|\nu x.S|\!\} \end{array}$$

The first equality expresses the essence of what is meant by a term with bound variables. We will outline (in §3) how the second equality can be treated by oriented rewriting modulo an *AC* theory.

Proposition 1. For any two CCS$^-$ terms p and q, $p \equiv q$ iff $\{\!|p|\!\} =_{\mathcal{A}} \{\!|q|\!\}$, where $\equiv$ denotes the standard notion of structural equivalence on CCS$^-$ terms.

3. Effective Structural Transformations

The above-mentioned intuitions for the heating-cooling and clean-up rules suggest that the rules should be *oriented* (rightwards) in the direction of heating and clean-up. If these oriented $\rightarrow_{\mathcal{A}}$-moves are confluent, they may be applied in any order and (if terminating) yield unique normal forms, which are more reactive than all other structurally equivalent forms. Note that confluence of heating implies the following commutation, which allows cooling to be postponed: $\rightharpoondown^*; \rightharpoonup^* \subseteq \rightharpoonup^*; \rightharpoondown^*$. Further, if heating/clean-up moves are not to prune away a potential reaction, then a series of heating/clean-up steps and any reaction step can commute. Combining these intuitions, we arrive at the following definition of *operational effectiveness*.

Definition 2 (Operational Effectiveness). A set of oriented structural rules (heating and clean-up rules of a CHAM) is said to be *operationally effective* if the following two properties hold:

1 ($\rightarrow_{\mathcal{A}}$-confluence) The relation $\rightarrow_{\mathcal{A}}$ is Church-Rosser: if $S \rightarrow_{\mathcal{A}}^* S_1$ and $S \rightarrow_{\mathcal{A}}^* S_2$, then $S_1 \rightarrow_{\mathcal{A}}^* S_3$ and $S_2 \rightarrow_{\mathcal{A}}^* S_3$ for some S_3.

2 ($\rightarrow_{\mathcal{A}}^* - \mapsto$-commutation or coherence) For all S, S_1, S_2 if $S \rightarrow_{\mathcal{A}}^* S_1$ and $S \mapsto S_2$, then there exists S_3 such that $S_1 \rightarrow_{\mathcal{A}}^* \mapsto S_3$ and $S_2 \rightarrow_{\mathcal{A}}^* S_3$.

The *coherence* condition may seem more general than needed for many instances, but even in our example CCS$^-$ CHAM, several suggested stronger versions are unable to handle adequately, *e.g.*, extrusion of the scope of a restriction by the (E) rule. *Confluence* is an essential requirement since without it, coherence is ineffective.
Immediate consequences of operational effectiveness are $=_{\mathcal{A}} \subseteq \rightarrow_{\mathcal{A}}^*; (\rightarrow_{\mathcal{A}}^{-1})^*$ and $(\rightarrow_{\mathcal{A}}^{-1})^*; \mapsto \;\subseteq\; \rightarrow_{\mathcal{A}}^*; \mapsto; (\rightarrow_{\mathcal{A}}^{-1})^*$, from which follows a standardization for reduction sequences.

Theorem 3 (Standardization). If a set of oriented structural rules is operationally effective then $\forall n \geq 0, \quad (=_{\mathcal{A}}; \mapsto; =_{\mathcal{A}})^n \subseteq \rightarrow_{\mathcal{A}}^*; (\mapsto; \rightarrow_{\mathcal{A}}^*)^n; (\rightarrow_{\mathcal{A}}^{-1})^*$

Proposition 4. The CHAM for CCS$^-$ is operationally effective.

This result follows from showing that the various rules commute as required. In fact, most pairs of structural rules commute strongly (strong diamond property), with the exception of the (E) rule.

We propose operational effectiveness as an important criterion for assessing a CHAM specification. We observe that some CHAMs in the literature (for the π-calculus and the Join calculus [FG96]) seem reasonable (effective), whereas the TCCS and the γ-calculus CHAMs in [BB90, BB92] are not, since the laws for restriction and the airlock law in the first, and the hatching and membrane laws in the second, lead to non-confluent heating.

Termination and strategy for implementation. In the CCS$^-$ CHAM given above, we can show that the administrative $\rightarrow_{\mathcal{A}}$-moves are strongly normalizing. The nontrivial aspect here involves treating extrusion of the scope of restriction by the rule (E).

Proposition 5 (Strong Normalization). The relations $\rightarrow_{\mathcal{A}}$ (heating+clean-up) and $\rightharpoondown$ (cooling) are strongly normalizing in the CHAM for CCS$^-$.

Standardization and termination yield a fairly simple but complete implementation strategy (even with guarded recursion): heat/clean-up a solution as much as possible using rules other than the recursion rule, then unfold *once* each recursive term, and then heat/clean-up as much as possible using the other rules.

3.1 Rewriting modulo equivalence

A crucial question is whether it is semantically correct to work with reduction (reaction) modulo oriented structural rules instead of reduction modulo structural equivalence. Our confluence-coherence conditions ensure that it is indeed so for effective CHAMs. We later found that in [Vir95], Viry has studied this issue in the general setting of *oriented rewrite theories* (ORTs). Technically, an equational theory is decomposed into a "core" notion of equality $\mathcal{E}$ (with respect to which matching is tractable) and a collection of oriented rewrite rules $\mathcal{A}$. The question is "when can $\mathcal{R}$ modulo $\mathcal{E} \cup \mathcal{A}^{\leftrightarrow}$ (the semantics) be simulated by $(\mathcal{A})^*\mathcal{R}(\mathcal{A})^*$ modulo $\mathcal{E}$ (the implementation)?" For CHAMs, $\mathcal{E}$ should capture only the essential equational theory for solutions. Viry has identified *coherence conditions* which suffice to establish that the implementation relations are *complete* with respect to the specified semantics (the other direction, *soundness*, is trivial). In the figure below, we depict (with solid lines quantified universally and dotted lines existentially) the following properties: (a) confluence of the oriented $\mathcal{A}$ rules, (b) our coherence property, and (c) Viry's *strong coherence* property.

Our coherence property implies Viry's strong coherence property, and therefore, ensures completeness of the implementation with respect to the semantics. Indeed, it does not need the extra $\mathcal{A}^*$ moves after the $\mathcal{R}$ move on the lower (existential) branch to complete the diagram. This stronger property slightly simplifies implementation and reasoning, *e.g.*, the proofs of full abstraction. Note that coherence does not require $\rightarrow_{\mathcal{A}}$, to be terminating (modulo $\mathcal{E}$) as, for instance, Noll does in his formalization of CCS [Nol99].

Next, we argue that the essence of an effective CHAM *is that it defines an operationally effective rewrite system modulo an AC equational theory.* Rewriting modulo arbitrary equational theories may not be tractable [Nol99]. Viry has given conditions for checking the coherence conditions (under the assumption that $\mathcal{A}$ is terminating), by checking a finite number of critical pairs modulo $\mathcal{E}$ when an instance of a *generic permutation lemma* holds for $\mathcal{E}$. Instances of this lemma are known for $\mathcal{E} = \emptyset$, $\mathcal{E} = A$ (associativity) and $\mathcal{E} = AC$ (associativity and commutativity). The last of these theories agrees well with the notion of multiset rewriting which is at the core of the CHAM framework. In the sequel, we illustrate that the salient concurrency combinators — restriction, external choice and synchronous parallel composition — can all be treated within an AC framework.

The identity laws for parallel composition and non-deterministic choice, and idempotence for the latter combinator are treated as rules in $\mathcal{A}$, namely as clean-up rules in the CHAM. The conditions on these clean-up rules ensure that there are no problematic critical pairs, thus avoiding the termination and completion related problems that may arise in rewriting modulo identity. Idempotence is dealt with a fairly simple commutation argument.

If we disregard α-conversion, which is uncontroversial and can anyway be treated in a first-order theory using an indexing scheme, the only equality that is not an AC property is the *(ν-swap)* equation introduced §1 for the CCS$^-$ CHAM. This was necessary to ensure commutation when using the (E) rule. It can be eliminated by the following mildly different treatment of restriction, one that highlights that restriction in some sense satisfies AC properties (based on those of set union).

Factoring the (E) rule. Instead of molecules of the form $\nu x.S$, we will write instead S_X, where X is a *set* of names, which are considered bound in S. The (M) rule is recast as $\{\!|\nu x.p|\!\} \rightleftharpoons \{\!|\{\!|p|\!\}_{\{x\}}|\!\}$. Now the (E) rule can now be factored into the two rules:

$$\{\!|S_X, p|\!\} \rightleftharpoons_{EM} \{\!|(S \uplus \{\!|p|\!\})_X|\!\} \quad X \cap fv(p) = \emptyset$$
$$\{\!|S_X, S'_Y|\!\} \rightleftharpoons_{EF} \{\!|(S \uplus S')_{X+Y}|\!\} \quad X \cap fv(S') = Y \cap fv(S) = \emptyset$$

With this factoring, the strong normalization property is preserved, and stronger statements can be made regarding rule commutation — (EF) commutes strongly, whereas (EM) commutes, but possibly weakly, with other rules.

3.2 Agreement with LTS semantics

What is the relationship between a calculus $\mathcal{P}$ equipped with a labelled transition system (LTS) $\rightarrow^\alpha$, and its purported CHAM formulation $\mathcal{C}$? We outline the key notions and a template for proving the correctness of the CHAMs in §4 and §5. First, we equip $\mathcal{C}$ with a *labelled transition relation* $\mapsto^\alpha$ based on a suitable notion of observability for solutions. Let $\Longrightarrow^\alpha = \rightarrow^*_{\mathcal{A}}; \mapsto^\alpha; \rightarrow^*_{\mathcal{A}}$. This will be the transition relation on $\mathcal{C}$.

Definition 6. Given a LTS $\langle \mathcal{G}, \rightarrow^\square \rangle$, a symmetric relation $\mathcal{R} \subseteq \mathcal{G} \times \mathcal{G}$ is called a bisimulation on $\mathcal{G}$ if whenever $(p, q) \in \mathcal{R}$ and $p \rightarrow^\alpha p'$, there exists $q' \in \mathcal{G}$ such that $q \rightarrow^\alpha q'$ and $(p', q') \in \mathcal{R}$.

Suppose $\sim_p$ and $\sim_c$ stand for bisimulation equivalence in $\mathcal{P}$ and $\mathcal{C}$ respectively. A translation $\langle . \rangle : \mathcal{P} \rightarrow \mathcal{C}$ is called *adequate* (sound) if $\langle p \rangle \sim_c \langle q \rangle$ implies $p \sim_p q$, and *fully abstract* if $p \sim_p q$ implies $\langle p \rangle \sim_c \langle q \rangle$ as well. (These properties also apply to reasonable notions of equivalence other than bisimulation.)

Lemma 7. If $\rightarrow_{\mathcal{A}}$-moves of a CHAM are operationally effective, then $=_{\mathcal{A}}$ is a bisimulation on CHAM configurations.

The crucial fact used here is that due to coherence, the (eventual) possibility of a reaction is preserved across $\rightarrow_{\mathcal{A}}$-moves.

Definition 8 (Forward and Backward Simulation). CHAM $\mathcal{C}$ *forward simulates* $\mathcal{P}$ if for all process $p, q \in \mathcal{P}$ such that $p \rightarrow^\alpha q$, there exists a CHAM configuration S such that $\langle p \rangle \Longrightarrow^\alpha S =_{\mathcal{A}} \langle q \rangle$. CHAM $\mathcal{C}$ *backward simulates* $\mathcal{P}$ if for any process p and CHAM configuration S, such that $\langle p \rangle \Longrightarrow^\alpha S$, there is a process p' such that $\langle p' \rangle =_{\mathcal{A}} S$ and $p \rightarrow^\alpha p'$.

Theorem 9 (Bisimulation). Let CHAM $\mathcal{C}$ be operationally effective and both forward and backward simulate $\mathcal{P}$. Then the following two relations are bisimulations on $\mathcal{C}$-configurations and processes in $\mathcal{P}$ respectively.

1 $\mathcal{B}_c = \{(S_1, S_2) \mid \exists p, q \text{ s.t. } p \sim_p q, S_1 =_{\mathcal{A}} \langle p \rangle, S_2 =_{\mathcal{A}} \langle q \rangle\}$

2 $\mathcal{B}_p = \{(p, q) \mid \exists S_1, S_2 \text{ s.t. } \langle p \rangle =_{\mathcal{A}} S_1, \langle q \rangle =_{\mathcal{A}} S_2, S_1 \sim_c S_2\}$

The forward and backward simulation conditions relate the $\rightarrow^\alpha$ moves of a process and the $\Longrightarrow^\alpha$-moves of its image under the translation. Lemma 7 allows us to find a suitable $\Longrightarrow^\alpha$-derivative of a given CHAM configuration to fulfil the bisimilarity requirements.

Corollary 10 (Full Abstraction). If the conditions of Theorem 9 hold for a CHAM, then $\langle p \rangle \sim_c \langle q \rangle$ if and only if $p \sim_p q$.

4. An Effective CHAM for TCCS

We now extend CCS$^-$ with external choice, and guarded recursion, *i.e.*, in $fix_i(\vec{x} = \vec{p})$, every occurrence of a process variable x_i in the p_i's is within an action-prefixed term. Guardedness is a vital condition for providing an effective treatment in the presence of recursion.

$$p ::= \ \ldots \mid p \Box p \mid fix_i(\vec{x} = \vec{p})$$

The standard semantics for TCCS is:

$$\frac{}{\alpha.p \mapsto^{\alpha} p} \quad \frac{p_1 \mapsto^{\alpha} p_1' \quad p_2 \mapsto^{\overline{\alpha}} p_2'}{p_1|p_2 \mapsto p_1'|p_2'} \quad \frac{p_1 \mapsto p_1'}{p_1|p_2 \mapsto p_1'|p_2} \quad \frac{p_2 \mapsto p_2'}{p_1|p_2 \mapsto p_1|p_2'}$$

$$\frac{p_1 \mapsto^{\alpha} p_1'}{p_1|p_2 \mapsto^{\alpha} p_1'|p_2} \quad \frac{p_2 \mapsto^{\alpha} p_2'}{p_1|p_2 \mapsto^{\alpha} p_1|p_2'} \quad \frac{p \mapsto p'}{\nu x.p \mapsto \nu x.p'} \quad \frac{p \mapsto^{\alpha} p' \ (\alpha \notin \{x, \overline{x}\})}{\nu x.p \mapsto^{\alpha} \nu x.p'}$$

$$\frac{p_1 \mapsto p_1'}{p_1 \Box p_2 \mapsto p_1' \Box p_2} \quad \frac{p_2 \mapsto p_2'}{p_1 \Box p_2 \mapsto p_1 \Box p_2'} \quad \frac{p_1 \mapsto^{\alpha} p_1'}{p_1 \Box p_2 \mapsto^{\alpha} p_1'} \quad \frac{p_2 \mapsto^{\alpha} p_2'}{p_1 \Box p_2 \mapsto^{\alpha} p_2'}$$

$$\frac{}{fix_i(\vec{x} = \vec{p}) \mapsto p_i[fix_j(\vec{x} = \vec{p}) \,/\, x_j]_{j=1}^{n}}$$

In [BB90, BB92], external choice was implemented using reversible rules for airlocks and *heavy ions*, which carry tags (l or r) memo-ing the component of a choice from which an action originated. Once choice is resolved by the context, irreversible projection rules eliminate the other alternatives. This treatment is quite awkward: it introduces a great deal of new syntax, and is rigid in tagging the heavy choice ions, contrary to the AC properties of choice. Furthermore the airlock law leads to non-confluence.

We generalize the tagging approach to a compositional treatment, while presenting an effective CHAM rewrite system. TCCS external choice is implemented using "speculative concurrent execution", *i.e.*, running the various (tagged) alternatives concurrently, until one is selected. Thereupon the others are culled away, using the tags to determine which components to retain or kill. Given any two sub-processes in a TCCS term, they are either in exclusive choice or in parallel with each other. We use an *unordered, finitely branching tree* of nodes alternatingly marked $\mathbf{P}$ and $\mathbf{C}$ (for parallel composition and choice respectively) to represent such relations between processes. The leaves are marked with the tags. This abstract data structure, called an *exclusion tree*, serves as a catalyst that mediates the non-local interaction necessary for external choice. While we present it as a "global" component, its manipulation may admit some parallelism. Let $\mathcal{L} = \{a_1, a_2, \ldots\}$ be an infinite set of labels. An exclusion tree, denoted by T, is defined by the following grammar.

$$T ::= T_p \quad T_p ::= a \mid \mathbf{P}(T_c, \ldots, T_c) \quad T_c ::= a \mid \mathbf{C}(T_p, \ldots, T_p)$$

$\mathbf{P}$ and $\mathbf{C}$ denote internal nodes of the tree with finite non-zero arity. Given an exclusion tree T, arbitrary nodes and subtrees rooted at those nodes are denoted by n and its decorated variants. Given a node n, the *type* of n is $\mathbf{P}$ (respectively $\mathbf{C}$) if the subtree rooted at n was produced from the non-terminal T_p (resp. T_c). Contexts for exclusion trees are denoted by C_T.

$$C_T ::= C_p \quad C_p ::= [\,] \mid \mathbf{P}(C_c, T_c, \ldots, T_c) \quad C_c ::= [\,] \mid \mathbf{C}(C_p, T_p, \ldots, T_p)$$

CHAM configurations are pairs, written $T \vdash S$, where T is an exclusion tree and S is a solution. It is assumed that all leaves in T are distinct; this property is preserved by the rewriting rules. TCCS terms in the solution S are labeled from the set $\mathcal{L}$. Molecules may now be redefined.

$$m ::= p^a \mid \nu x.S$$

A molecule p^a is termed *active* if its tag a is a leaf in the tree T. *Only active molecules are allowed to take part in a reaction.* The rest may be garbage collected.

The equational theory $\mathcal{E}$ on configurations $T \vdash S$ is obtained by "lifting" to configurations the equational theory $\mathcal{E}$ defined earlier for solutions, and adding the equations

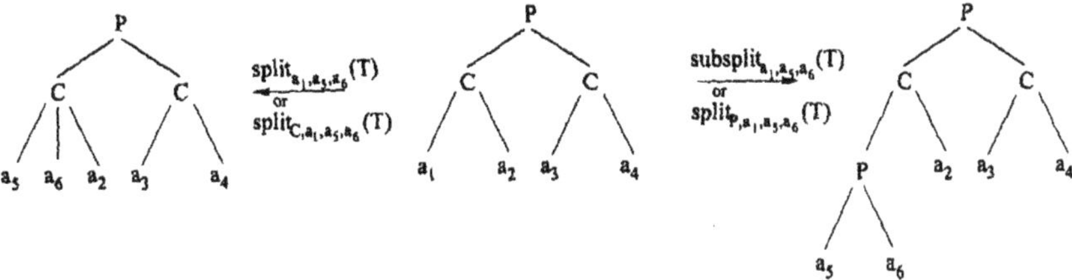

Figure 1. The *split* and *subsplit* operations

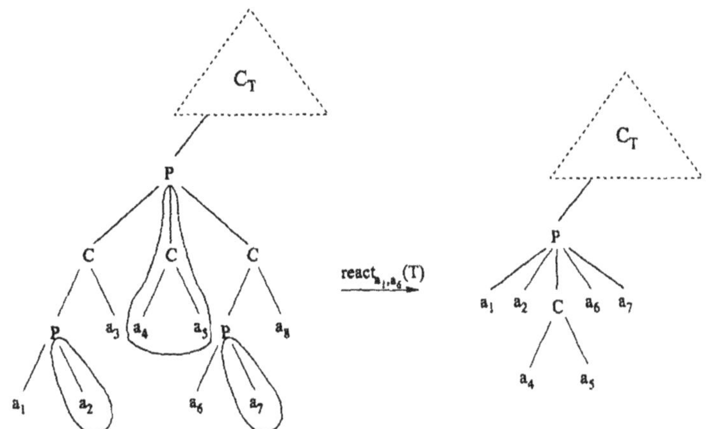

Figure 2. The *react* operation

$$\mathbf{P}(\ldots,T_i,\ldots,T_j,\ldots) = \mathbf{P}(\ldots,T_j,\ldots,T_i,\ldots)$$
$$\mathbf{C}(\ldots,T_i,\ldots,T_j,\ldots) = \mathbf{C}(\ldots,T_j,\ldots,T_i,\ldots)$$

to emphasize the unordered (*AC*) nature of the tree. In addition, $\mathcal{E}$ also contains the following renaming equality for labels.

$$T \vdash \mathcal{S} = T[a_2/a_1] \vdash \mathcal{S}[a_2/a_1] \quad a_2 \notin T, \mathcal{S}$$

Let C denote a *solution context* with a "solution-shaped" hole.

$$C ::= [\,] \mid C \uplus \mathcal{S} \mid \{\!|\nu x.C|\!\}$$

We say that $a \in T$ if the tree T has a leaf labeled a. Also, $(n_1 \leftarrow n_2) \in T$ if the parent of node n_1 in T is the node n_2. If n is a node with only one child n_1, $remove_n(T)$ is the tree T with the nodes n, n_1 removed and the children of n_1 connected to $parent(n)$; if n_1 is itself a leaf, it is connected to $parent(n)$. $T - (n_1 \leftarrow n_2)$ denotes tree T with the node n_1 and all its children removed provided $(n_1 \leftarrow n_2) \in T$. If $n_2 \in T$, $T + (n_1 \leftarrow n_2)$ is the tree T with the additional subtree n_1 added below n_2. Define $split_{a,a_1,a_2}(T) = ((T - (a \leftarrow n)) + (a_1 \leftarrow n)) + (a_2 \leftarrow n)$ when $(a \leftarrow n) \in T$ and $a_1, a_2 \in \mathcal{L}$ are not in T. Also, $subsplit_{a,a_1,a_2}(T) = ((T - (a \leftarrow n)) + (n' \leftarrow n)) + (a_1 \leftarrow n') + (a_2 \leftarrow n')$ if $(a \leftarrow n) \in T$. n' is a new internal node having a type different from n and $a_1, a_2 \in \mathcal{L}$ are labels not in T. Figure 1 depicts these operations graphically.
For $t \in \{\mathbf{P}, \mathbf{C}\}$ define

$$split_{t,a,a_1,a_2}(T) = \begin{cases} split_{a,a_1,a_2}(T) & \text{if } t = type(parent(a)) \\ subsplit_{a,a_1,a_2}(T) & otherwise \end{cases}$$

$$T \vdash C[\{\!|(p|q)^a|\!\}] \rightleftharpoons_P split_{\mathbf{P},a,a_1,a_2}(T) \vdash C[\{\!|p^{a_1}, q^{a_2}|\!\}] \qquad (a \in T)$$

$$T \vdash C[\{\!|(\nu x.p)^a|\!\}] \rightleftharpoons_M T \vdash C[\{\!|\nu x.\{\!|p^a|\!\}|\!\}] \qquad (a \in T)$$

$$T \vdash C[\{\!|m, \nu x.S|\!\}] \rightleftharpoons_E T \vdash C[\{\!|\nu x.(S \uplus \{\!|m|\!\})|\!\}] \qquad (x \notin fv(m))$$

$$T \vdash C[\{\!|(p[]q)^a|\!\}] \rightleftharpoons_C split_{\mathbf{C},a,a_1,a_2}(T) \vdash C[\{\!|p^{a_1}, q^{a_2}|\!\}] \qquad (a \in T)$$

$$T \vdash C[\{\!|fix_i(\vec{x} = \vec{p})^a|\!\}] \rightleftharpoons_F T \vdash C[\{\!|(p_i[fix_j(\vec{x} = \vec{p}) \,/\, x_j]_{j=1}^n)^a|\!\}] \quad (a \in T)$$

$$T \vdash C[\{\!|p^a|\!\}] \rightsquigarrow_{gc} T \vdash C[\{\!|\ |\!\}] \qquad \text{if } a \notin T$$

$$T \vdash C[\{\!|\nu x.S|\!\}] \rightsquigarrow_{\nu c} T \vdash C[S] \qquad \text{if } x \notin fv(S)$$

$$T \vdash C[\{\!|0^a|\!\}] \rightsquigarrow_{0c} T - (a \leftarrow n) \vdash C[\{\!|\ |\!\}] \qquad (a \leftarrow n) \in T$$

$$T + (n_1 \leftarrow n) \vdash S \rightsquigarrow_{aL} remove_n(T) \vdash S \qquad \text{if } n \text{ has only one child } n_1 \text{ in } T$$

$$T \vdash C[\{\!|(\alpha.p)^{a_1}, (\overline{\alpha}.q)^{a_2}|\!\}] \mapsto_R react_{a_1,a_2}(T) \vdash C[\{\!|p^{a_1}, q^{a_2}|\!\}]$$
$$\text{if } a_1, a_2 \in T \text{ and } react_{a_1,a_2}(T) \text{ is defined}$$

Figure 3. Rules for the TCCS CHAM.

Let $LCA_T(a_1, a_2)$ be the least common ancestor of the leaves a_1 and a_2 in T. Let $a_1, a_2 \in T$ and $n = LCA_T(a_1, a_2)$. Let n have type $\mathbf{P}$ and $T = C_T[T']$ where T' is the subtree of T rooted at n and C_T is the rest of the tree T. Define $react_{a_1,a_2}(T)$ to be the tree $C_T[\mathbf{P}(a_1, a_2, T_1, T_2, \ldots)]$ where $T_1, T_2, \ldots$ are all the subtrees of T whose roots were children of nodes of type $\mathbf{P}$ occurring on the unique paths from a_1 to n and a_2 to n in T. The *react* operation is depicted graphically in Figure 2, with the subtrees $T_1, T_2, \ldots$ circled.

The rewriting rules for TCCS CHAM configurations are given in Figure 3. The rules are presented as context-embedded rewrites, rather than specifying elementary rewrites and inductively propagating these steps via Chemical and Membrane laws. This is just a matter of technical convenience. Such an approach is often used for specifying reduction semantics for λ-calculi instead of inference rules for induction cases.

The heating-cooling rules (M), (E) are as before, except for the tag management. The (P) rule splits the leaf corresponding to the term where it is applied. The (C) rule deals with external choice and allows a term $p[]q$ to decompose into p and q tagged with leaves occurring as separate children of a $\mathbf{C}$ node. The rule (F) for fix-points allows recursive definitions to be unfolded in the heating direction, and is standard. The (gc) clean-up rule allows one to "garbage collect" *inactive* molecules, those whose tags are not in T. The (aL) clean-up rule removes nodes that represent a singleton term in a choice or parallel context. The rules $(0c)$ and (νc) are as before. The proviso on the reaction rule ensures that both reagent molecules are active, and not in mutual exclusion. The reaction eliminates from the exclusion tree all tags that marked terms mutually exclusive of either reacting molecule.

We define the administrative moves of the TCCS CHAM as the heating and cleanup rules: $\rightarrow_A = \rightharpoonup \cup \rightsquigarrow$. With a small extension of the earlier treatment, it is not difficult to show that $\rightarrow_A$ is strongly normalizing (since recursion is guarded, the use of $\rightharpoonup_F$ is bounded).

Definition 11 (LTS). A labelled transition relation $\mapsto^\alpha$ can be defined as:
$T \vdash C[\{\!|(\alpha.p)^a|\!\}] \mapsto^\alpha T' \vdash C[\{\!|p^a|\!\}]$ if $a \in T$ and $C[\ ]$ does not restrict α. Here $T' = \mathbf{P}(a, T_1, T_2, \ldots)$ where $T_1, T_2, \ldots$ are all the subtrees of T whose root is a child of a node of type $\mathbf{P}$ occurring on the path from a to the root of T.

Definition 12 (Translation). For p in TCCS, define $\langle p \rangle = a \vdash \{\!|p^a|\!\} \quad a \in \mathcal{L}$

Lemma 13 (TCCS-Administrative Moves). The administrative moves $\rightarrow_{\mathcal{A}}$ of TCCS CHAM are operationally effective for both the LTS ($\mapsto^{\alpha}$) and reduction ($\mapsto_R$).

Lemma 14 (TCCS-Simulation). The TCCS CHAM satisfies the properties of forward and backward simulation with respect to both the LTS and the reduction semantics.

The proof of this lemma employs an alternative formulation of the CHAM, which is closer to the inductive style followed in LTS semantics of TCCS. In fact, the CHAM we have presented was systematically derived from the equivalent alternative "inductive" LTS presentation. That formulation was first "closed" with contexts to yield a reduction system with inductive laws, and then "flattened" with respect to contexts to yield the present rewrite-rule form.

Theorem 15 (Standardization and Full Abstraction).

1 For the TCCS CHAM, $(=_{\mathcal{A}}; \rightarrow^{\alpha}; =_{\mathcal{A}})^n \subseteq \rightarrow^*_{\mathcal{A}}; (\rightarrow^{\alpha}; \rightarrow^*_{\mathcal{A}})^n; (\rightarrow^{-1}_{\mathcal{A}})^*$

2 For the TCCS CHAM, $(=_{\mathcal{A}}; \mapsto_R; =_{\mathcal{A}})^n \subseteq \rightarrow^*_{\mathcal{A}}; (\mapsto_R; \rightarrow^*_{\mathcal{A}})^n; (\rightarrow^{-1}_{\mathcal{A}})^*$

3 The TCCS CHAM is a fully abstract implementation.

We note in passing that in [Vir95], Viry had specified LOTOS semantics (which is closely related to CCS) as an oriented rewriting theory. We believe that his formulation is somewhat unsatisfactory since it includes the "Expansion Theorem" [Mil89] in the oriented structural rules $\mathcal{A}$. This amounts to embedding a *particular* notion of observation and program equivalence into the structural equivalence, which seems to run contrary to Milner's injunction on keeping structural equivalence independent of the dynamics.

5. An Effective CHAM for SCCS

We now consider a variant of SCCS [Mil83], a calculus in which process execution is *synchronous*. Assume that the set of actions Act forms an Abelian monoid, under the operation $\cdot$, with 1 denoting the identity element. Let $\alpha \in Act$, a set of actions, and let $X \subseteq Act$. For brevity, we write $\alpha\beta$ for $\alpha \cdot \beta$.
The syntax of the subset of SCCS we consider is given by the abstract grammar:

$$p ::= 0 \mid \alpha.p \mid p_1|p_2 \mid \nu X.p \mid fix_i(\vec{x} = \vec{p})$$

0 represents inability to execute, "." denotes prefixing, and "|" is now synchronous parallel composition. Due to space restrictions, in this paper, we omit the choice operator considered by Milner in his original presentation of SCCS. Further we assume that we have only guarded recursion. We must clarify that for continuity with the previous section, we employ a restriction operator νX similar in spirit to that in CCS. Our $\nu X.p$ can be defined as $p \wr (Act - X)$ in Milner's syntax.
The LTS semantics for this SCCS subset are:

$$\frac{}{\alpha.p \mapsto^{\alpha} p} \qquad \frac{p_1 \mapsto^{\alpha_1} p_1' \quad p_2 \mapsto^{\alpha_2} p_2'}{p_1|p_2 \mapsto^{\alpha_1\alpha_2} p_1'|p_2'}$$

$$\frac{p \mapsto^{\alpha} p'}{\nu X.p \mapsto^{\alpha} \nu X.p'} \ \alpha \notin X \qquad \frac{(p_i[fix_j(\vec{x} = \vec{p}) \,/\, x_j]_{j=1}^n) \mapsto^{\alpha} p'}{fix_i(\vec{x} = \vec{p}) \mapsto^{\alpha} p'}$$

In a synchronous calculus, all processes act in concert. At first blush, this suggests an alternative chemical law of the form:

$$\frac{S_1 \rightarrow S_1' \qquad S_2 \rightarrow S_2'}{S_1 \uplus S_2 \rightarrow S_1' \uplus S_2'}$$

In a CHAM, however, the processes must be structurally adjusted to be ready for synchronizing with one another. Since the number of administrative $\rightarrow_A$ moves can vary for different components, they cannot be performed in lockstep. Thus we continue with the old chemical law, at least for the structural rules, though we discuss below an alternative chemical law for the synchronization steps.

Since all terms in a SCCS process act together to produce a composite action, their individual actions need to be propagated upward on the structure of the term, and only at the top level is it decided whether an action can take place. Our CHAM implementation mimics this idea, but several implementation-level rewrite steps are needed to accomplish a semantic transition. We use tags to propagate actions. Let $\circ$ be an element not in Act (we call this element *"Notag"*, and it is used to mark molecules prior to ionization or after action propagation). Tags are elements of $Act \cup \{\circ\}$. We denote tags by the letter t and its decorated variants.

Molecules and solutions. Solutions (denoted by S) and molecules (denoted by m) are defined by the following grammar.

$$m ::= p \mid \nu X.S^t \qquad S ::= \{\!|m_1^{t_1}, \ldots, m_n^{t_n}|\!\} \quad n \geq 0$$

Tagged solutions and tagged molecules are solutions and molecules with a tag on them. The tag is written as a superscript on the solution or molecule. We define contexts for (untagged) solutions by the following grammar.

$$C ::= [\,]^t \mid (\{\!|(\nu X.C)^{t_1}|\!\} \uplus S)^{t_2}$$

Rules. The heating/cooling rules given below can be freely applied wherever permitted by a Chemical Law or Membrane Law. The (I) rule describes *ionization* of a prefixed term.

$$\{\!|(\alpha.p)^\circ|\!\} \rightleftharpoons_I \{\!|p^\alpha|\!\} \qquad \{\!|(\nu X.p)^\circ|\!\} \rightleftharpoons_M \{\!|(\nu X.\{\!|p^\circ|\!\}^\circ)^\circ|\!\}$$

$$\{\!|(p|q)^\circ|\!\} \rightleftharpoons_P \{\!|p^\circ, q^\circ|\!\} \quad \{\!|fix_i(\vec{x} = \vec{p})^\circ|\!\} \rightleftharpoons_F \{\!|(p_i[fix_j(\vec{x} = \vec{p}) \,/\, x_j]_{j=1}^n)^\circ|\!\}$$

Reaction. Reaction in SCCS is a LTS move $\quad S^\alpha \mapsto_R^\alpha S^\circ$. Reaction is a *top level* rewrite, to which the Membrane Law and Chemical Law do *not* apply.

Propagation Rules. The propagation rules given below propagate actions on molecules and solutions upwards on the structure of the system. Synchronisation is facilitated by the rule (PU). The rule (νU) allows actions to be propagated past a restriction.

$$\{\!|m_1^{\alpha_1}, \ldots, m_n^{\alpha_n}|\!\}^\circ \hookrightarrow_{PU} \{\!|m_1^\circ, \ldots, m_n^\circ|\!\}^{\alpha_1 \cdots \alpha_n}$$

$$\{\!|(\nu X.S^\alpha)^\circ|\!\} \hookrightarrow_{\nu U} \{\!|(\nu X.S^\circ)^\alpha|\!\} \quad \alpha \notin X$$

Both the chemical and membrane law may be used in conjunction with (νU). Observe that the rule (PU) works on *tagged* solutions. The usual chemical law does not apply to this rule. However the membrane law does. Contexts for tagged solutions are defined as follows.

$$C_t ::= [\,] \mid (\{\!|(\nu X.C_t)^{t_1}|\!\} \uplus S)^{t_2}$$

Alternative Chemical Law for (PU). As the (PU) rule is essentially about synchronizing actions from different components, the usual chemical law does not apply. However, the following alternative chemical law achieves (piecemeal) the synchronization of actions and upward propagation done by (PU):

$$\{\!|m^\alpha|\!\}^\circ \hookrightarrow_{PU} \{\!|m^\circ|\!\}^\alpha \qquad \frac{S_1^\circ \hookrightarrow_{PU} (S_1')^{\alpha_1} \quad S_2^\circ \hookrightarrow_{PU} (S_2')^{\alpha_2}}{(S_1 \uplus S_2)^\circ \hookrightarrow_{PU} (S_1' \uplus S_2')^{\alpha_1 \cdot \alpha_2}}$$

Results. The SCCS CHAM given here is also operationally effective, and is in agreement with its LTS semantics. This supports our case that synchronous operations can be dealt with in a disciplined CHAM framework.

Definition 16 (Administrative Moves). For the SCCS CHAM, $\rightarrow_{\mathcal{A}} = \rightharpoonup \cup \hookrightarrow$.

Definition 17 (Translation). For a SCCS process p, we define $\langle p \rangle = \{\!|p^{\circ}|\!\}^{\circ}$.

Lemma 18 (SCCS-Administrative Moves). The administrative moves $\rightarrow_{\mathcal{A}}$ of the SCCS CHAM are operationally effective for the LTS $(\mapsto^{\alpha}_{R})$.

Lemma 19 (SCCS Simulation). The SCCS CHAM forward and backward simulates the LTS semantics of SCCS.

Theorem 20 (Standardization and Full Abstraction).

1 For the SCCS CHAM, $(=_{\mathcal{A}}; \mapsto^{\alpha}_{R}; =_{\mathcal{A}})^{n} \subseteq \rightarrow^{*}_{\mathcal{A}}; (\mapsto^{\alpha}_{R}; \rightarrow^{*}_{\mathcal{A}})^{n}; (\rightarrow^{-1}_{\mathcal{A}})^{*}$

2 The SCCS CHAM is a fully abstract implementation.

6. Conclusion

We have argued that operational effectiveness is an important criterion for assessing any structural congruence or CHAM specification, since it ensures that the implementation is reasonable and in agreement with the intended semantics. The critical notions are those of confluence and coherence, which turn out to be valuable tools for reasoning about systems and in proofs of adequacy and full abstraction. We believe that the CHAM framework is worth extending beyond asynchronous systems to accommodate non-local interactions and (partial) synchronous operators. Accordingly, we have proposed an alternative "artificial chemistry" in which reactions are "mediated", and in which operational effectiveness provides a vital discipline. Indeed, we contend that the *locality principle* articulated by Banâtre, Boudol and others should relate not merely to the particular Chemical Law they presented (which works well for asynchronous systems) but to these notions of confluence and coherence, which are at the heart of any reasonable CHAM treatment.

In our two examples, we have considered limited subsets of TCCS and SCCS to illustrate the ideas, and for establishing standardization and full abstraction. This is not a serious limitation. For instance, internal choice can be treated by adding the following *reaction* rules. Since internal choice leads to non-confluent behaviour, it should not be a structural rule. These rules do not affect the properties of operational effectiveness.

$$T \vdash \{\!|(p_1 \oplus p_2)^{a}|\!\} \mapsto_{IC} T \vdash \{\!|p_i^{a}|\!\} \quad \text{if } a \in T \quad i \in \{1, 2\}$$

τ actions are invisible moves which resolve internal choice but not external choice. They can be treated by adding an extra reaction rule.

$$T \vdash \{\!|(\tau.p)^{a}|\!\} \mapsto_{R} T \vdash \{\!|p^{a}|\!\} \quad \text{if } a \in T$$

It is intuitive and satisfying that reasonable notions of structural equivalence arise from rule commutations. We believe that structural equivalences arise from permitted commutations in a framework such as rewriting logic. Indeed, the semantic foundations of CHAMs in conditional rewriting logic deserve greater study ([Mes92] shows how CHAMs can be expressed in that framework, though properties such as coherence of those rewriting rules have not been studied further there or in subsequent related work, *e.g.*, [VM00]). We also feel that rewriting logic can provide a framework for exploring the connections between asynchronous and synchronous calculi, since it can express both kinds of chemistry.

In summary, we tacitly identify the essential mechanism of a CHAM as being oriented rewriting modulo a collection of AC equational theories. We may posit that the essential aspects of good

CHAM formulations are: (a) The structural rules are factored into a "core" AC equality theory and an orientable set of rewrite rules. (b) The oriented structural rules $\twoheadrightarrow_{\mathcal{A}}$ satisfy commutation properties, thus exhibiting confluence and strong coherence of $\twoheadrightarrow_{\mathcal{A}}$ with $\mapsto$. (c) Establishing strong coherence is kept relatively simple by avoiding problematic critical pairs, particularly in non-superposition cases, *e.g.*, by disallowing reactions within molecules that are heatable.

Acknowledgement. This work was supported in part by MHRD projects RP01425 and RP01432 and a grant from SUN Microsystems.

References

[AP98] R. Amadio and S. Prasad. Modelling IP mobility. In *Proceedings of CONCUR '98*, *LNCS* vol. 146: 301–316. Springer, 1998.

[BB90] G. Berry and G. Boudol. The chemical abstract machine. In *Proceedings of PoPL'90*, pages 81–94. ACM, 1990.

[BB92] G. Berry and G. Boudol. The chemical abstract machine. *TCS*, 96:217–248, 1992.

[Bou94] G. Boudol. Some chemical abstract machines. In *A Decade of Concurrency*, *LNCS* vol. 803: 92–123. Springer, 1994.

[EG01] J. Engelfriet and T. Gelsema. Structural inclusion in the pi-calculus with replication. *TCS*, 258(1-2):131–168, 2001.

[FG96] C. Fournet and G. Gonthier. The reflexive chemical abstract machine and the join-calculus. In *Proceedings of PoPL'96*, pages 372–385. ACM, 1996.

[GS95] J. F. Groote and J. Springintveld. Focus points and convergent process operators. Logic Group Preprint Series 142, Department of Philosophy, Utrecht University, 1995.

[Mes92] J. Meseguer. Conditional rewriting logic as a unified model of concurrency. *TCS*, 96(1):73–155, 1992.

[Mil83] R. Milner. Calculi for synchrony and asynchrony. *TCS*, 25:267–310, 1983.

[Mil89] R. Milner. *Communication and Concurrency*. Prentice Hall International, 1989.

[Mil90] R. Milner. Functions as processes. In *Proceedings of ICALP'90*, *LNCS* vol. 443: 167–180. Springer-Verlag, 1990.

[Mil93] R. Milner. The polyadic π-calculus: A tutorial. In W. Brauer, F.L. Bauer, and H. Schwichtenberg, eds, *Logic and Algebra of Specification*. Springer, 1993.

[NH87] R. De Nicola and M. Hennessy. CCS without τ's. In *Proceedings of TAPSOFT'87*, *LNCS* vol. 249: 138–152. Springer, 1987.

[Nol99] T. Noll. On coherence properties in term rewriting models of concurrency. In *Proceedings of CONCUR '99*, *LNCS* vol. 1664: 478–493, Springer, 1999.

[NP96] U. Nestmann and B. C. Pierce. Decoding choice encodings. In *Proceedings of CONCUR '96*, *LNCS* vol. 1119: 179–194. Springer, 1996.

[Pal97] C Palamidessi. Comparing the expressive power of the synchronous and the asynchronous pi-calculus. In *Proceedings of PoPL'97*, pages 256–265. ACM, 1997.

[VM00] A. Verdejo and N. Martí-Oliet. Implementing CCS in Maude. In *Proceedings of FORTE 2000*, pages 351–366, Kluwer, 2000.

[Vir95] P. Viry. Rewriting modulo a rewrite system. Technical Report TR-95-20, Dipartimento di Informatica, Univ. Pisa, Dec 1995.

CONTROLLER SYNTHESIS FOR PROBABILISTIC SYSTEMS (EXTENDED ABSTRACT)

Christel Baier[1*], Marcus Größer[1**], Martin Leucker[2***], Benedikt Bollig[3], Frank Ciesinski[1*]

[1] *Institut für Informatik I, University of Bonn,* [baier|groesser|ciesinsk]@cs.uni-bonn.de
[2] *IT Department, Uppsala University,* leucker@it.uu.se
[3] *Lehrstuhl für Informatik II, RWTH Aachen,* bollig@cs.rwth-aachen.de

* Supported by the DFG-NWO-Project "VOSS".
** Supported by the DFG-Project "VERIAM" and the DFG-NWO-Project "VOSS".
*** Supported by the European Research Training Network "Games".

Abstract Controller synthesis addresses the question of how to limit the internal behavior of a given implementation to meet its specification, regardless of the behavior enforced by the environment. In this paper, we consider a model with probabilism and nondeterminism where the nondeterministic choices in some states are assumed to be controllable, while the others are under the control of an unpredictable environment. We first consider probabilistic computation tree logic as specification formalism, discuss the role of strategy-types for the controller and show the NP-hardness of the controller synthesis problem. The second part of the paper presents a controller synthesis algorithm for automata-specifications which relies on a reduction to the synthesis problem for PCTL with fairness.

1. Introduction

In system design, the general goal is to develop systems that satisfy user requirement specifications. To simplify this development process, it should be automated as far as possible. One goal is to *synthesize* a system based on the requirements. Another, practically important task is to synthesize only a *controller* that limits or controls the behavior of an existing system, usually called *plant*, to meet the given specification.

In such a framework, the plant acts usually in an *environment*. The goal is to find a *schedule* for the controllable events that guarantees the specification to be satisfied considering all possible environmental behaviors. One can also understand the controller and environment as two *players*. The plant constitutes to the game board and controller synthesis becomes the problem of finding a *strategy* for the controller that satisfies the specification whatever move the environment does, or in other words, under any *adversary*.

The requirement specification can either be given *internally* or *externally*. Internal specifications impose restrictions for example on the number of visits of a state of the plant. Examples for external specifications are temporal logic formulas that are supposed to be satisfied by the controlled plant.
The controller synthesis problem has attracted a lot of attention in recent years. For discrete systems, the problem is meanwhile well understood [Thomas, 2003]. Recently, the problem was studied for timed systems [Bouyer et al., 2003; de Alfaro et al., 2003]. Here, the plant is modeled as a timed transition system and requirement specifications are given in timed temporal logic or as ω-regular winning conditions on the system.
We study the problem in a probabilistic setting. Our underlying model for the plant are Markov Decision Processes (MDPs), in which we, however, distinguish states that are under control of the plant from those that are under the control of the environment. This model is also known as *turn-based stochastic* $2\frac{1}{2}$*-player games* [Condon, 1992; Condon, 1993; Filar and Vrieze, 1997; de Alfaro et al., 1998; de Alfaro and Henzinger, 2000; Chatterjee et al., 2003], and it is a popular model in planning, AI, and control problems. Several solutions have been suggested for ω-regular winning objectives (e.g. reachability, Büchi and coBüchi, Rabin chain, parity condition) with *qualitative* winning criteria (sure, almost sure, limit sure) in the turn-based and concurrent case [Condon, 1993; de Alfaro et al., 1998; de Alfaro and Henzinger, 2000; Jurdzinski et al., 2003; Chatterjee et al., 2003]. We are interested here in *quantitative winning criteria* stating that the probability to win the game meets a given lower (or upper) probability bound as studied in [de Alfaro and Majumdar, 2001] for concurrent games and in the recent paper [Chatterjee et al., 2004] for $1\frac{1}{2}$- and $2\frac{1}{2}$-player stochastic games.
Translating the players to *system* and *environment*, one can construct a lot of examples of similar spirit, for example in domain of security analysis. The environment acts as an intruder and random moves are used to model different nuances [Mitchell, 2001].
In our setting, we study the problem to find a strategy for the plant such that a given external specification formalized as a *probabilistic temporal logic formula* is fulfilled, no matter how the opponent (environment) behaves. In the first part of the paper, we consider the synthesis problem where the specification is provided by means of a formula of probabilistic computation tree logic PCTL [Hansson and Jonsson, 1994; Bianco and De Alfaro, 1995]. As for strategies, we discuss several choices: The system or the opponent has to choose deterministically (D) or can choose randomly (R). Furthermore, he or she might choose according to the current state (M), also called stationary or Markovian, or, is allowed to look at the history of the game played so far (H). From a practical point of view, it would be desirable to be able to synthesize controllers that do not require extra memory to keep track of a history and

do not depend on random number generators. However, we show that this is not always possible. For security analysis, this implies that adversaries that act according to the information obtained so far are stronger than those not using this information. For the synthesis algorithms, it means that any of the strategy-classes HD, HR, MD and MR requires its own synthesis algorithm. We then show the NP-completeness of the synthesis problem for PCTL and MD-strategies and the NP-hardness of the synthesis problem for PCTL and the strategy-classes HD, HR and MR. Moreover, we show that these results already hold in the setting of $1\frac{1}{2}$-player games (where all states are assumed to be controllable) and for the sublogics $\mathrm{PCTL}_{\setminus \bigcirc}$ and $\mathrm{PCTL}_{\setminus \mathcal{U}}$ that do not use the next step and until operator, respectively. This result stands in contrast to the PCTL model checking problem which is solvable in polynomial-time and for which the strategy-class is irrelevant [Bianco and De Alfaro, 1995].
The second part of the paper addresses the synthesis problem for linear time specifications formalized by LTL-formulas. We show that an optimal HD-strategy for $\mathcal{M}$ and LTL-formula φ can be derived from an optimal MD-strategy for the product-MDP $\mathcal{M} \times \mathcal{A}$, built from the original MDP $\mathcal{M}$ and a deterministic Rabin automaton $\mathcal{A}$ for φ, that maximizes the probability to reach a so-called *winning component* under certain *fairness* assumptions for the adversary. We thus obtain a triple-exponential solution for the HD-controller synthesis problem for MDPs and LTL-specifications that relies on a reduction to the HD-controller synthesis problem for MDPs and Rabin automaton specifications. The latter is solvable via a reduction to the MD-synthesis problem for PCTL with fairness [Baier and Kwiatkowska, 1998]. The recent paper [Chatterjee et al., 2004] establishes the same complexity result for quantitative stochastic $2\frac{1}{2}$-player parity games. In fact, the latter is equivalent to the HD-controller synthesis problem for MDPs and Rabin automaton specifications because both the parity and Rabin-chain condition have the expressiveness of ω-regular winning conditions [Thomas, 1990; Emerson and Jutla, 1991; de Alfaro and Henzinger, 2000]. Thus, our algorithm, which relies on applying a model checker for PCTL with fairness to the MDPs induced by the MD-strategies, can be seen as an alternative to the algorithm suggested in [Chatterjee et al., 2004], which applies an algorithm to solve the quantitative $1\frac{1}{2}$-player parity game to the MDPs induced by the MD-strategies. For a full version of this paper see *http://web.informatik.uni-bonn.de/I/baier/publikationen.html.*

2. Preliminaries

A *distribution* on a countable set X denotes a function $\mu : X \to [0,1]$ with $\sum_{x \in X} \mu(x) = 1$. $\mathsf{Distr}(X)$ denotes the set of all distributions on X. A MDP is a tuple $\mathcal{M} = (S, \mathsf{Act}, \mathsf{P}, s_{init}, \mathsf{AP}, L)$ where S is a countable set of *states*, Act a finite set of actions, $\mathsf{P} : S \times \mathsf{Act} \times S \to [0,1]$ is a three-dimensional transition probability matrix such that $\sum_{t \in S} \mathsf{P}(s, \alpha, t) \in \{0, 1\}$ for all states $s \in S$ and actions $\alpha \in \mathsf{Act}$, and $s_{init} \in S$ is the initial state. AP denotes a finite set of atomic propositions, and $L : S \to 2^{\mathsf{AP}}$ a labelling function which assigns to each state $s \in S$ the set $L(s)$ of atomic propositions that are (assumed to be) valid in s. For technical reasons, we require that none of the states is terminal, i.e., for each state s there exists an action α and a state s' with $\mathsf{P}(s, \alpha, s') > 0$. $\mathcal{M}$ is called finite if the state space S is finite. If $T \subseteq S$, then $\mathsf{P}(s, \alpha, T) = \sum_{t \in T} \mathsf{P}(s, \alpha, t)$ denotes the probability for s to move to a T-state, provided that action α has been selected in state s. We write $\mathsf{Act}_{\mathcal{M}}(s)$ or briefly $\mathsf{Act}(s)$ for the action-set $\{\alpha \in \mathsf{Act} \mid \mathsf{P}(s, \alpha, S) = 1\}$.

A *path* in $\mathcal{M}$ is a finite or infinite alternating sequence of states and actions $\sigma = s_1, \alpha_1, \ldots, \alpha_{n-1}, s_n$ or $\varsigma = s_1, \alpha_1, s_2, \alpha_2, \ldots$ such that $\mathsf{P}(s_i, \alpha_i, s_{i+1}) > 0$. $\sigma[i]$ denotes the i-th state of σ, $\mathsf{first}(\sigma) = \sigma[0]$, and $\mathsf{pref}(\sigma, i)$ denotes the i-th prefix of σ (ending in $\sigma[i]$). For finite paths, $\mathsf{last}(\sigma)$ denotes the last state of σ, while $\mathsf{length}(\sigma)$ stands for the number of transitions in σ. For infinite paths, $\mathsf{trace}(\varsigma)$ denotes the infinite word over the alphabet 2^{AP} which arises from ς by the projection of the induced state-sequence to the sequence of the labelings. If ς is as above then $\mathsf{trace}(\varsigma) = L(s_1), L(s_2), L(s_3), \ldots \in (2^{\mathsf{AP}})^{\omega}$. $\mathsf{Lim}(\varsigma)$ denotes the pair (T, A) where T is the set of states that occur infinitely often in ς and where $A : T \to \mathsf{Act}$ assigns to state $s \in T$ the set of actions $\alpha \in \mathsf{Act}(s)$ with $s = s_i$ and $\alpha = \alpha_i$ for infinitely many indices i. $\mathsf{Path}_{\mathcal{M}}(s)$ (briefly $\mathsf{Path}(s)$) stands for the set of infinite paths in $\mathcal{M}$ which start in state s. In the sequel, we assume that $\mathcal{M}$ is a finite MDP and S_0 a nonempty subset of S consisting of the states which are under the control of the system, i.e., where the system may decide which of the possible actions is executed. The states in $S \setminus S_0$ are controlled by the environment. By a *strategy* for $(\mathcal{M}, S_0)$, we mean any instance D that resolves the nondeterminism in the S_0-states. We distinguish four types of strategies for $(\mathcal{M}, S_0)$, where M stands for Markovian, H for history-dependent, D for deterministic and R for randomized.

- A MD-strategy is a function $D : S_0 \to \mathsf{Act}$ such that $D(s) \in \mathsf{Act}(s)$.
- A MR-strategy is a function $D : S_0 \to \mathsf{Distr}(\mathsf{Act})$ with $D(s) \in \mathsf{Distr}(\mathsf{Act}(s))$
- A HD-strategy is a function D that assigns to any finite path σ in $\mathcal{M}$ with $\mathsf{last}(\sigma) = s \in S_0$ an action $D(\sigma) \in \mathsf{Act}(s)$.
- A HR-strategy is a function D that assigns to any finite path σ with $\mathsf{last}(\sigma) = s \in S_0$ a distribution $D(\sigma) \in \mathsf{Distr}(\mathsf{Act}(s))$.

MD-strategies are often called *simple* or *purely memoryless*. A D-path denotes a path that can be generated by D. E.g., if D is a HD-strategy and σ as above then σ is a D-path iff for all indices $i \in \{1, \ldots, n-1\}$ where $s_i \in S_0$ the chosen action α_i in σ agrees with $D(\mathsf{pref}(\sigma, i))$. We refer to the strategies for the environment as *adversaries*. Formally, for X $\in$ {MD, MR, HD, HR}, a X-adversary for $(\mathcal{M}, S_0)$ denotes a X-strategy for $(\mathcal{M}, S \setminus S_0)$. The notion of *policy* will be used to denote a decision rule that resolves both the internal nondeterministic choices and the nondeterministic choices to be resolved by the environment. Thus, by a X-policy for $\mathcal{M}$ we mean a X-strategy for $(\mathcal{M}, S)$. We will use the letter D for strategies, E for adversaries and C for policies. Policies will often be written in the form $C = (D, E)$.

It is clear that the four strategy-types form a hierarchy. Each simple strategy can be viewed as a MR-strategy (which chooses for any state $s \in S_0$ a fixed action $\alpha \in \mathsf{Act}(s)$ with probability 1) and as a HD-strategy (which only looks for the last state of a path). Similarly, any HD-strategy can be viewed as a HR-strategy. Hence, the class of HR-strategies subsumes the other three strategy-classes MD, HD and MR.

The MDP induced by a strategy. Any strategy D for $(\mathcal{M}, S_0)$ induces a MDP $\mathcal{M}_D$ which arises through unfolding $\mathcal{M}$ into a tree-like structure where the nondeterministic choices in the S_0-states are resolved according to D. E.g., if D is a HD-strategy for $(\mathcal{M}, S_0)$ then the states in $\mathcal{M}_D$ are the finite D-paths. The initial state of $\mathcal{M}_D$ is s_{init}, viewed as a path of length 0. If σ is a finite D-path and $\mathsf{last}(\sigma) \in S_0$ then $\mathsf{Act}_{\mathcal{M}_D}(\sigma) = \{D(\sigma)\}$ and $\mathsf{P}_D(\sigma, D(\sigma), \sigma') = \mathsf{P}(\mathsf{last}(\sigma), D(\sigma), s)$ if $\sigma' = \sigma, \alpha, s$ where $\alpha = D(\sigma)$, and $\mathsf{P}_D(\sigma, \alpha, \sigma') = 0$ in all other cases. If $\mathsf{last}(\sigma) \notin S_0$ then $\mathsf{Act}_{\mathcal{M}_D}(\sigma) = \mathsf{Act}_{\mathcal{M}}(\mathsf{last}(\sigma))$ and $\mathsf{P}_D(\sigma, \alpha, \langle\sigma, \alpha, s\rangle) = \mathsf{P}(\mathsf{last}(\sigma), \alpha, s)$ for all $\alpha \in \mathsf{Act}$ and $s \in S$. The MDP $\mathcal{M}_D$ for HR-strategies is defined in the same way except that $\mathsf{P}_D(\sigma, \alpha, \langle\sigma, \alpha, s\rangle) = D(\sigma)(\alpha) \cdot \mathsf{P}(\mathsf{last}(\sigma), \alpha, s)$ if $\mathsf{last}(\sigma) \in S_0$.

Markov chains and probability measure for policies. If $S_0 = S$ and $D = C$ is a policy for $\mathcal{M}$ then all nondeterministic choices are resolved in $\mathcal{M}_C$. Hence, for any HR-policy C, the MDP $\mathcal{M}_C$ is an infinite-state discrete-time Markov chain. If C is a stationary Markovian policy then all finite C-paths σ, σ' (viewed as states of $\mathcal{M}_C$) with $\mathsf{last}(\sigma) = \mathsf{last}(\sigma')$ can be identified. Hence, $\mathcal{M}_C$ can be viewed as a (discrete-time) Markov chain with state space S. If C is a policy for $\mathcal{M}$, then we write $\mathrm{Pr}^C_{\mathcal{M}}$ or briefly Pr^C to denote the (standard) probability measure on $\mathcal{M}_C$.

Probabilistic Computation Tree Logic (PCTL). PCTL (and its extension PCTL*) [Hansson and Jonsson, 1994; Bianco and De Alfaro, 1995] is a branching-time temporal logic à la CTL/CTL* where state-formulas are interpreted over states of a MDP and path-formulas over its paths. It incorporates an operator to refer to the probability of the occurrence of particular paths (rather than quantification over paths as in CTL). In the sequel, we assume a fixed set AP of atomic propositions and use the letter a to denote an atomic proposition (i.e., $a \in \mathsf{AP}$). The letter p stands for a probability bound (i.e., $p \in [0, 1]$). The symbol $\bowtie$ is one of the comparison operators $\leqslant$ or $\geqslant$. The syntax of PCTL*-state formulas (denoted by Φ, Ψ) and path formulas (denoted by φ) is as follows:

$$\begin{aligned} \Phi &::= \mathsf{tt} \mid a \mid \Phi \wedge \Phi \mid \neg\Phi \mid \mathcal{P}_{\bowtie p}(\varphi) \\ \varphi &::= \Phi \mid \varphi \wedge \varphi \mid \neg\varphi \mid \bigcirc\varphi \mid \varphi\,\mathcal{U}\,\varphi \end{aligned}$$

Intuitively, $\mathcal{P}_{\bowtie p}(\varphi)$ asserts that the probability measure of the paths satisfying φ meets the bound given by $\bowtie p$. The path modalities $\bigcirc$ (next step) and $\mathcal{U}$ (Until) have the same meaning as in CTL*. Other boolean connectives (e.g. $\vee$) and the temporal operators $\Diamond$ (eventually) and $\Box$ (always) can be derived as in CTL* by $\Diamond\varphi = \mathrm{tt}\,\mathcal{U}\,\varphi$ and $\Box\varphi = \neg\Diamond\neg\varphi$. PCTL denotes the sublogic where only path formulas of the form $\bigcirc\Phi$ and $\Phi\,\mathcal{U}\,\Psi$ are allowed. The always-operator can be derived in PCTL using the duality of lower and upper probability bounds, e.g. $\mathcal{P}_{\geqslant p}(\Box\Phi) = \mathcal{P}_{\leqslant 1-p}(\Diamond\neg\Phi)$. $\mathrm{PCTL}_{\setminus\bigcirc}$ ($\mathrm{PCTL}_{\setminus\mathcal{U}}$) denotes the fragment of PCTL that does not use the next step (until) operator. LTL (linear time logic) denotes the path-formula fragment of PCTL* where atoms are atomic propositions (rather than arbitrary state formulas).

Given a MDP $\mathcal{M}$ as before, the formal definition of the satisfaction relation $\models$ for PCTL*-path formulas and propositional PCTL*-state formulas is exactly as for CTL* and omitted here. For the probabilistic operator, the semantics is defined by $s \models \mathcal{P}_{\bowtie p}(\varphi)$ iff for all policies C : $\Pr^C(s,\varphi) \bowtie p$ where $\Pr^C(s,\varphi) = \Pr^C\{\varsigma \in \mathsf{Path}(s) \mid \varsigma \models \varphi\}$. We shall use $\Pr^C(\varphi)$ as an abbreviation for $\Pr^C(s_{init},\varphi)$. To distinguish the satisfaction relation for different MDPs, we sometimes write $(\mathcal{M},s) \models \Phi$ instead of $s \models \Phi$. We write $\mathcal{M} \models \Phi$ iff Φ holds in the initial state of $\mathcal{M}$.

The satisfaction relation for PCTL does not depend on the chosen policy-type because maximal and minimal probabilities for PCTL-path formulas under all HR-policies are reached with simple policies [Bianco and De Alfaro, 1995].

Rabin automata. A *deterministic Rabin automaton* is a structure $\mathcal{A} = (Q,\Pi,\delta,q_0,\mathrm{Acc})$ where Q is a finite state space, Π the alphabet, $q_0 \in Q$ the starting state, and $\delta : Q \times \Pi \to Q$ the transition function. (To encode an LTL-formula by a Rabin automaton the alphabet $\Pi = 2^{\mathsf{AP}}$ is used.) The acceptance condition Acc is a set of tuples (H_i,K_i) consisting of subsets H_i and K_i of Q. The run for an infinite word $\pi = \pi[0],\pi[1],\ldots \in \Pi^\omega$ in $\mathcal{A}$ means the infinite sequence $q_0,q_1,q_2,\ldots$ of automata-states where $q_{i+1} = \delta(q_i,\pi[i])$. Acceptance of π under the Rabin condition $\mathrm{Acc} = \{(H_i,K_i) : i = 1,\ldots,m\}$ can be described by the LTL-formula $\mathrm{acc}(\mathcal{A}) = \bigvee_{1\leq i\leq m}\Diamond\Box(H_i \wedge \Diamond K_i)$. That is, a run $\rho = q_0,q_1,q_2,\ldots$ in $\mathcal{A}$ is accepting if there is at least one pair (H_i,K_i) in the acceptance condition Acc of $\mathcal{A}$ such that $\lim(\rho) \subseteq H_i$ and $\lim(\rho) \cap K_i \neq \varnothing$ where $\lim(\rho)$ denotes the set of all states in Q which appear infinitely often in ρ. $\mathcal{L}(\mathcal{A})$ denotes the accepted language of $\mathcal{A}$, i.e., the set of infinite words $\rho \in \Pi^\omega$ whose run in $\mathcal{A}$ is accepting. Given a MDP $\mathcal{M} = (S,\mathsf{Act},\mathsf{P},s_{init},\mathsf{AP},L)$, policy C for $\mathcal{M}$ and Rabin automaton $\mathcal{A} = (Q,2^{\mathsf{AP}},\delta,Q_0,\mathsf{Acc})$, we write $\Pr^C(s,\mathcal{A})$ for the probability measure of all C-paths that start in state s and that generate a trace which is accepted by $\mathcal{A}$, i.e., we put $\Pr^C(s,\mathcal{A}) = \Pr^C\{\varsigma \in \mathsf{Path}(s) : \mathsf{trace}(\varsigma) \in \mathcal{L}(\mathcal{A})\}$. $\Pr^C(\mathcal{A})$ stands short for $\Pr^C(s_{init},\mathcal{A})$.

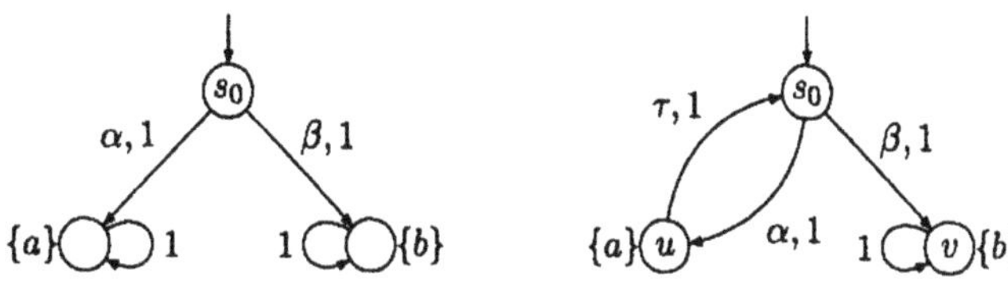

Fig. 1(a) randomization helps **Fig. 1(b)** history helps

3. The controller synthesis problem for PCTL

The controller synthesis problems discussed in this paper are formalized by triples $(\mathcal{M}, S_0, Spec)$ where $\mathcal{M}$ is a finite MDP, S_0 a set of controllable states in $\mathcal{M}$ and *Spec* a temporal-logical or ω-regular specification. The question is to find a strategy D for $(\mathcal{M}, S_0)$ such that *Spec* holds for the MDP $\mathcal{M}_D$, no matter how the environment (adversary) behaves.

This section addresses the case where *Spec* is a PCTL-state formula and first discusses the role of the strategy-type. Let $\mathrm{X} \in \{\mathrm{MD}, \mathrm{MR}, \mathrm{HD}, \mathrm{HR}\}$ be a strategy class. The X-controller synthesis problem for PCTL is as follows:

Given: a finite MDP $\mathcal{M}$, a subset S_0 of states and a PCTL-state formula Φ.

Wanted: a X-strategy D for $(\mathcal{M}, S_0)$ such that $\mathcal{M}_D \models \Phi$ (if one exists).

Clearly, any solution of the MD-strategy controller synthesis problem (i.e., any simple strategy D with $\mathcal{M}_D \models \Phi$) is at the same time a solution for the controller synthesis problem for any other strategy-class which subsumes the simple strategies (in particular, for the strategy-classes MR, HD and HR). With the same argument, if the HD- or MR-controller synthesis problem is solvable then so is the HR-controller synthesis problem.

The question arises whether (as for the PCTL satisfaction relation) e.g. simple strategies are as powerful as HD-strategies to solve the controller synthesis problem and the same question for other strategy-classes X_1 (instead of MD) and X_2 (instead of HD) with $\mathrm{X}_2 \not\subseteq \mathrm{X}_1$. The answer is *no* in either case (more precisely, for the strategy-classes MD, MR, HD and HR discussed here), even for the sublogics $\mathrm{PCTL}_{\backslash\bigcirc}$ and $\mathrm{PCTL}_{\backslash\mathcal{U}}$.

For the MDP $\mathcal{M}$ in Fig. 1(a) with $s_0 \in S_0$ and the $\mathrm{PCTL}_{\backslash\mathcal{U}}$-formula $\Phi = \mathcal{P}_{\geqslant 0.5}(\bigcirc a) \wedge \mathcal{P}_{\geqslant 0.5}(\bigcirc b)$ the HD-controller synthesis problem is not solvable for $\mathcal{M}$, S_0 and Φ. On the other hand, $(\mathcal{M}_D, s_0) \models \Phi$ for the MR-strategy D which assigns probability 1/2 to actions α and β in state s_0. Hence, the MR-controller synthesis problem is solvable for $\mathcal{M}$, S_0 and Φ. The same argument applies to the $\mathrm{PCTL}_{\backslash\bigcirc}$-formula $\mathcal{P}_{\geqslant 0.5}(\Diamond a) \wedge \mathcal{P}_{\geqslant 0.5}(\Diamond b)$. Thus, randomized strategies (MR, HR) can be more powerful than deterministic (MD, HD) strategies to solve the controller synthesis problem for $\mathrm{PCTL}_{\backslash\mathcal{U}}$ or $\mathrm{PCTL}_{\backslash\bigcirc}$.

The following shows that there are instances $(\mathcal{M}, S_0, \Phi)$ for which the controller synthesis problem for the strategy-class HD is solvable but not for the MR-strategies. For the MDP shown in Figure 1(b), with $s_0 \in S_0$, and $\Phi =$

$\mathcal{P}_{\geqslant 1}(\bigcirc a) \wedge \mathcal{P}_{\geqslant 1}(\bigcirc \Psi)$, with $\Psi = \mathcal{P}_{\geqslant 1}(\bigcirc \mathcal{P}_{\geqslant 1}(\bigcirc b))$ there is a HD-strategy D with $(\mathcal{M}_D, s_0) \models \Phi$. On the other hand, the only MR-strategy D which guarantees for s_0 that with probability 1 the next state is an a-state is given by $D(s_0)(\alpha) = 1$, and $D(s_{uu})(\beta) = 0$. For this MR-strategy D, we have $(\mathcal{M}_D, s_0) \not\models \mathcal{P}_{\geqslant 1}(\bigcirc \Psi)$, and hence, $(\mathcal{M}_D, s_0) \not\models \Phi$. The same argument applies to the PCTL$_{\setminus\bigcirc}$-formula $\mathcal{P}_{\geqslant 1}(\Diamond a) \wedge \mathcal{P}_{\geqslant 1}(\Diamond b)$ where the only chance for a MR-strategy to reach the a-state u with probability 1 is to select action α in state s_0 with probability 1.

The previous remarks show that the role of strategy-types for controller synthesis is completely different from the situation in PCTL model checking. While a single algorithm suffices for PCTL model checking, for controller synthesis, any strategy type requires its own synthesis algorithm!

The naïve idea to solve the MD-controller synthesis problem for $\mathcal{M}$, S_0 and PCTL-formula Φ is to consider all simple strategies D for $(\mathcal{M}, S_0)$ and to apply a standard PCTL model checking algorithm to $\mathcal{M}_D$ and Φ. The time complexity is linear in the length of Φ and exponential in size$(\mathcal{M})$, but we should not expect an algorithm which is efficient for all MDPs because of the following theorem which shows that the decision variant of the controller synthesis problem is NP-complete. The decision variant asks for the *existence* of a simple strategy D such that $\mathcal{M}_D \models \Phi$ but not for such a strategy. To prove membership in NP we need the existence of a polynomial-time algorithm that calculates the *precise* maximal or minimal probabilities for PCTL-path formulas under simple policies (rather than approximation algorithms). For instance, this is possible if all probabilities in the given MDP $\mathcal{M}$ and all probability bounds in the given PCTL formula Φ are rational. In this case, we may apply the PCTL model checking procedure à la Bianco and de Alfaro [Bianco and De Alfaro, 1995] using precise methods to solve linear programs.

THEOREM 1 *Under the above conditions, the decision variant of the MD-controller synthesis problem for PCTL and its sublogics* PCTL$_{\setminus\mathcal{U}}$ *and* PCTL$_{\setminus\bigcirc}$ *is NP-complete, even when we require all states in the MDP to be controllable.*

THEOREM 2 *The decision variant of the MR/HD/HR-controller synthesis for PCTL and its sublogics* PCTL$_{\setminus\bigcirc}$ *and* PCTL$_{\setminus\mathcal{U}}$ *is NP-hard, even when all states are required to be controllable.*

PCTL with fairness. In Section 4, we shall need a variant of the controller synthesis problem for PCTL where fairness assumptions about the adversaries are made. The X-controller synthesis problem for PCTL with fairness assumes a finite MDP $\mathcal{M} = (S, \mathsf{Act}, \mathsf{P}, s_{init}, \mathsf{AP}, L)$, a subset S_0 of S, a PCTL-formula Φ and, in addition, a fairness condition for the adversaries. It asks for a X-strategy D such that $\mathcal{M}_D \models_{fair} \Phi$ where the satisfaction relation $\models_{fair}$ is defined as the standard satisfaction relation $\models$, except for the probabilistic op-

erator: $s \models_{fair} \mathcal{P}_{\bowtie p}(\varphi)$ iff for all fair policies C: $\Pr^C(s,\varphi) \bowtie p$. Several fairness notions for MDPs have been suggested [Vardi, 1985; Pnueli and Zuck, 1986; Baier and Kwiatkowska, 1998]. In Section 4 we shall use the notion of a fair adversary (for a given strategy D) to denote an adversary F such that almost all (D,F)-paths are fair.
The NP-completeness established in Theorem 1 for PCTL without fairness carries over to PCTL with fairness. To solve the MD-controller synthesis problem for PCTL with fairness conditions, we may apply the model checking algorithm suggested in [Baier and Kwiatkowska, 1998] to each MDP $\mathcal{M}_D$ induced by a simple strategy D. For other strategy types (MR, HD or HR), the complexity or even the decidability of the controller synthesis problem for PCTL (without or with fairness) is an open problem.

4. HD-controller synthesis for automata-specifications

We now address the controller synthesis problem where the specification is provided by means of an ω-automaton and a probability bound "$\bowtie p$". Using an automata-representation for a given LTL-formula, the techniques suggested here also solve the controller synthesis problem for LTL.
In the rest of this section, $\mathcal{M} = (S, \mathsf{Act}, \mathsf{P}, s_{init}, \mathsf{AP}, L)$ is a finite MDP, $S_0 \subseteq S$, and $\mathcal{A} = (Q, 2^{\mathsf{AP}}, \delta, q_0, \mathsf{Acc})$ a deterministic Rabin automaton as in Sect. 2. The X-controller synthesis problem for $\mathcal{M}$, S_0, $\mathcal{A}$, "$\bowtie p$" asks whether there is a X-strategy D such that $\Pr^{(D,E)}(\mathcal{A}) \bowtie p$ for all HD-adversaries E.
To see the difference between the controller synthesis problems for the strategy-classes HD and MD resp. MR, consider the following. Let $\mathcal{M}$ be as in figure 1(b), $s_0 \in S_0$ and $\varphi = (\Diamond a \wedge \Diamond b)$ and $\varphi' = (\bigcirc a \wedge \bigcirc\bigcirc\bigcirc b)$ be $\mathrm{LTL}_{\setminus\bigcirc}$ and $\mathrm{LTL}_{\setminus\mathcal{U}}$ formulas respectively. The controller synthesis problem for $\mathcal{M}$, S_0, φ (resp. φ') and probability bound "$\geqslant 1$" is solvable for HD, but not for MD or MR strategies. The controller synthesis problem for $\mathcal{M}$, S_0, φ (resp. φ') and probability bound "$\geqslant p$" is solvable for MR, but not for MD strategies for $0 < p < 1$ (resp. $0 < p \leqslant \frac{1}{4}$). So any of the strategy types MD, MR, HD requires its own synthesis algorithm.
On the other hand, the two history-dependent strategy types HD and HR are equivalent for the controller synthesis problem for automata-specifications as HR-strategies can be viewed as convex combinations of (possibly infinitely many) HD-strategies, see e.g. [Derman, 1970; Puterman, 1994].
In the following, we present a solution for the HD-controller synthesis problem for $\mathcal{M}$, S_0, $\mathcal{A}$ and *lower* probability bounds "$\geqslant p$". Thus, our goal is the construction of a HD-strategy D such that $\Pr^{(D,E)}(s_{init}, \mathcal{A}) \geqslant p$ for all HD-adversaries E. Upper probability bounds can be treated in a similar way.

DEFINITION 3 (PRODUCT-MDP [DE ALFARO, 1997]) The MDP $\mathcal{M} \times \mathcal{A} = (S \times Q, \mathsf{Act}, \mathsf{P}, t_{init}, \mathsf{AP}', L')$ is defined as follows: The initial state t_{init} is

$\langle s_{init}, q_{init}\rangle$ where $q_{init} = \delta(q_0, L(s_{init}))$. The values of the transition probability matrix are given by $\mathsf{P}(\langle s,q\rangle,\alpha,\langle s',\delta(q,L(s'))\rangle) = \mathsf{P}(s,\alpha,s')$ and $\mathsf{P}(\cdot) = 0$ in all other cases. The set AP' is $\mathsf{AP} \cup (S \times Q) \cup Q$ where AP, $S \times Q$ and Q are supposed to be pairwise disjoint. The labeling function L' is given by $L'(\langle s,q\rangle) = L(s) \cup \{\langle s,q\rangle, q\}$. The "liftings" of the sets $H_i, K_i \subseteq Q$ in the acceptance condition of $\mathcal{A}$ are defined by $\bar{H}_i = S \times H_i$, and $\bar{K}_i = S \times K_i$. If $P \subseteq (S \times Q) \cup Q$ then we write P for the propositional formula $\bigvee_{q \in P} q$. ■

There is a one-to-one correspondence between the paths in $\mathcal{M}$ and $\mathcal{M} \times \mathcal{A}$. Given a (finite or infinite) path π in $\mathcal{M}$, we lift π to a path $\pi^{\times}$ in $\mathcal{M} \times \mathcal{A}$ by adding automata components which describe the run of π in $\mathcal{A}$. Vice versa, given a path π in $\mathcal{M} \times \mathcal{A}$, the projection $\pi|_{\mathcal{M}}$ of π to the state sequence in $\mathcal{M}$ is a path in $\mathcal{M}$ while the projection $\pi|_{\mathcal{A}}$ of π to the sequence of automata-states is the run for $\pi|_{\mathcal{M}}$ in $\mathcal{A}$. This observation yields a one-to-one correspondence between the HD-strategies for $(\mathcal{M}, S_0)$ and $(\mathcal{M} \times \mathcal{A}, S_0 \times Q)$ in the following sense. If D is a strategy for $(\mathcal{M}, S_0)$ then we may define a strategy $D^{\times}$ for $(\mathcal{M} \times \mathcal{A}, S_0 \times Q)$ by $D^{\times}(\sigma) = D(\sigma|_{\mathcal{M}})$. Vice versa, given a strategy D for $(\mathcal{M} \times \mathcal{A}, S_0 \times Q)$, we may define the "corresponding" strategy $D|_{\mathcal{M}}$ for $(\mathcal{M}, S_0)$ by $D|_{\mathcal{M}}(\sigma) = D(\sigma^{\times})$. The described transformation $D \mapsto D^{\times}$ is type-preserving in the sense that if D is a X-strategy for $(\mathcal{M}, S_0)$ then $D^{\times}$ is a X-strategy for $(\mathcal{M} \times \mathcal{A}, S_0 \times Q)$, while the converse transformation $D \mapsto D|_{\mathcal{M}}$ may yield a HD-strategy $D|_{\mathcal{M}}$ for $(\mathcal{M}, S_0)$ if D is a simple strategy for $(\mathcal{M} \times \mathcal{A}, S_0 \times Q)$. If C is a HD-policy for $\mathcal{M}$ and $C^{\times}$ the induced HD-policy in $\mathcal{M} \times \mathcal{A}$ then $\Pr^{C}_{\mathcal{M}}(\mathcal{A}) = \Pr^{C\times}_{\mathcal{M}\times\mathcal{A}}(\mathcal{A}) = \Pr^{C\times}_{\mathcal{M}\times\mathcal{A}}(\mathsf{acc}(\mathcal{A}))$. By the one-to-one-relation for both the adversaries E and strategies D, we get:

LEMMA 4 $\sup_D \inf_E \Pr^{(D,E)}_{\mathcal{M}}(\mathcal{A}) = \sup_D \inf_E \Pr^{(D,E)}_{\mathcal{M}\times\mathcal{A}}(\mathcal{A})$

Lemma 4 allows us to focus on the product-MDP. From now on, if not stated otherwise, by a strategy (an adversary) we mean a strategy (an adversary) for $(\mathcal{M} \times \mathcal{A}, S_0 \times Q)$. [de Alfaro, 1997] defines end components of the product-MDP as the MDP-analogue of recurrent sets in discrete-time Markov chains. Intuitively, end components are sub-MDPs for which a policy can be defined such that almost all paths in the end component visit any state of the end component infinitely often. Formally, an *end component* [de Alfaro, 1997] for the MDP $\mathcal{M} \times \mathcal{A}$ denotes a pair (T, A) consisting of a nonempty subset T of $S \times Q$ and a function $A : T \to \mathsf{Act}$ such that (i) $\varnothing \neq A(t) \subseteq \mathsf{Act}(t)$ for all states $t \in T$, (ii) $\mathsf{P}(t, \alpha, T) = 1$ for all $t \in T$ and $\alpha \in A(t)$ and (iii) the induced digraph $(T, \longrightarrow_A)$ is strongly connected. (Here, $t \longrightarrow_A t'$ iff $\mathsf{P}(t, \alpha, t') > 0$ for some $\alpha \in A(t)$.) An *accepting end component* (AEC) is an end component (T, A) such that $T \subseteq \bar{H}_i$ and $T \cap \bar{K}_i \neq \varnothing$ for some index $i \in \{1, \ldots, m\}$.

[de Alfaro, 1997] shows that for each policy C, the probability measure for the infinite paths ς where $\mathsf{Lim}(\varsigma)$ is an end component is 1. Hence, we have $\Pr^C_{\mathcal{M}\times\mathcal{A}}(\mathcal{A}) = \Pr^C_{\mathcal{M}\times\mathcal{A}}\{\varsigma : \mathsf{Lim}(\varsigma) \text{ is an AEC}\}$.
For our purposes, we need a variant of accepting end components, called winning components. The idea is that for any state t of a winning component there is a strategy such that—independent on how the adversary resolves the nondeterminism—almost all paths starting in t will eventually reach an AEC and stay there forever.

DEFINITION 5 (WINNING COMPONENT) A winning component denotes a pair (T, A) consisting of a nonempty subset T of $S \times Q$ and a function $A : T \to \mathsf{Act}$ such that (1) $A(t) \subseteq \mathsf{Act}(t)$ and $|A(t)| = 1$ for all $t \in T \cap (S_0 \times Q)$, (2) $A(t) = \mathsf{Act}(t)$ for all $t \in T \cap ((S \setminus S_0) \times Q)$, (3) $\mathsf{P}(t, \alpha, T) = 1$ for all $t \in T$ and $\alpha \in A(t)$ and (4) for any simple adversary E and any bottom strongly connected component U of the digraph $(T, \longrightarrow_E)$ with $t \longrightarrow_E t'$ iff $\mathsf{P}(t, E(t), t') > 0$ there exists an index $i \in \{1, \ldots, m\}$ such that $U \subseteq \bar{H}_i$ and $U \cap \bar{K}_i \neq \varnothing$. WC denotes the set of all states $t \in S \times Q$ that are contained in some winning component. ■

Our goal is now to show that the best strategy to generate $\mathcal{A}$-paths can be derived from the best strategy to reach a winning component.

LEMMA 6 *For any state* $t_0 \in (S \times Q) \setminus \mathsf{WC}$ *and HD-strategy* D, *there exists a HD-adversary* E *such that* $\Pr^{(D,E)}_{\mathcal{M}\times\mathcal{A}}(t_0, \mathcal{A}) < 1$.

We now show that any strategy can be improved by forcing the system to stay in WC as soon as WC is reached.

LEMMA 7 *There is a simple strategy* D_{WC} *such that* $\Pr^{(D_{\mathsf{WC}},E)}_{\mathcal{M}\times\mathcal{A}}(t, \mathcal{A}) = 1$ *for all HD-adversaries* E *and all states* $t \in \mathsf{WC}$. *and for any infinite* D_{WC}*-path* ς, *if* $\varsigma[i] \in \mathsf{WC}$ *then* $\varsigma[j] \in \mathsf{WC}$ *for all* $j \geqslant i$.

Lemma 6 and 7 yield:

COROLLARY 8 *For any state* $t \in \mathcal{M} \times \mathcal{A}$: $t \in \mathsf{WC}$ *iff there exists a HD-strategy* D *with* $\Pr^{(D,E)}_{\mathcal{M}\times\mathcal{A}}(t, \mathcal{A}) = 1$ *for all HD-adversaries* E.

LEMMA 9 *For any HD-strategy* D *there is a HD-strategy* $\widehat{D}$ *such that for all HD-adversaries* E:

(1) *For any infinite* $\widehat{D}$*-path* ς, *if* $\varsigma[i] \in \mathsf{WC}$ *then* $\varsigma[j] \in \mathsf{WC}$ *for all* $j \geqslant i$.

(2) $\Pr^{(\widehat{D},E)}_{\mathcal{M}\times\mathcal{A}}(\Diamond\mathsf{WC}) = \Pr^{(\widehat{D},E)}_{\mathcal{M}\times\mathcal{A}}(\Diamond\mathsf{WC} \wedge \mathsf{acc}(\mathcal{A}))$

(3) $\Pr^{(\widehat{D},E)}_{\mathcal{M}\times\mathcal{A}}(\mathcal{A}) \geqslant \Pr^{(D,E)}_{\mathcal{M}\times\mathcal{A}}(\mathcal{A})$

Our rough goal is to show $\sup\limits_D \inf\limits_E \Pr^{(D,E)}(\mathcal{A}) = \sup\limits_D \inf\limits_E \Pr^{(D,E)}(\Diamond\mathsf{WC})$.

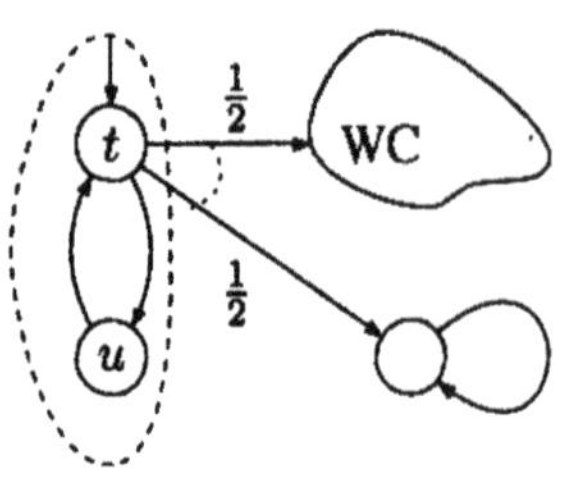

Lemma 9 yields "$\geqslant$". Unfortunately, "$\leqslant$" does not hold in general. For instance, in the MDP shown aside, we assume that states t and u build an AEC which is not contained in WC. If $t \notin S_0$ then the best adversary, $\widehat{E}$, chooses the transition that leaves the AEC $\{t, u\}$ and moves with probability 1/2 to WC. On the other hand, under the adversary E that forces the system to stay forever in the AEC $\{t, u\}$, WC is never reached, and thus, E minimizes the probability for $\Diamond$WC. However, any adversary, which—as in the example aside—forces the system to stay in an AEC that does not intersect with WC, can be improved by leaving the AEC, even if WC is reached under the modified adversary.

LEMMA 10 *For any HD-strategy $\widehat{D}$ which fulfills condition (1) and (2) of Lemma 9 and any HD-adversary E there exists a HD-adversary $\widehat{E}$ such that*

(4) $\Pr^{(\widehat{D},\widehat{E})}_{\mathcal{M}\times\mathcal{A}}(\Gamma) = 0$ *where Γ denotes the set of infinite paths ς that start in t_{init} and where* $\mathsf{Lim}(\varsigma) = (T, A)$ *is an AEC with $T \cap \mathsf{WC} = \varnothing$.*

(5) $\Pr^{(\widehat{D},E)}_{\mathcal{M}\times\mathcal{A}}(\mathcal{A}) \geqslant \Pr^{(\widehat{D},\widehat{E})}_{\mathcal{M}\times\mathcal{A}}(\mathcal{A}) = \Pr^{(\widehat{D},\widehat{E})}_{\mathcal{M}\times\mathcal{A}}(\Diamond\mathsf{WC})$

For policies $(\widehat{D}, \widehat{E})$ where (1), (2) and (4) hold, the probability to reach WC agrees with the probability for the $\mathcal{A}$-paths. Thus, using Lemma 7, 9 and 10, we obtain: $\sup_D \inf_E \Pr^{(D,E)}_{\mathcal{M}\times\mathcal{A}}(\mathcal{A}) = \sup_{\widehat{D}} \inf_{\widehat{E}} \Pr^{(D,\widehat{E})}_{\mathcal{M}\times\mathcal{A}}(\Diamond\mathsf{WC})$ where D, E range over all HD-strategies/HD-adversaries and $\widehat{D}$, $\widehat{E}$ over all HD-strategies/HD-adversaries satisfying (1), (2) and (4). We now show that the adversaries where (4) holds are exactly the adversaries that are fair in the following sense:

DEFINITION 11 (AEC-FAIRNESS) For any state $t \in ((S\backslash S_0)\times Q)\cap(\mathsf{AEC}\backslash \mathsf{WC})$, let $\mathsf{FairAct}(t)$ be the set of actions $\alpha \in \mathsf{Act}(t)$ such that $\mathsf{P}(t, \alpha, S \setminus \mathsf{AEC}) > 0$. Here, AEC denotes the set of all states that are contained in some AEC. For any other state $t \in S \times Q$, we put $\mathsf{FairAct}(t) = \varnothing$. An infinite path $\varsigma = s_1 \xrightarrow{\alpha_1} s_2 \xrightarrow{\alpha_2} \ldots$ is called AEC-fair iff for all $t \in ((S\backslash S_0)\times Q)\cap(\mathsf{AEC}\backslash \mathsf{WC})$ where $\mathsf{FairAct}(t) \neq \varnothing$: If t occurs infinitely often in ς then there are infinitely many indices i with $s_i = t$ and $\alpha_i \in \mathsf{FairAct}(s_i)$. An HD-adversary F is called AEC-fair for strategy D if $\Pr^{(D,F)}_{\mathcal{M}\times\mathcal{A}}\{\varsigma : \varsigma \text{ is AEC-fair}\} = 1$. ■

Given a strategy $\widehat{D}$ satisfying (1) and (2), any adversary $\widehat{E}$ that fulfills condition (4) in Lemma 10 is AEC-fair for $\widehat{D}$. Vice versa, (4) holds for any adversary F that is AEC-fair for $\widehat{D}$. Thus:

$$\inf_{E} \Pr^{(\widehat{D},E)}_{\mathcal{M}\times\mathcal{A}}(\mathcal{A}) = \inf_{F \text{ fair}} \Pr^{(\widehat{D},F)}_{\mathcal{M}\times\mathcal{A}}(\mathcal{A}) = \inf_{F \text{ fair}} \Pr^{(\widehat{D},F)}_{\mathcal{M}\times\mathcal{A}}(\Diamond\mathsf{WC})$$

LEMMA 12 $\sup_{D} \inf_{E} \Pr^{(D,E)}_{\mathcal{M}\times\mathcal{A}}(\mathcal{A}) = \sup_{D} \inf_{F \text{ fair}} \Pr^{(D,F)}_{\mathcal{M}\times\mathcal{A}}(\Diamond \mathsf{WC})$
where D ranges over all HD-strategies, E over all HD-adversaries and F over all HD-adversaries that are AEC-fair for D. This follows from Lemma 9.

According to Lemma 12, the HD-controller synthesis problem for Rabin-automata specifications is reducible to the HD-controller synthesis problem for PCTL with fairness. Although the controller synthesis problem for PCTL depends on the chosen strategy-type, for probabilistic reachability properties such as $\mathcal{P}_{\geqslant p}(\Diamond \mathsf{WC})$ we may switch from HD-strategies to simple strategies.

LEMMA 13 $\sup_{D} \inf_{F \text{ fair}} \Pr^{(D,F)}_{\mathcal{M}\times\mathcal{A}}(\Diamond \mathsf{WC}) = \max_{\widetilde{D} \text{ simple}} \inf_{F \text{ fair}} \Pr^{(\widetilde{D},F)}_{\mathcal{M}\times\mathcal{A}}(\Diamond \mathsf{WC})$

where D ranges over all HD-strategies, $\widetilde{D}$ over all simple strategies and F over all HD-adversaries that are AEC-fair for D resp. $\widetilde{D}$. And finally we get

THEOREM 14 *There is a HD-strategy D for $(\mathcal{M}, S_0)$ which solves the controller synthesis problem for $\mathcal{M}$, S_0, $\mathcal{A}$ and probability bound "$\geqslant p$" iff there is a simple strategy $\widetilde{D}$ for the MD-controller synthesis problem for $\mathcal{M} \times \mathcal{A}$, $S_0 \times Q$, the PCTL-formula $\mathcal{P}_{\geqslant p}(\Diamond \mathsf{WC})$ and AEC-fairness (Def. 11).*

In summary, the HD-controller synthesis problem for automata specifications and lower probability bounds can be solved by performing the following steps: (i) Built the product-MDP $\mathcal{M} \times \mathcal{A}$, (ii) calculate WC, (iii) check whether there is a simple strategy $\widetilde{D}$ for $(\mathcal{M} \times \mathcal{A}, S_0 \times Q)$ such that $(\mathcal{M} \times \mathcal{A})_{\widetilde{D}} \models_{fair} \mathcal{P}_{\geqslant p}(\Diamond \mathsf{WC})$ and (iv) if no such simple strategy $\widetilde{D}$ exists then return "No." Otherwise return the HD-scheduler D as in the proof of Theorem 14. In step (ii), we may make use of Corollary 8 which yields that WC is the set of states that have a winning strategy for the Rabin-chain winning objective (formalized by the LTL-formula $\mathsf{acc}(\mathcal{A})$) and the almost-sure winning criterion. Reformulating $\mathsf{acc}(\mathcal{A})$ as a parity winning condition, we may apply the reduction technique suggested in [Chatterjee et al., 2003] from qualitative stochastic $2\frac{1}{2}$-player parity games to (non-stochastic) 2-player parity games to calculate WC with known methods [Emerson et al., 1993; Jurdzinski, 2000; Vöge and Jurdzinski, 2000]. In step (iii), the naïve method that applies a model checking algorithm for PCTL with fairness [Baier and Kwiatkowska, 1998] to any of the MDPs $(\mathcal{M} \times \mathcal{A})_{\widetilde{D}}$, the space complexity is bounded by $\mathcal{O}(\mathsf{size}(\mathcal{M}) \cdot \mathsf{size}(\mathcal{A}))$, but the worst-case running time is exponential in $\mathsf{size}(\mathcal{M})$ and $\mathsf{size}(\mathcal{A})$. (Note that the number of simple strategies is $\prod_{s \in S_0} |\mathsf{Act}(s)|^{|Q|} \geqslant 2^{|S_0| \cdot |Q|}$ if $|\mathsf{Act}(s)| \geqslant 2$ for all states $s \in S_0$.)

References

Baier, C. and Kwiatkowska, M. (1998). Model checking for a probabilistic branching time logic with fairness. *Distributed Computing*, 11(3):125–155.

Bianco, A. and De Alfaro, L. (1995). Model checking of probabilistic and non-deterministic systems. In Proc. FST & TCS, LNCS 1026, pages 499–513.

Bouyer, P., D'Souza, D., Madhusudan, P., and Petit, A. (2003). Timed control with partial observability. In Proc. CAV LNCS 2725, pages 180–192.

Chatterjee, K., Jurdzinski, M., and Henzinger, T. (2003). Simple stochastic parity games. In Proc. CSL LNCS 2803, pages 100–113.

Chatterjee, K., Jurdzinski, M., and Henzinger, T. (2004). Quantitative simple stochastic parity games. In *Proceedings of the Annual Symposium on Discrete Algorithms (SODA)*. SIAM.

Condon, A. (1992). The complexity of stochastic games. *Inf. and Comp.*, 96:203–224.

Condon, A. (1993). On algorithms for simple stochastic games. DIMACS, 13:51–71.

de Alfaro, L. (1997). *Formal Verification of Probabilistic Systems*. PhD thesis, Stanford University. Technical report STAN-CS-TR-98-1601.

de Alfaro, L., Faella, M., Henzinger, T., Majumdar, R., and Stoelinga, M. (2003). The element of surprise in timed games. In *Proc. CONCUR*, LNCS 2761, pages 144–158.

de Alfaro, L. and Henzinger, T. (2000). Concurrent omega-regular games. In Proc. LICS, pages 141–154. IEEE Computer Society Press.

de Alfaro, L., Henzinger, T., and Kupferman, O. (1998). Concurrent reachability games. In Proc. FOCS, pages 564–575. IEEE Computer Society Press.

de Alfaro, L. and Majumdar, R. (2001). Quantitative solution of omega-regular games. In Proc. STOC'01, pages 675–683. ACM Press.

Derman, C. (1970). *Finite-State Markovian Decision Processes*. Academic Press.

Emerson, E. and Jutla, C. (1991). Tree automata, mu-calculus and determinacy. In Proc.FOCS, pages 368–377. IEEE Computer Society Press.

Emerson, E. A., Jutla, C. S., and Sistla, A. P. (1993). On model-checking for fragments of mu-calculus. In Courcoubetis, C., editor, Proc. CAV, LNCS 697, pages 385–396.

Filar, J. and Vrieze, K. (1997). *Competitive Markov Decision Processes*. Springer.

Hansson, H. and Jonsson, B. (1994). A logic for reasoning about time and reliability. *Formal Aspects of Computing*, 6:512–535.

Jurdzinski, M. (2000). Small progress for solving parity games. In *Proc. STACS*, volume 1770 of *LNCS*, pages 290–301.

Jurdzinski, M., Kupferman, O., and Henzinger, T. (2003). Trading probability for fairness. In Proc.CSL, LNCS 2471, pages 292–305.

Mitchell, J. C. (2001). Probabilistic polynomial-time process calculus and security protocol analysis. In Proc. ESOP LNCS 2028, pages 23–29.

Pnueli, A. and Zuck, L. (1986). Verification of multiprocess probabilistic protocols. *Distributed Computing*, 1:53–72.

Puterman, M. L. (1994). *Markov Decision Processes: Discrete Stochastic Dynamic Programming*. John Wiley & Sons, Inc., New York, NY.

Thomas, W. (1990). Automata on infinite objects. In van Leeuwen, J., editor, *Handbook of Theoretical Computer Science*, volume B, chapter 4, pages 133–191. Elsevier Science Publishers

Thomas, W. (2003). Infinite games and verification In Poc. CAV LNCS 2725, pages 58–64.

Vardi, M. Y. (1985). Automatic verification of probabilistic concurrent finite-state programs. In Proc. FOCS, pages 327–338, Portland, Oregon. IEEE.

Vöge, J. and Jurdzinski, M. (2000). A discrete strategy improvement algorithm for solving parity games. In Proc. CAV, LNCS 1855, pages 202–215.

HIGHLY UNDECIDABLE QUESTIONS FOR PROCESS ALGEBRAS*

Petr Jančar
Department of Computer Science, Technical University of Ostrava
17. listopadu 15, 708 33 Ostrava - Poruba, Czech Republic
Petr.Jancar@vsb.cz

Jiří Srba
BRICS†, *Department of Computer Science, University of Aalborg*
Fredrik Bajersvej 7B, 9220 Aalborg East, Denmark
srba@brics.dk

Abstract We show Σ_1^1-completeness of weak bisimilarity for PA (process algebra), and of weak simulation preorder/equivalence for PDA (pushdown automata), PA and PN (Petri nets). We also show Π_1^1-hardness of weak ω-trace equivalence for the (sub)classes BPA (basic process algebra) and BPP (basic parallel processes).

Keywords: Weak bisimilarity, simulation, trace preorder, high undecidability

1. Introduction

In the area of verification, the possibilities of checking behavioural equivalences and/or preorders of systems are a natural object to study, which includes various decidability and complexity questions. A part of research effort has been aimed at bisimulation equivalence (bisimilarity) and simulation preorder, since these had been recognized as fundamental notions. We are interested in infinite-state systems, for which recent surveys of results have been given, e.g., in [Burkart et al., 2001, Kučera and Jančar, 2002, Srba, 2002].

The systems we study can be uniformly defined by means of process rewrite systems (PRS) — see Figure 1 for the PRS-hierarchy from [Mayr, 2000]; the second and the third level from the bottom is the focus of our interest. We now

*Both authors are partly supported by the Grant Agency of the Czech Rep., grant No. 201/03/1161.
†Basic Research in Computer Science,
Centre of the Danish National Research Foundation.

provide a selection of some results relevant to our paper (all references can be found in [Srba, 2002]).

(Strong) bisimilarity is already well known to be decidable for the class BPA (basic process algebra, or basic sequential processes), i.e., the class of labelled transition systems generated by left-most derivations of context-free grammars in Greibach normal form; the states correspond to finite sequences of nonterminals which are composed sequentially and only the first one, say X, can be rewritten according to a rule $X \stackrel{a}{\longrightarrow} \alpha$ while emitting an action a (so for a state $X\beta$ we have $X\beta \stackrel{a}{\longrightarrow} \alpha\beta$). Bisimilarity is also known to be decidable for BPP (basic parallel processes); the only difference with BPA is that nonterminals are viewed as composed in parallel, i.e., each can be rewritten. (We can mention also the recent result [Jančar et al., 2003] showing the decidability for the union of BPA and BPP.) An involved result by Sénizergues (later strengthened and simplified by Stirling) showed the decidability even for PDA – labelled transition systems generated by pushdown automata (where a state (p, α) comprises a control state and a sequence of stack symbols). For PN (labelled place/transition Petri nets) bisimilarity is known to be undecidable; this even holds for the subclass PPDA (pushdown automata with stack symbols composed in parallel), which lies strictly between BPP and PN. For the class PA (where the right-hand sides of grammar rules can contain a mixture of sequential and parallel compositions), the decidability question is still open. *(Strong) simulation preorder* is undecidable (already) for both BPA and BPP – as well as classical language equivalence and its modification called *trace equivalence*.

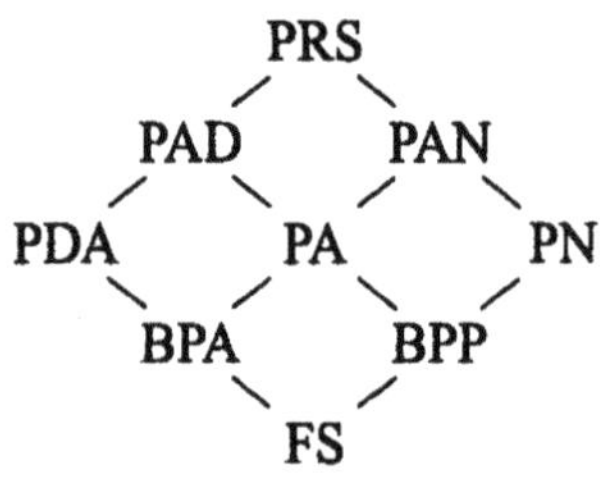

PRS
PAD PAN
PDA PA PN
BPA BPP
FS

Figure 1. PRS-hierarchy

We can naturally ask similar questions for models with silent (internal) actions, and explore weak bisimilarity and weak simulation. Decidability of *weak bisimilarity* is still open for both BPA and BPP. From [Srba, 2003a] it is known to be highly undecidable for PDA and PN, more precisely, complete for the level Σ^1_1 of the analytical hierarchy (i.e., it can be described by a formula $\exists X.\phi(\ldots, X, \ldots)$ where ϕ is a first-order arithmetical formula containing the predicate X; we refer to [Rogers, 1967] for further details about arithmetical and analytical hierarchies). For PA, weak bisimilarity was recently proved undecidable in [Srba, 2003b] but the absence of a control unit seemed to prevent a reduction showing Σ^1_1-hardness; so this problem was left open. In fact, such questions might not seem very relevant from the 'practical' point of view, nevertheless we believe that categorizing undecidable problems according to their degrees of undecidability is still useful for deeper understanding of the studied problems. We can also recall the general experience that the 'natural' undecidable problems (in computer science) are either on the lowest levels of the arithmetical hierarchy or on the lowest levels of the analytical hierarchy (see, e.g., [Harel, 1986]).

In this paper we succeeded in modelling a sufficient fragment of the (missing) finite-control unit, which enabled us to show Σ_1^1-completeness of weak bisimilarity also for PA. We then use some modifications of the developed reductions to show Σ_1^1-completeness of *weak simulation preorder/equivalence* for all the classes PDA, PA and PN (in fact, again even for PPDA).

Weak trace preorder/equivalence is easily shown to be in Π_1^0, i.e., (very) low in the arithmetical hierarchy. This seems to contradict the experience from the strong case (without silent actions) where the complexity increases in the direction: bisimulation – simulation – trace. We give some results indicating that when taking infinite traces (ω-traces) into account, the mentioned 'contradiction' disappears; in particular we show Π_1^1-hardness of *weak ω-trace preorder/equivalence* for both BPA and BPP.

We also show that *weak regularity checking* (checking if a given system is weakly bisimilar to some finite-state one) is 'easier', by which we mean at most hyperarithmetical, for any reasonable process algebra. Finally we add a few observations about Σ_1^1-completeness of *branching bisimilarity* for PDA and PPDA.

Note: a full version of this paper appears as [Jančar and Srba, 2004].

2. Basic Definitions

A *labelled transition system* (LTS) is a triple $(S, Act, \longrightarrow)$ where S is a set of *states* (or *processes*), Act is a set of *labels* (or *actions*), and $\longrightarrow \subseteq S \times Act \times S$ is a *transition relation*; for each $a \in Act$, we view $\stackrel{a}{\longrightarrow}$ as a relation on S where $\alpha \stackrel{a}{\longrightarrow} \beta$ iff $(\alpha, a, \beta) \in \longrightarrow$. We assume that Act contains a distinguished *silent action* τ. The *weak transition relation* $\Longrightarrow$ is defined by $\stackrel{a}{\Longrightarrow} \stackrel{\text{def}}{=} (\stackrel{\tau}{\longrightarrow})^* \circ \stackrel{a}{\longrightarrow} \circ (\stackrel{\tau}{\longrightarrow})^*$ for $a \in Act \smallsetminus \{\tau\}$, and $\stackrel{a}{\Longrightarrow} \stackrel{\text{def}}{=} (\stackrel{\tau}{\longrightarrow})^*$ for $a = \tau$.

Given $(S, Act, \longrightarrow)$, a binary relation $R \subseteq S \times S$ is a *weak simulation* iff for each $(\alpha, \beta) \in R$, $a \in Act$, and α' such that $\alpha \stackrel{a}{\longrightarrow} \alpha'$ there is β' such that $\beta \stackrel{a}{\Longrightarrow} \beta'$ and $(\alpha', \beta') \in R$. A *weak bisimulation* is a weak simulation which is a symmetric relation. We say that a process α *is simulated* by a process β, denoted $\alpha \sqsubseteq_s \beta$, if there is a weak simulation containing (α, β). Processes α and β are *simulation equivalent*, denoted $\alpha =_s \beta$, if $\alpha \sqsubseteq_s \beta$ and $\beta \sqsubseteq_s \alpha$. Processes α and β are *weakly bisimilar*, denoted $\alpha \approx \beta$, if there is a weak bisimulation containing (α, β).

We shall use standard game-theoretic characterizations of the introduced notions. A (weak) *bisimulation game* on a pair of processes α_1 and α_2 is a two-player game between 'Attacker' and 'Defender'. The game is played in *rounds*. In each round the players change the *current states* β_1 and β_2 (initially α_1 and α_2) according to the following rule:

1 Attacker chooses $i \in \{1,2\}$, $a \in Act$ and $\beta'_i \in S$ such that $\beta_i \xrightarrow{a} \beta'_i$.

2 Defender responds by choosing $\beta'_{3-i} \in S$ such that $\beta_{3-i} \xRightarrow{a} \beta'_{3-i}$.

3 States β'_1 and β'_2 become the current states.

A *play* is a maximal sequence of pairs of states formed by the players according to the rule described above, starting from the initial states α_1 and α_2. Defender is the winner in every infinite play. A finite play is lost by the player who is stuck. A (weak) *simulation game* is played similarly, the only change is that Attacker is bound to choose $i = 1$ (thus playing in the "left process" only).

PROPOSITION 1 *It holds that $\alpha_1 \approx \alpha_2$ (resp. $\alpha_1 \sqsubseteq_s \alpha_2$) iff Defender has a winning strategy in the bisimulation (resp. simulation) game from α_1 and α_2.*

PA-processes

Let *Const* be a set of *process constants*. The class of *process expressions* over *Const* is given by $E ::= \epsilon \mid X \mid E.E \mid E \| E$ where 'ϵ' is the *empty process*, X ranges over *Const*, '.' is the operator of *sequential composition*, and '$\|$' stands for a *parallel composition*. We do not distinguish between process expressions related by a *structural congruence*, which is the smallest congruence respecting that '.' is associative, '$\|$' is associative and commutative, and 'ϵ' is a unit for '.' and '$\|$'. We shall adopt the convention that the sequential operator binds tighter than the parallel one. Thus, for example, $X.Y \| Z$ means $(X.Y) \| Z$.

A *PA process rewrite system* ($(1, G)$-PRS in the terminology of [Mayr, 2000]) Δ is a finite set of *rules* of the form $X \xrightarrow{a} E$, where $X \in Const$, $a \in Act$ and E is a process expression. Let us denote the set of actions and the set of process constants that appear in Δ as $Act(\Delta)$ and $Const(\Delta)$, respectively. (Note that these sets are finite).

A PA system Δ determines a labelled transition system where the process expressions over $Const(\Delta)$ are the states and $Act(\Delta)$ is the set of labels. The *transition relation* is the least relation satisfying the following SOS rules (recall that '$\|$' is commutative):

$$\frac{(X \xrightarrow{a} E) \in \Delta}{X \xrightarrow{a} E} \qquad \frac{E \xrightarrow{a} E'}{E.F \xrightarrow{a} E'.F} \qquad \frac{E \xrightarrow{a} E'}{E \| F \xrightarrow{a} E' \| F}$$

A process constant $D \in Const(\Delta)$ is called a *deadlock* iff Δ contains no rule $D \xrightarrow{a} E$ for any E. In the usual presentation of PA it is often assumed that Δ contains no deadlocks.

PDA, PPDA, BPA and BPP processes

Let $Q = \{p, q, \ldots\}$, $\Gamma = \{X, Y, \ldots\}$ and $Act = \{a, b, \ldots\}$ be finite sets of *control states*, *stack symbols* and *actions*, respectively, such that $Q \cap \Gamma = \emptyset$ and $\tau \in Act$ is the distinguished silent action. A *PDA system* (or a pushdown automaton) Δ is a finite set of rewrite rules of the type $p \xrightarrow{a} q\alpha$ or $pX \xrightarrow{a} q\alpha$ where $a \in Act$, $p, q \in Q$, $X \in \Gamma$ and $\alpha \in \Gamma^*$. Such a PDA system generates a labelled transition system where $Q \times \Gamma^*$ is the set of states, Act is the set of actions, and the transition relation is defined by prefix-rewriting rules: $(p \xrightarrow{a} q\alpha) \in \Delta$ ($(pX \xrightarrow{a} q\alpha) \in \Delta$) implies $p\gamma \xrightarrow{a} q\alpha\gamma$ ($pX\gamma \xrightarrow{a} q\alpha\gamma$) for all $\gamma \in \Gamma^*$. A *PPDA system* (a parallel pushdown automaton) is defined in the same way as a PDA system but the composition of stack symbols is now viewed as commutative, i.e., 'parallel'. (So each symbol stored in the stack is directly accessible and the stack can be viewed as a multiset of stack symbols.) A PDA (resp. PPDA) system is called BPA for *basic process algebra* (resp. BPP for *basic parallel processes*) whenever the set of control states is singleton. The classes BPA, BPP, PDA and PA correspond directly to the classes from the PRS hierarchy in Figure 1. The class PPDA is positioned strictly between BPP and PN. Hence all the lower bounds we shall prove for PPDA immediately apply also to PN.

Defender's Choice Technique

In what follows we shall frequently use a technique called 'Defender's Choice' (abbreviated by DC). The idea is that Attacker in the (bi)simulation game starting from α and β can be forced by Defender to play a certain transition in the following sense: if Attacker takes any other available transition, Defender can answer in such a way that the resulting processes are guaranteed to be (bi)similar (and hence Attacker loses). A typical situation in the case of bisimilarity may look like in Figure 2 part a) where $\alpha_i \approx \beta_i$ for all $i \geq 1$ (very often α_i and β_i will be even syntactically equal). It is easy to see that in the bisimulation game starting from α and β Attacker is forced (DC) to take the transition $\alpha \xrightarrow{a} \alpha'$. In all other possible moves he loses.

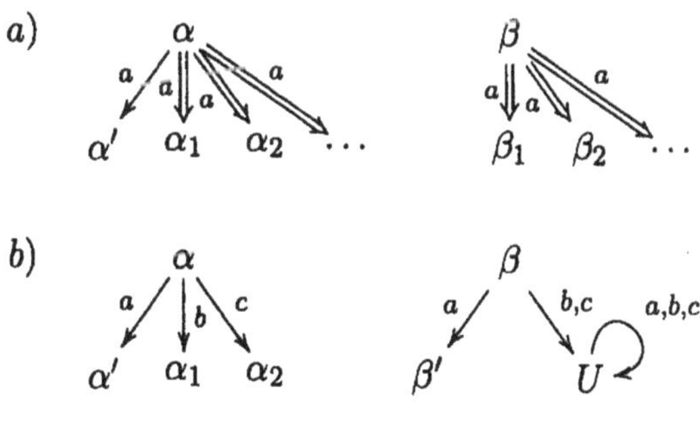

Figure 2. Defender's Choice

In the case of simulation game, Defender can also use another way to force Attacker to perform a certain move. Defender can threaten to enter a *universal state*, i.e., a state where all available actions are constantly enabled. The situation may look like in Figure 2 part b). Obviously Attacker who is playing in the left process is forced (DC) to perform the action a to which Defender can answer only by the same action; the players then continue from the pair α' and β'. Should Attacker play b or c in the first round, Defender answers by the same action and enters the universal state U. From now on Defender can answer to all Attacker's moves and clearly wins.

3. Σ_1^1-completeness of weak (bi)similarity problems

From [Srba, 2003a] we know that weak bisimilarity is Σ_1^1-complete on PDA and PPDA. For PA only undecidability was known [Srba, 2003b] and it was not clear how to simulate "finite-control unit features" which would allow to derive high undecidability as well. Here we answer this question by showing Σ_1^1-completeness also for PA. We then add the Σ_1^1-completeness results for weak simulation preorder (and equivalence) on all the classes PDA, PA and PPDA. Finally we sketch an extension of the results to branching bisimilarity on PDA and PPDA.

We first observe that the mentioned problems are in Σ_1^1: the expression "there exists a set of pairs which contains (P_1, P_2) and is a weak bisimulation (a weak simulation)" can be routinely transformed into a Σ_1^1-formula. For this, it is sufficient that the relations $\xrightarrow{a}$ and $\xRightarrow{a}$ are arithmetical (which is obviously true for any reasonable process algebra like PRS); in fact, these relations are even decidable for the classes PDA, PA and PPDA which we are primarily interested in.

The Σ_1^1-hardness results are achieved by (algorithmic) reductions from suitable problems which are known to be Σ_1^1-complete. One of them is the following:

> Problem: *Recurrent Post's correspondence problem (rPCP)*
> *Instance:* Two sequences $A = [u_1, u_2, \ldots, u_n]$, $B = [v_1, v_2, \ldots, v_n]$ $(n \geq 1)$ of nonempty words over an alphabet Σ such that $|u_i| \leq |v_i|$ for all i, $1 \leq i \leq n$.
> *Question:* Is there an infinite sequence of indices $i_1, i_2, i_3, \ldots$ from the set $\{1, 2, \ldots, n\}$ in which the index 1 appears infinitely often and for which the infinite words $u_{i_1} u_{i_2} u_{i_3} \cdots$ and $v_{i_1} v_{i_2} v_{i_3} \cdots$ are equal ?

Such an infinite sequence $i_1, i_2, i_3, \ldots$ is called a *solution* of the instance (A, B). Any finite sequence $i_1, i_2, \ldots, i_m$ is called a *partial solution* of (A, B) iff $u_{i_1} u_{i_2} \cdots u_{i_m}$ is a prefix of $v_{i_1} v_{i_2} \cdots v_{i_m}$.

REMARK 2 *The problem rPCP is usually defined without the condition $|u_i| \leq |v_i|$; we have included this additional requirement since it is technically convenient and can be easily shown not to affect the following theorem.*

THEOREM 3 *([Harel, 1986]) Problem rPCP is Σ_1^1-complete.*

Let us now fix an instance (A, B) of rPCP, over an alphabet Σ, where $A = [u_1, \ldots, u_n]$ and $B = [v_1, \ldots, v_n]$. A solution of (A, B), if it exists, can be naturally represented by an infinite sequence of process constants from $\{V_1, V_2, \ldots, V_n\}$; the sequence can be divided into finite segments, where a *segment* is defined as a sequence from $\{V_2, V_3, \ldots, V_n\}^* \cdot \{V_1\}$. We note that an infinite sequence composed from segments represents a solution of (A, B) iff all its finite prefixes represent partial solutions, which is equivalent to saying that infinitely many of its finite prefixes represent partial solutions.

A general idea behind our reductions can be described as the following game (which is then concretely implemented in the particular cases we study). Starting from the empty sequence (viewed as a partial solution), Attacker can repeatedly request Defender to prolong the so far constructed partial solution by adding a further segment (for which the implementations will use sequences of τ-moves). Besides the mentioned request, Attacker has also a possibility to enter a checking phase to verify that the (so far) constructed sequence indeed represents a partial solution – if it does not then Attacker wins, and if it does then Defender wins. This means that Defender has a winning strategy if and only if there is an (infinite) solution of the (A, B)-instance.

We now describe a concrete implementation for weak bisimilarity of PA. We show an (algorithmic) construction of a PA system Δ with a pair of processes P_1 and P_2 such that

$$(A, B) \text{ has a solution} \iff P_1 \approx P_2 . \qquad (1)$$

We present Δ in a stepwise manner, always giving a piece of it together with several useful observations (which should make the verification of the desired property straightforward).

In the construction we use a distinguished process constant D which is a *deadlock*, i.e., there are no rules with D on the left-hand side. Particularly useful for us is to note that $\alpha.D.\beta \parallel \gamma \approx \alpha \parallel \gamma$. Later on we show that using the deadlock is not essential (just technically convenient).

Our first intention is to arrange that the bisimulation game will start from the pair (X, X') and continue through some pairs $(X.\alpha_1, X'.\alpha_1)$, $(X.\alpha_2.\alpha_1, X'.\alpha_2.\alpha_1)$, $(X.\alpha_3.\alpha_2.\alpha_1, X'.\alpha_3.\alpha_2.\alpha_1)$, ...where α_i's are reversed segments which are chosen by Defender (using DC, i.e. Defender's Choice technique). Let us look at the rules in the groups I and II.

I	$X \xrightarrow{a} X_1'$	$X' \xrightarrow{a} X_1'$	
		$X_1' \xrightarrow{\tau} X_1'.V_i$	for each $i \in \{2, 3, \ldots, n\}$
	$X \xrightarrow{a} Y$	$X_1' \xrightarrow{\tau} Y'.V_1$	
II	$Y \xrightarrow{a} Y_1.D$	$Y' \xrightarrow{a} Y_1.D$	
	$Y_1 \xrightarrow{\tau} Y_1.V_i$		for each $i \in \{2, 3, \ldots, n\}$
	$Y_1 \xrightarrow{\tau} X.V_1$	$Y' \xrightarrow{a} X'$	

According to these rules, when starting from the pair $(X.\alpha, X'.\alpha)$, Attacker is forced (DC) to perform $X.\alpha \xrightarrow{a} Y.\alpha$, otherwise Defender can reach a syntactic equality. Defender can be then viewed as forced to respond by $X' \stackrel{a}{\Longrightarrow} Y'.\beta.\alpha$ for a (reversed) segment β of his choice. If he does not finish by using the rule $X'_1 \xrightarrow{\tau} Y'.V_1$, Attacker can perform a move according to this rule in the next round — thus installing a pair $(Y.\alpha, Y'.\beta.\alpha)$ anyway.

Rules in II make clear that Attacker is now forced (DC) to move $Y'.\beta.\alpha \xrightarrow{a} X'.\beta.\alpha$ and Defender can respond by $Y.\alpha \stackrel{a}{\Longrightarrow} X.\beta.\alpha.D.\alpha$; since D is a deadlock, we can view the installed pair as $(X.\beta.\alpha, X'.\beta.\alpha)$. Similarly as above, Defender cannot gain by not using the rule $Y_1 \xrightarrow{\tau} X.V_1$. As we shall see later, he neither can gain by installing $X.\gamma$ for $\gamma \neq \beta.\alpha$.

To enable Attacker to enter the checking phase, we add the following rules.

III	$X \xrightarrow{c} R_1.D$	$X' \xrightarrow{c} R_1.D$	
		$X' \xrightarrow{c} Z$	
	$R_1 \xrightarrow{\tau} R_1.U_i$	$R_1 \xrightarrow{\tau} R_2$	for all $i \in \{1, 2, \ldots, n\}$
	$R_2 \xrightarrow{\tau} R_2.L_s$	$R_2 \xrightarrow{\tau} Z$	for all $s \in \Sigma$

Having a pair $(X.\alpha, X'.\alpha)$, Attacker can thus also choose to play a c-action (instead of an a-action); in this case he is obviously forced (DC) to play $X'.\alpha \xrightarrow{c} Z.\alpha$. Defender can respond by $X.\alpha \stackrel{c}{\Longrightarrow} Z.\gamma.D.\alpha$ for some $\gamma \in \{L_s \mid s \in \Sigma\}^* \cdot \{U_1, U_2, \ldots, U_n\}^*$ where L_s and U_i are new process constants (we recall that Σ is the alphabet of the instance (A, B)). In the whole PA system Δ, there will be only one rule with the action d, namely $Z \xrightarrow{d} Z$ (in group V). By inspecting the rules it is easy to verify that if Defender chooses not to finish his move by using the rule $R_2 \xrightarrow{\tau} Z$, Attacker can play $Z \xrightarrow{d} Z$ in the next round and thus, in fact, force reaching a pair $(Z.\gamma.D.\alpha,\ Z.\alpha)$.

We now want to arrange that the above mentioned Defender's response $(X.\alpha \stackrel{c}{\Longrightarrow} Z.\gamma.D.\alpha)$ can be successful if and only if $\alpha = V_{i_m}.V_{i_{m-1}}.\cdots.V_{i_1}$ represents a partial solution; and in this case the response must be such that $\gamma = L_{a_\ell}.L_{a_{\ell-1}}.\cdots.L_{a_1}.U_{i_m}.U_{i_{m-1}}.\cdots.U_{i_1}$ where

$$u_{i_1} u_{i_2} \ldots u_{i_m} a_1 a_2 \ldots a_\ell = v_{i_1} v_{i_2} \ldots v_{i_m}. \tag{2}$$

In order to achieve that, we define the set $\mathcal{T} \stackrel{\text{def}}{=} \{T_w \mid w \text{ is a suffix of some } (u_i)^R \text{ or } (v_i)^R\}$ of new process constants (where $(.)^R$ denotes the reversal operation), and we add the following rules.

IV	$U_k \xrightarrow{t_k} \epsilon$	$V_k \xrightarrow{t_k} \epsilon$	for each $k \in \{1, 2, \ldots, n\}$
	$U_k \xrightarrow{\tau} T_{(u_k)^R}$	$V_k \xrightarrow{\tau} T_{(v_k)^R}$	for each $k \in \{1, 2, \ldots, n\}$
	$T_{sw} \xrightarrow{s} T_w$	$T_{sw} \xrightarrow{\tau} T_w$	for $T_{sw} \in \mathcal{T}$ and $s \in \Sigma$
		$T_\epsilon \xrightarrow{\tau} \epsilon$	
	$L_s \xrightarrow{s} \epsilon$	$L_s \xrightarrow{\tau} \epsilon$	for all $s \in \Sigma$

We can easily verify that a necessary condition for the processes $L_{a_\ell}.L_{a_{\ell-1}}.\cdots.L_{a_1}.U_{i_m}.U_{i_{m-1}}.\cdots.U_{i_1}$ and $V_{j_{m'}}.V_{j_{m'-1}}.\cdots.V_{j_1}$ to be weakly bisimilar is that $m = m'$, $i_1 = j_1, i_2 = j_2, \ldots, i_m = j_m$, and (2) holds. But due to the possible mixing of 'letter-actions' and 'index-actions', the condition is not sufficient. That is why the above processes are preceded by Z in our bisimulation game. If Z can be somehow used to implement a 'switch' for Attacker by which he binds himself to checking either only the index-actions or only the letter-actions then our goal is reached.

We first note that the outcomes of such switching can be modeled by composing in parallel either a process constant C_1 (which masks all letter-actions) or C_2 (which masks all index-actions). So we add the rules for C_1, C_2, and also all the rules for Z (whose meaning will become clear later).

V	$C_1 \xrightarrow{s} C_1$	for each $s \in \Sigma$
	$C_2 \xrightarrow{\iota_k} C_2$	for each $k \in \{1, 2, \ldots, n\}$
	$Z \xrightarrow{z} \epsilon$	
	$Z \xrightarrow{\tau} D$	
	$Z \xrightarrow{d} Z$	

The following propositions are now easy to verify.

PROPOSITION 4 *It holds that* $Z.L_{a_\ell}.L_{a_{\ell-1}} \cdots L_{a_1}.U_{i_m}.U_{i_{m-1}} \cdots U_{i_1} \| C_1 \approx Z.V_{j_{m'}}.V_{j_{m'-1}} \cdots V_{j_1} \| C_1$ *if and only if* $m = m'$ *and* $i_k = j_k$ *for all* k, $1 \leq k \leq m$.

PROPOSITION 5 *It holds that* $Z.L_{a_\ell}.L_{a_{\ell-1}} \cdots L_{a_1}.U_{i_m}.U_{i_{m-1}} \cdots U_{i_1} \| C_2 \approx Z.V_{j_{m'}}.V_{j_{m'-1}} \cdots V_{j_1} \| C_2$ *if and only if* $u_{i_1}u_{i_2} \ldots u_{i_m}a_1a_2 \ldots a_\ell = v_{j_1}v_{j_2} \ldots v_{j_{m'}}$.

In order to realize the above discussed 'switch', we add the final group of rules.

VI	$C \xrightarrow{c_1} C_1$	$C \xrightarrow{c_2} C_2$	$C \xrightarrow{z} C\|W$
	$W \xrightarrow{\tau} W.U_k$	$W \xrightarrow{\tau} W.V_k$	for each $k \in \{1, 2, \ldots, n\}$
	$W \xrightarrow{\tau} W.L_s$		for all $s \in \Sigma$
	$W \xrightarrow{\tau} \epsilon$		

Now the pair of processes $(X\|C, X'\|C)$ is the pair (P_1, P_2) we were aiming to construct according to equation (1). This is confirmed by the following two lemmas (the proofs are in the full version of the paper).

LEMMA 6 *If the rPCP instance* (A, B) *has no solution then* $X\|C \not\approx X'\|C$.

LEMMA 7 *If the rPCP instance* (A, B) *has a solution then* $X\|C \approx X'\|C$.

Now we state the main theorem, which assumes the usual class PA, i.e., without deadlocks.

THEOREM 8 *Weak bisimilarity on PA is Σ_1^1-complete.*

Proof. The membership in Σ_1^1 was already discussed; Σ_1^1-hardness follows from the construction we described and from Lemmas 6 and 7 – on condition that we handle the question of deadlocks. However, there is a straightforward (polynomial-time) reduction from weak bisimilarity of PA with deadlocks to PA without deadlocks (described in [Srba, 2003b]). ■

Combining with the results of [Srba, 2003a] (for PDA and PPDA), we can conclude that weak bisimilarity problems for all PRS-classes on the third level of the hierarchy (and above) are Σ_1^1-complete. Using a similar general strategy, we can show the same results also for weak simulation preorder and equivalence:

THEOREM 9 *Weak simulation preorder/equivalence on PDA, PA and PPDA is Σ_1^1-complete.*

The constructions are more straightforward in this case, where each player is given a fixed system to play in. Here Defender can influence Attacker's moves by threatening to enter a 'universal' process, which enables all actions forever. Problem rPCP is convenient for reductions in the cases of PDA and PA; in the case of PPDA, the recurrent problem for nondeterministic Minsky machines is more suitable. (It asks whether there is an infinite computation which uses a distinguished instruction infinitely often.) A detailed proof is given in the full version of the paper.

A natural conjecture is now that all relations subsuming weak bisimilarity and being subsumed in weak simulation preorder are also Σ_1^1-hard. Such claims, for general relations $R_1 \subseteq R_2$ are usually proven by reduction (from a suitable problem $\mathcal{P}$) constructing two processes P_1 and P_2 such that $(P_1, P_2) \in R_1$ if the answer (for the instance of $\mathcal{P}$ being reduced) is YES and $(P_1, P_2) \notin R_2$ if the answer is NO.

So far we do not see how to modify our constructions to satisfy this. However, in the case of PDA and PPDA, we could in this way derive Σ_1^1-hardness for all relations between weak bisimilarity and branching bisimilarity. A branching bisimulation (as introduced by van Glabbeek and Weijland, see, e.g., [van Glabbeek and Weijland, 1996]) is a symmetric relation R where, for each $(\alpha, \beta) \in R$, each (Attacker's) move $\alpha \stackrel{a}{\longrightarrow} \alpha'$ can be matched by a (Defender's) move $\beta \stackrel{\tau}{\longrightarrow}^* \beta_1 \stackrel{a}{\longrightarrow} \beta_2 \stackrel{\tau}{\longrightarrow}^* \beta'$ where we require $(\alpha', \beta') \in R$ and also $(\alpha, \beta_1) \in R$, $(\alpha', \beta_2) \in R$; Defender's move can be empty in the case $a = \tau$ (then $(\alpha', \beta) \in R$).

CLAIM 10 *All relations subsuming branching bisimilarity and being subsumed in weak bisimilarity are Σ_1^1-hard on PDA and PPDA.*

We do not provide a detailed proof since it would require to repeat the constructions used in [Srba, 2003a], with some slight modifications. The point is that the long τ-moves (of Defender) can be made reversible (e.g., for setting a counter value there are τ-actions for both increasing and decreasing). This can be achieved easily in the presence of a finite-control unit (like in case of PDA and PPDA). Such a reversibility is not present in our construction for PA, and it is unclear whether PA can model these features in an alternative way.

4. Other semantic equivalences

A natural question to ask is about the complexity of other well-known semantic equivalences (like those in [van Glabbeek, 2001] or, more relevantly for us, in [van Glabbeek, 1993]). Of particular interest is the question whether some other equivalences are also highly undecidable (i.e., beyond (hyper)arithmetical hierarchy). We provide a few results and notes about this.

For a finite or infinite $w = a_1 a_2 \dots$ we write $\alpha_0 \stackrel{w}{\Longrightarrow}$ iff there are $\alpha_1, \alpha_2, \dots$ such that $\alpha_i \stackrel{a_{i+1}}{\Longrightarrow} \alpha_{i+1}$ for all $i = 0, 1, 2, \dots$. The coarsest equivalence among the studied action-based semantic equivalences is the trace equivalence: two processes α and β are *weakly trace equivalent* iff $\forall w \in (Act \smallsetminus \{\tau\})^* : \alpha \stackrel{w}{\Longrightarrow} \Leftrightarrow \beta \stackrel{w}{\Longrightarrow}$ (i.e., α and β enable the same *finite* observable traces).

We can immediately see that the problem is at a very low level in the arithmetical hierarchy even for very general classes of labelled transition systems. We call a labelled transition system (LTS) *recursively enumerable* if the set of states S and the set of actions Act are both (represented as) recursively enumerable sets of strings in some finite alphabets and the set $\{ (\alpha, a, \beta) \mid \alpha, \beta \in S, a \in Act, \alpha \stackrel{a}{\longrightarrow} \beta \}$ is also recursively enumerable. The respective algorithms (Turing machines) can serve as finite descriptions of such an LTS.

We can easily observe that given a recursively enumerable LTS (where Act includes τ), the set $\{ (\alpha, w) \mid w \in (Act \smallsetminus \{\tau\})^*, \alpha \stackrel{w}{\Longrightarrow} \}$ is also recursively enumerable. More generally, the set of all triples (L, α, w), where L is (a description of) a recursively enumerable LTS, α one of its states and w a finite sequence of its (observable) actions such that $\alpha \stackrel{w}{\Longrightarrow}$ (in L), can be defined by some Σ_1^0-formula $\exists x. \phi(L, \alpha, w, x)$ where ϕ is recursive (with the parameters coded by natural numbers).

PROPOSITION 11 *The set of all triples (L, α, β), where L is (a description of) a recursively enumerable LTS and α, β two weakly trace equivalent states, is in Π_2^0.*

REMARK 12 *In fact, for the classes like PDA, PA and PN the set $\{(L, \alpha, w) \mid \alpha \stackrel{w}{\Longrightarrow}\}$ is even recursive. For PDA and PA this follows, e.g., from [Büchi, 1964] and [Lugiez and Schnoebelen, 2002] and for PN it can be decided by standard constructions from Petri net theory (reducing to the coverability problem). This means that weak trace equivalence for such classes is in Π_1^0.*

For other equivalences based on trace-like finite behaviours (sometimes called 'decorated traces'), i.e., failure equivalence, ready equivalence, ready-trace equivalence etc., we can make similar observations. This means that in fact all these (weak) equivalences are very low in the arithmetical hierarchy.

In some sense, this might seem as a surprising fact. In the strong case (without τ-actions), complexity of the equivalence problems is decreasing in the direction: trace – simulation – bisimulation. On the other hand in the weak case the situation now seems to look different. However, the right way for such a comparison is to take also infinite traces (i.e., ω-traces) into account. Then the above complexity-decreasing chain is restored as illustrated below.

REMARK 13 *For image-finite labelled transition systems (like those generated by PRS systems in the strong case), the finite-trace equivalence implies also the ω-trace equivalence. This is, however, not true for non-image-finite systems, which are easily generated by PRS systems in the weak case.*

We shall focus on the classes BPP and BPA. For BPP weak bisimilarity is known to be semidecidable [Esparza, 1997], so it belongs to the class Σ_1^0. In fact, it seems even well possible that the problem is decidable (see [Jančar, 2003] where PSPACE-completeness of strong bisimilarity is established). Simulation preorder/equivalence (as well as trace preorder/equivalence) is undecidable even in the strong case [Hüttel, 1994]. Weak simulation preorder/equivalence is surely in Σ_1^1 (the best estimate we can derive at the moment) while we can prove that weak ω-trace preorder/equivalence is Π_1^1-hard:

THEOREM 14 *Weak ω-trace preorder/equivalence on BPP is Π_1^1-hard.*

Given a nondeterministic Minsky machine, the nonexistence of an infinite computation using instruction 1 infinitely often can be reduced to the weak ω-trace preorder (equivalence) problem. In order to prove this we modify a known construction showing undecidability of trace preorder in the strong case (which can be found in [Hirshfeld, 1994]). A more detailed sketch of the proof is in the full version of the paper.

For BPA, the situation is roughly similar though a bit more unclear. Both weak bisimilarity and weak similarity are surely in Σ_1^1 but otherwise we only know that weak bisimilarity is EXPTIME-hard [Mayr, 2003] and weak similarity undecidable; the latter follows from undecidability of (even) strong similarity [Groote and Hüttel, 1994]. There are some reasons to conjecture that weak bisimilarity of BPA might be decidable. The (obvious) membership in Σ_1^1 thus seems to be a very rough upper bound, and one might start to try to strenghten this by showing that the problem is in the hyperarithmetical hierarchy, i.e., in the intersection of Σ_1^1 and Π_1^1. Nevertheless, it seems that a deeper insight would be needed even for this less ambitious goal.

The undecidability of strong trace equivalence for BPA follows easily from classical results for context-free langauges. Moreover, similarly as in the case of BPP, we can show:

THEOREM 15 *Weak ω-trace preorder/equivalence on BPA is Π^1_1-hard.*

The theorem holds even when one BPA-process is a fixed finite-state process. The proof uses the recurrent problem for nondeterministic Turing machines and builds on the classical context-free grammar generating all words which do not correspond to correct computations of a Turing machine (where all even configurations are written in the reverse order). More details are in the full version of the paper. We also add an analogy to Proposition 11:

PROPOSITION 16 *The set of all triples (L, α, β), where L is (a description of) a recursively enumerable LTS and α, β two weakly ω-trace equivalent states, is in Π^1_2.*

5. Regularity is in the hyperarithmetical hierarchy

Here we look at some more specialized problems, namely the question of equivalence (of a general process) with a given finite-state process, and the question of regularity, which asks whether a given (general) process is equivalent (weakly bisimilar in our case) to an (unspecified) finite-state process.

Denoting the collection of all sets which are recursively enumerable in *TA* (truth in mathematics) by $\Sigma^0_{\omega+1}$, we can show:

PROPOSITION 17 *The problem of weak regularity of recursively enumerable labelled transition systems is in $\Sigma^0_{\omega+1}$.*

Though the stated result is not too practical, it still separates weak bisimilarity checking from weak regularity checking for the classes like PDA, PA and PPDA (because $\Sigma^0_{\omega+1}$ is a proper subclass of $\Sigma^1_1 \cap \Pi^1_1$). Recalling the general experience that natural problems (in computer science) are either at low levels of the arithmetical hierarchy or at low levels of the analytical hierarchy, we have at least some indication in what direction the results for regularity can be possibly strengthened.

References

[Büchi, 1964] Büchi, J.R. (1964). Regular canonical systems. *Arch. Math. Logik u. Grundlagenforschung*, 6:91–111.

[Burkart et al., 2001] Burkart, O., Caucal, D., Moller, F., and Steffen, B. (2001). Verification on infinite structures. In Bergstra, J., Ponse, A., and Smolka, S., editors, *Handbook of Process Algebra*, chapter 9, pages 545–623. Elsevier Science.

[Esparza, 1997] Esparza, J. (1997). Petri nets, commutative context-free grammars, and basic parallel processes. *Fundamenta Informaticae*, 31:13–26.

[Groote and Hüttel, 1994] Groote, J.F. and Hüttel, H. (1994). Undecidable equivalences for basic process algebra. *Information and Computation*, 115(2):353–371.

[Harel, 1986] Harel, D. (1986). Effective transformations on infinite trees, with applications to high undecidability, dominoes, and fairness. *Journal of the ACM (JACM)*, 33(1):224–248.

[Hirshfeld, 1994] Hirshfeld, Y. (1994). Deciding equivalences in simple process algebras. Tech. report ECS-LFCS-94-294, Dept. of Computer Science, University of Edinburgh.

[Hüttel, 1994] Hüttel, H. (1994). Undecidable equivalences for basic parallel processes. In *Proc. of TACS'94*, volume 789 of *LNCS*, pages 454–464. Springer-Verlag.

[Jančar, 2003] Jančar, P. (2003). Strong bisimilarity on basic parallel processes is PSPACE-complete. In *Proc. of LICS'03*, pages 218–227. IEEE Computer Society Press.

[Jančar et al., 2003] Jančar, P., Kučera, A., and Moller, F. (2003). Deciding bisimilarity between bpa and bpp processes. In *Proc. of CONCUR'03*, volume 2761 of *LNCS*, pages 159–173. Springer-Verlag.

[Jančar and Srba, 2004] Jančar, P. and Srba, J. (2004). Highly undecidable questions for process algebras. Tech. Report RS-04-8, BRICS Research Series.

[Kučera and Jančar, 2002] Kučera, A. and Jančar, P. (2002). Equivalence-checking with infinite-state systems: Techniques and results. In *Proc. of SOFSEM'02*, volume 2540 of *LNCS*, pages 41–73. Springer-Verlag.

[Lugiez and Schnoebelen, 2002] Lugiez, D. and Schnoebelen, Ph. (2002). The regular viewpoint on pa-processes. *Theoretical Computer Science*, 274(1–2):89–115.

[Mayr, 2000] Mayr, R. (2000). Process rewrite systems. *Information and Computation*, 156(1):264–286.

[Mayr, 2003] Mayr, R. (2003). Weak bisimilarity and regularity of BPA is EXPTIME-hard. In *Proc. of EXPRESS'03*, pages 160–143.

[Rogers, 1967] Rogers, H. (1967). *Theory of Recursive Functions and Effective Computability*. McGraw-Hill.

[Srba, 2002] Srba, J. (2002). Roadmap of infinite results. *Bulletin of the European Association for Theoretical Computer Science (Columns: Concurrency)*, 78:163–175. Updated online version: http://www.brics.dk/~srba/roadmap.

[Srba, 2003a] Srba, J. (2003a). Completeness results for undecidable bisimilarity problems. In *Proc. of INFINITY'03*, pages 9–22.

[Srba, 2003b] Srba, J. (2003b). Undecidability of weak bisimilarity for PA-processes. In *Proc. of DLT'02*, volume 2450 of *LNCS*, pages 197–208. Springer-Verlag.

[van Glabbeek, 1993] van Glabbeek, R.J. (1993). The linear time – branching time spectrum II (the semantics of sequential systems with silent moves). In *Proc. of CONCUR'93*, volume 715 of *LNCS*, pages 66–81. Springer-Verlag.

[van Glabbeek, 2001] van Glabbeek, R.J. (2001). The linear time - branching time spectrum I: The semantics of concrete, sequential processes. In *Handbook of Process Algebra*, chapter 1, pages 3–99. Elsevier Science.

[van Glabbeek and Weijland, 1996] van Glabbeek, R.J. and Weijland, W.P. (1996). Branching time and abstraction in bisimulation semantics. *Journal of the ACM*, 43(3):555–600.

NEW-HOPLA

a higher-order process language with name generation

Glynn Winskel
Computer Laboratory, University of Cambridge, UK
Francesco Zappa Nardelli
INRIA & Computer Laboratory, University of Cambridge, UK

Abstract This paper introduces new-HOPLA, a concise but powerful language for higher-order nondeterministic processes with name generation. Its origins as a metalanguage for domain theory are sketched but for the most part the paper concentrates on its operational semantics. The language is typed, the type of a process describing the shape of the computation paths it can perform. Its transition semantics, bisimulation, congruence properties and expressive power are explored. Encodings are given of well-known process algebras, including π-calculus, Higher-Order π-calculus and Mobile Ambients.

1 The origins of new-HOPLA

This work is part of a general programme (reported in [8]), to develop a domain theory which scales up to the intricate languages, models and reasoning techniques used in distributed computation. This ambition led to a concentration on path based models, and initially on presheaf models because they can even encompass causal dependency models like event structures; so 'domains' is being understood more broadly than usual, to include presheaf categories.

The general methodology has been to develop domain theories with a rich enough life of their own to suggest powerful metalanguages. The point to emphasise is that in this way informative domain theories can have a pro-active role; they can yield new metalanguages, by their nature very expressive, accompanied by novel ways to deconstruct existing notions into more primitive ones, as well as new analysis techniques. A feature of presheaf models has been very useful: in key cases there is often a strong correspondence between elements of the presheaf denotation and derivations in an operational semantics. In the cases of HOPLA and new-HOPLA the presheaf models have led not only the core operations of the language, and a suitable syntax, but also to their operational semantics.

This paper reports on new-HOPLA, a compact but expressive language for higher-order nondeterministic processes with name generation. It extends the language HOPLA of Nygaard and Winskel [7] with name generation, and like its predecessor has its origins in a domain theory for concurrency. Specifically it arose out of the metalanguage implicitly being used in giving a presheaf semantics to the π-calculus [2]. But a sketch of its mathematical origins and denotational semantics does not require that heavy an investment, and can be based on path sets rather than presheaves.[1]

The key features of new-HOPLA hinge on its types and these can be understood independently of their origin as objects, and constructions on objects, in a category of domains—to be sketched shortly within the simple domain theory of path sets. A type $\mathbb{P}$ specifies the computations possible with respect to a given current set of names; if a process has type $\mathbb{P}$, then any computation path it performs with the current set of names s will be an element of $\mathbb{P}(s)$.

A central type constructor is that of prefix type $!\mathbb{P}$; at a current set of names s, a process of this type $!\mathbb{P}$, if it is to do anything, is constrained to first doing a prototypical action ! before resuming as a process of type $\mathbb{P}$. (Actions within sum or tensor types will come to be tagged by injections and so of a less anonymous character.)

In the category of domains, domains can be tensored together, a special case of which gives us types of the form $\mathbb{N} \otimes \mathbb{P}$, a kind of dynamic sum which at current names s comprises paths of $\mathbb{P}(s)$ tagged by a current name which serves as an injection function. There is also a more standard sum $\Sigma_{i \in I} \mathbb{P}_i$ of an indexed family of types $\mathbb{P}_i$ where $i \in I$; this time paths are tagged by indices from the fixed set I rather than the dynamic set of names.

The remaining type constructions are the formation of recursive types, and three forms of function space. One is a 'linear function space' $\mathbb{N} \multimap \mathbb{P}$, the type of processes which given a name return a process of type $\mathbb{P}$. Another is a 'continuous function space' $\mathbb{P} \to \mathbb{Q}$, the type of processes which given a process of type $\mathbb{P}$ return a process of type $\mathbb{Q}$. There is also a type $\delta\mathbb{P}$ associated directly with new-name generation. A process of type $\delta\mathbb{P}$ takes any new name (i.e. a name not in the current set of names) as input and returns a process of type $\mathbb{P}$. Name generation is represented by new name abstraction, to be thought of as picking a new name (any new name will do as well as any other), and resuming as a process in which that new name is current.

This summarises the rather economical core of new-HOPLA. Very little in the way of standard process algebra operations are built in—nothing beyond a prefix operation and nondeterministic sum. By being based on more fundamental primitives than usual, the language of new-HOPLA is remarkably expressive. As additional motivation we now turn to how these primitives arise from a mathematical model refining the intuitions we have just presented.

A domain theory If for the moment we ignore name generation, a suitable category of domains is that of **Lin**. Its objects, *path orders*, are preorders $\mathbb{P}$ consisting of computation paths with the order $p \leq p'$ expressing how a path p extends to a path p'. A path order $\mathbb{P}$ determines a domain $\widehat{\mathbb{P}}$, that of its *path sets*, left-closed sets w.r.t. $\leq_{\mathbb{P}}$, ordered by inclusion. (Such a domain is a prime-algebraic complete lattice, in which the complete primes are precisely those path sets generated by individual paths.) The arrows of **Lin**, linear maps, from $\mathbb{P}$ to $\mathbb{Q}$ are join-preserving functions from $\widehat{\mathbb{P}}$ to $\widehat{\mathbb{Q}}$.

[1] Path sets arise by 'flattening' presheaves, which can be viewed as characteristic functions to truth values given in the category of sets, as sets of realisers, to simpler characteristic functions based on truth values $0 \leq 1$ [8].

The category **Lin** is monoidal-closed with a tensor given by the product $\mathbb{P} \times \mathbb{Q}$ of path orders and a corresponding function space by $\mathbb{P}^{op} \times \mathbb{Q}$—it is easy to see that join-preserving functions from $\widehat{\mathbb{P}}$ to $\widehat{\mathbb{Q}}$ correspond to path sets of $\mathbb{P}^{op} \times \mathbb{Q}$. In fact **Lin** has enough structure to form a model of Girard's classical linear logic [4]. To exhibit its exponential ! we first define the category **Cts** to consist, like **Lin**, of path orders as objects but now with arrows the Scott-continuous functions between the domains of path sets. The inclusion functor $\mathbf{Lin} \hookrightarrow \mathbf{Cts}$ has a left adjoint $! : \mathbf{Cts} \to \mathbf{Lin}$ which takes a path order $\mathbb{P}$ to a path order consisting of finite subsets of $\mathbb{P}$ with order

$$P \leq_{!\mathbb{P}} P' \text{ iff } \forall p \in P\, \exists p' \in P' .\, p \leq_{\mathbb{P}} p'$$

—so $!\mathbb{P}$ can be thought of as consisting of compound paths associated with several runs.

The higher-order process language HOPLA is built around constructions in the category **Lin**. Types of HOPLA, which may be recursively defined, denote objects of **Lin**, path orders circumscribing the computation paths possible. As such all types support operations of nondeterministic sum and recursive definitions, both given by unions. Sum types are provided by coproducts, and products, of **Lin**, both given by the disjoint juxtaposition of path orders; they provide injection and projection operations. There is a type of functions from $\mathbb{P}$ to $\mathbb{Q}$ given by $(!\mathbb{P})^{op} \times \mathbb{Q}$, the function space of **Cts**; this gives the operation of application and lambda abstraction. To this the adjunction yields a primitive prefix operation, a continuous map $\mathbb{P} \to !\mathbb{P}$, given by the unit at $\mathbb{P}$; it is accompanied by a destructor, a prefix-match operation, obtained from the adjunction's natural isomorphism. For further details, encodings of traditional process calculi in HOPLA and a full abstraction result, the reader is referred to [7, 9].

A domain theory for name generation We are interested in extending HOPLA to allow name generation. We get our inspiration from the domain theory. As usual a domain theory for name generation is obtained by moving to a category in which standard domains are indexed functorially by the current set of names. The category $\mathcal{I}$ consists of finite sets of names related by injective functions. The functor category $\mathbf{Lin}^{\mathcal{I}}$ has as objects functors $\mathbb{P} : \mathcal{I} \to \mathbf{Lin}$, so path orders $\mathbb{P}(s)$, indexed by finite sets of names s, standing for the computation paths possible with that current set of names; its arrows are natural transformations $\alpha = \langle \alpha_s \rangle_{s \in \mathcal{I}} : \mathbb{P} \to \mathbb{Q}$, with components in **Lin**. One important object in $\mathbf{Lin}^{\mathcal{I}}$ is the object of names $\mathbb{N}$ providing the current set of names, so $\mathbb{N}(s) = s$ regarded as a discrete order, at name set s. Types of new-HOPLA will denote objects of $\mathbf{Lin}^{\mathcal{I}}$.

The category has coproducts and products, both given by disjoint juxtaposition at each component. These provide a *sum type* $\Sigma_{i \in I}\mathbb{P}_i$ from a family of types $(\mathbb{P}_i)_{i \in I}$. It has *injections* producing a term $i{:}t$ of type $\Sigma_{i \in I}\mathbb{P}_i$ from a term t of type $\mathbb{P}_i$, for $i \in I$. *Projections* produce a term $\pi_i t$ of type $\mathbb{P}_i$ from a term t of the sum type.

There is a tensor got pointwise from the tensor of **Lin**. Given $\mathbb{P}$ and $\mathbb{Q}$ in $\mathbf{Lin}^{\mathcal{I}}$ we define $\mathbb{P} \otimes \mathbb{Q}$ in $\mathbf{Lin}^{\mathcal{I}}$ so that $(\mathbb{P} \otimes \mathbb{Q})(s) = \mathbb{P}(s) \times \mathbb{Q}(s)$ at $s \in \mathcal{I}$. We will only use a special case of this construction to form tensor types $\mathbb{N} \otimes \mathbb{P}$, so $(\mathbb{N} \otimes \mathbb{P})(s) = s \times \mathbb{P}(s)$ at $s \in \mathcal{I}$. These are a form of 'dynamic sum', referred to earlier, in which the components and the corresponding injections grow with the availability of new names. There are term constructors producing a term $n \cdot t$ of type $\mathbb{N} \otimes \mathbb{P}$ from a term t of type $\mathbb{P}$ and a name n. There are projections $\pi_n t$ forming a term of type $\mathbb{P}$ from a term t of tensor type.

At any stage s, the current set of names, a new name can be generated and used in a term in place of a variable over names. This leads to the central idea of new-name abstractions of type $\delta\mathbb{P}$ where $\delta\mathbb{P}(s) = \mathbb{P}(s \dot\cup \{\star\})$ at name set s. As observed by Stark [14] the construction $\delta\mathbb{P}$ can be viewed as a space of functions from $\mathbb{N}$ to $\mathbb{P}$ but with the proviso that the input name is fresh. A new-name abstraction is written $new\alpha.t$ and has type $\delta\mathbb{P}$, where t is a term of type $\mathbb{P}$. New-name application is written $t[n]$, where t has type $\delta\mathbb{P}$, and requires that the name n is fresh w.r.t. the names of t.

The adjunction $\mathbf{Lin} \underset{\hookrightarrow}{\overset{!}{\underset{\bot}{\leftarrow}}} \mathbf{Cts}$ induces an adjunction $\mathbf{Lin}^{\mathcal{I}} \underset{\hookrightarrow}{\overset{!}{\underset{\bot}{\leftarrow}}} \mathbf{Cts}^{\mathcal{I}}$ where the left adjoint is got by extending the original functor $! : \mathbf{Cts} \to \mathbf{Lin}$ in a pointwise fashion. The unit of the adjunction provides a family of maps from $\mathbb{P}$ to $!\mathbb{P}$ in $\mathbf{Cts}^{\mathcal{I}}$. As with HOPLA, these yield a prefix operation $!t$ of type $!\mathbb{P}$ for a term t of type $\mathbb{P}$. A type of the form $!\mathbb{P}$ is called a prefix type; its computation paths at any current name set first involve performing a prototypical action, also called '!'.

To support higher-order processes we need function spaces $\mathbb{P} \multimap \mathbb{Q}$ such that

$$\mathbf{Lin}^{\mathcal{I}}(\mathbb{R}, \mathbb{P} \multimap \mathbb{Q}) \cong \mathbf{Lin}^{\mathcal{I}}(\mathbb{R} \otimes \mathbb{P}, \mathbb{Q})$$

natural in $\mathbb{R}$ and $\mathbb{Q}$. Such function spaces do not exist in general—the difficulty is in getting a path order $\mathbb{P} \multimap \mathbb{Q}(s)$ at each name set s. However a function space $\mathbb{P} \multimap \mathbb{Q}$ does exist in the case where $\mathbb{P}f$ preserves complete primes and $\mathbb{Q}f$ preserves non-empty meets for each map $f : s \to s'$ in $\mathcal{I}$. This suggests limiting the syntax of types to special function spaces $\mathbb{N} \multimap \mathbb{Q}$ and $!\mathbb{P} \multimap \mathbb{Q}$, the function space in $\mathbf{Cts}^{\mathcal{I}}$. The function spaces are associated with operations of application and lambda abstraction.

Related work and contribution The above domain theoretic constructions provide the basis of new-HOPLA. It resembles, and indeed has been inspired by, the metalanguages for domain theories with name generation used implicitly in earlier work [3, 14, 2], as well as the language of FreshML [11]. The language new-HOPLA is distinguished through the path-based domain theories to which it is fitted and, as we will see, in itself forming a process language with an operational semantics. For lack of space, in this extended abstract we omit the proofs of the theorems; these can be found in [16].

2 The language

Types The type of names is denoted by $\mathbb{N}$. The types of processes are defined by the grammar below.

$$\mathbb{P} ::= 0 \mid \mathbb{N}\otimes\mathbb{P} \mid !\mathbb{P} \mid \delta\mathbb{P} \mid \mathbb{N} \to \mathbb{P} \mid \mathbb{P} \to \mathbb{Q} \mid \Sigma_{i\in I}\mathbb{P}_i \mid \mu_j P_1 \dots P_k.(\mathbb{P}_1 \dots \mathbb{P}_k) \mid P$$

The sum type $\Sigma_{i\in I}\mathbb{P}_i$ when I is a finite set, is most often written $i_1{:}\mathbb{P} + \cdots + i_k{:}\mathbb{P}$. The symbol P is drawn from a set of type variables used in defining recursive types; closed type expressions are interpreted as path orders. The type $\mu_j P_1 \dots P_k.(\mathbb{P}_1 \dots \mathbb{P}_k)$ is interpreted as the j-component, for $1 \leq j \leq k$, of the 'least' solution to the defining equations $P_1 = \mathbb{P}_1, \dots, P_k = \mathbb{P}_k$, where the expressions $\mathbb{P}_1 \dots \mathbb{P}_k$ may contain the P_j's.

t, u, v	$::=$	$\mathbf{0}$	$!t$	inactive process and prototypical action
	$\mid$	$n \cdot t$	$\pi_n t$	tensor and projection
	$\mid$	$\lambda x.t$	tu	process abstraction and application
	$\mid$	$\lambda\alpha.t$	tn	name abstraction and application
	$\mid$	$new\alpha.t$	$t[n]$	new-name abstraction and application
	$\mid$	$rec x.t$	x	recursive definition and process variables
	$\mid$	$i{:}t$	$\pi_i t$	injection and projection
	$\mid$	$\Sigma_{i \in I} t_i$	$\Sigma_{\alpha \in \mathbf{N}} t$	sum and sum over names
	$\mid$	$[t > p(x) \Rightarrow u]$		pattern matching

Table 1. new-HOPLA: syntax of terms

Terms and actions We assume a countably infinite set of *name constants*, ranged over by $a, b, \ldots$ and a countably infinite set of *name variables*, ranged over by $\alpha, \beta, \ldots$ Names, either constants or variables, are ranged over by $m, n, \ldots$. We assume an infinite, countable, set of *process variables*, ranged over by $x, y, \ldots$

Every type is associated with actions processes of that type may do. The *actions* are defined by the grammar below:

$$p, q, r \quad ::= \quad x \mid !p \mid n \cdot p \mid i{:}p \mid new\alpha.p \mid n \mapsto p \mid u \mapsto p \mid p[n]\,.$$

As we will see shortly, well-typed actions are constructed so that they involve exactly one prototypical action ! and exactly one 'resumption variable' x. Whenever a term performs the action, the variable of the action matches the resumption of the term: the typings of an action thus relates the type of a term with the type of its resumption. According to the transition rules a process of prefix type $!\mathbb{P}$ may do actions of the form $!p$, while a process of tensor or sum type may do actions of the form $n \cdot p$ or $i{:}p$ respectively. A process of type $\delta\mathbb{P}$ does actions of the form $new\alpha.p$ meaning that at the generation of a new name, a say, as input the action $p[a/\alpha]$ is performed. Actions of function type $n \mapsto p$ or $u \mapsto p$ express the dependency of the action on the input of a name n or process u respectively. The final clause is necessary in building up actions because we sometimes need to apply a resumption variable to a new name.

The *terms* are defined by the grammar reported in Table 1.

In new-HOPLA actions are used as patterns in terms $[t > p(x) \Rightarrow u]$ where we explicitly note the resumption variable x. If the term t can perform the action p the resumption of t is passed on to u via the variable x.

We assume an understanding of the *free name variables* (the binders of name variables are $\lambda\alpha.-$, $new\alpha.-$, and $\Sigma_{\alpha\in\mathbf{N}}-$) and of the *free process variables* (the binders of process variables are $\lambda x.-$, and $[t > p(x) \Rightarrow -]$) of a term, and of substitutions. The *support* of a closed term, denoted $\mathsf{n}(t)$, is the set of its name constants. We say that a name n is *fresh* for a closed term t if $n \not\in \mathsf{n}(t)$.

Transition rules The behaviour of terms is defined by a transition relation of the form

$$s \vdash t \xrightarrow{p\,(x)} t'$$

where s is a finite set of name constants such that $\mathsf{n}(t) \subseteq s$. The transition above should be read as 'with current names s the term t can perform the action p and resume as t''. We generally note the action's resumption variable in the transitions;

$$\frac{}{!\mathbb{P}; s \vdash !t \xrightarrow{!x\,(x)} t} \qquad \frac{\mathbb{P}; s \vdash t_i \xrightarrow{p\,(x)} t'}{\mathbb{P}; s \vdash \Sigma_{i \in I} t_i \xrightarrow{p\,(x)} t'} \qquad \frac{\mathbb{P}; s \vdash t[a/\alpha] \xrightarrow{p\,(x)} u \quad a \in s}{\mathbb{P}; s \vdash \Sigma_{\alpha \in \mathbf{N}} t \xrightarrow{p\,(x)} u}$$

$$\frac{\mathbb{P}; s \vdash t \xrightarrow{p\,(x)} t' \quad a \in s}{\mathbf{N} \otimes \mathbb{P}; s \vdash a \cdot t \xrightarrow{a \cdot p\,(x)} t'} \qquad \frac{\mathbf{N} \otimes \mathbb{P}; s \vdash t \xrightarrow{a \cdot p\,(x)} t'}{\mathbb{P}; s \vdash \pi_a t \xrightarrow{p\,(x)} t'} \qquad \frac{\mathbb{P}; s \vdash t[rec\,y.t/y] \xrightarrow{p\,(x)} u}{\mathbb{P}; s \vdash rec\,y.t \xrightarrow{p\,(x)} u}$$

$$\frac{\mathbb{P}_i; s \vdash t \xrightarrow{p\,(x)} t'}{\Sigma_{i \in I} \mathbb{P}_i; s \vdash i{:}t \xrightarrow{i:p\,(x)} t'} \qquad \frac{\Sigma_{i \in I} \mathbb{P}_i; s \vdash t \xrightarrow{i:p\,(x)} t'}{\mathbb{P}_i; s \vdash \pi_i t \xrightarrow{p\,(x)} t'} \qquad \frac{\mathbb{Q}; s \vdash t[u/x] \xrightarrow{p\,(x)} v \quad s \vdash u : \mathbb{P}}{\mathbb{P} \to \mathbb{Q}; s \vdash \lambda x.t \xrightarrow{u \mapsto p\,(x)} v}$$

$$\frac{\mathbb{P} \to \mathbb{Q}; s \vdash t \xrightarrow{u \mapsto p\,(x)} v}{\mathbb{Q}; s \vdash tu \xrightarrow{p\,(x)} v} \qquad \frac{\mathbb{P}; s \vdash t[a/\alpha] \xrightarrow{p\,(x)} v \quad a \in s}{\mathbf{N} \to \mathbb{P}; s \vdash \lambda \alpha.t \xrightarrow{a \mapsto p\,(x)} v} \qquad \frac{\mathbf{N} \to \mathbb{P}; s \vdash t \xrightarrow{a \mapsto p\,(x)} v}{\mathbb{P}; s \vdash ta \xrightarrow{p\,(x)} v}$$

$$\frac{\mathbb{P}; s \dot{\cup} \{a\} \vdash t[a/\alpha] \xrightarrow{p[a/\alpha]\,(x)} u[a/\alpha]}{\delta\mathbb{P}; s \vdash new\alpha.t \xrightarrow{new\alpha.p[x'[\alpha]/x]\,(x')} new\alpha.u} \qquad \frac{\delta\mathbb{P}; s \vdash t \xrightarrow{new\alpha.p[x'[\alpha]/x]\,(x')} u}{\mathbb{P}; s \dot{\cup} \{a\} \vdash t[a] \xrightarrow{p[a/\alpha]\,(x)} u[a]}$$

$$\frac{\mathbb{P}; s \vdash t \xrightarrow{p\,(x)} t' \quad \mathbb{Q}; s \vdash u[t'/x] \xrightarrow{q\,(x')} v}{\mathbb{Q}; s \vdash [t > p(x) \Rightarrow u] \xrightarrow{q\,(x')} v}$$

In the rule for new name abstraction, the conditions $a \notin \mathsf{n}(p)$ and $a \notin \mathsf{n}(u)$ must hold.
Table 2. new-HOPLA: transition rules

this simplifies the transition rules in which the resumption variable must be explicitly manipulated.

So the transition relation is given at stages indexed by the set of current names s. The body of an abstraction over names $\lambda\alpha.t$ can only be instantiated with a name in s, and an abstraction over processes $\lambda x.t$ can only be instantiated with a process whose support is contained in s. As the transition relation is indexed by the current set of names, it is possible to generate new names at run-time. Indeed, the transition rule for new-name abstraction $new\alpha.t$ extends the set s of current names with a new name $a \notin s$; this name a is then passed to t via the variable α. The transition rules must respect the typings of actions and terms given in the next section. Formally:

Definition 1 (Transition relation) *For closed terms t such that $s \vdash t : \mathbb{P}$ and path patterns such that $s;;x{:}\mathbb{Q} \Vdash p : \mathbb{P}$ the rules reported in Table 2 define a relation $\mathbb{P}; s \vdash t \xrightarrow{p\,(x)} u$, called the* transition relation.

Typing judgements Consider a term $t = t'[\alpha]$. As we have discussed in the previous section, this denotes a new-name application: any name instantiating α should be fresh for the term t'. Consider now the context $C[-] = \lambda\alpha.-$. In the term $C[t] = \lambda\alpha.(t'[\alpha])$, the variable α is abstracted via a lambda abstraction, and may be instantiated with any current name. In particular it may be instantiated with names that belong to the support of t', thus breaking the hypothesis that t' has been applied to a fresh name. The same problem arises with contexts of the form $C[-] = \Sigma_{\alpha \in \mathbf{N}}-$.

Moreover, if the process variable x is free in t, a context like $C[-] = \lambda x.-$ might replace x with an arbitrary term u. As the name instantiating α might belong to the support of u, nothing ensures it is still fresh for the term $t[u/x]$.

The type system must sometimes ensure that name variables are instantiated by fresh names. To impose this restriction, the typing context contains not only typing assumptions about name and process variables, such as $\alpha{:}\mathbb{N}$ and $x{:}\mathbb{P}$, but also *freshness assumptions* about them, written (α, β) or (α, x). The intended meaning of (α, β) is that the names instantiating the variables α and β must be *distinct*. A freshness assumption like (α, x), where x is a process variable, records that in any environment the name instantiating α must be fresh for the term instantiating x.

Using this auxiliary information, the type system assumes that it is safe to abstract a variable, using lambda abstraction or sum over names, only if no freshness assumptions have been made on it.

The type system of new-HOPLA terms can be specified using judgements of the form:

$$A; \Gamma; d \vdash t : \mathbb{P}$$

where

- $A \equiv \alpha_1{:}\mathbb{N}, \ldots, \alpha_k{:}\mathbb{N}$ is a collection of name variables;
- $\Gamma \equiv x_1{:}\mathbb{P}_1, \ldots, x_k{:}\mathbb{P}_k$ is a partial function from process variables to types;
- d is a set of pairs $(\alpha, x) \in A \times \Gamma$, and $(\alpha, \beta) \in A \times A$, keeping track of the *freshness assumptions*.

Notation: We write $d \setminus \alpha$ for the set of freshness assumptions obtained from d by deleting all pairs containing α. The order in which variables appear in a distinction is irrelevant; we will write $(\alpha, \beta) \in d$ as a shorthand for $(\alpha, \beta) \in d$ *or* $(\beta, \alpha) \in d$. When we write $\Gamma \cup \Gamma'$ we allow the environments to overlap; the variables need not be disjoint provided the environments are consistent.

Actions are typed along the same lines, even if type judgements explicitly report the resumption variable:

$$A; \Gamma; d; ; x{:}\mathbb{R} \Vdash p : \mathbb{P}\,.$$

The meaning of the environment $A; \Gamma; d$ is exactly the same as above. The variable x is the resumption variable of the pattern p, and its type is $\mathbb{R}$.

The type system of new-HOPLA is reported in Table 3 and Table 4.

The rule responsible for generating freshness assumptions is the rule for new-name application. If the term t has been typed in the environment $A; \Gamma; d$ and α is a new-name variable (that is, $\alpha \notin A$), then the term $t[\alpha]$ is well-typed under the hypothesis that any name instantiating the variable α is distinct from all the names in terms instantiating the variables that can appear in t. This is achieved adding the set of freshness assumptions $\{\alpha\} \times (\Gamma \cup A)$ to d (when convenient, as here, we will confuse an environment with its domain). The rule for pattern matching also modifies the freshness assumptions. The operational rule of pattern matching substitutes a subterm of t, whose names are contained in A', for x. Accordingly, the typing rule initially checks that no name in A' belongs to the set of the variables supposed fresh for x. Our attention is then drawn to the term $u[t'/x]$, where t' is a subterm of t. A name variable $\alpha \in A$

$$\frac{}{A;\Gamma;d;;x{:}\mathbb{R} \Vdash !x : !\mathbb{R}} \qquad \frac{A;\Gamma;d;;x{:}\mathbb{R} \Vdash p : \mathbb{P}}{A;\Gamma;d;;x{:}\mathbb{R} \Vdash \alpha \cdot p : \mathbb{N} \otimes \mathbb{P}}\alpha \in A$$

$$\frac{\alpha{:}\mathbb{N}, A;\Gamma;d;;x{:}\mathbb{R} \Vdash p : \mathbb{P}}{A;\Gamma;(d \setminus \alpha);;x'{:}\delta\mathbb{R} \Vdash new\alpha.p[x'[\alpha]/x] : \delta\mathbb{P}} \qquad \frac{A;\Gamma;d;;x{:}\mathbb{R} \Vdash p : \mathbb{P}}{A;\Gamma;d;;x{:}\mathbb{R} \Vdash \alpha \mapsto p : \mathbb{P}}\alpha \in A$$

$$\frac{A;\Gamma;d \vdash u : \mathbb{Q} \quad A;\Gamma;d;;x{:}\mathbb{R} \Vdash p : \mathbb{P}}{A;\Gamma;d;;x{:}\mathbb{R} \Vdash u \mapsto p : \mathbb{Q} \to \mathbb{P}} \qquad \frac{A;\Gamma;d;;x{:}\mathbb{R} \Vdash p : \mathbb{P}_j \quad j \in I}{A;\Gamma;d;;x{:}\mathbb{R} \Vdash (j{:}p) : \Sigma_{i \in I}\mathbb{P}_i}$$

$$\frac{A;\Gamma;d;;x{:}\mathbb{R} \Vdash t : \mathbb{P}_j[\mu\vec{P}.\vec{\mathbb{P}}/\vec{P}]}{A;\Gamma;d;;x{:}\mathbb{R} \Vdash t : \mu_j P : \vec{\mathbb{P}}} \qquad \frac{A;\Gamma;d;;x{:}\mathbb{R} \Vdash p : \mathbb{P}}{A';\Gamma';d';;x{:}\mathbb{R} \Vdash p : \mathbb{P}} \begin{array}{l} A \subseteq A' \\ \Gamma \subseteq \Gamma' \\ d \subseteq d' \end{array}$$

Table 3. new-HOPLA: typing rules for actions

$$\frac{}{A;\Gamma;d \vdash \emptyset : \mathbb{P}} \qquad \frac{}{A;x{:}\mathbb{P},\Gamma;d \vdash x : \mathbb{P}} \qquad \frac{A;\Gamma;d \vdash t : \mathbb{P}}{A';\Gamma';d' \vdash t : \mathbb{P}} \begin{array}{l} A \subseteq A' \\ \Gamma \subseteq \Gamma' \\ d \subseteq d' \end{array} \qquad \frac{A;\Gamma;d \vdash t : \mathbb{P}}{A;\Gamma;d \vdash !t : !\mathbb{P}}$$

$$\frac{\alpha{:}\mathbb{N}, A;\Gamma;d \vdash t : \mathbb{P}}{A;\Gamma;d \vdash \Sigma_{\alpha \in \mathbb{N}}t : \mathbb{P}}\alpha \notin d \qquad \frac{\alpha{:}\mathbb{N}, A;\Gamma;d \vdash t : \mathbb{P}}{A;\Gamma;d \vdash \lambda\alpha.t : \mathbb{N} \to \mathbb{P}}\alpha \notin d \qquad \frac{A;x{:}\mathbb{Q},\Gamma;d \vdash t : \mathbb{P}}{A;\Gamma;d \vdash \lambda x.t : \mathbb{Q} \to \mathbb{P}}x \notin d$$

$$\frac{\alpha{:}\mathbb{N}, A;\Gamma;d \vdash t : \mathbb{P}}{A;\Gamma;(d \setminus \alpha) \vdash new\alpha.t : \delta\mathbb{P}} \qquad \frac{A;\Gamma;d \vdash t : \delta\mathbb{P}}{\alpha{:}\mathbb{N}, A;\Gamma;d \cup (\{\alpha\} \times (\Gamma \cup A)) \vdash t[\alpha] : \mathbb{P}}$$

$$\frac{A;\Gamma;d \vdash t : \mathbb{N} \to \mathbb{P}}{A;\Gamma;d \vdash t\alpha : \mathbb{P}}\alpha \in A \qquad \frac{A;\Gamma;d \vdash t : \mathbb{P} \to \mathbb{Q} \quad A;\Gamma;d \vdash u : \mathbb{P}}{A;\Gamma;d \vdash tu : \mathbb{Q}} \qquad \frac{A;\Gamma;d \vdash t : \mathbb{P}_i}{A;\Gamma;d \vdash i{:}t : \Sigma_{i \in I}\mathbb{P}_i}$$

$$\frac{A;\Gamma;d \vdash t : \Sigma_{i \in I}\mathbb{P}_i}{A;\Gamma;d \vdash \pi_i t : \mathbb{P}_i} \qquad \frac{A;x{:}\mathbb{P},\Gamma;d \vdash t : \mathbb{P}}{A;\Gamma;d \vdash rec x.t : \mathbb{P}}x \notin d \qquad \frac{A;\Gamma;d \vdash t_i : \mathbb{P} \quad \forall i \in I}{A;\Gamma;d \vdash \Sigma_{i \in I}t_i : \mathbb{P}}$$

$$\frac{A;\Gamma;d \vdash t : \mathbb{P}}{A;\Gamma;d \vdash \alpha \cdot t : \mathbb{N} \otimes \mathbb{P}}\alpha \in A \qquad \frac{A;\Gamma;d \vdash t : \mathbb{N} \otimes \mathbb{P}}{A;\Gamma;d \vdash \pi_\alpha t : \mathbb{P}}\alpha \in A \qquad \frac{A;\Gamma;d \vdash t : \mathbb{P}_j[\mu\vec{P}.\vec{\mathbb{P}}/\vec{P}]}{A;\Gamma;d \vdash t : \mu_j P : \vec{\mathbb{P}}}$$

$$\frac{A';\Gamma';d' \vdash t : \mathbb{P} \quad A';\Gamma';d';;x{:}\mathbb{R} \Vdash p : \mathbb{P} \quad A;x{:}\mathbb{R},\Gamma;d \vdash u : \mathbb{Q}}{A \cup A';\Gamma \cup \Gamma';\overline{d} \vdash [t > p(x) \Rightarrow u] : \mathbb{Q}} A' \cap \{\alpha \mid (\alpha,x) \in d\} = \emptyset$$

$$\text{where } \overline{d} = (d \setminus x) \cup d' \cup \{\{\alpha\} \times (A' \cup \Gamma') \mid (\alpha,x) \in d\}$$

Table 4. new-HOPLA: typing rules for processes

supposed fresh from x when typing u, must now be supposed fresh from all the free variables of t'. This justifies the freshness assumptions $\{\{\alpha\} \times (A' \cup \Gamma') \mid (\alpha, x) \in d\}$.

The rest of the type system follows along the lines of type systems for the simply typed λ-calculus.

The type system assumes that terms do not contain name constants. This is to avoid the complications in a type system coping with both name variables and constants at the same time. We write $s \vdash t : \mathbb{P}$ when there is a judgement $A;\emptyset;d \vdash \sigma t' : \mathbb{P}$ and a substitution σ for A respecting the freshness assumptions d such that t is $\sigma t'$. Similarly for patterns.

Proposition 1 *The judgement $s \vdash t : \mathbb{P}$ holds iff there is a canonical judgement $A; \emptyset; \{(\alpha, \beta) \mid \alpha \neq \beta\} \vdash t' : \mathbb{P}$, in which the substitution σ is a bijection between name variables and names and t is $\sigma t'$.*

We can now prove that the operational rules are type correct.

Lemma 2 (Substitution Lemma) *If $A'; \Gamma'; d' \vdash t : \mathbb{Q}$ and $A; x{:}\mathbb{Q}, \Gamma; d \vdash u : \mathbb{P}$, where $\Gamma \cup \Gamma'$ is consistent and $A' \cap \{\alpha \mid (\alpha, x) \in d\} = \emptyset$, then $A \cup A'; \Gamma \cup \Gamma'; \overline{d} \vdash u[t/x] : \mathbb{P}$ where $\overline{d} = (d \setminus x) \cup d' \cup \{\{\alpha\} \times (A' \cup \Gamma') \mid (\alpha, x) \in d\}$.*

Theorem 3 (Transitions preserve types) *If $s \vdash t : \mathbb{P}$ and $s;; x{:}\mathbb{R} \Vdash p : \mathbb{P}$ and $\mathbb{P}; s \vdash t \xrightarrow{p\,(x)} t'$, then $s \vdash t' : \mathbb{R}$.*

3 Equivalences

After introducing some notations regarding relations, we explore the bisimulation equivalence that arises from the transition semantics. A relation $\mathcal{R}$ between typing judgements is said to respect types if, whenever $\mathcal{R}$ relates $E_1 \vdash t_1 : \mathbb{P}_1$ and $E_2 \vdash t_2 : \mathbb{P}_2$, we have $E_1 \equiv E_2$ and $\mathbb{P}_1 \equiv \mathbb{P}_2$. We are mostly interested in relations between closed terms, and we write $s \vdash t \mathrel{\mathcal{R}} u : \mathbb{P}$ to denote $(s \vdash t : \mathbb{P}, s \vdash q : \mathbb{P}) \in \mathcal{R}$.

Definition 4 (Bisimilarity) *A symmetric type-respecting relation on closed terms, $\mathcal{R}$, is a* bisimulation *if whenever $s \vdash t \mathrel{\mathcal{R}} u : \mathbb{P}$ and $\mathbb{P}; s' \vdash t \xrightarrow{p(x)} t'$ for $s' \supseteq s$, there exists a term u' such that $\mathbb{P}; s' \vdash u \xrightarrow{p(x)} u'$ and $s' \vdash t' \mathrel{\mathcal{R}} u' : \mathbb{R}$; where $\mathbb{R}$ is the type of the resumption variable x in p. Let* bisimilarity, *denoted $\sim$, be the largest bisimulation.*

We say that two closed terms t and q are bisimilar if $s \vdash t \sim q : \mathbb{P}$ for some s and $\mathbb{P}$.

In the definition of bisimulation, the universal quantification on sets of names s' is required, otherwise we would relate $\{a\} \vdash \lambda\alpha.[\alpha!0 > a!x \Rightarrow !0] : \mathbb{N} \to !0$ and $\{a\} \vdash \lambda\alpha.!0 : \mathbb{N} \to !0$ while these two terms behave differently in a world where a is not the only current name.

Using an extension of Howe's method [6] as adapted by Gordon and Pitts to a typed setting [5, 10], we show that bisimilarity is preserved by well typed contexts.

Theorem 5 *Bisimilarity $\sim$ is an equivalence relation and a congruence.*

Proposition 2 *For closed, well-formed, terms the equations reported in Table 5 hold.*

Proposition 3 *Bisimilarity validates β-reduction on new-name abstraction:*

$$s \mathbin{\dot\cup} \{a\} \vdash (new\alpha.t)[a] \sim t[a/\alpha] : \mathbb{P}\,.$$

4 Examples

In this section, we illustrate how new-HOPLA can be used to give semantics to well-known process algebras.

We introduce an useful product type $\mathbb{P}\,\&\,\mathbb{Q}$, which is not primitive in new-HOPLA. It is definable as $1{:}\mathbb{P} + 2{:}\mathbb{Q}$. The projections are given by $fst(t) = \pi_1(t)$ and $snd(t) = \pi_2(t)$, while pairing is defined as $(t, u) = 1{:}t{+}2{:}u$. For actions $(p, -) = 1{:}p$, $(-, q) = 2{:}q$. It is then easy to verify that $s \vdash fst(t, u) \sim t : \mathbb{P}$, that $s \vdash snd(t, u) \sim u : \mathbb{Q}$, and that $s \vdash (fst(t, u), snd(t, u)) \sim (t, u) : \mathbb{P}\,\&\,\mathbb{Q}$, for all $s \supseteq \mathsf{n}(t) \cup \mathsf{n}(u)$.

$$s \vdash (\lambda x.t)u \sim t[u/x] : \mathbb{P} \qquad s \vdash (\lambda \alpha.t)a \sim t[a/\alpha] : \mathbb{P}$$
$$s \vdash \lambda x.(tx) \sim t : \mathbb{P} \to \mathbb{Q} \qquad s \vdash \lambda \alpha.(t\alpha) \sim t : \mathbb{N} \to \mathbb{P}$$
$$s \vdash \lambda x.(\Sigma_{i\in I} t_i) \sim \Sigma_{i\in I}(\lambda x.t_i) : \mathbb{P} \to \mathbb{Q} \qquad s \vdash \lambda \alpha.(\Sigma_{i\in I} t_i) \sim \Sigma_{i\in I}(\lambda \alpha.t_i) : \mathbb{N} \to \mathbb{P}$$
$$s \vdash (\Sigma_{i\in I} t_i)u \sim \Sigma_{i\in I}(t_i u) : \mathbb{P} \qquad s \vdash (\Sigma_{i\in I} t_i)a \sim \Sigma_{i\in I}(t_i a) : \mathbb{P}$$
$$s \vdash \pi_\beta(\beta \cdot t) \sim t : \mathbb{P} \qquad s \vdash \pi_\beta(\alpha \cdot t) \sim \mathbf{0} : \mathbb{P}$$
$$s \vdash \beta \cdot (\Sigma_{i\in I} t_i) \sim \Sigma_{i\in I} \beta \cdot t_i : \mathbb{P} \qquad s \vdash \pi_\beta(\Sigma_{i\in I} t_i) \sim \Sigma_{i\in I} \pi_\beta t_i : \mathbb{P}$$
$$s \vdash t \sim \Sigma_{\alpha \in \mathbb{N}} \alpha \cdot (\pi_\alpha t) : \mathbb{N} \otimes \mathbb{P} \qquad s \vdash [!u > !x \Rightarrow t] \sim t[u/x] : \mathbb{P}$$
$$s \vdash [\Sigma_{i\in I} u_i > !x \Rightarrow t] \sim \Sigma_{i\in I}[u_i > !x \Rightarrow t] : \mathbb{P}$$

Table 5. Proposition 2: equations

π-calculus We denote *name constants* with $a, b, \ldots$, and *name variables* with $\alpha, \beta, \ldots$; the letters $n, m, \ldots$ range over both name constants and name variables. The terms of the language are constructed according the following grammar:

$$P, Q \ ::= \ \mathbf{0} \mid P \mid Q \mid (\nu\alpha)P \mid \overline{n}m.P \mid n(\alpha).P\,.$$

The late labelled transition system (denoted $\xrightarrow{\alpha}_l$) and the definition of strong late bisimulation (denoted $\sim_l$) are standard [13].[2]

We can specify a type $\mathbb{P}$ as

$$\mathbb{P} \ = \ \tau{:}!\mathbb{P} \ + \ \mathsf{out}{:}\mathbb{N} \otimes \mathbb{N} \otimes !\mathbb{P} + \ \mathsf{bout}{:}\mathbb{N} \otimes !(\delta\mathbb{P}) \ + \ \mathsf{inp}{:}\mathbb{N} \otimes !(\mathbb{N} \to \mathbb{P})\,.$$

The terms of π-calculus can be expressed in new-HOPLA as the following terms of type $\mathbb{P}$:

$$[\![\mathbf{0}]\!] = 0 \qquad [\![\overline{n}m.P]\!] = \mathsf{out}{:}n \cdot m \cdot ![\![P]\!] \qquad [\![n(\beta).P]\!] = \mathsf{inp}{:}n \cdot !(\lambda\beta.[\![P]\!])$$
$$[\![(\nu\alpha)P]\!] = \mathit{Res}\,(\mathit{new}\alpha.[\![P]\!]) \qquad [\![P \mid Q]\!] = [\![P]\!] \parallel [\![Q]\!]$$

Here, $\mathit{Res} \, : \delta\mathbb{P} \to \mathbb{P}$ and $\parallel : \mathbb{P}\&\mathbb{P} \to \mathbb{P}$ (we use infix notation for convenience) and are abbrevations for the recursively defined processes reported in Table 6.

Informally, the restriction map $\mathit{Res} \, : \delta\mathbb{P} \to \mathbb{P}$ pushes restrictions inside processes as far as possible. The five summands correspond to the five equations below:

$$(\nu\alpha)\tau.P \sim_l \tau.(\nu\alpha)P$$
$$(\nu\alpha)\overline{m}n.P \sim_l \overline{m}n.(\nu\alpha)P \ \text{ if } \alpha \neq m, n \qquad (\nu\alpha)\overline{m}\alpha.P \sim_l \overline{m}(\alpha).P \ \text{ if } \alpha \neq m$$
$$(\nu\alpha)\overline{m}(\beta).P \sim_l \overline{m}(\beta).(\nu\alpha)P \ \text{ if } \alpha \neq m \qquad (\nu\alpha)m\beta.P \sim_l m\beta.(\nu\alpha)P \ \text{ if } \alpha \neq m$$

where $\overline{m}(\alpha)$ is an abbreviation to express bound-output, that is, $(\nu\alpha)\overline{m}\alpha$. The map Res implicitly also ensures that $(\nu\alpha)P \sim_l 0$ if none of the above cases applies. The parallel composition map $\parallel$ captures the *(late) expansion law* of π-calculus. There is a strong correspondence between actions performed by a closed π-calculus process and the actions of its encoding.

Theorem 6 *Let P a closed π-calculus process. If $P \xrightarrow{\tau}_l P'$ is derivable in π-calculus, then $\mathsf{n}([\![P]\!]) \vdash [\![P]\!] \xrightarrow{\tau:!} t$ for some t, and $\mathsf{n}(t) \vdash t \sim [\![P']\!] : \mathbb{P}$. Conversely, if*

[2] To avoid complicating proofs, we ignore replication; that can be encoded as $[\![!P]\!] = \mathit{rec}\, x.([\![P]\!] \parallel x)$.

$$\begin{array}{rcl}
Res\ t & = & [t > new\alpha.\tau{:}!(x[\alpha])) \Rightarrow \tau{:}!Res\ x] \\
& + & \Sigma_{\beta\in\mathbf{N}}\Sigma_{\gamma\in\mathbf{N}}[t > new\alpha.\mathsf{out}{:}\beta\cdot\gamma\cdot!(x[\alpha]) \Rightarrow \mathsf{out}{:}\beta\cdot\gamma\cdot!Res\ x] \\
& + & \Sigma_{\beta\in\mathbf{N}}[t > new\alpha.\mathsf{out}{:}\beta\cdot\alpha\cdot!(x[\alpha]) \Rightarrow \mathsf{bout}{:}\beta\cdot!x] \\
& + & \Sigma_{\beta\in\mathbf{N}}[t > new\alpha.\mathsf{bout}{:}\beta\cdot!(x[\alpha]) \Rightarrow \mathsf{bout}{:}\beta\cdot!new\gamma\cdot Res\,(new\eta.x[\eta][\gamma])] \\
& + & \Sigma_{\beta\in\mathbf{N}}[t > new\alpha.\mathsf{inp}{:}\beta\cdot!(x[\alpha]) \Rightarrow \mathsf{inp}{:}\beta\cdot!\lambda\gamma.Res\,(new\eta.x[\eta](\gamma))]
\end{array}$$

$$\begin{array}{rcl}
t \parallel u & = & [t > \tau{:}!x \Rightarrow \tau{:}!(x \parallel u)] \\
& + & \Sigma_{\beta\in\mathbf{N}}\Sigma_{\gamma\in\mathbf{N}}[t > \mathsf{out}{:}(\beta\cdot\gamma\cdot!x) \Rightarrow [u > \mathsf{inp}{:}(\beta\cdot!y) \Rightarrow \tau{:}!(x \parallel y\gamma)]] \\
& + & \Sigma_{\beta\in\mathbf{N}}[t > \mathsf{bout}{:}(\beta\cdot!x) \Rightarrow [u > \mathsf{inp}{:}(\beta\cdot!y) \Rightarrow \tau{:}!Res\,(new\eta.(x[\eta] \parallel y\eta))]] \\
& + & \Sigma_{\beta\in\mathbf{N}}\Sigma_{\gamma\in\mathbf{N}}[t > \mathsf{out}{:}\beta\cdot\gamma\cdot!x \Rightarrow \mathsf{out}{:}\beta\cdot\gamma\cdot!(x \parallel u)] \\
& + & \Sigma_{\beta\in\mathbf{N}}[t > \mathsf{bout}{:}\beta\cdot!x \Rightarrow \mathsf{bout}{:}\beta\cdot!new\eta.(x[\eta] \parallel u)] \\
& + & \Sigma_{\beta\in\mathbf{N}}[t > \mathsf{inp}{:}\beta\cdot!x \Rightarrow \mathsf{inp}{:}\beta\cdot!\lambda\eta.(x(\eta) \parallel u)] \quad + \text{symmetric cases}
\end{array}$$

where η is chosen to avoid clashes with the free name variables of u.

Table 6. Restriction and parallel composition for π-calculus

$\mathsf{n}([\![P]\!]) \vdash [\![P]\!] \xrightarrow{\tau:!} t$ *in new-HOPLA, then* $P \xrightarrow{\tau}_l P'$ *for some* P'*, and* $\mathsf{n}(t) \vdash t \sim [\![P']\!] : \mathbb{P}$.

The encoding also preserves and reflects late strong bisimulation.

Theorem 7 *Let P and Q be two closed π-calculus processes. If* $P \sim_l Q$ *then* $\mathsf{n}(P) \cup \mathsf{n}(Q) \vdash [\![P]\!] \sim [\![Q]\!] : \mathbb{P}$*. Conversely, if* $\mathsf{n}([\![P]\!]) \cup \mathsf{n}([\![Q]\!]) \vdash [\![P]\!] \sim [\![Q]\!] : \mathbb{P}$*, then* $P \sim_l Q$.

Along the same lines, new-HOPLA can encode the early semantics of π-calculus. The type of the input action assigned to π-calculus terms captures the difference between the two semantics. In the late semantics a process performing an input action has type $\mathsf{inp}{:}\mathbf{N} \otimes !(\mathbf{N} \to \mathbb{P})$: the type of the continuation $(\mathbf{N} \to \mathbb{P})$ ensures that the continuation is actually an *abstraction* that will be instantiated with the received name when interaction takes place. In the early semantics, the type of a process performing an input action is changed into $\mathsf{inp}{:}\mathbf{N} \otimes \mathbf{N} \to !\mathbb{P}$. Performing an input action now involves picking up a name before executing the prototypical action, and in the continuation (whose type is $\mathbb{P}$) the formal variable has been instantiated with the received name. Details can be found in [16].

Higher-Order π-calculus The language we consider can be found in [13]. Rather than introducing a unit value, we allow processes in addition to abstractions to be communicated. For brevity, we gloss over typing issues. The syntax of terms and values is defined below.

$$P ::= V \bullet V \mid n(x).P \mid \overline{n}(V).P \mid P \,|\, P \mid x \mid (\nu\alpha)P \mid 0 \qquad V ::= P \mid (x).P$$

The reduction semantics for the language is standard [13]; we only recall the axioms that define the reduction relation:

$$(x).P \bullet V \rightarrow P[V/x] \qquad \overline{n}(V).P \mid n(x).Q \rightarrow P \mid Q[V/x]\,.$$

Types for HOπ are given recursively by

$$\mathbb{P} = \tau{:}!\mathbb{P} + \mathsf{out}{:}\mathbf{N}\otimes!\mathbb{C} + \mathsf{inp}{:}\mathbf{N}\otimes!(\mathbb{F} \to \mathbb{P}) \qquad \mathbb{C} = 0{:}\mathbb{F}\&\mathbb{P} + 1{:}\delta\mathbb{C} \qquad \mathbb{F} = 2{:}\mathbb{P} + 3{:}\mathbb{F} \to \mathbb{P}\,.$$

Concretions of the form $(\nu\tilde{\alpha})\langle V\rangle P$ correspond to terms of type $\mathbb{C}$; recursion on types is used to encode the tuple of restricted names $\tilde{\alpha}$. The functions $[\![-]\!]_v$ and $[\![-]\!]$ translate respectively values into the terms of type $\mathbb{F}$, and processes into terms of type $\mathbb{P}$:

$$[\![P]\!]_v = 2{:}[\![P]\!] \qquad [\![(x).P]\!]_v = 3{:}\lambda x.[\![P]\!] \qquad [\![V \bullet W]\!] = \tau{:}!(\pi_3[\![V]\!]_v)(\pi_2[\![W]\!]_v + \pi_3[\![W]\!]_v)$$

$$[\![P \mid Q]\!] = [\![P]\!] \parallel [\![Q]\!] \qquad [\![(\nu\alpha)P]\!] = Res\, new\alpha.[\![P]\!] \qquad [\![x]\!] = x \qquad [\![0]\!] = 0$$

$$[\![n(x).P]\!] = \mathsf{inp}{:}n \cdot !(\lambda x.[\![P]\!]) \qquad [\![\overline{n}(V)]\!] = \mathsf{out}{:}n \cdot !([\![V]\!]_v, [\![P]\!])\,.$$

The restriction map $Res\ : \delta\mathbb{P} \to \mathbb{P}$ filters the actions that a process emits, blocking actions that refer to the name that is being restricted. Output actions cause names to be extruded: the third summand records these names in the appropriate concretion.

$$\begin{aligned}
Res\ t \ &= \ [t > new\alpha.\tau{:}!x[\alpha] \Rightarrow \tau{:}!Res\, x] \\
&+ \ \Sigma_{\beta\in\mathbf{N}}[t > new\alpha.\mathsf{inp}{:}(\beta \cdot !x[\alpha]) \Rightarrow \mathsf{inp}{:}(\beta \cdot !\lambda y.Res\,(new\gamma.x[\gamma](y)))] \\
&+ \ \Sigma_{\beta\in\mathbf{N}}[t > new\alpha.\mathsf{out}{:}(\beta \cdot !x[\alpha]) \Rightarrow \mathsf{out}{:}(\beta \cdot !3{:}x)]
\end{aligned}$$

Parallel composition is a family of mutually dependent operations also including components such as $\parallel_i$ of type $\mathbb{C}\&\mathbb{F} \to \mathbb{P}$ to say how values compose in parallel with concretions etc. All these components can be tupled together in a product and parallel composition defined as a simultaneous recursive definition:

— *Processes in parallel with processes:*

$$\begin{aligned}
t \parallel u \ &= \ \Sigma_{\beta\in\mathbf{N}}[t > \mathsf{out}{:}\beta \cdot !x \Rightarrow [u > \mathsf{inp}{:}\beta \cdot !y \Rightarrow \tau{:}!(x \parallel_i y)]] \\
&+ \ \Sigma_{\beta\in\mathbf{N}}[u > \mathsf{inp}{:}\beta \cdot !y \Rightarrow \mathsf{inp}{:}\beta \cdot !(t \parallel_a y)] \\
&+ \ \Sigma_{\beta\in\mathbf{N}}[u > \mathsf{out}{:}\beta \cdot !y \Rightarrow \mathsf{out}{:}\beta \cdot !(t \parallel_c y)] \\
&+ \ [u > \tau{:}!y \Rightarrow \tau{:}!(t \parallel y)] \quad + \text{symmetric cases}
\end{aligned}$$

— *Concretions in parallel with values*

$$\begin{aligned}
c \parallel_i f = snd(\pi_0 c) \parallel (\, &(\pi_3 f)(\pi_2(fst(\pi_0 c)) + \pi_3(fst(\pi_0 c))) \\
&+ Res\,(new\alpha.(((\pi_1 c)[\alpha]) \parallel_i f))\,)
\end{aligned}$$

— *Concretions in parallel with processes*

$$c \parallel_c t \ = \ 0{:}(fst(\pi_0 c), snd(\pi_0 c) \parallel t) + 1{:}(new\alpha.((\pi_1 c)[\alpha] \parallel_c t))$$

— *Values in parallel with processes*

$$f \parallel_a t \ = \ \lambda x.(((\pi_3 f)x) \parallel u)$$

The remaining cases are given symmetrically. The proposed encoding agrees with the reduction semantics of HOπ. The resulting bisimulation is analogous to the so called *higher-order bisimulation* [1, 15], and as such it is strictly finer than observational equivalence. It is an open problem whether it is possible to provide an encoding of HOπ that preserves and reflects the natural observational equivalence given in [12].

Polyadic π-calculus A natural and convenient extension to π-calculus is to admit processes that pass tuples of names: polyadicity is a good testing ground for the expressivity of our language. We can specify a type for polyadic π-calculus processes as:

$$\mathbb{P} \ = \ \tau{:}!\mathbb{P} + \mathsf{out}{:}\mathbf{N} \otimes \mathbb{C} + \mathsf{inp}{:}\mathbf{N} \otimes !\mathbb{F} \qquad \mathbb{C} \ = \ 0{:}\mathbf{N} \otimes \mathbb{C} + 1{:}\delta\mathbb{C} + 2{:}!\mathbb{P} \qquad \mathbb{F} = 3{:}\mathbf{N} \to \mathbb{F} + 4{:}\mathbb{P}$$

Recursive types are used to encode tuples of (possibly new) names in concretions, and sequences of name abstractions in abstractions.

Just as with the π-calculus, it is possible to write a restriction map $Res : \delta\mathbb{P} \to \mathbb{P}$ that pushes restrictions inside processes as far as possible, and a parallel map that captures the expansion law. The resulting semantics coincides with the standard late semantics of polyadic π-calculus. Details can be found in [16].

Mobile Ambients We sketch an encoding of the mobility core of the Ambient Calculus, extending the encoding of Mobile Ambients with public names into HOPLA given in [7]. Details can be found in [16].

Types reflect the actions that ambient processes can perform, and are given recursively by:

$$\begin{aligned} \mathbb{P} \;&=\; \tau{:}!\mathbb{P} + \mathsf{in}{:}\mathbb{N} \otimes !\mathbb{P} + \mathsf{out}{:}\mathbb{N} \otimes !\mathbb{P} + \mathsf{open}{:}\mathbb{N} \otimes !\mathbb{P} + \mathsf{mvin}{:}\mathbb{N} \otimes !\mathbb{C} \\ &\quad + \mathsf{mvout}{:}\mathbb{N} \otimes !\mathbb{C} + \overline{\mathsf{open}}{:}\mathbb{N} \otimes !\mathbb{P} + \overline{\mathsf{mvin}}{:}\mathbb{N} \otimes !\mathbb{F} \\ \mathbb{C} &= 0{:}\mathbb{P}\&\mathbb{P} + 1{:}\delta\mathbb{C} \qquad\qquad \mathbb{F} = \mathbb{P} \to \mathbb{P} \end{aligned}$$

The injections in, out, and open correspond to the basic capabilities a process can exercise, while their action on the enclosing ambients is registered by the components mvin and mvout. The injections $\overline{\mathsf{open}}$ and $\overline{\mathsf{mvin}}$ record the receptive interactions that an ambient can (implicitly) have with the environment. Again, recursive types are used in concretions to record the sequence of names that must be extruded. Terms are then translated as:

$$[\![\mathtt{in\_}n.P]\!] = \mathsf{in}\, n \cdot ![\![P]\!] \quad [\![\mathtt{out\_}n.P]\!] = \mathsf{out}\, n \cdot ![\![P]\!] \quad [\![\mathtt{open\_}n.P]\!] = \mathsf{open}\, n \cdot ![\![P]\!]$$

$$[\![0]\!] = 0 \quad [\![n[P]]\!] = \mathit{Amb}\,(n, [\![P]\!]) \quad [\![P \mid Q]\!] = [\![P]\!] \parallel [\![Q]\!] \quad [\![(\nu\alpha)P]\!] = \mathit{Res}\,(\mathit{new}\alpha.[\![P]\!])$$

The restriction map $Res : \delta\mathbb{P} \to \mathbb{P}$ filters the actions that a process emit, and blocks actions that refer to the name that is restricted. In fact, in Mobile Ambients, the only scope extrusions are caused by mobility, and not by pre-actions.

$$\mathit{Res}\ t \;=\; \cdots + \Sigma_{\beta\in\mathbb{N}}[t > \mathit{new}\alpha.\mathsf{in}{:}(\beta \cdot !x[\alpha]) \Rightarrow \mathsf{in}{:}(\beta \cdot !\mathit{Res}\, x)] + \cdots$$

Parallel composition is a family of operations, one of which is a binary operation between processes, $\|_{\mathbb{P}\&\mathbb{P}}\colon \mathbb{P}\&\mathbb{P} \to \mathbb{P}$. The most interesting cases are when two processes interact:

$$\begin{aligned} t \parallel u \;&=\; \Sigma_{\beta\in\mathbb{N}}[t > \overline{\mathsf{open}}{:}\ \beta \cdot !x \Rightarrow [u > \mathsf{open}{:}\ \beta \cdot !y \Rightarrow \tau{:}\cdot!(x \parallel_c y)]] \\ &\quad+\; \Sigma_{\beta\in\mathbb{N}}[t > \overline{\mathsf{mvin}}{:}\ \beta \cdot !f \Rightarrow [u > \mathsf{mvin}{:}\ \beta \cdot !c \Rightarrow \tau{:}\cdot!(c \parallel_i f)]] + \cdots \end{aligned}$$

Interaction between concretions, abstractions, and processes is analogous to that in the HOπ encoding. Finally, ambient creation can be defined recursively in new-HOPLA as an operation $Amb : \mathbb{N}\&\mathbb{P} \to \mathbb{P}$:

$$\begin{aligned} \mathit{Amb}\,(m,t) \;&=\; [t > \tau{:}!x \Rightarrow \tau{:}!\mathit{Amb}\,(m,x)] \\ &\quad+\; \Sigma_{\beta\in\mathbb{N}}[t > \mathsf{in}{:}\beta \cdot !x \Rightarrow \mathsf{mvin}{:}\beta \cdot !(\mathit{Amb}\,(m,x), 0) \\ &\quad+\; \Sigma_{\beta\in\mathbb{N}}[t > \mathsf{out}{:}\beta \cdot !x \Rightarrow \mathsf{mvout}{:}\beta \cdot !(\mathit{Amb}\,(m,x), 0) \\ &\quad+\; [t > \mathsf{mvout}{:}m \cdot !c \Rightarrow \tau{:}!\mathit{Extr}\,(m,c)] \\ &\quad+\; \overline{\mathsf{open}}{:}m \cdot !t + \overline{\mathsf{mvin}}{:}m \cdot !\lambda y.\mathit{Amb}\,(m, t \parallel y) \end{aligned}$$

where the map $Extr : \mathbb{N}\&\mathbb{C} \to \mathbb{P}$ extrudes names across ambient's boundary after a mvout action:

$$\mathit{Extr}(m,c) \;=\; \mathit{fst}(\pi_0 c) \parallel \mathit{Amb}\,(m, \mathit{snd}(\pi_0 c)) + \mathit{Res}\,(\mathit{new}\alpha.(\mathit{Extr}\,(m, (\pi_1 c)[\alpha]))) \,.$$

5 Conclusion

This paper has concentrated on the operational semantics of new-HOPLA, which despite its economy has been shown to be remarkably expressive. This is in part because only two of the usual process-algebra operations appear as primitives in new-HOPLA: a basic prefix operation and nondeterministic sum. The denotational semantics of new-HOPLA and the domain theories on which they rest will be explained more fully elsewhere. The path-set semantics sketched in the introduction suggests an analysis of adequacy and full abstraction, based on the basic observation of !-transitions, along the lines of [8, 9]. The more detailed presheaf semantics supports bisimulation, though at higher-order we do not understand how open-map bisimulation, intrinsic to presheaf models, relates to the bisimulation we have defined—in the case of the π-calculus the two bisimulations agree by [2]. Closer to the concerns of this paper are questions of exploiting the rich types of new-HOPLA to give 'fully-abstract' encodings of higher-order process calculi.

References

[1] G. Boudol. Towards a lambda calculus for concurrent and communicating systems. In *Proc. TAPSOFT '89*, volume 351 of *LNCS*, pages 149–161. Springer Verlag, 1989.

[2] G. L. Cattani, I. Stark, and G. Winskel. Presheaf models for the π-calculus. In *Proc. CTCS'97*, volume 1290 of *LNCS*. Springer Verlag, 1997.

[3] M. Fiore, E. Moggi, and D. Sangiorgi. A fully-abstract model for the π-calculus. In *Proc. 11th LICS*. IEEE Computer Society Press, 1996.

[4] J.Y. Girard. Linear logic. *Theoretical Computer Science*, 50:1–102, 1987.

[5] A. D. Gordon. Bisimilarity as a theory of functional programming: mini-course. Notes Series BRICS-NS-95-3, BRICS, Department of CS, University of Aarhus, July 1995.

[6] D. J. Howe. Proving congruence of bisimulation in functional programming languages. *Information and Computation*, 124(2):103–112, 1996.

[7] M. Nygaard and G. Winskel. Hopla—a higher-order process language. In *Proc. CONCUR '02*, volume 2421 of *LNCS*. Springer Verlag, 2002.

[8] M. Nygaard and G. Winskel. Domain theory for concurrency. To appear in *Theoretical Computer Science*, special issue on domain theory, accepted 2003.

[9] M. Nygaard and G. Winskel. Full abstraction for HOPLA. In *Proc. CONCUR '03*, LNCS. Springer Verlag, 2003.

[10] A. M. Pitts. Operationally-based theories of program equivalence. In P. Dybjer and A. M. Pitts, editors, *Semantics and Logics of Computation*, Publications of the Newton Institute, pages 241–298. Cambridge University Press, 1997.

[11] A. M. Pitts and M. J. Gabbay. A metalanguage for programming with bound names modulo renaming. In *Proc. MPC 2000*, volume 1837 of *LNCS*. Springer Verlag, 2000.

[12] D. Sangiorgi. Bisimulation in higher-order calculi. In *Proc. IFIP PROCOMET'94*, pages 207–224. North-Holland, 1994.

[13] D. Sangiorgi and D. Walker. *The π-calculus: a Theory of Mobile Processes*. Cambridge University Press, 2001.

[14] I. Stark. A fully-abstract domain model for the π-calculus. In *Proc. 11th LICS*. IEEE Computer Society Press, 1996.

[15] B. Thomsen. *Calculi for Higher Order Communicating Systems*. PhD thesis, Department of Computing, Imperial College, 1990.

[16] F. Zappa Nardelli. *De la sémantique des processus d'ordre supérieur*. PhD thesis, Université de Paris 7, 2003. Available in English from `http://www.di.ens.fr/~zappa`.

BEHAVIOURAL EQUIVALENCES FOR DYNAMIC WEB DATA

Sergio Maffeis and Philippa Gardner
Department of Computing, Imperial College London, UK.
{maffeis,pg}@doc.ic.ac.uk

Abstract We study behavioural equivalences for dynamic web data in X$d\pi$, a model for reasoning about behaviour found in (for example) dynamic web page programming, applet interaction, and web-service orchestration. X$d\pi$ is based on an idealised model of semistructured data, and an extension of the π-calculus with locations and operations for interacting with data. The equivalences are non-standard due to the integration of data and processes, and the presence of locations.

1 Introduction

Web data, such as XML, plays a fundamental rôle in the exchange of information between globally distributed applications. Applications naturally fall into some sort of mediator approach: systems are divided into peers, with mechanisms based on XML for interaction between peers. The development of analysis techniques, languages and tools for web data is by no means straightforward. In particular, although web services allow for interaction between processes and data, direct interaction between processes is not well-supported.

Peer-to-peer data management systems are decentralised distributed systems where each component offers the same set of basic functionalities and acts both as a producer and as a consumer of information. We model systems where each peer consists of an XML data repository and a working space where processes are allowed to run. Our processes can be regarded as agents with a simple set of functionalities; they communicate with each other, query and update the local repository, and migrate to other peers to continue execution. A process definition can be included in a document as an atomic piece of data, and can be selected for execution by other processes. These functionalities are enough to express most of the dynamic behaviour found in web data, such as web services, distributed (and replicated) documents [1], distributed query patterns [19], hyperlinks, forms, and scripting.

The X$d\pi$-calculus [7] provides a formal description of such systems. It is based on a network of locations (peers) containing a (semi-structured) data model, and π-like processes [17, 20, 10] for modelling process interaction, process migration, and interaction with data. The data model consists of unordered labelled trees, with embedded processes for querying and updating data, and explicit pointers for referring to other parts of the network: for example, a document with a hyperlink referring to another site, and a light-weight trusted process for retrieving information associated with the link.

A behavioural understanding of dynamic web data can serve as a starting point for the use of formal techniques. Moreover, the combination of web services and scripted processes provides the data engineer with many alternative patterns for exchanging information on the web [2, 19], and equational reasoning becomes useful to show, for example, that some complex data-exchange protocol conforms to its specification.

We study behavioural equivalences in Core X$d\pi$, which is a slight adaptation of X$d\pi$, where both the data and the process component of a network are explicitly located, and therefore easier to analyse independently. We identify two main notions of contextual equivalence for *open* networks, based on the observation of the data structure at each location, or of the capabilities of process to access data. We derive the corresponding process equivalences so that when two equivalent pieces of code are put in the same position in a network, the resulting networks cannot be distinguished by an observer. Process equivalences appear to be sensitive to the set of locations composing the network. This feature, together with having scripted processes as values, requires non trivial techniques for defining a labelled-bisimulation-based proof method. We address interested readers to the full paper [15] for all the technical details.

Related Work. Our model is related to the Active XML approach to data integration developed independently by Abiteboul et al. [2]. Several distributed query languages, such as [19, 14, 4], extend traditional query languages with facilities for distribution awareness. Our approach is closest to the ubQL query language of [19], partly motivated by ideas from the π-calculus [18]. Process calculi have also been used for example to study security properties of web services [8], and to program XML-based Home Area Networks devices [3].

In [7] we have defined a first notion of barbed equivalence, and we have sketched a proof method based on higher-order bisimulation. In this paper we study in detail behavioural equivalences, improving and extending significantly the previous results. Core X$d\pi$ uses ideas from [5], and the contextual equivalences are based on the reduction-closed framework of [12]. Our labelled transition system and bisimulation exploit a translation technique from higher-order to first-order actions proposed in [13], and based on [21]. Ours is the first attempt to study behavioural equivalences of web-based (higher-order) data-sharing applications, and is characterised by its emphasis on dynamic data.

2 Core X$d\pi$

In X$d\pi$, a peer-to-peer network is represented as a set of locations (we regard *location* and *peer* as synonyms), each containing a data-tree and some processes. In order to reason modularly on data and processes, we instead model a network in Core X$d\pi$ as a pair (D, P), where D is a set of located trees, each one representing the data component of a location, and P is a multiset of located-process, representing both the services provided by each peer and the agents in execution on behalf of other peers.

$$
\begin{array}{ll}
\text{(TREES)} & U \equiv U' \implies \mathsf{a}[U] \equiv \mathsf{a}[U'] \\
\text{(VALUES)} & v' \equiv w' \wedge \tilde{v} \equiv \tilde{w} \implies v', \tilde{v} \equiv w', \tilde{w} \qquad P \equiv Q \implies \Box P \equiv \Box Q \\
\text{(PROCESSES)} & (\nu c)(\nu c')P \equiv (\nu c')(\nu c)P \qquad (\nu c)0 \equiv 0 \\
& c \notin fn(P) \implies P \,|\, (\nu c)Q \equiv (\nu c)(P \,|\, Q) \\
& V \equiv V' \wedge P \equiv Q \implies l\cdot\mathsf{update}_p(\chi, V).P \equiv l\cdot\mathsf{update}_p(\chi, V').Q \\
\text{(STORES)} & \forall l.\, D(l) \equiv B(l) \implies D \equiv B \\
\text{(NETWORKS)} & D \equiv B \wedge P \equiv Q \implies (D, P) \equiv (B, Q)
\end{array}
$$

Table 1. Structural congruence for Core X$d\pi$ is the least congruence satisfying alpha-conversion, the commutative monoidal laws for $(0, |)$ on trees and processes, and the axioms reported above.

Trees. Our data model extends the unordered labelled rooted trees of [6], with leaves which can either be scripted processes or pointers to data. We use the following constructs: *edge labels* denoted by $\mathsf{a}, \mathsf{b}, \mathsf{c} \in \mathcal{A}$, *path expressions* denoted by $p, q \in \mathcal{E}$ and used to identify specific subtrees, and *location names* of the form $\circlearrowleft, l, m \in \mathcal{L}$, where the 'self' location $\circlearrowleft$ refers to the enclosing location. The set of data trees, denoted $\mathcal{T}$, is given by

$$T ::= 0 \mid T \,|\, T \mid \mathsf{a}[T] \mid \mathsf{a}[\Box P] \mid \mathsf{a}[@l{:}p]$$

Tree 0 denotes a rooted tree with no content. Tree $T_1 \,|\, T_2$ denotes the composition of T_1 and T_2, which simply joins the roots. A tree of the form $\mathsf{a}[\dots]$ denotes a tree with a single branch labelled a which can have three types of content: a subtree T; a *scripted process* $\Box P$, which is a static process awaiting a command to run; a *pointer* $@l{:}p$, which denotes a pointer to a set of subtrees identified by path expression p in the tree at location l. The structural congruence for trees states that trees are unordered, and scripted processes are identified up to the structural congruence for processes (see Table 1).

We regard a path p as a function from trees to sets of nodes (up to structural congruence): $p(T)$ denotes the tree T where the nodes identified by p are selected. For simplicity we do not show node identifiers explicitly, but we underline the selected nodes. We describe paths using a subset of XPath [16], where "a" denotes a step along an edge labelled a, "/" denotes path composition, ".." a step back, "//" any node, and ".", which can appear only in paths inside trees, denotes the path from the root to the current node. For example, in $\mathsf{a}[\underline{\mathsf{a}[S]} \,|\, \mathsf{b}[S'] \,|\, \mathsf{c}[T']]$ we have underlined the nodes selected by path //a.

Located Processes. Our processes are based on asynchronous π_2-processes [5] extended with an operation for manipulating the tree structure (update) and one for selecting a script for execution (run). Generic variables are x, y, z, channel names or channel variables are a, b, c, the meaning will be clear from the context, and values are

$$u, v, w ::= T \mid c \mid l \mid p \mid \Box P$$

We use the notation $\tilde{z}$ for vectors of variables, and $\tilde{v}$ for vectors of values and variables. Identifiers U, V range over scripted processes, pointers and trees. *Patterns* χ, ξ have the form $\chi ::= X \mid @x{:}y \mid \Box X$, where X denotes a tree or process variable. The set of processes, denoted by $\mathcal{P}$, is given by

$$P,Q,R ::= \quad 0 \mid P \mid P \mid \overline{l\cdot b}\langle\tilde{v}\rangle \mid l\cdot b(\tilde{z}).P \mid !l\cdot b(\tilde{z}).P \mid (\nu c)P$$
$$\mid l\cdot\mathsf{update}_p(\chi, V).P \mid l\cdot\mathsf{run}_p$$

The processes in the first line of the grammar are constructs arising from the π_2-calculus: the *output* process $\overline{l\cdot b}\langle\tilde{v}\rangle$ denotes a vector of values $\tilde{v}$ waiting to be sent via channel b at location l, the *input* process $l\cdot b(\tilde{z}).P$ is waiting to receive values from an output process via channel b at l, and the standard *nil, composition, restriction* and *replicated input.* Channel names C are partitioned into *public* and *session* channels, denoted C_p and C_s respectively. Public channels denote those channels that are intended to have the same meaning at each location, such as "finger", and cannot be restricted. Session channels are used for process interaction, and can be restricted. We assume the usual notions of *free* and *bound* names (fn, bn) for session channels. Scripted processes cannot have free session names. We assume a simple sorting discipline on channels.

Command $l\cdot\mathsf{run}_p$ activates the scripted processes selected by the path expression p in the tree at l. Command $l\cdot\mathsf{update}_p(\chi, V).P$ is used to interact with the data tree at l. In an update, V may contain variables and must have the same sort as χ. The variables free in χ are bound in V and P. The update command finds all the values V_i given by the path p, and pattern-matches these values with χ to obtain the substitution σ_i when it exists. For each successful pattern-matching, it replaces the V_i with $V\sigma_i$ and evolves to $P\sigma_i$. Below we give some basic commands derived from update:

$l\cdot\mathsf{copy}_p(X).P \triangleq l\cdot\mathsf{update}_p(X,X).P$	copy the tree at p and use it in P
$l\cdot\mathsf{cut}_p(X).P \triangleq l\cdot\mathsf{update}_p(X,0).P$	cut the tree at p and use it in P
$l\cdot\mathsf{paste}_p\langle T\rangle.P \triangleq l\cdot\mathsf{update}_p(X, X \mid T).P$	where X is not free in T or P, paste tree T at p and evolve to P

Networks and Stores. A network is represented by a pair (D, P) where the first component (the *store*) is a finite partial function from location names to trees, and the second component is a process. Interaction between processes and data is always local, as will be shown by rules (UPDATE) and (RUN) in Table 2, and consequently we regard the store as *distributed*. We write $dom(D)$ to denote the domain of store D. We write $D_1 \uplus D_2$ for the union of stores D_1 and D_2 with disjoint domains. The network (D, P) is well-formed if D and P contain no free variables, and all the scripted processes have no free session names.

Our reduction semantics on networks will be closed with respect to *network contexts* $(\mathcal{C}_\mathcal{S}, \mathcal{C}_\mathcal{P})$, where *store contexts* $\mathcal{C}_\mathcal{S}$ are defined by $\mathcal{C}_\mathcal{S} ::= - \mid \mathcal{C}_\mathcal{S} \uplus D$ and *process contexts* $\mathcal{C}_\mathcal{P}$ are defined by $\mathcal{C}_\mathcal{P} ::= - \mid \mathcal{C}_\mathcal{P} \mid P \mid (\nu c)\, \mathcal{C}_\mathcal{P}$. Given a network (D, P) and a context $\mathcal{C} = (\mathcal{C}_\mathcal{S}, \mathcal{C}_\mathcal{P})$, we write $\mathcal{C}\{(D,P)\}$ for their composition: for example, if $\mathcal{C}_\mathcal{S} = - \uplus B$, $\mathcal{C}_\mathcal{P} = (\nu c)-$ then $\mathcal{C}\{(D,P)\} = (D \uplus B, (\nu c)P)$. A composition involving stores is defined only for stores with disjoint domains. We will omit the subscripts from contexts when no ambiguity can arise.

Reduction Semantics. The reduction relation $\rightarrow$, relying on an updating function $\rightsquigarrow$, describes processes interaction, the interaction between processes and data, and (implicitly) the movement of processes across locations (Table 2).

(Com) $(\{l \mapsto T\}, \overline{l \cdot c}\langle \tilde{v} \rangle \mid l \cdot c(\tilde{x}).P) \rightarrow (\{l \mapsto T\}, P\{\tilde{v}/\tilde{x}\})$

(!Com) $(\{l \mapsto T\}, \overline{l \cdot c}\langle \tilde{v} \rangle \mid !l \cdot c(\tilde{x}).P) \rightarrow (\{l \mapsto T\}, !l \cdot c(\tilde{x}).P | P\{\tilde{v}/\tilde{x}\})$

(Update) $$\frac{p(T) \rightsquigarrow_{p,l,\chi,V} T', \{\sigma_1, \cdots, \sigma_n\}}{(\{l \mapsto T\}, l \cdot \mathsf{update}_p(\chi, V).P) \rightarrow (\{l \mapsto T'\}, P\sigma_1 \mid \cdots \mid P\sigma_n)}$$

(Run) $$\frac{p(T) \rightsquigarrow_{p,l,\Box X,\Box X} T, \{\{\Box P_1/\Box X\}, \cdots, \{\Box P_n/\Box X\}\}}{(\{l \mapsto T\}, l \cdot \mathsf{run}_p) \rightarrow (\{l \mapsto T\}, P_1 \mid \cdots \mid P_n)}$$

(Reduction) The reduction relation on processes is the smallest relation closed with respect to reduction contexts, structural congruence and the axioms above.

(Zero) $0 \rightsquigarrow_\Theta 0, \emptyset$ (Link) $\mathsf{a}[@m{:}q] \rightsquigarrow_\Theta \mathsf{a}[@m{:}q], \emptyset$

(Script) $\mathsf{a}[\Box Q] \rightsquigarrow_\Theta \mathsf{a}[\Box Q], \emptyset$ (Node) $\dfrac{T \rightsquigarrow_\Theta T', \Sigma}{\mathsf{a}[T] \rightsquigarrow_\Theta \mathsf{a}[T'], \Sigma}$

(Par) $$\frac{T \rightsquigarrow_\Theta T', \Sigma_1 \qquad S \rightsquigarrow_\Theta S', \Sigma_2}{T \mid S \rightsquigarrow_\Theta T' \mid S', \Sigma_1 \oplus \Sigma_2}$$

(Up) $$\frac{\mathsf{match}(U, \chi) = \sigma \qquad V\sigma \rightsquigarrow_\Theta V', \Sigma \qquad \Theta = p, l, \chi, V}{\mathsf{a}[\underline{U}] \rightsquigarrow_\Theta \mathsf{a}[V'], \{\sigma\{l/\circlearrowleft, p/.\}\} \oplus \Sigma}$$

(Updating Function) Above, Σ is a multiset of substitutions, and $\oplus$ is multiset union, and $\Theta = p, l, \chi, V$ are the parameters of an update or run command.

Table 2. Reduction axioms and updating function for Core Xdπ.

First we describe the reduction relation. Rules (Com) and (!Com) are basically the standard communication rules for the π-calculus, except that processes only communicate if they are at the same location l, and l is in the store. Rule (Update) provides interaction between processes and data. Given the command $l \cdot \mathsf{update}_p(\chi, V).P$ and the tree T at l in the store, the updating function $\rightsquigarrow$ takes $p(T)$ as an argument, matches each identifier U_i in $p(T)$ with the pattern χ to obtain the substitution σ_i, replaces each U_i with $V\sigma_i$ in T, and returns the continuation process $P_i\sigma_i$. Rule (Run) is a special case of update, where the tree is not modified, and the scripted processes $\Box P_i$ identified by $p(T)$ are activated in parallel to yield the continuation P_i.

We now describe the updating function $\rightsquigarrow$, which is parameterised by p, l, χ, V, the arguments of an update or run command. The first five rules define simply a traversal of the tree collecting the set of substitutions Σ, whereas rule (Up) is responsible for the actual update. It applies to the identified nodes (underlined), matching U with χ, to obtain substitution σ (in our case patterns are simple, and pattern-matching is trivial, but the approach can be extended to more complicated patterns). When σ exists, the process continues recursively updating $V\sigma$, until some subtree V' with a set of substitutions denoted by Σ is returned. At this point U is replaced with V', and Σ is returned, together with $\sigma\{l/\circlearrowleft, p/.\}$ (where any references to the current location $\circlearrowleft$ and position "." are substituted by the actual values l and p).

For example, consider $T = \mathsf{c}[\mathsf{a}[T_1] \mid \mathsf{a}[T_2] \mid \mathsf{b}[S]]$ and $T' = \mathsf{c}[\mathsf{a}[0] \mid \mathsf{a}[0] \mid \mathsf{b}[S]]$, and a $\mathsf{cut}_{\mathsf{c/a}}(X)$ command to remove the subtrees at $\mathsf{c/a}$. We have

$$(\{l \mapsto T\}, l \cdot \mathsf{cut}_{\mathsf{c/a}}(X).P) \rightarrow (\{l \mapsto T'\}, P\{T_1/X\} \mid P\{T_2/X\})$$

where the subtrees T_1 and T_2, identified by c/a, are removed from the store, and each is passed to a copy of P. As an example of command run and of the substitution of local references, consider $S = \mathsf{a}[\,\mathsf{b}[\,\Box\overline{\circlearrowleft\cdot a}\langle v\rangle\,]\,|\,\mathsf{b}[\,\Box m\cdot\mathsf{run}_{./../\mathsf{c}}\,]\,]$. We have

$$(\{l \mapsto S\}, \mathsf{run}_{\mathsf{a}/\mathsf{b}}) \rightarrow (\{l \mapsto S\}, \overline{l\cdot a}\langle v\rangle \,|\, m\cdot\mathsf{run}_{\mathsf{a}/\mathsf{b}/../\mathsf{c}})$$

The store S is unaffected by the run operation, which spawns the two processes identified by a/b, where the local path $./../\mathsf{c}$ is replaced by $\mathsf{a}/\mathsf{b}/../\mathsf{c}$, and $\circlearrowleft$ is replaced by l. Note that $m\cdot\mathsf{run}_{\mathsf{a}/\mathsf{b}/../\mathsf{c}}$ is located at m, which is not in the domain of the store. There is no reduction rule for such a process, which represents mobile code "lost" due to network partitioning, or to an invalid network address. In fact, in our model it is not possible for a process to create a new location. Processes represent either scripts or web services, none of which could realistically create new peers, hence the domain of a network is invariant under reduction. Nonetheless we consider open systems, since we admit network composition. Our approach differs from the one of e.g. [9], where process migration can have the effect of creating a new location. We will see in Section 3 how our choice requires new techniques for studying behavioural equivalences.

We conclude the section with an example on web services, see [7] for other motivating examples (other web services, XLink, e-forms). Consider, at location m, a web service `get` for downloading data which, given a path expression p, returns a stream of messages containing the subtrees denoted by p at m. The service is described by process $m\cdot\mathtt{get} = !m\cdot get(x,y,z).m\cdot\mathsf{copy}_x(Y).\overline{y\cdot z}\langle Y\rangle$, where channel get inputs a path x, a location y, and a channel z, and returns its results at y on z. The corresponding service invocation from l is

$$l\cdot\mathtt{call}(m, get, p) = (\nu c)(\overline{m\cdot get}\langle p, l, c\rangle \,|\, !l\cdot c(Y).R),$$

where R is some code handling each result. We will see in Section 4 that invoking $m\cdot\mathtt{get}$ with $l\cdot\mathtt{call}(m, get, p)$ is equivalent to running (from l) the specification $l\cdot\mathsf{spec} = m\cdot\mathsf{copy}_x(Y).R$.

3 Contextual Equivalences for Core X$d\pi$

In this section we study equivalences for networks and processes. In particular, we define when two processes are equivalent in such a way that when they are put in the same position in the network, the resulting networks are equivalent. In Section 4, we introduce a proof method for showing process equivalence.

Network Equivalences. We base our network equivalences on the reduction-closed framework of Honda and Yoshida [12]. The equivalences depend on the choice of observables, and we have studied several cases.

In the setting of dynamic web data, a natural criterion to decide when two systems are equivalent is to compare the structure of the data tree at each location without looking directly at processes, which can be seen as working in the background, and hence not directly observable. The analysis of processes is implicit in the reduction closure property. Below we will define *tree congruence* as the equivalence induced by tree observations. In the full paper [15], we show that tree congruence coincides with two other reduction congruences induced by different observables: one records whether a located tree is empty, the other records located output capabilities.

Another natural choice for observables, motivated by security concerns, is to consider the capabilities of a processes to access data. This notion of equivalence, defined later on as *barbed congruence*, proves to be more restrictive than tree congruence.

We begin with standard generic definitions, based on some observation relation $N \downarrow_\beta$ which states that network N exhibits the observable β. We then study specific observation relations.

DEFINITION 1 *The* weak observation relation *induced by* $\downarrow_\beta$*, denoted by* $\Downarrow_\beta$*, is defined by* $N \Downarrow_\beta \;\triangleq\; \exists N'. N \rightarrow N' \wedge N' \downarrow_\beta$. *The* reduction congruence induced by $\downarrow_\beta$*, denoted by* $\simeq$*, is the largest symmetric relation* $\dot{\simeq}$ *on networks such that* $N \dot{\simeq} M$ *implies*

- *N and M have the same observables:* $N \downarrow_\beta \Rightarrow M \Downarrow_\beta$;
- $\dot{\simeq}$ *is reduction-closed:* $N \rightarrow N' \Rightarrow (\exists M'.M \rightarrow^* M' \wedge N' \dot{\simeq} M')$;
- $\dot{\simeq}$ *is closed under network contexts:* $\forall C.C[N] \dot{\simeq} C[M]$.

We now define tree congruence. Comparing trees up to structural congruence would be overly restrictive, since scripted processes can be semantically equivalent without being structurally congruent. We consider a weaker notion of equivalence on trees which does not look at scripts or pointers. These can be analysed indirectly by suitable contexts.

DEFINITION 2 *We define* observation congruence $(\equiv^t)$*, as the structural congruence of Table 1 with the additional axioms* $\Box P \equiv^t \Box Q$ *and* $@l{:}p \equiv^t @m{:}q$.

As an example of observation congruence, consider $T = \mathtt{a}[\,\mathtt{b}[\Box P] \,|\, \mathtt{b}[T'] \,|\, \mathtt{c}[@l{:}p]\,]$ and $S = \mathtt{a}[\,\mathtt{c}[@m{:}q] \,|\, \mathtt{b}[S'] \,|\, \mathtt{b}[\Box Q]\,]$, with $T' \equiv^t S'$. We have $T \equiv^t S$.

DEFINITION 3 *A* tree observable *has the form* $l{\cdot}T$*, where* l *is a location name and* T *is a tree. We define the observation relation* $N \downarrow_{l \cdot T}$ *on networks and tree observables by* $N \downarrow_{l \cdot T} \triangleq \exists C, S.\ N = C\{(\{l \mapsto S\}, 0)\} \wedge S \equiv^t T$*: that is,* N *contains a location* l *with an* S *tree-congruent to* T. Tree congruence $(\simeq^t)$ *is the reduction congruence induced by tree observables.*

For example, consider the network $\mathtt{alt}(T,S) = (\{l \mapsto S\}, (\nu c)(\overline{l{\cdot}c}\langle T\rangle \,|\, \mathtt{swap}))$, and the process $\mathtt{swap} = !l{\cdot}c(X).l{\cdot}\mathsf{update}_{/}(Y,X).l{\cdot}\mathsf{update}_{/}(Z,Y).\overline{l{\cdot}c}\langle Z\rangle$, which records in Y the tree at l, replaces it by X, and then does the inverse action. We have that $\mathtt{alt}(T,S) \simeq^t \mathtt{alt}(S,T)$ for any T and S, since each process can mimic the other and swap the trees, even if the two networks start with different stores. As an example of non-equivalence, and of how scripts are analysed by contexts, consider the network $\mathtt{net}(P) = (\{l \mapsto \mathtt{a}[\Box P]\}, 0)$ and processes $P_1 = \circlearrowleft \cdot\mathsf{cut}_{/}(X)$ and $P_2 = \circlearrowleft \cdot\mathsf{paste}_{/}\langle \mathtt{b}[0]\rangle$. We have $\mathtt{net}(P_1) \not\simeq^t \mathtt{net}(P_2)$, since $\mathtt{test} = (-, - \,|\, l{\cdot}\mathsf{run}_{a})$ distinguishes $\mathtt{net}(P_1)$ from $\mathtt{net}(P_2)$: $\mathtt{test}\{\mathtt{net}(P_1)\} \Downarrow_{l \cdot 0}$ but $\mathtt{test}\{\mathtt{net}(P_2)\} \not\Downarrow_{l \cdot 0}$.

We now consider a different equivalence notion based on the observation of *barbs* revealing where a process can potentially read or write in a located tree.

DEFINITION 4 *A* barb *has the form* $l{\cdot}p$*, where* l *is a location name and* p *is a path expression. We define the observation relation* $N \downarrow_{l \cdot p}$ *on networks and barbs* *by* $N \downarrow_{l \cdot p} \triangleq \exists C, T, \chi, U, P.\, N \equiv C\{(\{l \mapsto T\}, l\cdot\mathsf{update}_p(\chi, U).P)\}$*: that is, N contains a location l with an* update$_p$ *command.* Barbed congruence *(*$\simeq^b$*) is the reduction congruence induced by barbs.*

For example, if $\mathtt{xch}(T_1, T_2) = (\nu c)(\overline{l\cdot c}\langle\rangle \mid !l\cdot c().l\cdot\mathsf{update}_p(X, T_1).l\cdot\mathsf{update}_p(X, T_2).\overline{l\cdot c}\langle\rangle)$ then we have $(\{l \mapsto S\}, \mathtt{xch}(T_1, T_2)) \simeq^b (\{l \mapsto S\}, \mathtt{xch}(T_2, T_1))$, for all T_1, T_2 and S. In fact, the processes have the same barbs, and if S contains a subtree at p, they can simulate each other.

Notice that a barb $l\cdot p$ merely records the location and the path at which some update command could take place, giving no information on *how* the data could be modified, and ignoring run commands. Again, this information can be observed indirectly using some context.

THEOREM 5 *Barbed congruence strictly implies tree congruence:* $\simeq^b \subsetneq \simeq^t$.

The inclusion is strict: for all D, $(D, 0) \simeq^t (D, l\cdot\mathsf{copy}_p(x))$, since the stores are equal and $l\cdot\mathsf{copy}_p(x)$ has no effect, but $(D, 0) \not\simeq^b (D, l\cdot\mathsf{copy}_p(x))$ since $l\cdot\mathsf{copy}_p(x) \downarrow_{l\cdot p}$. This correspond to the intuition that barbed congruence is more operational than tree congruence. Structural congruence for networks is included in $\simeq^b$, and therefore in $\simeq^t$.

Process Equivalences. We now analyse process behaviour, which is influenced by the locations present in the network (*network connectivity*). Consider replacing the definition of a service at location l, which uses only local data, with an equivalent one depending on data from another location m. If we can assume that m is always connected, then the behaviour of the services is the same. On the other hand, if location m should fail, the behaviour of the new one is affected. With network equivalences, the "reliable" locations are those in the domain of the store. With process equivalences, it is necessary to state explicitly the minimum set of reliable locations. For example, consider $\mathtt{oldS} = l\cdot\mathsf{cut}_/(X)$ and $m\cdot\mathtt{newS} = (\nu c)(\overline{m\cdot c}\langle/\rangle \mid m\cdot c(x).l\cdot\mathsf{cut}_x(X))$. The two processes are equivalent if m is reliable, otherwise they are not: in the context $(\{l \mapsto T\}, -)$ the first process can delete T, but the second one cannot move. As a consequence, in order for two processes to be equivalent, they must be equivalent in all possible network contexts, starting from a given domain.

DEFINITION 6 *Given a network equivalence* $\simeq$ *and a set of location names* Λ, *we define the induced* domain process equivalence *by* $\sim_\Lambda = \{(P, Q) \mid \forall D\,.\,\Lambda \subseteq dom(D) \Longrightarrow (D, P) \simeq (D, Q)\}$. Domain tree equivalence, *(*$\sim^t_\Lambda$*), is the domain process equivalence induced by* $\simeq^t$, *and* domain barbed equivalence *(*$\sim^b_\Lambda$*), is the one induced by* $\simeq^b$.

For example, for any Λ, $\mathtt{xch}(T_1, T_2) \sim^b_\Lambda \mathtt{xch}(T_2, T_1)$. Similarly to the case for network equivalences (Theorem 5), we have $\sim^b_\Lambda \subsetneq \sim^t_\Lambda$, with the same counterexample.

In order to be able to replace a process sub-term by an equivalent one, we extend process equivalences to *open* terms (terms with free variables).

DEFINITION 7 Full process contexts *are defined by*

$$C ::= - \mid C \mid P \mid (\nu c)\, C \mid l\cdot a(\tilde{x}).C \mid !l\cdot a(\tilde{x}).C \mid l\cdot\mathsf{update}_p(\chi, V).C$$

DEFINITION 8 *A substitution σ is a* closing substitution *for P iff $P\sigma$ is closed. Given an equivalence $\sim$ for closed processes, and two open processes P and Q, we say that $P \sim Q$ iff $P\sigma \sim Q\sigma$ for all closing substitutions σ.*

THEOREM 9 *For all Λ, (i) if $\Lambda \subset \Lambda'$ then $\sim^t_\Lambda \subset \sim^t_{\Lambda'}$ and $\sim^b_\Lambda \subset \sim^b_{\Lambda'}$; (ii) $\sim^t_\Lambda$ and $\sim^b_\Lambda$ (both on open and closed processes) are congruences over full contexts.*

As an example for the strict inclusion of (i), consider the processes `oldS` and m·`newS` given above. We have `oldS` $\sim^b_{l,m}$ m·`newS` but `oldS` $\not\sim^b_l$ m·`newS`. In the full paper [15], we show that process tree and barbed equivalences are in fact the largest congruences compatible with the corresponding network equivalences.

Core X$d\pi$ is an extension of the asynchronous π-calculus, and accordingly the *asynchrony law* – stating that the presence of a communication buffer cannot be observed – holds also in our setting: $!l{\cdot}a(x).\overline{l{\cdot}a}\langle x\rangle \sim^b_\Lambda 0$. On the other hand, the law for *equators* does not hold: let $l{\cdot}\mathrm{E}(a,b) = !l{\cdot}a(x).\overline{l{\cdot}b}\langle x\rangle \mid !l{\cdot}b(x).\overline{l{\cdot}a}\langle x\rangle$, then

$$l{\cdot}\mathrm{E}(a,b) \mid \overline{l{\cdot}c}\langle a\rangle \not\sim^b_\Lambda l{\cdot}\mathrm{E}(a,b) \mid \overline{l{\cdot}c}\langle b\rangle,$$

since a context can read b from c at l, and use it at some fresh location m where no equator is defined. In the next section we will show how using *distributed equators* it is possible regard different names interchangeably only on some designated locations.

4 A Proof Method for Process Equivalence

The process equivalence given in Definition 6, is hard to use in practice, because it requires closure under all store and process contexts. In this section we provide a coinductive equivalence which does not quantify over contexts.

The main difficulties involved in defining such an equivalence for Core X$d\pi$ are caused by having scripted processes among values, and by barbed equivalence being sensitive to the presence of locations. We solve the first problem by translating messages containing scripts into ones where each script is replaced by a uniquely named *trigger* (a placeholder), and placing in parallel some *definitions* associating each trigger with the code of the scripted process. Using this approach it is possible to analyse the interaction between scripts and their contexts. For a discussion of this technique see [13, 21], where it is used on the higher-order π-calculus. We solve the second problem using an adaptation of the bisimulation approach to families of relations indexed by sets of locations, which we call *domain-dependent bisimilarity*. Communication is asynchronous, hence we borrow techniques from the asynchronous π-calculus.

Labelled Transition System. Let $\mathcal{K}$, ranged over by i, j, k, be the set of *trigger* names, disjoint from the channel names in $\mathcal{C}$. We introduce a construct $\langle k \Leftarrow \Box P\rangle$, called a *definition*, which associates a scripted process to the trigger name k. There is no reduction rule for definitions, which are analysed only in the labelled transition system (lts). Parallel compositions of processes and definitions are called *configurations* K, L, and together with contexts C are given by

$$K, L ::= K \mid K \mid (\nu c)K \mid P \mid \langle k \Leftarrow \Box P\rangle \quad C ::= - \mid K \mid C \mid (\nu c)C$$

where the set of values appearing in processes are extended to contain also triggers where scripts were allowed. We let underlined letters $\underline{u}, \underline{v}$ range over *first-order* values

$$\frac{\begin{array}{c} F(v) = (v'; A; \tilde{k}) \\ F(\tilde{v}) = (\tilde{v'}; A'; \tilde{k'}) \\ \tilde{k} \cap (\tilde{k'} \cup fn(v) \cup fn(\tilde{v})) = \emptyset \\ \tilde{k'} \cap (\tilde{k} \cup fn(v) \cup fn(\tilde{v})) = \emptyset \end{array}}{F(v, \tilde{v}) = (v', \tilde{v'}; A \mid A'; \tilde{k}, \tilde{k'})} \qquad \frac{\begin{array}{c} F(U) = (U'; A; \tilde{k}) \\ F(\tilde{U}) = (\tilde{U}'; A'; \tilde{k'}) \\ \tilde{k} \cap (\tilde{k'} \cup fn(U) \cup fn(\tilde{U})) = \emptyset \\ \tilde{k'} \cap (\tilde{k} \cup fn(U) \cup fn(\tilde{U})) = \emptyset \end{array}}{F(U, \tilde{U}) = (U', \tilde{U}'; A \mid A'; \tilde{k}, \tilde{k'})}$$

$$F(c) = (c; 0; ()) \qquad F(k) = (k; 0; ())$$

$$F(l) = (l; 0; ()) \qquad F(p) = (p; 0; ())$$

$$F(@l{:}p) = (@l{:}p; 0; ()) \qquad F(0) = (0; 0; ())$$

$$F(\Box P) = (k; \langle k \Leftarrow \Box P \rangle; k)$$

$$\frac{F(T) = (T'; A; \tilde{k})}{F(\mathsf{a}[T]) = (\mathsf{a}[T']; A; \tilde{k})} \qquad \frac{\begin{array}{c} F(T_1) = (T_1'; A_1; \tilde{k_1}) \\ F(T_2) = (T_2'; A_2; \tilde{k_2}) \\ \tilde{k_1} \cap (\tilde{k_2} \cup fn(T_1) \cup fn(T_2)) = \emptyset \\ \tilde{k_2} \cap (\tilde{k_1} \cup fn(T_1) \cup fn(T_2)) = \emptyset \end{array}}{F(T_1 \mid T_2) = (T_1' \mid T_2'; A_1 \mid A_2; \tilde{k_1}, \tilde{k_2})}$$

Table 3. The relation F. The important rule is the axiom replacing scripted processes with triggers and generating the corresponding definition. The inductive rules have additional conditions to avoid clashes of trigger names.

(values not containing scripted processes), and we will omit the underlining when there is no ambiguity.

Structural congruence is extended to configurations in the obvious way. A configuration K is well-formed if its processes are well-formed, there is at most one $\langle k \Leftarrow \Box P \rangle$ for each k, and processes in definitions do not contain triggers. When an output or update transition takes place in the lts, we use a relation F to incorporate the triggers. F relates the potentially higher-order values $\tilde{v}$ with the triple $(\tilde{\underline{u}}; A; \tilde{k})$ consisting of the first order values $\tilde{\underline{u}}$, obtained by replacing each scripted process $\Box P$ in $\tilde{v}$ with a unique trigger k, the configuration A consisting of a parallel composition of definitions $\langle k \Leftarrow \Box P \rangle$, and the unique triggers $\tilde{k}$. The actual relation F is defined as a homomorphism on all terms, with $F(\Box P) = (k; \langle k \Leftarrow \Box P \rangle; k)$ for scripts (see Table 3).

Transition labels α_l are indexed with the location at which actions take place, and are defined by

$$\alpha_l ::= (\tilde{c}, \tilde{k})\overline{l{\cdot}c}\langle \tilde{\underline{v}} \rangle \mid l{\cdot}c(\tilde{\underline{v}}) \mid l{\cdot}\tau \mid (\tilde{k})l{\cdot}\mathsf{update}_p(\tilde{\underline{U}}, (\chi)\tilde{\underline{V}}) \mid l{\cdot}\mathsf{run}_p \mid l{\cdot}k(p)$$

Labels for input and output are standard, first-order labels. Label $l{\cdot}\tau$ denotes communication at l. The label for update contains a vector $\tilde{U}$ corresponding to the potential results of pattern-matching χ with values at path p in some tree (the range of Σ in the updating function) and treats $(\chi)\tilde{V}$ as an abstraction on the pattern variables (which are therefore subject to alpha-conversion). The vector $(\tilde{k})$ is used by the side conditions of the lts to enforce freshness of triggers, and binds the triggers $\tilde{k}$. Label run_p just records a run at p, and label $l{\cdot}k(p)$ signals that the script defined by k is selected for execution, with parameters l and p. Structural congruence extends to actions in the obvious way.

$$\text{(COM)} \quad \overline{l\cdot c}\langle\tilde{v}\rangle \mid l\cdot c(\tilde{x}).P \xrightarrow{l\cdot\tau} P\{\tilde{v}/\tilde{x}\}$$

$$\text{(COM!)} \quad \overline{l\cdot c}\langle\tilde{v}\rangle \mid !l\cdot c(\tilde{x}).P \xrightarrow{l\cdot\tau} !l\cdot c(\tilde{x}).P \mid P\{\tilde{v}/\tilde{x}\}$$

$$\text{(UPDATE)} \quad l\cdot\mathsf{update}_p(\chi, V).P \xrightarrow{(\tilde{k})l\cdot\mathsf{update}_p(\underline{\tilde{U}},(\chi)\underline{\tilde{V}}')} P\{\underline{U_1}/\chi\} \mid \cdots \mid P\{\underline{U_n}/\chi\} \mid A$$

for any $\underline{\tilde{U}} = \{\underline{U_1}, \ldots, \underline{U_n}\}$ with $\tilde{k}$ fresh, and $F(V_1, \ldots, V_n) = (\underline{\tilde{V}}'; A; \tilde{k})$, where each $V_i = V$

$$\text{(OUT)} \quad \overline{l\cdot c}\langle\tilde{v}\rangle \xrightarrow{(\tilde{k})\overline{l\cdot c}\langle\underline{\tilde{u}}\rangle} A \text{ where } F(\tilde{v}) = (\underline{\tilde{u}}; A; \tilde{k}) \qquad \text{(IN)} \quad 0 \xrightarrow{l\cdot c(\underline{\tilde{v}})} \overline{l\cdot c}\langle\underline{\tilde{v}}\rangle$$

$$\text{(TRIGGER)} \quad \langle k \Leftarrow \Box P\rangle \xrightarrow{l\cdot k(p)} \langle k \Leftarrow \Box P\rangle \mid P\{l/\circlearrowleft\}\{p/.\} \qquad \text{(RUN)} \quad l\cdot\mathsf{run}_p \xrightarrow{l\cdot\mathsf{run}_p} 0$$

$$\text{(RES)} \quad \frac{K \xrightarrow{\alpha_l} K'}{(\nu c)K \xrightarrow{\alpha_l} (\nu c)K'} \; c\notin n(\alpha_l) \qquad \text{(PAR)} \quad \frac{K \xrightarrow{\alpha_l} K'}{K \mid L \xrightarrow{\alpha_l} K' \mid L} \; bn(\alpha_l)\cap fn(L)=\emptyset$$

$$\text{(STRUCT)} \quad \frac{K \equiv L \xrightarrow{\alpha_l} L' \equiv K'}{K \xrightarrow{\alpha_l} K'} \qquad \text{(OPEN)} \quad \frac{K \xrightarrow{(\tilde{d},\tilde{k})\overline{l\cdot c}\langle\tilde{v}\rangle} K'}{(\nu b)K \xrightarrow{(b,\tilde{d},\tilde{k})\overline{l\cdot c}\langle\tilde{v}\rangle} K'} \; b\neq c,\, b\in fn(\tilde{v})\backslash\tilde{d}$$

Table 4. Labelled Transition System for Core X$d\pi$. The structural and communication rules are standard. The (OUT) rule uses relation F to replace scripts with triggers and produces a parallel composition of the associated definitions. The (IN) rule only allows first-order values, and the (UPDATE) rule can be regarded as a combination of input, output and communication.

We explain now the rules for the lts; the formal definition is given in Table 4. Labelled transitions are defined for well-formed configurations. We have standard contextual and communication rules in the asynchronous style of [11], with the side conditions adapted to avoid clashes of trigger names. The rule for input and output are

$$\text{(IN)} \quad 0 \xrightarrow{l\cdot c(\underline{\tilde{v}})} \overline{l\cdot c}\langle\underline{\tilde{v}}\rangle \qquad \text{(OUT)} \quad \overline{l\cdot c}\langle\tilde{v}\rangle \xrightarrow{(\tilde{k})\overline{l\cdot c}\langle\underline{\tilde{u}}\rangle} A$$

where $F(\tilde{v}) = (\underline{\tilde{u}}; A; \tilde{k})$. Any scripted process in v is replaced by a trigger in $\underline{\tilde{u}}$, and A is the parallel composition of all the definitions associated with $\tilde{k}$. In an input transition, values must necessarily be first-order. The rule for updates is

$$\text{(UPDATE)} \quad l\cdot\mathsf{update}_p(\chi, V).P \xrightarrow{(\tilde{k})l\cdot\mathsf{update}_p(\underline{\tilde{U}},(\chi)\underline{\tilde{V}}')} R \mid A$$

for any first-order vector $\underline{\tilde{U}} = \{\underline{U_1}, \cdots, \underline{U_n}\}$, $F(V_1, \ldots, V_n) = (\underline{\tilde{V}}'; A; \tilde{k})$ where each $V_i = V$, $\tilde{k}$ is fresh, and $R = P\{\underline{U_1}/\chi\} \mid \cdots \mid P\{\underline{U_n}/\chi\}$. These conditions are determined by viewing $\underline{\tilde{U}}$ as (first-order) parameters received in input, and $\tilde{V}$ as parameters of a subsequent output. We conclude with the rules for running a script and analysing its definition:

$$\text{(RUN)} \; l\cdot\mathsf{run}_p \xrightarrow{l\cdot\mathsf{run}_p} 0 \qquad \text{(TRIGGER)} \; \langle k \Leftarrow \Box P\rangle \xrightarrow{l\cdot k(p)} \langle k \Leftarrow \Box P\rangle \mid P\{l/\circlearrowleft\}\{p/.\}$$

The first rule simply records the location and path from which we run a script; the second one effectively executes a copy of a script, initialised with l and p.

Domain Bisimilarity. We introduce our bisimulation equivalence. The intuition is that when two processes are running in a domain Λ, we need to check that, if a process makes an action α_l with $l \in \Lambda$, then the other one can mimic it, possibly relying on the existence of other locations in Λ. If $l \notin \Lambda$ we need not worry about matching actions. But since the domain can be extended by composing networks, we need to make sure that actions not in Λ are also matched, this time in a different relation parameterised by $\Lambda \cup \{l\}$.

We use the notation $K \xrightarrow{\tau}_\Lambda K'$ if $K \xrightarrow{l\cdot\tau} K'$ for some $l \in \Lambda$, and $\xrightarrow{\alpha_l}\!\!\!\!\rightarrow_\Lambda \triangleq \xrightarrow{\tau^*}_\Lambda \circ \xrightarrow{\alpha_l} \circ \xrightarrow{\tau^*}_\Lambda$ if $l \in \Lambda, \alpha_l \neq l\cdot\tau$, and $\xrightarrow{\tau}\!\!\!\!\rightarrow_\Lambda \triangleq \xrightarrow{\tau^*}_\Lambda$. The function $bn(-)$ extends to triggers in the obvious way. We say that an action α_l is relevant to a configuration K, abbreviated by $rel(\alpha_l, K)$, if $bn(\alpha_l) \cap fn(K) = \emptyset$.

DEFINITION 10 *A family of symmetric relations on configurations (indexed with sets of locations)* $\dot{\approx} = \{\dot{\approx}_\Lambda | \Lambda \subseteq \mathcal{L}\}$ *is a* domain bisimulation *if* $K \dot{\approx}_\Lambda L$ *and* $K \xrightarrow{\alpha_l} K'$ *implies:*

1. *if* $l \in \Lambda$ *with* $rel(\alpha_l, L)$ *then* $L \xrightarrow{\alpha'_l}\!\!\!\!\rightarrow_\Lambda L'$ *where* $\alpha'_l \equiv \alpha_l$ *and* $K' \dot{\approx}_\Lambda L'$;
2. *if* $l \notin \Lambda$ *then* $K \dot{\approx}_{\Lambda \cup \{l\}} L$.

Domain bisimilarity ($\approx$) *is the pointwise largest domain bisimulation. Two open processes* P, Q *are* Λ*-bisimilar iff for all closing substitutions* σ, $P\sigma \approx_\Lambda Q\sigma$.

In the long version [15], we show that domain bisimilarity is defined as the largest fixpoint of a monotonic operator on families of relations. Showing that $K \approx_\Lambda L$ consists of exhibiting a domain bisimulation $\dot{\approx} = \{\dot{\approx}_\Delta | \Lambda \subseteq \Delta \subseteq \mathcal{L}\}$ such that $K \dot{\approx}_\Lambda L$. It is less burdensome than it may seem: the family is monotonic, and therefore starting from the pairs in $\dot{\approx}_\Lambda$, we can build each $\dot{\approx}_{\Delta \cup \{l\}}$ from $\dot{\approx}_\Delta$ adding only the pairs where the first component makes a move at l.

THEOREM 11 *For all* Λ, *(i) if* $\Lambda \subset \Lambda'$ *then* $\approx_\Lambda \subset \approx_{\Lambda'}$; *(ii)* $\approx_\Lambda$ *is a congruence on configurations, and the restriction of* $\approx_\Lambda$ *to processes is a congruence on processes.*

This theorem corresponds to Theorem 9, but point (ii) here is much harder to prove since the definition of $\approx_\Lambda$ does not require closure under contexts. The congruence property of $\approx_\Lambda$ plays a fundamental role in the theorem below, justifying the use of domain bisimilarity as a proof method for our process equivalences.

THEOREM 12 *Process bisimilarity is a sound approximation of process barbed congruence: for all* Λ, *if* $P \approx_\Lambda Q$ *then* $P \sim^b_\Lambda Q$.

The converse implication does not hold, as can be seen from $\mathtt{xch}(T, S) \sim^b_\Lambda \mathtt{xch}(S, T)$ and point (1) below. We leave to future work the study of complete characterisations of the contextual equivalences, which we believe could be based on a notion of weak bisimulation able to abstract away (partly) from update actions.

Examples. We start with an example of the proof method. We call the process $\mathtt{dE}(l\cdot a, m\cdot b) = !l\cdot a(\tilde{x}).\overline{m\cdot b}\langle\tilde{x}\rangle \,|\, !m\cdot b(\tilde{x}).\overline{l\cdot a}\langle\tilde{x}\rangle$ a *distributed equator*. It has the effect of making the use of channel a at l undistinguishable from the use of channel m at b, a key property to define optimisations for web services. Let $E_1 = \mathtt{dE}(l\cdot a, m\cdot b) \,|\, \overline{l\cdot a}\langle\tilde{v}\rangle$ and $E_2 = \mathtt{dE}(l\cdot a, m\cdot b) \,|\, \overline{m\cdot b}\langle\tilde{v}\rangle$. We show that $E_1 \approx_{\{l,m\}} E_2$. We need to give a domain bisimulation $\mathcal{R} = \{\mathcal{R}_\Delta\}_{\{l,m\} \subseteq \Delta}$ such that $\mathcal{R}_{\{l,m\}}$ contains the two processes. In this case, it suffices to take the family where $\mathcal{R}_\Delta = \{(E_1, E_2), (E_2, E_1)\} \cup I$ for all Δ, where I is the identity relation. In fact, if $E_1 \xrightarrow{\alpha_l} E_1'$ then $E_2 \xrightarrow{m\cdot\tau}\xrightarrow{\alpha_l} E_1'$, and similarly for m. The case for α_n with $n \notin \{l, m\}$ is analogous.

Using domain bisimilarity, we can also prove the following results referring to examples discussed in Section 2 and Section 3:

1. for any Λ, if $S \not\equiv^t T$ then $\mathtt{xch}(T, S) \not\approx_\Lambda \mathtt{xch}(S, T)$;
2. $\mathtt{oldS} \approx_\Lambda m{\cdot}\mathtt{newS}$ iff $m \in \Lambda$;
3. for any Λ, $!l{\cdot}a(\tilde{x}).\overline{l{\cdot}a}\langle\tilde{x}\rangle \approx_\Lambda 0$ and $l{\cdot}\mathtt{E}(a,b) \,|\, \overline{l{\cdot}c}\langle a\rangle \not\approx_\Lambda l{\cdot}\mathtt{E}(a,b) \,|\, \overline{l{\cdot}c}\langle b\rangle$;
4. $(\nu\, get)(m{\cdot}\mathtt{get} \,|\, l{\cdot}\mathtt{call}(m, get, p)) \approx_\Lambda (\nu\, get)(m{\cdot}\mathtt{get} \,|\, l{\cdot}\mathtt{spec})$ iff $m \in \Lambda$.

We conclude with an example on replication of web services. Consider the two services $\mathtt{s}_1$ and $\mathtt{s}_2$, meant to be interchangeable, defined as

$$\mathtt{s}_1 = !m{\cdot}b(\tilde{x}, y, z).(\overline{n{\cdot}a}\langle\tilde{x}, y, z\rangle \oplus_m S) \quad \mathtt{s}_2 = !n{\cdot}a(\tilde{x}, y, z).(\overline{m{\cdot}b}\langle\tilde{x}, y, z\rangle \oplus_n S)$$

where $P \oplus_l Q = (\nu c)(\overline{l{\cdot}c}\langle\rangle \,|\, l{\cdot}c().P \,|\, l{\cdot}c().Q)$. Both offer the same service S, but an internal choice determines whether the service will be provided locally, or delegated to the other location. It does not matter if we paste in the data a service call to $\mathtt{s}_1$ or one to $\mathtt{s}_2$, as justified by the equation

$$\mathtt{s}_1 \,|\, \mathtt{s}_2 \,|\, l{\cdot}\mathsf{paste}_p\langle\mathtt{sc}[\,\Box l{\cdot}\mathtt{call}(m, b, \tilde{v})\,]\rangle \approx_{\{m,n\}} \mathtt{s}_1 \,|\, \mathtt{s}_2 \,|\, l{\cdot}\mathsf{paste}_p\langle\mathtt{sc}[\,\Box l{\cdot}\mathtt{call}(n, a, \tilde{v})\,]\rangle$$

5 Conclusions

We have compared alternative notions of behavioural equivalences for Core X$d\pi$ networks, and we have derived corresponding notions of process equivalence which are useful to reason about web-related examples. We have defined a sound proof technique for these equivalences based on the notion of *domain bisimilarity*. Our work illustrates that a behavioural understanding of dynamic web data can be grounded on the existing techniques associated with process calculi, although the adaptation is by no means straightforward.

Acknowledgments. We thank Alex Ahern, Martin Berger, Cristiano Calcagno, Jonathan Hayman, Andrew Phillips, Iain Phillips, Maria Grazia Vigliotti, Nobuko Yoshida and Uri Zarfaty for useful comments and suggestions.

References

[1] Serge Abiteboul, Angela Bonifati, Grégory Cobena, Ioana Manolescu, and Tova Milo. Dynamic XML documents with distribution and replication. In *Proceedings of SIGMOD'03*, 2003.

[2] Abiteboul, S. et al. Active XML primer. INRIA, GEMO Report number 275.

[3] G. Bierman and P. Sewell. Iota: a concurrent XML scripting language with application to Home Area Networks. University of Cambridge Technical Report 557, jan 2003.

[4] Reinhard Braumandl, Markus Keidl, Alfons Kemper, Donald Kossmann, Alexander Kreutz, Stefan Seltzsam, and Konrad Stocker. Objectglobe: Ubiquitous query processing on the internet. To appear in the VLDB Journal: Special Issue on E-Services, 2002.

[5] Marco Carbone and Sergio Maffeis. On the expressive power of polyadic synchronisation in π-calculus. *Nordic Journal of Computing*, 10(2):70–98, 2003.

[6] Luca Cardelli and Giorgio Ghelli. A query language based on the ambient logic. In *Proceedings of ESOP'01*, volume 2028 of *LNCS*, pages 1–22. Springer, 2001.

[7] Philippa Gardner and Sergio Maffeis. Modeling dynamic Web data. In Georg Lausen and Dan Suciu, editors, *Proc. of DBPL'03*. LNCS, September 2003.

[8] Andrew Gordon and Riccardo Pucella. Validating a web service security abstraction by typing. In *Proceedings of the 2002 ACM Workshop on XML Security*, pages 18–29, 2002.

[9] M. Hennessy and J. Riely. Resource access control in systems of mobile agents. In *Proceedings of HLCL '98*, volume 16.3 of *ENTCS*, pages 3–17. Elsevier, 1998.

[10] K. Honda and M. Tokoro. An object calculus for asynchronous communication. In *Proceedings of ECOOP*, volume 512 of *LNCS*, pages 133–147, Berlin, Heidelberg, New York, Tokyo, 1991. Springer-Verlag.

[11] K. Honda and M. Tokoro. On asynchronous communication semantics. *LNCS*, 612:21–51, 1992.

[12] Kohei Honda and Nobuko Yoshida. On reduction-based process semantics. *Theoretical Computer Science*, 151(2):437–486, 1995.

[13] Alan Jeffrey and Julian Rathke. Contextual equivalence for higher-order pi-calculus revisited. Computer Science Report 04/2002, University of Sussex, 2002.

[14] Alfons Kemper and Christian Wiesner. Hyperqueries: Dynamic distributed query processing on the internet. In *Proceedings of VLDB'01*, pages 551–560, 2001.

[15] Sergio Maffeis and Philippa Gardner. Behavioural equivalences for dynamic web data. Draft available as `http://www.doc.ic.ac.uk/~maffeis/corexdpilong.pdf`. Forthcoming Imperial College London Technical Report, 2004.

[16] World Wide Web Consortium. XML Path Language (XPath) Version 1.0. available at `http://w3.org/TR/xpath`.

[17] R. Milner, J. Parrow, and J. Walker. A calculus of mobile processes, I and II. *Information and Computation*, 100(1):1–40,41–77, September 1992.

[18] Arnaud Sahuguet, Benjamin Pierce, and Val Tannen. Distributed Query Optimization: Can Mobile Agents Help? Unpublished draft.

[19] Arnaud Sahuguet and Val Tannen. Resource Sharing Through Query Process Migration. University of Pennsylvania Technical Report MS-CIS-01-10, 2001.

[20] D. Sangiorgi and D. Walker. *The π-calculus: a Theory of Mobile Processes*. Cambridge University Press, 2001.

[21] D. Sangirogi. Expressing mobility in process algebras: First-order and higher-order paradigms. PhD thesis, University of Edinburgh, 1992.

BEHAVIOURAL THEORY FOR MOBILE AMBIENTS

Massimo Merro
Dipartimento di Informatica, Università di Verona, Italy
Francesco Zappa Nardelli
INRIA & Computer Laboratory, University of Cambridge, UK

Abstract We study the behavioural theory of Cardelli and Gordon's *Mobile Ambients*, by focusing on a standard contextual equivalence, *reduction barbed congruence*. We prove a *context lemma* that allows the derivation of contextual equivalences by considering only contexts for *concurrency* and *locality*. We go further and give a characterisation of *reduction barbed congruence* over arbitrary processes in terms of a *labelled bisimilarity* defined over a restricted class of processes, called systems. This characterisation extends and completes an earlier result on bisimulation proof methods for Mobile Ambients, that was restricted to systems. The characterisation is then used to prove a collection of algebraic laws.

1 Introduction

The calculus of *Mobile Ambients* [5], abbreviated MA, has been introduced as a process calculus for describing *mobile agents*. In MA, the term $n[P]$ represents an agent, or *ambient*, named n, executing the code P. The ambient n is a bounded, protected, and (potentially) mobile space where the computation P takes place. In turn P may contain other ambients, may perform (local) *communications*, or may exercise *capabilities*, which allow entry to or exit from named ambients. *Ambient names*, such as n, are used to control access to the ambient's computation space and may be dynamically created as in the π-calculus, [17], using the construct $(\nu n)P$. A *system* in MA is a collection of ambients running in parallel, where the knowledge of certain names may be restricted.

Background Reduction barbed congruence [13] is a coinductive contextual relation widely adopted as a natural behavioural equivalence for process languages. It is defined as the largest equivalence relation that (i) is a congruence; (ii) preserves, in some sense, the reduction semantics of the language; (iii) preserves *barbs*, some simple observational property of terms. Reduction barbed congruence can be virtually applied to any process language, but the universal quantification over all contexts often represents a serious obstacle in proofs. Simpler proof techniques are traditionally based on labelled bisimilarities, which do not involve context quantification.

The work [16] focuses on MA systems, and its main result is the definition of a *labelled transition system* (*LTS*) and of a *labelled bisimilarity* over systems (denoted $\approx$) that coincides with *reduction barbed congruence over systems* (denoted $\cong_s$). The paper [16] also provide *up-to context and up-to expansion* proof techniques, which are used to prove a set of algebraic laws between systems. Those laws allows us to equate bigger systems starting from equivalent sub-systems. However, *they cannot be used to equate processes starting from equivalent sub-processes.*

The main reason why the paper [16] focuses on systems rather than processes is the fact that MA semantics suffers a phenomenon called *stuttering*, originated by ambients that may repeatedly enter and exit another ambient. In fact, as observed in [18], the two processes

$$P \stackrel{\text{def}}{=} \mathtt{in\_}n.\mathtt{out\_}n.\mathtt{in\_}n.R \text{ and } Q \stackrel{\text{def}}{=} \mathtt{in\_}n.\mathtt{out\_}n.\mathtt{in\_}n.R + \mathtt{in\_}n.R$$

are not distinguished by *reduction barbed congruence over processes* (denoted $\cong_p$).[1] Intuitively, a context can provide an ambient named n, that originates the reduction: $k[Q] \mid n[\,] \twoheadrightarrow n[k[R]]$. But the process P can match it performing three consecutive reductions: $k[P] \mid n[\,] \twoheadrightarrow\twoheadrightarrow\twoheadrightarrow n[k[R]]$. As stuttering cannot be observed, a labelled bisimilarity that successfully captures $\cong_p$ must be insensitive to stuttering. Characterising the interactions that a process has with its environment in a way insensitive to stuttering would make the definition of the LTS (and of the corresponding weak actions) quite complicated. Focusing on systems leads to definition of a simple and natural LTS; stuttering is then modelled in terms of standard weak actions.

Systems represent an expressive subset of MA processes, but the results of [16] only guarantee that the equivalence is preserved by *system contexts* (a subset of the static contexts). In particular, they leave open the question if the bisimulation proof methods are sound when all MA contexts are considered. Also, a proper treatment of processes is needed to fully understand the subtleties of MA algebraic theory.

Contributions This paper develops a behavioural theory of MA processes, extending and completing the results of [16]. The main contributions are:

- a *context lemma* for reduction barbed congruence over processes, that allows the derivation of contextual equivalences by considering only parallel composition and ambient nesting;
- a characterisation of reduction barbed congruence over processes in terms of a simple relation based on the bisimilarity over systems introduced in [16]. In particular, we show that $\cong_p$ coincides with the relation $\mathcal{S}$ below, defined on top of $\approx$:

  $$\mathcal{S} \stackrel{\text{def}}{=} \{(P,Q) : k[P \mid R] \approx k[Q \mid R] \text{ for all } k \text{ and } R\}.$$

  This result, combined with the up-to proof techniques for the labelled bisimilarity, gives an effective proof method to show the behavioural equality of two processes;
- we show that when comparing two *systems*, the labelled bisimilarity $\approx$ is a sound and complete technique for reduction barbed congruence over processes.

[1] For simplicity we use external choice *à la* CCS; the same phenomenon can be exhibited using replication.

As a consequence, all the algebraic laws given in [16] hold for reduction barbed congruence over processes;

- we extend our results to the calculus equipped with asynchronous communication of capabilities, and for the first time we give a complete semantic treatment of communication in MA;
- we prove a collection of algebraic laws on processes to be added to the laws on systems inherited from [16].

We believe that the proofs of the two main results of the paper, i.e. the context lemma (Theorem 9) and the labelled characterisation of reduction barbed congruence over processes (Theorem 10) are non-standard and interesting in their own. In fact, the proof of Theorem 10 requires sophisticated up-to proof techniques, whereas the proof of Theorem 9 relies on the characterisation of reduction barbed equivalence given in Theorem 10: a direct proof seems difficult.

Related work Higher-order LTSs for Mobile Ambients can be found in [4, 9, 20, 7]. But we are not aware of any form of bisimilarity defined using these LTSs. A simple first-order LTS for MA without restriction is proposed by Sangiorgi in [18]. Using this LTS the author defines an *intensional* bisimilarity for MA that separates terms on the basis of their internal structure. Other forms of labelled bisimilarity for higher-order distributed calculi, such as Safe Ambients [14], Distributed π-calculus [12], Safe Dπ [11] Seal [21], Nomadic Pict [19], a Calculus for Mobile Resources [8], can be found in [15, 10, 6, 19, 8, 3, 11], but only [15, 10, 8, 3, 11] prove labelled characterisations of a contextually defined notion of equivalence. In [9], Gordon and Cardelli give a context lemma for a Morris-style contextual equivalence. However, unlike ours, their context lemma closes the contextual equivalence also under restriction. In that paper, using the context lemma, the authors prove the correctness of the perfect firewall equation.

Outline In Section 2 we recall the definitions and results of [16]. In Section 3 we focus on processes, and we prove several properties of reduction barbed congruence over processes, including its characterisation in terms of the labelled bisimilarity over systems. In Section 4 we extend the results of the previous section to the full calculus with communication. Finally, in Section 5 we use our proof methods to prove a collection of algebraic laws.

2 A semantic theory for systems

Syntax and reduction semantics In Table 1 we report the syntax of MA processes, where $\mathbf{N}$ denotes an infinite set of names, ranged over by $n, h, \ldots$. We also define a subset of MA processes, called *systems*.

The syntax for processes is standard, [5], except for replication that is replaced by replicated prefixing, $!C.P$. As in the π-calculus, this simplifies the definition of the LTS. A system is a collection of ambients running in parallel, where the knowledge of certain ambient names may be restricted among two or more ambients.

We use a number of notational conventions. Parallel composition has the lowest precedence among the operators. The process $C.C'.P$ is read as $C.(C'.P)$. We omit trailing dead processes, writing C for $C.\mathbf{0}$, and $n[]$ for $n[\mathbf{0}]$. Restriction $(\nu n)P$ acts as binder for name n, and the set of *free names* of P, $\text{fn}(P)$, is defined accordingly.

Systems:		*Processes:*		*Capabilities:*		
M, N ::=	$\mathbf{0}$	P, Q, R ::=	$\mathbf{0}$	C ::=	$\mathtt{in}\_n$	may enter into n
	$M_1 \mid M_2$		$P_1 \mid P_2$		$\mathtt{out}\_n$	may exit out of n
	$(\nu n)M$		$(\nu n)P$		$\mathtt{open}\_n$	may open n
	$n[P]$		$n[P]$			
			$C.P$			
			$!C.P$			

Reduction Rules:

$$n[\mathtt{in}\_m.P \mid Q] \mid m[R] \twoheadrightarrow m[n[P \mid Q] \mid R] \qquad \mathtt{open}\_n.P \mid n[Q] \twoheadrightarrow P \mid Q$$

$$m[n[\mathtt{out}\_m.P \mid Q] \mid R] \twoheadrightarrow n[P \mid Q] \mid m[R] \qquad P \equiv Q,\ Q \twoheadrightarrow R,\ R \equiv S \text{ imply } P \twoheadrightarrow S$$

Table 1. The Mobile Ambients in Two Levels: Syntax and Reduction Rules

A *context* is a process not completely defined; we write $-$ for the hole. A *static context* is a context where the hole does not appear underneath prefix and replication. The dynamics of the calculus is specified by a *reduction relation*, $\twoheadrightarrow$, which is the least relation over processes closed under static contexts and satisfying the rules in Table 1. As systems are processes with a special structure, the rules of Table 1 also describe the evolution of systems. The reduction semantics relies on an auxiliary relation called *structural congruence*, $\equiv$, that brings the participants of a potential interaction into contiguous positions. Its definition is standard (see [5]). It is easy to check that systems always reduce to systems.

The behavioural theory of systems We focus on a generalisation of the *reduction barbed congruence*, a *contextual*, *reduction closed*, and *barb preserving* equivalence relation. We now explain what these properties mean.

A *system context* is a context generated by the following grammar:

$$C[-] ::= - \ \mid\ C[-] \mid M \ \mid\ M \mid C[-] \ \mid\ (\nu n)C[-] \ \mid\ n[C[-] \mid P] \ \mid\ n[P \mid C[-]]$$

where M is an arbitrary system, and P is an arbitrary process. A relation $\mathcal{R}$ over systems is *preserved by system contexts* if $M\ \mathcal{R}\ N$ implies $C[M]\ \mathcal{R}\ C[N]$ for all system contexts $C[-]$.

A relation $\mathcal{R}$ is *reduction closed* if whenever $P\ \mathcal{R}\ Q$ and $P \twoheadrightarrow P'$ there is some Q' such that $Q \twoheadrightarrow^* Q'$ and $P'\ \mathcal{R}\ Q'$, where $\twoheadrightarrow^*$ denotes the reflexive and transitive closure of $\twoheadrightarrow$.

In MA the observation predicate $P \downarrow_n$ denotes the possibility of the process P interacting with the environment via the ambient n. We write $P \downarrow_n$ if $P \equiv (\nu\tilde{m})(n[P_1] \mid P_2)$ with $n \notin \{\tilde{m}\}$. We write $P \Downarrow_n$ if there exists P' such that $P \twoheadrightarrow^* P'$ and $P' \downarrow_n$. A relation $\mathcal{R}$ is *barb preserving* if $P\ \mathcal{R}\ Q$ and $P \downarrow_n$ imply $Q \Downarrow_n$.

Definition 1 (Reduction barbed congruence over systems) *Reduction barbed congruence over systems, written $\cong_s$, is the largest symmetric relation over systems which is reduction closed, barb preserving, and preserved by system contexts.*

We briefly summarise the results of [16]. The main result is the definition of a LTS and of a labelled bisimilarity over systems that coincide with reduction barbed congruence over systems. The LTS is defined over processes, although the labelled bisimilarity only considers actions going from systems to systems. A distinction is made between *pre-actions* and *env-actions*: the former denote the possibility to exercise certain capabilities whereas the latter model the interaction of a system with its

Pre-actions: $\pi ::= \mathtt{in\_}n \mid \mathtt{out\_}n \mid \mathtt{open\_}n \mid \mathtt{enter\_}n \mid \mathtt{amb\_}n \mid \mathtt{exit\_}n$

Env-actions: $\mu ::= k.\mathtt{enter\_}n \mid k.\mathtt{exit\_}n \mid *.\mathtt{enter\_}n \mid *.\mathtt{exit\_}n \mid n.\overline{\mathtt{enter}}\mathtt{\_}k \mid k.\mathtt{open\_}n$

Actions: $\alpha ::= \mu \mid \tau$

Outcomes: $O ::= P \mid K$ *Concretions:* $K ::= (\nu\tilde{m})\langle P\rangle Q$

Table 2. Pre-actions, Env-actions, Actions, Concretions, and Outcomes

$$\frac{}{\pi.P \xrightarrow{\pi} P} \qquad \frac{}{!\pi.P \xrightarrow{\pi} P \mid !\pi.P} \qquad \frac{P \xrightarrow{\mathtt{out\_}n} P_1}{m[P] \xrightarrow{\mathtt{exit\_}n} \langle m[P_1]\rangle \mathbf{0}}$$

$$\frac{}{n[P] \xrightarrow{\mathtt{amb\_}n} \langle P\rangle \mathbf{0}} \qquad \frac{P \xrightarrow{\mathtt{in\_}n} P_1}{m[P] \xrightarrow{\mathtt{enter\_}n} \langle m[P_1]\rangle \mathbf{0}} \qquad \frac{P \xrightarrow{\pi} O \quad n \notin \mathrm{fn}(\pi)}{(\nu n)P \xrightarrow{\pi} (\nu n)O}$$

$$\frac{P \xrightarrow{\pi} O}{\begin{array}{c} P \mid Q \xrightarrow{\pi} O \mid Q \\ Q \mid P \xrightarrow{\pi} Q \mid O \end{array}}$$

Table 3. Labelled Transition System - Pre-actions

$$\frac{P \xrightarrow{\mathtt{enter\_}n} (\nu\tilde{p})\langle P_1\rangle P_2 \quad Q \xrightarrow{\mathtt{amb\_}n} (\nu\tilde{q})\langle Q_1\rangle Q_2{}^{(*)}}{\begin{array}{c} P \mid Q \xrightarrow{\tau} (\nu\tilde{p})(\nu\tilde{q})(n[P_1 \mid Q_1] \mid P_2 \mid Q_2) \\ Q \mid P \xrightarrow{\tau} (\nu\tilde{q})(\nu\tilde{p})(n[Q_1 \mid P_1] \mid Q_2 \mid P_2) \end{array}} \qquad \frac{P \xrightarrow{\tau} P'}{\begin{array}{c} P \mid Q \xrightarrow{\tau} P' \mid Q \\ Q \mid P \xrightarrow{\tau} Q \mid P' \end{array}}$$

$$\frac{P \xrightarrow{\mathtt{exit\_}n} (\nu\tilde{m})\langle k[P_1]\rangle P_2}{n[P] \xrightarrow{\tau} (\nu\tilde{m})(k[P_1] \mid n[P_2])} \qquad \frac{P \xrightarrow{\tau} Q}{n[P] \xrightarrow{\tau} n[Q]}$$

$$\frac{P \xrightarrow{\mathtt{open\_}n} P_1 \quad Q \xrightarrow{\mathtt{amb\_}n} (\nu\tilde{m})\langle Q_1\rangle Q_2}{\begin{array}{c} P \mid Q \xrightarrow{\tau} P_1 \mid (\nu\tilde{m})(Q_1 \mid Q_2) \\ Q \mid P \xrightarrow{\tau} (\nu\tilde{m})(Q_1 \mid Q_2) \mid P_1 \end{array}} \qquad \frac{P \xrightarrow{\tau} P'}{(\nu n)P \xrightarrow{\tau} (\nu n)P'}$$

(*) We require $(\mathrm{fn}(P_1) \cup \mathrm{fn}(P_2)) \cap \{\tilde{q}\} = (\mathrm{fn}(Q_1) \cup \mathrm{fn}(Q_2)) \cap \{\tilde{p}\} = \emptyset$

Table 4. Labelled Transition System - τ-actions

$$\frac{P \xrightarrow{\mathtt{enter\_}n} (\nu\tilde{m})\langle k[P_1]\rangle P_2{}^{(\dagger)}}{P \xrightarrow{k.\mathtt{enter\_}n} (\nu\tilde{m})(n[k[P_1] \mid \circ] \mid P_2)} \qquad \frac{P \xrightarrow{\mathtt{exit\_}n} (\nu\tilde{m})\langle k[P_1]\rangle P_2{}^{(\dagger)}}{P \xrightarrow{k.\mathtt{exit\_}n} (\nu\tilde{m})(k[P_1] \mid n[\circ \mid P_2])}$$

$$\frac{P \xrightarrow{\mathtt{amb\_}n} (\nu\tilde{m})\langle P_1\rangle P_2{}^{(\dagger)}}{P \xrightarrow{n.\overline{\mathtt{enter}}\mathtt{\_}k} (\nu\tilde{m})(n[P_1 \mid k[\circ]] \mid P_2)} \qquad \frac{P \xrightarrow{\mathtt{amb\_}n} (\nu\tilde{m})\langle P_1\rangle P_2}{P \xrightarrow{k.\mathtt{open\_}n} k[\circ \mid (\nu\tilde{m})(P_1 \mid P_2)]}$$

$$\frac{P \xrightarrow{\mathtt{enter\_}n} (\nu\tilde{m})\langle k[P_1]\rangle P_2{}^{(\ddagger)}}{P \xrightarrow{*.\mathtt{enter\_}n} (\nu\tilde{m})(n[k[P_1] \mid \circ] \mid P_2)} \qquad \frac{P \xrightarrow{\mathtt{exit\_}n} (\nu\tilde{m})\langle k[P_1]\rangle P_2{}^{(\ddagger)}}{P \xrightarrow{*.\mathtt{exit\_}n} (\nu\tilde{m})(k[P_1] \mid n[\circ \mid P_2])}$$

(†) We require $k \notin \tilde{m}$. (‡) We require $k \neq n$ and $k \in \tilde{m}$

Table 5. Labelled Transition System - Env-actions

environment. Internal computations are modelled by τ-*actions*. Only env-actions and τ-actions model the evolution of a system at run-time.

The pre-actions, defined in Table 3, are of the form $P \xrightarrow{\pi} O$ where the ranges of π and of O, the *outcomes*, are reported in Table 2. An outcome is a process Q, if π is a prefix of the language, or a *concretion*, of the form $(\nu\tilde{m})\langle P\rangle Q$, when an ambient boundary is somehow involved. In this case, intuitively, P represents the part of the system affected by the action while Q is not, and $\tilde{m}$ is the set of private names shared by P and Q. We adopt the convention that if K is the concretion $(\nu\tilde{m})\langle P\rangle Q$, then $(\nu r)K$ is a shorthand for $(\nu\tilde{m})\langle P\rangle(\nu r)Q$, if $r \notin \text{fn}(P)$, and for the concretion $(\nu r\tilde{m})\langle P\rangle Q$ otherwise. In the rule (π Par) we define $K \mid R$ to be the concretion $(\nu\tilde{m})\langle P\rangle(Q \mid R)$, where $\tilde{m}$ are chosen, using α-conversion if necessary, so that $\text{fn}(R) \cap \{\tilde{m}\} = \emptyset$. Similarly for $R \mid K$. Finally, $(\nu\tilde{m})\langle P\rangle(0 \mid R)$ is abbreviated by $(\nu\tilde{m})\langle P\rangle R$.

The τ-actions, defined in Table 4, model the internal evolution of processes. It can be shown that if $P \xrightarrow{\tau} P'$ then $P \twoheadrightarrow P'$; conversely if $P \twoheadrightarrow P'$ then $P \xrightarrow{\tau}\equiv P'$.

The env-actions, defined in Table 5, are of the form $M \xrightarrow{\mu} M'$, where the range of μ is given in Table 2. Roughly speaking, env-actions capture the interaction of a system with its environment. In practice, env-actions turn concretions into running systems by explicitly introducing the environment's ambient interacting with the process being considered. The content of this ambient is arbitrary; it is left unspecified in the LTS and is taken into account only in the definition of bisimulation. For convenience, the syntax of processes is extended with a special process $\circ$, used to pinpoint those ambients whose content must be instantiated in the bisimulation. Operationally, the process $\circ$ is analogous to the inactive process (it is simply a placeholder). Unlike pre-actions and τ-actions, env-actions do not have structural rules; this is because env-actions are supposed to be performed by systems that can directly interact with the environment.

The set of the *actions* is the set of env-actions extended with τ. As env-ctions capture the interaction of a system with its environment, the definition of bisimilation only takes into account actions (and not pre-actions). More explanations on the LTS can be found in [16].

The definition of weak actions is standard: $\Rightarrow$ denotes the reflexive and transitive closure of $\xrightarrow{\tau}$; $\xRightarrow{\alpha}$ denotes $\Rightarrow\xrightarrow{\alpha}\Rightarrow$; $\xRightarrow{\hat{\alpha}}$ denotes $\Rightarrow$ if $\alpha = \tau$ and $\xRightarrow{\alpha}$ otherwise.

Env-actions introduce a special process $\circ$ to pinpoint those ambients whose content will be specified in the bisimilarity. The $\bullet$ operator instantiates the placeholder with a process.

Definition 2 *Let T and T_i be either systems or processes. Then, for a process P, we define:*

$$0 \bullet P \stackrel{\text{def}}{=} 0 \qquad (T_1 \mid T_2) \bullet P \stackrel{\text{def}}{=} (T_1 \bullet P) \mid (T_2 \bullet P) \qquad \circ \bullet P \stackrel{\text{def}}{=} P$$
$$n[R] \bullet P \stackrel{\text{def}}{=} n[R \bullet P] \qquad (\nu n)T \bullet P \stackrel{\text{def}}{=} (\nu n)(T \bullet P) \text{ if } n \notin \text{fn}(P)$$
$$!C.R \bullet P \stackrel{\text{def}}{=} !C.(R \bullet P) \qquad C.R \bullet P \stackrel{\text{def}}{=} C.(R \bullet P)$$

Bisimilarity over systems is defined below.

Definition 3 (Bisimilarity) *A symmetric relation $\mathcal{R}$ is a* bisimulation *if $M \ \mathcal{R} \ N$ implies:*

- *if $M \xrightarrow{\alpha} M'$, $\alpha \notin \{*.\mathtt{enter\_}n, *.\mathtt{exit\_}n\}$, then there is a system N' such that $N \stackrel{\hat{\alpha}}{\Longrightarrow} N'$ and for all processes P it holds $M' \bullet P \ \mathcal{R} \ N' \bullet P$;*
- *if $M \xrightarrow{*.\mathtt{enter\_}n} M'$ then there is a system N' such that $N \mid n[\circ] \Rightarrow N'$ and for all processes P it holds $M' \bullet P \ \mathcal{R} \ N' \bullet P$;*
- *if $M \xrightarrow{*.\mathtt{exit\_}n} M'$ then there is a system N' such that $n[\circ \mid N] \Rightarrow N'$ and for all processes P it holds $M' \bullet P \ \mathcal{R} \ N' \bullet P$.*

Systems M and N are bisimilar, *denoted $M \approx N$, if $M \ \mathcal{R} \ N$ for a bisimulation $\mathcal{R}$.*

Theorem 4 *Reduction barbed congruence over systems and bisimilarity coincide.*

We end this section with a sound up-to proof technique for bisimilarity that generalises those presented in [16]. The *expansion* [2], written $\gtrsim$, is an asymmetric variant of $\approx$ such that $M \gtrsim N$ holds if $M \approx N$ and M has at least as many τ-moves as N.

Definition 5 (Bisimulation up to context and up to $\gtrsim \approx$) *A symmetric relation $\mathcal{R}$ over systems is a* bisimulation up to context and up to $\gtrsim \approx$ *if $M \ \mathcal{R} \ N$ implies:*

- *if $M \xrightarrow{\alpha} M''$, $\alpha \notin \{*.\mathtt{enter\_}n, *.\mathtt{exit\_}n\}$, then there exists a system N'' such that $N \stackrel{\hat{\alpha}}{\Longrightarrow} N''$, and for all processes P there is a system context $C[-]$ and systems M' and N' such that $M'' \bullet P \gtrsim C[M']$, $N'' \bullet P \approx C[N']$, and $M' \ \mathcal{R} \ N'$;*
- *if $M \xrightarrow{*.\mathtt{enter\_}n} M''$ then there exists a system N'' such that $N \mid n[\circ] \Rightarrow N''$, and for all processes P there is a system context $C[-]$ and systems M' and N' such that $M'' \bullet P \gtrsim C[M']$, $N'' \bullet P \approx C[N']$, and $M' \ \mathcal{R} \ N'$;*
- *if $M \xrightarrow{*.\mathtt{exit\_}n} M''$ then there exist a system N'' such that $n[\circ \mid N] \Rightarrow N''$, and for all processes P there is a system context $C[-]$ and systems M' and N' such that $M'' \bullet P \gtrsim C[M']$, $N'' \bullet P \approx C[N']$, and $M' \ \mathcal{R} \ N'$.*

Theorem 6 *If $\mathcal{R}$ is a bisimulation up to context and up to $\gtrsim \approx$ then $\mathcal{R} \subseteq \approx$.*

3 A semantic theory for processes

In this section we characterise reduction barbed congruence over processes.

Definition 7 Reduction barbed congruence over processes, *written $\cong_{\mathrm{p}}$, is the largest symmetric relation over processes which is reduction closed, barb preserving, and preserved by arbitrary single-hole contexts.*

In the definition above, the universal quantification over arbitrary contexts makes direct proofs of the equivalence of two systems difficult and error prone. Reducing the number of contexts to consider in the quantification is a first step towards the definition of a useful proof technique, and, broadly speaking, towards an understanding of the algebraic theory of processes.

We show that it is possible to work with a lighter definition of contextuality. In particular it suffices to close the contextual equivalence only under the two crucial constructions of MA: parallel composition (to model concurrency) and ambient nesting (to model locality).

Definition 8 Reduction barbed equivalence over processes, *written* $\cong^{e}_{p}$, *is the largest symmetric relation over processes which is reduction closed, barb preserving, and closed under parallel composition and ambient construct.*

Theorem 9 (Context Lemma) *The relations* $\cong_{p}$ *and* $\cong^{e}_{p}$ *coincide.*

Reduction barbed equivalence over processes still requires us to consider non-trivial contexts. More than that, a direct proof of the context lemma is surprisingly difficult. We look for a more operative characterisation of $\cong^{e}_{p}$, and we postpone the proof of the context lemma after Theorem 10.

Theorem 10 (Characterisation of $\cong^{e}_{p}$) *Let*

$$\mathcal{S} = \{(P,Q) : k[P \mid R] \approx k[Q \mid R], \textit{for all } k, R\} .$$

The relations $\cong^{e}_{p}$ *and* $\mathcal{S}$ *coincide.*

To prove Theorem 10 we need some technical lemmas. The next two lemmas are necessary for proving the completeness part of Theorem 10. In particular Lemma 11 says that reduction barbed equivalence over processes is preserved by restriction. This result will be also useful when proving the context lemma.

Lemma 11 *If* $P \cong^{e}_{p} Q$*, then* $(\nu n)P \cong^{e}_{p} (\nu n)Q$.

Lemma 12 $\cong^{e}_{p} \cap (\mathcal{M} \times \mathcal{M}) \; = \; \cong_{s}$, *where* $\mathcal{M}$ *is the set of all systems.*

Everything is now in place to prove Theorem 10. In the remainder of the paper, when working with a relation $\mathcal{R}$ over processes and/or systems, we denote $\mathcal{R}^{=}$ the symmetric closure of $\mathcal{R}$.

Proof of Theorem 10. We first prove that $P \cong^{e}_{p} Q$ implies $P \; \mathcal{S} \; Q$. For that, we must show that for all k, R, it holds $k[P \mid R] \approx k[Q \mid R]$. Both $k[P \mid R]$ and $k[Q \mid R]$ are systems, and it holds $k[P \mid R] \cong^{e}_{p} k[Q \mid R]$ because $\cong^{e}_{p}$ is closed under parallel composition and ambient construct. The result follows from Lemma 12 and Theorem 4.

It remains to prove that $\mathcal{S} \subseteq \cong^{e}_{p}$. For that, we must show that $\mathcal{S}$ is reduction closed, barb preserving, and closed under parallel composition and ambient construct.

1. $\mathcal{S}$ is reduction closed. Suppose $P \; \mathcal{S} \; Q$ and $P \rightarrow P'$. Let n be a name such that $n \notin \mathrm{fn}(P,Q)$. Then, by definition of $\mathcal{S}$, it holds $n[P] \approx n[Q]$. As $n \notin \mathrm{fn}(P,Q)$, and because of the correspondence between τ-transitions and reductions, there is a system M such that $n[P] \xrightarrow{\tau} M \equiv n[P']$. As $n[P] \approx n[Q]$, there is N such that $n[Q] \Rightarrow N$ and $M \approx N$. But $n \notin \mathrm{fn}(P,Q)$, and there must be Q' such that $Q \rightarrow^{*} Q'$ and $N \equiv n[Q']$; thus $n[P'] \approx n[Q']$.

Now, we prove that $P' \cong^{e}_{p} Q'$. By the completeness result, this suffices to conclude that $P' \; \mathcal{S} \; Q'$, as desired. The argument is by contradiction. Let us suppose that $P' \not\cong^{e}_{p} Q'$. From the definition of $\cong^{e}_{p}$, it follows that there is a context $C[-]$, containing only parallel composition and ambient constructs, such that at least one of the following conditions holds:

- there exists P'' such that $C[P'] \rightarrow^{*} P''$ and there is no Q'' such that $C[Q'] \rightarrow^{*} Q''$ and $P'' \cong^{e}_{p} Q''$;
- there exists Q'' such that $C[Q'] \rightarrow^{*} Q''$ and there is no P'' such that $C[P'] \rightarrow^{*} P''$ and $Q'' \cong^{e}_{p} P''$;
- there exists a such that $C[P'] \Downarrow_{a}$ and $C[Q'] \not\Downarrow_{a}$;
- there exists a such that $C[Q'] \Downarrow_{a}$ and $C[P'] \not\Downarrow_{a}$.

It is easy to verify that if one of these conditions holds, then the same condition holds also when we replace P' with $(\nu n)(n[P'] \mid \mathsf{open\_}n)$ and Q' with $(\nu n)(n[Q'] \mid \mathsf{open\_}n)$ for $n \notin \mathrm{fn}(P',Q')$.

For instance, in the first case there is P'' such that $C[(\nu n)(n[P'] \mid \text{open\_}n)] \rightarrow P''$ and there is no Q'' such that $C[(\nu n)(n[Q'] \mid \text{open\_}n)] \Rightarrow Q''$ and $P'' \cong^e_p Q''$.

By Lemma 11, the relation $\cong^e_p$ is closed under restriction. So we can take the context $C[(\nu n)(- \mid \text{open\_}n)]$ to conclude that $n[P'] \not\cong^e_p n[Q']$. By Lemma 12 it follows that $n[P'] \not\cong_s n[Q']$. By Theorem 4 we reach the contradiction that $n[P'] \not\approx n[Q']$.

2. $\mathcal{S}$ is barb preserving. Suppose that $P \; \mathcal{S} \; Q$ and $P \downarrow_n$. Consider the context

$$C[-] = b[- \mid a[\text{in\_}n.\text{out\_}n.\text{ok}[\text{out\_}a.\text{out\_}b]]]$$

where a, b and ok are fresh for both P and Q. Then $C[P] \approx C[Q]$ by definition of $\mathcal{S}$. As $P \downarrow_n$, the construction of $C[-]$ assures that $C[P] \Downarrow_{\text{ok}}$. Bisimilarity is barb preserving and $C[Q] \Downarrow_{\text{ok}}$ must hold. The construction of $C[-]$ guarantees that $Q \Downarrow_n$.

3. $\mathcal{S}$ is closed under parallel composition and ambient construct.

$P \; \mathcal{S} \; Q$ implies $P \mid R \; \mathcal{S} \; Q \mid R$: by definition of $\mathcal{S}$ we have $k[P \mid R'] \approx k[Q \mid R']$ for all k, R'. By taking $R' = R \mid R''$ for arbitrary R'' we have $k[P \mid R \mid R''] \approx k[Q \mid R \mid R'']$ for all R''. This implies $P \mid R \; \mathcal{S} \; Q \mid R$.

$P \; \mathcal{S} \; Q$ implies $n[P] \; \mathcal{S} \; n[Q]$: by definition of $\mathcal{S}$ we have $n[P] \approx n[Q]$ for all n. The result follows from the closure of $\approx$ under static contexts. □

The characterisation of $\cong^e_p$ is a fundamental tool to reason about processes. As a first application, we give the proof the context lemma.

Proof of Theorem 9. For that, we have to show that $\cong^e_p = \cong_p$. The inclusion $\cong_p \subseteq \cong^e_p$ is straightforward. For the converse we must prove that: (i) $\cong^e_p$ is reduction closed; (ii) $\cong^e_p$ is barb preserving; (iii) $\cong^e_p$ is closed under arbitrary contexts. Conditions (i) and (ii) hold by definition of $\cong^e_p$. It remains to show that the relation $\cong^e_p$ is preserved by all process contexts. The relation $\cong^e_p$ is preserved by parallel composition and ambient constructor by definition. It is also preserved by restriction by Lemma 11. It remains to prove that it is preserved by prefixing and replicated prefixing. We detail replicated prefixing.

We have to prove that if $P \cong^e_p Q$, then $!\pi.P \cong^e_p !\pi.Q$. Rather than working directly with $\cong^e_p$, we use Theorem 10 and we prove that $!\pi.P \; \mathcal{S} \; !\pi.Q$. For that, we show that $k[!\pi.P \mid R] \approx k[!\pi.Q \mid R]$ for all k and R. We perform a case analysis on π, and we detail the case $\pi = \text{in\_}o$. For this, we show that the relation

$$\mathcal{R} = \{(n[!\text{in\_}o.P \mid R], n[!\text{in\_}o.Q \mid R]) \; : \; P \cong^e_p Q\}^= \cup \approx$$

is a *bisimulation up to context and up to* $\gtrsim \approx$. The most interesting case is when the process $!\text{in\_}o.P$ exercises the capability $\text{in\_}o$. Suppose

$$n[!\text{in\_}o.P \mid R] \xrightarrow{n.\text{enter\_}o} o[n[P \mid !\text{in\_}o.P \mid R] \mid \circ] \, .$$

We have a matching transition

$$n[!\text{in\_}o.Q \mid R] \xrightarrow{n.\text{enter\_}o} o[n[Q \mid !\text{in\_}o.Q \mid R] \mid \circ] \, .$$

Since $P \cong^e_p Q$, we have $P \; \mathcal{S} \; Q$ and in turn, for all R', we have $n[P \mid R'] \approx n[Q \mid R']$. As $\approx$ is preserved by system contexts, for all instantiations of $\circ$ it holds $o[n[P \mid R'] \mid \circ] \approx o[n[Q \mid R'] \mid \circ]$. By taking $R' = !\text{in\_}o.Q \mid R$, we obtain

$$o[n[!\text{in\_}o.Q \mid R \mid P] \mid \circ] \approx o[n[Q \mid !\text{in\_}o.Q \mid R] \mid \circ] \, .$$

Then, for all processes S, the following hold:

$$\begin{aligned} o[n[P \mid !\text{in\_}o.P \mid R] \mid \circ] \bullet S \quad &\gtrsim \; C[n[!\text{in\_}o.P \mid R \mid P]] \\ o[n[Q \mid !\text{in\_}o.Q \mid R] \mid \circ] \bullet S \quad &\approx \; C[n[!\text{in\_}o.Q \mid R \mid P]] \end{aligned}$$

where $C[-] = o[- \mid S]$ (we can rearrange the terms using structural congruence because $\equiv \subseteq \gtrsim$ and $\equiv \subseteq \approx$). By construction of $\mathcal{R}$ we have

$$n[!\mathtt{in\_}o.P \mid R \mid P] \;\mathcal{R}\; n[!\mathtt{in\_}o.Q \mid R \mid P]$$

and we can conclude that up to context and up to $\gtrsim\, \approx$ we are still in $\mathcal{R}$. □

The result below is a consequence of Theorems 9 and 10.

Corollary 13 *The relations $\mathcal{S}$ and $\cong_{\mathrm{p}}$ coincide.*

The relation $\mathcal{S}$ still involves a universal quantification over all the processes R. Yet, it is built on top of a labelled bisimilarity, it can be coupled with the up-to proof techniques. In turn, it reveals a useful tool to reason about processes, as illustrated by the proof of the context lemma and by the other examples given in Section 5.

Systems, revisited In [16], we conjectured that when working with systems reduction barbed congruence over systems ($\cong_{\mathrm{s}}$) *is* "the right" equality. We are now in measure to close the conjecture. In fact, if we restrict our attention to systems, we can show that system contexts have the same discriminating power as arbitrary contexts.

Theorem 14 *Let M and N be two systems, then $M \cong_{\mathrm{s}} N$ if and only if $M \cong_{\mathrm{p}} N$.*

Proof $M \cong_{\mathrm{p}} N$ implies $M \cong_{\mathrm{s}} N$, by definition. For the converse, by Theorem 4, if $M \cong_{\mathrm{s}} N$ then $M \approx N$. As $\approx$ is preserved by system contexts, for all n and R $n[M \mid R] \approx n[N \mid R]$. By Theorems 10 and 9 it follows that $M \cong_{\mathrm{p}} N$. □

This in turn implies a strong result: $\approx$ completely characterises $\cong_{\mathrm{p}}$ on systems.

Corollary 15 *Let M and N be two systems, then $M \cong_{\mathrm{p}} N$ if and only if $M \approx N$.*

4 Adding communication

The basic idea is to have an *output process* such as $\langle E \rangle$, which outputs the message E, and an input process $(x).Q$ which on receiving a message binds it to x in Q which then executes; here occurrences of x in Q are bound. Messages are sequences of capabilities. This form of message is more restrictive than those given in [5], but much of the power of name transmission can still be captured in our language. The syntax of our extended language is given in Table 6. We assume an understanding of free and bound variables, and of *substitutions*. A process P is said to be *closed* if $\mathrm{fv}(P) = \emptyset$; otherwise is said to be *open*. The structural and reduction rules below define the semantics of communication:

$$E.(F.P) \equiv (E.F).P \qquad \varepsilon.P \twoheadrightarrow P \qquad (x).P \mid \langle E \rangle \twoheadrightarrow P\{^E/_x\}\,.$$

The LTS is extended by the introduction of two new pre-actions (E) for input, $\langle - \rangle$ for output, and a new form of concretions $(\nu\tilde{m})\langle E \rangle Q$. In Table 7 we give the rules that should be added to those of Table 3 and Table 4 to define the LTS $P \xrightarrow{\alpha} P'$ for the closed processes of the extended calculus. Note that in the structural rules of Table 3 we are now assuming that parallel composition and restriction distribute over the new form of concretions $(\nu\tilde{m})\langle E \rangle Q$ in the same manner as $(\nu\tilde{m})\langle P \rangle Q$. The unusual pre-action for output allows a uniform treatment of extrusion of names. Definition 3 and the extended LTS induce a bisimilarity relation, still denoted by $\approx$, over the closed systems of the message passing calculus.

For general terms, we define the *open extension* $\mathcal{R}^{\circ}$ of a relation $\mathcal{R}$ as: $P \;\mathcal{R}^{\circ}\; Q$ holds if and and only if for every closing substitution σ mapping from variables to expressions, we have $P\sigma \;\mathcal{R}\; Q\sigma$.

Names:	$a, b, \ldots, k, l, m, n, \ldots \in \mathbf{N}$	
Capabilities:		
$C ::=$	$\mathtt{in}\_n$	may enter into n
$\mid$	$\mathtt{out}\_n$	may exit out of n
$\mid$	$\mathtt{open}\_n$	may open n
Expressions:		
$E, F ::=$	x	variable
$\mid$	C	capability
$\mid$	$E.F$	path
$\mid$	ε	empty path
Guards:		
$G ::=$	E	expression
$\mid$	(x)	input

Systems:		
$M, N ::=$	$\mathbf{0}$	termination
$\mid$	$M_1 \mid M_2$	parallel composition
$\mid$	$(\nu n)M$	restriction
$\mid$	$n[P]$	ambient
Processes:		
$P, Q, R ::=$	$\mathbf{0}$	nil process
$\mid$	$P_1 \mid P_2$	parallel composition
$\mid$	$(\nu n)P$	restriction
$\mid$	$G.P$	prefixing
$\mid$	$n[P]$	ambient
$\mid$	$!G.P$	replication
$\mid$	$\langle E \rangle$	output

Table 6. The Message-passing Mobile Ambients in Two Levels

Pre-actions: $\pi ::= \ldots \mid (E) \mid \langle - \rangle$ *Concretions:* $K ::= (\nu \tilde{m})\langle P \rangle Q \mid (\nu \tilde{m})\langle E \rangle Q$

$$\frac{-}{\langle E \rangle \xrightarrow{\langle - \rangle} \langle E \rangle \mathbf{0}} \qquad \frac{-}{(x).P \xrightarrow{(E)} P\{^E/_x\}} \qquad \frac{E.(F.P) \xrightarrow{\pi} Q}{(E.F).P \xrightarrow{\pi} Q}$$

$$\frac{-}{\epsilon.P \xrightarrow{\tau} P} \qquad \frac{P \xrightarrow{\langle - \rangle} (\nu \tilde{m})\langle E \rangle P' \quad Q \xrightarrow{(E)} Q' \quad \mathrm{fn}(Q') \cap \{\tilde{m}\} = \emptyset}{P \mid Q \xrightarrow{\tau} (\nu \tilde{m})(P' \mid Q')}$$

Table 7. Pre-actions, Concretions and Labelled Transition System for Communication

Theorem 16 *Relations $\approx^{\circ}$ and $\cong_{\mathrm{s}}{}^{\circ}$ coincide over systems in the message-passing calculus.*

Proof [Sketch] It is straightforward to extend Theorem 2 of [16] to the message-passing calculus. The completeness results follows because these relations are defined over systems and communication cannot be observed at top-level. □

The open extension of the relation $\mathcal{S}$, written $\mathcal{S}^{\circ}$ can be shown equivalent to the relation

$$\mathcal{S}^{\circ} = \{(P, Q) : k[P \mid R] \approx^{\circ} k[Q \mid R], \text{ for all } k, R \text{ closed}\}\,.$$

Our characterisation of reduction barbed equivalence over processes lifts smoothly to the message passing calculus.

Theorem 17 (Characterisation of $\cong_{\mathrm{p}}^{\mathrm{e}\circ}$) *The relations $\cong_{\mathrm{p}}^{\mathrm{e}\circ}$ and $\mathcal{S}^{\circ}$ coincide over processes in the message-passing calculus.*

Proof [Sketch] It is easy to extend the proof of Theorem 10 to the closed terms of the message passing calculus. The result then follows from the definition of open extension. □

The context lemma can be rephrased for the message passing calculus.

Theorem 18 *Relations $\cong_{\mathrm{p}}^{\mathrm{e}\circ}$ and $\cong_{\mathrm{p}}{}^{\circ}$ coincide over processes in the message-passing calculus.*

Proof The proof is an extension of the proof in the case without communication. We detail the case of closure under input prefix and replicated input prefix (for all the other cases it is enough to consider close terms).

Suppose that $P \cong_{\mathrm{p}}^{\mathrm{eo}} Q$ and that $\mathrm{fn}(P) \cup \mathrm{fn}(Q) \subseteq \{x\}$. We want to show that $(x).P \cong_{\mathrm{p}}^{\mathrm{e}} (x).Q$. For that we use our characterisation of $\cong_{\mathrm{p}}^{\mathrm{e}}$ and we prove that for all n, R closed it holds $n[(x).P \mid R] \approx n[(x).Q \mid R]$. In particular, we prove that the relation

$$\mathcal{R} = \{(n[(x).P \mid R], n[(x).Q \mid R]) : P \cong_{\mathrm{p}}^{\mathrm{eo}} Q,\ \mathrm{fn}(P,Q) \subseteq \{x\},\ \forall n, R \text{ closed}\}^{=} \cup \approx$$

is a bisimulation up to context and up to structural congruence. The most interesting case is when $n[(x).P \mid R] \xrightarrow{\tau} n[(\nu\tilde{r})(P\{^E/_x\} \mid R')] \equiv (\nu\tilde{r})n[P\{^E/_x\} \mid R']$, where $n \notin \tilde{r}$. Observe that R sends the message E and resumes as R'. So we have a matching transition $n[(x).Q \mid R] \xrightarrow{\tau}\equiv (\nu\tilde{r})n[Q\{^E/_x\} \mid R']$. Since $P \cong_{\mathrm{p}}^{\mathrm{eo}} Q$, it holds $P\{^E/_x\} \cong_{\mathrm{p}}^{\mathrm{e}} Q\{^E/_x\}$. The characterisation of $\cong_{\mathrm{p}}^{\mathrm{e}}$ guarantees that $n[P\{^E/_x\} \mid R'] \approx n[Q\{^E/_x\} \mid R']$ and this allows us to conclude that up to context we are still in $\mathcal{R}$.

Suppose that $P \cong_{\mathrm{p}}^{\mathrm{eo}} Q$ and that $\mathrm{fn}(P) \cup \mathrm{fn}(Q) \subseteq \{x\}$. Now we want to show that $!(x).P \cong_{\mathrm{p}}^{\mathrm{e}} !(x).Q$. Reasoning as before, we prove that for all n, R closed it holds $n[!(x).P \mid R] \approx n[!(x).Q \mid R]$. In particular, we prove that the relation

$$\mathcal{R} = \{(n[!(x).P \mid R], n[!(x).Q \mid R)] : P \cong_{\mathrm{p}}^{\mathrm{eo}} Q,\ \mathrm{fn}(P,Q) \subseteq \{x\},\ \forall n, R \text{ closed}\}^{=} \cup \approx$$

is a bisimulation up to context and up to $\gtrsim\approx$. The most interesting case is when $n[!(x).P \mid R] \xrightarrow{\tau} n[(\nu\tilde{r})(P\{^E/_x\} \mid !(x).P \mid R)] \equiv (\nu\tilde{r})n[P\{^E/_x\} \mid !(x).P] \mid R'$, where $n \notin \tilde{r}$ and $\tilde{r} \cap \mathrm{fn}(P) = \emptyset$. Observe that R sends the message E and resumes as R'. So we have a matching transition $n[!(x).Q \mid R] \xrightarrow{\tau}\equiv (\nu\tilde{r})n[Q\{^E/_x\} \mid !(x).Q \mid R']$, where $\tilde{r} \cap \mathrm{fn}(Q) = \emptyset$. By construction of $\mathcal{R}$ we have $n[P\{^E/_x\} \mid !(x).P \mid R'] \ \mathcal{R}\ n[P\{^E/_x\} \mid !(x).Q \mid R']$. Since $P \cong_{\mathrm{p}}^{\mathrm{eo}} Q$, it holds $P\{^E/_x\} \cong_{\mathrm{p}}^{\mathrm{e}} Q\{^E/_x\}$. The characterisation of $\cong_{\mathrm{p}}^{\mathrm{e}}$ guarantees that $n[P\{^E/_x\} \mid !(x).Q \mid R'] \approx n[Q\{^E/_x\} \mid !(x).Q \mid R']$. Since bisimilarity is closed under restriction we have $(\nu\tilde{r})n[P\{^E/_x\} \mid !(x).Q \mid R'] \approx (\nu\tilde{r})n[Q\{^E/_x\} \mid !(x).Q \mid R']$. This allows us to conclude that up to context (we factor out the context $(\nu\tilde{r})(-)$) and up to $\gtrsim, \approx$ we are still in $\mathcal{R}$. □

Corollary 19 *Relations $\mathcal{S}^{\mathrm{o}}$ and $\cong_{\mathrm{p}}{}^{\mathrm{o}}$ coincide over processes in the message-passing calculus.*

A characteristic of working with systems deserves to be pointed out. Bisimilarity is defined over systems, and as such it cannot directly observe the exercise of communications capabilities (apart from internal communications). This allow us to avoid any special treatment for asynchronous communication. More than that, we can easily extend our results to a calculus equipped with *synchronous* communication (e.g., $\langle E\rangle.P$).

5 Algebraic theory

In this section we give a collection of algebraic laws for $\cong_{\mathrm{p}}$. First of all we recall the laws already proved in [16] with respect to $\cong_{\mathrm{s}}$. By Theorem 14 these laws also hold for $\cong_{\mathrm{p}}$:

Theorem 20 (System Laws)

1 $(\nu n)n[\langle E\rangle \mid (x).Q \mid M] \cong_{\mathrm{p}} (\nu n)n[Q\{^E/_x\} \mid M]$ *if* $n \notin \mathrm{fn}(M)$

2 $(\nu n)n[\langle E\rangle \mid (x).Q \mid \prod_{j\in J} \mathtt{open}\_k_j.R_j] \cong_{\mathrm{p}} (\nu n)n[Q\{^E/_x\} \mid \prod_{j\in J} \mathtt{open}\_k_j.R_j]$

3 $(\nu n)n[P] \cong_{\mathrm{p}} \mathbf{0}$ *if* $n \notin \mathrm{fn}(P)$

4 $(\nu n)((\nu m)m[\text{in\_}n.P] \mid n[M]) \cong_p (\nu n)n[(\nu m)m[P] \mid M]$ *if* $n \notin \text{fn}(M)$

5 $(\nu m,n)(m[\text{in\_}n.P] \mid n[\prod_{j\in J}\text{open\_}k_j.R_j]) \cong_p (\nu m,n)n[m[P] \mid \prod_{j\in J}\text{open\_}k_j.R_j]$

6 $(\nu n)n[(\nu m)m[\text{out\_}n.P] \mid M] \cong_p (\nu n)((\nu m)m[P] \mid n[M])$ *if* $n \notin \text{fn}(M)$

7 $(\nu n)n[m[\text{out\_}n.P] \mid \prod_{j\in J}\text{open\_}k_j.R_j] \cong_p (\nu n)(m[P] \mid n[\prod_{j\in J}\text{open\_}k_j.R_j])$
if $m \neq k_j$*, for* $j \in J$

8 $n[(\nu m)(\text{open\_}m.P \mid m[N]) \mid Q] \cong_p n[(\nu m)(P \mid N) \mid Q]$ *if* $Q \equiv M \mid \prod_{j\in J}(x).R_j$ *and* $m \notin \text{fn}(N)$

9 $(\nu n)n[(\nu m)(\text{open\_}m.P \mid m[Q]) \mid R] \cong_p (\nu n)n[(\nu m)(P \mid Q) \mid R]$ *if* $R \equiv \prod_{i\in I}(x).S_i \mid \prod_{j\in J}\text{open\_}k_j.R_j$ *and* $m,n \notin \text{fn}(Q)$

In Theorem 21 we give a collection of new algebraic laws involving processes. In Law 1 opening of private ambients containing arbitrary messages cannot be observed. Law 2 says that stuttering is not observable as well. Law 3 shows that processes prefixed by private capabilities are garbage. Law 4 says that two processes that differ only for having received different private capabilities cannot be distinguished. An instance of this law is

$$(\nu n)\langle C_n\rangle \cong_p (\nu n)\langle D_n\rangle$$

for $C_n, D_n \in \{\text{in\_}n, \text{out\_}n, \text{open\_}n\}$. Notice that the above private outputs are not equivalent to 0. Law 5 is the Mobile Ambient variant of the *asynchrony law* [1] due to asynchronous communication. Finally, Law 6 equates two different outputs by adding a special process. While this law reminds us of Honda and Yoshida's *equator* [13], it should be pointed out that Honda and Yoshida's equators hide the difference between two channels, whereas we equate messages.

Theorem 21 (Process Laws)

1 $(\nu n)(n[\prod_{j\in J}\langle E_j\rangle] \mid \text{open\_}n.P) \cong_p \prod_{j\in J}\langle E_j\rangle \mid P$ *if* $n \notin \text{fn}(P, E_j)$ *for all* j

2 $\text{in\_}n.\text{out\_}n.\text{in\_}n.P \cong_p \text{in\_}n.\text{out\_}n.\text{in\_}n.P \oplus \text{in\_}n.P$ *where* $\oplus$ *is internal choice*

3 $(\nu n)C_n.P \cong_p 0$ *if* $C_n \in \{\text{in\_}n, \text{out\_}n, \text{open\_}n\}$;

4 $(\nu n)P\{C_n/x\} \cong_p (\nu n)P\{D_n/x\}$ *if* $\text{fv}(P) \subseteq \{x\}$ *and* $n \notin \text{fn}(P)$,
for $C_n, D_n \in \{\text{in\_}n, \text{out\_}n, \text{open\_}n\}$

5 $(x).\langle x\rangle \cong_p 0$

6 $\langle E\rangle \mid Eq(E,F) \cong_p \langle F\rangle \mid Eq(E,F)$ *where* $Eq(E,F) \stackrel{\text{def}}{=} !(x).\langle E\rangle \mid !(x).\langle F\rangle$

Proof By Theorems 9 and 10, it suffices to show that

$$k[LHS \mid R] \approx k[RHS \mid R]$$

for all k and R, where LHS and RHS denote the left hand side, right hand side, of each law. In all cases, except 4, this can be proved by showing that the relation

$$\mathcal{R} = \{(k[LHS \mid R], k[RHS \mid R]) : \text{ for all } k \text{ and } R\}^{=} \cup \mathcal{I}$$

is a bisimulation up to context and up to $\gtrsim\ \approx$, where $\mathcal{I}$ represent the identity relation over systems.

In Law 4, the equality to prove is $k[(\nu n)P\{C_n/x\} \mid R] \approx k[(\nu n)P\{D_n/x\} \mid R]$, for all k and R. This can be proved by showing that the relation

$$\mathcal{R} = \{((\nu n)M\{C_n/x\}, (\nu n)M\{D_n/x\}) : \text{fv}(M) \subseteq \{x\} \text{ and } n \notin \text{fn}(M)\}^{=}$$

is a bisimulation. Notice that, as R is closed, up to α-conversion, to avoid name-capturing, we have $k[(\nu n)P\sigma \mid R] \equiv (\nu n)k[P \mid R]\sigma$. □

References

[1] R. Amadio, I. Castellani, and D. Sangiorgi. On bisimulations for the asynchronous π-calculus. *Theoretical Computer Science*, 195:291–324, 1998.

[2] S. Arun-Kumar and M. Hennessy. An efficiency preorder for processes. *Acta Informatica*, 29:737–760, 1992.

[3] M. Bugliesi, S. Crafa, M. Merro, and V. Sassone. Communication interference in mobile boxed ambients. To appear in Information & Computation 2004, an extended abstract appeared in Proc. FSTTCS'02, LNCS, Springer Verlag.

[4] L. Cardelli and A. Gordon. A commitment relation for the ambient calculus. 1996.

[5] L. Cardelli and A. Gordon. Mobile ambients. *Theoretical Computer Science*, 240(1):177–213, 2000. An extended abstract appeared in *Proc. of FoSSaCS '98*.

[6] G. Castagna and F. Zappa Nardelli. The seal calculus revisited: Contextual equivalence and bisimilarity. In *Proc. 22nd FSTTCS '02*, LNCS. Springer Verlag, 2002.

[7] G. Ferrari, U. Montanari, and E. Tuosto. A LTS semantics of ambients via graph synchronization with mobility. In *Proc. ICTCS*, LNCS, 2001.

[8] J.C. Godskesen, T. Hildebrandt, and V. Sassone. A calculus of mobile resources. In *Proc. 10th CONCUR '02*, LNCS, 2002.

[9] A. D. Gordon and L. Cardelli. Equational properties of mobile ambients. *Journal of Mathematical Structures in CS*, 12:1–38, 2002. Also in *Proc. FoSSaCs '99*.

[10] M. Hennessy, M. Merro, and J. Rathke. Towards a behavioural theory of access and mobility control in distributed system. In *Proc. 5th FoSSaCS '03*, LNCS, 2003.

[11] M. Hennessy, J. Rathke, and N Yoshida. safedpi: a language for controlling mobile code. In *Proc. FOSSACS 03*, LNCS, 2003.

[12] M. Hennessy and J. Riely. A typed language for distributed mobile processes. In *Proc. 25th POPL*. ACM Press, 1998.

[13] K. Honda and N. Yoshida. On reduction-based process semantics. *Theoretical Computer Science*, 152(2):437–486, 1995.

[14] F. Levi and D. Sangiorgi. Controlling interference in ambients. An extended abstract appeared in *Proc. 27th POPL*, ACM Press, 2000.

[15] M. Merro and M. Hennessy. Bisimulation congruences in safe ambients. In *Proc. 29th POPL*. ACM Press, 2002.

[16] M. Merro and F. Zappa Nardelli. Bisimulation proof methods for mobile ambients. In *Proc. ICALP 2003*, LNCS, Springer Verlag, 2003. An extended version is available as Computer Science Report 2003:01, University of Sussex.

[17] R. Milner, J. Parrow, and D. Walker. A calculus of mobile processes, (Parts I and II). *Information and Computation*, 100:1–77, 1992.

[18] D. Sangiorgi. Extensionality and intensionality of the ambient logic. In *Proc. 28th POPL*. ACM Press, 2001.

[19] A. Unyapoth and P. Sewell. Nomadic Pict: Correct communication infrastructures for mobile computation. In *Proc. 28th POPL*. ACM Press, 2001.

[20] M. G. Vigliotti. Transition systems for the ambient calculus. Master thesis, Imperial College of Science, Technology and Medicine (University of London), September 1999.

[21] J. Vitek and G. Castagna. Seal: A framework for secure mobile computations. In *Internet Programming Languages*, LNCS, pages 47–77. Springer Verlag, 1999.

NESTED COMMITS FOR MOBILE CALCULI: EXTENDING JOIN *

Roberto Bruni, Hernán Melgratti, Ugo Montanari
Dipartimento di Informatica, Università di Pisa, Italia.
{bruni, melgratt, ugo}@di.unipi.it

Abstract In global computing applications the availability of a mechanism for some form of committed choice can be useful, and sometimes necessary. It can conveniently handle, e.g., distributed agreements and negotiations with nested choice points. We propose a linguistic extension of the Join calculus for programming nested commits, called *Committed* Join (cJoin). It provides primitives for explicit abort, programmable compensations and interactions between negotiations. We give the operational semantics of cJoin in the *reflexive* CHAM style. Then we discuss its expressiveness on the basis of a few examples and encodings. Finally, we provide a big-step semantics for cJoin processes that can be typed as *shallow* and we show that shallow processes are serializable.

1. Introduction

In recent years, wide area network computing, web programming, and, more generally, *global computing* (GC) are attracting the interest of many researchers in an attempt of laying the foundations for largely distributed applications. Such applications often require a coordination layer to orchestrate their components, which are designed and implemented separately, run on different platforms and communicate asynchronously. Often, the components must agree on the activities they are carrying on (e.g. in terms of transactions, like in [16, 7]) by committing the results of long distributed decision processes as soon as the participants reach partial agreements. Applications can handle these situations in an ad hoc manner or they can rely on a fixed set of coordination primitives. In this work we are interested on studying suitable primitives for describing distributed commits in GC applications. Note that we use the term "*commit*" (also *contract* or *negotiation*) instead of "*transaction*" to emphasize the coordination aspects, which are orthogonal to ACID database transactions. For instance, in

* Research supported by the MSR Cambridge Project NAPI, by the FET-GC Project IST-2001-32747 AGILE, by the MIUR Projects COFIN COMETA and IS-MANET, and by the MURST-CNR 1999 Project.

the case of web services, the orchestration layer should provide the primitives for specifying transactional services and the valid interactions between them. Nevertheless, any service should be responsible for maintaining the consistency on their local data (i.e., assuring ACID properties on them).

Process description languages (PDLS) are mathematical models of computation designed for isolating and studying phenomena that occur in concurrent languages. In the spirit of PDL, it would be desirable to extend well-known calculi with primitives for distributed nested commits. Two key operations are the "abort with compensation" (e.g., to stop a negotiation when some participants withdraw their interest in carrying out the contract) and the "commit" (to store a partial agreement before moving to the next phase of a long negotiation). In this paper we introduce *Committed* Join (cJoin) as an extension of the Join calculus [12]. The features of cJoin are compared against two other paradigms with commit, namely AKL [13] and *Zero-Safe* nets [8].

The design of cJoin has been inspired by the requirements (i)–(vi) below. Contracts are decision processes distributed on several nodes, each with the possibility of consulting both local and global resources and generating local sub-contracts (e.g. modeling decisions internal to an organization). However: (i) each internal sub-decision should be stored locally and not made public before a common agreement is achieved; (ii) global resources might be made available to partners upon commits, marking the conclusion of some contract; (iii) decision processes can be aborted, in which case all participants should be informed and suitable compensation procedures activated (e.g., upon abort, new attempts for finding an agreement can be initiated) ; (iv) divergence is possible, but well designed GC applications should guarantee that each contract eventually leads to an abort or a commit; (v) when two processes involved in separate negotiations exchange some information, then their contracts should be merged into a unique one; (vi) it should be possible to have nested contracts. Though an internal abort can be compensated in such a way that the main contract can still be successfully completed, a failure of the main contract should cause the abort of all ongoing internal activities.

We define the small-step operational semantics of cJoin in the *reflexive* CHAM style [12]. We also give a big-step semantics for the sub-calculus of *shallow* processes and we show that shallow processes are serializable by proving a correspondence between their CHAM and big-step semantics. *Serializability* ensures the correctness of reasoning at different levels of abstractions when transactions become atomic transitions at the abstract level.

Synopsis. In § 2 we recall the principles of the CHAM and the syntax and semantics of Join. Committed Join is introduced in § 3. In § 4 we illustrate the main features of cJoin by showing a simple application for booking trips and the encoding of AKL. The implementation of ZS nets is presented in § 5. Finally, we study *serializability* in § 6.

2. Background: CHAM and Join

The Chemical Abstract Machine. In CHAM [3] states s (called *solutions*) are finite multisets of terms m (called *molecules*), and computations are multiset rewrites. Multisets are denoted by $m_1, \ldots, m_n$ and abbreviated with $\otimes_i m_i$. Solutions can be structured in a hierarchical way by using the operator *membrane* $\{\![.]\!\}$ to group a solution s into a molecule $\{\![s]\!\}$. In [3] molecules can be built also with the constructor *airlock*, but it is not needed in our presentation.

Transformations are described by a set of *chemical rules*, which specify how solutions react. In a CHAM there are two different kinds of chemical rules: *Heating / cooling* (or *structural*) rules $\rightleftharpoons$ representing syntactical rearrangements of molecules in a solution, and *reaction* rules $\rightarrow$. Structural rules are reversible: a solution obtained by applying a cooling rule can be heated back to the original state, and vice versa. Instead, reaction rules cannot be undone.

The laws governing CHAM computations state that whenever an instance of a left-hand-side of a rule is found into a solution, it can be replaced by the corresponding instance of the right-hand-side. Chemical rules $S_1 \rightarrow S_2$ have no premises and are purely local, specifying only the part of the solution that actually changes. Consequently, they can be applied in every larger solution $S, S_1 \rightarrow S, S_2$ (*chemical law*) and also in grouped sub-solutions, $\{\![S, S_1]\!\} \rightarrow \{\![S, S_2]\!\}$. In particular, they can be nested at any level of hierarchical solutions. Note that, since solutions are multisets, rules can be applied concurrently.

The Join calculus. The Join calculus [12] is a well-known PDL with asynchronous name-passing communication. It has the same expressive power as the asynchronous π-calculus and it has distributed running implementations, e.g. Jocaml [10] and Polyphonic C$^\sharp$ [1]. Join relies on an infinite set of names $x, y, u, v, \ldots$. Name tuples are written $\vec{u}$. Join processes, definitions and patterns are in Figure 1.a. A *process* is either the inert process 0, the asynchronous emission $x\langle\vec{y}\rangle$ of message $\vec{y}$ on port x, the process **def** D **in** P equipped with local ports defined by D, or a parallel composition of processes $P|Q$. A *definition* is a conjunction of elementary reactions $J \triangleright P$ that associate *join-patterns* J with *guarded processes* P. Names defined by D in **def** D **in** P are bound in P and in all the guarded processes contained in D. The sets of defined names dn, received names rn and free names fn are defined as usual.

The semantics of the Join calculus relies on the *reflexive* CHAM. It is called reflexive because active reaction rules are represented by molecules present in solutions, which are activated dynamically. Molecules correspond to terms of the Join calculus denoting processes or definitions. The chemical rules are shown in Figure 1.b. Rule STR-NULL states that 0 can be added or removed from any solution. Rules STR-JOIN and STR-AND stand for the associativity and commutativity of $|$ and $\wedge$, because $\_ , \_$ is such. STR-DEF denotes the activation

(PROC)
$P, Q ::= 0 \mid x\langle\vec{y}\rangle \mid \mathbf{def}\ D\ \mathbf{in}\ P \mid P|Q$

(DEF)
$D, E ::= J \triangleright P \mid D \wedge E$

(PAT)
$J, K ::= x\langle\vec{y}\rangle \mid J|K$

a. Syntax.

(STR-NULL) $0 \leftrightharpoons$

(STR-JOIN) $P \mid Q \leftrightharpoons P, Q$

(STR-AND) $D \wedge E \leftrightharpoons D, E$

(STR-DEF) $\mathbf{def}\ D\ \mathbf{in}\ P \leftrightharpoons D\sigma_{dn(D)}, P\sigma_{dn(D)}$ $(range(\sigma_{dn(D)})$ globally fresh)

(RED) $J \triangleright P, J\sigma \rightarrow J \triangleright P, P\sigma$

b. Semantics.

Figure 1. Join Calculus.

$$\begin{array}{lcl} M, N & ::= & 0 \mid x\langle\vec{y}\rangle \mid M|N \\ P, Q & ::= & M \mid abort \mid \mathbf{def}\ D\ \mathbf{in}\ P \mid [P : Q] \mid P|Q \\ D, E & ::= & J \triangleright P \mid J \blacktriangleright P \mid D \wedge E \\ J, K & ::= & x\langle\vec{y}\rangle \mid J|K \end{array}$$

Figure 2 Syntax of cJoin.

of a local definition, which implements a static scoping discipline by properly renaming defined ports by *globally fresh* names. A name x is fresh w.r.t. a process P (resp. a definition D) if $x \notin fn(P)$ (resp. $x \notin fn(D)$). Moreover, x is fresh w.r.t. a solution s if it is fresh w.r.t. every term in s. A set of names X is fresh if every name in X is such. We write the substitution of names $x_1 \ldots x_n$ by names $y_1 \ldots y_n$ as $\sigma = \{^{y_1 \ldots y_n}/_{x_1 \ldots x_n}\}$, with $dom(\sigma) = \{x_1, \ldots, x_n\}$ and $range(\sigma) = \{y_1, \ldots, y_n\}$. We indicate with σ_N an injective substitution σ such that $dom(\sigma) = N$. We require names to be globally fresh, i.e. fresh w.r.t the implicit context in which the rule is applied.

Consider, for instance, $s = \{\!\![z\langle x, z\rangle, \mathbf{def}\ x\langle y\rangle \triangleright z\langle y, x\rangle\ \mathbf{in}\ x\langle a\rangle]\!\!\}$, whose second molecule contains a definition of a local port x different from the homonym free port in the first molecule. When STR-DEF is applied, the local definition of x is renamed by using a fresh name, obtaining, for instance, the solution $s' = \{\!\![z\langle x, z\rangle, x_1\langle y\rangle \triangleright z\langle y, x_1\rangle, x_1\langle a\rangle]\!\!\}$.

Finally, RED describes the use of an active reaction rule ($J \triangleright P$) to consume messages forming an instance of J (for a suitable substitution σ, with $dom(\sigma) = rn(J)$), and produce a new instance $P\sigma$ of its guarded process P. By applying RED to s' for $\sigma = \{^a/_y\}$, we get $s' \rightarrow \{\!\![z\langle x, z\rangle, x_1\langle y\rangle \triangleright z\langle y, x_1\rangle, z\langle a, x_1\rangle]\!\!\}$. Note that the local port x_1 has been extruded on the free channel z.

3. Committed Join

Syntax. We extend the syntax of Join as in Figure 2. A negotiation is represented by $[P : Q]$, where P is the normal activity and Q is its compensation. The normal activity P is intended to execute in isolation until reaching either a commit or an abort decision. If P commits, the obtained result is delivered to the outside of the negotiation. Instead, Q is activated when P aborts. The abort decision is signaled with the special process *abort*.

A new kind of definitions $J \blacktriangleright P$, called *merge definitions*, is introduced to describe the interactions among negotiations. Merge definitions allow the

$$dn_o(D \wedge E) = dn_o(D) \cup dn_o(E) \quad dn_o(J \triangleright P) = dn(J) \quad dn_o(J \blacktriangleright P) = \emptyset$$
$$dn_m(D \wedge E) = dn_m(D) \cup dn_m(E) \quad dn_m(J \triangleright P) = \emptyset \quad dn_m(J \blacktriangleright P) = dn(J)$$

Figure 3. Ordinary and merge names.

(STR-NULL)	$0 \leftrightharpoons$
(STR-JOIN)	$P \mid Q \leftrightharpoons P, Q$
(STR-AND)	$D \wedge E \leftrightharpoons D, E$
(STR-DEF)	$\mathbf{def}\ D\ \mathbf{in}\ P \leftrightharpoons D\sigma_{dn(D)}, P\sigma_{dn(D)}$ ($range(\sigma_{dn(D)})$ globally fresh)
(RED)	$J \triangleright P, J\sigma \rightarrow J \triangleright P, P\sigma$
(STR-CONT)	$[P : Q] \leftrightharpoons \{\!\!\{P, \llcorner Q \lrcorner\}\!\!\}$
(COMMIT)	$\{\!\!\{M \mid \mathbf{def}\ D\ \mathbf{in}\ 0, \llcorner Q \lrcorner\}\!\!\} \rightarrow M$
(ABORT)	$\{\!\!\{abort \mid P, \llcorner Q \lrcorner\}\!\!\} \rightarrow Q$
(MERGE)	$\Pi_j J_j \blacktriangleright P, \bigotimes_i \{\!\!\{J_i\sigma, S_i, \llcorner Q_i \lrcorner\}\!\!\} \rightarrow \Pi_j J_j \blacktriangleright P, \{\!\!\{\bigotimes_i S_i, P\sigma, \llcorner \Pi_i Q_i \lrcorner\}\!\!\}$

Figure 4. Operational semantics of cJoin.

consumption of messages produced in the scope of different contracts by joining all participants in a unique larger negotiation. Moreover, usual definitions can be used to create negotiations dynamically. For instance, by firing $J \triangleright [P : Q]$ a new instance of the negotiation P with compensation Q is activated.

For convenience we introduce the syntactical category M of processes without definitions, i.e. a parallel composition of messages.

The definition of fn is extended with $fn(abort) = \emptyset$, $fn([P : Q]) = fn(P) \cup fn(Q)$ and $fn(J \blacktriangleright P) = dn(J) \cup (fn(P) \setminus rn(J))$. For a definition D, we redefine $dn(D) = dn_o(D) \cup dn_m(D)$, where dn_o denotes the *defined ordinary* names and dn_m the *defined merge* names (Figure 3). We assume $dn_o(D) \cap dn_m(D) = \emptyset$ for every definition D.

Operational Semantics. The operational semantics of cJoin is defined in the reflexive CHAM style. Molecules m and solutions S are defined below.

$$m ::= P \mid D \mid \llcorner P \lrcorner \mid \{\!\!\{S\}\!\!\} \qquad S ::= m \mid m, S$$

As in ordinary Join, processes and definitions are molecules. Additionally, a molecule $\llcorner P \lrcorner$ denotes a compensation that is frozen inside a solution. The chemical rules are in Figure 4. The first five rules are the ordinary ones for Join. Rule STR-CONT describes how a negotiation corresponds to a sub-solution of two molecules: the process P and its compensation Q, which is frozen (because the operator $\llcorner . \lrcorner$ forbids the enclosed process to react).

COMMIT can be executed only when all participants have done their tasks reaching a (local) state that does not contain locally defined names. This way, a commit means clean termination where all names denoting internal states of contracts have been consumed. Note that all definitions belonging to a contract are discarded at commit time because the messages that are being released do not contain those names (we recall that local names cannot be extruded). Similarly, the compensation is discarded at commit. Moreover, a negotiation cannot commit when *abort* is within the solution because *abort* is not a message. The abort is handled by rule ABORT, which activates the compensation procedure while discarding all terms in the solution. Compensations are not predefined to execute atomically, but they can be explicitly programmed as negotiations.

Interactions among contracts are specified by rule MERGE, which consumes messages $J_i\sigma$ from different contracts and creates a new larger negotiation by combining the existing contracts together with the new instance $P\sigma$, where $dom(\sigma) = rn(\Pi_j J_j)$. The compensation for the joint negotiation is the parallel composition of all the original compensations. When merging negotiations, clashes of locally defined names should be avoided by imposing the side condition $dn(S_i) \cap (dn(S_j) \cup fn(S_j)) = \emptyset$ for $i \neq j$. However, if we are guaranteed that STR-DEF generates globally fresh names (and not just locally fresh names) then this side condition can be safely omitted, as it is trivially satisfied.

PROPOSITION 1 *cJoin is a conservative extension of Join.*

Discussion. Sibling contracts can be merged only by using merge definitions introduced by their parent. In practice, it might be useful to apply a merge definition provided by any ancestor. To this aim, the rule STR-MOVE below might be added, so that merge definitions could float across contract boundaries.

$$\text{STR-MOVE} \quad J \blacktriangleright P, \{\!\{S\}\!\} \quad \leftrightharpoons \quad \{\!\{J \blacktriangleright P, S\}\!\}$$

Regarding deadlocks, note that stall negotiations are not discarded. For instance, the process $[\mathbf{def}\ x\langle\rangle | y\langle\rangle \triangleright 0\ \mathbf{in}\ x\langle\rangle\ :\ Q]$ cannot compute. Neither it can commit, because there is a message on the local port x. In this situation the contract is blocked and should be aborted. Some of these situations can be recognized and handled locally to promote the abort (i.e., when no local rules can be applied). These situations can be represented by ad hoc rules or by a general rule to generate nondeterministically the abort (situations that real implementations typically handle with timeouts). Nevertheless, we cannot expect to axiomatize stall situations because it would mean to write axioms recognizing non-termination, which is an undecidable problem. On the other hand, we do not want to limit the expressiveness of the language.

With respect to the requirements discussed in the Introduction, we have that, membranes are exploited to define the boundaries of negotiations. Process like $[P_1 \mid [P_2 : Q_2] \mid [P_3 : Q_3] : Q_1]$ straightforwardly model sub-negotiations. The decisions taken internally by P_2 can influence P_3 only if some merge definition is available at the level of P_1. In absence of merge definitions, global and local resources are kept separate in each sub-negotiation. The commit of P_2 can only happen when the internal state contains only global resources. At commit time, the result of the negotiation is made available to P_1. An abort generated in P_2 activates the compensation Q_2 at the level of P_1, neither forcing the abort of

$$
\begin{array}{l}
\mathrm{H} \equiv \mathbf{def}\ \ WaitBooking\langle\rangle \triangleright [\mathbf{def}\ \ request\langle o\rangle \triangleright o\langle\$\rangle \mid price\langle\$\rangle \\
\qquad\qquad\qquad\qquad\qquad \wedge\ price\langle\$\rangle \mid confirm\langle v\rangle \triangleright BookedRoom\langle v\rangle \\
\qquad\qquad\qquad\qquad\qquad \wedge\ price\langle\$\rangle \triangleright abort \\
\qquad\qquad\qquad\qquad\qquad \mathbf{in}\ \ offerRoom\langle request, confirm\rangle : Q] \\
\qquad \wedge\ BookedRoom\langle v\rangle \triangleright R \\
\qquad \mathbf{in}\ \ WaitBooking\langle\rangle \mid \ldots \\
\mathrm{C} \equiv \mathbf{def}\ \ BookHotel\langle\rangle \triangleright\ [\mathbf{def}\ HotelMsg\langle r, c\rangle \triangleright \\
\qquad\qquad\qquad\qquad \mathbf{def}\ offer\langle\$\rangle \triangleright c\langle visa\rangle \mid hotelOK\langle hConf\rangle \\
\qquad\qquad\qquad\qquad \wedge\ offer\langle\$\rangle \triangleright abort \\
\qquad\qquad\qquad\qquad \wedge\ hConf\langle\rangle \triangleright HotelFound\langle\rangle \\
\qquad\qquad\qquad\qquad \mathbf{in}\ \ r\langle offer\rangle\ \ \mathbf{in}\ searchRoom\langle HotelMsg\rangle : Q'] \\
\qquad \wedge\ BookFlight\langle\rangle \triangleright\ [\mathbf{def}\ FlightMsg\langle r, c\rangle \triangleright \\
\qquad\qquad\qquad\qquad \mathbf{def}\ offer\langle\$\rangle \triangleright c\langle visa\rangle \mid flightOK\langle fConf\rangle \\
\qquad\qquad\qquad\qquad \wedge\ offer\langle\$\rangle \triangleright abort \\
\qquad\qquad\qquad\qquad \wedge\ fConf\langle\rangle \triangleright FlightFound\langle\rangle \\
\qquad\qquad\qquad\qquad \mathbf{in}\ \ r\langle offer\rangle\ \ \mathbf{in}\ searchFlight\langle FlightMsg\rangle : Q''] \\
\qquad \wedge\ flightOK\langle fc\rangle \mid hotelOK\langle rc\rangle \blacktriangleright fc\langle\rangle \mid rc\langle\rangle \\
\qquad \mathbf{in}\ \ BookHotel\langle\rangle \mid BookFlight\langle\rangle \mid \ldots \\
\mathrm{Trip} \equiv \mathbf{def}\ searchRoom\langle hm\rangle \mid offerRoom\langle r, c\rangle \blacktriangleright hm\langle r, c\rangle \\
\qquad \wedge\ searchFlight\langle fm\rangle \mid offerFlight\langle r, c\rangle \blacktriangleright fm\langle r, c\rangle \qquad \mathbf{in}\ \mathrm{H} \mid \mathrm{A} \mid \mathrm{C}
\end{array}
$$

Figure 5. Trip booking example.

any other sub-negotiations (P_3) nor the abort of the main contract (P_1). Note that if $[P_2 : Q_2]$ was the result of the merging of several negotiations, then Q_2 is the union of all the compensations of the participants.

An important restriction is that local resources can neither cross negotiations boundaries nor be extruded to siblings negotiations. The only way to exchange information between siblings negotiations is by merging all participants into a unique negotiation that must then commit, or abort, or diverge as such.

4. Examples

Trip booking. Figure 5 shows the encoding of the application Trip that allows a user to book flights and accommodations. Trip is defined in term of three components: the hotel H, the airline A and the customer C. The component H is a process that activates (by firing the definition for *WaitBooking*) a negotiation to serve customer requests. Such negotiation starts by publishing on the merge port *offerRoom* (defined in Trip) the names of the services a client should use to reserve a room: *request* to ask for a quote; and *confirm* to accept an offer. The component A (omitted in Figure 5) is defined analogously, but it publishes services on port *offerFlight* instead of *offerRoom*.

The component C defines two rules for creating negotiations: one for booking rooms and the other for buying flight tickets. Both contracts are quite similar. In particular, the negotiation for booking a room starts by sending a message to the merge port *searchRoom* (defined in Trip) to obtain the names for interacting with a hotel. The first merge rule in Trip will associate an offer from a hotel with a request from a client by sending the names r and c to the corresponding port hm. Once received r and c on *HotelMsg*, C uses r to send a message to H for asking for a quote. Then, the hotel will answer with an offer on port offer. Whether the customer accepts or not a particular quote is modeled by the multiple definitions for the pattern $\mathit{offer}\langle\$\rangle$ in C. If the offer is not adequate then C can abort the negotiation, which will activate the compensation $Q \mid Q'$ (analogously for H and A). C can accept the offer by sending a confirmation message on port c. In this case, C also generates a message to the local port $\mathit{hotelOK}\langle \mathit{hConf}\rangle$. This message will be managed by the local merge rule defined by C. The contract will be blocked until a running negotiation for buying flight tickets generates a message on $\mathit{flightOK}$. At this time, the local merge definition can be fired and both contracts merged. Eventually the negotiation will commit by releasing the messages on *HotelFound* and *FlightFound*. Moreover, messages $\mathit{BookedRoom}\langle v\rangle$ and $\mathit{SoldFlight}\langle v\rangle$ generated by H and A to change their local states are released only at this time, when all participants have committed.

Andorra Kernel Language. As a second example, we sketch how merge definitions and nesting can be used to model some features of AKL [13], a concurrent logic programming language. We consider guarded rules $A \leftarrow G|B$, where the *head* A is an atom, the *guard* G and the *body* B are (possibly empty) conjunction of atoms, and | is the commit operator. An AKL program $\mathcal{P}$ is a list of guarded rules. An execution of $\mathcal{P}$ is initiated by providing a *goal* $\mathcal{G}$, which is a conjunction of atoms. A cJoin process that simulates $\mathcal{P}$ queried with $\mathcal{G}$ is:

$$\mathbf{def}\ \mathsf{D} \wedge [\![\mathsf{defs}(\mathcal{P})]\!] \wedge [\![\mathsf{undef}(\mathcal{P})]\!]\ \mathbf{in}\ [\![\mathbf{and}(\mathcal{G})]\!]_{\mathit{trueG},\mathit{falseG}} \mid \mathit{unif}\langle \mathit{final}, \mathtt{tt}\rangle$$

The definitions in D are needed to promote constraints computed locally. The rules in $\mathcal{P}$ are translated separately by grouping all rules defining the same atom A. Such partition is denoted by $\mathsf{defs}(\mathcal{P})$, while $\mathsf{undef}(\mathcal{P})$ denotes all atoms in $\mathcal{P}$ without defining rules, i.e., atoms whose proofs will always fail. Constraints θ are encoded conveniently as cJoin processes ($\mathtt{tt}$ is the empty constraint). In general, the term $\mathit{unif}\langle \mathit{final}, \theta\rangle$ stores the computed constraints of a running proof. At the end, a message on either port trueG or falseG will inform the environment about the outcome of the computation. The encoding of clauses and goals is in Figure 6.

An atom A is encoded as a merge rule that substitutes a message $A\langle t, f\rangle$ by the proof of its defining rules (rule DEF). An undefined atom is encoded as a rule that always fails (UNDEF). A conjunction (AND) corresponds to a process that activates a new negotiation containing the atoms $A_i\langle t_i, f_i\rangle$ to be proved and the initial local constraints $\mathit{unif}\langle w, \mathtt{tt}\rangle$. Every sub-proof initiated by $A_i\langle t_i, f_i\rangle$ will notify its termination by using ports t_i (success) and f_i (failure). If all sub-proofs end successfully, the second definition in the negotiation can be fired producing $t\langle\rangle$ (i.e., the signal of the successful proof of the conjunction) and

$$
\begin{array}{ll}
(\textsc{Def}) & [\![A \leftarrow B_1|C_1,\ldots,A \leftarrow B_n|C_n]\!] = A\langle t,f\rangle \blacktriangleright [\![\mathbf{choice}(B_1|C_1,\ldots,B_n|C_n)]\!]_{t,f} \\
(\textsc{Undef}) & [\![A]\!] = A\langle t,f\rangle \blacktriangleright f\langle\rangle \\
(\textsc{And}) & [\![\mathbf{and}(A_1,\ldots,A_n)]\!]_{t,f} = \mathbf{def}\ and\langle\rangle \triangleright [\mathbf{def}\quad w\langle\rangle \triangleright 0 \\
& \qquad \wedge\ \Pi_{i=1}^{n}\ t_i\langle\rangle \triangleright done\langle w\rangle \mid t\langle\rangle \\
& \qquad \bigwedge_{i=1}^{n}\ f_i\langle\rangle \triangleright and\langle\rangle \mid failed\langle\rangle \\
& \qquad \text{...Rules for handling abortion...} \\
& \qquad \mathbf{in}\ \Pi_{i=1}^{n} A_i\langle t_i, f_i\rangle | unif\langle w, \mathtt{tt}\rangle : f\langle\rangle] \\
& \quad \mathbf{in}\ and\langle\rangle \\
(\textsc{Choice}) & [\![\mathbf{choice}(A_1|B_1,\ldots,A_n|B_n)]\!]_{t,f} = \mathbf{def}\ \bigwedge_{i=1}^{n}\ i\langle\rangle \triangleright [\![\mathbf{and}(B_i)]\!]_{t,f} \\
& \quad \mathbf{in}\ [\mathbf{def}\ \ \Pi_{i=1}^{n}\ f_i\langle\rangle \mid proving\langle\rangle \triangleright abort \\
& \qquad \bigwedge_{i=1}^{n}\ t_i\langle\rangle \mid proving\langle\rangle \triangleright i\langle\rangle | chosen\langle\rangle \\
& \qquad \text{...Rules for handling abortion...} \\
& \quad \mathbf{in}\ \Pi_{i=1}^{n}\ [\![\mathbf{and}(A_i)]\!]_{t_i,f_i} | proving\langle\rangle : f\langle\rangle]
\end{array}
$$

Figure 6. Encoding of AKL committed rules.

$done\langle w\rangle$ that activates the promotion of computed constraints managed by D (omitted for space limitation). Note that $t\langle\rangle$ will be released outside only at commit, after constraints have been promoted. Instead, if a sub-atom fails, all running sub-contracts are aborted and the contract commits by releasing the activation of a new proof.

Rule CHOICE opens a negotiation for proving one of the guards of a multiple choice goal. When a guard is successful the negotiation can commit by releasing the message $i\langle\rangle$, which activates the body B_i of the chosen goal.

If there is an AKL refutation for the goal $\mathcal{G}$ with computed constraints $\mathbf{and}(\mathtt{tt}, \theta)$ then the messages $final\langle\theta\rangle$ and $trueG\langle\rangle$ can be released. On the other hand, $falseG\langle\rangle$ is generated only if $\mathcal{G}$ cannot be proved.

5. Encoding Zero-Safe nets

Zero-safe nets (ZS *nets*) [8] extends Place/Transition Petri nets (PT *nets*) with a mechanism for expressing concurrent transactions. Recently, they have been used in [7] to encode short-running transactions of Biztalk, a commercial workflow management system [16]. ZS nets additionally provides a "dynamic" specification of transactions boundaries supporting multiway transactions, which retain several entry and exit points, and admit a number of participants which is statically unknown. However, ZS nets are not suitable to express some interesting aspects, such as mobility, programmable compensations and nesting.

In this section we show that ZS nets can be straightforwardly encoded in cJoin. A distributed implementation of ZS nets in Join has been presented in [7], but there the encoding is complicated by the need of attaching a local transaction manager to each transition.

We recall that, in Petri nets, *places* are repositories of *tokens* and *transitions* fetch and produce tokens. Net configurations, called *markings*, are multisets of tokens. The places of ZS nets are partitioned into ordinary and transactional

(FIRING)
$$\frac{S+Z\,[\rangle\,S'+Z' \in T}{(S+S'',Z+Z'') \to_T (S'+S'',Z'+Z'')}$$

(STEP)
$$\frac{(S_1,Z_1)\to_T(S_1',Z_1') \quad (S_2,Z_2)\to_T(S_2',Z_2')}{(S_1+S_2,Z_1+Z_2)\to_T(S_1'+S_2',Z_1'+Z_2')}$$

(CONCATENATION)
$$\frac{(S_1,Z)\to_T(S_1',Z'') \quad (S_2,Z'')\to_T(S_2',Z')}{(S_1+S_2,Z)\to_T(S_1'+S_2',Z')}$$

(CLOSE)
$$\frac{(S,\emptyset)\to_T(S',\emptyset)}{(S,\emptyset)\Rightarrow_T(S',\emptyset)}$$

Figure 7. Operational semantics of ZS nets (+ denotes multiset union).

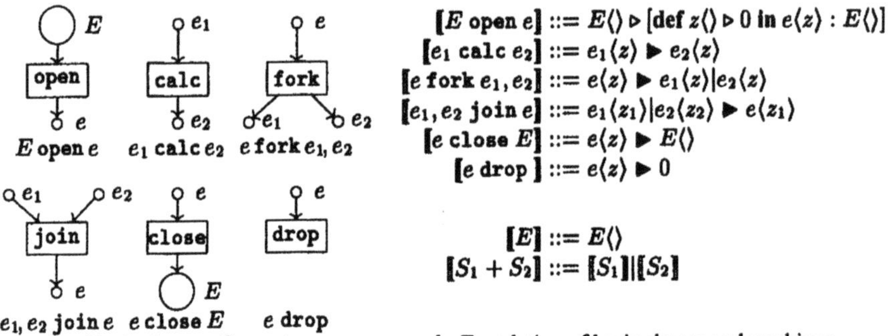

a. Basic shapes of ZS nets. b. Translation of basic shapes and markings.

Figure 8. Encoding of ZS nets in cJoin.

ones, called *stable* and *zero*, respectively. Correspondingly, markings U can be seen as pairs (S, Z) with $U = S + Z$, where S and Z are the multisets of stable and zero resources, respectively. Transitions are written $U[\rangle U'$. A *transaction* goes from a multiset of stable places (*stable marking*) to another stable marking. The key point is that stable tokens produced during a transaction are made available only at commit time, when no zero tokens are left. We write (T, S) for a ZS net with set of transitions T and initial stable marking S.

The operational semantics of ZS nets is defined by the two relations $\Rightarrow_T$ and $\to_T$ in Figure 7. Rules FIRING and STEP are the ordinary ones for Petri nets, for the execution of one/many transition(s). However, sequences of steps differ from the ordinary transitive closure of $\to_T$: The rule CONCATENATION composes zero tokens in series but stable tokens in parallel, hence stable tokens produced by the first step cannot be consumed by the second step. CLOSE selects the moves $(S,\emptyset) \Rightarrow_T (S',\emptyset)$, which defines the transactions of the net.

As done in [7], and without loss of generality, we restrict to ZS nets whose transitions have the basic shapes in Figure 8.a, for E any stable place and e, e_1, e_2 any zero places. The translation in Figure 8.b associates a cJoin definition to each basic shape. Places are seen as ports and tokens as messages. Tokens in stable places carry no value, while tokens in zero places carry the identifier of the transaction they belong to. The cJoin process associated to the ZS net (T, S) is **def** $[\![T]\!]$ **in** $[\![S]\!]$, where $[\![T]\!] = \bigwedge_{t \in T} [\![t]\!]$.

A transaction can be opened by firing a transition of the form E **open** e. In cJoin, this means opening a new negotiation whose internal state contains the definition of a fresh name z, the message $e\langle z\rangle$, and whose compensation, by default, gives back the stable resources $E\langle\rangle$. The dummy definition $z\langle\rangle \triangleright 0$ is the cJoin way of declaring a fresh identifier z for the transaction. When two transactions are merged by applying e.g. $e_1\langle z_1\rangle | e_2\langle z_2\rangle \blacktriangleright e\langle z_1\rangle$, then z_1 and z_2 become equivalent identifiers for the same larger negotiation. When computing inside a negotiation, each zero token carries one of the possibly many equivalent identifiers for that negotiation (e.g., z_1). If stable messages $E\langle\rangle$ are released inside the negotiation, e.g., by firing e **close** E, then they are frozen until commit, because the only rules that can fetch them are outside the negotiation boundaries, in the top chemical soup. The commit can happen if and only if the negotiation reaches a local state containing only stable messages (and dummy definitions). Then, the reaction COMMIT can close the negotiations and release all stable tokens to the environment. The following result assures the correctness and completeness of $[\![\_]\!]$.

THEOREM 2 $(S, \emptyset) \Rightarrow_T^* (S', \emptyset)$ *iff* $\mathbf{def}\ [\![T]\!]\ \mathbf{in}\ [\![S]\!] \rightarrow^* \mathbf{def}\ [\![T]\!]\ \mathbf{in}\ [\![S']\!]$.

The main behavioral difference between the cJoin encoding in Figure 8 and the Join encoding in [7] relies on the treatment of failures, as here no abort can be generated (and consequently compensations cannot be activated). A possible solution would be to add a *timeout* component each time a new negotiation is open, which is able to produce the abort via the rule $A = timeout\langle\rangle \blacktriangleright abort$. In this case, we should let $[\![E\ \mathbf{open}\ e]\!] = E\langle\rangle \triangleright [\mathbf{def}\ z\langle\rangle \triangleright 0\ \mathbf{in}\ e\langle z\rangle | timeout\langle\rangle : E\langle\rangle]$ and encode the net $N = (T, S)$ as $\mathbf{def}\ A \wedge [\![T]\!]\ \mathbf{in}\ [\![S]\!]$.

6. Serializability and Big-Step Semantics

The semantics of cJoin given in Figure 4 allows the cooperation among several negotiations. Nevertheless, we would like to reason about a process by analyzing interacting negotiations independently from the rest of the system. A concurrent execution $T_1 \parallel \ldots \parallel T_n$ of several transactions is said *serializable* if there exists a sequence $T_{i_1};\ T_{i_2}; \ldots ; T_{i_n}$ that executes all transactions one at a time (without interleaving their steps) and produces the same result [2]. Serializability is important because it allows to reason about the behavior of a system by considering one transaction at a time. In this section we introduce a syntactical restriction on processes, called *shallowness*, and show that it guarantees serializability.

The idea is to describe multi-party negotiations as abstract transitions that fetch the messages needed to initiate all sub-negotiations separately and produce the processes released at commit or abort. Consequently, serializable negotiations can postpone the activation of each sub-negotiation until all other cooperating sub-negotiations needed to commit can be activated.

(PAR)
$$\frac{\mathcal{D}\vdash\mathcal{P}\twoheadrightarrow\mathcal{D}\vdash\mathcal{P}' \quad \mathcal{D}\vdash\mathcal{Q}\twoheadrightarrow\mathcal{D}\vdash\mathcal{Q}'}{\mathcal{D}\vdash\mathcal{P}\mid\mathcal{Q}\twoheadrightarrow\mathcal{D}\vdash\mathcal{P}'\mid\mathcal{Q}'}$$

(SEQ)
$$\frac{\mathcal{D}\vdash\mathcal{P}\twoheadrightarrow\mathcal{D}\vdash\mathcal{P}'' \quad \mathcal{D}\vdash\mathcal{P}''\twoheadrightarrow\mathcal{D}\vdash\mathcal{P}'}{\mathcal{D}\vdash\mathcal{P}\twoheadrightarrow\mathcal{D}\vdash\mathcal{P}'}$$

(GLOBAL FIRING)
$$\mathcal{D}\wedge J\triangleright\mathcal{P}\vdash J\sigma\twoheadrightarrow\mathcal{D}\wedge J\triangleright\mathcal{P}\vdash\mathcal{P}\sigma$$

(LOCAL FIRING)
$$\frac{\tilde{\mathcal{B}}\vdash\mathcal{S}\twoheadrightarrow\tilde{\mathcal{B}}\vdash\mathcal{S}'}{\mathcal{D}\wedge\mathcal{B}\vdash[\mathcal{S}:\mathcal{Q}]\twoheadrightarrow\mathcal{D}\wedge\mathcal{B}\vdash[\mathcal{S}':\mathcal{Q}]}$$

(MERGE)
$$\mathcal{D}\wedge\Pi_i J_i \blacktriangleright \mathcal{S} \vdash \Pi_i[\mathcal{D}_i\vdash J_i\sigma \mid \mathcal{S}_i{:}\mathcal{Q}_i] \twoheadrightarrow \mathcal{D}\wedge\Pi_i J_i \blacktriangleright\mathcal{S} \vdash [\textstyle\bigwedge_i\mathcal{D}_i\vdash(\Pi_i\mathcal{S}_i)|\mathcal{S}\sigma : \Pi_i\mathcal{Q}_i]$$

(LOCAL COMMIT)
$$\mathcal{D}\vdash[M \mid \mathcal{D}'\vdash 0:\mathcal{S}]\twoheadrightarrow\mathcal{D}\vdash M$$

(ABORT)
$$\mathcal{D}\vdash[abort|\mathcal{P}:\mathcal{S}]\twoheadrightarrow\mathcal{D}\vdash\mathcal{S}$$

(IDLE)
$$\mathcal{D}\vdash\mathcal{P}\twoheadrightarrow\mathcal{D}\vdash\mathcal{P}$$

Figure 9. Big-step semantics of cJoin.

DEFINITION 3 (SHALLOWNESS) *The nesting* $nest(P)$ *of* P *is defined by:*

$nest(0) = nest(abort) = nest(x\langle y\rangle) = 0$ $\quad nest([P:Q]) = nest(P)+1$
$nest(\mathbf{def}\ D\ \mathbf{in}\ P) = nest(P)$ $\quad nest(P \mid Q) = \max\{nest(P), nest(Q)\}$

P *is* shallow *if any basic definition* D *in* P *satisfies one of the two conditions:*

1. $D \equiv J \triangleright P$, *where* $nest(P)=0$ *or* $P=[R:Q]$ *and* $nest(R|Q)=0$
2. $D \equiv J \blacktriangleright P$ *and* $nest(P)=0$

We refer definitions in shallow processes as *shallow definitions*. Moreover, we call a process P *stable* iff P is shallow and $nest(P)=0$. The shallow property imposes a discipline for activating negotiations. In particular, condition 1 assures that the firing of an ordinary rule increases the height of the nesting by at most one level (i.e., a definition produces either a stable process or one negotiation without nested sub-contracts). Condition 2 forbids the creation of sub-negotiations while merging. The absence of condition 2 would prevent the possibility of postponing the activation of some negotiations until all cooperating negotiations can be activated. Shallowness forbids rules such as $J_1 \triangleright P \mid [P_1:Q]$ and $J_2 \triangleright [[P_1:Q_1]:Q]$, which however can be encoded as shallow definitions by using new local ports, e.g. as $D_1 \equiv J_1 \triangleright x\langle\rangle|P \ \wedge\ x\langle\rangle \triangleright [P_1:Q]$ and $D_2 \equiv J_2 \triangleright [\mathbf{def}\ x\langle\rangle \triangleright [P_1 : Q_1]\ \mathbf{in}\ x\langle\rangle : Q]$, respectively. Moreover $\mathbf{def}\ D_2\ \mathbf{in}\ J_2\sigma$ reduces in two steps to $\mathbf{def}\ D_2\ \mathbf{in}\ [\mathbf{def}\ x\langle\rangle \triangleright [P_1\sigma : Q_1\sigma]\ \mathbf{in}\ [P_1\sigma : Q_1\sigma] : Q\sigma]$, which has nested negotiations.

In the following $\mathcal{P}$ and $\mathcal{Q}$ will denote shallow processes, $\mathcal{D}$ a shallow definition, $\mathcal{S}$ a stable process, and $\mathcal{B}$ a shallow definition containing just merge rules. We abbreviate $\mathbf{def}\ \mathcal{D}\ \mathbf{in}\ \mathcal{P}$ as $\mathcal{D}\vdash\mathcal{P}$, and $\vdash\mathcal{P}$ as $\mathcal{P}$. Terms are considered up-to structural equivalence generated by closure w.r.t the equations for the associativity and commutativity of $|$ and $\wedge$, 0 the unit for $|$, and

$$\mathcal{D}\vdash\mathcal{P} \mid \mathbf{def}\ \mathcal{D}'\ \mathbf{in}\ \mathcal{Q} \ \equiv\ \mathcal{D}\wedge\mathcal{D}'\sigma_{dn}\vdash\mathcal{P} \mid \mathcal{Q}\sigma_{dn}$$
$$range(\sigma_{dn}) \cap (fn(\mathcal{D}) \cup fn(\mathcal{P}) \cup fn(\mathbf{def}\ \mathcal{D}'\ \mathbf{in}\ \mathcal{Q})) = \emptyset$$

We characterize serializability by the big-step reduction relation between shallow processes presented in Figure 9.

Steps can be composed in parallel (PAR) and sequentially (SEQ), even with idle transitions (IDLE). Rule GLOBAL FIRING corresponds to the firing of an ordinary definition in a top-level process. Instead LOCAL FIRING states possible internal transitions of a running contract. LOCAL FIRING represents suitable sub-negotiations as ordinary transitions at an abstract level. In fact, the computations occurring at a lower level in the nesting hierarchy (premise of LOCAL FIRING) that are relevant to its containing negotiation are those relating stable processes, i.e., S and S'. A negotiation has available, in addition to its own definitions, the merge definitions introduced by its parent. In fact, a merge definition applied on a single contract behaves as an ordinary rule but defined in a global scope. The operator $\widetilde{\ }$ transforms merge definitions in ordinary ones: $\widetilde{J \blacktriangleright \mathcal{P}} \equiv J \triangleright \mathcal{P}$ and $\widetilde{B \wedge B'} \equiv \widetilde{B} \wedge \widetilde{B'}$. If the rule STR-MOVE is also considered for cJoin, then the premise of LOCAL FIRING must be $\widetilde{B} \wedge B \vdash S \twoheadrightarrow \widetilde{B} \wedge B \vdash S'$.

Rules LOCAL COMMIT and ABORT handle the termination of a negotiation, whereas MERGE describes the interaction among sibling negotiations. This time, negotiations can be joined only if they do not contain running contracts.

The big-step relation enforces serializability. In fact, the completed negotiations at a particular level become ordinary transitions at the upper level and all interacting transactions can be analyzed independently from the rest of the system. The following result states the correspondence between both semantics for shallow processes, proving that shallow processes are serializable.

THEOREM 4 *Let S, S' be stable processes. Then $S \rightarrow^* S'$ iff $\vdash S' \twoheadrightarrow \vdash S'$.*

7. Concluding remarks

We have proposed cJoin as a linguistic extension of Join with natural primitives for modeling nested negotiations. The expressiveness of cJoin has been demonstrated by means of an informal discussion about the satisfaction of the general requirements enumerated in the Introduction and three sample applications (trip booking and the encodings of AKL and ZS nets). Additionally, we have defined a syntactical restriction of processes that assures serializability.

Unlike *workflow systems*, cJoin does not fix a set of constructors to describe dependencies in the style of ConTracts [15]. The actual dependencies of a negotiation are known at execution time and are consequence of its interaction with other contracts. This feature distinguishes cJoin from [4], where processes running as transactions can interact freely with the environment. On the other hand, cJoin is aimed at providing a way to model multi-party transactions by describing their interacting agents and not their global structure, such as [6, 9]. Nevertheless, our language does not provide default mechanisms for undoing pre-committed activities of aborted transactions, differently from [9]. We leave as a future work the comparison with other calculi that models ACID transactions [17], long-running negotiations [4, 11], and exception handling [14].

Negotiations in cJoin have the flavour of multiway transactions in ZS nets, where participants are not statically fixed. We plan to reuse or to extend the D2PC proposed in [7] to have a full encoding of cJoin in Join itself. This would allow us to extend implementations of Join, such as Jocaml or Polyphonic C♯, by providing primitives for handling distributed negotiations. As a preliminary result, the encoding for the subcalculus of *flat* processes is in [5].

Acknowledgments. We thank Nick Benton, Luca Cardelli, Cédric Fournet and Cosimo Laneve with whom we discussed preliminary versions of cJoin.

References

[1] N. Benton, L. Cardelli, and C. Fournet. Modern concurrency abstractions for C♯. *Proc. of ECOOP 2002, LNCS* 2374, pp. 415–440. Springer Verlag, 2002.

[2] P.A. Bernstein, V. Hadzilacos, and N. Goodman. *Concurrency, Control and Recovery in Database Systems*. Addison-Wesley Longman, 1987.

[3] G. Berry and G. Boudol. The chemical abstract machine. *TCS*, 96(1):217–248, 1992.

[4] L. Bocchi, C. Laneve, and G. Zavattaro. A calculus for long-running transactions. *Proc. of FMOODS'03, LNCS* 2884, pp. 194–208. Springer Verlag, 2003.

[5] R. Bruni, H. Melgratti, and U. Montanari. Flat Committed Join in Join. *Proc. of COMETA 2003, ENTCS*. To appear.

[6] BPEL Specification, May 2003. `http://www-106.ibm.com/developerworks/webservices/library/ws-bpel/`.

[7] R. Bruni, C. Laneve, and U. Montanari. Orchestrating transactions in join calculus. *Proc. of CONCUR 2002, LNCS* 2421, pp. 321–336. Springer Verlag, 2002.

[8] R. Bruni and U. Montanari. Zero-safe nets: Comparing the collective and individual token approaches. *Inform. and Comput.*, 156(1-2):46–89, 2000.

[9] M. Butler, M. Chessell, C. Ferreira, C. Griffin, P. Henderson, and D. Vines. Extending the concept of transaction compensation. *IBM Systems Journal*, 41(4):743–758, 2002.

[10] S. Conchon and F. Le Fessant. Jocaml: Mobile agents for Objective-Caml. *Proc. of ASA'99/MA'99*, 1999.

[11] D. Duggan. Abstractions for Fault-Tolerant Global Computing. *TCS*. To appear.

[12] C. Fournet and G. Gonthier. The reflexive chemical abstract machine and the Join calculus. *Proc. of POPL'96*, pp. 372–385. ACM Press, 1996.

[13] S. Haridi, S. Janson, and C. Palamidessi. Structural operational semantics of AKL. *Journal of Future Generation Computer Systems*, 8:409–421, 1992.

[14] M. Mazzara and R. Lucchi. A framework for generic error handling in business processes. *Proc. of WS-FM'04, ENTCS*. To appear.

[15] A. Reuter and H. Wächter. The contract model. *Transaction Models for Advanced Applications*. Morgan Kaufmann, 1992.

[16] U. Roxburgh. Biztalk orchestration: transactions, exceptions, and debugging, 2001. `http://msdn.microsoft.com/library/en-us/dnbiz/html/btsorch.asp`.

[17] J. Vitek, S. Jagannathan, A. Welc, and A. L. Hosking. A Semantic Framework for Designer Transactions. *Proc. of ESOP'04, LNCS* 2986, pp. 249–263. Springer Verlag, 2004.

DYNAMIC AND LOCAL TYPING FOR MOBILE AMBIENTS

Mario Coppo[1*], Mariangiola Dezani-Ciancaglini[1†], Elio Giovannetti[1‡], and Rosario Pugliese[2§]

[1] *Dip. di Informatica, Univ. di Torino, Corso Svizzera 185, 10149 Torino, Italy*
{coppo,dezani,elio}@di.unito.it

[2] *Dip. di Sistemi e Informatica, Univ. di Firenze, v. Lombroso 6/17, 50134 Firenze, Italy*
pugliese@dsi.unifi.it

Abstract An ambient calculus with both static and dynamic types is presented, where the latter ones represent mobility and access rights that may be dynamically consumed and acquired in a controlled way. Novel constructs and operations are provided to this end. Type-checking is purely local, except for a global hierarchy that establishes which locations have the authority to grant rights to which: there is no global environment (for closed terms) assigning types to names. Each ambient or process move is subject to a double authorization, one static and the other dynamic: static type-checking controls (communication and) "active" mobility rights, i.e., where a given ambient or process has the right to go; dynamic type-checking controls "passive" rights, i.e., which ambients a given ambient may be crossed by and which processes it may receive.

Keywords: Ambient calculi, type systems for security, local type checking, dynamic exchange of rights.

1. Introduction

The ever growing importance, in the last decades, of forms of distributed and mobile computing over wide physical or virtual domains has prompted the design of new theoretical models of computing: in particular, distributed process calculi and ambient calculi, for example [Hennessy and Riely, 2002; Cardelli and Gordon, 2000; Levi and Sangiorgi, 2003; Bugliesi et al., 2004].

* Partially supported by EU FET - Global Computing initiative, project DART IST-2001-33477.
† Partially supported by EU FET - Global Computing initiative, project DART IST-2001-33477.
‡ Partially supported by EU FET - Global Computing initiative, project MIKADO IST-2001-32222.
§ Partially supported by EU FET - Global Computing initiative, project MIKADO IST-2001-32222.

All such models rely on (often sophisticated) type systems for expressing and checking behavioural properties concerning mobility, resource access, security, etc. In most of them, a system or component is represented by a term t of a given calculus, a type T assigned to t, and an environment Γ. In the standard view, as is well-known, the term t abstractly describes the implementation, its type T may express some behavioural properties, and the environment Γ is a set of assumptions on the outside world. Typically, these are assumptions on types of non-local names; there is thus the notion of a global environment, which is the abstract description of situations where all the interacting parties are known in advance to each other, so that static checks performed before execution ensure the correctness of the whole system.

When dealing with distributed and mobile computing in wide-area "open" systems, however, one is often confronted with a scenario where interaction may take place between parties whose respective properties are unknown or only partially known to each other. If stopping the execution for re-checking is to be avoided, each component must dynamically carry with it sufficient behavioural information that can be checked at runtime by the other ones interacting with it. This may correspond to a formal system where, like in the one proposed in [Bugliesi and Castagna, 2002], the typing judgment $\Gamma \vdash_a t{:}T$ is relative to a locality a, and may be "packed" into a new kind of term $a[t]^{\Gamma}_{T}$ that carries at runtime the typing information.

In this paper we address the same problem (of theoretically modelling such kind of scenarios) via a new approach that, though similar in spirit to the one of [Bugliesi and Castagna, 2002] just recalled, is nevertheless different from it in several aspects.

We present a typed ambient calculus where global type assumptions on ambient names are eliminated, and the only global assumptions left are those on the input variables which, owing to their nature, have only a limited scope and do not span the whole system.

Behavioural type assumptions are instead local to each ambient. Thus an ambient type, which in most calculi [Cardelli et al., 2000; Bugliesi and Castagna, 2002; Bugliesi et al., 2004; Coppo et al., 2003; Bugliesi et al., 2003] specifies the behaviour of all ambients with the same name or group and requires cross-reference type controls, is here attached to a single ambient occurrence: ambients with the same name or group, occurring in different parts of a system, can have different types. The absence of static global type information requires the introduction of runtime types, with dynamic controls which test the compatibility between different local assumptions.

Our calculus is based on $\mathbf{M}^3$ [Coppo et al., 2003], a variant of the Calculus of Mobile Ambients (MA) where the open primitive for dissolving ambient boundaries has been removed and its role in enabling component interaction is played by primitives for general process mobility. The new operators were inspired by the go primitive of Dπ [Hennessy and Riely, 2002], but they are tailored to the ambient nested structure, which is richer than the flat structure of Dπ locations.

As a matter of fact, the open primitive of MA has been considered by many researchers as potentially dangerous, because it could be inadvertently or maliciously used to destroy an ambient's individuality (by dissolving its boundary). Several variants of MA have therefore been proposed, which either are equipped with additional constructs for controlling the execution of open, like co-capabilities of Safe Ambients [Levi and Sangiorgi, 2003], or replace it with other mechanisms for interaction between ambients, such as the communication between nested ambients that characterizes Boxed Ambients [Bugliesi et al., 2004]. Process mobility, however, seems to be a more suitable mechanism for modelling code exchange and remote execution.

The rest of the paper is organized as follows. In the next section we describe the main features of our system. In sect. 3 a meaningful example, which illustrates the use of the different constructs of the calculus, is developed at length. In sect. 4 we draw some short conclusions.

Due to space limitation most technical details, like the proof of subject reduction, have been omitted. We refer the interested reader to the full paper [Coppo et al., 2004] for a detailed account. In it we also introduce, along with further examples, a behavioural semantics (i.e., barbed congruence) and some equivalence laws based on it. The soundness of the laws is proved through standard techniques by relying on a higher-order labelled transition system and on a labelled bisimulation (which is proved sound w.r.t. to the behavioural semantics).

2. The typed language and its reduction semantics

The syntax of the pre-terms of the language (where type constraints are ignored) is given in Fig. 1, the one of types in Fig. 2. The precise syntax of the language results from the typing rules given in Definition 3. Processes are built through the usual constructs of sequential action prefixing, parallel composition, and ambient construction. In the following a process of the form $m{:}g(G)[\mathsf{c},\mathsf{e}\|P]$, which corresponds, in our richer calculus, to the term $m[P]$ of standard ambient calculi, will be simply called an ambient, distinct from the mere ambient name m. Communication is only local (and synchronous), as in the original MA [Cardelli and Gordon, 2000]. Actions include the usual in and out primitives for ambient mobility, and the two new primitives down and up for moving processes between ambients; already taken into consideration in [Coppo et al., 2003], they replace the to primitive of $\mathbf{M}^3$.

The down action is analogous to the in action. Its (simplified) reduction rule (see [Coppo et al., 2003]) is: $\mathsf{down}\ m.P \,|\, Q \,|\, m[R] \;\rightarrow\; Q \,|\, m[P \,|\, R]$; i.e., the process $\mathsf{down}\ m.P$ enters an ambient named m where it continues as P. On the contrary, the up action is only partially analogous to out, since its argument is the name of the destination ambient and not that of the source ambient, like in the case of out. The corresponding (simplified) reduction rule is $m[n[\mathsf{up}\ m.P \,|\, R] \,|\, Q] \;\rightarrow\; m[P \,|\, n[R] \,|\, Q]$, also given in [Coppo et al., 2003]. The explicit mention of the target ambient allows more effective controls on the incoming process. In the present setting the four mobility primitives, though keeping their basic behaviours just recalled, come with richer syntactic forms that correspond to more sophisticated reduction rules, as we will see later in the section.

Types describe communication and mobility properties. With reference to an ambient, we distinguish between its active and passive mobility: by the former we intend which ambients the given ambient may cross or send processes to; by the latter, the ambients by which it may be crossed or sent processes. Of course, by directly specifying the active mobility of each ambient one indirectly specifies the passive mobility of all the concerned ambients, and vice versa. One of the main features of our system is

$\mathscr{A}$ denotes the set of *ambient names* and $\mathscr{G}$ denotes the set of *group names*.

α	::=	**ambients**		γ	::=	**groups**	
		$m, n, \ldots$	ambient names			$g, h, \ldots$	group names
		$x, y, \ldots$	variables			$x, y, \ldots$	variables

χ ::= **capabilities**

$\mathsf{in}\ \alpha{:}g$	moves the containing ambient into ambient α of group g
$\mathsf{out}\ \alpha{:}g$	moves the containing ambient out of ambient α of group g
$\mathsf{up}\ \alpha{:}g\ \mathsf{with}\ G$	moves the continuation process out from its ambient up to enclosing ambient α of group g requiring rights G
$\mathsf{down}\ \alpha{:}g\ \mathsf{with}\ G$	moves the continuation process from its ambient down to enclosed ambient α of group g requiring rights G
$\mathsf{add}^{\mathsf{c}}\ \gamma^{\varphi}\ \mathsf{in}\ \alpha{:}g$	adds the crossing right γ with multiplicity φ to ambient α of group g
$\mathsf{add}^{\mathsf{e}}\ \langle\gamma, G\rangle^{\varphi}\ \mathsf{in}\ \alpha{:}g$	adds the entering right $\langle\gamma, G\rangle$ with multiplicity φ to ambient α of group g
$\chi.\chi'$	path
$x, y, \ldots$	variables

M, N, L	::=	**messages**		ρ	::=	**guards**	
		α	ambients			χ	capabilities
		γ	groups			$\langle\overrightarrow{M}\rangle$	synchronous output
		χ	capabilities			$(x{:}\,\overrightarrow{W})$	typed input

P, Q, R ::= **processes**

$\mathbf{0}$	null
$\rho\,.\,P$	prefixing
$P \mid Q$	parallel composition
$\alpha{:}g(G)[\mathsf{c}, \mathsf{e} \| P]$	ambient
$!\,\rho\,.\,P$	guarded replication
$(\nu n)P$	name restriction

where c are multisets of groups, e are multisets of pairs $\langle g, G\rangle$; $\overrightarrow{W}$ and G are defined in Figure 2.

Figure 1. Syntax

		$\mathscr{C}, \mathscr{E}, \ldots$	sets of groups;
G	$::=$	$\mathsf{mc}(\mathscr{C}, \mathscr{E}, T)$	*mobcom* type: mobility rights and communication type
Pro	$::=$	$g(G)$	process type: processes that can stay in ambients of group g with rights G
Cap	$::=$	$g'(G') \rightsquigarrow g(G)$	capabilities that can be consumed by processes of type $g'(G')$ and leave processes of type $g(G)$ as continuations
W	$::=$		message type
		Cap	capability type
		group	group
		amb	ambient type
T	$::=$		communication type
		shh	no communication
		$\overrightarrow{W}$	communication of messages of type $\overrightarrow{W}$
Σ	$::=$	$\varnothing$	context
		$\Sigma, x : W$	

Figure 2. Types

that static types directly specify active mobility while dynamic types directly specify passive mobility, and the compatibility between them is tested by runtime checks.

The type system is based on *ambient groups*: a group is a name that represents (i.e., labels) a set of ambient name occurrences. Different ambient names may belong to the same group, but at the same time different occurrences of the same ambient name may be labelled with different group names, i.e., different ambients with the same name may belong to different groups. The mobility properties directly specified for each ambient are always expressed with reference to groups and not to individual ambients, so as to avoid a dependence of types from values.

In order to enable an ambient to check at runtime (i.e., during reduction) that the active types of the incoming processes are compatible with its own type, the primitives for moving processes between ambients carry with them the communication and mobility types of their continuations.

While local typing allows the control of the active mobility behaviour, the absence of global type information makes impossible a static control of the passive behaviour. This check has therefore also to be performed dynamically; for that reason, at runtime each ambient carries a specification of which (groups of) ambients can cross it and which can send it processes, and how many times.

Thus every mobility action becomes subject to a double authorization, one static and the other dynamic. The fact that "passive" permits are dynamically checked allows them to also be dynamically granted; to this end, we have introduced two new primitives through which a process may enrich the rights of another one thus enabling it to carry out a given task.

Static types and their packing for runtime use

The static type system is centered on the notion of process type, which consist *both* of a group name g *and* of a mobility and communication type (or *mobcom* type for short) G; following the notation of [Cardelli et al., 1999], we write it $g(G)$.

The mobcom type G is of the form $\mathsf{mc}(\mathscr{C}, \mathscr{E}, T)$, where $\mathscr{C}$ is the set of (groups of) ambients into which the process may drive (through an in or out action) its enclosing ambient, $\mathscr{E}$ the set of (groups of) ambients to which it may send (through a down or up action) a continuation process, and T is the process communication type. We use the notation $\mathscr{C}(G)$, $\mathscr{E}(G)$, $T(G)$ to respectively indicate the components $\mathscr{C}$, $\mathscr{E}$, T of G.

Like in most ambient calculi, all the (parallel) processes within an ambient must have the same process type $g(G)$, which is thus a sort of inner type of that ambient and, as we will see, is bound locally to it. Ambient names, on the other hand, only have the atomic type amb, and are therefore omitted in the environments. As a consequence, name restriction may be simply written as $(\nu m)P$. Similarly, group names have the atomic type group. Group names can be exchanged in communications but group variables can only be used in a limited way, as will be remarked later.

Ambient and process mobility actions must specify not only an ambient name, as in MA, but also a group name. For instance, the syntax of the usual in and out primitives becomes $\mathsf{in}\,\alpha{:}g$, $\mathsf{out}\,\alpha{:}g$ (with α ambient name or variable). A process may contain one such action (i.e., it may be well typed) only if its type allows it to drive its enclosing ambient across the boundary of ambients labelled with the group name g. Values exchanged in communications may be ambient names (of type amb), group names (of type group), or capabilities.

A capability type consists, as in [Coppo et al., 2003], of a pair of process types, written here with the notation $g'(G') \leadsto g(G)$. Capability types take into account the fact that, owing to the down or up actions, a process can move from one ambient to another, changing its type accordingly. A capability χ of type $g'(G') \leadsto g(G)$ drives a continuation process P from an ambient of (inner) type $g'(G')$ to an ambient of type $g(G)$. Obviously P must have the type $g(G)$ of the destination ambient while the resulting process $\chi.P$ has the type $g'(G')$ of the source ambient. This is formalized in the rule (PREFIX) of Fig. 3. The type of a sequence of in- or out-capabilities has the form $g(G) \leadsto g(G)$, because in executing in or out actions a process remains in the same ambient.

The meaning of types, informally described in the body of this section, is formally defined by the set of the typing rules shown in Fig. 3.

Dynamic types

Type controls no longer statically performed must of course be done dynamically. To this end, the inner type $g(G)$ of an ambient named m is bound to it with the notation $m{:}g(G)[\ldots]$. An ambient is also characterized by two components c and e that record by which ambient or process groups it may be entered and how many times. The complete notation is $\alpha{:}g(G)[\mathsf{c}, \mathsf{e} \| P]$, with α variable or ambient name.

$$\frac{n \in \mathscr{A}}{\mathcal{O};\Sigma \vdash n : \mathsf{amb}} \text{ (AMB CONST)} \qquad \frac{g \in \mathscr{G}}{\mathcal{O};\Sigma \vdash g : \mathsf{group}} \text{ (GRP CONST)}$$

$$\frac{x : W \in \Sigma}{\mathcal{O};\Sigma \vdash x : W} \text{ (ENV)} \qquad \frac{}{\mathcal{O};\Sigma \vdash 0 : ((g)G)} \text{ (NULL)}$$

$$\frac{\mathcal{O};\Sigma \vdash \alpha : \mathsf{amb} \quad g \in \mathscr{C}(G)}{\mathcal{O};\Sigma \vdash \mathsf{in}\ \alpha{:}g : g'(G) \rightsquigarrow g'(G)} \text{ (IN)} \qquad \frac{\mathcal{O};\Sigma \vdash \alpha : \mathsf{amb} \quad g \in \mathscr{C}(G)}{\mathcal{O};\Sigma \vdash \mathsf{out}\ \alpha{:}g : g'(G) \rightsquigarrow g'(G)} \text{ (OUT)}$$

$$\frac{\mathcal{O};\Sigma \vdash \alpha : \mathsf{amb} \quad g \in \mathscr{E}(G')}{\mathcal{O};\Sigma \vdash \mathsf{down}\ \alpha{:}g\ \mathsf{with}\ G : g'(G') \rightsquigarrow g(G)} \text{ (DOWN)}$$

$$\frac{\mathcal{O};\Sigma \vdash \alpha : \mathsf{amb} \quad g \in \mathscr{E}(G')}{\mathcal{O};\Sigma \vdash \mathsf{up}\ \alpha{:}g\ \mathsf{with}\ G : g'(G') \rightsquigarrow g(G)} \text{ (UP)}$$

$$\frac{\langle g, g' \rangle \in \mathcal{O} \quad \mathcal{O};\Sigma \vdash \alpha : \mathsf{amb} \quad \mathcal{O};\Sigma \vdash \gamma : \mathsf{group}}{\mathcal{O};\Sigma \vdash \mathsf{add}^{\mathsf{c}}\ \gamma^{\varphi}\ \mathsf{in}\ \alpha{:}g : g'(G) \rightsquigarrow g'(G)} \text{ (ADD-C)}$$

$$\frac{\langle g, g' \rangle \in \mathcal{O} \quad \mathcal{O};\Sigma \vdash \alpha : \mathsf{amb} \quad \mathcal{O};\Sigma \vdash \gamma : \mathsf{group}}{\mathcal{O};\Sigma \vdash \mathsf{add}^{\mathsf{e}}\ \langle \gamma, G \rangle^{\varphi}\ \mathsf{in}\ \alpha{:}g : g'(G') \rightsquigarrow g'(G')} \text{ (ADD-E)}$$

$$\frac{\mathcal{O};\Sigma \vdash \chi : g'(G') \rightsquigarrow g''(G'') \quad \mathcal{O};\Sigma \vdash \chi' : g''(G'') \rightsquigarrow g(G)}{\mathcal{O};\Sigma \vdash \chi.\chi' : g'(G') \rightsquigarrow g(G)} \text{ (PATH)}$$

$$\frac{\mathcal{O};\Sigma \vdash \chi : g'(G') \rightsquigarrow g(G) \quad \mathcal{O};\Sigma \vdash P : g(G)}{\mathcal{O};\Sigma \vdash \chi.P : g'(G')} \text{ (PREFIX)}$$

$$\frac{\mathcal{O};\Sigma, \overrightarrow{x : W} \vdash P : g(G) \quad G \equiv \mathsf{mc}(\mathscr{C}, \mathscr{E}, \overrightarrow{W})}{\mathcal{O};\Sigma \vdash (\overrightarrow{x : W}).P : g(G)} \text{ (INPUT)}$$

$$\frac{\mathcal{O};\Sigma \vdash P : g(G) \quad \mathcal{O};\Sigma \vdash \overrightarrow{M} : \overrightarrow{W} \quad G \equiv \mathsf{mc}(\mathscr{C}, \mathscr{E}, \overrightarrow{W})}{\mathcal{O};\Sigma \vdash \langle \overrightarrow{M} \rangle.P : g(G)} \text{ (OUTPUT)}$$

$$\frac{\mathcal{O};\Sigma \vdash \alpha : \mathsf{amb} \quad \mathcal{O};\Sigma \vdash P : g(G) \quad \langle g'', G'' \rangle \in \mathsf{e} \implies G'' \leq G}{\mathcal{O};\Sigma \vdash \alpha{:}g(G)[\mathsf{c}, \mathsf{e} \| P] : g'(G')} \text{ (AMB)}$$

$$\frac{\mathcal{O};\Sigma \vdash P : g(G) \quad \mathcal{O};\Sigma \vdash Q : g(G)}{\mathcal{O};\Sigma \vdash P \mid Q : g(G)} \text{ (PAR)} \qquad \frac{\mathcal{O};\Sigma \vdash \rho.P : g(G)}{\mathcal{O};\Sigma \vdash !\,\rho.P : g(G)} \text{ (REPL)}$$

$$\frac{\mathcal{O};\Sigma \vdash P : g(G)}{\mathcal{O};\Sigma \vdash (\nu n)P : g(G)} \text{ (AMB RES)}$$

Figure 3. Typing rules

More precisely, in a given ambient the component c is the multiset of groups of ambients that are allowed to cross its external boundary, while e is the multiset of groups of ambients that are allowed to send processes to it. In e each element is actually a pair $\langle g, G\rangle$ consisting of a group and a mobcom type; its meaning is that a process coming from an ambient of group g is given the entrance permit if it respects the behavioural constraints specified by the type G. In an ambient $m{:}g_m(G_m)[\mathsf{c}, \mathsf{e} \| P]$ all the pairs $\langle g, G\rangle$ occurring in e must therefore be such that G is a subtype of G_m.

Each execution of an in or out action consumes one element of c and each execution of a down or up action consumes one element of e, with the exception of *starred* elements, which represent permanent permits, i.e., elements with infinite multiplicity. The control of the mobility constraints represented by c and e is performed dynamically during process reduction. A reduction rule cannot fire if the corresponding side conditions on c and e are not satisfied.

In the following we give the formal definition of a multiset with possibly infinite multiplicities, and we define the operations of addition and removal of elements.

DEFINITION 1

- *A multiset over a set of elements S is a function from S to the set of multiplicities $\omega \cup \{*\}$ (ranged over by f); $\omega \cup \{*\}$ is the set of natural numbers ω extended with the extra element $*$ denoting the infinity;*
- *If f is a multi-set on S, $s, r \in S$, $\varphi \in \omega \cup \{*\}$ we define:*
  - $s \in f$ *iff* $f(s) \neq 0$;
  - $(f \cup s^{\varphi})(r) = \begin{cases} f(s) + \varphi & \text{if } r = s, \\ f(r) & \text{otherwise.} \end{cases}$
  - $(f \downarrow s)(r) = \begin{cases} f(s) - 1 & \text{if } r = s, \\ f(r) & \text{otherwise.} \end{cases}$

  where $* \pm \varphi = *$.

A partial order on mobcom types is naturally defined via set inclusion, and so is the notion of glb of mobcom types. Communication subtyping is characterized only by the fact that shh is smaller than any other communication type.

DEFINITION 2

- $T \leq T'$ *if either* $T = \mathsf{shh}$ *or* $T = T'$.
- $\mathsf{mc}(\mathscr{C}, \mathscr{E}, T) \leq \mathsf{mc}(\mathscr{C}', \mathscr{E}', T')$ *if* $\mathscr{C} \subseteq \mathscr{C}'$ *and* $\mathscr{E} \subseteq \mathscr{E}'$ *and* $T \leq T'$.
- $T \sqcap T' = \begin{cases} \mathsf{shh} & \text{if } T = \mathsf{shh} \text{ or } T' = \mathsf{shh} \\ T & \text{if } T = T' \\ \text{undefined} & \text{otherwise} \end{cases}$
- $\mathsf{mc}(\mathscr{C}, \mathscr{E}, T) \sqcap \mathsf{mc}(\mathscr{C}', \mathscr{E}', T') = \mathsf{mc}(\mathscr{C} \cap \mathscr{C}', \mathscr{E} \cap \mathscr{E}', T \sqcap T')$
  if $T \sqcap T'$ *is defined and is undefined otherwise.*

The elements of c and e are similar to the co-capabilities of Safe Ambients [Levi and Sangiorgi, 2003], with starred elements corresponding to banged co-capabilities.

Dynamic modification of mobility rights

The components c and e of an ambient process may allow or forbid movements at runtime; they can therefore be changed dynamically without breaking the subject reduction. As a matter of fact, this is achieved:

- by automatically removing a (consumable) permit when a movement action is performed;
- by adding to c or to e an element with a multiplicity, by means of one of the two newly introduced permit-adding primitives add^c and add^e.

Action $\mathsf{add}^c\ g^{\varphi}$ in $m{:}g_m$ dynamically adds the group g with multiplicity φ to the c component of a local ambient named m of group g_m (see the reduction rule (R-add^c)); as usual, by "local ambient" we intend one that is found in the same enclosing ambient. Action $\mathsf{add}^e\ \langle g, G_1\rangle^{\varphi}$ in $m{:}g_m$ dynamically adds the group/type pair $\langle g, G_1\rangle$ with multiplicity φ to the e component of a local ambient m (rule (R-add^e)). In a term $m{:}g_m(G_m)[\mathsf{c},\mathsf{e}\|P]$ all mobcom types occurring in e are subtypes of G_m. This property is preserved by the reduction rule (R-add^e) since the $\mathsf{add}^e\ \langle g, G_1\rangle^{\varphi}$ in $m{:}g_m$ action can be performed only if $G_1 \sqcap G_m$ is defined.

A process may perform a permit-adding operation on an ambient only if its group is higher than the target's group in a global administrative hierarchy, represented by a partial order relation $\mathcal{O}$ over group names. Such hierarchy is the only global environment of our calculus; it might be thought of as some general (not necessarily centralized) coordination and administration structure of the network. The typing rules (ADD-C), (ADD-E) assure that this hierarchy is always respected.

Mobility actions and dynamic type-checking

Process mobility actions must specify, in addition to the ambient and group name of the destination, the mobcom type G of the continuation process (i.e., of the process that will run within the target ambient). The complete syntax of the down action is down $m{:}g_m$ with G, that of up is similar. Of course, the type G needs to be compatible (via subtyping) with the mobcom type G_m of the destination ambient. More precisely, if a process down $m{:}g_m$ with G' . P is of group g (i.e., is typed with a type $g(G)$) the e component of the target ambient m must contain the group g paired with a type G'' such that $G' \leq G''$. The typing rule (AMB), along with the reduction rule (R-add^e), ensures that $G'' \leq G_m$ and so $G' \leq G'' \leq G_m$. Hence, the migrating process P is guaranteed not to require more rights than those specified by the inner type $g_m(G_m)$ of the destination ambient, which was statically checked.

Reduction rules are thus dependent on the typing assumptions and the reduction relation is labelled with the process type $g(G)$, even though the group name g is only involved in the (R-down) rule and the type G never plays any role in reduction. In fact reduction rules are only defined for well typed terms, i.e., for processes that are typed with some type $g(G)$. The complete set of rules is given in Fig. 4.

A basic property of the system is that typing is preserved by $\leq$ on mobcom types.

LEMMA 3 *If* $\mathcal{O};\Sigma \vdash P : g(G)$ *and* $G \leq G'$ *then* $\mathcal{O};\Sigma \vdash P : g(G')$

Basic reduction rules:

(R-in) $n{:}g_n(G_n)[\mathsf{c}_n, \mathsf{e}_n \| \text{in } m{:}g_m \,.\, P \mid Q] \mid m{:}g_m(G_m)[\mathsf{c}_m, \mathsf{e}_m \| R]$
$\rightarrow_{g,G}\ m{:}g_m(G_m)[\mathsf{c}_m \downarrow g_n, \mathsf{e}_m \| \, n{:}g_n(G_n)[\mathsf{c}_n, \mathsf{e}_n \| P \mid Q] \mid R]$
if $g_n \in \mathsf{c}_m$

(R-out) $m{:}g_m(G_m)[\mathsf{c}_m, \mathsf{e}_m \| \, n{:}g_n(G_n)[\mathsf{c}_n, \mathsf{e}_n \| \text{out } m{:}g_m \,.\, P \mid Q] \mid R]$
$\rightarrow_{g,G}\ n{:}g_n(G_n)[\mathsf{c}_n, \mathsf{e}_n \| P \mid Q] \mid m{:}g_m(G_m)[\mathsf{c}_m \downarrow g_n, \mathsf{e}_m \| R]$
if $g_n \in \mathsf{c}_m$

(R-down) $\text{down } m{:}g_m \text{ with } G' \,.\, P \mid m{:}g_m(G_m)[\mathsf{c}_m, \mathsf{e}_m \| Q]$
$\rightarrow_{g,G}\ m{:}g_m(G_m)[\mathsf{c}_m, \mathsf{e}_m \downarrow \langle g, G'' \rangle \| P \mid Q]$
if $\langle g, G'' \rangle \in \mathsf{e}_m \;\&\; G' \leq G''$

(R-up) $m{:}g_m(G_m)[\mathsf{c}_m, \mathsf{e}_m \| n{:}g_n(G_n)[\mathsf{c}_n, \mathsf{e}_n \| \text{up } m{:}g_m \text{ with } G' \,.\, P \mid R] \mid Q]$
$\rightarrow_{g,G}\ m{:}g_m(G_m)[\mathsf{c}_m, \mathsf{e}_m \downarrow \langle g_n, G'' \rangle \| n{:}g_n(G_n)[\mathsf{c}_n, \mathsf{e}_n \| R] \mid Q \mid P]$
if $\langle g_n, G'' \rangle \in \mathsf{e}_m \;\&\; G' \leq G''$

(R-add^{c}) $\text{add}^{\mathsf{c}}\ g'^{\varphi} \text{ in } m{:}g_m \,.\, P \mid m{:}g_m(G_m)[\mathsf{c}_m, \mathsf{e}_m \| R]$
$\rightarrow_{g,G}\ P \mid m{:}g_m(G_m)[\mathsf{c}_m \cup g'^{\varphi}, \mathsf{e}_m \| R]$

(R-add^{e}) $\text{add}^{\mathsf{e}}\ \langle g', G' \rangle^{\varphi} \text{ in } m{:}g_m \,.\, P \mid m{:}g_m(G_m)[\mathsf{c}_m, \mathsf{e}_m \| R]$
$\rightarrow_{g,G}\ P \mid m{:}g_m(G_m)[\mathsf{c}_m, \mathsf{e}_m \cup \langle g', G' \sqcap G_m \rangle^{\varphi} \| R]$
if $G' \sqcap G_m$ is defined

(R-comm) $(\overrightarrow{x{:}\,W}) \,.\, P \mid \langle \overrightarrow{M} \rangle \,.\, Q \ \rightarrow_{g,G}\ P\{\vec{x} := \overrightarrow{M}\} \mid Q$

Structural reduction rules:

(R-par) $P \rightarrow_{g,G} Q \quad \Rightarrow \quad P \mid R \rightarrow_{g,G} Q \mid R$

(R-amb) $P \rightarrow_{g,G} Q \quad \Rightarrow \quad n{:}g(G)[\mathsf{c}, \mathsf{e} \| P] \rightarrow_{g',G'} n{:}g(G)[\mathsf{c}, \mathsf{e} \| Q]$

(R-≡) $P' \equiv P',\ P \rightarrow_{g,G} Q,\ Q \equiv Q' \quad \Rightarrow \quad P' \rightarrow_{g,G} Q'$

(R-ν) $P \rightarrow_{g,G} Q \quad \Rightarrow \quad (\nu n)P \rightarrow_{g,G} (\nu n)Q$

Structural Congruence: $(\,|\,, 0)$ is a commutative monoid.

$$(\nu n)(P \mid Q) \equiv (\nu n)P \mid Q \quad (n \notin \text{fn}(Q)) \qquad (\nu n)(\nu m)P \equiv (\nu m)(\nu n)P$$

$$n{:}g(G)[\mathsf{c}, \mathsf{e} \| (\nu m)P] \equiv (\nu m)n{:}g(G)[\mathsf{c}, \mathsf{e} \| P] \quad (n \neq m) \qquad !P \equiv P \mid !P$$

Figure 4. Reduction

Using Lemma 3 a property of subject reduction, which ensures that static typing is preserved by computation, can be proved with standard techniques.

THEOREM 4 (SUBJECT REDUCTION) *If* $\mathcal{O};\Sigma \vdash P : g(G)$ *and* $P \rightarrow_{g,G} Q$ *then* $\mathcal{O};\Sigma \vdash Q : g(G)$.

Finally, observe that group variables may only occur as first arguments of $\mathsf{add}^{\mathsf{c}}$ and $\mathsf{add}^{\mathsf{e}}$, so that they never occur in G or within the c and e components, since otherwise their role in allowing a safe name restriction would be defeated.

3. An example

Our main example is the modelling of a public transportation system, the *train* introduced by [Cardelli, 1999] as a nice pictorial illustration of the issues related to the control of mobility.

We want to represent a railway network connecting a set of different places (e.g., cities) in the world. Trains move between stations, travellers may get into and off trains only at stations and cannot drive them (no hijacking possible). The number of passengers in a train at any given instant cannot exceed the number of seats; a passenger takes a seat on boarding and releases it on getting off. Each train has a fixed route.

For the sake of simplicity, we assume that:

- There is a top-level untrusted ambient *world*, which includes stations, travellers, and some other unspecified process R (e.g., other means of transport); it has group and mobcom type $g_w(G_w)$, but no assumption can be made on G_w. Also, c_{world}, e_{world} and R are unknown.

- In our intended representation different stations should be found within different cities or localities, and moving from one city to another would only be possible by train. The presence of cities would however increase the size of the example in a trivial manner, without providing more insights; we therefore place stations directly within *world*, although in this way travellers appear to use a train to end up in the same ambient *world* where they started from.

- There are only two stations *stA* and *stB*, and one train TRAIN commuting between them. Initially, the train is within *stA*.

Stations and trains are represented by ambient processes; travellers are represented by simple processes; the number of free seats in a train is represented by the multiplicity of the right to get into the train.

Stations are ambients $stA{:}g_{st}(G_{st})[\ldots]$ and $stB{:}g_{st}(G_{st})[\ldots]$, of group g_{st} and mobcom type G_{st}. They are immobile, and can have travellers both going down into the trains or up into the world; they can be crossed by trains, and can receive travellers both from train and from the outside world. Correspondingly:

$$G_{st} = \mathsf{mc}(\varnothing, \{g_{tr}, g_w\}, \mathsf{shh}) \quad \mathsf{c}_{st} = \{g_{tr}^{*}\} \quad \mathsf{e}_{st} = \{\langle g_{tr}, G_{to}\rangle^{*}, \langle g_w, G_{from}\rangle^{*}\}$$

where $G_{from} = \mathsf{mc}(\varnothing, \{g_{tr}\}, \mathsf{shh})$ and $G_{to} = \mathsf{mc}(\varnothing, \{g_w\}, \mathsf{shh})$. Note that $G_{from} \leq G_{st}$ and $G_{to} \leq G_{st}$, i.e., both G_{from} and G_{to}, which represent two accepted behaviours for processes entering the station, are compatible with G_{st}, as is required by the typing rule (AMB).

The train is an ambient of group g_{tr}, which can cross stations and world, send traveller processes into stations, and receive a maximum number n of passengers from stations, provided they behave as good passengers (and not, for example, as drivers):

$$\text{TRAIN} \triangleq tr{:}g_{tr}(G_{tr})[\mathsf{c}_{tr}, \mathsf{e}_{tr} \| \,!\,\mathsf{out}\; stA{:}g_{st} \,.\, \mathsf{in}\; stB{:}g_{st} \,.\, \mathsf{out}\; stB{:}g_{st} \,.\, \mathsf{in}\; stA{:}g_{st}]$$
$$\text{where } G_{tr} = \mathsf{mc}(\{g_{st}\}, \{g_{st}\}, \mathsf{shh}) \quad \mathsf{c}_{tr} = \varnothing \quad \mathsf{e}_{tr} = \{\langle g_{st}, G_{psng}\rangle^{\mathsf{n}}\}$$
$$\text{with } G_{psng} = \mathsf{mc}(\varnothing, \{g_{st}\}, \mathsf{shh})$$

A traveller is represented by a parametric process TRAVELLER(src, dst) which from some unspecified place in the world enters the station src to become a passenger of a train that takes it to the station dst:

$$\text{TRAVELLER}(src, dst) \triangleq \mathsf{down}\; src{:}g_{st} \text{ with } G_{from} \,.\, \text{PSNG}$$
$$\text{where PSNG} \triangleq \mathsf{down}\; tr{:}g_{tr} \text{ with } G_{psng} \,.\, \mathsf{up}\; dst{:}g_{st} \text{ with } G_{to}$$
$$.\, \mathsf{add}^{\mathsf{e}}\, \langle g_{st}, G_{psng}\rangle \text{ in } tr : g_{tr} \,.\, \mathsf{up}\; world{:}g_w \text{ with } G_w \,.\, \mathrm{P}$$

The mobcom types G_{from} and G_{to} specify the behaviours of a passenger respectively in the departure station, going to board a train, and in the arrival station, going to exit the station into the outside world or city.

The initial configuration is:

$$(\nu\; stA, stB) world{:}g_w(G_w)[\mathsf{c}_w, \mathsf{e}_w \| R \mid \text{TRVLRS}(stA, stB)$$
$$\mid stA{:}g_{st}(G_{st})[\mathsf{c}_{st}, \mathsf{e}_{st} \| \text{TRAIN}] \mid stB{:}g_{st}(G_{st})[\mathsf{c}_{st}, \mathsf{e}_{st} \| 0]$$
$$\mid \text{TRVLRS}(stB, stA)\,]$$

where TRVLRS(src, dst) is a parallel composition of processes TRAVELLER.

Our specification satisfies many properties of interest; some of them immediately follow from the definitions. For instance, from the definition of e_{tr} it follows that no traveller can get into the train tr when this is outside a station: any action to such purpose from a process in *world* will be dynamically blocked. Also, by the definition of e_{tr} and of the PSNG process[1] it follows that at most n PSNG processes can be within the train tr at the same time.

A *bad* passenger willing to get off the train when this is not in a station, though it maybe statically well typed, is dynamically not allowed to do so. Suppose the bad passenger be represented by the process

$$\text{BADPSNG} \triangleq \mathsf{down}\; tr{:}g_{tr} \text{ with } G_{bad} \,.\, \mathsf{up}\; world{:}g_w \text{ with } G_w \,.\, \text{BP}$$

By assuming $\mathcal{O}; \Sigma \vdash \text{BP} : g_w(G_w)$ one may derive the typing

$$\mathcal{O}; \Sigma \vdash \mathsf{up}\; world{:}g_w \text{ with } G_w \,.\, \text{BP} : g_{tr}(G_{bad}) \;\text{ with } G_{bad} \triangleq \mathsf{mc}(\varnothing, \{g_w\}, \mathsf{shh})$$

Observe that the process type $g_{tr}(G_{bad})$ characterizes a process that might stay within the train and go from it directly into the world. From the above we may infer the typing $\mathcal{O}; \Sigma \vdash$ BADPSNG : $g_{st}(G_{st})$, since for that it is enough that G_{st} allows the process to get into the train, i.e., $g_{tr} \in \mathcal{E}(G_{st})$.

[1]The present specification does not prevent a passenger to add more than one pair to e_{tr}.

The process BADPSNG is therefore statically allowed to stay within a station, as for example in the well-typed term $stA : g_{st}(G_{st})[\mathsf{c}_{st}, \mathsf{e}_{st} \| \text{BADPSNG} \mid \text{TRAIN}]$. Nevertheless, when trying at runtime to get into the train, the process is blocked because $\mathsf{e}_{tr} = \{\langle g_{st}, G_{psng}\rangle^{n}\}$ (with $G_{psng} \leq G_{tr}$). As a matter of fact, for the action down $tr{:}g_{tr}$ with G_{bad} to fire, it is required that $G_{bad} \leq G_{psng}$, which is not the case since $G_{bad} = \mathsf{mc}(\varnothing, \{g_w\}, \mathsf{shh})$ while $G_{psng} = \mathsf{mc}(\varnothing, \{g_{st}\}, \mathsf{shh})$: G_{bad} allows going into the world while G_{psng} does not.

This should have been somehow expected, because in our calculus the dynamic checks performed by an ambient are assigned the task of controlling that mobile processes willing to get in do respect some fixed policies expressed through types and, if this is not the case, of preventing them from getting in. Notice that all the previous properties are guaranteed by only exploiting in the operational semantics information local to the involved processes/ambients.

A similar scenario has already been modelled in [Cardelli, 1999; Ferrari et al., 2002]. In both cases, the mobility control is implemented by informing the passenger when the train has reached the station at which he wants to get off. More specifically, in [Cardelli, 1999] a new primitive for *ambient renaming* is exploited. Intuitively, the train ambient takes a suitable name to implicitly inform the passengers when it has arrived at a certain station, while it takes a name unknown to passengers when it is moving (in this way passengers cannot get in or off the train). In [Ferrari et al., 2002] a suitable ambient called *announcement* is generated by the train when it arrives at a station. This ambient informs the passengers of the arrival at a certain station.

4. Conclusions

The calculus we presented is a first attempt to model the interplay of static and dynamic type-checking when handling the security requirements of global computing applications. In particular, the packing of a mobility and communication type within a mobile process and its subsequent check at destination may be considered as an abstract modelling of the proof-carrying code approach.

Due to the absence of static ambient types (apart from the atomic type amb), static typing rules may be easily translated into a simple type inference algorithm that, given a term in whose body all the mobcom types are left unspecified, reconstructs the minimal such type allowing the term to be well typed. The algorithm will merely build a type by recording the capabilities occurring in the term. The groups assigned to ambient occurrences, on the other hand, as well as the dynamic components c and e, define the policy and the mobility constraints established by the designer of the application, and cannot be sensibly inferred.

A still unsatisfactory aspect of our model is that the authority (specified by the partial order $\mathcal{O}$) granting dynamic rights to ambients is a too coarse-grain notion: either an ambient is authorized to grant a right with any (even infinite) multiplicity, or the ambient may grant none. It would be useful that this authority could have different degrees, related to maximal multiplicities of granted rights. As noticed by one referee, another useful extension would be the introduction of a primitive for group restriction as in [Cardelli et al., 2000; Coppo et al., 2003]. This could provide protection from external untrusted agents, but the interaction with the partial order $\mathcal{O}$ representing the administrative hierarchy requires a careful handling. A modification of the calculus in this sense, along with a possible increasing of the expressivity of types, is currently under investigation.

Acknowledgements We gratefully acknowledge the anonymous referees for careful reading and useful suggestions.

References

Bugliesi, Michele and Castagna, Giuseppe (2002). Behavioral typing for Safe Ambients. *Computer Languages*, 28(1):61 – 99.

Bugliesi, Michele, Castagna, Giuseppe, and Crafa, Silvia (2004). Access control for mobile agents: The calculus of boxed ambients. *ACM Transactions on Programming Languages and Systems*, 26(1):57–124.

Bugliesi, Michele, Crafa, Silvia, Merro, Massimo, and Sassone, Vladimiro (2003). Communication and Mobility Control in Boxed Ambients. To appear in *Information and Computation*. Extended and revised version of M. Bugliesi, S. Crafa, M. Merro, and V. Sassone. Communication Interference in Mobile Boxed Ambients. In FSTTCS'02, volume 2556 of LNCS, pages 71-84. Springer-Verlag, 2002.

Cardelli, Luca (1999). Abstractions for mobile computation. In Vitek, Jan and Jensen, Christian, editors, *Secure Internet Programming: Security Issues for Mobile and Distributed Objects*, volume 1603 of *LNCS*, pages 51–94. Springer-Verlag.

Cardelli, Luca, Ghelli, Giorgio, and Gordon, Andrew D. (1999). Mobility types for mobile ambients. In Wiedermann, Jiri, van Emde Boas, Peter, and Nielsen, Mogens, editors, *ICALP'99*, volume 1644 of *LNCS*, pages 230–239. Springer-Verlag.

Cardelli, Luca, Ghelli, Giorgio, and Gordon, Andrew D. (2000). Ambient groups and mobility types. In van Leeuwen, Jan, Watanabe, Osamu, Hagiya, Masami, and Peter D. Mosses, Takayasu Ito, editors, *International Conference IFIP TCS 2000*, volume 1872 of *LNCS*, pages 333–347. Springer-Verlag. Extended version to appear in Information and Computation, special issue on TCS'2000.

Cardelli, Luca and Gordon, Andrew D. (2000). Mobile ambients. *Theoretical Computer Science*, 240(1):177–213. Special Issue on Coordination, Daniel Le Métayer Editor.

Coppo, Mario, Dezani-Ciancaglini, Mariangiola, Giovannetti, Elio, and Pugliese, Rosario (2004). Dynamic and local typing for mobile ambients. Research report, Dipartimento di Sistemi e Informatica, Università di Firenze. Available at `http://www.dsi.unifi.it/~pugliese /DOWNLOAD/dltma-full.pdf`.

Coppo, Mario, Dezani-Ciancaglini, Mariangiola, Giovannetti, Elio, and Salvo, Ivano (2003). M3: Mobility types for mobile processes in mobile ambients. In Harland, James, editor, *CATS 2003*, volume 78 of *ENTCS*. Elsevier.

Ferrari, Gianluigi, Moggi, Eugenio, and Pugliese, Rosario (2002). Guardians for ambient-based monitoring. In Sassone, Vladimiro, editor, *F-WAN*, volume 66 of *ENTCS*. Elsevier.

Hennessy, Mattew and Riely, James (2002). Resource Access Control in Systems of Mobile Agents. *Information and Computation*, 173:82–120.

Levi, Francesca and Sangiorgi, Davide (2003). Controlling interference in Ambients. *Transactions on Programming Languages and Systems*, 25(1):1–69.

POLYA: TRUE TYPE POLYMORPHISM FOR MOBILE AMBIENTS

Torben Amtoft[†]
Kansas State University

Henning Makholm
Heriot-Watt University

J. B. Wells
Heriot-Watt University

Abstract Previous type systems for mobility calculi (the original Mobile Ambients, its variants and descendants, e.g., Boxed Ambients and Safe Ambients, and other related systems) offer little support for generic mobile agents. Previous systems either do not handle communication at all or globally assign fixed communication types to ambient names that do not change as an ambient moves around or interacts with other ambients. This makes it hard to type examples such as a messenger ambient that uses communication primitives to collect a message of non-predetermined type and deliver it to a non-predetermined destination.

In contrast, we present our new type system PolyA. Instead of assigning communication types to ambient names, PolyA assigns a type to each process P that gives upper bounds on (1) the possible ambient nesting shapes of any process P' to which P can evolve, (2) the values that may be communicated at each location, and (3) the capabilities that can be used at each location. Because PolyA can type generic mobile agents, we believe PolyA is the first type system for a mobility calculus that provides type polymorphism comparable in power to polymorphic type systems for the λ-calculus. PolyA is easily extended to ambient calculus variants. A restriction of PolyA has principal typings.

1 Introduction

Whereas the π-calculus [15] is probably the most widely known calculus for communicating processes, the ambient calculus [6] has recently become important, because it adds reasoning about locations and mobility. In the ambient calculus, pro-

---

*Partially supported by EC FP5 grant IST-2001-33477, EPSRC grant GR/R41545/01, NSF grants 9806745 (EIA), 9988529 (CCR), and 0113193 (ITR), and Sun Microsystems equipment grant EDUD-7826-990410-US.

[†]Much of the work was done while Amtoft was at Heriot-Watt University paid by EC FP5 grant IST-2001-33477.

cesses are located in *ambients*, locations which can be nested, forming a tree. Ambients can move, making the tree dynamic. Furthermore, only processes that are "close" to each other can exchange values.

1.1 The problem with ambient calculus type systems

Consider this process:

$$\mathtt{m}[\mathsf{in}\ \mathtt{s}.0 \mid \mathsf{open}\ \mathtt{t}.(\mathtt{p},\mathtt{v}).\mathtt{p}.\langle \mathtt{v}\rangle.0] \mid \mathtt{s}[\mathtt{t}[\mathsf{in}\ \mathtt{m}.\langle \mathsf{in}\ \mathtt{r},\mathtt{d}\rangle.0] \mid \mathtt{r}[\mathsf{open}\ \mathtt{m}.(\mathtt{v}).\mathsf{out}\ \mathtt{v}.0]]$$

The example ambient named m is perhaps the simplest kind of *generic mobile agent*, namely a *messenger*. That is, m first goes somewhere looking for messages to deliver, then m collects a destination and a payload, and then m goes to that destination and delivers that payload.

Nearly all type systems for ambient calculi follow the example of the seminal system of Cardelli and Gordon [7] and assign to each ambient name a a description of the communication that can happen within ambients named a. Unfortunately, type systems based on this principle are inflexible about generic functionality. Consider the example process extended to have *two* possible execution paths, in that m can enter either of two senders:

$$\begin{array}{lll} & \mathtt{m}[\mathsf{in}\ \mathtt{s}.0 \mid \mathsf{open}\ \mathtt{t}.(\mathtt{p},\mathtt{v}).\mathtt{p}.\langle \mathtt{v}\rangle.0] & \\ \mid & \mathtt{s}[\mathtt{t}[\mathsf{in}\ \mathtt{m}.\langle \mathsf{in}\ \mathtt{r},\mathtt{d}\rangle.0] \mid \mathtt{r}[\mathsf{open}\ \mathtt{m}.(\mathtt{v}).\mathsf{out}\ \mathtt{v}.0]] & (\mathtt{v}\ \textit{must be a name}) \\ \mid & \mathtt{s}[\mathtt{t}[\mathsf{in}\ \mathtt{m}.\langle \mathsf{in}\ \mathtt{q},\mathsf{out}\ \mathtt{d}\rangle.0] \mid \mathtt{q}[\mathsf{open}\ \mathtt{m}.(\mathtt{v}).\mathtt{v}.0]] & (\mathtt{v}\ \textit{must be a capability}) \end{array}$$

Here, the messenger m must be able to deliver two different types of payloads, *both* an ambient name *and* a capability. None of the previous type systems for ambient calculi allow this. In general, the previous type systems do not support the possibility that a mobile agent may carry non-predetermined types of data from location to location and deliver this data using communication primitives.

In previous type systems for ambient calculi, generic mobile agents can be encoded by using extra ambient wrappers, one for each type of data to be delivered. However, this encoding is awkward and also loses the ability to predict whether the correct type of data is being delivered to each location, avoiding stuck states.

In solving this problem, a key observation is that the possible communication within m depends on which of the s's the ambient m is found inside.

1.2 Our solution – overview

To overcome the weaknesses of previous type systems for generic functionality, we present a new type system, PolyA. Types indicate the possible positions of capabilities, inputs, and outputs, and also represent upper bounds on the possible ambient nesting tree into which a process can evolve. Thus they look much like processes, as is also the case, e.g., for the types of [9].

Our type system's basic concept is the *shape predicate*. The actual definition is somewhat involved, partly due to the need of handling communication, so let us introduce the concept gently with a toy system where the only capability is "in":

$$\text{Toy shape predicates: } \sigma \ ::= \ 0 \quad (\sigma \mid \sigma) \quad a[\sigma] \quad \mathsf{in}\ a$$

A shape predicate's meaning is a set of terms, given by this matching relation:

$$\frac{\vdash P : \sigma}{\vdash a[P] : (\cdots \mid a[\sigma] \mid \cdots)} \qquad \frac{\vdash P : \sigma \quad \vdash Q : \sigma}{\vdash P \mid Q : \sigma}$$

$$\frac{}{\vdash \mathsf{in}\ a.0 : (\cdots \mid \mathsf{in}\ a \mid \cdots)} \qquad \frac{}{\vdash 0 : \sigma}$$

With these rules we can derive the judgement $\vdash P_0 : \sigma_0$, where

$$P_0 = \mathsf{a[in\ b.0 \mid in\ c.0] \mid b[d[in\ a.0]] \mid c[e[in\ a.0]]}$$
$$\sigma_0 = \mathsf{a[in\ b \mid in\ c] \mid b[d[in\ a]] \mid c[e[in\ a]]}$$

But we can also derive, say,

$$\vdash \mathsf{a[in\ b.0] \mid a[in\ c.0]} : \sigma_0$$

— the matching rules do not care that the b and c on the top level are missing, nor that the a[in b | in c] part of the shape predicate is used twice.

PolyA *types* are shape predicates such that the set of terms matching a type is closed under reduction. The shape predicate σ_0 above is not a type, because

$$P_0 \hookrightarrow P_1 = \mathsf{b[a[in\ c.0] \mid d[in\ a.0]] \mid c[\cdots]}$$

yet $\not\vdash P_1 : \sigma_0$. One type that P_0 does have is

$$\sigma_1 = \mathsf{a[in\ b \mid in\ c] \mid b[a[in\ b \mid in\ c \mid d[in\ a]] \mid d[in\ a]]}$$
$$\mathsf{\mid c[a[in\ b \mid in\ c \mid e[in\ a]] \mid e[in\ a]]}$$

The a[⋯] predicate inside b still allows the in b. This must be so because shape predicates do not care about the number of identical items (unlike what is the case in [19]), so one of the terms matched by σ_1 is a[in b.0 | in b.0] | b[0], which reduces to b[a[in b]].

A more subtle point about σ_1 is that it *disallows* having an e inside an a inside a b, or a d inside an a inside a c. This example therefore illustrates the most basic kind of polymorphism possible: The same initial a ambient can evolve differently in different possible futures, and the type system can prove that those different futures do not interfere with each other.

PolyA lets any supertype (i.e., a type that is matched by a larger set of terms) be used as a *polymorphic variant* if it appears in the right place of the overall typing. The overall typing contains all of the polymorphic variants that will ever be needed for each ambient in the particular context it is being typed in.

Some readers might think that this does not *look* like type polymorphism, because the various types for a are not substitution instances of a *parameterised* type. However, how one technically expresses the relation between the type for some generic code and the types for its concrete uses is not essential to the concept of genericity or polymorphism. What is important is that the type system supports reasoning about distinct uses of the same generic code. We achieve what Cardelli and Wegner [8] called "the purest form of polymorphism: the same object or function can be used uniformly in different type context without changes, coercions or any kind of run-time tests or special encodings of representations".

PolyA can optionally track the sequencing of actions, a possibility pioneered by Amtoft et al. [1, 2]. For example, a[in b.in c.0] | b[c[0]] | c[open a.0] has a PolyA type proving that a will never be opened.

PolyA can assign the following type to the example containing the generic messenger and two clients:

```
letrec Xm8 = in s.0 | open t.(p,v).p.⟨{v}⟩.0
in m[Xm8]
 | s[letrec Xm7 = (Xm8) | (Xt3) | ⟨{d}⟩.0 | (p,v).p.⟨{v}⟩.0
                | in r.⟨{d}⟩.0 | m[Xm7] | r[Xr1] | t[Xt3]
           Xr1= (Xm7) | (v).out v.0 | out d.0 | open m.(v).out v.0
           Xt3= ⟨<in r>,{d}⟩.0 | in m.⟨<in r>,{d}⟩.0
     in m[Xm7] | r[Xr1] | t[in m.⟨<in r>,{d}⟩.0] end]
 | s[letrec Xm3 = (Xm8) | (Xt1) | ⟨<out d>⟩.0 | (p,v).p.⟨{v}⟩.0
                | in q.⟨<out d>⟩.0 | m[Xm3] | q[Xq1] | t[Xt1]
           Xq1= (Xm3) | (v).v.0 | out d.0 | open m.(v).v.0
           Xt1= ⟨<in q>,<out d>⟩.0 | in m.⟨<in q>,<out d>⟩.0
     in m[Xm3] | q[Xq1] | t[in m.⟨<in q>,<out d>⟩.0] end]
end
```

This type proves that the example process has only well defined behaviour, something which no previous type system for ambients can do. The type may appear complex compared to the term it types. This is partly because we constructed it with the help of a type inference algorithm [14] which strives to create a very precise (and thus information-rich) type. It is possible to construct visually smaller but less precise types that also prove well defined behaviour for the messenger example.

1.3 Other related work

Although not type-based, several papers have explored letting the analysis of an ambient subprocess depend on its possible contexts — a task which requires an estimate of the possible shapes of the ambient tree structure. None of these handle communication, however, so none can prove the safety of our example polymorphic messenger. With shape grammars [17], a set of grammars is returned such that at any step, the current process can be described by one of these grammars. The analysis is very precise, but potentially also very expensive. In Kleene analysis [16], a 3-valued logic is used to estimate the possible shapes. The framework allows for trade-offs w.r.t. precision versus costs. The abstract interpretation system of [11] keeps track of the context "one level up". This is sufficient to achieve a quite precise analysis, yet is "only" polynomial (n^7).

Polymorphic type systems already exist for the π-calculus [20, 18], but do not generalise easily to the spatial nature of our messenger example.

1.4 Summary of contributions (conclusion)

- We present PolyA, the first type system for the ambient calculus that is flexible enough to type generic mobile agents.
- We explain how PolyA types can be used not just to check basic type safety but also to give precise answers to various questions about process behaviour of interest for other reasons, e.g., security.

- We prove subject reduction (Thm. 16) and the decidability of type checking (Prop. 6) for PolyA.
- We prove principal typings (Thm. 23) for a useful restriction of PolyA.
- We illustrate how to extend PolyA to support the cross-ambient communication of Boxed Ambients [4], the co-capabilities of Safe Ambients [12], and the process (not ambient) mobility capability of M^3 [10].

The proofs of most propositions and theorems have been omitted here for space reasons. They can be found in an extended online version of this paper [3].

In other work [14] we have developed a type inference algorithm for a useful restriction of PolyA. Space limitations prevent including a further description here.

Acknowledgements The design of PolyA benefited from helpful discussions with Mario Coppo, Mariangiola Dezani, and Elio Giovannetti.

2 The ambient calculus

For space reasons, we present the system for a calculus without name restriction. In [3] we present a straightforward way to handle name restriction. In later work it may be possible to combine PolyA with more advanced treatments of name restriction, such as the "abstract names" of Lhoussaine and Sassone [13].

Fig. 1 defines the syntax and semantics of our base calculus. Whenever it has been defined that some (meta)variable letter, say "x", ranges over a given set of objects, the notation $\boxed{x}$ shall mean that set of objects.

The syntactic category of *prefixes* is not in traditional ambient calculus formulations. Our calculus treats ambient boundaries as capabilities; "amb a" is the capability that creates an ambient named a when executed. In our formulation, an ambient with contents P is written "amb $a.P$". The traditional notation "$a\,[P]$" is syntactic sugar for amb $a.P$; we use this whenever convenient. The capability amb a can in principle be passed in a message. We allow this more because it is syntactically convenient than because we expect processes to actually do it. Our main results do not fully support programs that *use* this possibility.

The special capability "•" is not supposed to be found in the initial term. It signifies a substitution result that would otherwise be syntactically invalid. For example, the term ⟨in c⟩ | (b).in a.open b.0 reduces to in a.•.0 instead of the (hypothetical) "in a.open (in c).0". Traditional ambient calculus accounts usually leave such a communication result undefined, implicitly understanding that the system would crash either at the communication time or when the ill-formed capability executes after the in a capability has fired.

The symbol • does not have any reduction rules associated with it. As far as our theory is concerned it just sits there. Likewise, there are no reduction rules for placeholder capabilities of the form "a". A PolyA type conservatively approximates *whether* and *where* one of these capabilities may occur, but the type system user must decide whether or not to consider it an error if this happens.

CONVENTION 1 *A term P is* **well formed** *iff its free names are distinct from the names bound by any "$(\vec{a})$" within the term and it does not contain any nested bindings of the same name. We consider only well formed terms.*

Syntax:

$$
\begin{array}{lrcl}
\text{Names:} & a,b & ::= & \mathsf{a} \mid \mathsf{b} \mid \mathsf{c} \mid \cdots \\
\text{Opcodes:} & O & ::= & \mathsf{in} \mid \mathsf{out} \mid \mathsf{open} \mid \mathsf{amb} \\
\text{Capabilities:} & C & ::= & a \mid Oa \mid \bullet \\
\text{Messages:} & M,N & ::= & C \mid M.N \mid \varepsilon \\
\text{Prefixes:} & p & ::= & M \mid \langle \vec{M} \rangle \mid (\vec{a}) \\
\text{Processes:} & P,Q,R & ::= & p.P \mid\ !P \mid (P \mid Q) \mid 0
\end{array}
$$

See main text for further syntactic restrictions (scoping).

Process equivalence:

$$\frac{}{P \mid Q \equiv Q \mid P} \qquad \frac{}{P \mid (Q \mid R) \equiv (P \mid Q) \mid R} \qquad \frac{}{0 \mid P \equiv P} \qquad \frac{}{!P \equiv P \mid\ !P}$$

$$\frac{}{!0 \equiv 0} \qquad \frac{}{(M.N).P \equiv M.(N.P)} \qquad \frac{}{\varepsilon.P \equiv P} \qquad \frac{}{P \equiv P}$$

$$\frac{P \equiv Q}{p.P \equiv p.Q} \qquad \frac{P \equiv Q}{P \mid R \equiv Q \mid R} \qquad \frac{P \equiv Q}{!P \equiv\ !Q} \qquad \frac{Q \equiv P}{P \equiv Q} \qquad \frac{P \equiv Q \quad Q \equiv R}{P \equiv R}$$

Substitution:

A **term substitution** $\mathcal{S}$ is a (total) function from names to messages such that $\mathcal{S}(a) \neq a$ for only finitely many a's. We often notate it $\mathcal{S} = [a_1 \mapsto M_1, \ldots, a_k \mapsto M_k]$, understanding implicitly that $\mathcal{S}(a) = a$ when a is not one of the a_i's. Shorter notations are $[a_i \mapsto M_i]_{1 \leq i \leq k}$ or $[a \mapsto M_a]_{a \in A}$.

For messages:

$$\mathcal{S}(M.N) = (\mathcal{S}M).(\mathcal{S}N) \qquad \mathcal{S}\varepsilon = \varepsilon$$

$$\mathcal{S}a = \mathcal{S}(a) \qquad \mathcal{S}\bullet = \bullet$$

$$\mathcal{S}(Oa) = \begin{cases} O\,\mathcal{S}(a) & \text{if } \mathcal{S}(a) \text{ is a name} \\ \bullet & \text{otherwise} \end{cases}$$

For other prefixes:

$$\mathcal{S}\langle M_1, \ldots, M_k \rangle = \langle \mathcal{S}M_1, \ldots, \mathcal{S}M_k \rangle$$

$$\mathcal{S}(a_1, \ldots, a_k) = \begin{cases} (a_1, \ldots, a_k) & \text{if } \mathcal{S}(a_i) = a_i \text{ for all } i \\ \bullet & \text{otherwise} \end{cases}$$

For terms:

$$\mathcal{S}(p.P) = (\mathcal{S}p).(\mathcal{S}P) \qquad \mathcal{S}(!P) = !(\mathcal{S}P)$$

$$\mathcal{S}(P \mid Q) = (\mathcal{S}P) \mid (\mathcal{S}Q) \qquad \mathcal{S}0 = 0$$

Reduction rules:

$$\frac{}{a[\mathsf{in}\ b.P \mid Q] \mid b[R] \hookrightarrow b[a[P \mid Q] \mid R]}$$

$$\frac{}{b[a[\mathsf{out}\ b.P \mid Q] \mid R] \hookrightarrow a[P \mid Q] \mid b[R]} \qquad \frac{}{a[P] \mid \mathsf{open}\ a.Q \hookrightarrow P \mid Q}$$

$$\frac{}{\langle M_1, \ldots, M_n \rangle.P \mid (a_1, \ldots, a_n).Q \hookrightarrow P \mid [a_i \mapsto M_i]_{1 \leq i \leq n} Q}$$

$$\frac{P \hookrightarrow Q}{a[P] \hookrightarrow a[Q]} \qquad \frac{P \hookrightarrow Q}{P \mid R \hookrightarrow Q \mid R} \qquad \frac{P \equiv P' \quad P' \hookrightarrow Q' \quad Q' \equiv Q}{P \hookrightarrow Q}$$

Figure 1. Syntax and semantics of the ambient calculus

Conv. 1 does not limit expressiveness. Any program (term) in a more conventional ambient calculus formulation that allows α-conversion has a well formed α-variant which can be used in our type system.

The convention ensures that our reduction rules will never perform a substitution where there is a risk of name capture by $(\vec{a})$ bindings. Reductions preserve well-formedness, because it is syntactically impossible for a substitution to inject a $(\vec{a})$ within the body of another $(\vec{a})$. (This is in contrast to the λ-calculus, where substitutions routinely insert λ-abstractions into other abstractions). Because of this, we do not need to recognise α-equivalence for $(\vec{a}).P$. This is a significant technical simplification, because for many purposes we can treat $(\vec{a})$ as any other action, without needing special machinery for α-equivalence of the bound names.

Fig. 1 contains no provisions for avoiding name capture in $\mathcal{S}(\vec{a})$ — this is handled by Convention 1. The • possibility for $\mathcal{S}(\vec{a})$ is never supposed to be used; substitutions leading to it will not arise by our rules.

3 Shape predicates

The following pseudo-grammar defines the (abstract) syntax of our type system:

$$
\begin{array}{llll}
\text{Message types:} & \mu & ::= \{C_1, C_2, \cdots, C_k\}* & (C_i\text{'s all different}, k \geq 1) \\
 & & \mid \ \lessdot C_1.C_2.\cdots.C_k \gtrdot & (C_i\text{'s all different}, k \geq 0) \\
 & & \mid \ \{a\} & \\
\text{Prefix types:} & \pi & ::= C \quad (\vec{a}) \quad \langle\vec{\mu}\rangle & \\
\text{Shape predicates:} & \sigma & ::= (\pi_1.\sigma_1 \mid \cdots \mid \pi_k.\sigma_k) & (k \geq 1) \\
 & & \mid \ 0 &
\end{array}
$$

DEFINITION 2 (MATCHING OF SHAPE PREDICATES) *These rules define the relations $\vdash M : \mu$, $\vdash p : \pi$, and $\vdash P : \sigma$:*

$$\frac{M \notin \boxed{a} \qquad M.0 \equiv C'_1.\cdots.C'_n.0 \qquad \{C'_1,\ldots,C'_n\} \subseteq \{C_1,\ldots,C_k\}}{\vdash M : \{C_1,\ldots,C_k\}*}\ \textsf{KleeneStar}$$

$$\frac{M \notin \boxed{a} \qquad M.0 \equiv C_1.\cdots.C_k.0}{\vdash M : \lessdot C_1.\cdots.C_k \gtrdot}\ \textsf{Sequenced} \qquad \frac{}{\vdash a : \{a\}}\ \textsf{Name}$$

$$\frac{}{\vdash C : C}\ \textsf{Cap} \qquad \frac{}{\vdash (\vec{a}) : (\vec{a})}\ \textsf{Recv} \qquad \frac{\vdash M_1 : \mu_1 \quad \cdots \quad \vdash M_k : \mu_k}{\vdash \langle M_1,\ldots,M_k\rangle : \langle \mu_1,\ldots,\mu_k\rangle}\ \textsf{Send}$$

$$\frac{\vdash p : \pi \qquad \vdash P : \sigma}{\vdash p.P : (\cdots \mid \pi.\sigma \mid \cdots)}\ \textsf{Pfx} \qquad \frac{\vdash M.(N.P) : \sigma}{\vdash (M.N).P : \sigma}\ \textsf{Seq} \qquad \frac{\vdash P : \sigma}{\vdash \varepsilon.P : \sigma}\ \textsf{Nop}$$

$$\frac{\vdash P : \sigma \qquad \vdash Q : \sigma}{\vdash P \mid Q : \sigma}\ \textsf{Par} \qquad \frac{}{\vdash 0 : \sigma}\ \textsf{Null} \qquad \frac{\vdash P : \sigma}{\vdash !P : \sigma}\ \textsf{Bang}$$

The side conditions $M \notin \boxed{a}$ and $M.0 \equiv C_1.\cdots.C_k.0$ on rules KleeneStar and Sequenced amount to specifying that these two forms of message types are matched modulo associativity of "." and neutrality of "ε" — with the exception that messages that are raw names (i.e., "a" as opposed to "$a.\varepsilon$" or "in a") are handled specially. They are matched only by the message type $\{a\}$.

THEOREM 3 *If $P \equiv Q$ then $\vdash P : \sigma \Leftrightarrow \vdash Q : \sigma$ for all σ.*

DEFINITION 4 *The **meaning** of a shape predicate (message type, prefix type) is the set of terms (messages, prefixes) that match it:*

$$[\![\mu]\!] = \{M \mid \vdash M : \mu\} \qquad [\![\pi]\!] = \{p \mid \vdash p : \pi\} \qquad [\![\sigma]\!] = \{P \mid \vdash P : \sigma\}$$

DEFINITION 5 *Define the following **containment** relations:*

$$\mu \leq \mu' \iff [\![\mu]\!] \subseteq [\![\mu']\!] \qquad \pi \leq \pi' \iff [\![\pi]\!] \subseteq [\![\pi']\!] \qquad \sigma \leq \sigma' \iff [\![\sigma]\!] \subseteq [\![\sigma']\!]$$

Each of the three containment relations is a preorder (transitive and reflexive). Containment of shape predicates is not antisymmetric, however. For example, the shape predicates amb a.amb b.0 and amb a.amb b.0 | amb a.0 have the same meaning, but it would be technically inconvenient (and not give any real benefit) to insist on equating shape predicates with equal meanings.

3.1 Recursive shape predicates

Our strategy in analysing a term is to look for a shape predicate describing all of its possible computational futures. Because many terms can create arbitrarily deep nestings of ambients (e.g., !a[!in a.0]), the finite trees we have used for shape predicates so far are not up to the task[1]. We need infinite shape predicates. We should, however, restrict ourselves to infinite shape predicates with finite *representations* — in other words, regular trees.

There are several regular tree representations that we could have used. We believe it is technically most convenient (and intuitive) to view regular trees as *graphs*. Therefore, we retroactively replace the abstract syntax for shape predicates with:

Node identifiers:	X,Y,Z	$::=$	X1 X2 X3 $\cdots$
Edges:	e	$::=$	$X \xrightarrow{\pi} Y$
Shape graphs:	G	$\in$	$\mathcal{P}_{\text{fin}}(\boxed{e})$
Shape predicates:	σ	$::=$	$\langle X \mid G\rangle$

A shape predicate is now a shape graph together with a pointer to a distinguished *root* node. The version of the Pfx rule that works with this notation is

$$\frac{\vdash p : \pi \qquad X \xrightarrow{\pi} Y \in G \qquad \vdash P : \langle Y \mid G\rangle}{\vdash p.P : \langle X \mid G\rangle}\ \text{Pfx}$$

Thm. 3 is still true with this formulation, because it was proven by induction on term equivalence rather than shape-predicate structure.

This graph-based formulation is the basis for our formal development. However, even though graphs are an intuitive way of *thinking* about regularly infinite shape predicates, they are less convenient for *writing down* shape predicates. Figure 2 defines a more tree-like textual notation for shape graphs for use in examples.

[1]This happens even for terminating terms such as b[in a.0] | a[open b.0], which shape predicates cannot distinguish from !b[!in a.0] | !a[open b.0]. Thus, nearly every nontrivial use of open will need recursive σ's. As already observed by [5], open often complicates analysis significantly.

This is the syntax of **shape expressions**:

Shape expressions: $V \ ::= \ X \mid U \mid \mathsf{letrec}\, X_1 = U_1; \ldots; X_n = U_n \;\mathsf{in}\; X_i$
Shape summands: $U \ ::= \ 0 \mid (U \mid U) \mid \pi \mid (\pi_1 \mid \cdots \mid \pi_n).V \mid (X)$

As additional syntactic sugar, $\mathsf{letrec} \cdots \mathsf{in}\; U$ stands for $\mathsf{letrec} \cdots; X = U \;\mathsf{in}\; X$ where X is fresh. $\pi.V$ stands for $(\pi).V$, and $a[V]$ stands for $(\mathsf{amb}\; a).V$.

To convert a shape expression to a graph-shaped shape predicate, first replace each U of the form (X) with the right-hand side of the innermost in-scope letrec binding for X. It is an error if no such binding exist, of if the unfolding does not terminate. (V's of the form X are not touched at this stage). Then α-rename the entire shape expression such that no X is bound by two different letrec's, and apply the function $(\cdot)^*$ defined by:

a) V^* is a shape predicate:

$X^* = \langle X \mid \varnothing \rangle \qquad U^* = \langle X \mid U_X^* \rangle$ where X is fresh

$(\mathsf{letrec}\, X_1 = U_1; \ldots; X_n = U_n \;\mathsf{in}\; X_i)^* = \langle X_i \mid U_{1X_1}^* \cup \cdots \cup U_{nX_n}^* \rangle$

b) U_X^* is a shape graph:

$0_X^* = \varnothing \qquad (U_1 \mid U_2)_X^* = (U_1)_X^* \cup (U_2)_X^*$

$\pi_X^* = \{X \xrightarrow{\pi} X\} \qquad ((\pi_1 \mid \cdots \mid \pi_n).V)_X^* = \{X \xrightarrow{\pi_i} X' \mid 1 \leq i \leq n\} \cup G$

where $\langle X' \mid G \rangle = V^*$

Note that the parentheses in $U ::= (X)$ are important; they distinguish between "$\pi.X$", which stands for an edge going to node X itself, and "$\pi.(X)$", which stands for an edge to a fresh node that happens to behave like X. This can influence whether the shape graph is "modest" (or "discrete"); see Sect. 4.3.

Figure 2. Shape expressions: a tree-like notation for recursive shape predicates

In general, defining some property for shape graphs implicitly defines it for shape predicates: The shape predicate $\langle X \mid G \rangle$ has the property iff G has.

PROPOSITION 6 *The relations of Defn. 2 are effectively (and efficiently) decidable when shape predicates are given as graphs.*

DEFINITION 7 *Two shape graphs G_1 and G_2 are **equivalent**, written $G_1 \approx G_2$, iff $[\![\langle X \mid G_1 \rangle]\!] = [\![\langle X \mid G_2 \rangle]\!]$ for all X.*

3.2 Effective characterisation of containment

DEFINITION 8 *Let R be a relation between shape predicates. R is a **shape simulation** iff $\langle X \mid G \rangle \; R \; \langle X' \mid G' \rangle$ and $X \xrightarrow{\pi} Y \in G$ imply that there is $\pi' \geq \pi$ and Y' such that $X' \xrightarrow{\pi'} Y' \in G'$ and $\langle Y \mid G \rangle \; R \; \langle Y' \mid G' \rangle$.*

THEOREM 9 *Shape containment $\leq$ is the largest shape simulation; it is the union of all shape simulations.*

Thus, to prove that $\sigma \leq \sigma'$ it is sufficient to find a shape simulation R such that $\sigma \; R \; \sigma'$. This strategy leads directly to:

PROPOSITION 10 *The relation* $\langle X \mid G\rangle \le \langle X' \mid G'\rangle$ *can be decided effectively (actually, in polynomial time).*

It is worth noticing that shape simulations treat $(\vec{a})$ just like any other prefix type. Thus $\le$ treats the "result" type covariantly (like [22]), whereas the input position in PolyA is a list of names and thus essentially invariant.

3.3 Type substitutions

DEFINITION 11 *A **type substitution** $\mathcal{T}$ is a function from names to message types such that $\mathcal{T}(a) \neq \{a\}$ for only finitely many a's. Like term substitutions, type substitutions may be written as $[a_1 \mapsto \mu_1, \ldots, a_k \mapsto \mu_k]$ or $[a \mapsto \mu_a]_{a \in A}$.*

A type substitution can be applied to capabilities, message types, shape graphs, and shape predicates as follows:

Type substitution for capabilities: $\mathcal{T}C$ is a message type, not a capability.

$$\mathcal{T}a = \mathcal{T}(a) \qquad \mathcal{T}(Oa) = \begin{cases} <Ob> & \text{if } \mathcal{T}(a) = \{b\} \\ <\bullet> & \text{otherwise} \end{cases} \qquad \mathcal{T}\bullet = <\bullet>$$

Substitution for message types: $\mathcal{T}\mu$ is a message type given by:

To compute $\mathcal{T}\{C_1,\ldots,C_k\}*$, let $\mu_i = \mathcal{T}C_i$ for $1 \le i \le k$. If $\mu_i = <>$ for all i, then the result is also $<>$. Otherwise, the result is $\{C'_1,\ldots,C'_n\}*$, where the C'_js are all capabilities that occur in any of the μ_i's, with duplicates removed (and in some canonical order).

To compute $\mathcal{T}<C_1.\cdots.C_k>$, let $\mu_i = \mathcal{T}C_i$ for $1 \le i \le k$. If any μ_i has the form $\{\cdots\}*$, or if any C appears in more than one μ_i, then the result is the same as the result of $\mathcal{T}\{C_1,\ldots,C_k\}*$. Otherwise, each μ_i has the form $<\cdots>$. Concatenate all of the capability lists (in the order of the i's) and return <the concatenated list>.

Finally, $\mathcal{T}\{a\}$ is simply $\mathcal{T}(a)$.

Substitution for shape graphs: $\mathcal{T}G$ is a shape graph. To construct $\mathcal{T}G$, first construct an intermediate graph G_ε which can contain special null edges written $X \xrightarrow{\varepsilon} Y$. G_ε contains contributions from each edge $Y_1 \xrightarrow{\pi} Y_2 \in G$:

1 When $\pi = a$ and $\mathcal{T}(a) = \{C_1,\ldots,C_k\}*$, choose a fresh node Z, and add to G_ε the edges: $Y_1 \xrightarrow{\varepsilon} Z \xrightarrow{C_1} Z \xrightarrow{C_2} \ldots \xrightarrow{C_k} Z \xrightarrow{\varepsilon} Y_2$

2 When $\pi = a$ and $\mathcal{T}(a) = <C_1.\cdots.C_k>$, choose fresh nodes Z_0 through Z_k, and add to G_ε the edges $Y_1 \xrightarrow{\varepsilon} Z_0 \xrightarrow{C_1} Z_1 \xrightarrow{C_2} \cdots Z_k \xrightarrow{\varepsilon} Y_2$

3 When $\pi = a$ and $\mathcal{T}(a) = \{b\}$, add to G_ε the edge $Y_1 \xrightarrow{b} Y_2$.

4 When $\pi = Oa$, $\mathcal{T}(Oa)$ will always have the form $<C'>$. Add to G_ε the edge $Y_1 \xrightarrow{C'} Y_2$.

5 When $\pi = (a_1,\ldots,a_k)$, check that $\mathcal{T}a_i = \{a_i\}$ for all i, and then add the edge $Y_1 \xrightarrow{\pi} Y_2$ to G_ε. Otherwise, add $Y_1 \xrightarrow{\bullet} Y_2$.

6 When $\pi = \langle \mu_1,\ldots,\mu_k\rangle$, add to G_ε the edge $Y_1 \xrightarrow{\langle \mathcal{T}\mu_1,\ldots,\mathcal{T}\mu_k\rangle} Y_2$.

Now set $\mathcal{T}G = \{X_k \xrightarrow{\pi} Y \mid (X_k \xrightarrow{\varepsilon} X_{k-1} \xrightarrow{\varepsilon} \cdots \xrightarrow{\varepsilon} X_0 \xrightarrow{\pi} Y) \in G_\varepsilon, k \ge 0\}$.

Substitution for shape predicates: $\mathcal{T}\sigma$ is a shape predicate given by:

$$\mathcal{T}\langle X \mid G\rangle = \langle X \mid \mathcal{T}G\rangle$$

THEOREM 12 *Assume that* $\vdash P : \sigma$ *and* $\vdash \mathcal{S}(a) : \mathcal{T}(a)$ *for all* a. *Then* $\vdash \mathcal{S}P : \mathcal{T}\sigma$.

4 Shape predicates as types

4.1 Closed shape predicates

DEFINITION 13 *The shape predicate* σ *is* ***semantically closed*** *iff its meaning is closed under reduction, i.e., if* $\vdash P : \sigma$ *and* $P \hookrightarrow Q$ *imply* $\vdash Q : \sigma$.

This definition is intuitively appealing, but it is not immediately clear how to decide it. However, we have local rules that imply semantic closure:

DEFINITION 14 *The shape graph* G *is* ***locally closed*** *at* X_0 *iff*

1 $\{(X_0 \xrightarrow{\mathsf{amb}\,a} X), (X \xrightarrow{\mathsf{in}\,b} Y), (X_0 \xrightarrow{\mathsf{amb}\,b} Z)\} \subseteq G$
$\Rightarrow \exists X' : Z \xrightarrow{\mathsf{amb}\,a} X' \in G \wedge \langle X \mid G\rangle \leq \langle X' \mid G\rangle \wedge \langle Y \mid G\rangle \leq \langle X' \mid G\rangle$,

2 $\{(X_0 \xrightarrow{\mathsf{amb}\,a} X), (X \xrightarrow{\mathsf{amb}\,b} Y), (Y \xrightarrow{\mathsf{out}\,a} Z)\} \subseteq G$
$\Rightarrow \exists Y' : X_0 \xrightarrow{\mathsf{amb}\,b} Y' \in G \wedge \langle Y \mid G\rangle \leq \langle Y' \mid G\rangle \wedge \langle Z \mid G\rangle \leq \langle Y' \mid G\rangle$,

3 $\{(X_0 \xrightarrow{\mathsf{amb}\,a} X), (X_0 \xrightarrow{\mathsf{open}\,a} Y)\} \subseteq G$
$\Rightarrow \langle X \mid G\rangle \leq \langle X_0 \mid G\rangle \wedge \langle Y \mid G\rangle \leq \langle X_0 \mid G\rangle$, *and*

4 $\{(X_0 \xrightarrow{\langle \mu_1,\ldots,\mu_k\rangle} Y), (X_0 \xrightarrow{(a_1,\ldots,a_k)} Z)\} \subseteq G$
$\Rightarrow \langle Y \mid G\rangle \leq \langle X_0 \mid G\rangle \wedge [a_i \mapsto \mu_i]_{1 \leq i \leq k}\langle Z \mid G\rangle \leq \langle X_0 \mid G\rangle$.

DEFINITION 15 *Let* $\sigma = \langle X \mid G\rangle$ *be a shape predicate. The* ***active nodes*** *in* σ, *written* $\mathsf{active}(\sigma)$, *is the least set of node names such that*

$$\mathsf{active}(\sigma) = \{X\} \cup \{Z \mid \exists Y \in \mathsf{active}(\sigma) : \exists a : Y \xrightarrow{\mathsf{amb}\,a} Z \in G\}.$$

The predicate σ *is* ***syntactically closed*** *iff* G *is locally closed at every* $X \in \mathsf{active}(\sigma)$.

THEOREM 16 *Every syntactically closed shape predicate is also semantically closed.*

4.2 Types

DEFINITION 17 *A* ***type*** τ *is a syntactically closed shape predicate. Given a type* τ, *the term* P *has type* τ *iff* $\vdash P : \tau$.

This notion of types has the basic properties expected of any type system: It enjoys subject reduction (Thm. 16), it can be effectively decided whether a given term has a given type (Prop. 6), and types can be distinguished from non-types (using Prop. 10).

Given an algorithm to compute precise types, (such as the one we present in [14]), one can approximate various properties of a term's computational behaviour:

- If P has the type $\sigma = \langle X \mid G\rangle$ and G contains no edge $Y \xrightarrow{\bullet} Z$ with $Y \in \mathsf{active}(\sigma)$, then P will never *execute* the result of a bad substitution such as $[a \mapsto M.N](\mathsf{in}\,a)$.
- If P has the type $\langle X \mid G\rangle$ and G contains no edge $Y \xrightarrow{\bullet} Z$, then executing P will never create such a malformed substitution result.

- Any **security policy** can be checked if it can be stated as a condition on configurations that must not arise. For example, the policy "no ambient a must ever directly contain an ambient named b" is satisfied by P if it has a type $\langle X \mid G \rangle$ such that G does not contain a sequence $X_1 \xrightarrow{\mathsf{amb\,a}} X_2 \xrightarrow{\mathsf{amb\,b}} X_3$.

PROPOSITION 18 *Every term P has a type (although the type may contain • and thus not prove that the term "cannot go wrong").*

Our notion of types is very expressive — it *allows* a very fine-grained approximation to important questions. However, it is not known whether principal types always exist; we have neither proved nor disproved this. Thus, we now define a syntactically restricted type system for which we *do* prove that principal types exist.

4.3 Modest and discrete types; existence of principal types

DEFINITION 19 *Define the relation* $=_{(\leq)}$ *on prefix types as the least equivalence relation that contains* $\leq$.

DEFINITION 20 *Define the* ***stratification function*** **S** *by*

$$\mathbf{S}((\vec{a})) = \mathbf{S}(\langle\vec{\mu}\rangle) = 3 \qquad \mathbf{S}(\mathsf{amb}\ a) = 2 \qquad \mathbf{S}(C) = 1 \text{ when } C \neq \mathsf{amb}\ a$$

DEFINITION 21 *The shape graph G is* ***modest*** *iff for each* π, *one of the following conditions hold:*

1. ***Finite depth.*** *There is a number* n_π *such that whenever G contains a chain* $X_0 \xrightarrow{\pi_1} X_1 \xrightarrow{\pi_2} \cdots \xrightarrow{\pi_k} X_k$ *with every* $\mathbf{S}(\pi_i) \leq \mathbf{S}(\pi)$, *there are at most* n_π *different i's such that* $\pi_i =_{(\leq)} \pi$.
2. ***Monomorphic recursion.*** *Whenever G contains a chain* $X_0 \xrightarrow{\pi_1} X_1 \xrightarrow{\pi_2} \cdots \xrightarrow{\pi_k} X_k$ *with every* $\mathbf{S}(\pi_i) \leq \mathbf{S}(\pi)$ *and* $\pi_1 =_{(\leq)} \pi =_{(\leq)} \pi_k$, *then* $X_1 = X_k$.

DEFINITION 22 *The shape graph G is* ***discrete*** *iff both of these hold:*

1. *For each capability C that is not* amb *a for some a, whenever G contains a chain* $X_0 \xrightarrow{C} X_1 \xrightarrow{C} \cdots \xrightarrow{C} X_k$ *of edges all decorated with C and any two of the* X_i*'s are identical, then* $X_0 = X_1 = \cdots = X_k$.
2. *G does not contain any message type of the shape* $\{C_1, \ldots, C_k\}*$ *such that one of the* C_i*'s is* amb *a*.

Allowing only modest *and* discrete types yields **principal typings** (defined in [21]):

THEOREM 23 *For every term P which has at least one modest discrete type, there is a modest discrete type* τ *that is minimal among P's modest discrete types.*

The restriction to modest discrete type may feel somewhat artificial; indeed these properties have been designed specifically to allow the theorem to hold. While it is easy to construct terms where non-modest types allow a more precise analysis, they do not seem to correspond to natural programming styles. We conjecture that the restriction of expressive power entailed by requiring modesty and discreteness does not seriously impede PolyA's ability to analyse real-world software designs.

The proof of Theorem 23 is non-constructive and does not point to an effective procedure for *finding* a principal type. In [14] we have defined (and implemented) a practical type inference algorithm for a yet more restricted version of PolyA, but its principality properties are not yet well understood.

Requiring discreteness of types loses Prop. 18: There exist terms having no discrete type. However, all (ν-free) terms of the original ambient calculus have types:

PROPOSITION 24 *Any term P that does not contain* amb *a inside* $\langle\vec{M}\rangle$ *has a modest discrete type, and so also a principal such.*

5 Extended and modified ambient calculi

Our framework is strong enough to handle many ambient calculus variants with different reduction rules. In most cases, PolyA can be extended to deal with such variation simply by adjusting Defn. 14 with conditions systematically derived from the changed or new reduction rules. If this is done correctly and the new or changed rules are straightforward rewriting steps, then it is simple to extend the proof of Thm. 16. The rest of our theory will then carry through unchanged, including the existence of principal types. We illustrate this principle with examples of such extensions.

Boxed Ambients [4] removes the open capability; instead processes can communicate across ambient boundaries with directional communication actions:

$$\text{Prefixes: } p ::= M \quad \langle\vec{M}\rangle^{\uparrow} \quad \langle\vec{M}\rangle^{\star} \quad \langle\vec{M}\rangle^{\downarrow a} \quad (\vec{a})^{\uparrow} \quad (\vec{a})^{\star} \quad (\vec{a})^{\downarrow a}$$

There are corresponding reduction rules such as:

$$\overline{\langle\vec{M}\rangle^{\downarrow b}.P \mid b[Q \mid (\vec{a})^{\star}.R] \hookrightarrow P \mid b[Q \mid [a_i \mapsto M_i]_i R]}$$

Our prefix type syntax is easily extended to include the new actions. The new reduction rules can be used to derive local closure conditions such as:

$$\{(X_0 \xrightarrow{\langle\mu_1,\ldots,\mu_k\rangle^{\downarrow b}} X), (X_0 \xrightarrow{\mathsf{amb}\,b} Y), (Y \xrightarrow{(a_1,\ldots,a_k)^{\star}} Z)\} \subseteq G$$
$$\Rightarrow \langle X \mid G\rangle \leq \langle X_0 \mid G\rangle \land [a_i \mapsto \mu_i]_{1\leq i\leq k}\langle Z \mid G\rangle \leq \langle Y \mid G\rangle$$

Safe Ambients [12] introduces *co-capabilities* where both interaction parties must present a capability. The reduction rules are amended to require this, e.g.:

$$\overline{a[\overline{\mathsf{open}}\, a.P \mid Q] \mid \mathsf{open}\, a.R \hookrightarrow P \mid Q \mid R}$$

It is straightforward to extend PolyA to systems with co-capabilities. For example, condition 3 of Defn. 14 would be replaced by:

$$\{(X_0 \xrightarrow{\mathsf{amb}\,a} X), (X_0 \xrightarrow{\mathsf{open}\,a} Y), (X \xrightarrow{\overline{\mathsf{open}}\,a} Z)\} \subseteq G$$
$$\Rightarrow \langle X \mid G\rangle \leq \langle X_0 \mid G\rangle \land \langle Y \mid G\rangle \leq \langle X_0 \mid G\rangle \land \langle Z \mid G\rangle \leq \langle X_0 \mid G\rangle.$$

The $\mathbf{M}^3$ calculus [10] introduces a new method of inter-ambient communication; a new capability to can move a process into a neighbour ambient:

$$\overline{a[P \mid \mathsf{to}\, b.Q] \mid b[R] \hookrightarrow a[P] \mid b[Q \mid R]}$$

This, too, is easily expressed as a closure condition:

$$\{(X_0 \xrightarrow{\mathsf{amb}\,b} X), (X_0 \xrightarrow{\mathsf{amb}\,a} Y), (Y \xrightarrow{\mathsf{to}\,b} Z)\} \subseteq G$$
$$\Rightarrow \langle Z \mid G\rangle \leq \langle X \mid G\rangle$$

References

[1] T. Amtoft, A. J. Kfoury, S. M. Pericas-Geertsen. What are polymorphically-typed ambients? In D. Sands, ed., *ESOP 2001, Genova*, vol. 2028 of *LNCS*. Springer-Verlag, 2001. An extended version appears as Technical Report BUCS-TR-2000-021, Comp.Sci. Department, Boston University, 2000.
[2] T. Amtoft, A. J. Kfoury, S. M. Pericas-Geertsen. Orderly communication in the ambient calculus. *Computer Languages*, 28, 2002.
[3] T. Amtoft, H. Makholm, J. B. Wells. PolyA: True type polymorphism for Mobile Ambients. Technical Report HW-MACS-TR-0015, Heriot-Watt Univ., School of Math. & Comput. Sci., 2004.
[4] M. Bugliesi, G. Castagna, S. Crafa. Boxed ambients. In *4th International Conference on Theoretical Aspects of Computer Science (TACS'01)*, vol. 2215 of *LNCS*. Springer-Verlag, 2001.
[5] L. Cardelli, G. Ghelli, A. D. Gordon. Mobility types for mobile ambients. In J. Wiedermann et al., eds., *ICALP'99*, vol. 1644 of *LNCS*. Springer-Verlag, 1999. Extended version appears as Microsoft Research Technical Report MSR-TR-99-32, 1999.
[6] L. Cardelli, A. D. Gordon. Mobile ambients. In M. Nivat, ed., *FoSSaCS'98*, vol. 1378 of *LNCS*. Springer-Verlag, 1998.
[7] L. Cardelli, A. D. Gordon. Types for mobile ambients. In *POPL'99, San Antonio, Texas*. ACM Press, 1999.
[8] L. Cardelli, P. Wegner. On understanding types, data abstraction, and polymorphism. *Computing Surveys*, 17(4), 1985.
[9] M. Coppo, M. Dezani-Ciancaglini. A fully abstract model for higher-order mobile ambients. In *VMCAI 2002*, vol. 2294 of *LNCS*, 2002.
[10] M. Coppo, M. Dezani-Ciancaglini, E. Giovannetti, I. Salvo. M3: Mobility types for mobile processes in mobile ambients. In *CATS 2003*, vol. 78 of *ENTCS*, 2003.
[11] F. Levi, S. Maffeis. An abstract interpretation framework for analysing mobile ambients. In *SAS'01*, vol. 2126 of *LNCS*. Springer-Verlag, 2001.
[12] F. Levi, D. Sangiorgi. Controlling interference in ambients. In *POPL'00, Boston, Massachusetts*. ACM Press, 2000.
[13] C. Lhoussaine, V. Sassone. A dependently typed ambient calculus. In *Programming Languages & Systems, 13th European Symp. Programming*, vol. 2986 of *LNCS*. Springer-Verlag, 2004.
[14] H. Makholm, J. B. Wells. Type inference for PolyA. Technical Report HW-MACS-TR-0013, Heriot-Watt Univ., School of Math. & Comput. Sci., 2004.
[15] R. Milner. *Communicating and Mobile Systems: The π-Calculus*. Cambridge Press, 1999.
[16] F. Nielson, H. R. Nielson, M. Sagiv. A Kleene analysis of mobile ambients. In *Programming Languages & Systems, 9th European Symp. Programming*, vol. 1782 of *LNCS*. Springer-Verlag, 2000.
[17] H. R. Nielson, F. Nielson. Shape analysis for mobile ambients. *Nordic Journal of Computing*, 8, 2001. A preliminary version appeared at POPL'00.
[18] B. C. Pierce, D. Sangiorgi. Behavioral equivalence in the polymorphic pi-calculus. *Journal of the ACM*, 47(3), 2000.
[19] D. Teller, P. Zimmer, D. Hirschkoff. Using ambients to control resources. In *CONCUR'02*, vol. 2421 of *LNCS*. Springer-Verlag, 2002.
[20] D. N. Turner. *The Polymorphic Pi-Calculus: Theory and Implementation*. PhD thesis, University of Edinburgh, 1995. Report no ECS-LFCS-96-345.
[21] J. B. Wells. The essence of principal typings. In *Proc. 29th Int'l Coll. Automata, Languages, and Programming*, vol. 2380 of *LNCS*. Springer-Verlag, 2002.
[22] P. Zimmer. Subtyping and typing algorithms for mobile ambients. In *FOSSACS 2000, Berlin*, vol. 1784 of *LNCS*. Springer-Verlag, 2000.

RECOVERING RESOURCES IN THE π-CALCULUS (DRAFT)*

David Teller – David.Teller@ens-lyon.fr
LIP (UMR CNRS, ENS Lyon, INRIA, Univ. Claude Bernard Lyon 1) - ENS Lyon - 46, alle d'Italie 69364, Lyon Cedex 07, France

Abstract Although limits of resources such as memory or disk usage are one of the key problems of many communicating applications, most process algebras fail to take this aspect of mobile and concurrent systems into account. In order to study this problem, we introduce the Controlled π-calculus, an extension of the π-calculus with a notion of recovery of unused resources with an explicit (parametrized) garbage-collection and dead-process elimination. We discuss the definition of garbage-collection and dead-process elimination for concurrent, communicating applications, and provide a type-based technique for statically proving resource bounds. Selected examples are presented and show the potential of the Controlled π-calculus.

1 Introduction

Virtually every piece of software or hardware in use nowadays relies on some form of communication. Whether a communication takes place between a program and the underlying operating system, between an application and a user, between the video board and the central processing unit or between several distant computers, it involves the concurrent emission and reception of information along a of *communication medium*. As no actual device has infinite resources, neither in memory limited-systems such as cellphones nor in enterprise-level webservers, only a finite number of communications may be performed simultaneously without failing, sometimes critically. Indeed, the problems of resource usage and resource awareness are crucial as this kind of failure may arise as a consequence of erroneous user-interaction, internal accidents or Denial of Service-like attacks.

A number of process algebras hold emissions and receptions as a primitive construction. Unfortunately, these calculi fail to address the problem of resource boundedness. This aspect of resource usage may be seen as closely re-

*This work is partially supported by IST Global Computing PROFUNDIS.

lated to the creation/restriction of fresh names, a construction shared between the class of process calculi known as *nominal process calculi* [3]. In this class of calculi, *names* are used to access resources while interaction is programmed by letting processes exercise some capabilities they have on names. Moreover, in nominal calculi, *names themselves may be seen as resources.*

In this paper, we study the crucial problem of resource boundedness using the π-calculus as a representative of nominal process calculi and as a base for our work. To achieve our goal, we revisit the operator ν (the Greek letter 'nu', pronounced 'new') of name creation/restriction in nominal process calculi from two distinct points of view. In our setting, ν is both:

- the action of creating a new name whose identity is given by an agreed-upon identifier – hence using some of the available resources;
- an indication of scope, limiting the definition domain of a name *in space as well as in time* – hence also limiting the usage of resources.

Based on this notion of resources, in order to permit the design of resource-aware protocols, we enrich the π-calculus with the ability to wait for the recovery of now-unused resources by introducing a new capability ᒣ (the Hebrew letter 'daleth', to be pronounced 'delete'). In this Controlled π-calculus, for instance,

$$(\nu x)((\daleth x).P|Q) \longrightarrow^{*} P|Q \text{ when } x \text{ is not free in } P \text{ or } Q.$$

In other words, when x is not used anymore, its *finalizer* P may be triggered and the resources occupied by x may be recovered. This operator, somewhat dual to ν, is very close to the `Gc.finalise` function in OCaml or to finalizer methods in Java or C#. Although much safer than `free` or `delete` in traditional programming languages, the definition of finalization requires care to avoid problems such as resurrection of previously garbage-collectable resources – problems which may be easily witnessed in the aforementioned languages, and which is considered bad programming as it may lead to unpredictable behaviors, especially when in distributed or cross-language settings (see e.g. [1]).

In turn, resource recovery requires some form of garbage-collection mechanism, which may be more or less automated, to recover resources which cannot be accessed anymore although they may still appear syntactically in a term. For example, let us consider a process Q defined by

$$Q \triangleq (\nu r)r(x).P \tag{1}$$

Q creates a new (secret) channel name r then immediately waits for an input on r. Since r is secret, no other process can possibly communicate using this channel, hence Q shall wait forever. Consequently, the resource r is unnecessary and could be recovered, as well as some of the resources which may appear in P, since P will never be actually executed.

In (1), a garbage-collector could rewrite Q into $\mathbf{0}$, possibly in several steps, hence releasing r. However, different garbage-collectors might take different approaches to remove Q and may or may not be able to analyze complex situations such as deadlocks or even livelocks. In order to deal with any possible garbage-collection method, we first define a relation $\mathcal{GC}$ between garbage-collectable processes and their garbage-collected counterparts using barbed simulations. We then introduce in the operational semantics of Controlled π a rule

$$\text{R-GC}\ \frac{P \longrightarrow_{GC} Q}{P \longrightarrow Q}$$

where $\longrightarrow_{GC}$ is a parametric relation on processes and included in $\mathcal{GC}$.

Although this enrichment of the π-calculus is not meant to add expressivity[1], it permits both dynamic reactivity to resources allocation and deallocation and easy reasoning the usage of resources. The possibility for processes to synchronize on resource recovery may be used to write resource-aware protocols which may be run with statically provable bounded amounts of resources. In order to prove these bounds, we introduce a resource-aware type system for the Controlled π-calculus, more powerful than our previous type systems of [10], for it does not require to replace replication by recursion.

In section 2, we introduce the Controlled π-calculus, starting with a simple language with only a simple form of garbage-collection (Core language) then expanding the definition to add garbage-collection mechanisms (Full language). We then present in section 3 a type system for resource-bounds guarantees. We conclude this paper by an overview of related works and future developments. Due to space limitations, proofs are not included in this document. They may be found in a companion technical annex [11].

2 The Controlled π-calculus

As the full definition of Controlled π-calculus (Cπ for short) requires a complex definition of dead-process elimination which in turn relies on the definition of the other parts of the calculus, we present Cπ in two steps. We start by defining the core of Cπ.

Core Cπ

Syntax The syntax of Core Cπ is presented on Figure 1. Although the syntax itself includes type annotations denoted by N in $(\nu x : N)$, we delay presenting a possible type system until Section 3. It is almost identical to that of the π-calculus, with the addition of $\urcorner$ and the special name $\diamond$ which denotes a special channel on which communications never actually occur and which cannot be bound. Process $(\urcorner x).P$, a finalizer for x, waits for name x to become unused then proceeds as P. Based on this syntax, we define the set of free names, fn and the set of bound names, bn, as in the π-calculus, with the addition of $(\urcorner x)$ - $(\urcorner x)$ is not a binder, rather x is a free name in $(\urcorner x).P$. Substitution, written $P\{a \leftarrow b\}$, is standard with the addition of rules for $\urcorner$: $((\urcorner x).P)\{a \leftarrow b\} = (\urcorner b).(P\{a \leftarrow b\})$ if $x = a$, $((\urcorner x).P)\{a \leftarrow b\} = (\urcorner x).(P\{a \leftarrow b\})$ otherwise.

[1] Actually, we believe $\urcorner$ is encodable in π-calculus, although the encoding itself is way too complicated to permit the relatively simple proofs of Section 3.

Processes			
P, Q	$::=$	$\mathbf{0}$	Terminated process
	$\mid$	$P \mid Q$	Parallel composition
	$\mid$	$\alpha.P$	Action
	$\mid$	$!\alpha.P$	Guarded replication
	$\mid$	$P + Q$	Non-deterministic choice
	$\mid$	$(\nu x : N)P$	Resource creation/restriction
	$\mid$	$(\urcorner x).P$	Resource finalization

Prefixes			
α	$::=$	$x(y)$	Input
	$\mid$	$\overline{x}\langle y\rangle$	Output

Figure 1. Syntax of Controlled π-calculus.

S-PAR-ASSOC	$P\|(Q\|R) \equiv (P\|Q)\|R$	S-PAR-COMM	$P\|Q \equiv Q\|P$
S-PAR-NIL	$P\|\mathbf{0} \equiv P$	S-BANG	$!P \equiv P\|!P$
S-SUM-COMM	$P + Q \equiv Q + P$	S-SUM-NIL	$P + \mathbf{0} \equiv P$
S-SUM-ASSOC	$P + (Q + R) \equiv (P + Q) + R$		
S-NEW-REN	$(\nu x : N)P \equiv (\nu y : N).P\{x \leftarrow y\}$		if $y \notin fn(P)$
S-RCV-REN	$c(x).P \equiv c(y).P\{x \leftarrow y\}$		if $y \notin fn(P)$
S-NEW-COMM	$(\nu x : N)(\nu y : U)P \equiv (\nu y : U)(\nu x : N)P$		if $x \neq y$
S-NEW-PAR	$(\nu x : N)(P\|Q) \equiv P\|(\nu x : N)Q$		if $x \notin fn(P)$
S-FIN-PAR	$(\urcorner x).P\|(\urcorner x).Q \equiv (\urcorner x).(P\|Q)$		
S-STRUCT-PAR	$P \equiv Q \Longrightarrow P\|R \equiv Q\|R$		

Figure 2. Structural congruence in Cπ

In order to simplify the definition of the language, we shall only take into account terms in which no name is bound twice (i.e. there is no P such that $P \triangleq a(x)Q$ or $P \triangleq (\nu x : T)Q$ with x bound in Q). It is a standard result that, through appropriate renamings, we may keep the names unique, in any term, hence preventing the presence of names bound twice.

Structural congruence Structural congruence is the smallest equivalence verifying the relations of Figure 2. The rules are mostly identical to their counterparts from the π-calculus. Actually, rule S-NEW-COMM is slightly more precise than its counterpart in the standard π-calculus, as it preserves type information[2].

Also note that the only rule specific to $\urcorner$ is S-FIN-PAR, which states that triggering two processes by either one or two identical finalizations does not change the behavior of the system. The only other difference is the absence of the usual rule $(\nu x)\mathbf{0} \equiv \mathbf{0}$. In C$\pi$, this congruence is not true since $(\nu x : T)\mathbf{0}$ is a process holding resource x, although it does not use it, while $\mathbf{0}$ is a process holding no resource.

Similarly, we do not have $(\nu x : T)\alpha.P \equiv \alpha.(\nu x : T)P$, a rule found in several variants of the π-calculus, which states that the time of allocation of a resource is not important. In fact, this rule would not make sense in Cπ, for the time of allocation of a resource is important, as may be seen in the following process:

$$Q \triangleq c(x).(\nu y : T)P$$

[2]This is actually not needed as long as we avoid names bound twice.

Communication			
R-COMM-SUM	$(\overline{a}\langle b\rangle.P+Q) \vert (a(x).R+S)$	$\longrightarrow$	$P \vert R\{x \leftarrow b\} \quad (a \neq \diamond)$

Structure			
R-PAR	$\dfrac{P \longrightarrow Q}{P\vert R \longrightarrow Q\vert R}$	R-NEW	$\dfrac{P \longrightarrow Q}{(\nu n:T)P \longrightarrow (\nu n:T)Q}$
R-EQUIV	$\dfrac{P \equiv P' \; P' \longrightarrow Q' \; Q' \equiv Q}{P \longrightarrow Q}$		

Resource recovery			
R-AUTOCLEAN	$(\nu x:N)\mathbf{0}$	$\longrightarrow$	$\mathbf{0}$
R-FINALIZE	$(\nu x:N)(\urcorner x).P$	$\longrightarrow$	$P\{x \leftarrow \diamond\}$

Figure 3. Reduction rules for Base $C\pi$

Q acquires resource y only if reception $c(x)$ actually takes place. If no other process ever emits anything on channel c, the allocation will not take place.

Reduction rules Reduction rules of *Base* $C\pi$ are defined in Figure 3.

R-COMM and R-SUM differ from their counterparts in the traditional π-calculus only insofar as communication cannot take place on the special channel named $\diamond$. This may be seen as processes trying to dereference a `null` pointer: the process is immediately stopped by the operating system. In other words, the communication never occurs. R-PAR, R-NEW and R-EQUIV are standard.

R-AUTOCLEAN takes the place of $(\nu x:T)\mathbf{0} \equiv \mathbf{0}$ in the traditional π-calculus. It means that a terminated process may release the resources it is holding. R-FINALIZE states that a name which appears only as a finalizer may actually be finalized. This is comparable to the behavior of garbage-collectors in traditional languages: if the only reference to an object is a finalizer, then the object has become unreachable and should be finalized then garbage-collected. Finalization of name x ensures that x shall never be used again by substituting special name $\diamond$ (once again similar to a `null` pointer) to possible occurrences of x. Without this substitution, x could appear after $(\urcorner x)$, which would mean that x still lives after having been garbage-collected. Note that we could have specified either that $(\urcorner x).P$ is incorrect when x is free in P or that $(\nu x)(\urcorner x).P$ may only be reduced whenever x is free in P. We preferred our formulation with $\diamond$ as we may wish, at a later stage, to use $\urcorner$ and $\diamond$ to reason about some notions of secrecy (we briefly discuss this perspective in the conclusion) as well as about erroneous deallocations.

Example: a Bounded Resources Manager

Under most operating systems, in order for an agent (such as a Un*x-like process) to allocate a resource, it must request it through a system call such as `malloc`, `fork` or `fopen`. In turn, the operating system is responsible for limiting the actual amount of resources used by each agent.

One possible model for such a bounded resources manager is presented on Figure 4. Each $\square$ offers a slot: at any time, the number of resources available for clients is equal to the number of concurrent $\square$ in the resource manager.

Conversely, each $\triangledown.P$ consumes a slot then proceeds as P. In order to allocate a resource, a client agent must request it on channel *alloc*. Whenever the resource manager receives a request, it waits for a slot to become available, consumes it by exerting $\triangledown$, creates the appropriate resource by exerting $(\nu c : N_c)$ and sends it to the client with $\overline{r}\langle c\rangle$. Whenever a resource c becomes unused and is garbage-collected, a new $\square$ is created, hence keeping track of released resources.

$$\square \triangleq \bar{l}\langle\diamond\rangle \qquad \triangledown.P \triangleq l(x).P \text{ with } x \notin fv(P)$$
$$BRM_n \triangleq (\nu l : N_l)\ (\ !alloc(r).\triangledown.(\nu c : N_c)(\overline{r}\langle c\rangle|(\urcorner c).\square)\ \mid\ \underbrace{\square|\square|\ldots|\square}_{n \text{ resources}}\ )$$

Figure 4. Bounded resources manager

This bounded resources manager models the behaviour of operating systems' memory allocation, process creation, file opening, network access opening... Also note that several bounded resources managers may coexist, each handling a different kind of resources. We shall return to this example to prove several of its properties in the following sections.

Do note that this service only works whenever c is garbage-collected, which may not happen if a client is faulty. Let us consider

$$ROGUE \triangleq (\nu r)\overline{alloc}\langle r\rangle.r(c).c(x).\mathbf{0}$$

A purely syntactic examination of *ROGUE* leads to believe that c is used as a channel to receive some value and should not be recovered. However, in $ROGUE|BRM_n$, no process will ever emit anything on channel c.

Other circumstances, such as deadlocks or communication attempts on channel $\diamond$, may hide the fact that a channel c is, in fact, unused. In each case, c falsely appears to be used because the name c appears syntactically in a process which will actually never be executed. Discovering and removing these occurences so as to recover unneeded resources is the task of the dead-processes eliminator.

Full $C\pi$

As in programming languages, for most systems, the actual set of dead processes not only changes during execution but also depends on non-deterministic choices made during the reduction of processes. For example, let us consider

$$(\nu a)(\nu c)(\ \overline{c}\langle\diamond\rangle.\mathbf{0} \mid c(x).P \mid c(x).Q\ )$$

where P uses a, Q does not and neither P nor Q ever use c. Since c is only used once, either P or Q will be triggered while the other process will end up dead. If P is triggered, a will be used, possibly infinitely often. If Q is triggered, a will become unused.

Therefore, we cannot consider dead process elimination (DPE for short) a static task. Instead, we must define it as a way to rewrite some processes whenever they are not needed anymore. Our intuition is that a process P may be replaced by $\mathbf{0}$ whenever P is triggered by some name a and the behavior of the whole scope of a is unaffected by the removal of P. We now define formally "P is triggered by some name a" (formally, "process P is guarded by a") and "the behavior [...] is unaffected" (formally, this is a barbed simulation).

$$\text{GC-NULL}\ \frac{Q_{[\diamond]}}{(Q, \mathbf{0}) \in \mathcal{GC}} \qquad \text{GC-REMOVE}\ \frac{(\nu a : N)(P|Q) \ll (\nu a : N)P \qquad Q_{[a]}}{(\ (\nu a : N)(P|Q),\ (\nu a : N)P\ ) \in \mathcal{GC}}$$

$$\text{GC-SUM}\ \frac{(\ (\nu a : N)(P|Q),\ (\nu a : N)P\ ) \in \mathcal{GC}}{(\ (\nu a : N)(P|(Q+R)),\ (\nu a : N)(P|R)\ ) \in \mathcal{GC}}$$

$$\text{GC-REPL}\ \frac{(\ (\nu a : N)(P|Q),\ (\nu a : N)P\ ) \in \mathcal{GC}}{(\ (\nu a : N)(P|!Q),\ (\nu a : N)P\ ) \in \mathcal{GC}}$$

Figure 5. Definition of $\mathcal{GC}$

DEFINITION 1 (GUARD) *We write $P_{[a]}$ ("P is guarded by a") whenever*

- $P = a(x).Q$, $P = \overline{a}\langle x\rangle.Q$, $P = (\urcorner a).Q$,
- $P = !P'$ *where* $P'_{[a]}$ *or*
- $P = (\nu b : N)P'$ *where* $P'_{[a]}$ *and* $a \neq b$.

DEFINITION 2 (BARB) *We write $P \downarrow_{\overline{a}}$ ("P has a barb $\overline{a}$") whenever $P \equiv (\nu b_1 : N_1)\ldots(\nu b_n : N_n)(\overline{a}\langle b\rangle.Q + R|S)$ and $P \downarrow_a$ ("P has a barb a") whenever $P \equiv (\nu b_1 : N_1)\ldots(\nu b_n : N_n)(a(x).Q + R|S)$ (with $a \notin \{b_1, \ldots, b_n\}$ in both cases).*

DEFINITION 3 (BARBED SIMULATION) *Let $\mathcal{R}$ be a relation on processes. If, for any processes P and Q such that $P\mathcal{R}Q$ and for any guard ζ we have $P \downarrow_\zeta \Rightarrow Q \downarrow_\zeta$ and $P \longrightarrow P' \Rightarrow Q \longrightarrow Q'$ with $P'\mathcal{R}Q'$, then $\mathcal{R}$ is a barbed simulation. If $P\mathcal{R}Q$ for some barbed simulation we say that Q simulates P, written $P \ll Q$.*

Figure 5 contains our definition for the Elimination of Dead Processes. Recall that we examine the scope of a name and only remove processes guarded by that name – with the exception of $\diamond$. Rule GC-NULL states that any process guarded by $\diamond$ can be safely removed, while rule GC-REMOVE formalizes our intuition: within the scope of name a, if Q is guarded by a and the process obtained by removing Q from the scope can simulate the original process, then Q is dead and may be removed. Rules GC-SUM and GC-REPL extend removing respectively to sums and replications. Note that, since replicated processes are always guarded, $!(\overline{a}\langle x\rangle.P + a(y).Q)$ is not a valid process and therefore causes no garbage-collection problems.

DEFINITION 4 (ELIMINATION OF DEAD PROCESSES) *Let $\mathcal{GC}$ be the smallest relation defined by the rules of Figure 5. If $(A, B) \in \mathcal{GC}$, we say that A is* garbage-collectable *into B by Dead Process Elimination.*

Note that, in defining $\mathcal{GC}$, we chose to focus on a relation which only requires the examination of a given term. Although some more powerful relations exist, this restriction actually corresponds to the fact that examining a whole network is not an option for a garbage-collector. Also note that we chose not to encompass all mechanisms for rewriting processes by removing bits without affecting the outcome. While it would have been relatively easy to define a larger relation $\mathcal{GC}$, we consider that, say, removing prefixes or allocations or removing processes before they get a chance to become active, rather than being garbage-collectors, are other forms of compile-time or run-time optimizations.

A simple example Let us consider $A \triangleq (\nu a : N)!a(x).B$. Since B may hinder resource recovery, we may wish to garbage-collect A into $\mathbf{0}$. From GC-REMOVE, we see that a term such as A is garbage-collectable into $A' \triangleq (\nu a)\mathbf{0}$ by dead process elimination. Since $A' \longrightarrow \mathbf{0}$ by R-AUTOCLEAN, this term is, in fact, "as good as $\mathbf{0}$". Hence, replacing A by A' corresponds to what we wish to do.

Garbage-collecting a deadlock Similarly, let us define $A \triangleq a(x).\bar{b}\langle x\rangle.P$ and $B \triangleq b(x).\bar{a}\langle x\rangle.Q$ and let us consider $C \triangleq (\nu a : N_a)(\nu b : N_b)(A|B)$. Since C is deadlocked, we may also wish to garbage-collect it into $\mathbf{0}$.

Let us then define a relation $\mathcal{R}$ by $(\nu b : N_b)(A|B)\mathcal{R}(\nu b : N_b)A$. Since the only ζ such that $(\nu b : N_b)(A|B) \downarrow_\zeta$ is a, since we also have $(\nu b : N_b)A \downarrow_a$ and since there is no process D such that $(\nu b : N_b)(A|B) \longrightarrow D$, $\mathcal{R}$ is a barbed simulation. Hence, by GC-REMOVE, we have $((\nu b : N_b)(A|B), (\nu b : N_b)A) \in \mathcal{GC}$. Similarly, we have $((\nu a : N_a)A, (\nu a : N_a)\mathbf{0}) \in \mathcal{GC}$. Hence, once again, using $\mathcal{GC}$ to provide a garbage-collected version of C corresponds to what we wish to do.

As we have seen, $\mathcal{GC}$ gives us a notion of garbage-collectable terms. However, as this relation is undecidable, no compiler or runtime support could track $\mathcal{GC}$-related terms. Therefore, we now present a mechanism to include a number of simple rules whose role is to approximate $\mathcal{GC}$.

DEFINITION 5 (GARBAGE-COLLECTOR) *A garbage-collector $\longrightarrow_{GC}$ is a relation between processes such that $P \longrightarrow_{GC} Q \Longrightarrow (P, Q) \in \mathcal{GC}$.*

Rather than specifying a garbage-collection algorithm, we leave the actual garbage-collection mechanism as a parameter of the language. Let us write $\longrightarrow_{GC}$ for this parameter, which must be a garbage-collector. To obtain full Cπ, with respect to core Cπ, the only addition is the following rule:

$$\text{R-GC}\ \frac{P \longrightarrow_{GC} Q}{P \longrightarrow Q}$$

Do note that, informally, compositional type systems with a subject reduction property for core Cπ in which $\mathbf{0}$ is always typable, with any type, also have a subject reduction property in full Cπ.

Examples

In these examples, we write $P \hookleftarrow x$ whenever all occurences of name x in P have the form $(\urcorner x).R$. Let us consider the smallest relation $\longrightarrow_{GC1}$ defined by the set of rules of Figure 6. Relation $\longrightarrow_{GC1}$ is a simple garbage-collector which could be easily and efficiently implemented and which, although limited, is powerful enough to collect some simple examples.

$$(1)\ \diamond(x).P \longrightarrow_{GC1} \mathbf{0} \quad (3)\ (\nu a : N)(P|a(x).Q) \longrightarrow_{GC1} (\nu a : N)P \text{ IF } P \hookleftarrow a$$
$$(2)\ \overline{\diamond}\langle x\rangle.P \longrightarrow_{GC1} \mathbf{0} \quad (4)\ (\nu a : N)(P|\overline{a}\langle x\rangle.Q) \longrightarrow_{GC1} (\nu a : N)P \text{ IF } P \hookleftarrow a$$
$$(5)\ \frac{(\nu a : N)(P|Q) \longrightarrow_{GC1} (\nu a : N)P}{(\nu a : N)(P|!Q) \longrightarrow_{GC1} (\nu a : N)P}$$

Figure 6. A garbage-collector.

GC1 is a garbage-collector Due to space constraints, we shall only give an outline of the proof. We prove by induction that for all A and B, $A \longrightarrow_{GC1} B$ implies $(A, B) \in \mathcal{GC}$. Let us start by proving this property for rule (3).

Let us consider $\mathcal{R}$, the smallest relation such that, for all P such that $P \hookleftarrow a$, if $(\nu a : N)(P|a(x)Q) \longrightarrow^* R$ and $R \equiv (\nu a_1 : N_1, \ldots, a : N, \ldots, a_n : N_n)(P'|a(x)Q)$ then $(R, (\nu a_1 : N_1, \ldots, a : N, \ldots, a_n : N_n)P') \in \mathcal{R}$. One shows that $\mathcal{R}$ is a barbed simulation. Consequently, for a, b, x P and Q such that rule (3) holds, we have $((\nu a : N)(P|a(x).Q), (\nu a : N)P) \in \mathcal{R}$, hence $(\nu a : N)(P|a(x).Q) \ll (\nu a : N)P$. By GC-REMOVE, $((\nu a : N)(P|a(x).Q), (\nu a : N)P)$ is in $\mathcal{GC}$. This proves that only garbage-collectable terms are garbage-collected.

Proof for rule (4) is almost identical. The other proofs are trivial.

Putting GC1 to work In the following example, we shall use an instanciation of $C\pi$ using rule GC1 as our garbage-collection parameter.

Let us consider the bounded memory manager BRM_n and its bad client $ROGUE$ as defined in Section 4. $BRM_n|ROGUE$ may be reduced in several steps into $(\nu c)(BRM'_n|c(x))$, where BRM'_n is the bounded memory manager with one resource locked and awaiting release, namely c. By definition of BRM_n, we have $BRM'_n \hookleftarrow c$. Hence, by rule (3), $(\nu c)(BRM'_n|c(x)) \longrightarrow_{GC1} (\nu c)BRM'_n$. By definition of BRM_n, we then have $(\nu c)BRM'_n \longrightarrow^* BRM_n$. In other words, although the bad client froze while holding resource c, GC1 was powerful enough to eventually recover c.

3 Type-based proofs for resource-bounds

The type system

Now that we have extended the π-calculus so as to make it aware of resources being released, we may define a type system which permits us to prove that resources are properly used. Namely, we intend to prove that systems which properly balance allocation and deallocation of resources have finite resource usage. Remember that, in $C\pi$, $(\nu c : N)$ stands for the allocation of some of the available resources while $(\urcorner c)$ permits to wait for the recovery of these resources. We will thus write $(\nu c : K, e)$ where K is some type information on the created name and e is the number of allocated resources. This lets us define formally the resource usage of a process:

DEFINITION 6 (RESOURCE USAGE) *We write $Res(P)$ for the number of resources process P currently uses, as defined by*

- *if $P = (\nu c : K_c, e_c)Q$ then $Res(P) = e_c + Res(Q)$*
- *if $P = Q + R$ then $Res(P) = max(Res(Q), Res(R))$*

Processes	T	$::=$	t	$t \in \mathbb{N}$	Communications	K	$::=$	$[N, z]$	$z \in \mathbb{Z}$
Names	N	$::=$	K, e	$e \in \mathbb{N}$			$\mid$	Ssh	

Figure 7. Grammar for the resource types

- *if $P = Q|R$ then $Res(P) = Res(Q) + Res(R)$*
- *in all other cases, $Res(P) = 0$*

Do note that the resource usage of $c(x).(\nu d)P$ is zero as this process has not allocated any memory yet.

Full grammar for the type system is given on Figure 7. It includes entries for the type of processes and names. *Typing environments*, ranged over with Γ, are lists of associations of the form $c : N$, where c is a name and N a type. We write $\Gamma(c) = N$ to represent the fact that name c is associated to type N while $\Gamma, c' : N'$ stands for environment Γ extended with $c' : N'$. By convention, we have $\Gamma(\diamond) = N$ for any N. For any name c, $\Gamma(c) = K, e$ expresses the fact that the nature of c is K and that c occupies e resources until it is deallocated. K may be either $[V, z]$ if c is a channel which may be used to communicate names of type V or Ssh if c is not a channel. In the first case, z is used to balance the accounting of the effects of processes triggered by the communication.

Deallocation strategies, ranged over with Λ, are lists of names. The typing judgement for a process is of the form $\Gamma; \Lambda \vdash P : t$ and expresses the fact that P may use up to t resources under assumptions Γ and provided the deallocation in P of names appearing in Λ is taken into account. Keeping track of deallocations prevents erroneously counting that two finalizers registered for the same name deallocate the resources twice.

The typing rules are given on Figure 8. While T-NIL specifies that $\mathbf{0}$ may always be typed and may take into account the deallocation of any number of names, T-REPL specifies that $!P$ may be typed if and only if P does not require any resource and does take into account any deallocation – in other words, if the effect of P is accounted for somewhere else, presumably by taking advantage of communication cost balancing. T-NEW may only be applied whenever the deallocation of the allocated name has somehow already been taken into account and it specifies the fact that $(\nu x : K, e).P$ requires e more resources than P. T-SUM is applicable only when both processes may be typed under the same environments and strategies, and the number of resources occupied corresponds to the worst case scenario. T-PAR, on the other hand, sums the contributions of both processes to the amount of resources allocated, as well as the list of names whose deallocation has been taken into account – the deallocation of one name may be taken into account only once. T-FINALIZE1 and T-FINALIZE2 permit the typing of finalizations. While the first of these rules does take into account the deallocation of a name, both by decreasing the number of necessary resources and by specifying into Λ that the deallocation has been taken into account, the second rule does neither, so as to allow the typing of several finalizers for the same name or of a finalizer for a name which will only be

$$\text{T-NIL } \Gamma;\Lambda \vdash \mathbf{0} : t \qquad \text{T-NEW } \frac{\Gamma, x : (K,e);\Lambda, x \vdash P : t_P}{\Gamma;\Lambda \vdash (\nu x : K,e)P : t_P + e}\ x \notin \Lambda$$

$$\text{T-REPL } \frac{\Gamma;\emptyset \vdash P : 0}{\Gamma;\Lambda \vdash !P : t} \qquad \text{T-SUM } \frac{\Gamma;\Lambda \vdash P : t \qquad \Gamma;\Lambda \vdash Q : t}{\Gamma;\Lambda \vdash P + Q : t}$$

$$\text{T-PAR } \frac{\Gamma;\Lambda_P \vdash P : t_P \qquad \Gamma;\Lambda_Q \vdash Q : t_Q}{\Gamma;\Lambda_P \cup \Lambda_Q \vdash P|Q : t_P + t_Q}\ \Lambda_P \cap \Lambda_Q = \emptyset$$

$$\text{T-FINALIZE1 } \frac{\Gamma;\Lambda \vdash P : t_P \qquad \Gamma(x) = \_, e}{\Gamma;\Lambda, x \vdash (\urcorner x).P : t_P - e}\ t_P \geq e, x \notin \Lambda$$

$$\text{T-FINALIZE2 } \frac{\Gamma;\Lambda \vdash P : t_P \qquad \Gamma(x) = \_, \_}{\Gamma;\Lambda \vdash (\urcorner x).P : t_P}\ x \notin \Lambda$$

$$\text{T-READ } \frac{\Gamma(c) = [N, z], \_ \qquad \Gamma, x : N;\Lambda \vdash P : t_P}{\Gamma;\Lambda \vdash c(x).P : t_P + z}\ x \notin \Lambda, t_P + z \geq 0$$

$$\text{T-WRITE } \frac{\Gamma(c) = [N, z], \_ \qquad \Gamma;\Lambda \vdash Q : t_Q \qquad \Gamma(y) = N}{\Gamma;\Lambda \vdash \bar{c}\langle y\rangle.Q : t_Q - z}\ t_Q - z \geq 0$$

Figure 8. Typing rules for resource-bounds checking

known at runtime. For instance, T-FINALIZE2 will be used to type $a(x).(\urcorner x).P$ as the actual name which will be deallocated depends on the context. Similarly, when typing $(\urcorner a).P \mid (\urcorner a).Q$, using T-FINALIZE1 on either $(\urcorner a).P$ or $(\urcorner a).Q$ will force a into Λ, hence forcing us to use T-FINALIZE2 to type the rest of the process – hence counting only once the resources set free during $(\urcorner a)$. Rules T-READ and T-WRITE permit the typing of communications. Note first that T-READ may only be applied when the deallocation of x has not been taken into account as x is dynamically bound and we do not know whether its deallocation may already have been accounted for under another name. Let us now consider a communication between $A = c(x).P$ and $B = \bar{c}\langle y\rangle.Q$. As either A or B may be enclosed within a replication, we may use z to make sure $t_P + t_Q$ appears in the typing of A (if $z = -t_P$), in that of B (if $z = t_Q$), or balanced between these processes. Note that T-SUM, T-FINALIZE1, T-READ and T-WRITE rely on a resource expansion property (Theorem 7) to ensure that effects remain positive.

Properties We then have the following properties:

THEOREM 7 (RESOURCE EXPANSION) *If we have* $\Gamma;\emptyset \vdash P : t$*, then for any* $u \geq t$*, we also have* $\Gamma;\emptyset \vdash P : u$*.*

THEOREM 8 (RESOURCE CONTROL) *If we have* $\Gamma;\emptyset \vdash P : t$ *and* $P \longrightarrow^* Q$ *then we also have* $Res(Q) \leq t$*.*

In other words, this type system permits us to find bounds on resources used by processes. This results are comparable to Resource control theorems in [10, 12] or to the Absence of over/under-flow theorem in [2].

Examples

Balancing costs Let us consider once again processes $A \triangleq c(x).P$ and $B \triangleq \overline{c}\langle y\rangle.Q$. Let us suppose we have $\Gamma(c) = [N_c, z_c],\_$, $\Gamma(y) = N_c$, $\Gamma, x : N_c; \emptyset \vdash P : t_P$ and $\Gamma; \emptyset \vdash Q : t_Q$.

Depending on the exact process we wish to type, we may need different values of z_c. For instance, if we wish to type $A \mid B$, with $z_c = 0$, we simply have $\Gamma; \emptyset \vdash A \mid B : t_P + t_Q$. Let us now consider rather process $A \mid !B$. Although B is enclosed under a replication, Q will probably not be triggered an infinite number of times. Actually, Q will be triggered at most as many times as $\overline{c}\langle y\rangle.Q$ may be actually reduced, in other words as many times as there are receptions on channel c. Therefore, in this case, instead of accounting for the cost of Q in B, it is preferable to consider that each reception on channel c costs an additional t_Q. To do this, it is sufficient to have $z = t_Q$. We then have $\Gamma; \emptyset \vdash A : t_P + t_Q$ and $\Gamma; \emptyset \vdash B : 0$. Hence, $\Gamma; \emptyset \vdash A \mid !B : t_P + t_Q$.

Note that z does not have actually to be exactly equal to t_Q: the operation is also possible with $z \geq t_Q$, albeit at the cost of a greater approximation, as we have $\Gamma; \emptyset \vdash A \mid !B : t_P + z$. Of course, by symmetry, we could have handled $!A \mid B$ in the same fashion.

Bounded Memory Manager Recall that the expression of the bounded resources manager BRM_n uses names l (the placeholder for resources, with type N_l), c (the actual resource being created, with type N_c) and *alloc* (the channel used to communicate requests, with type $\Gamma(alloc)$). By convention, we will assume that both c and l occupy 1 resource. The actual value of N_l, N_c and $\Gamma(alloc)$, however, depends on the property we wish to prove.

For example, a desirable property is that BRM_n must be bounded in its resource usage while the action of requesting a name through *alloc* does not induce any cost for a client. To prove this, we may use the types as in the *First typing* of Figure 9. With such types, we have $\Gamma; \emptyset \vdash BRM_n : n + 1$, which proves that BRM_n is bounded indeed. The fact that requesting a name through *alloc* is "free" is specified in the type of *alloc* by the fact that $z = 0$.

We may also wish to prove that BRM_n actually occupies at most 1 resource while requesting a name through *alloc* costs 1 resource to the client. This property corresponds to the *Second typing* of Figure 9. With such types, we have $\Gamma; \emptyset \vdash BRM_n : 1$, which proves that BRM_n occupies at most 1 resource. The fact that requesting a name through *alloc* costs 1 resource is specified in the type of *alloc* by the fact that $z = -1$.

4 Conclusion

We have introduced the Controlled π-calculus in order to permit the design and modelling of resource-aware protocols. Beyond adding to the π-calculus the ability to wait for the recovery of resources, we have presented a defini-

	Resource usage is bounded	Each request costs 1
N_l	$[\_, \mathbf{1}], 1$	$[\_, \mathbf{0}], 1$
N_c	$\_, 1$	$\_, 1$
$\Gamma(alloc)$	$[[N_c, 0], \_, \mathbf{0}], \_$	$[[N_c, 0], \_, -\mathbf{1}], \_$

Figure 9. Typing BRM_n.

tion of garbage-collection and dynamic dead processes elimination in parallel systems. We have enhanced this calculus with a type system created to allow simple proofs on resource-bounds – a type system which may handle traditional replication, not just recursion as in our earlier works [10, 12].

Note that, although our type grammar only permits integer costs, it should be quite easy to rework the type system so as to permit variables. We could then obtain results such as "this process requires $3 \cdot e_a + 7 \cdot e_b - 2 \cdot e_c$ resources", where e_a, e_b and e_c are the resources required by the allocation of a, b and c. This would permit us to refine the information on the costs of protocols and systems.

We are also currently trying to expand Cπ to handle explicit distribution, as this kind of extension seems natural. In order to obtain semantics of finalization close to that of Java, OCaml or C♯, we are investigating the use of type systems with causality [4, 13] so as to prevent the appearance of name $\diamond$. We also wish to try and apply our results to existing implementations of the π-calculus.

Another aspect we are planning to study is the possibility of using finalization as an element of specification for secrecy: as $(\urcorner x).P$ guarantees that P will not be triggered as long as name x is still present somewhere in the system, this kind of property may be used to model protocols which must guarantee that they do forget informations (e.g. unless the user specifically asks that her password must be remembered, her webbrowser must forget it).

Related works Many works consider names as resources in the π-calculus and offer different mechanisms for protecting resources from being exposed or misused, without trying to account for allocation or deallocation [8, 9]. Other works [6] use linear types to prove bounds on the number of communications on channels in the π-calculus without considering allocation, deallocation or garbage-collection.

Garbage-collection for functional languages has been investigated in [7], although without finalization or guarantees on resource-bounds. On the other hand, a primitive similar to $\urcorner$ has been proposed along with a type system to design memory-bounded functional programs [5], with no extension to concurrency. This $@\_$ primitive, however, is related to manual deallocation rather than automatic garbage-collection. Process algebras have also been designed by us and others [2, 10, 12] with explicit allocation and deallocation of cells (ambients, agents, ...) and type systems to offer resource-bounds guarantees. However, these calculi are specifically designed for this purpose, the main resource entity is a cell rather than a name and there is no notion of dead processes or finalization. Note that the main idea of BoCa [2] is actually quite close to our bounded resources manager with the addition of distribution. It is, however, built in the language and seems limited to only one kind of resources. Also note BoCa uses a different, dynamically typed, mechanism of guarded replication for preventing uncontrolled spawning of processes.

Our work is also related to some attempts at designing and modelling garbage-collectors for distributed calculi. Among these, a work on groups in π-calculus [14] offers a definition of dead process elimination close to ours. However, to the best of our knowledge, no such work provides either synchronization and reuse of resources or resource-bounds guarantees.

Acknowledgements We would like to thank Daniel Hirschkoff and Tom Hirschowitz for their time and their insightful suggestions during this work.

References

[1] K. Arnold and J. Gosling. *The Java Programming Language.* Addison-Wesley, 1998.

[2] F. Barbanera, M. Bugliesi, M. Dezani-Ciancaglini, and V. Sassone. A calculus of bounded capacities. In *ASIAN'03*, number 2896 in LNCS, pages 205–223. Springer-Verlag, 2003.

[3] A. Gordon. Notes on nominal calculi for security and mobility. In R. Focardi and R. Gorrieri, editors, *FOSAD*, volume 2171 of *LNCS*, pages 262–330. Springer-Verlag, 2002.

[4] A. Igarashi and N. Kobayashi. A generic type system for the pi-calculus. In *POPL*, pages 128–141, 2001.

[5] S. Jost. `lfd_infer`: an implementation of a static inference on heap space usage. In *Proceedings of SPACE 2004*, 2004.

[6] Naoki Kobayashi, Benjamin C. Pierce, and David N. Turner. Linearity and the Pi-Calculus. *ACM Transactions on Programming Languages and Systems*, 21(5):914–947, 1999.

[7] Greg Morrisett, Matthias Felleisen, and Robert Harper. Abstract models of memory management. In *Proceedings of FPCA 1995*, pages 66–77. ACM Press, 1995.

[8] N.Yoshida and M. Hennessy. Subtyping and locality in distributed higher order processes. In *CONCUR'99*, volume 1664 of *LNCS*, pages 557–572. Springer-Verlag, 1999.

[9] B. Pierce and D. Sangiorgi. Typing and subtyping for mobile processes. In *8th IEEE Logics in Computer Science*, pages 376–385, Montreal, Canada, 1993.

[10] D. Teller. Formalisms for mobile resource control. In *FGC'03*, volume 85 of *ENCS*. Elsevier, 2003.

[11] D. Teller. Resource recovery in pi-calculus – technical annex. 2004. available at `http://perso.ens-lyon.fr/david.teller/recherche/Publications/cpita.pdf`.

[12] D. Teller, P. Zimmer, and D. Hirschkoff. Using Ambients to Control Resources. In *Proc. of CONCUR'02*, volume 2421 of *LNCS*. Springer-Verlag, 2002.

[13] N. Yoshida. Graph types for monadic mobile processes. In *Foundations of Software Technology and Theoretical Computer Science*, pages 371–386, 1996.

[14] S. Dal Zilio and A. D. Gordon. Region analysis and a π-calculus with groups. In *MFCS 2000: 25th ISMFCS*, 2000.

ENSURING TERMINATION BY TYPABILITY

Yuxin Deng[1] and Davide Sangiorgi[2]
[1] *INRIA and University Paris 7,* [2] *University of Bologna*

Abstract A term terminates if all its reduction sequences are of finite length. We show four type systems that ensure termination of well-typed π-calculus processes. The systems are obtained by successive refinements of the types of the simply typed π-calculus. For all (but one of) the type systems we also present upper bounds to the number of steps well-typed processes take to terminate. The termination proofs use techniques from term rewriting systems.

We show the usefulness of the type systems on some non-trivial examples: the encodings of primitive recursive functions, the protocol for encoding separate choice in terms of parallel composition, a symbol table implemented as a dynamic chain of cells.

Keywords: Concurrency, the π-calculus, type system, termination

1. Introduction

A term terminates if all its reduction sequences are of finite length. As far as programming languages are concerned, termination means that computation in programs will eventually stop. In computer science termination has been extensively investigated in term rewriting systems [5, 3] and λ-calculi [7, 2] (where strong normalization is a synonym more commonly used). Termination has also been discussed in process calculi, notably the π-calculus [12, 17], a formalism widely used to address issues related to concurrency.

Indeed, termination is interesting in concurrency. For instance, if we interrogate a process, we may want to know that an answer is eventually produced (termination alone does not guarantee this, but termination would be the main ingredient in a proof). Similarly, when we load an applet we would like to know that the applet will not run for ever on our machine, possibly absorbing all the computing resources (a 'denial of service' attack). In general, if the lifetime of a process can be infinite, we may want to know that the process does not remain alive simply because of non-terminating internal activity, and that, therefore, the process will eventually accept interactions with the environment.

Languages of terminating processes are proposed in [19] and [16]. In both cases, the proofs of termination make use of logical relations, a well-known technique from functional languages. The languages of terminating processes so obtained are however rather 'functional', in that the structures allowed are similar to those derived when encoding functions as processes. In particular, the languages are very restrictive on nested inputs (that is, the possibility of having free inputs underneath other inputs), and recursive inputs (that is, replications $!a(x).P$ in which the body P can recursively call the guard a of the replication). Such patterns are entirely forbidden in [19]; nested inputs are allowed in [16] but in a very restricted form. For example, the process

$$a(x).!b.\bar{x} \mid \bar{a}c \tag{1}$$

is legal neither for [19] nor for [16]. The restrictions in [19, 16] actually rule out also useful functional processes, for instance

$$F \equiv !a(n,b).\ \mathtt{if}\ n = 1\ \mathtt{then}\ \bar{b}\langle 1\rangle\ \mathtt{else}\ \nu c(\bar{a}\langle n-1, c\rangle \mid c(m).\bar{b}\langle m * n\rangle) \tag{2}$$

which represents the factorial function.

In this paper, we consider several type systems and well-typed processes under each system are ensured to terminate. First, in Section 3, we present a core type system, which adds level information to the types of the simply typed π-calculus. Then, in Sections 4 to 6 we show three refinements of the core system. Nested inputs and recursive inputs are the main patterns we focus on. For all the type systems (except for the second one, which can capture primitive recursive functions) we also present upper bounds to the number of steps well-typed processes take to terminate. Such bounds depend on the structures of the processes and on the types of the names in the processes. We show the usefulness of the type systems on some non-trivial examples: the encodings of primitive recursive functions, the protocol for encoding separate choice in terms of parallel composition from [13, 17], a symbol table implemented as a dynamic chain of cells from [8, 15].

Roughly, for each type system to prove termination we choose a measure which decreases after finite steps of reductions. To compare two measures, we exploit *lexicographic* and *multiset orderings*, well-known techniques in term rewriting systems [5, 4]. For the core type system, the measure is just a vector recording, for each level, the number of outputs (unguarded by replicated inputs) at channels with that level in the type. For the extended type systems, the ideas are similar, but the measures become more sophisticated since we allow them to decrease after some finite (unknown and variable) number of reductions, up-to some commutativities of reductions and process manipulations.

2. The simply typed π-calculus

We begin with a brief overview of the simply typed π-calculus [17]. In this work we only study type systems *à la Church*, and each name is assigned a type a priori. We write $x : T$ to mean that the name x has type T. A judgment $\vdash P$ says that P is a well-typed process, and $\vdash v : T$ says that v is a well-typed value of type T. The syntax of types and processes as well as the typing rules are shown in Table 1. We use the usual constructors of monadic π-calculus. Recall that in the input prefix $a(x)$ and output prefix $\bar{a}v$, name a is the *subject* and x, v are the *objects* of the prefixes. We assume α-conversion implicitly in order to avoid name capture and keep the uniqueness of every bound name. The transition rules are standard, in the early style.

Table 1. Processes, types and typing rules of the simply typed π-calculus

S, T	$::=$	$V \mid L$	types
V	$::=$	$L \mid \texttt{bool} \mid \texttt{Nat}$	value types
L	$::=$	$\sharp V$	link types
v, w	$::=$	$x \mid true, false \mid 0, 1, 2, \cdots$	values
P, Q	$::=$	$0 \mid a(x).P \mid \bar{a}v.P \mid P \mid P \mid P + P \mid \nu aP \mid !a(x).P$	processes

$$\text{T-in}\ \frac{\vdash a : \sharp T \quad x : T \quad \vdash P}{\vdash a(x).P} \qquad \text{T-out}\ \frac{\vdash a : \sharp T \quad \vdash v : T \quad \vdash P}{\vdash \bar{a}v.P} \qquad \text{T-nil}\ \frac{}{\vdash 0}$$

$$\text{T-par}\ \frac{\vdash P \quad \vdash Q}{\vdash P \mid Q} \qquad \text{T-sum}\ \frac{\vdash P \quad \vdash Q}{\vdash P + Q} \qquad \text{T-res}\ \frac{a : L \quad \vdash P}{\vdash \nu aP}$$

$$\text{T-rep}\ \frac{\vdash a : \sharp T \quad x : T \quad \vdash P}{\vdash !a(x).P}$$

For simplicity we only consider two basic types: `bool`, for boolean values, and `Nat`, for natural numbers. Values of basic types are said to be of first-order because, unlike channels (names of link type), they cannot carry other values. We also assume some basic operations on first-order values. For example, we may use addition $(n + m)$, subtraction $(n - m)$, multiplication $(n * m)$ for `Nat` expressions. To avoid being too specific, we do not give a rigid syntax and typing rules for first-order expressions. We just assume a separate mechanism for evaluating expressions of type `Nat`.

Next we introduce some notations about vectors, partial orders and multisets. We write $\mathbf{0}_i$ as the abbreviation of a vector $\langle n_k, \cdots, n_1 \rangle$ where $n_i = 1$ and $n_j = 0$ for all $j \neq i$, and $\mathbf{0}$ for a vector with all 0 components. The binary operator *sum* can be defined between two vectors. Let $\varphi_1 \equiv \langle n_k, n_{k-1}, \cdots, n_1 \rangle$, $\varphi_2 \equiv \langle m_l, m_{l-1}, \cdots, m_1 \rangle$ and $k \geq l$. First we extend the length of φ_2 to k by inserting $(k - l)$ zeros to the left of m_l to get an equivalent vector φ_2'. Then we do pointwise addition over two vectors with equal length. We also define an order between two vectors of equal length as follows: $\langle n_k, n_{k-1}, \cdots, n_1 \rangle \prec \langle m_k, m_{k-1}, \cdots, m_1 \rangle$ iff $\exists i \leq k$ with $n_j = m_j$ for $j > i$ and $n_i < m_i$.

Let S be a set and $>$ a strict partial order on S. Following [1], we write a multiset $\mathcal{M}$ *over* S in the form $\mathcal{M} = [x_1, \ldots, x_n]$, where $x_i \in S$ for $1 \leq$

$i \leq n$; we use $(\mathcal{M} \uplus \mathcal{M}')$ for the *union* of $\mathcal{M}$ and $\mathcal{M}'$, and write $>_{mul}$ for the multiset ordering (on multisets over S) induced by $>$. A multiset becomes smaller, in the sense of $>_{mul}$, by replacing one or more of its elements by any finite number (including zero) of smaller elements. It can indeed be shown that $>_{mul}$ is well-founded [1].

In this paper we restrict our attention to the termination property of closed processes, i.e., processes without free names of bool or Nat types.

3. The core system: the simply typed π-calculus with levels

Our first type system for termination is obtained by making mild modifications to the types and typing rules of the simply typed π-calculus. We assign a level, which is a natural number, to each channel name and incorporate it into the type of the name. Now the syntax of link type takes the new form:

$$\begin{array}{lcll} L & ::= & \sharp^n V & \text{link types} \\ n & ::= & 1, 2, \cdots & \text{levels} \end{array}$$

The typing rules in Table 1 are still valid (by obvious adjustments for link types), with the exception of rule T-rep, which takes the new form:

$$\text{T-rep} \ \frac{\vdash a : \sharp^n T \quad x : T \quad \vdash P \quad \forall b \in os(P), lv(b) < n}{\vdash !a(x).P}$$

where $os(P)$ is a set collecting all names in P which appear as subjects of those outputs that are not underneath any replicated input (we say this kind of outputs are *active*). The function $lv(b)$ calculates the *level* of channel b from its type. If $b : \sharp^n T$ then $lv(b) = n$.

The purpose of using levels is to rule out recursive inputs as, for instance, in the process $\bar{a} \; | !a.\bar{b} \; | !b.\bar{a}$ the two replicated processes can call each other thus producing a divergence. It is ruled out by our type system because $!a.\bar{b}$ requires $lv(a) > lv(b)$ while $!b.\bar{a}$ requires $lv(b) > lv(a)$. With levels, we also have a concise way of handling nested inputs. For example, let $a : \sharp^1 \sharp^1 \texttt{Nat}, b : \sharp^2 \texttt{Nat}, c : \sharp^1 \texttt{Nat}$, then process (1) is well-typed. We call $\mathcal{T}$ this type system and write $\mathcal{T} \vdash P$ to mean that P is a well-typed process under $\mathcal{T}$. The subject reduction theorem of the simply typed π-calculus can be easily adapted to $\mathcal{T}$.

To prove the termination property of well-typed processes, we need to define a measure for processes. The measure that we choose in this section is the *weight*, $wt(P)$, of a process P. It is a vector determined by the levels of subject names which appear in active outputs. Specifically,

$$\begin{array}{rclcrcl} wt(0) & = & \mathbf{0} & & wt(\bar{a}v.P) & = & wt(P) + \mathbf{0}_{lv(a)} \\ wt(!a(x).P) & = & \mathbf{0} & & wt(P \mid Q) & = & wt(P) + wt(Q) \\ wt(a(x).P) & = & wt(P) & & wt(P + Q) & = & max\{wt(P), wt(Q)\} \\ wt(\nu a P) & = & wt(P) & & & & \end{array}$$

In the next theorem, clause (i) says that weight is a good measure because it decreases at each reduction step, which leads naturally to the termination property of well-typed processes (clause (ii)), by the well-foundedness of weight.

THEOREM 1 *(i) Suppose* $\mathcal{T} \vdash P$ *and* $P \xrightarrow{\tau} P'$*, then* $wt(P') \prec wt(P)$*.*
(ii) If $\mathcal{T} \vdash P$*, then* P *terminates.*

It is easy to see that the weight of a process gives us a bound on the time that the process takes to terminate.

PROPOSITION 2 *Let* n *and* k *be the size and the highest level in a well-typed process* P*, respectively. Then* P *terminates in polynomial time* $\mathcal{O}(n^{k-1})$*.*

As a consequence we are not able to encode the simply typed λ-calculus, according to the known result that computing the normal form of a non-trivial λ-term cannot be finished in elementary time [18, 9]. We shall see in the next section an extension of $\mathcal{T}$ that makes it possible to encode all primitive recursive functions (some of which are not representable in the simply typed λ-calculus).

4. Allowing limited forms of recursive inputs

The previous type system allows nesting of inputs but forbids all forms of recursive inputs. In this and the following sections we study how to relax this restriction.

4.1 The type system

Let us consider a simple example. Process P below has a recursive input: underneath the replication at a there are two outputs at a itself. However, the values emitted at a are "smaller" than the value received. This, and the fact that the "smaller than" relation on natural numbers is well-founded, ensures the termination of P. In other words, the termination of P is ensured by the relation among the subjects and objects of the prefixes – rather the subjects alone as it was in the previous system.

$$\begin{array}{rl} P \equiv & \bar{a}\langle 10\rangle \mid !a(n).\,\texttt{if}\ n > 0\ \texttt{then}\ (\bar{a}\langle n-1\rangle \mid \bar{a}\langle n-1\rangle) \\ \longrightarrow & \bar{a}\langle 9\rangle \mid \bar{a}\langle 9\rangle \mid !a(n).\,\texttt{if}\ n > 0\ \texttt{then}\ (\bar{a}\langle n-1\rangle \mid \bar{a}\langle n-1\rangle) \end{array}$$

For simplicity, the only well-founded values that we consider are naturals. But the arguments below apply to any data type on whose values a well-founded relation can be defined.

We use function $out(P)$ to extract all active outputs in P. The definition is similar to that of $os(P)$ in Section 3. The main difference is that each element of $out(P)$ is a complete output prefix, including both subject and object names. For example, we have $out(!a(x).P) = \emptyset$ and $out(\bar{a}v.P) = \{\bar{a}v\} \cup out(P)$.

In the typing rule, in any replication $!a(x).P$ we compare the active outputs in P with the input $a(x)$ using the relation $\lhd$ below. We have that $\bar{b}v \lhd a(x)$ holds in two cases: (1) b has a lower level than a; (2) b and a have the same level, but the object v of b is provably smaller than the object x of a. For this, we assume a mechanism for evaluating (possibly open) integer expressions that allows us to derive assertions such as $x - i < x$ if $i > 0$, or $x + 2 - 3 + 1 \leq x$. We adopt an eager reduction strategy, thereby the expression in an output is evaluated before the output fires.

DEFINITION 3 *Let $a : \sharp^n S$ and $b : \sharp^m T$. We write $\bar{b}v \lhd a(x)$ if one of the two cases holds: (i) $m < n$; (ii) $m = n$, $S = T = \mathtt{Nat}$ and $v < x$.*

By substituting the following rule for T-rep in Table 1, we get the extended type system $\mathcal{T}'$. The second condition in the definition of $\lhd$ allows us to include some recursive inputs and gives us the difference from $\mathcal{T}$.

$$\text{T-rep} \quad \frac{\vdash a : \sharp^n T \quad x : T \quad \vdash P \quad \forall \bar{b}v \in out(P'), \bar{b}v \lhd a(x)}{\vdash !a(x).P}$$

The termination property of $\mathcal{T}'$ can also be proved with a schema similar to the proof in last section. However, the details are more complex because we need to be clear about how the first-order values in which we are interested evolve with the reduction steps. So we use a measure which records, for each output prefix, the value of the object and the level information of the subject. More precisely, the measure is a *compound vector*, which consists of two parts: the *Nat-multiset* and the weight, corresponding to each aspect of information that we wish to record.

To a given process P and level i, with $0 < i \leq k$, we assign a unique Nat-multiset $\mathcal{M}_{P,i} = [n_1, \cdots, n_l]$, with $n_j \in \mathbb{N} \cup \{\infty\}$ for all $j \leq l$. (Here we consider ∞ as the upper bound of the infinite set $\mathbb{N}$.) Intuitively, this multiset is obtained as follows. For each active output $\bar{b}v$ in P with $lv(b) = i$, there are two possibilities. If v is a constant value ($v \in \mathbb{N}$), then v is recorded in $\mathcal{M}_{P,i}$. If v contains variables of type $\mathtt{Nat}$, then a ∞ is recorded in $\mathcal{M}_{P,i}$. For instance, suppose $a : \sharp^3\mathtt{Nat}, b : \sharp^2\mathtt{Nat}, c : \sharp^1\mathtt{Nat}$ and $P \equiv \bar{a}\langle 1\rangle \mid \bar{a}\langle 1\rangle \mid \bar{b}\langle 2\rangle \mid\, !a(n).\bar{b}\langle n+1\rangle \mid b(n).\bar{c}\langle n\rangle$, then $\mathcal{T}' \vdash P$ and there are three Nat-multisets: $\mathcal{M}_{P,3} = [1, 1]$, $\mathcal{M}_{P,2} = [2]$ and $\mathcal{M}_{P,1} = [\infty]$. We define an operator $\searrow$ to combine a set of Nat-multisets $\{\mathcal{M}_{Q,i} \mid 0 < i \leq k\}$ with the weight of Q (as defined in the previous section), $wt(Q) = \langle n_k, \cdots, n_1\rangle$, so as to get a *compound vector* $t_Q = \langle(\mathcal{M}_{Q,k}; n_k), \cdots, (\mathcal{M}_{Q,1}; n_1)\rangle$. The order $\prec$ is extended to compound vectors as follows:

DEFINITION 4 *Suppose $t_P = \langle(v_k), \cdots, (v_1)\rangle$ and $t_Q = \langle(u_k), \cdots, (u_1)\rangle$, where $v_i = \mathcal{M}_{P,i}; n_i$ and $u_i = \mathcal{M}_{Q,i}; n'_i$ for $0 < i \leq k$.*
(i) $v_i \prec u_i$ if $\mathcal{M}_{P,i} <_{mul} \mathcal{M}_{Q,i} \vee (\mathcal{M}_{P,i} = \mathcal{M}_{Q,i} \wedge n_i < n'_i)$
(ii) $t_P \prec t_Q$ if $\exists i \leq k, v_j = u_j$ for $j > i$ and $v_i \prec u_i$

THEOREM 5 *(i) If $\mathcal{T}' \vdash P$ and $P \xrightarrow{\tau} P'$ then $t_{P'} \prec t_P$.*
(ii) If $\mathcal{T}' \vdash P$ then P terminates.

The measure used here is more powerful than that in Section 3. With weights, we only prove the termination of processes which always terminate in polynomial time. By using compound vectors, however, as we shall see immediately, we are able to capture the termination property of some processes which terminate in time $\mathcal{O}(f(n))$, where $f(n)$ a is primitive recursive function. For example, we can write a process to encode the *repeated exponentiation*, where $E(0) = 1$, $E(n+1) = 2^{E(n)}$. Once received a number n, the process does internal computation in time $\mathcal{O}(E(n))$ before sending out its result.

4.2 Example: primitive recursive functions

For simplicity of presentation, we have concentrated mainly on monadic communication. It is easy to extend our calculus and type system to allow polyadic communications and an if-then-else construct, which are needed in this example.

PROPOSITION 6 *All primitive recursive functions can be represented as terminating processes in the π-calculus.*

We represent each function $f(\widetilde{x})$ as a process with replicated inputs like $!p(\widetilde{x}, r).R$, where name p has type $T_{m,n} = \sharp^m(\widetilde{\mathtt{Nat}}, \sharp^n\mathtt{Nat})$ with $m > n$. After receiving via p some arguments $\widetilde{x}$ and a return channel r, process R does some computation, and finally the result is delivered at r. This style of encoding is a straightforward adaptation of Milner's encoding of λ-terms into π-processes [10]. Furthermore, the resulting processes are well typed in $\mathcal{T}'$. For instance, the process F in (2) is typable if we give name a the type $\sharp^2(\mathtt{Nat}, \sharp^1\mathtt{Nat})$. By contrast, the encoding of functions that are not primitive recursive may not be typable. An example is Ackermann's function.

5. Asynchronous names

In this section we start a new direction for extending our core type system of Section 3: we prove termination by exploiting the structure of processes instead of the well-foundedness of first-order values. The goal of the new type systems (in this and in the next section) is to gain more flexibility in handling nested inputs. In the previous type systems, we required that in a replicated process $!a(x).P$, the highest level should be given to a. This condition appears rigid when we meet a process like $!a.b.\bar{a}$ because we do not take advantage of the level of b. This is the motivation for relaxing the requirement. The basic idea is to take into account the sum of the levels of two input subjects a, b, and compare it with the level of the output subject a. However, this incurs another problem. Observe the following reductions:

$$
\begin{array}{rl}
P \equiv & \bar{a} \mid \bar{b} \mid !a.b.\bar{a} \\
\longrightarrow & \bar{b} \mid b.\bar{a} \mid !a.b.\bar{a} \\
\longrightarrow & \bar{a} \mid !a.b.\bar{a}
\end{array}
$$

The weight of P does not decrease after the first step of reduction (we consume a copy of $\bar{a}$ but liberate another one). Only after the second reduction does the weight decrease. Further, P might run in parallel with another process, say Q, that interferes with P and prevents the second reduction from happening. This example illustrates two new problems that we have to consider: the weight of a process may not decrease at every step; because of interferences and interleaving among the activities of concurrent processes, consecutive reductions may not yield "atomic blocks" after which the weight decreases.

In the new type system we allow the measure of a process to decrease after a finite number of steps, rather than at every step, and up-to some commutativities of reductions and process manipulations. This difference has a strong consequence in the proofs. For technical reasons related to the proofs, we require certain names to be asynchronous.

5.1 Proving termination with asynchronous names

A name a is *asynchronous* if all outputs with subject a are followed by 0. That is, if $\bar{a}v.P$ appears in a process then $P \equiv 0$. A convenient way of distinguishing between synchronous and asynchronous names is using Milner's sorts [11]. Thus we assume two sorts of names, AN and SN, for asynchronous and synchronous names respectively, with the requirement that all names in AN are syntactically used as asynchronous names. We assume that all processes are well-sorted in this sense and will not include the requirements related to sorts in our type systems. (We stick to using both asynchronous and synchronous names instead of working on asynchronous π-calculus, because synchronous π-calculus is sometimes useful – see for instance the example in Section 6.2 – and it is more expressive [14]. However, all the results in this paper are valid for asynchronous π-calculus as well.)

We make another syntactic modification to the calculus by adding a construct to represent a sequence of inputs underneath a replication:

$$
\begin{array}{lll}
\kappa & ::= & a_1(x_1).\cdots.a_n(x_n) \qquad n \geq 1 \text{ and } \forall i < n, a_i \in AN \\
P & ::= & \ldots \mid !\kappa.P
\end{array}
$$

This addition is not necessary – it only simplifies the presentation. It is partly justified by the usefulness of input sequences in applications. (It also strongly reminds us of the input pattern construct of the Join-calculus [6]). We call κ an input pattern. Note that all but the last name in κ are required to be asynchronous. As far as termination is concerned, we believe that the constraint – and therefore the distinction between asynchronous and synchronous names – can be lifted. However, we do not know how to prove Theorem 7 without it.

The usual form of replication $!a(x).P$ is now considered as a special case where the input pattern has length 1, i.e., it is composed of just one input prefix. We extend the definition of weight to input patterns by taking account of the levels of input subjects: $wt(a_1(x_1).\cdots.a_n(x_n)) = \mathbf{0}_{k_1} + \cdots + \mathbf{0}_{k_n}$ where $lv(a_i) = k_i$. The typing rule T-rep in Table 1 is replaced by the following one.

$$\text{T-rep}\ \frac{\vdash \kappa.P \quad wt(\kappa) \succ wt(P)}{\vdash !\kappa.P}$$

Intuitively, this rule means that we consume more than what we produce. That is, to produce a new process P, we have to consume all the prefixes from $a_1(x_1)$ to $a_n(x_n)$ on the left of P, which leads to the consumption of corresponding outputs at $a_1, \cdots, a_n$. Since the sum of weights of all the outputs is larger than the weight of P, the whole process has a tendency to decrease its weight. Although the idea behind this type system ($\mathcal{T}''$) is simple, the proof of termination is non-trivial because we need to find out whether and when a whole input pattern is consumed and thus the measure decreases.

THEOREM 7 *If* $\mathcal{T}'' \vdash P$ *then* P *terminates.*

Below we briefly explain the structure of the proof and proceed in four steps. Firstly, we decorate processes and transition rules with tags, which indicate the origin of each reduction: whether it is caused by calling a replicated input, a non-replicated input or it comes from an if-then-else structure. This information helps us to locate some points, called *landmarks*, in a reduction path. If a process performs a sequence of reductions that are locally ordered (that is, all and only the input prefixes of a given input pattern are consumed), then the process goes from a landmark to the next one and decreases its weight. (This is not sufficient to guarantee termination, since in general the reductions of several input patterns may interleave and some input patterns may be consumed only partially.) Secondly, by taking advantage of the constraint about asynchronous names, we show a limited form of commutativity of reductions. Thirdly, by commuting consecutive reductions, we adjust a reduction path and establish on it some locally ordered sequences separated by landmarks. Moreover, when an input pattern is not completely consumed, we perform some manipulations on the derivatives of processes and erase some inert subprocesses. Combining all of these with the result of Step 1, we are able to prove the termination property of tagged processes. Finally, the termination of untagged processes follows from the operational correspondence between tagged and untagged processes, which concludes our proof of Theorem 7.

PROPOSITION 8 *For a process* P *well-typed under* $\mathcal{T}''$, *let* n *and* k *be its size and the highest level, respectively. Then* P *terminates in polynomial time* $\mathcal{O}(n^k)$.

5.2 Example: the protocol of encoding separate choice

Consider the following protocol which is used for encoding separate choice by parallel composition [13], [17, Section 5.5.4]. One of the main contributions in [13] is the proof that the protocol does not introduce divergence. Here we prove it using typability.

$$
\begin{array}{l}
[\Sigma_{i=1}^{n} \bar{x}_i d_i.P_i] \equiv \nu s\ (\ \bar{s}\langle true\rangle \\
\qquad\qquad\qquad\quad \mid \Pi_{i=1}^{n} \nu a \bar{x}_i\langle d_i, s, a\rangle.a(x).\ \mathtt{if}\ x\ \mathtt{then}\ [P_i]\ \mathtt{else}\ 0) \\
[\Sigma_{i=1}^{m} y_i(z).Q_i] \equiv \\
\nu r\ (\ \bar{r}\langle true\rangle \\
\quad \mid \Pi_{i=1}^{m} \nu g\ (\ \bar{g} \\
\qquad\qquad \mid\ !g.y_i(z, s, a).r(x).\ \mathtt{if}\ x\ \mathtt{then} \\
\qquad\qquad\qquad\qquad (\ s(y).\ \mathtt{if}\ y\ \mathtt{then} \\
\qquad\qquad\qquad\qquad\qquad (\ \bar{r}\langle false\rangle \mid \bar{s}\langle false\rangle \mid \bar{a}\langle true\rangle \mid [Q_i]) \\
\qquad\qquad\qquad\qquad\quad \mathtt{else} \\
\qquad\qquad\qquad\qquad\qquad (\ \bar{r}\langle true\rangle \mid \bar{s}\langle false\rangle \mid \bar{a}\langle false\rangle \mid \bar{g})) \\
\qquad\qquad\qquad\quad \mathtt{else} \\
\qquad\qquad\qquad\quad \bar{r}\langle false\rangle \mid \bar{y}_i\langle z, s, a\rangle))
\end{array}
$$

where r, s and a are fresh and $\Pi_{i=1}^{n} P_i$ means $P_1 \mid \cdots \mid P_n$.

The protocol uses two locks s and r. When one input branch meets a matching output branch, it receives a datum together with lock s and acknowledge channel a. Then the receiver tests r and s sequentially. If r signals failure, because another input branch has been chosen, the receiver is obliged to resend the value just received. Otherwise, it continues to test s. When s also signals success, the receiver enables the acknowledge channel and let the sender proceed. At the same time, both r and s are set to $false$ to prevent other branches from proceeding. If the test of s is negative, because the current output branch has committed to another input branch, the receiver should restart from the beginning and try to catch other send-requests. This backtracking is implemented by recursively triggering a new copy of the input branch.

Usually when a protocol employs a mechanism of backtracking, it has a high probability to give rise to divergence. The protocol in this example is an exception. However, to figure out this fact is non-trivial, one needs to do careful reasoning so as to analyze the possible reduction paths in all different cases. With the aid of type system $\mathcal{T}''$, we reduce the task to a routine type-checking problem. Simply taking $g.y_i(z, s, a)$ as an input pattern, one can check that the typability of $[P_i]$ and $[Q_i]$ implies that of $[\Sigma_{i=1}^{n} \bar{x}_i d_i.P_i]$ and $[\Sigma_{i=1}^{m} y_i(z).Q_i]$, which means that the protocol does not have infinite loops.

6. Partial orders

The purpose of our final type system is to type processes even if they contain replications whose input and output parts have the same weight. Of course not all such processes can be accepted. For instance, $!a.b.(\bar{a} \mid \bar{b})$ should not be accepted, since it does not terminate when running together with $\bar{a} \mid \bar{b}$. However, we might want to accept

$$!p(a, b).a.(\bar{p}\langle a, b\rangle \mid \bar{b}) \tag{3}$$

where a and b have the same type. Processes like (3) are useful. For instance they often appear in systems composed of several "similar" processes (an example is the chain of cells in Section 6.2). In (3) the input pattern $p(a, b).a$ and the continuation $\bar{p}\langle a, b\rangle \mid \bar{b}$ have the same weight, which makes rule T-rep of $\mathcal{T}''$ inapplicable. In the new system, termination is proved by incorporating partial orders into certain link types. For instance, (3) will be accepted if the partial order extracted from the type of p shows that b is below a.

6.1 The type system

We present the new type system $\mathcal{T}'''$. The general structure of the associated termination proof goes along the same line as the proof in Section 5.1. But now we need a measure which combines lexicographic and multiset orderings.

To begin with, we introduce some preliminary notations. Let $\mathcal{A}$ be a set and $\mathcal{R} \subseteq \mathcal{A} \times \mathcal{A}$ be a partial order on elements of $\mathcal{A}$. The set of names appearing in elements of $\mathcal{R}$ is $n(\mathcal{R}) = \{a \mid a\mathcal{R}b \vee b\mathcal{R}a \text{ for some } b\}$. Let $\widetilde{x}$ be a tuple of names $x_1, \cdots, x_n$. The partial order $\mathcal{S}$ on the index set $\{1, \ldots, n\}$ induces a partial order on $\widetilde{x}$, defined as $\mathcal{S} * \widetilde{x} = \{(x_i, x_j) \mid i\mathcal{S}j\}$.

Remark: In this paper we use partial order in a very narrow sense. Formally, for a partial order on names to be well defined, we require that it satisfies the following two conditions: (i) mathematically it is a strict partial order (irreflexive, antisymmetric and transitive); (ii) all names in $n(\mathcal{R})$ are of the same type (this type is written $T_{\mathcal{R}}$).

The operator $os(\cdot)$ of Section 3 is now refined to be $mos_{\mathcal{R}}(\cdot)$, which defines a multiset recording all subject occurrences of names in active outputs and with type $T_{\mathcal{R}}$. The operator $mos_{\mathcal{R}}(\cdot)$ can be extended to input patterns by defining: $mos_{\mathcal{R}}(\kappa) = mos_{\mathcal{R}}(\bar{a}\widetilde{x}_1 \mid \cdots \mid \bar{a}\widetilde{x}_n)$ if $\kappa = a_1(\widetilde{x}_1). \cdots .a_n(\widetilde{x}_n)$.

Let $\mathcal{R}$ be a partial order and $\mathcal{R}_{mul}$ be the induced multiset ordering on multisets over $n(\mathcal{R})$. The binary relation $\widehat{\mathcal{R}}$ defined below will act as the second component of our measure, which is a lexicographic ordering with weight of processes as its first component.

DEFINITION 9 *Suppose that $\mathcal{R}$ is a partial order, Q is a process, P is either an input pattern or a process. It holds that $P \ \widehat{\mathcal{R}}\ Q$ if the following three conditions are satisfied, for some multisets $\mathcal{M}_1, \mathcal{M}_2$ and $\mathcal{M}$: (i) $mos_{\mathcal{R}}(P) = \mathcal{M} \uplus \mathcal{M}_1$; (ii) $mos_{\mathcal{R}}(Q) = \mathcal{M} \uplus \mathcal{M}_2$; (iii) $\mathcal{M}_1\ \mathcal{R}_{mul}\ \mathcal{M}_2$.*

Essentially the relation $\widehat{\mathcal{R}}$ is an extension of the multiset ordering $\mathcal{R}_{mul}$. So it is also well-founded: if $\mathcal{R}$ is finite, then there exists no infinite sequence $P_0 \ \widehat{\mathcal{R}}\ P_1 \ \widehat{\mathcal{R}}\ P_2 \ \widehat{\mathcal{R}} \cdots$

Now we are well-prepared to present our types and type system. Here we consider polyadic π-calculus and redefine link type as follows.

$$L ::= \natural^n_S \widetilde{T} \quad \text{where} \quad \forall i, j \in n(S),\ T_i = T_j$$

where $S \subseteq \mathtt{Nat} \times \mathtt{Nat}$ is a partial order on the indexes of $\widetilde{T}$. If i and j are two indexes related by S, then the i-th and j-th components of $\widetilde{T}$ have the same type. Suppose $\kappa = a_1(\widetilde{x}_1).\cdots.a_n(\widetilde{x}_n)$ and each a_i has type $\natural^{m_i}_{S_i}\widetilde{T}$. We extract a partial order from κ by defining $\mathcal{R}_\kappa = S_1 * \widetilde{x}_1 \cup \cdots \cup S_n * \widetilde{x}_n$. It is well defined as all the bound names are assumed to be different from each other.

If νaP is a subprocess of Q, we say that the restriction νa is *unguarded* if νaP is not underneath any input or output prefix. Besides the two sorts AN and SN introduced in the beginning of Section 5.1, now we need another sort RN. It requires that if a name of sort RN appears in the subject position of a prefix, then the continuation process has no unguarded restrictions. This technical condition facilitates the presentation of the definition below.

DEFINITION 10 *Let $\kappa = a_1(\widetilde{x}_1).\cdots.a_n(\widetilde{x}_n)$. The relation $\kappa \succ P$ holds if one of the following two cases holds: (i) $wt(\kappa) \succ wt(P)$; (ii) $wt(\kappa) = wt(P)$, $\kappa\, \widehat{\mathcal{R}_\kappa}\, P$ and $a_n \in RN$.*

The second condition indicates the improvement of $\mathcal{T}'''$ over $\mathcal{T}''$. We allow the input pattern to have the same weight as that of the continuation, as long as there is some partial order to reflect a tendency of decrement. The constraint imposed on a_n prohibits dangerous extension of partial orders underneath an input pattern and also simplifies our proof of Theorem 11. For the new type system $\mathcal{T}'''$, the most important rule is the following one:

$$\text{T-rep}\ \frac{\mathcal{R} \vdash \kappa.P \quad \kappa \succ P}{\mathcal{R} \vdash !\kappa.P}$$

Now the judgment $\mathcal{R} \vdash P$ means that P is a well-typed process under $\mathcal{T}'''$ and the free names in P respect the (possibly empty) partial order $\mathcal{R}$. All other rules are easily adapted from $\mathcal{T}''$ by adding some appropriate partial order information to the type environment. Finally we have the following termination theorem for $\mathcal{T}'''$. The proof heavily relies on the well-foundedness of $\widehat{\mathcal{R}}$.

THEOREM 11 *If $\mathcal{R} \vdash P$ then P terminates. Moreover, let n and k be its size and the highest level, then P terminates in polynomial time $\mathcal{O}(n^{k+2})$.*

6.2 Example: symbol table

This example comes from [8, 15]. It implements a symbol table as a chain of cells. Below: G is a generator for cells; ST_0 is the initial state of the symbol table with only one cell; ST_m is the system in which the symbol table has m pending requests.

Every cell of the chain stores a pair (n, s), where s is a string and n is a key identifying the position of the cell in the chain. A cell is equipped with two channels so as to be connected to its left and right neighbors. The first cell has a public left channel a to communicate with the environment and the last cell has a right channel nil to mark the end of the chain. Once received a query for string t, the table lets the request ripple down the chain until either t is found in a cell, or the end of the chain is reached, which means that t is a new string and thus a new cell is created to store t. In both cases, the key associated to t is returned as a result. There is parallelism in the system: many requests can be rippling down the chain at the same time.

$$
\begin{array}{rcl}
G & \equiv & !p(a,b,n,s).a(t,x). \\
 & & \quad\quad\quad\quad \mathtt{if}\ t = s\ \mathtt{then} \\
 & & \quad\quad\quad\quad\quad \bar{x}\langle n\rangle.\bar{p}\langle a,b,n,s\rangle \\
 & & \quad\quad\quad\quad \mathtt{else}\ \ \mathtt{if}\ b = nil\ \mathtt{then} \\
 & & \quad\quad\quad\quad\quad\quad\quad \bar{x}\langle n+1\rangle.\nu c(\bar{p}\langle c, nil, n+1, t\rangle \mid \bar{p}\langle a,c,n,s\rangle) \\
 & & \quad\quad\quad\quad\quad\quad \mathtt{else}\ \bar{b}\langle t,x\rangle.\bar{p}\langle a,b,n,s\rangle \\
ST_0 & \equiv & \nu p(G \mid \bar{p}\langle a, nil, 1, s_0\rangle) \\
ST_m & \equiv & ST_0 \mid \bar{a}\langle t_1, x_1\rangle \mid \cdots \mid \bar{a}\langle t_m, x_m\rangle
\end{array}
$$

As to termination, the example is interesting for at least two reasons. (1) The chain exhibits a syntactically challenging form. The replicated process G has a sophisticated structure of recursive inputs: the input pattern has inputs at p and a, while the continuation has a few outputs at p and one output at b, which should have the same type as a. (2) Semantically, the chain is a dynamic structure, which can grow to finite but unbounded length, depending on the number of requests it serves. Moreover, the chain has a high parallelism involving independent threads of activities. The number of steps that the symbol table takes to serve a request depends on the length of the chain, on the number of internal threads in the chain, and on the value of the request.

Suppose $T \equiv \sharp^2_\emptyset(\mathsf{String}, \sharp^1\mathtt{Nat})$, $S \equiv \{(1,2)\}$ and let the type of p be $\sharp^1_S(T, T, \mathtt{Nat}, \mathsf{String})$. We consider nil as a constant name of the language studied in this section and take it for the bottom element of any partial order $\mathcal{R} \subseteq \mathcal{N}_2 \times \mathcal{N}_2$ with $T_\mathcal{R} = T$. For any $m \in \mathbb{N}$, process ST_m is well typed under $\mathcal{T}'''$ and thus terminating.

7. Final remarks

Since we are not able to encode the simply typed λ-calculus, our systems do not include those of [16] and [19]. Nevertheless, a large class of processes (including all examples analyzed in this paper) are excluded by the above two works. One way of interpreting the results of this paper is to consider combinatory approach (on which this paper is based) as a complementary technique to logical relations (on which [16] and [19] are based) for showing termination of processes. It would be interesting to see whether the two approaches can be successfully combined.

References

[1] M. Bezem. Mathematical background. In M. Bezem, J. Klop, and R. de Vrijer, editors, *Term Rewriting Systems*, pages 790–825. Cambridge University Press, 2003.

[2] G. Boudol. On strong normalization in the intersection type discipline. *LNCS*, 2701:60–74, 2003.

[3] N. Dershowitz and C. Hoot. Natural termination. *Theoretical Computer Science*, 142(2):179–207, 1995.

[4] N. Dershowitz and J.-P. Jouannaud. Rewrite systems. In J. van Leeuwen, editor, *Handbook of Theoretical Computer Science*, chapter 6, pages 243–320. North-Holland, Amsterdam, 1990.

[5] N. Dershowitz and Z. Manna. Proving termination with multiset orderings. *Communications of the ACM*, 22(8):465–476, 1979.

[6] C. Fournet. *The Join-Calculus: A Calculus for Distributed Mobile Programming*. PhD thesis, Ecole Polytechnique, Paris, France, 1998.

[7] R. O. Gandy. Proofs of strong normalization. In *To H.B. Curry: Essays on Combinatory Logic, Lambda Calculus and Formalism*. Academic Press, 1980.

[8] C. Jones. A π-calculus semantics for an object-based design notation. In E. Best, editor, *Proc. CONCUR '93*, volume 715 of *LNCS*, pages 158–172. Springer, 1993.

[9] R. Loader. Notes on simply typed lambda calculus. Technical Report 381, LFCS, University of Edinburgh, 1998.

[10] R. Milner. Functions as processes. *Journal of Mathematical Structures in Computer Science*, 2(2):119–141, 1992.

[11] R. Milner. The polyadic π-calculus: A tutorial. In F. L. Bauer, W. Brauer, and H. Schwichtenberg, editors, *Logic and Algebra of Specification*, volume 94 of *Series F*. NATO ASI, Springer, 1993.

[12] R. Milner. *Communicating and Mobile Systems: the π-Calculus*. Cambridge University Press, May 1999.

[13] U. Nestmann. What is a 'good' encoding of guarded choice? *Journal of Information and Computation*, 156:287–319, 2000.

[14] C. Palamidessi. Comparing the expressive power of the synchronous and asynchronous π-calculi. *Mathematical Structures in Computer Science*, 13:685–719, 2003.

[15] D. Sangiorgi. The typed π-calculus at work: A proof of Jones's parallelisation theorem on concurrent objects. *Theory and Practice of Object-Oriented Systems*, 5(1), 1999.

[16] D. Sangiorgi. Termination of processes, Dec. 2001. Available from `ftp://ftp-sop.inria.fr/mimosa/personnel/davides`.

[17] D. Sangiorgi and D. Walker. *The π-calculus: a Theory of Mobile Processes*. Cambridge University Press, 2001.

[18] R. Statman. The typed λ-calculus is not elementary recursive. *Theoretical Computer Science*, 9(1):73–81, 1979.

[19] N. Yoshida, M. Berger, and K. Honda. Strong normalisation in the pi-calculus. In *Logic in Computer Science*, pages 311–322, 2001.

THE SIMPLY-TYPED PURE PATTERN TYPE SYSTEM ENSURES STRONG NORMALIZATION

Benjamin Wack
LORIA & Université Henri Poincaré, Nancy, France
Benjamin.Wack@loria.fr

Abstract Pure Pattern Type Systems (P^2TS) combine in a unified setting the capabilities of rewriting and λ-calculus. Their type systems, adapted from Barendregt's λ-cube, are especially interesting from a logical point of view. Strong normalization, an essential property for logical soundness, had only been conjectured so far: in this paper, we give a positive answer for the simply-typed system.

The proof is based on a translation of terms and types from P^2TS into the λ-calculus. First, we deal with untyped terms, ensuring that reductions are faithfully mimicked in the λ-calculus. For this, we rely on an original encoding of the pattern matching capability of P^2TS into the λ-calculus.

Then we show how to translate types: the expressive power of System Fω is needed in order to fully reproduce the original typing judgments of P^2TS. We prove that the encoding is correct with respect to reductions and typing, and we conclude with the strong normalization of simply-typed P^2TS terms.

1 Introduction

The λ-calculus and term rewriting provide two fundamental computational paradigms that had a deep influence on the development of programming and specification languages, and on proof environments. The idea that having computational power at hand makes deduction significantly easier and safer is widely acknowledged (Dowek et al., 2003; Werner, 1994). Many frameworks have been designed with a view to integrate these two formalisms: either by enriching first-order rewriting with higher-order capabilities (Klop et al., 1993) or by adding algebraic features to the λ-calculus (*case* expressions with dependent types (Coquand, 1992), a typed pattern calculus (Kesner et al., 1996) and calculi of algebraic constructions (Blanqui, 2001)).

The *rewriting calculus*, or ρ-calculus, by unifying the λ-calculus and the rewriting, makes all the basic ingredients of rewriting explicit objects, in particular the notions of *rule application* and *result*. A rewrite rule becomes a first-class object which can be created and manipulated in the calculus, whereas in works like (Blanqui, 2001), the rewriting remains a bit external to the calculus.

In (Cirstea et al., 2001), a collection of type systems for the ρ-calculus was presented, extending Barendregt's λ-cube to a ρ-cube. Later, these type systems have been studied deeper for the similar formalism of P^2TS (Barthe et al., 2003). Yet, the rewriting calculus has also been assigned some type systems that do *not* prevent infinite reductions (Cirstea et al., 2004). Thus, strong normalization did remain an open problem for P^2TS. In this paper, we give a first positive answer to this problem. Since consistency is related to termination, this result makes P^2TS a good candidate for a proof-term language integrating deduction and computation at the same level.

The main contributions of this paper are:

- a more recent version of P^2TS, enhanced with a signature for the types of constants and some corrections on the product rules;
- a concise encoding of pattern matching in the λ-calculus, which has other potential applications for the encoding of term rewriting systems;
- a translation of the simply-typed system of P^2TS into System Fω emphasizing some particular typing mechanisms of P^2TS;
- a proof of strong normalization for simply-typed P^2TS terms.

This paper is organized as follows. In Section 2, we recall the syntax and the small-step semantics of P^2TS. In Section 3, we give an untyped version of the translation, showing how pattern matching is encoded. In Sections 4 and 5, we present the type systems of P^2TS and System Fω. In Sections 6 and 7, we give the fully typed translation and we outline a proof of correctness for three important elements of the typed translation: variables, constants and delayed matching constraints. In Section 8, we state the key lemmas used in the full strong normalization proof.

We assume the reader is reasonably familiar with the notations and results of typed λ-calculi (Barendregt, 1992), of the ρ-calculus (Cirstea et al., 2004) and of P^2TS (Barthe et al., 2003).

Conventions and notations Generally, the reader can assume that every capital letter denotes an object belonging to P^2TS, and every small letter denotes an object belonging to the λ-calculus (except for constants and their arity). For instance, in P^2TS: X, Y, Z are variables; A, B, C are terms; P, Q are patterns; a, f, g are constants; Φ, Ψ are types; Ξ is an atomic type. In System Fω: w, x, y, z are variables; t, u are terms; β, γ are type variables; σ, τ are types; k is a kind. Moreover, we will use the notations: α, α_i for an arity; θ for a substitution; Γ, Δ for contexts (mainly in P^2TS); Σ for a signature.

Syntactic equivalence of terms will be denoted by $\equiv$. If a substitution θ has domain $X_1 \ldots X_n$ and $\forall i,\ X_i\theta \equiv A_i$, we will also write it $[X_1 := A_1 \ldots X_n := A_n]$. We assume that the signature Σ of constants that can be used in P^2TS is finite, which is legitimate since a given (finite) term only uses a finite number of constants. Therefore, we will number the constants $f_1, \ldots, f_S$, where S is the cardinal of Σ. To denote a tuple of terms $B_k \ldots B_n$, we will use the vector notation $\overrightarrow{B}_{(k..n)}$, or simply $\overrightarrow{B}$ when k and n are obvious from the context. This notation will be used in combination with operators according to their default associativity: for instance, in System Fω, $A\overrightarrow{B} \triangleq AB_1 \ldots B_n$ and $\lambda\overrightarrow{x}.A \triangleq \lambda x_1 \ldots \lambda x_n.A$. To avoid confusion between symbols, we will use bold $\boldsymbol{\lambda}$ and $\boldsymbol{\Pi}$ for P^2TS and roman λ and Π for System Fω.

2 P^2TS: dynamic semantics

In this section, we recall the syntax of P^2TS and their evaluation rules. The syntax of P^2TS extends that of the typed λ-calculus with structures and patterns (Barthe et al., 2003). Several choices can be made for the set of patterns P: in this paper, *we only consider algebraic patterns*, whose shape is defined below. The main reason for this restriction is that patterns containing symbols such as λ require higher-order matching, which seems difficult to encode in a typed λ-calculus.

$$
\begin{array}{lll}
\textit{Signature} & \Sigma ::= \emptyset \mid \Sigma, f : A & \qquad \textit{Context} \quad \Gamma ::= \emptyset \mid \Gamma, X : A \\
\textit{Pattern} & P ::= X \mid f \bullet \overrightarrow{P} & \\
\textit{Term} & A ::= f \mid X \mid \lambda(P : \Delta).A \mid \Pi(P : \Delta).A \mid [P \ll_\Delta A]A \mid A \bullet A \mid A ; A &
\end{array}
$$

A term with shape $\lambda(P : \Delta).A$ is an *abstraction* with pattern P, body A and context Δ. The term $[P \ll_\Delta B]A$ is a *delayed matching constraint* with pattern P, body A, argument B and context Δ. A term $\Pi(P : \Delta).A$ is a *dependent product*, and will be used as a type; finally, $(A; B)$ is a *structure* and $A \bullet B$ is an *application*. The application of a constant symbol, say f, to a term A will be denoted by $f \bullet A$ too; it follows that the usual algebraic notation of a term is currified, *e.g.* $f(A_1, \ldots, A_n) \triangleq f \bullet A_1 \bullet \cdots \bullet A_n \triangleq f \bullet \overrightarrow{A}$.

DEFINITION 1 (FREE VARIABLES $\mathcal{FV}$ OF A TERM)

$$
\begin{array}{lcl}
\mathcal{FV}(A;B) = \mathcal{FV}(A \bullet B) & \triangleq & \mathcal{FV}(A) \cup \mathcal{FV}(B) \qquad\quad \mathcal{FV}(X) \ \triangleq \ \{X\} \\
\mathcal{FV}(\lambda(P : \Delta).A) & \triangleq & \mathcal{FV}(\Pi(P : \Delta).A) \ \triangleq \ (\mathcal{FV}(A) \cup \mathcal{FV}(\Delta)) \setminus \mathcal{D}om(\Delta) \\
\mathcal{FV}([P \ll_\Delta B]A) & \triangleq & (\mathcal{FV}(A) \cup \mathcal{FV}(\Delta)) \setminus \mathcal{D}om(\Delta) \\
\mathcal{FV}(\Gamma, X : A) & \triangleq & \mathcal{FV}(\Gamma) \cup \mathcal{FV}(A) \qquad\quad \mathcal{FV}(f) \ \triangleq \ \emptyset
\end{array}
$$

In this paper, extending Church's notation, the context Δ in $\lambda(P : \Delta).B$ (resp. $[P \ll_\Delta B]A$ or $\Pi(P : \Delta).B$) contains the type declarations of the free variables appearing in the pattern P, *i.e.* $\mathcal{D}om(\Delta) = \mathcal{FV}(P)$. These variables are bound in the abstraction. The context Δ will be omitted when we consider untyped terms. As usual, we work modulo *α-conversion* and we use Barendregt's "*hygiene-convention*" (Barendregt, 1992), *i.e.* free and bound variables have different names.

For the purpose of this paper, we consider only syntactic pattern matching; a syntactic matching equation $P \ll A$ has either no solution or a unique solution noted $\theta_{(P \ll A)}$. In fact, it seems difficult to encode more elaborated matching theories: for instance, associative matching can generate an arbitrary high number of distinct solutions. Thus, to give a faithful account of all matching solutions in the λ-calculus, one would probably need a fixed point.

$$
\begin{array}{llcl}
(\rho) & (\lambda(P : \Delta).A) \bullet B & \to_\rho & [P \ll_\Delta B]A \\
(\sigma) & [P \ll_\Delta B]A & \to_\sigma & A\theta_{(P \ll B)} \\
(\delta) & (A;B) \bullet C & \to_\delta & A \bullet C ; B \bullet C
\end{array}
$$

Figure 1. Top-level rules of P^2TS

The top-level rules are presented in Fig. 1. By the (ρ) rule, the application of a term $\lambda(P : \Delta).A$ to a term B reduces to the delayed matching constraint $[P \ll_\Delta B]A$; the application of the (σ) rule consists in solving the matching equation $P \ll B$ and applying the obtained substitution (if it exists) to the the term A. If no solution exists, the (σ) rule is not fired and the term $[P \ll_\Delta B]A$ is not reduced. As usual, $\mapsto_{\rho\sigma\delta}$ denotes the congruent closure of $\rightarrow_\rho \cup \rightarrow_\sigma \cup \rightarrow_\delta$, and $\mapsto\!\!\!\!\to_{\rho\sigma\delta}$ (resp. $=_{\rho\sigma\delta}$) is defined as the reflexive and transitive (resp. reflexive, symmetric and transitive) closure of $\mapsto_{\rho\sigma\delta}$.

3 Untyped encoding

In this section we translate the untyped P^2TS with algebraic patterns. The process of syntactic pattern matching consists in discriminating whether the argument begins with the expected constant, and recursively use pattern matching on subterms. It is this (quite simple) algorithm that we encode in the λ-calculus. We use the following notations: S is the number of symbols appearing in the signature. The ith symbol of Σ is denoted by f_i.

To build the encoding of pattern matching, we need three conditions:

1 each constant f_i has a "maximal" arity α_i, in the sense that f_i is never applied to more than α_i arguments;
2 in every matching equation $f_i \bullet \overrightarrow{P}_{(1..p)} \ll f_j \bullet \overrightarrow{B}_{(1..q)}$, we have $\alpha_i - p = \alpha_j - q$;
3 each term $(A; B)$ has a maximal arity α.

In particular, when $i = j$, the second condition reduces to $p = q$, which is an essential condition for resolving this matching equation.

In this section, we assume these properties. In Section 4, we will see that typing enforces the three conditions. They remain true in some untyped situations too: for instance, if we were to encode a Term Rewriting System, the arity of the constants would be given, and partial application of a constant would be forbidden, ensuring that in every matching equation $\alpha_i - p = \alpha_j - q = 0$.

The translation is given in Fig. 2, by a recursive function $[\![\cdot]\!]$ mapping P^2TS terms to λ-terms. We use a fresh variable $x_\perp$; if a closed term is needed, we add an abstraction "$\lambda x_\perp$" once the whole P^2TS term is translated.

$$
\begin{aligned}
[\![X]\!] &\triangleq X \\
[\![f_i]\!] &\triangleq \lambda \overrightarrow{x}_{(1..\alpha_i)}.(\lambda \overrightarrow{z}_{(1..S)}.(z_i\, \overrightarrow{x}_{(1..\alpha_i)})) \\
[\![A;B]\!] &\triangleq \lambda \overrightarrow{x}_{(1..\alpha)}.\Big(\lambda z.(z([\![A]\!]\overrightarrow{x}_{(1..\alpha)})([\![B]\!]\overrightarrow{x}_{(1..\alpha)}))\Big) \\
[\![\lambda X.A]\!] &\triangleq \lambda X.[\![A]\!] \\
[\![\lambda(f_i \bullet \overrightarrow{P}_{(1..p)}).A]\!] &\triangleq \lambda y.(y\overrightarrow{x_\perp}_{(p+1..\alpha_i)}\, \overrightarrow{x_\perp}_{(1..i-1)}[\![\lambda \overrightarrow{P}_{(1..p)}.\lambda \overrightarrow{x}'_{(p+1..\alpha_i)}.A]\!]\, \overrightarrow{x_\perp}_{(i+1..S)}) \\
[\![A \bullet B]\!] &\triangleq [\![A]\!][\![B]\!] \\
[\![[P \ll B]A]\!] &\triangleq \text{the term obtained by head-}\beta\text{-reducing } [\![(\lambda P.A) \bullet B]\!]
\end{aligned}
$$

Figure 2. Untyped term translation

Let us briefly explain this translation:

- In $[\![f_i]\!]$, the variables $x_1 \ldots x_{\alpha_i}$ will be instantiated by the arguments $\overrightarrow{B}$ of f_i (which explains why we had to bound the arity of f_i). Then, among the variables $z_1 \ldots z_S$, the one corresponding to the head constant of P is selected.
- $[\![A;B]\!]$ is translated into the usual pair encoding of the λ-calculus, and the abstractions $\lambda\overrightarrow{x}$ distribute the arguments to both elements of the pair.

- In $[\![\lambda X.A]\!]$, the abstraction over a single variable is straightforwardly translated into a λ-abstraction.
- In $[\![\lambda(f_i \bullet \overrightarrow{P}_{(1..p)}).A]\!]$, the variable y will be instantiated by the argument of this function (for instance $[\![f_j \bullet \overrightarrow{B}]\!]$). If necessary, the $\alpha_i - p$ first occurrences of the variable $x_\perp$ instantiate the remaining variables $x_{q+1} \ldots x_{\alpha_j}$ which can appear in $[\![f_j]\!]$: this is where we use the condition $\alpha_i - p = \alpha_j - q$. Then, if $f_i = f_j$, the $z_1 \ldots z_S$ select $[\![\lambda \overrightarrow{P}_{(1..p)}.\lambda \overrightarrow{x'}_{(p+1..\alpha_i)}.A]\!]$ and the encoding of pattern matching can then go on (pointwise) with the sub-patterns $P_1 \ldots P_p$ and the subterms $B_1 \ldots B_p$; if matching fails, $x_\perp$ is selected, witnessing the failure. The fresh variables $x'_{p+1} \ldots x'_{\alpha_i}$ will be instantiated by $x_\perp$'s, but they do not appear in $[\![A]\!]$. If a variable X has multiple occurrences in the pattern, by α-conversion, only one of the subpatterns P_i will get the "original" variable, and the other X's are renamed to fresh variables not occurring in $[\![A]\!]$ (so matching failures due to non-linearity are not detected by the encoding).
- $[\![A \bullet B]\!]$ is translated into standard λ-calculus application.
- $[\![[P \ll B]A]\!]$ is $[\![(\lambda P.A) \bullet B]\!]$ where y has been instantiated by $[\![B]\!]$.

LEMMA 1 (CLOSURE BY SUBSTITUTION)
For any P^2TS terms A and $B_1, \ldots, B_n$, for any variables $X_1, \ldots X_n$,

$$[\![A[X_1 := B_1 \ldots X_n := B_n]]\!] = [\![A]\!][X_1 := [\![B_1]\!] \ldots X_n := [\![B_n]\!]]$$

THEOREM 1 (FAITHFUL REDUCTIONS)
For any terms A and B, if $A \mapsto_{\rho\delta} B$, then $[\![A]\!] \mapsto\!\!\!\rightarrow_\beta [\![B]\!]$ in at least one step.

EXAMPLE 1 (TRANSLATION OF A SUCCESSFUL DELAYED MATCHING)

$$\begin{array}{rcl} (\lambda Y.\underline{(\lambda(f \bullet X).X) \bullet Y}) \bullet (f \bullet a) & \mapsto_b & \underline{(\lambda Y.[f \bullet X \ll Y]X) \bullet (f \bullet a)} \\ & \mapsto_b & \underline{[Y \ll f \bullet a][f \bullet X \ll Y]X} \\ & \mapsto_b & \underline{[f \bullet X \ll f \bullet a]X} \\ & \mapsto_b & a \end{array}$$

The inner delayed matching constraint is essential here because it has to "wait" for the instantiation of Y before performing matching. For the translation, we consider $\Sigma = \{a_1, f_2\}$ with $\alpha_1 = 0$ and $\alpha_2 = 1$. The reductions are shown on Fig. 3. The selected λ-abstraction and its argument are underlined.

4 The typed P^2TS: static semantics

This section presents a version of the type systems of P^2TS with some minor adaptations. The inference rules are given in Fig. 4. For a detailed explanation of these rules, the reader can refer to (Barthe et al., 2003); here, we will only discuss some differences with regard to previous type systems for the ρ-calculus and P^2TS:

- In (Cirstea and Kirchner, 2000), a first strongly normalizing type system for the ρ-calculus was introduced; however, the proof of normalization is mainly based on a heavy restriction over the types of constants.

$$
\begin{array}{ll}
& (\lambda Y.(\overbrace{(\underline{\lambda y}.(y x_\perp (\lambda X.X)))}^{[\![\lambda(f\bullet X).X]\!]}\underline{Y})) ((\overbrace{(\lambda x_1.\lambda z_1 \lambda z_2.(z_2 x_1))}^{[\![f]\!]} \overbrace{(\lambda u_1 \lambda u_2.u_1)}^{[\![a]\!]})) \quad \text{with } \overbrace{}^{[\![\lambda Y.(\lambda(f\bullet X).X)\bullet Y]\!]} \text{ over the first part}\\
\mapsto_\beta & (\lambda Y.(Y x_\perp (\lambda X.X)))((\underline{\lambda x_1}.\lambda z_1 \lambda z_2.(z_2 x_1))\underline{(\lambda u_1 \lambda u_2.u_1)})\\
\mapsto_\beta & (\underline{\lambda Y}.(Y x_\perp (\lambda X.X)))\underline{(\lambda z_1 \lambda z_2.(z_2(\lambda u_1 \lambda u_2.u_1)))}\\
\mapsto_\beta & (\underline{\lambda z_1}\lambda z_2.(z_2(\lambda u_1 \lambda u_2.u_1)))\underline{x_\perp}(\lambda X.X)\\
\mapsto_\beta & (\underline{\lambda z_2}.(z_2(\lambda u_1 \lambda u_2.u_1)))\underline{(\lambda X.X)}\\
\mapsto_\beta & (\underline{\lambda X}.X)\underline{(\lambda u_1 \lambda u_2.u_1)}\\
\mapsto_\beta & (\lambda u_1 \lambda u_2.u_1)\\
= & [\![a]\!]
\end{array}
$$

Figure 3. Translation of a successful delayed matching

- In (Cirstea et al., 2004), we studied a more permissive type system, still enforcing subject reduction, but allowing to typecheck some terms with infinite reductions. Therefore, this type system was not fit for using the ρ-calculus as a proof-term language.
- The type systems of (Cirstea et al., 2001; Barthe et al., 2003) were designed in order to provide a strongly normalizing calculus where there was no restriction on the type of the constants (apart those imposed by the type system). Until now, strong normalization was an open problem for these systems. Here, we show this property for a slight variation of (Barthe et al., 2003). We have introduced a signature Σ which prevents the type of a constant to depend on free variables.

  In rules (MSORT) and (PROD), the first premise avoids a collapse of the P^2TS-cube. If we had just taken $\Psi_0 : s_1$, with $\vdash_\rho f : \Pi(\beta : *).\beta$, the pattern $f\bullet\gamma$ would have sort $*$ but could be used to instantiate the type variable γ, enabling polymorphism in the simply-typed system.
  In the rule (Var), we use $\Gamma_\Box \triangleq \{X : \Phi \in \Gamma \mid \Sigma, \Gamma \vdash_\rho \Phi : \Box\}$ to avoid free *term* variables occuring in the type of a variable. It is mainly because we want to keep the system "simply-typed", in the sense that matching constraints occurring in types do not yield types depending on terms. For the type systems allowing terms depending on types, this restriction will have to be relaxed.

  Finally, the rule (STRUCT) can seem quite restrictive, since case-dependent expressions such as $\lambda(0 : nat).0 \,; \lambda(s\bullet X : nat).X$ are forbidden. However, it is non-trivial to weaken this rule. For example, if we had typed $\lambda(0 : nat).0 \,; \lambda(s\bullet X : nat).X$ with $\Pi(N : nat).nat$, we could have built a typed term with infinite reductions as in (Cirstea et al., 2004).

The notion of arity we have assumed in the untyped encoding can be properly defined here using types: if f_i has type Φ_i, then α_i is defined as $\alpha(\Phi_i)$:

$$
\begin{array}{rcl}
\alpha(\Xi) & \triangleq & 0\\
\alpha(\Pi P.\Psi) & \triangleq & 1+\alpha(\Psi)\\
\alpha([P \ll B]\Psi) & \triangleq & \alpha(\Psi)
\end{array}
$$

$$\frac{}{\emptyset \vdash_\rho * : \Box} \text{(AXIOM)} \qquad \frac{\Sigma, \Gamma \vdash_\rho A : \Phi \qquad \Sigma, \Gamma \vdash_\rho B : \Phi}{\Sigma, \Gamma \vdash_\rho A; B : \Phi} \text{(STRUCT)}$$

$$\frac{\Sigma, \Gamma_\Box \vdash_\rho \Phi : s \qquad X \notin \mathcal{D}om(\Gamma)}{\Sigma, \Gamma, X{:}\Phi \vdash_\rho X : \Phi} \text{(VAR)} \qquad \frac{\Sigma \vdash_\rho \Phi : s \qquad f \notin \mathcal{D}om(\Sigma)}{\Sigma, f : \Phi \vdash_\rho f : \Phi} \text{(CONST)}$$

$$\frac{\Sigma, \Gamma \vdash_\rho A : \Phi \qquad \Sigma, \Gamma \vdash_\rho \Psi : s \qquad X \notin \mathcal{D}om(\Gamma)}{\Sigma, \Gamma, X{:}\Psi \vdash_\rho A : \Phi} \text{(WEAK}\Gamma\text{)}$$

$$\frac{\Sigma \vdash_\rho A : \Phi \qquad \Sigma \vdash_\rho \Psi : s \qquad f \notin \mathcal{D}om(\Sigma)}{\Sigma, f{:}\Psi \vdash_\rho A : \Phi} \text{(WEAK}\Sigma\text{)}$$

$$\frac{\Sigma, \Gamma \vdash_\rho A : \Psi \qquad \Sigma, \Gamma \vdash_\rho \Phi : s \qquad \Phi =_{\rho\delta} \Psi}{\Sigma, \Gamma \vdash_\rho A : \Phi} \text{(CONV)}$$

$$\frac{\Sigma, \Gamma, \Delta \vdash_\rho A : \Phi \qquad \Sigma, \Gamma \vdash_\rho \Pi(P : \Delta).\Phi : s}{\Sigma, \Gamma \vdash_\rho \lambda(P : \Delta).A : \Pi(P : \Delta).\Phi} \text{(ABS)}$$

$$\frac{\Sigma, \Gamma \vdash_\rho A : \Pi(P : \Delta).\Phi \qquad \Sigma, \Gamma \vdash_\rho [P \ll_\Delta B]\Phi : s}{\Sigma, \Gamma \vdash_\rho A \bullet B : [P \ll_\Delta B]\Phi} \text{(APPL)}$$

$$\frac{\Sigma, \Gamma, \Delta \vdash_\rho A : \Phi \qquad \Sigma, \Gamma \vdash_\rho [P \ll_\Delta B]\Phi : s}{\Sigma, \Gamma \vdash_\rho [P \ll_\Delta B]A : [P \ll_\Delta B]\Phi} \text{(MATCH)}$$

$$\frac{\forall (X{:}\Psi) \in \Delta,\ \Sigma, \Gamma, \Delta \vdash_\rho \Psi : s_1 \qquad \Sigma, \Gamma, \Delta \vdash_\rho P : \Psi_0 \qquad \Sigma, \Gamma, \Delta \vdash_\rho \Phi : s_2}{\Sigma, \Gamma \vdash_\rho \Pi(P : \Delta).\Phi : s_2} \text{(PROD)}$$

$$\frac{\begin{array}{c}\forall (X{:}\Psi) \in \Delta,\ \Sigma, \Gamma, \Delta \vdash_\rho \Psi : s_1 \\ \Sigma, \Gamma, \Delta \vdash_\rho P : \Psi_0 \qquad \Sigma, \Gamma \vdash_\rho B : \Psi_0 \qquad \Sigma, \Gamma, \Delta \vdash_\rho \Phi : s_2\end{array}}{\Sigma, \Gamma \vdash_\rho [P \ll_\Delta B]\Phi : s_2} \text{(MSORT)}$$

In the simply-typed system, $(s_1, s_2) = (*, *)$.

Figure 4. The typing rules of P^2TS

One is easily convinced that a term $f_i \bullet \overrightarrow{A}$ where $\overrightarrow{A}$ contains more than α_i elements can not be correctly typed. Similarly, in a term $(A; B) \bullet \overrightarrow{C}$, A and B have a common type Φ so $\overrightarrow{C}$ can not contain more than $\alpha(\Phi)$ elements.

The second condition on arities is enforced too: in a given matching equation $f_i \bullet \overrightarrow{P}_{(1..p)} \ll f_j \bullet \overrightarrow{B}_{(1..q)}$, typing enforces that $f_i \bullet \overrightarrow{P}_{(1..p)}$ and $f_j \bullet \overrightarrow{B}_{(1..q)}$ have the same type, which immediately imposes $\alpha_i - p = \alpha_j - q$.

Some properties of these calculi, proved in (Barthe et al., 2003), are:

LEMMA 2 (SUBSTITUTION) *If* $\Gamma, X : \Phi, \Delta \vdash_\rho A : \Psi$ *and* $\Gamma \vdash_\rho B : \Phi$, *then* $\Gamma, \Delta[X := B] \vdash_\rho A[X := B] : \Psi[X := B]$.

THEOREM 2 (SUBJECT REDUCTION)
If $\Gamma \vdash_\rho A : \Phi$ *and* $A \mapsto\!\!\!\!\to_{\rho\delta} A'$, *then* $\Gamma \vdash_\rho A' : \Phi$.

LEMMA 3 (UNIQUENESS OF TYPES UP TO SECOND ORDER)
If $(s_1, s_2) \in \{(*, *), (\Box, *)\}$, *if* $\Gamma \vdash_\rho A : \Phi_1$ *and* $\Gamma \vdash_\rho A : \Phi_2$, *then* $\Phi_1 =_{\rho\delta} \Phi_2$.

In this paper, we only treat the case of the simply typed calculus, corresponding to $(s_1, s_2) = \{(*, *)\}$. In particular, this implies uniqueness of types.

As a conclusion to this section, let us briefly explain why usual reducibility techniques seem to fail for this typed calculus. Roughly speaking, the interpretation of a type $\Pi(P : \Delta).\Phi$ should be a function space whose domain is defined not only as the interpretation of the type of P but also as terms matching with P and whose suitable subterms belong to the interpretations of the types appearing in Δ. Quickly, this imbrication of interpretations leads to circularities in the definition of interpretations. Thus, it seems really tricky to obtain a proper definition of the reducibility candidates.

5 The System Fω

In this section, we shortly recall the type system Fω, first introduced and studied in (Girard, 1972). The formalism and its properties have been generalized to the Calculus of Constructions (Coquand and Huet, 1988), and later on to Pure Type Systems. Here, we follow the generic presentation of (Barendregt, 1992). The inference rules are given in Fig. 5. Here, the possible product rules are $\{(*,*), (\Box,*), (\Box,\Box)\}$.

$$\frac{}{\emptyset \vdash_{F\omega} * : \Box}\ (\text{AXIOM}) \qquad \frac{\Gamma, x:\sigma \vdash_{F\omega} t : \tau \qquad \Gamma \vdash_{F\omega} \Pi(x:\sigma).\tau : s}{\Gamma \vdash_{F\omega} \lambda(x:\sigma).t : \Pi(x:\sigma).\tau}\ (\text{ABS})$$

$$\frac{\Gamma \vdash_{F\omega} \sigma : s \qquad x \notin \mathcal{D}om(\Gamma)}{\Gamma, x{:}\sigma \vdash_{F\omega} x : \sigma}\ (\text{VAR}) \qquad \frac{\Gamma \vdash_{F\omega} t : \Pi(x:\sigma).\tau \qquad \Gamma \vdash_{F\omega} u : \sigma}{\Gamma \vdash_{F\omega} t\,u : \tau[x := u]}\ (\text{APPL})$$

$$\frac{\Gamma \vdash_{F\omega} t : \sigma \qquad \Gamma \vdash_{F\omega} \tau : s \qquad x \notin \mathcal{D}om(\Gamma)}{\Gamma, x{:}\tau \vdash_{F\omega} t : \sigma}\ (\text{WEAK})$$

$$\frac{\Gamma \vdash_{F\omega} t : \tau \qquad \Gamma \vdash_{F\omega} \sigma : s \qquad \sigma =_\beta \tau}{\Gamma \vdash_{F\omega} t : \sigma}\ (\text{CONV})$$

$$\frac{\Gamma \vdash_{F\omega} \sigma : s_1 \qquad \Gamma, x:\sigma \vdash_{F\omega} \tau : s_2 \qquad (s_1, s_2) \in \{(*,*), (\Box,*), (\Box,\Box)\}}{\Gamma \vdash_{F\omega} \Pi(x:\sigma).\tau : s_2}\ (\text{PROD})$$

Figure 5. The typing rules of Fω

In all the remaining, for a type $\Pi(x : \sigma).\tau$, we will use the usual type arrow abbreviation $\sigma \rightarrow \tau$ whenever $x \notin \mathcal{FV}(\tau)$, *i.e.* for terms depending on terms (product rule $(*,*)$) and for types depending on types (product rule $(\Box,\Box)$).

Some well-known properties of this calculus are (Girard, 1972; Barendregt, 1992):

LEMMA 4 (SUBSTITUTION) *If* $\Gamma, x : \sigma, \Delta \vdash_{F\omega} t : \tau$ *and* $\Gamma \vdash_{F\omega} u : \sigma$, *then* $\Gamma, \Delta[x := u] \vdash_{F\omega} t[x := u] : \tau[x := u]$.

THEOREM 3 (SUBJECT REDUCTION)
If $\Gamma \vdash_{F\omega} t : \sigma$ *and* $t \mapsto\!\!\!\rightarrow_\beta t'$, *then* $\Gamma \vdash_{F\omega} t' : \sigma$.

LEMMA 5 (UNIQUENESS OF TYPES)
If $\Gamma \vdash_{F\omega} t : \sigma_1$ *and* $\Gamma \vdash_{F\omega} t : \sigma_2$, *then* $\sigma_1 =_\beta \sigma_2$.

THEOREM 4 (STRONG NORMALIZATION)
If $\Gamma \vdash_{F\omega} t : \sigma$, *then t is strongly normalizing.*

6 The typed translation algorithm

Here, instead of translating a term to a term, we translate a typed term into a (typable) term. For simplicity of presentation, we still write $[\![A]\!]$ but, as one can see on

Fig. 6, the translation of a term A is generally based on the fact that A is typable. Supposing we are given a type derivation for a judgment $\Sigma, \Gamma \vdash_\rho A : \Phi$, we recursively build a term $[\![A]\!]$ typable in $[\![\Gamma]\!]$. There is no translation for Σ since, as we will see in Section 7, the context $x_\perp : \perp.$ is sufficient to type $[\![f]\!]$ for any constant $f \in \Sigma$.

For the rest of the paper, we adopt the following abbreviations, for any types σ, σ_1, ..., σ_n, τ in Fω. The third definition is a special case of the second one with $\alpha = 0$:

$$
\begin{array}{ll}
[\sigma]^S \to \tau & \triangleq \underbrace{\sigma \to \ldots \to \sigma}_{S} \to \tau \\
\{\sigma_1, \ldots, \sigma_\alpha\} & \triangleq \Pi(\beta : *).([\sigma_1 \to \ldots \sigma_\alpha \to \beta]^S \to \beta) \\
\{\emptyset\} & \triangleq \Pi(\beta : *).([\beta]^S \to \beta)
\end{array}
$$

For each variable X appearing in a P^2TS term, we add in the corresponding λ-term a type variable β_X which appears in the type of $[\![X]\!]$. This variable β_X is common to every occurrence of X in the term, and if X is bound, we bind β_X at the same point as X in the translation. If X is free, then in the translation of the context, the type variable β_X appears just before X. The need for β_X is explained in Section 7.

First we define the translation of types (*i.e.* terms such that $\Gamma \vdash_\rho \Phi : *$) by four mutually dependent definitions:

$[\![\Phi]\!]^X_{\vec{\gamma}}$ translates the type Φ, supposing it is the type of the variable X depending on the list of type variables $\vec{\gamma}$. The free type variable β_X (univocally corresponding to X) appears in this translation.

$$
\begin{array}{rcl}
[\![\Xi]\!]^X_{\vec{\gamma}} & \triangleq & \beta_X \vec{\gamma} \quad \text{(where } \Xi \text{ is atomic)} \\
[\![\Pi(P : \Delta).\Psi]\!]^X_{\vec{\gamma}} & \triangleq & \overrightarrow{\prod_{(Y:\Phi_Y)\in\Delta} \beta_Y : \mathbb{K}(\Phi_Y)_\emptyset}.\, (\ulcorner P \urcorner_\Delta \to [\![\Psi]\!]^X_{\vec{\gamma} \cup \vec{\beta_Y}}) \\
[\![[P \ll_\Delta B]\Psi]\!]^X_{\vec{\gamma}} & \triangleq & \overrightarrow{\prod_{(Y:\Phi_Y)\in\Delta} \beta'_Y : \mathbb{K}(\Phi_Y)_\emptyset}.\, \left((\sigma \to \ulcorner P \urcorner_\Delta) \to [\![\Psi]\!]^X_{\vec{\gamma} \cup \vec{\beta'_Y}}\right) \\
& & \text{where } [\![\Gamma]\!] \vdash_{F\omega} [\![B]\!] : \sigma
\end{array}
$$

$[\![\Phi]\!]^f_{\vec{\tau}}$ translates the type Φ, supposing it is the type of the constant f depending on the list of types $\vec{\tau}$.

$$
\begin{array}{rcl}
[\![\Xi]\!]^f_{\vec{\tau}} & \triangleq & \{\vec{\tau}\} \quad \text{(where } \Xi \text{ is atomic)} \\
[\![\Pi(P : \Delta)\Psi]\!]^f_{\vec{\tau}} & \triangleq & \overrightarrow{\prod_{(Y:\Phi_Y)\in\Delta} \beta_Y : \mathbb{K}(\Phi_Y)_\emptyset}.\, (\ulcorner P \urcorner_\Delta \to [\![\Psi]\!]^f_{\vec{\tau} \cup \ulcorner P \urcorner_\Delta}) \\
[\![[P \ll_\Delta B]\Psi]\!]^f_{\vec{\tau}} & \triangleq & \overrightarrow{\prod_{(Y:\Phi_Y)\in\Delta} \beta'_Y : \mathbb{K}(\Phi_Y)_\emptyset}.\, \left((\sigma \to \ulcorner P \urcorner_\Delta) \to [\![\Psi]\!]^f_{\vec{\tau}}\right) \\
& & \text{where } [\![\Gamma]\!] \vdash_{F\omega} [\![B]\!] : \sigma
\end{array}
$$

The only free variable appearing in $[\![\Phi]\!]^X_\emptyset$ is β_X, and the arguments $\vec{\gamma}$ of β_X are the bound variables whose scope extends to this subterm of the type. Similarly, in $[\![\Phi]\!]^f_\emptyset$, no variable is free, and all the bound variables whose scope extends to the subterm $\{\vec{\tau}\}$ are represented in this subterm.

$\ulcorner P \urcorner_\Delta$ flattens a pattern P with $\mathcal{FV}(P) \subseteq \mathcal{Dom}(\Delta)$. Since patterns appear in the P^2TS types, the translation at the type level must be accurate.

$$\ulcorner f_i \bullet \overrightarrow{P} \urcorner_\Delta \triangleq [\![\Pi(P'_{p+1} : \Delta_{p+1}) \ldots \Pi(P'_{\alpha_i} : \Delta_{\alpha_i}) \,.\, \Xi]\!]^{f}_{\overrightarrow{\ulcorner P \urcorner_\Delta}}$$

$$\text{where } \Sigma \vdash_\rho f_i : \Pi(P'_1 : \Delta_1) \ldots \Pi(P'_{\alpha_i} : \Delta_{\alpha_i}) \,.\, \Xi$$

$$\ulcorner X \urcorner_\Delta \triangleq [\![\Phi]\!]^X_\emptyset \qquad \text{if } X : \Phi \in \Delta$$

$\mathbb{K}(\Phi)_{\overrightarrow{k}}$ computes the kind of β_X if X has type Φ.

$$\begin{aligned} \mathbb{K}(\Xi)_{\overrightarrow{k}} &\triangleq \overrightarrow{k} \rightarrow * \\ \mathbb{K}(\Pi(P : \Delta).\Psi)_{\overrightarrow{k}} &\triangleq \mathbb{K}(\Psi)_{\overrightarrow{k} \cup \bigcup_{(Y:\Phi_Y) \in \Delta} \mathbb{K}(\Phi_Y)_\emptyset} \\ \mathbb{K}([P \ll_\Delta B]\Psi)_{\overrightarrow{k}} &\triangleq \mathbb{K}(\Psi)_{\overrightarrow{k} \cup \bigcup_{(Y:\Phi_Y) \in \Delta} \mathbb{K}(\Phi_Y)_\emptyset} \end{aligned}$$

We can extend this translation to contexts, the base case being given by $x_\perp$:

$$\begin{aligned} [\![\emptyset]\!] &\triangleq x_\perp : \perp \\ [\![\Gamma, X : \Phi]\!] &\triangleq [\![\Gamma]\!],\ \beta_X : \mathbb{K}(\Phi)_\emptyset,\ X : [\![\Phi]\!]^X_\emptyset \qquad (\text{if } \Gamma \vdash_\rho \Phi : *) \\ [\![\Gamma, X : *]\!] &\triangleq [\![\Gamma]\!], X : * \end{aligned}$$

Finally, we can translate typed terms. The translation is given in two distinct parts: in Fig. 6, we give all the cases that are simply adapted from the untyped case. In Fig. 7, we deal with the trickiest situations: matching constraints and conversion in the types. These last cases are further explained in Section 7.

7 Rationale of the typed translation

In this section we treat three key constructs of the typed translation:

1 the type of a translated constant (accounting for the use of System F);

2 the type of a variable (requiring types depending on types);

3 the translation of matching constraints appearing in the P^2TS types.

Typing the translation of a constant

First, let us study how constants and their translation affect typing. In order to get a typed translation, in the previous section, we have added to the untyped term $[\![f_i]\!]$ some type abstractions. The type abstractions $\lambda(\beta_Y : \mathbb{K}(\Phi_Y)_\emptyset)$ are needed for correctly typing the variables, as we will see in the next subsection. Here, we are interested in the type abstraction $\lambda(\beta : *)$ appearing in $[\![f_i]\!]$.

To explain the modifications we made, let us start from the untyped translation. We suppose $\vdash f_i : \Pi P_1 \ldots \Pi P_{\alpha_i} \,.\, \Xi$ where Ξ is an atomic type, and we assume that each P_n is translated to a certain type σ_n. Then we have:

$$x_\perp : \beta \vdash [\![f_i]\!] : \sigma_1 \rightarrow \ldots \rightarrow \sigma_\alpha \rightarrow [\sigma_1 \rightarrow \ldots \rightarrow \sigma_\alpha \rightarrow \beta]^S \rightarrow \beta$$

What remains unclear is the meaning of β. The type of a translated abstraction is:

$$\vdash [\![\lambda(f_i \bullet \overrightarrow{X}_{(1..p)}).A]\!] : \Big(\sigma_{p+1} \rightarrow \ldots \rightarrow \sigma_\alpha \rightarrow [\sigma_1 \rightarrow \ldots \rightarrow \sigma_\alpha \rightarrow \tau]^S \rightarrow \gamma \Big) \rightarrow \gamma$$

$$
\begin{aligned}
[\![X]\!] &\triangleq X \\
[\![f_i]\!] &\triangleq \lambda\overrightarrow{\beta_Y}_1.\lambda x_1 \ldots \lambda\overrightarrow{\beta_Y}_{\alpha_i}.\lambda x_{\alpha_i}.\lambda(\beta : *)\ (\lambda \overrightarrow{z}_{(1..S)}.(z_i \overrightarrow{x}_{(1..\alpha_i)})) \\
&\quad \text{where } \Sigma \vdash_\rho f_i : \boldsymbol{\Pi}(P_1 : \Delta_1)\ldots\boldsymbol{\Pi}(P_{\alpha_i} : \Delta_{\alpha_i})\,.\,\Xi \\
&\quad \text{and } \overrightarrow{\beta_Y}_n \text{ correspond to } \overrightarrow{(Y : \Phi_Y)} \in \Delta_n, \text{ with } \overrightarrow{\beta_Y : \mathbb{K}(\Phi_Y)_\emptyset}. \\
[\![A; B]\!] &\triangleq \overrightarrow{\lambda\overrightarrow{\beta_Y}.\lambda x_{(1..\alpha)}}.\Big(\lambda z.\big(z([\![A]\!]\overrightarrow{\overrightarrow{\beta_Y} x_{(1..\alpha)}})([\![B]\!]\overrightarrow{\overrightarrow{\beta_Y} x_{(1..\alpha)}})\big)\Big) \\
&\quad \text{where } \Sigma, \Gamma \vdash_\rho A; B : \boldsymbol{\Pi}(P_1 : \Delta_1)\ldots\boldsymbol{\Pi}(P_{\alpha_i} : \Delta_{\alpha_i})\,.\,\Xi \\
&\quad \text{and } \overrightarrow{\beta_Y}_n \text{ are the type variables corresponding to } \mathcal{FV}(P_n). \\
[\![\boldsymbol{\lambda}(X : \Phi).A]\!] &\triangleq \lambda(\beta_X : \mathbb{K}(\Phi)_\emptyset).\lambda(X : [\![\Phi]\!]^X_\emptyset).[\![A]\!] \\
&\quad \text{where } \Sigma, \Gamma \vdash_\rho \boldsymbol{\lambda}(X : \Phi).A : \boldsymbol{\Pi}(X : \Phi).\Psi \\
[\![\boldsymbol{\lambda}(f_i \bullet \overrightarrow{P}_{(1..p)} : \Delta).A]\!] &\triangleq \lambda_{X \in \Delta}(\overrightarrow{\beta_X : \mathbb{K}(\Phi_X)}).\lambda y.(y \overrightarrow{\bot}\,\overrightarrow{(x_\bot\ \ulcorner P' \urcorner_\Delta [\beta_Y := \bot])}_{(p+1..\alpha_i)} \\
&\qquad \tau\ \overrightarrow{(x_\bot \tau_0)}\ [\![\boldsymbol{\lambda}\overrightarrow{P{:}\Delta}_{(1..p)}.\boldsymbol{\lambda}\overrightarrow{x'{:}\ \ulcorner P' \urcorner_\Delta}_{(p+1..\alpha_i)}.A]\!]\ \overrightarrow{(x_\bot \tau_0)}) \\
&\quad \text{where } \Sigma, \Gamma \vdash_\rho \boldsymbol{\lambda}(f_i \bullet \overrightarrow{P}_{(1..p)} : \Delta).A : \boldsymbol{\Pi}(f_i \bullet \overrightarrow{P}_{(1..p)} : \Delta).\Psi \\
&\quad \text{and } \Sigma \vdash_\rho f_i : \boldsymbol{\Pi}\overrightarrow{(P' : \Delta)}_{(1..\alpha_i)}).\Xi \quad \text{and } [\![\Gamma]\!] \vdash_{\mathsf{F}\omega} [\![A]\!] : \tau \\
&\quad \text{and } [\![\Gamma]\!] \vdash_{\mathsf{F}\omega} [\![\boldsymbol{\lambda}\overrightarrow{P}_{(1..p)}.\boldsymbol{\lambda}\overrightarrow{x'}_{(p+1..\alpha_i)}.A]\!] : \tau_0 \\
[\![A \bullet B]\!] &\triangleq [\![A]\!]\ \overrightarrow{\tau_X}\ [\![B]\!] \qquad \text{if } [\![\Gamma]\!] \vdash_{\mathsf{F}\omega} [\![B]\!] : \ulcorner P \urcorner_\Delta\,[\overrightarrow{\beta_X := \tau_X}]_{X \in \Delta} \\
&\quad \text{where } \Sigma, \Gamma \vdash_\rho A \bullet B : [P \ll_\Delta B]\Psi \\
[\![[P \ll_\Delta B]A]\!] &\triangleq \text{the term obtained by head-}\beta\text{-reducing } [\![(\boldsymbol{\lambda}(P : \Delta).A)\bullet B]\!]
\end{aligned}
$$

Figure 6. Typed term translation without matching constraints

Therefore, the λ-term $[\![\boldsymbol{\lambda}(f_i \bullet \overrightarrow{X}_{(1..p)}).A]\!]\ ([\![f_i]\!][\![B_1]\!] \ldots [\![B_p]\!])$ has a valid type only if $[\sigma_1 \to \ldots \to \sigma_\alpha \to \tau]^S \to \gamma = [\sigma_1 \to \ldots \to \sigma_\alpha \to \beta]^S \to \beta$, *i.e.* $\tau = \beta = \gamma$ and $\vdash [\![B_1]\!]{:}\sigma_1\ \ldots \vdash [\![B_p]\!]{:}\sigma_p$. The types β and γ should be replaced by the return type τ of the function which is applied to $[\![f_i \bullet \overrightarrow{B}]\!]$. Since one can not guess what function will be applied to a given term, we introduce the polymorphism of Girard's System F in the target language. The resulting modification can be seen on Fig. 6: in $[\![f_i]\!]$, we abstract over the type variable β, which is instantiated with τ by $[\![\boldsymbol{\lambda}(f_i \bullet \overrightarrow{P}).A]\!]$.

Thanks to polymorphism, the variable $x_\bot$ can get type $\Pi(\iota : *).\iota$, which is usually noted $\bot$. Then, if we need an arbitrary term with type σ, we use $x_\bot \sigma$. This means that all the λ-terms we build are typable in a context containing $x_\bot{:}\bot$; again, we can add an abstraction "$\lambda(x_\bot{:}\bot)$" to get a closed term.

The types $[\![\Phi]\!]^f_\emptyset$ have been built to fit with the new translation of constants: a translated constant $[\![f_i]\!]$ with arity α_i takes α_i arguments with types $\sigma_1 \ldots \sigma_{\alpha_i}$ and returns a term with type $\{\sigma_1, \ldots \sigma_{\alpha_i}\}$. The types $\ulcorner P \urcorner_\Delta$ extend this notion to nested patterns: for instance $[\![f \bullet (g \bullet x_1) \bullet x_2]\!]$ will have type $\{\{\sigma_1\}, \sigma_2\}$. This flattening process keeps the shape of the pattern but forgets the constants used.

Typing a variable

In this subsection, we explain why we need a new type variable β_X for each variable X appearing in a P^2TS term (including bound variables appearing in a type).

DEFINITION 2 (TREE AUTOMATON) *A (non-deterministic) tree automaton (NDTA) is a pair* $\mathcal{A} = (R, \delta)$ *where R is a finite set of* nodes, *and* $\delta \subseteq (\Sigma \times R) \cup (R \times R \times R)$.

Each node r in a NDTA defines a subset $\mathcal{A}[\![r]\!]$ of $\mathcal{V}$. These sets can be defined by the following mutually recursive equations:

$$\mathcal{A}[\![r]\!] = \{a \in \Sigma \mid (a, r) \in \delta\} \cup \bigcup_{(r_1, r_2, r) \in \delta} \mathcal{A}[\![r_1]\!] \times \mathcal{A}[\![r_2]\!]$$

We write $\mathcal{A}[\![r]\!]^2 = \mathcal{A}[\![r]\!] \cap (\mathcal{V} \times \mathcal{V})$. By definition, a regular language is a subset of the form $\mathcal{A}[\![r]\!]$ for some NDTA $\mathcal{A}$ and some node r. We say that this language is *defined* by $\mathcal{A}$. There are two classical notions of deterministic tree automata: (1) Top-down deterministic automata (TDDTA) satisfy the property: $\{(r_1, r_2) \mid (r_1, r_2, r) \in \delta\}$ has at most one element for any node r. These automata are strictly weaker than NDTA in terms of expressive power (they cannot define all the regular languages). (2) Bottom-up deterministic automata (DTA) satisfy the property: $\{r \mid (r_1, r_2, r) \in \delta\}$ has at most one element for any pair of nodes (r_1, r_2), and similarly for the sets $\{r \mid (a, r) \in \delta\}$ with $a \in \Sigma$. These automata have the same expressive power as NDTA.

REMARK 3 *We use a non-standard terminology of nodes instead of states. The reason is that we are going to split this notion in two: results and control states. Results will correspond to nodes in a DTA, and control states will correspond to nodes in TDDTA.*

In order to motivate the use of a different kind of automaton, let us introduce different notions of context. During the traversal of a tree, an automaton computes and gathers information. The amount of extracted information can only depend on the context of the current location in the tree. A top-down recognizer (for TDDTA) can only propagate information downwards: the context of a location is thus the path from the root to the location ("upward context"). A bottom-up recognizer propagates information upwards: the context is the whole subtree rooted at the current location ("downward context").

Top-down algorithms are more efficient when the relevant information is located near the root. For instance, going back to the CDuce example in the introduction, we see easily that the function g should be implemented by starting the traversal from the root of the tree, since looking only at the root tag is enough. Patterns in CDuce tend to look in priority near the root of the trees instead of their leafs. However, because of their lack of expressive power, pure TDDTA cannot be used in general. Also, since they perform independant computations of the left and the right children of a location in a tree, they cannot use information gathered in the left subtree to guide the computation in the right subtree.

information. In P^2TS, this process is initiated by the matching constraints appearing in types, and carried on by the conversion rule.

In System Fω, we can not encode pattern matching in the types, so matching constraints must be treated at the meta-level, *i.e.* during the translation. Let us study the two kinds of matching constraints appearing in the types:

$[P \ll_\Delta B]\Psi$ with $\exists\theta,\ B =_{\rho\sigma\delta} P\theta$: By successive application of Lemmas 2, 1 and 4, we can prove that the same equality holds for the types in System Fω: if $[\![B]\!]$ has type σ, then $\exists\overrightarrow{\tau_X},\ \sigma =_\beta \ulcorner P \lrcorner_\Delta\ [\overrightarrow{\beta_X := \tau_X}]$ where $\vec{X} = \mathcal{FV}(P)$. The proof of Theorem 5 is constructive: it gives an algorithm for computing the $\overrightarrow{\tau_X}$.

$[P \ll_\Delta B]\Psi$ with $\forall\theta,\ B \neq_{\rho\sigma\delta} P\theta$: In this case, a new postponement variable w is created with type $\sigma \to \ulcorner P \lrcorner_\Delta$, where σ is the type of $[\![B]\!]$. The type of w appears in $[\![[P \ll B]\Psi]\!]^X_\emptyset$, accounting for the delayed matching constraint in the type. The term $w[\![B]\!]$ is used so that the λ-term is well-typed, since $[\![\lambda(P : \Delta).A]\!]$ expects a term of type $\ulcorner P \lrcorner_\Delta$. Suppose some subsequent applications instantiate some free variables in B (replacing it with a term $B\theta_0$) such that $\exists\theta, B\theta_0 =_{\rho\sigma\delta} P\theta$. Then, we should instantiate the free type variables $\overrightarrow{\beta_X}$ of $\ulcorner P \lrcorner_\Delta$ with suitable types $\overrightarrow{\tau_X}$ and instantiate w with the identity since we had translated B into $w[\![B]\!]$.
From a typing point of view, it is sound: because of the substitutions θ_0 and θ, the type of w is now $\sigma[\![\theta_0]\!] \to \ulcorner P \lrcorner_\Delta\ [\overrightarrow{\beta_X := \tau_X}]$ and the equality $B\theta_0 =_{\rho\sigma\delta} P\theta$ ensures that $\sigma[\![\theta_0]\!] =_\beta \ulcorner P \lrcorner_\Delta\ [\overrightarrow{\beta_X := \tau_X}]$, which means w has a suitable type for identity. The subtle point is that w can be located quite deep in the term we are considering: this is why we use the function $solve(\cdot,\cdot)$ given in Fig. 7, which performs a kind of η-expansion to instantiate w.

8 Strong normalization

In this section, we give the properties of our typed encoding.

PROPOSITION 1 (FAITHFUL REDUCTIONS) *Lemma 1 and Theorem 1 are still valid with the typed translation: each $\rho\sigma\delta$-reduction can be mimicked by at least one β-reduction (and the postponement variables w only prevent unsuccessful matchings).*

LEMMA 6 (WELL-KINDEDNESS)
$\forall\Sigma, \forall\Gamma, \forall\Phi,\quad \Sigma, \Gamma \vdash_\rho \Phi : * \ \Rightarrow\ [\![\Gamma]\!], \beta_X : \mathbb{K}(\Phi)_\emptyset \vdash_{F\omega} [\![\Phi]\!]^X_\emptyset : *$

THEOREM 5 (WELL-TYPED TRANSLATION) $\forall\Sigma, \Gamma, A, \Phi,$ *if* $\Sigma, \Gamma \vdash_\rho A{:}\Phi$ *then, for a fresh variable Z,* $\exists\tau_A,\quad [\![\Gamma]\!] \vdash_{F\omega} [\![A]\!] : [\![\Phi]\!]^Z_\emptyset [\beta_Z := \tau_A]$

THEOREM 6 (STRONG NORMALIZATION OF TYPABLE P^2TS TERMS)
$\forall\Sigma, \Gamma, A, \Phi,$ *if* $\Sigma, \Gamma \vdash_\rho A : \Phi$ *then A is strongly normalizing.*

Proof: A P^2TS-typable term A is translated into an Fω-typable term which has no infinite reduction, so by Proposition 1, A is strongly normalizing. □

9 Conclusion and perspectives

We have proved strong normalization of the simply-typed P^2TS by translating it into System Fω. First, we have shown how to encode untyped syntactic pattern matching in the λ-calculus. Introducing types in the translation then proved an interesting challenge. One difficulty comes from the pattern matching occuring in the P^2TS types, which calls for accurate adjustments in the translation. Another remarkable point is that the typing mechanisms of P^2TS can be expressed only with the expressive power of System Fω, which is rather surprising since we only deal with the simply-typed P^2TS. This fact leads us to think that, with the same product rules, the expressive power of P^2TS is greater than the one of the λ-calculus.

An interesting development of this work would be to adapt the proof for the other type systems of P^2TS. In the long term, we expect to use P^2TS as the base language for a powerful proof assistant combining the logical soundness of the λ-calculus and the computational power of the rewriting. This proof of strong normalization is a main stepstone for this research direction, since logical soundness is deeply related to strong normalization.

Acknowledgements Thanks to H. Cirstea, C. Kirchner and L. Liquori for the constant support and interest they put in this work; P. Blackburn for some useful insights about the typed λ-calculus; S. Salvati for many fruitful informal discussions about System F; F. Blanqui, G. Dowek and anonymous referees for their valuable comments.

Long version A detailed version of this article containing proofs and type derivations can be found at `http://www.loria.fr/~wack/papers/rhoSN.ps.gz`.

References

Barendregt, H. P. (1992). Lambda calculi with types. In Abramsky, S., Gabbay, D., and Maibaum, T., editors, *Handbook of Logic in Computer Science*. Clarendon Press.

Barthe, G., Cirstea, H., Kirchner, C., and Liquori, L. (2003). Pure Patterns Type Systems. In *POPL 2003, New Orleans, USA*. ACM.

Blanqui, F. (2001). Definitions by rewriting in the calculus of constructions. In *LICS*, pages 9–18.

Cirstea, H. and Kirchner, C. (2000). The typed rewriting calculus. In *Third International Workshop on Rewriting Logic and Application*, Kanazawa (Japan).

Cirstea, H., Kirchner, C., and Liquori, L. (2001). The Rho Cube. In Honsell, F., editor, *FOSSACS*, volume 2030 of *LNCS*, pages 166–180, Genova, Italy.

Cirstea, H., Liquori, L., and Wack, B. (2004). Rewriting calculus with fixpoints: Untyped and first-order systems. In *TYPES'03*, LNCS, Torino. To be published.

Coquand, T. (1992). Pattern matching with dependent types. In *Informal proceedings workshop on types for proofs and programs*, pages 71 – 84. Båstad, Suède.

Coquand, T. and Huet, G. (1988). The calculus of constructions. *Information and Computation*, 76:95 – 120.

Dowek, G., Hardin, T., and Kirchner, C. (2003). Theorem proving modulo, revised version. Rapport de Recherche 4861, INRIA.

Girard, J.-Y. (1972). *Interprétation fonctionnelle et élimination des coupures de l'arithmétique d'ordre supérieur*. PhD thesis, Université Paris VII.

Kesner, D., Puel, L., and Tannen, V. (1996). A typed pattern calculus. *Information and Computation*, 124(1):32–61.

Klop, J., van Oostrom, V., and van Raamsdonk, F. (1993). Combinatory reduction systems: introduction and survey. *TCS*, 121:279–308.

Werner, B. (1994). *Une Théorie des Constructions Inductives*. PhD thesis, Université Paris VII.

TERMINATION IN MODAL KLEENE ALGEBRA

Jules Desharnais[1], Bernhard Möller[2] and Georg Struth[2*]

[1] *Département d'informatique, Université Laval, Québec QC G1K 7P4 Canada*
Jules.Desharnais@ift.ulaval.ca

[2] *Institut für Informatik, Universität Augsburg, Universitätsstr. 14, D-86135 Augsburg, Germany*
{moeller,struth}@informatik.uni-augsburg.de

Abstract Modal Kleene algebras (MKAs) are Kleene algebras with forward and backward modal operators defined via domain and codomain operations. The paper formalizes and compares different notions of termination, including Löb's formula, in MKA. It studies exhaustive iteration and gives calculational proofs of two fundamental termination-dependent statements from rewriting theory: the well-founded union theorem by Bachmair and Dershowitz and Newman's lemma. These results are also of general interest for the termination analysis of programs and state transition systems.

1. Introduction

Kleene algebras, initially conceived as algebras of regular events [5, 12], have by now applications ranging from program development and analysis to rewriting theory and concurrency control. Recently, they have been extended to comprise infinite iteration [4] and abstract domain and codomain operations [6]. The latter extension leads to modal Kleene algebras: forward and backward boxes and diamonds are definable "semantically" in terms of domain and codomain operations.

We propose MKAs as a useful tool for termination analysis. It allows a simple and calculational style of reasoning that is also well-suited for mechanization. Induction with respect to "external" measures is avoided in favour of "internal" fixed-point reasoning and contraction law. Point-

*Partially supported by DFG Project InopSys (Interoperability of System Calculi).

free proofs in the algebra of modal operators introduce a new level of abstraction and conciseness.

Our main results are as follows. First, we investigate notions of Noethericity and well-foundedness in MKA, abstracted from set-theoretic relations (cf. [8]). We compare this notion with two alternatives. The first models termination as absence of proper infinite iteration. We show that this notion is not equivalent to the previous one, even under natural additional assumptions. It turns out that the notion of termination induced by MKA is the more natural and useful one. The second alternative arises in modal logic as Löb's formula [3] and is essentially equivalent to the first one. MKA can serve as an algebraic semantics for modal logics, allowing simple calculational correspondence proofs for second-order frame properties. Note however, that the star operation of Kleene algebra is usually not available in classical modal logic.

Second, we continue our research on abstract rewriting in Kleene algebra [16, 17]. We prove Bachmair's and Dershowitz's well-founded union theorem [2] and a variant of Newman's lemma (cf. [1]) in MKA. These proofs are simpler than previous results in related structures [8, 14]. Moreover, MKA provides an algebraic semantics for the usual rewrite diagrams; the algebraic proofs immediately reflect their diagrammatic counterparts. Together with our earlier results this shows that a large part of abstract rewriting is indeed conveniently modelled by MKA.

Because of space limitations we suppress some details and additional results that, however, can be found in [7].

2. Modal Kleene Algebra

A *semiring* is a structure $(K, +, \cdot, 0, 1)$ such that $(K, +, 0)$ is a commutative monoid, $(K, \cdot, 1)$ is a monoid, multiplication distributes over addition from the left and right and zero is a left and right annihilator, i.e., $a0 = 0 = 0a$ for all $a \in K$ (the operation symbol $\cdot$ is omitted here and in the sequel). The semiring is *idempotent* if it satisfies $a + a = a$ for all $a \in K$. Then K has a *natural ordering* $\leq$ defined for all $a, b \in K$ by $a \leq b$ iff $a + b = b$. It induces a semilattice with $+$ as join and 0 as the least element; addition and multiplication are isotone w.r.t. $\leq$.

A *Kleene algebra* [12] is a structure $(K, ^*)$ such that K is an idempotent semiring, and the *star* * satisfies, for $a, b, c \in K$, the *unfold* and *induction laws*

$$1 + aa^* \leq a^*, \quad (*\text{-}1) \qquad b + ac \leq c \Rightarrow a^*b \leq c, \quad (*\text{-}3)$$

$$1 + a^*a \leq a^*, \quad (*\text{-}2) \qquad b + ca \leq c \Rightarrow ba^* \leq c. \quad (*\text{-}4)$$

Therefore, a^* is the least pre-fixpoint and the least fixpoint of the mappings $\lambda x.ax + b$ and $\lambda x.xa + b$ and the star is $\leq$-isotone.

Models of KA are for instance the set-theoretic relations under set union, relational composition and reflexive transitive closure, the sets of regular languages (regular events) over some finite alphabet, the algebra of path sets in a directed graph under path concatenation and the algebra of imperative programs with angelic choice, composition and iteration.

A *Boolean algebra* is a complemented distributive lattice. A *test semiring* is a structure $(K, \mathsf{test}(K))$, where K is an IL-semiring and $\mathsf{test}(K) \subseteq K$ is a Boolean algebra embedded into K, such that join and meet in $\mathsf{test}(K)$ coincide with the restrictions of $+$ and $\cdot$ of K to $\mathsf{test}(K)$, resp., and such that 0 and 1 are the least and greatest elements of $\mathsf{test}(K)$. Hence $p \leq 1$ for all $p \in \mathsf{test}(K)$. But in general, $\mathsf{test}(K)$ is only a subalgebra of the subalgebra of all elements below 1 in K.

We will consistently use the letters $a, b, c \ldots$ for semiring elements and $p, q, r, \ldots$ for Boolean elements. The symbol $\neg$ denotes complementation in $\mathsf{test}(K)$. We will also use relative complement $p - q = p\neg q$ and implication $p \rightarrow q = \neg p + q$ with their standard laws.

A *Kleene algebra with tests* [13] is a test semiring (K, B) such that K is a KA. For all $p \in \mathsf{test}(K)$ we have that $p^* = 1$.

Let now a semiring element a describe an action or abstract program and a test p a proposition or assertion. Then pa describes a restricted program that acts like a when the initial state satisfies p and aborts otherwise. Symmetrically, ap describes a restriction of a in its possible final states. We now introduce an abstract domain operator $\ulcorner$ that assigns to a the test that describes precisely its enabling states.

An *semiring with domain* [6] (a $\ulcorner$-semiring) is a structure $(K, \ulcorner)$, where K is an idempotent semiring and the *domain operation* $\ulcorner : K \rightarrow \mathsf{test}(K)$ satisfies for all $a, b \in K$ and $p \in \mathsf{test}(K)$

$$a \leq (\ulcorner a)a, \quad \text{(d1)} \qquad \ulcorner(pa) \leq p, \quad \text{(d2)} \qquad \ulcorner(a\ulcorner b) \leq \ulcorner(ab) \quad \text{(d3)}$$

If K is a KA, we speak of a *KA with domain*, briefly $\ulcorner$*-KA*. To explain (d1) and (d2) we note that their conjunction is equivalent to each of

$$\ulcorner a \leq p \Leftrightarrow a \leq pa, \quad \text{(llp)} \qquad \ulcorner a \leq p \Leftrightarrow \neg pa \leq 0, \quad \text{(gla)}$$

which constitute elimination laws for $\ulcorner$. (llp) and (gla) say that $\ulcorner a$ is the least left preserver and $\neg\ulcorner a$ is the greatest left annihilator of a, resp. Both properties obviously characterize domain for set-theoretic relations. (d3) states that the domain of ab is not determined by the inner structure of b or its codomain; information about $\ulcorner b$ in interaction with a suffices.

Many natural properties follow from the axioms. Domain is uniquely defined. It is strict ($\ulcorner a = 0 \Leftrightarrow a = 0$), additive ($\ulcorner(a + b) = \ulcorner a + \ulcorner b$), isotone ($a \leq b \Rightarrow \ulcorner a \leq \ulcorner b$), local ($\ulcorner(ab) = \ulcorner(a\ulcorner b)$) and stable on tests ($\ulcorner p = p$). Domain satisfies an import/export law ($\ulcorner(pa) = p\ulcorner a$), and an induction law ($\ulcorner(ap) \le p \Rightarrow \ulcorner(a^*p) \le p$). Finally, domain commutes with all existing suprema. See [6] for further information.

A codomain operation $\urcorner$ is easily defined as a domain operation in the opposite semiring in which the order of multiplication is swapped. We call a semiring K with domain and codomain also a *modal semiring*; if K in addition is a KA, we call it a *modal KA (MKA)*.

Let K be a modal semiring. We introduce forward and backward diamond operators via abstract preimage and image.

$$|a\rangle p = \ulcorner(ap), \qquad (1) \qquad\qquad \langle a|p = (pa)\urcorner, \qquad (2)$$

for all $a \in K$ and $p \in \mathsf{test}(K)$. It follows that diamond operators are strict additive mappings (or *hemimorphisms*) on the algebra of tests.

Forward and backward diamonds satisfy the *exchange law*

$$|a\rangle p \le \neg q \Leftrightarrow \langle a|q \le \neg p \qquad (3)$$

for all $a \in K$ and $p, q \in \mathsf{test}(K)$. De Morgan duality transforms diamonds into boxes and vice versa, for instance $|a]p = \neg|a\rangle\neg p$ and $|a\rangle p = \neg|a]\neg p$. This yields Galois connections: for all $a \in K$ and $p, q \in \mathsf{test}(K)$,

$$|a\rangle p \le q \Leftrightarrow p \le [a|q, \qquad (4) \qquad\qquad \langle a|p \le q \Leftrightarrow p \le |a]q. \qquad (5)$$

Hence diamonds (boxes) commute with all existing suprema (infima) of the test algebra and thus are isotone.

In the sequel, when the direction of diamonds and boxes does not matter, we will use the notation $\langle a\rangle$ and $[a]$. For a test p we have $\langle p\rangle q = pq$ and $[p]q = p \to q$. Hence, $\langle 1\rangle = [1]$ is the identity function on tests. Moreover, $\langle 0\rangle p = 0$ and $[0]p = 1$.

We now study the modal operators as objects with their own algebra. We use the pointwise ordering $f \le g \Leftrightarrow \forall p\,.\, fp \le gp$ between functions $f, g : \mathsf{test}(K) \to \mathsf{test}(K)$, and the pointwise liftings of join and meet,

$$(f+g)(p) = f(p) + g(p), \quad (6) \qquad\qquad (f \sqcap g)(p) = f(p)g(p). \quad (7)$$

We also use the pointwise liftings of $-$ and $\to$ to the operator level.

Many properties of modal operators can now be presented much more succinctly in the respective algebra of operators. First, modalities distribute through the semiring operators as follows.

$$\begin{array}{rclrclrcl} \langle a+b\rangle & = & \langle a\rangle + \langle b\rangle, & |ab\rangle & = & |a\rangle|b\rangle, & \langle ab| & = & \langle b|\langle a|, \\ [a+b] & = & [a] \sqcap [b], & |ab] & = & |a]|b], & [ab| & = & [b|[a|. \end{array}$$

Note that the decomposition with respect to multiplication is covariant for forward modalities and contravariant for backward modalities. The decomposition can be used to transform expressions into normal form and to reason entirely at the level of modal oOperators. These laws imply that diamonds are isotone, i.e., $a \le b$ implies $\langle a\rangle \le \langle b\rangle$, and boxes are antitone, i.e., $a \le b$ implies $[b] \le [a]$.

Next, the test-level Galois connections can be lifted to operators f, g : $\mathsf{test}(K) \to \mathsf{test}(K)$ by setting, for all $a \in K$,

$$|a\rangle f \leq g \Leftrightarrow f \leq [a|g, \qquad \langle a|f \leq g \Leftrightarrow f \leq |a]g.$$

Finally, we obtain the following unfold and induction laws (cf. [6]):

$$|1\rangle + |a\rangle|a^*\rangle = |a^*\rangle, \qquad |1\rangle + |a^*\rangle|a\rangle = |a^*\rangle, \tag{8}$$

$$|b\rangle + |a\rangle|c\rangle \leq |c\rangle \Rightarrow |a^*\rangle|b\rangle \leq |c\rangle. \tag{9}$$

3. Termination in Modal Kleene Algebra

We now abstract a notion of termination from the theory of partial orders. A similar characterization has been used in [10].

According to the standard definition, a relation R on a set A is well-founded iff every non-empty subset of A has an R-minimal element. In a $\ulcorner$- semiring K the minimal part of $p \in \mathsf{test}(K)$ w.r.t. some $a \in K$ can algebraically be characterized as $p - \langle a|p$, i.e., as the set of points that have no a-predecessor in p. So, by contraposition, the well-foundedness condition holds iff for all $p \in \mathsf{test}(K)$ one has $p - \langle a|p \leq 0 \Rightarrow p \leq 0$. Abstracting to a modal semiring K (and using Boolean algebra) we say that a is *well-founded* or *Noetherian*, resp., if for all $p \in \mathsf{test}(K)$,

$$p \leq \langle a|p \Rightarrow p \leq 0. \tag{10}$$

$$p \leq |a\rangle p \Rightarrow p \leq 0. \tag{11}$$

Note that by de Morgan duality a is Noetherian iff, for all $p \in \mathsf{test}(K)$,

$$|a]p \leq p \Rightarrow 1 \leq p. \tag{12}$$

The set of Noetherian elements in K is denoted by $\mathcal{N}(K)$.

We now state abstract algebraic variants of some simple and well-known properties of well-founded and Noetherian relations. Because of symmetry we only treat Noethericity; for algebraic proofs see [6].

LEMMA 1 *Let K be a $\ulcorner$-semiring with $0 \neq 1$ and $a, b \in K$, $p \in \mathsf{test}(K)$.*

(i) $0 \in \mathcal{N}(K)$.
(ii) $p \notin \mathcal{N}(K)$, *if* $p \neq 0$ *and in particular* $1 \notin \mathcal{N}(K)$.
(iii) $b \in \mathcal{N}(K)$ *and* $a \leq b$ *imply* $a \in \mathcal{N}(K)$.
(iv) $a \in \mathcal{N}(K)$ *implies* $a \sqcap 1 \leq 0$, *i.e., a is irreflexive.*
(v) $a \not\leq 0$ *and* $a \in \mathcal{N}(K)$ *imply* $a \not\leq aa$, *that is a is not dense.*
(vi) $a \in \mathcal{N}(K)$ *iff* $a^+ \in \mathcal{N}(K)$, *for K a* $\ulcorner$*-KA.*
(vii) $a^* \notin \mathcal{N}(K)$, *for K a KA with domain.*
(viii) $a + b \in \mathcal{N}(K)$ *implies* $a \in \mathcal{N}(K)$ *and* $b \in \mathcal{N}(K)$.

In general, $a \in \mathcal{N}(K)$ and $b \in \mathcal{N}(K)$ do not imply $a + b \in \mathcal{N}(K)$, so that $\mathcal{N}(K)$ is not a semilattice-ideal. A trivial counterexample is given by the relations $a = \{(0,1)\}$ and $b = \{(1,0)\}$. In Section 7 we will present commutativity conditions that enforce this implication.

4. Termination in Modal Logics

We now give two equational characterizations of Noethericity. The first one uses the star, the second one does not. It holds for the special case of a *transitive* Kleenean element a, i.e., when $aa \leq a$.

Let K be a $^{\ulcorner}$-semiring or a $^{\ulcorner}$-KA, resp. Consider the equations

$$|a\rangle \leq |a\rangle^{+}(|1\rangle - |a\rangle), \quad (13) \qquad\qquad |a\rangle \leq |a\rangle(|1\rangle - |a\rangle). \quad (14)$$

The equation (14) is a translation of Löb's formula from modal logic (cf. [3]) that expresses well-foundedness in Kripke structures. We say that a is *pre-Löbian* if it satisfies (13). We say that a is *Löbian* if it satisfies (14). The sets of pre-Löbian and Löbian elements of K are denoted by $p\mathcal{L}(K)$ and $\mathcal{L}(K)$, resp.

In the relational model, Löb's formula states that a is transitive and that there are no infinite a-chains. We will now relate Löb's formula and Noethericity.

THEOREM 2 *Let T be the set of transitive elements of a $^{\urcorner}$-KA K.*
(i) $\mathcal{L}(K) \subseteq \mathcal{N}(K)$.
(ii) $p\mathcal{L}(K) \subseteq \mathcal{N}(K)$.
(iii) $\mathcal{N}(K) \subseteq p\mathcal{L}(K)$.
(iv) $\mathcal{N}(T) \subseteq \mathcal{L}(T)$.

Properties (i) and (iv) already hold in $^{\ulcorner}$-semirings. A calculational proof of (iii) based on [10] can be found in [6].

The calculational translation between the Löb-formula and our definition of Noethericity is quite interesting for the correspondence theory of modal logic. In this view, our property of Noethericity expresses a frame property, which is part of semantics, whereas the Löb formula stands for a modal formula, which is part of syntax. In modal semirings, we are able to express syntax and semantics in one and the same formalism. Moreover, while the traditional proof of the correspondence uses model-theoretic semantic arguments based on infinite chains, the algebraic proof is entirely calculational and avoids infinity. This is quite beneficial for instance for mechanization.

5. Termination via Infinite Iteration

Cohen has extended KA with an $^{\omega}$ operator for modeling infinite iteration [4]; he has also shown applications in concurrency control. In [17], this algebra has been used for calculating proofs of theorems from abstract rewriting that use simple termination assumptions.

An *ω-algebra* is a structure (K, ω) where K is a KA and

$$a^{\omega} \leq aa^{\omega}, \quad (15) \qquad\qquad c \leq ac + b \Rightarrow c \leq a^{\omega} + a^{*}b, \quad (16)$$

for all $a, b, c \in K$. Hence a^{ω} is also the greatest fixpoint of $\lambda x \,.\, ax$.

Like in Section 2, for a $^{\ulcorner}$-KA K it seems interesting to lift (15) and (16) to operator algebras, similar to the laws (8), and (9) for the star. This is very simple for (15): for $a \in K$,

$$|a^\omega\rangle \leq |a\rangle|a^\omega\rangle. \tag{17}$$

However, as we will see below, there is no law corresponding to (9) and (16). The proof of (9) uses (llp) and works, since the star occurs at the left-hand sides of inequalities. There is no similar law that allows us to handle $^\omega$ which occurs at right-hand sides of inequalities.

Instead one can axiomatize the greatest fixpoint $\nu|a\rangle$ of $|a\rangle$ for $a \in K$:

$$\nu|a\rangle \leq |a\rangle\, \nu|a\rangle, \quad (18) \qquad\qquad p \leq |a\rangle p + q \Rightarrow p \leq \nu|a\rangle + |a^*\rangle q. \quad (19)$$

For complete $\mathsf{test}(K)$, by the Knaster-Tarski theorem $\nu|a\rangle$ always exists, since $|a\rangle$ is isotone. Then one can use a weaker axiomatization (see [10]) from which (19) follows by greatest fixpoint fusion.

Since $|a\rangle p = \neg|a]\neg p$, existence of $\nu|a\rangle$ also implies existence of the least fixpoint $\mu|a]$ of $|a]$, since $\mu|a] = \neg\nu|a\rangle$. In the modal μ-calculus, $\mu|a]$ is known as the *halting predicate* (see, e.g., [11]). With the help of $\nu|a\rangle$ we can rephrase Noethericity more concisely as

$$a \in \mathcal{N}(K) \Leftrightarrow \nu|a\rangle = 0. \tag{20}$$

COROLLARY 3 *Define, for fixed $q \in \mathsf{test}(K)$ and $a \in K$, the function $f : \mathsf{test}(K) \to \mathsf{test}(K)$ by $fp = q + |a\rangle p$. If $\nu|a\rangle$ exists and $a \in \mathcal{N}(K)$ then f has the unique fixpoint $|a^*\rangle q$.*

Proof. The star axioms imply that that the least fixpoint of f is $|a^*\rangle q$. But by the assumption and (19) this is also the greatest fixpoint of f so that all fixpoints coincide with it. □

It turns out that $\nu|a\rangle$ is more suitable for termination analysis than a^ω. In ω-algebra one defines guaranteed termination as the absence of infinite iteration. We call a *ω-Noetherian* if $a^\omega \leq 0$, and denote by $\mathcal{N}_\omega(K)$ the set of all ω-Noetherian elements. To study the relation between $\mathcal{N}$ and $\mathcal{N}_\omega$, we call a $^{\ulcorner}$-KA K *extensional*, if $|a\rangle \leq |b\rangle \Rightarrow a \leq b$ for all $a, b \in K$. E.g., the language model is not extensional. The following lemma shows, somewhat surprisingly, that the connection between Noethericity and ω-Noethericity does not depend on extensionality, although the two notions coincide for the extensional relational model.

LEMMA 4 *Let K be an ω-algebra with domain.*
(i) $\mathcal{N}(K) \subseteq \mathcal{N}_\omega(K)$.
(ii) $\mathcal{N}_\omega(K) \not\subseteq \mathcal{N}(K)$, *for K suitably chosen.*
(iii) $\mathcal{N}_\omega(K) \not\subseteq \mathcal{N}(K)$, *for extensional K suitably chosen.*
(iv) $\mathcal{N}_\omega(K) \subseteq \mathcal{N}(K)$, *for non-extensional K suitably chosen.*

Proof. (i) Let a be Noetherian. By isotonicity, for all $p \in \mathsf{test}(K)$,

$$|a^\omega\rangle p \leq |aa^\omega\rangle p = |a\rangle|a^\omega\rangle p.$$

Hence Noethericity of a implies that $|a^\omega\rangle p = 0$ for all $p \in \mathsf{test}(K)$. But, by strictness of domain, this is the case iff $a^\omega = 0$.

(ii) In the language model we have $a^\omega = 0$ if $1 \sqcap a = 0$, but also $a \neq 0 \Rightarrow \forall p \,.\, |a\rangle p = p$.

(iii) We use an *atomic* KA, in which every element is the sum of *atoms*, i.e., minimal nonzero elements. There are 4 atoms and hence 2^4 elements; it is order-isomorphic to the power set of the set of atoms under inclusion. The atoms of the test algebra are p and q, i.e., $1 = p + q$. The domain of an element x is the sum of all atomic tests t such that $tx \neq 0$. Composition is given by a table for the atoms only; it extends to the other elements through disjunctivity, thus satisfying this axiom by construction. E.g., for atoms w, x, y, z we set $(w+x)(y+z) = wy + wz + xy + xz$. The algebra is extensional. Moreover, it is easily checked that 0 is the only fixpoint of the function $\lambda x \,.\, (a+b)x$, so that $(a+b)^\omega = 0$. But $1 \leq |a+b\rangle 1$.

$\cdot$	p	q	a	b
p	p	0	a	0
q	0	q	0	b
a	0	a	0	0
b	b	0	0	0

(iv) Consider the KA K from [5], p. 101. It consists of elements $0 < 1 < a$; the ordering defines the addition table. The only non-trivial relation in the multiplication table is $aa = a$. The star is defined by $a^* = a$ and $0^* = 1^* = 1$. We extend K to an ω-algebra by setting $0^\omega = 0$ and $1^\omega = a^\omega = a$. Moreover, we define domain by $\ulcorner 0 = 0$ and $\ulcorner 1 = \ulcorner a = 1$. Since $x^\omega = 0 \Leftrightarrow x = 0$ holds in K, i.e., $\mathcal{N}_\omega(K) = \{0\}$, we have to verify $\mathcal{N}_\omega(K) \subseteq \mathcal{N}(K)$ only for the zero. But $0 \in \mathcal{N}(K)$ was already stated in Lemma 1(i). □

By the following corollary, (16) cannot in general be lifted to (19).

COROLLARY 5 *There exists a* $\ulcorner$*-KA* K *such that* $\nu|a\rangle \leq 0$, *but* $a^\omega > 0$ *for some* $a \in K$.

Thus ω-algebra does not entirely capture the notion of termination.

6. Termination of Exhaustive Iteration

We now study the exhaustive finite iteration of an element $a \in K$,

$$\mathsf{exh}\, a = \mathsf{while}\ulcorner a\, \mathsf{do}\, a = a^*\neg\ulcorner a\ .$$

Then the set of points from which a terminal point can be reached via a-steps is represented by

$$\ulcorner(\mathsf{exh}\, a) = \ulcorner(a^*\neg\ulcorner a) = |a^*\rangle\neg\ulcorner a. \tag{21}$$

PROPOSITION 6 *If* $a \in \mathcal{N}(K)$ *then* $\ulcorner(\mathsf{exh}\, a) = 1$, *i.e., from* every *starting point a terminal point can be reached.*

Proof. We calculate a recursion equation for $\ulcorner(\mathsf{exh}\,a)$ as follows:

$$\ulcorner(\mathsf{exh}\,a) = |a^*\rangle\neg\ulcorner a = (|1\rangle + |a\rangle|a^*\rangle)\neg\ulcorner a$$
$$= \neg\ulcorner a + |a\rangle|a^*\rangle\neg\ulcorner a = \neg\ulcorner a + |a\rangle\ulcorner(\mathsf{exh}\,a)\ .$$

The first step uses (21), the second star unfold, the third distributivity and neutrality of 1, the fourth again (21).

So $\ulcorner(\mathsf{exh}\,a)$ has to be a fixpoint of $f(p) = \neg\ulcorner a + |a\rangle p$ which by Noethericity of a and Corollary 3 is unique. Hence our claim is shown if 1 also is a fixpoint of f. This holds, since $f(1) = \neg\ulcorner a + |a\rangle 1 = \neg\ulcorner a + \ulcorner a = 1$. □

This theorem shows again that MKA is more adequate for termination analysis than ω-algebra. To see this, consider the algebra LAN of formal languages which is both an ω-algebra and a $\ulcorner$-KA with complete test algebra $\mathbf{test}(\mathrm{LAN}) = \{0,1\}$. In LAN we have $|a\rangle 1 = \ulcorner a = 1 \neq 0$ when $a \neq 0$ and hence $\mathcal{N}(a) \Leftrightarrow a = 0$. Moreover, distinguishing the cases $a = 0$ and $a \neq 0$, easy calculations show that in LAN we have $\mathsf{exh}\,a = \neg\ulcorner a$. This mirrors the fact that by totality of concatenation a nonempty language can be iterated indefinitely without reaching a terminal element. But we also have $a^\omega = 0$ whenever $1 \sqcap a = 0$. Therefore, unlike in the relational model, $a^\omega = 0 \;\not\Rightarrow\; \ulcorner(\mathsf{exh}\,a) = 1$, while still $\nu|a\rangle = 0 \Rightarrow \ulcorner(\mathsf{exh}\,a) = 1$.

7. Additivity of Termination

Many statements of abstract rewriting that depend on termination assumptions can be proved in ω-algebra [17], among them an abstract variant of Bachmair's and Dershowitz's well-founded union theorem [2]. For comparison, we prove that here in MKA.

Consider a KA K and $a, b \in K$. We say that a *semi-commutes* over b, if $ba \leq a^+b^*$. a *quasi-commutes* over b, if $ba \leq a(a+b)^*$. We write $sc(a,b)$ if a semi-commutes over b and $qc(a,b)$, iff a quasi-commutes over b. Semi-commutation and quasi-commutation state conditions for permuting certain steps to the left of others. In general, sequences with a-steps and b-steps can be split into a "good" part with all a-steps occurring to the left of b-steps and into a "bad" part where both kinds of steps are mixed. The following lemma lifts semi-commutation and quasi-commutation to sequences of b-steps and states a separation law.

LEMMA 7 *For a KA K and all $a, b \in K$,*
(i) $sc(a,b) \Leftrightarrow b^*a \leq a^+b^*$,
(ii) $qc(a,b) \Leftrightarrow b^+a \leq a(a+b)^*$,
(iii) $(a+b)^* = a^*b^* + a^*b^+a(a+b)^*$.

A proof of this lemma can be found in [17]. The following lemma compares quasi-commutation and semi-commutation.

LEMMA 8 *Consider a KA K and $a, b \in K$.*
(i) $sc(a,b) \Rightarrow qc(a,b)$.
(ii) *If K is extensional and $a \in \mathcal{N}(K)$ then* $qc(a,b) \Rightarrow sc(a,b)$.

Proof. (i) Let a semi-commute over b. By Kleene algebra,

$$a^+b^* = a(a^*b^*) \leq a(a+b)^*.$$

(ii) Let a quasi-commute over b and let a be Noetherian. First,

$$\begin{aligned} a(a+b)^* &= a(a^*b^* + a^*b^+a(a+b)^*) = a^+b^* + a^+b^+a(a+b)^* \\ &\leq a^+b^* + a^+a(a+b)^*(a+b)^* = a^+b^* + a^+a(a+b)^*. \end{aligned}$$

The first step uses Lemma 7(iii), the second distributivity and the definition of a^+, the third Lemma 7 (ii), the fourth $x^*x^* = x^*$.

To apply Noethericity, we now pass to the modal operator level. To enhance readability, we write α for $|a\rangle$ and β for $|b\rangle$ and ζ for $|0\rangle$.

$$\begin{aligned} \alpha(\alpha+\beta)^* - \alpha^+\beta^* &\leq (\alpha^+\beta^* + \alpha^+\alpha(\alpha+\beta)^*) - \alpha^+\beta^* \\ &= (\alpha^+\beta^* - \alpha^+\beta^*) + (\alpha\alpha^+(\alpha+\beta)^* - \alpha^+\beta^*) \\ &\leq \alpha\alpha^+(\alpha+\beta)^* - \alpha^+\alpha^+\beta^* \\ &= \alpha^+(\alpha(\alpha+\beta)^* - \alpha^+\beta^*). \end{aligned}$$

The first step uses isotonicity of minus in its first argument. The second step uses $(p+q)-r = (p-r)+(q-r)$. The third step uses $p-p=0$, $a^+a^+ \leq a^+$ and antitonicity of subtraction in its second argument. The fourth step uses $aa^+ = a^+a$ and distributivity.

By Lemma 1(vi) we know that a is Noetherian iff a^+ is. Therefore $\alpha^+(\alpha+\beta)^* - \alpha^+\beta^* \leq \zeta$, whence $\alpha^+(\alpha+\beta)^* \leq \alpha^+\beta^*$. The claim then follows from $\alpha \leq \alpha^+$ and extensionality. □

LEMMA 9 *Let K be a $\ulcorner$-KA.*
(i) *For all $a \in \mathcal{N}(K)$ and $b \in K$,* $qc(a,b) \Rightarrow b^*a \leq a^+b^*$.
(ii) *For all $a, b \in K$, $qc(a,b)$ and $a \in \mathcal{N}(K)$ imply $b^*a \in \mathcal{N}(K)$.*
(iii) *For all $b, b^*a \in \mathcal{N}(K)$, $(a+b) \in \mathcal{N}(K)$.*

Proof. We use the same abbreviations as in the previous proof.

(i) Immediate from Lemma 8 and Lemma 7 (i).

(ii) Let $a \in \mathcal{N}(K)$ and $\alpha\beta \leq (\alpha+\beta)^*\alpha$. Then by (i), $\alpha\beta^* \leq \beta^*\alpha^+$. Now let $p \leq \beta^*\alpha p$, whence $p \leq \alpha^+\beta^*p$ and in particular $\beta^*p \leq \alpha^+\beta^*p$. Since by Lemma1 (vi) a is Noetherian iff a^+ is, we have that $\beta^*p \leq 0$ by assumption. This can only be the case if $p \leq 0$.

(iii) We calculate $(a+b)^+ = (b^*a)^*b^*(a+b) \leq (b^*a)^+ + b^+$. Now $a+b$ is Noetherian if $(a+b)^+$ is. Let $p \leq (\alpha+\beta)^+p$. Then $p \leq (\beta^*\alpha)^+p + \beta^+p$ and $p \leq 0$ follows from the assumptions. □

Lemma 9 (ii) and (iii) immediately imply the main theorem of this section. It generalizes the Bachmair-Dershowitz well-founded union theorem from relations to MKA.

THEOREM 10 *Let K be an extensional $\ulcorner$-KA and $a, b \in K$ with $qc(a,b)$. Then $(a+b) \in \mathcal{N}(K)$ iff $a, b \in \mathcal{N}(K)$.*

These results show that MKA provides proofs for abstract rewriting that are as simple as those in ω-algebra. Note that the original proofs in [2] are rather informal, while also previous diagrammatic proofs (e.g. [9]) suppress many elementary steps. In contrast, our algebraic proofs are complete, formal and still simple. For an extensive discussion of the relation between the proofs in ω-algebra and their diagrammatic counterparts see [17]. In particular, the algebraic proofs mirror precisely the diagrammatic; this also holds for the modal proofs given here.

8. Newman's Lemma and Normal Forms

We now turn from semi-commutation to commutation and confluence. For their direct algebraic characterization one either has to use converse at the element level or a combination of forward and backward modalities at the operator level. Since converse is not available in MKA, we have to choose the second alternative.

We say that $a, b \in K$ *commute* if $\langle b^*||a^*\rangle \leq |a^*\rangle\langle b^*|$, and *commute locally* if $\langle b||a\rangle \leq |a^*\rangle\langle b^*|$. These definitions can be visualized as

Then $a \in K$ is *(locally) confluent* if it (locally) commutes with itself.

In the relational setting, the generalization from confluence to commutation has been used in [15] for a theory of term-rewriting with pre-congruences that extends the traditional equational case. This also yields generalizations of the Church-Rosser theorem and of Newman's lemma. While the former has already been proved in Kleene algebra in [16], it has been argued in [17] that a proof of Newman's lemma does not work in pure Kleene or ω-algebra.

For the equational case, [14] gives a calculational proof of Newman's lemma in relation algebra. But it cannot be adapted to our case, since it uses a notion of unique normal form that does not exist in the commutation-based setting. Moreover, conceptually it is nicer to completely uncouple confluence from normal forms.

We will faithfully reconstruct the diagrammatic proof using Noetherian induction [15]; it turns out that MKA is very well suited for this. A calculational proof that is close in spirit occurs in [8]. However, it is more complex in that it uses full residuation, whereas we can make do with the much weaker concept of modal operators. (The modal box operator corresponds to the monotype factor that is also used in [8].) Also, the theorem there is more restricted, since it only covers the relational case, whereas our result also applies to e.g. the path algebra. Now we are ready for our generalization of Newman's lemma.

THEOREM 11 *Let K be a modal KA with complete test algebra. If $a+b \in \mathcal{N}(K)$ and a and b commute locally then a and b commute.*

Proof. The central idea of our proof is to use a generalized predicate that characterizes the set of all points on which a and b commute and to retrieve full commutation as a special case. If we can show that this predicate is contracted by $|a+b]$ then, by the second form (12) of Noethericity, we are done. So let us define (rc stands for "restricted commutation")

$$rc(p,a,b) \Leftrightarrow \langle b^*|\langle p\rangle|a^*\rangle \leq |a^*\rangle\langle b^*| \ .$$

$rc(p,a,b)$ states that a and b commute on all points in p. The notation $\langle p\rangle$ enhances the symmetry of the formulation; it is justified, since $|p\rangle = \langle p|$ for all tests p. Clearly, a and b commute iff $rc(1,a,b)$. Moreover, rc is downward closed, i.e., $rc(p,a,b) \wedge q \leq p \Rightarrow rc(q,a,b)$. We now define $r = \sup\{p \mid rc(p,a,b)\}$ which exists by completeness of $\mathsf{test}(K)$. This represents the set of all points on which a and b commute. Completeness of $\mathsf{test}(K)$ implies that $\cdot$ distributes over all suprema in $\mathsf{test}(K)$, so that $|r\rangle = \sup\{|p\rangle \mid rc(p,a,b)\}$. Moreover, composition with diamonds is universally disjunctive in both arguments, so that we may infer $rc(r,a,b)$. Together with downward closure of rc we therefore obtain

$$p \leq r \Leftrightarrow rc(p,a,b) \ . \tag{22}$$

We now show that r is contracted by $|a+b]$, so that $a+b \in \mathcal{N}(K)$ implies $r=1$. For this we first calculate

$$\begin{aligned}
(|a+b]r \leq r) &\Leftrightarrow (\forall p \,.\, p \leq |a+b]r \Rightarrow p \leq r) \\
&\Leftrightarrow (\forall p \,.\, \langle a+b|p \leq r \Rightarrow p \leq r) \\
&\Leftrightarrow (\forall p \,.\, \langle a|p \leq r \wedge \langle b|p \leq r \Rightarrow p \leq r) \\
&\Leftrightarrow (\forall p \,.\, rc(p_a,a,b) \wedge rc(p_b,a,b) \Rightarrow rc(p,a,b)).
\end{aligned}$$

The first step uses order theory, the second the Galois connection (5), the third distributivity and Boolean algebra, the fourth (22) and the definition $p_x = \langle x|p$.

So assume $rc(p_a,a,b) \wedge rc(p_b,a,b)$. By the star fixpoint law (8) and distributivities, $\langle b^*|\langle p\rangle|a^*\rangle \leq \langle b^*|\langle p\rangle + \langle b^*|\langle b|\langle p\rangle|a\rangle|a^*\rangle + \langle p\rangle|a^*\rangle$. The outer two of these summands are below $|a^*\rangle\langle b^*|$ by isotonicity, $p \leq 1 \leq x^*$ and neutrality of $|1\rangle$. For the middle summand we first state

$$\langle p\rangle|x\rangle = \langle p\rangle|x\rangle\langle p_x\rangle \leq |x\rangle\langle p_x\rangle \ , \quad \langle x|\langle p\rangle = \langle p_x\rangle\langle x|\langle p\rangle \leq \langle p_x\rangle\langle x| \ . \tag{23}$$

This follows by isotonicity, since the definition of p_a and right neutrality of codomain imply $px = px\langle p_x\rangle \leq x\langle p_x\rangle$. Now we calculate, illustrating this by a diagram in which the bottom point is in p and the two points in the next higher layer are in p_b and p_a, resp.

$$
\begin{array}{ll}
& \langle b^*|\langle b|\langle p\rangle|a\rangle|a^*\rangle \\
\leq & \langle b^*|\langle p_b\rangle\langle b||a\rangle\langle p_a\rangle|a^*\rangle \\
\leq & \langle b^*|\langle p_b\rangle|a^*\rangle\langle b^*|\langle p_a\rangle|a^*\rangle \\
\leq & |a^*\rangle\langle b^*|\langle b^*|\langle p_a\rangle|a^*\rangle \\
\leq & |a^*\rangle\langle b^*|\langle p_a\rangle|a^*\rangle \\
\leq & |a^*\rangle|a^*\rangle\langle b^*| \\
\leq & |a^*\rangle\langle b^*|.
\end{array}
$$

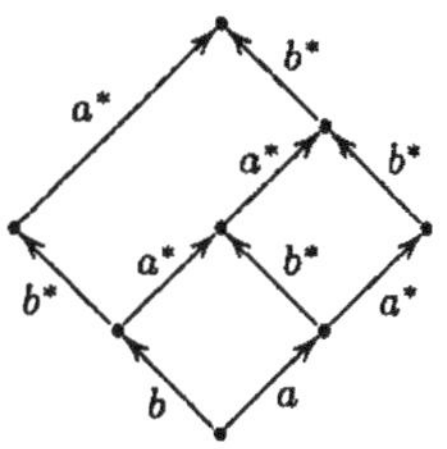

The first step uses idempotence of $\langle p\rangle$, codomain propagation (23) twice and compositionality, the second $\mathrm{LC}(a,b)$, the third the assumption $rc(p_a,a,b)$, the fourth idempotence of star and compositionality, the fifth the assumption $rc(p_b,a,b)$, the sixth idempotence of star and compositionality. □

We conclude this section by showing that confluence implies uniqueness of normal forms. As in Section 6, for $a \in K$ the element $\mathsf{exh}\, a = a^*\neg\ulcorner a$ describes the exhaustive iteration of a, the points in $(\mathsf{exh}\, a)\urcorner$ being the *normal forms*. Now, a Kleene element b assigns to each point in its domain at most one point in its codomain iff b is *deterministic*, i.e., iff $\langle b||b\rangle \leq \langle 1\rangle$. This formula corresponds to the relational characterization $b\breve{}b \leq 1$ of determinacy of b (where $\breve{}$ is converse). Now we can show

LEMMA 12 *If a is confluent then* $\mathsf{exh}\, a$ *is deterministic.*
Proof. Plugging in the definition of $\mathsf{exh}\, a$ we calculate

$$
\begin{array}{rcl}
\langle a^*\neg\ulcorner a||a^*\neg\ulcorner a\rangle & = & \langle\neg\ulcorner a\rangle\langle a^*||a^*\rangle\langle\neg\ulcorner a\rangle \leq \langle\neg\ulcorner a\rangle|a^*\rangle\langle a^*|\langle\neg\ulcorner a\rangle \\
& = & |\neg\ulcorner aa^*\rangle\langle\neg\ulcorner aa^*| = |\neg\ulcorner a\rangle\langle\neg\ulcorner a| \leq \langle 1\rangle.
\end{array}
$$

The first step uses compositionality, the second confluence of a, the third compositionality again, the fourth the star fixpoint law, distributivity and (gla), the fifth isotonicity and idempotence of $\langle 1\rangle$. □

9. Conclusion

We have used modal KA for termination analysis, introducing and comparing different notions of termination that arise in this context and applying our techniques to two examples from abstract rewriting. All proofs are abstract, concise and entirely calculational. Together with previous work [16, 17] our case study in abstract rewriting shows that large parts of this theory can be reconstructed in MKA. By its simplicity, our approach has considerable potential for mechanization. There are strong connections with automata-theoretic decision procedures.

From the proof of Newman's lemma and the associated diagram it becomes clear that MKA allows one to perform induction in the middle of an expression. This is not possible in pure Kleene or ω-algebra due to the shape of the star and omega induction rules. Hence MKA allows "context-free" induction, whereas pure Kleene or ω-algebra admit only "regular" induction. Therefore, in [8] residuals are used to move the point of induction from inside an expression to its ends and back.

The results of this paper contribute to establishing modal Kleene algebra as a formalism for safe cross-theory reasoning and therefore interoperability between different calculi for program analysis. We envision three main lines of further work. First, the integration of our results into Hoare-style reasoning and into Kleene algebras for the weakest precondition semantics, second, a further exploitation of the mentioned connection with the modal μ-calculus and third, further applications of our technique to the analysis of programs and protocols.

References

[1] F. Baader, T. Nipkow. *Term rewriting and all that.* Cambridge University Press 1998.

[2] L. Bachmair, N. Dershowitz. Commutation, transformation, and termination. In J.H. Siekmann (ed.), *8th International Conference on Automated Deduction.* LNCS 230. Springer 1986, 5–20.

[3] B.F. Chellas. *Modal Logic: An Introduction.* Cambridge University Press 1980.

[4] E. Cohen. Separation and reduction. In R. Backhouse, J.N. Oliveira (eds.), *Proc. Mathematics of Program Construction, 5th International Conference, MPC 2000.* LNCS 1887. Springer 2000, 45–59.

[5] J.H. Conway. *Regular Algebra and Finite State Machines.* Chapman & Hall 1971.

[6] J. Desharnais, B. Möller, G. Struth. Kleene algebra with domain. Technical Report 2003-07, Universität Augsburg, Institut für Informatik, June 2003.

[7] J. Desharnais, B. Möller, G. Struth. Termination in modal Kleene algebra. Technical Report 2004-04, Universität Augsburg, Institut für Informatik, January 2004.

[8] H. Doornbos, R. Backhouse, J. van der Woude. A calculational approach to mathematical induction. *Theoretical Computer Science*, 179:103–135 (1997).

[9] A. Geser. *Relative termination.* PhD thesis, Fakultät fur Mathematik und Informatik, Universität Passau 1990.

[10] R. Goldblatt., R. An algebraic study of well-foundedness. *Studia Logica*, 44(4):422–437 (1985).

[11] D. Harel, D. Kozen, J. Tiuryn. *Dynamic Logic.* MIT Press 2000.

[12] D. Kozen. A completeness theorem for Kleene algebras and the algebra of regular events. *Information and Computation*, 110(2):366–390 (1994).

[13] D. Kozen. Kleene algebra with tests. *Trans. Programming Languages and Systems*, 19(3):427–443 (1997).

[14] G. Schmidt, T. Ströhlein. *Relations and Graphs.* EATCS Monographs in Computer Science. Springer 1993.

[15] G. Struth. Non-symmetric rewriting. Technical Report MPI-I-96-2-004, Max-Planck-Institut für Informatik Saarbrücken 1996.

[16] G. Struth. Calculating Church-Rosser proofs in Kleene algebra. In H.C.M. de Swart (ed.), *Relational Methods in Computer Science, 6th International Conference.* LNCS 2561. Springer 2002, 276–290.

[17] G. Struth. An algebraic study of commutation and termination. Technical Report 2003-18, Institut für Informatik, Universität Augsburg, December 2003.

REGULAR TREE LANGUAGE RECOGNITION WITH STATIC INFORMATION

Alain Frisch
École Normale Supérieure
Alain.Frisch@ens.fr

Abstract This paper presents our compilation strategy to produce efficient code for pattern matching in the CDuce compiler, taking into account static information provided by the type system.

1. Introduction

Emergence of XML[BPSM98] has given tree automata theory a renewed importance[Nev02]. Indeed, XML schema languages such as DTD, XML-Schema[TBMM01, SW03], Relax-NG describe more or less regular languages of XML documents (considered as trees). Consequently, recent XML-oriented typed programming languages such as XDuce [Hos00, HP02], CDuce [BCF03, FCB02], Xtatic [GP03] have type algebras where types denote regular tree languages. An essential ingredient of these languages is a powerful pattern matching operation. A pattern is a declarative way to extract information from an XML tree. Because of this declarative nature, language implementors have to propose efficient execution models for pattern matching.

This paper describes our approach in implementing pattern matching in CDuce[1]. To simplify the presentation, the paper studies only a restricted form of pattern matching, without capture variables and with a very simple kind of trees. Of course, our implementation handles capture variables and the full set of types and patterns constructors in CDuce. In the simplified form, the pattern matching problem is a recognition problem, namely deciding whether a tree v belongs to a regular tree language X or not. If the regular language is given by a tree automaton, a top-down recognition algorithm may have to backtrack, and the recognition time is not linear in the size of the input tree. It is well-known that any tree automaton can be transformed into an equiva-

[1] CDuce is available for download at `http://www.cduce.org/`.

lent bottom-up deterministic automaton, which ensures linear execution time. However, the size of the automaton may be huge even for simple languages, which can make this approach unfeasible in practice.

The static type system of the language provides an upper approximation for the type of the matched tree v, that is some regular language X_0 such that v is necessarily in X_0. Taking this information into account, it should be possible to avoid looking at some subtree of v. However, classical bottom-up tree automata are bound to look at the whole tree, and they cannot take this kind of static knowledge into account. Let us give an example to illustrate this point. Consider the following CDuce program:

```
type A = <a>[ A* ]
type B = <b>[ B* ]

let f ((A|B)->Int) A    ->0 | B ->1
let g ((A|B)->Int) <a>_->0 | _ ->1
```

The first lines introduce two types A and B. They denote XML documents with only <a> (resp. <b>) tags and nothing else. Then two functions f and g are defined. Both functions take an argument which is either a document of type A or of type B. They return 1 when the argument is of type A, and 0 when the argument is of type B. The declaration of g suggests an efficient execution schema: one just has to look at the root tag to answer the question. Instead, if we consider only the body of f, we have to look at the whole argument, and check that every node of the argument is tagged with <a> (resp. with <b>); whatever technique we use - deterministic bottom-up or backtracking top-down - it will be less efficient than g.

But if we use the information given by the function interface, we know that the argument is necessarily of type A or of type B, and we can compile f exactly as we compile g. This example demonstrates that taking static information into account is crucial to provide efficient execution for declarative patterns as in f.

Contributions. The main contributions of this paper are the definition of a new kind of deterministic bottom-up tree automata, called NUA (non-uniform automata) and a compilation algorithm that produces an efficient NUA equivalent to a given non-deterministic (classical) automaton, taking into account static knowledge about the matched trees.

A central idea in XDuce-like languages is that XML documents live in an untyped world and that XML types are structural. This is in contrast with the XML Schema philosophy, whose data model (after validation) attaches type *names* to XML nodes. Moreover, in XML Schema, the context and the tag of an element are enough to know the exact XML Schema type of the element. In XDuce-like languages, in general, one may have to look deep inside the elements to check type constraints. Our work shows how an efficient compilation of pattern matching can avoid this costly checks: our compilation algorithm detects when the context and the tag are enough to decide of the type of an element without looking at its content. This work supports the claim that a structural data model *à la* XDuce can be implemented as efficiently as a data model with explicit type names *à la* XML Schema.

Related work. Levin [Lev03] also addresses the implementation of pattern matching in XDuce-like programming languages. He introduces a general framework (intermediate language, matching automata) to reason about the compilation of patterns, and he proposes several compilation strategies. He leaves apart the issue of using static types for compilation, which is the main motivation for our work. So the two works are complementary: our compilation algorithm could probably be re-cast in his formalism.

Neumann and Seidl [NS98] introduce push-down automata to locate efficiently nodes in an XML tree. Our automata share with push-down automata the idea of threading a control-state through the tree. The formalisms are quite different because we work with simpler kind of automata (binary trees with labeled leaves, whereas they have unranked labeled forests), and we explicitly distinguish betwen control states (threaded through the tree) and results (used in particular to update the state). However, using an encoding of unranked trees in binary trees, we believe that the two notions of automata are isomorphic. But again, they don't address the issue of using static information to improve the automata, which is our main technical contribution. It should be possible to adapt our compilation algorithm to their push-down automata setting, but it would probably result in an extremely complex technical presentation. This motivates us working with simpler kinds of tree and automata.

2. Technical framework

In this section, we introduce our technical framework. We consider one of the simplest form of trees: binary trees with labeled leafs and unlabeled nodes. Any kind of ordered trees (n-ary, ranked, unranked; with or without labeled nodes) can be *encoded*, and the notion of regular language is invariant under these encodings. (Note that the encodings change the expressive power of top-down deterministic tree automata, but this is not the case for the "non-uniform" automata we are going to define.) Using this very simple kind of trees simplifies the presentation.

2.1 Trees and classical tree automata

DEFINITION 1 *Let Σ be a (fixed) finite set of symbols. A tree v is either a symbol $a \in \Sigma$ or a pair of trees (v_1, v_2). The set of trees is written $\mathcal{V}$.*

DEFINITION 2 (TREE AUTOMATON) *A (non-deterministic) tree automaton (NDTA) is a pair $\mathcal{A} = (R, \delta)$ where R is a finite set of* nodes, *and $\delta \subseteq (\Sigma \times R) \cup (R \times R \times R)$.*

Each node r in a NDTA defines a subset $\mathcal{A}[\![r]\!]$ of $\mathcal{V}$. These sets can be defined by the following mutually recursive equations:

$$\mathcal{A}[\![r]\!] = \{a \in \Sigma \mid (a, r) \in \delta\} \cup \bigcup_{(r_1, r_2, r) \in \delta} \mathcal{A}[\![r_1]\!] \times \mathcal{A}[\![r_2]\!]$$

We write $\mathcal{A}[\![r]\!]^2 = \mathcal{A}[\![r]\!] \cap (\mathcal{V} \times \mathcal{V})$. By definition, a regular language is a subset of the form $\mathcal{A}[\![r]\!]$ for some NDTA $\mathcal{A}$ and some node r. We say that this language is *defined* by $\mathcal{A}$. There are two classical notions of deterministic tree automata: (1) Top-down deterministic automata (TDDTA) satisfy the property: $\{(r_1, r_2) \mid (r_1, r_2, r) \in \delta\}$ has at most one element for any node r. These automata are strictly weaker than NDTA in terms of expressive power (they cannot define all the regular languages). (2) Bottom-up deterministic automata (DTA) satisfy the property: $\{r \mid (r_1, r_2, r) \in \delta\}$ has at most one element for any pair of nodes (r_1, r_2), and similarly for the sets $\{r \mid (a, r) \in \delta\}$ with $a \in \Sigma$. These automata have the same expressive power as NDTA.

REMARK 3 *We use a non-standard terminology of nodes instead of states. The reason is that we are going to split this notion in two: results and control states. Results will correspond to nodes in a DTA, and control states will correspond to nodes in TDDTA.*

In order to motivate the use of a different kind of automaton, let us introduce different notions of context. During the traversal of a tree, an automaton computes and gathers information. The amount of extracted information can only depend on the context of the current location in the tree. A top-down recognizer (for TDDTA) can only propagate information downwards: the context of a location is thus the path from the root to the location ("upward context"). A bottom-up recognizer propagates information upwards: the context is the whole subtree rooted at the current location ("downward context").

Top-down algorithms are more efficient when the relevant information is located near the root. For instance, going back to the CDuce example in the introduction, we see easily that the function g should be implemented by starting the traversal from the root of the tree, since looking only at the root tag is enough. Patterns in CDuce tend to look in priority near the root of the trees instead of their leafs. However, because of their lack of expressive power, pure TDDTA cannot be used in general. Also, since they perform independant computations of the left and the right children of a location in a tree, they cannot use information gathered in the left subtree to guide the computation in the right subtree.

The idea behind push-down automata is to traverse each node twice. A location is first entered in a given context, some computation is performed on the subtree, and the location is entered again with a new context. When a location is first entered, the context is the path from the root, but also all the "left siblings" of these locations and their subtrees (we call this the "up/left context" of the location). After the computation on the children, the context also includes the subtree. The notion of non-uniform automata we are going to introduce is a slight variation on this idea: a location is entered three times. Indeed, when computing on a tree which is a pair, the automaton considers the left and right subtrees sequentially. Between the two, the location is entered again to update its context, and the automaton uses the information gathered on the left subtree to guide the computation on the right subtree. This richer notion of context allows to combine the advantages of DTA and TDDTA, and more.

2.2 Non-uniform automata

We now introduce a new kind of tree automaton: non-uniform automata (NUA in short). They can be seen as (a generalization of) a merger between DTA and TDDTA. Let us call "results" (resp. "control states") the nodes of DTA (resp. TDDTA). We are going to use these two notions in parallel. A current "control state" is threaded and updated during a depth-first left-to-right traversal of the tree (this control generalizes the one of TDDTA, where the state is only propagated downwards), and each control state q has its own set of results $R(q)$. Of course, the transition relation depends on q.

When the automaton has to deal with a tree (v_1, v_2) in a state q, it starts with some computation on v_1 using a new state $q_1 = \texttt{left}(q)$ computed from the current one, as for a TDDTA. This gives a result r_1 which is immediately used to compute the state $q_2 = \texttt{right}(q, r_1)$. Note that contrary to TDDTA, q_2 depends not only on q, but also on the computation performed on the left subtree. The computation on v_2 is done from this state q_2, and it returns a result r_2. As for classical bottom-up deterministic automata, the result for (v_1, v_2) is then computed from r_1 and r_2 (and q). Let us formalize the definition of non-uniform automata. We define only the deterministic version.

DEFINITION 4 *A non-uniform automaton $\mathcal{A}$ is given by a finite set of states Q, and for each state $q \in Q$:*

- *A finite set of results $R(q)$.*
- *A state $\texttt{left}(q) \in Q$.*
- *For any result $r_1 \in R(\texttt{left}(q))$, a state $\texttt{right}(q, r_1) \in Q$.*

- *For any result* $r_1 \in R(\texttt{left}(q))$, *and any result* $r_2 \in R(\texttt{right}(q, r_1))$, *a result* $\delta^2(q, r_1, r_2) \in R(q)$.
- *A* partial *function* $\delta^0(q, \_) : \Sigma \to R(q)$.

The *result* of the automaton from a state q on an input $v \in \mathcal{V}$, written $\mathcal{A}(q, v)$, is the element of $R(q)$ defined by induction on v:

$$\begin{array}{lcl} \mathcal{A}(q,a) & = & \delta^0(q,a) \\ \mathcal{A}(q,(v_1,v_2)) & = & \delta^2(q,r_1,r_2) \text{ where } \end{array} \left\{ \begin{array}{lcl} r_1 & = & \mathcal{A}(\texttt{left}(q), v_1) \\ r_2 & = & \mathcal{A}(\texttt{right}(q,r_1), v_2) \end{array} \right.$$

Because the functions $\delta^0(q, \_)$ are partial, so are the $\mathcal{A}(q, \_)$. We write $\texttt{Dom}(q)$ for the set of trees v such that $\mathcal{A}(q, v)$ is defined.

Our definition of NUAs (and more generally, the class of push down automata [NS98]) is flexible enough to simulate DTA and TDDTA (without explosion of size). Indeed, the definition of a NUA boils down to that of a DTA when Q is a singleton $\{q\}$: the set of results of the NUA (for the only state) corresponds to the set of nodes of the DTA. It is also possible to convert a TDDTA to a NUA of the same size: The set of states of the NUA corresponds to the set of nodes of the TDDTA, and all the states have a single result.

A pair (q, r) with $q \in Q$ and $r \in R(q)$ is called a *state-result* pair. For such a pair, we write $\mathcal{A}[\![q; r]\!] = \{v \mid \mathcal{A}(q, v) = r\}$ for the set of trees yielding result r starting from initial state q. The reader is invited to check that a NUA can be interpreted as a non-deterministic tree automata whose nodes are state-result pairs. Consequently, the expressive power of NUAs (that is the class of languages of the form $\mathcal{A}[\![q; r]\!]$) is the same as NDTAs (ie: they can define only regular languages). The point is that the definition of NUAs gives an efficient execution strategy.

Running a NUA. The definition of $\mathcal{A}(q, v)$ defines an efficient algorithm that operates in linear time with respect to the size of v. We will only run this algorithm for trees v which are known *a priori* to be in $\texttt{Dom}(q)$. This is because of the intended use of the theory (compilation of CDuce pattern matching): indeed, the static type system in CDuce ensures exhaustivity of pattern matching.

An important remark: the flexibility of having a different set of results for each state makes it possible to short-cut the inductive definition and completely ignore subtrees. Indeed, as soon as the algorithm reaches a subtree v' in a state q' such that $R(q')$ is a singleton, it can directly return without even looking at v'.

3. The algorithm

Different NUA can perform the same computation with different complexities (that is, they can ignore more or fewer subtrees of the input). To obtain efficient NUA, the objective is to keep the set of results $R(q)$ as small as possible, because when $R(q)$ is a singleton, we can drop the corresponding subtree (and having $R(q)$ small will help "subsequent" $R(q')$ to be singletons).

Also, we want to build NUAs that take static information about the input trees into account. Hopefully, we have the opportunity of defining *partial* states, whose domain is not the whole set of trees.

In this section, we present an algorithm to build an efficient NUA to solve the dispatch problem under static knowledge.

Given a regular language X_0 (the input domain) and given regular languages $X_1, \ldots, X_n$ (the dispatch alternatives), we want to compute efficiently for any tree $v \in X_0$ the set $\{i \mid i \in \{1, \ldots, n\}, v \in X_i\}$.

3.1 Intuitions

Let us consider four regular languages X_1, X_2, X_3, X_4, and let $X = (X_1 \times X_2) \cup (X_3 \times X_4)$. Imagine we want to recognize the language X without static information ($X_0 = \mathcal{V}$). If we are given a tree (v_1, v_2), we must first perform some computation on v_1. Namely, it is enough to know, after this computation, if v_1 is in X_1 or not, and similarly for X_3. It is not necessary to do any other computation; for instance, we don't care whether v_1 is in X_2 or not. According to the presence of v_1 in X_1 and/or X_3, we continue with different computations of v_2:

- It v_1 is neither in X_1 nor in X_3, we already know that v is not in X without looking at v_2. We can stop the computation immediately.
- If v_1 is in X_1 but not in X_3, we have to check whether v_2 is in X_2.
- If v_1 is in X_3 but not in X_1, we have to check whether v_2 is in X_4.
- If v_1 is in X_1 and in X_3, we must check whether v_2 is in X_2 or not, and in X_4 or not. But actually, this is too much. We only have to find out whether it is in $X_2 \cup X_4$ or not, and this can be easier to do (for instance, if $X_2 \cup X_4 = \mathcal{V}$, we don't have anything to do at all).

This is the general case, but in some special cases, it is not necessary to know both whether v_1 is in X_1 *and* whether it is in X_3. For instance, imagine that $X_2 = X_4$. Then we don't have to distinguish the three cases $v_1 \in X_1 \backslash X_3$, $v_1 \in X_3 \backslash X_1$, $v_1 \in X_1 \cap X_3$. Indeed, we only need to check whether v_1 is in $X_1 \cup X_3$ or not. We could as well have merged $X_1 \times X_2$ and $X_3 \times X_4$ into $(X_1 \cup X_3) \times X_2$ in this case. We can also merge $X_1 \times X_2$ and $X_3 \times X_4$ if one of them is a subset of the other.

Now consider the case where X_0 is a proper subset of V (non trivial static information). If for instance, $X_0 \cap (X_1 \times X_2) = \varnothing$, we can simply ignore the rectangle $X_1 \times X_2$. Also, in general, we deduce some information about

v_1: it belongs to $\pi_1(X_0) = \{v_1^0 \mid (v_1^0, v_2^0) \in X_0\}$. After performing some computation on v_1, we get more information. For instance, we may deduce $v_1 \in X_1 \backslash X_3$. Then we know that v_2 is in $\pi_2(X_0 \cap (X_1 \backslash X_3) \times \mathcal{V})$. In general, we can combine the static information and the results we get for the a left subtree to get a better static information for the right subtree. Propagating a more precise information allows to ignore more rectangles.

The static information allows us to weaken the condition to merge two rectangles $X_1 \times X_2$ and $X_3 \times X_4$. Indeed, it is enough to check whether $\pi_2(X_0 \cap (X_1 \times X_2)) = \pi_2(X_0 \cap (X_3 \times X_4))$ (which is strictly weaker than $X_2 = X_4$).

In some cases, there are decisions to make. Imagine that $X_0 = X_1 \times X_2 \cup X_3 \times X_4$, and we want to check if a tree (v_1, v_2) is in $X_1 \times X_2$. If we suppose that $X_1 \cap X_3 = \varnothing$ and $X_2 \cap X_4 = \varnothing$, we can work on v_1 to see if it is in X_1 or not, or we can work on v_2 to see if it is in X_2 or not. We don't need to do both, and we must thus choose which one to do. We always choose to perform some computation on v_1 if it allows to gain useful knowledge on v. This choice allows to stop the top-down left-to-right traversal of the tree as soon as possible. This choice is relevant when considering the way CDuce encodes sequences and XML trees as binary trees. Indeed, the choice corresponds to: (1) extracting information from an XML tag to guide the computation on the content of the element, and (2) extracting information from the first children before considering the following ones.

3.2 Types

We have several regular languages $X_0, X_1, \ldots, X_n$ as inputs, and our algorithm produces other languages as intermediate steps. Instead of working with several different NDTA to define these languages, we assume that all the regular languages we will consider are defined by the same fixed NDTA $\mathcal{A}$ (each language is defined by a specific state of this NDTA). This assumption is not restrictive since it is always possible to take the (disjoint) union of several NDTA. Moreover, we assume that this NDTA has the following properties:

- **Boolean-completeness.** The class of languages defined by $\mathcal{A}$ (that is, the languages of the form $\mathcal{A}[\![r]\!]$), is closed under boolean operations (union, intersection, complement with respect to $\mathcal{V}$).
- **Canonicity.** If $(r_1, r_2, r) \in \delta$, then: $\mathcal{A}[\![r_1]\!] \neq \varnothing, \mathcal{A}[\![r_2]\!] \neq \varnothing$. Moreover, if we consider another pair $(r_1', r_2') \neq (r_1, r_2)$ such that $(r_1', r_2', r) \in \delta$, then $\mathcal{A}[\![r_1]\!] \cap \mathcal{A}[\![r_1']\!] = \varnothing$ and $\mathcal{A}[\![r_2]\!] \neq \mathcal{A}[\![r_2']\!]$.

It is well-known that the class of all regular tree languages is closed under boolean operations. The first property says that the class of languages defined by the fixed NDTA $\mathcal{A}$ is closed under these operations. Starting from an arbitrary NDTA, it is possible to extend it to a Boolean-complete one [2]. If r_1, r_2 are two nodes, we write $r_1 \vee r_2$ (resp. $r_1 \wedge r_2$, $\neg r_1$) for some node r such that $\mathcal{A}[\![r]\!] = \mathcal{A}[\![r_1]\!] \cup \mathcal{A}[\![r_2]\!]$ (resp. $\mathcal{A}[\![r_1]\!] \cap \mathcal{A}[\![r_2]\!]$, $\mathcal{V} \backslash \mathcal{A}[\![r_1]\!]$).

The Canonicity property forces a canonical way to decompose the set $\mathcal{A}[\![r]\!]^2$ as a finite union of rectangles of the form $\mathcal{A}[\![r_1]\!] \times \mathcal{A}[\![r_2]\!]$. For instance, it disallows the following situation: $\{(r_1, r_2) \mid (r_1, r_2, r) \in \delta\} = \{(a, c), (b, c)\}$. In that case, the decomposition of $\mathcal{A}[\![r]\!]^2$ given by δ would have two rectangles with the same second component. To eliminate this situation, we can merge the two rectangles, to keep only $(a \vee b, c)$. We also want to avoid more complex situations, for instance where a rectangle in the decomposition of $\mathcal{A}[\![r]\!]^2$ is covered by the union of others rectangles in this decomposition. It is always possible to modify the transition relation δ of a Boolean-complete NDTA to enforce the Canonicity property (first, by splitting the rectangles to enforce non-intersecting first-components, and then by merging rectangles with the same second component). This process does not break Boolean completeness since it doesn't change the class of languages defined by the automaton. The definition of Canonicity is asymmetric with respect to r_1 and r_2; this corresponds to the fixed traversal order of a tree during the run of a NUA (left-to-right).

We will use the word "type" to refer to the nodes of our fixed NDTA $\mathcal{A}$. Indeed, they correspond closely to the types of the CDuce (internal) type algebra, which support boolean operations and a canonical decomposition of products. Note that the set of types is finite, here. In what follows, we use t, t_1, t_2, $\ldots$ to range over nodes of the given NDTA, and r, r_1, r_2, $\ldots$ to range over nodes of the generated NUA. We also write $[\![t]\!]$ instead of $\mathcal{A}[\![t]\!]$. We define $\Delta^2(t) = \{(t_1, t_2) \mid (t_1, t_2, t) \in \delta\}$, and $\Delta^0(t) = \{a \mid (a, t) \in \delta\}$.

3.3 Filters

Even if we start with a single check to perform ("is the tree in X?"), several checks may have to be performed in parallel on a subtree ("is v_1 in X_1 and/or in X_3?"); we will call any finite set of such checks a *filter*.

A filter is intended to be applied to any tree v from a given language; for such a tree, the filter must compute which of its elements contain v.

DEFINITION 5 *Let τ be a type. A τ-filter is a set of types ρ such that $\forall t \in \rho.\ [\![t]\!] \subseteq [\![\tau]\!]$.*
The result of a τ-filter ρ for a tree $v \in [\![\tau]\!]$, written v/ρ, is defined by:

$$v/\rho = \{t \in \rho \mid v \in [\![t]\!]\}$$

[2] The proof is outside the scope of this paper. In a nutshell, this can be done by adding nodes that represent formal boolean combinations of existing nodes (using a finite syntax for combinations, like disjunctive normal forms). See for instance [FCB02]. This process induces an exponential blowup of the size of the automaton, but this is not an issue in practice since we don't need to compute the whole automaton.

DEFINITION 6 *Let ρ be a τ-filter. If $\rho' \subseteq \rho$, we write $\rho'|\rho$ for the type:*

$$\tau \wedge \bigwedge_{t \in \rho'} t \wedge \bigwedge_{t \in \rho \setminus \rho'} \neg t$$

(the τ in this formula is only useful for the case $\rho' = \varnothing$)

LEMMA 7 *Let ρ be a τ-filter and v a tree in $[\![\tau]\!]$. Then v/ρ is the only subset $\rho' \subseteq \rho$ such that $v \in [\![\rho'|\rho]\!]$.*

Our construction consists of building a NUA whose states are pairs (τ, ρ) of a type τ and a τ-filter ρ. Note that the set of all these pairs is finite, because we are working with a fixed NDTA to define all the types, so there is only a finite number of them.

3.4 Discussion

The type τ represents the static information we have about the tree, and ρ represents the tests we want to perform on a tree v which is known to be in τ. The expected behavior of the automaton is:

$$\forall v \in [\![\tau]\!].\ \mathcal{A}((\tau, \rho), v) = v/\rho$$

Moreover, the state (τ, ρ) can simply reject any tree outside $[\![\tau]\!]$. Actually, we will build a NUA such that $\mathtt{Dom}((\tau, \rho)) = [\![\tau]\!]$.

The rest of the section describes how the NUA should behave on a given input. It will thus mix the description of the expected behavior of the NUA at runtime and the (compile-time) construction we deduce from this behavior.

Results. In order to minimize the set of possible results for a state (τ, ρ), we consider only the $\rho' \subseteq \rho$ that can be obtained for an input in τ:

$$R((\tau, \rho)) = \{\rho' \subseteq \rho \mid [\![\rho'|\rho]\!] \neq \varnothing\}$$

Note that ρ' is in this set if and only if there is a $v \in [\![\tau]\!]$ such that $v/\rho = \rho'$.

Left. Assume we are given a tree $v = (v_1, v_2)$ which is known to be in a type τ. What can we say about v_1? Trivially, it is in one of the sets $[\![t_1]\!]$ for $(t_1, t_2) \in \Delta^2(\tau)$. We define:

$$\pi_1(\tau) = \bigvee_{(t_1, t_2) \in \Delta^2(\tau)} t_1$$

It is the best information we can find about v_1 (we use the assumption that the rectangles in the decomposition are not empty - this is part of the Canonicity property). Note that: $[\![\pi_1(\tau)]\!] = \{v_1 \mid (v_1, v_2) \in [\![\tau]\!]\}$.

Now assume we are given a τ-filter ρ that represents the tests we have to perform on v. Which tests do we have to perform on v_1? It is enough to consider those tests given by the $\pi_1(\tau)$-filter:

$$\pi_1(\rho) = \{t_1 \mid (t_1, t_2) \in \Delta^2(t),\ t \in \rho\}$$

This set is indeed a $\pi_1(\tau)$-filter. It corresponds to our choice of performing any computation on v_1 which can potentially simplify the work we have to do later on v_2. Indeed, two different rectangles in $\Delta^2(t)$ for some $t \in \rho$ have different second projections because of the Canonicity property. This discussion suggests to take:

$$\texttt{left}((\tau, \rho)) = (\pi_1(\tau), \pi_1(\rho))$$

Right. Let us continue our discussion with the tree $v = (v_1, v_2)$. The NUA performs some computation on v_1 from the state (τ_1, ρ_1) with $\tau_1 = \pi_1(\tau)$ and $\rho_1 = \pi_1(\rho)$. Let ρ'_1 be the returned result, which is the set of all the types $t_1 \in \rho_1$ such that $v_1 \in [\![t_1]\!]$. What can be said about v_2? It is in the following type:

$$\pi_2(\tau; \rho'_1) = \bigvee_{(t_1,t_2)\in\Delta^2(\tau)\ \mid\ [\![t_1 \wedge (\rho'_1 | \rho_1)]\!] \neq \varnothing} t_2$$

This type represents the best information we can get about v_2 knowing that $v \in [\![\tau]\!]$ and $v_1 \in [\![\rho'_1 | \rho_1]\!]$. Indeed, its interpretation is:

$$\{v_2 \mid (v_1, v_2) \in [\![\tau]\!], \rho'_1 = v_1/\rho_1\}$$

Now we must compute the checks we have to perform on v_2. Let us consider a given type $t \in \rho$. If $(t_1, t_2) \in \Delta^2(t)$, we have $t_1 \in \rho_1$, so we know if $v_1 \in [\![t_1]\!]$ or not (namely, $v_1 \in [\![t_1]\!] \iff t_1 \in \rho'_1$). There is at most one pair $(t_1, t_2) \in \Delta^2(t)$ such that $v_1 \in [\![t_1]\!]$. Indeed, two rectangles in the decomposition $\Delta^2(t)$ have non-intersecting first projection (Canonicity). If there is such a pair, we must check if v_2 is in $[\![t_2]\!]$ or not, and this will be enough to decide if v is in $[\![t]\!]$ or not. We thus take:

$$\pi_2(\rho; \rho'_1) = \{t_2 \mid (t_1, t_2) \in \Delta^2(t), t \in \rho, t_1 \in \rho'_1\}$$

This set has at most as many elements as ρ by the remark above. Finally, the "right" transition is:

$$\texttt{right}((\tau, \rho), \rho'_1) = (\pi_2(\tau; \rho'_1), \pi_2(\rho; \rho'_1))$$

Computing the result. We write $\tau_2 = \pi_2(\tau; \rho'_1)$ and $\rho_2 = \pi_2(\rho; \rho'_1)$. We can run the NUA from this state (τ_2, ρ_2) on the tree v_2, and get a result $\rho'_2 \subseteq \rho_2$ collecting the $t_2 \in \rho_2$ such that $v_2 \in [\![t_2]\!]$. For a type $t \in \rho$, and a rectangle (t_1, t_2) in its decomposition $\Delta^2(t)$, we have:

$$v \in [\![t_1]\!] \times [\![t_2]\!] \iff (t_1 \in \rho'_1) \wedge (t_2 \in \rho'_2)$$

So the result of running the NUA from the state (τ, ρ) on the tree v is:

$$\delta^2((\tau,\rho),\rho'_1,\rho'_2) = \{t \in \rho \mid \Delta^2(t) \cap (\rho'_1 \times \rho'_2) \neq \varnothing\}$$

Result for symbols. Finally, we must consider the case when the tree v is a symbol $a \in \Sigma$. The NUA has only to accept for the state (τ, ρ) trees in the set $[\![\tau]\!]$; so if $a \notin \Delta^0(\tau)$, we can let $\delta^0((\tau,\rho), a)$ undefined. Otherwise, we take:

$$\delta^0((\tau,\rho),a) = \{t \in \rho \mid a \in \Delta^0(t)\}$$

3.5 Formal construction, soundness

We can summarize the above discussion by an abstract construction of the NUA:

- the set of states are the pairs (τ, ρ) where τ is a type and ρ a τ-filter;
- $R((\tau,\rho)) = \{\rho' \subseteq \rho \mid [\![\rho' | \rho]\!] \neq \varnothing\}$;
- $\texttt{left}((\tau,\rho)) = (\pi_1(\tau), \pi_1(\rho))$ where:
  $\pi_1(\tau) = \bigvee\{t_1 \mid (t_1,t_2) \in \Delta^2(\tau)\}$ and
  $\pi_1(\rho) = \{t_1 \mid (t_1,t_2) \in \Delta^2(t),\ t \in \rho\}$;
- $\texttt{right}((\tau,\rho),\rho'_1) = (\pi_2(\tau;\rho'_1), \pi_2(\rho;\rho'_1))$ where:
  $\rho_1 = \pi_1(\rho)$,
  $\pi_2(\tau;\rho'_1) = \bigvee\{t_2 \mid (t_1,t_2) \in \Delta^2(\tau), [\![t_1 \wedge (\rho'_1|\rho_1)]\!] \neq \varnothing\}$ and
  $\pi_2(\rho;\rho'_1) = \{t_2 \mid (t_1,t_2) \in \Delta^2(t), t \in \rho, t_1 \in \rho'_1\}$;
- $\delta^2((\tau,\rho),\rho'_1,\rho'_2) = \{t \in \rho \mid \Delta^2(t) \cap (\rho'_1 \times \rho'_2) \neq \varnothing\}$;
- $\delta^0((\tau,\rho),a) = \{t \in \rho \mid a \in \Delta^0(t)\}$ if $a \in \Delta^0(\tau)$ (undefined otherwise)

This equations give explicitly for each state q the set of results $R(q)$ and the transition functions for this state. This opens the door to a lazy construction of the NUA from an initial state, so as to build only the part of the NUA that is effectively used in a run. The abstract presentation however has the advantage of simplicity (exactly as for the abstract subset construction for the determinization of automata).

The construction has a nice property: the efficiency of the constructed NUA (that is, the positions where it will ignore subtrees of an input) does not depend on the type τ and the types in ρ (which are syntactic objects), but only on the languages denoted by these types. This is because of the Canonicity property. As a consequence, there is no need to "optimize" the types before running the algorithm.

The following theorem states that the constructed NUA computes what it is supposed to compute.

THEOREM 8 *The above construction is well defined and explicitly computable. The resulting NUA satisfies the following properties for any state* (τ, ρ):

- $\mathsf{Dom}((\tau, \rho)) = [\![\tau]\!]$
- $\forall v \in [\![\tau]\!].\ \mathcal{A}((\tau, \rho), v) = v/\rho$
- $\forall \rho' \in R((\tau, \rho)).\ \exists v.\ \mathcal{A}((\tau, \rho), v) = \rho'$

The third point simply states that there are no "useless" result (a result is useless if it cannot be obtained for a value in the domain). The proof of the theorem is by induction on trees, and follows the lines of the discussion above.

3.6 An example

In this section, we give a very simple example of a NUA produced by our algorithm. We assume that Σ contains at least two symbols a,b and possibly others. We consider a type t_a (resp. t_b) which denotes all the trees with only a leaves (resp. b leaves). Our static information τ_0 is $t_a \vee t_b$, and the filter we are interested in is $\rho_0 = \{t_a, t_b\}$. Assuming proper choices for the NDTA that defines the types, the construction gives for the initial state $q_0 = (\tau_0, \rho_0)$:

- $R(q_0) = \{\{t_a\}, \{t_b\}\}$
- $\texttt{left}(q_0) = q_0$
- $\texttt{right}(q_0, \{t_a\}) = (t_a, \{t_a\})$; $\texttt{right}(q_0, \{t_b\}) = (t_b, \{t_b\})$
- $\delta^2(q_0, \{t_a\}, \{t_a\}) = \{t_a\}$; $\delta^2(q_0, \{t_b\}, \{t_b\}) = \{t_b\}$
- $\delta^0(q_0, a) = \{t_a\}$; $\delta^0(q_0, b) = \{t_b\}$; $\delta^0(q_0, c)$ undefined if $c \neq a, c \neq b$

There is no need to give the transition functions for the states $q_a = (t_a, \{t_a\})$ and $q_b = (t_b, \{t_b\})$ because they each have a single result ($R(q_a) = \{\{t_a\}\}$ and $R(q_b) = \{\{t_b\}\}$), so the NUA will simply skip the corresponding subtrees. The behavior of the NUA is simple to understand: it goes directly to the leftmost leaf and returns immediately. In particular, it traverses a single path from the root to a leaf and ignores the rest of the tree.

3.7 Implementation

We rely a lot on the possibility of checking emptiness of a type ($[\![t]\!] = \varnothing$). For instance, the definition of $R((\tau, \rho))$ requires to check a lot of types for emptyness. All the techniques developed for the implementation of XDuce and CDuce subtyping algorithms can be used to do it efficiently. In particular, because of caching, the total cost for all the calls to the emptiness checking procedure does not depend on the number of calls (there is a single exponential cost), so they are "cheap" and we can afford a lot of them. CDuce also demonstrates an efficient implementation of the "type algebra" with boolean combinations and canonical decomposition.

The number of states (τ, ρ) is finite, but it is huge. However, our construction proceeds in a top-down way: starting from a given state (τ, ρ), it defines its set of results and its transitions explicitly. Hence we are able to build the NUA "lazily" (either by computing all the reachable states, or by waiting to consume inputs - this is how the CDuce implementation works).

We haven't studied the theoretical complexity of our algorithm, but it is clearly at least as costly as the inclusion problem for regular tree languages. However, in practice, the algorithm works well. It has been successfully used to compile non-trivial CDuce programs.

Preliminary benchmarks [BCF03] suggest very good runtime performances, and we believe that our compilation strategy for pattern matching is the main reason for that.

Acknowledgments

I would like to express my best gratitude to Haruo Hosoya for his help to improve the presentation of the paper. The referees of PLANX 2004 and ICALP 2004 also suggested significant improvements to the presentation.

References

[BCF03] Véronique Benzaken, Giuseppe Castagna, and Alain Frisch. CDuce: an XML-centric general-purpose language. In *ICFP*, 2003.

[BPSM98] Tim Bray, Jean Paoli, and C. M. Sperberg-McQueen. Extensible markup language (XML) 1.0. In *W3C Recommendation*, 1998.

[FCB02] Alain Frisch, Giuseppe Castagna, and Véronique Benzaken. Semantic subtyping. In *LICS*, 2002.

[GP03] Vladimir Gapeyev and Benjamin Pierce. Regular object types. In *FOOL*, 2003.

[Hos00] Haruo Hosoya. Regular expression types for XML. *Ph.D thesis. The University of Tokyo*, 2000.

[HP02] Haruo Hosoya and Benjamin Pierce. Regular expression pattern matching for XML. *Journal of Functional Programming*, 2002.

[Lev03] Michael Levin. Compiling regular patterns. In *ICFP*, 2003.

[Nev02] Frank Neven. Automata theory for XML researchers. In *SIGMOD Record, 31(3), 2002.*, 2002.

[NS98] Andreas Neumann and Helmut Seidl. Locating matches of tree patterns in forests. In *Foundations of Software Technology and Theoretical Computer Science*, pages 134–145, 1998. Extended abstract available at `http://www.informatik.uni-trier.de/~seidl/conferences.html`.

[SW03] Jerome Simeon and Philip Wadler. The essence of XML. In *POPL*, 2003.

[TBMM01] Henri S. Thompson, David Beech, Murray Maloney, and N. Mendelsohn. XML Schema part 1: Structures. In *W3C Recommendation*, 2001.

Author Index

GPSR Compliance
The European Union's (EU) General Product Safety Regulation (GPSR) is a set of rules that requires consumer products to be safe and our obligations to ensure this.

If you have any concerns about our products, you can contact us on

ProductSafety@springernature.com

In case Publisher is established outside the EU, the EU authorized representative is:

Springer Nature Customer Service Center GmbH
Europaplatz 3
69115 Heidelberg, Germany

www.ingramcontent.com/pod-product-compliance
Ingram Content Group UK Ltd.
Pitfield, Milton Keynes, MK11 3LW, UK
UKHW022317190726
13856UKWH00001B/55
* 9 7 8 1 4 7 5 7 8 0 2 1 5 *